THE STRATEGY PROCESS

THE STRATEGY PROCESS

European Edition

Henry Mintzberg, James Brian Quinn and
Sumantra Ghoshal

Prentice Hall

London   New York   Toronto   Sydney   Tokyo   Singapore
Madrid   Mexico City   Munich

First published 1995 by
Prentice Hall International (UK) Limited
Campus 400, Maylands Avenue
Hemel Hempstead
Hertfordshire, HP2 7EZ
A division of
Simon & Schuster International Group

Typeset in 10/12pt Times
by P&R Typesetters, Salisbury

Printed and bound in Great Britain by the Bath Press.

Library of Congress Cataloging-in-Publication Data

Mintzberg, Henry.
    The strategy process / Henry Mintzberg, James Brian Quinn,
Sumantra Ghoshal. - - European ed.
      p.   cm.
    Quinn's name appears first on the earlier ed.
    Includes bibliographical references and index.
    ISBN 0-13-149626-3
      1. Strategic planning - - Case studies.   I. Quinn, James Brian,
1928-   .   II. Ghoshal, Sumantra. III. Title.
HD30.28.Q53   1995b
658.4'012- -dc20   95-1818
                                                CIP

British Library Cataloguing in Publication Data

A catalogue record for this book is available from
the British Library

ISBN 0-13-149626-3

---

1 2 3 4 5   99 98 97 96 95

CONTENTS

SECTION TWO ORGANIZATION

SECTION TWO CASES

SECTION THREE CONTEXT

INTRODUCTION

In the first edition of *The Strategy Process*, two of the three authors of the present volume set out to produce a different kind of textbook in the field of business policy or, as it is now more popularly called, strategic management. We sought to provide the reader with a richness of theory, a richness of practice and a strong basis for linkage between the two. We had rejected the strictly case study approach, which left theory out altogether or soft-pedalled it, and thereby denied the accumulated benefits of many years of careful research and thought about management processes. We had also rejected an alternative approach, which forced on readers a highly rationalistic model of how the strategy process *should* function. We collaborated on the book because of a shared belief that in this complex world of organizations, a range of concepts was needed to cut through and illuminate particular aspects of that complexity. There is no 'one best way' to create strategy, nor is there 'one best form' of organization. Quite different forms work well in particular contexts. The book was a product of our conviction that exploring a fuller variety systematically would create a deeper and more useful appreciation of the strategy process.

The first two editions of *The Strategy Process* have sold well in Europe. But it was the belief of the two co-authors, Henry Mintzberg and James Brian Quinn, that an edition especially geared to Europe was necessary, especially in the case material. Accordingly, Sumantra Ghoshal of the London Business School, well-known for his incisive articles on strategy and international business as well as many award-winning cases on European companies, was invited to take the lead in preparing the book for a European audience.

This revised edition remains loyal to the beliefs and objectives of the original book, which are fully shared by the new co-author. While maintaining the basic outline, a great many of its specific components have been replaced, added or revised, with the aim of making the result more relevant to our European audience. The most significant impact has been on our choice of cases: 18 of the 24 cases in this book focus on companies based in Europe or on the European operations of companies that have their headquarters elsewhere. Yet managers in Europe have to compete in an international context no less, and probably more, than managers is some other parts of the world. Thus, the remaining cases, two on North American companies and four on companies based in Japan, complement the European focus with a broader international orientation.

In revising the readings, our objective has been to include new ideas rather than necessarily European ones: good ideas, we believe, are good irrespective of their source. Yet the proportion of Europe-based authors has increased significantly in the text. This may in part reflct the fact that Henry Mintzberg is now a faculty member of a European institution, INSEAD, as is the new co-author of the book. But, this is also because of the impact other Europe-based authors, such as Gary Hamel, John Stopford and Charles Baden-Fuller, have recently been having in the strategy field.

The text, therefore, is even more eclectic than in the last edition. Each author has his or her own ideas and his or her own best way of expressing them – ourselves included. As in the earlier editions, we have presented these ideas as originally published by the authors rather than filtering them through our minds and pens. Had they been summarized by us, the readings would have lost a good deal of their richness.

We do not apologize for contradictions among the ideas of leading thinkers; the world is full of contradictions. The real danger lies in using pat solutions to a nuanced reality, not in opening up perspectives to different interpretations. The effective strategist is one who can live with contradictions, learn to appreciate their causes and effects, and reconcile them sufficiently for effective action. The readings have, none the less, been ordered by chapter to suggest some ways in which that reconciliation can be considered. Our introductions are also intended to assist in this task and to help place the readings themselves in perspective.

ON THEORY

A word on theory is in order. We do not consider theory a dirty word; nor do we apologize for making it a major component of this book. To some, to be theoretical is to be detached, impractical. But as a bright social scientist once said, 'There is nothing so practical as a good theory.' And every successful doctor, engineer and physicist would have to agree: they would be unable to practise without a theoretical framework. Theories are useful because they avoid the need to store masses of data. It is easier to remember a simple framework about a phenomenon than it is to consider every detail you have ever observed. In a sense, theories are a bit like a library cataloguing system: the world would be impossibly confusing without them. They enable you to store and conveniently access your own experiences, as well as those of others.

One can, however, suffer not just from an absence of theories, but also from unwittingly being dominated by them. To paraphrase John Maynard Keynes, most 'practical men' are the slaves of some defunct theorist. Whether we realize it or not, our behaviour is guided by the system of ideas we have internalized over the years. Much can be learned by bringing these out in the open, examining them more carefully and comparing them with alternative ways to view the world – including ones based on systematic study, that is, research. One of our prime intentions in this book is to expose the limitations of conventional theories and to offer alternative explanations, which can be superior guides to understanding and taking actions in specific contexts.

Prescriptive Versus Descriptive Theory

Unlike many textbooks in this field, this one tries to explain the world as it is rather than as someone thinks it is *supposed* to be. Although there has sometimes been a tendency to disdain such *descriptive* theories, *prescriptive* (or normative) ones have often been the problem, rather than the solution, in the field of management. There is no one best way in management; no prescription works for all organizations. Even when a prescription seems effective in some context, it requires a sophisticated understanding of exactly what the context is and how it functions. In other words, one cannot decide reliably what should be done in a system as complicated as a contemporary organization without a genuine understanding of how that organization really works. In engineering, no student ever questions having to learn physics, or in medicine, having to learn anatomy. Imagine an engineering student's hand shooting up in a physics class: 'Listen, sir, it's fine telling us how the atom works. But what we really want to know is how the atom *should* work!' Why should a management student's similar demand in the realm of strategy or structure be considered any more appropriate? How can people manage complex systems they do not understand?

Nevertheless, we have not ignored prescriptive theory when it appears useful. A number of prescriptive techniques (industry analysis, portfolio analysis, experience curves, etc.) are discussed. But these are associated both with other readings and with cases that will help you understand the context and limitations of their usefulness. Both cases and readings offer opportunities to pursue the full complexity of strategic situations. You will find a wide range of issues and perspectives addressed. One of our main goals is to integrate a variety of views, rather than allow strategy to be fragmented into just 'human issues' and 'economic issues'. The text and cases provide a basis for treating the full complexity of strategic management.

ON SOURCES

How were the readings selected and edited? One popular textbook boasted a few years ago that all its readings had been published since 1980 (except one dated 1979!). We make no such claim; indeed, we would like to make quite a different boast: many of our readings have been around quite a while – long enough to mature, like fine wine. Our criterion for inclusion was not the novelty of the article so much as the quality of its insight – that is, its ability to explain some aspect of the strategy process better than any other article. Time does not age the really good articles; quite the opposite – it distinguishes their quality (even if sometimes it brings us back to the old habits of masculine gender, for which we apologize to our readers). We are, of course, not biased towards old articles, just towards good ones. Hence, the materials in this book range from classics of the 1960s to some published just before our final selection was made. You will find articles from the most serious academic journals, the best practitioner magazines, books, and some very obscure sources. The best can sometimes be found in strange places!

We have opted to include many shorter readings rather than fewer longer ones, and we have tried to present as wide a variety of good ideas as possible while maintaining clarity. To do so we have often had to edit the readings. We have, in fact, put a great deal of effort into the editing in order to extract the key messages of each reading in as brief, concise and clear a manner as possible. Unfortunately, our cuts sometimes forced us to eliminate interesting examples and side-issues. (In the readings, as well as some of the case materials from published sources, ellipses (. . .) signify portions that have been deleted from the original, while square brackets [ ] signify our own insertions of minor clarifications into the original text.) We apologize to you, the reader, as well as to the authors, for having done this, but hope that the overall result has rendered these changes worthwhile.

We have also included a number of our own works. Perhaps we are biased, having less objective standards by which to judge what we have written. But we have messages to convey too, and our own writings do examine the basic themes that we feel are important in policy and strategy courses today.

ON CASES

A major danger of studying the strategy process – probably the most enticing subject in the management curriculum and the most comprehensive of organizational processes – is that students and professors can become detached from the basics of the enterprise. The 'Don't bore me with the operating details; I'm here to tackle the really big issues' syndrome has been the death of many business policy or strategy courses, not to mention managerial practices! The big issues *are* rooted in little details. We have tried to recognize this in both the readings and the cases. Effective strategy processes always come down to specifics. The cases and the industry reference notes provide a rich soil for investigating strategic realities. Their complexities always extend well below the surface. Each layer peeled back can reveal new insights and rewards.

As useful as they are, however, cases are not really the ideal way to understand strategy: involving oneself in the hubbub of a real organization is. We harbour no illusions that reading 20 pages on an organization will make you an expert. But cases remain the most convenient way to introduce practice into the classroom, to tap a wide variety of experiences and to involve student actively in analysis and decision-making. Our cases consciously contain both their prescriptive and descriptive aspects. On the one hand, they provide the data and background for making a major decision. Students can appraise the situation in its full context, suggest what future directions would be best for the organization in question and discuss how their solutions can realistically be implemented. On the other hand, each case is also an opportunity to understand the dynamics of an organization – the historical context of the problems it faces, the influence of its culture, its probable reactions to varying solutions, and so on. Unlike many cases which focus only on the analytical aspects of a decision, ours constantly force you to consider the messy realities of arriving at decisions in organizations and obtaining a desired response to any decision. In these respects, case study involves a good deal of descriptive *and* prescriptive analysis.

Linking Cases and Readings

The cases in this book are not intended to emphasize any particular theories, any more than the theoretical materials are included because they explain particular cases.

Each case presents a slice of some specific reality, each reading a conceptual interpretation of some phenomenon. The readings are placed in particular groupings because they approach some common aspects or issues in theory.

We have deliberately avoided linking particular cases to specific readings because we believe each case must be analyzed for its own sake. Cases are intrinsically richer than readings. Each contains a wide variety of issues – many awfully messy – in no particular order. The readings, in contrast, are usually neat and tidy, professing one or a few basic conceptual ideas and providing some specific vocabulary. When the two connect – sometimes through direct effort, more often indirectly as conceptual ideas are recalled in the situation of a particular case – some powerful learning can take place in the form of clarification or, we hope, revelation.

Try to see how particular theories can help you to understand some of the issues in the cases and provide useful frameworks for drawing conclusions. Perhaps the great military theorist, Von Clausewitz, expressed it best over a century ago (to borrow a quotation from one of our readings of Chapter 1):

> All that theory can do is give the artist or soldier points of reference and standards of evaluation . . . with the ultimate purpose not of telling him how to act but of developing his judgment. (1976: 15)

In applying the theory to cases, please do not assume that it is only the readings in the same section that matter. We have designed the book so that the textual materials develop as the chapters unfold. Concepts introduced in earlier chapters become integrated in the later ones; and early cases tend to build knowledge for those appearing later. Problems and their organizational context move from the simple to the more complex. Space limitations and the structured nature of theories require some compartmentalization. But don't take that compartmentalization too literally. In preparing each case, use whatever concepts you find helpful from chapters of this book and your personal knowledge. The cases themselves deal with real people in real companies. The reality they present is enormously complicated: their dynamics extend to today's newspapers and *Who's Who*, or any other reference you can imagine. Use any sound source of information that helps you to deal with them. Part of the excitement of policy or strategy courses is understanding how major decisions happened to be made and what were their subsequent consequences – local, national, international.

These are living cases. In the strictest sense they have no beginning or end. They have been written in as lively a style as possible: we do not believe business school cases need be dull. Each case deals with a major transition point in the history of an enterprise. Each can be used in a variety of ways to emphasize a particular set of concepts at a particular time in the course. Many lend themselves to sophisticated financial, industry, portfolio and competitive analyses as well as discerning organizational, behavioural and managerial practice inquiries. And many contain entrepreneurial and technological dimensions rarely found in strategy cases. Trying to figure out what is going on should be challenging as well as fun!

Case Discussion

Management cases provide a concrete information base for students to analyze and share as they discuss management issues. Without this focus, discussions of theory can become quite confusing. You may have in mind an image of an organization or situation that is very different from that of other discussants. As a result, what appears to be a difference in theory will, after much argument, often turn out to be no more than a difference in perception of the realities surrounding these examples.

In this text we try to provide three levels of learning: first, a chance to share the generalized insights of leading theoreticians (in the readings); second, an opportunity to test the applicability and limits of these theories in specific (case) situations; and third, the capacity to develop one's own special blend of insights based on empirical observations and inductive reasoning (from case analyses). All are useful approaches. But some students and teachers will find one mix more productive for their special level of experience or mind set, while others will prefer a quite different mix. Hence, we include a wide selection of cases and readings.

The cases are not intended as *examples* of either weak or exceptionally good management practices, nor, as we noted, do they provide *examples* of the concepts in Simon & Schuster: The Strategy Process — Mintzberg & Quinn of various approaches. And they are analytical vehicles for applying and testing concepts and tools developed in your education and experience. Almost every case has its marketing, operations, accounting, financial, human relations, planning and control, external environment, ethical, political and quantitative dimensions. Each dimension should be addressed in preparations and classroom discussions, although some aspects will inevitably emerge as more important in one situation than another.

In each case you should look for several sets of issues. First, you should understand what was happening in that situation. Why did things turn out that way? What are the strong or weak features of what happened? What could have been changed to advantage? How? Why? Second, there are always issues of what should be done next. What are the key issues to be resolved? What are the major alternatives available? What outcomes could the organization expect from each? Which alternative should it select? Why? Third, there will almost always be 'hard' quantitative data and 'soft' qualitative impressions about each situation. Both deserve attention. Because the cases deal with real companies and real people in real situations, their data-bases can be *extended* as far as students and teachers wish. They only have to consult their libraries and daily newspapers.

But remember, no realistic strategy situation is just an organization behaviour problem, or just a financial or economic analytical one. Both sets of information should be considered and an *integrated* solution developed. Our cases are consciously constructed for this. Given their complexity, we have tried to keep the cases as brief as possible. And we have tried to capture some of the flavour of the real organization. Moreover, we have sought to mix product and services cases, technological and 'non-tech' cases, entrepreneurial and large enterprise situations. In this cross-section, we have tried to capture some of the most important and exciting issues, concepts and products of our times. We believe management is both fun and important. The cases try to convey this.

There is no 'correct' answer to any case. There may be several 'good' answers and many poor ones. The purpose of a strategy course should be to help you understand the nature of these 'better' answers, what to look for, how to analyze alternatives and how to see through the complexities of reaching solutions and implementing them in real organizations. A strategy course can only improve your probability of success; it cannot ensure it. The total number of variables in a real strategy situation is typically beyond the control of any one person or group. Hence another caveat: don't rely on what a company actually did as a guide to effective action. The company may have succeeded or failed, not because of its specific decisions, but because of luck, an outstanding personality, the bizarre action of an opponent, international events over which it had no control, and so on. One of the outcomes of a successful strategy course should be a little humility.

Not Formulation, Then Implementation

The first edition of this book offered a chapter format that was new in the policy or strategy field. Unlike most others, it had no specific chapter or section devoted to 'implementation' *per se*. The assumption in other texts is that strategy is formulated and then implemented, with organizational structures, control systems and the like following obediently in its wake. In this text, as in real life, formulation and implementation are intertwined as complex interactive processes in which politics, values, organizational culture and management styles determine or constrain particular strategic decisions. And strategy, structure and systems comingle in complicated ways to influence outcomes. While strategy formulation and implementation may be separated in some situations – perhaps in crises, in some totally new ventures, as well as in organizations facing predictable futures – these events are particular. We certainly do not believe in building a whole book (let alone a whole field) about this conceptual distinction.

But Concepts, then Contexts

The readings are divided approximately into two parts. The first deal with *concepts*; the second with *contexts*. We introduce strategy and structure as well as power, culture and several other concepts early in the text as equal partners in the complex web of ideas which make up what we call 'the strategy process'. In the second half of the text we weave these concepts together in a number of distinct situations, which we call contexts.

   Our theme diagram illustrates this. Concepts, shown at the top, are divided into two groups – strategy and organization – to represent the first two sections of the book. Contexts draw all these concepts together, in a variety of situations (covered in the third section), which we consider the key ones in the field of strategy today (although hardly the only ones). The outline of the text, chapter by chapter, proceeds as follows.

Section One: Strategy

The first section is called 'Strategy'. It comprises four chapters (two introductory in nature, and two on the processes by which strategy making takes place). Chapter 1 introduces the *strategy concept* and probes the meaning of this important word to broaden your view of it. Here the pattern is to challenge you to question conventional views, especially when these act to narrow perspectives. The themes introduced in this chapter recur throughout the book and are worth care in understanding.

   Chapter 2 introduces a very important character in this book, *the strategist* as

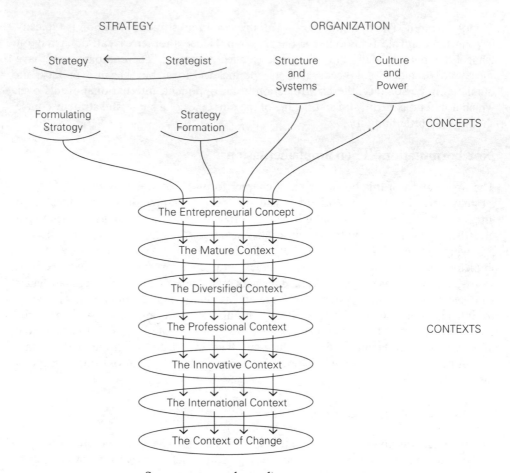

Strategy process theme diagram

general manager. This person may not be the only one who makes strategy in an organization, but he or she is clearly a key player. In examining the work of the general manager and the nature of his or her job, we shall perhaps upset a number of widely accepted notions. We do this to help you understand the very real complexities and difficulties of making strategy and managing in contemporary organizations.

Chapters 3 and 4 take up a theme that is treated extensively in the text to the point of being reflected in its title: the development of an understanding of the processes by which strategies are made. Chapter 3 looks at *strategy formulation*, specifically at some widely accepted prescriptive models of how organizations should go about developing and testing their strategies. While readings in later chapters will challenge some of these precepts, what will not be questioned is the importance of having to understand them. They are fundamental to appreciating the strategy process today.

Chapter 4 switches from a prescriptive to a descriptive approach. Concerned with understanding *strategy formation*, it considers how strategies are actually formed in organizations (not necessarily by being formulated) and why different processes may be effective in specific circumstances. This text takes an unconventional stand by viewing planning and other formal approaches as not the only – and often indeed not even the most desirable – ways to make strategy. You will find our emphasis on the descriptive process – as an equal partner with the more traditional concerns for technical and analytical issues – to be one of the unifying themes of this book.

Section Two: Organization

In Section One the readings introduced strategy, the strategist and various ways in which strategy might be formulated and does in fact form. In Section Two, entitled *Organization,* we introduce other concepts, which constitute part of the strategy process.

In Chapter 5, we consider *structure and systems* where particular attention is paid to the various forms that structure can take as well as the mechanisms that comprise it. In Chapter 6 we consider *culture and power,* and how they impact on organizations and their strategies and so influence their effectiveness.

Section Three: Context

Section Three is called Context. We consider how all the elements introduced so far – strategy, the processes by which it is formulated and gets formed, the strategist, structure, systems, culture and power – combine to suit particular contexts, seven in all.

Chapter 7 deals with the *entrepreneurial context,* where a rather simple organization comes under the close control of a strong leader, often a person with vision. Chapter 8 examines the *mature context,* one common to many large business and government organizations involved in the mass production or distribution of goods or services. Chapter 9 introduces the *diversified context,* and deals with organizations that have diversified their product or service lines and usually divided their structures to deal with the greater varieties of environments they face.

Chapters 10 and 11 develop the contexts of professionalism and innovation, both involving organizations of high expertise. In the *professional context,* the experts work relatively independently in rather stable conditions, while in the *innovation context,* they combine in project teams under more dynamic conditions. What these two contexts have in common, however, is that they act in ways that upset many of the widely accepted notions about how organizations should be structured and make strategy. Chapter 12 focuses on the *international context,* dealing with the special complexities in the strategy process of multinational companies. This is a special case of the diversified context, but one whose importance, we believe, deserves special attention.

In considering each of these different contexts, we seek to discuss (where appropriate material is available) the situations in which each is most likely to be found, the structures most suited to it, the kinds of strategy that tend to be pursued, the processes by which these strategies tend to be formed and might be formulated, and the social issues associated with the context.

Chapter 14 is devoted not so much to a specific context as to managing change, between contexts or within a context (which we characterize as the *context of change*). The major concerns are how organizations can cope with crises, turnarounds, revitalizations and new stages in their own lifecycles or those of their key products.

Well, there you have it. We have worked hard on this book, in both the original and this European edition, to get it right. We have tried to think things through from the basics, with a resulting text that in style, format and content is unusual for the field of policy or strategy. Our product may not be perfect, but we believe it is good – indeed, better than any other text available. Now it's your turn to find out if you agree. Have fun doing so!

SECTION ONE

STRATEGY

THE STRATEGY CONCEPT

We open this text on its focal point: Strategy. The first section is called Strategy, the first chapter, the strategy concept. Later chapters in this section describe the roles of the general manager as strategist and consider the processes by which strategies are made from two perspectives: deliberate formulation through systematic analysis, and emergent formation through the interactive learning of people. But in the opening chapter, we consider the central concept strategy itself.

What is strategy anyway? There is no single, universally accepted definition. Different authors and managers use the term differently: for example, some include goals and objectives as part of strategy, while others make firm distinctions between the two. Our intention in including the following readings is not to promote any one view of strategy, but rather to suggest a number that seem useful. As will be evident throughout this text, our wish is not to narrow perspectives but to broaden them, by trying to clarify issues. In pursuing these readings, it will be helpful to think about the meaning of strategy, to try to understand how different people have used the term, and, later, to see if certain definitions hold up better in particular contexts.

We have taken the opportunity to include in this first chapter readings by two of the authors of the book. As you will see, the two views are similar but certainly not identical; indeed, in places they differ somewhat: for example, on the word 'tactics'. But overall, we believe you will find their views complementary.

The first reading, by James Brian Quinn of the Amos Tuck Business School, Dartmouth College, provides a general overview by clarifying some of the vocabulary used in this field and introducing a number of the themes that will appear throughout the text. In this reading from his book *Strategies for Change: Logical incrementalism*, Quinn places special emphasis on the military uses of the term and draws from this domain a set of essential 'dimensions' or criteria for successful stategies. To derive these, he goes back to Philip and Alexander of Macedonia for his main example; he also provides a brief kaleidoscope of how smilar concepts have influenced later military and diplomatic strategists.

Discussion of the military aspects of strategy must surely be among the oldest continuous literatures in the world. In fact, the origins of the word 'strategy' go back even further than this experience in Macedonia, to the Greeks whom Alexander and his father defeated. As Quinn notes and Roger Evered, in another article, elaborates:

> Initially *strategos* referred to a role (a general in command of an army). Later it came to mean 'the art of the general', which is to say the psychological and behavioral skills with which he occupied the role. By the time of Pericles (450 BC) it came to mean managerial skill (administration, leadership oration, power). And by Alexander's time (330 BC) it referred to the skill of employing forces to overcome opposition and to create a unified system of global governance. (1980: 3)

The second reading, by Henry Mintzberg, who holds positions in the Faculty of Management at McGill University in Canada and at INSEAD in France, serves to open up the concept of stategy to a variety of views, some very different from traditional military or business writings, but suggested briefly in the Quinn reading. Mintzberg focuses on various distinct definitions of strategy – as plan (as well as ploy), pattern, position and perspective. He uses the first two of these definitions to take us beyond deliberate strategy – beyond the traditional views of the term – to the notion of emergent strategy. This introduces the idea that strategies can *form* in an organization without being consciously intended; that is, without being *formulated*. This may seem to run counter to the whole thrust of the strategy literature, but Mintzberg argues that many people implicitly use the term this way, even though they would not so define it.

Upon completion of thse readings, we hope that you will be less sure of how the word strategy is used, but more ready to tackle the study of the strategy process with a broadened perspective and an open mind. There are no universally right answers in this field, any more than there are in most other fields, but there are interesting and constructive orientations. Our expectation is that by the time you have absorbed the ideas of all the different authors represented in this book and have tested these ideas against the expediences of the different companies in the cases, you will be in a position to develop your own personal perspective on strategy and also the judgement and skills to understand how you may be able to shape the direction and performance of the organization with which you are, or eventually will be, associated.

• STRATEGIES FOR CHANGE*

JAMES BRIAN QUINN

SOME USEFUL DEFINITIONS

Because the words *strategy, objectives, goals, policy* and *programmes* . . . have different meanings to individual readers or to various organizational cultures, I [try] to use certain definitions consistently . . . For clarity – not pedantry – these are set forth as follows:

A **strategy** is the *pattern* or *plan* that *integrates* an organization's *major* goals, policies and action sequences into a *cohesive* whole. A well-formulated strategy helps to *marshal* and *allocate* an organization's resources into a *unique and viable posture* based on its relative *internal competencies* and *shortcomings,* anticipated *changes in the environment* and contingent moves by *intelligent opponents*.

Goals (or **objectives**) state *what* is to be achieved and *when* results are to be accomplished, but they do not state *how* the results are to be achieved. All organizations have multiple goals existing in a complex hierarchy (Simon, 1964): from value objectives, which express the broad value premises towards which the company is to strive; through overall organizational objectives, which establish the intended *nature* of the enterprise and the *directions* in which it should move; to a series of less permanent goals that define targets for each organizational unit, its subunits, and finally all major programme activities within each subunit. Major goals – those that affect the entity's overall direction and viability – are called *strategic goals*.

Policies are rules or guidelines that express the *limits* within which action should occur. These rules often take the form of contingent decisions for resolving conflicts among specific objectives. For example: 'Don't exceed three months' inventory in any item without corporate approval.' Like the objectives they support, policies exist in a hierarchy throughout the organization. Major policies – those that guide the entity's overall direction and posture or determine its viability – are called *strategic policies*.

Programmes specify the *step-by-step sequence of actions* necessary to achieve major objectives. They express *how* objectives will be achieved within the limits set by policy. They ensure that resources are committed to achieve goals, and they provide the dynamic track against which progress can be measured. Those major programmes that determine the entity's overall thrust and viability are called *strategic programmes*.

Strategic decisions are those that determine the overall direction of an enterprise and its ultimate viability in light of the predictable, the unpredictable and the unknowable changes that may occur in its most important surrounding environments. They intimately shape the true goals of the enterprise. They help delineate the broad limits within which the enterprise operates. They dictate both the resources the

---

*Excerpted from James Brian Quinn. *Strategies for Change. Logical Incrementalism* (copyright © Richard D. Irwin, Inc, 1980), Chs. 1 and 5; reprinted by permission of the publisher.

enterprise will have accessible for its tasks and the principal patterns in which these resources will be allocated. And they determine the effectiveness of the enterprise – whether its major thrusts are in the right directions given its resource potentials – rather than whether individual tasks are performed efficiently. Management for efficiency, along with the myriad decisions necessary to maintain the daily life and services of the enterprise, is the domain of operations.

Strategies Versus Tactics

Strategies normally exist at many different levels in any large organization. For example, in government there are world trade, national economic, treasury department, military spending, investment, fiscal, monetary supply, banking, regional development and local re-employment strategies – all related to each other somewhat hierarchically yet each having imperatives of its own. Similarly, businesses have numerous strategies from corporate levels to department levels within divisions. Yet if strategies exist at all these levels, how do strategies and tactics differ? Often the primary difference lies in the scale of action or the perspective of the leader. What appears to be a 'tactic' to the chief executive officer (or general) may be a 'strategy' to the marketing head (or lieutenant) if it determines the ultimate success and viability of his or her organization. In a more precise sense, tactics can occur at either level. They are the short-duration, adaptive, action–interaction realignments, which opposing forces use to accomplish limited goals after their initial contact. Strategy defines a continuing basis for ordering these adaptations towards more broadly conceived purposes.

A genuine strategy is always needed when the potential actions or responses of intelligent opponents can seriously affect the endeavour's desired outcome – regardless of that endeavour's organizational level in the total enterprise. This condition almost always pertains to the important actions taken at the top level of competitive organizations. However, game theorists quickly point out that some important top-level actions – for example, sending a peacetime fleet across the Atlantic – merely require elaborate coordinative plans and programmes (Von Neumann and Morgenstern, 1944; McDonald, 1950; Shubik, 1975). A whole new set of concepts, a true strategy, is needed if some people or nations decide to oppose the fleet's purposes. And it is these concepts that in large part distinguish strategic formulation from simpler programmatic planning.

Strategies may be looked at as either *a priori* statements to guide action or *a posteriori* results of actual decision behaviour. In most complex organizations . . . one would be hardpressed to find a complete *a priori* statement of a total strategy that actually is followed. Yet often the existence of a strategy (or strategy change) may be clear to an objective observer, although it is not yet apparent to the executives making critical decisions. One, therefore, must look at the actual emerging *pattern* of the enterprise's operant goals, policies and major programmes to see what its true strategy is (Mintzberg, 1972). Whether it is consciously set forth in advance or is simply a widely held understanding resulting from a stream of decisions, this pattern becomes the real strategy of the enterprise. And it is changes in this pattern – regardless of what any formal strategic documents may say – that either analysts or strategic decision-makers must address if they wish to comprehend or alter the concern's strategic posture . . .

THE CLASSICAL APPROACH TO STRATEGY

Military-diplomatic strategies have existed since prehistoric times. In fact, one function of the earliest historians and poets was to collect the accumulated lore of these successful and unsuccessful life-and-death strategies and convert them into wisdom and guidance for the future. As societies grew larger and conflicts more complex, generals, statesmen and captains studied, codified and tested essential strategic concepts until a coherent body of principles seemed to emerge. In various forms these were ultimately distilled into the maxims of Sun Tzu (1963), Machiavelli (1950), Napoleon (1940), Von Clausewitz (1976), Foch (1970), Lenin (1927), Hart (1954), Montgomery (1958) and Mao Tse-Tung (1967). Yet with a few exceptions – largely introduced by modern technology – the most basic principles of strategy were in place and recorded long before the Christian era. More modern institutions primarily adapted and modified these to their own special environments.

Although one could choose any number of classical military-diplomatic strategies as examples, Philip and Alexander's actions at Chaeronea (in 338 BC) contain many currently relevant concepts (Green, 1970; Varner and Alger, 1978) . . .

A Classical Strategy

A Grand Strategy

Philip and his young son, Alexander, had very *clear goals*. They sought to rid Macedonia of influence by the Greek city-states and to *establish dominance* over what was then essentially northern Greece. They also wanted Athens to *join a coalition* with them against Persia on their eastern flank. *Assessing their resources,* they *decided to avoid* the overwhelming superiority of the Athenian fleet and *chose to forgo* attack on the powerful walled cities of Athens and Thebes where their superbly trained phalanxes and cavalry would not *have distinct advantages.*

Philip and Alexander *used an indirect approach* when an invitation by the Amphictyonic Council brought their army south to punish Amphissa. In a *planned sequence of actions and deceptive manoeuvres,* they cut away from a direct line of march to Amphissa, *bypassed the enemy,* and *fortified a key base,* Elatea. They then took steps to *weaken their opponents politically and morally* by pressing restoration of the Phoenician communities earlier dispersed by the Thebans and by having Philip declared a champion of the Delphic gods. Then *using misleading messages* to make the enemy believe they had moved north to Thrace and also *using developed intelligence sources,* the Macedonians, in a *suprise attack,* annihilated the Greeks' positions near Amphissa. This *lured their opponents away from their defensive positions* in the nearby mountain passes to *consolidate their forces* near the town of Chaeronea.

There, *assessing the relative strengths* of their opponents, the Macedonians first *attempted to negotiate* to achieve their goals. When this was unsuccessful they had a *well-developed contingency plan* on how to *attack and overwhelm* the Greeks. Prior to this time of course, the Macedonians had *organized* their troops into the famed phalanxes, and had *developed the full logistics* needed for their field support including a longer spear, which helped the Macedonian phalanxes penetrate the solid shield wall of the heavily massed Greek formations. *Using the natural advantages* of their grassy terrain, the Macedonians had developed cavalry support for their phalanxes' movements far beyond the Greek capability. Finally, using a *relative advantage* – the *command structure* their hierarchical *social system* allowed – against the more democratic Greeks, the

Macedonian nobles had *trained their personnel* into one of the most *disciplined and highly motivated forces* in the world.

The Battle Strategy

Supporting this was the battle strategy at Chaeronea, which emerged as follows. Philip and Alexander first *analyzed their specific strengths and weaknesses and their opponents' current alignments and probable moves*. The Macedonian strength lay in their new spear technology, the *mobility* of their superbly disciplined phalanxes and the powerful cavalry units led by Alexander. Their weaknesses were that they were badly outnumbered and faced – in the Athenians and the Theban Band – some of the finest foot troops in the world. However, their opponents had two weak points. One was the Greek left flank with lightly armed local troops placed near the Chaeronean Acropolis and next to some more heavily armed but hastily assembled hoplites bridging to the strong centre held by the Athenians. The famed Theban Band anchored the Greek right wing near a swamp on the Cephissus River [see Figure 1].

Philip and Alexander *organized their leadership to command key positions;*

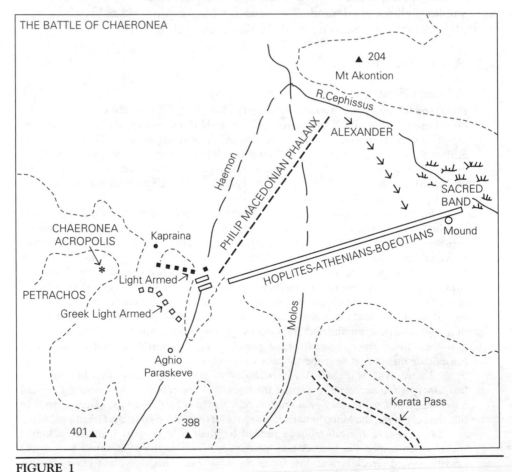

FIGURE 1

The Battle of Chaeronea

Source: Modified with permission from P. Green, *Alexander the Great*. (New York: Praeger 1970).

Philip took over the right wing and Alexander the cavalry. They *aligned their forces into a unique posture* which *used their strengths* and *offset their weaknesses.* They decided on those spots at which they would *concentrate their forces,* what *positions to concede,* and what *key points* they *must take and hold.* Starting with their units angled back from the Greek lines (see Figure), they developed a *focused major thrust* against the Greek left wing and *attacked their opponents' weakness* – the troops near Chaeronea–with the most disciplined of the Macedonian units, the guards' brigade. After building up pressure and stretching the Greek line to its left, the guards' brigade abruptly began a *planned withdrawal.* This *feint* caused the Greek left to break ranks and rush forward, believing the Macedonians to be in full retreat. This *stretched the opponents' resources* as the Greek centre moved left to *maintain contact* with its flank and to attack the 'fleeing' Macedonians.

Then *with predetermined timing,* Alexander's cavalry *attacked the exposure of* the stretched line at the same moment Philip's phalanxes *re-formed as planned* on the high ground at the edge of the Heamon River. Alexander *broke through* and *formed a bridgehead* behind the Greeks. He *refocused his forces against a segment* of the opponents' line; his cavalry *surrounded and destroyed* the Theban Band as the *overwhelming power* of the phalanxes poured through the gap he had created. From its *secured position,* the Macedonian left flank then turned an *attacked the flank* of the Athenians. With the help of Philip's *planned counterattack,* the Macedonians *expanded their dominance and overwhelmed the critical target,* i.e. the Greek centre . . . .

Modern Analogies

Similar concepts have continued to dominate the modern era of formal strategic thought. As this period begins, Scharnhorst still points to the need to *analyze social forces and structures* as a basis for *understanding effective command styles* and *motivational stimuli* (Von Clausewitz, 1976: 8). Frederick the Great proved this point in the field. Presumably based on such analyses, he adopted *training, discipline* and *fast manoeuvres* as the central concepts for a tightly disciplined German culture which had to be constantly ready to fight on two fronts (Phillips, 1940). Von Bülow (1806) continued to emphasize the dominant strategic roles of *geographical positioning* and *logistical support systems* in strategy. Both Jomini (1971) and Von Bülow (1806) stressed the concepts of *concentration, points of domination* and *rapidity of movement* as central strategic themes, and even tried to develop them into mathematically precise principles for their time.

Still later, Von Clausewitz expounded on the paramountcy of *clear major objectives* in war and on developing war strategies as a component of the nation's *broader goals* with *time horizons* extending beyond the war itself. Within this context he postulated that an effective strategy should be focused around a relatively *few central principles,* which can *create, guide and maintain dominance* despite the enormous frictions that occur as one tries to position or manoeuvre large forces in war. Among these he included many of the concepts operant in Macedonian times: *spirit or morale, suprise, cunning, concentration in space, dominance of selected positions, use of strategic reserves, unification over time, tension and release,* and so on. He showed how these broad principles applied to a number of specific attack, defence, flanking and retreat situations; but he always stressed the intangible of *leadership.* His basic positioning and organizational principles were to be mixed with boldness, perseverance and genius. He constantly emphasized – as did Napoleon – the need for *planned flexibility* once the battle was joined.

Later strategic analysts adapted these classic themes for larger-scale conflicts. Von Schlieffen linked together the huge numerical and production *strengths* of Germany and the vast *manoeuvring capabilities* of Flanders fields to pull the nation's might together conceptually behind a *unique alignment of forces* ('a giant hayrake'), which would *outflank* his French opponents, *attack weaknesses* (their supply lines and rear), capture and *hold key political centres* of France, and *dominate or destroy* its weakened army in the field (Tuchman, 1962). On the other side, Foch and Grandmaison saw *morale* ('élan'), *nerve* ('cran') and continuous *concentrated attack* ('attaque à outrance') as *matching the values* of a volatile, recently defeated and vengeful French nation, which had decided (for both moral and *coalition* reasons) to *set important limits* on its own actions in World War I – that is, not to attack first or through Belgium.

As these two strategies lost shape and became the head-on slaughter of trench warfare, Hart (1954) revitalized the *indirect approach*, and this became a central theme of British strategic thinking between the wars. Later in the United States, Martloff and Snell (1953) began to stress planning for *large-scale coalitions* as the giant forces of World War II developed. The Enigma group *moved secretly to develop the intelligence network* that was so crucial in the war's outcome (W. Stevenson, 1976). But once engaged in war, George Marshall still saw the only hope for Allied victory in *concentrating overwhelming forces* against one enemy (Germany) first, then after *conceding early losses* in the Pacific, *refocusing Allied forces* in a gigantic *sequential coordinated movement* against Japan. In the eastern theatre, MacArthur first *fell back, consolidated a base* for operations, *built up his logistics, avoided his opponent's strengths, bypassed* Japan's established defensive positions, and in a *gigantic flanking manoeuvre* was ready to invade Japan after *softening its political and psychological will* through saturation bombing (James, 1970).

All these modern thinkers and practitioners utilized classical principles of strategy dating back to the Greek era, but perhaps the most startling analogies of World War II lay in Patton's and Rommel's battle strategies, which were almost carbon copies of the Macedonians' concepts of planned concentration, rapid breakthrough, encirclement and attack on the enemy's rear (Essame, 1974; Farago, 1964; Young, 1974; Irving, 1977).

Similar concepts still pervade well-conceived strategies – whether they are government, diplomatic, military, sports or business strategies. What could be more direct than the parallel between Chaeronea and a well-developed business strategy which first probes and withdraws to determine opponents' strengths, forces opponents to stretch their commitments, then concentrates resources, attacks a clear exposure, overwhelms a selected market segment, builds a bridgehead in that market, and then regroups and expands from that base to dominate a wider field? Many companies have followed just such strategies with great success . . . .

DIMENSIONS OF STRATEGY

Analysis of military-diplomatic strategies and similar analogies in other fields provides some essential insights into the basic dimensions, nature and design of formal strategies.

First, effective formal strategies contain three essential elements: (1) the most important *goals* (or objectives) to be achieved, (2) the most significant *policies* guiding or limiting actions, and (3) the major *action sequences* (or programmes) that are to accomplish the defined goals within the limits set. Since strategy determines the overall direction and action focus of the organization, its formulation cannot be regarded as the mere generation and alignment of programmes to meet predetermined goals. Goal development is an integral part of strategy formulation . . . .

Second, effective strategies develop around a *few key concepts and thrusts,* which give them cohesion, balance and focus. Some thrusts are temporary; others are carrid through to the end of the strategy. Some cost more per unit gain than others. Yet resources must be *allocated in patterns* that provide sufficient resources for each thrust to succeed regardless of its relative cost/gain ratio. And organizational units must be coordinated and actions controlled to support the intended thrust pattern or else the total strategy will fail . . . .

Third, strategy deals not just with the unpredictable but also with the *unknowable.* For major enterprise strategies, no analyst could predict the precise ways in which all impinging forces could interact with each other, be distorted by nature or human emotions, or be modified by the imaginations and purposeful counteractions of intelligent opponents (Braybrooke and Lindblom, 1963). Many have noted how large-scale systems can respond quite counterintuitively (Forrester, 1971) to apparently rational actions, or how a seemingly bizarre series of events can conspire to prevent or assist success (Lindblom, 1959; White, 1978) . . . .

Consequently, the essence of strategy – whether military, diplomatic, business, sports, (or) political . . . – is to *build a posture* that is so strong (and potentially flexible) in selective ways that the organization can achieve its goals despite the unforeseeable ways external forces may actually interact when the time comes.

Fourth, just as military organizations have multiple echelons of grand, theatre, area, battle, infantry and artillery strategies, so should other complex organizations have a number of hierarchically related and mutually supporting strategies (Vancil and Lorange, 1975; Vancil, 1976). Each such strategy must be more or less complete in itself, congruent with the level of decentralization intended. Yet each must be shaped as a cohesive element of higher-level strategies. Although, for reasons cited, achieving total cohesion among all a major organization's strategies would be a superhuman task for any chief executive officer, it is important that there be a systematic means for testing each component strategy and seeing that it fulfils the major tenets of a well-formed strategy.

The criteria derived from military-diplomatic strategies provide an excellent framework for this, yet too often one sees purported formal strategies at all organizational levels that are not strategies at all. Because they ignore or violate even the most basic strategic principles, they are little more than aggregates of philosophies or agglomerations of programmes. They lack the cohesiveness, flexibility, thrust, sense of positioning against intelligent opposition and other criteria that historical analysis suggests effective strategies must contain. Whether formally or incrementally derived, strategies should be at least intellectually tested against the proper criteria.

Criteria for Effective Strategy

In devising a strategy to deal with the unknowable, what factors should one consider? Although each strategic situation is unique, are there some common criteria that tend to define a good strategy? The fact that a strategy worked in retrospect is not a sufficient criterion for judging any strategy. Was Grant really a greater strategist than Lee? Was Foch's strategy better than Von Schlieffen's? Was Xerxes's strategy superior to that of Leonidas? Was it the Russians' strategy that allowed them to roll over the Czechoslovaks in 1968? Clearly other factors than strategy – including luck, overwhelming resources, superb or stupid implementation and enemy errors – help determine ultimate results. Besides, at the time one formulates a strategy, one cannot use the criterion of ultimate success because the outcome is still in doubt. Yet one clearly needs some guidelines to define an effective strategic structure.

A few studies have suggested some initial criteria for evaluating a strategy (Tilles, 1963; Christensen *et al.*, 1978). These include its clarity, motivational impact, internal consistency, compatibility with the environment, appropriateness in light of resources, degree of risk, match to the personal values of key figures, time horizon and workability .... In addition, historical examples, from both business and military-diplomatic settings, suggest that effective strategies should at a minimum encompass certain other critical factors and structural elements ....

- *Clear, decisive objectives:* Are all efforts directed towards clearly understood, decisive and attainable overall goals? Specific goals of subordinate units may change in the heat of campaigns or competition, but the overriding goals of the strategy for all units must remain clear enough to provide continuity and cohesion for tactical choices during the time horizon of the strategy. All goals need not be written down or numerically precise, but they must be understood and be decisive – that, is if they are achieved, they should ensure the continued viability and vitality of the entity *via-à-vis* its opponents.

- *Maintaining the initiative:* Does the strategy preserve freedom of action and enhance commitment? Does it set the pace and determine the course of events rather than reacting to them? A prolonged reactive posture breeds unrest, lowers morale and surrenders the advantage of timing and intangibles to opponents. Ultimately, such a posture increases costs, decreases the number of options available and lowers the probability of achieving sufficient success to ensure independence and continuity.

- *Concentration:* Does the strategy concentrate superior power at the place and time likely to be decisive? Has the strategy defined precisely what will make the enterprise superior in power – that is, 'best' in critical dimensions – in relation to its opponents. A distinctive competency yields greater success with fewer resources and is the essential basis for higher gains (or profits) than competitors ....

- *Flexibility:* Has the strategy purposely built in resource buffers and dimensions for flexibility and manoeuvre? Reserved capabilities, planned manoeuvrability and repositioning allow one to use minimum resources while keeping opponents at a relative disadvantage. As corollaries of concentration and concession, they permit the strategist to re-use the same forces to overwhelm selected positions at different times. They also force less flexible opponents to use more resources to hold predetermined positions, while simultaneously requiring minimum fixed commitment of one's own resources for defensive purposes.

- *Coordinated and committed leadership:* Does the strategy provide responsible, committed leadership for each of its major goals? . . . [Leaders] must be so chosen and motivated that their own interests and values match the needs of their roles. Successful strategies require commitment, not just acceptance.

- *Surprise:* Has the strategy made use of speed, secrecy and intelligence to attack exposed or unprepared opponents at unexpected times? With surprise and correct timing, success can be achieved out of all proportion to the energy exerted and can decisively change strategic positions . . . .

- *Security:* Does the strategy secure resource bases and all vital operating points for the enterprise? Does it develop an effective intelligence system sufficient to prevent surprises by opponents? Does it develop the full logistics to support each of its major thrusts? Does it use coalitions effectively to extend the resource base and zones of friendly acceptance for the enterprise? . . .

These are critical elements of strategy, whether in business, government or warfare.

• FIVE Ps FOR STRATEGY*

HENRY MINTZBERG

Human nature insist on *a* definition for every concept. But the word *strategy* has long been used implicitly in different ways even if it has traditionally been defined in only one. Explicit recognition of multiple definitions can help people to manoeuvre through this difficult field. Accordingly, five definitions of strategy are presented here – as plan, ploy, pattern, position and perspective – and some of their interrelationships are then considered.

STRATEGY AS PLAN

To almost anyone you care to ask, **strategy is a plan** – some sort of *consciously intended* course of action, a guideline (or set of guidelines) to deal with a situation. A kid has a 'strategy' to get over a fence, a corporation has one to capture a market. By this definition, strategies have two essential characteristics: they are made in advance of the actions to which they apply, and they are developed consciously and

*Originally published in the *California Management Review* (Fall, 1987). © 1987 by the Regents of the University of California. Reprinted with deletions by permission of the *California Management Review*.

purposefully. A host of definitions in a variety of fields reinforce this view. For example:

- *In the military:* Strategy is concerned with 'draft[ing] the plan of war ... shap[ing] the individual campaigns and within these, decid[ing] on the individual engagements' (Von Clausewitz, 1976: 77).

- *In Game Theory:* Strategy is 'a complete plan: a plan which specifies what choices [the player] will make in every possible situation' (von Newman and Morgenstern, 1944: 79).

- *In management:* 'Strategy is a unified, comprehensive, and integrated plan ... designed to ensure that the basic objectives of the enterprise are achieved' (Glueck, 1980: 9).

As plans, strategies may be general or they can be specific. There is one use of the word in the specific sense that should be identified here. As plan, **a strategy can be a ploy,** too, really just a specific 'manoeuvre' intended to outwit an opponent or competitor. The kid may use the fence as a ploy to draw a bully into his yard, where his Doberman pinscher awaits intruders. Likewise, a corporation may threaten to expand plant capacity to discourage a competitor from building a new plant. Here the real strategy (as plan, that is, the real intention) is the threat, not the expansion itself, and as such is a ploy.

In fact, there is a growing literature in the field of strategic management, as well as on the general process of bargaining, that views strategy in this way and so focuses attention on its most dynamic and competitive aspects. For example, in his popular book, *Competitive Strategy,* Porter (1980) devotes one chapter to 'Market signals' (including discussion of the effects of announcing moves, the use of 'the fighting brand', and the use of threats of private antitrust suits) and another to 'Competitive Moves' (including actions to pre-empt competitive response). And Schelling (1980) devotes much of his famous book, *The Strategy of Conflict,* to the topic of ploys to outwit rivals in a competitive or bargaining situation.

STRATEGY AS PATTERN

But if strategies can be intended (whether as general plans or specific ploys), surely they can also be realized. In other words, defining strategy as a plan is not sufficient; we also need a definition that encompasses the resulting behaviour. Thus a third definition is proposed: **strategy is a pattern** – specifically, a pattern in a stream of actions (Mintzberg and Waters, 1985). By this definition, when Picasso painted in blue for a time, that was a strategy, just as was the behaviour of the Ford Motor Company when Henry Ford offered his Model T only in black. In other words, by this definition, strategy is *consistency* in behaviour, *whether or not* intended.

This may sound like a strange definition for a word that has been so bound up with free will ('strategos' in Greek, the art of the army general[1]). But the fact of

---

[1] Evered (1983) discusses the Greek origins of the word and traces its entry into contemporary Western vocabulary through the military.

tho matter is that while haidly anyone defines strategy in this way, many people seem at one time or another to so use it. Consider this quotation from a business executive: 'Gradually the successful approaches merge into a pattern of action that becomes our strategy. We certainly don't have an overall strategy on this' (quoted in Quinn, 1980: 35). This comment is inconsistent only if we restrict ourselves to one definition of strategy: what this man seems to be saying is that his firm has strategy as pattern, but not as plan. Or consider this comment in *Business Week* on a joint venture between General Motors and Toyota:

> The tentative Toyota deal may be most significant because it is another example of how GM's strategy boils down to doing a little bit of everything until the market decides where it is going. (*Business Week,* 31 October 1983)

A journalist has inferred a pattern in the behaviour of a corporation and labelled it strategy.

The point is that every time a journalist imputes a strategy to a corporation or to a government, and every time a manager does the same thing to a competitor or even to the senior management of his own firm, they are implicitly defining strategy as pattern in action – that is, inferring consistency in behaviour and labelling it strategy. They may, of course, go further and impute intention to that consistency – that is, assume there is a plan behind the pattern. But that is an assumption, which may prove false.

Thus, the definitions of strategy as plan and pattern can be quite independent of each other: plans may go unrealized, while patterns may appear without preconception. To paraphrase Hayek, strategies may result from human actions but not human designs (see Malone, 1976–7). If we label the first definition *intended* strategy and the second *realized* strategy, as shown in Figure 2, then we can distinguish *deliberate* strategies, where intentions that existed previously were realized, from

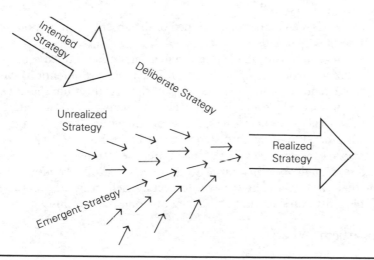

FIGURE 2
Deliberate and emergent strategies

Table 1   Various Kinds of Strategies, from Rather Deliberate to Mostly Emergent*

Planned Strategy: Precise intentions are formulated and articulated by a central leadership, and backed up by formal controls to ensure their surprise-free implementation in an environment that is benign, controllable or predictable (to ensure no distortion of intentions); these strategies are highly deliberate.

Entrepreneurial Strategy: Intentions exist as the personal, unarticulated vision of a single leader, and so are adaptable to new opportunities; the organization is under the personal control of the leader and located in a protected niche in its environment; these strategies are relatively deliberate but can emerge too.

Ideological Strategy: Intentions exist as the collective vision of all the members of the organization, controlled through strong shared norms; the organization is often proactive *vis-à-vis* its environment; these strategies are rather deliberate.

Umbrella Strategy: A leadership in partial control of organizational actions defines strategic targets or boundaries within which others must act (for example, that all new products be high priced and at the technological cutting edge, although what these actual products are to be is left to emerge); as a result, strategies are partly deliberate (the boundaries) and partly emergent (the patterns within them); this strategy can also be called deliberately emergent, in that this leadership purposefully allows others the flexibility to manoeuvre and form patterns within the boundaries.

Process Strategy: The leadership controls the process aspects of strategy (who gets hired and so gets a chance to influence strategy, what structures they work within, etc.), leaving the actual content of strategy to others; strategies are again partly deliberate (concerning process) and partly emergent (concerning content), and deliberately emergent.

Disconnected Strategy: Members or subunits loosely coupled to the rest of the organization produce patterns in the streams of their own actions in the absence of, or in direct contradiction to the central or common intentions of the organization at large; the strategies can be deliberate for those who make them.

Consensus Strategy: Through mutual adjustment, various members converge on patterns that pervade the organization in the absence of central or common intentions; these strategies are rather emergent in nature.

Imposed Strategy: The external environment dictates patterns in actions, either through direct imposition (say, by an outside owner or by a strong customer) or through implicitly pre-empting or bounding organizational choice (as in a large airline that must fly jumbo jets to remain viable); these strategies are organizationally emergent, although they may be internalized and made deliberate.

* Adapted from Mintzberg and Waters (1985: 270).

emergent strategies, where patterns developed in the absence of intentions, or despite them (which went *unrealized*).

For a strategy to be truly deliberate – that is, for a pattern to have been intended *exactly* as realized – would seem to be a tall order. Precise intentions would have had to be stated in advance by the leadership of the organization; these would have had to be accepted as is by everyone else, and then realized with no interference by market, technological or political forces, and so on. Likewise, a truly emergent strategy is again a tall order, requiring consistency in action without any hint of intention. (No consistency means *no* strategy, or at least unrealized strategy). Yet some strategies do come close enough to either form, while others – probably most – sit on the continuum that exists between the two, reflecting deliberate as well as emergent aspects. Table 1 lists various kinds of strategies along this continuum.

Strategies About What?

Labelling strategies as plans or patterns still begs one basic question: *Strategies about what?* Many writers respond by discussing the deployment of resources, but the question remains: Which resources and for what purposes? An army may plan to reduce the number of nails in its shoes, or a corporation may realize a pattern of marketing only products painted black, but these hardly meet the lofty label 'strategy'. Or do they?

As the word has been handed down from the military, 'strategy' refers to the important things, 'tactics' to the details (more formally, 'tactics teaches the use of armed forces in the engagement, strategy the use of engagements for the object of the war'; von Clausewitz, 1976: 128). Nails in shoes, colours of cars; these are certainly details. The problem is that in retrospect details can sometimes prove 'strategic'. Even in the military: 'For want of a Nail, the Shoe was lost; for want of a Shoe the Horse was lost . . .', and so on through the rider and general to the battle, 'all for want of Care about a Horseshoe Nail' (Franklin, 1977: 280). Indeed, one of the reasons Henry Ford lost his war with General Motors was that he refused to paint his cars anything but black.

Rumelt (1979) notes that 'one person's strategies are another's tactics – that what is strategic depends on where you sit'. It also depend on *when* you sit; what seems tactical today may prove strategic tomorrow. The point is that labels should not be used to imply that some issues are *inevitably* more important than others. There are times when it pays to manage the details and let the strategies emerge for themselves. Thus there is good reason to refer to issues are more or less 'strategic', in other words, more or less 'important' in some context, whether as intended before acting or as realized after it. Accordingly, the answer to the question, strategy about what, is: potentially about anything. About products and processes, customers and citizens, social responsibilities and self-interests, control and colour.

Two aspects of the content of strategies must, however, be singled out because they are of particular importance.

STRATEGY AS POSITION

The fourth definition is that **strategy is a position** – specifically, a means of locating an organization in what organization theorists like to call an 'environment'. By this definition, strategy becomes the mediating force – or 'match', according to Hofer and Schendel (1978: 4) – between organization and environment, that is, between the internal and the external context. In ecological terms, strategy becomes a 'niche'; in economic terms, a place that generates 'rent' (that is 'returns to [being] in a "unique" place' (Bowman, 1974: 47); in management terms, formally, a product-market 'domain' (J.D. Thompson, 1967), the place in the environment where resources are concentrated.

Note that this definition of strategy can be compatible with either (or all) of the preceding ones; a position can be pre-selected and aspired to through a plan (or ploy) and/or it can be reached, perhaps even found, through a pattern of behaviour.

In military and game theory views of strategy, it is generally used in the context of what is called a 'two-person game', better known in business as head-on competition (where ploys are especially common). The definition of strategy as position, however, implicitly allows us to open up the concept, to so-called *n*-person games (that is, many players), and beyond. In other words, while position can always be defined with respect to a single competitor (literally so in the military, where position becomes the site of battle), it can also be considered in the context of a large number of competitors or simply with respect to markets or an environment at large. But strategy as position can extend beyond competition too, economic and otherwise. Indeed, what is the meaning of the word 'niche' but a position that is occupied to *avoid* competition? Thus, we can move from the definition employed by General Ulysses Grant in the 1860s, 'Strategy [is] the deployment of one's resources in a manner which is most likely to defeat the enemy', to that of Professor Richard Rumelt in the 1980s, 'Strategy is creating situations for economic rents and finding ways to sustain them',[2] that is, any viable position, whether or not directly competitive.

Astley and Fombrun (1983), in fact, take the next logical step by introducing the notion of 'collective' strategy, that is, strategy pursued to promote cooperation between organizations, even would-be competitors (equivalent in biology to animals herding together for protection). Such strategies can range 'from informal arrangements and discussions to formal devices such as interlocking directorates, joint ventures, and mergers' (p. 577). In fact, considered from a slightly different angle, these can sometimes be described as *political* strategies, that is strategies to subvert the legitimate forces of competition.

STRATEGY AS PERSPECTIVE

While the fourth definition of strategy looks out, seeking to locate the organization in the external environment, and down to concrete positions, the fifth looks inside the organization, indeed inside the heads of the collective strategist, but up to a broader view. Here, **strategy is a perspective,** its content consisting not just of a chosen position, but of an ingrained way of perceiving the world. There are organizations that favour marketing and build a whole ideology around that (an IBM); Hewlett-Packard has developed the 'H-P way', based on its engineering culture, while McDonald's has become famous for its emphasis on 'quality, service, cleanliness and value'.

Strategy in this respect is to the organization what personality is to the individual. Indeed, one of the earliest and most influential writers on strategy (at least as his ideas have been reflected in more popular writings) was Philip Selznick (1957: 47), who wrote about the 'character' of an organization – distinct and integrated 'commitments to ways of acting and responding' that are built right into it. A variety of concepts from other fields also capture this notion; anthropologists refer to the 'culture' of a society and sociologists to its 'ideology'; military theorists write of the 'grand strategy' of armies while management theorists have used terms such as the 'theory of the business' and its 'driving force' (Drucker, 1974; Tregoe and Zimmerman, 1980); and Germans perhaps capture it best with their word *Weltanschauung*, literally 'worldview', meaning collective intuition about how the world works.

This fifth definition suggests above all that strategy is a *concept*. This has one important implication, namely, that all strategies are abstractions which exist only in the minds of interested parties. It is important to remember that no one has ever

---

[2] Expressed at the Strategic Management Society Conference, Montreal, October 1982.

seen a strategy or touched one; every strategy is an invention, a figment of someone's imagination, whether conceived of as intentions to regulate behaviour before it takes place or inferred as patterns to describe behaviour that has already occurred.

What is of key importance about this fifth definition, however, is that the perspective is *shared*. As implied in the words *Weltanschauung*, culture and ideology (with respect to a society), but not the word personality, strategy is a perspective shared by the members of an organization, through their intentions and/or by their actions. In effect, when we are talking of strategy in this context, we are entering the realm of the *collective mind* – individuals united by common thinking and/or behaviour. A major issue in the study of strategy formation becomes, therefore, how to read that collective mind – to understand how intentions diffuse through the system called organization to become shared and how actions come to be exercised on a collective yet consistent basis.

INTERRELATING THE Ps

As suggested above, strategy as both position and perspective can be compatible with strategy as plan and/or pattern. But, in fact, the relationships between these different definitions can be more involved than that. For example, while some consider perspective to *be* a plan (Lapierre (1980) writes of strategies as 'dreams in search of reality'), others describe it as *giving rise* to plans (for example, as positions and/or patterns in some kind of implicit hierarchy). But the concept of emergent strategy is that a pattern can emerge and be recognized so that it gives rise to a formal plan, perhaps within an overall perspective.

We may ask how perspective arises in the first place. Probably through earlier experiences: the organization tried various things in its formative years and gradually consolidated a perspective around what worked. In other words, organizations would appar to develop 'character' much as people develop personality – by interacting with the world as they find it through the use of their innate skills and natural propensities. Thus pattern can give rise to perspective too. And so can position. Witness Perrow's (1970: 161) discussion of the 'wool men' and 'silk men' of the textile trade, people who developed an almost religious dedication to the fibers they produced.

No matter how they appear, however, there is reason to believe that while plans and positions may be dispensable, perspectives are immutable (Brunsson, 1982). In other words, once they are established, perspectives become difficult to change. Indeed, a perspective may become so deeply ingrained in the behaviour of an organization that the associated beliefs can become subconscious in the minds of its members. When that happens, perspective can come to look more like pattern than like plan – in other works, it can be found more in the consistency of behaviours than in the articulation of intentions.

Of course, if perspective is immutable, then change in plan and position within perspective is easy compared to change outside perspective. In this regard, it is interesting to take up the case of Egg McMuffin. Was this product when new – the American breakfast in a bun – a strategic change for the McDonald's fast-food chain? Posed in MBA classes, this earth-shattering (or at least stomach-shattering) question inevitably evokes heated debate. Proponents (usually people sympathetic to fast food) argue that of course it was: it brought McDonald's into a new market, the breakfast one, extending the use of existing facilities. Opponents retort that this is nonsense; nothing changed but a few ingredients: this was the same old pap in a new package. Both sides are, of course, right – and wrong. It simply depends on how you define strategy. Position changed; perspective remained the same. Indeed – and this is the point – the position could be changed easily because it was compatible with the existing perspective. Egg McMuffin is pure McDonald's, not only in product and package, but also in production and propagation. But imagine a change of position at McDonald's that would require a change of perspective – say, to introduce candlelight dining with personal service (your McDuckling à l'Orange cooked to order) to capture the late evening market. We needn't say more, except perhaps to label this the 'Egg McMuffin syndrome'.

THE NEED FOR ECLECTICISM IN DEFINITION

While various relationships exist among the different definitions, no one relationship, nor any single definition for that matter, takes precedence over the others. In some ways, these definitions compete (in that they can substitute for each other), but in perhaps more important ways, they complement. Not all plans become patterns, nor are all patterns that develop planned; some ploys are less than positions, while other strategies are more than positions yet less than perspectives. Each definition adds important elements to our understanding of strategy, indeed encourages us to address fundamental questions about organizations in general.

As plan, strategy deals with how leaders try to establish direction for organizations, to set them on predetermined courses of action. Strategy as plan also raises the fundamental issue of cognition – how intentions are conceived in the human brain in the first place, indeed, what intentions really mean. The road to hell in this field can be paved with those who take all stated intentions at face value. In studying strategy as plan, we must somehow get into the mind of the strategist, to find out what is really intended.

As ploy, strategy takes us into the realm of direct competition, where threats and feints and various other manoeuvres are employed to gain advantage. This places the process of strategy formation in its most dynamic setting, with moves provoking countermoves and so on. Yet ironically, strategy itself is a concept rooted not in change but in stability – in set plans and established patterns. How then to reconcile the dynamic notions of strategy as ploy with the static ones of strategy as pattern and other forms of plan?

As pattern, strategy focuses on action, reminding us that the concept is an empty one if it does not take behaviour into account. Strategy as pattern also introduces the notion of convergence, the achievement of consistency in an organization's behaviour. How does this consistency form, where does it come from? Realized strategy, when considered alongside intended strategy, encourages us to consider the notion that strategies can emerge as well as be deliberately imposed.

As position, strategy encourages us to look at organizations in their competitive environments – how they find their positions and protect them in order to meet competition, avoid it or subvert it. This enables us to think of organizations in ecological terms, as organisms in niches that struggle for survival in a world of hostility and uncertainty as well as symbiosis.

And finally as perspective, strategy raises intriguing questions about intention and behaviour in a collective context. If we define organization as collective action in the pursuit of common mission (a fancy way of saying that a group of people under a common label – whether a General Motors or a Luigi's Body Shop – somehow find the means to cooperate in the production of specific goods and services), then strategy as perspective raises the issue of how intentions diffuse through a group of people to become shared as norms and values, and how patterns of behaviour become deeply ingrained in the group.

Thus, strategy is not just a notion of how to deal with an enemy or a set of competitors or a market, as it is treated in so much of the literature and in its popular usage. It also draws us into some of the most fundamental issues about organizations as instruments for collective perception and action.

To conclude, a good deal of the confusion in this field stems from contradictory and ill-defined uses of the term strategy. By explicating and using various definitions, we may be able to avoid some of this confusion, and thereby enrich our ability to understand and manage the processes by which strategies form.

CHAPTER

2

THE STRATEGIST

Every conventional strategy or policy textbook focuses on the job of the general manager as a main ingredient in understanding the process of strategy formation. The discussion of emergent strategy in the last chapter suggests that we do not take such a narrow view of the strategist. Anyone in the organization who happens to control key or precedent setting actions can be a strategist; the strategist can be a collection of people as well. Nevertheless, managers – especially senior general managers – are obviously prime candidates for such a role because their perspective is generally broader than any of their subordinates and because so much power naturally resides with them. Hence we focus in this chapter on the general manager as strategist.

We present three readings that describe the work of the manager. The one by Mintzberg challenges the conventional view of the manager as planner, organizer, coordinator and controller. The point is not that managers do not do these things; it is that these words are too vague to capture the daily reality of managerial work. The image presented in this article is a very different one; a job characterized by pressure, interruption, orientation to action, oral rather than written communication and working with outsiders and colleagues as much as with so-called subordinates. While the issue is not addressed at this point in any detail, one evident and important conclusion is that managers who work in such ways cannot possibly function as traditionally depicted strategists supposedly do – as leaders directing their organizations the way conductors direct their orchestras (at least the way it looks on the podium). We shall develop this point further in Chapter 4, when we consider how strategies really form in organizations.

The article by Gary Hamel of the London Business School and C.K. Prahalad of the University of Michigan presents a view of the management role that is consistent with the military analogy of strategy in Quinn's article in the preceding chapter. The challenge of building global leadership, according to Hamel and Prahalad, is to embed the ambition for such leadership throughout the company, and to create 'an obsession with winning', which will energize the collective action of all employees. The manager's role is to build such an ambition, to help people develop faith in their own ability to deliver on tough goals, to motivate them to do so and to channel their energies into a step-by-step progression that they compare with 'running the marathon in 400-metre sprints'.

The last reading in this section is by Peter Senge of MIT. Senge views the ability to learn as the primary source of a company's competitive advantage and argues that facilitating organizational learning is the principal task of the strategist. Like Hamel and Prahalad, Senge sees a long-term vision as the key source of tension in the organization and, therefore, of energy in the learning process. The manager must be the designer, the teacher and the steward of the learning organization and, to play these roles, he or she must develop a new set of skills, which Senge describes in the article.

How do you reconcile these different views on the role of the strategist? At one level, perhaps you do not need a grand theory that integrates across all of them. There are different kinds of managers, different beliefs and styles, and different kinds of authors, and different lenses capture different aspects of managerial work. Some of you may also observe many similarities in the roles and tasks of the strategist described in the three readings, despite the very different languages the authors use. You may, for instance, think about how the advocacies of Hamel and Prahalad and Senge relate to the nine managerial roles Mintzberg describes. And you may like to carry over the debate to later sessions, testing these views against the roles played by senior managers in some of the cases you will discuss.

● THE MANAGER'S JOB: FOLKLORE AND FACT*

HENRY MINTZBERG

If you ask managers what they do, they will most likely tell you that they plan, organize, coordinate and control. Then watch what they do. Don't be surprised if you can't relate what you see to these four words.

When they are called and told that one of their factories has just burned down, and they advise the caller to see whether temporary arrangements can be made to supply customers through a foreign subsidiary, are they planning, organizing, coordinating or controlling? How about when they present a gold watch to a retiring employee? Or when they attend a conference to meet people in the trade? Or on

*Originally published in the *Harvard Business Review* (July–August 1975) and winner of the McKinsey prize for the best article in the *Review* in 1975. Copyright © 1975 by the President and Fellows of Harvard College: all rights reserved. Reprinted with deletions by permission of the *Harvard Business Review*.

returning from that conference, when they tell one of their employees about an interesting product idea they picked up there?

The fact is that these four words, which have dominated management vocabulary since the French industrialist Henri Fayol first introduced them in 1916, tell us little about what managers actually do. At best, they indicate some vague objectives managers have when they work.

My intention in this article is simple: to break the reader away from Fayol's words and introduce him or her to a more supportable, and what I believe to be a more useful, description of managerial work. This description derives from my review and synthesis of the available research on how various managers have spent their time.

In some studies, managers were observed intensively ('shadowed' is the term some of them used); in a number of others, they kept detailed diaries of their activities; in a few studies, their records were analyzed. All kinds of managers were studied – foremen, factory supervisors, staff managers, field sales managers, hospital administrators, presidents of companies and nations, and even street gang leaders. These 'managers' worked in the United State, Canada, Sweden and Great Britain.

A synthesis of these findings paints an interesting picture, one as different from Fayol's classical view as a cubist abstract is from a Renaissance painting. In a sense, this picture will be obvious to anyone who has ever spent a day in a manager's office, either in front of the desk or behind it. Yet, as the same time, this picture may turn out to be revolutionary, in that it throws into doubt so much of the folklore that we have accepted about the manager's work.

I first discuss some of this folklore and contrast it with some of the findings of systematic research – the hard facts about how managers spend their time. Then I synthesize those research findings in a description of ten roles that seem to describe the essential content of all managers' jobs. In a concluding section, I discuss a number of implications of this synthesis for those trying to achieve more effective management.

SOME FOLKLORE AND FACTS ABOUT MANAGERIAL WORK

There are four myths about the manager's job that do not bear up under careful scrutiny of the facts.

Folklore: The manager is a reflective, systematic planner. The evidence on this issue is overwhelming, but not a shred of it supports this statement.

Fact: Study after study has shown that managers work at an unrelenting pace, that their activities are characterized by brevity, variety and discontinuity, and that they are strongly oriented to action and dislike reflective activities. Consider this evidence:

- Half the activities engaged in by the five [American] chief executives [that I studied in my own research (Mintzberg, 1973a)] lasted less than 9 minutes, and only 10 per cent exceeded 1 hour. A study of 56 US foremen found that they averaged 583 activities per 8-hour shift, an average of 1 every 48 seconds (Guest, 1956: 478). The workpace for both chief executives and foremen was unrelenting. The chief executives met a steady stream of callers and mail from the moment they arrived in the morning until they left in the evening. Coffee breaks and lunches were inevitably work-related, and ever-present subordinates seemed to usurp any free moment.

- A diary study of 160 British middle and top managers found that they worked for a half hour or more without interruption only about once every two days (Stewart, 1967).

- Of the verbal contacts of the chief executives in my study, 93 per cent were arranged on an *ad hoc* basis. Only 1 per cent of the executives' time was spent in open-ended observational tours. Only 1 out of 368 verbal contacts was unrelated to a specific issue and could be called general planning. Another researcher finds that 'in *not one single case* did a manager report the obtaining of important external information from a general conversation or other undirected personal communication' (Aguilar, 1967: 102).

- No study has found important patterns in the way managers schedule their time. They seem to jump from issue to issue, continually responding to the needs of the moment.

Is this the planner that the classical view describes? Hardly. How, then, can we explain their behaviour? The manager is simply responding to the pressures of the job. I found that my chief executives terminated many of their own activities, often leaving meetings before the end and interrupted their desk work to call in subordinates. One president not only placed his desk so that he could look down a long hallway but also left his door open when he was alone – an invitation for subordinates to come in and interrupt him.

Clearly, these managers wanted to encourage the flow of current information. But more significantly, they seemed to be conditioned by their own workloads. They appreciated the opportunity cost of their own time, and they were continually aware of their ever-present obligations – mail to be answered, caller to attend to, and so on. It seems that no matter what he or she is doing, the manager is plagued by the possibilities of what he or she might do and must do.

When the manager must plan, he or she seems to do so implicitly in the context of daily actions, not in some abstract process reserved for two weeks in the organization's mountain retreat. The plans of the chief executives I studied seemed to exist only in their heads, as flexible, but often specific, intentions. The traditional literature notwithstanding, the job of managing does not breed reflective planners; the manager is a real-time responder to stimuli, an individual who is conditioned by his or her job to prefer live to delayed action.

Folklore: The effective manager has no regular duties to perform. Managers are constantly being told to spend more time planning and delegating, and less time seeing customers and engaging in negotiations. These are not, after all, the true tasks of the manager. To use the popular analogy, the good manager, like the good conductor, carefully orchestrates everything in advance, then sits back to enjoy the fruits of his or her labour, responding occasionally to an unforeseeable exception . . ..

Fact: In addition to handling exceptions, managerial work involves performing a number of regular duties, including ritual and ceremony, negotiations and processing of soft information that links the organization with its environment. Consider some evidence from the research studies:

- A study of the work of the presidents of small companies found that they engaged in routine activities because their companies could not afford staff specialists and were so thin on operating personnel that a single absence often required the president to substitute (Choran, in Mintzberg, 1973).

- One study of field sales managers and another of chief executives suggest that it is a natural part of both jobs to see important customers, assuming the manager wish to keep those customers (Davis, 1957: Copeman, 1963).

- Someone, only half in jest, once described the manager as that person who sees visitors so that everyone else can get his or her work done. In my study, I found that certain ceremonial duties – meeting visiting dignitaries, giving out gold watches, presiding at Christmas dinners – were an intrinsic part of the chief executive's job.

- Studies of managers' information flow suggest that managers play a key role in securing 'soft' external information (much of it available only to them because of their status) and in passing it along to their subordinates.

Folklore: The senior manager needs aggregated information, which a formal management information system best provides. In keeping with the classical view of the manager as that individual perched on the apex of a regulated, hierarchical system, the literature's manager was to receive all important information from a giant, comprehensive MIS.

But this never proved true at all. A look at how managers actually process information makes the reason quite clear. Managers have five media at their command – documents, telephone calls, scheduled and unscheduled meetings and observational tours.

Fact: Managers strongly favour the verbal media – namely, telephone calls and meetings. The evidence comes from every single study of managerial work. Consider the following:

- In two British studies, managers spent an average of 66 per cent and 80 per cent of their time in verbal (oral) communication (Burns, 1954: Stewart, 1967). In my study of five American chief executives, the figure was 78 per cent.

- These five chief executives treated mail processing as a burden to be dispensed with. One came in Saturday morning to process 142 pieces of mail in just over 3 hours, to 'get rid of all the stuff'. This same manager looked at the first piece of 'hard' mail he had received all week, a standard cost report, and put it aside with the comment, 'I never look at this'.

- These same five chief executives responded immediately to 2 of the 40 routine reports they received during the five weeks of my study and to four items in the 104 periodicals. They skimmed most of these periodicals in seconds almost ritualistically. In all, these chief executives of good-sized organizations initiated on their own – that is, not in response to something else – a grand total of 25 pieces of mail during the 25 days I observed them.

An analysis of the mail the executives received reveals an interesting picture – only 13 per cent was of specific and immediate use. So now we have another piece in the puzzle: not much of the mail provides live, current information – the action of a competitor, the mood of a government legislator, or the rating of last night's television show. Yet this is the information that drove the managers, interrupting their meetings and rescheduling their workdays.

Consider another interesting finding. Managers seem to cherish 'soft' information, especially gossip, hearsay and speculation. Why? The reason is its timeliness: today's gossip may be tomorrow's fact. The manager who is not accessible for the telephone call informing him or her that the firm's biggest customer was seen golfing with its main competitor may read about a dramatic drop in sales in the next quarterly report. But then it's too late.

Consider the words of Richard Neustadt, who studied the information-collecting habits of Presidents Roosevelt, Truman and Eisenhower:

> It is not information of a general sort that helps a President see personal stakes; not summaries, not surveys, not the *bland amalgams*. Rather ... it is the odds and ends of *tangible detail* that pieced together in his mind illuminate the underside of issues put before him. To help himself he must reach out as widely as he can for every scrap of fact, opinion, gossip, bearing on his interests and relationships as President. He must become his own director of his own central intelligence. (1960: 153–4; italics added)

The manager's emphasis on the verbal media raises two important points:

First, verbal information is stored in the brains of people. Only when people write this information down can it be stored in the files of the organization – whether in metal cabinets or on magnetic tape – and managers apparently do not write down much of what they hear. Thus the strategic data bank of the organization is not in the memory of its computers but in the minds of its managers.

Second, the managers' extensive use of verbal media helps to explain why they are reluctant to delegate tasks. When we note that most of the managers' important information comes in verbal form and is stored in their heads, we can well appreciate their reluctance. It is not as if they can hand a dossier over to someone; they must take the time to 'dump memory' – to tell that someone all they know about the subject. But this could take so long that the managers may find it easier to do the task themselves. Thus the managers are damned by their own information systems to a 'dilemma of delegation' – to do too much themselves or to delegate to their subordinates with inadequate briefing.

Folklore: Management is, or at last is quickly becoming, a science and a profession. By almost any definitions of *science* and *profession,* this statement is false. Brief observation of any manager will quickly lay to rest the notion that managers practise a science. A science involves the enaction of systematic, analytically determined procedures or programmes. If we do not even know what procedures managers use, how can we prescribe them by scientific analysis? And how can we call management a profession if we cannot specify what managers are to learn?

Fact: The managers' programmes – to schedule time, process information, make decisions, and so one – remain locked deep inside their brains. Thus, to describe these programmes, we rely on words like *judgement* and *intuition,* seldom stopping to realize that they are merely labels for our ignorance.

I was struck during my study by the fact that the executives I was observing – all very competent by any standard – are fundamentally indistinguishable from their counterparts of a hundred years ago (or a thousand years ago, for that matter). The information they need differs, but they seek it in the same way – by word of mouth. Their decisions concern modern technology, but the procedures they use to make them are the same as the procedures of the nineteenth-century manager. In fact, the manager is in a kind of loop, with increasingly heavy work pressures but no aid forthcoming from management science.

Considering the facts about managerial work, we can see that the manager's job is enormously complicated and difficult. The manager is overburdened with obligations; yet he or she cannot easily delegate tasks. As a result, he or she is driven to overwork and is forced to do many tasks superficially. Brevity, fragmentation and verbal communication characterize the work. Yet these are the very characteristics of managerial work that have impeded scientific attempts to improve it. As a result, the management scientists have concentrated their efforts on the specialized functions of the organization, where they could more easily analyze the procedures and quantify the relevant information. Thus the first step in providing managers with some help is to find out what their job really is.

BACK TO A BASIC DESCRIPTION OF MANAGERIAL WORK

Now let us try to put some of the pieces of this puzzle together. Earlier, I defined the manager as that person in charge of an organization or one of its subunits. Besides chief executive officers, this definition would include vice-presidents, bishops, foremen, hockey coaches and prime ministers. Can all these people have anything in common? Indeed they can. For an important starting point, all are vested with formal authority over an organizational unit. From formal authority comes status, which leads to various interpersonal relations, and from these comes access to information. Information, in turn, enables the manager to make decisions and strategies for his or her unit.

The manager's job can be described in terms of various 'roles', or organized sets of behaviours identified with a position. My description, shown in Figure 1, comprises ten roles.

Interpersonal Roles

Three of the manager's roles arise directly from formal authority and involve basic interpersonal relationships.

1. First is the *figurehead* role. By virtue of his or her position as head of an organizational unit, every manager must perform some duties of a ceremonial nature. The president greets the touring dignitaries, the foreman attends the wedding of a lathe operator and the sales manager takes an important customer to lunch.

The chief executives of my study spend 12 per cent of their contact time on ceremonial duties: 17 per cent of their incoming mail dealt with acknowledgements and requests related to their status. For example, a letter to a company president requested free merchandise for a crippled school child; diplomas were put on the desk of the school superintendent for his signature.

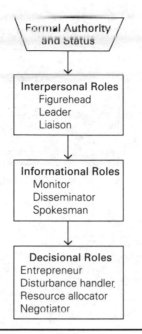

FIGURE 1
The manager's roles

Duties that involve interpersonal roles may sometimes be routine, involving little serious communication and no important decision-making. Nevertheless, they are important to the smooth functioning of an organization and cannot be ignored by the manager.

2. Because he or she is in charge of an organizational unit, the manager is responsible for the work of the people of that unit. His or her actions in this regard constitute the *leader* role. Some of these actions involve leadership directly – for example, in most organizations the manager is normally responsible for hiring and training his or her own staff.

In addition, there is the indirect exercise of the leader role. Every manager must motivate and encourage his or her employees, somehow reconciling their individual needs with the goals of the organization. In virtually every contact the manager has with these employees, subordinates seeking leadership clues probe his or her actions: 'Does he approve?' 'How would she like the report to turn out?' 'Is he more interested in market share than high profits?'

The influence of managers is most clearly seen in the leader role. Formal authority vests them with great potential power; leadership determines in large part how much of it they will realize.

3. The literature of management has always recognized the leader role, particularly those aspects of it related to motivation. In comparison, until recently it has hardly mentioned the *liaison* role, in which the manager makes contacts outside his or her vertical chain of command. This is remarkable in light of the finding of virtually every study of managerial work that managers spend as much time with peers and other people outside their units as they do with their own subordinates – and,

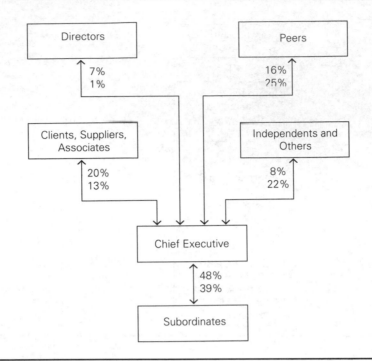

FIGURE 2
The Chief executives' contacts

surprisingly, very little time with their own superiors (generally on the order of 45 per cent, 45 per cent and 10 per cent respectively).

The contacts the five CEOs made were with an incredibly wide range of people: subordinates; clients, business associates and suppliers; and peers – managers of similar organizations, government and trade organization officials, fellow directors on outside boards and independents with no relevant organizational affiliations. The chief executives' time with and mail from these groups is shown in Figure 2.

As we shall see shortly, the manager cultivates such contacts largely to find information. In effect, the liaison role is devoted to building up the manager's own external information system – informal, private, verbal, but, nevertheless, effective.

Informational Roles

By virtue of their interpersonal contacts, both with subordinates and with their network of contacts, managers emerge as the nerve centres of their organizational units. They may not know everything, but they typically know more than any other member of their unit.

Studies have shown this relationship to hold for all managers, from street gange leaders to US presidents. In *The Human Group,* George C. Homans (1950) explains how, because they were at the centre of the information flow in their own gangs and were also in close touch with other gang leaders, street gang leaders were better informed than any of their followers. And Richard Neustadt describes the following account from his study of Franklin D. Roosevelt:

> The essence of Roosevelt's technique for information-gathering was competition. 'He would call you in,' one of his aides once told me, 'and he'd ask you to get the story on some complicated business, and you'd come back after a couple of days of hard labour and present the juicy morsel you'd uncovered under a stone somewhere, and *then* you'd find out he knew all about it, along with something else you *didn't* know. Where he got his information from he wouldn't mention, usually, but after he had done this to you once or twice you got damn careful about *your* information.' (1960: 157)

We can see where Roosevelt 'got this information' when we consider the relationship between the interpersonal and informational roles. As leaders, managers have formal and easy access to every member of their units. Hence, as noted earlier, they tend to know more about their own unit than anyone else does. In addition, their liaison contacts expose the managers to external information to which their subordinates often lack access. Many of these contacts are with other managers of equal status, who are themselves nerve centres in their own organization. In this way managers develop powerful databases of information.

The processing of information is a key part of the manager's job. In my study, the chief executives spent 40 per cent of their contact time on activities devoted exclusively to the transmission of information; 70 per cent of their incoming mail was purely informational (as opposed to requests for action). The manager does not leave meetings or hang up the telephone in order to get back to work. In large part, communication *is* his or her work. Three roles describe these informational aspects of managerial work.

4.　As *monitor,* the manager perpetually scans the environment for information, interrogates his or her liaison contacts and subordinates, and receives unsolicited information, much of it as a result of the network of personal contacts he or she has developed. Remember that a good part of the information the manager collects in the monitor role arrives in verbal form, often as gossip, hearsay and speculation. By virtue of his or her contacts, the manager has a natural advantage in collecting this soft information.

5.　Managers must share and distribute much of this information. Information gleaned from outside personal contacts may be needed within the unit. In their *disseminator* roles, managers pass some of their privileged information directly to their subordinates, who would otherwise have no access to it. When their subordinates lack easy contact with one another, managers will sometimes pass information from one to another.

6.　In their *spokesperson* roles, managers send some of their information to people outside their units – a president makes a speech to lobby for an organization cause, or a foreman suggests a product modification to a supplier. In addition, as part of their roles as spokesperson, every manager must inform and satisfy the influential people who control his or her organizational unit. Chief executives especially may spend great amounts of time with hosts of influencers. Directors and shareholders must be advised about financial performance; consumer groups must be assured that the organization is fulfilling its social responsibilities, and so on.

Decisional Roles

Information is not, of course, an end in itself; it is the basic input to decision-making. One thing is clear in the study of managerial work: managers play the major role in their unit's decision-making system. As its formal authority, only they can commit the unit to important new courses of action; and as its nerve centre, only they have full and current information to make the set of decisions that determine the unit's strategy. Four roles describe the manager as decision-maker:

7.   As *entrepreneur*, the manager seeks to improve the unit, to adapt it to changing conditions in the environment. In the monitor role, the president is constantly on the lookout for new ideas. when a good one appears, he or she initiates a development project that he or she may supervise himself or delegate to an employee (perhaps with the stipulation that he or she must approve the final proposal).

There are two interesting features about these development projects at the chief executive level. First, these projects do not involve single decisions or even unified clusters of decisions. Rather, they emerge as a series of small decisions and actions sequenced over time. Apparently, chief executives prolong each project so that they can fit it bit by bit into their busy, disjointed schedules and so that they can gradually come to comprehend the issue, if it is a complex one.

Second, the chief executives I studied supervised as many as 50 of these projects at the same time. Some projects entailed new products or processes; others involved public relations campaigns, improvement of the cash position, reorganization of a weak department, resolution of a morale problem in a foreign division, integration of computer operations, various acquisitions at different stages of development, and so on.

The chief executive appears to maintain a kind of inventory of the development projects that he or she supervises – projects that are at various stages of development, some active and some in limbo. Like a juggler, he or she keeps a number of projects in the air; periodically, one comes down, is given a new burst of energy, and is sent back into orbit. At various intervals, he or she puts new projects on-stream and discards old ones.

8.   While the entrepreneur role describes the manager as the voluntary initiator of change, the *disturbance handler* role depicts the manager involuntarily responding to pressures. Here change is beyond the manager's control. A strike looms, a major customer has gone bankrupt, or a supplier reneges on his contract.

It has been fashionable, I noted earlier, to compare the manager to an orchestra conductor, just as Peter F. Drucker wrote in *The Practice of Management*:

> The manager has the task of creating a true whole that is larger than the sum of its parts, a productive entity that turns out more than the sum of the resources put into it. One analogy is the conductor of a symphony orchestra, through whose effort, vision and leadership individual instrumental parts that are so much noise by themselves become the living whole of music. But the conductor has the composer's score: he is only interpreter. The manager is both composer and conductor. (1954: 341–2)

Now consider the words of Leonard R. Sayles, who has carried out systematic research on the manager's job:

> [The manager] is like a symphony orchestra conductor, endeavouring to maintain a melodious performance in which the contributions of the various instruments are coordinated and sequenced, patterned and paced, while the orchestra members are having various personal difficulties, stage hands are moving music stands, alternating excessive heat and cold are creating audience and instrument problems, and the sponsor of the concert is insisting on irrational changes in the program. (1964: 162)

In effect, every manager must spend a good part of his or her time responding to high-pressure disturbances. No organization can be so well run, so standardized, that it has considered every contingency in advance. Disturbances arise not only because poor managers ignore situations until they reach crisis proportions, but also because good managers cannot possibly anticipate all the consequences of the actions they take.

9.   The third decisional role is that of *resource allocater*. To the manager falls the responsibility of deciding who will get what in his or her organizational unit. Perhaps the most important resource the manager allocates is his or her own time. Access to the manager constitutes exposure to the unit's nerve centre and decision-maker. The manager is also charged with designing the unit's structure, that pattern of formal relationships that determines how work is to be divided and coordinated.

Also, in his or her role as resource allocater, the manager authorizes the important decisions of the unit before they are implemented. By retaining this power, the manager can ensure that decisions are interrelated; all must pass through a single brain. To fragment this power is to encourage discontinuous decision-making and a disjoined strategy.

10.   The final decisional role is that of *negotiator*. Studies of managerial work at all levels indicate that managers spend considerable time in negotiations: the president of the football team is called in to work out a contract with the holdout superstar; the corporation president leads her company's contingent to negotiate a new stock issue; the foreman argues a grievance problem to its conclusion with the shop steward. As Leonard Sayles puts it, negotiations are a 'way of life' for the sophisticated manager.

These negotiations are duties of the manager's job; perhaps routine, they are not to be shirked. They are an integral part of the job, for only the manager has the authority to commit organizational resources in 'real time', and only he or she has the nerve centre information that important negotiations require.

The Integrated Job

It should be clear by now that the ten roles I have been describing are not easily separable. In the terminology of the psychologist, they form a Gestalt, an integrated whole. No role can be pulled out of the framework and the job be left intact. For example, a manager without liaison contacts lacks external information. As a result, he or she can neither disseminate the information employees need nor make decisions that adequately reflect external conditions. (In fact, this is a problem for the new person in a managerial position, since he or she cannot make effective decisions until he or she has built up his network of contacts.)

To say that the ten roles form a Gestalt is not to say that all managers give equal attention to each role. In fact, I found in my review of the various research studies that

> ... sales managers seem to spend relatively more of their time in the interpersonal roles, presumably a reflection of the extrovert nature of the marketing activity;
> ... production managers give relatively more attention to the decisional roles, presumably a reflection of their concern with efficient work flow;
> ... staff managers spend the most time in the informational roles, since they are experts who manage departments that advise other parts of the organization.

Nevertheless, in all cases the interpersonal, informational, and decisional roles remain inseparable.

CONCLUSION

No job is more vital to our society than that of the manager. It is the manager who determines whether our social institutions serve us well or whether they squander our talents and resources. It is time to strip away the folklore about managerial work, and time to study it realistically so that we can begin the difficult task of making significant improvements in its performance.

● STRATEGIC INTENT*

BY Gary Hamel and C.K. Prahalad

Today managers in many industries are working hard to match the competitive advantages of their new global rivals. They are moving manufacturing offshore in search of lower labour costs, rationalizing product lines to capture global scale conomies, instituting quality circles and just-in-time production, and adopting Japanese human resource practices. When competitiveness still seems out of reach, they form strategic alliances – often with the very companies that upset the competitive balance in the first place.

Important as these initiatives are, few of them go beyond mere imitation .... For these executives and their companies, regaining competitiveness will mean rethinking many of the basic concepts of strategy .... The new global competitors approach strategy from a perspective that is fundamentally different from that which underpins western management thought ....

Companies that have risen to global leadership over the past 20 years invariably began with ambitions that were out of all proportion to their resources and capabilities. But they created an obsession with winning at all levels of the organization and then sustained that obsession over the 10- to 20-year quest for global leadership. We term this obsession 'strategic intent'.

*Originally published in *Harvard Business Review* (May–June 1989). Copyright © 1989 by the President and Fellows of Harvard College: all rights reserved. Reprinted with deletions by permission of the *Harvard Business Review*.

On the one hand, strategic intent envisions a desired leadership position and establishes the criterion the organization will use to chart its progress. Komatsu set out to 'Encircle Caterpillar'. Canon sought to 'Beat Xerox'. Honda strove to become a second Ford – an automotive pioneer. All are expressions of strategic intent.

At the same time, strategic intent is more than simply unfettered ambition. (Many companies possess an ambitious strategic intent yet fall short of their goals.) The concept also encompasses an active management process that includes: focusing the organization's attention on the essence of winning; motivating people by communicating the value of the target; leaving room for individual and team contributions; sustaining enthusiasm by providing new operational definitions as circumstances change; and using intent consistently to guide resource allocations.

Strategic intent captures the essence of winning. The Apollo programme – landing a man on the moon ahead of the Soviets – was as competitively focused as Komatsu's drive against Caterpillar. The space programme became the scorecard for America's technology race with the USSR . . . . For Coca-Cola, strategic intent has been to put a Coke within 'arm's reach' of every consumer in the world.

Strategic intent is stable over time. In battles for global leadership, one of the most critical tasks is to lengthen the organization's attention span. Strategic intent provides consistency to short-term action, while leaving room for reinterpretation as new opportunities emerge . . . .

Strategic intent sets a target that deserves personal effort and commitment. Ask the chairmen of many American corporations how they measure their contributions to their companies' success and you're likely to get an answer expressed in terms of shareholder wealth. In a company that possesses a strategic intent, top management is more likely to talk in terms of global market leadership. Market share leadership typically yields shareholder wealth, to be sure. But the two goals do not have the same motivational impact. It is hard to imagine middle managers, let alone blue-collar employees, waking up each day with the sole thought of creating more shareholder wealth. But mightn't they feel different given the challenge to 'Beat Benz' – the rallying cry at one Japanese car producer? Strategic intent gives employees the only goal that is worthy of commitment: to unseat the best or remain the best, worldwide . . . .

Just as you cannot plan a 10- to 20-year quest for global leadership, the chance of falling into a leadership position by accident is also remote. We don't believe that global leadership comes from an undirected process of intrapreneurship. Nor is it the product of a skunkworks or other techniques for internal venturing. Behind such programme lies a nihilistic assumption: the organization is so hidebound, so orthodox-ridden, that the only way to innovate is to put a few bright people in a dark room, pour in some money and hope that something wonderful will happen. In this 'Silicon Valley' approach to innovation, the only role for top managers is to retrofit their corporate strategy to the entrepreneurial successes that emerge from below. Here the value-added of top management is low indeed . . . .

In companies that overcame resource constraints to build leadership positions, we see a different relationship between means and ends. While strategic intent is clear about ends, it is flexible as to means – it leaves room for improvization. Achieving strategic intent requires enormous creativity with respect to means . . . . But this creativity comes in the service of a clearly prescribed end. Creativity is unbridled, but not uncorralled, because top management establishes the criterion against which employees can pre-test the logic of their initiatives. Middle managers must do more than deliver on promised financial targets; they must also deliver on the broad direction implicit in their organization's strategic intent.

Strategic intent implies a sizeable stretch for an organization. Current capabilities and resources will not suffice. This forces the organization to be more inventive, to make the most of limited resources. Whereas the traditional view of strategy focuses on the degree of fit between existing resources and current opportunities, strategic intent creates an extreme misfit between resources and ambitions. Top management then challenges the organization to close the gap by systematically building new advantages. For Canon this meant first understanding Xerox's patents, then licensing technology to create a product that would yield early market experience, then gearing up internal R&D efforts, then licensing its own technology to other manufacturers to fund further R&D, then entering market segments in Japan and Europe where Xerox was weak, and so on.

In this respect, strategic intent is like a marathon run in 400-metre sprints. No one knows what the terrain will look like at mile 26, so the role of top management is to focus the organization's attention on the ground to be covered in the next 400 metres. In several companies, management did this by presenting the organization with a series of corporate challenges, each specifying the next hill in the race to achieve strategic intent. One year the challenge might be quality, the next total customer care, the next entry into new markets, the next a rejuvenated product line. As this example indicates, corporate challenges are a way to stage the acquisition of new competitive advantages, a way to identify the focal point for employees' efforts in the near to medium term. As with strategic intent, top management is specific about the ends (reducing product development times by 75 per cent, for example) but less prescriptive about the means.

Like strategic intent, challenges stretch the organization. To pre-empt Xerox in the personal copier business, Canon set its engineers a target price of $1,000 for a home copier. At the time, Canon's least expensive copier sold for several thousand dollars . . .. Canon engineers were challenged to reinvent the copier – a challenge they met by substituting a disposable cartridge for the complex image-transfer mechanism used in other copiers . . . .

For a challenge to be effective, individuals and teams throughout the organization must understand it and see its implications for their own jobs. Companies that set corporate challenges to create new competitive advantages (as Ford and IBM did with quality improvement) quickly discover that engaging the entire organization requires top management to:

Create a sense of urgency, or quasi-crisis by amplifying weak signals in the environment which point up the need to improve, instead of allowing inaction to precipitate a real crisis . . . .

Develop a competitor focus at every level through widespread use of competitive intelligence. Every employee should be able to benchmark his or her efforts against best-in-class competitors so that the challenge becomes personal . . ..

Provide employees with the skills they need to work effectively – training in statistical tools, problem-solving, value engineering and team-building, for example.

Give the organization time to digest one challenge before launching another. When competing initiatives overload the organization, middle managers often try to protect their people from the whipsaw of shifting priorities. But this 'wait and see if they're serious this time' attitude ultimately destroys the credibility of corporate challenges.

Establish clear milestones and review mechanisms to track progress and ensure that internal recognition and rewards reinforce desired behaviour. The goal is to make the challenge inescapable for everyone in the company . . . .

However, direct labour costs in manufacturing accounted for less than 15 per cent of total value-added. The company thus succeeded in demoralizing its entire blue-collar workforce for the sake of a 1.5 per cent reduction in total costs. Ironically, further analysis showed that their competitors' most significant cost savings came not from lower hourly wages but from better work methods invented by employees. You can imagine how eager the US workers were to make similar contributions . . . at Nissan when the yen strengthened: top management took a big pay cut and then asked middle managers and line employees to sacrifice relatively less.

Reciprocal responsibility means shared gain and shared pain. In too many companies, the pain of revitalization falls almost exclusively on the employees least responsible for the enterprise's decline . . . . This one-sided approach to regaining competitiveness keeps many companies from harnessing the intellectual horsepower of their employees.

Creating a sense of reciprocal responsibility is crucial because competitiveness ultimately depends on the pace at which a company embeds new advantages deep within its organization, not on its stock of advantages at any given time. Thus we need to expand the concept of competitive advantage beyond the scorecard many managers now use: Are my costs lower? Will my product command a price premium?

Few competitive advantages are long-lasting. Uncovering a new competitive advantage is a bit like getting a hot tip on a stock: the first person to act on the insight makes more money than the last . . . .

Keeping score of existing advantages is not the same as building new advantages. The essence of strategy lies in creating tomorrow's competitive advantages faster than competitors mimic the ones you possess today. In the 1960s, Japanese producers relied on labour and capital cost advantages. As Western manufacturers began to move production offshore, Japanese companies accelerated their investment in process technology and created scale and quality advantages. Then as their US and European competitors rationalized manufacturing they added another string to their bow by accelerating the rate of product development. They they built global brands. Then they deskilled competitors through alliances and outsourcing deals. The moral? An organization's capacity to improve existing skills and learn new ones is the most defensible competitive advantage of all.

To achieve a strategic intent, a company must usually take on larger, better financed competitors. That means carefully managing competitive engagements so that scarce resources are conserved. Managers cannot do that simply by playing the same game better – making marginal improvements to competitors' technology and business practices. Instead, they must fundamentally change the game in ways that disadvantage incumbents – devising novel approaches to market entry, advantage building and competitive warfare. For smart competitors, the goal is not competitive imitation but competitive innovation, the art of containing competitive risks within manageable proportions.

Four approaches to competitive innovation are evident in the global expansion of Japanese companies. These are: building layers of advantage, searching for loose bricks, changing the terms of engagement and competing through collaboration.

The wider a company's portfolio of advantages, the less risk it faces in competitive battles. New global competitors have built such portfolios by steadily expanding their arsenals of competitive weapons. They have moved inexorably from less defensible advantages such as low wage costs to more defensible advantages like global brands . . . .

Another approach to competitive innovation – searching for loose bricks – exploits the benefits of surprise, which is just as useful in business battles as it is in war. Particularly in the early stages of a war for global markets, successful new competitors work to stay below the response threshold of their larger, more powerful rivals. Staking out underdefended territory is one way to do this.

To find loose bricks, managers must have few orthodoxies about how to break into a market or challenge a competitor . . . .

The search for loose bricks begins with a careful analysis of the competitor's conventional wisdom: How does the company define its 'served market'? What activities are most profitable? Which geographic markets are too troublesome to enter? The objective is not to find a corner of the industry (or niche) where larger competitors seldom tread but to build a base of attack just outside the market territory that industry leaders currently occupy. The goal is an uncontested profit sanctuary, which could be a particular product segment (the 'low end' in motorcycles), a slice of the value chain (components in the computer industry), or a particular geographic market (Eastern Europe) . . . .

Changing the terms of engagement – refusing to accept the front runner's definition of industry and segment boundaries – represents still another form of competitive innovation. Canon's entry into the copier business illustrates this approach . . . .

While Xerox built a wide range of copiers, Canon standardized machines and components to reduce costs. Canon chose to distribute through office-product dealers rather than try to match Xerox's huge direct sales force. It also avoided the need to create a national service network by designing reliability and serviceability into its product and then delegating service responsibility to the dealers. Canon copiers were sold rather than leased, freeing Canon from the burden of financing the lease base. Finally, instead of selling to the heads of corporate duplicating departments, Canon appealed to secretaries and department managers who wanted distributed copying. At each stage, Canon neatly sidestepped a potential barrier to entry . . . .

Competitive innovation works on the premise that a successful competitor is likely to be wedded to a 'recipe' for success. That's why the most effective weapon new competitors possess is probably a clean sheet of paper. And why an incumbent's greatest vulnerability is its belief in accepted practice.

Through licensing, outsourcing agreements and joint ventures, it is sometimes possible to win without fighting. For example, Fujitsu's alliances in Europe with Siemens and STC (Britain's largest computer maker) and in the United States with Amdahl yield manufacturing volume and access to Western markets .... In fighting larger global rivals by proxy, Japanese companies have adopted a maxim as old as human conflict itself: my enemy's enemy is my friend.

Hijacking the development efforts of potential rivals is another goal of competitive collaboration. In the consumer electronics war, Japanese competitors attacked traditional businesses like TVs and hi-fis while volunteering to manufacture 'next generation' products like VCRs, camcorders and compact disc players for Western rivals. They hoped their rivals would ratchet down development spending, and in most cases that is precisely what happened. But companies that abandoned their own development efforts seldom re-emerged as serious competitors in subsequent new product battles.

Collaboration can also be used to calibrate competitors' strengths and weaknesses. Toyota's joint venture with GM, and Mazda's with Ford, give these automakers an invaluable vantage point for assessing the progress their US rivals have made in cost reduction, quality and technology. They can also learn how GM and Ford compete – when they will fight and when they won't. Of course, the reverse is also true: Ford and GM have an equal opportunity to learn from their partner-competitors.

The route to competitive revitalization we have been mapping implies a new view of strategy. Strategic intent assures consistency in resource allocation over the long term. Clearly articulated corporate challenges focus the efforts of individuals in the medium term. Finally, competitive innovation helps reduce competitive risk in the short term. This consistency in the long term, focus in the medium term and inventiveness and involvement in the short term provide the key to leveraging limited resources in pursuit of ambitious goals ....

Business schools ... have perpetuated the notion that a manager with net present value calculations in one hand and portfolio planning in the other can manage any business anywhere.

In many diversified companies, top management evaluates line managers on numbers alone because no other basis for dialogue exists. Managers move so many times as part of their 'career development' that they often do not understand the nuances of the businesses they are managing. At GE, for example, one fast-track manager heading an important new venture had moved across five businesses in five years. His seris of quick successes finally came to an end when he confronted a Japanese competitor whose managers had been plodding along in the same business for more than a decade.

Regardless of ability and effort, fast-track managers are unlikely to develop the deep business knowledge they need to discuss technology options, competitors' strategies and global opportunities substantively. Invariably, therefore, discussions gravitate to 'the numbers', while the value-added of managers is limited to the financial and planning savvy they carry from job to job. Knowledge of the company's internal planning and accounting systems substitutes for substantive knowledge of the business, making competitive innovation unlikely.

When managers know that their assignments have a 2–3-year time frame, they feel great pressure to create a good track record fast. This pressure often takes one of two forms. Either the manager does not commit to goals whose time line extends beyond his or her expected tenure. Or ambitious goals are adopted and squeezed into an unrealistically short time frame. Aiming to be No. 1 in a business is the essence of strategic intent; but imposing a 3–4-year horizon on the effort simply invites disaster. Acquisitions are made with little attention to the problems of integration. The organization becomes overloaded with initiatives. Collaborative ventures are formed without adequate attention to competitive consequences.

Almost every strategic management theory and nearly every corporate planning system is premised on a strategy hierarchy in which corporate goals guide business unit strategies and business unit strategies guide functional tactics. In this hierarchy, senior management makes strategy and lower levels execute it. The dichotomy between formulation and implementation is familiar and widely accepted. But the strategy hierarchy undermines competitiveness by fostering an elitist view of management which tends to disenfranchise most of the organization. Employees fail to identify with corporate goals or involve themselves deeply in the work of becoming more competitive.

The strategy hierarchy isn't the only explanation for an elitist view of management, of course. The myths that grow up around successful top managers . . . perpetuate it. So does the turbulent business environment. Middle managers buffeted by circumstances that seem to be beyond their control desperately want to believe that top management has all the answers. And top management, in turn, hesitates to admit it does not for fear of demoralizing lower level employees . . . .

Unfortunately, a threat that everyone perceives but no one talks about creates more anxiety than a threat that has been clearly identified and made the focal point for the problem-solving efforts of the entire company. That is one reason honesty and humility on the part of top management may be the first prerequisite of revitalization. Another reason is the need to make participation more than a buzzword.

Programmes such as quality circles and total customer service often fall short of expectations because management does not recognize that successful implementation requires more than administrative structures. Difficulties in embedding new capabilities are typically put down to 'communication' problems, with the unstated assumption that if only downward communication were more effective – 'if only middle management would get the message straight' – the new programme would quickly take root. The need for upward communication is often ignored, or assumed to mean nothing more than feedback. In contrast, Japanese companies win, not because they have smarter managers, but because they have developed ways to harness the 'wisdom of the anthill'. They realize that top managers are a bit like the astronauts who circle the earth in the space shuttle. It may be the astronauts who get all the glory, but everyone knows that the real intelligence behind the mission is located firmly on the ground . . . .

Developing faith in the organization's ability to deliver on tough goals, motivating it to do so, focusing its attention long enough to internalize new capabilities – this is the real challenge for top management. Only by rising to this challenge will senior managers gain the courage they need to commit themselves and their companies to global leadership.

THE LEADER'S NEW WORK: BUILDING LEARNING ORGANIZATIONS*

PETER M. SENGE

Human beings are designed for learning. No one has to teach an infant to walk, or talk or master the spatial relationships needed to stack eight building blocks that don't topple. Children come fully equipped with an insatiable drive to explore and experiment. Unfortunately, the primary institutions of our society are oriented predominantly towards controlling rather than learning, rewarding individuals for performing for others rather than for cultivating their natural curiosity and impulse to learn. The young child entering school discovers quickly that the name of the game is getting the right answer and avoiding mistakes – a mandate no less compelling to the aspiring manager.

'Our prevailing system of management has destroyed our people', writes W. Edwards Deming, leader in the quality movement.[1]

> People are born with intrinsic motivation, self-esteem, dignity, curiosity to learn, joy in learning. The forces of destruction begin with toddlers – a prize for the best Halloween costume, grades in school, gold stars, and on up through the university. On the job, people, teams, divisions are ranked – reward for the one at the top, punishment at the bottom. MBO, quotas, incentive pay, business plans, put together separately, division by division, cause further loss, unknown and unknowable.

Ironically, by focusing on performing for someone else's approval, corporations create the very conditions that predestine them to mediocre performance. Over the long run, superior performance depends on superior learning. A Shell study showed that ... [the long-term] key to the survival [of the large industrial enterprise] was the ability to run 'experiments in the margin', continually to explore new business and organizational opportunities that create potential new sources of growth.[2]

If anything, the need for understanding how organizations learn and accelerating that learning is greater today than ever before. The old days when a Henry Ford, Alfred Sloan or Tom Watson *learned for the organization* are gone. In an increasingly dynamic, interdependent and unpredictable world, it is simply no longer possible for anyone to 'figure it all out at the top'. The old model, 'the top think and the local acts', must now give way to integrating thinking and acting at all levels ....

ADAPTIVE LEARNING AND GENERATIVE LEARNING

The prevailing view of learning organizations emphasizes increased adaptability.

But increasing adaptiveness is only the first stage in moving towards learning organizations. The impulse to learn in children goes deeper than desires to respond

*Originally published in *Sloan Management Review* 7 (Autumn 1990). Reprinted with deletions by permission of the *Review*.
[1] P. Senge, *The Fifth Discipline: The art and practice of the learning organization* (New York: Doubleday/Currency, 1990).
[2] A.P. de Geus, 'Planning as learning,' *Harvard Business Review,* March–April 1988, pp. 70–4.

and adapt more effectively to environmental change. The impulse to learn, at its heart, is an impulse to be generative, to expand our capability. This is why leading corporations are focusing on *generative* learning, which is about creating, as well as *adaptive* learning, which is about coping . . . .

Generative learning, unlike adaptive learning, requires new ways of looking at the world, whether in understanding customers or in understanding how to better manage a business. For years, US manufacturers sought competitive advantage in aggressive controls on inventories, incentives against overproduction and rigid adherence to production forecasts. Despite these incentives, their performance was eventually eclipsed by Japanese firms who saw the challenges of manufacturing differently. They realized that eliminating delays in the production process was the key to reducing instability and improving cost, productivity and service. They worked to build networks of relationships with trusted suppliers and to redesign physical production processes so as to reduce delays in materials procurement, production and in-process inventory – a much higher leverage approach to improving both cost and customer loyalty.

As Boston Consulting Group's George Stalk has observed, the Japanese saw the significance of delays because they saw the process of order entry, production scheduling, materials procurement, production and distribution *as an integrated system*. 'What distorts the system so badly is time', observed Stalk – the multiple delays between events and responses. 'These distortions reverberate throughout the system, producing disruptions, waste and inefficiency.'[3] Generative learning requires seeing the systems that control events. When we fail to grasp the systemic source of problems, we are left to 'push on' symptoms rather than eliminate underlying causes. The best we can ever do is adaptive learning.

THE LEADER'S NEW WORK

. . . Our traditional view of leaders – as special people who set the direction, make the key decisions and energize the troops – is deeply rooted in an individualistic and non-systemic worldview. Especially in the West, leaders are *heroes* – great men (and occasionally women) who rise to the fore in times of crisis. So long as such myths prevail, they reinforce a focus on short-term events and charismatic heroes rather than on systemic forces and collective learning.

Leadership in learning organizations centres on subtler and ultimately more important work. In a learning organization, leaders' roles differ dramatically from that of the charismatic decision-maker. Leaders are designers, teachers and stewards. These roles require new skills: the ability to build shared vision, to bring to the surface and challenge prevailing mental models and to foster more systemic patterns of thinking. In short, leaders in learning organizations are responsible for *building organizations* where people are continually expanding their capabilities to shape their future – that is, leaders are responsible for learning.

---

[3] G. Stalk Jr, 'Time: The next source of competitive advantage,' *Harvard Business Review*, July–August 1988, pp. 41–51.

CREATIVE TENSION: THE INTEGRATING PRINCIPLE

Leadership in a learning organization starts with the principle of creative tension.[4] Creative tension comes from seeing clearly where we want to be, our 'vision', and telling the truth about where we are, our 'current reality'. The gap between the two generates a natural tension. . . .

Creative tension can be resolved in two basic ways: by raising current reality towards the vision, or by lowering the vision towards current reality. Individuals, groups and organizations who learn how to work with creative tension learn how to use the energy it generates to move reality more reliably toward their visions . . . .

Without vision there is no creative tension. Creative tension cannot be generated from current reality alone. All the analysis in the world will never generate a vision. Many who are otherwise qualified to lead fail to do so because they try to substitute analysis for vision. They believe that, if only people understood current reality, they would surely feel the motivation to change. They are then disappointed to discover that people 'resist' the personal and organizational changes that must be made to alter reality. What they never grasp is that the natural energy for changing reality comes from holding a picture of what might be that is more important to people than what is.

But creative tension cannot be generated from vision alone; it demands an accurate picture of current reality as well. Just as [Martin Luther] King had a dream, so too did he continually strive to 'dramatize the shameful conditions' of racism and prejudice so that they could not longer be ignored. Vision without an understanding of current reality will more likely foster cynicism that creativity. The principle creative tension teaches that *an accurate picture of current reality is just as important as a compelling picture of a desired future*.

Leading through creative tension is different from solving problems. In problem-solving, the energy for change comes from attempting to get away from an aspect of current reality that is undesirable. With creative tension, the energy for change comes from the vision, from what we want to create, juxtaposed with current reality. While the distinction may seem small, the consequences are not. Many people and organizations find themselves motivated to change only when their problems are bad enough to cause them to change. This works for a while, but the change process runs out of steam as soon as the problems driving the change become less pressing. With problem-solving, the motivation for change is extrinsic. With creative tension, the motivation is intrinsic. This distinction mirrors the distinction between adaptive and generative learning.

NEW ROLES

The traditional authoritarian image of the leader as 'the boss calling the shots' has been recognized as oversimplified and inadequate for some time. According to Edgar Schein, 'Leadership is intertwined with culture formation.' Building an organization's culture and shaping its evolution is the 'unique and essential function' of leadership.[5]

---

[4] The principle of creative tension comes from Robert Fritz's work on creativity. See R. Fritz, *The Path of Least Resistance* (New York: Ballantine, 1989) and *Creating* (New York: Ballantine, 1990).
[5] E. Schein, *Organizational Culture and Leadership* (San Francisco: Jossey-Bass, 1985).

In a learning organization, the critical roles of leadership – designer, teacher and steward – have antecedents in the ways leaders have contributed to building organizations in the past. But each role takes on new meaning in the learning organization and, as will be seen ... demands new skills and tools.

Leader as Designer

Imagine that your organization is an ocean liner and that you are 'the leader'. What is your role?

I have asked this question of groups of managers many times. The most common answer, not surprisingly, is 'The captain'. Others say, 'The navigator, setting the direction'. Still others say, 'The helmsman, actually controlling the direction', or 'The engineer down there stoking the fire, providing energy' or 'The social director, making sure everybody's enrolled, involved and communicating'. While these are legitimate leadership roles, there is another which, in many ways, eclipses them all in importance. Yet rarely does anyone mention it.

The neglected leadership role is the *designer* of the ship. No one has a more sweeping influence than the designer. What good does it do for the captain to say, 'Turn starboard 30 degrees' when the designer has built a rudder that will only turn to port, or which takes 6 hours to turn to starboard? It's fruitless to be the leader in an organization that is poorly designed.

The functions of design, or what some have called 'social architecture', are rarely visible; they take place behind the scenes. The consequences that appear today are the result of work done long in the past, and work today will show its benefits far in the future. Those who aspire to lead out of a desire to control, or gain fame, or simply to be at the contre of the action, will find little to attract them to the quiet design work of leadership.

But what, specifically, is involved in organizational design? 'Organization design is widely misconstrued as moving around boxes and lines,' says Hanover [Insurance Company CEO, William] O'Brien. 'The first task of organization design concerns designing the governing ideas of purpose, vision and core values by which people will live.' Few acts of leadership have a more enduring impact on an organization than building a foundation of purpose and core values ....

If governing ideas constitute the first design task of leadership, the second design task involves the policies, strategies and structures that translate guiding ideas into business decisions. Leadership theorist Philip Selznick calls policy and structure the 'institutional embodiment of purpose'.[6] 'Policy-making (the rules that guide decisions) ought to be separated from decision-making,' says Jay Forrester.[7] 'Otherwise, short-term pressures will usurp time from policy creation.'

Traditionally, writers like Selznick and Forrester have tended to see policy-making and implementation as the work of a small number of senior managers. But that view is changing. Both the dynamic business environment and the mandate of the learning organization to engage people at all levels now make it clear that this

---

[6] P. Selznick, *Leadership Administration* (New York: Harper & Row, 1957).

[7] J.W. Forrester, 'A new corporate design,' *Sloan Management Review* (formerly *Industrial Management Review*), Autumn 1965, pp. 5–17.

second design task is more subtle. Henry Mintzberg has argued that strategy is less a rational plan arrived at in the abstract and implemented throughout the organization than an 'emergent phenomenon'. Successful organizations 'craft strategy' according to Mintzberg, as they continually learn about shifting business conditions and balance what is desired and what is possible.[8] The key is not getting the right strategy but fostering strategic thinking. 'The choice of individual is only part of ... the policy-maker's need,' according to Mason and Mitroff.[9] 'More important is the need to achieve insight into the nature of the complexity and to formulate concepts and world views for coping with it.'

Behind appropriate policies, strategies and structures are effective learning processes; their creation is the third key design responsibility in learning organizations. This does not absolve senior managers of their strategic responsibilities. Actually, it deepens and extends those responsibilities. Now, they are not only responsible for ensuring that an organization has well-developed strategies and policies, but also for ensuring that processes exist whereby these are continually improved.

In the early 1970s, Shell was the weakest of the big seven oil companies. Today, Shell and Exxon are arguably the strongest, both in size and financial health. Shell's ascendance began with frustration. Around 1971 members of Shell's 'Group Planning' in London began to foresee dramatic change and unpredictability in world oil markets. However, it proved impossible to persuade managers that the stable world of steady growth in oil demand and supply they had known for 20 years was about to change. Despite brilliant analysis and artful presentation, Shell's planners realized, in the words of Pierre Wack, that they 'had failed to change behavior in much of the Shell organization'.[10] Progress would probably have ended there, had the frustration not given way to a radically new view of corporate planning.

As they pondered this failure, the planners' view of their basic task shifted: 'We no longer saw our task as producing a documented view of the future business environment five or ten years ahead. Our real target was the microcosm (the "mental model") of our decision makers.' Only when the planners reconceptualized their basic task as fostering learning rather than devising plans did their insights begin to have an impact. The initial tool used was 'scenario analysis', through which planners encouraged operating managers to think through how they would manage in the future under different possible scenarios. In mattered not that the managers believed the planners' scenarios absolutely, only that they became engaged in ferreting out the implications. In this way, Shell's planners conditioned managers to be mentally prepared for a shift from low prices to high prices and from stability to instability. The results were significant. When OPEC became a reality, Shell quickly responded by increasing local operating company control (to enhance manoeuvrability in the new political environment), building buffer stocks and accelerating development of non-OPEC sources – actions that its competitors took much more slowly, or not at all.

Somewhat inadvertently, Shell planners had discovered the leverage of designing institutional learning processes, whereby, in the words of former planning director de Geus, 'Management teams change their shared mental models of their company,

---

[8] See, for example, H. Mintzbrtg, 'Crafting strategy,' *Harvard Business Review*, July–August 1987, pp. 66–75.
[9] R. Mason and I. Mitroff, *Challenging Strategic Planning Assumptions* (New York: John Wiley & Sons, 1981), p. 16.
[10] P. Wack, 'Scenarios: Uncharted waters ahead,' *Harvard Business Review*, September–October 1985, pp. 73–89.

their markets, and their competitors.'[11] Since then, 'planning as learning' has become a byword at Shell, and Group Planning has continually sought out new learning tools that can be integrated into the planning process. Some of these are described below.

Leader as Teacher

'The first responsibility of a leader', writes retired Herman Miller CEO Max de Pree, 'is to define reality.'[12] Much of the leverage leaders can actually exert lies in helping people achieve more accurate, more insightful and more *empowering* views of reality.

Leader as teacher does *not* mean leader as authoritarian expert whose job it is to teach people the 'correct' view of reality. Rather, it is about helping everyone in the organization, oneself included, to gain more insightful views of current reality. This is in line with a popular emerging view of leaders as coaches, guides or facilitators …. In learning organizations, this teaching role is developed further by virtue of explicit attention to people's mental models and by the influence of the systems perspective.

The role of leader as teacher starts with bringing to the surface people's mental models of important issues. No one carries an organization, a market or a state of technology in his or her head. What we carry in our heads are assumptions. These mental pictures of how the world works have a significant influence on how we perceive problems and opportunities, identify courses of action and make choices.

One reason that mental models are so deeply entrenched is that they are largely tacit. Ian Mitroff, in his study of General Motors, argues that an assumption that prevailed for years was that, in the United States, 'Cars are status symbols. Styling is therefore more important than quality.'[13] The Detroit carmakers didn't say, 'We have a *mental model* that all people care about is styling.' Few actual managers would even say publicly that all people care about is styling. So long as the view remained unexpressed, there was little possibility of challenging its validity or forming more accurate assumptions.

But working with mental models goes beyond revealing hidden assumptions. 'Reality,' as perceived by most people in most organizations, means pressures that must be borne, crises that must be reacted to and limitations that must be accepted. Leaders as teachers help people *restructure their views of reality* to see beyond the superficial conditions and events into the underlying causes of problems – and therefore to see new possibilities for shaping the future.

Specifically, leaders can influence people to view reality at three distinct levels: events, patterns of behaviour, and systemic structure.

Systemic Structure
(Generative)
↓

---

[11] de Geus (1988).

[12] M. de Pree, *Leadership is an Art* (New York: Doubleday, 1989), p. 9.

[13] I. Mitroff, *Break-Away Thinking* (New York: John Wiley & Sons, 1988), pp. 66–7.

Patterns of Behaviour
(Responsive)
↓
Events
(Reactive)

The key question becomes: *Where do leaders predominantly focus their own and their organization's attention?*

Contemporary society focuses predominantly on events. The media reinforces this perspective, with almost exclusive attention to short-term, dramatic events. This focus leads naturally to explaining what happens in terms of those events: 'The Dow Jones average went up 16 points because high fourth-quarter profits were announced yesterday.'

Pattern of behaviour explanations are rarer in contemporary culture than event explanations, but they do occur. 'Trend analysis' is an example of seeing patterns of behaviour. A good editorial that interprets a set of current events in the context of long-term historical changes is another example. Systemic, structural explanations go even further by addressing the question, 'What causes the patterns of behaviour?'

In some sense, all three levels of explanation are equally true. But their usefulness is quite different. Event explanations – who did what to whom – doom their holders to a reactive stance towards change. Pattern of behaviour explanations focus on identifying long-term trends and assessing their implications. They at least suggest how, over time, we can respond to shifting conditions. Structural explanations are the most powerful. Only they address the underlying causes of behaviour at a level such that patterns of behaviour can be changed.

By and large, leaders of our current institutions focus their attention on events and patterns of behaviour, and, under their influence, their organizations do likewise. That is why contemporary organizations are predominantly reactive, or at best responsive – rarely generative. On the other hand, leaders in learning organizations pay attention to all three levels, but focus especially on systemic structure; largely by example, they teach people throughout the organization to do likewise.

Leader as Steward

This is the subtlest role of leadership. Unlike the roles of designer and teacher, it is almost solely a matter of attitude. It is an attitude critical to learning organizations.

While stewardship has long been recognized as an aspect of leadership, its source is still not widely understood. I believe Robert Greenleaf came closest to explaining real stewardship, in his seminal book *Servant Leadership*.[14] There, Greenleaf argues that 'The servant leader *is* servant first . . . . It begins with the natural feeling that one wants to serve, to serve *first*. This conscious choice brings one to aspire to lead. That person is sharply different from one who is leader first, perhaps because of the need to assuage an unusual power drive or to acquire material possessions.'

---

[14] R.K. Greenleaf, *Servant Leadership: A journey into the nature of legitimate power and greatness* (New York: Paulisi Press, 1977).

Leaders' sense of stewardship operates on two levels: stewardship for the people they lead and stewardship for the larger purpose or mission that underlies the enterprise. The first type arises from a keen appreciation of the impact one's leadership can have on others. People can suffer economically, emotionally and spiritually under inept leadership. If anything, people in a learning organization are more vulnerable because of their commitment and sense of shared ownership. Appreciating this naturally instils a sense of responsibility in leaders. The second type of stewardship arises from a leader's sense of personal purpose and commitment to the organization's larger mission. People's natural impulse to learn is unleashed when they are engaged in an endeavour they consider worthy of their fullest commitment. Or, as Lawrence Miller puts it, 'Achieving return on equity does not, as a goal, mobilize the most noble forces of our soul.'[15]

Leaders engaged in building learning organizations naturally feel part of a larger purpose that goes beyond their organization. They are part of changing the way businesses operate, not from a vague philanthropic urge, but from a conviction that their efforts will produce more productive organizations, capable of achieving higher levels of organizational success and personal satisfaction than more traditional organizations . . . .

NEW SKILLS

New leadership roles require new leadership skills. These skills can only be developed, in my judgement, through a lifelong commitment. It is not enough for one or two individuals to develop these skills. They must be distributed widely throughout the organization. This is one reason that understanding the *disciplines* of a learning organization is so important. These disciplines embody the principles and practices that can widely foster leadership development.

Three critical areas of skills (disciplines) are building shared vision, surfacing and challenging mental models and engaging in systems thinking.[16]

Building Shared Vision

How do individual visions come together to create shared visions? A useful metaphor is the hologram, the three-dimensional image created by interacting light sources.

If you cut a photograph in half, each half shows only part of the whole image. But if you divide a hologram, each part, no matter how small, shows the whole image intact. Likewise, when a group of people come to share a vision for an organization, each person sees an individual picture of the organization at its best. Each shares responsibility for the whole, not just for one piece. But the component pieces of the

---

[15] L. Miller, *American Spirit: Visions of a new corporate culture* (New York: William Morrow, 1984), p. 15.
[16] These points are condensed from the practices of the five disciplines examined in Senge (1990).

hologram are not identical. Each represents the whole image from a different point of view. It's something like poking holes in a window shade; each hole offers a unique angle for viewing the whole image. So, too, is each individual's vision unique.

When you add up the pieces of a hologram, something interesting happens. The image becomes more intense, more lifelike. When more people come to share a vision, the vision becomes more real in the sense of a mental reality that people can truly imagine achieving. They now have partners, co-creators; the vision no longer rests on their shoulders alone. Early on, when they are nurturing an individual vision, people may say it is 'my vision'. But, as the shared vision develops, it becomes both 'my vision' and 'our vision'.

The skills involved in building shared vision include the following:

- *Encouraging personal vision:* Shared visions emerge from personal visions. It is not that people only care about their own self-interest – in fact, people's values usually include dimensions that concern family, organization, community, and even the world. Rather, it is that people's capacity for caring is *personal*.

- *Communicating and asking for support:* Leaders must be willing to share continually their own vision, rather than being the official representative of the corporate vision. They also must be prepared to ask, 'Is this vision worthy of your commitment?' This can be difficult for a person used to setting goals and presuming compliance.

- *Visioning as an ongoing process:* Building shared vision is a never-ending process. At any one point there will be a particular image of the future that is predominant, but that image will evolve. Today, too many managers want to dispense with the 'vision business' by going off and writing the Official Vision Statement. Such statements almost always lack the vitality, freshness and excitement of a genuine vision that comes from people asking, 'What do we really want to achieve?'

- *Blending extrinsic and intrinsic visions:* Many energizing visions are extrinsic – that is, they focus on achieving something relative to an outsider, such as a competitor. But a goal that is limited to defeating an opponent can, once the vision is achieved, easily become a defensive posture. In contrast, intrinsic goals like creating a new type of product, taking an established product to a new level, or setting a new standard for customer satisfaction can call forth a new level of creativity and innovation. Intrinsic and extrinsic visions need to coexist; a vision solely predicated on defeating an adversary will eventually weaken an organization.

- *Distinguishing positive from negative visions:* Many organizations only truly pull together when their survival is threatened. Similarly, most social movements aim at eliminating what people don't want: for example, anti-drugs, anti-smoking or anti-nuclear arms movements. Negative visions carry a subtle message of powerlessness: people will only pull together when there is sufficient threat. Negative visions also tend to be short term. Two fundamental sources of energy can motivate organizations: fear and aspiration. Fear, the energy source behind negative visions, can produce extraordinary changes in short periods, but aspiration endures as a continuing source of learning and growth.

Surfacing and Testing Mental Models

Many of the best ideas in organizations never get put into practice. One reason is that new insights and initiatives often conflict with established mental models. The leadership task of challenging assumptions without invoking defensiveness requires reflection and inquiry skills possessed by few leaders in traditional controlling organizations.[17]

- *Seeing leaps of abstraction:* Our minds literally move at lightning speed. Ironically, this often slows our learning, because we leap to generalizations so quickly that we never think to test them. We then confuse our generalizations with the observable data upon which they are based, treating the generalizations *as if they were data.*

- *Balancing inquiry and advocacy:* Most managers are skilled at articulating their views and presenting them persuasively. While important, advocacy skills can become counterproductive as managers rise in responsibility and confront increasingly complex issues that require collaborative learning among different, equally knowledgeable people. Leaders in learning organizations need to have both inquiry *and* advocacy skills . . . .

- *Distinguishing espoused theory from theory in use:* We all like to think that we hold certain views, but often our actions reveal deeper views. For example, I may proclaim that people are trusthworthy, but never lend friends money and jealously guard my possessions. Obviously, my deeper mental model (my theory in use) differs from my espoused theory. Recognizing gaps between espoused views and theories in use (which often requires the help of others) can be pivotal to deeper learning.

- *Recognizing and refusing defensive routines:* As one CEO in our research programme puts it, 'Nobody ever talks about an issue at the 8:00 business meeting exactly the same way they talk about it at home that evening or over drinks at the end of the day.' The reason is what Chris Argyris calls 'defensive routines', entrenched habits used to protect ourselves from the embarrassment and threat that come with exposing our thinking. For most of us, such defences began to build early in life in response to pressures to have the right answers in school or at home. Organizations add new levels of performance anxiety and thereby amplify and exacerbate this defensiveness. Ironically, this makes it even more difficult to expose hidden mental models, and thereby lessens learning.

  The first challenge is to recognize defensive routines, then to inquire into their operation. Those who are best at revealing and defusing defensive routines operate with a high degree of self-disclosure regarding their own defensiveness (e.g. I notice that I am feeling uneasy about how this conversation is going. Perhaps I don't understand it or it is threatening to me in way I don't yet see. Can you help me see this better?)

---

[17]The ideas below are based to a considerable extent on the work of Chris Argyris, Donald Schon and their Action Science colleagues: C. Argyris and D. Schon, *Organizational Learning: A theory-in-action perspective* (Reading, MA: Addison-Wesley, 1978); C. Argyris, R. Putnam and D. Smith, *Action Science* (San Francisco: Jossey-Bass, 1985); C. Argyris, *Strategy, Change and Defensive Routines* (Boston: Pitman, 1985); and C. Argyris, *Overcoming Organizational Defenses* (Englewood Cliffs, NJ: Prentice-Hall, 1990).

Systems Thinking

We all know that leaders should help people see the big picture. But the actual skills whereby leaders are supposed to achieve this are not well understood. In my experience, successful leaders often *are* 'systems thinkers' to a considerable extent. They focus less on day-to-day events and more on underlying trends and forces of change. But they do this almost completely intuitively. The consequence is that they are often unable to explain their intuitions to others and feel frustrated that others cannot see the world the way they do.

One of the most significant developments in management science today is the gradual coalescence of managerial systems thinking as a field of study and practice. This field suggests some key skills for future leaders:

- *Seeing interrelationships, not things, and processes, not snapshots:* Most of us have been conditioned throughout our lives to focus on things and to see the world in static images. This leads us to linear explanations of systemic phenomenon. For instance, in an arms race each party is convinced that the other is *the cause* of problems. They react to each new move as an isolated event, not as part of a process. So long as they fail to see the interrelationships of these actions, they are trapped.

- *Moving beyond blame:* We tend to blame each other or outside circumstances for our problems. But it is poorly designed systems, not incompetent or unmotivated individuals, that cause most organizational problems. Systems thinking shows us that there is no outside – that you and the cause of your problems are part of a single system.

- *Distinguishing detail complexity from dynamic complexity:* Some types of complexity are more important strategically than others. Detail complexity arises when there are many variables. Dynamic complexity arises when cause and effect are distant in time and space, and when the consequences over time of interventions are subtle and not obvious to many participants in the system. The leverage in most management situations lies in understanding dynamic complexity, not detail complexity.

- *Focusing on areas of high leverage:* Some have called systems thinking the 'new dismal science' because it teaches that most obvious solutions don't work – at best, they improve matters in the short run, only to make things worse in the long run. But there is another side to the story. Systems thinking also shows that small, well-focused actions can product significant, enduring improvements, if they are in the right place. Systems thinkers refer to this idea as the principle of 'leverage'. Tackling a difficult problem is often a matter of seeing where the high leverage lies, where a change – with a minimum of effort – would lead to lasting, significant improvement.

- *Avoiding symptomatic solutions:* The pressures to intervene in management systems that are going awry can be overwhelming. Unfortunately, given the linear thinking that predominates in most organizations, interventions usually focus on symptomatic fixes, not underlying causes. This results in only temporary relief, and it tends to create still more pressures later on for further, low-leverage intervention. If leaders acquiesce to these pressures, they can be sucked into an endless spiral of increasing intervention. Sometimes the most difficult leadership acts are to refrain from intervening through popular quick fixes and to keep the pressure on everyone to identify more enduring solutions.

While leaders who can articulate systemic explanations are rare, those who *can* will leave their stamp on an organization . . . .

The consequence of leaders who lack systems thinking skills can be devastating. Many charismatic leaders manage almost exclusively at the level of events. They deal in visions and in crises, and little in between. Under their leadership, an organization hurtles from crisis to crisis. Eventually, the worldview of people in the organization becomes dominated by events and reactiveness. Many, especially those who are deeply committed, become burned out. Eventually, cynicism comes to pervade the organization. People have no control over their time, let alone their destiny.

Similar problems arise with the 'visionary strategist', the leader with vision who sees both patterns of change and events. This leader is better prepared to manage change. He or she can explain strategies in terms of emerging trends, and thereby foster a climate that is less reactive. But such leaders still impart a responsive orientation rather than a generative one.

Many talented leaders have rich, highly systemic intuitions but cannot explain those intuitions to others. Ironically, they often end up being authoritarian leaders, even if they don't want to, because only they see the decisions that need to be made. They are unable to conceptualize their strategic insights so that these can become public knowledge, open to challenge and further improvement . . . .

. . . .

I believe that [a] new sort of management development will focus on the roles, skills and tools for leadership in learning organizations. Undoubtedly, the ideas offered above are only a rough approximation of this new territory. The sooner we begin seriously exploring the territory, the sooner the initial map can be improved – and the sooner we will realize an age-old vision of leadership:

> The wicked leader is he who the people despise.
> The good leader is he who the people revere.
> The great leader is he who the people say, 'We did it ourselves.'

Lao Tsu

CHAPTER

3

STRATEGY FORMULATION

Much of the work in the strategy field has focused on how strategy should be designed or consciously formulated. Kenneth Andrews of the Harvard Business School is associated with one of the earliest and more influential conceptual frameworks on strategy formulation. His work, commonly known as SWOT analysis and summarized in the first reading in this chapter, introduced the basis idea that, ultimately, a company's strategy must achieve a fit between the internal capability (strengths and weakness) and the external situation (opportunities and threats). As you will observe, Andrews' framework builds directly on some of the military concepts in earlier chapters. Both seek to leverage the impact of resources by concentrating efforts within a defined zone of dominance while attempting to anticipate the effects of potentially damaging external forces. Both also imply a clear distinction between strategy formulation and strategy implementation – the belief that strategy (or at least intended strategy) should be made explicit, and that strategy emanates from the formal leadership of the organization. This model of strategy formulation has proved very useful in many circumstances as a general way to analyze a strategic situation and to think about making strategy. A careful strategist should certainly touch all the bases suggested in this approach. However, there are circumstances when this model cannot or should not be followed to the letter, a point we return to in Chapter 4.

While the Andrews framework dominated the field in the 1970s, the 1980s ushered in an era of a more analytical approach to strategy formulation, which was pioneered by Michael Porter, also of the Harvard Business School. By building intellectual bridges between the fields of business strategy and industrial organization economics, Porter further developed the work of Andrews but focused on the structure of the industry – a component of the external context of opportunities and threats in Andrews' model – to provide a more formal approach for developing a company's competitive strategy. As presented in his award-winning *Harvard Business Review* article, the second reading in this chapter, Porter's framework of industry and competitive analysis argues that five basic forces define the structure and attractiveness of an industry – the bargaining power of existing suppliers and buyers, the threat of substitutes and new entrants, and the intensity of competitive rivalry. Formulating strategy requires a careful analysis of each of these forces so as to position the company in such as way that it can defend against these forces, influence the balance of the forces in its favour and exploit opportunities created by changes in any one of the forces or in their interactions.

Porter is known for a number of other frameworks as well – for example, his concept of 'generic strategies', of which he argues there are three in particular; cost leadership, differentiation and focus (or scope); his discussion of the 'value chain' as a way of decomposing the activities of a business to apply strategy analyses of various kinds; his notion of strategic groups where firms with like sets of strategies compete in sub-segments of an industry; and his concept of 'generic industry environments', such as 'fragmented' or 'mature', which reflect similar characteristics.

We shall return to Porter on the last of these in Section Three. In this chapter, his three generic strategies as well as his value chain will be summarized in the third reading, by Mintzberg, which seeks to present a more comprehensive picture of the various strategies that firms commonly pursue. Mintzberg's overall framework considers these at five levels – (1) locating the core business; (2) distinguishing the core business (the heart of what is often referred to a 'business'-level strategy, where Porter's three generic strategies are found and where his value chain is best introduced); (3) elaborating the core business; (4) extending the core business (where so-called corporate-level strategies are found); and (5) reconceiving the core business. Of these five levels, the article in this chapter focuses on the first three, which relate more at the business level, leaving the last two for a reading in Chapter 9, where we deal with the issues of corporate-level strategy.

The fourth reading is another *Harvard Business Review* award-winning article, by Gary Hamel and C.K. Prahalad, the authors of 'Strategic intent' in Chapter 2. If the Porter framework dominated thinking about strategy formulation in the 1980s, this article on core competence of a company appears to be doing so in the 1990s. While Porter elaborated the external threats and opportunities dimension in the Andrews model, the argument of core competence focuses on and elaborates the dimension of internal strengths and weaknesses. As Hamel and Prahalad argue, a company is not only a portfolio of businesses and products, it must also be seen by its managers as a portfolio of competences which lie at the root of its competitiveness in the different businesses and products. The article describes how companies can identify their existing competences, develop new ones and exploit them both to strengthen existing businesses and to enter new ones,

In Hamel and Prahalad's exposition, the concept of core competences may appear as an alternative to Porter's view of building competitive strategy with industry analysis as the starting point. Reflecting back on the Andrews framework, you may find that the two approaches to strategy may be relatively more complementary, representing two different kinds of analysis both of which must be brought to bear for improving the quality of strategic thinking and analysis. This complementarity is manifest in the last reading in this chapter on strategy evaluation by Richard Rumelt, a professor at INSEAD. While the Andrews article contains a discussion on strategy evaluation, Rumelt develops this a particularly useful and elegant way, which also ties up all the different ideas and frameworks we have included in this chapter.

● THE CONCEPT OF CORPORATE STRATEGY*

KENNETH R. ANDREWS

THE STRATEGY CONCEPT

What Strategy Is

Corporate strategy is the pattern of decisions in a company that determines and reveals its objectives, purposes or goals, produces the principal policies and plans for achieving those goals, and defines the range of business the company is to pursue, the kind of economic and human organization it is or intends to be and the nature of the economic and non-economic contribution it intends to make to its shareholders, employees, customers and communities. . . .

The strategic decision contributing to this pattern is one that is effective over long periods of time, affects the company in many different ways and focuses and commits a significant portion of its resources to the expected outcomes. The pattern resulting from a series of such decisions will probably define the central character and image of a company, the individuality it has for its members and various publics, and the position it will occupy in its industry and markets. It will permit the specification of particular objectives to be attained through a timed sequence of investment and implementation decisions and will govern directly the deployment or redeployment of resources to make these decisions effective.

Some aspects of such a pattern of decision may be in an established corporation unchanging over long periods of time, like a commitment to quality, or high technology, or certain raw materials, or good labour relations. Other aspects of a strategy must change as or before the world changes, such as product line, manufacturing process or merchandising and styling practices. The basic determinants of company character, if purposefully institutionalized, are likely to persist through and shape the nature of substantial changes in product-market choices and allocation of resources. . . .

It is important, however, not to take the idea apart in another way, that is, to separate goals from the policies designed to achieve those goals. The essence of the definition of strategy I have just recorded is *pattern*. The interdependence of purposes, policies and organized action is crucial to the particularity of an individual strategy and its opportunity to identify competitive advantage. It is the unity, coherence and internal consistency of a company's strategic decisions that position the company in

*Excerpted from Kenneth R. Andrews, *The Concept of Corporate Strategy:* rev edn (copyright © by Richard D. Irwin, Inc., 1980). Chs. 2 and 3; reprinted by permission of the publisher.

its environment and give the firm its identity, its power to mobilize its strengths and its likelihood of success in the marketplace. It is the interrelationship of a set of goals and policies that crystallizes from the formless reality of a company's environment a set of problems an organization can seize upon and solve.

What you are doing, in short, is never meaningful unless you can say or imply what you are doing it *for*: the quality of administrative action and the motivation lending it power cannot be appraised without knowing its relationship to purpose. Breaking up the system of corporate goals and the character-determining major policies for attainment leads to narrow mechanical conceptions of strategic management and endless logic chopping. . . .

Summary Statements of Strategy

Before we proceed to clarification of this concept by application, we should specify the terms in which strategy is usually expressed. A summary statement of strategy will characterize the product line and services offered or planned by the company, the markets and market segments for which products and services are now or will be designed, and the channels through which these markets will be reached. The means by which the operation is to be financed will be specified, as will the profit objectives and the emphasis to be placed on the safety of capital versus level of return. Major policy in central functions such a marketing, manufacturing, procurement, research and development, labour relations and personnel, will be stated where they distinguish the company from others, and usually the intended size, form and climate of the organization will be included.

Each company, if it were to construct a summary strategy from what it understands itself to be aiming at, would have a different statement with different categories of decision emphasized to indicate what it wanted to be or do. . . .

Formulation of Strategy

Corporate strategy is an organization process, in many ways inseparable from the structure, behaviour and culture of the company in which it takes place. Nevertheless, we may abstract from the process two important aspects, interrelated in real life but separable for the purposes of analysis. The first of these we may call *formulation,* the second *implementation*. Deciding what strategy should be may be approached as a rational undertaking, even if in life emotional attachments . . . may complicate choice among future alternatives. . . .

The principal subactivities of strategy formulation as a logical activity include identifying opportunities and threats in the company's environment and attaching some estimate or risk to the discernible alternatives. Before a choice can be made, the company's strengths and weaknesses should be appraised, together with the resources on hand and available. Its actual or potential capacity to take advantage of perceived market needs or to cope with attendant risks should be estimated as objectively as possible. The strategic alternative which results from matching opportunity and corporate capability at an acceptable level of risk is what we may call an *economic strategy*.

The process described thus far assumes that strategists are analytically objective in estimating the relative capacity of their company and the opportunity they see or anticipate in developing markets. The extent to which they wish to undertake low or high risk presumably depends on their profit objectives. The higher they set the latter, the more willing they must be to assume a correspondingly high risk that the market opportunity they see will not develop or that the corporate competence required to excel competition will not be forthcoming.

So far we have described the intellectual processes of ascertaining what a company *might do* in terms of environmental opportunity, of deciding what it *can do* in terms of ability and power, and of bringing these two considerations together in optimal equilibrium. The determination of strategy also requires consideration of what alternatives are preferred by the chief executive and perhaps by his or her immediate associates as well, quite apart from economic considerations. Personal values, aspirations and ideals do, and in our judgement quite properly should, influence the final choice of purposes. Thus what the executive of a company *want to do* must be brought into the strategic decision.

Finally strategic choice has an ethical aspect – a fact much more dramatically illustrated in some industries than in others. Just as alternatives may be ordered in terms of the degree of risk that they entail, so may they be examined against the standards of responsiveness to the expectations of society that the strategist elects. Some alternatives may seem to the executive considering them more attractive than others when the public good or service to society is considered. What a company *should do* thus appears as a fourth element of the strategic decision. . . .

The Implementation of Strategy

Since effective implementation can make a sound strategic decision ineffective or a debatable choice successful, it is as important to examine the processes of implementation of strategy is comprised of a series of subactivities which are primarily administrative. If purpose is determined, then the resources of a company can be mobilized to accomplish it. An organizational structure appropriate for the efficient performance of the required tasks must be made effective by information systems and relationships permitting coordination of subdivided activities. The organizational processes of performance measurement, compensation, management development – all of them enmeshed in systems of incentives and controls – must be directed towards the kind of behaviour required by organizational purpose. The role of personal leadership is important and sometimes decisive in the accomplishment of strategy. Although we know that organization structure and processes of compensation, incentives, control and management development influence and constrain the formulation of strategy, we should look first at the logical proposition that structure should follow strategy in order to cope later with the organizational reality that strategy also follows structure. When we have examined both tendencies, we will understand and to some extent be prepared to deal with the interdependence of the formulation and implementation of corporate purpose. Figure 1 may be useful in understanding the analysis of strategy as a pattern of interrelated decisions. . . .

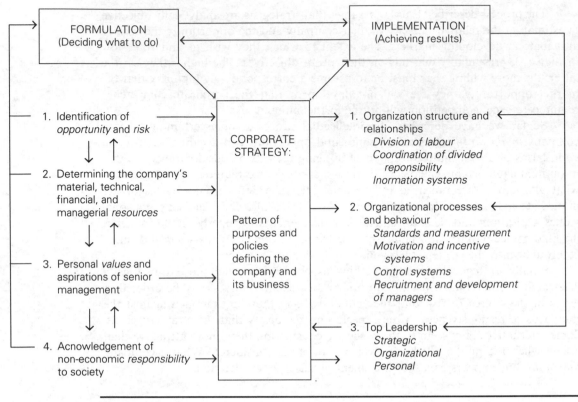

Figure 1

RELATING OPPORTUNITIES TO RESOURCES

Determination of a suitable strategy for a company begins in identifying the opportunities and risks in its environment. This [discussion] is concerned with the identification of a range of strategic alternatives, the narrowing of this range by recognizing the constraints imposed by corporate capability, and the determination of one or more economic strategies at acceptable levels of risk....

The Nature of the Company's Environment

The environment of an organization in business, like that of any other organic entity, is that pattern of all the external conditions and influences that affect its life and development. The environmental influences relevant to strategic decision operate in a company's industry, the total business community, its city, its country and the world. They are technological, economic, physical, social and political in kind. The corporate strategist is usually at least intuitively aware of these features of the current environment. But in all these categories change is taking place at varying rates – fastest in technology, less rapidly in politics. Change in the environment of business necessitates continuous monitoring of a company's definition of its business, lest it falter, blur or become obsolete. Since by definition the formulation of strategy is performed with the future in mind, executives who take part in the strategic planning process must be aware of those aspcts of their company's environment especially susceptible to the kind of change that will affect their company's future.

Technology

From the point of view of the corporate strategist, technological developments are not only the fastest unfolding but the most far-reaching in extending or contracting opportunity for an established company. They include the discoveries of science, the impact of related product development, the less dramatic machinery and process improvements, and the progress of automation and data processing. . . .

Ecology

It used to be possible to take for granted the physical characteristics of the environment and find them favourable to industrial development. Plant sites were chosen using criteria like availability of process and cooling water, accessibility to various forms of transportation and stability of soil conditions. With the increase in sensitivity to the impact on the physical environment of all industrial activity, it becomes essential, often to comply with law, to consider how planned expansion and even continued operation uner changing standards will affect and be perceived to affect the air, water, traffic density and quality of life generally of any area which a company would like to enter. . . .

Economics

Because business is more accustomed to monitoring economic trends than those in other spheres, it is less likely to be taken by surprise by such massive developments as the internationalization of competition, the return of China and Russia to trade with the West, the slower than projected development of the Third World countries, the Americanization of demand and culture in the developing countries and the resulting backlash of nationalism, the increased importance of the large multinational corporations and the consequences of host-country hostility, the recurrence of recession and the persistence of inflation in all phases of the business cycle. The consequences of world economic trends need to be monitored in much greater detail for any one industry or company.

Industry

Although the industry environment is the one most company strategists believe they know most about, the opportunities and risks that reside there are often blurred by familiarity and the uncritical acceptance of the established relative position of competitors. . . .

Society

Social development of which strategists keep aware include such influential forces as the quest for equality for minority groups, the demand of women for opportunity and recognition, the changing patterns of work and leisure, the effects of urbanization upon the individual, family and neighbourhood, the rise of crime, the decline of conventional morality and the changing composition of world population.

Politics

The political forces important to the business firm are similarly extensive and complex – the changing relations between communist and non-communist countries (East and West) and between prosperous and poor countries (North and South), the relation between private enterprise and government, between workers and management, the impact of national planning on corporate planning, and the rise of what George Lodge (1975) calls the communitarian ideology. . . .

Although it is not possible to know or spell out here the significance of such technical, economic, social and political trends, and possibilities for the strategist of a given business or company, some simple things are clear. Changing values will lead to different expectations of the role business should perform. Business will be expected to perform its mission not only with economy in the use of energy but with sensitivity to the ecological environment. Organizations in all walks of life will be called upon to be more explicit about their goals and to meet the needs and aspirations (for example, for education) of their membership.

In any case, change threatens all established strategies. We know that a thriving company – itself a living system – is bound up in a variety of interrelationships with larger systems comprising its technological, economic, ecological, social and political environment. If environmental developments are destroying and creating business opportunities, advance notice of specific instances relevant to a single company is essential to intelligent planning. Risk and opportunity in the last quarter of the twentieth century require of executives a keen interest in what is going on outside their companies. More than that, a practical means of tracking developments promising good or ill, and profit or loss, needs to be devised. . . .

For the firm that has not determined what its strategy dictates it needs to know or has not embarked upon the systematic surveillance of environmental change, a few simple questions kept constantly in mind will highlight changing opportunity and risk. In examining your own company, or one you are interested in, these questions should lead to an estimate of opportunity and danger in the present and predicted company setting.

1. What are the essential economic, technical and physical characteristics of the industry in which the company participates?. . .

2. What trends suggesting future change in economic and technical characteristics are apparent?. . .

3. What is the nature of competition both within the industry and across industries?. . .

4. What are the requirements for success in competition in the company's industry?. . .

5. Given the technical, economic, social and political developments that most directly apply, what is the range of strategy available to any company in this industry?. . .

Identifying Corporate Competence and Resources

The first step in validating a tentative choice among several opportunities is to determine whether the organization has the capacity to prosecute it successfully. The capability of an organization is its demonstrated and potential ability to accomplish, against the opposition of circumstance or competition, whatever it sets out to do. Every organization has actual and potential strengths and weaknesses. Since it is prudent in formulating strategy to extend or maximize the one and contain or minimize the other, it is important to try to determine what they are and to distinguish one from the other.

It is just as possible, though much more difficult, for a company to know its own strengths and limitations as it is to maintain a workable surveillance of its changing environment. Subjectivity, lack of confidence and unwillingness to face reality may make it hard for organizations as well as for individuals to know themselves. But just as it is essential, though difficult, that a maturing person achieve reasonable self-awareness, so an organization can identify approximately its central strength and critical vulnerability. . . .

To make an effective contribution to strategic planning, the key attributes to be appraised should be identified and consistent criteria established for judging them. If attention is directed to strategies, policy commitments and past practices in the context of discrepancy between organization goals and attainment, an outcome useful to an individual manager's strategic planning is possible. The assessment of strengths and weaknesses associated with the attainment of specific objectives becomes in Stevenson's (1976) words a 'key link in a feedback loop' which allows managers to learn from the success or failures of the policies they institute.

Although [a] study by Stevenson did not find or establish a systematic way of developing or using such knowledge, members of organizations develop judgements about what the company can do particularly well – its core of competence. If consensus can be reached about this capability, no matter how subjectively arrived at, its application to identified opportunity can be estimated.

Sources of Capabilities

The powers of a company constituting a resource for growth and diversification accrue primarily from experience in making and marketing a product line or providing a service. They inhere as well in (1) the developing strengths and weaknesses of the individuals comprising the organization, (2) the degree to which individual capability is effectively applied to the common task, and (3) the quality of coordination of individual and group effort.

The experience gained through successful execution of a strategy centred on one goal may unexpectedly develop capabilities which could be applied to different ends. Whether they should be so applied is another question. For example, a manufacturer of salt can strengthen his competitive position by offering his customers salt-dispensing equipment. If, in the course of making engineering improvements in this equipment, a new solenoid principle is perfected which has application to many industrial switching problems, should this patentable and marketable innovation be exploited? The answer would turn not only on whether economic analysis of the opportunity shows this to be a durable and profitable possibility, but also on whether the organization can muster the financial, manufacturing and marketing strength to exploit the discovery and live with its success. The former question is likely to have a more positive answer than the latter. In this connection, it seems important to remember that individual and unsupported flashes of strength are not as dependable as the gradually accumulated product and market-related fruits of experience.

Even where competence to exploit an opportunity is nurtured by experience in related fields, the level of that competence may be too low for any great reliance to be placed upon it. Thus a chain of children's clothing stores might well acquire the administrative, merchandising, buying and selling skills that would permit it to add departments in wormen's wear. Similarly, a sales force effective in distributing typewriters might gain proficiency in selling office machinery and supplies. But even here it would be well to ask what *distinctive* ability these companies could bring to the retailing of soft goods or office equipment to attract customers away from a plethora of competitors.

Identifying Strengths

The distinctive competence of an organization is more than what it can do; it is what is can do particularly well. To identify the less obvious or by-product strengths of an organization that may well be transferable to some more profitable new opportunity, one might well begin by examining the organization's current product line and by defining the functions it serves in its markets. Almost any important consumer product has functions which are related to others into which a qualified company might move. The typewriter, for example, is more than the simple machine for mechanizing handwriting that it once appeared to be when looked at only from the point of view of its designer and manufacturer. Closely analyzed from the point of view of the potential user, the typewriter is found to contribute to a broad range of information processing functions. Any one of these might have suggested an area to be exploited by a typewriter manufacturer. Tacitly defining a typewriter as a replacement for a fountain pen as a writing instrument rather than as an input–output device for word processing is the explanation provided by hindsight for the failure of the old-line typewriter companies to develop before IBM did the electric typewriter and the computer-related input–output devices it made possible. The definition of product which would lead to identification of transferable skills must be expressed in terms of the market needs it may fill rather than the engineering specifications to which it conforms.

Besides looking at the uses or functions to which present products contribute, the would-be diversifier might profitably identify the skills that underlie whatever success has been achieved. The qualifications of an organization efficient at performing its long-accustomed tasks come to be taken for granted and considered humdrum, like the steady provision of first-class service. The insight required to identify the essential strength justifying new ventures does not come naturally. Its cultivation can probably be helped by recognition of the need for analysis. In any case, we should look beyond the company's capacity to invent new products. Product leadership is not possible for a majority of companies, so it is fortunate that patentable new products are not the only major highway to new opportunities. Other avenues include new marketing services, new methods of distribution, new values in quality–price combinations and creative merchandising. The effort to find or to create a competence that is truly distinctive may hold the real key to a company's success or even to is future development. For example, the ability of a cement manufacturer to run a truck fleet more effectively than its competitors may constitute one of its principal competitive strengths in selling an undifferentiated product.

Matching Opportunity and Competence

The way to narrow the range of alternatives, made extensive by imaginative identification of new possibilities, is to match opportunity to competence, once each has been accurately identified and its future significance estimated. It is this combination which establishes a company's economic mission and its position in its environment. The combination is designed to minimize organizational weakness and to maximize strength. In every case, risk attends it. And when opportunity seems to outrun present distinctive competence, the willingness to gamble that the latter can be built up to the required level is almost indispensable to a strategy that challenges the organization and the people in it. Figure 2 shows the matching of opportunity and resources that results in an economic strategy.

Before we leave the creative act of putting together a company's unique internal

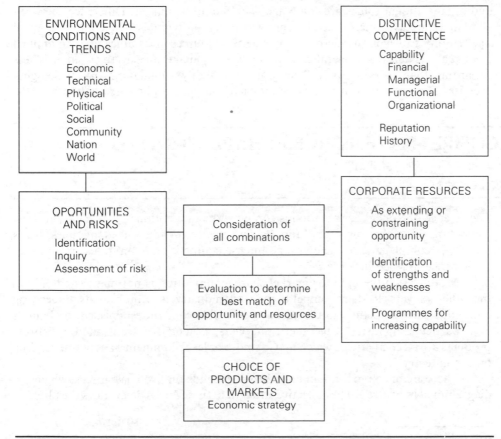

FIGURE 2
Schematic development of economic strategy

capability and opportunity evolving in the external world, we should note that – aside from distinctive competence – the principal resources found in any company are money and people – technical and managerial people. At an advanced stage of economic development, money seems less a problem than technical comptence, and the latter less critical than managerial ability. Do not assume that managerial capacity can rise to any occasion. The diversification of American industry is marked by hundreds of instances in which a company strong in one endeavour lacked the ability to manage an enterprise requiring different skills. The right to make handsome profits over a long period must be earned. Opportunism without competence is a path to fairyland.

Besides equating an appraisal of market opportunity and organizational capability, the decision to make and market a particular product or service should be accompanied by an identification of the nature of the business and the kind of company its management desires. Such a guiding concept is a product of many considerations, including the managers' personal values. . . .

Uniqueness of Strategy

In each company, the way in which distinctive competence, organizational resources and organizational values are combined is or should be unique. Differences between companies are as numerous as differences between individuals. The combinations of opportunity to which distinctive competences, resources and values may be applied are equally extensive. Generalizing about how to make an effective match is less rewarding than working at it. The effort is a highly stimulating and challenging exercise. The outcome will be unique for each company and each situation.

• HOW COMPETITIVE FORCES SHAPE STRATEGY*

Michael E. Porter

The essence of strategy formulation is coping with competition. Yet it is easy to view competition too narrowly and too pessimistically. While one sometimes hears executives complaining to the contrary, intense competition in an industry is neither coincidence nor bad luck.

Moreover, in the fight for market share, competition is not manifested only in the other players. Rather, competition in an industry is rooted in its underlying economics, and competitive forces exist that go well beyond the established combatants in a particular industry. Customers, suppliers, potential entrants and substitute products are all competitors which may be more or less prominent or active depending on the industry.

The state of competition in an industry depends on five basic forces, which are diagrammed in Figure 1. The collective strength of these forces determines the ultimate

*Originally published in the *Harvard Business Review* (March–April 1979) and winner of the McKinsey prize for the best article in the *Review* in 1979. Copyright © 1979 by the President and Fellows of Harvard College: all rights reserved. Reprinted with deletions by permission of the *Harvard Business Review*.

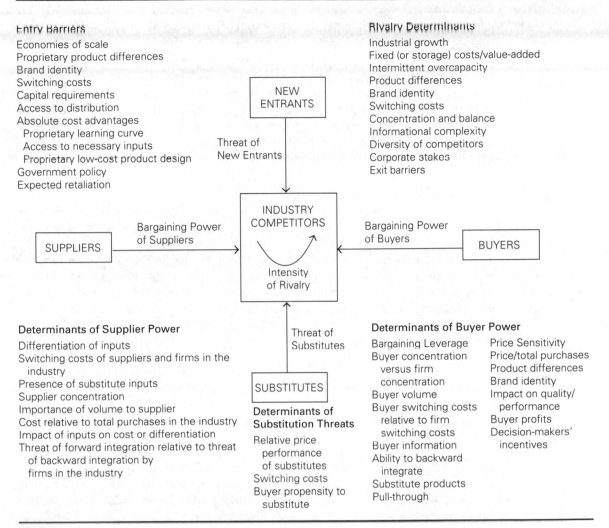

Entry Barriers

Economies of scale
Proprietary product differences
Brand identity
Switching costs
Capital requirements
Access to distribution
Absolute cost advantages
  Proprietary learning curve
  Access to necessary inputs
  Proprietary low-cost product design
Government policy
Expected retaliation

Rivalry Determinants

Industrial growth
Fixed (or storage) costs/value-added
Intermittent overcapacity
Product differences
Brand identity
Switching costs
Concentration and balance
Informational complexity
Diversity of competitors
Corporate stakes
Exit barriers

NEW ENTRANTS

Threat of
New Entrants

INDUSTRY
COMPETITORS

Intensity
of Rivalry

Bargaining Power
of Suppliers

SUPPLIERS

Bargaining Power
of Buyers

BUYERS

Determinants of Supplier Power

Differentiation of inputs
Switching costs of suppliers and firms in the
  industry
Presence of substitute inputs
Supplier concentration
Importance of volume to supplier
Cost relative to total purchases in the industry
Impact of inputs on cost or differentiation
Threat of forward integration relative to threat
  of backward integration by
  firms in the industry

Threat of
Substitutes

SUBSTITUTES

**Determinants of
Substitution Threats**

Relative price
  performance
  of substitutes
Switching costs
Buyer propensity to
  substitute

Determinants of Buyer Power

Bargaining Leverage
Buyer concentration
  versus firm
  concentration
Buyer volume
Buyer switching costs
  relative to firm
  switching costs
Buyer information
Ability to backward
  integrate
Substitute products
Pull-through

Price Sensitivity
Price/total purchases
Product differences
Brand identity
Impact on quality/
  performance
Buyer profits
Decision-makers'
  incentives

FIGURE 1
Elements of industry structure

profit potential of an industry. It ranges from *intense* in industries like tyres, metal cans and steel, where no company earns spectacular returns on investment, to *mild* in industries like oil field services and equipment, soft drinks and toiletries, where there is room for quite high returns.

In the economists' 'perfectly competitive' industry, jockeying for position is unbridled and entry to the industry very easy. This kind of industry structure, of course, offers the worst prospect for long-run profitability. The weaker the forces collectively, however, the greater the opportunity for superior performance.

Whatever their collective strength, the corporate strategist's goal is to find a position in the industry where his or her company can best defend itself against these forces or can influence them in its flavour. The collective strength of the forces may be painfully apparent to all the antagonists; but to cope with them, the strategist must delve below the surface and analyze the sources of each. For example, what makes the industry vulnerable to entry? What determines the bargaining power of suppliers?

Knowledge of these underlying sources of competitive pressure provides the groundwork for a strategic agenda of action. They highlight the critical strengths and weaknesses of the company, animate the positioning of the company in its industry, clarify the areas where strategic changes may yield the greatest payoff and highlight the places where industry trends promise to hold the greatest significance as either opportunities or threats. Understanding these sources also proves to be of help in considering areas for diversification.

CONTENDING FORCES

The strongest competitive force or forces determine the profitability of an industry and so are of greatest importance in strategy formulation. For example, even a company with a strong position in an industry unthreatened by potential entrants will earn low returns if it faces a superior or lower-cost substitute product – as the leading manufacturers of vacuum tubes and coffee percolators have learned to their sorrow. In such a situation, coping with the substitute product becomes the number one strategic priority.

Different forces taken on prominence, of course, in shaping competition in each industry. In the ocean-going tanker industry the key force is probably the buyers (the major oil companies), while in tyres it is powerful OEM buyers coupled with tought competitors. In the steel industry the key forces are foreign competitors and substitute materials.

Every industry has an underlying structure, or a set of fundamental economic and technical characteristics, which gives rise to these competitive forces. The strategist, wanting to position his company to cope best with its industry environment or to influence that environment in the company's favour, must learn what makes the environment tick.

This view of competition pertains equally to industries dealing in services and to those selling products. To avoid monotony in this article, I refer to both products and services as 'products'. The same general principles apply to all types of business.

A few characteristics are critical to the strength of each competitive force. I shall discuss them in this section.

Threat of Entry

New entrants to an industry bring new capacity, the desire to gain market share and often substantial resources. Companies diversifying through acquisition into the industry from other markets often leverage their resources to cause a shakeup, as Philip Morris did with Miller beer.

The seriousness of the threat of entry depends on the barriers present and on the reaction from existing competitors that the entrant can expect. If barriers to entry are high and a newcomer can expect sharp retaliation from the entrenched competitors, obviously he will not pose a serious threat to entering.

There are six major sources of barriers to entry:

1. *Economies of scale:* These economies deter entry by forcing the aspirant either to come in on a large scale or to accept a cost disadvantage. Scale economies in production, research, marketing and service are probably the key barriers to entry in the mainframe computer industry, as Xerox and GE sadly discovered. Economies of scale can also act as hurdles in distribution, utilization of the sales force, financing and nearly any other part of a business.

2. *Product differentiation:* Brand identification creates a barrier by forcing entrants to spend heavily to overcome customer loyalty. Advertising, customer service, being first in the industry and product differences are among the factors fostering brand identification. It is perhaps the most important entry barrier in soft drinks, over-the-counter drugs, cosmetics, investment banking and public accounting. To create high fences around their businesses, brewers couple brand identification with economies of scale in production, distribution and marketing.

3. *Capital requirements:* The need to invest large financial resources in order to compete creates a barrier to entry, particularly if the capital is required for unrecoverable expenditures in up-front advertising or R&D. Capital is necessary not only for fixed facilities but also for customer credit, inventories and absorbing start-up losses. While major corporations have the financial resources to invade almost any industry, the huge capital requirements in certain fields, such as computer manufacturing and mineral extraction, limit the pool of likely entrants.

4. *Cost disadvantages independent of size:* Entrenched companies may have cost advantages not available to potential rivals, no matter what their size and attainable economies of scale. These advantages can stem from the effects of the learning curve (and of its first cousin, the experience curve), proprietary technology, access to the best raw materials sources, assets purchased at pre-inflation prices, government subsidies or favourable locations. Sometimes cost advantages are legally enforceable, as they are through patents. . . .

5. *Access to distribution channels:* The new kid on the block must, of course, secure distribution of his product or service. A new food product, for example, must displace others from the supermarket shelf via price breaks, promotions, intense selling efforts or some other means. The more limited the wholesale or retail channels are and the more that existing competitors have these tied up, obviously the tougher that entry into the industry will be. Sometimes this barrier is so high that, to surmount it, a new contestant must create its own distribution channels, as Timex did in the watch industry in the 1950s.

6. *Government policy:* The government can limit or even foreclose entry to industries with such controls as licence requirements and limits on access to raw materials. Regulated industries like road freight, alcohol retailing and freight forwarding are noticeable examples; more subtle government restrictions operate in fields like ski-area development and coal mining. The government also can play a major indirect role by affecting entry barriers through controls such as air and water pollution standards and safety regulations.

The potential rival's expectations about the reaction of existing competitors also will influence its decision on whether to enter. The company is likely to have second thoughts if incumbents have previously lashed out at new entrants or if:

- The incumbents possess substantial resources to fight back, including excess cash and unused borrowing power, productive capacity or clout with distribution channels and customers.
- The incumbents seem likely to cut prices because of a desire to keep market shares or because of industrywide excess capacity.
- Industry growth is slow, affecting its ability to absorb the new arrival and probably causing the financial performance of all the parties involved to decline.

Changing Conditions

From a strategic standpoint there are two important additional points to note about the threat of entry.

First, it changes, of course, as these conditions change. The expiration of Polaroid's basic patents on instant photography, for instance, greatly reduced its absolute cost entry barrier built by proprietary technology. It is not surprising that Kodak plunged into the market. Product differentiation in printing has all but disappeared. Conversely, in the car industry economies of scale increased enormously with post-World War II automation and vertical integration – virtually stopping successful new entry.

Second, strategic decisions involving a large segment of an industry can have a major impact on the conditions determining the threat of entry. For example, the actions of many US wine producers in the 1960s to step up product introduction, raise advertising levels and expand distribution nationally surely strengthened the entry road blocks by raising economies of scale and making access to distribution channels more difficult. Similarly, decisions by members of the recreational vehicle industry to integrate vertically in order to lower costs have greatly increased the economies of scale and raised the capital cost barriers.

Powerful Suppliers and Buyers

Suppliers can exert bargaining power on participants in an industry by raising prices or reducing the quality of purchased goods and services. Powerful suppliers can thereby squeeze profitability out of an industry unable to recover cost increases in its own prices. By raising their prices, soft drink concentrate producers have contributed to the erosion of profitability of bottling companies because the bottlers, facing intense competition from powdered mixes, fruit drinks and other beverages, have limited freedom to raise *their* prices accordingly. Customers likewise can force down prices, demand higher quality or more service, and play competitors off against each other – all at the expense of industry profits.

The power of each important supplier or buyer group depends on a number of characteristics of its market situation and on the relative importance of its sales or purchases to the industry compared with its overall business.

A *supplier* group is powerful if:

- It is dominated by a few companies and is more concentrated than the industry it sells to.

- Its product is unique or at least differentiated, or if it has built up switching costs (i.e. fixed costs buyers face in changing suppliers). These arise because, among other things, a buyer's product specifications tie it to particular suppliers, it has invested heavily in specialized ancillary equipment or in learning how to operate a supplier's equipment (as in computer software), or its production lines are connected to the supplier's manufacturing facilities (as in some manufacture of beverage containers).

- It is not obliged to contend with other products for sale to the industry. For instance, the competition between the steel companies and the aluminium companies to sell to the can industry checks the power of each supplier.

- It poses a credible threat of integrating forward into the industry's business. This provides a check against the industry's ability to improve the terms on which it purchases.

- The industry is not an important customer of the supplier group. If the industry *is* an important customer, suppliers' fortunes will be closely tied to the industry, and they will want to protect the industry through reasonable pricing and assistance in activities like R&D and lobbying.

A *buyer* group is powerful if:

- It is concentrated or purchases in large volumes. Large-volume buyers are particularly potent forces if heavy fixed costs characterize the industry – as they do in metal containers, corn refining and bulk chemicals, for example – which raise the stakes to keep capacity filled.

- The products it purchases from the industry are standard or undifferentiated. The buyers, sure that they can always find alternative suppliers, may play one company against another, as they do in aluminium extrusion.

- The products it purchases from the industry form a component of its product and represent a significant fraction of its cost. The buyers are likely to shop for a favourable price and purchase selectively. Where the product sold by the industry in question is a small fraction of buyers' costs buyers are usually much less price-sensitive.

- It earns low profits, which create great incentive to lower its purchasing costs. Highly profitable buyers, however, are generally less price-sensitive (that is, of course, if the item does not represent a large fraction of their costs).

- The industry's product is unimportant to the quality of the buyers' products or services. Where the quality of the buyers' products is very much affected by the industry's product, buyers are generally less price-sensitive. Industries in which this situation obtains include oil field equipment, where a malfunction can lead to large losses, and enclosures for electronic medical and test instruments, where the quality of the enclosure can influence the user's impression about the quality of the equipment inside.

- The industry's product does not save the buyer money. Where the industry's product or service can pay for itself many times over, the buyer is rarely price sensitive; rather, he is interested in quality. This is true in services like investment banking and public accounting, where errors in judgement can be costly and embarrassing, and in businesses like the logging of oil wells, where an accurate survey can save thousands of dollars in drilling costs.

- The buyers pose a credible threat of integrating backward to make the industry's product. The Big Three car producers and major buyers of cars have often used the threat of self-manufacture as a bargaining lever. But sometimes an industry engenders a threat to buyers that its members may integrate forward.

Most of these sources of buyer power can be attributed to consumers as a group as well as to industrial and commercial buyers; only a modification of the frame of reference is necessary. Consumers tend to be more price-sensitive if they are purchasing products that are undifferentiated, expensive relative to their incomes and of a sort where quality is not particularly important.

The buying power of retailers is determined by the same rules, with one important addition. Retailers can gain significant bargaining power over manufacturers when they can influence consumers' purchasing decisions, as they do in audio components, jewellery, applicances, sporting goods and other goods.

Strategic Action

A company's choice of suppliers to buy from or buyer groups to sell to should be viewed as a crucial strategic decision. A company can improve its strategic posture by finding suppliers or buyers who possess the least power to influence it adversely.

Most common is the situation of a company being able to choose to whom it will sell – in other words, buyer selection. Rarely do all the buyer groups a company sells to enjoy equal power. Even if a company sells to a single industry, segments usually exist within that industry which exercise less power (and which are therefore less price-sensitive) than others. For example, the replacement market for most products is less price-sensitive than the overall market.

As a rule, a company can sell to powerful buyers and still come away with above-average profitability only if it is a low-cost producer in its industry or if its product enjoys some unusual, if not unique, features. In supplying large customers with electric motors, Emerson Electric earns high returns because its low-cost position permits the company to meet or undercut competitors' prices.

If the company lacks a low-cost position or a unique product, selling to everyone is self-defeating because the more sales it achieves, the more vulnerable it becomes. The company may have to muster the courage to turn away business and sell only to less potent customers.

Buyer selection has been a key to the success of National Can and Crown Cork & Seal. They focus on the segments of the can industry where they can create product differentiation, minimize the threat of backward integration and otherwise mitigate the awesome power of their customers. Of course, some industries do not enjoy the luxury of selecting 'good' buyers.

As the factors creating supplier and buyer power change with time or as a result of a company's strategic decisions, naturally the power of these groups rises or declines. In the ready-to-wear clothing industry, as the buyers (department stores and clothing stores) have become more concentrated and control has passed to large chains, the industry has come under increasing pressure and suffered falling margins.

The industry has been unable to differentiate its product or engender switching costs that lock in its buyers enough to neutralize these trends.

Substitute Products

By planing a ceiling on prices it can charge, substitute products or services limit the potential of an industry. Unless it can upgrade the quality of the product or differentiate it somehow (as via marketing), the industry will suffer in earnings and possibly in growth.

Manifestly, the more attractice the price-performance trade-off offered by substitute products, the firmer the lid placed on the industry's profit potential. Sugar producers confronted with the large-scale commercialization of high-fructose corn syrup, a sugar substitute, are learning this lesson today.

Substitutes not only limit profits in normal times; they also reduce the bonanza an industry can reap in boom times. In 1978 the producers of fiberglass insulation enjoyed unprecedented demand as a result of high energy costs and severe winter weather. But the industry's ability to raise prices was tempered by the plethora of insulation substitutes, including cellulose, rock wool and polystyrene. These substitutes arc bound to become an even stronger force once the current round of plant additions by fiberglass insulation producers has boosted capacity enough to meet demand (and then some).

Substitute products that deserve the most attention strategically are those that (1) are subject to trends improving their price-performance trade-off with the industry's product, or (2) are produced by industries earning high profits. Substitutes often come rapidly into play if some development increases competition in their industries and causes price reduction or performance improvement.

Jockeying for Position

Rivalry among existing competitors takes the familiar form of jockeying for position – using tactics like price competition, product introduction and advertising slugfests. Intense rivalry is related to the presence of a number of factors:

- Competitors are numerous or are roughly equal in size and power. In many US industries . . . foreign contenders, of course, have become part of the competitive picture.

- Industry growth is slow, precipitating fights for market share that involve expansion-minded members.

- The product or service lacks differentiation or switching costs, which lock in buyers and protect one combatant from raids on its customers by another.

- Fixed costs are high or the product is perishable, creating strong temptation to cut prices. Many basic materials businesses, like paper and aluminium, suffer from this problem when demand slackens.

- Capacity is normally augmented in large increments. Such additions, as in the chlorine and vinyl chloride businesses, disrupt the industry's supply–demand balance and often lead to periods of overcapacity and price-cutting.

- Exit barriers are high. Exit barriers, like very specialized assets or management's loyalty to a particular business, keep companies competing even though they may be earning low or even negative returns on investment. Excess capacity remains functioning, and the profitability of the healthy competitors suffers as the sick ones hang on. If the entire industry suffers from overcapacity, it may seek government help – particularly if foreign competition is present.

- The rivals are diverse in strategies, origins and 'personalities'. They have different ideas about how to compete and continually run head on into each other in the process. . . .

While a company must live with many of these factors – because they are built into industry economics – it may have some latitude for improving matters through strategic shifts. For example, it may try to raise buyers' switching costs or increase product differentiation. A focus on selling efforts in the fastest-growing segments of the industry or on market areas with the lowest fixed costs can reduce the impact of industry rivalry. If it is feasible, a company can try to avoid confrontation with competitors having high exit barriers and can thus sidestep involvement in bitter price-cutting.

FORMULATION OF STRATEGY

Once the corporate strategist has assessed the forces affecting competition in his industry and their underlying causes, he can identify his company's strengths and weaknesses. The crucial strengths and weaknesses from a strategic standpoint are the company's posture *vis-à-vis* the underlying causes of each force. Where does it stand against substitutes? Against the sources of entry barriers?

Then the strategist can devise a plan of action that may include (1) positioning the company so that its capabilities provide the best defense against the competitive force; and/or (2) influencing the balance of the forces through strategic moves, thereby improving the company's position; and/or (3) anticipating shifts in the factors underlying the forces and responding to them, with the hope of exploiting change by choosing a strategy appropriate for the new compeitive balance before opponents recognize it. I shall consider each strategic approach in turn.

Positioning the Company

The first approach takes the structure of the industry as given and matches the company's strengths and weaknesses to it. Strategy can be viewed as building defences against the competitive forces or as finding positions in the industry where the forces are weakest.

Knowledge of the company's capabilities and of the causes of the competitive forces will highlight the areas where the company should confront competition and where avoid it. If the company is a low-cost producer, it may choose to confront powerful buyers while it takes care to sell them only products not vulnerable to competition from substitutes. . . .

Influencing the Balance

When dealing with the forces that drive industry competition, a company can devise a strategy that takes the offensive. This posture is designed to do more than merely cope with the forces themselves; it is meant to alter their causes.

Innovations in marketing can raise brand identification or otherwise differentiate the product. Capital investments in large-scale facilities or vertical integration affect entry barriers. The balance of forces is partly a result of external factors and partly in the company's control.

Exploiting Industry Change

Industry evolution is important strategically because evolution, of course, brings with it changes in the sources of competition I have identified. In the familiar product lifecycle pattern, for example, growth rates change, product differentiation is said to decline as the business becomes more mature, and the companies tend to integrate vertically.

These trends are not so important in themselves: what is critical is whether they affect the sources of competition. . . .

The framework for analyzing competition that I have described can also be used to predict the eventual profitability of an industry. In long-range planning the task is to examine each competitive force, forecast the magnitude of each underlying cause and then construct a composite picture of the likely profit potential of the industry. . . .

The key to growth – even survival – is to stake out a position that is less vulnerable to attack from head-to-head opponents, whether established or new, and less vulnerable to erosion from the direction of buyers, suppliers, and substitute goods. Establishing such a position can take many forms – solidifying relationships with favourable customers, differentiating the product either substantively or psychologically through marketing, integrating forward or backward, establishing technological leadership.

• GENERIC BUSINESS STRATEGIES*

HENRY MINTZBERG

Almost every serious author concerned with 'content' issues in strategic management, not to mention strategy consulting 'boutique', has his, her or its own list of strategies commonly pursued by different organizations. The problem is that these lists almost always either focus narrowly on special types of strategies or else aggregate arbitrarily across all varieties of them with no real order.

---

*Abbreviated version prepared for this book of Henry Mintzberg, 'Generic strategies toward a comprehensive framework', in *Advances in Strategic Management*. Vol. 5 (Greenwich, CT: JAI Press, 1988), pp. 1–67.

In 1965, Igor Ansoff proposed a matrix of four strategies which became quite well known – market penetration, product development, market development and diversificaton (1965: 109). But this was hardly comprehensive. Fifteen years later, Michael Porter (1980) introduced what became the best-known list of 'generic strategies': cost leadership, differentiation and focus. But the Porter list was also incomplete: while Ansoff focused on *extensions* of business strategy, Porter focused on *identifying* business strategy in the first place.

We believe that families of strategies may be divided into five broad groupings. These are:

1.   Locating the core business.
2.   Distinguishing the core business.
3.   Elaborating the core business.
4.   Extending the core business.
5.   Reconceiving the core business.

This reading examines the first three, locating, distinguishing and elaborating the core business, since they are more relevant for business-level strategy. A companion reading in Chapter 9 discusses the two more relevant for corporate-level strategy – extending and reconceiving the core business. These five groupings of strategies are presented as a logical hierarchy, although it should be emphasized that strategies do not necessarily develop that way in organizations.

LOCATING THE CORE BUSINESS

A business can be thought to exist at a junction in a network of industries that take raw materials and through selling to and buying from each other produce various finished products (or services). Figure 1, for example, shows a hypothetical canoe business in such a network. Core location strategies can be described with respect to the stage of the business in the network and the particular industry in question.

Strategies of Stage of Operations

Traditionally, industries have been categorized as being in the primary (raw materials extraction and conversion), secondary (manufacturing) or tertiary (delivery or other service) stage of operations. More recently, however, stage in the 'stream' has been the favoured form of description:

Upstream Business Strategy
Upstream businesses function close to the raw material. The flow of product tends to be divergent, from a basic material (wood, aluminium) to a variety of uses for it. Upstream business tends to be technology and capital-intensive rather than people-intensive, and more inclined to search for advantage through low costs than through high margins and to favour sales push over market pull (Galbraith, 1983: 65–6).

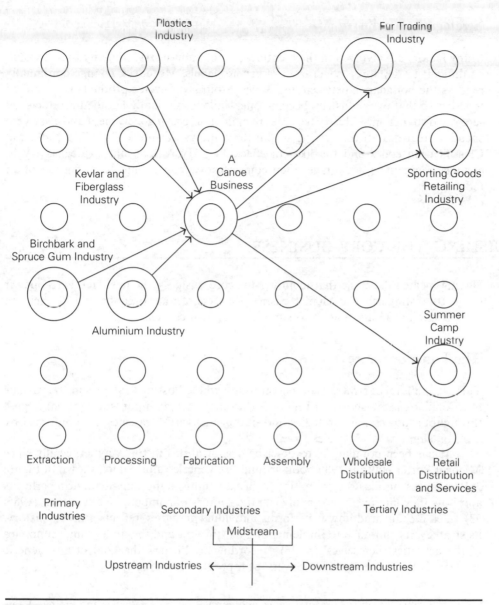

FIGURE 1
Locating a core business as a junction in a network of industries

Midstream Business Strategy

Here the organization sits at the neck of an hour-glass, drawing a variety of inputs into a single production process out of which flows the product to a variety of users, much as the canoe business is shown in Figure 1.

Downstream Business Strategy

Here a wide variety of inputs converge into a narrow funnel, as in the many products sold by a department store.

Strategies of Industry

Many factors are involved in the identification of an industry, so many that it would be difficult to develop a concise set of generic labels. Moreover, change continually renders the boundaries between 'industries' arbitrary. Diverse products get bundled together so that two industries become one, while traditionally bundled products get separated so that one industry becomes two. Economists in government and elsewhere spend a great deal of time trying to pin these things down, via Standard Industrial Classification codes and the like. In effect, they try to fix what strategists try to change: competitive advantage often comes from reconceiving the definition of an industry.

DISTINGUISHING THE CORE BUSINESS

Having located the circle that identifies the core business, the next step is to open it up – to distinguish the characteristics that enable an organization to achieve competitive advantage and so to survive in its own context.

The Functional Areas

This second level of strategy can encompass a whole host of strategies in the various functional areas. As shown in Figure 2, they may include input 'sourcing' strategies, throughput 'processing' strategies and output 'delivery' strategies, all reinforced by a set of 'supporting' strategies.

It has been popular ... to describe organizations in this way, especially since Michael Porter built his 1985 book around the 'generic value chain', shown in Figure 3. Porter presents it as 'a systematic way of examining all the activities a firm performs and how they interact ... for analyzing the sources of competitive advantage' (1985: 33). Such a chain, and how it performs individual activities, reflects a firm's 'history, its strategy, its approach to implementing its strategy, and the underlying economies of the activities themselves' (p. 36). According to Porter, 'the goal of any generic strategy' is to 'create value for buyers' at a profit. Accordingly,

> The value chain displays total value, and consists of *value activities* and *margin*. Value activities are the physically and technologically distinct activities a firm performs. These are the building blocks by which a firm creates a product valuable to its buyers. Margin is the difference between total value and the collective cost of performing the value activities. ...
>
> Value activities can be divided into two broad types, *primary* activities and *support* activities. Primary activities, listed along the bottom of Figure 3 are the activities involved in the physical creation of the product and its sale and transfer to the buyer as well as after-sale assistance. In any firm, primary activities can be divided into the five generic categories shown in Figure 3. Support activities support the primary activities and each other by providing purchased inputs, technology, human resources, and various firmwide functions. (p. 38)[1]

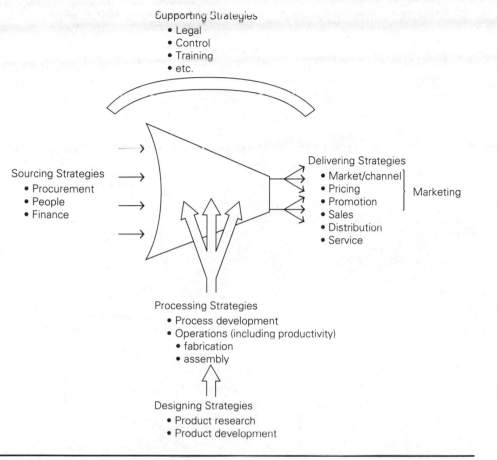

Supporting Strategies
• Legal
• Control
• Training
• etc.

Sourcing Strategies
• Procurement
• People
• Finance

Delivering Strategies
• Market/channel
• Pricing   } Marketing
• Promotion
• Sales
• Distribution
• Service

Processing Strategies
• Process development
• Operations (including productivity)
  • fabrication
  • assembly

Designing Strategies
• Product research
• Product development

FIGURE 2
Functional areas, in systems terms

Porter's Generic Strategies

Porter's framework of 'generic strategies' has also become quite widely used. In our terms, these constitute strategies to distinguish the core business. Porter believes there are but two 'basic types of competitive advantage a firm can possess: low costs or differentiation' (1985: 11). These combine with the 'scope' of a firm's operation (the

---

[1] Our figure differs from Porter's in certain ways. Because he places his major emphasis on the flow of physical materials (for example, referring to 'inbound logistics' as encompassing 'materials handling, warehousing, inventory control, vehicle scheduling, and returns to suppliers'), he shows procurement and human resource management as support activities, whereas by taking more of a general system orientation, our Figure 2 shows them as inputs, among the sourcing strategies. Likewise, he considers technology development as support whereas Figure 2 considers it as part of processing. (Among the reasons Porter gives for doing this is that such development can pertain to 'outbound logistics' or delivery as well as processing. While true, it also seems true that far more technology development pertains to operations than to delivery, especially in the manufacturing firms that are the focus of Porter's attention. Likewise, Porter describes procurement as pertaining to any of the primary activities, or other support activities for that matter. But in our terms that does not make it any less an aspect of sourcing on the inbound side.) In fact, Porter's description would relegate engineering and product design (not to mention human resources and purchasing) to staff rather than line activities, a place that would certainly be disputed in many manufacturing firms (with product design, for example, being mentioned only peripherally in his text (p. 42) alongside other 'technology development' activities such as media research and servicing procedures).

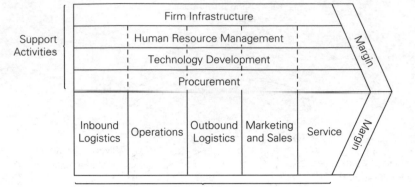

FIGURE 3
The generic value chain
Source: Porter (1985:37).

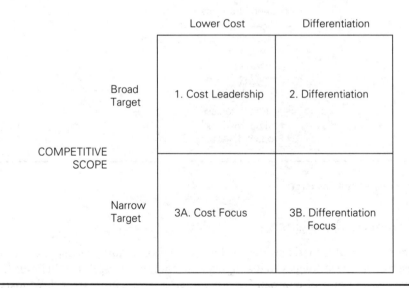

FIGURE 4
Porter's generic strategies
Source: Porter (1985:12).

range of market segments targeted) to produce 'three *generic strategies* for achieving above-average performance in an industry: cost leadership, differentiation, and focus' (namely, narrow scope), shown in Figure 4.

To Porter, firms that wish to gain competitive advantage must 'make a choice' among these: 'being "all things to all people" is a recipe for strategic mediocrity and below-average performance' (p. 12). Or in words that have become more controversial, 'a firm that engages in each generic strategy but fails to achieve any of them is "stuck in the middle" '(p. 16).

The strategies we describe in this section take their lead from Porter, but depart in some respects. We shall distinguish scope and differentiation, as Porter did in his 1980 book (focus being introduced as narrow scope in his later book), but we shall include cost leadership as a form of differentiation (namely, with regard to low price). If, as Porter argues, the intention of generic strategies is to seize and sustain competitive advantage, then it is not taking the leadership on cutting costs that matters so much as using that cost leadership to underprice competitors and so to attract buyers.[2]

Thus two types of strategy for distinguishing a core business are presented here. First, is a set of increasingly extensive strategies of *differentiation,* shown on the face of the circle. These identify what is fundamentally distinct about a business in the marketplace, in effect as perceived by its customers. Second, is a set of decreasingly extensive strategies of *scope,* shown as a third dimension, which converts the circle into a cylinder. These identify what markets the business is after, as perceived by itself.

Strategies of Differentiation

As is generally agreed in the literature of strategic management, an organization distinguishes itself in a competitive marketplace by differentiating its offerings in some way – by acting to distinguish its product and services from those of its competitors .... Hence, differentiation fills the face of the circle used to identify the core business. An organization can differentiate its offerings in six basic ways:

Price Differentiation Strategy

The most basic way to differentiate a product (or service) is simply to charge a lower price for it. All things being equal, or not too unequal, some people at least will always beat a path to the door of the cheaper product. Price differentiation may be used with a product undifferentiated in any other way – in effect, a standard design, perhaps a commodity. The producer simply absorbs the lost margin, or makes it up through a higher volume of sales. But other times, backing up price differentiation is a strategy of design intended to create a product that is intrinsically cheaper.

---

[2] In other words, it is the differentiation of price that naturally drives the functional strategy of reducing costs just as it is the differentiation of product that naturally drives the functional strategies of enhancing quality or creating innovation. (To be consistent with the label of 'cost leadership', Porter would have had to call his differentiation strategy 'product leadership'.) A company could, of course, cut costs while holding prices equivalent to competitors. But often that means less service, lower quality, fewer features, etc., and so the customers would have to be attracted by lower prices. (See Mintzberg (1988: 14–17) for a fuller discussion of this point.)

Image Differentiation Strategy

Marketing is sometimes used to feign differentiation where it does not otherwise exist – an image is created for the product. This can also include cosmetic differences to a product that do not enhance its performance in any serious way, for example, putting fins on an automobile or a fancier package around yogurt. (Of course, if it is the image that is for sale, in other words if the product is intrinsically cosmetic, as, say, in 'designer' jeans, then cosmetic differences would have to be described as design differentiation.)

Support Differentiation Strategy

More substantial, yet still having no effect on the product itself, is to differentiate on the basis of something that goes alongside the product, some basis of support. This may have to do with selling the product (such as special credit or 24-hour delivery), servicing the product (such as exceptional after-sales service), or providing a related product or service alongside the basic one (paddling lessons with the canoe you buy). In an article entitled 'Marketing success through differentiation – of anything', Theodore Levitt has argued the interesting point that 'there is no such thing as a commodity' (1980: 8). His basic point is that no matter how difficult it may be to achieve differentiation by design, there is always a basis to achieve another substantial form of differentiation, especially by support.

Quality Differentiation Strategy

Quality differentiation has to do with features of the product that make it better – not fundamentally different, just better. The product performs with (1) greater initial reliability, (2) greater long-term durability, and/or (3) superior performance.

Design Differentiation Strategy

Last but certainly not least is differentiation – the basis of design – offering something that is truly different, that breaks away from the 'dominant design' if there is one, to provide unique features. When everyone else was making cameras whose pictures could be seen next week, Edward and went off and made one whose pictures could be seen in the next minute.

Undifferentiation Strategy

To have no basis for differentiation is a strategy too, indeed by all observation a common one, and in fact one that may be pursued deliberately. Hence there is a blank space in the circle. Given enough room in a market, and a management without the skill or the will to differentiate what it sees, there can be place for copycats.

Scope Strategies

The second dimension to distinguish the core business is by the *scope* of the products and services offered, in effect the extent of the markets in which they are sold. Scope is essentially a demand-driven concept, taking its lead from the market in what exists out there. Differentiation, in contrast, is a supply-driven concern, rooted in the nature of the product itself – what is offered to the market (W.E. Smith, 1956). Differentiation, by concentrating on the product offered, adopts the perspective of the customer, existing only when that person perceives some characteristic of the product that adds value. And scope, by focusing on the market served, adopts the perspective of the producer, existing only in the collective mind of the organization – in terms of how it diffuses and disaggregates its markets (in other words, what marketing people call segmentation). . . .

Unsegmentation Strategy

'One size fits all': the Ford Model T, table salt. In fact, it is difficult to think of any product today that is not segmented in some way. What the unsegmented strategy really means then is that the organization tries to capture a wide chunk of the market with a basic configuration of the product.

Segmentation Strategies

The possibilities for segmentation are limitless, as are the possible degrees. We can, however, distinguish a range of this, from a simple segmentation strategy (three basic sizes of paper clips) to a hyperfine segmentation strategy (as in designer lighting). Also, some organizations seek to be *comprehensive,* to serve all segments (department store, large cigarette manufacturers), others to be *selective,* targeting carefully only certain segments (e.g. 'clean' mutual funds).

Niche Strategy

Niche strategies focus on a single segment. Just as the panda bear has found its biological niche in the consumption of bamboo shoots, so too is there the canoe company that has found its market niche in the fabrication of racing canoes, or the many firms which are distinguished only by the fact that they provide their highly standardized offerings in a unique place, a geographical niche – the corner grocery store, the regional cement producer, the national Red Cross office. All tend to follow 'industry' recipes to the letter, providing them to their particular community. In a sense, all strategies are in some sense niche, characterized as much by what they exclude as by what the include. No organization can be all things to all people. The all-encompassing strategy is no strategy at all.

Customizing Strategies

Customization is the limiting case of segmentation: disaggregation of the market to the point where each customer constitutes a unique segment. *Pure* customization, in which the product is developed from scratch for each customer, is found in the architecturally designed house and the special purpose machine. It infiltrates the entire value chain: the product is not only delivered in a personalized way, not only assembled and even fabricated to order, but is also designed for the individual customer in the first place. Less ambitious but probably more common is *tailored* customization: a basic design is modified, usually in the fabrication stage, to the customer's needs or specifications (certain housing, protheses modified to fit the bone joints of each customer, and so on). *Standardized* customization means that final products are assembled to individual request for standard components – as in automobiles in which the customer is allowed to choose colour, engine and various accessories. Advances in computer-aided design and manufacturing (CAD, CAM) will doubtlessly cause a proliferation of standardized customization, as well as tailored customization.

ELABORATING THE CORE BUSINESS

An organization can elaborate a business in a number of ways. It can develop its product offerings within that business, it can develop its market via new segments, new channels or new geographical areas, or it can simply push the same products more vigorously through the same markets. Back in 1965, Igor Ansoff showed these strategies (as well as one to be discussed in Chapter 9) as presented in Figure 5.

Penetration Strategies

Penetration strategies work from a base of existing products and existing markets, seeking to penetrate the market by increasing the organization's share of it. This may be done by straight *expansion* or by the *takeover* of existing competitors. Trying to expand sales with no fundamental change in product or market (buying market share through more promotion, etc.) is at one and the same time the most obvious thing to do and perhaps the most difficult to succeed at, because, at least in a relatively stable market, it means extracting market share from other firms, which logically leads to increased competition. Takeover, where possible, obviously avoids this, but perhaps at a high cost. The harvesting strategy, popularized in the 1970s by the Boston Consulting Group, in some ways represents the opposite of the penetration strategies. The way to deal with 'cash cows' – businesses with high market shares but low growth potential – was to harvest them, cease investment and exploit whatever potential remained. The mixing of the metaphors may have been an indication of the dubiousness of the strategy since to harvest a cow is, of course, to kill it.

Market Development Strategies

A predominant strategy here is *market elaboration,* which means promoting existing products in new markets – in effect broadening the scope of the business by finding new market segments, perhaps served by new channels. Product substitution is a particular case of market elaboration, where uses for a product are promoted which enable it to substitute for other products. *Market consolidation* is the inverse of market elaboration, namely reducing the number of segments. But this is not just a strategy of failure. Given the common tendency to proliferate market segments, it makes sense for the healthy organization to rationalize them periodically, to purge the excesses.

	Existing Product	New Product
Existing Market	Penetration Strategies	Product Development Strategies
New Market	Market Development Strategies	Diversification Strategies

FIGURE 5
Ways to elaborate a given business
Source: From Ansoff (1965:109), with minor modifications; see also Johnson and Jones (1957:52).

Geographic Expansion Strategies

An important form of market development can be geographic expansion – carrying the existing product offering to new geographical areas, anywhere from the next block to across the world. When this also involves a strategy of geographic rationalization – locating different business functions in different places – it is sometimes referred to as a 'global strategy'. The IKEA furniture company, for example, designs in Scandinavia, sources in Eastern Europe among other places and markets in Western Europe and North America.

Product Development Strategies

Here we can distinguish a simple *product extension* strategy from a more extensive *product line proliferation* strategy, and their counterparts, *product line rationalization*. Offering new or modified products in the same basic business is another obvious way to elaborate a core business – from cornflakes to bran flakes and rice crispies, eventually offering every permutation and combination of the edible grains. This may amount to differentiation by design, if the products are new and distinctive, or else to no more than inreased scope through segmentation, if standardized products are added to the line. Product line proliferation means aiming at comprehensive product segmentation – the complete coverage of a given business. Rationalization means culling products and thinning the line to get rid of overlaps or unprofitable excesses. Again we might expect cycles of product extension and rationalization, at least in businesses (such as cosmetics and textiles) predisposed to proliferation in their product lines.

• THE CORE COMPETENCE OF THE CORPORATON*

C.K. Prahalad and Gary Hamel

The most powerful way to prevail in global competition is still invisible to many companies. During the 1980s, top executives were judged on their ability to restructure, declutter and delayer their corporations. In the 1990s, they'll be judged on their ability to identify, cultivate and exploit the core competencies that make growth possible – indeed, they'll have to rethink the concept of the corporation itself.

Consider . . . GTE and NEC. In the early 1980s, GTE was well positioned to become a major player in the evolving information technology industry. It was active in telecommunications. Its operations spanned a variety of businesses. . . .

In 1980, GTE's sales were $9.98 billion, and net cash flow was $1.73 billion. NEC, in contrast, was much smaller, at $3.8 billion in sales. It had a comparable technological base and computer businesses, but it had no experience as an operating telecommunications company.

Yet look at the positions of GTE and NEC in 1988. GTE's 1988 sales were $16.46 billion, and NEC's sales were considerably higher at $21.89 billion. GTE has,

---

in effect, become a telephone operating company with a position in defence and lighting products. . . . Non-US revenue as a per cent of total revenue dropped from 20 per cent to 15 per cent between 1980 and 1988.

NEC has emerged as the world leader in semiconductors and as a first-tier player in telecommunications products and computers. It has consolidated its position in mainframe computers. It has moved beyond public switching and transmission to include such lifestyle products at mobile telephones, facsimile machines and laptop computers – bridging the gap between telecommunications and office automation. NEC is the only company in the world to be in the top five in revenue in telecommunications, semiconductors and mainframes. Why did these two companies, starting with comparable business portfolios, perform so differently? Largely because NEC conceived of itself in terms of 'core competencies', and GTE did not.

RETHINKING THE CORPORATION

Once, the diversified corporation could simply point its business units at particular end-product markets and admonish them to become world leaders. But with market boundaries changing ever more quickly, targets are elusive and capture is at best temporary. A few companies have proved themselves adept at inventing new markets, quickly entering emerging markets and dramatically shifting patterns of customer choice in established markets. These are the one to emulate. The critical task for management is to create an organization capable of infusing products with irresistible functionality or, better yet, creating products that customers need but have not yet even imagined.

This is a deceptively difficult task. Ultimately, it requires radical change in the management of major companies. . . . Early in the 1970s, NEC articulated a strategic intent to exploit the convergence of computing and communications, what it called 'C&C'. Success, top management reckoned, would hinge on acquiring *competencies,* particularly in semiconductors. Management adopted an appropriate 'strategic architecture,' summarized by C&C, and then communicated its intent to the whole organization and the outside world during the mid-1970s.

NEC constituted a 'C&C Committee' of top managers to oversee the development of core products and core competencies. NEC put in place coordination groups and committees that cut across the interests of individual businesses. Consistent with its strategic architecture, NEC shifted enormous resources to strengthen its position in components and central processors. By using collaborative arrangements to multiply internal resources, NEC was able to accumulate a broad array of core competencies.

NEC carefully identified three interrelated streams of technological and market evolution. Top management determined that computing would evolve from large mainframes to distributed processing components from simple ICs to VLSI, and communications from mechanical cross-bar exchange to complex digital systems we now call ISDN. As things evolved further, NEC reasoned, the computing, communications and components businesses would so overlap that it would be very hard to distinguish among them, and that there would be enormous opportunities for any company that had built the competencies needed to serve all three markets.

NEC top management determined that semiconductors would be the company's most important 'core product'. It entered into myriad strategic alliances – over 100 as of 1987 – aimed at building competencies rapidly and at low cost. In mainframe computers, its most noted relationship was with Honeywell and Bull. Almost all the collaborative arrangements in the semiconductor component field were oriented towards technology access. . . .

No such clarity of strategic intent and strategic architecture appeared to exist at GTE. Although senior executives discussed the implications of the evolving information technology industry, no commonly accepted view of which competencies would be required to compete in that industry were communicated widely. While significant staff work was done to identify key technologies, senior line managers continued to act as if they were managing independent business units.

THE ROOTS OF COMPETITIVE ADVANTAGE

. . . The diversified corporation is a large tree. The trunk and major limbs are core products, the smaller branches are business units; the leaves, flowers and fruit are

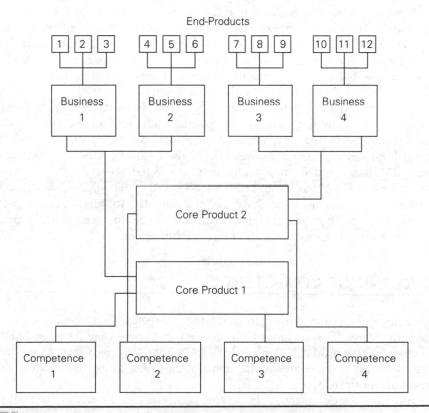

FIGURE 1
Competencies: The roots of competitiveness

end-products. The root system that provides nourishment, sustenance and stability is the core competence. You can miss the strength of competitors by looking only at their end-products, in the same way you miss the strength of a tree if you look only at its leaves.

Core competencies are the collective learning in the organization, especially how to coordinate diverse production skills and integrate multiple streams of technologies. . . .

If core competence is about harmonizing streams of technology, it is also about the organization of work and the delivery of value. Among Sony's competencies is miniaturization. To bring miniaturization to its products, Sony must ensure that technologists, engineers and marketers have a shared understanding of customer needs and of technological possibilities. . . .

Core competence is communication, involvement and a deep commitment to working across organizational boundaries. It involves many levels of people and all functions. World-class research in, for example, lasers or ceramics can take place in corporate laboratories without having an impact on any of the businesses of the company. The skills that together constitute core competence must coalesce around individuals whose efforts are not so narrowly focused that they cannot recognize the opportunities for blending their functional expertise with those of others in new and interesting ways.

Core competence does not diminish with use. Unlike physical assets, which do deteriorate over time, competencies are enhanced as they are applied and shared. But competencies still need to be nurtured and protected; knowledge fades if it is not used. Competencies are the glue that binds existing businesses. They are also the engine for new business development. Patterns of diversification and market entry may be guided by them, not just by the attractiveness of markets.

Consider 3M's competence with sticky tape. In dreaming up businesses as diverse as 'Post-it' notes, magnetic tape, photographic film, pressure-sensitive tapes and coated abrasives, the company has brought to bear widely shared competencies in substrates, coatings and adhesives and devised various ways to combine them. Indeed, 3M has invested consistently in them. What seems to be an extremely diversified portfolio of businesses belies a few shared core competencies. In contrast, there are major companies that have had the potential to build core competencies but failed to do so because top management was unable to conceive of the company as anything other than a collection of discrete businesses. . . .

HOW NOT TO THINK OF COMPETENCE

Since companies are in a race to build the competencies that determine global leadership, successful companies have stopped imagining themselves as bundles of businesses making products. Canon, Honda, Casio or NEC may seem to preside over portfolios of businesses unrelated in terms of customers, distribution channels and merchandising strategy. . . .

But looks are deceiving. . . . In the core competencies underlying them, disparate businesses become coherent. It is Honda's core competence in engines and power trains that gives it a distinctive advantage in car, motorcycle, lawn mower and generator businesses. Canon's core competencies in optics, imaging and microprocessor controls have enabled it to enter, even dominate, markets as seemingly diverse as copiers, laser printers, cameras and image scanners. . . .

Unlike the battle for global brand dominance, which is visible in the world's broadcast and print media and is aimed at building global 'share of mind', the battle to build world-class competencies is invisible to people who aren't deliberately looking for it. . . .

Let us be clear. Cultivating core competence does *not* mean outspending rivals on research and development. In 1983, when Canon surpassed Xerox in worldwide unit market share in the copier business, its R&D budget in reprographics was but a small fraction of Xerox's. Over the past 20 years, NEC has spent less on R&D as a percentage of sales than almost all of its American and European competitors.

Nor does core competence mean shared costs, as when two or more SBUs use a common facility – a plant, service facility or sales force – or share a common component. The gains of sharing may be substantial, but the search for shared costs is typically a *post hoc* effort to rationalize production across existing businesses, not a premeditated effort to build the competencies out of which the businesses themselves grow.

Building core competencies is more ambitious and different than integrating vertically, moreover. Managers deciding whether to make or buy will start with end-products and look upstream to the efficiencies of the supply chain and downstream toward distribution and customers. They do not take inventory of skills and look forward to applying them in non-traditional ways. (Of course, decisions about competencies *do* provide a logic for vertical integration. Canon is not particularly integrated in its copier business, except in those aspects of the vertical chain that support the competencies it regards as critical.)

IDENTIFYING CORE COMPETENCIES – AND LOSING THEM

As least three tests can be applied to identify core competencies in a company. First, a core competence provides potential access to a wide variety of markets. . . . Second, a core competence should make a significant contribution to the perceived customer benefits of the end product. Clearly, Honda's engine expertise fills this bill.

Finally, a core competence should be difficult for competitors to imitate. And it *will* be difficult if it is a complex harmonization of individual technologies and production skills. A rival might acquire some of the technologies that comprise the core competence, but will find it more difficult to duplicate the more or less comprehensive pattern of internal coordination and learning. . . .

Few companies are likely to build world leadership in more than five or six fundamental competencies. A company that compiles a list of 20–30 capabilities has probably not produced a list of core competencies. Still, it is probably a good discipline to generate a list of this sort and to see aggregate capabilities as building blocks. This tends to prompt the search for licensing deals and alliances through which the company may acquire, at low cost, the missing pieces.

. . . In our view, too many companies have unwittingly surrendered core competencies when they cut internal investment in what they mistakenly thought were just 'cost centres' in favour of outside suppliers. Consider Chrysler. Unlike Honda, it has tended to view engines and power trains as simply one more component. . . . It is difficult to imagine Honda yielding manufacturing responsibility, much less design, of so critical a part of a car's function to an outside company – which is why Honda has made such an enormous commitment to Formula One auto racing. Honda has been able to pool its engine-related technologies; it has parlayed these into a corporate-wide competency from which it develops world-beating products, despite R&D budgets smaller than those of GM and Toyota. . . . Outsourcing can provide a shortcut to a more competitive product, but it typically contributes little to building the people-embodied skills that are needed to sustain product leadership.

Nor is it possible for a company to have an intelligent alliance or sourcing strategy if it has not made a choice about where it will build competence leadership. . . .

Another way of losing is forgoing opportunities to establish competencies that are evolving in existing businesses. In the 1970s and 1980s, many American and European companies – like GE, Motorola, GTE, Thorn and GEC – chose to exit the colour television business, which they regarded as mature. If by 'mature' they meant that they had run out of new product ideas at precisely the moment global rivals had targeted the TV business for entry, then yes, the industry was mature. But it certainly wasn't mature in the sense that all opportunities to enhance and apply video-based competencies had been exhausted.

In ridding themselves of their television businesses, these companies failed to distinguish between divesting the business and destroying their video media-based competencies. They not only got out of the TV business but they also closed the door on a whole stream of future opportunities reliant on video-based competencies . . . .

There are two clear lessons here. First, the costs of losing a core competence can be only partly calculated in advance. The baby may be thrown out with the bathwater in divestment decisions. Second, since core competencies are built through a process of continuous improvement and enhancement that may span a decade or longer, a company that has failed to invest in core competence building will find it very difficult to enter an emerging market, unless, of course, it will be content simply to serve as a distribution channel. . . .

FROM CORE COMPETENCIES TO CORE PRODUCTS

The tangible link between identified core competencies and end-products is what we call the core products – the physical embodiments of one or more core competencies. Honda's engines, for example, are core products, lynchpins between design and development skills that ultimately lead to a proliferation of end-products. Core products are the components or subassemblies that actually contribute to the value of the end-products. Thinking in terms of core products forces a company to distinguish between the brand share it achieves in end product markets (for example, 40 per cent of the US refrigerator market) and the manufacturing share it achieves in any particular core product (for example, 5 per cent of the world share of compressor output). Canon is reputed to have an 84 per cent world manufacturing share in desktop laser printer 'engines', even though its brand share in the laser printer business is minuscule. . . .

It is essential to make this distinction between core competencies, core products and end-products because global competition is played out by different rules and for different stakes at each level. To build or defend leadership over the long term, a corporation will probably be a winner at each level. At the level of core competence, the goal is to build world leadership in the design and development of a particular class of product functionality – be it compact data storage and retrieval, as with Philips's optical-media competence, or compactness and ease of use, as with Sony's micromotors and microprocessor controls.

To sustain leadership in their chosen core competence areas, these companies *seek to maximize their world manufacturing share in core products*. The manufacture of core products for a wide variety of external (and internal) customers yields the revenue and market feedback that, at least partly, determines the pact at which core competencies can be enhanced and extended. . . .

Control over core products is critical for other reasons. A dominant position in core products allows a company to shape the evolution of applications and end markets. . . . As a company multiplies the number of application arenas for its core products, it can consistently reduce the cost, time and risk in new product development. In short, well-targeted core products can lead to economies of scale *and* scope.

THE TYRANNY OF THE SBU

The new terms of competitive engagement cannot be understood using analytical tools devised to manage the diversified corporation of 20 years ago, when competition was primarily domestic (GE versus Westinghouse; General Motors versus Ford) and all the key players were speaking the language of the same business schools and consultancies. Old prescriptions have potentially toxic side-effects. The need for new principles is most obvious in companies organized exclusively according to the logic of Strategic Business Unit, or SBU.

Obviously, diversified corporations have a portfolio of products and a portfolio of businesses. But we believe in a view of the company as a portfolio of competencies as well. US companies do not lack the technical resources to build competencies, but their top management often lacks the vision to build them and the administrative means for assembling resources spread across multiple businesses. A shift in commitment will inevitably influence patterns of diversification, skill deployment, resource allocation priorities and approaches to alliances and outsourcing.

We have described the three different planes on which battles for global leadership are waged: core competence, core products and end-products. A corporation has to know whether it is winning or losing on each plane. By sheer weight of investment, a company might be able to beat its rivals to blue-sky technologies yet still lose the race to build core competence leadership. If a company is winning the race to build core competencies (as opposed to building leadership in a few technologies), it will almost certainly outpace rivals in new business development. If a company is winning the race to capture world manufacturing share in core product, it will probably outpace rivals in improving product features and the price/performance ratio. . . .

When you think about this reconceptualization of the corporation, the primacy of the SBU – an organizational dogma for a generation – is now clearly an anachronism. Where the SBU is an article of faith, resistance to the seductions of decentralization can seem heretical. In many companies, the SBU prism means that only one plane of the global competitive battle, the battle to put competitive products on the shelf *today*, is visible to top management. What are the costs of this distortion?

Underinvestment in Developing Core Competencies and Core Products

When the organization is conceived of as a multiplicity of SBUs, no single business may feel responsible for maintaining a viable position in core products nor be able to justify the investment required to build world leadership in some core competency....

Imprisoned Resources

As an SBU evolves, it often develops unique competencies. Typically, the people who embody this competence are seen as the sole property of the business in which they grew up. The manager of another SBU who asks to borrow talented people is likely to get a cold rebuff. SBU managers are not only unwilling to lend their competence carriers, but they may actually hide talent to prevent its redeployment in the pursuit of new opportunities. This may be compared to residents of an underdeveloped country hiding most of their cash under their mattresses. The benefits of competencies, like the benefits of the money supply, depend on the velocity of their circulation as well as on the size of the stock the company holds....

Bounded Innovation

If core competencies are not recognized, individual SBUs will pursue only those innovation opportunities that are close at hand – marginal product-line extensions or geographic expansions. Hybrid opportunities like fax machines, laptop computers, hand-held televisions or portable music keyboards will emerge only when managers take off their SBU blinkers. Remember, Canon appeared to be in the camera business at the time it was preparing to become a world leader in copiers. Conceiving of the corporation in terms of core competencies widens the domain of innovation.

DEVELOPING STRATEGIC ARCHITECTURE

We believe that senior management should spend a significant amount of its time developing a corporate-wide strategic architecture that establishes objectives for competence building. A strategic architecture is a road map of the future that identifies which core competencies to build and their constituent technologies.

By providing an impetus for learning from alliances and a focus for internal development efforts, a strategic architecture like NEC's C&C can dramatically reduce the investment needed to secure future market leadership....

Of course, all of this begs the question of what a strategic architecture should look like. The answer will be different for every company. But it is helpful to think again of that tree, of the corporation organized around core products and, ultimately, core competencies. To sink sufficiently strong roots, a company must answer some fundamental questions: How long could we preserve our competitiveness in this business if we did not control this particular core competence? How central is this core competence to perceived customer benefits? What future opportunities would be foreclosed if we were to lose this particular competence? . . .

The strategic architecture should make resource allocation priorities transparent to the entire organization. It provides a template for allocation decisions by top management. It helps lower-level managers understand the logic of allocation priorities and disciplines senior management to maintain consistency. In short, it yields a definition of the company and the markets it serves. . . .

It is consistency of resource allocation and the development of an administrative infrastructure appropriate to it that breathes life into a strategic architecture and creates a managerial culture, teamwork, a capacity to change and a willingness to share resources, to protect proprietary skills and to think long term. That is also the reason the specific architecture cannot be copied easily or overnight by comptitors. Strategic architecture is a tool for communicating with customers and other external constituents. It reveals the broad direction without giving away every step.

REDEPLOYING TO EXPLOIT COMPETENCIES

If the company's core competencies are its critical resource and if top management must ensure that competence carriers are not held hostage by some particular business, then it follows that SBUs should bid for core competencies in the same way they bid for capital. We've made this point glancingly. It is important enough to consider more deeply.

Once top management (with the help of divisional and SBU managers) has identified overarching competencies, it must ask businesses to identify the projects and people closely connected with them. Corporate officers should direct an audit of the location, number, and quality of the people who embody competence.

This sends an important signal to middle managers: core competencies are *corporate* resources and may be reallocated by corporate management. An individual business doesn't own anybody. SBUs are entitled to the services of individual employees so long as SBU management can demonstrate that the opportunity it is pursuing yields the highest possible pay-off on the investment in their skills. This message is further underlined if each year in the strategic planning or budgeting process, unit managers must justify their hold on the people who carry the company's core competencies. . . .

Finally, there are ways to wean key employees off the idea that they belong in perpetuity to any particular business. Early in their careers, people may be exposed to a variety of businesses through a carefully planned rotation programme. At Canon, critical people move regularly between the camera business and the copier business and between the copier business and the professional optical-products business. In mid-career, periodic assignments to cross-divisional project teams may be necessary, both for diffusing core competencies and for loosening the bonds that might tie an individual to one business even when brighter opportunities beckon elsewhere. Those who embody critical core competencies should know that their careers are tracked and guided by corporate human resource professionals. In the early 1980s at Canon, all engineers under 30 were invited to apply for membership on a seven-person committee that was to spend two years plotting Canon's future direction, including its strategic architecture.

Competence carriers should be regularly brought together from across the corporation to trade notes and ideas. The goal is to build a strong feeling of community among these people. To a great extent, their loyalty should be to the integrity of the core competence area they represent and not just to particular businesses. In travelling regularly, talking frequently to customers, and meeting with peers, competence carriers may be encouraged to discover new market opportunities.

Core competencies are the wellspring of new business development. They should constitute the focus for strategy at the corporate level. Managers have to win manufacturing leadership in core products and capture global share through brand-building programmes aimed at exploiting economies of scope. Only if the company is conceived of as a hierarchy of core competencies, core products, and market-focused business units will it be fit to fight.

Nor can top management be just another layer of accounting consolidation, which it often is in a regime of radical decentralization. Top management must add value by enunciating the strategic architecture that guides the competence acquisition process. We believe an obsession with competence building will characterize the global winners of the 1990s. With the decade underway, the time for rethinking the concept of the corporation is already overdue.

● EVALUATING BUSINESS STRATEGY*

RICHARD P. RUMELT

Strategy can neither be formulated nor adjusted to changing circumstances without a process of strategy evaluation. Whether performed by an individual or as part of an organization review procedure, strategy evaluation forms an essential step in the process of guiding an enterprise.

For many executives strategy evaluation is simply an appraisal of how well a business performs. Has it grown? Is the profit rate normal or better? If the answers to these questions are affirmative, it is argued that the firm's strategy must be sound. Despite its unassailable simplicity, this line of reasoning misses the whole point of strategy – that the critical factors determining the quality of long-term results are often not directly observable or simply measured, and that by the time strategic opportunities or threats do directly affect operating results, it may well be too late for an effective response. Thus, strategy evaluation is an attempt to look beyond the obvious facts regarding the short-term health of a business and appraise instead those more fundamental factors and trends that govern success in the chosen field of endeavour.

*This paper is a revised and updated version for this book of 'The evaluation of business strategy', originally published in William F. Glueck, *Strategic Management and Business Policy* (New York: McGraw-Hill, 1980). New version printed here by permission of the author.

THE CHALLENGE OF EVALUATION

However it is accomplished, the products of a business strategy evaluation are answers to these three questions:

- Are the objectives of the business appropriate?
- Are the major policies and plan appropriate?
- Do the results obtained to date confirm or refute critical assumptions on which the strategy rests?

Devising adequate answers to these questions is neither simple nor straightforward. It requires a reasonable store of situation-based knowledge and more than the usual degree of insight. In particular, the major issues which make evaluation difficult and with which the analyst must come to grips are these:

- Each business strategy is unique. For example, one paper manufacturer might rely on its vast timber holdings to weather almost any storm while another might place primary reliance in modern machinery and an extensive distribution system. Neither strategy is 'wrong' nor 'right' in any absolute sense; both may be right or wrong for the firms in question. Strategy evaluation must, then, rest on a type of situational logic that does not focus on 'one best way' but which can be tailored to each problem as it is faced.
- Strategy is centrally concerned with the selection of goals and objectives. Many people, including seasoned executives, find it much easier to set or try to achieve goals than to evaluate them. In part this is a consequence of training in problem-solving rather than in problem-structuring. It also arises out of a tendency to confuse values, which are fundamental expressions of human personality, with objectives, which are devices for lending coherence to action.
- Formal systems of strategic review, while appealing in principle, can create explosive conflict situations. Not only are there serious questions as to who is qualified to give an objective evaluation, the whole idea of strategy evaluation implies management by 'much more than results' and runs counter to much of currently popular management philosophy.

THE GENERAL PRINCIPLES OF STRATEGY EVALUATION

The term 'strategy' has been so widely used for different purposes that it has lost any clearly defined meaning. For our purposes a strategy is a set of objective, policies and plans that, taken together, define the scope of the enterprise and its approach to survival and success. Alternatively, we could say that the particular policies, plans and objectives of a business express its strategy for coping with a complex competitive environment.

One of the fundamental tenets of science is that a theory can never be proven to be absolutely true. A theory can, however, be declared absolutely false if it fails to stand up to testing. Similarly, it is impossible to demonstrate conclusively that a particular business strategy is optimal or even to guarantee that it will work. One can, nevertheless, test it for critical flaws. Of the many tests which could be justifiably applied to a business strategy, most will fit within one of these broad criteria:

- *Consistency:* The strategy must not present mutually inconsistent goals and policies.

- *Consonance:* The strategy must represent an adaptive response to the external environment and to the critical changes occurring within it.

- *Advantage:* The strategy must provide for the creation and/or maintenance of a competitive advantage in the selected area of activity.

- *Feasibility:* The strategy must neither overtax available resources nor create unsolvable subproblems.

A strategy that fails to meet one or more of these criteria is strongly suspect. It fails to perform at least one of the key functions that are necessary for the survival of the business. Experience within a particular industry or other setting will permit the analyst to sharpen these criteria and add others that are appropriate to the situation at hand.

Consistency

Gross inconsistency within a strategy seems unlikely until it is realized that many strategies have not been explicitly formulated but have evolved over time in an *ad hoc* fashion. Even strategies that are the result of formal procedures may easily contain compromise arrangements between opposing power groups.

Inconsistency in strategy is not simply a flaw in logic. A key function of strategy is to provide coherence to organizational action. A clear and explicit concept of strategy can foster a climate of tacit coordination that is more efficient than most administrative mechanisms. Many high-technology firms, for example, face a basic strategic choice between offering high-cost products with high custom-engineering content and lower-cost products that are more standardized and sold at higher volume. If senior management does not enunciate a clear consistent sense of where the corporation stands on these issues, there will be continuing conflict between sales, design, engineering and manufacturing people. A clear consistent strategy, by contrast, allows a sales engineer to negotiate a contract with a minimum of coordination; the trade-offs are an explicit part of the firm's posture.

Organizational conflict and interdepartmental bickering are often symptoms of a managerial disorder but may also indicate problems of strategic inconsistency. Here are some indicators that can help sort out these two different problems:

- If problems in coordination and planning continue despite changes in personnel and tend to be issue- rather than people-based, they are probably due to inconsistencies in strategy.

- If success for one organizational department means, or is interpreted to mean, failure for another department, either the basic objective structure is inconsistent or the organizational structure is wastefully duplicative.

- If, despite attempts to delegate authority, operating problems continue to be brought to the top for the resolution of policy issues, the basic strategy is probably inconsistent.

A final type of consistency that must be sought in strategy is between organizational objectives and the values of the management group. Inconsistency in this area is more of a problem in strategy formulation than in the evaluation of a strategy that has already been implemented. It can still arise, however, if the future direction of the business requires changes that conflict with managerial values. The most frequent source of such conflict is growth. As a business expands beyond the scale that allows an easy informal method of operation, many executives experience a sharp sense of loss. While growth can of course be curtailed, it often will require special attention to a firm's competitive position if survival without growth is desired. The same basic issues arise when other types of personal or social values come into conflict with existing or apparently necessary policies: the resolution of the conflict will normally require an adjustment in the competitive strategy.

Consonance

The way in which a business relates to its environment has two aspects: the business must both match and be adapted to its environment and it must at the same time compete with other firms that are also trying to adapt. This dual character of the relationship between the firm and its environment has its analogue in two different aspects of strategic choice and two different methods of strategy evaluation.

The first aspect of it deals with the basic mission or scope of the business and the second with its special competitive position or 'edge'. Analysis of the first is normally done by looking at changing economic and social conditions over time. Analysis of the second, by contrast, typically focuses on the differences across firms at a given time. We call the first the *generic* aspect of strategy and the second *competitive* strategy. Generic strategy deals with the creation of social value – with the question of whether the products and services being created are worth more than their cost. Competitive strategy, by contrast, deals with the firm's need to capture some of the social value as profit. Table 1 summarizes the differences between these concepts.

TABLE 1   Generic versus competitive strategy

	Generic Strategy	**Competitive Strategy**
Value Issue	Social Value	Corporate Value
Value Constraint	Customer Value > Cost	Price > Cost
Success Indicator	Sales Growth	Increased Corporate Worth
Basic Strategic Task	Adapting to Change	Innovating, Impeding Imitation, Deterring Rivals
How Strategy is Expressed	Product Market Definition	Advantage, Position and Policies Supporting Them
Basic Approach to Analysis	Study of an Industry over Time	Comparison across Rivals

The notion of consonance, or matching, therefore, invites a focus on generic strategy. The role of the evaluator in this case is to examine the basic pattern of economic relationships that characterize the business and determine whether or not sufficient value is being created to sustain the strategy. Most macroanalysis of changing economic conditions is oriented towards the formulation or evaluation of generic strategies. For example, a planning department forecasts that within six years flat-panel liquid crystal displays will replace CRT-based video displays in computers. The basic message here to makers of CRT-based video dispays is that their generic strategies are becoming obsolete. Note that the threat in this case is not to a particular firm, competitive position, or individual approach to the marketplace but to the basic generic mission.

One major difficulty in evaluating consonance is that most of the critical threats to a business are those that come from without, threatening an entire group of firms. Management, however, is often so engrossed in competitive thinking that such threats are only recognized after the damage has reached considerable proportions.

Another difficulty in appraising the fit between a firm's mission and the environment is that trend analysis does not normally reveal the most critical changes – they are the result of interactions among trends. The supermarket, for example, comes into being only when home refrigeration and the widespread use of private cars allow shoppers to buy in significantly larger volumes. The supermarket, the automobile and the move to suburbia together form the nexus which gives rise to shopping centres. These in turn change the nature of retailing and, together with the decline of urban centres, create new forms of enterprise, such as the suburban film theatre with four screens. Thus, while gross economic or demographic trends might appear steady for many years, there are waves of change going on at the institutional level.

The key to evaluating consonance is an understanding of why the business, as it currently stands, exists at all and how it assumed its current pattern. Once the analyst obtains a good grasp of the basic economic foundation that supports and defines the business, it is possible to study the consequences of key trends and changes. Without such an understanding, there is no good way of deciding what kinds of changes are most crucial and the analyst can be quickly overwhelmed with data.

Advantage

It is no exaggeration to say that competitive strategy is that art of creating or exploiting those advantages that are most telling, enduring and most difficult to duplicate.

Competitive strategy, in contrast with generic strategy, focuses on the differences among firms rather than their common missions. The problem it addresses is not so much 'How can this function be performed' but 'how can we perform it either better than, or at least instead of, our rivals?' The chain supermarket, for example, represents a successful generic strategy. As a way of doing business, of organizing economic transactions, it has replaced almost all the smaller owner-managed food shops of an earlier era. Yet a potential or actual participant in the retail food business must go beyond this generic strategy and find a way of competing in this business. As another illustration, IBM's early success in the PC industry was generic – other firms soon copied the basic product concept. Once this happened, IBM had to try either to forge a strong competitive strategy in this area or seek a different type of competitive arena.

Competitive advantages can normally be traced to one of three roots:

- Superior skills.
- Superior resources.
- Superior position.

In examining a potential advantage, the critical question is 'What sustains this advantage, keeping competitors from imitating or replicating it?' A firm's skills can be a source of advantage if they are based on its own history of learning-by-doing and if they are rooted in the coordinated behaviour of many people. By contrast, skills that are based on generally understood scientific principles, on training that can be purchased by competitors, or which can be analyzed and replicated by others are not sources of sustained advantage.

The skills that compose advantages are usually organizational, rather than individual, skills. They involve the adept coordination or collaboration of individual specialists and are built through the interplay of investment, work, and learning. Unlike physical assets, skills are enhanced by their use. Skills that are not continually used and improved will atrophy.

Resources include patents, trademark rights, specialized physical assets and the firm's working relationships with suppliers and distribution channels. Resources that constitute advantages are specialized to the firm, are built up slowly over time through the accumulated exercise of superior skills, or are obtained through being an insightful first mover, or by just plain luck. For example, Nucor's special skills in mini-mill construction are embodied in superior physical plants. Goldman Sachs' reputation as the premier US investment banking house has been built up over many years and is now a major resource in its own right.

A firm's *position* consists of the products or services it provides, the market segments it sells to and the degree to which it is isolated from direct competition. In general, the best positions involve supplying very uniquely valuable products to price-insensitive buyers, whereas poor positions involve being one of many firms supplying marginally valuable products to very well informed price-sensitive buyers.

Positional advantage can be gained by foresight, superior skill and/or resources, or just plain luck. Once gained, a good position is defensible. This means that it (1) returns enough value to warrant its continued maintenance, and (2) would be so costly to capture that rivals are deterred from full-scale attacks on the core of the business. Position, it must be noted, tends to be self-sustaining as long as the basic environmental factors that underlie it remain stable. Thus, entrenched firms can be almost impossible to unseat, even if their raw skill levels are only average. And when a shifting environment allows position to be gained by a new entrant or innovator, the results can be spectacular.

Positional advantages are of two types: (1) first mover advantages, and (2) reinforcers. The most basic first mover advantage occurs when the minimum scale to be efficient requires a large (sunk) investment relative to the market. Thus, the first firm to open a large discount retail store in a rural area precludes, through its relative scale, close followers. More subtle first mover advantages occur when standardization effects 'lock in' customers to the first-mover's product (e.g. Lotus 123). Buyer learning and related phenomena can increase the buyer's switching costs, protecting an incumbent's customer base from attack. Frequent flyer programmes are aimed in this direction. First movers may also gain advantages in building distribution channels, in typing up specialized suppliers or in gaining the attention of customers. The first product of a class to engage in mass advertising, for example, tends to impress itself more deeply in people's minds than the second, third, or fourth. In a careful study of frequently-purchased consumer products, Urban *et al.* (1986) found that (other things being equal) the first entrant will have a market share that is $\sqrt{n}$ times as large as that of the nth entrant.

Reinforcers are policies or practices acting to strengthen or preserve a strong market position and which are easier to carry out because of the position. The idea that certain arrangements of one's resources can enhance their combined effectiveness, and perhaps even put rival forces in a state of disarray, is at the heart of the traditional notion of strategy. It is reinforcers that provide positional advantage: the strategic quality familiar to military theorists, chess players and diplomats.

A firm with a larger market share, due to being an early mover or to having a technological lead, can typically build a more efficient production and distribution system. Competitors with less demand simply cannot cover the fixed costs of the larger more efficient facilities, so for them larger facilities are not an economic choice. In this case, scale economies are a reinforcer of market position, not the cause of market position. The firm that has a strong branch can use it as a reinforcer in the introduction of related brands. A company that sells a speciality coating to a broader variety of users may have better data on how to adapt the coating to special conditions than a competitor with more limited sales – properly used, this information is a reinforcer. A famous brand will appear on TV and in films because it is famous, another reinforcer. An example given by Porter (1985: 145) is that of Steinway and Sons, the premier US maker of fine pianos. Steinway maintains a dispersed inventory of grand pianos which approved pianists are permitted to use for concerts at very low rental rates. The policy is less expensive for a leader than for a follower and helps maintain leadership.

The positive feedback provided by reinforcers is the source of the power of position-based advantages – the policies that act to enhance position may not require unusual skills; they simply work most effectively for those who are already in the position in the first place.

While it is not true that larger businesses always have the advantages, it is true that larger businesses will tend to operate in markets and use procedures that turn their size to advantage. Large national consumer-products firms, for example, will normally have an advantage over smaller regional firms in the efficient use of mass advertising, especially network TV. The larger firm will, then, tend to deal in those products where the marginal effect of advertising is most potent, while the smaller firms will seek product/market positons that exploit other types of advantage.

Other position-based advantages follow from such factors as:

- The ownership of special raw material sources or advantageous long-term supply contracts.

- Being geographically located near key customers in a business involving significant fixed investment and high transport costs.

- Being a leader in a service field that permits or requires the building of a unique experience base while serving clients.

- Being a full-line producer in a market with heavy trade-up phenomena.

- Having a wide reputation for providing a needed product or service trait reliably and dependably.

In each case, the position permits competitive policies to be adopted that can serve to reinforce the position. Whenever this type of positive-feedback phenomena is encountered, the particular policy mix that creates it will be found to be a defensible business position. The key factors that sparked industrial success stories such as IBM and Eastman Kodak were the early and rapid domination of strong positions opened up by new technologies.

Feasibility

The final broad test of strategy is its feasibility. Can the strategy be attempted within the physical, human and financial resources available? The financial resources of a business are the easiest to quantify and are normally the first limitation against which strategy is tested. It is sometimes forgotten, however, that innovative approaches to financing expansion can both stretch the ultimate limitations and provide a competitive advantage, even if it is only temporary. Devices such as captive finance subsidiaries, sale–leaseback arrangements, and tying plant mortgages to long-term contracts have all been used effectively to help win key positions in suddenly expanding industries.

The less quantifiable but actually more rigid limitation on strategic choice is that imposed by the individual and organizational capabilities that are available.

In assessing the organization's ability to carry out a strategy, it is helpful to ask three questions:

1. Has the organization demonstrated that it possesses the problem-solving abilities and/or special competencies required by the strategy? A strategy, as such, does not and cannot specify in detail each action that must be carried out. Its purpose is to provide structure to the general issue of the business's goals and approaches to coping with its environment. It is up to the members and departments of the organization to carry out the tasks defined by strategy. A strategy that requires tasks to be accomplished which fall outside the realm of available or ... obtainable skill and knowledge cannot be accepted. It is either unfeasible or incomplete.

2. Has the organization demonstrated the degree of coordinative and integrative skill necessary to carry out the strategy? The key tasks required of a strategy not only require specialized skill, but often make considerable demands on the organization's ability to integrate disparate activities. A manufacturer of standard office furniture may find, for example, that its primary difficulty in entering the new market for modular office systems is a lack of sophisticated interaction between its field sales offices and its manufacturing plant. Firms that hope to span national boundaries with integrated worldwide systems of

production and marketing may also find that organizational process, rather than functional skill *per se* or isolated competitive strength, becomes the weak link in the strategic posture.

3.   Does the strategy challenge and motivate key personnel and is it acceptable to those who must lend their support? The purpose of strategy is effectively to deploy the unique and distinctive resources of an enterprise. If key managers are unmoved by a strategy, not excited by its goals or methods, or strongly support an alternative, it fails in a major way.

THE PROCESS OF STRATEGY EVALUATION

Strategy evaluation can take place as an abstract analytical task, perhaps performed by consultants. But most often it is an integral part of an organization's processes of planning, review and control. In some organizations, evaluation is informal, only occasional, brief and cursory. Others have created elaborate systems containing formal periodic strategy review sessions. In either case, the quality of strategy evaluation and, ultimately, the quality of corporate performance, will be determined more by the organization's capacity for self-appraisal and learning than by the particular analytical technique employed.

In their study of organizational learning, Argyris and Schon (1978) distinguish between single-loop and double-loop learning. They argue that normal organizational learning is of the feedback-control-type deviations between expected and actual performance lead to a problem-solving which brings the system back under control. They note that

> [Single-loop learning] is concerned primarily with effectiveness that is, with how best to achieve existing goals and objectives and how best to keep organizational performance within the range specified by existing norms. In some cases, however, error correction requires a learning cycle in which organizational norms themselves are modified.... We call this sort of learning 'double-loop'. There is ... a double feedback loop which connects the detection of error not only to strategies and assumptions for effective performance but to the very norms which define effective performance. (1978: 20)

These ideas parallel those of Ashby, a cyberneticist. Ashby (1954) has argued that all feedback systems require more than a single-loop error control for stability; they also need a way of monitoring certain critical variables and changing the system 'goals' when old control methods are no longer working.

These viewpoints help to remind us that the real strategic processes in any organization are not found by looking at those things that happen to be labelled 'strategic' or 'long range'. Rather, the real components of the strategic process are, by definition, those activities which most strongly affect the selection and modification of objectives and which influence the irreversible commitment of important resources. They also suggest that appropriate methods of strategy evaluation cannot be specified in abstract terms. Instead, an organization's approach to evaluation must fit its strategic posture and work in conjunction with its methods of planning and control.

In most firms comprehensive strategy evaluation is infrequent and, if it occurs, is normally triggered by a change in leadership or financial performance. The fact that comprehensive strategy evaluation is neither a regular event nor part of a formal system tends to be deplored by some theorists, but there are several good reasons for this state of affairs. Most obviously, any activity that becomes an annual procedure is bound to become more automatic. While evaluating strategy on an annual basis might lead to some sorts of efficiencies in data collection and analysis, it would also tend strongly to channel the types of questions asked and inhibit broad-ranging reflection.

Second, a good strategy does not need constant reformulation. It is a framework for continuing problem-solving, not the problem-solving itself. One senior executive expressed it this way: 'If you play from strength, you don't always need to be rethinking the whole plan; you can concentrate on details. So when you see us talking about slight changes in tooling it isn't because we forgot the big picture, its because we took care of it.'

Strategy also represents a political alignment within the firm and embodies the past convictions and commitments of key executives. Comprehensive strategy evaluation is not just an analytical exercise; it calls into question this basic pattern of commitments and policies. Most organizations would be hurt rather than helped to have their mission's validity called into question on a regular basis. Zero-based budgeting, for example, was an attempt to get agencies to rejustify their existence each time a new budget is drawn up. If this were literally true, there would be little time or energy remaining for any but political activity.

Finally, there are competitive reasons for not reviewing the validity of a strategy too freely! There are a wide range of rivalrous confrontations in which it is crucial to be able to convince others that one's position, or strategy, is fixed and unshakable. Schelling's (1963) analysis of bargaining and conflict shows that a great deal of what is involved in negotiating is finding ways to bind or commit oneself convincingly. This is the principle underlying the concept of deterrence and what lies behind the union leader's tactics of claiming that while he would go along with management's desire for moderation, he cannot control the members if the less moderate demands are not met. In business strategy, such situations occur in classic oligopoly, plant capacity duels, new product conflicts, and other situations in which the winner may be the party whose policies are most credibly unswayable. Japanese electronics firms, for example, have gained such strong reputations as low-cost committed players that their very entry into a market has come to induce rivals to give up. If such firms had instead the reputation of continually reviewing the advisability of continuing each product, they would be much less threatening, and thus less effective, competitors. . . .

CONCLUSIONS

Strategy evaluation is the appraisal of plans and the results of plans that centrally concern or affect the basic mission of an enterprise. Its special focus is the separation between obvious current operating results and those factors which underlie success or failure in the chosen domain of activity. Its result is the rejection, modification or ratification of existing strategies and plans. . . .

In most medium to large firms, strategy evaluation is not a purely intellectual task. The issues involved are too important and too closely associated with the distribution of power and authority for either strategy formulation or evaluation to take place in an ivory tower environment. In fact, most firms rarely engage in explicit formal strategy evaluation. Rather, the evaluation of current strategy is a continuing process and one that is difficult to separate from the normal planning, reporting, control, and reward systems of the firm. From this point of view, strategy evaluation is not so much an intellectual task as it is an organizational process. . . .

Ultimately, a firm's ability to maintain its competitive position in a world of rivalry and change may be best served by managers who can maintain a dual view of strategy and strategy evaluation; they must be willing and able to perceive the strategy within the welter of daily activity and to build and maintain structures and systems that make strategic factors the object of current activity.

CHAPTER

4

STRATEGY FORMATION

The readings in the last two chapters described how strategies are supposed to be made and thereby illustrated the prescriptive side of the field. This chapter presents readings that describe how strategies really do seem to be made, the descriptive side. We call this chapter 'Strategy formation' to emphasize the point introduced in Chapter 1 that strategies can form implicitly as well as be formulated explicitly.

The preceding chapters may seem to deal with an unreachable utopia, this one with an imperfect reality. But there may be a better conclusion: that prescription offers useful guidelines for thinking about ends and how to order physical resources efficiently to achieve them, while description provides a useful frame of reference for considering how this must be related to real-world patterns of behaviour in organizations. Another way to say this is that while the analytical tools and models prescribed earlier are vital to thinking about strategy intelligently, they must also be rooted in a genuine understanding of the realities of organizations. Unfortunately, management writers, especially in traditional strategy textbooks, have often been quick to prescribe, without offering enough appreciation of why managers and organizations act in the ways they do.

Brian Quinn opens with a sharp focus on how managers really do seem to behave when they create strategy. This reading is drawn from his book *Strategies for Change: Logical incrementalism,* and it develops a particular view of the strategy-making process based on intensive interviews in some of America's and Europe's best-known corporations. Planning does not capture the essence of strategy formation according to Quinn, although it does play an important role in developing new data and in confirming strategies derived in other ways. The traditional view of incrementalism does not fit observed behaviour patterns either. The processes Quinn observed seem incremental on the surface, but a powerful logic underlies them. And unlike the other incremental processes, these are not so much reactive as subtly proactive. Executives use incremental approaches to deal simultaneously with the informational, motivational and political aspects of creating a strategy.

Above all, Quinn depicts strategy formation as a managed interactive learning process in which the chief strategist gradually works out strategy in his or her mind and orchestrates the organization's acceptance of it. In emphasizing the role of a central strategist – or small groups managing 'subsystems' of strategy – Quinn often seems close to Andrews' view. But the two differ markedly in other important respects. In his emphasis on the learning dimension of strategy, Quinn is much closer to Senge, both in his views on how a company should go about its strategy-making process and the role that senior managers must play within that process.

The following reading by Mintzberg complements Quinn's. Called 'Crafting strategy' and another winner of the *Harvard Business Review* McKinsey award, it shows how managers mould strategies the way craft workers mould their clay. This reading also builds on Mintzberg's reading of Chapter 1 on the different forms of strategy, developing further the concept of emergent strategy.

In a chapter that challenges many of the accepted notions about how strategy should be made, the next reading may be the most upsetting of all. Here Richard Pascale, a well-known consultant, writer and lecturer, challenges head-on not only the whole approach to strategy analysis (as represented in Chapter 3), especially as practised by the Boston Consulting Group (one of the better known 'strategy boutiques', whose ideas will be discussed in Chapter 9), but also the very concept of strategy formulation itself.

As his point of departure, Pascale quotes from a BCG study carried out for the British government to explain how manufacturers in that country lost the American motorcycle market to the Japanese, and to the Honda Company in particular. The analysis seems impeccable and eminently logical: the Japanese were simply more clever, by thinking through a brilliant strategy before they acted. But then Pascale flew to Japan and interviewed those clever executives who pulled off this coup. We shall save the story for Pascale, who recounts it with a great deal of colour, except to note here its basic message: an openness to learning and a fierce commitment to an organization and its markets may count for more in strategy-making than all the brilliant analysis one can imagine. (Ask yourself while reading these accounts how the strategic behaviour of the British motorcycle manufacturers who received the BCG report might have differed if instead they had received Pascale's second story.) Pascale in effect takes the arguments for incrementalism and strategy-making as a crafting and learning process to their natural conclusions (or one of them, at least).

No one who reads Pascale's account can ever feel quite so smug about rational strategy analysis again. We include this reading, however, not to encourage rejection of that type of analysis, or the very solid thinking that has gone into the works of Andrews, Porter and others. Rather, we wish to balance the message conveyed in so much of the strategy literature with the practical lessons from the field. The point is that successful strategists can no more rely exclusively on such analysis than they can do without it. Effective strategy formation, one must conclude from all these readings, is a sometimes deceptive and multifaceted affair, its complexity never to be underestimated.

• STRATEGIC CHANGE: 'LOGICAL INCREMENTALISM'*

JAMES BRIAN QUINN

> When I was younger I always conceived of a room where all these [strategic] concepts were worked out for the whole company. Later I didn't find any such room.... The strategy [of the company] may not even exist in the mind of one man. I certainly don't know where it is written down. It is simply transmitted in the series of decisions made. (Interview quote)

When well-managed major organizations make significant changes in strategy, the approaches they use frequently bear little resemblance to the rational-analytical systems so often touted in the planning literature. The full strategy is rarely written down in any one place. The processes used to arrive at the total strategy are typically fragmented, evolutionary and largely intuitive. Although one can usually find embedded in these fragments some very refined *pieces* of formal strategic analysis, the real strategy tends to *evolve* as internal decisions and external events flow together to create a new, widely shared consensus for action among key members of the top management team. Far from being an abrogation of good management practice, the rationale behind this kind of strategy formulation is so powerful that it perhaps provides the normative model for strategic decision-making – rather than the step-by-step 'formal systems planning' approach so often espoused.

THE FORMAL SYSTEMS PLANNING APPROACH

A strong normative literature states what factors *should* be included in a systematically planned strategy and how to analyze and relate these factors step by step. While this approach is excellent for some purposes, it tends to focus unduly on measurable quantitative factors and to underemphasize the vital qualitative, organizational and power-behavioural factors which so often determine strategic success in one situation versus another. In practice, such planning is just one building-block in a continuous stream of events that really determine corporate strategy.

THE POWER-BEHAVIOURAL APPROACH

Other investigators have provided important insights on the crucial psychological, power and behavioural relationships in strategy formulation. Among other things, these have enhanced understanding about: the *multiple goal structures* of organizations, the *politics* of strategic decisions, executive *bargaining* and *negotiation* processes, *satisficing* (as opposed to maximizing) in decision-making, the role of *coalitions* in strategic management and the practice of 'middling' in the public sphere. Unfortunately,

---

*Excerpted from an article originally published in *Sloan Management Review* 1, no. 20 (Autumn 1978), pp. 7–21. Copyright © 1978 by Sloan Management Review; reprinted by permission of the *Review*.

however, many power-behavioural studies have been conducted in settings far removed from the realities of strategy formulation. Others have concentrated solely on human dynamics, power relationships and organizational processes and ignored the ways in which systematic data analysis shapes and often dominates crucial aspects of strategic decisions. Finally, few have offered much normative guidance for the strategist.

THE STUDY

Recognizing the contributions and limitations of both approaches, I attempted to document the dynamics of actual strategic change processes in some ten major companies as perceived by those most knowledgeably and intimately involved in them. These companies varied with respect to products, markets, time horizons, technological complexities and national versus international dimensions. . . .[1]

SUMMARY FINDINGS

Several important findings have begun to emerge from these investigations:

- Neither the 'power-behavioural' nor the 'formal systems planning' paradigm adequately characterizes the way successful strategic processes operate.
- Effective strategies tend to emerge from a series of 'strategic subsystems', each of which attacks a specific class of strategic issue (e.g. acquisitions, divestitures or major reorganizations) in a disciplined way, but which is blended incrementally and opportunistically into a cohesive pattern that becomes the company's strategy.
- The logic behind each 'subsystem' is so powerful that, to some extent, it may serve as a normative approach for formulating these key elements of strategy in large companies.
- Because of cognitive and process limits, almost all of these subsystems – and the formal planning activity itself – must be managed and linked together by an approach best described as 'logical incrementalism'.
- Such incrementalism is not 'muddling'. It is a purposeful, effective, proactive management technique for improving and integrating *both* the analytical and behavioural aspects of strategy formulation.

CRITICAL STRATEGIC ISSUES

Although certain 'hard data' decisions (e.g. on product market position or resource allocations) tend to dominate the analytical literature (Ansoff, 1965; Katz, 1970),

---

[1] Cooperating companies included General Motors Corp., Chrysler Corp., Volvo (AB), General Mills, Pilsbury Co., Xerox Corp., Texas Instruments, Exxon, Continental Group, and Pilkington Brothers.

executives identified other 'soft' changes that have at least as much importance in shaping their concern's strategic posture. Most often cited were changes in the company's:

1. Overall organizational structure or its basic management style.
2. Relationships with the government or other external interest groups.
3. Acquisition, divestiture or divisional control practices.
4. International posture and relationships.
5. Innovative capabilities or personnel motivations as affected by growth.
6. Worker and professional relationships reflecting changed social expectations and values.
7. Past or anticipated technological environments.

When executives were asked to 'describe the processes through which their company arrived at its new posture' *vis-à-vis* each of these critical domains, several important points emerged. First, few of these issues lent themselves to quantitative modelling techniques or perhaps even formal financial analyses. Second, successful companies used a different 'subsystem' to formulate strategy for each major class of strategic issues, yet these 'subsystems' were quite similar among companies even in very different industries (see Figure 1). Finally, no single formal analytical process could handle all strategic variables simultaneously on a planned basis. Why?

Precipitating Events

Often external or internal events, over which managements had essentially no control, would precipitate urgent, piecemeal, interim decisions which inexorably shaped the company's future strategic posture. One clearly observes this phenomenon in: the decisions forced on General Motors by the 1973–4 oil crisis, the shift in posture pressed upon Exxon by sudden nationalizations, or the dramatic opportunities allowed for Haloid Corporation and Pilkington Brothers, Ltd by the unexpected inventions of xerography and float glass.

In these cases, analyses from earlier formal planning cycles did contribute greatly, as long as the general nature of the contingency had been anticipated. They broadened the information base available (as in Exxon's case), extended the options considered (Haloid-Xerox), created shared values to guide decisions about precipitating events in consistent directions (Pilkington), or built up resource bases, management flexibilities or active search routines for opportunities whose specific nature could not be defined in advance (General Mills, Pillsbury). But no organization – no matter how brilliant, rational or imaginative – could possibly foresee the timing, severity or even the nature of all such precipitating events. Further, when these events did occur there might be neither time, resources nor information enough to undertake a full formal strategic analysis of all possible options and their consequences, Yet early decisions made under stress conditions often meant new thrusts, precedents, or lost opportunities that were difficult to reverse later.

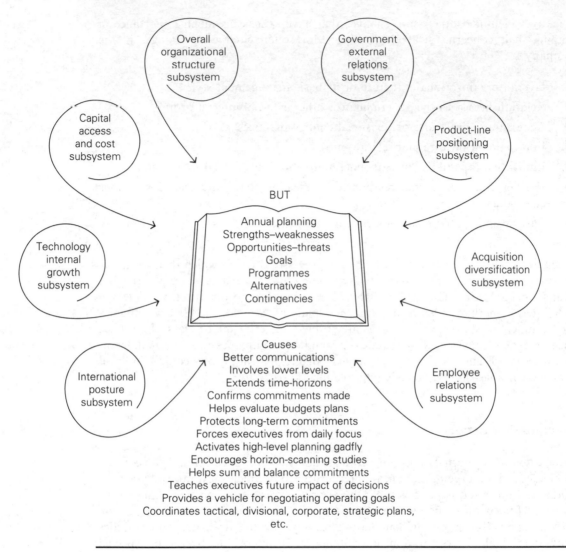

Figure 1

An Incremental Logic

Recognizing this, top executives usually consciously tried to deal with precipitating events in an incremental fashion. Early commitments were kept broadly formative, tentative and subject to later review. In some case neither the company nor the external players could understand the full implications of alternative actions. All parties wanted to test assumptions and have an opportunity to learn from and adapt to the others' responses. Such behaviour clearly occurred during the 1973–4 oil crisis; the ensuing interactions improved the quality of decisions for all. It also recurred frequently in other widely different contexts. For example, neither the potential producer nor user of a completely new product or process (like xerography or float glass) could fully conceptualize its ramifications without interactive testing. All parties benefited from procedures which purposely delayed decisions and allowed mutual feedback. Some companies, like IBM or Xerox, have formalized this concept into 'phase programme planning' systems. They make concrete decisions only on individual phases (or stages) of new product developments, establish interactive testing procedures with customers and postpone final configuration commitments until the latest possible moment.

Similarly, even under pressure, most top executives were extremely sensitive to organizational and power relationships and consciously managed decision processes to improve these dynamics. They often purposely delayed initial decisions, or kept such decisions vague, in order to encourage lower-level participation, to gain more information from specialists, or to build commitment to solutions. Even when a crisis atmosphere tended to shorten time horizons and make decisions more goal-oriented than political, perceptive executives consciously tried to keep their options open until they understood how the crisis would affect the power bases and needs of their key constituents. . . .

Conscious incrementalism helps to (1) cope with both the cognitive and process limits on each major decision, (2) build the logical-analytical framework these decisions require, and (3) create the personal and organizational awareness, understanding, acceptance and commitment needed to implement the strategies effectively.

The Diversification Subsystem

Strategies for diversification, either through R&D or acquisitions, provide excellent examples. The formal analytical steps needed for successful diversification are well documented (Mace and Montgomery, 1962). However, the precise directions that R&D may project the company can only be understood step by step as scientists uncover new phenomena, make and amplify discoveries, build prototypes, reduce concepts to practice and interact with users during product introductions. Similarly, only as each acquisition is sequentially identified, investigated, negotiated for and integrated into the organization can one predict its ultimate impact on the total enterprise.

A step-by-step approach is clearly necessary to guide and assess the strategic fit of each internal or external diversification candidate. Incremental processes are also required to manage the crucial psychological and power shifts that ultimately determine the programme's overall direction and consequences. These processes help unify both the analytical and behavioural aspects of diversification decisions. They create the broad conceptual consensus, the risk-taking attitudes, the organizational and resource flexibilities and the adaptive dynamism that determine both the timing and direction of diversification strategies. Most important among these processes are:

- *Generating a genuine, top-level psychological commitment to diversification:* General Mills, Pillsbury and Xerox all started their major diversification programmes with broad analytical studies and goal-setting exercises designed both to build top-level consensus around the need to diversify and to establish the general directions for diversification. Without such action, top-level bargaining for resources would have continued to support only more familiar (and hence apparently less risky) old lines, and this could delay or undermine the entire diversification endeavour.

- *Consciously preparing to move opportunistically:* Organizational and fiscal resources must be built up in advance to exploit candidates as they randomly appear. And a 'credible activist' for ventures must be developed and backed by someone with commitment power. All successful acquirers created the potential for 'profit-centred' divisions within their organizational structures, strengthened their financial-controllership capabilities, took action to create low-cost capital access and maintained the shortest possible communication lines from the 'acquisitions activist' to the resource-committing authority. All these actions integrally determined which diversifications actually could be made, the timing of their accession and the pace they could be absorbed.

- *Building a 'comfort factor' for risk-taking:* Perceived risk is largely a function of one's knowledge about a field. Hence well-conceived diversification programmes should anticipate a trial-and-error period during which top managers reject early proposed fields or opportunities until they have analyzed enough trail candidates to 'become comfortable' with an initial selection. Early successes tend to be 'sure things' close to the companies' past (real or supposed) expertise. After a few successful diversifications, managements tend to become more confident and accept other candidates – farther from traditional lines – at a faster rate. Again the way this process is handled affects both the direction and pace of the actual programme.

- *Developing a new ethos:* If new divisions are more successful than the old – as they should be – they attract relatively more resources and their political power grows. Their most effective line managers move into corporate positions, and slowly the company's special competency and ethos change. Finally, the concepts and products which once dominated the company's culture may decline in importance or even disappear. Acknowledging these ultimate consequences to the organization at the beginning of a diversification programme would clearly be impolitic, even if the manager both desired and could predict the probable new ethos. These factors must be handled adaptively, as opportunities present themselves and as individual leaders and power centres develop.

Each of the above processes interacts with all others (and with the random appearance of diversification candidates) to affect action sequences, elapsed time and ultimate results in unexpected ways. Complexities are so great that few diversification programmes end up as initially envisioned. Consequently, wise managers recognize the limits to systematic analysis in diversification, and use formal planning to build the 'comfort levels' executives need for risk-taking and to guide the programme's early directions and priorities. They then modify these flexibly, step by step, as new opportunities, power centres and developed competencies merge to create new potentials.

The Major Reorganization Subsystem

It is well recognized that major organizational changes are an integral part of strategy (Chandler, 1962). Sometimes they constitute a strategy themselves, sometimes they precede and/or precipitate a new strategy, and sometimes they help to implement a strategy. However, like many other important strategic decisions, macro-organizational moves are typically handled incrementally *and* outside of formal planning processes. Their effects on personal or power relationships preclude discussion in the open forums and reports of such processes.

In addition, major organizational changes have timing imperatives (or 'process limits') all their own. In making any significant shifts, the executive must think through the new roles, capabilities and probable individual reactions of the many principals affected. He may have to wait for the promotion or retirement of a valued colleague before consummating any change. He then frequently has to bring in, train or test new people for substantial periods before he can staff key posts with confidence. During this testing period he may substantially modify his original concept of the reorganization, as he evaluates individuals' potentials, their performance in specific roles, their personal drives and their relationships with other team members.

Because this chain of decisions affects the career development, power, affluence and self-image of so many, the executive tends to keep close counsel in his discussions, negotiates individually with key people and makes final commitments as late as possible in order to obtain the best matches between people's capabilities, personalities and aspirations and their new roles. Typically, all these events do not come together at one convenient time, particularly the moment annual plans are due. Instead the executive moves opportunistically, step by step, selectively moving people towards a broadly conceived organizational goal, which is constantly modified and rarely articulated in detail until the last pieces fit together.

Major organizational moves may also define entirely new strategies the guiding executive cannot fully foresee. For example when Exxon began its regional decentralization on a worldwide basis, the Executive Committee placed a senior officer and board member with a very responsive management style in a vaguely defined 'coordinative role' *vis-à-vis* its powerful and successful European units. Over a period of two years this man sensed problems and experimented with voluntary coordinative possibilities on a pan-European basis. Only later, with greater understanding by both corporate and divisional officers, did Exxon move to a more formal 'line' relationship for what became Exxon Europe. Even then the move had to be coordinated in other areas of the world. All of these changes together led to an entirely new internal power balance toward regional and non-US concerns and to a more responsive worldwide posture for Exxon. . . .

In such situations, executives may be able to predict the broad direction, but not the precise nature, of the ultimate strategy which will result. In some cases, such as Exxon, the rebalance of power and information relationships *becomes* the strategy, or at least its central element. In others, organizational shifts are primarily means of triggering or implementing new strategic concepts and philosophies. But in all cases, major organizational changes create unexpected new stresses, opportunities, power bases, information centres and credibility relationships that can affect both previous plans and future strategies in unanticipated ways. Effective reorganizaton decisions, therefore, allow for testing, flexibility and feedback. Hence, they should, and usually do, evolve incrementally.

FORMAL PLANNING IN CORPORATE STRATEGY

What role do classical formal planning techniques play in strategy formulation? All companies in the sample do have formal planning procedures embedded in their management direction and control systems. These serve certain essential functions. In a process sense they:

- Provide a discipline forcing managers to take a careful look ahead periodically.
- Require rigorous communications about goals, strategic issues and resource allocations.
- Stimulate longer-term analyses than would otherwise be made.
- Generate a basis for evaluating and integrating short-term plans.
- Lengthen time horizons and protect long-term investments such as R&D.
- Create a psychological backdrop and an information framework about the future against which managers can calibrate short-term or interim decisions.

In a decision-making sense they:

- Fine-tune annual commitments.
- Formalize cost reduction programmes.
- Help implement strategic changes once decided on (for example, coordinating all elements of Exxon's decision to change its corporate name).

In fact, formal planning practices actually institutionalize incrementalism. There are two reasons for this. First, in order to utilize specialized expertise and to obtain executive involvement and commitment, most planning occurs 'from the bottom up' in response to broadly defined assumptions or goals, many of which are long-standing or negotiated well in advance. Of necessity, lower-level groups have only a partial view of the corporation's total strategy, and command only a fragment of its resources. Their power bases, identity, expertise and rewards also usually depend on their existing products or processes. Hence, these products or processes, rather than entirely new departures, should and do receive their primary attention. Second, most managements purposely design their plans to be 'living' or 'ever green'. They are intended only as 'frameworks' to guide and provide consistency for future decisions made incrementally. To act otherwise would be to deny that further information could have a value. Thus, properly formulated formal plans are also a part of an incremental logic.

In each case there were also important precursor events, analyses and political interactions, and each was followed by organizational, power and behavioural changes. But interestingly, such special strategic studies also represent a 'subsystem' of strategy formulation distinct from both annual planning activities and the other subsystems exemplified above. Each of these develops some important aspect of strategy, incrementally blending its conclusions with those of other subsystems, and it would be virtually impossible to force all these together to crystallize a completely articulated corporate strategy at any one instant.

Total Posture Planning

Occasionally, however, managements do attempt very broad assessments of their companies' total posture. James McFarland of General Mills did this through taking the company's topmost managers away for a three-day retreat to answer the questions on what defined a 'great company' from the viewpoints of stockholders, employees, suppliers, the public and society; how did the company's strengths and weaknesses compare with the defined posture of 'greatness', and finally how should they proceed to overcome the company's weaknesses and move it from 'goodness to greatness'. The strategies that characterized the McFarland era at General Mills flowed from these assessments.

Yet even such major endeavours are only portions of a total strategic process. Values which have been built up over decades stimulate or constrain alternatives. Precipitating events, acquisitions, divestitures, external relations and organizational changes develop important segments of each strategy incrementally. Even the strategies articulated leave key elements to be defined as new information becomes available, policies permit, particular opportunities appear or major product thrusts prove unsuccessful. Actual strategies therefore evolve as each company overextends, consolidates, makes errors and rebalances various thrusts over time. And it is both logical and expected that this should be the case.

LOGICAL INCREMENTALISM

Strategic decisions do not lend themselves to aggregation into a single massive decision matrix where all factors can be treated relatively simultaneously in order to arrive at a holistic optimum. Many have spoken of the 'cognitive limits' (March and Simon, 1958) which prevent this. Of equal importance are the 'process limits' – that is, the timing and sequencing imperatives necessary to create awareness, build comfort levels, develop consensus, select and train people, and so on – which constrain the system, yet ultimately determine the decision itself.

A Strategy Emerges

Successful executives link together and bring order to a series of strategic processes and decisions spanning years. At the beginning of the process it is literally impossible to predict all the events and forces which will shape the future of the company. The best executives can do is to forecast the most likely forces which will impinge on the company's affairs and the ranges of their possible impact. They then attempt to build a resource base and a corporate *posture* that are so strong in selected areas that the enterprise can survive and prosper despite all but the most devastating events. They consciously select market/technological/product segments which the concern can 'dominate' given its resource limits, and place some 'side bets' (Ansoff, 1965) in order to decrease the risk of catastrophic failure or to increase the company's flexibility for future options.

They then proceed incrementally to handle urgent matters, start longer-term sequences whose specific future branches and consequences are perhaps murky, respond to unforeseen events as they occur, build on successes, and brace up or cut losses on failures. They constantly reassess the future, find new congruencies as events unfurl and blend the organization's skills and resources into new balances of dominance and risk-aversion as various forces intersect to suggest better — but never perfect – alignments. The process is dynamic, with neither a real beginning nor end. . . .

CONCLUSION

Strategy deals with the unknowable, not the uncertain. It involves forces of such great number, strength and combinatory powers that one cannot predict events in a probabilistic sense. Hence logic dictates that one proceed flexibly and experimentally from broad concepts towards specific commitments, making the latter concrete as late as possible in order to narrow the bands of uncertainty and to benefit from the best available information. This is the process of 'logical incrementalism'.

'Logical incrementalism' is not 'muddling', as most people use that word. It is conscious, purposeful, proactive, good management. Properly managed, it allows the executive to bind together the contributions of rational systematic analyses, political and power theories, and organizational behaviour concepts. It helps the executive achieve cohesion and identity with new directions. It allows him to deal with power relationships and individual behavioural needs, and permits him to use the best possible informational and analytical inputs in choosing his major courses of action. . . .

● CRAFTING STRATEGY*

HENRY MINTZBERG

Imagine someone planning strategy. What likely springs to mind is an image of orderly thinking: a senior manager, or a group of them, sitting in an office formulating courses of action that everyone else will implement on schedule. The keynote is reason – rational control, the systematic analysis of competitors and markets, of company strengths and weaknesses, the combination of these analyses producing clear, explicit, full-blown strategies.

Now imagine someone *crafting* strategy. A wholly different image likely results, as different from planning as craft is from mechanization. Craft evokes traditional skill, dedication, perfection through the mastery of detail. What springs to mind is not so much thinking and reason as involvement, a feeling of intimacy and harmony with the materials at hand, developed through long experience and commitment. Formulation and implementation merge into a fluid process of learning through which creative strategies evolve.

*Originally published in the *Harvard Business Review* (July–August 1987) and winner of McKinsey prize for second best article in the *Review* 1987. Copyright © 1987 by the President and Fellows of Harvard College; all rights reserved. Reprinted with deletions by permission of the *Harvard Business Review*.

My thesis is simple: the crafting image better captures the process by which effective strategies come to be. The planning image, long popular in the literature, distorts these processes and thereby misguides organizations that embrace it unreservedly.

In developing this thesis, I shall draw on the experiences of a single craftsman, a potter, and compare them with the results of a research project that tracked the strategies of a number of corporations across several decades. Because the two contexts are so obviously different; my metaphor, like my assertion, may seem far-fetched at first. Yet if we think of a craftsman as an organization of one, we can see that he or she must also resolve one of the great challenges the corporate strategist faces: knowing the organization's capabilities well enough to think deeply enough about its strategic direction. By considering strategy-making from the perspective of one person, free of all the paraphernalia of what has been called the strategy industry, we can learn something about the formation of strategy in the corporation. For much as our potter has to manage her craft, so too managers have to craft their strategy.

At work, the potter sits before a lump of clay on the wheel. Her mind is on the clay, but she is also aware of sitting between her past experiences and her future prospects. She knows exactly what has and has not worked for her in the past. She has an intimate knowledge of her work, her capabilities and her markets. As a craftsman, she senses rather than analyzes these things; her knowledge is 'tacit'. All these things are working in her mind as her hands are working the clay. The product that emerges on the wheel is likely to be in the tradition of her past work but she may break away and embark on a new direction. Even so, the past is no less present, projecting itself into the future.

In my metaphor, managers are craftsmen and strategy is their clay. Like the potter, they sit between the past of corporate capabilities and a future of market opportunities. And if they are truly craftsmen, they bring to their work an equally intimate knowledge of the materials at hand. That is the essence of crafting strategy.

STRATEGIES ARE BOTH PLANS FOR THE FUTURE AND PATTERNS FROM THE PAST

Ask almost anyone what strategy is, and they will define it as a plan of some sort, an explicit guide to future behaviour. Then ask them what strategy a competitor or a government or even they themselves have actually pursued. Chances are they will describe consistency in *past* behaviour – a pattern in action over time. Strategy, it turns out, is one of those words that people define in one way and often use in another, without realizing the difference.

The reason for this is simple. Strategy's formal definition and its Greek military origins notwithstanding, we need the word as much to explain past actions as to describe intended behaviour. After all, if strategies can be planned and intended, they can also be pursued and realized (or not realized, as the case may be). And pattern in action, or what we call realized strategy, explains that pursuit. Moreover, just as a plan need not produce a pattern (some strategies that are intended are simply not realized), so too a pattern need not result from a plan. An organization can have a pattern (or realized strategy) without knowing it, let alone making it explicit.

Patterns, like beauty, are in the mind of the beholder, of course. But finding them in organizations is not very difficult. But what about intended strategies, those formal plans and pronouncements we think of when we use the term *strategy*? Ironically, here we run into all kinds of problems. Even with a single craftsman, how can we know what her intended strategies really were? If we could go back, would we find expressions of intention? And if we could, would we be able to trust them? We often fool ourselves, as well as others, by denying our subconscious motives. And remember that intentions are cheap, at least when compared with realizations.

Reading the Organization's Mind

If you believe all this has more to do with the Freudian recesses of a craftsman's mind than with the practical realities of producing automobiles, then think again. For who knows what the intended strategies of an organization really mean, let alone what they are? Can we simply assume in this collective context that the company's intended strategies are represented by its formal plans or by other statements emanating from the executive suite? Might these be just vain hopes or rationalizations or ploys to fool the competition? And even if expressed intentions do exist, to what extent do various people in the organization share them? How do we read the collective mind? Who is the strategist anyway?

The traditional view of strategic management resolves these problems quite simply, by what organizational theorists call attribution. You see it all the time in the business press. When General Motors acts, it's because its CEO has made a strategy. Given realization, there must have been intention, and that is automatically attributed to the chief.

In a short magazine article, this assumption is understandable. Journalists don't have a lot of time to uncover the origins of strategy, and GM is a large, complicated organization. But just consider all the complexity and confusion that gets tucked under this assumption – all the meetings and debates, the many people, the dead ends, the folding and unfolding of ideas. Now imagine trying to build a formal strategy-making system around that assumption. Is it any wonder that formal strategic planning is often such a resounding failure?

To unravel some of the confusion – and move away from the artifical complexity we have piled around the strategy-making process – we need to get back to some basic concepts. The most basic of all is the intimate connection between thought and action. That is the key to craft and so also to the crafting of strategy.

STRATEGIES NEED NOT BE DELIBERATE – THEY CAN ALSO EMERGE, MORE OR LESS

Virtually everything that has been written about strategy-making depicts it as a deliberate process. First we think, then we act. We formulate, then we implement. The progression seems so perfectly sensible. Why would anybody want to proceed differently?

Our potter is in the studio, rolling the clay to make a waferlike sculpture. The clay sticks to the rolling pin, and a round form appears. Why not make a cylindrical vase? One idea leads to another, until a new pattern forms. Action has driven thinking, a strategy has emerged.

Out in the field, a salesman visits a customer. The product isn't quite right, and together they work out some modifications. The salesman returns to his company and puts the changes through; after two or three more rounds, they finally get it right. A new product emerges, which eventually opens up a new market. The company has changed strategic course.

In fact, most salespeople are less fortunate than this one or than our craftsman. In an organization of one, the implementor is the formulator, so innovations can be incorporated into strategy quickly and easily. In a large organization, the innovator may be ten levels removed from the leader who is supposed to dictate strategy and may also have to sell the idea to dozens of peers doing the same job.

Some salespeople, of course, can proceed on their own, modifying products to suit their customers and convincing skunkworks in the factory to produce them. In effect, they pursue their own strategies. Maybe no one else notices or cares. Sometimes, however, their innovations do get noticed, perhaps years later, when the company's prevalent strategies have broken down and its leaders are groping for something new. Then the salesperson's strategy may be allowed to pervade the system, to become organizational.

Is this story farfetched? Certainly not. We've all heard stories like it. But since we tend to see only what we believe, if we believe that strategies have to be planned, we're unlikely to see the real meaning such stories hold.

Consider how the National Film Board of Canada (NFB) came to adopt a feature-film strategy. The NFB is a federal government agency, famous for its creativity and expert in the production of short documentaries. Some years back, it funded a film-maker on a project that unexpectedly ran long. To distribute his film, the NFB turned to theatres and so inadvertently gained experience in marketing feature-length films. Other film-makers caught on to the idea, and eventually the NFB found itself pursuing a feature-film strategy – a pattern of producing such films.

My point is simple, deceptively simple: strategies can *form* as well as be *formulated*. A realized strategy can emerge in response to an evolving situation, or it can be brought about deliberately, through a process of formulation followed by implementation. But when these planned intentions do not produce the desired actions, organizations are left with unrealized strategies.

Today we hear a great deal about unrealized strategies, almost always in concert with the claim that implementation has failed. Management has been lax, controls have been loose, people haven't been committed. Excuses abound. At times, indeed, they may be valid. But often these explanations prove too easy. So some people look beyond implementation to formulation. The strategists haven't been smart enough.

While it is certainly true that many intended strategies are ill conceived, I believe that the problem often lies one step beyond, in the distinction we make between formulation and implementation, the common assumption that thought must be independent of and precede action. Sure, people could be smarter – but not only by conceiving more clever strategies. Sometimes they can be smarter by allowing their strategies to develop gradually, through the organization's actions and experiences. Smart strategists appreciate that they cannot always be smart enough to think through everything in advance.

Hands and Minds

No craftsman thinks some days and works others. The craftsman's mind is going constantly, in tandem with her hands. Yet large organizations try to separate the work of minds and hands. In so doing, they often sever the vital feedback link between the two. The salesperson who finds a customer with an unmet need may possess the most strategic bit of information in the entire organization. But that information is useless if he or she cannot create a strategy in response to it or else convey the information to someone who can – because the channels are blocked or because the formulators have simply finished formulating. The notion that strategy is something that should happen way up there, far removed from the details of running an organization on a daily basis, is one of the great fallacies of conventional strategic management. And it explains a good many of the most dramatic failures in business and public policy today.

Strategies like the NFB's that appear without clear intentions – or in spite of them – can be called emergent. Actions simply converge into patterns. They may become deliberate, of course, if the pattern is recognized and then legitimated by senior management. But that's after the fact.

All this may sound rather strange, I know. Strategies that emerge? Managers who acknowledge strategies already formed? Over the years, we have met with a good deal of resistance from people upset by what they perceive to be our passive definition of a word so bound up with proactive behaviour and free will. After all, strategy means control – the ancient Greeks used it to describe the art of the army general.

Strategic Learning

But we have persisted in this usage for one reason: learning. Purely deliberate strategy precludes learning once the strategy is formulated; emergent strategy fosters it. People take actions one by one and respond to them, so that patterns eventually form.

Our craftsman tries to make a freestanding sculptural form. It doesn't work, so she rounds it a bit here, flattens it a bit there. The result looks better, but still isn't quite right. She makes another and another and another. Eventually, after days or months or years, she finally has what she wants. She is off on a new strategy.

In practice, of course, all strategy-making walks on two feet, one deliberate, the other emergent. For just as purely deliberate strategy making precludes learning, so purely emergent strategy-making precludes control. Pushed to the limit, neither approach makes must sense. Learning must be coupled with control. That is why we used the word *strategy* for both emergent and deliberate behaviour.

Likewise, there is no such thing as a purely deliberate strategy or a purely emergent one. No organization – not even the ones commanded by those ancient Greek generals – knows enough to work everything out in advance, to ignore learning *en route*. And no one – not even a solitary potter – can be flexible enough to leave everything to chance, to give up all control. Craft requires control just as it requires responsiveness to the material at hand. Thus deliberate and emergent strategy form the end points of a continuum along which the strategies that are crafted in the real world may be found. Some strategies may approach either end, but many more fall at intermediate points.

EFFECTIVE STRATEGIES DEVELOP IN
ALL KINDS OF STRANGE WAYS

Effective strategies can show up in the strangest places and develop through the most unexpected means. There is no one best way to make strategy.

The form for a ceramic cat collapses on the wheel, and our potter sees a bull taking shape. Clay sticks to a rolling pin, and a line of cylinders results. Wafers come into being because of a shortage of clay and limited kiln space while visiting a studio in France. Thus errors become opportunities and limitations stimulate creativity. The natural propensity to experiment, even boredom, likewise stimulates strategic change.

Organizations that craft their strategies have similar experiences. Recall the National Film Board with its inadvertently long film. Or consider its experiences with experimental films, which made special use of animation and sound. For 20 years, the NFB produced a bare but steady trickle of such films, In fact, every film but one in that trickle was produced by a single person, Norman McLaren, the NFB's most celebrated film-maker. McLaren pursued a *personal strategy* of experimentation, deliberate for him perhaps (though who can know whether he had the whole stream in mind or simply planned one film at a time?) but not for the organization. Then 20 years later, others followed his lead and the trickle widened, his personal strategy becoming more broadly organizational.

While the NFB may seem like an extreme case, it highlights behaviour that can be found, albeit in muted form, in all organizations. Those who doubt this might read Richard Pascale's account of how Honda stumbled into its enormous success in the American motorcycle market. [See 'The Honda Effect', pp 125–34.]

Grass-roots Strategy-Making

These strategies all reflect, in whole or part, what we like to call a grass-roots approach to strategic management. Strategies grow like weeds in a garden. They take root in all kinds of places, wherever people have the capacity to learn (because they are in touch with the situation) and the resources to support that capacity. These strategies become organizational when they become collective, that is, when they proliferate to guide the behaviour of the organization at large.

Of course, this view is overstated. But it is no less extreme than the conventional view of strategic management, which might be labelled the hothouse approach. Neither is right. Reality falls between the two. Some of the most effective strategies we uncovered in our research combined deliberation and control with flexibility and organizational learning.

Consider first what we call the *umbrella strategy*. Here senior management sets out broad guidelines (say, to produce only high-margin products at the cutting edge of technology or to favour products using bonding technology) and leaves the specifics (such as what these products will be) to others lower down in the organization. This strategy is not only deliberate (in its guidelines) and emergent (in its specifics), but it is also deliberately emergent, in that the process is consciously managed to allow strategies to emerge *en route*. IBM used the umbrella strategy in the early 1960s with the impending 360 series, when its senior management approved a set of broad criteria for the design of a family of computers later developed in detail throughout the organization.

Deliberately emergent, too, is what we call the *process strategy*. Here management controls the process of strategy formation – concerning itself with the design of the structure, its staffing, procedures, and so on – while leaving the actual content to others.

Both process and umbrella strategies seem to be especially prevalent in businesses that require great expertise and creativity – a 3M, a Hewlett-Packard, a National Film Board. Such organizations can be effective only if their implementors are allowed to be formulators, because it is people way down in the hierarchy who are in touch with the situation at hand and have the requisite technical expertise. In a sense, these are organizations peopled with craftsmen, all of whom must be strategists.

STRATEGIC REORIENTATIONS HAPPEN IN BRIEF QUANTUM LEAPS

The conventional view of strategic management, especially in the planning literature, claims that change must be continuous: the organization should be adapting all the time. Yet this view proves to be ironic because the very concept of strategy is rooted in stability, not change. As this same literature makes clear, organizations pursue strategies to set direction, to lay out courses of action, and to elicit cooperation from their members around common, established guidelines. By any definition, strategy imposes stability on an organization. No stability means no strategy (no course to the future, no pattern from the past). Indeed, the very fact of having a strategy, and especially of making it explicit (as the conventional literature implores managers to do), creates resistance to strategic change!

What the conventional view fails to come to grips with, then, is how and when to promote change. A fundamental dilemma of strategy-making is the need to reconcile the forces for stability and for change – to focus efforts and gain operating efficiencies on the one hand, yet adapt and maintain currency with a changing external environment on the other.

Quantum Leaps

Our own research and that of colleagues suggests that organizations resolve these opposing forces by attending first to one and then to the other. Clear periods of stability and change can usually be distinguished in any organization: while it is true that particular strategies may always be changing marginally, it seems equally true that major shifts in strategic orientation occur only rarely.

In our study of Steinberg, Inc., a large Quebec supermarket chain headquartered in Montreal, we found only two important reorientations in the 60 years from its founding to the mid-1970s: a shift to self-service in 1933 and the introduction of shopping centres and public financing in 1953. At Volkswagenwerk, we saw only one between the late 1940s and the 1970s, the tumultuous shift from the traditional Beetle to the Audi-type design. And at Air Canada, we found none over the airline's first four decades, following its initial positioning.

Our colleagues at McGill, Danny Miller and Peter Friesen (1984), found this pattern of change so common in their studies of large numbers of companies (especially the high-performance ones) that they built a theory around it, which they labelled the quantum theory of strategic change. Their basic point is that organizations adopt two distinctly different modes of behaviour at different times.

Most of the time they pursue a given strategic orientation. Change may seem continuous, but it occurs in the context of that orientation (perfecting a given retailing formula, for example) and usually amounts to doing more of the same, perhaps better as well. Most organizations favour these periods of stability because they achieve success not by changing strategies but by exploiting the ones they have. They, like craftsmen, seek continuous improvement by using their distinctive competencies on established courses.

While this goes on, however, the world continues to change, sometimes slowly, occasionally in dramatic shifts. Thus gradually, or suddenly, the organization's strategic orientation moves out of sync with its environment. Then what Miller and Friesen call a strategic revolution must take place. That long period of evolutionary change is suddenly punctuated by a brief bout of revolutionary turmoil in which the organization quickly alters many of its established patterns. In effect, it tries to leap to a new stability quickly to re-establish an integrated posture among a new set of strategies, structures and culture.

But what about all those emergent strategies, growing like weeds around the organization? What the quantum theory suggests is that the really novel ones are generally held in check in some corner of the organization until a strategic revolution becomes necessary. Then, as an alternative to having to develop new strategies from scratch or having to import generic strategies from competitors, the organization can turn to its own emerging patterns to find its new orientation. As the old, established strategy disintegrates, the seeds of the new one begin to spread.

This quantum theory of change seems to apply particularly well to large established, mass-production companies, like a Volkswagenwerk. Because they are especially reliant on standardized procedures, their resistance to strategic reorientation tends to be especially fierce. So we find long periods of stability broken by short, disruptive periods of revolutionary change. Strategic reorientations really are cultural revolutions.

In more creative organizations we see a somewhat different pattern of change and stability, one that is more balanced. Companies in the business of producing novel outputs apparently need to run off in all directions from time to time to sustain their creativity. Yet they also need to settle down after such periods to find some order in the resulting chaos – convergence following divergence.

Whether through quantum revolutions or cycles of convergence and divergence, however, organizations seem to need to separate in time the basic forces for change and stability, reconciling them by attending to each in turn. Many strategic failures can be attributed either to mixing the two or to an obsession with one of these forces at the expense of the other.

The problems are evident in the work of many craftsmen. On the one hand, there are those who seize on the perfection of a single theme and never change. Eventually the creativity disappears from their work and the world passes them by – much as it did Volkswagenwerk until the company was shocked into its strategic revolution. And then there are those who are always changing, who flit from one idea to another and never settle down. Because no theme or strategy ever emerges in their work, they cannot exploit or even develop any distinctive competence. And because their work lacks definition, identity crises are likely to develop, with neither the craftsmen nor their clientele knowing what to make of it. Miller and Friesen (1978: 921) found this behaviour in conventional business too; they label it 'the impulsive firm running blind'. How often have we seen it in companies that go on acquisition sprees?

TO MANAGE STRATEGY, THEN, IS TO CRAFT THOUGHT AND ACTION, CONTROL AND LEARNING, STABILITY AND CHANGE

The popular view sees the strategist as a planner or as a visionary, someone sitting on a pedestal dictating brilliant strategies for everyone else to implement. While recognizing the importance of thinking ahead and especially of the need for creative vision in this pedantic world, I wish to propose an additional view of the strategist – as a pattern recognizer, a learner if you will – who manages a process in which strategies (and visions) can emerge as well as be deliberately conceived. I also wish to redefine that strategist, to extend that someone into the collective entity made up of the many actors whose interplay speaks an organization's mind. This strategist *finds* strategies no less than creates them, often in patterns that form inadvertently in its own behaviour.

What, then, does it mean to craft strategy? Let us return to the words associated with craft: dedication, experience, involvement with the material, the personal touch, mastery of detail, a sense of harmony and integration. Managers who craft strategy do not spend much time in executive suites reading MIS reports or industry analyses. They are involved, responsive to their materials, learning about their organizations and industries through personal touch. They are also sensitive to experience, recognizing that while individual vision may be important, other factors must help determine strategy as well.

Manage Stability

Managing strategy is mostly managing stability, not change. Indeed, most of the time senior managers should not be formulating strategy at all; they should be getting on with making their organizations as effective as possible in pursuing the strategies they already have. Like distinguished craftsmen, organizations become distinguished because they master the details.

To manage strategy, then, at least in the first instance, is not so much to promote change as to know *when* to do so. Advocates of strategic planning often urge managers to plan for perpetual instability in the environment (for example, by rolling over five-year plans annually). But this obsession with change is dysfunctional. Organizations that reassess their strategies continuously are like individuals who reassess their jobs or their marriages continuously – in both cases, they will drive themselves crazy or else reduce themselves to inaction. The formal planning process repeats itself so often and so mechanically that it desensitizes the organization to real change, programmes it more and more deeply into set patterns and thereby encourages it to make only minor adaptations.

So-called strategic planning must be recognized for what it is: a means, not to create strategy, but to programme a strategy already created – to work out its implications formally. It is essentially analytical in nature, based on decomposition, while strategy creation is essentially a process of synthesis. That is why trying to create strategies through formal planning most often leads to extrapolating existing ones or copying those of competitors.

This is not to say that planners have no role to play in strategy formation. In addition to programming strategies created by other means, they can feed *ad hoc* analyses into the strategy-making process at the front end to be sure that the hard data are taken into consideration. They can also stimulate others to think strategically. And of course, people called planners can be strategists too, so long as they are creative thinkers who are in touch with what is relevant. But that has nothing to do with the technology of formal planning.

Detect Discontinuity

Environments do not change on any regular or orderly basis. And they seldom undergo continuous dramatic change, claims about our 'age of discontinuity' and environmental 'turbulence' notwithstanding. (Tell people who lived through the Great Depression or survivors of the seige of Leningrad during World War II that ours are turbulent times.) Much of the time, change is minor and even temporary and requires no strategic response. Once in a while there is a truly significant discontinuity or, even less often, a Gestalt shift in the environment, where everything important seems to change at once. But these events, while critical, are also easy to recognize.

The real challenge in crafting strategy lies in detecting the subtle discontinuities that may undermine a business in the future. And for that, there is no technique, no programme, just a sharp mind in touch with the situation. Such discontinuities are unexpected and irregular, essentially unprecedented. They can be dealt with only by minds that are attuned to existing patterns yet able to perceive important breaks in them. Unfortunately, this form of strategic thinking tends to atrophy during the long periods of stability that most organizations experience. So the trick is to manage within a given strategic orientation most of the time yet be able to pick out the occasional discontinuity that really matters. The ability to make that kind of switch in thinking is the essence of strategic management. And it has more to do with vision and involvement than it does with analytical technique.

Know the Business

Note the kind of knowledge involved in strategic thinking: not intellectual knowledge, not analytical reports or abstracted facts and figures (though these can certainly help), but personal knowledge, intimate understanding, equivalent to the craftsman's feel for the clay. Facts are available to anyone; this kind of knowledge is not. Wisdom is the word that captures it best. But wisdom is a word that has been lost in the bureaucracies we have built for ourselves, systems designed to distance leaders from operating details. Show me managers who think they can rely on formal planning to create their strategies, and I'll show you managers who lack intimate knowledge of their businesses or the creativity to do something with it.

Craftsmen have to train themselves to see, to pick up things other people miss. The same holds true for managers of strategy. It is those with a kind of peripheral vision who are best able to detect and take advantage of events as they unfold.

Manage Patterns

Whether in an executive suite in Manhattan or a pottery studio in Montreal, a key to managing strategy is the ability to detect emerging patterns and help them take shape. The job of the manager is not just to preconceive specific strategies but also to recognize their emergence elsewhere in the organization and intervene when appropriate.

Like weeds that appear unexpectedly in a garden, some emergent strategies may need to be uprooted immediately. But management cannot be too quick to cut off the unexpected, for tomorrow's vision may grow out of today's aberration. (Europeans, after all enjoy salads made from the leaves of the dandelion, America's most notorious weed.) Thus some patterns are worth watching until their effects have more clearly manifested themselves. Then those that prove useful can be made deliberate and be incorporated into the formal strategy, even if that means shifting the strategic umbrella to cover them.

To manage in this context, then, is to create the climate within which a wide variety of strategies can grow. In more complex organizations, this may mean building flexible structures, hiring creative people, defining broad umbrella strategies, and watching for the patterns that emerge.

Reconcile Change and Continuity

Finally, managers considering radical departures need to keep the quantum theory of change in mind. As Ecclesiastes reminds us, there is a time to sow and a time to reap. Some new patterns must be held in check until the organization is ready for a strategic revolution, or at least a period of divergence. Managers who are obsessed with either change or stability are bound eventually to harm their organizations. As pattern recognizer, the manager has to be able to sense when to exploit an established crop of strategies and when to encourage new strains to displace the old.

While strategy is a word that is usually associated with the future, its link to the past is no less central. As Kierkegaard once observed, life is lived forward but understood backward. Managers may have to live strategy in the future, but they must understand it through the past.

Like potters at the wheel, organizations must make sense of the past if they hope to manage the future. Only by coming to understand the patterns that form in their own behaviour do they get to know their capabilities and their potential. Thus crafting strategy, like managing craft, requires a natural synthesis of the future, present and past.

THE HONDA EFFECT*

Richard T. Pascale

At face value, 'strategy' is an innocent noun. Webster defines it as the large-scale planning and direction of operations. In the business context, it pertains to a process by which a firm searches and analyzes its environment and resources in order to (1) select opportunities defined in terms of markets to be served and products to serve them, and (2) make discrete decisions to invest resources in order to achieve identified objectives (Bower, 1970: 7–8).

But for a vast and influential population of executives, planners, academics and consultants, strategy is more than a conventional English noun. It embodies an implicit model of how organizations should be guided and consequently, pro-configures our way of thinking. Strategy formulation (1) is generally assumed to be driven by senior management whom we expect to set strategic direction, (2) has been extensively influenced by empirical models and concepts, and (3) is often associated with a laborious strategic planning process that, in some companies, has produced more paper than insight.

A $500-million-a-year 'strategy' industry has emerged in the United States and Europe comprised of management consultants, strategic planning staffs and business school academics. It caters to the unique emphasis that American and European companies place upon this particular aspect of managing and directing corporations.

Words often derive meaning from their cultural context. *Strategy* is one such word and nowhere is the contrast of meanings more pronounced than between Japan and the United States. The Japanese view the emphasis we place on 'strategy' as we might regard their enthusiasm for Kabuki or sumo wrestling. They note our interest not with an intent of acquiring similar ones but for insight into our peculiarities. The Japanese are somewhat distrustful of a single 'strategy' for in their view any idea that focuses attention does so at the expense of peripheral vision. They strong believe that *peripheral vision* is essential to discerning changes in the customer, the technology or competition, and is the key to corporate survival over the long haul. They regard any prospensity to be driven by a single-minded strategy as a weakness.

The Japanese have particular discomfort with strategic concepts. While they do not reject ideas such as the experience curve or portfolio theory outright they regard them as a stimulus to perception. They have often ferreted out the 'formula' of their concept-driven American competitors and exploited their inflexibility. In musical instruments, for example (a mature industry facing stagnation as birthrates in the United States and Japan declined), Yamaha might have classified its products as 'cash cows' and gone on to better things (as its chief US competitor, Baldwin United, had done). Instead, beginning with a negligible share of the US market, Yamaha ploughed ahead and destroyed Baldwin's seemingly unchallengeable dominance. YKK's success in zippers against Talon (a Textron division) and Honda's

---

*Excerpted from an article originally entitled 'Perspectives on strategy: The real story behind Honda's success', *California Management Review XXVI*, no. 3, pp. 47–72. Copyright © 1984 by the Regents of the University of California. Reprinted by permission of the Regents.

outflanking of Harley-Davidson (a former AMF subsidiary) in the motorcycle field provide parallel illustrations. All three cases involved American conglomerates, wedded to the portfolio concept, that had classified pianos, zippers and motorcycles as mature businesses to be harvested rather than nourished and defended. Of course, those who developed portfolio theory and other strategic concepts protest that they were never intended to be mindlessly applied in setting strategic direction. But most would also agree that there is a widespread tendency in American corporations to misapply concepts and to otherwise become strategically myopic – ignoring the marketplace, the customer and the problems of execution. This tendency towards misapplication, being both pervasive and persistent over several decades, is a phenomenon that the literature has largely ignored (for exceptions, see Hayes and Abernathy, 1980: 67; Hayes and Garvin, 1982: 71). There is a need to identify explicitly the factors that influence how we conceptualize strategy – and that foster its misuse.

HONDA: THE STRATEGY MODEL

In 1975, Boston Consulting Group (BCG) presented the British government its final report: *Strategy Alternatives for the British Motorcycle Industry*. This 120-page document identified two key factors leading to the British demise in the world's motorcycle industry:

1. Market share loss and profitability declines.
2. Scale economy disadvantages in technology, distribution and manufacturing.

During the period 1959 to 1973, the British share of the US motorcycle industry had dropped from 49 per cent to 9 per cent. Introducing BCG's recommended strategy (of targeting market segments where sufficient production volumes could be attained to be price-competitive) the report states:

> The success of the Japanese manufacturers originated with the growth of their domestic market during the 1950s. As recently as 1960, only 4 percent of Japanese motorcycle production was exported. By this time, however, the Japanese had developed huge production volumes in small motorcycles in their domestic market, and volume-related cost reductions had followed. This resulted in a highly competitive cost position which the Japanese used as a springboard for penetration of world markets with small motorcycles in the early 1960s. (BCG, 1975: xiv)

The BCG study was made public by the British government and rapidly disseminated in the United States. It exemplifies the necessary (and, I argue, insufficient) strategist's perspective of:

- examining competition primarily from an intercompany perspective,
- at a high level of abstraction,
- with heavy reliance on microeconomic concepts (such as the experience curve).

Case writers at Harvard Business School, UCLA, and the University of Virginia quickly condensed the BCG report for classroom use in case discussions. It currently enjoys extensive use in first-term courses in business policy.

Of particular note in the BCG study, and in the subsequent Harvard Business School rendition, is the historical treatment of Honda:

The mix of competitors in the U.S. motorcycle market underwent a major shift in the 1960s. Motorcycle registrations increased from 575,000 in 1960 to 1,382,000 in 1965. Prior to 1960 the U.S. market was served mainly by Harley-Davidson of U.S.A., BSA, Triumph and Norton of U.K. and Moto-Guzzi of Italy. Harley was the market leader with total 1959 sales of $16.6 million. After the second world war, motorcycles in the U.S.A. attracted a very limited group of people other than police and army personnel who used motorcycles on the job. While most motorcyclists were no doubt decent people, groups of rowdies who went around on motorcycles and called themselves by such names as 'Hell's Angels,' 'Satan's Slaves' gave motorcycling a bad image. Even leather jackets which were worn by motorcyclists as a protective device acquired an unsavory image. A 1953 movie called 'The Wild Ones' starring a 650 cc Triumph, a black leather jacket and Marlon Brando gave the rowdy motorcyclists wide media coverage. The stereotype of the motorcyclist was a leather-jacketed, teenage troublemaker.

Honda established an American subsidiary in 1959 – American Honda Motor Company. This was in sharp contrast to other foreign producers who relied on distributors. Honda's marketing strategy was described in the 1963 annual report as 'With its policy of selling, not primarily to confirmed motorcyclists by rather to members of the general public who had never before given a second thought to a motorcycle. . . .' Honda started its push in the U.S. market with the smallest, lightweight motorcycles. It had a three-speed transmission, an automatic clutch, five horsepower (the American cycle only had two and a half), an electric starter and step through frame for female riders. And it was easier to handle. The Honda machines sold for under $250 in retail compared with $1,000–$1,500 for the bigger American or British machines. Even at that early date Honda was probably superior to other competitors in productivity.

By June 1960 Honda's Research and Development effort was staffed with 700 designers/engineers. This might be contrasted with 100 engineers/draftsmen employed by . . . (European and American competitors). In 1962 production per man-year was running at 159 units (a figure not reached by Harley-Davidson until 1974). Honda's net fixed asset investment was $8170 per employee . . . (more than twice its European and American competitors). With 1959 sales of $55 million Honda was already the largest motorcycle producer in the world.

Honda followed a policy of developing the market region by region. They started on the West Coast and moved eastward over a period of four–five years. Honda sold 2,500 machines in the U.S. in 1960. In 1961 they lined up 125 distributors and spent $150,000 on regional advertising. Their advertising was directed to the young families, their advertising theme was 'You Meet the Nicest People on a Honda.' This was a deliberate attempt to dissociate motorcycles from rowdy, Hell's Angels type people.

Honda's success in creating demand for lightweight motorcycles was phenomenal. American Honda's sales went from $500,000 in 1960 to $77 million in 1965. By 1966 the market share data showed the ascendancy of Japanese producers and their success in selling lightweight motorcycles. [Honda had 63% of the market.] . . . Starting from virtually nothing in 1960, the lightweight motorcycles had clearly established their lead. (Purkayastha, 1981: 5, 10, 11, 12)

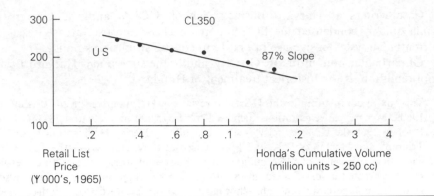

FIGURE 1
Source: BCG (1973), 'Strategy alternatives for the British motorcycle industry'.

Quoting from the BCG report:

> The Japanese motorcycle industry, and in particular Honda, the market leader, present a [consistent] picture. The basic philosophy of the Japanese manufacturers is that high volumes per model provide the potential for high productivity as a result of using capital intensive and highly automated techniques. Their marketing strategies are therefore directed towards developing these high model volumes, hence the careful attention that we have observed them giving to growth and market share.
>
> The overall result of this philosophy over time has been that the Japanese have now developed an entrenched and leading position in terms of technology and production methods. . . . The major factors which appear to account for the Japanese superiority in both these areas are . . . (specialized production systems, balancing engineering and market requirements, and the cost efficiency and reliability of suppliers). (BCG, pp. 59, 40)

As evidence of Honda's strategy of taking position as low-cost producer and exploiting economies of scale, other sources cite Honda's construction in 1959 of a plant to manufacture 30,000 motorcycles per month well ahead of existing demand at the time (up until then Honda's most popular models sold 2,000–3,000 units per month) (Sakiya, 1982: 119).

The overall picture as depicted by the quotes exemplifies the 'strategy model'. Honda is portrayed as a firm dedicated to being the low-price producer, utilizing its dominant market position in Japan to force entry into the US market, expanding that market by redefining a leisure class ('Nicest People') segment and exploiting its comparative advantage via aggressive pricing and advertising. Richard Rumelt, writing the teaching note for the UCLA adaptation of the case states: 'The fundamental contribution of BCG is not the experience curve per se but the ever-present assumption that differences in cost (or efficiency) are the fundamental components of strategy' (Rumelt, 1980: 2).

THE ORGANIZATIONAL PROCESS PERSPECTIVE

On 10 September 1982, the six Japanese executives responsible for Honda's entry into the US motorcycle market in 1959 assembled in Honda's Tokyo headquarters.

They had gathered at my request to describe in fine-grain detail the sequence of events that had led to Honda's ultimate position of dominance in the US market. All were in their sixties; three were retired. The story that unfolded, greatly abbreviated below, highlights miscalculation, serendipity and organizational learning – counterpoints to the streamlined 'strategy' version related earlier. . . .

Any account of Honda's successes must grasp at the outset the unusual character of its founder, Soichiro Honda, and his partner, Takeo Fujisawa. Honda was an inventive genius with a large ego and mercurial temperament, given to bouts of 'philandering' (to use his expression) (Sakiya, 1979). . . .

Postwar Japan was in desperate need of transportation. Motorcycle manufacturers proliferated, producing clip-on engines that converted bicycles into makeshift 'mopeds'. Honda was among these, but it was not until he teamed up with Fujisawa in 1949 that the elements of a successful enterprise began to take shape. Fujisawa provided money as well as financial and marketing strengths. In 1950 their first D-type motorcycle was introduced. They were, at that juncture, participating in a fragmented industry along with 247 other manufacturers. Other than its sturdy frame, this introductory product was unnoteworthy and did not enjoy great commercial success (Sakiya, 1979; 1982).

Honda embodied a rare combination of inventive ability and ultimate self-confidence. His motivation was not primarily commercial. Rather, the company served as a vehicle to give expression to his inventive abilities. A successful company would provide a resource base to pursue, in Fujisawa's words, his 'grandiose dream'. Fujisawa continues, 'There was no end to his pursuit of technology' (Sakiya, 1982).

Fujisawa, in an effort to save the faltering company, pressed Honda to abandon their noisy two-stroke engine and pursue a four-stroke design. The quieter four-stroke engines were appearing on competitive motorcycles, therefore threatening Honda with extinction. Mr Honda balked. But a year later, Honda stunned Fujisawa with a breakthrough design that doubled the horsepower of competitive four-stroke engines. With this innovation, the firm was off and putting, and by 1951 demand was brisk. There was no organization, however, and the plant was chaotic (Sakiya, 1982). Strong demand, however, required early investment in a simplified mass production process. As a result, *primarily* due to design advantages, and secondarily to production methods, Honda became one of the four or five industry leaders by 1954 with 15 per cent market share (data provided by company). . . .

For Fujisawa, the engine innovation meant increased sales and easier access to financing. For Mr Honda, the higher horsepower engine opened the possibility of pursuing one of his central ambitions in life – to race his motorcycle and win. . . .

Fujisawa, throughout the 1950s, sought to turn Honda's attention from his enthusiasm with racing to the more mundane requirements of running an enterprise. By 1956, as the innovations gained from racing had begun to pay off in vastly more efficient engines, Fujisawa pressed Honda to adapt this technology for a commercial motorcycle (Sakiya, 1979; 1982). Fujisawa had a particular segment in mind. Most motorcyclists in Japan were male and the machines were used primarily as an alternative form of transportation to trains and buses. There were, however, a vast number of small commercial establishments in Japan that still delivered goods and ran errands on bicycles. Trains and buses were inconvenient for these activities. The pursestrings of these small enterprises were controlled by the Japanese wife – who resisted buying conventional motorcycles because they were expensive, dangerous and hard to handle. Fujisawa challenged Honda: Can you use what you've learned from racing to come up with an inexpensive, safe-looking motorcycle that can be driven with one hand (to facilitate carrying packages).

In 1958, the Honda 50 cc Supercub was introduced – with an automatic clutch, three-speed transmission, automatic starter and the safe, friendly look of a bicycle (without the stigma of the outmoded mopeds). Owing almost entirely to its high horsepower but *lightweight 50 cc engine* (not to production efficiencies), it was affordable. Overnight, the firm was overwhelmed with orders. Engulfed by demand, they sought financing to build a new plant with a 30,000 unit per month capacity. 'It wasn't a speculative investment,' recalls one executive. 'We had the proprietary technology, we had the market, and the demand was enormous.' (The plant was completed in mid-1960.) Prior to its opening, demand was met through makeshift, high-cost, company-owned assembly and farmed-out assembly through subcontractors. By the end of 1959, Honda had skyrocketed into first place among Japanese motorcycle manufacturers. Of its total sales that year of 285,000 units, 168,000 were Supercubs.

Fujisawa utilized the Supercub to restructure Honda's channels of distribution. For many years, Honda had rankled under the two-tier distribution system that prevailed in the industry. These problems had been exacerbated by the fact that Honda was a late entry and had been carried as secondary line by distributors whose loyalties lay with their older manufacturers. Further weakening Honda's leverage, all manufacturer sales were on a consignment basis.

Deftly, Fujisawa had characterized the Supercub to Honda's distributors as 'something much more like a bicycle than a motorcycle'. The traditional channels, to their later regret, agreed. Under amicable terms Fujisawa began selling the Supercub directly to retailers – and primarily through bicycle shops. Since these shops were small and numerous (approximately 12,000 in Japan), sales on consignment were unthinkable. A cash-on-delivery system was installed, giving Honda significantly more leverage over its dealerships than the other motorcycle manufacturers enjoyed.

The stage was now set for exploration of the US market. Mr Honda's racing conquests in the late 1950s had given substance to his convictions about his abilities. . . .

Two Honda executives – the soon-to-be-named president of American Honda, Kihachiro Kawashima, and his assistant – arrived in the United States in late 1958. Their itinerary: San Francisco, Los Angeles, Dallas, New York and Columbus. Mr Kawashima recounts his impressions:

> My first reaction after travelling across the United States was: How could we have been so stupid as to start a war with such a vast and wealthy country! My second reaction was discomfort. I spoke poor English. We dropped in on motorcycle dealers who treated us discourteously and in addition, gave the general impression of being motorcycle enthusiasts who, secondarily, were in business. There were only 3,000 motorcycle dealers in the United States at the time and only 1,000 of them were open five days a week. The remainder were open on nights and weekends. Inventory was poor, manufacturers sold motorcycles to dealers on consignment, the retailers provided consumer financing; after-sales service was poor. It was discouraging.
>   My other impression was that everyone in the United States drove an automobile – making it doubtful that motorcycles could ever do very well in the market. However, with 450,000 motorcycle registrations in the US and 60,000 motorcycles imported from

Europe each year it didn't seem unreasonable to shoot for 10 per cent of the import market. I returned to Japan with that report.

In truth, we had no strategy other than the idea of seeing if we could sell something in the United States. It was a new frontier, a new challenge, and it fit the 'success against all odds' culture that Mr Honda had cultivated. I reported my impressions to Fujisawa – including the seat-of-the-pants target of trying, over several years, to attain a 10 per cent share of US imports. He didn't probe that target quantitatively. We did not discuss profits or deadlines for breakeven. Fujisawa told me if anyone could succeed, I could and authorized $1 million for the venture.

The next hurdle was to obtain a currency allocation from the Ministry of Finance. They were extraordinarily skeptical. Toyota had launched the Toyopet in the US in 1958 and had failed miserably. 'How could Honda succeed?' they asked. Months went by. We put the project on hold. Suddenly, five months after our application, we were given the go-ahead – but at only a fraction of our expected level of commitment. 'You can invest $250,000 in the US market,' they said, 'but only $110,000 in cash.' The remainder of our assets had to be in parts and motorcycle inventory.

We moved into frantic activity as the government, hoping we would give up on the idea, continued to hold us to the July 1959 start-up timetable. Our focus, as mentioned earlier, was to compete with the European exports. We knew our products at the time were good but not far superior. Mr Honda was especially confident of the 250 cc and 305 cc machines. The shape of the handlebar on these larger machines looked like the eyebrow of Buddha, which he felt was a strong selling point. Thus, after some discussion and with no compelling criteria for selection, we configured our start-up inventory with 25 per cent of each of our four products – the 50 cc Supercub and the 125 cc, 250 cc and 305 cc machines. In dollar value terms, of course, the inventory was heavily weighted toward the larger bikes.

The stringent monetary controls of the Japanese government together with the unfriendly reception we had received during our 1958 visit caused us to start small. We chose Los Angeles where there was a large second and third generation Japanese community, a climate suitable for motorcycle use, and a growing population. We were so strapped for cash that the three of us shared a furnished apartment that rented for $80 per month. Two of us slept on the floor. We obtained a warehouse in a run-down section of the city and waited for the ship to arrive. Not daring to spare our funds for equipment, the three of us stacked the motorcycle crates three high by hand, swept the floors, and built and maintained the parts bin.

We were entirely in the dark the first year. We were not aware the motorcycle business in the United States occurs during a seasonable April-to-August window – and our timing coincided with the closing of the 1959 season. Our hard-learned experiences with distributorships in Japan convinced us to try to go to the retailers direct. We ran ads in the motorcycle trade magazine for dealers. A few responded. By spring of 1960, we had forty dealers and some of our inventory in their stores – mostly larger bikes. A few of the 250 cc and 305 cc bikes began to sell. Then disaster struck.

By the first week of April 1960, reports were coming in that our machines were leaking oil and encountering clutch failure. This was our lowest moment. Honda's fragile reputation was being destroyed before it could be established. As it turned out, motorcycles in the United States are driven much farther and much faster than in Japan. We dug deeply into our precious cash reserves to air freight our motorcycles to the Honda testing lab in Japan. Through the dark month of April, Pan Am was the only enterprise in the US that was nice to us. Our testing lab worked twenty-four-hour days bench testing the bikes to try to replicate the failure. Within a month, a redesigned head gasket and clutch spring solved the problem. But in the meantime, events had taken a surprising turn.

Throughout our first eight months, following Mr Honda's and our own instincts, we had not attempted to move the 50 cc Supercubs. While they were a smash success in Japan (and manufacturing couldn't keep up with demand there), they seemed wholly unsuitable for the US market where everything was bigger and more luxurious. As a clincher, we had our sights on the import market – and the Europeans, like the American manufacturers, emphasized the larger machines.

We used the Honda 50s ourselves to ride around Los Angeles on errands. They attracted a lot of attention. One day we had a call from a Sears buyer. While persisting in our refusal to sell through an intermediary, we took note of Sears' interest. But we still hesitated to push the 50 cc bikes out of fear they might harm our image in a heavily macho market. But when the larger bikes started breaking, we had no choice. We let the 50 cc bikes move. And surprisingly, the retailers who wanted to sell them weren't motorcycle dealers, they were sporting goods stores.

The excitement created by the Honda Supercub began to gain momentum. Under restrictions from the Japanese government, we were still on a cash basis. Working with our initial cash and inventory, we sold machines, reinvested in inventory, and sunk the profits into additional inventory and advertising. Our advertising tried to straddle the market. While retailers continued to inform us that our Supercub customers were normal everyday Americans, we hesitated to target toward this segment out of fear of alienating the high margin end of our business – sold through the traditional motorcycle dealers to a more traditional 'black leather jacket' customer.

Honda's phenomenal sales and share gains over the ensuing years have been previously reported. History has it that Honda 'redefined' the US motorcycle industry. In the view of American Honda's start-up team, this was an innovation they backed into – and reluctantly. It was certainly not the strategy they embarked on in 1959. As late as 1963, Honda was still working with its original Los Angeles advertising agency, its ad campaigns straddling all customers so as not to antagonize one market in pursuit of another.

In the spring of 1963, an undergraduate advertising major at UCLA submitted, in fulfilment of a routine course assignment, an ad campaign for Honda. Its theme: 'You Meet the Nicest People on a Honda'. Encouraged by his instructor, the student passed his work on to a friend at Grey Advertising. Grey had been soliciting the Honda account – which with a $5 million a year budget was becoming an attractive potential client. Grey purchased the student's idea – on a tightly kept non-disclosure basis. Grey attempted to sell the idea to Honda.

Interestingly, the Honda management team, which by 1963 had grown to five Japanese executives, was badly split on this advertising decision. The president and treasurer favoured another proposal from another agency. The director of sales, however, felt strongly that the Nicest People campaign was the right one, and his commitment eventually held sway. Thus, in 1963, through an inadvertent sequence of events, Honda came to adopt a strategy that directly identified and targeted that large untapped segment of the marketplace that has since become inseparable from the Honda legend.

The Nicest People campaign drove Honda's sales at an even greater rate. By 1964, nearly one out of every two motorcycles sold was a Honda. As a result of the influx of medium-income, leisure-class consumers, banks and other consumer credit companies began to finance motorcycles, shifting away from dealer credit, which had been the traditional purchasing mechanism available. Honda, seizing the opportunity of soaring demand for its products, took a courageous and seemingly risky position. Late in 1964, they announced that thereafter, they would cease to ship on a consignment basis but would require cash on delivery. Honda braced itself for revolt. While nearly every dealer questioned, appealed or complained, none relinquished his franchise. In one fell swoop, Honda shifted the power relationship from the dealer to the manufacturer. Within three years, this would become the pattern for the industry.

THE 'HONDA EFFECT'

The preceding account of Honda's inroads into the US motorcycle industry provides more than a second perspective on reality. It focuses our attention on different issues and raises different questions. What factors permitted two men as unlike one another as Honda and Fujisawa to function effectively as a team? What incentives and understandings permitted the Japanese executives at American Honda to respond to the market as it emerged rather than doggedly pursue the 250 cc and 305 cc strategy that Mr Honda favoured? What decision process permitted the relatively junior sales director to overturn the bosses' preferences and choose the Nicest People campaign? What values or commitment drove Honda to take the enormous risk of alienating its dealers in 1964 in shifting from a consignment to cash? In hindsight, these pivotal events all seem ho-hum common sense. But each day, as organizations live out their lives without the benefit of hindsight, few choose so well and so consistently.

The juxtaposed perspectives reveal what I shall call the 'Honda Effect'. Western consultants, academics and executives express a preference for oversimplifications of reality and cognitively linear explanations of events. To be sure, they have always acknowledged that the 'human factor' must be taken into account. But extensive reading of strategy cases at business schools, consultants' reports, strategic planning documents as well as the coverage of the popular press, reveals a widespread tendency to overlook the process through which organizations experiment, adapt and learn. We tend to impute coherence and purposive rationality to events when the opposite may be closer to the truth. How an organization deals with miscalculation, mistakes and serendipitous events *outside its field of vision is often crucial to success over time*. It is this realm that requires better understanding and further research if we are to enhance our ability to guide an organization's destiny. . . .

An earlier section has addressed the shortcomings of the narrowly defined microeconomic strategy model. The Japanese avoid this pitfall by adopting a broader notion of 'strategy'. In our recent awe of things Japanese, most Americans forget that the original products of the Japanese automotive manufacturers badly missed the mark. Toyota's Toyopet was square, sexless and mechanically defective. It failed miserably, as did Datsun's first several entries into the US market. More recently, Mazda miscalculated badly with its first rotary engine and nearly went bankrupt. Contrary to myth, the Japanese did not from the onset embark on a strategy to seize the high quality, small car market. They manufactured what they were accustomed to building in Japan and tried to sell it abroad. Their success, as any Japanese automotive executive will readily agree, did not result from a bold insight by a few big brains at the top. On the contrary, success was achieved by senior managers humble enough not to take their initial strategic positions too seriously. What saved

Japan's near-failures was the cumulative impact of 'little brains' in the form of salesmen and dealers and production workers, all contributing incrementally to the quality and market position these companies enjoy today. Middle and upper management saw their primary task as guiding and orchestrating this input from below rather than steering the organization from above along a predetermined strategic course.

The Japanese don't use them term 'strategy' to describe a crisp business definition or competitive master plan. They think more in terms of 'strategic accommodation', or 'adaptive persistence', underscoring their belief that corporate direction evolves from an incremental adjustment to unfolding events. Rarely, in their view, does one leader (or a strategic planning group) produce a bold strategy that guides a firm unerringly. Far more frequently, the input is from below. It is this ability of an organization to move information and ideas from the bottom to the top and back again in continuous dialogue that the Japanese value above all things. As this dialogue is pursued, what in hindsight may be 'strategy' evolves. In sum, 'strategy' is defined as 'all the things necessary for the successful functioning of organization as an adaptive mechanism'. . . .

ROBIN HOOD*

It was in the spring of the second year of his insurrection against the High Sheriff of Nottingham that Robin Hood took a walk in Sherwood forest. As he walked he pondered the progress of the campaign, the disposition of his forces, the Sheriff's recent moves and the options that confronted him.

The revolt against the Sheriff had begun as a personal crusade, it erupted out of Robin's conflict with the Sheriff and his administration. However, alone Robin Hood could do little. He therefore sought allies, men with grievances and a deep sense of injustice. Later he welcomed all who came, asking few questions and only demanding a willingness to serve. Strength, he believed, lay in numbers.

He spent the first year forging the group into a disciplined band, united in enmity against the Sheriff, and willing to live outside the law. The band's organization was simple. Robin ruled supreme, making all important decisions. He delegated specific tasks to his lieutenants. Will Scarlett was in change of intelligence and scouting. His main job was to shadow the Sheriff and his men, always alert to their next move. He also collected information on the travel plans of rich merchants and tax collectors. Little John kept discipline among the men, and saw to it that their archery was at the high peak that their profession demanded. Scarlock took care of the finances, converting loot to cash, paying shares of the take and finding suitable hiding places for the surplus. Finally, Much the Miller's son had the difficult task of provisioning the ever-increasing band of Merrymen.

The increasing size of the band was a source of satisfaction for Robin, but also

*Prepared by Joseph Lampel, New York University.
Copyright Joseph Lampel © 1985, revised 1991.

a source of concern. The fame of his Merrymen was spreading, and new recruits poured in from every corner of England. As the band grew larger, their small bivouac became a major encampment. Between raids the men milled about, talking and playing games. Vigilance was in decline, and discipline was becoming harder to enforce. 'Why?' Robin reflected, 'I don't know half the men I run into these days.'

The growing band was also beginning to exceed the food capacity of the forest. Game was becoming scarce, and supplies had to be obtained from outlying villages. The cost of buying food was beginning to drain the band's financial reserves at the very moment when revenues were in decline. Travellers, especially those with the most to lose, were now giving the forest a wide berth. This was costly and inconvenient to them, but it was preferable to having all their goods confiscated.

Robin believed that the time had come for the Merrymen to change their policy of outright confiscation of goods to one of a fixed transit tax. His lieutenants strongly resisted this idea. They were proud of the Merrymen's famous motto: 'Rob the rich and give to the poor.' 'The farmers and the townspeople', they argued, 'are our most important allies.' 'How can we tax them, and still hope for their help in our fight against the Sheriff?'

Robin wondered how long the Merrymen could keep to the ways and methods of their early days. The Sheriff was growing stronger and better organized. He now had the money and the men, and was beginning to harass the band, probing for its weaknesses. The tide of events was beginning to turn against the Merrymen. Robin felt that the campaign must be decisively concluded before the Sheriff had a chance to deliver a mortal blow. 'But how', he wondered, 'could this be done?'

Robin had often entertained the possibility of killing the Sheriff, but the chances for this seemed increasingly remote. Besides, killing the Sheriff might satisfy his personal thirst for revenge, but it would not improve the situation. Robin had hoped that the perpetual state of unrest, and the Sheriff's failure to collect taxes, would lead to his removal from office. Instead, the Sheriff used his political connections to obtain reinforcement. He had powerful friends at court, and was well regarded by the regent, Prince John.

Prince John was vicious and volatile. He was consumed by his unpopularity among the people, who wanted the imprisoned King Richard back. He also lived in constant fear of the barons, who had first given him the regency, but were now beginning to dispute his claim to the throne. Several of these barons had set out to collect the ransom that would release Richard the Lionheart from his jail in Austria. Robin was invited to join the conspiracy in return for future amnesty. It was a dangerous proposition. Provincial banditry was one thing, court intrigue another. Prince John's spies were everywhere. If the plan failed the pursuit would be relentless, and retribution swift.

The sound of the supper horn startled Robin from his thoughts. There was the smell of roasting venison in the air. Nothing was resolved or settled. Robin headed for camp promising himself that he would give these problems his utmost attention after tomorrow's raid.

1-2

THE EUROPEAN TRUCK INDUSTRY IN 1990: PREPARING FOR THE POST–1992 ERA*

Europe in the late 1980s was a rapidly changing business environment. The impact of the Single European Market, the deregulation it involved and the harmonization of product and technical standards allowed companies to take better advantage of the benefits of efficient, large-scale operation and had already unleashed an impressive joint venture and merger activity in many industries.

The truck industry was clearly influenced by all these changes. In recent years the Dutch-based DAF had merged with Leyland from the UK (in 1987), and MAN from Germany had taken over the Austrian manufacturer Steyr (in 1989). In early 1990 Volve and Renault took significant cross-holdings in each other's shares, declaring the intention of complete integration of the companies in the medium term. In the second half of the same year the Italian producer Iveco acquired Enasa from Spain, after an earlier acquisition of Enasa by a Man/Mercedes-Benz consortium had to be dissolved on order of the German anti-trust office.

This case describes the situation and developments of the European truck industry in the late 1980s and the likely impact of the completion of the internal market in this industry.

*This case was prepared by Frank de Haan and Hubert Thomassen, both IESE MBA, class of 1990 under the supervision of professor Paul Verdin. It is intended to be used as a basis for class discussion rather than to illustrate either effective or ineffective handling of an administrative situation.

TRUCKS

During the last centuries the world's growing and integrating economies had shown an increasing demand for transport of goods and people. Transport could be through the air, over water or over land. Land transport could either be by rail or road.

The vehicles used for road transport were supplied by the automotive industry and included: cars, vans, trucks and buses. The latter three were also categorized as commercial vehicles (CVs). In this note the attention will be focused mainly on trucks, but some statistics on the other segments of the CV industry have also been included (see Exhibit 1 for an exact definition of the different types of CVs).

For description and analytical purposes the truck industry was most often divided in segments according to Gross Vehicle Weight (GVW). GVW was the weight of the truck and its maximum payload together. Segmentations varied by source and country. In Europe the most common segmentations included a van segment and light, medium and heavy weight truck segments. (See Exhibit 2 for the segmentation of the truck market.)

TRUCK DEMAND

The total world demand for commercial vehicles was around 14 million units in 1989. Most of this unit demand was for vans and light weight trucks. Sales in the medium and heavy truck segment only amounted to around 1.5 million units. (See Exhibit 3.)

The world truck market was usually divided in three regions: Western Europe with its main export markets in the Middle East and Africa, United States with its main export markets in South America and Japan with its main export markets in Southeast Asia. Between the regions truck trade was limited. In the van and light truck segments import penetrations were usually below 20 per cent, while the medium and heavy truck segments imports were, due to the different product standards, even more limited. China, the Soviet Union and some Eastern European countries had also a significant truck industry but their trade outside communist countries was negligible. (See Exhibit 4.)

The sales of commercial vehicles in Western Europe had gone through a deep crisis in the early 1980s followed by a steady recovery. (See Exhibit 5.) In 1989 the demand in the Western European countries was at record heights and amounted to almost 1.4 million units for vans and light trucks and about 260,000 units for trucks above 6 tons GVW. (See Exhibit 6.)

TRUCK SUPPLY

In 1988 the West European manufacturers produced 1,250,000 vans and 400,000 trucks. Of the vans 150,000 were destined for exports. The rest covered 80 per cent of West European demand. The remaining 20 per cent was imported, mainly from Japan. The truck sector had almost no imports (2 per cent) but quite significant exports. Of the 400,000 trucks produced, 88,000 were destined for customers outside Europe.

The market was served by a rapidly decreasing number of producers. In the medium and heavy truck segments Daimler-Benz was market leader, with a unit market share of 23 per cent, followed by Fiat/Iveco with 20 per cent. Five more competitors had market shares of around 10 per cent each (Renault, Volvo, MAN, DAF and Scania). Some smaller specialized producers served the rest of the market.

The van and the light truck segment showed a similar division of marketshares. Leader was Renault with 20 per cent unit market share followed by PSA (Peugeot/ Citroën) with 16 per cent. PSA was one example of a car company which was successfully present in the van and light weight truck segments but had no presence in the medium and heavy weight truck segments. Some Japanese producers (Toyota, Nissan) had a similar strategy. (See Exhibits 7-9 for more market share data.)

TRUCK USERS

Vans and smaller trucks were mainly used for regional delivery, while larger trucks were used for longer distance transportation and for heavy jobs like construction. Transportation services were performed by company-owned fleets as well as contracted parties.

The size and sophistication of an in-house shipping department varied and depended on the type of activities in which a company was involved. A small furniture retailer for example could own one marginally used truck for occasional customer deliveries. On the other hand, a major industrial group could maintain a well-managed fleet of over 100 trucks for interplant transportation and distribution.

Dedicated transportation firms ranged from single truck owner/drivers to companies with several hundreds of trucks. Some larger companies had full line fleets owning heavy trucks as well as vans. Other firms were offering services in a particular segment of the transportation market (for example, only long haul or only door-to-door delivery) and employed corresponding fleets. Trucking companies could also specialize in a certain type of goods like liquids, containers or even smaller niches, such as the transportation of hanging clothes and secured art delivery.

For a trucking department or firm an important requirement for success was to minimize its costs per ton per kilometre for each specific transport task. This implied a good logistical planning (e.g. use the right truck for the right task) and an effective management of each truck's operational costs.

The main operational costs of a truck were: labour, amortization and interest, fuel and maintenance. Obviously, the exact amount of these costs varied widely for different trucks, but even for an identical truck operated by different owners or for different purposes, the cost per ton per kilometre could vary considerably, both for the total amount and in composition. (See Exhibit 10 for a cost analysis of a tractor/trailer combination for a specific fleet owner.)

TRUCK MANUFACTURERS

Most truck manufacturers in Europe divided their operations in the following units:

- research and development,
- manufacturing,
- marketing, sales and distribution,
- truck leasing and financing.

Research and Development

Research and development costs were significant in the truck industry. Expenditures varied from 4 to 8 per cent on sales, depending on the size and the degree of vertical integration of a producer. The development of a new product would typically take 4–7 years and involve huge capital outlays. Once developed a product would be produced for the next 10–15 years and only require small investments for gradual improvements.

Technological innovation and increasing sophistication of trucks in terms of fuel efficiency, ergonomy and electronics content had gradually pushed up development costs and seemed to favour competitors with large corporate scopes for cost-efficient research. Smaller players had been forced to focus their R&D on particular components and enter into strategic alliances, aimed at sharing the R&D costs.

Manufacturing

The main components of a truck were: axles, chassis, motor, gearbox and cabin. The manufacturing of a truck involved the production of these parts and their assembly. In the United States, most truck manufacturers were mainly assemblers, buying their components from producers like Cummins (engines), Eaton (gearboxes) and Rockwell (axles). In Europe the choices with respect to the degree of vertical integration varied among competitors. Producers with a high degree of vertical integration, like Volvo and Scania, created up to 60 per cent of sales value in-house. This percentage could go down to as low as 30 per cent for mere assemblers like Fiat/Iveco.

Industry observers disagreed on the exact efficient scales for production plants for the different components and the final assembly. However, it was widely accepted that the production of the motor and the gearbox involved the largest economies of scale (estimates varied from 50,000 to 100,000 units yearly output for an efficient facility). The production of cabin, axles, chassis and the final assembly were decreasingly sensitive to scale effects.

The make/buy decisions in the industry partly reflected the impact of scale effects. Another criterion for these decisions was how much a certain component added to product differentiation. In addition, some truck producers also regarded vertical integration as an essential instrument to control quality.

An example reflecting this type of consideration was that some manufacturers bought their gearboxes and axles, but produced their motors in-house. The in-house motor production was often supported by additional sales in the component market, to niche producers of trucks and for other uses (for example, ships and yachts). This in turn increased the production quantity.

Marketing, Sales and Distribution

The people in the marketing department of a truck manufacturer were usually involved in two types of activities. First, they had to create brand and product awareness with the potential customer; and secondly, they had to establish a dealer network which could take care of the final sales, distribution and service for the manufacturer's products.

The amount of time and money invested in the creation of brand and product awareness varied between producers and markets. Some producers profited from brand images established in other businesses (e.g. Mercedes-Benz, Volvo) and the specific outlays to promote their brand in the truck world could be rather limited. Due to their long presence and large market shares, the spending of most manufacturers in their home markets was small when compared to sales. Only when a producer entered a new market, advertising and promotion spending could be a considerable cost element.

Manufacturers concentrated their promotional spending on trade fairs and trucking journals. However on specific occasions, such as new product introductions, they also used newspapers, popular magazines and even television advertising to increase the impact of their publicity efforts.

For sales and service, most truck manufacturers utilized a two-tier distribution system. A national importer or distributor was responsible for marketing and the development of the dealer and service network. The dealers in their turn were responsible for the individual client contacts and execution of maintenance and repair work.

The size and distribution of the European dealer networks varied per producer. Some manufacturers had a very dense network in their home markets and almost no dealers outside, while others had a more general presence throughout Europe. Volvo, for example, had a European network of approximately 400 dealers and 800 service points relatively equally distributed over Europe, while Leyland-DAF had around 1,200 which were largely concentrated in the Dutch, Belgian and UK market.

All European truck manufacturers considered their dealer and service network as an important strategic ingredient to their operations. While a marked decline in the number of manufacturers had taken place, a similar decline was not observed in the number of dealers and service centres. In addition, most of the dealers were committed to the sales of only one brand. The wide range of fleet compositions made it attractive for the dealers to be able to offer and service a full range of truck sizes.

Truck Leasing and Financing

As in many industries involved in the production of capital goods (e.g. aeroplanes, production machines, etc.), the truck manufacturers also had become engaged in the financing of their products. These type of engagements could vary in size and degree. While some of the larger companies had set up complete financial services divisions, borrowing money on the capital markets and lending it to their truck customers, others had limited themselves to coordinating the contacts between their dealers, final customers and banks, effectively only providing a stream of referrals and information.

THE ENVIRONMENT

European industries in the late 1980s were repositioning themselves for the post-1992 era, in which the internal frontiers would be eliminated. There was a general tendency to rationalize the manufacturing function and obtain scale efficiencies by centralizing production in fewer, more specialized locations. This resulted in an increased average distance between the location of production and consumption.

Consequently, international distribution systems evolved which supplied local distribution centres with products from different production centres scattered throughout Europe. The overall logistic system became an increasingly important competitive factor, and demand for the transportation industry was expected to increase.

Within the transportation industry the formation of a united Europe was expected to increase productivity of both drivers and trucks. The formalities and delays at the customs posts had already been reduced by the introduction of a 'Single Administrative Document' which replaced the numerous country-specific documents on 1 January 1988. In addition, the strict system of quotas which limited the number of trips that haulers of one country could make into other EC countries in a given year had been relaxed in June 1987. The EC member nations had agreed to increase these quotas by 40 per cent per year in 1988 and 1989 and to abolish all quotas by 1 January 1993. As a result of these two changes, industry analysts expected a 30–50 per cent increase in the transportation industry's intra-EC trade by the year 2000.

Furthermore, the European Commission was pushing for unrestricted cabotage.[1] In 1989, restrictions on cabotage were partially responsible for 35 per cent of all trucks on EC roads travelling empty. After deregulation took place in the United States their empty mile ratio had dropped to 6–9 per cent.

On the other hand, a growing congestion of roads in some of the most important industrial areas in Europe and an increasing concern about air pollution caused by road transport had induced investigations in alternative modes of transport. It was especially rail and intermodal transport (involving a combination of road, rail and shipping) which received attention. (See Exhibit 11 for some statistics on the relative importance of road and rail transport.)

Another effect of this increase in environmental concern was that gas and noise emission standards were expected to become stricter. Important non-EC transit countries like Switzerland and Austria had already incorporated measures to decrease noise and other pollution. EC legislation was expected to follow.

The regulatory control on the safety of transportion was also expected to increase. Some countries already were checking the speed of trucks and the time the chauffeur had been driving without resting, through the use of board computers.

For the truck manufacturers all of these developments implied an increasing demand for the sophistication of their products and an increasing technology content. On the other hand, due to EC regulation, the need for special models complying with country-specific legislation declined. In addition to the elimination of tariffs, this further reduced the protection some producers had enjoyed in their home markets.

THE COMPETITORS

The Europeans

Most European competitors belonged to large industrial corporations. Some of these corporations were active in a lot of different industries, but others concentrated mainly in the automotive industry. The players in the industry showed a wide variation in international presence, in the scope of their product line and in the degree of vertical integration. As a result, various strategic groups could be defined on the basis of a variety of criteria. (See Exhibits 12 and 13 for two examples.)

The industry players also showed a wide variation in their involvement in research joint ventures and marketing agreements (see Exhibit 14 for an overview of the linkages).

Daimler-Benz

The truck division of Daimler-Benz formed part of one of the largest conglomerates of West Germany. Daimler-Benz had interests in cars (Mercedes), aircraft (Dornier) and electronics (AEG).

Daimler-Benz was not only the truck market leader in Europe, but also leader at world level. It was present in the United States with a fully owned branch, under the name Freightliner. In Europe it marketed a full line of products and its presence was especially strong in the medium range of trucks.

Daimler-Benz produced medium and heavy trucks in West Germany and vans and light trucks in Spain. In 1989 it had acquired DTV, an originally independent supplier of diesel engines, thereby increasing its already high degree of vertical integration.

Iveco

Since the early 1980s Iveco belonged to the Fiat group, which was the main force in the automotive industry in Italy. It marketed a full line of products and almost completely controlled the Italian market. Iveco had a low degree of vertical integration. However, it had many cooperation agreements with suppliers like Eaton and Rockwell.

Due to the acquisition of Magirius Deutz (West Germany) in 1982 and the formation of a joint venture with Ford (UK) in 1986, Iveco had obtained a relatively strong position in these markets. In late 1990 Iveco took over Pegaso from Spain after an earlier association of Pegaso with Man from Germany had to be dissolved by order of the German anti-trust office.

Renault

Renault Vehicles Industries (RVI) was part of Regie Renault, the French state-controlled automotive corporation. The group was also a main force in the European car industry. During the 1980s Regie Renault had received large amounts of government support. However, under EC legislation this support had to be discontinued.

Renault was also active in the United States with a 45 per cent participation in Mack and had a strong export presence in the African market. In early 1990, Renault and Volvo had taken considerable cross-holdings in each other's shares and announced the intention to merge the companies completely in the medium term. Renault was a full line producer with very high market shares in its home market. Within Europe, Renault was the overall market leader in the van and light truck segment.

It had an average degree of vertical integration. Apart from France, Renault also owned plants in Spain and the United Kingdom. The latter plant was bought from Dodge which had decided to withdraw from the European market.

Volvo

Volvo had a worldwide presence in the medium and the heavy truck segment and was also active in the car business. Although Sweden was not an EC member, Volvo still profited from all intra-European Community advantages because of its major plants in Belgium and Scotland.

In the United States, Volvo was present through its joint venture with White/GM. Furthermore, it had some smaller production facilities in Latin America and Australia. In early 1990 Volvo had entered in the abovementioned relationship with Renault. Volvo was a producer with a high degree of vertical integration.

MAN/Steyr

In 1989, MAN acquired the Austrian truck manufacturer Steyr. In the following year it tried, in consortium with Daimler-Benz, to take over the Spanish producer of Pegaso trucks Enasa. However, as mentioned, this combination had to be dissolved, thus limiting MAN's presence to the central part of Europe.

Besides this strong presence in the medium and the heavy truck segment, MAN also had access to the van and the light truck segment, through its cooperation with Volkswagen. This allowed MAN to offer a full line of trucks to their dealers.

In the industry MAN was considered to be a producer with a relatively low degree of vertical integration. For some parts MAN and Daimler-Benz used the same suppliers. The terms of these joint purchases were unknown and led to speculation about the level of cooperation between these two producers.

DAF

In 1987 the Dutch company DAF acquired the formerly state-owned UK company Leyland. This merger gave DAF an improved access to the UK market and provided an extension of its product line, originally focused on the medium and the heavy segment, to a full range.

Earlier DAF had already courted Pegaso, during a joint venture aimed at developing a new generation of truck cabins (Cabtech, formed in 1984), thus sharing the high cost of development involved. However, further integration had never taken place and Pegaso was acquired by Iveco in 1990. DAF was considered to have a relatively low degree of vertical integration.

Scania

Scania was a Swedish producer with many similarities to Volvo both in terms of its product strategy and in its degree of vertical integration. However their market area was essentially confined to Western Europe.

US Manufacturers

The Americans had been present on the European market through their subsidiaries in the United Kingdom. However, the crisis of the truck industry in the early 1980s made them close down their plants or sell their interests, thereby effectively implying a retreat to their own continent. Due to the completely different truck standards in the United States, exports from the United States to Europe were negligible.

The Japanese

The Japanese were present only in the van segment. They lacked the products to enter the heavy segment. The truck market in Japan, like the market in the United States had its own specific type of heavy trucks which were not suited for the European market. The Japanese also lacked a dealer network to market heavy trucks.

Eastern Europe

The Eastern European producers had no significant presence on the Western European market. Companies like Tatra (Czechoslovakia), ROMAN (Romania) and Zil (Soviet Union) could certainly use Western European technology, and the recent move of Eastern Europe towards free market economies created interesting options for joint ventures and acquisitions.

CONCLUDING OBSERVATIONS

In view of the increasing concentration, the European Commission had started looking more closely into the question of competition within the sector. On the one hand, the increasing concentration caused growing concern from an anti-trust point of view. One the other hand, the technological developments that were under way required large scale operation or cooperation in a sector that had clearly the potential of becoming a truly global industry – one in which European manufacturers had a strong position, if not a head start.

EXHIBIT 1
Products of the commercial vehicle industry.

Articulated trucks:

Definition	CV for freight transport with articulated body (tractor-trailer or truck-trailer combination).
Use	For national and international long distance transport. Also for short-distance transport of heavy loads (e.g. earth movement).
Weight	Between 20 and 40 ton for truck, trailer and payload together.
Engine	Between 200 and 600 horsepower.
Price	Up to 130,000 ECU for a complete combination.
Examples	Tractor-trailer combination for long distance transport:

Truck-trailer combination for long distance transport:

Rigid trucks:

Definition	CV for freight transport with non articulated body.
Use	For short and medium-distance transport.
Weight	Between 3.5 and 25 ton for truck, trailer and payload together.
Engine	Between 100 and 400 horsepower.
Price	From 20,000 to 80,000 ECU.
Examples	Heavy truck equipped with cement mixer:

Medium weight truck for freight transport:

Coaches and buses:

Definition	CV for transport of people.
Use	For long (usually denominated coach) and short-distance (bus) transport of people.
Weight	Between 10 and 20 tons for transport of 40–120 people.
Engine	Between 200 and 400 horsepower.
Price	From 30,000 to 80,000 ECU.

Vans:

Definition	CV with a weight of vehicle and payload of less than 3.5 tons for the transport of freight or people.
Use	Short distance transport of freight or transport of small groups of people.
Weight	Less than 3.5 tons.
Engine	Between 60 and 140 horsepower.
Price	From 10,000 to 20,000 ECU.

Source: Company brochures and pricelists.

EXHIBIT 2
Segmentation of the C V market.

Heavy weight CV	
Definition	GVW over 15 or 16* tons
Includes	Articulated and rigid trucks and large buses
Medium weight CV	
Definition	GVW over 6, 7.5 or 9 tons but below 15 or 16 tons
Includes	Some articulated but mostly rigid trucks and medium size buses
Light weight CV	
Definition	GVW over 3.5 tons but below 6, 7.5 or 9 tons
Includes	Rigid trucks and small buses
Vans	
Definition	GVW below 3.5 tons
Includes	Car derived vans, normal vans and minibuses

*In the literature the exact boundaries vary from source to source. The boundaries here indicated are the most common ones.

EXHIBIT 3
World demand for automotive industry in units, 1989 data.

	Demand in units
Trucks (GVW > 6 tons)	1,400,000
Buses (GVW > 6 tons)	100,000
Light trucks, minibuses and vans (GVW < 6 tons)	12,500,000
Total demand commercial vehicles	14,000,000
Cars	37,000,000
TOTAL DEMAND AUTOMOTIVE INDUSTRY	51,000,000

Source: Compiled from various annual reports.

EXHIBIT 4
World demand for C V industry by regions, 1989 data.

	Share of world demand %
US region:	
North America	22
South America	8
European region:	
Western Europe	19
Africa	3
Middle East	1
Eastern Europe and Soviet Union	17
Japanese region:	
Japan and Far East countries	15
China	15

Source: Compiled from expert interviews.

EXHIBIT 5
Truck demand in the 1980s.

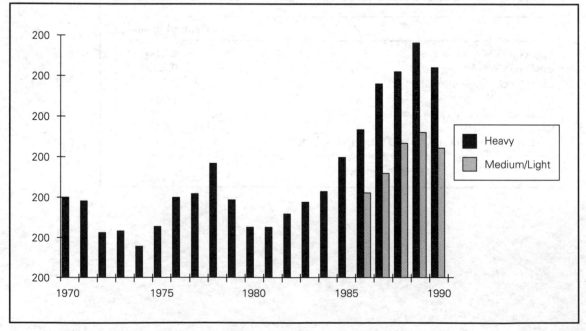

Note: Medium and light trucks 3.5–16 tons, data available from 1986 on.
Source: Compiled from various annual reports.

EXHIBIT 6
New registrations: Estimated figures (000s) by country and segment, 1989 data.

	Vans & Trucks < 6T	Trucks > 6T
Germany	190	51
France	390	49
United Kingdom	280	65
Italy	150	28
Spain	200	27
Netherlands	50	14
Belgium	30	10
Sweden	35	6
Switzerland	25	4
Austria	20	6
Denmark	15	3
TOTAL	1,385	263

Source: Compiled from various annual reports.

EXHIBIT 7
Market share of European new truck unit sales by manufacturer and by segment, 1989 data.

	Vans & Trucks < 6T	Trucks > 6T
Daimler-Benz	6	23
Iveco	11	20
Renault	20	12
Man-Pegaso[1]	–	12
Leyland-DAF	2	11
Volvo	–	10
Scania	–	6
PSA	16	–
Ford	13	–
Nissan	4	–
Others	18	6

1. In 1989 the statistics considered Man-Pegaso as one company.
2. In many countries Volkswagen had a marketing agreement with Man to market its vans and light trucks.
Source: Compiled from various statistical and annual reports.

EXHIBIT 8
Selected market share data by manufacturer and by country >3.5T, 1987 data.

	West Germany	France	Italy	Holland
Daimler-Benz	48	20	12	23
Renault	2	40	0	2
Iveco	16	15	68	5
Volvo	4	10	4	16
Leyland-DAF	2	6	2	27
Scania	4	5	8	9
MAN	20	3	2	10
Others	4	1	4	8

Source: Dealer and manufacturer interviews.

EXHIBIT 9
Percentage of production exported outside Europe by manufacturer, 1989 estimates.

	Export sales (% of total sales)
Scania	39
Volvo	35
Volkswagen	19
Daimler-Benz	17
PSA	17
Leyland-DAF	15
Ford	12
Nissan	10
MAN-Pegaso	9
Renault	4
Iveco	*

*No data available, but estimated to be below 5 per cent.
Source: Compiled from various annual reports.

EXHIBIT 10
Example of a cost breakdown for a tractor-trailer combination for long-distance transport.

Cost components	Cost in ECU per km	Percentage of Total Cost per km
Salary driver	0.304	32
Fuel	0.228	24
Depreciation & interest	0.209	22
Tyres	0.048	5
Insurance	0.048	5
Maintenance & repairs	0.029	3
Other variable costs	0.028	3
Allocation of administrative overhead	0.057	6
TOTAL	0.950	100
Total per ton per km (24 tons)	0.040	
Total per m^3 per km (60 m^3)	0.016	

Source: Dealer interviews.

EXHIBIT 11
National rail and road transport in five EC markets in milliard ton/km.

	1979	1982	1987	1993
France				
Road transport	94.6	77.1	89.9	102.9
Rail transport	70.0	53.9	51.3	50.4
West Germany				
Road transport	123.9	119.8	142.7	164.7
Rail transport	66.3	57.4	59.1	60.0
Italy				
Road transport	81.6	94.9	108.9	125.6
Rail transport	18.4	17.7	19.3	21.5
Spain				
Road transport	92.2	91.5	95.7	114.0
Rail transport	10.3	10.5	11.5	12.2
United Kingdom				
Road transport	104.6	96.8	107.0	118.5
Rail transport	19.9	16.5	15.6	15.3

Sources: National statistics, Forecasts BIPE, IFO, PROMETEIA.

EXHIBIT 12
Strategic map of competitor positon: product line and degree of vertical intgration of the commercial vehicles manufacturers.

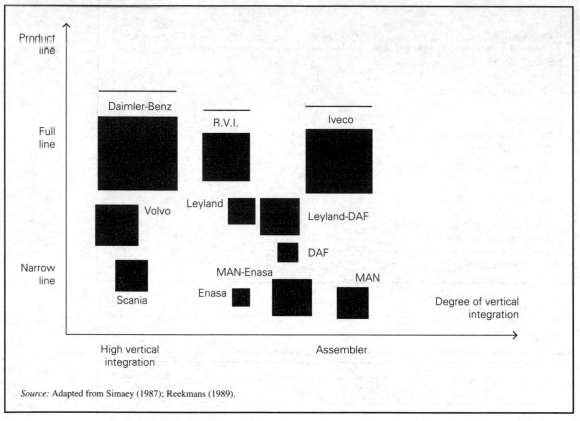

Source: Adapted from Simaey (1987); Reekmans (1989).

EXHIBIT 13
Strategic map of competitor position: product line and geographical spread of the European commercial vehicles manufacturers.

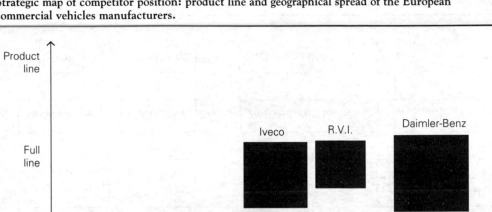

Source: Adapted from Simaey (1987); Reekmans (1989).

EXHIBIT 14
Linkages between the European truck manufacturers.

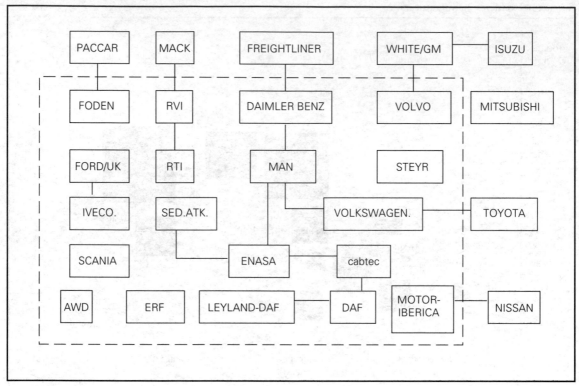

1-3

DAF IN 1991: PREPARING FOR THE POST–1992 ERA*

When in March 1991 the annual report of 1990 was published it became clear how heavily DAF had been hit by the downturn in the UK truck market. From a record profit of Dfl. 171.6 million[1] in 1989, the result had turned into an unprecedented loss of Dfl. 227.6 million in 1990. Management had reacted with drastic measures: the total workforce had been reduced by 1,390 people (8 per cent) and an important programme to improve profitability had been initiated. Further, the company was increasing its efforts to enter the German market, the only market which had shown significant demand growth in 1990 and also was reinforcing its marketing activities outside Europe, especially in some of the booming Far East economies.

This case gives an overview of DAF's activities in the 1980s and focuses on the post-1987 period after the merger with Leyland from the United Kingdom.

HISTORY

The DAF organization as it existed in 1990 had been the result of a merger of the independent truck manufacturer DAF from The Netherlands with the Leyland truck division of the Rover group from the United Kingdom. Both companies had long

*This case was prepared by Frank de Haan, student of MBA 1990, under the supervision of Professors Joan Enric Ricart and Paul Verdin. It is intended to be used as a basis for class discussion rather than to illustrate either effective or ineffective handling of an administrative situation.

histories and considerable positions in their home markets, but the heavy losses of Leyland in the early 1980s and DAF's wish to expand from the medium and heavy segments into the van and light weight segments of the truck market, had led to the merger in early 1987.

Since its foundation in 1928 in Eindhoven by the two brothers Hub and Wim Van Doorne, as a machine shop for the production of bicycle frames and steel windows, DAF had grown through a number of different periods. In 1931 the company started to produce trailers and it is from this period that the company derives its name (DAF is the Dutch acronym for Van Doorne's trailer factories). In 1948, the reconstruction period after World War II, the company started to assemble complete trucks and from 1957 on, it also produced engines, axles and cabs, thus developing into an integrated truck manufacturer.

In 1958 the company had, based on Hub Van Doorne's invention of the Variomatic, an automatic gearbox especially suited for light cars, diversified into car production. A separate plant was established in Borne, a small city in the mining region of Holland where the progressive closing of coal mines had created a growing labour surplus. During the 1960s this company was quite successful. In 1972 it started a cooperative venture with Volvo from Sweden to widen its base. In 1976 this cooperation resulted in a complete acquisition of DAF's car division by Volvo.

Meanwhile, the truck division went through its own period of foreign influence. In 1972 International Harvester from the United States acquired a 33 per cent stake in DAF. However, integration of the companies never took place and when in the crisis of the early 1980s International Harvester got into serious problems, the shares were sold back to a consortium of Dutch governmental investment organizations and the original Van Doorne family. From this time on (1983) DAF was on its own again.

Leyland had gone through its own history, full of acquisitions and mergers. Founded in 1896 as a producer of steam lorries, it had grown, through the production for two world wars, to one of the most important truck manufacturers in the UK. In 1951, it started a number of acquisitions and subsequently acquired the independent truck manufacturers: Albion (1951), Seammel (1955) and AEC (1962).

In 1961 Leyland also got involved in the car business by the acquisition of Triumph, followed in 1967 by the acquisition of Rover Alvis. Finally, in 1968, the merger of the Leyland Group with British Motor Holding resulted in a corporate giant with over 200,000 employees and a collection of brands (Austin, Triumph, Rover) and factories which would prove difficult to control.

In the recession of 1973/4 following the first big oil shock, the renamed British Leyland Motor Corporation took its first hit. In 1974 the heavy losses resulted in a nationalization by the British government to protect employment. After reorganization in 1975 and 1976 the truck division seemed to do well, until the 1980/2 recession, after the second oil shock, made painfully clear how weak the company, then almost completely dependent on the British market, still was.

The subsequent years of the early 1980s showed some revival, but when in late 1986 the chairman of the renamed Rover Group, Mr Graham Day, met his counterpart in DAF, Mr Aart van der Padt, both parties seemed quite keen on developing a previous existing marketing agreement (in 1984 DAF started to market Leyland vans through its channels on the continent) into a complete merger.

AFTER THE MERGER

The negotiation of the merger took place at surprising speed. The British Government agreed to absorb the Dfl. 600 million of debt corresponding to Leyland trucks, which was approved by the EC. The unions accepted a drastic restructuring and closing of some British plants and Rover agreed to minority positions in both the board of directors (2 out of 11) and the executive board (1 out of 6) of the new company. The new DAF company, in turn, had to commit to invest a minimum of Dfl. 500 million in the United Kingdom over the five years following the merger.

The new company was incorporated on 1 April 1987 and subsequently went through three years of prosperity. (See Exhibits 1 and 2 for selected financial data and ratios.) In 1989 it was introduced on the Amsterdam and London stock exchanges and welcomed warmly by the investors. The stock was introduced at Dfl. 47 and traded shortly afterwards at Dfl. 61 but prices fell rapidly when at the end of the year recessionary forecasts for the truck market were published. When in 1990 the full implications of the recession in the UK market, the stagnation in some other markets and DAF's exposure to it became clear, DAF's stock dropped as low as Dfl. 17.5, well below its book value of Dfl. 34.0 per share.

ORGANIZATION

In 1990 DAF's organization showed a quite even distribution of units on both sides of the North Sea.

The legal structure consisted of a DAF holding incorporated in The Netherlands and four main subsidiaries: DAF B.V., owner of the Dutch and Belgian operations, Leyland-DAF Ltd for the UK, DAF Special Products for the production of special, most often military, parts (e.g. the front landing gear for F16 fighter jets) and vehicles and DAF Finance Company which supported DAF's sales & marketing department by providing truck financing for their clients. (See Exhibit 3.)

DAF's operating structure was also divided across the North Sea. The production, product development and sales & marketing department all had units in both the UK and in The Netherlands and/or Belgium. (See Exhibit 4 for a more detailed overview.)

DAF's management structure was mainly organized along the traditional functional lines. The six men executive board was formed by the chairman and the heads of the marketing & sales, production, product development, finance and corporate strategy departments.

MARKETING AND SALES

In 1990 DAF had a market share of 8.6 per cent in the truck and 2.8 per cent in the van segment of the West European market for commercial vehicles. Most of the sales were concentrated in the UK, Dutch and Belgian markets. (See Exhibit 5 for geographic spread of sales and some more detailed market size and share information.) In 1990 DAF had delivered a total of 53,800 vehicles compared with 58,700 in 1989 and gross margins, especially for heavy trucks, had been under pressure from increasing competition. (See Exhibit 6 for market shares and unit sales per segment.) This decrease in unit sales was only partly explained by the decrease of truck turnover in Western Europe. Other reasons were the deconsolidation of DAF's bus division which accounted for a decrease of 1,200 units and the downturn in military sales.

The marketing and sales department of DAF operated out of Eindhoven (trucks and general supervision), Birmingham (vans) and Manchester (DAF International for the markets outside Europe). In Western Europe it operated through fully owned subsidiaries in the United Kingdom, The Netherlands, Belgium, France, Spain, Germany, Austria, Switzerland, Norway and Sweden. Seven other European countries were served through independent importers. Outside Europe DAF owned twelve more sales subsidiaries and had relations with over 60 importers, thus extending its presence to almost 90 countries.

DAF's marketing and sales department faced the tough task of keeping up sales and margins in declining markets and, at same time, implementing a programme of rapid expansion in some booming markets like those in the united Germany and some of the Far East countries. The responsibilities of the marketing & sales department included the development of a sales and service network and the marketing and communication strategy for DAF products and services.

In Europe, DAF had a dealer network with a total of 1,300 sales and service points. The geographic distribution of this network was quite uneven. The weak position in Germany, where DAF had only 48 dealers in 1989, had made it impossible to profit from this rapidly growing market. In 1990, however, DAF had made considerable progress and added a total of 94 new German dealers to its network, an effort expected to pay off with increased turnover in 1991.

The dealer and service network also played an important role in maintaining DAF's image of quality, reliability and service. To underline its concern for these matters, DAF had set up a special organization to guarantee service to any DAF truck which would break down on any place in Europe. DAF called this service ITS (International Truck Service) and promoted it extensively, especially to international transporters.

The promotion of DAF also stressed its new product innovations. In recent years DAF had introduced trucks with extra noise reduction, low emission engines and electronic log devices, thereby maintaining its reputation as a technologically advanced producer.

DAF International supervised sales outside Europe. During the 1970s DAF had sold quite significant numbers of trucks in Africa and the Middle East. However in the early 1980s those markets had lost in importance, and in recent years it was more the Far East which had the attention. In 1989 DAF had started a cooperation venture in Thailand to assemble trucks locally, and further in 1990 it had appointed new importers in Brunei, Malaysia, The Philippines and Indonesia. Total sales for DAF International amounted to 3,547 vehicles in 1990.

DAF FINANCE COMPANY N.V.

The goal of DAF Finance Company was to support the sales of DAF products by providing financial services. DAF Finance offered a range of products. For DAF's clients its offer consisted of: financial and operational leases, long-term rental of equipment and insurance. For the dealers it offered credit facilities to finance their stock.

The activities of DAF Finance had experienced important growth over recent years. Finance contracts for new DAF vehicles had increased from 4,620 in 1988 to 6,380 in 1990 and total assets had grown from Dfl. 1,870 million in 1988 to Dfl. 2,400 million in 1990. The problems of 1990 were, although to a much lesser extent, also reflected in the results of DAF Finance. Growth had been less spectacular and net profit had decreased from Dfl. 20.1 million in 1989 to Dfl. 17.9 million in 1990. (See Exhibit 7 for further financial data of DAF Finance.) Management attributed this loss in profitability to increased competitive pressure on interest margins and to the extra expenses incurred for expansion of the activities in the German market.

DAF Finance worked through subsidiaries in the United Kingdom, The Netherlands, Belgium, France, Spain, Italy, Switzerland and Germany. To improve its position in the German market DAF had recently (1989) acquired GKB (Gewerbekreditbank), a small commercial bank located in Dusseldorf. This bank had already been involved in the financing of DAF products. To maintain an efficient size the bank had to continue its involvement in financing of non-DAF products.

PRODUCT DEVELOPMENT

In recent years DAF's product development department had been working on the integration of the Leyland and DAF product lines, the development of low emission engines, drive-by noise reduction and, together with Renault, the development of a new van generation. Furthermore, DAF was involved in joint ventures to develop support systems for truck management and systems to facilitate communication between a truck driver and the home office.

DAF product development department had facilities in the United Kingdom and the Netherlands. Its total staff of 1,300 people were divided over three locations. In Eindhoven a staff of 475 people had access to a newly constructed office and a test circuit in nearby St Oedenrode. The rest of the staff was divided over the UK locations of Leyland, where the company also had a test circuit available, and Birmingham, which was dedicated to the development of vans.

Since 1987 DAF had made considerable progress to integrate its product lines. On the date of the merger Leyland produced a complete product line ranging from vans to heavy weight trucks. DAF had concentrated on the medium and heavy weight trucks, which meant that, after the merger, the company had a dual range in this segments. Since then the introduction of DAF's engines and axles in the Leyland range and the application of DAF's technology in Leyland cabins had been important steps to integration. However, there were still significant differences in the offer of Leyland-DAF to the UK market and the offer of DAF on the European continent.

This was partly due to market requirements but there was still further work to be done in product integration.

DAF's investments in diesel engine technology had resulted in the development of ATi technology (Advanced Turbo intercooling), which allowed the company to develop trucks with greater fuel efficiency and lower exhaust emissions. The further development of clean diesel technology had led to the introduction of the so-called '9 NOx' engine line. These engines complied with even the strictest emission standards to be expected in the near future and allowed transporters in some markets (The Netherlands) to take advantage of special government investment subsidies for the use of clean technologies.

Another development in response to environmental concern was the development of trucks which could meet stricter standards for drive-by noise. This type of research had been induced by Austria, an important transit country, which had already introduced regulation to limit noise emission for trucks which wished to travel by night. DAF had responded with the introduction of a special model of its 95 series which could meet Austrian standards, thus enabling transporters to avoid delays when a truck wished to cross Austria at night.

In 1989 DAF had announced the formation of a joint venture with Renault Vehicle Industry to develop a new van generation to replace the existing van range of Leyland origins.

Other development programmes addressed improvements for truck management and communication between driver and home office. The introduction of the Logic system had been a first step. This system consisted of a simple board computer which automatically recorded the most important parameters of truck usage: driving time, fuel consumption, engine hours, etc. and supported the driver in his administrative tasks like recording expenses. At the end of the journey the collected data could be exchanged with the transport companies administrative computers, by means of a memory card, thus saving a considerable quantity of paperwork and data entry.

The work on improvement of communication systems for trucks was undertaken in a joint venture with Dutch Telecom and a number of other specialized electronic firms. The aim was to develop a system which would allow direct communication between truck and home office, independent of the truck's location in Europe. This type of communication was expected to increase efficiency of truck use by enabling the transport firm's office to order a driver to pick up extra freight and by improved knowledge of expected arrival times of each truck, thus allowing for better scheduling of loading and unloading.

PRODUCTION

Since the merger of 1987 DAF's and Leyland's manufacturing plants had gone through an important reorganization. In 1990 the downturn in demand had required a reduction of the production level, which resulted in a cut in the workforce of 1,390 people. (See Exhibit 8 for production and employment statistics.) Even so, the company had still ended the year with more stock than at the end of 1989. The high interest in the United Kingdom made this too expensive, and in early 1991 management was continuing its talk with employee representatives and the unions to reduce the workforce further.

The reorganization of plants had mainly involved the concentration of the production of most components and models in one location. Important moves had been the increase in the production level of heavy engines in Eindhoven supplying the Leyland heavy range and the translation of the assembly of most medium weight trucks to Leyland. This had left Eindhoven with more capcity for the assembly of heavy range trucks.

Further, DAF had started to study its supplier relations in some more depth. Currently, DAF bought parts with a total value of Dfl. 3,000 million from nearly 2,000 different suppliers. Plans to implement Just In Time production methods, requiring direct delivery to production lines, and a desire to increase the amount of research and development executed by suppliers, implied the need to work closer with a smaller number of higher qualified suppliers. This type of demand to suppliers had already made DAF's purchase horizon widen and led to the use of parts produced by companies located in Spain and the Far East.

EXPECTATIONS FOR THE 1990s

DAF management seemed confident that DAF's strategy would enable it to survive as an independent truck manufacturer in the 1990s. On the other hand, it stated explicitly that it would continue to consider any forms of cooperation which are in the interest of the further development of the company and all those involved in it.

Industry observers wondered if this type of cooperation would be limited to further development joint ventures like those with Renault, or whether rumours that DAF and Scania were talking could lead to a further concentration in the European truck industry. The reduced value of DAF on the stock exchange had made some people speculate about what could happen if somebody were to launch a takeover bid. Dutch law allowed for extensive protection of a sitting management but a party with long-term interests might still consider such a move.

EXHIBIT 1
Selected financial data.

Profit and Loss Account:	1990	1989	1988	1987
Turnover	4,828	5,266	5,201	3,776
Cost of Sales	4,157	4,279	4,234	3,073
Gross Result	671	987	967	703
Distribution Expenses	721	693	685	536
General Administrative Expenses	67	91	94	77
Other Operating Income		9	5	16
Operating Result	(108)	212	193	106
Net interest Payable	95	39	39	51
Result before Taxation	(207)	173	154	55
Taxation	(27)	22	23	6
Result after Taxation	(176)	151	131	49
Result of Non-consolidated				
Companies and Minority Interests	26	21	16	14
Extraordinary Items	(78)	–	–	–
Net Result	(228)	172	147	63
Balance Sheet:				
Tangible Assets	1,137	1,064	1,056	1,000
Financial Assets	351	283	280	237
Total Fixed Assets	1,488	1,347	1,336	1,237
Stocks	1,336	1,219	1,154	1,128
Debtors	835	755	670	577
Cash	30	268	329	218
Total Assets	3,089	3,589	3,489	3,160
Creditors – due within one year	1,668	1,511	1,414	1,289
Total Assets less Current Liabilities	2,021	2,078	2,075	1,871
Creditors – due after one year	861	669	678	676
Provisions for Liabilities and Charges	144	202	200	195
Total Long-term Liabilities	1,005	871	878	871
Minority Interests	28	28	28	27
Capital and Reserves	988	1,179	1,169	973
Net Capital Employed	2,021	2,078	2,075	1,871

The 1987 income statement numbers are not comparable to the other numbers due to the merger in April 1987.
In 1990 the company recorded an extraordinary loss for reorganization expenses.
Source: DAF 1990 Annual report.

EXHIBIT 2
Selected financial ratios.

Data per Share	1990	1989	1988	1987
Cash Flow	(2.66)	11.38	10.51	6.55
Net Result before Extraordinary				
Items	(5.14)	5.91	5.17	2.22
Net Result	(7.82)	5.91	5.17	2.22
Dividend	–	2.50	–	–
Capital and Reserves	33.98	40.62	41.07	34.17
Share Price: – highest	43.40	61.00	–	–
– lowest	17.50	40.50	–	–
– year end	18.00	43.20	–	–
No. of Shares Outstanding				
(× 1,000,000)	29.09	29.03	28.47	28.47
Ratios				
Operating Result as a Percentage				
of Turnover	(2.2%)	4.0%	3.7%	2.8%
Net Result as a Percentage of				
Average Capital and Reserves	(21.0%)	14.6%	13.7%	7.8%
Group Capital and Reserves as a				
Percentage of Total Net Capital				
Employed	50%	58%	58%	53%
As a Percentage of Total Assets	28%	34%	34%	32%
Other data				
Capital Expenditure (Dfl. million)	213	260	203	210
Depreciation (Dfl. million)	150	159	152	123
Workforce	15,390	16,782	16,491	16,631
Wages, Salaries and Social				
Security cost (Dfl. million)	1,038	1,060	963	842

Source: DAF 1990 Annual report.

EXHIBIT 3
DAF's legal structure.

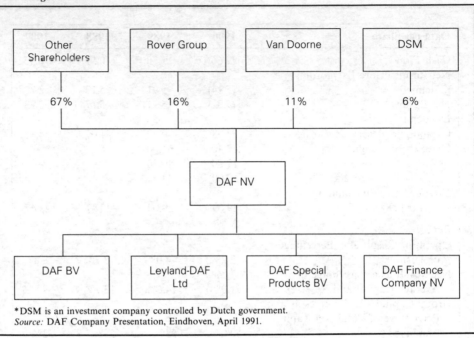

*DSM is an investment company controlled by Dutch government.
Source: DAF Company Presentation, Eindhoven, April 1991.

EXHIBIT 4
Geographical distribution of DAF operations.

United Kingdom	The Netherlands and Belgium
Production	
Leyland	*Eindhoven*
6.2 l diesel engines	8.25 and 11.6 l diesel engines
Components for trucks.	Components for trucks.
Assembly of light, medium	Assembly of medium and heavy
and heavy range trucks.	range trucks.
Glasgow	*Westerlo*
Axles.	Axles and cabs.
Birmingham	
Assembly of vans.	
Development Department	
Leyland	*Eindhoven*
General development work.	General development work.
Test circuit facilities.	Test circuit facilities.
	Development of engine technology.
Birmingham	
Development of vans.	
Marketing and Sales	
Manchester	*Eindhoven*
DAF International for markets	European markets.
outside of Europe.	
Birmingham	
Special task force for marketing	
and sales of vans.	

Source: DAF 1989 and 1990 Annual reports.

EXHIBIT 5
Geographical distribution of DAF sales.

	1989	1990
United Kingdom	42%	31%
Benelux	22%	27%
Rest of Europe	28%	34%
Rest of World	8%	8%
TOTAL SALES (Dfl. million)	5,266	4,828

Market Shares across Europe

	1989			1990		
	Total Market Size	DAF Market Share	DAF Unit Sales	Total Market Size	DAF Market Share	DAF Unit Sales
Trucks > 3.5 ton GVW:						
United Kingdom	69	21.1%	14.7	50	22.9%	11.3
Netherlands	14	28.2%	3.9	13	30.4%	4.0
Belgium	12	17.3%	2.1	13	17.0%	2.2
France	52	5.9%	3.1	49	6.9%	3.4
Spain	42	4.8%	2.0	37	5.9%	2.2
Germany	67	0.8%	0.5	80	0.9%	0.7
Rest of Western Europe	75	3.8%	2.9	74	4.5%	3.3
TOTAL WESTERN EUROPE	332	8.8%	29.2	315	8.6%	27.1
Vans between 2.0 and 3.5 ton GVW:						
TOTAL WESTERN EUROPE	803	2.5%	20.1	776	2.8%	21.7

Source: Geographical distribution of sales and market shares from DAF Company Presentation, Eindhoven, April 1991.
Market sizes are compiled from various truck manufacturer annual reports and government statistics.

EXHIBIT 6
DAF market shares per segment, Western Europe.

	1990	1989	1988	1987
DAF Market Shares:				
Light (3.5–9 ton GVW)	6.2%	6.2%	8.5%	7.8%
Medium (9–15 ton GVW)	8.5%	8.5%	8.5%	7.8%
Heavy (>15 ton GVW)	9.8%	10.1%	11.4%	10.8%
TOTAL TRUCKS	8.6%	8.8%	9.5%	8.7%
TOTAL VANS	2.8%	2.5%	2.6%	2.6%
Segment Sizes:				
(× 1,000)				
Light (3.5–9 ton GVW)	90	93	90	
Medium (9–15 ton GVW)	43	45	44	
Heavy (>15 ton GVW)	182	194	179	
TOTAL TRUCKS	315	331	314	
TOTAL VANS	776	803	745	

Source: DAF Company Presentation, Eindhoven, April 1991.

EXHIBIT 7
DAF Finance Company N.V.: selected financial data.

	1990	1989	1988	1987
Total Assets	2,403	2,204	1,871	1,402
Retail Portfolio	1,847	1,859	1,515	991
Retail Portfolio as Percentage of Total Assets	77%	84%	81%	71%
Capital and Reserves	146	126	121	97
Subordinated Loans	70	55	40	25
Interest Bearing External Borrowing/ Capital and Reserves and Subordinated Loans	9.6	10.7	10.1	9.5
Net Profit	17.9	20.1	18.2	15.5
Net Profit as a Percentage of Average Capital and Reserves	13.1%	15.8%	16.2%	16.2%

Source: DAF 1990 Annual report.

EXHIBIT 8
Selected employment and production statistics.

	1990	1989
Employment:		
United Kingdom	6,491	7,095
The Netherlands	6,037	6,676
Belgium	1,938	2,046
Other countries	924	965
TOTAL WORKFORCE	15,390	16,782
Production Statistics Trucks:		
United Kingdom	12,786	16,310
The Netherlands and Belgium	17,207	18,432
TOTAL TRUCKS	29,993	34,742
Vans:		
United Kingdom	24,575	23,616

Source: DAF 1990 Annual report.

1-4

NOTE ON THE SPANISH BANKING INDUSTRY

INTRODUCTION

This case is to be read in conjunction with the Banco Popular Español case (p. 532). It is divided into two parts, the first covering the recent history of banking in Spain until 1988, and the second covering the structure of and competitive influences in the banking arena after 1988, a year which marked a turning point for Spanish banking.

RECENT HISTORY UNTIL 1988

The Spanish Economic Environment

Prior to Spain's membership of the EC, which became effective on 1 January 1987, the economy had been relatively closed and productive assets underpriced in European terms. The year 1987 saw a rapid acceleration in GDP growth (from 3.3 per cent in 1986 to 5.5 per cent in 1987), fuelled by a surge in domestic demand, which began attracting large-scale foreign investment. The result was a revaluation of real assets in the Spanish economy.

*This case has been written by Christina Johnson, Research Associate, and Christopher Taubmann, Research Assistant, under the supervision of Dominique Héau, Professor of Business Policy and Associate Dean of the Executive Development Programme, and of Philippe Haspeslagh, Associate Professor of Business Policy.

Increased domestic demand contributed to a deterioration in the level of private domestic savings, which fell from 22 per cent of GDP in 1986 to 20 per cent in early 1988, amounting to 7.3 billion pesetas. This resulted in a rapid expansion of lending to the private sector to finance growing domestic investment. It also caused a worsening of Spain's trade balance, which was further aggravated by an appreciation of the peseta[1] (another consequence of foreign capital inflows). The appreciating currency, in conjunction with the existing high level of domestic interest rates, in turn attracted speculative financial investment, thereby triggering a growth in the complexity of Spain's financial markets.

The Spanish Financial System

The Spanish financial system in 1988 was characterized by a relatively well-organized market for short- to medium-term public debt, but less developed markets for long-term bonds. The stockmarkets had traditionally been illiquid and inefficient, with only a small proportion of large firms listed. Approximately 60 per cent of all private wealth was held in the form of cash or bank deposits. The Spanish interbank market had grown rapidly since its establishment in 1971. However, there was no organized market for options or futures.

With the comparative illiquidity of the long-term capital markets, companies had generally relied on the banking sector for funding. In addition to loans, many of the large commercial banks had amassed substantial equity positions in their industrial clients, partly as compensation for loans which turned bad during the 1960s and 1970s. As a result, the banking sector accounted for approximately 30 per cent of total market capitalization by the late 1980s.[2] Responsibility for supervision of the financial system lay with the Bank of Spain, which had become increasingly interventionist since the banking crisis of 1978–85. The Bank of Spain also conducted monetary policy, which in recent years had centred on fighting inflation.

The Banking Sector

Like the financial system, Spanish banking had been highly regulated and protected from external competition. Interest rates on deposits and loans had traditionally been tied to the discount rate offered by the Bank of Spain, allowing banks generous interest rate margins. On the other hand, the banks were required to fund public projects through investment requirements, as well as providing loans to certain priority sectors. In addition, reserve requirements were introduced in 1970 as an instrument of monetary policy and maintained at a relatively high level of around 15–18 per cent during the 1980s. In spite of the extent of regulation, there were signs of progressive liberalization, notably the relaxation of formal interest rate restrictions which began in 1969 and was completed by 1987.

Spanish banks were of two distinct types: 'private' commercial banks and 'public' savings banks. Other players in the Spanish banking sector were the foreign banks and the credit cooperatives.

Commercial Banks

Commercial banks operated on the '*banca mixta*' model, providing a range of commercial and investment banking services on a national basis, often through subsidiaries or associates. They had traditionally provided retail services to middle and upper-class personal customers as well as medium- to large-sized businesses. The sector was dominated by the so-called 'Big Seven' private banks – Banco de Bilbao, Banco Español de Crédito ('Banesto'), Banco Central, Banco Hispano Americano, Banco Santander, Banco de Vizcaya and Banco Popular – and Banco Exterior, a large, state-owned 'export' bank.

Notwithstanding the power of the 'Big Seven', the commercial banking sector had experienced declining concentration in terms of loans and deposits since the late 1950s, owing to a higher rate of growth of small and medium-sized banks. This trend was interrupted by the Spanish banking crisis of 1978–85, during which the cumulative effects of a severe industrial crisis, bad management, fraud and inadequate monitoring by the Bank of Spain were manifested in the failure of 51 domestic commercial banks.[3] Included in these were 20 banks from the RUMASA Group, a private industrial group representing 46 per cent of the existing banks in 1977. These failed banks were taken over by a newly formed Deposit Guarantee Fund, and subsequently sold – principally to the large commercial and foreign banks. Many of these were operated as 'second-name' merchant or regional banks within the acquiring banking groups.[4] After the crisis and the absorption of these banks, the trend towards declining market concentration continued afresh, with the large commercial banks losing 6 per cent of the market in deposits and 5 per cent of the market in loans between 1984 and 1987, principally to the two largest savings banks and the foreign banks.[5]

Savings Banks

Savings banks, known as '*cajas de ahorro*', had traditionally offered a more limited range of retail banking services than the commercial banks to a less affluent client base. A high proportion of their deposits took the form of savings accounts,[6] which were lent out for community-related projects, private mortgages (where they had held a monopoly until 1983), and as interbank loans. Savings bank depositors were less price-sensitive than those of the commercial banks, and the average financial cost of *caja* deposits had been 0.5–2.0 per cent lower. The conservative nature of their asset portfolios translated into lower margins on loans than the commercial banks, but greater security – as became apparent during the banking crisis, when not a single *caja* failed.

Restrictions on *caja* branch locations were relaxed in 1975, shortly after this restriction was lifted for commercial banks. However, unlike the commercial banks the *cajas* were confined until 1988 to their own geographic regions, albeit with a limited ability to operate through subsidiaries in other regions. Interestingly, they were permitted to expand overseas from 1980, and by early 1988 a number of the larger savings banks had, or were planning to establish, branches in the larger European capitals.

In 1988, 81 savings banks with 12,600 branches were chiefly engaged at a regional level in the highly profitable business of relending deposits received from the fast-growing savings of private households. In spite of geographic limitations on their operations, the savings banks held over 42 per cent of Spanish banking system deposits (up from 33 per cent in 1985). Approximately 54 per cent of these savings bank deposits were in the hands of the ten largest *cajas*, three of which ranked among Spain's ten largest deposit-taking financial institutions. The challenge posed by these savings banks to the commercial banking sector is best indicated by their deposits, which grew at an average rate of 5.27 per cent in 1987, slightly more than that achieved by Banco de Vizcaya, the fastest growing of the 'Big Seven' commercial banks. Indeed, other large commercial banks, including Banco de Bilbao, had recorded a fall in deposits during that year.

Much of the *cajas*' success could be attributed to their regional ties with the fast-growing small- and medium-sized business sectors, and a head start over the commercial banks in establishing a nationwide electronic interbank funds transfer system, direct salary payment systems and debit card facilities. They also employed a lower number of employees per branch, averaging 5.9 in 1988 as opposed to an average of 9.2 people per commercial bank branch.

Foreign Banks

Foreign banks had been prohibited from operating in Spain, with the exception of four long-standing institutions, which had a comparatively minor presence.[7] In 1978, a new regulation permitted foreign banks to enter, but subject to restrictions serving to minimize their participation in the retail market. They were prevented from establishing more than three branches in Spain including the head office, forbidden (until 1986) to invest in non-Spanish government securities and limited in their local deposit financing to 40 per cent of credits made to Spanish residents. However, a foreign bank could avoid these restrictions entirely by acquiring a domestic bank, which, if approved, meant that the acquirer technically assumed the acquired bank's domestic status. Thereafter, the new banking entity was entitled to establish new branches under any name that it chose. For example, Barclays Bank established a retail presence by purchasing the ailing 38-branch Banco de Valladolid in 1981. By mid-1987, Barclays had a total of 70 branches, albeit still a far cry from the thousands of branches operated by the large commercial banks.

By 1988, a total of 36 foreign banks were operating in Spain: Exhibit 5 lists some of the major foreign banks. In view of the severe limitations on their retail operations, these banks relied on the interbank market for funding, concentrating their efforts on expanding and developing the wholesale and capital markets. For example, Manufacturers Hanover initiated the bond market while Midland Bank helped to launch the commercial paper market. In 1985, Barclays became the first bank to offer its customers interest on their current account in Spain, a feature that was subsequently copied by other non-Spanish banks.

Nevertheless, reliance on interbank funds entailed significant risks for the foreign banks, as became particularly apparent during the first half of 1987 when interbank deposit rates skyrocketed; to take a striking example, one-month interbank deposit rates rose from 12 per cent in December 1986 to over 20 per cent in May 1987. The result was large losses for many foreign banks, particularly those that held large quantities of public sector paper. These conditions made acquisitions of local banks with retail deposit bases an attractive strategy, albeit an elusive one prior to 1992: in 1987 the Governor of the Bank of Spain warned that it did not favour foreign attempts to establish control over Spanish banks, while the large banking groups were thought to have reached a pact with the Bank of Spain not to sell any of their subsidiaries to foreigners.

Credit Cooperatives

Credit cooperatives, operating around 3,000 branches, had captured market shares of approximately 5 per cent of customer deposits and 3 per cent of customer loans in 1988. Like the savings banks, their share of deposits had been rising, but was too small to pose a significant threat to the private banks.

Comparison with European and International Banks in Early 1988

At the beginning of 1988, Spain boasted a total of 138 registered commercial banks,[8] which accounted for the majority of banking system accounts, employees and offices (see Exhibit 2). However, 64 of these 138 banks formed part of either the 'Big Seven' banking groups or the state-owned Banco Exterior, in large part a legacy of the banking crisis. Exhibit 7 presents a comparison of these largest banks, which together controlled over 50 per cent (and whose banking groups controlled over 80 per cent) of all commercial banks deposits in 1987.

In spite of these statistics, bank concentration in Spain was not that dissimilar to that in other EC countries. It was higher than in the United Kingdom and Luxembourg, but considerably lower than in Belgium, Denmark, the Netherlands, Portugal or Greece, where the largest five institutions recorded total market shares of 80 per cent on average.[9] On the other hand, Spain boasted the highest per capita concentration of bank branches in Europe (with the exception of Luxembourg): its 17,000 commercial and 12,600 savings bank branches represented one branch for every 1,191 Spaniards, compared with total bank branch ratios of 1:1,896 in Great Britain, 1:2,176 in France and 1:1,530 in the Federal Republic of Germany.[10]

After Denmark, Spanish banks enjoyed the highest interest rate margins in Europe, the spread between the bank borrowing rate and the prime lending rate (all averages) being 6.1 per cent compared with an EC average of 4.1 per cent. In fact, the spreads enjoyed by the large commercial banks were even more impressive, because of an informal interest rate cartel,[11] which had survived fierce interbank rivalry and formal interest rate deregulation. In February 1988, retail depositors were offered an average of 5.2 per cent p.a. There were, however, significant differences between the low rates publicly offered by the large private banks, and higher rates offered by the same large banks to special clients as well as by the smaller independent and second-name banks. By way of comparison, overnight interbank rates averaged 12.13 per cent in February 1988, while prime lending rates averaged 15.86 per cent on terms of 1–3 years.[12] This combination of high interest rate margins and dense branch networks translated to the highest profitability ratios as well as some of the highest costs of any European banking sector (see Exhibit 6). These ratios reflected the heavily retail nature of the Spanish banking industry. In contrast, countries like Germany, Switzerland and The Netherlands were characterized by relatively low profitability and low costs, reflecting a greater emphasis on wholesale banking (e.g. corporate in Germany, interbank in Switzerland).

These ratios also reflected the inefficiencies inherited by the sector from its highly regulated and protected environment. As the banks could not compete on price they competed (fiercely at that) in 'quality', defined as proximity to the customer. This explains the rapid growth in the 'Big Seven' branch networks following the removal of restrictions on branching in 1974, their extensive Automated Teller Machine (ATM) networks, and low branch 'productivity' – average credits per branch were little more than one fifth of the EC average. Moreover, none of the Spanish banks had achieved prominence in international terms: a 1988 survey ranked them between 100 and 213 in the world on the basis of recorded assets.[13] This was a matter of concern to Felipe González's socialist government in the lead-up to 1992, following which EC banks would have unrestricted access to the Spanish market.[14]

Distinguishing Features of the 'Big Seven' in early 1988

Banco Central

The largest private bank at year-end 1987, Banco Central was distinctive for its huge portfolio of industrial holdings. It was the most conservative and bureaucratic of the 'Big Seven', providing traditional corporate and retail banking services through its network of 2,044 branches. The majority of its retail clients were from rural areas with low incomes and basic needs, while the companies in which it held equity participations accounted for a majority of its corporate clients. Consequently, the bank had little incentive to offer innovative, high value-added products.

Banco Español de Crédito (Banesto)

Banesto boasted the largest network of the 'Big Seven'. Like Banco Central, Banesto had extensive industrial holdings, which distinguished it from the other banks. Notwithstanding its size, it had been weakened by a history of feuding among the families that controlled its board, along with $581 million worth of losses incurred by an affiliate, Banco Garriga Nogues. The latter, which it wrote off in 1986, completely wiped out its profit for that year. 1987 marked a turning point for Banesto. Mario Conde, who had risen from nothing, took the helm of Banesto at the age of 39. One of the youngest and most aggressive CEOs in Spain's banking industry, he was determined to change Banesto's image, building a solid, modern, professional institution with a strong market orientation.

Banco Hispano Americano

Hispano Americano's customers were typically private borrowers and small- to medium-sized companies ('PYME'), mostly in the industrial sector. Like Banesto, it had suffered major losses from the failure in 1984 of a subsidiary, Banco Urquijo, although profits had subsequently improved. In recent years the bank had been actively pursuing small retail accounts, and offering a top quality electronic banking service. In the course of 1987 it installed electronic payments systems, improved its ATM network and offered its customers a videotex service. International operations included 23 overseas offices, including six branches, and the Europartner link-up with Banco di Roma, Credit Lyonnais and Commerzbank.

Banco de Bilbao

Founded in 1857, Banco de Bilbao was one of Spain's oldest banks. It was perceived as a conservative, stable bank. Approximately 60 per cent of Banco de Bilbao's lending activity was to the PYME sector, although increasing attention was being paid to consumer and mortgage financing. Bilbao had also turned focusing more heavily on wholesale banking business, offering a wide range of capital markets, portfolio management and corporate advisory and consultancy services through its newly incorporated Bilbao Merchant Bank. It had a strategy of establishing links with the European Community, acquiring a 5 per cent equity participation in Hambros, a German merchant bank as well as acting as the ECU Banks Association's clearing bank in Spain for ECU transactions. Banco de Bilbao's Chaiman, José Asiaín, had for some years been a major proponent of a major bank merger in Spain.

Banco Santander

Santander, the only large family controlled bank, had the most innovative and aggressive management style of the large Spanish banks. It strove to be at the forefront of competition in the Spanish financial markets, and to this end was constantly developing new and higher value-added products including home banking for its increasingly sophisticated clientele. Santander was also the most international Spanish bank, boasting 169 foreign branches and representative offices. Its international strategy was to establish a strong presence in the European market by acquiring equity holdings in established European institutions – notably Bankhaus Central Credit (CC-Bank) in West Germany, which it acquired from Bank of America in April 1987. It was also entering into strategic alliances with overseas organizations like the major US insurance company, Metropolitan Life.

Banco de Vizcaya

Formed in 1901, Banco de Vizcaya had developed a reputation for young, aggressive management and tight internal controls, largely inspired by Pedro Toledo, who became chairman in 1987. Through a series of acquisitions during the banking crisis, notably that of the large Banca Catalana, it had achieved spectacular growth. However, Toledo emphasized bank management rather than mergers, as the key to competitive success of Spanish banks. By the end of 1987, the bank's policies were characterized by strict cost control procedures and a strong treasury department focused on large business transactions. This contrasted with Banco de Bilbao's traditional PYME clientele focus, although Vizcaya had a smaller international presence than Bilbao.

Banco Popular

The smallest of the 'Big Seven', Banco Popular was also the closest to being a pure commercial bank, dedicated to providing retail services to individuals and PYME clients. It was one of the most profitable private banks, recording a return on equity of 31.2 per cent. Popular's major strength lay in its ability to offer overall service to homogeneous groups. It intended to remain very much a domestic player, prepared to engage in strategic alliances with other European entities but with the key objective of acquiring expertise to expand the range of products and services offered to its domestic customers.

SPANISH BANKING INDUSTRY AND COMPETITIVE TRENDS AFTER 1988

The Spanish 'Big Bang'

July 1989 marked the beginning of a major reform of the Spanish equity markets. Whilst the large commercial banks had been major players in the Spanish stockmarkets, they had been required to deal through licensed '*agentes de cambio*'. Beginning in July, stock exchange membership became generally available to companies satisfying minimal capital requirements and brokerage rates were deregulated. Minimum ownership of these new exchange-member firms was initially set at 70 per cent, but this requirement would be progressively reduced, and finally eliminated by 1992. Each of the major commercial banks subsequently applied for membership.

The Large Commercial Banks

General Developments

With the progressive liberalization of Spain's financial sector and the aggressive moves of the foreign banks, the banking industry in Spain was undergoing rapid change. The foreign banks had shaken 'the foundations of the Spanish financial system' and had 'provoked a sink-or-swim atmosphere' in the industry. To ward off increasing competition, the commercial banks were forced to modernize, not only in terms of products offered, but also in terms of management. 'Traditionally Spanish banks were run like family businesses with top positions frequently inherited.' This was changing. For example, Banesto, 'one of Spain's most decrepit banks', had undergone a considerable transformation since Mario Conde, aged 42, had taken over the presidency in late 1987. He weeded out members and sympathizers of the old families that ruled the bank, and implemented a drastic restructuring and modernization programme, which comprised a cohesive marketing strategy and a huge investment in technology. This virtual revolution in the industry triggered aggressive financial innovation and a 'series of mega-mergers among leading financial institutions'.[15]

Merger Activity

In November 1987, the Spanish prime minister, Felipe González, told reporters of his preference for a pairing off of six of the 'Big Seven' private banks, in preparation for 1992. Mariano Rubio, Governor of the Bank of Spain, and José Angel Asiaín, president of Banco de Bilbao, were likewise openly advocating a merger between two 'Big Seven' banks. Besides the traditional arguments of achieving economies of scale and scope, the rationale for such a merger (or mergers) was based on the fact that Spain's banks were still quite small relative to the banks in other European nations. In order to compete in the European banking arena, these banks would require a certain size in terms of assets and capital, and would have to merge in order to achieve this. There was also a question of 'vanity', as Luis Valls, president of Banco Popular, put it.

On 19 November 1987 Banco de Bilbao announced that it was offering merger talks with Banesto. This came as a surprise to Banesto's CEO and the rest of the

Spanish financial community. Following a lukewarm response from Banesto, Bilbao rapidly announced a hostile bid for the bank, offering a combination of shares and cash. Hostile bids among Spanish banks had been without precedent in recent history. However, in early December three of the four Spanish stock exchanges rejected the bid, on the grounds that the Bilbao board lacked shareholder approval to create the shares offered as consideration. Bilbao withdrew its bid the following day in what was seen as an embarrassing setback for the Spanish government.

Bilbao's CEO, José Angel Sánchez Asiaín, anxious to merge with one of the 'Big Seven', continued looking for a suitable match. In early January 1988 he sent an expression of interest to Banco de Vizcaya's CEO, Pedro Toledo, who readily agreed. The merger was formally announced on 21 January, forming Banco Bilbao-Vizcaya ('BBV'), the largest bank in Spain with assets of Ptas 6.8 billion in December of 1988. From that day on the 'Big Seven' private commercial banks became the 'Big Six'.[16] It was established that the merger was to be 'voluntary, friendly and enthusiastic' and that there would be equality between the two banks in all respects, including customers shareholders and employees. During its first four years the merged bank would be administered by a board comprising the boards of the two banks, the former chairmen of both banks acting as co-chairmen. As a further application of the principle of equality the executive management of the merged bank would comprise equal numbers of managers from each bank. This supposed equality generated one of the biggest and most scandalous power struggles in the history of Spanish banking.

With the untimely death of Pedro Toledo in December 1989, a crisis, which had long been brewing, came to the fore. The men from Vizcaya, younger and more aggressive than their counterparts at Bilbao, had manoeuvred their way into key positions before Toledo's demise. These men did not want to accept Asiaín, co-chairman, as their new leader, and tried to elect a new co-chairman to replace Toledo. The Bilbao managers, in their turn, argued that the meticulous division of power need not be maintained at the top level once Vizcaya's original signatory was dead. With the body of a co-president still unburied, the BBV board showed itself bitterly divided over the future management structure of the bank. When the conflict went public, it deeply embarrassed the Spanish government, which had pressed hard for bank mergers.

Shortly after the BBV merger was announced, another merger was attempted, between Banco Central and Banesto. On 17 May 1988, these banks announced their plans to merge, basing their rationale for the merger on their massive industrial holdings – together they owned, controlled or 'influenced' over 1,000 Spanish companies.[17] The proposal came from Mr Escámez, the chairman of Banco Central, who had been worried by Cartera Central – a joint venture of the Kuwait Investment Office and two Spanish entrepreneurs known as Los Albertos. The latter had acquired seats on the Banco central board and made clear their intention of gaining control of the bank. Under the terms of the agreement worked out between Escámez and the Banesto president Mario Conde, the two banks would merge over a period of three years. A holding company would be formed, of which Escámez would be president until his retirement, when Mario Conde would take over. Prime minister González enthusiastically proclaimed the merger, which would have created Spain's biggest bank, as 'possibly the biggest economic event of the century.'[18] However, Los

Albertos continued to oppose the merger and took steps to prevent it. Using their persuasive abilities, they were able to convince a large part of the Banesto board that Mario Conde had manipulated the bank's 1988 results in order to keep Banesto's share price equal to that of Banco Central (a condition of the merger agreement). Faced with continuing hostility and adverse publicity, Mario Conde and Alfonso Escámez agreed, in late February 1989, to bring the 9-month-long merger process to an end.

In May 1991 two more mergers were announced. The first involved the absorption of Spain's publicly owned banks by Banco Exterior, to form Corporación Bancaria Expañola, the biggest bank in Spain with assets of Ptas 8.3 billion. This announcement triggered a quick response from the private banks, notably Banco Central, which proposed a merger with Banco Hispano Americano. The new bank, Banco Central Hispanoamericano, would surpass the Banco Exterior conglomerate and become Spain's largest financial institution with assets of Ptas 8.8 billion. Felipe González's government applauded these moves, which would place Spain's banks on a more 'competitive' footing with the large European banks. The successful completion of these mergers would mean that the Spanish banking sector would be dominated by the 'Big Five' private banks and Banco Exterior.

'Super Accounts'

As mentioned earlier, the deregulation of interest rate ceilings on deposits triggered a move towards offering deposit accounts earning higher rates of interest. However, the 'Big Six' banks at first refrained from publicizing these accounts, maintaining a tacit agreement of avoiding price competition. The position became less tenable after June 1989, when the Spanish government promoted a series of treasury bills yielding 13.75 per cent, which were available to individuals through retail banks. In the second half of 1989, the banking industry was also anticipating a significant reduction in the Bank of Spain's liquidity reserve ratio,[19] which would reduce the effective cost of raising deposits. On 13 September 1989, Banco de Santander made a shock announcement: a 'Super current account' payment 11 per cent p.a. interest monthly on current account balance in excess of Ptas 500,000 ($4,065), compared with an average interest rate of 7.72 per cent on private bank current accounts. The account was launched with a Ptas 700 million publicity campaign offering to transfer standing orders in other banks witin 24 hours. The result was nothing short of spectacular: the total value of Santander's current accounts virtually doubled from Ptas 376,000 million in August 1989 to Ptas 658,000 million in December 1989 as against an average increase of Ptas 37,000 million recorded by Santander's 'Big Six' competitor banks.

The other large commercial banks counterattacked with publicity campaigns contrasting their continued policies of 'free' account-keeping services with the fees which Santander had begun to charge on its new accounts. In late February 1990 the Bank of Spain announced that it would be cutting the liquidity reserve ratio from 17 per cent (9.5 per cent of which earned 7.5 per cent with the balance paying no interest) to 5 per cent (interest free). However, in the interest of restricting consequent money supply growth, freed reserves on existing deposits (including the deposits raised by Santander) were required to be invested in long-term certificates of deposit issued by the Bank of Spain and yielding just 6 per cent.

February and March 1990 saw the public launching of 'Super accounts' by nine other commercial banks, including Banesto, Exterior, Hispano Americano and BBV. Then, in April 1990, BBV launched an account offering 5 per cent interest and regular lottery prizes on deposits of just Ptas 50,000. This left only two of the 'Big Six' private banks holding out against the 'Super account' market, Banco Central and Banco Popular.

The success of Santander's strategy was confirmed by a 19 per cent rise in its net profits for 1990, which accompanied an increase in its share of total commercial and savings bank deposits from 3.51 to 5.25 per cent.[20]

International Expansion

In addition to its aggressive competition in the domestic Spanish market, Santander stood out as the most international of Spanish banks, being the sole Spanish commercial bank actively to pursue a strategy of entering other European retail banking markets. Its strategy was to penetrate these markets through associations with well-established local institutions, including Crédit du Nord Belge in Belgium (which it acquired in 1988), the Royal Bank of Scotland (in which it acquired a 9.9 per cent shareholding in late 1988) and Istituto Bancario Italiano, the eleventh largest Italian bank (in which it acquired a 30 per cent stake in early 1989).

The Savings Banks

Until 1988 the *cajas* had been organized as mutual rather than private institutions, controlled by large bodies comprised of depositors, staff members, local personalities and government representatives. As such, they were prevented from issuing equity, thereby forcing them to rely on retained earnings for expansion. However, in 1988 regulations were introduced permitting savings banks to issue '*cuotas participativas*', non-voting shares paying dividends varying with the level of profits. In the same year regulations restricting the *cajas*' geographic expansion beyond their traditional regions were lifted. These two measures represented a culmination of the earlier trend to savings bank deregulation, as they now could establish a presence in other regions and could raise the necessary capital to do so.

Interestingly, however, the *cajas* did not rush to issue shares. Moreover, all but the largest *cajas* continued to face difficulties in penetrating other geographical regions with loyal client bases. A logical alternative to internal expansion was merger, two significant instances of which occurred in 1989–90. In July 1989 the Caja de Pensiones and the Caixa de Barcelona announced their merger, forming the Caja de Ahorros y Pensiones, or less formally 'La Caixa', the largest depository institution in Spain. Then, in 1990 a merger was announced between Caja de Ahorros Municipal de Bilbao and the Caja Vizcaína to form the Caja de Bilbao Bizkaia Kutxa. This new savings bank ranked fourth in Spain in terms of loans.[21] Most of these *caja* mergers were intra-regional. Inter-regional mergers seemed a more difficult proposition, as local political and economic interests did their best to inhibit this type of activity.

In addition to merger activity, many of the larger savings banks like La Caixa and Caja de Madrid were actively involved in international expansion. The objective was to protect their domestic market by bringing in new products and serving Spanish customers abroad. For example, La Caixa (through Caixa de Barcelona) was among the most vigorous banks in foreign exchange trading, whilst the Caja de Madrid was the leading savings bank for international business with a share of about 25 per cent of this market in 1987. Since then Caja de Madrid had moved to expand this market and improve its market share by entering into strategic alliances with European partners, in particular with a German commercial bank, as well as taking equity stakes in other related entities in Italy and Morocco.[22]

At a more general level, in October 1990 the Spanish confederation of savings banks (CECA) (with 77 member savings banks) entered into a two-year cooperation agreement with its German counterpart (with 577 member savings banks) under which each would provide financial advice and services to the other's clients on both private and business matters.[23] In a further move, ten Spanish savings banks set up Savings International Trade (along with eight chambers of commerce and the Consejo Superior de las Cámaras de Comercio, Industria y Navegación), a trading concern that would act as an intermediary and take stakes in companies established abroad by Spanish firms.

In addition to their international expansion, many savings banks were posing a significant competitive threat to the big commercial banks domestically, as the differences between the two were progressively narrowing. Not only were the *cajas* expanding geographically, but they had begun aggressively targeting small- to medium-sized companies, a traditional customer base of the commercial banks. They were able to expand and diversify their customer base by offering newer and more sophisticated financial products. For example in 1990 both Caja de Madrid and Caja de Bilbao Bizcaia Kutxa introduced their own 'supercuentas'.[24] In fact, the savings banks belonging to CECA showed a rised in profit in 1989 that was triple that of the big conventional banks, primarily due to their policy of diversification into new financial products and opening new branches.[25]

The Foreign Banks

1989 and 1990 saw increased foreign bank presence in Spain. The 'Actualidad Económica' of 3 June 1990 noted that six new banks had opened branches: Industrial Bank of Japan, Banco de Fomento Exterior (Portugal), Banco de Espirito Santo (Portugal), San Paolo di Torino (Italy) and WestDeutsche Landesbank (FRG). In addition, foreign banks were acquiring interests in domestic Spanish banks. For example, Dresdner Bank, which already had a retail presence in Spain through Banco Comercial Transatlántico, moved to acquire a 5 per cent stake in Banesto in December 1990.[26]

By February 1991, there were 62 foreign banks operating in Spain with a combined market share of 16.1 per cent in terms of assets. The leading foreign bank was Barclays, with a branch network expanded to 200 offices, followed by Banque Nationale de Paris (BNP España), Citibank (Citibank España), Deutsche Bank (Bancotrans) and Crédit Lyonnais.[27]

EXHIBIT 1
Spanish financial market segmentation.

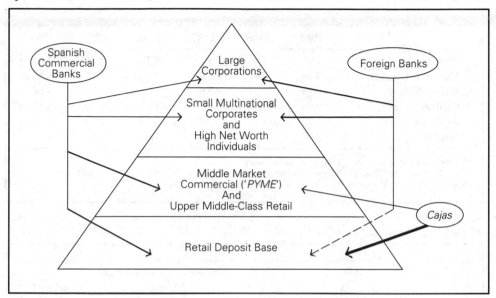

Source: Adapted from Salomon Brothers, 'The Spanish Commercial Banks', Sept. 1989.

EXHIBIT 2
The Spanish banking system (1988).

	Deposits	Loans	Offices	Employees
Commercial Banks*	48%	55%	17,000	157,000
Savings Banks	28%	35%	12,600	74,000

*Includes foreign banks.

EXHIBIT 3
Market shares – domestic (early 1990).

	Total Assets	%	Loans	%	Deposits	%
Commercial Banks*	32,332	58.38	16,410	62.78	12,816	48.82
Savings Banks	21,753	39.28	8,954	34.25	12,107	46.12
Credit Cooperatives	1,791	3.23	777	2.97	1,330	5.07
TOTAL	55,382	100.00	26,140	100.00	26,253	100.00

*Includes foreign banks.
Source: Kleinwort Benson Securities, 'The Big Six Spanish Banks', June 1990.

EXHIBIT 4
Evolution of the profitability of the Big Six*.

	1985	1986	1987	1988	1989	1990
Popular	1.60	1.80	2.24	2.54	2.16	2.94
Hispano Americano	0.39	0.63	0.02	1.70	1.11	1.53
Bilbao Vizcaya	0.99	2.37	1.61	1.70	1.63	1.68
Central	0.74	1.02	1.19	1.59	1.50	1.50
Santander	1.11	1.32	1.40	1.99	1.76	1.76
Banesto	0.90	–	1.26	1.49	1.37	1.37

*Net profit divided by average total assets (in per cent).
Note: The results for Bilbao Vizcaya before the merger are a combination of the results of Bilbao and Vizcaya.
Source: Expansion, 'Evolucion de la Rentabilidad de la Gran Banca', May 1991.

EXHIBIT 5
Major foreign banks in Spain (31 December 1987).

	Assets*	Average Total Intermed. Margin	Branches**
Barclays	246,593	3.59%	186
BNP España	258,347	1.99%	48
Citibank España	326,814	2.28%	104
Bancotrans (Deutsche)	168,388	4.39%	108
Crédit Lyonnais	189,369	1.08%	19

*In Ptas millions.
**At 31 December 1989.
Sources: El Nuevo Lunes, 'Rating', June 1988; El Pais, 'Ranking de Bancos', 9 October 1990.

EXHIBIT 6
Top European banks: profitability in 1989.

Gross Income/ Average Assets	Net Int. Income/ Average Assets	Net Op. Income/ Average Assets	Total Costs/ Average Assets*
Popular (6.98)	Popular (5.98)	Popular (3.80)	TSB Group (4.91)
TSB Group (6.78)	Hispano Am. (4.80)	Bankinter (2.93)	Lloyds (4.21)
Lloyds (6.62)	BBV (4.67)	Santander (2.64)	Midland (3.90)
Hispano Am. (5.75)	Santander (4.41)	BBV (2.43)	Hispano Am. (3.39)
Santander (5.52)	Lloyds (4.03)	Lloyds (2.41)	NatWest (3.32)
BBV (5.48)	Central (4.02)	Hispano Am. (2.36)	Popular (3.32)
Midland (5.38)	Banesto (3.99)	Central (1.95)	Exterior (3.06)
Exterior (5.01)	Bankinter (3.99)	TSB Group (1.87)	BBV (3.05)
Bankinter (4.77)	Exterior (3.97)	Bank of Scotland (1.82)	Barclays (3.03)
Barclays (4.77)	TSB Group (3.80)	Banesto (1.74)	Banesto (2.93)

*Bottom ten.
Source: Merrill Lynch & Co., 'European banks: measuring and comparing profitability', November 1990 (corrected).

EXHIBIT 7
The Big Seven banks (31 December 1987).
(Ptas thousands of millions)

	Total Assets	Deposits	Loans	Equity	Net Profit	Interest Margin	ROA*	ROE*
Central	2,912	2,041	1,287	185	32	4.02%	1.20%	18.90%
Banesto	2,517	1,966	1,033	137	24	4.19%	0.97%	17.93%
Hispano Americano	2,299	1,536	1,089	142	0	4.71%	0.00%	0.00%
Bilbao	2,466	1,649	1,249	122	24	5.61%	1.00%	20.70%
Vizcaya	1,854	1,079	667	121	23	4.80%	1.30%	20.00%
Santander	2,103	1,356	918	173	21	4.05%	1.00%	14.30%
Popular	1,164	845	489	89	17	6.03%	1.50%	22.40%

*Net profit over average total assets and average equity.
Source: Annual reports.

EXHIBIT 8
The Big Six banks (31 December 1990).
(Ptas thousands of millions)

	Total Assets	Deposits	Loans	Equity	Net Profit	Interest Margin	ROA*	ROE*
Bilbao Vizcaya	6,111	3,575	2,510	377	71	4.29%	1.20%	18.38%
Banesto	4,294	2,701	1,974	223	40	3.50%	1.01%	17.85%
Central	3,792	2,507	1,874	253	36	4.32%	1.02%	17.82%
Santander	3,798	2,314	1,408	237	42	3,60%	1.24%	17.96%
Hispano Americano	3,356	1,937	1,720	178	31	4.53%	0.97%	18.16%
Popular	1,452	1,067	714	103	28	6.57%	1.98%	27.33%

*Net profit over average total assets and average equity.
Source: Annual reports.

BSN GROUPE – EUROPE 1992*

BSN's objective for 1992 is to be among the major multiproduct food groups of Europe, to serve the world's largest market, with a population of over 320 million.

We will continue to seize all the opportunities for acquisition that present themselves in other parts of the world – provided they do not divert our energies from our first priority, Europe.

BSN has the means appropriate to its ambitions . . . to anticipate the future and offer the best products to the largest number of consumers.

Antoine Riboud, Chairman, BSN

So states BSN's 1988 annual report. The company set its goal to be the third player in the European food industry, behind Nestlé and Unilever, and to build a global presence in the food industry by purchasing or developing other worldwide operations. Through 1989, BSN had made several acquisitions to implement its strategy, most notably, its acquisition of Nabisco Europe, but with the food industry consolidating, company price tags were increasing rapidly. To capitalize on European unification, BSN believed its organization must be in place by 1992, but it still had to find and acquire complementary companies, invest in research and development and joint ventures, and secure funds to finance these activities – all within three years. In addition, BSN had to be wary of potential predators wanting to purchase the company for its European presence. BSN faced many challenges to the achievement of its goals, yet Antoine Riboud and his management team were confident they would succeed.

---

*This case was prepared by Janet Shaner under the supervision of Professor Roy Goldberg as the basis for class discussion rather than to illustrate either effective or ineffective handling of an administrative situation.

THE ACQUISITION OF NABISCO INTERNATIONAL

Monday, 5 June 1989. Antoine Riboud was at the Evian festival, acting as usual among his friends and guests. Joking, teasing, talking. Riboud was hosting this annual festival, among other reasons to promote BSN, and he didn't deny that fact.

Riboud sat down at the lunch table, only to be interrupted by Michel David-Weill, the 'godfather' of Lazard Frères, and one of Riboud's confidants. David-Weill was informing Riboud that Riboud would lunch the following day with Henry Kravis, of Kohlberg Kravis Roberts. The lunch was all or nothing. It had been exactly one month since KKR announced its intention to sell Nabisco's five European businesses, and BSN wanted to purchase them. At about 1 or 2, Riboud left his guests, took Concorde from London, and lunched in New York. At dessert, Kravis was convinced, BSN would have Nabisco-Europe. It was BSN who would take it away, before the German company Bahlsen, among others. The Crédit Lyonnais had loaned BSN $2.5 billion in 2 hours.[1] Thirty days later, BSN announced it would sell Nabisco's two potato crisp businesses, Walkers and Smiths, to Pepsi for approximately $1.3 billion.

Over dessert, BSN had spent $2.5 billion, or approximately 27 times its earnings, for Nabisco's five European operations, increasing BSN's debt to FF22 billion from FF5.9 billion. The purchase was expensive, but if BSN wanted to be strong in its core segments it needed a concentrated distribution network and the brands to push through that network. BSN realized that in ten years there would be no more opportunities like Nabisco, and developing brands and markets might be more expensive and would take more time than the 1992 EC unification deadline allowed. 'A strategic acquisition doesn't have a price,' commented Riboud.[2]

With this single purchase, BSN had become the No. 1 European biscuit manufacturer with a 18–20 per cent market share, ahead of United Biscuit and Bahlsen, and No. 2 worldwide. BSN also had attained a presence in the Italian and British biscuit markets, where it had none before. (Exhibit 1 details the Nabisco purchase.) This No. 1 position was particularly impressive considering that until BSN's 1986 purchase of Générale Biscuit, BSN had no presence in the biscuit market. In three years, BSN had risen from nothing to No. 1.

BSN – THE COMPANY

The biscuit segment wasn't the first time that BSN had risen from nothing to become a major player in the food industry. BSN started as a glass manufacturing company, Souchon Neuvesel, of which Antoine Riboud was appointed general manager in 1958. For most of the next ten years, Riboud stayed in glass businesses, diversifying only from glass containers into flat glass for auto windshields and housing by merging with the Boussois flat glass company in 1966. In 1968, Riboud attempted a takeover of Saint Gobain, then a far larger glassmaker. BSN's proposal to swap BSN convertible bonds for Saint Gobain stock, at the time a novel approach in France, failed, in the process causing so much stir that a terrorist gang opposed to the bid bombed Riboud's

Paris apartment. While his tactics offended France's conservative business establishment, Riboud became something of a cult figure among younger managers eager for change. Virtually overnight, BSN acquired a new image, and youthful executives flocked to join Riboud's banner.[3]

The rebuff by Saint Gobain helped Riboud to spot a trend: 'I saw it would be better to fill the bottles rather than just make them.'[4] Throughout the 1970s and 1980s BSN made a series of bold acquisitions and began diversifying into mineral water, baby foods, beer, dairy products, grocery products and biscuits. (Exhibit 2 lists BSN's purchases, Exhibit 3 shows the company structure in 1988, and Exhibit 5 illustrates its geographic locations.)

To enter these new businesses BSN needed executives with brand marketing expertise. In 1969, Riboud hired Francis Gautier, formerly chairman and first executive officer of Colgate-Palmolive France. Since that time, BSN's decentralized organization had grown into three concentric circles (Exhibit 4). The outside ring included the 50 subsidiary heads and the middle ring contained the nine general division heads. Four key executives occupied the inner circle: Antoine Riboud, chairman; Georges Lecallier, vice-chairman and president, 58; Francis Gautier, vice-chairman, 66; and Pierre Bonnet, senior executive, vice-president, 61.

THE FOOD INDUSTRY

Branding. No. 1 or No. 2 position in market share. Line extension. New product development. Critical mass. Cash flow. These were the food industry buzzwords in the late 1980s. In prior decades, major food companies had invested significant sums to build production facilities, develop new products and establish distribution networks. These companies had built critical mass to spread fixed costs over many production units, and they had fine-tuned their corporate machines for efficient operations. By 1989, these investments were paying out huge cash flows.

Food consumption was growing at only 1–2 per cent annually, which meant that food companies desiring higher growth had to increase market share. To achieve this growth, they could invest spare cash in one of two ways: by building market share with new product development and heavy advertising expenditures or by buying market share with purchases of established brands.

Successful 1980s food companies needed strong brands (those holding the No. 1 or No. 2 position in market share) to gain and retain customer loyalty and supermarket shelf space. Consumers, with more disposable income and less time to learn about food products, trusted the quality and value of branded products. Strong brand loyalty and No. 1 or No. 2 market position generated several benefits for food companies, including greater pricing flexibility and supplier power with retailers, improved chances of success for subsequent product introductions, and greater production efficiencies. To gain and retain these market positions, food companies were increasing advertising and promotion expenditures significantly, both to pull customers into the stores, and to push their products through the distribution channels.

Driven by this need for critical mass and the lack of market growth, the food industry was consolidating. Developing brands was expensive and time-consuming.

Purchasing existing brands was much faster, although competition for strong brands was bidding up prices rapidly. In 1988, several significant acquisitions occurred including Philip Morris's purchase of Kraft for $12.9 billion (P/E 24), Kohlberg Kravis Roberts's leveraged buyout of RJR/Nabisco for $25 billion (P/E 18), and Nestlé's purchase of Rowntree MacIntosh for $3.8 billion (P/E 23).

European Consolidation

The 1992 market unification was driving consolidation of the European food industry. The EC ministers had written approximately 300 directives to make the necessary changes to intra-EC trade, creating the Single European Market. Prior to unification, individual country trade barriers required food manufacturers to locate plants and distribution networks in each country, reducing a manufacturer's ability to realize economies of scale. Examples of these trade barriers include:

- Restrictions on the use of specific ingredients, such as France's aspartame ban for non-alcoholic beverages.
- Regulations relating to content and its description, such as the purity law on pasta in Italy or beer in Germany.
- Packaging and labelling.
- Tax discrimination, such as specific taxes on beer in the United Kingdom and Italy.
- Specific import restrictions.

The 1992 directives would eliminate all trade barriers, taxes, etc., between the EC countries. The direct benefits would come from three sources:

1. The use of less expensive ingredients.
2. The reduction in packaging and labelling costs.
3. The removal of bureaucratic obstacles to imports.

Both producers and consumers would benefit from the elimination of these restrictions. Producers could consolidate their operations to gain economies of scale and thus lower costs. Consumers should receive lower prices and also have a greater product selection. Exhibit 6 lists the economic benefits from removing the non-tariff barriers in food processing.

An extremely fragmented European food industry had emerged because of the trade barriers, with most producers operating in only their home country. The 1992 unification would create the opportunity for truly European companies, and BSN wanted to be one of the top three. But it had to act now to achieve that goal.

COMPETITION

Nestlé and Unilever dominated the European food industry. Grand Metropolitan, a British food and drink company, held the No. 3 position in terms of total sales, while

BSN ranked fourth following its Nabisco acquisition. Nestlé and Unilever had deep roots in the food business, extending over 100 years. In comparison, BSN and Grand Met had entered the industry a mere 20 years ago. In addition to the 'big boys', many regional food companies existed in their respective countries and competed with BSN in specific market segments. (Exhibit 7 lists the major players in the food industry and comparative financial statistics.)

Nestlé

Nestlé, the 'giant among food giants', was founded in Switzerland in 1866. From the beginning it processed milk and had since expanded into almost every segment of the food business, including chocolate, coffee, frozen foods, infant foods and pet foods. Constrained by the boundaries of the small Swiss market, Nestlé expanded early in life so that by 1989, Nestlé was the world's largest producer of coffee, powdered milk, frozen dinners, and confectionary with operations in more than 60 countries on all parts of the globe (Exhibit 8).

Nestlé had adopted a patient, long-term strategy during its quest for food industry supremacy. The company typically built manufacturing facilities for its dairy operations, penetrating slowly at first, but gradually accelerating branded product introductions. Nestlé's patience allowed it to learn the intricacies of country management through its simpler dairy operations, analyze the country's needs and introduce the products to meet those needs. In addition, research and development was crucial to Nestlé's success. The 3,000 scientist research staff worldwide had created innovations such as Nestlé's *Quick* and *Nescafé*, creations which competition had failed to match. In 1988, it spent approximately SFr 375 million ($253 million) or 0.9 per cent of sales on R&D.

Once characterized as a sleepy giant, Nestlé, under the leadership of Helmut Maucher, had transformed itself into an aggressive, dynamic company. The company operated within a decentralized organization structure, each subsidiary reporting to headquarters monthly on a single sheet of paper. To strengthen its industry position, Nestlé had made several strategic acquisitions, including Carnation, an American food company, for $3 billion in 1985; Rowntree, a British chocolate manufacturer, for $3.8 billion, and Buitoni, an Italian pasta maker, for $1.3 billion in 1989. Maucher claimed the major part of his acquisition programme was complete and that Nestlé was prepared for 1992. With its huge cash flow of SFr 3.3 billion ($2.2 billion), however, Nestlé could finance practically any purchase out of its own pocket, and outsiders believed future acquisitions were probable, particularly in the United States.

Unilever

Unilever, formed by the 1930 merger between the British soap company Lever Brothers and the Dutch margarine company Unie, was Nestlé's greatest rival. The company, like Nestlé, had built its business by locating industrial operations, in this case in fat and oil processing facilities, and then expanding its sales and market share in a country by introducing value-added products such as Imperial Margarine, Close-Up toothpaste, Lipton soup and Pond's hand lotion. By 1988, Unilever was involved in six business segments: margarine, edible fats and oils and dairy products; frozen foods and ice cream; detergents; personal products; specialty chemicals; and agribusiness. Its 1988 sales of $31 billion included $15.4 billion or almost 50 per cent from the food sector (Exhibit 9).

Unilever spent $601 million, or 2 per cent of sales, on research and development in 1988, and its experiments included biotechnological studies. The company operated under a product and regional manager matrix structure, so that each country's product manager reported to two bosses.

Grand Metropolitan

Grand Metropolitan was a rapidly emerging player in the food industry. The company had started in 1962 as a small hotel and restaurant business, had diversified into the wines and spirits business, and by 1989 had set its strategic focus on the food, drinks and retailing businesses in Western Europe, the United States, and Japan. Grand Met, like BSN, was acquiring food companies to build its brands and increase its critical mass. Most notably, Grand Met had purchased Pillsbury for $5.7 billion (P/E 31) in late 1988. The company strove for lean, efficient operations and maintained a decentralized organization structure. (Exhibit 10 illustrates financial results.)

BSN IN 1989

BSN entered the food industry in 1970 with a specific strategy, and during its 20-year quest to become a major industry player, BSN had deviated little from that strategy. BSN focused its business activities on high value-added, individually packaged products. It intentionally avoided commodity products such as coffee and chocolate which have low margins and price-sensitive sales. In addition, BSN focused on segments where it could be No. 1 or No. 2 in the market. Intensifying competition for shelf space among branded products was squeezing out marginal brands, and this drive for the No. 1 or 2 position was becoming increasingly critical in 1989 (Exhibit 11 presents BSN's financial performance.)

A focus on four specific areas had helped BSN achieve its strategies: marketing, human resources, research and development, and efficient operations. BSN was one of the most respected and desirable companies for marketing employment in France because of its creative and innovative approaches, and BSN was renowned for its excellent union relations as well. BSN encouraged personal development with training classes, and provided a generous profit participation programme which nearly equalled the profit received by shareholders. BSN maintained a decentralized organization structure, and it was working to 'internationalize' its workforce, training managers to lead the company in its new global environment.

A commitment to research and development had provided BSN with innovative new products to sell in the marketplace. In 1988, BSN spent approximately FF 250 million ($43 million) or 0.6 per cent of sales on research and development. New products included 'Dannon Light' yogurt, 'Kronenbourg Light' low calorie beer, 'Tourtel Brune' non-alcoholic beer, Lea & Perrins sauces in tomato, curry and pimento flavours, and unique combinations of prepared pasta dishes and pastries. In addition, BSN's research staff, composed of several hundred people worldwide, was studying biotechnology. Although biotechnology had been controversial in other spheres, BSN believed its product innovations would be accepted:

> BSN believes its research group can make significant production process improvements and develop new products with biotechnology applied to the fermentation process [in yogurt, beer and vinegar]. Regulation for this kind of innovation is very strict in most European countries, and before putting this type of new product on the market, proof must be demonstrated that the products do not harm human health. Consequently, it seems that European consumers, and more specifically 'the greens', do not react to biotechnological innovation the way they do in the United States. BSN does not feel that they will face nonacceptance for the biotechnical innovations.

BSN believed these biotechnology developments would decrease costs or create unique products, thus giving the company a competitive advantage.

Finally, BSN believed it had achieved highly efficient operations. The company was confident that it could translate this efficiency, resulting from its attitude of minimum bureaucracy, to acquired companies in terms of lower production costs and, as a result, create additional synergistic value.

SIX MARKET SEGMENTS

BSN focused its strategy on six key segments in 1989: dairy products, grocery products, biscuits, beer, champagne and mineral water, and containers. (Exhibit 12 details BSN's market segments and Exhibit 13 illustrates major competitors and market shares within each segment.) The segments had shifted over the years with BSN's acquisitions and divestitures. For example, the acquisition of Générale Biscuit in 1986, put BSN in the biscuit segment where it had no presence previously. In addition, BSN had gradually diversified out of the flat glass business to concentrate on food. (Exhibit 14 illustrates Salomon Brothers' financial projections through 1994. Exhibits 15 to 17 illustrate European and US consumption trends.)

Dairy Products

BSN entered the dairy segment through the acquisition of Gervais-Danone in 1972. By 1989 BSN was the world's largest refrigerated dairy products producer, with sales of FF11 billion compared to FF6.1 billion of Nestlé, its closest competitor. BSN's particular strengths were yogurt (45.2 per cent of total segment sales), natural cheeses (33.2 per cent), desserts (15.8 per cent) and other products (5.8 per cent). Its major brands included Dannon, Gervais and Bio. The company saw tremendous worldwide growth opportunities in this segment.

To build the size and profitability of dairy products, BSN had invested in a state-of-the-art processing plant near Lyons in May 1987, designed to service the French, German, Italian and Spanish markets. By 1989 the new factory had contributed significantly to division margins. In addition, BSN purchased 35 per cent of Galbani in 1989 for FF3.8 billion. (Galbani's 1988 sales were FF6.8 billion with FF575 million earnings and 1 billion cash available.) Galbani was Italy's No. 1 cheese company with 17 per cent market share, and it was BSN's first entry into Italian choose technology. BSN believed it could push Galbani's products through BSN's distribution channels in other European countries, and it could push existing BSN dairy products through Galbani's 120,000-outlet distribution network, both creating additional synergistic value.

Yogurt consumption was among the fastest growing segments in the European food industry (Exhibit 16c), and BSN saw opportunities to increase sales both in the United States and Japan where yogurt consumption per capita was significantly less than in Europe. In addition, BSN was attempting to build a market for yogurt in countries like China by establishing joint ventures with local companies.

Grocery Products

Since 1980, the Grocery Division had been a rapidly growing part of the BSN Group and it was the largest contributor to operating income. Originally almost entirely French, this segment had undergone intense Europeanization through a number of acquisition. For example, BSN had purchased HP Foods/Lea & Perrins and the jam division of Soparind in 1988.

By 1989 the segment produced revenues of more than FF10 billion from products including pasta and prepared foods (38.2 per cent of total division sales); sauces, soups, mustards and condiments (29.8 per cent); confectionary/jams (13.9 per cent); baby food (11.0 per cent); and other products (7.1 per cent). Particularly in pasta, baby food, soup and prepared foods, BSN seemed to be positioned in higher growth segments of both the European and American markets (Exhibit 16).

BSN was continuing to add to the division with the 1989 purchase of 35 per cent of Star and Starlux, the No. 1 tomato sauce producer in Italy and Spain. The deal gave BSN expansion opportunities in high-growth southern European markets; new products for pastas, prepared dishes and biscuits; and additional distribution outlets for marketing Star's products. The acquisition cost BSN FF1.5 billion for a company generating 1988 sales of FF4.1 billion. The Fossati family owned Star, and IFIL (Fiat) had joined BSN by purchasing an additional 10 per cent of the company.

BSN seemed to be in a strong competitive position in this segment. Its acquisitions of local companies offered production and research economies of scale while retaining the ability to tailor products to satisfy local needs. Analysts believed BSN was well placed to expand into ready-to-serve food with its experience in pastas and sauces combined with its established chilled dairy distribution network. Nestlé and Unilever could threaten BSN's position, however, by introducing products from non-European markets and subsidizing these products with earnings from other geographic segments. BSN would have to pre-empt this threat by creating strong brands and efficient operations, making new entry too expensive for global competitors.

Biscuits

BSN had no presence in the biscuit market before it purchased Générale Biscuit in 1986. By 1989, prior to the Nabisco acquisition, BSN was the leading maker of biscuits and packaged toasts in continental Europe and in third place worldwide. The Biscuits Division accounted for more than FF7 billion in sales of which half was outside of France. BSN produced a range of products under brand names such as

'Lu', 'L'Alsacienne' and 'Heudebert', and competed with United Biscuit (1988 sales, FF9.1 billion) and Bahlsen (1987 sales, FF5.2 billion) for European consumers.

Before BSN's Nabisco purchase, the division lacked a truly international network. Nabisco supplied that distribution strength. BSN, having no other presence in potato chips, did not want to keep these British operations. Consequently, it sold these businesses to Pepsi and reduced its debt load. To summarize the transaction:

	Price	Earnings	P/E
	(FF bn)	(FF m)	
Bought: Nabisco Europe	16.8	620	27.1
Sold: Snack businesses	9.0	325	27.7
Retained: Biscuit businesses	7.8	295	26.4

Source: Prudential Bache estimates.

Integration of the Nabisco businesses offered significant synergies with BSN's existing operations. France's Belin (1988 sales FF1.8 billion, earnings FF100 million) offered the greatest synergistic opportunities. It was the market leader in baked snacks, salted biscuits and frozen pastries, and No. 2 to BSN in sweet biscuits. The acquisition strengthened BSN's position in salted biscuits, and it provided opportunities for considerable administrative, distribution and production synergies between the two companies. Prudential Bache analysts estimated that pre-tax savings could be as much as FF140 million per year.

Of the other two companies, Italy's Saiwa (1988 sales FF790 million) held 10 per cent market share, second to Barilla's 23 per cent, and Prudential Bache analysts believed BSN could achieve administrative and distribution synergies worth approximately FF40 million per year. The UK company, Jacob's Bakery (1988 sales FF1.8 billion), held just 16 per cent of the biscuit market, far behind United Biscuits' 48 per cent overall share, but Jacob's was well placed in plain crackers (45 per cent share) and salted biscuits (23 per cent share). Prudential Bache believed it could achieve savings of FF70 million per year.

Beer

With its Kronenbourg and Kanterbrau brands, BSN (sales 21.5 billion hl) was second only to Heineken (sales 23 billion hl) in the European brewing market. BSN held 48 per cent market share in France and nearly 30 per cent in Europe through affiliations with companies in Belgium (Alken-Kronenbourg), Spain (Mahou), Italy (Wuhrer and Peroni) and Greece (Henninger Hellas). By 1989, BSN's beer production was divided as follows: France (42.0 per cent, 10.3 hl), Italy (19.6 per cent), Spain (17.1 per cent), Belgium (8.6 per cent), Exports/Franchise (8.2 per cent) and Greece (4.5 per cent).

In northern European countries, with the exception of the United Kingdom, per capita beer consumption was declining slightly. However, BSN saw growth opportunities in the southern European countries such as Spain, Italy and Greece where traditionally wine-drinking consumers were purchasing more beer. Competitors also spotted this growth opportunity, and like BSN, were establishing relationships with local beer producers.

Champagne and Mineral Water

BSN believed its quality product and innovative packaging had allowed it to become the No. 1 worldwide bottler of mineral water (Perrier was second). Evian was the world's largest exporter of non-carbonated mineral water, and in France, Evian held 24 per cent market share. Spain's market growth was 'spectacular' and BSN's Font Vella retained market leadership. Italy was Europe's largest mineral water market and was growing at 4 per cent annually. BSN's 1988 purchase of 35 per cent of Sangemini, the leading Italian mineral water company, gave BSN an Italian distribution network for Evian and its other mineral water products. Because of an underdeveloped European non-alcoholic industry and declining alcohol consumption, analysts expect dramatic change in the non-alcoholic drink segment. Competitors such as Coca-Cola, PepsiCo and Cadbury Schweppes could enter the market and challenge BSN's leadership position.

In champagne, BSN (5.7 per cent share) was the world's third largest bottler behind Moët (20 per cent) and Seagram (6.5 per cent). BSN believed its 'Pommery' and 'Lanson' brands symbolized high quality, the force of tradition and worldwide distribution – all valuable elements facilitating the company's expansion. In 1989, BSN had purchased Scharffenberger Cellars, a California producer of wine by the champagne method, to grow its champagne segment.

Containers

The container division was all that remained of the original BSN. In 1988, the company was Europe's largest bottle manufacturer with annual production of more than 6.2 billion units (75.1 per cent of total division sales). The division sold 18.6 per cent of its products to other BSN divisions, and it also produced flasks (13.8 per cent) and plastic packaging materials (11.1 per cent) in France, the Netherlands and Spain. BSN also had a minority interest in France in a company producing jars and glass tableware. The company's presence in this segment improved its marketing flexibility by reducing packaging costs (as much as 60 per cent of the delivered cost of mineral water, for example). A logical complement to BSN's food activities, the oldest of the company's divisions remained faithful to the tradition of glass. Technological progress and vigorous competitive pressures had forced BSN to stress constant adaptation of its manufacturing activities and continuing product innovation.

GROWTH STRATEGY

As BSN looked to the future, it believed growth was the key not only for success but for survival. BSN was one fourth the size of the giant food companies like Nestlé, Unilever, Philip Morris and Nabisco. To compete successfully against these giants, BSN needed the critical mass and the No. 1 and 2 brands in its chosen segments to generate cash flow, retain and grow shelf space, fund research and development, and finance future acquisitions. BSN saw growth as the key to financing innovation, solidifying the company's long-term position, and preventing attack from one of the giants.

To maintain its goal of at least 10 per cent earnings per share growth per year, BSN had a two pronged strategy of acquiring companies for short-term growth while developing new markets to provide sustained long-term growth. BSN sought to acquire or develop high value-added products. Geographically it focused first on Europe. It wanted bases in all principal European markets in preparation for the 1992 EC unification. As Antoine Riboud stated, 'We must construct Europe as quickly as possible. The Belgian, German, English, Italian, etc. vacationers must be able to find my products everywhere. Our consumer is becoming European.'[5] After Europe, BSN's priorities were, in order, the United States, Asia, South America, Eastern Europe and Africa.

In evaluating new countries, BSN examined the number of mouths to feed, the political stability of the country, and the disposable income levels to determine the most attractive markets. (Exhibit 18 presents demographic statistics for selected countries.) New markets took time, patience and often partners to satisfy local investment regulations. For example, Indian law requires a maximum foreign control of 40 per cent of a company. In France, BSN wanted 100 per cent ownership in the companies it owned, but in other countries like Italy and Japan, it recognized that joint ventures would be the only way to penetrate the markets.

BSN had expanded into new countries. It had established joint ventures with companies like Ajinomoto in Japan and a local company in China to sell Dannon yogurt, and it had signed agreements with new producers in Canada and Australia where it had no previous presence. Internal expansion was slow, however, and competitive pressures did not give BSN the luxury of time.

Recognizing that 1992 was just three years away, Antoine Riboud embarked on an acquisition spree, which had accelerated since the 1986 Générale Biscuit acquisition. Riboud and his staff searched diligently and patiently for companies whose products fit with BSN's core segments and who could benefit from the company's efficient operations. After identifying an appropriate candidate, BSN wasted no time – it bid for and acquired its target. From 1986 to 1989, BSN purchased 23 companies, most notably its whirlwind acquisition of Nabisco Europe.

COMPETITIVE CHALLENGE

BSN had set its course. It would stay at home and conquer its own European market before embarking on overseas journeys. BSN understood the battleground and knew it contained several potential land mines. These included the increasing power of large supermarket chains, decreased alcohol consumption, threats of purchase or competition from larger European or American players desiring a presence in Europe, limited resources for future acquisitions, and the timing of European unification.

Supermarkets

Large European supermarket chains such as Leclerc, Intermarche and Carrefour in France, Tesco and Sainsbury in England and Tengelmann and Aldi in Germany, had become powerful forces in the European food industry. These chains controlled significant market share (Exhibit 19), and consequently, held great buyer power in negotiating prices and terms with food producers. In addition, retailers were developing their own in-house brands to compete directly with branded products.

Initially, many store brands were discount/generic products designed to attract the price-sensitive consumer in the early 1970s. By 1989, however, the store brands' image communicated good consumer value. Supermarkets had established their own sophisticated research and sourcing groups to develop high-quality products at a reasonable price. Supermarkets hoped to achieve several goals with store brands. First, they wanted to create customer loyalty to store brands thus inducing customers to shop specifically at their chain to purchase those brands. Second, the supermarkets wanted to increase margins by controlling the product's input costs and eliminating the food company as middleman. Finally, supermarkets saw the opportunity to increase customer satisfaction by providing a 'good value' product which customers could trust. Store brands were reaching, in some cases, up to 30 per cent of the total market.

Higher margins meant that supermarkets wanted to allocate as much shelf space as possible to their own brands, squeezing out less profitable products. Supermarkets needed the No. 1 or 2 food company brands to attract consumers to the store and add credibility to the store's quality. Less popular brands risked losing shelf space to top brands which attracted customers and paid larger slotting allowances or to store brands which increased margins and built store loyalty.

Decreased Alcohol Consumption

BSN derived 15 per cent of its 1988 revenues from beer sales. Although beer consumption was stable in the northern European countries, the company saw growth opportunities in countries like Italy and Spain which had been wine drinkers traditionally. As the population aged and the fear of alcohol increased, however, per capita consumption was declining (Exhibit 16d). BSN had introduced low calorie and non-alcoholic beer to address these trends.

Industry Consolidation

BSN wanted to ensure that it was not swallowed by one of the giant companies looking to purchase a presence in the European market. BSN believed its best defence was shareholder satisfaction, so it concentrated on building a strong European food and beverage group and satisfying shareholders with above-average earnings. To provide additional protection, BSN had implemented several anti-takeover measures.

The company first forged a relationship with the Agnelli group whereby Agnelli owns 5 per cent of BSN and BSN owns 35 per cent in IFIL Partecipazioni, an IFIL subsidiary which, in turn owns 6.7 per cent of Fiat. With this alliance, BSN achieves two objectives: it obtains a friendly shareholder and it builds credibility in Italian markets with Italian business relationships. The partnership's ventures were expanding rapidly and included purchases of Sangemini (Italian mineral water), Gruppo Star (Italian and Spanish tomato sauce and pasta), Galbani (Italian cheese) and Peroni (Italian beer). More deals were expected.

Additionally, BSN had built a core group of supportive investors. This core group consisted primarily of Lazard Frères (5.8 per cent), the Agnelli family (5.0 per cent), the Fossati family (Italian owners of Starlux, 4.0 per cent), UAP (4.0 per cent) and the Saint-Louis Group (a French sugar and oil manufacturer, 2.7 per cent). As a further defence, BSN had issued 1.2 million warrants, exercisable into 12.24 million shares of 19 per cent of the diluted capital, to Gemofim, a holding company owned by a wide range of financial institutions friendly to BSN. The key members of this consortium are Paribas, Lazard Frères, Crédit Lyonnais, BNP, Société Générale, Demachy, Deutsche Bank and Sofina.

Finally, at the end of 1988, BSN acquired Alfabanque, a small private French bank from Lazard Frères. Under French law, any potential acquirer of more than 10 per cent of a French bank, or a company that owns more than 10 per cent of a French bank, can only do so with the approval of the Minister of Finance and the Comité des Etablissements de Crédit. Commenting on the likelihood of a foreign takeover, Antoine Riboud remarked that 'BSN was like a cathedral, and what state in its right mind would allow one of its national monuments to be sold to a foreign country?'[6]

Limited Resources

BSN had to develop supplementary financing sources to fund future acquisitions. In the past, BSN had issued convertible bonds, bonds with warrants attached and stock to finance its activities (Exhibits 20 and 21). Additional options could include injecting capital, converting part of the Gemofin options to shares, issuing new stock, or selling certain businesses. In 1988, BSN generated a FF4.2 billion cash flow. It needed to determine how much it would need to finance future acquisitions, the optimal supplementary financing sources, and when each should be utilized.

Unification Achievement

BSN based its Europeanization strategy on the 1992 goal for Community unification, but the 300 specific directives required to implement that goal were complicated and politically charged. These directives included the elimination of all border taxes and trade barriers, free access by all Community members to any Community country, Community-wide recognition of educational institutions, and the development of a European currency. BSN believed the European Community eventually would be fully integrated, but it had no guarantee that unification would proceed as scheduled. Delays in implementing 1992 changes might impact BSN's ability to achieve its own goals.

THE FUTURE

Antoine Riboud believed the role of a CEO was 'to have one idea in his head: what will happen in five years?'[7] He thought of the future daily, and in that future Riboud wanted BSN to be the 'French Nestlé'. BSN was at a crucial point in its quest to achieve that goal. Riboud realized that decisions he and his management team made during the next few years would determine whether BSN survived and prospered in the new, unified Europe, or if instead it was devoured by one of the larger food sharks. Looking into the crystal ball, BSN saw expansion and acquisition opportunities – in what countries and which companies? It saw threats from the giant food companies – how could it prevent them? And it saw changes in the European market structure and consumer preference – which products would maximize BSN's return from these changes? Finally, BSN had to wonder if being European was a sustainable strategy or if only large global companies like Nestlé and Unilever would survive. Twenty years ago, Antoine Riboud's vision had shifted BSN from a glass manufacturer to that of a major European food company. He and his management team didn't know all the answers to these puzzles, but they would find the pieces. They had succeeded before. They were determined to succeed again.

EXHIBIT 1
Details of Nabisco companies purchased.

Segment	Walkers (UK)	Smiths (UK)	Jacob's Bakery (UK)	Belin (France)	Saiwa (Italy)
Sales (FF 000s)	1,400,000	1,600,000	2,000,000	1,900,000	850,000
Market Position	Crisps: No. 1 Snacks: No. 3	Snacks: No. 1 Crisps: No. 3 (behind Walkers and United Biscuit) Salted nuts: No. 2 (behind United Biscuit)	Sweet biscuits: No. 2 (behind United Biscuit) Chocolate bars: No. 3 (behind Rowntree and United Biscuit) Crackers: No. 1 (support for cheese) Salted biscuits: No. 2 (behind United Biscuit)	Sweet biscuits: No. 2 (behind BSN) Salted biscuits: No. 1 Snacks: No. 2 (behind Bahlsen) Frozen pastries: No. 1	Sweet biscuits: No. 3 (behind Barilla and Alivar SME) Salted biscuits: No. 1 Snacks: No. 2 (behind Ferrero)
Brands	Crisps: Walkers Snacks: French fries, Snaps, Bitza Pizza	Snacks: Quavers, Square, Monster Munch Crisps: Tudor Crisps, Salt 'n' Shake, Jackets Salted nuts: Planters, Big D	Sweet biscuits: Huntley & Palmers, Peek Freans Chocolate: Club, Trio Crackers: Jacob's Salted biscuits: Ritz, Twiglets, Cheeselets	Sweet biscuits: Pepito, Petits coeurs, Cookies de Belin Salted biscuits: Crackers Belin Snacks: Chipster Frozen pastries: Belin Lenotre	Sweet biscuits: Oro saiwa Vafer saiwa Salted biscuits: Premium, Ritz Snack: Chipste-, Urra
Workforce	1,585	3,653	3,825	2,667	1,175
Factories	3	6	2	7	3
Proportion of Sales	Crisps: 92% Snacks: 8%	Snacks: 50% Crisps: 44% Nuts: 6%	Sweet biscuits: 18.3% Chocolate bars: 18.3% Party products: 10.6% Crackers: 14.1% Salted biscuits: 8.5% Others: 30.2%	Sweet biscuits: 37.0% Salted biscuits: 22.0% Snacks: 5.0% Frozen pastries: 10.3% Others: 30.2%	Sweet biscuits: 42.0% Salted biscuits: 26.0% Snacks: 15.0% Others: 17.0%

Source: Company press release.

EXHIBIT 2
BSN list of acquisitions.

1968	Takeover bid for Saint-Gobain, fails.
1970	Acquires Kronenbourg, Evian.
1972	Acquires Glaverbel, glass manufacturer.
1973	Acquires Font Vella, Spanish mineral water.
	Merges with Gervais Danone, yogurt.
1978–9	Acquires Spanish brewery, Mahou.
	Divestiture of some flat glass operations.
1980	Acquires several French food companies.
	Creates Japanese joint venture.
1981	Divests more flat glass businesses.
	Acquires Dannon, USA.
1982	Sale of last of flat glass operations.
	Purchases Liebig, European packaged food businesses.
1983	Acquires Pommery and Lanson, French mineral water and champagne.
1986	Acquires Générale Biscuit. No. 1 in Europe, No. 3 worldwide.
	Acquires Sonnen-Basserman, German pasta maker.
	Purchases interest in Italian pasta maker.
1987	Purchases additional interests in previous acquisitions.
1988	Creates Guangzhou Danone Yoghurt Company Ltd, a Chinest yogurt manufacturer.
	Acquires Saratoga mineral water, United States.
	Acquires HP Foods in the United Kingdom, and Lea & Perrins in the United States.
	Acquires Soparind, French jam maker.
	Acquires Spanish glass container manufacturer.
	Merges with Belgian brewer, Kronenbourg.
1989	Acquires 35 per cent of grocery products companies, Star (Italy) and Starlux (Spain).
	Acquires majority interest in Scharffenberger Cellars (California) producers of sparkling wine by the champagne method.
	Acquires La Familia, Spanish pasta producer.
	Purchases Nabisco's European businesses.
	Sell Walkers and Smiths to Pepsi.
	Acquires Hanniger Hellas, Greek brewery.
	Acquires Galbani, Italian dairy company.

EXHIBIT 3

DAIRY PRODUCTS	GROCERY PRODUCTS	BISCUITS	BEER	CHAMPAGNE MINERAL WATER	EMBALLAGE
GERVAIS DANONE *France*	AMORA *France*	L'ALSACIENNE *France*	KRONENBOURG *France*	EVIAN *France*	SEPROSY *France*
LAITERIE DE VILLECOMTAL *France*	DIÉPAL *France*	HEUDEBERT *France*	KANTERBRÄU S.A. *France*	LANSON *France*	VERRERIES DE MASNIÈRES *France*
STENVAL *France*	CALLIA-H-PH *France*	LU *France*	ALKEN-MAES *Belgium*	POMMERY *France*	VERRERIES SOUCHON NEUVESEL *France*
DANONE S.A. *Spain*	LENZBOURG *France*	GENERAL BISCUIT GmbH *West Germany*	BIRRA PERONI INDUSTRIALE *Italy*	SEAT *France*	VMC *France*
GERVAIS DANONE A.C *West Germany*	LEREBOURG *France*	GENERAL BISCUITS ÖSTERREICH *Austria*	MAHOU *Spain*	FONT VELLA *Spain*	GIRALT LAPORTA *Spain*
GERVAIS DANONE AUSTRIA *Austria*	PANZANI S.A. *France*	GENERAL BISCUITS BELGIE *Belgium*		SANGEMINI *Italy*	VIDRIERIA VILELLA *Spain*
GERVAIS DANONE BELGIQUE *Belgium*	ROSSIGNOL-GÉNÉRALE TRAITEUR *France*	GENERAL BISCUITS ESPAÑA *Spain*		SARATOGA *United States*	VEREENIGDE GLASFABRIEKEN *Netherlands*
GERVAIS DANONE ITALIANA *Italy*	SEGMA-LIBBIG-MAILLE *France*	SIRO *Spain*		SCHARFFENBERGER CELLARS *United States*	
GERVAIS DANONE NEDERLAND *Netherlands*	STOEFFLER *France*	GENERAL BISCUITS NEDERLAND *Netherlands*			
AJINOMOTO DANONE *Japan*	VANDAMME PIE QUI CHANTE *France*	ITALU *Italy*			
THE DANNON COMPANY *United States*	HP FOODS *United Kingdom*	GENERAL BISCUITS OF AMERICA *United States*			
DANONE DE MEXICO *Mexico*	LIEBIG BENELUX *Belgium*				
GUANGZHOU DANONE YOGHURT COMPANY *China*	PANZANI PONTE LIEBIG *Italy*				
LPC INDUSTRIAS ALIMENTICIAS *Brazil*	SONNEB-BASSERMANN *West Germany*				
	LEA & PERRINS *United States*				

EXIIIBIT 4

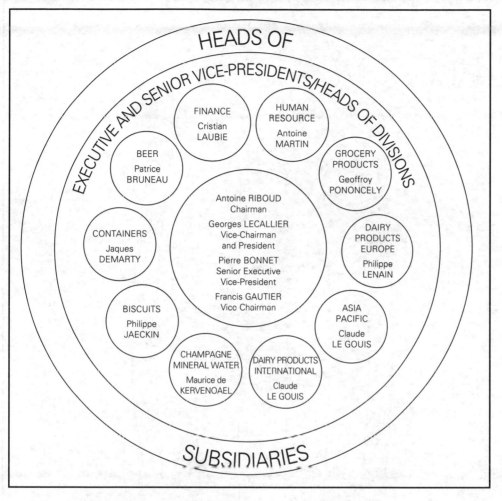

HEADS OF

EXECUTIVE AND SENIOR VICE-PRESIDENTS/HEADS OF DIVISIONS

FINANCE

Cristian LAUBIE

HUMAN RESOURCE

Antoine MARTIN

BEER

Patrice BRUNEAU

GROCERY PRODUCTS

Geoffroy PONONCELY

CONTAINERS

Jaques DEMARTY

Antoine RIBOUD
Chairman

Georges LECALLIER
Vice-Chairman
and President

Pierre BONNET
Senior Executive
Vice-President

Francis GAUTIER
Vice Chairman

DAIRY PRODUCTS EUROPE

Philippe LENAIN

BISCUITS

Philippe JAECKIN

ASIA PACIFIC

Claude LE GOUIS

CHAMPAGNE MINERAL WATER

Maurice de KERVENOAEL

DAIRY PRODUCTS INTERNATIONAL

Claude LE GOUIS

SUBSIDIARIES

EXHIBIT 5
BSN around the World.

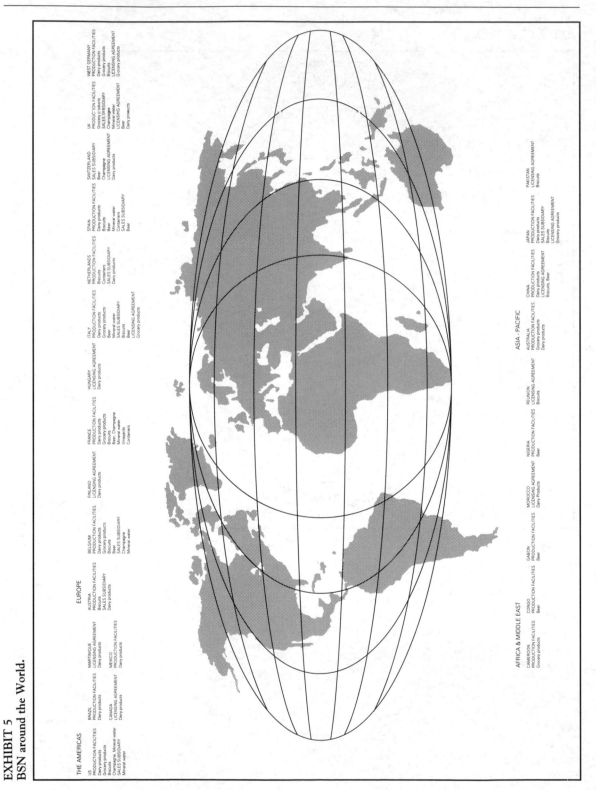

THE AMERICAS

US
PRODUCTION FACILITIES
Dairy products
Grocery products
Biscuits
Champagne, Mineral water
SALES SUBSIDIARY
Mineral water

BRAZIL
PRODUCTION FACILITIES
Dairy products
CANADA
LICENSING AGREEMENT
Dairy products

MARTINIQUE
LICENSING AGREEMENT
Dairy products
MEXICO
PRODUCTION FACILITIES
Dairy products

EUROPE

AUSTRIA
PRODUCTION FACILITIES
Biscuits
SALES SUBSIDIARY
Dairy products

BELGIUM
PRODUCTION FACILITIES
Dairy products
Grocery products
Biscuits
Beer
SALES SUBSIDIARY
Champagne
Mineral water

FINLAND
LICENSING AGREEMENT
Dairy products

FRANCE
PRODUCTION FACILITIES
Dairy products
Grocery products
Biscuits
Beer, Champagne
Mineral water
Vineyards
Containers

HUNGARY
LICENSING AGREEMENT
Dairy products

ITALY
PRODUCTION FACILITIES
Dairy products
Grocery products
Biscuits
Mineral water
SALES SUBSIDIARY
Beer
LICENSING AGREEMENT
Grocery products

NETHERLANDS
PRODUCTION FACILITIES
Biscuits
Containers
SALES SUBSIDIARY
Dairy products

SPAIN
PRODUCTION FACILITIES
Dairy products
Biscuits
Beer
Mineral water
Containers
SALES SUBSIDIARY
Beer

SWITZERLAND
SALES SUBSIDIARY
Beer
Champagne
LICENSING AGREEMENT
Dairy products

UK
PRODUCTION FACILITIES
Grocery products
SALES SUBSIDIARY
Champagne
Mineral water
LICENSING AGREEMENT
Beer
Dairy products

WEST GERMANY
PRODUCTION FACILITIES
Dairy products
Grocery products
Biscuits
LICENSING AGREEMENT
Grocery products

AFRICA & MIDDLE EAST

CAMEROON
PRODUCTION FACILITIES
Grocery products

CONGO
PRODUCTION FACILITIES
Beer

GABON
PRODUCTION FACILITIES
Beer

MOROCCO
LICENSING AGREEMENT
Dairy Products

NIGERIA
PRODUCTION FACILITIES
Beer

REUNION
LICENSING AGREEMENT
Biscuits

ASIA - PACIFIC

AUSTRALIA
PRODUCTION FACILITIES
Grocery products
Dairy products

CHINA
PRODUCTION FACILITIES
Dairy products
LICENSING AGREEMENT
Biscuits, Beer

JAPAN
PRODUCTION FACILITIES
Dairy products
SALES SUBSIDIARY
Biscuits
LICENSING AGREEMENT
Grocery products

PAKISTAN
LICENSING AGREEMENT
Biscuits

EXHIBIT 6

Economic implications of removing trade barriers on the European food processing industry.

Barrier	Total Benefit (million ECU/year)
1. Purity Law on Beer	105–235
2. Purity Law on Pasta	35–100
3. Aspartame	0–10
4. Vegetable Fat – chocolate	190–235
5. Vegetable Fat – ice cream	75–100
6. Recycling of Containers	<1
7. 'Worth' Tax on Beer	<1
8. Health Regulations	<1
9. Bulk Transport	<1
10. Saccharine	20–45
11. Chlorine	<1
12. Labelling	<5
13. 'German' Water	<1
14. Plastic Containers	15–50
15. Double Inspection	<1
Other 200 Barriers	0–200
TOTAL	440–975

Note: The total economic benefit from removal of nontariff barriers includes both direct benefits and indirect benefits including increased competition, restructuring, and increased trade.
Source: European Economy, The Economics of 1992 (March 1988).

EXHIBIT 7
Food industry comparisons for 1987 financial results.

Company	Country	Sales	Operating Margin	Net Margin	ROE	Cash Flow/Sales	Sales/Employ. US$	Asset Turnover	Debt/Total Assets	P/E	5-year growth Sales	5-year growth EPS
Nestlé SA	Switzerland	22,770.0	10.4%	5.2%	15.0	8.5%	139,692	1.4	8.6%	10.2	5.0%	8.4%
Philip Morris	USA	22,279.0	18.3	8.3	32.6	12.5	197,200	1.2	43.4	11.0	19.6	20.0
RJR Nabisco	USA	15,766.0	16.2	7.7	22.2	13.5	131,000	0.9	38.5	9.0	10.3	15.3
Unilever PLC	UK	10,242.6	7.1	4.9	15.4	7.4	66,045	1.4	18.1	13.9	-0.1	11.3
Kraft	USA	9,675.7	8.0	5.4	29.7	6.2	212,400	1.8	32.0	14.4	-0.2	8.9
Grand Metropolitan	UK	9,274.3	9.9	8.1	22.7	8.3	83,217	1.2	39.9	14.9	6.2	13.7
Sara Lee	USA	9,154.6	5.6	2.9	22.8	5.5	99,100	52.2	29.8	13.6	9.7	13.4
ConAgra Inc.	USA	9,001.6	3.6	1.7	28.9	2.6	214,300	3.6	36.8	13.7	32.5	16.8
Anheuser-Busch	USA	8,258.4	13.7	7.4	29.5	12.1	198,800	1.3	32.6	16.4	8.1	17.7
Dalgety FLC	UK	8,092.4	2.2	1.5	26.6	2.9	374,006	4.1	27.2	14.1	9.6	6.1
Coca-Cola Company	USA	7,658.3	17.8	12.0	26.1	12.5	440,100	0.9	19.9	15.7	4.1	15.8
BSN Groupe	France	6,989.0	8.9	4.2	17.8	9.1	169,290	1.1	22.4	12.7	11.2	9.1
Taiyo Fishery Co.	Japan	6,608.3	1.8	nom	0.6	nc	2,112,674	2.3	48.1	601.6	-0.3	nc
Borden Inc.	USA	6,514.4	0.1	4.1	18.6	11.9	165,300	1.6	41.3	13.7	9.6	13.3
KF Group	Sweden	6,511.0	0.4	0.4	7.7	2.4	234,329	2.4	64.0	nc	12.0	nc
Pillsbury	USA	6,127.8	7.3	3.0	13.8	7.5	58,400	1.6	40.8	14.5	10.9	11.5
Ralston Purina	USA	5,868.0	12.2	8.9	52.0	9.1	100,700	1.5	59.3	12.7	3.8	36.1
Archer Daniels Midland	USA	5,744.6	6.6	4.6	12.8	8.1	546,200	1.5	21.7	11.1	9.6	20.5
Allied Lyons	UK	5,593.9	9.1	5.3	10.4	12.1	87,934	0.8	40.7	11.2	9.9	22.3
Bass PLC	UK	5,241.1	11.1	8.1	18.2	10.5	76,424	0.9	9.1	13.1	11.5	19.7
General Mills	USA	5,189.3	9.0	4.3	32.5	6.9	79,100	2.3	28.1	17.0	-1.4	5.1
Elders IXL	Australia	5,187.9	5.8	4.8	14.3	7.1	0	0.8	57.5	12.5	21.1	15.1
CPC International	USA	4,903.0	9.5	7.2	37.1	10.0	156,100	1.5	41.0	9.3	3.2	21.2
Jacobs Suchard	Switzerland	4,809.8	7.7	4.3	18.3	6.9	299,598	2.0	29.5	15.9	8.5	17.4
HJ Heinz	USA	4,639.5	10.4	7.3	24.9	11.1	94,700	1.4	29.6	15.0	7.0	14.1
Guinness	UK	4,568.6	16.0	17.4	79.8	7.8	171,906	1.0	38.8	9.4	22.0	19.1
Campbell Soup	USA	4,490.4	9.5	5.5	16.1	10.3	91,200	1.5	17.8	14.4	8.1	7.9
Quaker Oats	USA	4,420.6	10.2	5.5	29.3	9.4	143,500	1.4	32.7	15.8	15.3	14.9
Cadbury Schweppes	UK	3,832.5	8.5	5.5	24.0	10.2	139,449	1.5	17.0	12.3	6.3	11.6
Kellogg	USA	3,793.0	18.4	10.4	44.1	14.5	213,500	1.4	19.3	16.4	9.9	16.5
Nippon Suisan	Japan	3,576.7	1.7	0.5	4.0	nc	1,089,209	1.8	27.3	61.2	1.9	5.9
Associated British Foods	UK	3,539.6	5.5	20.5	49.2	8.5	76,801	1.1	1.0	11.5	-7.6	7.8

	Country												
Kirin Brewery	Japan	3,351.0	18.1	6.5	12.7	12.0	569,123	0.7	4.5	46.7	7.1	11.6
Ajinomoto Co.	Japan	3,301.2	5.4	3.4	6.0	7.9	461,978	0.8	19.4	126.8	0.6	5.1
United Brands	USA	3,268.0	3.4	1.8	14.6	3.1	81,700	2.9	27.3	11.5	-3.8	nc
Heineken	Netherlands	3,190.5	9.1	5.1	12.8	12.5	112,263	0.9	16.7	11.2	11.2	13.4
Unigate PLC	UK	3,167.6	5.2	3.6	21.1	8.0	110,390	2.5	14.5	12.5	5.4	14.4
Beghin Say	France	2,941.0	9.5	4.7	31.6	nc	216,710	0.8	40.3	5.0	7.7	31.6
Rowntree	UK	2,693.9	9.1	6.2	22.6	9.9	81,330	1.5	36.1	11.0	13.1	11.1
United Biscuits (86)	UK	2,671.2	7.5	4.2	18.3	5.3	85,859	1.7	33.8	11.4	12.1	7.6
Rank Hovis McDougal	UK	2,517.9	8.4	5.6	29.2	7.8	81,707	1.8	42.3	13.6	0.4	22.9
LVMH Moët-Hennessy	France	2,491.8	23.9	10.1	32.0	14.0	202,396	0.7	41.6	13.4	23.6	17.2
Hershey Foods	USA	2,433.8	12.1	6.1	20.4	8.6	150,200	1.5	28.9	14.9	4.9	10.8
Booker PLC	UK	2,384.4	4.3	3.3	27.8	5.0	189,644	2.5	13.0	11.7	5.5	26.8
Saint Louis	France	2,375.9	-1.8	13.3	143.9	16.7	199,612	1.3	9.2	3.2	23.2	55.7
Ferruzzi (86)	Italy	2,374.4	8.9	2.4	20.3	8.4	1,597,217	0.8	33.4	8.0	38.8	nc
Northern Foods	UK	2,167.2	5.7	5.2	31.4	5.7	92,463	3.0	3.5	13.0	-4.9	6.3
Industriaalfin	Italy	1,790.1	6.1	1.5	35.3	6.0	236,719	1.3	59.8	12.0	21.3	18.2
Barilla	Italy	1,197.7	3.1	4.3	42.1	nc	245,429	2.0	35.1	nc	18.9	18.6
Nabisco Group	UK	1,099.1	7.8	6.1	22.7	10.2	99,256	1.5	6.1	nc	46.0	31.6
Deutsches Milch Kont	West Germany	1,052.2	-0.3	0.1	9.0	nc	9,478,774	5.3	0.0	nc	-0.4	nc
Suedzucker AG	West Germany	823.0	4.5	1.9	9.9	10.4	334,669	1.2	6.7	19.2	-1.4	3.4
Grancis Moulins de Paris	France	789.3	0.5	0.1	1.1	nc	212,741	1.9	55.8	361.1	3.4	nc
Brau und Brunnen	West Germany	726.9	-4.4	-1.9	-7.1	nc	145,641	1.4	0.9	def	-0.8	nc
Maizena GMBH	West Germany	607.2	nc	nom	nom	nc	322,882	2.4	0.0	nc	-1.9	nc
Star Stablimento	Italy	544.2	5.5	3.2	16.3	6.8	217,202	1.7	8.1	nc	5.9	17.2
Elosua (86)	Spain	472.7	4.6	1.8	25.4	nc	357,081	2.3	53.2	nc	nc	nc
Arnot's Ltd.	Australia	462.9	10.3	17.8	73.6	10.2	0	1.5	12.9	18.6	9.3	13.1
Brasserie Piedboeuf	Belgium	362.8	-5.0	2.3	10.5	nc	192,250	1.1	65.0	nc	5.2	nc
Koipe (86)	Spain	281.9	1.8	2.0	6.7	3.4	248,148	1.7	0.3	21.1	18.7	5.8
Country Comparisons												
Australia		316.7	14.0	9.2	20.2	11.0	287,483	1.0	28.2	11.8	0.7	26.5
France		1,752.5	8.3	6.5	30.5	12.6	158,192	1.1	27.9	8.8	10.6	20.9
Italy		1,538.3	10.7	3.5	29.0	9.0	178,016	1.1	43.3	5.0	23.8	46.9
Japan		2,574.6	4.7	1.9	8.2	9.3	722,399	1.5	20.4	64.9	3.1	-0.8
United Kingdom		2,939.9	5.9	5.3	24.1	6.9	103,974	1.8	19.9	10.6	4.8	20.1
United States		3,316.4	8.3	5.2	21.2	8.8	170,700	1.6	31.1	12.0	4.8	10.1
West Germany		3,892.0	2.3	1.5	7.0	14.9	159,721	0.5	60.4	31.8	2.0	26.4

Source: WorldScope Industrial Company Profiles.

EXHIBIT 8
Nestlé financial results, 1978–87 (SFr millions).

	1988	1987	1986	1985	1984	1983
Sales	40,685	35,241	38,050	42,225	31,141	27,943
Operating Income	4,288	3,651	3,671	4,315	3,206	2,883
Net Income	2,038	1,827	1,789	1,750	1,487	1,261
EPS	582	537	526	515	480	430
Total Assets	33,169	25,143	25,095	25,188	24,474	20,489
Cash Flow	3,345	3,011	2,946	3,081	2,491	2,171
Capital Investments	1,950	1,588	1,533	1,748	1,339	1,122
Employees	198,000	163,050	162,078	155,000	138,000	140,000
SFr Exchange Rate	1.48	1.49	1.80	2.45	2.35	2.10
Sales by Division as % of Total						
Drinks	27.5%	30.0%	31.5%	29.7%	31.6%	
Cereals, Milks & Dietetics	20.5	22.7	22.7	25.7	25.4	
Culinary Products	12.1	11.8	11.3	12.2	12.6	
Frozen Foods and Ice Cream	10.3	10.5	10.2	10.5	10.8	
Chocolate and Confectionery	12.4	7.8	7.4	7.6	8.7	
Refrigerated Products	8.8	9.1	8.3	4.5	5.6	
Petfoods	4.3	4.3	4.0	4.2	0.0	
Pharmaceutical Products and Cosmetics	2.0	2.1	2.0	2.2	2.5	
Capital Investments by Division						
Cereals, Milks and Dietetics	324	285				
Drinks	260	254				
Culinary Products	223	147				
Frozen Foods and Ice Cream	198	164				
Chocolate and Confectionery	171	107				
Refrigerated Products	184	123				
Other Group	215	176				
Research and Development	375	332				
Capital Investments by Geography						
Europe	883	751	627	622	562	501
North America	643	483	512	672	383	267
Asia	146	141	164	145	109	153
Latin America and Caribbean	166	141	163	206	195	110
Africa	46	28	34	54	63	54
Oceania	66	44	33	49	27	37
Stock Market Data						
Stockholders' Equity	11,358	15,774	12,201	11,238	12,989	11,120
Net Dividend (per share)	175.00	150.00	145.00	145.00	135.80	127.00
Bearer Stock Price High	9.025	11.450	9.875	9.200	5.600	4.899
Bearer Stock Price Low	6.350	7.200	7.325	5.600	4.524	3.697

Source: Annual reports.

EXHIBIT 9
Unilever financial results, 1983 – 88 (US $ millions).

	1988	1987	1986	1985	1984	1983
Sales	30,980	39,948	25,368	24,205	18,760	19,410
Operating Income	2,743	2,567	1,664	1,376	1,078	1,085
Net Income	1,584	1,483	1,037	805	622	604
EPS	5.39	5.04	3.5	2.67	2.08	1.99
Total Assets	19,909	18,699	20,413	13,521	11,236	11,206
Capital Investments	1,505	1,336	1,029	961	693	712
Employees	291,000	294,000	298,000	304,000	319,000	267,000
Sales by Division as % of Total						
Food Products	49.8%	49.4%	49.7%	50.8%	50.2%	47.9%
Detergents	21.8	21.7	22.0	19.2	20.6	20.6
Personal Products	9.5	9.1	6.1	5.1	5.4	5.3
Specialty Chemicals	8.5	7.9	7.6	7.2	7.5	6.8
Other Operations	10.4	11.9	14.6	17.7	16.3	19.3
Operating Margin by Division						
Food Products	9.0%	8.6%	7.2%	5.8%	6.0%	5.7%
Detergents	6.5	7.5	5.0	3.9	6.1	7.0
Personal Products	10.2	9.2	5.9			
Specialty Chemicals	14.0	12.6	10.5	10.6	10.6	10.7
Other Operations	7.7	4.9	5.0	5.3	2.5	
Capital Investments by Division						
Food Products	613	590	458	383	289	276
Detergents	362	271	213	187	159	159
Personal Products	100	77	54	36	37	29
Specialty Chemicals	186	181	127	165	69	67
Other Operations	244	217	177	190	139	181
	1,505	1,336	1,029	961	693	712
Sales by Geography as % of Total						
Europe	60.3%	62.5%	62.1%	64.3%	61.4%	64.3%
North America	20.0	18.6	17.6	17.3	19.2	16.1
Rest of World	19.7	18.9	20.4	18.4	19.3	19.6
Operating Margin by Geography						
Europe	8.6%	7.6%	6.2%	5.1%	4.3%	4.0%
North America	8.2	7.8	3.8	3.7	6.1	6.5
Rest of World	10.3	11.0	10.0	9.6	9.8	10.1
Capital Investments by Geography						
Europe	872	841	644	558	381	419
North America	366	287	207	255	190	145
Rest of World	267	208	178	148	122	148
	1,505	1,336	1,029	961	693	712
Stock Market Data						
Stockholders' Equity	5,451	5,317	5,313	4,635	3,750	4,315
Net Dividend (per share)	2.15	2.03	1.41	1.07	0.79	0.85
Market Capitalization	16,097	15,952	12,713	7,803	4,786	5,028
P/E	10	11	12	10	8	8

Source: Annual reports.

EXHIBIT 10
Grand Metropolitan financial results 1984–88 (£ millions).

	1988	1987	1986	1985	1984
Sales	6,028.8	5,705.5	5,291.3	5,589.5	5,075.0
Operating Income	653.6	571.6	487.4	453.2	443.9
Net Income	420.3	336.0	275.9	246.9	235.2
EPS	0.48	0.39	0.32	0.35	0.32
Total Assets	4,189.4	3,731.6	3,124.2	3,088.1	2,739.0
Employees	89,753	129,436	131,493	137,195	125,074
Pound Exchange Rate	1.78	1.64	1.47	1.30	1.34
Dollar Sales	10,731.3	9,357.0	7,778.2	7,266.4	6,800.5
Sales by Division					
Food	1,252.6	1,046.9			
Drinks	2,581.2	2,177.7			
Retailing	1,670.9	1,467.4			
	5,504.7	4,692.0			
Operating Income by Division					
Food	84.0	69.2			
Drinks	315.8	256.9			
Retailing	178.8	159.8			
	578.6	485.9			
Capital Employed					
Food	310.2	260.2			
Drinks	1,478.5	1,503.5			
Retailing	1,898.3	1,290.3			
	3,687.0	3,054.0			
Sales by Geography					
UK	3,835.5	3,558.6			
Continental Europe	220.7	214.2			
United States	1,758.3	1,720.3			
Rest of North America	54.1	57.5			
Africa and Middle East	127.0	120.5			
Rest of World	33.2	34.4			
	6,028.8	5,705.5			
Operating Income by Geography					
UK	363.9	330.9			
Continental Europe	46.2	36.1			
United States	217.6	185.4			
Rest of North America	13.8	12.8			
Africa and Middle East	6.5	5.9			
Rest of World	5.6	0.5			
	653.6	571.6			
Capital Employed by Geography					
UK	2,699.6	1,944.6			
Continental Europe	384.1	385.8			
United States	1,033.6	1,316.1			
Rest of North America	50.0	60.8			
Africa and Middle East	17.9	18.5			
Rest of World	4.2	5.8			
	4,189.4	3,731.6			

Source: Annual reports.

EXHIBIT 11
BSN Groupe financial results 1979–88 (FF millions).

	1988	1987	1986	1985	1984	1983	1982	1981	1980	1979
Sales	42,177	37,156	33,623	28,475	27,293	24,889	21,890	19,256	18,233	16,439
Operating Income	4,490	3,296	2,724	1,863	1,660	1,653	1,532	1,455	1,389	1,178
Operating Cash Flow	4,249	3,378	3,160	2,338	2,135	2,140	1,788	1,620	1,547	1,331
Net Income	2,189	1,550	1,081	798	755	741	574	446	331	247
EPS (1989 10/1 split)	41.70	34.00	27.00	21.00	20.30	22.40	22.70	18.60	14.40	10.70
Total Assets	38,839	34,349	28,061	21,063	20,646	17,137	15,089	13,892	13,650	12,943
Capital Investments	2,403	2,371	2,155	2,205	2,417	1,505	1,216	1,198	1,203	1,544
Number of Employees	42,234	41,285	42,780	33,447	37,340	38,007	39,914	41,751	47,969	55,895
FF Exchange Rate	5.96	6.00	6.93	8.98	8.74	7.62	6.58	5.44	4.22	4.26
Sales by Division as % of Total										
Dairy Products	25.6%	25.7%	28.8%	32.9%	33.3%	32.1%	32.8%	28.3%	24.0%	22.2%
Grocery Products	23.7	23.1	21.6	22.9	19.7	20.0	19.1	17.3	14.7	9.5
Biscuits	16.7	16.7	12.3	0.0	0.0	0.0	0.0	0.0	0.0	0.0
Beer	14.5	14.6	15.8	19.6	22.2	30.0	30.2	26.9	23.8	23.5
Champagne, Mineral Water	8.0	7.8	7.7	8.4	7.4	0.0	0.0	0.0	0.0	0.0
Containers	11.5	12.1	13.9	16.2	17.4	17.9	17.9	17.9	16.8	15.7
Flat Glass	0.0	0.0	0.0	0.0	0.0	0.0	0.0	9.5	20.7	29.2
Operating Income/Segment Sales										
Dairy Products	7.5%	5.5%	6.4%	4.5%	3.9%	1.1%				
Grocery Products	9.9	10.0	10.1	9.7	9.2	3.4				
Biscuits	9.9	10.4	8.6							
Beer	9.7	9.4	5.6	3.4	4.2	3.4				
Champagne, Mineral Water	15.1	15.8	14.4	10.9	7.8					
Containers	11.2	8.9	6.5	6.1	6.1	1.8				
Flat Glass										

EXHIBIT 11 (Continued)
BSN Groupe financial results 1979–88 (FF millions).

Operating Cash Flow by Division

Division										
Dairy Products	777	585	776	631	557	433	428	319	195	173
Grocery Products	730	642	536	453	373	370	333	255	165	99
Biscuits	541	482	274	598	500	737	605	572	488	507
Beer	960	730	664	190	114					
Champagne, Mineral Water	358	300	275							
Containers	683	510	425	310	404	375	262	254	271	178
Flat Glass								150	384	360

Capital Investments by Division as % of Sales

Division										
Dairy Products	3.8%	3.9%	3.9%	6.5%	9.0%	5.7%	4.1%	4.4%	4.3%	4.7%
Grocery Products	3.8	3.9	3.8	3.8	3.9	3.2	4.1	2.5	4.2	3.1
Biscuits	3.4	6.9	8.4	13.8	12.2	6.9	6.7	7.5	10.9	11.5
Beer	8.7	9.7	10.3	7.3	8.8					
Champagne, Mineral Water	7.9	7.1	5.7							
Containers	9.7	9.6	6.8	7.3	7.4	6.7	6.4	8.3	6.0	6.5
Flat Glass								7.0	4.9	13.5

Sales by Geography

Region										
France	66.3%	68.0%	69.6%	72.6%	73.3%	73.6%	72.8%	75.1%	67.4%	57.9%
Europe Outside France	24.0	22.4	19.8	17.5	18.0	19.2	18.4	19.2	29.8	39.3
Outside Europe	9.7	9.6	10.6	10.0	8.7	7.2	8.9	5.7	2.8	2.9

Operating Margin by Geographic Segment

Region										
France	11.5%	10.6%	8.4%	7.1%	6.6%	3.0%	2.6%	2.5%	2.0%	1.9%
Europe Outside France	7.6	7.9	7.8	3.6	4.8	5.5	4.6	2.6	1.6	0.6
Outside Europe	6.7	4.3	7.5	5.7	3.3	−3.9	−1.1	−1.7	−0.6	5.1

Capital Investments by Geography as % of Sales

Region										
France	6.5%	6.6%	7.0%	8.4%	9.8%	6.5%	5.9%	5.6%	6.7%	8.6%
Europe Outside France	4.3	6.2	5.5	6.4	6.5	4.8	5.5	8.7	6.2	10.8
Outside Europe	3.8	5.5	4.2	5.1	5.7	4.6	3.0	5.8	8.9	7.0

Operating Cash Flow by Geography

Region										
France	2,873	2,347	1,942	1,651	1,477	1,602	1,307	1,236	1,021	778
Europe Outside France	897	759	765	365	389	522	401	318	492	517
Outside Europe	279	143	243	166	82	16	80	66	34	36

Source: Annual reports.

EXHIBIT 11 (Continued)
Consolidated Balance Sheet at 31 December (FF millions).

Assets	1988	1987
Current Assets		
Cash and Time Deposits	1,265	1,209
Marketable Securities	464	347
Trade Accounts and Notes Receivable	7,536	6,273
Short-term Loans Receivable	329	143
Inventories	5,289	4,891
Other Accounts Receivable and Pre-paid Expenses	1,579	2,227
	16,462	15,090
Fixed Assets		
Property, Plant and Equipment	23,782	21,168
Less: Accumulated Depreciation	(11,355)	(9,702)
	12,427	11,466
Intangible Assets	1,714	1,629
Less: Amortization	(795)	(718)
	919	911
Other Assets		
Goodwill	4,698	3,144
Long-term Loans	439	508
Trade Investments	1,686	1,395
Equity in Affiliated Companies	1,893	1,558
Other	315	277
	9,031	6,882
TOTAL ASSETS	38,839	34,349

Liabilities and Stockholders' Equity (FF millions)

	1988	1987
Current Liabilities		
Short-term Debt and Bank Overdrafts	1,856	1,855
Trade Accounts and Notes Payable	5,933	4,903
Other Accounts Payable and Accrued Expenses	4,433	4,497
Current Liabilities	12,222	11,255
Deferred Taxes	1,526	1,439
Provision for Retirement Indemnities and Pensions	1,113	1,224
Provisions for Other Risks and Charges	1,601	1,345
Long-term Debt	5,288	4,148
Consigned Containers	674	594
Minority Interests	715	494
	10,917	9,244
Stockholders' Equity		
Capital Stock	521	520
Capital Surplus	8,173	8,160
Retained Earnings	7,072	5,230
	15,766	13,910
Treasury Stock	(66)	(60)
Total Stockholders' Equity	15,700	13,850
Total Liabilities and Stockholders' Equity	38,839	34,349

EXHIBIT 11 (Continued)
Consolidated Balance Sheet at 31 December (FF millions).

Stock Market Data (Paris Bourse–Monthly Settlement Market)
(FF millions unless otherwise indicated)

	1984	1985	1986	1987	1988
Market Capitalization, Year-end	8,652	9,964	17,253	22,584	33,309
Average Daily Amount of Transactions	9.2	13.8	10.0	38.4	31.90
Number of Shares Traded (units)	895,530	1,454,547	2,501,507	2,443,767	1,646,960
High (FF)	2,885	2,760	4,750	5,420	6,500
Low (FF)	2,350	1,965	2,720	3,710	3,761

BSN Interim Results
(FF million)

	30 June 1989	30 June 1988
Revenues	23,184	20,706
Income before Amortization, Interest and Taxes	3,615	3,251
Amortization	(1,065)	(952)
Operating Income	2,550	2,299
Interest Expense	(330)	(252)
Income before Taxes	2,220	2,047
Net Income to Groups	1,413	1,257

Segment Results

	30 June 1989		30 June 1988	
	Sales	Operating Income	Sales	Operating Income
Dairy Products	6,344	537	5,454	418
Grocery Products	5,039	444	4,371	460
Biscuits	4,183	522	4,239	421
Beer	3,284	496	3,090	414
Champagne/Mineral Water	2,039	316	1,649	286
Containers	2,857	339	2,531	357
Internal Transfers	(562)	(104)	(628)	(57)
Groupe	23,184	2,550	20,706	2,299

EXHIBIT 12
BSN segment detail.

Segment	Dairy Products	Grocery Products	Biscuits	Beer	Champagne, Mineral Water	Containers
Sales	1,115,000 tons worldwide 445,000 tons – France 440,000 tons – other European countries 230,000 tons – ROW	220,000 tons – pasta 95,000 tons – mustard vinegar and condiments 85,000 tons – prepared dishes 50,000 tons – baby foods	315,000 tons – cookies 60,000 tons – crackers	10.5 Mhl – France 4.2 Mhl – Spain 4.9 Mhl – Italy 2.1 Mhl – Belgium	13.2 mm bottles champagne 2.5b litres mineral water	1,050,000 tons bottles France 67,000 tons flasks
Market Position	First worldwide First in the Americas First in Europe First in France First in Germany First in Belgium First in Spain First in the United States First in Brazil First in Mexico	Pasta: Second in Europe First in France Mustards, vinegar and condiments: Second in Italy First in France Baby Foods: First in France Packaged Confectionery: First in France	Third in the world First in Continental Europe Fourth in the United States	Second in Europe First in France First in Italy Second in Belgium Fourth in Spain	World's largest mineral water bottler World's third largest champagne producer	Largest bottle producer France
Production Facilities	10 plants – France 10 plants – other Europe 11 plants outside Europe	31 plants – France 14 plants – other Europe 3 plants outside Europe	31 plants – France 14 plants – other Europe 2 plants outside Europe	4 breweries – France 14 breweries – other Europe 5 breweries outside Europe	2 vineyards in Champagne 2 bottlers – France 6 bottlers – other Europe 2 bottlers – United States	13 plants – France 7 plants – other Europe
Workforce	8,935	8,999	9,698	4,217	2,571	7,458
Main Brands	Dannon Gervais Bio	HP, Lea & Perrins Amora, La Pie Qui Chante LaFamilia, Panzani	L'Alsacienne Lu DeBeukelaer	Kronenbourg, Kanterbrau Maes, Mahou Peroni	Evian, Font Vella Pommery, Saratoga Scharffenberger	Glass bottles Glass jars Glass tableware

Source: Company reports.

EXHIBIT 13
Market shares (in value) and competitors.

France			*Belgium*		
Dairy products	BSN	31.4	Dairy products	BSN	29
	Yoplait	18.5		Jacky	20
	Chambourcy (Nestlé)	16.9		Stassano	11
Biscuits	BSN	30.3	Biscuits	BSN	29
	Nabisco France (now BSN)	14		Store brands	19
	Biscuiterie Nantaise	6		Corona Lotus	10
Beer	BSN	47.6	Beer	Interbrew	55
	Frabra (=Heineken)	25.3		BSN	16
Mineral Water			*Spain*		
– still water	BSN	21.1	Dairy products	BSN	60
	Vittel	18		no significant competitors	
	Contrex	18			
– sparkling water	BSN	35.2	Biscuits	Cuetara	23
	Perrier	26.3		Fontanedo	19
	St. Yorre	22.9		BSN	12
Pasta	BSN	34.7	Beer	Cruz Campo	21
	Rivoire & Carret	14		El Aguila	19
	Lustucru	9		Damm	17
	Store brands	21.5		BSN	15.5

Glass bottles	BSN	38
	Saint Gobain	33
	Import	16.5
Germany		
Dairy products	BSN	9
	Bauer	8
	Südmilch	7
Biscuits	Bahlsen	40
	BSN	11
Italy		
Dairy products	BSN	26
	Yomo	26
	Parmalat	7
Biscuits	Barilla	23
	Alivar	17
	Nabisco Italy (now BSN)	10
	BSN	<1
Beer	BSN	34
	Dreher + Henninger	26
Mineral Water	BSN	20
	San Pellegrino	14
	San Benedetto	10

Mineral Water		
– still water	BSN	37
	Bezoya	12
	Vichy Catalan	63
– sparkling water	BSN	16
Glass bottles	Vicasa	50
	BSN	22
	Alava	11
United Kingdom		
Biscuits	United Biscuits	48
	Nabisco (now BSN)	16.3
United States		
Dairy products	BSN	29
	Kraft	12
	Yoplait	12

Source: Company records.

EXHIBIT 14
Financial forecasts (FF millions).

Pre-tax, Earnings and Dividends Forecasts, 1989–94(E)

	1989	1990	Percentage Change 1990–4(E)	1994(E)
Net Sales	48,267	55,102	10%	79,161
Operating Income	5,024	5,863	12	9,292
Net Interest	1,000	1,900	(8)	1,350
Pre-tax Income	4,024	3,963	20%	7,942
Taxation	1,650	1,585	20%	3,256
Tax Rate	41.0%	40.0%	(NM)	41.0%
Minority Interests	82	91	12%	143
Equity Consolidated Net Income	336	725	18	1,408
Net Income	2,628	3,011	19%	5,951
Average Shares in Issue (millions)	52.2	52.2	(NC)	52.2
Basic EPS	50.4	57.8	19%	114.0
Diluted EPS	48.6	54.0	18	104.9
Dividend	11.5	13.2	14%	22.3
Dividend Cover	4.4	4.4	(NM)	5.1
Interest Cover	5.0	3.1	(NM)	6.9

[a] Except per-share amounts.
E = Estimate. NC = No change. NM = Not meaningful.

Forecast Balance Sheet, 1989–90(E)

	1989(E)	1990(E)
Fixed Assets	12,900	13,250
Working Capital	7,443	8,039
Goodwill	10,198	9,943
Net Borrowings	16,415	15,680
Provisions	2,985	3,284
Shareholders' funds[a]	20,155	22,855

[a] Including minorities.
E = Estimate.

Source: Salomon Brothers European Equity Research.

Estimated Operating and Free Cash Flow, 1988–94(E)
(FF millions)

	1988	1989(E)	1990(E)	1991(E)	1992(E)	1993(E)	1994(E)	Compound Annual Growth 1988(E)–1994(E)
Operating Income	4,490	5,024	5,863	6,518	7,321	8,115	9,292	13%
Depreciation and Amortization	2,039	2,450	2,900	3,219	3,573	3,966	4,402	14
Operating Cash Flow	6,529	7,474	8,763	9,737	10,894	12,081	13,694	13
Net Interest Expense	589	1,000	1,900	1,800	1,700	1,550	1,350	15
Pre-tax Cash Flow	5,940	6,474	6,863	7,937	9,194	10,531	12,344	13
Less								
Cash Taxes	1,461	1,685	1,967	2,187	2,456	2,722	3,023	13%
Capital Expenditures	2,403	2,667	2,961	3,286	3,648	4,049	4,495	11
Dividends	456	525	605	690	786	896	1,022	14
Working Capital Increase	631	551	595	643	695	750	810	14
Free Cash Flow	989	1,045	735	1,132	1,609	2,113	2,994	20%

EXHIBIT 14 (Continued)

Sales and Operating Income Forecasts, 1989–94(E)
(FF millions)

	1989(E)	1990(E)	Percent Change			1994(E)
			1988–9(E)	1989–90(E)	1990–4(E)	
Sales						
Dairy	12,672	14,192	15%	12%	13%	23,140
Grocery	10,722	11,901	5	11	11	18,066
Biscuit	9,772	12,874	36	32	6	16,274
Beer	6,636	6,967	6	5	5	8,469
Mineral Water/Champagne	4,070	4,640	18	14	15	8,115
Packaging/Other	4,396	4,527	8	3	13	5,096
TOTAL	48,267	55,102	14%	14%	10%	79,161
Operating Income						
Dairy	1,026	1,221	23%	19%	17%	2,314
Grocery	1,126	1,309	11	16	11	1,987
Biscuit	889	1,223	24	38	12	1,952
Beer	657	704	8	7	26	889
Mineral Water/Champagne	610	673	16	10	14	1,136
Packaging/Other	715	734	(9)	3	8	1,013
TOTAL	5,024	5,863	12%	17%	12%	9,292
Operating Margin						
Dairy	8.1%	8.6%	(NM)	(NM)	(NM)	10.0%
Grocery	10.5	11.0	(NM)	(NM)	(NM)	11.0
Biscuit	9.1	9.5	(NM)	(NM)	(NM)	12.0
Beer	9.9	10.1	(NM)	(NM)	(NM)	10.5
Mineral Water/Champagne	15.0	14.5	(NM)	(NM)	(NM)	14.0
Packaging/Other	16.3	16.2	(NM)	(NM)	(NM)	19.9
TOTAL	10.4%	10.6%	(NM)	(NM)	(NM)	11.7%
Equity Consolidated Income	336	725	(NM)	115%	18%	1,408

E = Estimate. NM = Not meaningful.
Source: Salomon Brothers.

Continental Biscuit Business, 1988–94(E)
(FF millions)

	1988	1989(E)	1990(E)	1991(E)	1992(E)	1993(E)	1994(E)
Sales							
Existing Activity	5,605	5,940	9,033	9,575	10,150	10,800	11,400
Nabisco Activities	2,530	1,400[a]	–	–	–	–	–
TOTAL	8,185	7,340	9,033	9,575	10,150	10,800	11,400
Operating Profits							
Existing Activity	560	595	860	960	1,115	1,290	1,490
Nabisco Activity	142	65	–	–	–	–	–
TOTAL	702	659	860	960	1,115	1,240	1,435
Operating Assets							
Existing Activity	2,600	2,800	3,700	3,800	4,000	4,200	4,400
Nabisco Activity	1,000	1,000	–	–	–	–	–
TOTAL OPERATING ASSETS	3,600	3,800	3,700	3,800	4,000	4,200	4,400
TOTAL OPERATING MARGINS	8.6%	9.1%	9.5%	10.0%	11.0%	11.5%	12.6%
TOTAL RETURN ON OPERATING ASSETS	19.5%	17.3%	23.2%	25.2%	27.9%	29.5%	32.7%

Note: All figures are SBIL estimates.
[a] Assuming consolidation for six months only.
E = Estimate.
Source: Salomon Brothers.

EXHIBIT 15
European food consumption
(US$ billions, current prices).

	1983	1988	1993	CAGR 1983–8	CAGR 1988–93
Belgium	10.2	16.7	23.8	10.4%	7.3%
Denmark	5.2	9.0	11.9	11.6	5.7
France	54.7	91.9	136.9	10.9	8.3
Greece	8.5	11.3	17.0	5.9	8.5
Ireland	2.8	4.3	6.2	9.0	7.6
Italy	60.1	101.1	146.9	11.0	7.8
Luxembourg	0.3	0.6	0.8	14.9	5.9
Netherlands	12.1	19.3	27.6	9.8	7.4
Portugal	4.5	6.9	9.4	8.9	6.4
Spain	26.4	51.4	71.9	14.3	6.9
UK	40.0	60.3	81.2	8.6	6.1
West Germany	80.7	129.0	182.1	9.8	7.1
TOTAL	305.5	501.8	715.7		

European Non-Alcoholic Beverage Consumption
($m current prices)

	1983	1988	1993	CAGR 1983–8	CAGR 1988–93
Belgium	606	1,100	1,741	12.7%	9.6%
Denmark	178	336	484	13.5	7.6
France	1,543	2,816	4,480	12.8	9.7
Greece	213	329	580	9.1	12.0
Ireland	162	271	427	10.8	9.5
Italy	803	1,640	2,980	15.4	12.7
Luxembourg	11	22	35	14.9	9.7
Netherlands	477	660	935	6.7	7.2
Portugal	43	106	200	19.8	13.5
Spain	438	741	1,130	11.1	8.8
UK	1,524	3,200	5,086	16.0	9.7
West Germany					
TOTAL	5,998	11,221	18,078		

EXHIBIT 15 (Continued)

European Alcoholic Beverage Consumption
($bn current prices)

	1983	1988	1993	CAGR 1983–8	CAGR 1988–93
Belgium	1.8	2.5	3.4	6.8%	6.3%
Denmark	1.2	1.9	2.5	9.6	5.6
France	7.1	11.2	15.3	9.5	6.4
Greece	0.6	1.0	1.7	10.8	11.2
Ireland	1.3	2.1	3.2	10.1	8.8
Italy	3.8	6.0	8.0	9.6	5.9
Luxembourg		0.1	0.1		0.0
Netherlands	1.6	2.4	3.4	8.4	7.2
Portugal	0.4	0.8	1.2	14.9	8.4
Spain	1.2	2.5	3.7	15.8	8.2
UK	5.2	8.9	13.2	11.3	8.2
West Germany					
TOTAL	24.2	39.4	55.7		

Source: Consumer Spending Patterns in the European Community, 1989.

EXHIBIT 16a
European consumption trends – bakery products (kg/capita).

Country	Bread — Per Capita Consumption 1986	Breakfast Cereals — Per Capita Consumption 1986	Breakfast Cereals — 5-Year Volume Growth %	Pasta — Per Capita Consumption 1986	Pasta — 5-Year Volume Growth %	Biscuits — Per Capita Consumption 1986	Biscuits — 5-Year Volume Growth %
EC members:							
Belgium	82.9	0.2	12.2	1.5	−8.2	5.2	−3.6
Denmark	29.5	3.0	9.2	1.4	14.0	4.3	3.7
France	67.3	0.4	30.4	6.6	1.6	6.0	3.6
West Germany	59.9	0.5	8.3	4.5	1.8	3.1	1.7
Greece	37.2			7.0	−2.4	7.3	6.9
Ireland	57.9	5.6	5.5			5.9	2.5
Italy	139.0	0.1	13.3	21.2	−2.4	7.3	6.5
Netherlands	60.0	0.3	30.8	1.1	11.7	2.7	−0.6
Portugal	13.9		−0.9	6.1	−2.7	1.5	−6.9
Spain	26.0	0.1	−0.9	3.9	−0.7	6.1	3.7
United Kingdom	43.7	7.0	5.1	3.2	7.7	8.3	−0.6
EFTA members:							
Austria	50.1	0.1	3.4	3.4	1.5	4.8	0.7
Finland	35.4	4.3	3.1	2.1	3.2	3.5	3.2
Norway	53.4	1.7	−1.0	0.3	4.7	3.6	0.0
Sweden	53.4	2.3	6.1	3.4	6.9	3.7	0.0
Switzerland	23.8	3.6	12.9	5.7	2.9	5.7	3.7
Weighted Average Growth			11.3%		2.0%		2.3%

Source: Consumer Europe 1988, European Marketing Data and Statistics (1988/1989).

EXHIBIT 16b
European consumption trends – convenience and miscellaneous
(kg/capita).

Country	Frozen Foods		Canned Foods		Baby Foods	
	Per Capita Consumption 1986	5-Year Volume Growth	Per Capita Consumption 1986	5-Year Volume Growth	Per Capita Consumption 1986	5-Year Volume Growth
EC members:		%		%		%
Belgium	10.5	12.0	31.4	−0.4		
Denmark	31.4	7.6	20.3	−1.2		
France	16.0	12.4	27.2	3.1	1.7	5.7
West Germany	19.7	5.3	26.0	−2.5	1.3	−2.2
Greece	5.4	10.0	25.5	0.9		
Ireland	21.3	5.7	25.7	2.3		
Italy	5.2	10.1	26.4	1.6	0.9	5.7
Netherlands	14.7	0.9	18.4	0.0		
Portugal	5.4	10.4	12.3	6.5		
Spain	5.4	10.1	22.6	4.7		
United Kingdom	21.2	5.2	24.7	1.6	1.4	1.3
EFTA members:						
Austria	10.2	6.8	15.0	0.4	0.7	2.7
Finland	11.3	4.1	11.6	3.9		
Norway	17.1	8.8	17.6	−5.9		
Sweden	26.3	1.7	20.9	−3.9		
Switzerland	20.2	6.7	17.0	0.5	0.4	−2.6
Weighted Average Growth		8.0%		1.2%		2.4%

EXHIBIT 16b (Continued)

Country	Pet Foods		Soups		Sugar	
	Per Capita Consumption 1986	5-Year Volume Growth	Per Capita Consumption 1986	5-Year Volume Growth	Per Capita Consumption 1986	5-Year Volume Growth
EC members:		%		%		%
Belgium	6.8				35.0	−1.2
Denmark	7.8				39.3	−2.2
France	13.6	8.3	6.3	8.7	12.7	−1.6
West Germany	6.6	10.8	12.9	2.0	33.4	−5.0
Greece	0.8				29.6	18.5
Ireland	6.8				30.5	−11.6
Italy	1.7	13.9	5.5	21.1	21.6	−4.9
Netherlands	14.1				39.5	−1.0
Portugal	0.8				34.5	4.0
Spain	1.0				29.0	−1.7
United Kingdom	19.9	6.5			11.6	−6.4
EFTA members:						
Austria	1.4				47.2	−1.7
Finland			1.2	0.4	37.3	0.0
Norway					40.9	5.0
Sweden			8.1	−4.9	46.3	1.5
Switzerland	6.0				44.6	−1.0
Weighted Average Growth		9.9%		9.5%		−2.7%

Source: Consumer Europe 1988, *European Marketing Data and Statistics* (1988/9).

EXHIBIT 16c
European consumption trends – dairy products
(kg/capita; milk, litres).

Country	Eggs		Butter		Cheese	
	Per Capita Consumption 1986	5-Year Volume Growth	Per Capita Consumption 1986	5-Year Volume Growth	Per Capita Consumption 1986	5-Year Volume Growth
EC members:		%		%		%
Belgium	14.6	0.7	10.1	2.1	12.6	−0.4
Denmark	14.5	0.7	6.5	−4.7	11.7	2.2
France	15.7	1.6	9.1	−0.3	21.2	2.8
West Germany	16.9	−0.8	7.9	3.1	9.6	2.2
Greece	11.6	0.2	0.9	6.5	21.2	2.1
Ireland	13.6	0.5	6.8	−13.1	5.1	8.5
Italy	11.7	0.8	2.6	3.9	16.4	1.7
Luxembourg	16.0		6.3	−2.1	6.8	0.0
Netherlands	11.8	−0.4	4.2	4.6	13.1	1.2
Portugal	6.6	−0.4	0.8	3.4	4.5	4.9
Spain	15.0	−4.3	0.5	0.0	4.6	6.9
United Kingdom	13.4	−0.2	3.2	−8.3	5.9	2.0
EFTA members:						
Austria	14.5	1.4	5.2	0.0	10.1	4.8
Finland	8.8	6.8	8.8	−6.0	11.0	5.9
Norway	12.7	1.5	4.6	−1.3	13.0	1.9
Sweden	12.9	3.5	7.1	2.2	15.8	3.1
Switzerland	12.3	0.6	7.1	−0.5	14.5	1.7
CMEA members:						
Bulgaria	12.4		2.7		11.9	
Czechoslovakia	17.7					
East Germany	15.4		15.6		9.0	
Hungary	15.5		2.8		4.1	
Poland	10.1		7.5		2.9	
Romania	12.9		1.3		3.7	
USSR	13.3					
Weighted Average Growth		0.0%		0.1%		2.8%

EXHIBIT 16c (Continued)

Country	Cream		Yogurt		Milk	
	Per Capita Consumption 1986	5-Year Volume Growth	Per Capita Consumption 1986	5-Year Volume Growth	Per Capita Consumption 1986	5-Year Volume Growth
EC members:		%		%		%
Belgium	2.5	7.1	5.6	2.9	69.0	−0.5
Denmark	8.8	3.6	8.8	−2.6	71.2	−4.5
France	2.7	6.3	12.9	4.3	49.8	−0.9
West Germany	5.8	4.9	8.1	3.6	54.7	−0.1
Greece	0.6	0.0	6.2	5.0	66.0	2.6
Ireland	2.3	3.4	3.4	7.5	178.1	−1.3
Italy	1.2	5.0	2.6	−1.4	67.6	−1.6
Luxembourg	10.9	7.5	8.2	10.7	92.6	5.9
Netherlands	2.5	−1.3	8.2	2.2	63.5	−1.5
Portugal	1.1	8.3	6.3	5.3	36.4	−9.7
Spain	1.1	9.4	6.3	5.0	101.4	0.6
United Kingdom	2.2	0.4	3.3	14.0	126.0	−0.8
EFTA members:						
Austria	5.0	4.4	8.7	3.3	111.4	−2.2
Finland	8.6	2.5	8.3	1.3	104.3	−10.5
Norway	7.9	1.6	2.4	2.7	114.9	−7.2
Sweden	8.3	2.7	4.9	3.3	98.1	−0.9
Switzerland	7.1	4.9	18.4	5.5	102.7	−1.0
CMEA members:						
Bulgaria					195.0	
Czechoslovakia						
East Germany					108.0	
Hungary					80.0	
Poland						
Romania						
USSR						
Weighted Average Growth		4.5%		4.7%		−1.2%

Source: Consumer Europe 1988, *European Marketing Data and Statistics* (1988/1989).

EXHIBIT 16d
European consumption trends–drinks
(litres/capita).

Country	Carbonated Drinks		Mineral Water		Fruit Juices	
	Per Capita Consumption 1986	5-Year Volume Growth	Per Capita Consumption 1986	5-Year Volume Growth	Per Capita Consumption 1986	5-Year Volume Growth
EC members:		%		%		%
Belgium	66.4	3.0	63.7	4.2	13.2	−0.6
Denmark	44.4	0.3	9.4	6.7	17.2	5.1
France	19.9	1.1	58.0	3.0	3.7	−0.2
West Germany	77.5	−0.2	62.3	6.4	26.7	5.1
Greece	34.3	3.2	10.0	15.8	3.8	7.0
Ireland	63.0	3.3	1.1	41.4	8.5	10.7
Italy	46.5	9.3	50.4	3.6	4.3	10.8
Luxembourg						
Netherlands	58.9	0.8	10.7	6.8	17.0	−0.6
Portugal	24.6	3.8	22.2	−0.4	2.4	4.7
Spain	65.2	6.5	26.2	2.7	3.6	4.7
United Kingdom	90.8	2.5	1.5	14.8	15.6	10.4
EFTA members:						
Austria	53.3	6.2	57.0	5.6	4.0	0.0
Finland	30.8	0.0	7.5	−1.9	29.3	1.6
Norway	70.7	6.3	5.1	2.5	7.7	−0.8
Sweden	34.5	3.6	8.9	4.9	14.6	−1.0
Switzerland	58.8	3.2	54.1	5.9	13.6	1.5
CMEA members:						
Bulgaria	61.3					
Czechoslovakia						
East Germany	96.3					
Hungary						
Poland						
Romania						
USSR						
Weighted Average Growth		3.5%		6.5%		5.3%

EXHIBIT 16d (Continued)

Country	Beer		Wine		Spirits	
	Per Capita Consumption 1986	5-Year Volume Growth	Per Capita Consumption 1986	5-Year Volume Growth	Per Capita Consumption 1986	5-Year Volume Growth
EC members:		%		%		%
Belgium	123.8	−1.2	20.1	−0.6	3.3	−6.6
Denmark	14.2	2.2	19.7	4.1	3.9	−1.2
France	40.4	−1.5	98.0	−4.7	5.2	−0.8
West Germany	147.2	−0.4	23.3	−1.8	6.3	−2.2
Greece	31.5	2.4	31.2	−7.9	14.8	0.7
Ireland	101.3	−1.0	3.1	0.0	4.2	0.0
Italy	2.3	3.1	79.5	−1.6	3.7	−2.2
Luxembourg	118.5	−1.0				
Netherlands	85.8	1.5	13.9	1.7	7.3	−2.4
Portugal	37.8	0.7	28.0	−24.3	1.8	−2.6
Spain	60.2	1.4	45.1	−1.8	6.9	1.6
United Kingdom	108.3	0.0	11.3	6.7	1.7	2.2
EFTA members:						
Austria	119.2	2.4	37.7	0.3	3.8	0.0
Finland	62.7	4.6	4.9	−5.4	11.6	−1.3
Norway	51.3	2.5	5.1	10.7	3.6	
Sweden	46.5	0.0	12.1	3.5	5.0	
Switzerland	67.5	−1.0	48.6	−0.2	35.2	
CMEA members:						
Bulgaria	97.0		23.0		3.0	
Czechoslovakia	131.0		14.0		3.4	
East Germany	142.0		10.0		4.9	
Hungary	93.0		25.0		5.4	
Poland	30.0		8.0		4.6	
Romania	43.0		29.0		2.0	
USSR	24.0		12.0		3.0	
Weighted Average Growth		0.6%		−1.1%		−0.8%

Source: Consumer Europe 1988, *European Marketing Data and Statistics* (1988/9).

EXHIBIT 16e
European consumption trends – snack foods (kg/capita).

Country	Chocolate Confectionery		Sugar Confectionery		Ice Cream		Savoury Snacks	
	Per Capita Consumption 1986	5-Year Volume Growth	Per Capita Consumption 1986	5-Year Volume Growth	PerCapita Consumption 1986	5-Year Volume Growth	Per Capita Consumption 1986	5-Year Volume Growth
		%		%		%		%
EC members:								
Belgium	6.2	2.4	4.7	3.9	8.7	12.3	3.0	9.7
Denmark	5.8	4.6	5.7	3.5	8.2	0.4		
France	4.1	0.8	2.6	−2.0	4.2	3.5	1.2	8.5
West Germany	6.3	0.7	5.8	0.0	6.9	0.3	2.9	4.0
Greece	2.1	6.0	2.3	1.6	4.9	3.7		
Ireland	7.4	2.4	6.6	6.7	7.9	3.9		
Italy	1.4	6.0	2.0	1.6	6.8	3.1	1.1	21.2
Netherlands	5.9	4.0	5.0	0.1	4.5	0.3		5.4
Portugal	0.4	−4.6	2.2	1.9	1.6	4.9	3.8	
Spain	2.0	4.7	2.2	1.6	2.5	−3.6		
United Kingdom	8.5	4.0	5.0	0.1	7.1	0.8	3.8	2.4
EFTA members:								
Austria	4.7	3.2		0.0		−1.8		
Finland	10.4	2.0		1.3		1.8		
Norway	11.5	3.2		3.9		5.1		
Sweden	14.3	4.0		2.3		2.3		
Switzerland	7.5	2.5		1.7		1.3		
Weighted Average Growth		3.0%		0.6%		1.6%		8.9%

Source: Consumer Europe 1988, European Marketing Data and Statistics (1988/1989).

EXHIBIT 17
US supermarket sales, 1988.

Category Performance

Category Name	1988 Sales Volume	% Change '88 vs. '87	5-Year CAGR
Baby foods	1,409.66	10.17	7.34
Bakery foods, packaged	8,170.63	5.70	4.42
Baking needs	4,102.19	2.46	−0.39
Beer and wine	7,054.84	3.35	3.11
Breakfast foods	5,754.12	9.94	8.88
Candy and gum	2,727.11	1.05	4.14
Canned fish	1,922.26	7.52	2.85
Canned fruit	1,247.02	4.83	2.99
Canned meat and specialty foods	1,381.90	3.54	4.12
Canned vegetables	2,574.41	2.77	1.57
Coffee and tea	3,815.49	−5.41	0.40
Cookies and crackers	5,061.84	5.82	5.99
Dairy products	19,162.22	2.35	2.74
Deli	6,114.49	11.30	8.00
Desserts and toppings	676.88	4.83	6.27
Diet and low-calorie foods	989.13	8.34	6.42

Rankings

	Sales	
1	Meat	40,981.89
2	Produce	22,625.32
3	Dairy products	19,162.22
4	Frozen foods	14,925.65
5	Soft drinks and mixes	9,584.21
6	Bakery foods, packaged	8,170.63
7	Beer and wine	7,054.84
8	Deli	6,114.49
9	Breakfast foods	5,754.12
10	Cookies and crackers	5,061.84

One-Year Growth

1	Rice and dried vegetables	19.39
2	In-store bakery	12.71

Category			
Dried fruit	534.11	1.11	12.03
Frozen foods	14,925.65	4.96	4.94
Ice cream	2,294.39	–1.00	4.14
In-store bakery	3,637.72	12.71	0.00
Juice (grocery)	3,333.87	3.59	5.95
Meat	40,981.89	6.37	3.64
Nuts	858.60	–3.84	3.13
Pasta	1,465.44	10.03	8.59
Pickles and olives	923.21	3.78	1.37
Produce	22,625.32	7.33	7.84
Rice and dried vegetables	894.33	19.39	6.69
Sauces and dressings	3,895.58	5.59	5.90
Snacks	3,620.63	4.74	7.07
Soft drinks and mixes	9,584.21	6.84	6.12
Soup	1,784.23	5.45	5.49
Spices and extracts	846.88	3.63	3.77
Spreads and syrups	1,620.00	1.65	3.02
Non-edibles	54,409.75		
TOTAL SUPERMARKET	240,400.00	5.21	4.91

3	Deli	11.30
4	Baby foods	10.17
5	Pasta	10.03
6	Breakfast foods	9.94
7	Diet and low-calorie food	8.34
8	Canned fish	7.52
9	Produce	7.33
10	Soft drinks and mixes	6.84

Five-Year Growth

1	Dried fruit	12.03
2	Breakfast foods	8.88
3	Pasta	8.59
4	Deli	8.00
5	Produce	7.84
6	Baby foods	7.34
7	Snacks	7.07
8	Rice and dried vegetables	6.69
9	Diet and low-calorie food	6.42
10	Desserts and toppings	6.27

Source: Progressive Grocer, July 1989.

EXHIBIT 18
World population and income statistics.

Country	Population 1985	Population 1995	Population 2010	% of Population, 1995 15–64 %	% of Population, 1995 65+ %	Consumer Expense Food, Drinks and Tobacco (%)	Income/Capita (1986, $)
EC members:							
Belgium	9,857	9,729	9,406	65.8	16.0	22.9	8,707
Denmark	5,111	5,108	5,019	67.6	15.7	20.3	11,510
France	55,062	56,338	57,939	66.3	13.9	19.4	9,835
West Germany	61,049	59,983	57,200	68.4	15.8	21.2	10,558
Greece	9,919	10,168	10,523	63.3	13.6	39.8	3,455
Ireland	3,540	4,083	4,759	62.0	9.5	53.6	4,694
Italy	57,080	57,506	55,800	67.9	15.9	30.3	6,340
Luxembourg	366	373	369	67.8	13.1	18.1	9,974
Netherlands	14,454	15,028	15,148	68.7	13.6	17.3	9,131
Portugal	10,129	10,819	11,423	67.1	13.2	44.6	1,861
Spain	38,495	40,022	41,205	66.8	14.1	27.8	3,680
United Kingdom	56,618	58,144	59,500	64.3	15.8	20.9	5,891
EC TOTAL	321,680	327,301	328,281	66.7	14.9		
EFTA members:							
Austria	7,558	7,621	7,537	66.8	15.7	21.3	10,240
Finland	4,894	5,054	5,048	66.9	14.5	22.8	10,551
Iceland	241	256	272	66.4	11.3	30.4	10,476
Norway	4,146	4,273	4,346	65.2	16.4	22.8	13,661
Sweden	8,343	8,498	8,514	64.4	17.9	21.7	11,747
Switzerland	6,456	6,485	6,430	67.0	15.4	24.9	16,492
EFTA TOTAL	31,638	32,187	32,147	66.0	16.1		

Eastern Europe:							
Bulgaria	8,960	9,392	9,760	64.6	14.0	30.7	
Czechoslovakia	15,500	16,155	17,307	66.5	12.1	32.6	
East Germany	16,671	16,998	17,431	66.8	12.9	36.8	
Hungary	10,657	10,561	10,703	67.3	14.4	38.6	1,813
Poland	37,063	39,552	42,943	65.0	11.1	50.9	
Romania	22,725	24,690	27,073	65.0	11.4	28.0	2,004
USSR	277,537	303,517	337,120	64.3	11.1	41.3	
EASTERN EUROPE TOTAL	389,113	421,065	462,337	64.7	11.4		
Argentina	30,564	35,073	41,507	60.6	9.4	34.0	2,676
Australia	15,698	17,693	20,319	66.6	11.2	20.8	9,019
Brazil	135,564	165,083	207,454	61.3	5.1	27.3	1,716
Canada	25,426	27,917	30,739	67.2	11.9	15.7	11,472
China						52.4	226
Colombia	28,714	34,940	43,840	61.1	4.3	49.2	1,157
Hong Kong	5,548	6,458	7,205	68.2	9.3	19.2	6,200
India	758,927	896,676	1,086,344	62.6	5.1	54.4	215
Indonesia	166,440	196,361	238,605	62.3	4.3	56.8	460
Israel	4,252	4,965	5,952	62.6	8.6	29.4	3,452
Japan	120,742	126,782	133,049	68.6	13.2	22.6	11,248
Kuwait	1,811	2,630	3,769	58.1	2.2	43.5	16,063
Malaysia	15,557	18,987	23,349	62.0	4.1	25.8	1,610
New Zealand	3,318	3,611	3,968	66.9	11.1	37.8	5,909
Nigeria	85,198	135,451	227,539	48.7	2.4	17.6	731
Philippines	54,498	67,591	86,344	60.1	3.6	54.5	473
Singapore	2,559	2,947	3,141	71.3	6.3	53.4	
South Africa	32,392	41,623	58,525	55.1	4.0	24.6	1,551
South Korea	41,258	48,059	55,942	66.4	5.0	31.8	1,793
Taiwan						37.7	2,780
Thailand	51,411	60,509	74,795	64.9	4.3	41.8	5,044
United States	238,020	258,651	286,294	65.4	12.3	17.8	15,621
Venezuela	17,317	22,212	30,006	59.4	4.0	54.6	2,526
Zimbabwe	8,777	12,612	21,456	49.1	2.7	15.7	

Sources: Business International, *European Marketing Data and Statistics* (1938/1989), *International Marketing Data and Statistics* (1988/1989).

EXHIBIT 19
Consolidation challenge food/beverage industry Europe: top five multiples.

	1982 Total bn (Local currency)	1982 Domestic %	1987 Total bn (Local currency)	1987 Domestic %	Source:
France			**France**		
1. Leclerc	28.8	28.7	1. Leclerc	58.7	58.7	Panorama
2. Auchan	17.4	17.4	2. Intermarche	57.0	57.0	Le Nouvel Economiste
3. Carrefour	29.1	16.4	3. Carrefour	56.6	43.9	
4. Promodes	17.7	17.7	4. Promodes	35.0	35.0	
5. Casino	16.9	16.9	5. Casino	33.6	33.6	
	109.9	97.1		240.9	228.2	
Total Grocery Sales	320.0		Total Grocery Sales	500.0		INSEE
Conc.		30.3	Conc.		45.7	
Germany			**Germany**		
1. Aldi	15.0E	13.5	1. Aldi	23.9E	19.4	G&L (without Metro
2. Tengelmann	29.9E	9.4	2. REWE	15.1	15.1	department stores)
3. COOP	8.6	8.6	3. Tengelmann	32.9E	12.5	
4. REWE	7.8	7.8	4. Asko/Schaper	11.3	11.3	
5. Schaper	3.8	3.8	5. COOP	10.3	10.3	
(Metro		10.7	(Metro		11.4)	
	65.1	43.1		93.5	68.6	
Total Grocery Sales	130.3		Total Grocery Sales	145.4		G&L adj.
Conc.		33.1	Conc.		47.2	
United Kingdom			**United Kingdom**		
1. Sainsbury	1.9	1.9	1. Tesco	4.4	4.4	Verdict
2. Tesco	1.9	1.9	2. Sainsbury	4.3	4.3	
3. Asda	1.1	1.1	3. DEE/Gateway	3.6	3.6	
4. Argyll	0.9	0.9	4. Asda	2.4	2.4	
5. Fine Fare	0.8	0.8	5. Argyll	2.1	2.1	
	6.6	6.6		17.8	16.8	
Total Grocery Sales	19.2		Total Grocery Sales	31.0		
Conc.		34.4	Conc.		57.4	

Source: Company records.

EXHIBIT 20
Consolidated capitalization of the Group
(FF millions).

	As at 31 December 1988[a]
Shareholders' Equity	
Issued and fully paid shares of FF 100 each	521
Capital surplus	8,173
Retained earnings	7,072
	15,766
Less: Treasury stock	66
	15,700
Minority interests	715
Total Shareholders' Equity	16,415
Short-term Bank Loans	1,856
Long-term Debts	
Convertible loan stock	
9.75 per cent convertible debentures due 1993	86
Other loan stock	
11.80 per cent non-convertible debentures due 1980–90	60
TAM + 0.25 per cent non-convertible debentures due 1986–96	120
8.00 per cent non-convertible debentures due 1988–96	1,332
Redeemable warrants 1989–93	373
Credit National	
Bank loans	3,317
Other	
TOTAL LONG-TERM DEBTS	5,288

[a] There has been no material change in the indebtedness of the group since 31 December 1988 except the 9% FF1,000,000,000 1989–97 now being issued.
Source: Company prospectus.

EXHIBIT 21
Changes in share capital[a].

Year	Operations Resulting in Changes in Capital During Past Five Years	Amounts of Changes in Capital				Amount of Capital	Cumulative[a] Total Number of Shares
		Sales of New Stock; Bond Conversion		Exchange			
		Par Value	Premium over Par Value	Par Value	Premium over Par Value		
1983[b]	Conversion of Convertible Bonds	12,825,100	93,323,300			249,971,600	24,997,150
1983	Sales of New Shares	65,699,100	459,893,700			262,796,700	26,279,670
1984	Exchange for Pommery and Lanson Shares			16,676,400	375,219,000	328,495,800	32,849,580
1984[b]	Conversion of Convertible Bonds	8,441,800	61,832,600			345,172,200	34,517,220
1985[b]	Conversion of Convertible Bonds	6,984,100	45,690,700			353,614,000	35,361,400
1985	Shares Issued in Gerdafrance and Somivet Mergers			32,100	615,540	360,598,100	36,059,810
1986[b]	Conversion of Convertible Bonds	6,552,200	46,896,400			360,630,200	36,063,020
1987[b]	Conversion of Convertible Bonds and Exercise of Warrants	29,449,400	542,518,653			367,182,200	36,718,220
1987	Shares Issued in Générale Biscuit Merger			30,000,000	1,173,540,760	396,631,600	39,663,160
1987	Exchange for Cofinda Shares			28,385,500	1,362,504,537	426,631,600	42,663,160
1987	Fusion and Absorption of SOGIM			4,833,800	231,869,863	455,017,100	45,501,710
				(−13,774,000, due to cancellation and retirement of BSN shares held by SOGIM)		446,076,900	44,607,690
1987	Merger and Absorption of Copab Fluxine			559,800	26,870,400	446,636,700	44,663,670
1987	Conversion of Convertible Bonds and Exercise of Warrants (recorded from 1 Jan. 1987 to 22 May 1987)	5,153,900	37,079,676			451,790,600	45,179,060
1987	Sale of New Shares for Cash	45,179,000	1,536,086,000			496,969,600	49,696,560
1987	Exchange for One IFIL Share			22,020,200	1,050,144,277	518,989,800	51,898,580
1987	Merger with Roginvest			500	24,002	518,990,300	51,899,030
1988[b]	Conversion of Convertible Bonds and Exercise of Warrants	1,370,000	13,117,341			520,360,300	52,036,030
1989[b]	Conversion of Convertible Bonds and Exercise of Warrants	646,100	13,356,638			521,007,100	52,100,710

[a] After the ten-for-one stock split approved on 9 January 1989.
[b] As verified at the first board of directors meeting during the year.
Source: Company prospectus.

BENETTON S.p.A.*

I should say the new strategy relates to our intention of structuring Benetton as a proper multinational company. That means we plan to create a complex global manufacturing system to advance our mission to reach the two-thirds of the world where we do not have a presence. It is in this light that our recent choice to diversify into the field of financial services must be interpreted. The financial services companies that we operate – generally in partnership with important banks and financial institutions – have to be considerate and provide the necessary support for Benetton's new development policy. In addition, the new and more sophisticated system that we are going to build in the field of services (not only financial services but the service industry overall) may help us in our attempts to implement the entrepreneurial formula that I have tried to explain to you.[1]

With these words, Mr Aldo Palmeri, general manager of Benetton, S.p.A., outlined the strategy for the future development of Benetton, a strategy designed to keep the outstanding rate of growth the company had enjoyed since its inception.

HISTORY OF THE COMPANY

The Benetton story was a tale of huge success built from humble origins. Started some 25 years ago, the company had reached $1 billion in worldwide sales, building

*This case was written by J. Carlos Jarillo and Jon I. Martínez, with the economic support of the European Foundation for Entrepreneurial Research. The casewriters gratefully acknowledge the assistance of Mr Franco Furnò, manager of Organizational Development at Benetton S.p.A., in the preparation of this case.

from its strengths in one of the most mature, labour-intensive industries in labour-expensive Western Europe.

The firm was a typically Italian family concern, with four siblings – Guiliana, Luciano, Gilberto and Carlo – involved from the beginning in the company operations. The eldest brother, Luciano, was born in 1935, and spent his childhood through the harsh times that Second World War brought to north-eastern Italy. On his father's death, he had to leave school at the age of 15 to take a job in a men's outfitters. In 1955, Luciano, who had just turned 20, told Giuliana he was convinced that he could market the bright-coloured, original sweaters she used to make as a hobby, so why shouldn't they leave their jobs and start a business?

With 30,000 lire, obtained from the sale of Luciano's accordion and Carlo's bicycle, Luciano and Giuliana bought a knitting machine, and soon afterwards Giuliana put together a collection of eighteen items. Luciano was immediately able to sell them to local stores. Sales increased steadily over the next few years, until Giuliana had a group of young women working for her, and Luciano had bought a minibus to carry these employees to and from a small workshop the Benettons had set up near their home.

In the early 1960s, Luciano Benetton put into practice several innovative ideas that helped turn the company from a small enterprise into a giant. The first idea was to sell only through specialized knitwear stores (as opposed to department stores and boutiques selling a wide range of clothes), whose owners would presumably be more interested in pushing sales of his particular product. Luciano made use of another idea unusual at that time: to offer retailers a 10 per cent discount if they paid in cash on delivery of his product. At that point, Benetton sweaters did not bear the family name (they used foreign names, like 'Lady Godiva' or 'Très Jolie'), but they already had the Benetton characteristics of medium-high quality and stylish design at a very reasonable price.

Two more new ideas emerged, this time for lowering production costs. The first was a novel technique for making wool soft, like cashmere; it was based on a method Luciano had observed while visiting factories in Scotland, where rudimentary machines with wooden paddles beat raw wool in water. The other idea was to buy and adapt obsolete hosiery-knitting machines, at a price of $5,000 apiece, a fraction of the cost of a new machine. The refurbished machines did their new job perfectly.[2]

Benetton was formally incorporated in 1965 as 'Maglificio di Ponzano Veneto dei Fratelli Benetton'. The small enterprise consisted of Luciano, Giuliana and their younger brothers, Gilberto and Carlo. Gilberto was placed in charge of financial issues, while Carlo headed the production system. In the same year, the first Benetton factory went up in the village of Ponzano, a few kilometres outside Treviso, in north-east Italy.

In 1968, the company opened the first independent outlet in the mountain village of Belluno, not far from Venice. With its appealing merchandise and its spare, intimate interior, the shop was an immediate success. The store occupied only about 400 square feet, in part because of limited Benetton product line at the time, but it set the pattern for the stores to follow. 'It was conceived on the idea of the specialized store, the desire for an alternative to the department store,' said Luciano Benetton to an American journalist. He added: 'From the beginning, we wanted to create an image – the right people to open our stores, the décor, the colours.'[3]

Through the late 1960s and early 1970s the Benettons concentrated their efforts on capturing the domestic market. By 1975, the distinctive white and green Benetton knitting-stitch logo had become the symbol of a phenomenon in the Italian commercial scene. Approximately 200 Benetton shops had opened in Italy; many of them, but not all bore the Benetton name. The idea of having other names – Sisley, Tomato, Merceria, 012 – with a different decoration and selection of Benetton clothes, grew out of the intention of appealing to different segments of the market and of avoiding mass flops: if one Benetton store was a failure, others in the same area wouldn't bear the stigma. Over the years, however, none of these names had achieved much importance, and many of them were being folded back into the Benetton brand.

In spite of the early opening of their first foreign outlet in Paris, in 1969, international sales had remained negligible for the company for most of the 1970s. In 1978, 98 per cent of the company's sales of $80 million were in Italy, where opportunities for continued high growth were diminishing. Consequently, the firm launched a major expansion campaign into the rest of Europe, always following their system of only selling through specialized, Benetton-named outlets. Sales boomed as the network of shops spread north into France, West Germany, Britain, Switzerland and the Scandinavian countries. In the early 1980s, most young women in Europe seemed to be buying Benetton sportswear, including Princess Caroline of Monaco and Diana, Princess of Wales, which gave Benetton worldwide publicity. By 1982, sales had grown to roughly $311 million. In 1983, Benetton had sales of $351 million, from 2,600 stores in Europe.

Though the Benettons still expected some growth in Europe, they saw greater opportunity further afield. By the end of 1983, the company had already placed 31 shops in department stores throughout Japan, and 27 shops in major cities of the United States. Interviewed by an American magazine, Luciano Benetton confessed: 'Being in America is like a dream – it is so big, so prestigious. If we do well, it will help us in Japan because they like whatever is big in the US.'[4] Progress in both countries had been difficult at the beginning, however. Instead of opening European-style shops, 18 of the 27 US shops were in department stores, like Macy's, where Benetton had small boutiques from which it obtained a percentage of the profits. The joint venture was short-lived, perhaps due to the Macy's practice of quickly marking down prices on slow-moving items, which went completely against Benetton's philosophy.

The company set up some manufacturing units outside Italy. The existing factories in France, Scotland and Spain were joined by an American facility in North Carolina in 1985. However, production outside Italy was not started for economic or technical reasons, but to bypass protectionism in those countries.

The complexity of handling an ever-expanding network of shops, production volumes, materials flows and employees kept increasing. By the late 1970s, everybody in the company felt that something had to be done. The decision was made in 1981 to recruit professional managers. Aldo Palmeri, 36, a highly regarded executive at the Bank of Italy (Italy's central bank) in Rome, was hired as a consultant and after a year became the new managing director. Although he had several ideas for reorganizing Benetton, his limited experience in industrial companies obliged him to recruit an experienced manager to put them into practice. This man, in charge of personnel and organization, was Mr Cantagalli, who joined Benetton in 1983 from a similar position with 3M, a large American multinational in Italy.

They proceeded to recruit experienced managers from other large companies to form a 'professional team'. The newly created organization department had to implement an organization development programme to bridge the old 'handshake management' culture with the new and more formal one. This process of creating new functions and written procedures lasted three years, and finished in October 1986.

The board of directors was composed of the four members of the Benetton family and Mr Palmeri. However, the Benettons did not play the conventional, distant role of members of the board and took part in many day-to-day decisions. Although it didn't appear in the organization chart, most of the senior functional managers had two reporting relationships: a formal one to Aldo Palmeri, an informal one to a member of the Benetton family. Hence, there were two different groups of young adults that had to coexist at the top: the self-made Benetton siblings, and the well-educated ex-multinational executives. The main task of the organization development department was to join both cultures. According to Mr Franco Furnò, manager of this department, 'There has been a lot of improvement in this mutual understanding process in the last three years, but the job is not finished yet.'

Until July 1986, the four Benetton siblings shared 100 per cent of the company's equity. After reporting strong 1985 results (see Exhibit 1), the company offered a total of 15.6 million common shares to the public. Eleven million were listed in the Milan and Venice stock exchanges, 4.48 million in the Euromarkets, and the rest was offered to Benetton's employees, agents and clients. The total stock issue represented about 10 per cent of the company. In addition, the company sold lira- (L70bn) and Deutschmark-denominated bonds (DM200m) with warrants. It was estimated that the whole financial operation represented about 20 per cent of the company's equity, bringing in a minimum of $330 million of fresh capital.

THE COMPANY IN 1987: AN OVERALL DESCRIPTION

Benetton was a vertically deintegrated company, not only in manufacturing, but also in the three other main activities that constituted its value chain: styling and design, logistics and distribution, and sales. The company relied on external people and companies for the major part of these crucial activities. It employed some 1,500 people at the end of 1987.

The styling or design of the garments was done outside the company by a number of international freelance stylists. Giuliana Benetton, with a staff of about 20 people in the Product Development Department, interpreted the 'look' created by the stylists and performed the modelling phase.

More than 80 per cent of manufacturing was done outside the company, by 350 subcontractors that employed about 10,000 people. In-house production accounted for the remaining less than 20 per cent (mainly dyeing) and was performed by 700–800 people.

Logistics and distribution activities were also performed mainly by outsiders. The company did the storage phase by using a single, huge warehouse for finished products. In addition, the Logistics Department at Benetton was in charge of delivering the finished garments to the stores all over the world.

Finally, the company utilized an external sales organization of almost 80 agents which took care of a retailing system of nearly 4,000 shops spread all over the world. The internal part of this activity was performed by seven area managers, who coordinated the selling system as a whole divided by territories.

The Operating Cycle

There were basically two fashion seasons: spring/summer, beginning in February and ending in July, and autumn/winter, beginning in September and ending in December. The large volume of business done by the company required that production planning for woollen and cotton articles began far in advance of shipment to the stores. Roughly, 21 months elapsed from the preparation of clothing designs for a particular selling season to the final payment of commissions to Benetton agents.

Basic steps in the operating cycle were: preparation of final designs; assembly of a few samples of each of the 600 items in the total collection; a 'pre-presentation' meeting was then held between Giuliana Benetton, manufacturing managers and some of the company's 80 agents, which eliminated about a fourth of the models; the remaining were then produced in small quantities for presentation by area managers to agents and by agents to store owners; upon receipt of the first orders, the planning department 'exploded' a rough production plan for the season, by fabrics and styles; purchases were made according to this plan, and capacity with the subcontractors negotiated; finally, production was started and deliveries begun just in time for the selling season. They were scheduled so that each store could present 80–90 per cent of all items (fabrics, styles and colours) in its basic collection to its customers at the outset of the selling season.

Although shops committed orders 7 months before the selling season, giving Benetton time to schedule, produce and deliver, the production plan did allow some flexibility for the retailer in three ways. First, from August through to early December, as they gathered more information about colour preferences, shopowners were allowed to specify colours for woven items that had been held in 'grey' up to that point, with a limit of 30 per cent of the total orders for the woollen items on such orders. Given the popularity of colourful weaves and jacquards in the last 3-4 years, 'grey' stock had only represented about 15–20 per cent of all orders. This trend was expected to change in the coming years, which would mean a return to more 'grey' orders.

The basic production plan was also adjusted through the presentation of a 'flash collection' just before the season. The flash collection corrected styling mistakes in the basic product line and usually included about 50 new designs based on 'hit styles' presented by fashion houses (competitors) during the two main seasonal shows.

Finally, orders could be adjusted through 'reassortment', which was the most critical phase in the production plan, requiring great coordination and follow-through by retailers, agents and producers. Reassortment occurred during the last third of each selling season, when retailers were allowed to add orders to their original ones based on sell-through of popular items. Juggling retail orders to match manufacturing capacity for thousands of shops in a 5-week period was not an easy task. There was a minimum economical production batch, so sometimes when the reassortment order was not enough to fill the minimum batch, the marketing people would get in touch with shop managers to propose some alternatives. As Benetton moved into new geographic areas the complexity of reassortment grew incessantly, because the best sellers for different areas tended to vary widely,

Payments to subcontractors, representing a major cash outflow, were made 70 days after the end of the month in which production occurred or, in the case of the spring–summer collection, in October. Collections from retail stores were based on a season beginning date of 30 March for the spring/summer season, with one third of payment due 30, 60 and 90 days after that date or the date of actual receipt of merchandise. This was designed to minimize retailer's investment in inventories.

Manufacturing Activities

The company was divided into three divisions: wool, cotton and jeans. In 1983, Benetton had seven plants in Italy. In 1985, the number of plants decreased to five, and in 1987 the company owned just three production units, one for each division. The reason for this reduction was simply a matter of the company's philosophy of vertical deintegration and external production as a mode of organization. All those divested plants acted in 1987 as Benetton subcontractors.

As shown in Exhibit 2, Benetton utilized three different kinds of raw material. In the wool division the raw material was basically thread, no matter whether it was acrylic, cotton or real wool. In the other two plants, the raw materials were basically textiles or fabrics. The wool division's technology was mainly knitting, while the other two divisions' technology was essentially cutting.

Benetton was the biggest purchaser of wool thread in the world. It purchased about 9 million kg of thread per year. The other two divisions bought raw materials (fabrics) from 80 to 90 different suppliers. The company centralized all the purchasing activities as this was perhaps the main source of economies of scale in the industry. In 1987, 37 tons of yarn and 40 tons of fabrics entered the production system daily, to be transformed into 180,000 garments, adding up to 40–45 million garments per year.

The wool division worked with 200 external production units. Because some of them were quite large, Benetton kept control over them through a percentage of their equities. The cotton and jeans divisions worked with other 150 external production units.

Benetton gave the external contractors the exact amount of raw materials (calculated by computer), technical documents, an idea of the time needed to perform each single production activity, etc. Therefore, although these production units were external, they were technically run by Benetton as most of them worked exclusively for the company. In addition, Benetton advised subcontractors about the required machinery to buy, and offered them financial aid through its own leasing and factoring companies. The contact with the subcontractors was also facilitated by the fact that, according to an Italian journalist, it could be said that there was no manager at Benetton who was not at the same time owner, president or direction of a leading subcontracting company in the Lombardia–Veneto area.

Although most of the manufacturing activities were externally performed, some were centralized at headquarters in Ponzano, Veneto. Among these were all purchasing, production planning, technical research, product development, acquisition and exploitation of patents and rights, cutting by computer and dyeing.

Even allowing for the added costs of shuttling raw materials and semi-finished products among subcontractors and Benetton's factories, the savings brought by decentralization resulted in total production costs for woollen items almost 20 per cent below those of garments of comparable quality made in Europe and on a par with those made in the Far East. The following pages explain in detail how the wool division worked to achieve those results.

The Wool Division

The wool division consumed 55 per cent of all raw materials used by the company, and woollen garments represent about 47 per cent of total sales in units. Three out of four woollen garments (that is, 15 million garments) were sold in the autumn/winter season. The remaining 25 per cent were sold during the spring/summer season. They were manufactured following a process made up of four sequential phases: knitting, assembling, dyeing and finishing.

Knitting

Once the agents had collected the orders from the stores and sent them to headquarters, the technical department prepared the portfolio order for each of the three divisions. Thus the manager of the wool plant received an order portfolio that only included the articles to be manufactured in that plant.

The proportion of internal work in the knitting phase had decreased in the last five years. In 1982, only 40 per cent of the knitting of wool had been performed externally. As shown in Exhibit 3, just 1 per cent of the knitting phase was done internally 1987, and 90 per cent of that 1 per cent was concentrated in a very specific type of knitting machine. Benetton had decided to keep in-house that kind of machine because it has a lot of problems finding those machines in external companies. That machine was very expensive and, therefore, risky for external contractors. The company also used its internal production to have first-hand information on the productivity and costing of the knitting phase.

Benetton worked with 70–80 subcontractors in the knitting phase, and nearly 90 per cent of them worked exclusively for Benetton. Mr Morelli, plant manager for the wool division, argued that there were pros and cons to that exclusivity: 'The main advantage is that the company can count on them to plan its production, as it knows their production capacity, kind of machines, number of shifts, etc. But the main disadvantage is that the company has to assure the saturation of their machines, which is risky for both Benetton and the external contractors.'

Assembly

This phase of the manufacturing process was completely performed outside the company by more than 100 external contractors, who worked exclusively for Benetton. In 1982, only 60 per cent of this activity had been done externally. The average number of employees of these contractors was 14–15 or multiples of these figures because, as they had to work on a continuous basis, this was the ideal number of workers for an assembly chain.

According to Mr Morelli, Benetton didn't perform the assembling phase internally because 'First of all, it goes against the philosophy of the company, that looks for deintegration and flexibility. Secondly, there are some economies in doing this job externally because these small subcontractors have to pay less in terms of social costs according to Italian law, although the salary level is almost the same.'

Dyeing

The early 1970s saw the development of Benetton's perhaps most widely publicized production technique: the dyeing of assembled garments rather than yarn, for single-colour garments. Up to then, it was the yarn that was dyed, and then the parts knit and the sweater assembled. The Benettons discovered that, to a some extent, the critical fashion factor was colour, not shape. They decided, therefore, to knit and assemble a large part of their production undyed ('grey') and wait until fashion trends for colours became clearer to make the final colour decision. They thus avoided overproduction of sweaters in non-appealing colours and ensured they could meet demand for the 'best hits' of the season. The process was slightly more expensive but had the advantage of allowing production to respond quickly to public demand. It also allowed the company to maintain almost no inventory, and to produce mainly to order.

The company kept 100 per cent of the dyeing phase internally. In 1982, half this phase had been performed outside the company. The whole process was concentrated at home because of the great importance of the dyeing phase for a company whose main distinctive product characteristic was its colourful style, and the ability of its garments to produce colour-coordinated sets of clothing. In addition, dyeing was both the most complex and the most capital-intensive process, which made it risky for external subcontractors.

Before the dyeing phase, every article had to pass through a chemical treatment to soften and wax the wool. The pieces that used already coloured threads had to pass through this chemical treatment, too. This phase was also a capital-intensive one but, technically speaking, was not as sophisticated as dyeing. The main part of this chemical process (70–5 per cent) was performed outside the company by three external companies. Two of these plants had belonged to Benetton until 1985, when it sold them to their plant managers. These plants became joint ventures between these new entrepreneurs and Benetton. These plants employed about 100 people each.

Finishing

Only 5 per cent of this phase was performed in-house, in contrast to the 80 per cent done internally in 1982. The 20 subcontractors that performed the other 95 per cent worked exclusively for Benetton. This phase was labour-intensive and didn't require particular machinery. It was split in two parts: quality control of each single garment and packaging.

Some Problems in the Benetton-Subcontractors Relationship

Mr Luigi Muzio, managing director of one of the largest external firms in which Benetton had an important equity position, commented: 'The main problem in working for Benetton is the great number of changes in articles, colours, etc, they do in a very short time. We have to adjust the machines weekly or even nightly to follow all these changes. This means a large number of different articles produced in small batches each, which, from a manufacturing point of view, is very inefficient.' This subcontractor also complained about the machinery suggested by Benetton. In his opinion, they had a 'final product orientation' instead of a 'process orientation', not taking into account the productivity or the suitability of the machinery to the subcontractor's characteristics. Thus, he maintained that the machinery suggested by the company was often more suitable to a craftsman than to an industrial concern.

Subcontractors ran a big risk when they decided on the purchase of a certain type of machine. The key factor that decided the usefulness of the knitting machines was the thickness of the thread. Fortunately, it didn't vary so rapidly as the styles, colours or fashion in general. However, the company had experienced some problems of this type in the past, for some subcontractors had been stuck with machines that were useless for the current fashion trends. The firm had facilitated the change of the machines both by buying them or by allowing the contractors wide earnings so they could reinvest this money in new machinery. For this reason, Benetton tried to concentrate in-house the most expensive and fashion-dependent activities.

Mr Muzio realized that working exclusively for Benetton involved a risk, but on the other hand it had the advantage of allowing them to dispense with a sales and marketing department: 'The constant work provided by Benetton enables this company to concentrate in manufacturing, with just a few people in charge of administrative and financial tasks. Working only for Benetton means one invoice per month, fixed payment conditions, etc. We often receive requests from potential clients, but I'd rather work this way.' Mr Morelli, head of the wool division, pointed out that 'one of the main problems in working with external firms is to achieve the required flexibility in them. They have to completely adapt to Benetton demands in terms of working periods, vacation, etc.' Another Benetton executive voiced this concern: 'This is neither a "just in time" system nor a very scheduled one.'

Subcontractors normally worked 8 hours a day, but when the company was in a hurry they had to work over the weekend, and 12 or more hours a day. Nearly 10 per cent of all subcontractors were released every year because they didn't meet quality standards.

One of the highlights of the company's network of subcontractors was described by Mr Morelli: 'Benetton maintains a sort of "umbilical cord" with external contractors. They are considered part of our family, and feel confident in telling us their problems.' Plant managers knew personally each subcontractor and some of them became friends, to the point that they talked about their personal problems and asked for advice. Manufacturing people visited subcontractors very often. In addition, they were permanently in touch by phone. This daily communication allowed them to work in real-time, solving little problems and making production adjustments.

According to the firm, the less experienced the subcontractor in the clothing industry, the better it would adjust to Benetton's philosophy. It was more difficult to create this 'umbilical cord' with people that had previously worked for other clients. The experienced contractor tried to impose its conditions before starting the relationship.

Finally, there was a strong identification with Benetton, not only within the company, but also among subcontractors' employees. Luigi Muzio said: 'Workers in my company are fully identified with Benetton. They feel very proud of belonging to a worldwide-known group born in an ignored province of Italy. It is the first time that a clothing producer of this region develops into a world-class company, and this means a lot for these people.'

High-Tech Production Processes

Many experts in the clothing industry agreed that the Benetton success formula was based on the company's ability to combine fashion with industry, using advanced technology. Luciano Benetton confirmed this to an American business magazine: 'There are many elements to our success, but the real point is that we have kept the same strategy all along – to put fashion on an industrial level. Most of the rest of Italian fashion is still on an artisan level.'[5]

For production, Benetton used numeric control knitting machines linked to Apricot (a British firm) computer-aided-design personal computer terminals. Designers using the ten CAD terminals could play around with knitwear colours and patterns on a video screen. Once a designer decided on a particular pattern, the computer prepared a tape that would direct the knitting machine to produce the fabric automatically, in an easy-to-assemble form of pieces. Since 1980, they had also used a Gerber Camsco CAD system which they had connected to a Spanish-made Investronica automatic cutter, turning the system into a CAD–CAM unit. The CAD–CAM system's automatic cutter followed pattern pieces stored in the computer's memory, which turned out 15,000 full garments every 8 hours, wasting less than 15 per cent of the cloth.

The dyeing phase was a high-tech process too. At the factory, workers could dye unbleached wool garments in 270 different colours for quick stock replenishments which were then despatched round the world within days.

Logistics

Logistics played an important role in the Benetton strategy. Stores carrying Benetton products were designed with limited storage space for back-up stocks. Upon arrival at the store direct from the company, merchandise often was checked and placed directly on the display shelves. This required both a carefully prepared schedule of shipments to stores, and a large and efficient warehouse to store finished products at headquarters.

The new robotized warehouse in Castrette, the main symbol of Benetton's high technology, became fully operational in February 1986. With a cost of over 42 billion lire (about $32 million) to build and outfit, the warehouse was a huge automatic box run by a Digital Equipment Corp. minicomputer which directed several robots via remote control. The robots could read bar codes on boxes, and then sort and store them. The operation of the warehouse was totally automatic and there was no human handling in the whole process. A staff of five specialists just monitored the movements via computer.

Selling Activities

There were three groups of actors involved in selling activities: the company, the agents and the shop owners and managers.

Although nominally a member of the board, the real marketing manager was Luciano Benetton, who in the past had formally occupied this position many times. Under him, the commercial director and the area managers composed the marketing department. Nearly all the members of the commercial organization had been hired by him, and were used to working directly with him. Area managers were company employees in charge of territories run by a number of agents. There were seven area managers for the nearly 80 agents. All the area managers were Italians.

Riccardo Weiss, the area manager in charge of the United States, Canada, Japan and countries of the Eastern bloc, described one of the tasks of an area manager: 'He does every month what agents do every day: have a look at each shop and its problems. We are always watching the movement store by store. Sometimes we talk directly with shopowners, although agents don't like that. But they need to hear the voice of the company from time to time.' Mr Weiss went once a month to the United States and talked almost daily with every agent by phone.

Another important task an area manager performed was the collection of the money from the shops. On average, an area manager devoted 30–5 per cent of his time to follow payment problems. His rush periods were May–June for the spring/summer collection, and October–November for the autumn/winter one.

Agents

As shown in Exhibit 4, the agents constituted the interface between Benetton and the shops. They were not Benetton employees, and had exclusive rights over a sales territory. Luciano Benetton had personally hand-picked most of the 80 agents. Right from the start, Luciano looked for a new king of agent, who could fit with the particular philosophy of the emerging company. He wanted 'personal attitudes, rather than business experience'. As an executive put it, 'The thing that really strikes Luciano is the entrepreneurial spirit in an agent, rather than anything else.' The company's relationship with its agents was managed largely on a verbal basis of trust: only in 1984 had formal contracts begun to be written between Benetton and the agents. Agents rarely had had to be replaced for failure to meet expectations.

Twice a year, all agents had to spend one week at headquarters getting to know the new collection for the season and selecting a sample of 30–40 per cent of the 600 items of the total collection. After this, every agent went back to his territory and took about 30–40 days to present the sample collection to each shop owner. Then the agent helped the shop owner in selecting the most suitable articles for each particular shop, and asked for orders. At the end of each day, the agent sent the orders collected in that day to headquarters. Articles were shipped directly to the shops from the central warehouse, without passing through the agent. During the season, the shop owner sent the money directly to Benetton, dividing the total payment in three quotas, which were paid 30, 60 and 90 days from the date of actual receipt of the merchandise. After this, the company paid the agent a 4 per cent commission on the value of goods shipped from the factories.

Mr Manlio Tonolo was the agent for the north-east region of Italy. He had joined the company in 1969 as the manager of the second shop opened by the company in Padova. He had worked with Luciano Benetton in a men's clothing store when they were teenagers. Mr Tonolo explained the criteria for selecting an agent at that time: 'The candidate had to have an enthusiastic predisposition towards the work itself. Luciano was looking for people who could be potential consumers rather than agents, who could understand the product – the multicoloured sweater, which back then was completely unconventional – and believe in it.'

The main responsibilities of the agents were: (1) To select the location of new shops. (2) To find and select potential investors for new shops. (3) To help new clients in starting shops and train them, usually in the agent's stores. (4) To look at the shops and help owners to manage and control their shops. (5) To present the collection to shop managers and help them in choosing goods. (6) To collect orders and transmit them to headquarters. (7) To encourage image competition among shops.

Agents were also encouraged to reinvest part of their commissions in opening new shops, thus becoming clients themselves. This mechanism produced a 'self-multiplying effect' in the retailing network. This policy of encouraging agents to have and run their own shops helped them to get first-hand knowledge of the retail business and its problems in practice. For instance, Mr Tonolo owned 35–40 shops out of the 200 he supervised in north-east Italy. More than competitors, the shops owned by him served as examples to the shops recently opened in such things as window dressing, products display, overall image, etc. Besides this, according to Mr Tonolo, the concentration of shops in an area of a town, instead of reducing the sales of each one, tended to increase them.

Agents had normally a small organization to perform their multiple activities. Although agents visited the shops regularly, they usually hired young assistants who controlled the shops' overall image and problems on a weekly basis. In addition, the assistants helped the agent in the task of monitoring the new trends in young people's culture. They had to visit the places where they met (discotheques, bars, etc.) and see how they behaved, not only what they wore.

The majority of European agents were Italians, and so were almost 50 per cent of the US agents. Some of these had started in Europe and then moved to America. Benetton had found it difficult to find agents with the 'right mentality' in America, so they had to replace them with Italians, already familiar with the firm. These had had their share of difficulties to penetrate the American market, because of their ignorance of laws and regulations. 'They had too much of the Italian mentality,' as one executive pointed out.

Shops

Fewer than ten of the Benetton stores worldwide were owned and operated by the company. These were located in key cities such as Milan, New York, Rome and Düsseldorf. The rest were set up by independent entrepreneurs, who often owned several shops in the same area. Benetton approved location of the shops and Luciano personally oversaw the more strategic sites.

Shop owners were not retail experts. As Luciano Benetton put it: 'We have caused a new type of retailer to become important who until the day before was perhaps a florist or a hairdresser. His prior career was of no importance, but he had to have the right spirit to work in a Benetton shop.' Mr Weiss, area manager for North America, Japan and Eastern Europe, commented: 'Experts in retailing are not good shop owners (and managers) because they don't understand very well the particular Benetton system.' When asked about this 'system', he mentioned the following characteristics: (1) New window display every week. (2) Good sales people in stores, good service. (3) competition of image among shops (window decoration, garments diversity and display). (4) 150 items per shop. (5) No price competition. (6) Initial prices set at factory or 'strongly suggested' (US case). (7) Markdowns discussed with agents.

Turnover among shop owners was low. For example, of the 200 shops controlled by Mr Tonolo in the northeast of Italy, which were owned by 50–60 people, only 5 or 6 shop owners had been replaced in a period of 10 years. The growth of the network of shops had been enormous, as can been seen in Exhibit 5.

Retailers didn't sign franchise agreements (Luciano Benetton hated bureaucracy and found that the current arrangement 'stimulates the full capacity of the owners'). Also, they were neither required to pay Benetton a fee for use of its name nor a royalty based on a percentage of sales or profits. Therefore, the term 'franchising' in describing the Benetton retailing network was a misnomer.

All Benetton outlets were required to follow basic merchandising concepts, the most important among them being that all merchandise must be displayed on open shelves accessible to customers, who could touch it and try it on. The open displays in an otherwise undecorated space create an impression of great colour and fashion to the window-shopping customer. Important also was the selection of adequate salespeople; they must be young and very customer-oriented. They had to be able to advise the customer on which garments coordinated well and what were the best colours for a particular person to wear. Benetton used five mechanisms to control its 'identity' in spite of the dramatic increase in the number of shops:

1. Standardization of the shop image. Retailers had to choose among 12 basic layouts and fixture selections. This furniture must be provided by only three Italian suppliers, located near headquarters.

2. Central supply of advertising material, which was produced at headquarters and shipped to the shops all over the world. Shops were allowed to do some advertising in local media (mainly newspapers) after the company had checked the advertisement.

3. A strict pricing policy. The computer back at Benetton printed the price in local currencies in each tag attached to every article. For the US market it was a 'suggested' price.

4. Benetton shops could only sell Benetton products.

5. Assistance to new clients.

Many people had called Benetton 'the fast food of the fashion industry', a comparison Luciano Benetton didn't disagree with: 'I like the idea that we are similar to fast food in the sense of organization, the efficiency, the cleanliness of image, the publicity.'[6]

Promotion Strategy

Employing one agency in Paris for France (Eldorado) and another in New York (J. Walter Thompson) for the rest of the world, the company had coordinated its advertising worldwide. Since the product was the same all over the world, the company had been able to maintain the consistency and international character of its ads. The themes, 'Benetton – All the Colours in the World', in 1983–4; and 'United Colours of Benetton', from 1985 on, had appeared on outdoor billboards and in numerous magazines all over the world, always in English. These campaigns were the results of brainstorming sessions held by Luciano Benetton and several friend/consultants including photographers and designers, such as Oliviero Toscani.

About 4 per cent of Benetton's sales was spent on direct advertising. Additionally, the company sponsored sports events, including rugby and basketball teams, and a Formula 1 racing team.

Global Outlook

When Luciano Benetton was asked if he wanted Benetton to become another McDonald's, he commented:

> 'Not McDonald's for the same level of goods, the same consumer, but, yes, for the distribution all over the world. I would like us to be everywhere. Another company we might compare ourselves to might be Coca-Cola or Pepsi-Cola, since we aim our product at young people. The idea behind Benetton – which was basically that of mass-produced, medium priced fashion that moves with the trends yet maintains something classic – had not changed since our clothing started to become not just a strictly European product but a product for the whole world. In America, in Australia, in Japan – where we envision having two hundred shops – it has been consistently accepted. In all these countries, the prototype client remains the same – young and female. Naturally, there are regional differences. In America, for example, we reach a public a little different from that in Europe – a more sophisticated public, which travels, and might have seen the product first in Europe.'[7]

In spite of their general success entering new markets, there were certain countries where the company had found serious difficulties due to tariffs, import quotas and other protectionist barriers. Benetton decided to invest in local facilities in order to avoid current or potential protectionism. Benetton Sarl. in France; Benetton S.A. in Spain; Tabando Ltd in Scotland; and Benetton USA Inc., were the four foreign manufacturing subsidiaries set up by Benetton International N.V., based in Holland. There was no international manufacturing network at Benetton: these manufacturing units outside Italy produced only to satisfy local needs, and they didn't supply all the goods needed in those countries. For example, the plant located in North Carolina produced only about 5 per cent of what was sold in the US market.

In other countries – where Benetton couldn't enter through exports and wasn't interested in building manufacturing facilities or in developing joint ventures with local partners – licensing agreements to use the Benetton trademarks were signed. Thus, local companies in Brazil, Mexico, Japan, Portugal, India and Argentina paid royalties to Benetton for each item they produced and sold. There were a total of 183 licensed operations in these six countries. Although these operations generated only a 5 per cent licence profit for the firm, they must adhere to Benetton standards.

The range of products and the manufacturing technology were exactly those of Benetton, because all these licensees visited Ponzano Veneto's factories, bought the machinery under the firm's supervision, etc.

Information Systems

The company had committed itself to using the best information systems available and to improving them when they could. Benetton spent about 1.2 per cent of its annual turnover on this, including hardware, software and personnel. As the company was growing at a rapid rate each year the information system was always being restructured to cope with the new demands.

The most important of these systems was the connection between the agents and the firm. They had started with a dedicated network of minicomputers located in seven European cities, which acted as nodes, connected to the company's mainframes in Italy. As retail operations had grown, this dedicated network became increasingly expensive. Then, after a successful test in North America, agents were connected to the Mark III General Electric Information System's value-added network service available round the clock in 250 cities in 25 countries. The service provided network access and data filing software. All application software was Benetton's own. Mark III replaced the need to operate the Information System Centre at headquarters 24 hours a day and relieved the burden of long distance, often transcontinental, telephone charges for data transmissions. Use of Mark III was indispensable during reassortment.

'Keeping track of the financial information of each one of the 4,000 shops in the world is completely mad and useless,' argued Bruno Zuccaro, the manager of information systems at Benetton, and former executive of Zanussi and Honeywell. This had been an information systems project in the past, but had failed due to administrative and technical problems. The project consisted of having a cash register in each single shop to keep track of the shop's sales and financial situation. This would have allowed the company to know the cash flow of each shop and the money it had. However, it was neither accepted by shop owners nor by the Italian law that specified a certain type of cash register for tax purposes.

The Information Systems Department was working on a project to connect a sample of a few representative shops all over the world. The sample contained shops that started selling early in each season due to their condition of international centres where innovative people went, such as upscale ski resorts. By installing a computerized point of sale (POS) system in each of these shops, the company could gather information about fashion trends in design, colours, etc., well in advance of the season, which was critical for planning and producing the reassortment articles. This project was being tested in five Italian shops to see how it worked and how well it was accepted by shop owners and agents.

Each shop owner was free to manage his or her shops as he or she pleased, but the Information Systems' staff had developed a software package for retail shop management which it planned to encourage retail shops to buy. The software ran on an IBM personal computer equipped with a bar code reader, for all garment tags came from the factory with critical information printed in bar code. The system processed sales, inventory, orders and receipt of goods.

The Information Systems Department had not done much to connect the subcontractors' network. The department was waiting for the moment when the company would deal with just a few of them, the bigger ones. In 1987, the firm felt that they were too many and most of them too small for attempting this task. The company knew the production capacity of every subcontractor, but the production scheduling and the allocation process of the production plan to each contractor was not done by computer. Therefore, Benetton didn't know the exact amount of work that each subcontractor had in a given moment.

IDEAS FOR THE FUTURE

Changes in the Subcontractors' Network

Benetton was working with a constellation of 350 subcontracted production units. The idea was to simplify the complex problem of being in touch with so many external firms, and deal only with the 9 or 10 largest subcontractors. These in turn would be in touch with all the medium-sized and small contractors. To control those big contractors better, Benetton private owners – not the company – would own shares in all of them.

The US Subsidiary

Benetton was planning to increase the production volume and the range of products in the US subsidiary located in North Carolina. It was currently making T-shirts and classic trousers there, which only accounted for 5 per cent of the total US consumption of Benetton products.

There were two main reasons to manufacture in this overseas facility: to avoid protectionism problems, and the fact that some Americans preferred garments 'made in USA'. Other reasons for producing locally rather than importing from Italy were the wild gyrations of exchange rates, and the tariffs and transportation costs the company had to bear. As a result of this last factor, final prices to consumers were 35–40 per cent higher in the United States than in Europe. Benetton had to pay 24–25 per cent in tariffs and 7–8 per cent in transportation.

Financial Matters

The company was planning to go public in the New York Stock Exchange, because it wanted to reinforce its international image and to secure funds for a planned diversification process, although the company had already accumulated a substantial amount of financial resources in the last years.

Diversification of the Benetton Group

In December 1985 the holding company changed its name from INVEP S.p.A. to Benetton Group S.p.A. and increased its capital stock from 8 billion lire to 70 billion lire by capitalizing reserves.

The INVEP holding, created in 1981, encompassed all the business activities controlled equally by the four Benettons. The main business of the group had traditionally been Benetton S.p.A., accounting for about two-thirds of the group sales. In December 1985, the three different companies named Benetton Lana S.p.A., Benetton Cotone S.p.A. and Benetton Jeans S.p.A., were merged into Benetton S.p.A. becoming its three manufacturing divisions.

The group invested from the beginning in related business activities, such as the 50 per cent share in Fiorucci S.p.A., the Milan-based design firm, acquired in 1981, and the 70 per cent of Calzaturificio di Varese, an Italian shoe manufacturer, bought in 1982. The first investment allowed the company to enter into the more rarefied realms of European fashion, and the second provided them with shoes for sale along with sweaters and shirts in Benetton shops around the world.

However, both investments were only marginally profitable. At the end of 1983, Luciano Benetton commented about Calzaturificio di Varese: 'As an experiment it has been quite interesting, but the factory is old and there have been many problems.'[8] However, after two or three years of operations, this company began to show positive results and it was considered a success. On the other hand, the investment in Fiorucci S.p.A. was sold in 1985. At the time of that sale, Benetton purchased 5 per cent of Nolan Norton Italia S.r.l., a company in the computer industry.

Benetton had taken advantage of its well-known trademark in licensing agreements covering a wide range of consumer products, like cosmetics, perfumes, socks, toys, household linen, etc. It had also arranged successful alliances with Bulova to sell watches with the Benetton name, and with Polaroid for the manufacture of Benetton sunglasses.

The diversification process of the company had gone beyond related business activities and entered into the financial services sector. Some of these investments were: 70 per cent of In Factor S.p.A., a factoring subsidiary with a capital stock of 5 billion lire; a 50 per cent stake in two leasing companies; Leasing S.p.A. and Finleasing Italia S.p.A.; 20 per cent of the private *Banco di Trento e Bolzano* in northern Italy; and a 10 per cent stake in leasing companies in France and West Germany, which were run by *Banca Nazionale del Lavoro,* Italy's biggest bank.

Luciano Benetton had announced new projects for the coming years: 'The future will include diversification in retailing, financial services in banking and elsewhere, in Italy and abroad.'[9] According to Aldo Palmeri: 'Benetton's plan to develop financial services will call for the company to achieve, within two years, a 50–50 per cent mix in group turnover between industrial and financial revenues.'[10] Benetton was planning to:

- Expand its factoring and leasing subsidiaries both in Italy and abroad. It had received authorization from the Ministry of Foreign Trade in Rome to operate in the factoring business outside of Italy.

- Form a financial services and venture capital company in Milan that would engage in currency swaps, syndicated loans, corporate finance, underwriting, and other investment banking activities for the clothing and textile sector, in partnership with another big Italian clothing manufacturer.

Carlo Gilardi, Benetton's finance director admitted that 'although we have a handful of citicorp specialists in currency swaps, factoring and leasing, it will be necessary to enlarge our human and managerial resources substantially to reach our goal.'[11]

EXHIBIT 1
Financial highlights
(Italian lire millions).

Consolidated Balance Sheet as of 31 December		
Assets	1986	1985
Current Assets	833,192	494,891
Investments and Other		
Non-current Assets	5,431	6,372
Fixed Assets (net)	134,636	80,335
Intangible Assets	15,548	10,215
TOTAL ASSETS	988,807	591,813
Liabilities and Stockholders' Equity		
Current Liabilities	373,663	317,203
Long-term Liabilities	251,148	76,730
Capital Gains Roll-over Reserve	–	130
Minority Interest in		
Consolidated Subsidiaries	2,437	4,742
Stockholders' Equity	361,559	193,008
TOTAL	988,807	591,813

Consolidated Statements of Income		
	1986	1985
Revenue	1,079,060	879,535
Cost of sales	701,818	558,501
Gross profit	377,242	321,034
Selling, general and		
administrative expenses	169,303	150,653
Income from operations	207,939	170,381
Other (income) expenses	1,878	6,368
Gain from Disposal of treasury stock	–	3,198
Income taxes	(87,008)	(69,788)
Deferred income taxes	(5,468)	–
Income before minority interest	113,585	97,423
Income to minority interest	(556)	(1,226)
NET INCOME FOR THE YEAR	113,029	96,197

EXHIBIT 2
Flow of materials.

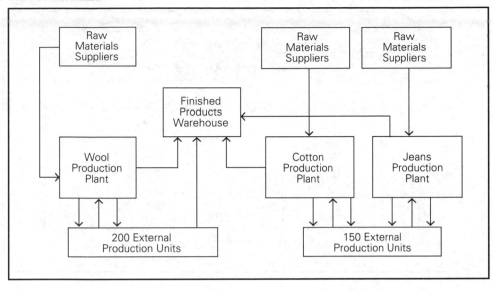

EXHIBIT 3
Summary chart of the manufacturing process in the wool division.

Production Phase	% Performed Internally	% Performed Externally	Number of Contractors	% Degree of Exclusiveness
Knitting	1	9	70–80	90
Assembling	0	100	100	100
Chemical Treatment	25–30	70–5	3	100
Dyeing	100	0	–	–
Finishing	5	95	20	100

EXHIBIT 4
Distribution network.

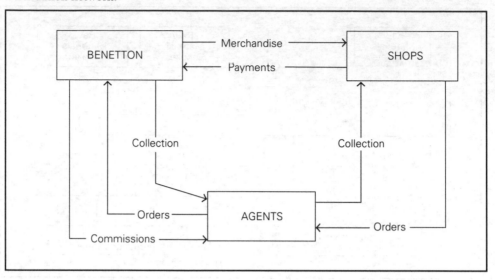

EXHIBIT 5
Stores in operation at year-end (not including licenses).

Year-End	1982	1983	1984	1985	1986	1987*	1988*	1989*	1990*
Stores	1,917	2,296	2,644	3,200	3,893	4,650	5,300	6,200	7,000
Change	n/a	379	348	556	693	757	650	900	800

*Morgan Stanley Research Estimates

1-7

CANON: COMPETING ON CAPABILITIES*

In 1961, following the runaway success of the company's model 914 office copier, Joseph C. Wilson, President of Xerox Corporation, was reported to have said, 'I keep asking myself, when am I going to wake up? Things just aren't this good in life.' Indeed, the following decade turned out to be better than anything Wilson could have dreamed. Between 1960 and 1970, Xerox increased its sales 40 per cent per year from $40 million to $1.7 billion and raised its after-tax profits from $2.6 million to $187.7 million. In 1970, with 93 per cent market share worldwide and a brand name that was synonymous with copying, Xerox appeared as invincible in its industry as any company ever could.

When Canon, 'the camera company from Japan', jumped into the business in the late 1960s, most observers were sceptical. Less than a tenth the size of Xerox, Canon had no direct sales or service organization to reach the corporate market for copiers, not did it have a process technology to bypass the 500 patents that guarded Xerox's Plain Paper Copier (PPC) process. Reacting to the spate of recent entries in the business including Canon, Arthur D. Little predicted in 1969 that no company would be able to challenge Xerox's monopoly in PPCs in the 1970s because its patents presented an insurmountable barrier.

Yet, over the next two decades, Canon rewrote the rule book on how copiers were supposed to be produced and sold as it built up $5 billion in revenues in the business, emerging as the second largest global player in terms of sales and surpassing

---

*This case was prepared by Mary Ackenhusen, Research Associate, under the supervision of Sumantra Ghoshal, Associate Professor at INSEAD. It is intended to be used as a basis for class discussion rather than to illustrate either effective or ineffective handling of an administrative situation.

Xerox in the number of units sold. According to the Canon Handbook, the company's formula for success as displayed initially in the copier business is 'synergistic management of the total technological capabilities of the company, combining the full measure of Canon's know how in fine optics, precision mechanics, electronics and fine chemicals'. Canon continues to grow and diversify using this strategy. Its vision, as described in 1991 by Ryuzaburo Kaku, president of the company, is 'to become a premier global company of the size of IBM combined with Matsushita'.

INDUSTRY BACKGROUND

The photocopying machine has often been compared with the typewriter as one of the few triggers that have fundamentally changed the ways of office work. But, while a mechanical Memograph machine for copying had been introduced by the A.B. Dick Company of Chicago as far back as 1887, it was only in the second half of this century that the copier market exploded with Xerox's commercialization of the 'electrophotography' process invented by Chester Carlson.

Xerox

Carlson's invention used an electrostatic process to transfer images from one sheet of paper to another. Licensed to Xerox in 1948, this invention led to two different photocopying technologies. The Coated Paper Copying (CPC) technology transferred the reflection of an image from the original directly to specialized zinc-oxide coated paper, while the Plain Paper Copying (PPC) technology transferred the image indirectly to ordinary paper through a rotating drum coated with charged particles. While either dry or liquid toner could be used to develop the image, the dry toner was generally preferable in both technologies. A large number of companies entered the CPC market in the 1950s and 1960s based on technology licensed from Xerox or RCA (to whom Xerox had earlier licensed this technology). However, PPC remained a Xerox monopoly since the company had refused to license any technology remotely connected to the PPC process and had protected the technology with over 500 patents.

Because of the need for specialized coated paper, the cost per copy was higher for CPC. Also, this process could produce only one copy at a time, and the copies tended to fade when exposed to heat or light. PPC, on the other hand, produced copies at a lower operating cost that were also indistinguishable from the original. The PPC machines were much more expensive, however, and were much larger in size. Therefore, they required a central location in the user's office. The smaller and less expensive CPC machines, in contrast, could be placed on individual desks. Over time, the cost and quality advantages of PPC, together with its ability to make multiple copies at high speed, made it the dominant technology and, with it, Xerox's model of centralized copying, the industry norm.

This business concept of centralized copying required a set of capabilities that Xerox developed and which, in turn, served as its major strengths and as key barriers to entry to the business. Given the advantages of volume and speed, all large companies found centralized copying highly attractive and they became the key customers for photocopying machines. In order to support this corporate customer base, Xerox's product designs and upgrades emphasized economies of higher volume copying. To market the product effectively to these customers, Xerox also built up an extensive direct sales and service organization of over 12,000 sales representatives and 15,000 service people. Forty per cent of the sales reps' time was spent 'hand holding' to prevent even minor dissatisfaction. Service reps, dressed in suits and carrying their tools in briefcases, performed preventative maintenance and prided themselves on reducing the average time between breakdown and repair to a few hours.

Further, with the high cost of each machine and the fast rate of model introductions, Xerox developed a strategy of leasing rather than selling machines to customers. Various options were available, but typically the customers paid a monthly charge on the number of copies made. The charge covered not only machine costs but also those of the paper and toner that Xerox supplied and the service visits. This lease strategy, together with the carefully cultivated service image, served as key safeguards from competition, as they tied the customers into Xerox and significantly raised their switching costs.

Unlike some other American corporations, Xerox had an international orientation right from the beginning. Even before it had a successful commercial copier, Xerox built up an international presence through joint ventures which allowed the company to minimize its capital investment abroad. In 1956, it ventured with the Rank Organization Ltd in the United Kingdom to form Rank Xerox. In 1962, Rank Xerox became a 50 per cent partner with Fuji Photo to form Fuji Xerox which sold copiers in Japan. Through these joint ventures, Xerox built up sales and service capabilities in these key markets similar to those it had in the United States. There were some 5,000 sales people in Europe, 3,000 in Japan and over 7,000 and 3,000 service reps, respectively. Xerox also built limited design capabilities in both the joint ventures for local market customization, which developed into significant research establishments in their own rights in later years.

Simultaneously, Xerox maintained high levels of investment in both technology and manufacturing to support its growing market. It continued to spend over $100 million a year in R&D, exceeding the total revenues from the copier business that any of its competitors were earning in the early 1970s, and also invested heavily in large-size plants not only in the United States, but also in the United Kingdom and Japan.

Competition in the 1970s

Xerox's PPC patents began to expire in the 1970s, heralding a storm of new entrants. In 1970, IBM offered the first PPC copier not sold by Xerox, which resulted in Xerox suing IBM for patent infringement and violation of trade secrets. Canon marketed a PPC copier the same year through the development of an independent PPC technology which they licensed selectively to others. By 1973, competition had expanded to include players from the office equipment industry (IBM, SCM, Litton, Pitney Bowes), the electronics industry (Toshiba, Sharp), the reprographics industry (Ricoh, Mita, Copyer, 3M, AB Dick, Addressograph/Multigraph), the photographic equipment industry (Canon, Kodak, Minolta, Konishiroku) and the suppliers of copy paper (Nashua, Dennison, Saxon). By the 1980s many of these new entrants, including IBM, had lost large amounts of money and quit the business. A few of the newcomers managed to achieve a high level of success, however, and copiers became a major business for them. Specifically, copiers were generating 40 per cent of Canon's revenues by 1990.

CANON

Canon was founded in 1933 with the ambition to produce a sophisticated 35 mm camera to rival that of Germany's world-class Leica model. In only two years' time, it had emerged as Japan's leading producer of high-class cameras. During the war, Canon utilized its optics expertise to produce an X-ray machine which was adopted by the Japanese military. After the war, Canon was able to market its high-end camera successfully, and by the mid-1950s it was the largest camera manufacturer in Japan. Building off its optics technology, Canon then expanded its product line to include a mid-range camera, an 8 mm video camera, television lenses and micrographic equipment. It also began developing markets for its products outside of Japan, mainly in the United States and Canada.

Diversification was always very important to Canon in order to further its growth, and a new products R&D section was established in 1962 to explore the fields of copy machines, auto-focusing cameras, strobe-integrated cameras, home VCRs and electronic calculators. A separate, special operating unit was also established to introduce new non-camera products resulting from the diversification effort.

The first product to be targeted was the electronic calculator. This product was challenging because it required Canon engineers to develop new expertise in microelectronics in order to incorporate thousands of transistors and diodes in a compact, desk model machine. Tekeshi Mitarai, president of Canon at that time, was against developing the product because it was seen to be too difficult and risky. Nevertheless, a dedicated group of engineers believed in the challenge and developed the calculator in secrecy. Over a year later, top management gave their support to the project. In 1964, the result of the development effort was introduced as the Canola 130, the world's first 10-key numeric pad calculator. With this product line, Canon dominated the Japanese electronic calculator market in the 1960s.

Not every diversification effort was a success, however. In 1956, Canon began development of the synchroreader, a device for writing and reading with a sheet of paper coated with magnetic material. When introduced in 1959, the product received high praise for its technology. But, because the design was not patented, another firm introduced a similar product at half the price. There was no market for the high priced and incredibly heavy Canon product. Ultimately, the firm was forced to disassemble the finished inventories and sell off the usable parts in the 'once-used' components market.

Move into Copiers

Canon began research into copier technology in 1959, and, in 1962, it formed a research group dedicated to developing a plain paper copier (PPC) technology. The only known PPC process was protected by hundreds of Xerox patents, but Canon felt that only this technology promised sufficient quality, speed, economy and ease of maintenance to successfully capture a large portion of the market. Therefore, corporate management challenged the researchers to develop a new PPC process which would not violate the Xerox patents.

In the meantime, the company entered the copier business by licensing the 'inferior' CPC technology in 1965 from RCA. Canon decided not to put the name of the company on this product and marketed it under the brand name Confax 1000 in Japan only. Three years later, Canon licensed a liquid toner technology from an Australian company and combined this with the RCA technology to introduce the CanAll Series. To sell the copier in Japan, Canon formed a separate company, International Image Industry. The copier was sold as an OEM to Scott Paper in the United States, who sold it under its own brand name.

Canon's research aiming at developing a PPC technical alternative to xerography paid off with the announcement of the 'New Process' (NP) in 1968. This successful research effort not only produced an alternative process but also taught Canon the importance of patent law: how not to violate patents and how to protect new technology. The NP process was soon protected by close to 500 patents.

The first machine with the NP technology, the NP1100, was introduced in Japan in 1970. It was the first copier sold by Canon to carry the Canon brand name. It produced ten copies per minute and utilized dry toner. As was the standard in the Japanese market, the copier line was sold outright to customers from the beginning. After two years of experience in the domestic market, Canon entered the overseas market, except North America, with this machine.

The second generation of the NP system was introduced in Japan in 1972 as the NPL7. It was a marked improvement because it eliminated a complex fusing technology, simplified developing and cleaning, and made toner supply easier through a new system developed to use liquid toner. Compared with the Xerox equivalent, it was more economical, more compact, more reliable and still had the same or better quality of copies.

With the NP system, Canon began a sideline which was to become quite profitable: licensing. The first generation NP system was licensed to AM, and Canon also provided it with machines on an OEM basis. The second generation was again licensed to AM as well as to Saxon, Ricoh and Copyer. Canon accumulated an estimated $32 million in licence fees between 1975 and 1982.

Canon continued its product introductions with a stream of state-of-the-art technological innovations throughout the 1970s. In 1973 it added colour to the NP system; in 1975, it added laser beam printing technology. Its first entry into high volume copiers took place in 1978 with a model which was targeted at the Xerox 9200. The NP200 was introduced in 1979 and went on to win a gold medal at the Leipzig Fair for being the most economical and productive copier available. By 1982, copiers had surpassed cameras as the company's largest revenue generator. (See Exhibits 1 and 2 for Canon's financial and sales by product line.)

The Personal Copier

In the late 1970s, top management began searching for a new market for the PPC copier. They had recently experienced a huge success with the introduction of the

AE-1 camera in 1976 and wanted a similar success in copiers. The AE-1 was a very compact single-lens reflex camera, the first camera that used a microprocessor to control electronically functions of exposure, film rewind and strobe. The product had been developed through a focused, cross-functional project team effort which had resulted in a substantial reduction in the number of components, as well as in automated assembly and the use of unitized parts. Because of these improvements, the AE-1 enjoyed a 20 per cent cost advantage over competitive models in the same class.

After studying the distribution of offices in Japan by size (see Exhibit 3), Canon decided to focus on a latent segment that Xerox had ignored. This was the segment comprised of small offices (segment E) who could benefit from the functionality offered by photocopiers but did not require the high-speed machines available in the market. Canon management believed that a low-volume 'value for money' machine could generate a large demand in this segment. From this analysis emerged the business concept of a 'personal side desk' machine which could not only create a new market in small offices, but potentially also induce decentralization of the copy function in large offices. Over time, the machine might even create demand for a personal copier for home use. This would be a copier that up to now no one had thought possible. Canon felt that, to be successful in this market, the product had to cost half the price of a conventional copier (target price $1,000), be maintenance-free, and provide ten times more reliability.

Top management took their 'dream' to the engineers, who, after careful consideration, took on the challenge. The machine would build on their previous expertise in microelectronics but would go much further in terms of material, functional component, design and production engineering technologies. The team's slogan was 'Let's make the AE-1 of copiers!', expressing the necessity of know-how transfer between the camera and copier divisions as well as their desire for a similar type of success. The effort was led by the director of the Reprographic Production Development Centre. His cross-functional team of 200 was the second largest ever assembled at Canon (the largest had been that of the AE-1 camera).

During the development effort, a major issue arose concerning the paper size that the new copier would accept. Canon Sales (the sales organization for Japan) wanted the machine to use a larger-than-letter-size paper which accounted for 60 per cent of the Japanese market. This size was not necessary for sales outside of Japan and would add 20–30 per cent to the machine's cost as well as make the copier more difficult to service. After much debate worldwide, the decision was made to forgo the ability to utilize the larger paper size in the interest of better serving the global market.

Three years later the concept was a reality. The new PC (personal copier) employed a new-cartridge-based technology, which allowed the user to replace the photoreceptive drum, charging device, toner assembly and cleaner with a cartridge every 2,000 copies, thus eliminating the need to maintain the copier regularly. This enabled Canon engineers to meet the cost and reliability targets. The revolutionary product was the smallest, lightest copier ever sold, and created a large market which had previously not existed. Large offices adjusted their copying strategies to include decentralized copying, and many small offices and even homes could now afford a personal copier. Again, Canon's patent knowledge was utilized to protect this research, and the cartridge technology was not licensed to other manufacturers. Canon has maintained its leadership in personal copiers into the 1990s.

BUILDING CAPABILITIES

Canon is admired for its technical innovations, marketing expertise and low-cost quality manufacturing. These are the result of a long-term strategy to become a premier company. Canon has frequently acquired outside expertise so that it could better focus internal investments on skills of strategic importance. This approach of extensive outsourcing and focused internal development has required consistent direction from top management and the patience to allow the company to become well grounded in one skill area before tasking the organization with the next objective.

Technology

Canon's many innovative products, which enabled the company to grow quickly in the 1970s and 1980s are in large part the result of a carefully orchestrated use of technology and the capacity for managing rapid technological change. Attesting to its prolific output of original research is the fact that Canon has been among the leaders in number of patents issued worldwide throughout the 1980s.

These successes have been achieved in an organization that has firmly pursued a strategy of decentralized R&D. Most of Canon's R&D personnel are employed by the product divisions where 80–90 per cent of the company's patentable inventions originate. Each product division has its own development centre which is tasked with short- to medium-term product design and improvement of production systems. Most product development is performed by cross-functional teams. The work of the development groups is coordinated by an R&D headquarters group.

The Corporate Technical Planning and Operation centre is responsible for long-term strategic R&D planning. Canon also has a main research centre which supports state-of-the-art research in optics, electronics, new materials and information technology. There are three other corporate research centres which apply this state-of-the-art reseach to product development.

Canon acknowledges that it has neither the resources nor the time to develop all necessary technologies and has therefore often traded or bought specific technologies from a variety of external partners. Furthermore, it has used joint ventures and technology transfers as a strategic tool for mitigating foreign trade tensions in Europe and the United States. For example, Canon had two purposes in mind when it made an equity participation in CPF Deutsch, an office equipment marketing firm in Germany. Primarily, it believed that this move would help develop the German market for its copiers; but it did not go unnoticed among top management that CPF owned Tetras, a copier maker who at that time was pressing dumping charges against Japanese copier makers. Canon also used Burroughs as an OEM for office automation equipment in order to acquire Burroughs software and know-how and participated in joint development agreements with Eastman Kodak and Texas Instruments. Exhibit 4 provides a list of the company's major joint ventures.

Canon also recognizes that its continued market success depends on its ability to exploit new research into marketable products quickly. It has worked hard to reduce the new product introduction cycle through a cross-functional programme called TS 1/2 whose purpose is to cut development time by 50 per cent on a continuous basis. The main thrust of this programme is the classification of development projects by total time required and the critical human resources needed so that these two parameters can be optimized for each product depending on its importance for Canon's corporate strategy. This allows product teams to be formed around several classifications of product development priorities of which 'best sellers' will receive the most emphasis. These are the products aimed at new markets or segments with large potential demands. Other classifications include products necessary to catch up with competitive offerings, product refinements intended to enhance customer satisfaction, and long-run marathon products which will take considerable time to develop. In all development classifications, Canon emphasizes three factors to reduce time to market: the fostering of engineering ability, efficient technical support systems and careful reviews of product development at all stages.

Canon is also working to divert its traditional product focus into more of a market focus. To this end, Canon R&D personnel participate in international product strategy meetings, carry out consumer research, join in marketing activities and attend meetings in the field at both domestic and foreign sales subsidiaries.

Marketing

Canon's effective marketing is the result of step-by-step, calculated introduction strategies. Normally, the product is first introduced and perfected in the home market before being sold internationally. Canon has learned how to capture learning from the Japanese market quickly so that the time span between introduction in Japan and abroad is as short as a few months. Furthermore, the company will not simultaneously launch a new product through a new distribution channel – its strategy is to minimize risk by introducing a new product through known channels first. New channels will only be created, if necessary, after the product has proven to be successful.

The launch of the NP copier exemplifies this strategy. Canon initially sold these copiers in Japan by direct sales through its Business Machines Sales organization, which had been set up in 1968 to sell the calculator product line. This sales organization was merged with the camera sales organization in 1971 to form Canon Sales. By 1972, after three years of experience in producing the NP product line, the company entered into a new distribution channel, that of dealers, to supplement direct selling.

The NP copier line was not marketed in the United States until 1974, after production and distribution were running smoothly in Japan. The US distribution system was similar to that used in Japan, with seven sales subsidiaries for direct selling and a network of independent dealers.

By the late 1970s, Canon had built up a strong dealer network in the United States which supported both sales and service of the copiers. The dealer channel was responsible for rapid growth in copier sales, and, by the early 1980s, Canon copiers were sold almost exclusively through this channel. Canon enthusiastically supported the dealers with attractive sales incentive programmes, management training and social outings. Dealers were certified to sell copiers only after completing a course in service training. The company felt that a close relationship with its dealers was a vital asset that allowed it to understand and react to customers' needs and problems in a timely manner. At the same time, Canon also maintained a direct selling mechanism through wholly owned sales subsidiaries in Japan, the United States and Europe in order to target large customers and government accounts.

The introduction of its low-end personal copier in 1983 was similarly planned to minimize risk. Initially, Canon's NP dealers in Japan were not interested in the product due to its low maintenance needs and inability to utilize large paper sizes. Thus, PCs were distributed through the firm's office supply stores who were already selling its personal calculators. After seeing the success of the PC, the NP dealers began to carry the copier.

In the United States, the PC was initially sold only through existing dealers and direct sales channels due to limited availability of the product. Later, it was sold through competitors' dealers and office supply stores, and, eventually, the distribution channels were extended to include mass merchandisers. Canon already had considerable experience in mass merchandising from its camera business.

Advertising has always been an integral part of Canon's marketing strategy. President Kaku believes that Canon must have a corporate brand name which is outstanding to succeed in its diversification effort. 'Customers must prefer products because they bear the name Canon,' he says. As described by the company's finance director, 'If a brand name is unknown, and there is no advertising, you have to sell it cheap. It's not our policy to buy share with a low price. We establish our brand with advertising at a reasonably high price.'

Therefore, when the NP-200 was introduced in 1980, 10 per cent of the selling price was spent on advertising; for the launch of the personal copier, advertising expenditure was estimated to be 20 per cent of the selling price. Canon has also sponsored various sporting events including World Cup football, the Williams motor racing team, and the ice dancers Torvill and Dean. The company expects its current expansion into the home automation market to be greatly enhanced by the brand image it has built in office equipment. (See Exhibit 1 for Canon's advertising expenditures through 1990.)

Manufacturing

Canon's goal in manufacturing is to produce the best quality at the lowest cost with the best delivery. To drive down costs, a key philosophy of the production system is to organize the manufacture of each product so that the minimum amount of time, energy and resources are required. Canon therefore places strong emphasis on tight inventory management through a stable production planning process, careful material planning, close supplier relationships and adherence to the *kanban* system of inventory movement. Additionally, a formal waste elimination programme saved Canon 177 billion yen between 1976 and 1985. Overall, Canon accomplished a 30 per cent increase in productivity per year from 1976 to 1982 and over 10 per cent thereafter through automation and innovative process improvements.

The workforce is held in high regard at Canon. A philosophy of 'stop and fix it' empowers any worker to stop the production line if he or she is not able to perform a task properly or observes a quality problem. Workers are responsible for their own machine maintenance governed by rules which stress prevention. Targets for quality and production and other critical data are presented to the workers with on-line feedback. Most workers also participate in voluntary 'small group activity' for problem-solving. The result of these systems is a workforce that feels individually responsible for the success of the products it manufactures.

Canon sponsors a highly regarded suggestion programme for its workers in order to directly involve those most familiar with the work processes in improving the business. The programme was originally initiated in 1952 with only limited success, but in the early 1980s, participation soared with more than 70 suggestions per employee per year. All suggestions are reviewed by a hierarchy of committees with monetary prizes awarded monthly and yearly depending on the importance of the suggestion. The quality and effectiveness of the process are demonstrated by a 90 per cent implementation rate of the suggestions offered and corporate savings of $202 million in 1985 (against a total expenditure of $2 million in running the programme, over 90 per cent of it in prize money).

Canon chooses to backward integrate only on parts with unique technologies. For other components, the company prefers to develop long-term relationships with its suppliers and it retains two sources for most parts. In 1990, over 80 per cent of Canon's copiers were assembled from purchased parts, with only the drums and toner being manufactured in-house. They company also maintains its own in-house capability for doing pilot production of all parts so as to understand better the technology and the vendors' costs.

Another key to Canon's high quality and low cost is the attention given to parts commonality between models. Between some adjacent copier models, the commonality is as high as 60 per cent.

Copier manufacture was primarily located in Toride, Japan, in the early years but then spread to Germany, California and Virginia (USA), France, Italy and Korea. In order to mitigate trade and investment friction, Canon is working to increase the local content of parts as it expands globally. In Europe it exceeds the EC standard by 5 per cent. It is also adding R&D capability to some of its overseas operations. Mr Kaku emphasizes the importance of friendly trading partners:

> Frictions cannot be erased by merely transferring our manufacturing facilities overseas. The earnings after tax must be reinvested in the country; we must transfer our technology to the country. This is the only way our overseas expansion will be welcomed.

LEVERAGING EXPERTISE

Canon places critical importance on continued growth through diversification into new product fields. Mr Kaku observed:

> Whenever Canon introduced a new product, profits surged forward. Whenever innovation lagged, on the other hand, so did the earnings .... In order to survive in the coming era of extreme competition, Canon must possess at least a dozen proprietary state-of-the-art technologies that will enable it to develop unique products.

While an avid supporter of diversification, Mr Kaku was cautious:

> In order to ensure the enduring survival of Canon, we have to continue diversifying in order to adapt to environmental changes. However, we must be wise in choosing ways toward diversification. In other words, we must minimize the risks. Entering a new business which requires either a technology unrelated to Canon's current expertise or a different marketing channel than Canon currently uses incurs a 50 per cent risk. If Canon attempts to enter a new business which requires both a new technology and a new marketing channel which are unfamiliar to Canon, the risk entailed in such ventures

would be 100 per cent. There are two prerequisites that have to be satisfied before launching such new ventures. First, our operation must be debt-free; second, we will have to secure the personnel capable of competently undertaking such ventures. I feel we shall have to wait until the twenty-first century before we are ready.

Combining Capabilities

Through its R&D strategy, Canon has worked to build up specialized expertise in several areas and then link them to offer innovative, state-of-the-art products. Through the 1950s and 1960s, Canon focused on products related to its main business and expertise, cameras. This prompted the introduction of the 8 mm movie camera and the Canon range of mid-market cameras. There was minimal risk because the optics technology was the same and the marketing outlet, camera shops, remained the same.

Entrance into the calculator market pushed Canon into developing expertise in the field of microelectronics, which it later innovatively combined with its optics capability to introduce one of its most successful products, the personal copier. From copiers, Canon utilized the replaceable cartridge system to introduce a successful desktop laser printer.

In the early 1970s, Canon entered the business of marketing micro-chip semiconductor production equipment. In 1980, the company entered into the development and manufacture of unique proprietary ICs in order to strengthen further its expertise in electronics technology. This development effort was expanded in the late eighties to focus on opto-electronic ICs. According to Mr Kaku:

> We are now seriously committed to R&D in ICs because our vision for the future foresees the arrival of the opto-electronic era. When the time arrives for the opto-electronic IC to replace the current ultra-LSI, we intend to go into making large-scale computers. Presently we cannot compete with the IBMs and NECs using the ultra-LSIs. When the era of the opto-electronic IC arrives, the technology of designing the computer will be radically transformed; that will be our chance for making entry into the field of the large-scale computer.

Creative Destruction

In 1975 Canon produced the first laser printer. Over the next 15 years, laser printers evolved as a highly successful product line under the Canon brand name. The company also provides the 'engine' as an OEM to Hewlett Packard and other laser printer manufacturers which when added to its own branded sales supports a total of 84 per cent of worldwide demand.

The biggest threat to the laser printer industry is substitution by the newly developed bubble jet printer. With a new technology which squirts out thin streams of ink under heat, a high-quality silent printer can be produced at half the price of the laser printer. The technology was invented accidentally in the Canon research labs. It keys on a print head which has up to 400 fine nozzles per inch, each with its own heater to warm the ink until it shoots out tiny ink droplets. This invention utilizes Canon's competencies in fine chemicals for producing the ink and its expertise in semiconductors, materials and electronics for manufacturing the print heads. Canon is moving full steam forward to develop the bubble jet technology, even though it might destroy a business that the company dominates. The new product is even more closely tied to the company's core capabilities, and management believes that successful development of this business will help broaden further its expertise in semiconductors.

Challenge of the 1990s

Canon sees the office automation business as its key growth opportunity for the 1990s. It already has a well-established brand name in home and office automation products through its offerings of copiers, facsimiles, electronic typewriters, laser printers, word processing equipment and personal computers. The next challenge for the company is to link these discrete products into a multifunctional system which will perform the tasks of a copier, facsimile, printer, and scanner and interface with a computer so that all the functions can be performed from one keyboard. In 1988, with this target, Canon introduced a personal computer which incorporated a PC, a fax, a telephone and a word processor. Canon has also introduced a colour laser copier which hooks up to a computer to serve as a colour printer. A series of additional integrated OA offerings are scheduled for introduction in 1992, and the company expects these products to serve as its growth engine in the first half of the 1990s.

MANAGING THE PROCESS

Undergirding this impressive history of continuously building new corporate capabilities and of exploiting those capabilities to create a fountain of innovative new products lies a rather unique management process. Canon has institutionalized corporate entrepreneurship through its highly autonomous and market focused business unit structure. A set of powerful functional committees provide the bridge between the entrepreneurial business units and the company's core capabilities in technology, manufacturing and marketing. Finally, an extraordinarily high level of corporate ambition drives this innovation engine, which is fuelled by the creativity of its people and by top management's continuous striving for ever higher levels of performance.

Driving Entrepreneurship: The Business Units

Mr Kaku had promoted the concept of the entrepreneurial business unit from his earliest days with Canon, but it was not until the company had suffered significant losses in 1975 that his voice was heard. His plan was implemented shortly before he became president of the company.

Mr Kaku believed that Canon's diversification strategy could only succeed if the business units were empowered to act on their own, free of central controls. Therefore, two independent operating units were formed in 1978, one for cameras and one for office equipment, to be managed as business units. Optical Instruments, the third business unit, had always been separate. Since that time, an additional three business units have been spun off. The original three business units were then given clear profitability targets, as well as highly ambitious growth objectives, and were allowed the freedom to devise their own ways to achieve these goals. One immediate result of this decentralization was the recognition that Canon's past practice of mixing production of different products in the same manufacturing facility would no longer work. Manufacturing was reorganized so that no plant produced more than one type of product.

Mr Kaku describes the head of each unit as a surrogate of the CEO empowered to make quick decisions. This allows him, as president of Canon, to devote himself exclusively to his main task of creating and implementing the long-term corporate strategy. In explaining the benefits of the system, he said:

> Previously, the president was in exclusive charge of all decision-making; his subordinates had to form a queue to await their turn in presenting their problems to him. This kind of system hinders the development of the young managers' potential for decision-making.
>
> Furthermore, take the case of the desktop calculator. Whereas, I can devote only about two hours each day on problems concerning the calculator, the CEO of Casio Calculator could devote 24 hours to the calculator . . . . In the fiercely competitive market, we lost out because our then CEO was slow in coping with the problem.

In contrast to the Western philosophy of stand-alone SBUs encompassing all functions including engineering, sales, marketing and production. Canon has chosen to separate its product divisions from its sales and marketing arm. This separation allows for a clear focus on the challenges that Canon faces in selling products on a global scale. Through a five-year plan initiated in 1977, Seiichi Takigawa, the president of Canon Sales (the sales organization for Japan), stressed the need to 'make sales a science'. After proving the profitability of this approach, Canon Sales took on the responsibility for worldwide marketing, sales and service. In 1981, Canon Sales was listed on the Tokyo stock exchange, reaffirming its independence.

Canon also allows its overseas subsidiaries free rein, though it holds the majority of stock. The philosophy is to create the maximum operational leeway for each subsidiary to act on its own initiative. Kaku describes the philosophy through an analogy:

> Canon's system of managing subsidiaries is similar to the policy of the Tokugawa government, which established secure hegemony over the warlords, who were granted autonomy in their territory. I am 'shogun' [head of the Tokugawa regime] and the subsidiaries' presidents are the 'daimyo' [warlords]. The difference between Canon and the Tokugawa government is that the latter was a zero-sum society; its policy was repressive. On the other hand, Canon's objective is to enhance the prosperity of all subsidiaries through efficient mutual collaboration.

Canon has also promoted the growth of intrapreneurial ventures within the company by spinning these ventures off as wholly owned subsidiaries. The first venture to be spun off was Canon Components, which produces electronic components and devices, in 1984.

Building Integration: Functional Committees

As Canon continues to grow and diversify, it becomes increasingly difficult but also ever more important to link its product divisions in order to realize the benefits possible only in a large multiproduct corporation. The basis of Canon's integration is a three-dimensional management approach in which the first dimension is the independent business unit, the second a network of functional committees, and the third the regional companies focused on geographic markets (see Exhibit 5).

Kaku feels there are four basic requirements for the success of a diversified business: (1) a level of competence in research and development; (2) quality, low-cost manufacturing technology; (3) superior marketing strength; and (4) an outstanding corporate identity, culture and brand name. Therefore, he has established separate functional committees to address the first three requirements of development, production and marketing, while the fourth task has been kept as a direct responsibility of corporate management. The three functional committees, in turn, have been made responsible for company-wide administration of three key management systems:

1. The Canon Development System (CDS) whose objectives are to foster the research and creation of new products and technologies by studying and continuously improving the development process.

2. The Canon Production System (CPS) whose goal is to achieve optimum quality by minimizing waste in all areas of manufacturing.

3. The Canon Marketing System (CMS), later renamed the Canon International Marketing System (CIMS), which is tasked to expand and strengthen Canon's independent domestic and overseas sales networks by building a high quality service and sales force.

Separate offices have been created at headquarters for each of these critical committees, and over time their role has broadened to encompass general improvement of the processes used to support their functions. The chairpersons of the committees are members of Canon's management committee, which gives them the ability to ensure consistency and communicate process improvements throughout the multi-product, multinational corporation.

Using information technology to integrate its world-wide operations, Canon began development of the Global Information System for Harmonious Growth Administration (GINGA) in 1987. The system will consist of a high-speed digital communications network to interconnect all parts of Canon into a global database and allow for the timely flow of information among managers in any location of the company's world-wide organization. GINGA is planned to include separate but integrated systems for computer-integrated manufacturing, global marketing and distribution, R&D and product design, financial reporting and personnel database tracking, as well as some advances in intelligent office automation. As described by Mr Kaku, the main objective of this system is to supplement Canon's efficient vertical communications structure with a lateral one that will facilitate direct information exchange among managers across businesses, countries, and functions on all operational matters concerning the company. The system is being developed at a total cost of 20 billion yen and it is targeted for completion in 1992.

Managing Renewal: Challenges and Change

Mr Kaku was very forthright about some of the management weaknesses of Canon prior to 1975:

In short, our skill in management – the software of our enterprise – was weak. Management policy must be guided by a soundly created software on management; if the software is weak, the firm will lack clearly defined ideals and objectives. In the beginning we had a clearly defined objective, to overtake West Germany's Leica. Since then our management policy has been changing like the colours of a chameleon.

In the past our management would order employees to reach the peak of Mount Fuji, and then before the vanguard of climbers had barely started climbing, they would be ordered to climb Mount Tsukuba far to the north. Then the order would again be suddenly changed to climb Mount Yatsugatake to the west. After experiencing these kind of shifts in policy, the smarter employees would opt to take things easy by taking naps on the bank of the river Tamagawa. As a result, vitality would be sapped from our workforce – a situation that should have been forestalled by all means.

Mr Kaku's first action as president of Canon was to start the firm on the path to global leadership through establishing the first 'premier company plan', a six-year plan designed to make Canon a top company in Japan. The plan outlined a policy for diversification and required consistently recurring profits exceeding 10 per cent on sales:

> The aim of any Japanese corporation is ensuring its perpetual survival. Unlike the venture businesses and US corporations, our greatest objective is not to maximize short-term profits. Our vital objective is to continually earn profits on a stable basis for ensuring survival. To implement this goal, we must diversify.

By the time the original six-year plan expired in 1981, Canon had become a highly respected company in Japan. The plan was then renewed through 1986 and then again into the 1990s. The challenge was to become a premier global company, defined as having recurring profits exceeding 15 per cent of sales. R&D spending was gradually increased from 6 per cent of sales in 1980 to 9 per cent in 1985 as a prerequisite for global excellence. As described by Mr Kaku:

> By implementing our first plan for becoming a premier company we have succeeded in attaining the allegorical top of Mount Fuji. Our next objective is the Everest. With a firm determination, we could have climbed Fuji wearing sandals. However, sandals are highly inappropriate for climbing Everest; it may cause our death.

According to Mr Kaku, such ambitions also require a company to build up the ability to absorb temporary reversals without panic; ambition without stability makes the corporate ship lose its way. To illustrate, he described the situation at Canon during the time the yen depreciated from 236 to the dollar in 1985 to 168 to the dollar in 1986. With 74 per cent of Canon's Japanese production going to export markets, this sudden change caused earnings to fall to 4.6 billion yen, one tenth of the previous year. Some board members at Canon sought drastic action such as a major restructuring of the company and cutting the R&D budget. Mr Kaku had successfully argued the opposite:

> What I did was calm them down. If a person gets lost in climbing a high mountain, he must avoid excessive use of his energy; otherwise his predicament will deepen .... Our ongoing strategy for becoming the premier company remains the best, even under this crisis; there is no need to panic. Even if we have to forgo dividends for two or three times, we shall surely overcome this crisis.

While celebrating the company's past successes, Mr Kaku also constantly reminds his colleagues that no organizational form or process holds the eternal truth. The need to change with a changing world is inevitable. For example, despite being the creator of the product division-marketing company split, he was considering rejoining these two in the nineties:

> In the future, our major efforts in marketing must be concentrated on clearly defining and differentiating the markets of the respective products and creating appropriate marketing systems for them. In order to make this feasible, we may have to recombine our sales subsidiaries with the parent company and restructure their functions to fully meet the market's needs.

While constantly aware of the need to change, Kaku also recognizes the difficulties managers face in changing the very approaches and strategies that have led to past successes:

> In order for a company to survive forever, the company must have the courage to be able to deny at one point what it has been doing in the past; the biological concept of 'ecdysis' – casting off the skin to emerge to new form. But it is difficult for human beings to deny and destruct what they have been building up. But if they cannot do that, it is certain that the firm can not survive forever. Speaking about myself, it is difficult to deny what I've done in the past. So when such time comes that I have to deny the past, I inevitably would have to step down.

EXHIBIT 1
Canon Inc. – ten-year financial summary
(Yen millions, except per share amounts).

	1990	1989	1988	1987	1986	1985	1984	1983	1982	1981
Net Sales:										
Domestic	508,747	413,824	348,462	290,382	274,174	272,966	240,656	198,577	168,178	144,898
Overseas	1,219,201	937,063	757,548	686,329	615,043	682,814	589,732	458,748	412,322	326,364
TOTAL	1,727,948	1,350,917	1,106,010	976,711	889,217	955,780	830,388	657,325	580,500	471,262
Percentage to Previous Year	127.9%	122.1	113.2	109.8	93.0	115.1	126.3	113.2	123.2	112.5
Net Income	61,408	38,293	37,100	13,244	10,728	37,056	35,029	28,420	22,358	16,216
Percentage to Sales	3.6%	2.8	3.4	1.4	1.2	3.9	4.2	4.3	3.9	3.4
Advertising Expense	72,234	54,394	41,509	38,280	37,362	50,080	51,318	41,902	37,532	23,555
Research and Development	86,008	75,566	65,522	57,085	55,330	49,461	38,256	28,526	23,554	14,491
Depreciation	78,351	64,681	57,627	57,153	55,391	47,440	39,995	30,744	27,865	22,732
Capital Expenditure	137,298	107,290	83,069	63,497	81,273	91,763	75,894	53,411	46,208	54,532
Long-term Debt	262,886	277,556	206,083	222,784	166,722	134,366	99,490	60,636	53,210	39,301
Stockholders' Equity	617,566	550,841	416,465	371,198	336,456	333,148	304,310	264,629	235,026	168,735
Total Assets	1,827,945	1,636,350	1,299,843	1,133,881	1,009,504	1,001,044	916,651	731,642	606,101	505,169
Per Share Data:										
Net Income:										
Common and Common Equivalent Share	78.29	50.6	51.27	19.65	16.67	53.38	53.63	46.31	41.17	34.04
Assuming Full Dilution	78.12	49.31	51.26	19.64	16.67	53.25	53.37	45.02	38.89	33.35
Cash Dividends Declared	12.50	11.93	11.36	9.09	11.36	11.36	9.88	9.43	8.23	7.84
Stock Price:										
High	1,940	2,040	1,536	1,282	1,109	1,364	1,336	1,294	934	1,248
Low	1,220	1,236	823	620	791	800	830	755	417	513
Average Number of Common and Common Equivalent Shares (000s)	788,765	783,546	747,059	747,053	746,108	727,257	675,153	645,473	564,349	515,593
Number of Employees	54,381	44,401	40,740	37,521	35,498	34,129	30,302	27,266	25,607	24,300
Average Exchange Rate ($1 =)	143	129	127	143	167	235	239	238	248	222

Source: Canon 1990 Annual Report.

EXHIBIT 2
Sales by product
(¥ millions).

Year	Cameras	Copiers	Other Business Machines	Optical & Other Products	Total
1981	201,635	175,389	52,798	40,222	470,044
1982	224,619	242,161	67,815	45,905	580,500
1983	219,443	291,805	97,142	48,665	657,325
1984	226,645	349,986	180,661	73,096	830,388
1985	197,284	410,840	271,190	76,466	955,780
1986	159,106	368,558	290,630	70,923	889,217
1987	177,729	393,581	342,895	62,506	976,711
1988	159,151	436,924	434,634	75,301	1,106,010
1989	177,597	533,115	547,170	93,035	1,350,917
1990	250,494	686,077	676,095	115,282	1,727,948

Source: Canon Annual Report, 1981–90.

EXHIBIT 3
Office size distribution, Japan 1979.

Copier Market Segment	Number of Office Workers	Number of Offices	Working Population
A	300+	200,000	9,300,000
B	100–299	30,000	4,800,000
C	30–99	170,000	8,300,000
D	5–29	1,820,000	15,400,000
E	1–4	4,110,000	8,700,000

Source: 'Breakthrough: The development of the Canon personal copier,' Teruo Yamanouchi, *Long Range Planning*, Vol. 22, October 1989, p. 4.

EXHIBIT 1
Canon's major international joint ventures.

Category	Partner	Description
Office Equipment	Eastman Kodak (US)	Distributes Kodak medical equipment in Japan; exports copiers to Kodak
	CPF Germany	Equity participation in CPF which markets Canon copiers
	Olivetti (Italy) Lotte (Korea)	Joint venture for manufacture of copier
Computers	Hewlett-Packard (US)	Receives OEM mini-computer from HP; supplies laser printer to HP
	Apple Computer (US)	Distributes Apple computers in Japan; supplies laser printer to Apple
	Net, Inc. (US)	Equity participation; Canon has marketing rights for Asia
Semiconductors	National Semiconductor (US)	Joint development of MPU & software for Canon office equipment
	Intel (US)	Joint development for LSI for Canon copier, manufactured by Intel
Telecommunications	Siemens (Germany)	Development of ISDN interface for Canon facsimile; Siemens supplies Canon with digital PBX
	DHL (US)	Equity participation; Canon suppllies terminals to DHL
Camera	Kinsei Seimitsu (Korea)	Canon licenses technology on 35 mm camera
Other	ECD (US)	Equity participation because Canon values its research on amorphous materials

Source: Canon Asia, Nomura Management School.

EXHIBIT 5
Organizational chart.

CANON ORGANIZATION CHART

Board of Directors

President

Executive Committee
- Canon Into the Future Committee
- Canon Development System Committee
- Canon Production System Committee
- Canon International Marketing System Committee

- Auditor's office
- Secretarial office
- Internal Auditing Office
- Canon Advancement Centre
- Canon Events Advancement Centre
- China Division

- Corporate Planning Headquarters
- Corporate Communications Centre
- General Affairs Headquarters
- Personnel & Organization Headquarters
- Finance & Accounting Headquarters
- Traffic and Distribution Headquarters

Product Quality Assurance Centre

Product Quality Assurance Centre

Product Quality Assurance Centre
- Production Planning Centre
- Purchasing and Materials Management Centre
- Production Engineering Research Laboratory
- Seiki Manufacturing Equipment Plant

R & D Headquaters
- Corporate Technical Planning & Operation Centre
- Canon Research Centre
- Applied Research and development Centre
- Information Systems Laboratory
- Component Development Centre
- Audio & visual Aids Division

Camera Operations

Business Machines Operations

Optical Products Operations

Canon Sales Co Inc
- Canon Eiden Co Inc
- Canon System Sales Co Inc
- Canon Software Inc
- Canon Copyer Sales Co Ltd
- Nippon Typewriter Co Ltd

Canon USA Inc
- Canon Canada Inc
- MCS Business Machines Inc
- Astro Office Products Ltd
- Ambassador Office Equpment Inc
- Canon Virginia Inc

Canon Europe NV — Canon SA Geneva

Canon Latin America Inc
- Canon Panama SA
- Canon Overseas Trading SA
- Canon do Brasil Industria e Comercio Limitada
- Canon de Mexico SA

Canon Australia Pty Ltd

Canon Singapore Pte Ltd
- Canon Hongkong Trading Co Ltd
- Canon Marketing Service Ptd Ptd

Canon Electronics Inc
- Minon Electronics Inc
- Yorii Electronics Inc
- Ogano Electronics Inc

Copyer Co Ltd

Canon Precision Inc
- Hanawa Precision Inc
- Hirosaki Precision Inc

- Canon Seika Co Ltd
- Oita Canon Inc
- Canon Inc Taiwan
- Danish Seiki Kegyo Co Ltd
- Canon Chemical Co Ltd
- Canon Greschen GmbH
- Canon Bretagna SA
- Canon Business Machines Inc
- Optron Inc
- Canon Insurance Centre
- Canon Battery Co

Canon (UK) Ltd — Canon Scotland Business Machines Ltd

Canon France SA
- Canon France Photo Cinema SA
- Canon france Grand Publc SA

Canon Italia SpA

Canon Copylux GmbH — Canon Euro-Photo Handelsgesellschaft mbH
Canon Svenska AB
- Canon Optics AG
- Canon Verkooporganisatie Nederland BV
- Canon Gesellshaft mbH
- Canon Rechner Deutschland GmbH
- Canon Business Machines Belgium NV/SA
- Canon España SA

Source: Canon Handbook, published by Canon, Inc.

EXHIBIT 5 (Continued)

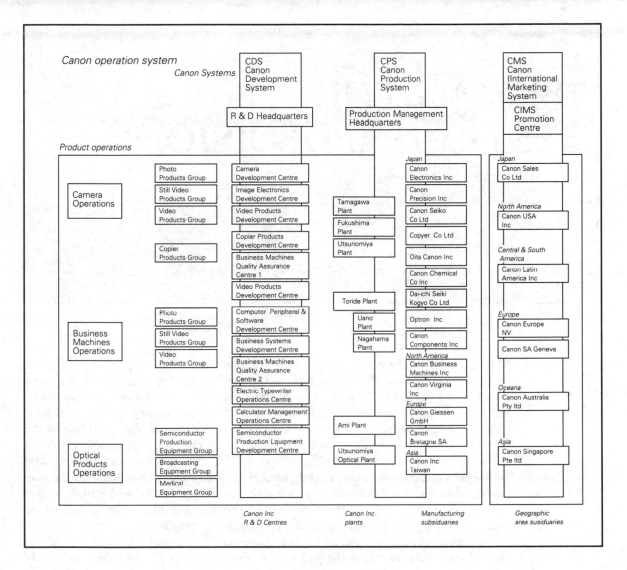

1–8

IBM (A): THE SYSTEM/360 DECISION*

The decision by the management of the International Business Machines Corp. to produce a new family of computers, called the System/360, was one of the most crucial and portentous – as well as perhaps the riskiest – business judgements of recent times. The decision committed IBM to laying out money in sums that read like the federal budget – some $5 billion over a period of four years. To launch the 360, IBM was forced into sweeping organizational changes, with executives rising and falling with the changing tides of battle. The very character of this large and influential company was significantly altered by the ordeal of the 360, and the way it thought about itself changed, too. Bob Evans, the line manager who had the major responsibility for designing this gamble of a corporate lifetime, was only half joking when he said: 'We called this project "You bet your company".'

Evans insisted that the 360 'was a damm good risk, and a lot less risk than it would have been to do anything else, or to do nothing at all', and there is a lot of evidence to support him. . . . A long stride ahead in the technology of computers in commercial use was taken by the 360. So sweeping were the implications that it required ten years before there were enough data to evaluate the wisdom of the whole undertaking.

---

*Case compilation copyright © 1983 by James Brian Quinn. All sections drawn from a two-part series: T. A. Wise. 'IBM's $5 billion gamble', and 'The rocky road to the marketplace', *Fortune*, September–October 1966. Copyright © 1966 Time Inc.
All rights reserved to original copyright holder. Reproduced by permission. Questions at end added by Professor Quinn. Verb tenses have been edited to clarify time relationships. Minor sections have been deleted (. . .) when peripheral.

The new System/360 was intended to obsolete virtually all other existing computers – including those being offered by IBM itself. Thus, the first and most extraordinary point to note about this decision was that it involved a challenge to the marketing structure of the computer industry – an industry that the challenger itself had dominated overwhelmingly for nearly a decade. It was roughly as though General Motors had decided to scrap its existing makes and models and offer in their place one new line of cars, covering the entire spectrum of demand, with a radically redesigned engine and an exotice fuel. . . .

[In 1966] there were perhaps 35,000 computers in use, and it was estimated that there would be 85,000 by 1975. IBM sat astride this exploding market, accounting for something like two-thirds of the worldwide business – that is, the dollar value of general-purpose computers then installed or on order. IBM's share of this market [in 1965] represented about 77 per cent of the company's $3.6 billion gross revenues [and $477 million of profits].

Several separate but interrelated steps were involved in the launching of System/360. Each one of the steps involved major difficulties, and taking them all meant that IBM was accepting a staggering challenge to its management capabilities. First, the 360 depended heavily on microcircuitry, an advance technology in the field of computers. In a 1952 vacuum-tube model of IBM's first generation of computers, there were about 2,000 components per cubic foot. In a second-generation machine, which used transistors instead of tubes, the figure was 5,000 per cubic foot. The System/360 model 75 computer, using hybrid microcircuitry, involved 30,000 components per cubic foot. The old vacuum-tube computer could perform approximately 2,500 multiplications per second; the 360 model 75 was designed to perform 375,000 per second. The cost of carrying out 100,000 computations on the first-generation model was $1.38; the 360 reduced the cost to $3\frac{1}{2}$ cents.

The second step was the provision for compatibility – that is, as the users' computer requirements grew they could move up from one machine to another without having to discard or rewrite already existing programs. Limited compatibility had already been achieved by IBM, and by some of its competitors too, for that matter, on machines of similar design but different power. But it had never been achieved on a broad line of computers with a wide range of powers, and achieving this compatibility depended as much on developing compatible programs or 'software' as it did on the hardware. All the auxiliary machines – 'peripheral equipment' as they are called in the trade – had to be designed so that they could feed information into or receive information from the central processing unit; this meant that the equipment had to have timing, voltage and signal levels matching those of the central unit. In computerese, the peripheral equipment was to have 'standard interface'. The head of one competing computer manufacturing company acknowledges that at the time of the System/360 announcement he regarded the IBM decision as sheer folly and doubted that IBM would be able to produce or deliver a line that was completely compatible.

Finally – and this was the boldest and most perilous part of the plan – it was decided that six main units of the 360 line, originally designated models 30, 40, 50, 62 and 70, should be announced and made available simultaneously. (Models at the lower and higher ends of the line were to be announced later.) This meant that all parts of the company would have to adhere to a meticulous schedule.

UP IN MANUFACTURING, DOWN IN CASH

The effort involved in the programme was enormous. IBM spent over half a billion dollars on research and development programmes associated with the 360. This involved a tremendous hunt for talent: by the end of 1966, one-third of IBM's 190,000 employees had been hired since the new programme was announced. Between that time, 7 April 1964, and the end of 1967, the company opened five new plants in the United States and abroad and had budgeted a total of $4.5 billion for rental machines, plants, and equipment. Not even the Manhattan Project, which produced the atomic bomb in World War II, cost so much (the government's costs up to Hiroshima are reckoned at $2 billion), nor, probably, had any other privately financed commercial project in history.

Such an effort changed IBM's nature in several ways:

The company, which was essentially an assembler of computer components and a business-service organization, became a major manufacturing concern as well. It became the world's largest maker of integrated circuits, producing as estimated 150 million of the hybrid variety annually in the late 1960s.

After some ambivalence, IBM abandoned any notion that it was simply another American company with a large foreign operation. The view now is that IBM is a fully integrated company, in which the managers of overseas units are presumed to have the same capabilities and responsibilities as those in the US. The company's World Trade subsidiary stopped trying to develop its own computers; instead, it marketed the 360 overseas, and helped in the engineering and manufacturing of the 360.

The company's table of organization was restructured significantly at least three times during the 360's development cycle. Several new divisions and their executives emerged, while others suffered total or partial eclipse. An old maxim of the IBM organization was that few men rose to line executive positions unless they had spent some time selling. A new group of technically oriented executives came to the forefront for the first time, diluting some of the traditional power of the marketing men in the corporation.

The Missionaries and the Scientists

Oddly enough, the upheaval at IBM went largely unnoticed. The company was able to make itself over more or less in private. It was able to do so partly beccause IBM is so widely assumed to be an organization in which the unexpected simply doesn't happen. Outsiders viewing IBM presume it to be a model of rationality and order – a presumption related to the company's products which are, of course, instruments that enable (and require) their users to think clearly about management.

This image of IBM, moreover, had been furthered over the years by the styles of the two Watsons. Tom Watson Sr combined an intense devotion to disciplined thinking with formal, rather Victorian attitudes about conduct, clothes and courtesy. The senior Watson's hostility towards drinking, and his demand that employees dedicate themselves totally to the welfare of the corporation, created a kind of evangelical atmosphere. When Tom Watson Jr took over from his father in 1956, the manner and style shifted somewhat, but the missionary zeal remained – now overlaid by a new dedication to the disciplines of science. The overlay reinforced the image of IBM as a chillingly efficient organization, one in which plans were developed logically and executed with crisp efficiency. It was hard to envision the company in a gambling role.

The dimensions of the 360 gamble are difficult to state precisely. The company's executives, who are men used to thinking of risks and payoffs in hard quantitative terms, insist that no meaningful figure could ever be put on the gamble – that is, on the odds that the programme would be brought off on schedule, or on the costs involved if it failed.

Outsailing the Boss

At the time, it scarcely seemed that any gamble at all was necessary. IBM was way out ahead of the competition, and looked as if it could continue smoothly in its old ways forever. Below the surface, though, IBM's organization didn't fit the changing markets so neatly anymore, and there really was, in Evans's phrase, a risk involved in doing nothing.

No one understood this more thoroughly, or with more sense of urgency, than one of the principal decision-makers of the company, T. Vincent Learson. His entire career at IBM, which began in 1935, had been concerned with getting new products to market. In 1954 he was tapped by young Tom Watson as the man to spearhead the company's first big entry into the commercial computer field – with the 702 and 705 models. His success led to his promotion to vice-president and group executive in 1956. In 1959 he took over both of the company's computer development and manufacturing operations, the General Products Division and the Data Systems Division.

Learson stood 6'6" and was a tough and forceful personality. When he was managing any major IBM programme, he tended to be impatient with staff reports and committees, and to operate outside the conventional chain of command; if he wanted to know why a programme was behind schedule, he was apt to call directly on an executive at a much lower level who might help him find out. But he often operated indirectly, too, organizing major management changes without his own hands being visible to the men involved. Though he lacked the formal scientific background that is taken for granted in many areas of IBM, Learson had a reputation as a searching and persistent questioner about any proposals brought before him; executives who had not done their homework might find their presentations falling apart under his questions – and might also find that he would continue the inquisition in a way that made their failure an object lesson to any spectators. And Learson was the most vigorous supporter of the company's attitude that a salesman who had lost an order without exhausting all the resources the company had to back him up deserved to be drawn and quartered.

At IBM, Learson was known as demanding, domineering and direct – given to calling people anywhere in the company to find out firsthand what was going on. But Learson was also known as a friendly and whimsical man who was IBM's number one cheerleader. He delighted in showing up unannounced, whether in a hospital to cheer up one of his sick secretaries or at a retirement dinner in Boston for a lady who ran a course in keypunching there when Learson was a young salesman. For all the diverging views of Learson, the man, as a top executive the degree of loyalty that Learson inspired was remarkable. Said one former executive, who was forced out of IBM, 'I admire the man. He's like General Patton – someone you follow into battle.'

Learson's personal competitiveness was something of a legend at IBM. It was significantly demonstrated in the Newport-to-Bermuda yacht race, in which Learson entered his own boat, the *Thunderbird*. He boned up on the history of the race in past years, and managed to get a navigator who had been on a winning boat three different times. He also persuaded Bill Lapworth, the famous boat designer, to be a crewman. Learson travelled personally to California to get one of the best spinnaker men available. All these competitive efforts were especially fascinating to the people at IBM because Tom Watson Jr also had an entry in the Bermuda race; he'd, in fact, been competing in it for years. Before the race Watson good-humouredly warned Learson at a board meeting that he'd better not win if he expected to stay at IBM. Learson's answer was not recorded. But Learson won the race. Watson's *Palowan* finished twenty-fourth on corrected time.

When Learson took over the computer group he found himself supervising two major engineering centres that had been competing with each other for some time. The General Products Division's facility in Endicott, New York, produced the low-priced 1401 model, by far the most popular of all IBM's computers – or of anyone else's to that date; something like 10,000 of them had been installed by the mid-1960s. Meanwhile, the Data Systems Division in Poughkeepsie made the more glamorous 7000 series, of which the 7090 was the most powerful. Originally, IBM had intended that the two centres operate in separate markets, but as computer prices came down in the late 1950s and as more versions of each model were offered, their markets came to overlap – and they entered a period in which they were increasingly penetrating each other's markets, heightening the feeling of rivalry. Each had its own development programme, although any decision to produce or market a new computer, of course, had to be ratified at corporate headquarters. The rivalry between the two divisions was to become an element in, and be exacerbated by, the decision to produce the 360.

Both the 1401 and the 7000 series were selling well in 1960. But computer engineers and architects are a restless breed; they are apt to be thinking of improvements in design or circuitry five minutes after the specifications of their latest machines are frozen. In the General Products Division, most such thinking in 1960 and 1961 was long term; it was assumed that the 1401 would be on the market until about 1968. The thinking at the Data Systems Division concerned both long-range and more immediate matters.

A $20 Million Stretch

One of the immediate matters was the division's 'Stretch' computer, which was already on the market but having difficulties. The computer had been designed to dwarf all others in size and power, and it was priced around $13,500,000. But it never met more than 70 per cent of the promised specifications, and not many of them were sold. In May 1961, Tom Watson made the decision that the price of Stretch should be cut to $8 million to match the value of its performance – at which level Stretch was plainly uneconomic to produce. He had to make the decision, it happened, just before he was to fly to California and address an industry group on the subject of progress in the computer field.

Before he left for the coast, an annoyed Watson made a few tart remarks about the folly of getting involved in large and overambitious projects that you couldn't deliver on. In his speech, he admitted that Stretch was a flop. 'Our greatest mistake in Stretch', he said, 'is that we walked up to the plate and pointed at the left-field stands. When we swung, it was not a homer but a hard line drive to the outfield. We're going to be a good deal more careful about what we promise in the future.' Soon after he returned the programme was quietly shelved; only seven of the machines were ultimately put in operation. IBM's overall loss on the programme was about $20 million.

The Stretch fiasco had two consequences. One was that the company practically ignored the giant computer field during the next two years – and thereby enabled Control Data to get a sizeable headstart in the market. Customers were principally government and university research centres, where the most complex scientific problems are tackled and computers of tremendous power are required. Eventually, in 1963, Watson pointed out that his strictures against overambitious projects had not been meant to exclude IBM from this scientific market, and the company later tried to get back into it. Its entry was to be the 360–90, the most powerful machine of the new line.

A second consequence of the Stretch fiasco was that Learson and the men under him, especially those in the Data Systems Division, were under special pressure to be certain that the next big project was thought out more carefully and that it worked exactly as promised. As it happened, the project the division had in mind in 1960–1 was a fairly ambitious one: it was for a line of computers, tentatively called the 8000 series, that would replace the 7000 series, and would also provide a limited measure of compatibility among the four models projected. The 8000 series was based on transistor technology, and therefore still belonged to the second generation; however, there had been so much recent progress in circuitry design and transistor performance that the series had considerably more capability than anything being offered by IBM at that time.

The principal sponsor of the 8000 concept was Fred Brooks, head of systems planning for the Poughkeepsie division. An imaginative, enthusiastic 29-year-old North Carolinian with a considerable measure of southern charm, Brooks became completely dedicated to the concept of the new series, and beginning in late 1960 he began trying to enlist support for it. He had a major opportunity to make his case for the 8000 programme at a briefing for the division's management, which was held at Poughkeepsie in January 1961.

By all accounts, he performed well: he was relaxed, confident, informed on every aspect of the technology involved, and persuasive about the need for a change. Data Systems' existing product line, he argued, was a mixed bag. The capability of some models overlapped that of others, while still other capabilities were unavailable in any model. The 8000 series would end all this confusion. One machine was already built, cost estimates and a market forecast had been made, a pricing schedule had been completed, and Brooks proposed announcing the series late that year or early in 1962. It could be the division's basic product line until 1968, he added. Most of Brooks' audience found his case entirely persuasive.

Enter the Man from Headquarters

Learson, however, was not ready to be sold so easily. The problems with Stretch must have been on his mind, and probably tended to make him look hard at any big new proposals. Beyond that, he was sceptical that the 8000 series would minimize the confusion in the division's product line, and he wondered whether the concept might not even *contribute* to the confusion. Learson had received a long memorandum from his chief assistant, Don Spaulding, on the general subject of equipment proliferation. Spaulding argued that there were already too many different computers in existence, and that they required too many supporting programs and too much peripheral equipment; some drastic simplification of the industry's merchandise was called for.

With these thoughts in mind, Learson was not persuaded that Brooks' concept was taking IBM in the right direction. Finally, he was not persuaded that the company should again invest heavily in second-generation technology. Along with a group of computer users, he had recently attended a special course on industrial dynamics that was being given at the Massachusetts Institute of Technology. Much of the discussion had been over his head, he later recalled, but from what his classmates were saying he came away with the clear conviction that computer applications would soon be expanding rapidly, and that what was needed was a bold move away from 'record-keeping' and towards more sophisticated business applications.

There was soon direct evidence of Learson's scepticism about the 8000 series. Shortly after the briefing Bob Evans, who was then manager of processing systems in the General Products Division, was dispatched to Poughkeepsie as head of Data Systems' planning and development. He brought along a number of men who had worked with him in Endicott. Given the rivalry between the two divisions, it is not very surprising that he received a cool welcome. His subsequent attitude towards the 8000 concept ensured that his relations with Brooks would stay cool.

Evans made several different criticisms of the concept. The main one was that the proposed line was 'non-homogeneous' – that is, it was not designed throughout to combine scientific and business applications. Further, he contended that it lacked sufficient compatibility within the line . It would compound the proliferation problem. He also argued that it was time to turn to the technologies associated with integrated circuits.

Blood on the Floor

For various reasons, including timing, Brooks was opposed, and he and Evans fought bitterly for several months. At one point Evans called him and quietly mentioned that Brooks was getting a raise in salary. Brooks started to utter a few words of thanks when Evans said flatly, 'I want you to know I had nothing to do with it.'

In March 1961, Brooks had a chance to make a presentation to the corporate management committee, a group that included Tom Watson, his brother, A. K. Watson, who headed the World Trade Corp., Albert Williams, who was then president of the corporation (later chairman of the executive committee), and Learson. Brooks made another effective presentation, and for a while he and his allies thought that the 8000 might be approved after all.

But early in May it booamo cloar that Evans was the winner. His victory was formalized in a meeting, at the Gideon Putnam Hotel in Saratoga, of all the key people who had worked on the 8000. There, on 15 May, Evans announced that the 8000 project was dead and that he now had the tough job of reassigning them all to other tasks. In the words of one participant, 'There was blood all over the floor.'

Evans now outlined some new programmes for the Data Systems Division. His short-term programme called for an extension of the 7000 line, both upward and downward. At the lower end of the line there would be two new models, the 7040 and 7044. At the upper end there would be a 7094 and a 7094 II. This programme was generally non-controversial, except for the fact that the 7044 had almost exactly the same capabilities as a computer called Scamp, which was being proposed by another part of IBM. It would obviously make no sense to build both computers; and, as it happened, Scamp had some powerful support.

Scamp was a small scientific computer developed originally for the European market. Its principal designer was John Fairclough, a young man (he was then 30) working in the World Trade Corp.'s Hursley Laboratory, 60 miles south-west of London. The subsidiary had a sizeable stake in Scamp. It had been trying for many years to produce a computer tailored to the needs of its own markets, but had repeatedly failed, and had therefore been obliged to sell American-made machines overseas.

But Scamp looked especially promising, and the subsidiary's executives, including Fairclough and A.K. Watson, were confident that it would meet American standards. It had previously tested well and attracted a fair amount of attention in IBM's American laboratories. Evans himself came to Hursley to look at it, and was impressed. But its similarity to the 7044 finally took Fairclough and some associates to the United States to test their machine against a 7044 prototype.

Mere Equality Won't Do

As things turned out, Scamp did about as well as the 7044 – but, also as things turned out, that wasn't good enough. Evans and Learson were resolved to stretch out the 7000 line, but opposed to anything that would add to proliferation. In principle, A.K. Watson, who had always run World Trade as a kind of personal fiefdom, could have stepped in and ordered the production of Scamp on his own authority. In practice, he decided the argument against proliferation was a valid one. And so, in the end, he personally gave the order to drop Scamp. Fairclough got the news one day soon after he had returned to England, and he found himself with a sizeable staff that had to be reassigned. He says that he considered resigning, but instead worked off his annoyance by sipping Scotch and brooding much of the night.

Evans and Learson had also agreed that Data Systems should try its hand at designing a computer line that would blanket the market. The General Products Division was asked to play a role in the new design, but its response was lukewarm, so the bulk of the work at this stage fell to Data Systems. The project was dubbed NPL, for new product line; the name System/360 was not settled on until much later. To head the project, Evans selected his old adversary Brooks – a move that surprised a large number of IBM executives, including Brooks himself.

Still smarting over the loss of the 8000 project, and suspicious that the NPL was just a 'window-dressing' operation, Brooks accepted the job only tentatively. To work with him, and apparently to ensure the NPL did not end up as the 8000 under a new name, Evans brought Gene Amdahl, a crack designer whom the company had called on to work on several earlier computers. However, Amdahl's influence was offset by that of another designer, Gerrit Blaauw, a veteran and past supporter of the 8000 project. Brooks' group received enough money to show that the company took NPL seriously (the first-year appropriation was $3,800,000), but Amdahl and Blaauw disagreed on design concepts, and the project floundered until November 1961.

Even to the trained eye IBM's main divisions appeared to be in excellent health in the summer of 1961. The General Products Division, according to Evans, was 'fat and dumb and happy' in the lower end of the market, selling the 1401 at a furious rate, and still feeling secure about its line through about 1968. The World Trade Corp. was growing rapidly, although it had suffered its third major setback on getting a computer line of its own. The Data Systems Division was extending its old 7000 line to meet the competition, and working on the NPL.

THE PROLIFERATING PRODUCTS

But it was around this time that Tom Watson and Learson – then a group executive vice-president, and nominally at least working under Albert Williams, the company president – developed several large concerns. There was the absence of any clear, overall concept of the company's product line; 15 or 20 different engineering groups scattered throughout the company were generating different computer products, and while the products were in most cases superior, the proliferation was putting overwhelming strains on the company's ability to supply programming for customers. The view at the top was that IBM required some major changes if it expected to stay ahead in the computer market when the third generation came along.

Between August and October 1961, Watson and Learson initiated a number of dialogues with their divisional lieutenants in an effort to define a strategy for the new era. By the end of October, though, neither of them believed that any strategy was coming into focus. At this point Learson made a crucial decision. He decided to set up a special committee, composed of representatives from every major segment of the company, to formulate some policy guidance. The committee was called SPREAD – an acronym for systems programming, research, engineering and development. Its chairman was John Haanstra, then a vice-president of the General Products Division. There were 12 other members, including Evans, Brooks and Fairclough.

The SPREAD Committee – Autumn 1961

The SPREAD Committee was conducted informally, but with a good amount of spirited discussion. For the same purposes it broke up into separate committees, such as one on programming capability. Haanstra, as one member put it, acted as a hammer on the committee anvil, forcing ideas into debate and demanding definitions. Still, there was some feeling that Haanstra was bothered by the fact that the group was heavily represented by 'big machine'-oriented men.

The progress of the committee during November was steady, but it was also, in Learson's view, 'hellishly slow'. Suddenly Haanstra found himself promoted to the presidency of the General Products Division and Bob Evans took over as chairman of SPREAD. The committee meetings were held in the New Englander Motor Hotel, just north of Stamford, Connecticut. In effect, although not quite literally, Learson locked the doors and told the members that they couldn't get out until they had reached some conclusions.

While Evans accelerated the pact of the sessions somewhat, Fred Brooks increasingly emerged as the man who was shaping the direction of the committee recommendations. This was not very surprising, for he and his group had had a headstart in thinking out many of the issues. By 28 December 1961, the SPREAD Committee had hammered out an 80-page statement of its recommendations. On 4 January 1962, the committee amplified the report for the benefit of the 50 top executives of the corporation.

Brooks was assigned the role of principal speaker on this occasion. The presentation was split into several parts and took an entire day. The main points of the report were:

> There was a definite need for a single, compatible family of computers ranging from one with the smallest existing core memory, which would be below the 1401 line, to one as powerful as IBM's biggest – at that time the 7094. In fact, the needs were said to extend beyond the IBM range, but the report expressed doubt that compatibility could be extended that far.
>
> The new line should not be aimed simply at replacing the popular 1401 or 7000 series, but at opening up whole new fields of computer applications. At that time compatibility between those machines and the new line was not judged to be of major importance, because the original timetable on the appearance of the various members of the new family of computers stretched out for several years.
>
> The System/360 must have both business and scientific applications. This dual purpose was a difficult assignment because commercial machines accept large amounts of data but have little manipulative ability, while scientific machines work on relatively small quantities of data that are endlessly manipulated. To achieve duality the report decided that each machine in the new line would be made available with core memories of varying sizes. In addition, the machine would provide a variety of technical and esoteric features to handle both scientific and commercial assignments.
>
> Information input and output equipment, and all other peripheral equipment, must have 'standard interface' – so that various types and sizes of peripheral equipment could be hitched to the main computer without missing a beat. This too was to become an important feature of the new line.

Learson recalled the reaction when the presentation ended. 'There were all sorts of people up there and while it wasn't received too well, there were no real objections. So I said to them, "All right, we'll do it." The problem was, they thought it was too grandiose. The report said we'd have to spend $125 million on programming the system at a time when we were spending only about $10 million a year for programming. Everybody said you just couldn't spend that amount. The job just looked too big to the marketing people, the financial people, and the engineers. Everyone recognized it was a gigantic task that would mean all our resources were tied up in one project – and we knew that for a long time we wouldn't be getting anything out of it.'

APRIL 1964 – PUBLIC ANNOUNCEMENT

When Tom Watson Jr made what he called 'the most important product announcement in the company's history', he created quite a stir. International Business Machines is not a corporation given to making earth-shaking pronouncements casually, and the declaration that it was launching an entirely new computer line, the System/360, was headline news. The elaborate logistics that IBM worked out in order to get maximum press coverage – besides a huge assembly at Poughkeepsie, IBM staged press conferences on the same day in 62 cities in the United States and in 14 foreign countries – underscored its view of the importance of the event. And the fact that the move until then had been a closely guarded secret added an engaging element of surprise. . . . In the scattered locations where IBM plans, builds, and sells its products, there was, on that evening of 7 April 1964, a certain amount of dancing in the streets. . . .

But the managerial and organizational changes that were brought about by the company's struggle to settle on, and then to produce and market, the new line [had very long-term] effects. In each of these several aspects, past, present and future were closely intertwined.

The Rising Cost of Asking Questions

No part of the whole adventure of launching System/360 was as tough, as stubborn or as enduring as the programming. Early in 1966, talking to a group of IBM customers, Tom Watson Jr said ruefully: 'We are investing nearly as much in System/360 programming as we are in the entire development of System/360 hardware. A few months ago the bill for 1966 was going to be $40 million. I asked Vin Learson last night before I left what he thought it would be for 1966 and he said $50 million. Twenty-four hours later I met Watts Humphrey, who is in charge of programming production, in the hall here and said, "Is this figure about right? Can I use it?" He said it's going to be $60 million. You can see that if I keep asking questions we won't pay a dividend this year.'

Watson's concern about programming went back to the beginning of the System/360 affair. By late 1962 he was sufficiently aware of the proportions of the question to invite the eight top executives of IBM to his ski lodge in Stowe, Vermont, for a three-day session on programming. The session was conducted by Fred Brooks, the corporate manager for the design of the 360 project, and other experts; they went into the programming in considerable detail. While the matter can become highly technical, in general IBM's objective was to devise an 'operating system' for its computer line, so that the computers would schedule themselves, without manual interruption, and would be kept working continuously at or near their capacity. At the time it announced System/360, IBM promised future users that it would supply them with such a command system.

Delivery on that promise was agonizingly difficult. Even though Tom Watson and the other top executives knew the critical importance of programming, the size of the job was seriously underestimated. The difficulty of coordinating the work of hundreds of programmers was enormous. The operating system IBM was striving for required the company to work out many new ideas and approaches; as one company executive said, 'We were trying to schedule inventions, which is a dangerous thing to do in a committed project.' Customers came up with more extensive programming tasks than the company had expected, and there were inevitable delays and slowdowns. The difficulties of programming prevented some users from getting the full benefits from their new machines for years. The company didn't have most of the bugs out of the larger systems' programming until at least mid-1967 – well behind its expectations.

The Cold Realities of Choice

In technology, IBM was also breaking new ground. During the formative years of the decisions about the technology of System/360, a lengthy report on the subject was prepared by the *ad hoc* Logic Committee, headed by Erich Bloch, a specialist in circuitry for IBM. Eventually, the Logic Committee report led to the company's formal commitment to a new hybrid kind of integrated-circuit technology – a move that, like many other aspects of the 360 decision, is still criticized by some people in the computer industry, both inside and outside of IBM.

The move, though, was hardly made in haste. The whole computer industry had raced through two phases of electronic technology – vacuum tubes and transistors – between 1951 and 1960. By the late 1950s it was becoming apparent that further technological changes of sweeping importance were in the offing. At that time, however, IBM was not very much of a force in scientific research, its strengths lying in the assembling and marketing of computers, not in their advanced concepts. The company's management at the time had the wit to recognize the nature of the corporate deficiency, and to see the importance of correcting it. In 1956, IBM hired Dr Emanuel Piore, formerly chief scientist of US naval research. Piore became IBM's director of research and a major figure in the technological direction that the company finally chose for its System/360.

In the end, the choice narrowed to two technologies. One was monolithic integrated circuitry: putting all the elements of a circuit – transistors, resistors and diodes – on one chip at one time. The other was hybrid integrated circuitry – IBM rather densely termed it 'solid logic technology' – which means making transistors and diodes separately and then soldering them into place. In 1961 the Logic committee decided that the production of monolithic circuits in great quantities would be risky, and in any case would not meet the schedule for any new line of computers to be marketed by 1964.

There was little opposition to this recommendation initially, except among a few engineering purists. Later, however, the opposition strengthened. The purists believed that monolithic circuits were sure to come, and that the company in a few years would find itself frozen into a technology that might be obsolete before the investment could be recovered. However, the Logic Committee's recommendation on the hybrid approach was accepted; since that time, Watson has referred to the acceptance as 'the most fortunate decision we ever made'.

THE SECRETS CIRCUITS HIDE

The decision to move into hybrid integrated technology accelerated IBM's push into component manufacturing, a basic change in the character of the company. In the day of vacuum tubes and transistors, IBM had designed the components for its circuits, ordered them from other companies (a principal supplier: Texas Instruments), then assembled them to its own specifications. But with the new circuitry, those specifications would have to be built into the components from the outset. 'Too much proprietary information was involved in circuitry production,' said Watson. 'Unless we did it ourselves, we could be turning over some of the essentials of our business to another company. We had no intention of doing that.' In addition, of course, IBM saw no reason why it should not capture some of the profit from the manufacturing that it was creating on such a large scale.

The company's turn to a new technology jibed neatly with a previous decision made in 1960 by Watson at the urging of the man who was then IBM president, Al Williams, that the company should move into component manufacturing. By the time the decision to go into hybrid circuits was made, IBM already had started putting together a component manufacturing division. Its general manager was John Gibson, a Johns Hopkins PhD in electrical engineering. Under Gibson, the new division won the authority, hitherto divided among other divisions of the company, to designate and to buy the components for computer hardware, along with a new authority to manufacture them when Gibson thought it appropriate.

This new assignment of responsibility was resented by managers in the Data Systems and General Products divisions, since it represented a limitation of their authority. Also, they protested that they would be unable to compare the price and quality of inhouse components with those made by an outside supplier if they lost their independence of action. But Vincent Learson, then group executive vice-president, feared that if they kept their independence they would continue to make purchases outside the company, and that IBM as a consequence would have no market for its own component output. He therefore put the power of decision in Gibson's hands. IBM's board, in effect, ruled in Gibson's favour when, in 1962, it authorized the construction of a new manufacturing plant, and the purchase of its automatic equipment, at a cost of over £100 million.

Systems Design: Worldwide

While IBM was making up its corporate mind about the technology for System/360, the delegation of specific responsibilities was going ahead. Learson designated Bob Evans, now head of the Federal Systems Division, to manage the giant undertaking. Under Evans, Fred Brooks was put in charge of all the System/360 work being done at Poughkeepsie, where four of the original models were designed; he was also made manager of the overall design of the central processors. The plant at Endicott was given the job of designing the model 30, successor to the popular 1401, which had been developed there. And John Fairclough, a systems designer at World Trade, was assigned to design the model 40 at the IBM lab at Hursley, England.

Out of the Hursley experience came an interesting byproduct that had significant implications for IBM's future. With different labs engaged in the 360 design, it was vital to provide for virtually instant communication between them. IBM therefore leased a special transatlantic line between its home offices and the engineers in England, and later in Germany. The international engineering group was woven together with considerable effectiveness, giving IBM the justifiable claim that the 360 computer was probably the first product of truly international design.

In a Tug-of-War, Enough Rope to Hang Yourself

Even in a corporation inured to change, people resist change. By 1963, with the important decisions on the 360 being implemented, excitement about the new product line began to spread through the corporation – at least among those who were privy to the secret. But this rising pitch of interest by no means meant that the struggle inside the company was settled. The new family of computers cut across all the old lines of authority and upset all the old divisions. The System/360 concepts plunged IBM into an organizational upheaval.

Resistance came in only a mild form from the World Trade Corp., whose long-time boss was A. K. Watson, Tom's brother. World Trade managers always thought of European markets as very different from those in the United States, and as requiring special considerations that US designers, would not give them. Initially they had reservations about the concept of a single computer family, which they thought of as fitted only to US needs. But when IBM laboratories in Europe were included in the formulation of the design of some of the 360 models, the grumblings from World Trade were muted. Later, A. K. Watson was made vice-chairman of the corporation and Gilbert Jones, formerly the head of domestic marketing of computers for the company, took over World Trade. These moves further integrated the domestic and foreign operations, and gave World Trade assurance that its voice would be heard at the top level of the corporation.

The General Products Division, for its part, really bristled with hostility. Its output, after all, accounted for two-thirds of the company's revenues for data processing. It had a popular and profitable product in the field, the 1401, which the 360 threatened to replace. The executive in charge of General Products, John Haanstra, fought against some phases of the 360 programme. Haanstra thought the new line would hit his division hard. He was concerned, from the time the System/360 program was approved, about the possibility that it would undermine his division's profits. Specifically, he feared that the cost of providing compatibility in the lower end of the 360 line (which would be General Products' responsibility) might price the machines out of the market. Later he was to develop some more elaborate arguments against the programme.

Long after the company's SPREAD Committee had outlined the System/360 concept, and it had been endorsed by IBM's top management, there were numerous development efforts going on inside the company that offered continuing alternatives to the concept – and they were taken seriously enough, in some cases, so that there were fights for jurisdiction over them. Early in 1963, for example, there was a row over development work at IBM's San Jose Laboratory, which belonged to the General Products Division. It turned out that San Jose – which had been explicitly told to stop the work – was still developing a low-power machine similar to the one being worked on in World Trade's German lab. When he heard about the continuing effort,

A. K. Watson went to the lab, along with Emanuel Piore, and seems to have angrily restated his demand that San Jose cut it out. Some people from San Jose were then transferred to Germany to work on the German machine, and the General Products effort was stopped. In the curious way of organizations, though, things turned out well enough in the end; the German machine proved to be a good one, and the Americans who came into the project contributed a lot to its salability. With some adaptations, the machine was finally incorporated into the 360 line, and, as the model 20 it later sold better than probably any other in the series.

TOP MANAGEMENT SHIFTS

In the autumn of 1963, Tom Watson . . . made some new management assignments that reflected the impact of the 360 programme on the corporation. Learson was shifted away from supervising product development and given responsibility for marketing, this being the next phase of the 360 programme. Gibson took over Learson's former responsibilities. The increasing development of IBM into a homogeneous international organization was reflected in the move up of A. K. Watson from World Trade to corporate vice-chairman. He was succeeded by Gilbert Jones, former head of domestic marketing. Piore became a group vice-president in charge of research and several other activities.

One reason for Watson's interest in speeding up the 360 programme in late 1963 was an increasing awareness that the IBM product line was running out of steam. The company was barely reaching its sales goals in this period. Some of this slowdown, no doubt, was due to mounting rumours about the new line. But there was another, critical reason for the slowdown: major customers were seeking ways of linking separate data-processing operations on a national basis, and IBM had limited capability along that line. Finally, IBM got a distinctly unpleasant shock in December 1963, when the Honeywell Corp. announced a new computer. Its model 200 had been designed along the same lines as the 1401 – a fact Honeywell cheerfully acknowledged – but it used newer, faster and cheaper transistors than the 1401 and was therefore priced 30 per cent below the IBM model. To make matters worse, Honeywell's engineers had figured out a means by which customers interested in reprogramming from an IBM 1401 to a Honeywell 200 could do so inexpensively. The vulnerability of the 1401 line was obvious, and so was the company's need for the new line of computers.

It was around this time that some IBM executives began to argue seriously for simultaneous introduction of the whole 360 family. There were several advantages to the move. One was that it would have a tremendous public relations impact and demonstrate the distinctive nature of IBM's new undertaking. Customers would have a clear picture of where and how they could grow with the computer product line, and so would be more inclined to wait for it. Finally, there might be an antitrust problem in introducing the various 360 models sequentially. The Justice Department might feel that an IBM salesman was improperly taking away competitors' business if he urged customers not to buy their products because of an impending announcement of his own company's new model. IBM had long had a company policy under which no employee was allowed to tell a customer of any new product not formally announced by the management. (Several employees have, in fact, been fired or disciplined for violating the rule.) Announcing the whole 360 line at once would dispose of the problem.

Learson Stages a Shoot-Out

Beginning in late 1963, then, the idea of announcing and marketing the 360 family all at once gained increasing support. At the same time, by making the 360 programme tougher to achieve, the idea gave Haanstra some new arguments against the programme. His opposition now centred on two main points. First, he argued that the General Products manufacturing organization would be under pressure to build in a couple of years enough units of the model 30 to replace a field inventory of the 1401 that had been installed over a five-year period. He said that IBM was in danger of acquiring a huge backlog, one representing perhaps two or three years' output, and that competitors, able to deliver in a year or less, would steal business away.

But Haanstra's argument was countered to some extent by a group of resourceful IBM engineers. They believed that the so-called 'read-only' storage device could be adapted to make the 360–30 compatible with the 1401. The read-only technique, which involved the storing of permanent electronic instructions in the computer, could be adapted to make the model 30 act like a 1401 in many respects: the computer would be slowed down, but the user would be able to employ his 1401 programs. IBM executives had earlier been exposed to a read-only device by John Fairclough, the head of World Trade's Hursley Laboratory in England, when he was trying (unsuccessfully) to win corporate approval for his Scamp computer.

Could the device really be used to meet Haanstra's objections to the 360–30? To find out, Learson staged a 'shoot-out' in January 1964, between the 1401-S and the model 30. The test proved that the model 30, 'emulating' the 1401, could already operate at 80 per cent of the speed of the 1401-S – and could improve that figure with other adaptations. That was good enough for Learson. He notified Watson that he was ready to go, and said that he favoured announcing the whole System/360 family at once.

'Going... Going... Gone!'

Haanstra was still not convinced. He persisted in his view that his manufacturing organization probably could not gear up to meet the production demand adequately. On 18 and 19 March, a final 'risk-assessment' session was held at Yorktown Heights to review once again every debatable point of the programme. Tom Watson Jr, president Al Williams and 30 top executives of the corporation attended. This was to be the last chance for the unpersuaded to state their doubts or objections on any aspect of the new programme – patent protection, policy on computer returns, the company's ability to hire and train an enormous new workforce in the time allotted, and so on. Haanstra himself was conspicuously absent from this session. In February he had been relieved of his responsibilities as president of the General Products Division and assigned to special duty – monitoring a project to investigate the possibility of IBM's getting into magnetic tape. (He later became a vice-president of the Federal Systems Division.) At the end of the risk-assessment meeting, Watson seemed satisfied that all the objections to the 360 had been met. Al Williams, who had been presiding, stood up before the group, asked if there were any last dissents, and then, getting no response, dramatically intoned, 'Going . . . going . . .gone!'

The 7 April 1964 announcement of the programme unveiled details of six separate compatible computer machines; their memories would be interchangeable, so that a total of 19 different combination would be available. The peripheral equipment was to consist of 40 different input and output devices, including printers, optical scanners and high-speed tape drives. Delivery of the new machines would start in April 1965.

The Nature of the Risk

The basic announcement of the new line brought a mixed reaction from the competition. The implication that the 360 line would make obsolete all earlier equipment was derided and minimized by some rival manufacturers, who seized every opportunity to argue that the move was less significant than it appeared . . . [or claimed it was unfeasible or uneconomic for customers].

But some of the competition was concerned enough about the System/360 to respond to its challenge on a large scale. During the summer of 1964, General Electric announced that its 600 line of computers would have time-sharing capabilities. The full import of this announcement hit IBM that Autumn, when MIT, a prime target of several computer manufacturers, announced that it would buy a GE machine. IBM had worked on a time-sharing programme back in 1960 but had abandoned the idea when the cost of the terminals involved seemed to make it uneconomic. GE's success caught IBM off base and in 1964 and 1965 it was scrambling madly to provide the same capability in the 360 line. Late in 1964, RCA announced it would use pure monolithic integrated circuitry (i.e. as opposed to IBM's hybrid circuitry) in some models of its new Spectra 70 line. This development probably led to a certain amount of soul-searching at IBM.

In the end . . .the company felt that the turn to monolithic circuitry did not involve capabilities that threatened the 360 line; furthermore, if and when monolithic circuitry ever did prove to have decisive advantages over IBM's hybrid circuitry, the company was prepared – the computers themselves and some three-quarters of the component manufacturing equipment could be adapted fairly inexpensively to monolithics. As for time-sharing, any anxieties IBM had about that were eased in March 1965, when Watts Humphrey, a systems expert who had been given the assignment of meeting the time-sharing challenge, got the job done. . . .

IBM announced additions to the 360 line in 1964 and 1965. One was the model 90, a supercomputer type, designed to be competitive with Control Data's 6800. Another was the 360–44, designed for special scientific purposes. Also, there was the 360–67, a large time-sharing machine. Another, the 360–20, represented a pioneering push into the low end of the market. None of these was fully compatible with the models originally announced, but they were considered part of the 360 family.

System/360 underwent many changes after the concept was originally brought forth back in 1962 and even after Watson's announcement in 1964. More central processors were later offered in the 360 line; some of them had memories that were much faster than those originally offered. The number of input–output machines [increased several times]. . . .

'Major Reshufflements'

IBM had several managers trying to keep the 360 programme on track in 1964–5. Gibson, who had succeeded Learson in the job, was replaced late in 1964. His successor, Paul Knaplund, lasted about another year.... In 1965 there was one item of unalloyed bad news; the company had suffered heavy setbacks at the high end of the 360 line – that is, in its efforts to bring forth a great supercomputer in the tradition of Stretch. In 1964 it wrote off $15 million worth of parts and equipment developed specifically for the 360–90.

There were signs at about this time that the 360 programme was still generating other reshufflements of divisions and personnel. Dr Piore had been freed from operational duties and responsibilities and given a licence to roam the company checking on just about all technical activities. Some of his former duties were placed in a division headed by Eugene Fubini, a former Assistant Secretary of Defence and the Pentagon's deputy director of research and engineering before he joined IBM in 1965. Fubini was one of the first outsiders ever brought into the company at such a high executive level. Another change represented a comeback for Stephen Dunwell, who had managed the Stretch programme and had been made the scapegoat for its expensive failure to perform as advertised. When IBM got into the 360 programme, its technical group discovered that the work done on Stretch was immensely valuable to them; and Watson personally gave Dunwell an award as an IBM fellow (which entitled him to work with IBM backing, for five years, on any project of his choosing).

In 1971 58-year-old Tom Watson Jr, slowed by poor health, turned over the chairmanship of the company to T. Vincent Learson. While Learson was taking on the top job, computer makers were rattled by a recession and shaken by a series of corporate crises. 1970–2 saw General Electric Co. and RCA withdraw from the field, cutting the number of US computer makers from nine to seven. The industry was struck by a backlash from oversold customers, a new generation of computers, and a switch in government expenditures away from R&D and towards social services. Customers became sales resistant and cost-conscious. *Business Week* commented,

> The Learson era in the computer business promises to be vastly different from the preceding two decades of frantic growth, during which IBM's yearly revenues increased more than thirty-fold – from $226 million in 1951 to $8.2 billion this year. The outlook for the industry is for a lower rate of growth from a bigger base. But the growth will still be a very healthy 10% to 12% annually, depending on the state of the general economy. If IBM merely holds its present share of the market, this pace of growth would mean annual increments in its revenues of around half a billion dollars....

On his sixtieth birthday in 1972, T. V. Learson surprised nearly everyone by announcing his retirement after only 18 months as chairman. Said Learson, 'We believe very strongly that in a business as technical and competitive as this, the interests of IBM will be best served by management teams of younger upcoming men and women...' Learson's successor as chairman, 52-year-old Frank Cary, was a quieter and more amiable executive, yet few observers felt the management shuffle heralded any significant departure from the vigorous marketing oriented practices of the Learson era.

QUESTIONS

1. What stimulated the change in strategy at the time of the 360? Evaluate the process by which change was brought about.
2. Evaluate Mr Learson as a change manager. Why does he act this way?
3. How could other companies have taken advantage of IBM's 360 strategy? What should IBM do about these?

1–9

THE HONDA MOTOR COMPANY*

In the post-World War II era Honda Motor Co. (Ltd) was a major force in revolutionizing the motorcycle and small car industries of the world. What were the keys to success for this unique Japanese company? What were its relationships to the national planning systems so often given credit for the emergence of the modern Japanese auto industry? And where should Honda look for its future successes in the mid- to late 1990s?

THE YOUNGEST ENTREPRENEUR

Mr Soichiro Honda began his career at Arto Shokai, a car repair shop in Tokyo. At the age of 16, during the Great Kanto earthquake of 1923, the young apprentice who had never driven a car leapt to the wheel of a customer's vehicle and in a bit of daring-do manoeuvred it to safety. Unlike his fellow apprentices Honda stayed on to help Arto Shokai's master mechanic recover from the disaster. Soon the owner-'master' set up the rapidly experienced Honda as head of a branch of Arto Shokai in Hamamatsu, Honda's home town. There Honda patented cast-metal spokes to replace all wooden ones – like those that burned out, almost wrecking his car, during the earthquake episode – and gathered the first of over 100 personal patents

---

*Case copyright © 1990 by James Brian Quinn.
Research associate, Penny C. Paquette. Numbers in parentheses indicate the reference and page number for material from a previously footnoted source.

in his lifetime. The Japanese trading companies soon began exporting his spokes all over the Far East.

By the age of 25, Honda was one of the youngest Japanese entrepreneurs around. He became *the* Hamamatsu playboy, not only plying from one geisha house to the next, but piling geishas into his own car for wild drives and drunken revels around the town. In one such escapade his car full of geishas went off a bridge, but landed safely in the mud – no injuries. In another, he tossed a geisha from a second-storey window. She landed on some electric wires below – from which a suddenly sobered Honda carefully extracted her – again, fortunately, no injuries. These are only some of the many colourful stories about the young Mr Honda.

Motors and Mechanics

Honda also loved motors and engines. When the head of Arto Shokai suggested Honda might build a racer (on his own time), Honda spent months of midnight hours to build a car from spare parts and war surplus aircraft engines. He soon began to drive his products himself, to win races and to extend his reputation for wild eccentricity into other areas.

Honda started making basic changes in racing car designs and soon set new speed records. But in the All Japan Speed Rally of 1936, travelling at 120 kph – a record not exceeded for years – another car jumped in front of Honda, demolishing Honda's car and leaving him with lifetime injuries. This incident as much as anything directed his energies from racing towards engineering. Seeing more opportunities in manufacturing than repairs, Honda formed Tokai Heavy Industries in 1937 to make piston rings for cars.

Piston Rings and War

But Honda knew nothing about the complex, casting processes involved. For months he and his assistant lived in their factory, day and night. Honda became a working hermit, complete with uncut hair and bristling chin. His limited savings wasted away. He sold his wife's jewellery to keep on, but he persisted, knowing his family would starve if he failed. After many frustrating failures, Honda sought the specialized technical knowledge he lacked because he had dropped out of school. After painfully gaining entry to the Hamamatsu High School of Technology – ten years older than his classmates, an unprecedented act in age- and class-conscious Japan – Honda promptly upset the authorities by attending only classes of interest to him, listening carefully to what interested him and not even taking notes on the rest. He refused to take examinations, saying that a diploma was worth less than a cinema ticket; at least the ticket guaranteed you got in to see the film.[1]

As Honda began to understand the technicalities of his product, he sold rings to the low end of the market, but could not meet Toyota's high quality standards. When he tried to expand his plant, the government refused to permit him a cement allotment in its carefully controlled pre-war economic strategy. Honda not only figured out how to make his own cement, he developed special automated equipment that let him meet the major manufacturers' quality standards for rings and later for aircraft propellers. But during the war American bombings and an earthquake destroyed much of his operation. Honda sold off the rest of his assets as the war ended. With the proceeds he bought a huge drum of medical alcohol, made his own sake, and spent an inebriated year visiting friends and trying to decide what to do next.

HONDA MOTORS BEGINS

The post-war era was terrible. Japan's cities were destroyed. City-dwellers had to sortie into the country to buy their daily food. Trains were overcrowded and petrol was in short supply. Honda later said, 'I happened on the idea of fitting an engine to a bicycle simply because I didn't want to ride the incredibly crowded trains and buses myself and it became impossible for me to drive my car because of the petrol shortage.'[2] Using small, war-surplus petrol-powered motors which had provided electricity for military radios, Honda made motor bikes that were an instant hit. When Honda exhausted his supply of surplus motors, he designed his own motor which could use an economical pine-resin fuel combination. He bought a pine forest to obtain the resin for his fuel mixture, but almost burned this down while trying to blast a hole in the base of a tree to get the resin.

Honda realized that his simple motorbikes would not last long once Japan began its post-war recovery. In 1949 he raised some $3,800 from friends and designed a longer-range two-stroke, 3 hp (98 cc) machine – the Type D with a superior stamped metal frame, christened the 'Dream'. Soon Honda was selling 1,000 bikes and motorcycles a month to black marketeers and small bicycle shops. But Honda's bill collectors often found their customers had disappeared or gone bankrupt before they paid the company. Honda was more interested in the product and its engineering than in profits. Production and sales were doing well, but the company was facing imminent bankruptcy. Honda welcomed the recommendation of an acquaintance that he take on Takeo Fujisawa as his head of finance and marketing. Fujisawa's heavy and ponderous style contrasted sharply with Honda's waspish, impatient, even rude directness, but the two became friends for life.

They moved the company from sleepy, gossipy, Hamamatsu – where the neighbours objected to Honda's flamboyant, noisy, sake-filled 3 a.m. returns on his motorcycle – to Tokyo and promptly applied for government support to produce 300 motorcycles per month. MITI – Japan's coordinating agency for industry, technology and trade affairs – thought no one could sell that many motorcycles, and denied its support. Ignoring MITI's scepticism, Fujisawa wrote an impassioned letter to all of the 18,000 bicycle shops in Japan, presenting Honda's product as their wave of the future and promising to train them in its sale and repair. While Japan's largest producers typically had only regional distribution, Honda soon had a national network of 5,000 dedicated dealers.

Next, instead of emulating the 4-stroke, side-valve machine competitors had Honda created a 146 cc 4-stroke, overhead valve (OHV) engine with 5.5 horsepower. The Type E doubled available horsepower with no added weight, and became the basis for Honda's appeal to the high performance marketplace. Honda integrated the production of the key components, engines, frames, chains and drives essential to such performance. But it outsourced non-critical parts as much as possible, and purchased a relatively small, old, sewing machine plant for assembly operations.

Lacking large-scale production facilities, Honda and his people designed special small-scale assembly equipment – and simply stayed at work each day as long as it took to meet orders.

Technology and Quality

While other manufacturers milked a single winning design in the domestic marketplace, Honda thought Type E did not hit a wide enough market. 'I racked my brain to contrive a two-wheeler with an engine which would be in high demand. I concluded I must make a motorcycle that would substitute for the bicycle.'[2] Honda developed a new 50 cc engine from the gound up, and coupled this with a small friendly-looking frame for informal users. Sensing an untapped market niche for local delivery vehicles for small businesses, he designed in a step-through frame, an automatic transmission and one-hand controls that allowed riders to carry a package in the other hand. The market for the 'Cub' boomed, and Honda moved into large volume manufacturing for the first time.

In 1951, top officials of the larger Japanese manufacturers invited Honda and Fujisawa to attend a private meeting to determine incentive policies for Japanese exports. Honda refused to attend, thus beginning a long pattern of non-participation with the central political and business forces directing Japan's economic recovery. He felt that high quality goods needed no such supports and knew no national boundaries.

Whatever his political prowess, Honda attacked any mechanical problems before him with energy and persistence. If he thought of a new concept in the middle of the night, he would get up and make notes so as not to forget it. Honda was talkative, energetic, gregarious – always excited by the technology and his products, never (according to Mr Fujisawa) 'by the profits we would make next year'. But Honda earned the nickname Kaminari-san – 'Mr. Thunder' – because of his instantaneous temper and sometimes erratic behaviour. He spent most of his time in the factory or development shop working side-by-side with his workers. Employees from his early years remember his shouting at engineers or pounding himself on the head when they made a mistake. On one occasion, after finding some bolts improperly tightened, he grabbed a wrench from a technician, did the job right and then popped the technician with the wrench while shouting, 'You damned fool. This is how you are supposed to tighten bolts.'[1,72] People later avoided close contact when Honda was carrying a wrench.

Expanding Investments

Honda's financial problems were solved in a unique way. Once they saw the Honda Cub, dealers were so impressed that they came to the company to buy whatever inventory they could. This was in sharp contrast to their usual practice of selling whatever models the big manufacturers had been able to force on them. Fujisawa cleverly used this demand to his advantage. He allocated production to those who could pay in advance and began weeding out slow-paying distributors and dealers. Soon Honda had not only the widest, but the strongest, motorcycle dealer network in Japan.

As sales expanded, Honda Motors pushed investments upward even faster. Fujisawa purchased some large, key plots of land for future expansion. And Soichiro Honda insisted on the highest quality machinery for his plants. The two travelled to the United States to evaluate the US industry, and engaged in a machine tool buying spree. Although total corporate capital was only $165,000, they bought over $1 million in imported tools; between 1952 and 1954 Honda's total capital expenditures outweighed those of the much larger Toyota and Nissan units. How did they finance this phenomenon? Unable and unwilling to obtain government financing, and lacking access to Japan's closely controlled equity markets, Mr Fujisawa again had to use clever – though high-risk – trade financing to see the company through.

EXPANSION TO WORLD MARKETS

About this time Honda decided that motorcycle racing could assert to the world his company's true expertise in motorcycle design. After some disappointing initial entries in international races, Honda realized that the key to success was lighter, more efficient engines, getting more power from more thorough combustion. Honda engineers ultimately designed an engine with the cam shaft at the top – the then unique overhead cam (OHC) engine – and made crucial discoveries about mixing gases in the combustion chamber that led to the CVCC engines of its later automobiles. Honda's motorcycles won the Manufacturers' Team Prize for the company in 1959 and the first five places (in both 125 and 255 cc sizes) at the Isle of Man races in 1961. These were considered the 'Olympics of racing' at the time.

Time for Strategy

While Mr Honda was mesmerized by the sheer technological questions of these 'racing years', Mr Fujisawa was concerned with the company's longer-term strategy. He thought there was a large untapped market for smaller, safer 'bikes', geared to customers who resisted larger motorcycles as expensive, dangerous and associated with the 'black leather jacket' crowd. He wanted a small 50 cc bike for novices, youthful executives or young couples. At first Mr Honda ignored his colleague's unusual vision. Then around 1958, Honda designed and built a full-sized example of a 'scooter' that would do the trick. Fujisawa was immediately excited by the product and soon predicted sales of 30,000 units per month – a bit ambitious in a Japanese market, which then constituted only 20,000 per month for all two-wheelers.

Now considered to be the Model T of two-wheeled vehicles and probably Honda's masterpiece, the new motorbike was called the Supercub. Revolutionary in design, the Supercub had a light, carefree image, a step-through configuration which made it easier for women to ride, and a graceful, stylish appearance. But the new model also sported a 3-speed transmission, an automatic clutch and a 50 cc OHC engine which, based on Honda's racing experience, generated 4.5 horsepower.

By the end of 1959 the Supercub had enabled Honda to assume the No. 1 position among Japanese motorcycle manufacturers, with 60 per cent of its sales being Supercubs. The company's best selling earlier model had sold only 3,000 units

The first Super Cub ("stepthrough") inaugurated in 1958
Source: Honda Motor Corporation

per month. Honda invested 10 billion yen in a single factory to build 30,000 Supercubs a month, with no guarantee of maintaining that level of sales. Fujisawa intuitively pushed ahead. He described the Supercub to retailers as 'more like a bicycle than a motorcycle', and began to sell the vehicles directly to retailers, mostly bicycle shops. By 1959 Honda was the largest motorcycle producer in the world.

American Honda

Honda and Fujisawa thought the time now had come to pursue the world market actively. Honda executives regarded Europe and Southeast Asia as the best markets to target, since Americans were so tied to the automobile and held an unattractive image of motorcycles and their riders. They argued that a small company like Honda would struggle to penetrate the US market where only 60,000 motorcycles were imported yearly and where only 3,000 dealers existed – scarcely 1,000 of which were even open five days a week – took motorcycles on consignment, and gave spotty after-sales service. After several years of trying to pry open the underdeveloped country markets of Asia, Mr Fujisawa – thinking that American preferences could set the trends for the rest of the world – targeted the United States as crucial.

Like most foreign producers, Honda at first relied on an agent for distribution in the United States but quickly dropped it as ineffective. Fujisawa established an overseas unit reporting directly to corporate headquarters to give Honda a better presence in the market, especially in post-sale servicing. Despite onerous exchange restrictions by the Japanese government, American Honda Motor Co. was formed in June 1959 with a Los Angeles headquarters and its own executive vice president, Mr. Kihachiro Kawashima.

The company had gone to MITI for a currency allocation, but was rebuffed. MITI reasoned that if the giant Toyota had earlier failed at the same venture, how could Honda succeed? Its meagre $110,000 currency allocation meant Honda had to start its UK operations with only $250,000 of paid-in capital. Initially, it appeared that the sceptics were right. Honda's cycles did not sell in the United States; the negative image associated with motorcycles might be too entrenched for even Honda to overcome. But Kawashima and his two associates dug in, shared an apartment for $80 a month, rented a warehouse in a run-down area of Los Angeles, and personally stacked motorcycle crates, swept the floors and built and maintained the parts bin.

Early 1960 became disastrous when customers reported Honda's larger motorcycles frequently leaked oil or experienced serious clutch failures on the longer, harder and faster roads and tracks of the United States. In a move that presaged later policies, Kawashima air-freighted the motorcycles to Japan where engineering teams, working night and day, found a way to fix the problem in one short month.

Then events took a surprising turn. Up to this point, executives of American Honda had promoted sales of the larger, more luxurious motorcycles because they seemed more suited to the US market. Although they had not attempted to sell the 50 cc Supercubs through US dealers, the executives rode them around Los Angeles themselves and noticed the bikes attracted considerable attention. With the larger bikes facing engineering problems, American Honda decided to increase emphasis on its 50 cc line, just to generate cash flows.

The Supercub created genuine excitement and enthusiasm in the American market primarily because it retailed for less than $250, compared with $1,000 to $1,500 for the bigger American or British motorcycles. American Honda was extremely concerned that it not lose the 'black leather jacket' customers which comprised the high margin portion of the business.[3] But Honda's retailers continually reported that Supercub customers were normal everyday Americans. Because of Japanese government restrictions, however, American Honda had to operate on a cash basis, building its inventory, advertising and distribution systems without using Japanese generated yen. The division was extremely limited on cash. Yet by 1962–3 Honda's export earnings (from motorcycles) surpassed those of Nissan or Toyota. And by 1965, Honda America's motorcycle sales had jumped to $77 million and a whopping 63 per cent market share.

DECISION POINT

How should Honda develop its US presence? What should its advertising, pricing, distribution, inventory, product and service policies be in the United States? How should these be related to its Japanese prices, production facilities, development activities, and the continuing restriction by the Ministry of Finance on exports of Japanese yen?

FOUR WHEELS FOR HONDA

In the 1950s Japan had intensified its now famous programmes for coordinating the development of selected high-priority industries. Early on, MITI had targeted the steel, textile, shipbuilding and petrochemical industries for such development. In the 1960s it began to encourage selected mass-production industries including automobiles and optical devices, although it never 'targeted' these as it had other sectors. In later years semiconductors, software and computers were given priorities.

MITI announced in 1960 that it planned to divide the existing passenger car manufacturers into three groups (a mass-production car group, a mini-car group and a special-purpose vehicle group) and that no other manufacturers would be permitted to enter. The government reasoned that the move would reduce destructive domestic competition and allow the industry to achieve scale economies for world penetration. But Honda, who would have been foreclosed from the market, was outraged. Fortunately, some leftist riots forced postponement of the hearings on the proposal and it was never officially enacted. But it did stimulate Mr Honda, who had dreamed since childhood of building automobiles, to move rapidly.

Racers and Instincts

To enter the car market, Honda determined that the company must: (1) design and build racing cars capable of competing with the world's best, and (2) ensure that any passenger cars derived from these would be of the world's highest quality. Although MITI actively opposed Honda's entry into automobiles, at the 1962 Tokyo Motor Show, Honda revealed a light-duty (T-360) truck and a (S-500) sports car prototype. The T-360 performed like a sports car and was the first truck of its class to permit high speeds. High horsepower, high rpms and outstanding combustion efficiency comprised the critical engineering technologies which went into these first vehicles.

Mr Honda's basic approach had always been to develop a special engine to solve each specific problem. Since he was strapped for cash, he had designed efficient small engines which were compact but powerful. As he moved to automobile engines, Honda adapted the technology he had created for his previous motorcycle designs. Replicating their motorcycle strategy, Honda engineers by 1964 had developed a Formula 1 racer. The company's 1965 Formula 1 entry won Honda's first Grand Prix victory in Mexico City. In 1966 Jack Brabham drove to eleven straight victories in a Honda Formula II equipped with a 4 cylinder 1,000 cc (160 hp) water-cooled engine. But within a few years Honda withdrew his cars (and later his motorcycles) from racing, saying the company had gained all the technology and publicity it could from that source.

Honda's car racing technology was soon transferred to mass production passenger cars – first in the 1967 N–360 mini car, with an air-cooled, two-cylinder engine, and a front-wheel drive (FWD) system unprecedented in automobile design. The N–360 was an instant success and captured 31.2 per cent of Japan's total sales in its class, a mere two months after its introduction.

A Clean New Engine

In 1970 the US Congress amended the Clean Air Act, requiring a 90 per cent reduction in the emission of hydrocarbons, carbon monoxide and nitrogen oxides by 1976. Honda executives had begun research on a 'clean' automobile engine in the mid-1960s. From the beginning they sought an engine that Mr Honda demanded, offering both the highest internal efficiency and greatest 'external merit' in terms of its cleanliness and safety. Recognizing that any system which used an after-treatment device inherently wasted the potential energy of fuel, Honda had started several major projects on different efficient engines that burned exhaust gases more thoroughly.

Ultimately, in early 1971, the company chose its CVCC (compound vortex controlled combustion) engine, an engineering concept that was surprisingly simple yet decidedly effective. Tasuka Date, a top Honda engineer, had conceived of igniting a much richer fuel mixture (about 4.5:1) in an auxiliary chamber and letting the explosion expand into the main chamber, which had the desired lean (18:1 or 20:1) mixture to keep operating temperature low within the engine, yet minimize exhausts.

The CVCC engine was adaptable to both small and large cars. Detroit executives initially held that such 'stratified charge' engines could only be put on small cars. But Honda proved its principle by modifying two 8-cylinder Chevy Impala engines to its design and improving their engine efficiency, petrol mileage and emission characteristics sufficiently to meet promulgated 1975 air quality standards. Despite Detroit's continued opposition, the CVCC was the only engine in the world which, operating in its normal mode in the early 1970s, could meet the proposed US Air Quality Standards.

A TECHNOLOGY FOCUS

The parent company backed its strong technological presence in its markets with many times more engineers than its non-Japanese competitors. Yet the company enjoyed the lowest rates of R&D cost to sales among the Japanese majors.

The Expert System

Recognizing that neither he nor Mr Honda would have prospered in a typical pyramidal organization, Mr Fujisawa had developed what became known as Honda Motor's 'expert system' in which creative people – experts – could fully utilize their skills and be rewarded appropriately. He wanted a flat or 'paperweight' oganization in which a promising person was not dependent upon or restrained by his immediate superior. He envisioned the organization as a kind of web 'with engineers lined up sideways instead of top to bottom'. According to Dr Kowomoto of Honda R&D, any number of people could have top engineering positions based solely on their technical 'expert' qualifications, even with no one reporting to them.

Fujisawa's organization recognized that fundamental research was unique. It needed to concentrate on technological understanding, faced many non-commercializable failures and rarely worked well in a structured environment. By contrast production/ development had to be carefully controlled, financially driven and error-free. Honda's researchers could define their own research themes and pursue their projects to conclusion. Research focused on product activities in small teams, typically 2–10 people. Engineering was independent of Research and concentrated on process development.

Integrated Designs

Once development began, projects were managed across research, design, product engineering and early production stages. Each person in a project group both maintained his own specialty and worked directly with other team members. Dr Kowomoto emphasized that few risks were taken once a product or process was prototyped. Using its special coordination techniques, Honda operated on a 2–3-year cycle from development to production, as compared with a worldwide average of over 4 years for the car industry.

Honda's development process centred on its SED (Sales, Production Engineering and Development) system. Through constant reviews and their own training, engineers were encouraged to 'think like customers'. Each group on a team advanced its arguments based on its own analysis of the potentials, requirements and constraints it saw for the new product. Interactions among the groups was based on a principle that the company characterized as 'mutual aggression'. Each was strongly encouraged to pursue its individual position all the way until a final decision was reached. Within R&D different subgroups pursued competing technical solutions until the most appropriate one was selected by the team. The R&D organization developing new products had 'no pyramidal or hierarchical organization, just engineers and chief engineers'. On a project team, titles did not influence decisions: even the newest engineers were to 'argue frankly' with senior people, including vice-presidents who might be on or visit their team. One person – like a metallurgy specialist – might be on many different teams simultaneously, developing completely different new products in parallel for each.

A very specific schedule was set for each project early on, and no deviations from the schedule were allowed despite problems which might develop. People were expected to work as hard as necessary to maintain planned progress, which was reviewed every three months by an SED oversight group where each function presented its views as vigorously as possible. Development people argued for the best technological solution, Engineering for the best quality-cost solution, and Sales to see that the design fitted market trends. Since Honda first introduced its cars in Japan, they had to be successful in the Japanese market. But the same car – modified only for local safety, right-hand driving or environmental standards – had to meet other countries' market demands as well. Although Honda, as a smaller manufacturer, outsourced many of its raw materials, sheet metal and fabricated parts, through the early 1980s, it had been reluctant to share its design information with outside suppliers until final specifications were set.

Honda Motors was quick to point out that its process was one of 'trial and error'. For example, in 1970 Honda's 1300 cc model introduced with considerable confidence by Marketing had suffered a terrible market failure. In contrast, the Civic had an unstylish look, which many feared would not sell well. Instead it became a popular product and Honda's stable-volume production model with a potential for long product life. The first marketed model of the Honda Prelude had so little power that it was sometimes called the 'Quaalude'. But the company quickly restyled it, increased the power of its engine, gave it a much more 'macho' appeal and made it a success.

A unique aspect of Honda's design process was the fact that workers could suggest and implement process changes themselves right on the production line. A visitor would see small areas (20′ × 20′) out on the factory floor where workers were building their own new prototype processes. When asked if they were supervised by engineers, the answer would be, 'No! If they need engineers they will find them.'

Changes were not limited to single work stations. Workers had automated whole body-panel and body-assembly sections this way. Each year Honda sponsored an 'idea contest' and gave awards for its employees' most ingenious ideas, both for company use and for sheer inventiveness. One winner was a three-wheeled 'all terrain' powered bike that became a major product line.

Production Organization

Honda enjoyed some unique policies in the production area. In its foreign operations, it encouraged employees to wear uniforms, like its Japanese employees. Most did. Each individual was called an 'associate', a term which described how each person related to other members of the organization and conveyed a feeling of respect for the individual. Overseas, Honda preferred to develop its own people in order to reduce the chances of employees bringing bad work habits with them. Newly hired associates were often rotated to other tasks and dispatched to Honda plants in Japan where they learned Honda's methodologies of producing to exact specifications.

Once trained, Honda promoted the best qualified person to do a job. Unlike other companies in Japan, seniority never had a high priority in determining advancement. Even in its US operations, where other companies stressed seniority, young Honda managers often occupied high positions that would take 5–10 years more to achieve in other companies.

Everyone was treated as an equal. Even the ubiquitous, identical uniforms of Honda employees emphasized equality, rather than rank. Everyone ate in the same cafeteria. No one had a private office. Honda facilities featured open areas where managers, coordinators, staff and clerical workers worked side by side at plain desks. Managers and engineers routinely handled parts and equipment on the shop floor. Soichiro Honda believed that good leaders should perform even the most undesirable jobs willingly, and at least once. Accordingly, he was known to sweep factory floors, empty ashtrays and pick up paper towels from bathroom floors wherever he went.

On matters which affected them, associates were asked their opinion. In the United States they voluntarily suggested cutting the lunch hour to 30 minutes and shortening the work day. They chose how to expand production during pressing times and which days of a holiday week would be work days or free. Disciplined associates could appeal their cases to a court of peers selected at random from cohorts on another shift. The peer group's decision was by secret ballot and was binding on all parties.

Dr Robert Guest, a world authority on automotive organizations, described Honda's organization practices this way:

> Almost all members of Honda's operating management started in the shop itself, as did 65 per cent of its Japanese sales personnel. There is frequent movement of workers laterally and through promotions. Everyone understands that automation will be targeted first at the most onerous tasks. Much of the machinery at Honda is built by a Honda engineering subsidiary, which was set up because of the many new ideas that were originated by the workforce themselves. No one fears problems of technological unemployment, as growth continues.
>
> Work standards are written up by the employees themselves, in conjunction with their foremen. Honda threw out American-style scientific management systems when

they found that their workers slowed down while being timed and objected to the process. Mr. Honda, by skill and temperament, was a 'shop man' who was always concerned about the product, production details, and more importantly about the role played by people on the shop floor and their creative potentials.[4]

Organization Structure

True to his stated policy of 'proceed always with ambition and youthfulness', Soichiro Honda (aged 68) and Takeo Fujisawa (aged 62) retired from active management of the company on its 25th anniversary in 1973, becoming 'advisors' to the firm. Mr Kowashima, then Tadashi Kume became president of Honda Motor Company. The top management group was assembled on the third floor of Honda's Tokyo headquarters office – using an open-plan executive suite where 32 directors worked together in a single open room. Just as in Honda's factories, senior executives like Kume occupied desks in an open office with chairs scattered around. Junior managers bustled in and out visiting dealers and suppliers. While decisions at this level were widely discussed in the room, Mr Kume, an engineer who had earlier opposed and defeated Honda in a showdown over the development of air-cooled engines, was clearly the first among equals. He was 'a passionate man in the Honda tradition, a man who, like the founder, sometimes shouted to make himself heard. . . . He listed as his hobby drinking sake, but cars, and more particularly engines in them were, still his passion.'

The company's management structure had three levels. At the top was a board of directors, consisting of 24 company officers, including its two 'supreme advisors'. Within the board were a senior managing director's group, a decision-making body consisting of the president, two executive vice-presidents and four senior management directors. The president's expertise was in technology; one vice-president's was in sales; and the other, responsible for the company's financial policies, was an engineer by training and a generalist by experience at Honda.

At the corporate level, this group controlled three specialist groups, each made up of managing directors and ordinary directors and joined as needed by the heads of semi-independent affiliated companies. The three specialist groups were responsible for matters relating to 'people, things, and money'. The individual sections and divisions responsible for day-to-day operations and for specific areas of profit-making reported to the 'president's office'. They were under the general oversight of the specialist groups, which did not represent any specific section with daily responsibilities for profit. Among other things, these specialist groups were responsible for overseeing major new projects of the company. An example was the deployment of a task force in 1977 to select a site for its US motorcycle (and later, automobile) assembly operations.

At the operational level, Honda utilized basically a worldwide functional organization for its line activities. For example, a North American Sales Division reported directly to the headquarters Sales group, overseas Production divisions to the headquarters Manufacturing group, and small overseas R&D units to corporate R&D. However, engine R&D, engine manufacture, and manufacture of some key subassemblies were kept in Japan. Some products were designed and built in Japan directly for export; some were built in Japan and modified for export; others were built entirely in overseas operations.

HONDA IN THE LATE 1980s

In the late 1980s Honda had become the fourth largest maker of American cars. Honda decided in 1979 to build a 150,000 unit US car assembly plant alongside its Marysville, Ohio motorcycle plant. Accords began rolling off in December 1982. When the plant's capacity became seriously strained in 1985, Honda moved quickly to double it. The new space was used to produce Honda's popular Civic, the smallest and least expensive car Honda sold in the United States.

Honda had aggressively built its image in the United States through a quiet sophisticated advertising programme. According to professional analysts, American consumers perceived the Honda name as being synonymous with quality, just as they perceived the Sony brand. The quality of Japanese-made Honda cars was legendary. Engineering and automotive magazine ratings of the world's best cars almost always included the Honda Accord. For example, testers for *Road and Track* had paired the Mercedes-Benz 190E with the Accord SE-i; the Mercedes at $23,000 scored 166 points, the Accord at $13,000 scored 163.[5] And the US operation was determined to equal that record.

Honda in Japan

In 1983 Honda eased past Mazda to take over the No. 3 sales position with 8 per cent of Japan's market, following Toyota's 41 per cent share and Nissan's 26 per cent. While the rest of the Japanese industry was having difficulty in its home market, Honda sales boomed upward by 18 per cent, the highest growth among major car makers. Honda launched a new mini-car in Japan called the Citi, whose sales immediately soared to 99,000 units, almost double those of the Civic, Honda's next most popular car there. Honda's partly-plastic bodied, CRX two-seater car won the 1983 Car of the Year Award in Japan, leading all contenders by a big margin. And in America, EPA gave the CRX its highest rating for fuel economy – 51 miles per gallon.

Although motorcycles accounted for only about 25 per cent of Honda's $10 billion in early 1980s sales, the company was dominated by people who grew up in that fiercely competitive business. The great flexibility and cost-consciousness of motorcycle manufacturing penetrated all aspects of Honda. And its top management was the youngest in the Japanese auto industry. Unfortunately, however – like its rivals – Honda had not been able to make much money in Japan. In the mid-1980s, the Japanese market was barely growing, and heavy competition among ten car makers kept prices low. While Japanese manufacturers discounted their cars heavily in Japan, they sold at premium prices in America. For example, Honda's 1984 Prelude, initially priced at $9,995 in America, went for about half that in Japan. Honda made higher operating profits (8.6 per cent on consolidated sales in 1983) than either Toyota (6.9 per cent) or Nissan (5.8 per cent). But in the voluntary quota system to the United States, Honda was allowed only 350,000 cars for shipment, compared with 500,000 for Toyota and 450,000 for Nissan.

Honda in America

Worldwide, Toyota was clearly Honda's most formidable Japanese competitor.

Toyota was the world's third largest car company (half the size of Ford and a third the size of G.M.) and had recently decided to lay down new plants in the United States and Canada. (See Exhibit 1.)

Despite its position as the No. 1 foreign car maker selling in the United States, Toyota had previously made all its cars abroad. Toyota's public references to its mid-1980s strategy was 'Global 10' symbolizing its intent to capture 10 per cent of the world vehicle market. But insiders said the company had raised that target to 12 per cent.[6] Toyota backed that intention with a war chest of some $5 billion in cash equivalent assets. Toyota's new US factory, unlike its joint venture with GM in California, would be aimed at the 'upscale' US market with its $9,378 Camry. And Toyota brought a number of its most crucial Japanese suppliers to the United States to manufacture near its plants. Backed by the lowest-cost production system in Japan, Toyota was adding dealerships, boosting advertising and lowering its cycle times for model changes. It was also bringing its dealers into its just-in-time inventory systems, pressing ahead with 'the same kind of ruthlessness in sales and distribution that it had pioneered in the factory'.[6]

Not content with having entered the US market directly, various Asian car makers were also entering through Canada. Lured by huge Canadian incentives, South Korea's Hyundai and Japan's Toyota and Suzuki had announced plans for some $600 million in capacity in Canada. (See Exhibit 1.) These would add 23 per cent to Canada's capacity of 1.1 million units per year by the late 1980s. Under a 1965 US–Canadian agreement, a manufacturer in Canada could ship cars to the United States duty-free as long as 50 per cent of the value had been added in North America.

Canadian provinces competed hotly for the new Asian plants. Experts estimated that Hyundai's tariff exemptions alone would cost the Canadian government $150 million in lost taxes per year. Canadian manufacturing costs had fallen sharply since 1980 because of Canada's weak currency. In addition, Canada's national health system created an (approximately) $8/hour labour cost advantage over the United States.

US Operations

Although some claimed Honda's ultimate goal was to be Japan's biggest car maker, its top management remained silent on this point. Nevertheless the press consistently reported that Honda's target was to sell one million cars a year in the United States in the early 1990s. In this competition, the $250 million Honda had invested in its Marysville plant compared favourably with the $660 million Nissan had spent for a similar capacity plant in the United States[7] or the $500 million Toyota was preparing to spend on its new 200,000 unit Camry facility.[6]

Honda had attacked all its costs in the United States aggressively. By using labour practices similar to its Japanese units, it had got the total compensation of its non-unionized US workers to about $14/hour compared with some $23 at the Big Three's unionized plants. Honda had also used less expensive components than US makers – and often got better quality for its money. About half the value of a Honda's parts was imported from Japan. Some were made to order by the parent company (especially for the Accord) but others were cheaper than US parts or of higher quality. Honda said it had planned to use a higher proportion of US-made parts, 'But the attitude of some suppliers was that their job was only to give us the parts, and that we must check the quality ourselves.... We told them that wasn't enough, we expected 100 per cent good parts.' Some suppliers responded, others did not. Honda could build a fully equipped 1985 Accord for about $8,000, some $1,000–$1,500 less than it cost General Motors to build a comparably equipped version of its Buick or Olds line. And by 1988 it could ship the cars to Japan from the United States at a profit.

After some initial problems (dominantly with paint, rust, brakes and air conditioning) in early models, Honda's US products were given an overwhelmingly high rating by Consumer's Union. The automobile press said the redesigned 1985 Accord built in America was 'a great improvement on one of the classic modern cars', and its successor became the best selling single mark in the United States during the late 1980s.

What is the Future?

Under Mr Kume, technology continued to receive the same high priority it had under Mr Honda. For example, while the body of the CRX sports car still contained 60 per cent metal in 1984, Kume said his goal was to build the car with a 100 per cent plastic shell. Further into the future was the possibility of the 'ceramic engine', currently being pursued by all Japanese manufacturers because of its high thermal efficiency, high compression ratios and low fuel consumption. Ceramic engines also offered opportunities for getting rid of water-cooled radiators and much of the other weight and complexity associated with the cast steel engine blocks which had been the standby of the industry for years. Automobile design and manufacture were undergoing their most radical changes in some 60 years.

Exhibit 2 offers some comparative and trend data concerning the major US and Japanese car makers' sales, production and export of cars. Exhibit 3 gives some comparative financials for these companies in the late 1980s. Exhibit 4 indicates the structure of the European and world markets for cars.

Sales of cars in Japan had been limited by government policy constraining credit, by the scarcity of roadways, and the very expensive parking facilities needed in most areas. In 1988 Japan had only 243 cars per 1,000 people as compared with 370 in Britain, 454 in West Germany and 588 in the United States. However, Japan's shift towards a domestic, consumer economy was expected to ease credit restrictions and to expand major motorways (from 2,700 miles to 8,700 miles by 2010). Japan's export of autos was constrained by its 'voluntary restraint' agreements with the United States.

Although Honda had been the first Japanese producer to manufacture cars in America, Nissan, Toyota, Mazda, Mitsubishi, Suzuki and Subaru were expected to follow. Honda's plant expansions would allow it to produce 500,000 cars per year, from which it expected to export 50,000 cars per year by 1991 from America to Japan. Nissan was expanding its Smyrna facility and would be producing some 450,000 cars per year by 1992. Total Japanese car manufacture in the United States was expected to reach 2.9 million vehicles per year in 1991 in addition to another 2 million direct exports from Japan. Ford and General Motors were expanding their plants to produce over 4.3 million compact and sub-compact cars annually during the early 1990s.

Although US manufacturers had made substantial progress, the average Japanese plant turned out a car with 20.3 hours of labour versus 24.4 hours for the average US facility. The rapidly appreciating yen had decreased the Japanese domestic manufacturing cost advantages to only $300 on the average. Wages and fringe benefits at the US Big Three cost about $30 per hours versus $24 at even Toyota's plants. And experts estimated that some of the Big Three's health care programmes alone cost $300–$500 more per car than Japanese manufacturers'. US manufacturers had responded by moving towards the up-market, but government-mandated 'fleet fuel economy' standards of 27.5 miles per gallon were beginning to create serious problems for American-owned producers.

The European Market

In contrast to its US strategy, Honda had been reluctant to invest heavily in Europe, apart from its motorcycle plants. It had undertaken a joint production arrangement with British Leyland for a new 2-litre car, bigger than any Honda had ever built. Total Japanese penetration of European markets was also not nearly as great. (See charts in Exhibit 4.) No one knew how Europe 1992 would affect car production in the EC. Quotas had restricted imports of Japanese cars into individual countries in the past. However, Spain and some of the 'Mediterranean countries' with low labour costs were pressing to break these quotas in 1992. Building sales in Europe would be difficult against the well-known, high quality and accepted European brands. However, many European producers had not updated their plants as dramatically as the Americans, and some of the great European cars had not won a 'car of the year' award in over a decade.

On the positive side, Japan's car industry, which had been barely a quarter the size of Britain's in 1965, was now seven times larger. However, like the Japanese and American markets, over-capacity (of about 20 per cent) plagued the European marketplace. Because of such considerations, France, Italy and Spain (which together accounted for about 40 per cent of total European sales) were virtually closed to Japanese producers, and other countries had applied ceilings to Japanese imports. These were largely offset by exports of the upper-line European cars, like BMW, Daimler-Benz, Jaguar, Saab and Volvo, mostly to the United States. Few of the 'lower-end' European cars enjoyed a substantial export market.

Cost structures in the automobile industry were changing rapidly in the late 1980s. Components and materials comprised about 50–60 per cent, and labour about 20 per cent, of an auto's factory cost. Plants for sophisticated components like engines, gear trains or trans-axles might cost $500–$800 million, while assembly plants were decreasing in size but increasing in the complexity of their flexible automation. In addition, about 30 per cent of the pre-tax price of a car was accounted for by marketing and distribution.

While US-owned companies had a strong presence in Europe, individual Japanese companies did not. (See Exhibit 4.) Japanese car companies' strategy problems were compounded by vastly increased price-cutting and retail competition in Japan. Toyota and Nissan seemed strong enough to withstand any onslaught, but both Mitsubishi and Mazda were plagued with scale problems, despite some fine individual products.

Given the massive capital requirements of the automobile industry, few would have thought a new entrant like Honda could have survived, much less prospered, in the 1960s and 1970s. But as *Fortune* concluded, 'A few years ago when Japanese cars flooded the American market, Detroit appeared frozen by indecision. The established Japanese companies, by comparison, seemed invincible. Now relative newcomer Honda is making the other Japanese car makers look ponderous and timid . . . against a company willing to take risks and move fast.'[7] But the markets of the 1990s posed formidable new challenges for Japan's No. 3 car producer.

QUESTIONS

1. What important patterns have guided Honda's strategy in the past? How do these affect its future strategy? What do you think of its organizational structure and practices? What lessons can be learned from Honda?

2. What were the critical factors for Honda's success during its early entrepreneurial development? Compare and contrast this pattern with that of other entrepreneurial Japanese and US companies. What are the most important similarities and differences?

3. How should Honda position itself in the early 1990s? Why? How should Detroit respond to this positioning?

4. What implications does Honda's past history have for the future of the car industry?

EXHIBIT 1
New capacity in Canada.

Company	Start-up date	Investment ($ millions)	Annual planned production units
Hyundai	1988	$220	100,000
Toyota	1988	$220	50,000
Suzuki*	1989	$300	300,000

*Joint venture with General Motors.
Source: Business Week, 4 November 1985.

EXHIBIT 2
Market shares of major producers.

	Honda	Toyota	Nissan	Mazda	Mitsubishi	GM	Ford	Chrysler[a]
US Car Sales (000s)								
1978	275	442	339	n/a	n/a	5,405	2,663	1,421
1983	401	556	522	n/a	n/a	4,054	1,571	1,178
1988	769	689	514	n/a	n/a	3,822	2,290	1,191
US Car Production (000s)								
1982	2	0	0	0	0	3,173	1,104	710
1985	145	0	44	0	0	4,822	1,636	1,377
1988	366	19[b]	110	167	0	3,427	1,807	1,073
US Market Share (%)								
1978	2.4	3.9	3.0	n/a	n/a	47.8	23.5	12.6
1983	4.4	6.1	5.7	n/a	n/a	44.2	17.1	12.3
1988	7.2	6.5	4.8	n/a	n/a	35.9	21.5	11.2
Japanese Car Sales (000s)								
1977	166	892	755	176	218	7	7	1
1982	240	1,174	822	247	226	2	1	<1
1987	337	1,454	765	199	158	3	1	<1
Japanese Car Production (000s)								
1978	653	2,039	1,733	493	629	0	0	0
1983	956	2,569	1,859	815	571	0	0	0
1988	1,073	2,983	1,731	880	640	0	0	0
Japanese Market Share (%)								
1977	10.6	34.7	29.8	9.2	9.0	<0.1	<0.1	<0.1
1982	12.7	31.9	26.6	11.8	8.5	<0.1	<0.1	<0.1
1987	16.2	32.1	21.7	11.5	7.2	<0.1	<0.1	<0.1
Car Exports (000s)								
1978	488	900	855	341	321	d	d	c
1983	900	1,365	1,179	674	432	d	d	c
1988	675	1,232	849	643	410	d	d	c
Car Production (000s) (outside of home country)								
1987	340	88[c]	213	4	n/a	2,002	2,170	77

[a] Includes AMC.
[b] Excludes NUMMI.
[c] Includes NUMMI.
[d] 1987 exports of cars from the United States totalled only 633,000 (with 562,000 of those being to Canada).
Source: Compiled from *Ward's Automotive Yearbook,* 1989 edition; *World Motor Vehicle Data,* 1989 edition.

EXHIBIT 3
Comparative financials – fiscal year 1989
($ millions).

	Honda[a]	Nissan[b]	Mazda[c]	Toyota[d]	Ford[e]
Sales	26,434	36,452	6,532	54,254	82,193
Other Income	121	276	12	203	11,148
Total Revenues					
Cost of Sales	19,274	28,651	5,840	45,032	68,233
S, G & A Expense	4,427	6,393	560	5,705	3,452
Interest Expense	186	752	39	168	354
Other Expenses	70	–	–	–	–
Income before Taxes	1,304	1,462	106	4,588	8,343
Income Taxes	611	608	69	2,369	2,999
Net Income	737	868	54	133	5,300
Cash Dividends	85	250	30	371	1,114
Inventories	3,600	3,814	1,254	1,968	4,396
TOTAL ASSETS	17,306	35,922	9,964	40,980	143,367
Long-term Debt and Other Obligations	2,543	6,163	1,946	4,179	6,175
Shareholders' Equity	6,829	12,495	2,614	24,701	21,529

[a] Honda Motor Co. Ltd. manufactures and sells motorcycles, cars, pumps, lawn mowers, power tillers, etc.
[b] Nissan Motor Co. Ltd. manufactures and sells cars, rockets, forklifts, textile machinery, boats, etc.
[c] Mazda Motor Corp. manufactures passenger cars, trucks, buses, machine tools, etc.
[d] Toyota Motor Co. Ltd. manufactures passenger cars, commercial vehicles, prefabricated housing units, etc. Merged with Toyota Motor Sales Co. Ltd. July 1982.
[e] Ford Motor Co. manufactures, assembles, and sells cars, trucks and related parts and accessories. Subsidiary businesses include Aerospace and Communications, steel, Ford Motor Credit Co., Leasing, Land Development. Ford owns 25 per cent interest in Mazda Motor Corp.
Source: Compiled from Moody's *Industrial Manual* and Moody's *International*, 1989 edition.

EXHIBIT 4
World vehicle production (000s).

Company	1982 Cars	1982 Total	1987 Cars	1987 Total
1. General Motors (USA)	4,870	6,150	5,605	7,497
2. Ford (USA)	2,890	4,027	4,000	5,892
3. Toyota (Japan)	2,258	3,147	2,796	3,730
4. Nissan (Japan)	1,864	2,512	2,017	2,658
5. Peugeot Group (France)	1,673	1,489	2,301	2,512
6. VW Group (W. Germany)	1,903	2,079	2,338	2,475
7. Chrysler (USA)	789	1,041	1,186	2,188
8. Renault (France)	1,844	2,105	1,742	2,053
9. Fiat Group (Italy)	1,343	1,635	1,675	1,880
10. VAZ (USSR)			725	1,605
11. Honda (Japan)	861	1,022	1,362	1,581
12. Mitsubishi (Japan)	573	969	595	1,231
13. Mazda (Japan)	824	1,110	858	1,202
14. Suzuki (Japan)	114	603	297	868
15. Daimler-Benz (W. Germany)	466	690	596	823
16. Hyundai (Korea)	78	91	545	607
17. Fuji-Subaru (Japan)	201	514	267	605
18. Daihatsu (Japan)	128	464	142	598
19. Isuzu (Japan)	113	405	204	542
20. Rover Group (UK)	405	509	472	537
Top 40 Manufacturers	26,077	34,221	32,727	44,609
North American Cos	8,869	11,501	10,792	15,663
Western European Cos	8,432	9,766	10,371	11,759
Japanese Cos	6,937	10,808	8,536	13,080
Eastern European Cos	1,925	1,989	2,086	2,975
Korean Cos	n/a	n/a	790	966
TOTAL WORLD PRODUCTION	29,776	39,750	33,007	45,914

Source: Compiled by the Motor Vehicle Manufacturers Association of the US. Inc. from reports of various overseas motor vehicle associations. Published in *Facts and Figures, 1985 and 1989.*

Free World Passenger Car Demand By Region (millions)

	1985	1987	1992	1997
United States	11.0	10.3	10.5	11.1
Canada	1.1	1.1	1.1	1.2
Europe	10.6	12.4	12.9	13.7
Latin America	1.2	1.1	1.6	2.0
Mid-East	0.4	0.3	0.6	0.7
Africa	0.3	0.3	0.5	0.7
Asia-Pacific	4.2	4.4	5.3	6.1
TOTAL	28.8	29.9	32.5	35.5

Source: 1992 Ward's Automotive Yearbook, p. 77.

EXHIBIT 4 (Continued)

European New Car Registrations By Manufacturer

	1985		1988	
	Units (000s)	%	Units (000s)	%
VW Group	1,529	14.4	1,930	14.9
Fiat Group	1,304	12.3	1,916	14.8
Ford Total[a]	1,268	11.9	1,466	11.3
Peugeot Group	1,226	11.5	1,672	12.9
GM Total[b]	1,212	11.4	1,375	10.6
Renault	1,139	10.7	1,326	10.2
Mercedes	394	3.7	445	3.4
Austin Rover	420	3.9	448	3.5
Nissan	307	2.9	378	2.9
Toyota	248	2.6	349	2.7
BMW	290	2.7	355	2.7
Volvo	255	2.4	265	2.0
Mazda	203	1.9	245	1.9
Alfa Romeo	161	1.5	213	1.6
Mitsubishi	116	1.1	156	1.2
Honda	n/a	n/a	140	1.1

[a] Of which more than 99 per cent is sold by Ford Europe.
[b] Of which more than 98 per cent is sold by Opel/Vauxhall.
Source: 1989 *Ward's Automotive Yearbook*, p. 87.

European Car Sales By Country

	New Car Sales (000s)	Japanese Import Penetration (%)	
	1988	1977	1987
W. Germany	2,808	2.5	15.1
France	2,217	2.6	2.9
United Kingdom	2,216	10.6	11.2
Italy	2,184	0.1	0.7
Spain	877	0.0	0.2
Netherlands	483	19.8	25.9
Belgium	427	19.3	20.8
Sweden	344	10.4	21.7
Switzerland	319	12.1	28.9
Austria	253	5.7	31.2
Portugal	206	15.2	8.5
Finland	174	21.8	41.8
Other	470	n/a	n/a
TOTAL	12,978	n/a	11.2

Source: 1988 Car sales from 1989 *Ward's Automotive Yearbook*, p. 87; Japanese import penetration figures compiled by the Motor Vehicle Manufacturers Association of the US, Inc. from reports of various overseas motor vehicle associations. Published in *Facts and Figures, 1989.*

EXHIBIT 4 (Continued)

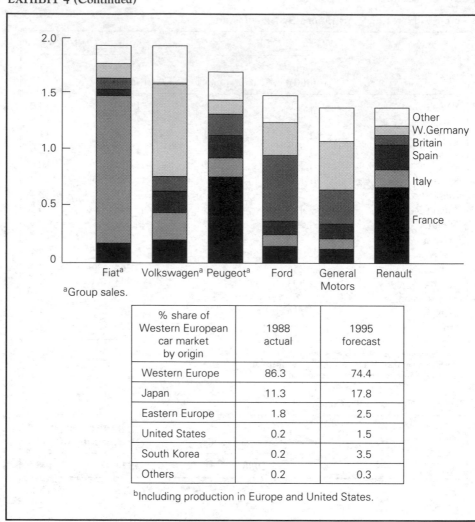

ᵃGroup sales.

% share of Western European car market by origin	1988 actual	1995 forecast
Western Europe	86.3	74.4
Japan	11.3	17.8
Eastern Europe	1.8	2.5
United States	0.2	1.5
South Korea	0.2	3.5
Others	0.2	0.3

ᵇIncluding production in Europe and United States.

Source: The Economist. 23 September 1989

In June 1991, Jack Schmuckli, chairman of European Operations at Sony Europa GmbH in Germany, recalled the evening of 9 November 1989, when the Berlin wall was opened:

> Suddenly, one of the most potent symbols of Europe's political and economic division was breached. As I watched television and saw the crowds streaming from East into West Berlin, it was evident that we were confronted with a significant business opportunity and needed to rethink our strategy regarding the Comecon countries.[1] Imagine, a region comprising some 400 million consumers, 20 per cent more than Western Europe, was at last opening up. In 1989, the Comecon markets accounted for roughly 1 per cent of our DM 7.7 billion in sales for all of Europe. This region, which we once considered low priority and best served by intermediaries, was at last joining the world of free markets. Sales of consumer electronics in these markets, estimated to be worth nearly $40 billion by the turn of the century, had to be looked at in a new perspective. How was Sony to enter this world and serve these countries?
>
> I immediately called Kazuo Matsuzaki, general manager of Sony's European Operations Office, and urged him to accelerate Sony's development in Eastern Europe. At the time, he reminded me that we were in the midst of a major expansion with Center, an Austrian trading company that acted as the distributor of our products to Poland, Hungary and Czechoslovakia, through those countries' foreign trade organizations (FTOs). He was quick to point out, however, that with the collapse of the wall, Center's value as a distributor became questionable. For that matter, we had to reconsider our

*This case was prepared as a basis for class discussion rather than to illustrate either effective or ineffective handling of a business situation. The support of Sony Europa GmbH executives in the development of this material is gratefully acknowledged.

trading arrangements throughout the region, and ask whether they would hold up or whether we should begin to build national subsidiaries immediately. Our initial focus concentrated on Poland which accounted for some 40 per cent of our 1989 East European sales. Moreover, Poland, with over 40 million inhabitants was the first country in the former East bloc to attain a non-Communist government and to implement market reforms.

For Sony, the most important of these reforms was the move towards a free market, enabling the country's retailing entrepreneurs to begin legitimate operations. A part of this move was currency convertibility. Prior to 1989, only those citizens who had worked abroad or with relatives in foreign countries were allowed to possess hard currency. Thus, for companies such as Sony, retail distribution was limited to hard currency outlets, and sales were restricted to tourists and the few Poles with access to hard currency. In mid-1989, the government had relaxed its currency restrictions, making it legal for all Poles to possess hard currency. Sony's 1988 sales of DM 9.8 million subsequently climbed to DM 31 million for 1989.[2] On 1 January 1990, in a first step towards having a convertible currency,[3] Poland devalued the zloty by nearly 60 per cent. Even though the devaluation made Western goods more expensive for those paying in zlotys, by the end of the year, Sony's sales had reached DM 41.6 million.

Despite increased supply, demand for consumer electronics exceeded the official supply available through Pewex, the FTO used by Center in Poland. To meet this demand, Polish entrepreneurs, or private dealers, began selling Sony products on the grey market,[4] independent of Pewex. Matthew Lang, assistant manager in Sony's Corporate Strategy Department, felt that the mere existence of a grey market implied something was wrong with the current channel arrangement. 'Was Sony supplying enough product to the market? Were its products priced too high? Were existing channels ineffective?' he asked.

In devising a future strategy for Poland, Matsuzaki and Lang had two major objectives: increasing sales through legitimate sales channels; and establishing an authorized sales and service network in an intermediate step towards a national company. Because a national subsidiary implied terminating agreements with Center and Pewex, some managers were reluctant to invest any more time and energy into upgrading the existing Center–Pewex distribution channel, and wanted to establish a Sony-owned network as soon as possible. In part, the desire to establish a fully-owned distribution ntwork stemmed from Sony's 30+ years of experience in Western Europe. On more than one occasion, local distributors had become so powerful that they were able to influence the distribution policy to a greater extent than Sony preferred. Not surprisingly, deciding when and how to alter distribution agreements was of paramount concern to Sony management. In Poland, where Pewex, a representative of the 'old' system, already accounted for nearly 100 per cent of Sony's sales, some managers believed that it was in the company's best interest to build a 'counterbalance' to Pewex's market presence by developing business with Poland's emerging private dealers.

By contrast, some other managers believed it was too soon for Sony to invest independently in Poland, and that extricating itself from Center and Pewex could not be accomplished quickly, due to Pewex's dominant position. Moreover, this same group of managers cited Pewex's extensive retail chain in Poland as another reason to stick with, or modify, the existing distribution agreement. Ideally, Matsuzaki and Lang sought a solution that would satisfy Poland's demand for consumer electronics and preserve the company's goodwill with each stakeholder. As the two resumed their discussions, they were keenly aware that any decisions and actions in Poland would be viewed as an indication of how, or how not, Sony might approach other markets in Eastern Europe and the USSR.

SONY IN EUROPE

One of Sony's stated objectives was to achieve share leadership in all major product categories in each national market. To achieve its goal, the company nurtured each market segment with strong competitive products and an excellent sales and service network.

Sony had begun marketing its products in Europe during the 1960s through Sony Overseas SA (SOSA), a subsidiary based in Switzerland. From the 1960s on, SOSA expanded the company's sales and service activities throughout Europe by appointing national distributors. By 1970, these distributor organizations were taken over or changed to Sony's own subsidiaries so that, by 1990, Sony had ten national organizations in Europe, plus two regional organizations – Sony Scandinavia and Sony Europe International (SEI); the latter served Eastern Europe and the USSR. Each organization reported to the European headquarters and normally consisted of three main marketing divisions: Consumer Products, Professional Products and Magnetic Products.

In this evolution, SOSA typically identified a country distributor which, at a later date, might become a joint venture partner. Some years after that, these same entities might become wholly owned Sony subsidiaries. Sony devoted significant energy to managing the relationships with its distributors, especially during the transition period to joint venture partner and/or wholly owned subsidiary. Matsuzaki emphasized that how and when Sony made these transitions was key and represented a part of the company's corporate ethic. He added 'Sony's image works both for and against us. If we cut links to a distributor abruptly, we may find it difficult to recruit distributors in other parts of the world thereafter. With long-standing distributorships, Sony typically does not simply terminate agreements, but offers phaseout periods with generous compensation.'

In planning the company's approach to Eastern Europe, and Poland in particular, Matsuzaki and Lang had to keep these points in mind. At the same time, however, the two also had to consider the challenge of managing distributor relationships in Europe. As an example, Lang cited Nissan's problems in the United Kingdom. When Nissan had first entered the UK market, it had sold its cars through Nissan UK, an independent, privately owned distributor. In 1990, executives from Nissan and Nissan UK began arguing over the pricing policy for the Nissan Primera. According to Octav Botnar, chairman and managing director of Nissan UK, Nissan's pricing was unfair to British consumers because UK-built Nissan cars sold more cheaply in Germany, the Netherlands and Belgium, where the distributors were owned by Nissan Motor Company itself. Eventually, the relationship between Botnar and

Nissan management became so strained that Nissan chose to establish a wholly owned distributorship with a view to disenfranchising Botnar. Throughout the process, both parties became involved in highly publicized legal proceedings. At Sony, management was loathe to become involved in such disputes.

Sales and Service in Europe

Within Sony Corporation, management was proud of its after-sales service. According to Lang, Sony's products had one of the lowest failure rates in the industry but, none the less, service was considered an integral part of the marketing mix and the company's 'customer satisfaction' philosophy. He added that the key elements for providing service were reliability and speed, and that together the two maintained Sony's image and brand reputation. Therefore, training for Sony personnel, from the telephone operator at a service centre through to the service technician, emphasized a customer orientation.

Apart from training, each national sales organization decided the best way to handle service in its particular market. As a result, no standard Sony service concept existed Europe-wide. Generally speaking, though, Sony sold its products through authorized dealers who, typically, also sold competing brands. Sony service, on the other hand, fell into one of three categories: fully owned service departments, authorized service stations or a combination of both.

Fully Owned Service Departments

As noted, Sony established sales and service organizations in Europe from 1968 on. Initially, national subsidiaries identified and authorized dealers to sell, but not repair, Sony products. Customers faced with a repair problem in these markets could return the product to the dealer who, in turn, sent the product to the service department at the country subsidiary. A customer could, of course, take the product directly to the service department himself.

Authorized Service Stations

With the growth of sales in larger markets, some subsidiaries authorized dealers to service, as well as sell, Sony products. Typically, an authorized service station repaired Sony as well as other brands of consumer electronics. Customers seeking repair in these markets could take their products to an authorized Sony service station.

Mixed Service Organizations

More recently, some markets had established mixed service organizations. In these markets, a customer could go to a fully owned service department directly, or to a dealer who sold, but did not repair, Sony products. Alternatively, a customer could go to an independent authorized dealer who sold as well repaired Sony and other brands of consumer electronics.

In addition to repairing locally purchased products, Sony's West European subsidiaries were obliged to service Sony products purchased in other markets. Aside from these service options, customers in any market could take a chance with an unauthorized service station. Those willing to do so ran the risk of having non-Sony components installed in their products or, worse, untrained personnel damaging their products. It was this very scenario which Matsuzaki and Lang wanted to avoid in Poland, lest Sony's brand image be damaged. None the less, the two remained uncertain whether to adopt a fully owned service department, authorized service stations, or a mixed service organization in Poland.

Eastern Europe

In the near future, Sony management believed that the opening of Eastern Europe would be one of the most important events to influence their business. Indeed, with most of the consumer electronics markets in the developed world at or near saturation, Sony's competitors had already begun to focus on Eastern Europe's emerging markets. According to one market research firm,[5] the market for consumer electronics in Eastern Europe was forecast to reach $38 billion by the year 2000 based on the 50 per cent penetration of electronic consumer goods achieved in Western countries.

In addition to the companies active in Poland, other companies in Eastern Europe included Philips, the large Dutch electronic and electrical goods company. In mid-1990, Philips announced plans to establish offices in Poland, Czechoslovakia and Hungary, in order to identify opportunities for cooperation and to serve as the nucleus for future sales organizations in those countries. In Czechoslovakia, with 1991 sales of its consumer electronic products expected to reach Sch 150 million,[6] the company announced plans for a network of 75 retail shops. In the USSR, Philips had established a sales and service organization, and had announced joint manufacturing plans for videocassette recorders (VCRs).

Additional companies building an East European presence included Nokia Consumer Electronics, Europe's third largest consumer electronics manufacturer. Specifically, Nokia announced plans to supply and assemble kits, in former East Germany, for distribution throughout Eastern Europe. Following the reunification of East and West Germany, Grundig, the German consumer electronics firm based in Fuerth, concentrated its East European sales efforts on the former DDR. In mid-1991, a Grundig spokesman said the company had targeted a turnover in excess of DM 100 million in the former East Germany. To achieve its goal, the company established a marketing outlet in Boehlitz-Ehrenberg, in what was previously East Germany, to supply retail dealers with its consumer goods.

Other companies involved in manufacturing deals were Akai with videocassette recorders in Bulgaria, Samsung with colour television in Hungary, and Thomson with colour television and VCRs in Hungary and the USSR. Regardless of the company, each of these joint venture activities was building a local manufacturing presence in Eastern Europe. For the management of Sony, who saw Eastern Europe as a natural extension of their presence in Western Europe, success in Poland played a key role in securing its place in an increasingly volatile global battle.

DOING BUSINESS IN POLAND

In 1991, Poland celebrated the 200th anniversary of a constitution proclaimed on 3 May 1791 by Stanislaus Augustus, King of Poland. During those 200 years, Poland had been subjected to a number of wars and territorial revisions which had positioned the country substantially west of its traditional boundaries. Because of these geographical changes, significant Polish minorities still lived in Lithuania, Byelorussia and the Ukraine. For example, in Lithuania, roughly 8 per cent of the population in the Vilnius areas was Polish. Likewise, in Byelorussia, approximately 12 per cent of the population was of Polish extraction. One analyst commented that, because of this distribution of minorities, there was a certain 'artificiality' to Poland's borders. Moreover, Polish, Lithuanian, Byelorussian, Ukrainian and Russian belonged to the same sub-group of languages, and thus shared many common words and expression, In brief, because of its historical, economic and cultural place in Europe, Poland was seen by many as a springboard for future investment into the neighbouring republics of the USSR. (See Exhibit 1 for maps depicting the changes in Poland's borders from the eighteenth century through World War II.)

Excluding the USSR, Poland was the single biggest market in Eastern Europe, with a population of 37.9 million. With a growth rate of 5.7 per cent between 1980 and 1988, Poland had one of the fastest growing populations on the continent, most of which was concentrated in urban communities. And, unlike other countries in Central and Eastern Europe, such as Czechoslovakia or Yugoslavia with their many ethnic groups, Poland had a more homogeneous population, a factor many analysts believed would contribute to future political as well as economic stability. Indeed, in 1990, the Polish government's statistical office estimated that the output of private industry grew by 50 per cent and accounted for 18 per cent of national income, up from 11 per cent in 1989. Moreover, the number of people employed in private enterprise grew by more than 500,000 in 1989, bringing the total to between 1.8 and 2 million people.[7]

One journalist, commenting on Polish behaviour, went so far as to say that no other group in Eastern Europe rivalled the Poles for being the most business-minded, and that Polish merchants were favoured for their bold and widespread commercial activities.[8] Typically, he added, merchants bought low-priced commodities in Poland and earned a substantial gain in foreign currency by selling these commodities in the West. Profits were easily doubled by using the gain to purchase western merchandise for resale back in Poland. Normally, these goods were sold through private enterprises, instead of Poland's FTOs.

For Sony, product demand was driven by the company's outstanding brand image and by the unexpected volume of zlotys and dollars circulating in Poland. To clarify, a survey in five European countries rated Sony number three after IBM and Mercedes-Benz in terms of popularity, dynamism and corporate image.[9] In another survey, Sony was considered number one in Poland and the USSR in 'image power'.[10] With respect to currency, one spokeswoman commented that Poles had been saving their money for yeas and were a lot more Western in their thinking than others in the former Eastern bloc. Then, too, hard currency remittances to Poles from relatives living abroad were estimated at over $3 billion in 1990.

Despite the growth of private industry, other factors – such as the lack of effective communications – hindered business conduct in Poland. According to one businessman, Poland had one of the worst telecommunications infrastructures in Central and Eastern Europe. With only seven phones per 100 people, it was extremely difficult to perform tasks taken for granted in the West. Fax machines, mobile phones, data transmission and other advanced services were equally, if not more, scarce than telephones. Yet another burden was the lack of local managers with experience in accounting, finance and other western business practices. In summary, the poor infrastructure and shortage of managerial talent in Poland could prolong the country's transition from a centrally planned to a market economy.

Foreign Trade Organizations

As of mid-1991, most foreign trade in Poland was still carried out by specialized foreign trade organizations (FTOs) with monopoly positions. Typically, an FTO acted as the main authority for foreign trade transactions dealing with any one product or related group of products. FTOs were responsible for all commercial activity with foreign partners in that product area, including negotiating and signing contracts, preparing and implementing cooperations agreements, conducting market research, organizing sales and purchases, advertising and participating in international trade fairs. After-sales service, however, was strictly limited to products purchased within the country and from a particular FTO.

Of the 86 FTOs in Poland, Pewex (see below, p. 327) and Baltona were the two largest that specialized in consumer electronics. With roughly 350 outlets throughout Poland, Baltona was the second largest of the two consumer electronics FTOs and sourced its products primarily from Hitachi and other smaller less well-known Japanese companies.

From 1990 onwards, there as increasing talk of privatization of state-owned enterprises in Poland. Retailing was at the forefront of the government's privatization programme and, according to one ministry official, roughly 90 per cent of the 120,000 state stores were expected to be transferred to private owners by 1996. It was hoped that the largest of these, including Pewex and Baltona, would be privatized before the end of 1991. In an interview on the eventual privatization of Pewex, Managing Director Marian Zacharski proposed allocating 49 per cent of Pewex's shares to Western companies, 20 per cent to employees and the rest to domestic investors. Despite this insight about Pewex's possible future owners, Pewex was still 100 per cent state-owned as of mid-1991.

COMPETITION IN POLAND

Matsushita Electric Industrial Co. Ltd

With 1990 sales of nearly $38 billion, Matsushita was by far the world's largest consumer electronics company. Within the industry, Matsushita was considered to be less innovative than its competitors, although it was renowned for its manufacturing skills. With the help of 25,000 company-owned shops in Japan, Matshushita usually flooded the domestic market and crushed the competition before repeating the exercise in overseas markets. In contrast to Sony, whose goods tended to appeal to more affluent consumers, Matsushita's products were geared for the mass market, for families of modest means with little technical interest.[11]

Additional brands owned by Matsushita included Panasonic, Quasar, Technics and National. Also, JVC was 51 per cent owned by Matsushita. The Panasonic brand was distributed exclusively by the Mitsubishi Trading Company (MTC) in Poland. MTC worked through Pewex; however, Panasonic was unofficially reputed to be looking for private dealers, independent of MTC.

To reinforce Panasonic's brand awareness in Poland, second to Sony in 1990, Panasonic began a massive promotion campaign using posters on buses and trams. In this way, the company hoped to strengthen its image position and, at the same time, maintain its 2:1 lead, in unit terms, against Sony. To service Panasonic's products, the MTC had established two service stations in Poland and planned to open ten more in the near future. Although the service network was fully owned by MTC, Panasonic provided technical assistance. As part of their ongoing cooperation, Panasonic and Mitsubishi announced plans in early 1991 to form a joint manufacturing venture in Poland. They had not disclosed, however, which products would be made.

Hitachi

Hitachi had conducted its business in Poland for nine years through International Trade & Investment (ITI), a trading company founded by two Poles, which sold Hitachi products through Baltona. In contrast to Sony or Matsushita, however, which had approached private dealers directly, Hitachi had allowed ITI to manage such contacts in Poland. Then, so as not to miss out on the growing opportunity with entrepreneurs, in the spring of 1991, ITI started offering Hitachi products to private dealers, supported by an office building ITI was constructing for Hitachi in Warsaw. According to one industry participant, ITI's competitive advantage in consumer electronics was its having the best service network in Poland.

Philips

One analyst commented that, with the exception of Philips, which sold its products through Brabok, a private dealer with only two shops, non-Japanese brands were not nearly as popular in Poland as Japanese products. He added that Philips had jointly produced videocassette recorders in Poland since 1986 and, more recently, had concluded a deal with a local company, Pratork, to assemble televisions in Poland bearing the Philips brand name.

Others

Aside from Sony, Matsushita's Panasonic brand and, to a lesser extent, Hitachi, Sanyo and Sharp were the only other significant Japanese brands sold in Poland. Although Sanyo and Sharp were sold through Pewex, both had also been offered to private dealers, independently of Pewex.

DISTRIBUTION AND SERVICE OF CONSUMER ELECTRONICS IN POLAND

As noted, the political and economic changes in Poland since 1989 had given birth to a significant grey market in consumer electronics. Sony management, eager to preserve and expand its share of the Polish market, felt an arrangement was needed to balance the interests of Center, Pewex and Poland's private dealers, to shift distribution away from the grey channels.

Center

Center was an affiliate of an Austrian holding company based in Vienna and, from the 1960s on, played an important role in supplying Sony products to the Polish as well as the Hungarian and Czechoslovakian markets, through the monopolies of the countries' state-owned foreign trade organizations. One part of the holding company, Center Technische GmbH, looked exclusively after Sony and had established representative offices in Warsaw, Prague and Budapest, as well as service stations in Budapest and Warsaw.

As noted, prior to the collapse of the Berlin wall, Sony considered Eastern Europe to be a minor part of its business, best handled by an intermediary – namely, Center. One manager pointed out, however, that Center was not a typical distributor. That is, unlike other Sony distributors, with operations in the country they served, Center was based in Austria. As a result, once the wall fell, Center offered little to Sony as a joint venture partner or acquisition candidate. On the other hand, some executives believed Center's role was still valuable. In particular, this group of executives emphasized that Center carried the risk of non-payment from Pewex, not an insignificant point given the volume of Sony's sales and the pace of change in Poland.

Pewex

Pewex, based in Warsaw, was Poland's largest and best run retail operation with approximately 1,010 outlets across the country. In 1990, Pewex reported sales of $936 million, up 68 per cent over 1989 with profits averaging 7–9 per cent of sales when expressed in Western accounting terms. According to Marian Zacharski, Managing Director of Pewex, sales in 1991 were forecast to reach nearly $2 billion. Traditionally, Pewex had been known for luxury goods but, with Poland's move towards a market economy, it added thousands of items to its product offering – including toys, clothing, drugs and foodstuffs. At the same time, Zacharski expanded Western-style displays and self-service. In addition, contrary to Polish shopping customs of the past, customers were no longer required to stand in separate queues for each purchase category. One Pewex customer commented, 'In my local store, if I want bread, beer, meat and candy, I must queue four times. Pewex is undoubtedly worth the extra money.'

Like Pewex customers, Pewex employees were highly motivated. On 31 December 1990, Pewex employees stayed after hours to convert pricing to the Polish zloty so the stores could open on time 2 January 1991. By contrast, Baltona was closed on 2 January to re-price. To maintain and improve its position in Poland, Pewex spent $30 million on a fully computerized accounting and inventory control system.

In Poland, all after-sales service requests for Sony products sold through Pewex were handled by Center's Warsaw-based service organization, Centropol, which received all spare parts and training from Center Technische GmbH in Vienna. Despite the proliferation of goods sold at Pewex, the retail chain was slow in building its service network. Specifically, customers seeking after-sales service for consumer electronics in Poland had to go to Pewex's one service station in Warsaw. Alternatively, customers could deposit their products at one of eight Pewex outlets in Poland. Once a week, all products in need of repair were sent to the central service station in Warsaw. For Sony products bought outside Poland, or for productss bought inside Poland but outside the Pewex chain, Polish customers had no alternative but to take their chances with an unauthorized service station.

After visiting Centropol, Lang commented that the Pewex staff members were familiar with technology on traditional products such as stereos, but were not well qualified to service products such as compact disc players or camcorders, based on more sophisticated digital and optical technologies. In a move to upgrade the repair skills of Pewex's staff and, at the same time, minimize any damage unauthorized services stations might do to Sony products and the company's image, he and Matsuzaki proposed organizing a training programme in Warsaw. Although seen as a first step, both knew full well that the training initiative would eventually have to be followed by a more comprehensive service organization.

Poland's Retailing Entrepreneurs

Matsuzaki described those in control of the grey market as typical entrepreneurs – dynamic individuals quick to identify and capitalize on an opportunity. He went on to say that one group of three university colleagues owned their own trading company, Digital, based in Gdansk. It had a staff over over 300. The group was clever and hard-working, and had franchised businesses across Poland. Moreover, the group was well versed in Western business methods and approaches, using western-style advertising to sell imported personal computers and satellite antennas, as well as Sony products (purchased from Sony Deutschland GmbH). For all these products, Digital paid hard currency and resold in zlotys.

By comparison, a newspaper journalist described an individual who sold Polish commodities in Germany, then used the DM proceeds to buy videocassette recorders for resale in Poland. After purchasing 20 VCRs, the individual would re-enter Poland at an obscure border crossing where a small bribe to the border guards secured his passage with the goods, at a customs fee below the goods' true value. Under this system, the private dealer earned a profit of roughly $1,000 per month – approximately 15 times the monthly salary of an average worker in Poland.

Lastly, Matsuzaki mentioned a Polish company called Selko, whose owner bought personal computers in Berlin and resold them in Poland, the Ukraine and Lithuania. According to Matsuzaki, this entrepreneur had become so successful that he had purchased a near bankrupt bookshop in Warsaw, transformed it into a profitable business, and was planning to convert the same building to a personal computer outlet. To top it all off, this same individual, unable to source sufficient product from Sony Deutschland, obtained container loads of Sony products from Singapore, shipped directly to his warehouse in Poland. Like other entrepreneurs, Selko paid for its purchases in hard currency, which it resold for zlotys in Poland.

Unauthorized Service Stations

Aside from selling products on the grey market, several entrepreneurs in Poland had started service stations for consumer electronics. On one visit to Warsaw, a Sony representative identified five unauthorized Sony service stations in the telephone directory. Although each station claimed they could repair Sony products, none had in fact received training; not did they use Sony parts. For Sony, the possibility of faulty product repair by unauthorized stationss posed a serious threat to its brand image.

Sony Europe International

Within the Sony European operations, Sony Europe International (SEI) was responsible for trading with Poland. Strictly speaking, Pewex placcd its orders through Center which, in turn, passed the orders on to SEI. Once received, SEI instructed its warehouse in Holland to ship the products directly to Pewex's main office in Warsaw, where they were then distributed to Pewex's 1,010 outlets across the country for sale to the Polish consumer. Payment occurred in two steps: first, Pewex converted zlotys into hard currency; then it paid Center, which in turn paid SEI.

As Poland moved towards a market economy, SEI proceeded to establish contact with 15 private dealers in Poland. Normally, these dealers contacted the SEI sales manager with product requests. Unlike its arrangement with Center, however, SEI would not ship from its warehouse to these dealers until it was paid in full, in hard currency. (See Exhibit 2 for a summary of the flow of orders, products and capital between Poland and the Sony organization.)

OPTIONS

To establish a direct presence in Poland meant renegotiating Sony's distribution agreement with Center. Based on past experience, any renegotiation would prove lengthy and, according to one manager, could cost up to DM 10 million. All the same, some managers favoured making the transition from distributor to local subsidiary sooner rather than later, based on experiences in both North America and Europe. As Matsuzaki and Lang continued their discussions, they concentrated on four options, all focused on Poland. In a larger context, however, the two were also aware that their decision, and the results that followed, would be scrutinized as an indication of how, or how not, to approach Sony's other markets in Central and Eastern Europe.

Continue Present Arrangements

Until the end of 1992, Sony was obliged to honour its exclusive agreement with Center as the distributor to all state-owned organizations in Poland. Sony was permitted, however, under the terms of the agreement, to develop its own network with private companies. Thus, Sony could wait until its agreement with Center expired at the end of 1992 and, simultaneously, allow the parallel imports to continue.

On the plus side, Lang mentioned that maintaining the status quo was the easiest option as it obviated any immediate renegotiation and/or compensation to Center. Also, under the present agreement, Center would continue to bear the risk of Pewex's non-payment. On the other hand, taking a *laissez-faire* stance would increase Sony's reliance on Center to expand the sales and service network in Poland, and thus did little to enhance Sony's control over sales and marketing policy.

Allowing the parallel imports to continue did not mean taking no action. On the contrary, if Sony chose to continue its arrangement with Center, it was also intent on furthering its cooperation with some of Poland's private dealers in preparation for the post-1992 era. By waiting until its agreement with Center expired, Sony would have 18 months to select some of Poland's entrepreneurs, and develop them as local sales and service representatives. Because many of these entrepreneurs had already demonstrated their ability to market Sony's products, via the grey market, Matsuzaki believed that with the proper incentives, these same individuals could be persuaded to join a future Sony Poland organization. In so doing, Sony might be able to unify its parallel markets in Poland and, at the same time, nurture a pool of talent for an eventual Polish subsidiary.

Supply Directly with Pewex

As one alternative to maintaining the status quo, Sony could terminate its agreement with Center and deal directly with Pewex, an idea proposed by Marian Zacharski. As Poland's largest retailer, Pewex clearly had an established sales network and possessed formidable buying power. With one-third of Pewex's nearly $1 billion 1990 sales attributed to consumer electronics, direct cooperation entailed serious consideration. Specifically, direct cooperation with Pewex would allow Sony to exercise more control over the sales and marketing of its products. As an example, Lang mentioned that Pewex, with Center acting as an intermediary, was unwilling to cut its margins by lowering prices, a factor which may have contributed to the grey market. Pewex's intransigence, he added, was in part due to Center, which lacked the clout of a Sony or other manufacturer, to persaude Pewex to reduce prices. Some managers believed that, in a direct relationship, Pewex would be more cooperative.

On the other hand, direct cooperation with Pewex implied that Sony would have to renegotiate its agreement with Center. Aside from any settlement costs, direct cooperation with Pewex meant that Sony would also be fully exposed to the non-payment risk now borne by Center. Then, too, with the growth of private dealers in Poland, there was no guarantee that Pewex could maintain or grow its impressive $1 billion in sales revenue. Furthermore, Matsuzaki pointed out, cutting the supply line to Poland's FTOs via Center might jeopardize Sony's access to the Hungarian and Czechoslovakian markets, one-quarter and one-third the size of the Polish market, respectively.

While keeping the above in mind, Sony management was also keeping a close eye on privatization in Poland. If Pewex were privatized before the end of 1992, Sony would be free to supply Pewex directly and cut Center out of the picture, without violating its agreement. Short of negating any settlement costs with Center, the advantages of a privatized Pewex were the same as with the existing state-owned FTO.

Supply Directly to Private Dealers from SEI

In a third option, Sony could sever its current channels, through Center and Pewex, and supply Poland's private dealers directly, via SEI. As advantages, dealing with Poland's private dealers would enable Sony to control its sales and service network directly. As disadvantages, however, Sony would have to carry the risk of non-payment and disentangle itself from Center, with the aforementioned cost problem and distribution risks to Hungary and Czechoslovakia. Furthermore, there was no guarantee that private dealers could maintain the country's current sales volume. Finally, despite the existence to date of private dealers in Poland, Sony management was uncertain about the total number of such private dealers or their capacity to perform after-sales service.

Establish Sony Poland

As a fourth option, the management of Sony could initiate its ultimate, longer-term, objective and establish a Sony Poland subsidiary. Aside from providing immediate control over its sales and service network, a local subsidiary would also be able to closely monitor any risk of non-payment. Most importantly, a Polish subsidiary could well enhance Sony's local image and would coincide with the company's philosophy of global localization.

To implement this option, Sony would have to renegotiate its agreement with Center with the same disadvantages cited above. Moreover, Matsuzaki and Lang did not believe a Sony Poland could support itself below a sales volume of DM 150 million per year. Below that level, a subsidiary would be certain to incur losses for an indefinite period. Then, too, although the management of Sony believed they could select a few future employees from among Poland's private dealers, the same possibility did not apply to someone capable of heading up a subsidiary. In Matsuzaki's opinion, the managing director of a Sony Poland would, in addition to speaking Polish, need to speak English to communicate within Sony, and be comfortable with Lithuanian, Byelorussian and Ukrainian to cultivate the neighbouring markets in the USSR.

EXHIBIT 1
Order, product and capital flows for Sony products sold in Poland.

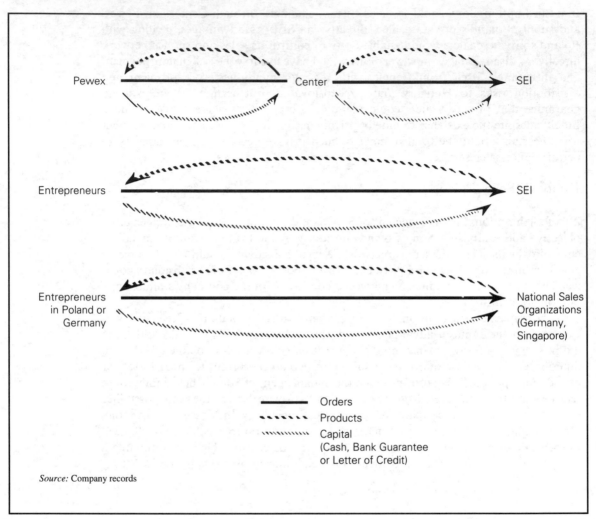

Source: Company records

ORGANIZATION

DEALING WITH STRUCTURE AND SYSTEMS

Chapter 4 completed Section One, which introduced the concepts related to our central theme, strategy – what it is, how it should and does get made, and the nature of the work of one of its key makers, the general manager. Section Two begins with Chapter 5 and deals with another set of concepts that every student of general management must come to understand. We group these under the title *Organization*, because they all pertain to the basic design and running of the organization.

In Chapter 5 we examine the design of organizational structure and development of systems for coordination and control. In Chapter 6, we consider culture, the ideological glue that holds organizations together, enhancing their ability to pursue strategies on one hand, but sometimes impeding strategic change on the other, and power, how it flows within the organization and how the organization uses it in its external environment.

Structure, in our view, no more follows strategy than the left foot follows the right in walking. The two exist interdependently, each influencing the other. There are certainly times when a structure is redesigned to carry out a new strategy. But the choice of any new strategy is similarly influenced by the realities and potentials of the existing structure. Indeed, the classical model of strategy formulation (discussed in Chapter 3) implicitly recognizes this by showing the strengths and weaknesses of the organization as an input to the creation of strategies. Surely these strengths and weaknesses are deeply rooted within the existing structure, indeed are often part and parcel of it. Hence we introduce here structure and the associated administrative systems as essential factors to consider in the strategy process. Later, when we present the various contexts within which organizations function, we shall consider the different ways in which strategy and structure interact.

All the readings of this chapter reinforce these points. The Waterman, Peters and Philips article, originally published under the title 'Structure is not organization', introduces the well-known '7-S' framework, which was developed at the consulting firm McKinsey, where all three authors worked when this article was published. (This framework was, in fact, one of the antecedents of the best-selling management book *In Search of Excellence* by two of these authors.) This framework explicitly considers how structure, systems, style, and other organizational factors interrelate with strategy. As such, many practising executives and students have found this a most valuable construct in thinking about organizations.

The subject of the second reading by Quinn, Doorley and Paquette is a rather new concept of organization for the 1990s, facilitated by new information technologies – what the authors call the 'intellectual holding company'. By concentrating strategic analyses on each element in the value chain, companies can target their own resources towards those things they do best, and outsource those activities others can perform better. In this way they can lower their investments, flatten their organizations and improve the quality and flexibility of their outputs.

The third reading, excerpted originally from Mintzberg's *The Structuring of Organizations*, comprehensively probes the design of organizational structures, including their formal systems. It seeks to do two things: first, to delineate the basic dimensions of organizations, and then to combine these to identify various basic types of organizations, called 'configurations'. The dimensions introduced include mechanisms used to coordinate work in organizations, parameters to consider in designing structures and situational factors which influence choices among these design parameters. This reading also introduces a somewhat novel diagram to depict organizations, not as the usual organizational chart or cybernetic flow process, but as a visual combination of the critical parts of an organization. This reading then clusters all these dimensions into a set of configurations, each introduced briefly here and discussed at length in later chapters. In fact, the choice of the chapters on context – entrepreneurial, mature, diversified, professional and innovative (leaving aside the last two on the international dimension and on strategic change) – was really based on five of these types, so that reading the conclusion to this article will help to introduce you to Section Three.

● THE 7-S FRAMEWORK*

Robert H. Waterman Jr, Thomas J. Peters and Julien R. Phillips

The Belgian surrealist René Magritte painted a series of pipes and titled the series *Ceci n'est pas une pipe*: this is not a pipe. The picture of the thing is not the thing. In the same way, a structure is not an organization. We all know that, but like as not, when we reorganize, what we do is to restructure. Intellectually, all managers and consultants know that much more goes on in the process of organizing than the charts, boxes, dotted lines, position descriptions and matrices can possibly depict.

*Originally published as 'Structure is not organization', *Business Horizons* (June 1980): copyright © 1980 by the Foundation for the School of Business at Indiana University: all rights reserved. Reprinted with deletions by permission of the publisher.

But all too often we behave as though we didn't know it; if we want change we change the structure....

Our assertion is that productive organization change is not simply a matter of structure, although structure is important. It is not so simple as the interaction between strategy and structure, although strategy is critical too. Our claim is that effective organizational change is really the relationship between structure, strategy, systems, style, skills, staff and something we call superordinate goals. (The alliteration is intentional: it serves as an aid to memory.)

Our central idea is that organization effectiveness, stems from the interaction of several factors – some not especially obvious and some underanalyzed. Our framework for organization change, graphically depicted in Figure 1, suggests several important ideas:

- First is the idea of a multiplicity of factors that influence an organization's ability to change and its proper mode of change. Why pay attention to only one or two, ignoring the others? Beyond structure and strategy, there are at least five other identifiable elements. The division is to some extent arbitrary, but it has the merit of acknowledging the complexity identified in the research and segmenting it into manageable parts.

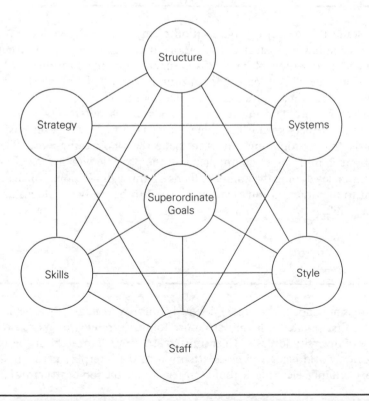

FIGURE 1
A new view of organization

- Second, the diagram is intended to convey the notion of the interconnectedness of the variables – the idea is that it's difficult, perhaps impossible, to make significant progress in one area without making progress in the others as well. Notions of organization change that ignore its many aspects or their interconnectedness are dangerous.

- In [an] article on strategy, *Fortune* commented that perhaps as many as 90 per cent of carefully planned strategies don't work. If that is so, our guess would be that the failure is a failure in execution, resulting from inattention to the other S's. Just as a logistics bottleneck can cripple a military strategy, inadequate systems or staff can make paper tigers of the best-laid plans for clobbering competitors.

- Finally, the shape of the diagram is significant. It has no starting point or implied hierarchy. *A priori*, it isn't obvious which of the seven factors will be the driving force in changing a particular organization at a particular point in time. In some cases, the critical variable might be strategy. In others, it could be systems or structure.

STRUCTURE

To understand this model of organization change better, let us look at each of its elements, beginning – as most organization discussions do – with structure. What will the new organization of the 1980s be like? If decentralization was the trend of the past, what is next? Is it matrix organization? What will 'Son of Matrix' look like? Our answer is that those questions miss the point. . . .

The central problem in structuring today . . . is not the one on which most organization designers spend their time – that is, how to divide up tasks. It is one of emphasis and coordination – how to make the whole thing work. The challenge lies not so much in trying to comprehend all the possible dimensions of organization structure as in developing the ability to focus on those dimensions which are currently important to the organization's evolution – and to be ready to refocus as the crucial dimensions shift.

STRATEGY

If structure is not enough, what is? Obviously, there is strategy. It was Alfred Chandler (1962) who first pointed out that structure follows strategy, or more precisely, that a strategy of diversity forces a decentralized structure. Throughout the past decade, the corporate world has given close attention to the interplay between strategy and structure. Certainly, clear ideas about strategy make the job of structural design more rational.

By 'strategy' we mean those actions that a company plans in response to or anticipation of changes in its external environment – its customers, its competitors.

Strategy is the way a company aims to improve its position *vis-à-vis* competition perhaps through low-cost production or delivery, perhaps by providing better value to the customer, perhaps by achieving sales and service dominance. It is, or ought to be, an organization's way of saying: 'Here is how we will create unique value.'

As the company's chosen route to competitive success, strategy is obviously a central concern in many business situations – especially in highly competitive industries where the game is won or lost on share points. But 'structure follows strategy' is by no means the be-all and end-all of organization wisdom. We find too many examples of large, prestigious companies around the world that are replete with strategy and cannot execute any of it. There is little if anything wrong with their structures; the causes of their inability to execute lie in other dimensions of our framework. When we turn to non-profit and public sector organizations, moreover, we find that the whole meaning of 'strategy' is tenuous – but the problem of organizational effectiveness looms as large as ever.

Strategy, then, is clearly a critical variable in organization design – but much more is at work.

SYSTEMS

By systems we mean all the procedures, formal and informal, that make the organization go, day by day and year by year: capital budgeting systems, training systems, cost accounting procedures, budgeting systems. If there is a variable in our model that threatens to dominate the others, it could well be systems. Do you want to understand how an organization really does (or doesn't) get things done? Look at the systems. Do you want to change an organization without disruptive restructuring? Try changing the systems.

A large consumer goods manufacturer was recently trying to come up with an overall corporate strategy. Textbook portfolio theory seemed to apply: find a good way to segment the business, decide which segments in the total business portfolio are most attractive, invest most heavily in those. The catch: reliable cost data by segment were not to be had. The company's management information system was not adequate to support the segmentation. . . .

[One] intriguing aspect of systems is the way they mirror the state of an organization. Consider a certain company we'll call International Wickets. For years management has talked about the need to become more market-oriented. Yet astonishingly little time is spent in their planning meetings on customers, marketing, market share or other issues having to do with market orientation. One of their key systems, in other words, remains *very* internally oriented. Without a change in this key system, the market orientation goal will remain unattainable no matter how much change takes place in structure and strategy.

To many business managers the word 'systems' has a dull, plodding, middle management sound. Yet it is astonishing how powerfully systems changes can enhance organizational effectiveness – without the disruptive side-effects that so often ensue from tinkering with structure.

STYLE

It is remarkable how often writers, in characterizing a corporate management for the business press, fall back on the word 'style' . . . The trouble we have with style is not in recognizing its importance, but in doing much about it. Personalities don't change, or so the conventional wisdom goes.

We think it is important to distinguish between the basic personality of a top management team and the way that team comes across to the organization. Organizations may listen to what managers say, but they believe what managers do. Not words, but patterns of actions are decisive. The power of style, then, is essentially manageable.

One element of a manager's style is how he or she chooses to spend time. As Henry Mintzberg has pointed out, managers don't spend their time in the neatly compartmentalized planning, organizing, motivating and controlling modes of classical management theory. Their days are a mess – or so it seems. There's a seeming infinity of things they might devote attention to. No top executive attends to all of the demands of his time; the median time spent on any one issue is 9 minutes.

What can a top manager do in 9 minutes? Actually, a good deal. He can signal what's on his mind; he can reinforce a message; he can nudge people's thinking in a desired direction. Skilful management of his inevitably fragmented time is, in fact, an immensely powerful change lever. . . .

Another aspect of style is symbolic behaviour. Companies most successful in finding mineral deposits typically have more people on the board who understand exploration or have headed exploration departments. Typically they fund exploration more consistently (that is, their year-to-year spending patterns are less volatile). They define fewer and more consistent exploration targets. Their exploration activities typically report at a higher organizational level. And they typically articulate better reasons for exploring in the first place.

STAFF

Staff (in the sense of people, not line/staff) is often treated in one of two ways. At the hard end of the spectrum, we talk of appraisal systems, pay scales, formal training programmes, and the like. At the soft end, we talk about morale, attitude, motivation and behaviour.

Top management is often, and justifiably, turned off by both these approaches. The first seems too trivial for their immediate concern ('Leave it to the personnel department'), the second too intractable ('We don't want a bunch of shrinks running around, stirring up the place with more attitude surveys').

Our predilection is to broaden and redefine the nature of the people issue. What do the top-performing companies do to foster the process of developing managers? How, for example, do they shape the basic values of their management cadre? Our reason for asking the question at all is simply that no serious discussion of organization can afford to ignore it (although many do). Our reason for framing the question around the development of managers is our observation that the superbly performing companies pay extraordinary attention to managing what might be called the socialization process in their companies. This applies especially to the way they introduce young recruits into the mainstream of their organizations and to the way they manage their careers as the recruits develop into tomorrow's managers. . . .

Considering people as a pool of resources to be nurtured, developed, guarded and allocated is one of the many ways to turn the 'staff' dimension of our 7-S framework into something not only amenable to, but worthy of practical control by senior management.

We are often told, 'Get the structure "right" and the people will fit' or 'Don't compromise the "optimum" organization for people considerations.' At the other end of the spectrum we are earnestly advised, 'The right people can make any organization work.' Neither view is correct. People do count, but staff is only one of our seven variables.

SKILLS

We added the notion of skills for a highly practical reason: It enables us to capture a company's crucial attributes as no other concept can do. A strategic description of a company, for example, might typically cover markets to be penetrated or types of products to be sold. But how do most of us characterize companies? Not by their strategies or their structures. We tend to characterize them by what they do best. We talk of IBM's orientation to the marketplace, its prodigious customer service capabilities or its sheer market power. We talk of Du Pont's research prowess, Procter & Gamble's product management capability, ITT's financial controls, Hewlett-Packard's innovation and quality, and Texas Instruments' project management. These dominating attributes, or capabilities, are what we mean by skills.

Now why is this distinction important? Because we regularly observe that organizations facing big discontinuities in business conditions must do more than shift strategic focus. Frequently they need to add a new capability, that is to say, a new skill. . . . These dominating capability needs, unless explicitly labelled as such, often get lost as the company 'attacks a new market' (strategy shift) or 'decentralizes to give managers autonomy' (structure shift).

Additionally, we frequently find it helpful to *label* current skills, for the addition of a new skill may come only when the old one is dismantled. Adopting a newly 'flexible and adaptive marketing thrust', for example, may be possible only if increases are accepted in certain marketing or distribution costs. Dismantling some of the distracting attributes of an old 'manufacturing mentality' (that is, a skill that was perhaps crucial in the past) may be the only way to ensure the success of an important change programme. Possibly the most difficult problem in trying to organize effectively is that of weeding out old skills – and their supporting systems, structures, and so on – to ensure that important new skills can take root and grow.

SUPERORDINATE GOALS

The word 'superordinate' literally means 'of higher order'. By superordinate goals, we mean guiding concepts – a set of values and aspirations, often unwritten, that goes beyond the conventional formal statement of corporate objectives.

Superordinate goals are the fundamental ideas around which a business is built. They are its main values. But they are more as well. They are the broad notions of future direction that the top management team wants to infuse throughout the organization. They are the way in which the team wants to express itself, to leave its own mark. Examples would include Theodore Vail's 'universal service' objective, which has so dominated AT&T; the strong drive to 'customer service' which guides IBM's marketing. . . .

In a sense, superordinate goals are like the basic postulates in a mathematical system. They are the starting points on which the system is logically built, but in themselves are not logically derived. The ultimate test of their value is not their logic but the usefulness of the system that ensues. Everyone seems to know the importance of compelling superordinate goals. The drive for their accomplishment pulls an organization together. They provide stability in what would otherwise be a shifting set of organization dynamics.

Unlike the other six S's, superordinate goals don't seem to be present in all, or even most, organizations. They are, however, evident in most of the superior performers.

To be readily communicated, superordinate goals need to be succinct. Typically, therefore, they are expressed at high levels of abstraction and may mean very little to outsiders who don't know the organization well. But for those inside, they are rich with significance. Within an organization, superordinate goals, if well articulated, make meanings for people. And making meanings is one of the main functions of leadership.

CONCLUSION

We have passed rapidly through the variables in our framework. What should the reader have gained from the exercise?

We started with the premise that solutions to today's thorny organizing problems that invoke only structure – or even strategy and structure – are seldom adequate. The inadequacy stems in part from the inability of the two-variable model to explain why organizations are so slow to adapt to change. The reasons often lie among the other variables: systems that embody outdated assumptions, a management style that is at odds with the stated strategy, the absence of a superordinate goal that binds the organization together in pursuit of a common purpose, the refusal to deal concretely with 'people problems' and opportunities.

At its most trivial, when we merely use the framework as a checklist, we find that it leads into new terrain in our efforts to understand how organizations really operate or to design a truly comprehensive change programme. At a minimum, it gives us a deeper bag in which to collect our experiences.

More importantly, it suggests the wisdom of taking seriously the variables in organizing that have been considered soft, informal or beneath the purview of top management interest. We believe that style, systems, skills, superordinate goals can be observed directly, even measured – if only they are taken seriously. We think that these variables can be at least as important as strategy and structure in orchestrating major change, indeed, that they are almost critical for achieving necessary, or desirable change. A shift in systems, a major retraining programme for staff, or the generation of top-to-bottom enthusiasm around a new superordinate goal could take years. Changes in strategy and structure, on the surface, may happen more quickly. But the pace of real change is geared to all seven S's.

At its most powerful and complex, the framework forces us to concentrate on interactions and fit. The real energy required to redirect an institution comes when all the variables in the model are aligned. One of our associates looks at our diagram as a set of compasses. 'When all seven needles are all pointed the same way,' he comments, 'you're looking at an *organized* company.'

• THE INTELLECTUAL HOLDING COMPANY: STRUCTURING AROUND CORE ACTIVITIES*

JAMES BRIAN QUINN, THOMAS I. DOORLEY AND PENNY C. PAQUETTE

Most companies primarily produce a chain of services and integrate these into a form most useful to certain customers. So dominant is this consideration that one questions whether many companies – like those in pharmaceuticals, computers, clothing, oil and gas, foods, office or automation equipment – should really be classified as 'manufacturers' anymore. The vast majority of their system costs, value-added profits and competitive advantage grows out of service activities.

For example, the strategies of virtually all pharmaceutical companies are critically dependent on service functions. This is especially true of the top performers like $5 billion Merck and $1.7 billion Glaxo, and less true for lower profit generic drug producers. The direct manufacturing cost of most patented ethical drugs is trivial relative to their sale price. Value is added primarily by service activities – discovery of a drug through R&D, a carefully constructed patent and legal defence, rapid and thorough clinical clearance through regulatory bodies, or a strong pre-emptive distribution system. Recognizing this, in recent years Merck's strategy has focused on one portion of the value chain, a powerful research-based patent position. Glaxo has successfuly targeted rapid clinical clearance as its key activity. Both strategies rest primarily on adding value through service activities. Merck and Glaxo outperform the industry in gross margins (71.5 per cent and 79.6 per cent versus an industry composite of 66.9 per cent), in operating income margins (27.1 per cent and 38.2 per cent versus 21.2 per cent), and in profits as a percentage of shareholders' equity (48 per cent of 35 per cent versus an industry average of 23 per cent).

As manufacturing becomes more universally automated, the major value added to a product increasingly moves away from the point where raw materials are converted into useful form (that is, steel into an auto 'body in white' or grain into edible cereals) and toward the styling features, perceived quality, subjective taste, and marketing presentation that service activities provide at all levels of the value chain.

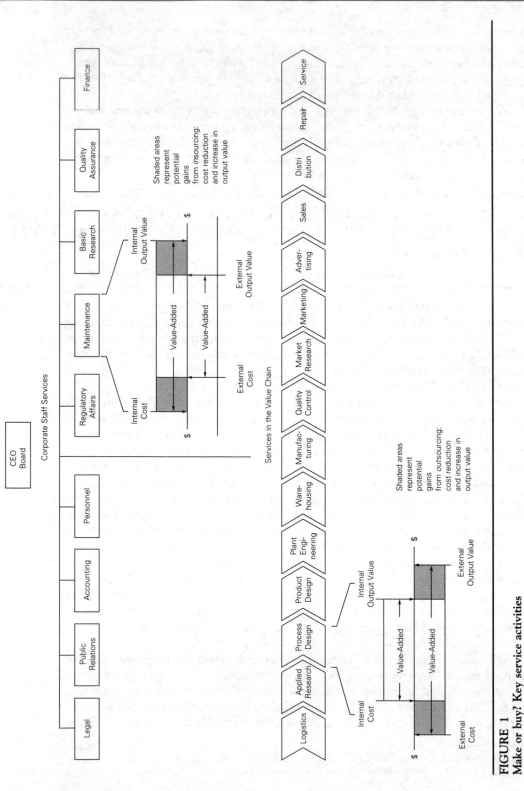

FIGURE 1
Make or buy? Key service activities

At each stage, technology had increased the relative power of services to the point where they dominate virtually all companies' value chains (see Figure 1).

THE 'INTELLECTUAL HOLDING COMPANY'

The fact is that many large companies, like Apple Computer and IBM, initially succeeded by recognizing and leveraging this concept – becoming essentially 'intellectual holding companies', purposely manufacturing or producing as little product internally as possible. For example, until the early 1960s IBM was known as an 'assembler', outsourcing up to 80 per cent of its manufacturing costs. And Apple succeeded by masterminding the highly sophisticated interconnection of architectural, design, software and hardware supply relationships that became its explosively successful Apple II system. This strategy may have been essential for Apple in its early years when it lacked both the time and capital to build factories or hire a salesforce. But even today – with 3-4 times the sales per employee and a third to a quarter the fixed investment per sales dollar of its competitors – Apple is structured less like a traditional 'manufacturing' company and more like a $4 billion 'service' company that happens to have three manufacturing facilities (see Table 1).

SMASHING OVERHEADS THROUGH OUTSOURCING

Because of the scale economies they permit, new service technologies also make it possible to achieve major economies of scale by purchasing not just manufactured parts, but also crucial services, externally – and also to manage such outsourcing effectively on a global basis.

Outside service groups can often provide greater economies of scale, flexibility and levels of expertise for specialized overhead services than virtually any company can achieve internally. To develop these potentials thoroughly one should consider each overhead category whether in the value chain or in a staff function – as a service that the company could either 'make' internally or 'buy' externally. This perspective will, at a minimum, introduce a new objectivity into overhead evaluations and create some strong competitive pressures for internal productivity. In many cases, companies find that specialized outside service sources can be much more cost effective

TABLE 1 **Apple, which outsources extensively, is structured less like a manufacturing than like a service company**

	Apple	IBM	DEC	Data General
Sales per employee	$369,593	$139,250	$84,972	$81,243
Net plant, property, and equipment as per cent of sales[a]	18.4	63.0	44.6	56.7

[a] Net property, plant and equipment figures have been adjusted to account for leased assets by multiplying the annual rental expense by 8.

than their internal groups. And they start outsourcing to lower costs or to improve value-added.

For example, $3 billion ServiceMaster Company can take over many of its customers' equipment and facilities maintenance functions, simultaneously improving the quality and lowering the costs of these activities through system economies and specialized management skills. So effective are its systems that ServiceMaster can not only lower absolute maintenance costs, it can often joint-invest in new equipment with its customers, sharing productivity gains to the benefit of both parties.

Whenever a company produces a service internally that others buy or produce more efficiently or effectively externally, it sacrifices competitive advantage. Conversely, the key to strategic success for many firms has been their coalitions with the world's best service providers – their external product desigerns, advertising agencies, distribution channels, financial houses, and so on. How can companies best exploit such opportunities?

LEARNING TO LOVE THE 'HOLLOW CORPORATION'

Considering the enterprise as an intellectual holding company (à la Apple Computer) restructures the entire way one attacks strategy. One needs to ask, activity by activity, 'Are we really competitive with the world's best here? If not, can intelligent outsourcing improve our long-term position?' Competitive analyses of service activities should not consider just the company's own industry, but should benchmark each service against 'best in class' performance among all potential service providers and industries that might cross-compete within the analyzed category – both in the United States and abroad.

As companies begin to outsource non-strategic activities – particularly overheads – they often discover important secondary benefits. Managements concentrate more on their businesses' core strategic activities. Other internal costs and time delays frequently drop as long-standing bureaucracies disappear and political pressures decrease for annual increments to each department's budget. All this leads to a more compact organization, with fewer hierarchical levels. It also leads to a much sharper focus on recruiting, developing and motivating the people who create most value in those areas where the company has special competencies.

DOMINATING THOSE ACTIVITIES CRUCIAL TO STRATEGY

Many have expressed concerns about the hollowing out and loss of strategic capability outsourcing could cause (*Business Week*, 1986). However, if the process is approached properly, careful outsourcing should increase both productivity and strategic focus. A company must maintain command of those activities crucial to its strategic position. If it does not, it has essentially redefined the business it is in. For all other activities, if the company cannot see its way to strategic superiority, or if the activity is not essential to areas where it can attain such superiority, the company should consider outsourcing. But it is essential that the company plan and manage its outsourcing coalitions so that it does not become overly dependent on – and hence dominated by – its partner. In some cases this means consciously developing and maintaining alternative competitive sources or even strategically controlling critical states in an overall process that might otherwise be totally outsourced.

HIGHEST ACTIVITY SHARE, NOT MARKET SHARE, FOR PROFITS

Once a company develops great depth in certain selected service activities as its strategic focus, many individual products can spring off these 'core' activities to give the firm a consistent corporate strategy for decades. Unfortunately, the true nature of these core capabilities is usually obscured by the tendency of organizations to think of their strengths in product – not activity or service – terms. The key point is that a few *selected activities should drive strategy*. Knowledge bases, skills sets and service activities are the things that generally can create continuing added value and competitive advantage.

Too much strategic attention has been paid to having a high share of the market. High share can be bought by inappropriate pricing or other short-term strategies. High market share and high profitability together come from having the highest relevant *activity* share in the marketplace – in other words, having the most effective presence in a service activity the market desires and thus gaining the experience curve and other benefits accruing to that high activity share.

To be most effective, this service activity dominance needs truly global development. As noted, the major value-added in most products today comes not from direct production or conversion processes, but from the technological improvements, styling, quality, marketing, timing and financing contributions of service activities. Since these are knowledge-based intangibles that can be shipped cost-free anywhere, producers who expand their scope worldwide to tap the best knowledge and service sources available anywhere can obtain significant competitive advantage.

AVOIDING VERTICAL INTEGRATION

Since most firms cannot afford to own or internally dominate all needed service activities, they tend to form coalitions, linking their own and their partners' capabilities through information, communication and contract arrangements – rather than through ownership (that is, vertical or horizontal integration). Because of their high value-added potentials, service companies and service activities within companies are central to many of these coalitions. An entirely new form of enterprise seems to be emerging with a carefully conceived and limited set of 'core strategic activities' (usually services) at its centre, which allows a company to command and coordinate a constantly changing network of the world's best production and service suppliers on a global basis. This is a logical and most powerful extension of the Kieretsu concept (linked networks of banks, producers, suppliers, and support distribution companies) that has long been at the heart of Japan's trading success.

Given today's rapid technological advances, many enterprises find they can lower their risks and leverage their assets substantially by *avoiding* investments in vertical integration and managing 'intellectual systems' instead of workers and machines. The core strategy of a coordinating or systems company becomes: 'Do only those things in-house that contribute to your competitive advantage, and try to source the rest from the world's best suppliers.'

MANUFACTURING INDUSTRIES BECOME 'SERVICE NETWORKS'

Many industries are becoming loosely structured networks of service enterprises that join together temporarily for one purpose – yet are each other's suppliers, competitors or customers elsewhere.

Biotechnology, where highly specialized companies are developing at each level, providing 'service' activities for one another and the industry, is becoming structured as a number of multiple-level consortia, offers an interesting example of this phenomenon. The semiconductor and electronics industries are moving towards a similar structure. Independent design, foundry, packaging, assembly, industrial distribution, kitting, configuration, systems analysis, networking and value-added distributor groups do more than $15 billion worth of customized development, generating almost $140,000 of revenue per employee (*Electronic Business,* 1988). Even large OEMs are finding that these groups' specialization, fast turnarounds, advanced designs and independent perspectives can lower costs, decrease investments and increase value at all levels.

STRATEGICALLY REDEFINING THE 'FOCUSED COMPANY'

Given the vast changes being wrought by new technologies, and the resulting potential for worldwide strategic outsourcing, the whole notion of what constitutes an 'industry' or a 'focused company' needs to be re-examined. True focus in strategy means the capacity to bring more power to bear on a selected sector than anyone else can.

Properly developed, a broad product or service line does not necessarily signify loss of focus if a firm can deploy especially potent service skills against selected marketplaces in a coordinated fashion. (In fact, a broad line may represent the leveraging of a less obvious strategic focus.) They key question is whether a company dominates a set of service skills that has importance to its customers – in other words, can bring more power to bear on this activity than anyone in the world. If so, the company can be a strategic success, provided it focuses its attention on that activity, obtains at least strategic parity through outsourcing elsewhere, and then blocks others from entering its markets by leveraging its skills across as broad a product line or customer base as it can dominate. Competitors must be defined as those with substitutable skill bases, not those with similar product lines. Product lines can be remarkably broad when the service skill base is deep enough to be dominating. Toys R Us, Procter & Gamble, McKesson, Matsushita and 3M provide only a few of many excellent cases in point.

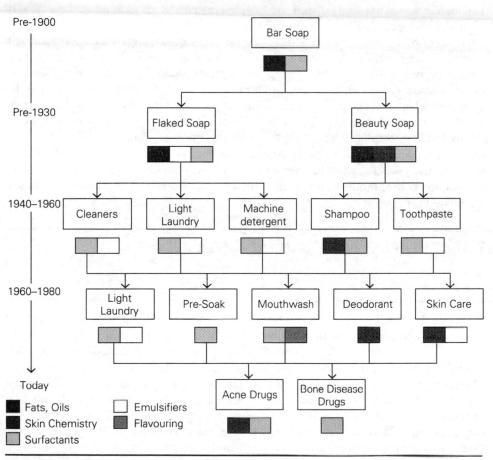

FIGURE 2
Proctor and Gamble: technology activity profile
Source: Braxton Associates

For example, Procter and Gamble (P&G) created a $15 billion corporation largely based on two central sets of service skills: its R&D capabilities in eight core technologies, and its superb marketing distribution skills. Today its extremely broad product line flows naturally from the interaction of these two service activities. Figure 2 shows how skills associated with bar soap could lead P&G naturally to flaked soaps, Tide detergent, and many of its later products. P&G's research depth in surfactant chemistry provided the central linkage among products apparently as diverse as soap and acne or bone disease control drugs, while its marketing and distribution strength allowed P&G to move powerfully, but incrementally, from market to market.

CONCLUSIONS

Most companies create a major portion of their incremental value and gain their real competitive advantage from a relatively few – generally service – activities. Much of the remaining enterprise exists primarily to permit these activities to take place.

Yet managements typically spend an inordinate amount of their time, energy and company resources dealing with these latter support functions – all of which decrease their attention to the company's truly crucial areas of strategic focus. Virtually all managers can benefit from a more carefully structured approach to managing their service activities strategically. Doing so involves defining each activity in the value creation system as a service, carefully analyzing each such service activity to determine whether the company can become the best in the world at it; and eliminating, outsourcing, or joint venturing the activity to achieve 'best in world' status when this is impossible internally. Perhaps most important, managers must recognize the cold reality that *not* achieving a strong enough competitive performance in each critical service activity will relegate the company to an inevitable loss of strategic advantage, provide lower profitability, and create a higher risk of takeover by those who do see the missed potentials.

● THE STRUCTURING OF ORGANIZATIONS*

HENRY MINTZBERG

The 'one best way' approach has dominated our thinking about organizational structure since the turn of the century. There is a right way and a wrong way to design an organization. A variety of failures, however, has made it clear that organizations differ, that, for example, long-range planning systems or organizational development programs are good for some but not others. And so recent management theory has moved away from the 'one best way' approach, towards an 'it all depends' approach, formally known as 'contingency theory'. Structure should reflect the organization's situation – for example, its age, size, type of production system, the extent to which its environment is complex and dynamic.

This reading argues that the 'it all depends' approach does not go far enough, that structures are rightfully designed on the basis of a third approach, which might be called the 'getting it all together' or 'configuration' approach. Spans of control, types of formalization and decentralization, planning systems and matrix structures should not be picked and chosen independently, the way a shopper picks vegetables at the market. Rather, these and other elements of organizational design should logically configure into internally consistent groupings.

When the enormous amount of research that has been done on organizational structure is looked at in the light of this conclusion, much of its confusion falls away, and a convergence is evident around several configurations, which are distinct in their structural designs, in the situations in which they are found, and even in the periods of history in which they first developed.

To understand these configurations, we must first understand each of the elements that make them up. Accordingly, the first four sections of these reading

*Excerpted originally from *The Structuring of Organizations* (Prentice Hall, 1979), with added sections from *Power in and Around Organizations* (Prentice Hall, 1983). This chapter was rewritten for this edition of the text, based on two other excerpts: 'A typology of organizational structure', published as Chapter 3 in Danny Miller and Peter Friesen, *Organizations: A quantum view* (Prentice Hall, 1984) and 'Deriving configurations', Chapter 6 in *Mintzberg on Management: Inside Our Strange World of Organizations* (Free Press, 1989).

discuss the basic parts of organizations, the mechanisms by which organizations coordinate their activities, the parameters they use to design their structures, and their contingency, or situational, factors. The final section introduces the structural configurations, each of which will be discussed at length in Section Three of this text.

SIX BASIC PARTS OF THE ORGANIZATION

At the base of any organization can be found its operators, those people who perform the basic work of producing the products and rendering the services. They form the *operating care*. All but the simplest organizations also require at least one full-time manager, who occupies what we shall call the *strategic apex,* where the whole system is overseen. And as the organization grows, more managers are needed – not only managers of operators but also managers of managers. A *middle line* is created, a hierarchy of authority between the operating core and the strategic apex.

As the organization becomes still more complex, it generally requires another group of people, whom we shall call the analysts. They, too, perform administrative duties – to plan and control formally the work of others – but of a different nature, often labelled 'staff'. These analysts form what we shall call the *techno-structure,* outside the hierarchy of line authority. Most organizations also add staff units of a different kind, to provide various internal services, from a cafeteria or mailroom to a legal counsel or public relations office. We call these units and the part of the organization they form the *support staff*.

Finally, every active organization has a sixth part, which we call its *ideology* (by which is meant a strong 'culture'). Ideology encompasses the traditions and beliefs of an organization that distinguish it from other organizations and infuse a certain life into the skeleton of its structure.

This gives us six basic parts of an organization. As shown in Figure 1, we have a small strategic apex connected by a flaring middle line to a large, flat operating core at the base. These three parts of the organization are drawn in one uninterrupted sequence to indicate that they are typically connected through a single chain of formal authority. The technostructure and the support staff are shown off to either side to indicate that they are separate from this main line of authority, influencing the opening core only indirectly, The ideology is shown as a kind of halo that surrounds the entire system.

These people, all of whom work inside the organization to make its decisions and take its actions – full-time employees or, in some cases, committed volunteers – may be thought of as *influencers* who form a kind of *internal coalition*. By this term, we mean a system within which people vie among themselves to determine the distribution of power.

In addition, various outside people also try to exert influence on the organization, seeking to affect the decisions and actions taken inside. These external influencers, who create a field of forces around the organization, can include owners, unions and other employee associations, suppliers, clients, partners, competitors and all kinds of publics, in the form of governments, special interest groups, and so forth. Together they can all be thought to form an *external coalition.*

Sometimes the external coalition is relatively *passive* (as in the typical behaviour

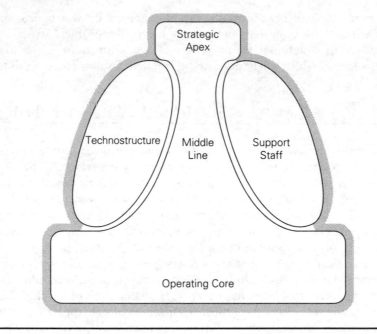

FIGURE 1
The six basic parts of the organization

of the shareholders of a widely held corporation or the members of a large union). Other times it is *dominated* by one active influencer or some group of them acting in concert (such as an outside owner of a business firm or a community intent on imposing a certain philosophy on its school system). And in still other cases, the external coalition may be *divided,* as different groups seek to impose contradictory pressures on the organization (as in a prison buffeted between two community groups, one favouring custody, the other rehabilitation).

SIX BASIC COORDINATING MECHANISMS

Every organized human activity – from the making of pottery to the placing of a man on the moon – gives rise to two fundamental and opposing requirements: the *division of labour* into various tasks to be performed and the *coordination* of those tasks to accomplish the activity. The structure of an organization can be defined simply as the total of the ways in which its labour is divided into distinct tasks and then its coordination achieved among those tasks.

1. *Mutual adjustment* achieves coordination of work by the simple process of information communication. The people who do the work interact with one another to coordinate, much as two canoeists in the rapids adjust to one another's actions. Figure 2a shows mutual adjustment in terms of an arrow between two operators. Mutual adjustment is obviously used in the simplest or organizations – it is the most obvious way to coordinate. But, paradoxically, it is also used

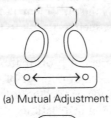

(a) Mutual Adjustment

(b) Direct Supervision

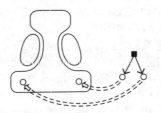

(c) Standardization of Work

(d) Standardization of Outputs

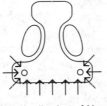

(e) Standardization of Skills

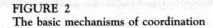

(f) Standardization of Norms

FIGURE 2
The basic mechanisms of coordination

in the most complex, because it is the only means that can be relied upon under extremely difficult circumstances, such as trying to figure out how to put a man on the moon for the first time.

2. *Direct supervision* in which one person coordinates by giving orders to others, tends to come into play after a certain number of people must work together. Thus, fifteen people in a war canoe cannot coordinate by mutual adjustment; they need a leader who, by virtue of instructions, coordinates their work, much as a football team requires a quarterback to call the plays. Figure 2b shows the leader as a manager with the instructions as arrows to the operators.

Coordination can also be achieved by *standardization* – in effect, automatically, by virtue of standards that predetermine what people do and so ensure that their work is coordinated. We can consider four forms – the standardization of the work processes themselves, of the outputs of the work, of the knowledge and skills that serve as inputs to the work, or of the norms that more generally guide the work.

3. *Standardization of work processes* means the specification – that is, the programming – of the content of the work directly, the procedures to be followed, as in the case of the assembly instructions that come with many children's toys. As shown in Figure 2c, it is typically the job of the analysts to so programme the work of different people in order to coordinate it tightly.

4. *Standardization of outputs* means the specification not of what is to be done but of its results. In that way, the interfaces between jobs is predetermined, as when a machinist is told to drill holes in a certain place on a fender so that they will fit the bolts being welded by someone else, or a division manager is told to achieve a sales growth of 10 per cent so that the corporation can meet some overall sales target. Again, such standards generally emanate from the analysts, as shown in Figure 2d.

5. *Standardization of skills,* as well as knowledge, is another, though looser way to achieve coordination. Here, it is the worker rather than the work or the outputs that is standardized. He or she is taught a body of knowledge and a set of skills which are subsequently applied to the work. Such standardization typically takes place outside the organization – for example, in a professional school of a university before the worker takes his or her first job – indicated in Figure 2e. In effect, the standards do not come from the analyst; they are internalized by the operator as inputs to the job he or she takes. Coordination is then achieved by virtue of various operators' having learned what to expect of each other. When an anaesthetist and a surgeon meet in the operating theatre to remove an appendix, they need hardly communicate (that is, use mutual adjustment, let alone direct supervision); each knows exactly what the other will do and can coordinate accordingly.

6. *Standardization of norms* means that the workers share a common set of beliefs and can achieve coordination based on it, as implied in Figure 2f. For example, if every member of a religious order shares a belief in the importance of attracting converts, then all will work together to achieve this aim.

These coordinating mechanisms can be considered the most basic elements of structure, the glue that holds organizations together. They seem to fall into a rough order: As organizational work becomes more complicated, the favoured means of coordination seems to shift from mutual adjustment (the simplest mechanism) to direct supervision, then to standardization, preferably of work processes or norms, otherwise of outputs or of skills, finally reverting back to mutual adjustment. But no organization can rely on a single one of those mechanisms; all will typically be found in every reasonably developed organization.

Still, the important point for us here is that many organizations do favour one mechanism over the others, at least at certain stages of their lives. In fact, organizations that favour none seem most prone to becoming politicized, simply because of the conflicts that naturally arise when people have to vie for influence in a relative vacuum of power.

THE ESSENTIAL PARAMETERS OF DESIGN

The essence of organizational design is the manipulation of a series of parameters that determine the division of labour and the achievement of coordination. Some of these concern the design of individual positions, others the design of the superstructure (the overall network of subunits, reflected in the organizational chart), some the design of lateral linkages to flesh out that superstructure, and a final group concerns the design of the decision-making system of the organization. Listed as follows are the main parameters of structural design, with links to the coordinating mechanisms.

● *Job specialization* refers to the number of tasks in a given job and the worker's control over these tasks. A job is *horizontally* specialized to the extent that it encompasses a few narrowly defined tasks, *vertically* specialized to the extent that the worker lacks control of the tasks performed. *Unskilled* jobs are typically highly specialized in both dimensions; skilled or *professional* jobs are typically specialized horizontally but not vertically. 'Job enrichment' refers to the enlargement of jobs in both the vertical and horizontal dimension.

● *Behaviour formalization* refers to the standardization of work processes by the imposition of operating instructions, job descriptions, rules, regulations, and the like. Structures that rely on any form of standardization for coordination may be defined as *bureaucratic,* those that do not as *organic.*

● *Training* refers to the use of formal instructional programmes to establish and standardize in people the requisite skills and knowledge to do particular jobs in organizations. Training is a key design parameter in all work we call professional. Training and formalization are basically substitutes for achieving the standardization (in effect, the bureaucratization) of behaviour. In one, the standards are learned as skills, in the other they are imposed on the job as rules.

● *Indoctrination* refers to programmes and techniques by which the norms of the members of an organization are standardized, so that they become responsive to its ideological needs and can thereby be trusted to make its decisions and take its actions. Indoctrination too is a substitute for formalization, as well as for skill training, in this case the standards being internalized as deeply rooted beliefs.

● *Unit grouping* refers to the choice of the bases by which positions are grouped together into units, and those units into higher-order units (typically shown on the organization chart). Grouping encourages coordination by putting different jobs under common supervision, by requiring them to share common resources and achieve common measures of performance, and by using proximity to facilitate mutual adjustment among them. The various bases for grouping – by work process, product, client, place, and so on – can be reduced to two fundamental ones – the *function* performed and the *market* served. The former (illustrated in Figure 3) refers to means, that is to a single link in the chain of processes by which products or services are produced, the latter (in Figure 4) to ends, that is, the whole chain for specific end-products, services, or markets. On what criteria should the choice of a basis for grouping be made? First, there is the consideration of workflow linkages, or 'interdependencies'. Obviously, the more tightly linked are positions or units in the workflow, the more desirable that they be grouped together to facilitate their coordination. Second, there is the consideration of process interdependencies – for example, across people doing the same kind of work but in different workflows (such as maintenance men working on different machines). It sometimes make sense to group them together to facilitate their sharing of equipment or ideas, to encourage the improvement of their skills, and so on. Third is the question of scale interdependencies. For example, all maintenance people in a factory may have to be grouped together because no single department has enough maintenance work for one person. Finally, there are the social interdependencies, the need to group people together for social reasons, as in coal mines where mutual support under dangerous working conditions can be a factor in deciding how to group people. Clearly, grouping by functions is favoured by process and scale interdependencies, and to a lesser extent by social interdependencies (in the sense that people who do the same kind of job often tend to get along better). Grouping by function also encourages specialization, for example, by allowing specialists to come together under the supervision of one of their own kind. The problem with functional grouping, however, is that it narrow perspectives, encouraging a focus on means instead of ends – the way to do the job instead of the reason for doing the job in the first place. Thus grouping by market is used to favour coordination in the workflow at the expense of process and scale specialization. In general, market grouping reduces the ability to do specialized or repetitive tasks well and is more wasteful, being less able to take advantage of economies of scale and often requiring the duplication of resources. But it enables the organization to accomplish a wider variety of tasks and to change its tasks more easily to serve the organization's end-markets. And so if the workflow interdependencies are the important ones and if the organization cannot easily handle them by standardization, then it will tend to favour the market bases for grouping in order to encourage mutual adjustment and direct supervision. But if the workflow is irregular (as in a 'job shop'), if standardization can easily contain the important workflow interdependencies, or if the process or scale interdependencies are the important ones, then the organization will be inclined to seek the advantages of specialization and group on the basis of function

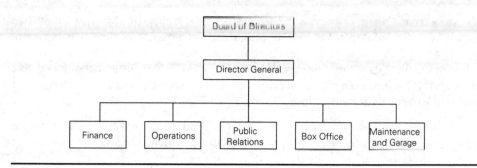

FIGURE 3
Grouping by function: a cultural centre

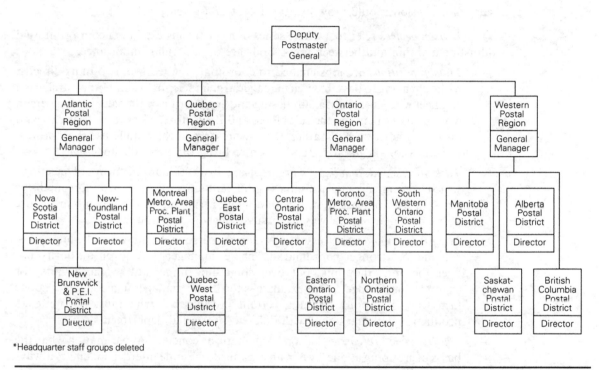

*Headquarter staff groups deleted

FIGURE 4
Grouping by market: The Candian Post Office

instead. Of course, in all but the smallest organizations, the question is not so much *which* basis of grouping, but in what *order*. Much as fires are built by stacking logs first one way and then the other, so too are organizations built by varying the different bases for grouping to take care of various interdependencies.

● *Unit size* refers to the number of positions (or units) contained in a single unit. The equivalent term, *span of control*, is not used here, because sometimes units are kept small despite an absence of close supervisory control. For example, when experts coordinate extensively by mutual adjustment, as in an engineering team in a space agency, they will form into small units. In this case, unit size is small and span of control is low despite a relative absence of direct supervision. In contrast, when work is highly standardized (because of either formalization or training), unit size can be very large, because there is little need for direct supervision. One foreman can supervise dozens of assemblers, because they work according to very tight instructions.

● *Planning and control systems* are used to standardize outputs. They may be divided into two types: *action planning* systems, which specify the results of specific actions before they are taken (for example, that holes should be drilled with diameters of 3 centimetres): and *performance control* systems, which specify the desired results of whole ranges of actions after the fact (for example, that sales of a division should grow by 10 per cent in a given year).

● *Liaison devices* refer to a whole series of mechanisms used to encourage mutual adjustment within and between units. Four are of particular importance:

– *Liaison positions* are jobs created to coordinate the work of two units directly, without having to pass through managerial channels, for example, the purchasing engineer who sits between purchasing and engineering or the sales liaison person who mediates between the sales force and the factory. These positions carry no formal authority *per se*; rather, those who serve in them must use their powers of persuasion, negotiation, and so on to bring the two sides together.

– *Task forces and standing committees* are institutionalized forms of meetings, which bring members of a number of different units together on a more intensive basis, in the first case to deal with a temporary issue, in the second, in a more permanent and regular way to discuss issues of common interest.

– *Integrating managers* – essentially liaison personnel with formal authority – provide for stronger coordination. These 'managers' are given authority not over the units they link, but over something important to those units, for example, their budgets. One example is the brand manager in a consumer goods firm who is responsible for a certain product but who must negotiate its production and marketing with different functional departments.

– *Matrix structure carries* liaison to its natural conclusion. No matter what the bases of grouping at one level in an organization, some interdependencies always remain. Figure 5 suggests various ways to deal with these 'residual interdependencies': a different type of grouping can be used at the next level in the hierarchy; staff units can be formed next to line units to advise on the problems; or one of the liaison devices already discussed can be overlaid on the grouping. But in each case, one basis of grouping is favoured over the others. The concept of matrix structure is balance between the two (or more) bases of grouping, for example functional with market (or for that matter, one kind of market with another – say, regional with product). This is done by the creation of a dual authority structure – two (or more) managers, units or individuals are made jointly and equally responsible for the same decisions. We can distinguish a *permanent* form of matrix structure, where the units and the people in them remain more or less in place, as shown in the example of a whimsical multinational firm in Figure 6, and a *shifting* form, suited to project work,

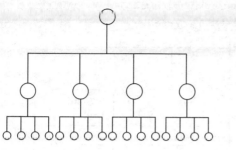

(a) Hierarchical Structure

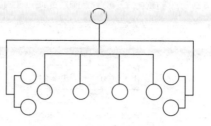

(b) Line and Staff Structure

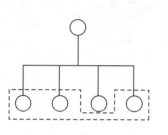

(c) Liaison Overlay Structure
(e.g. Task Force)

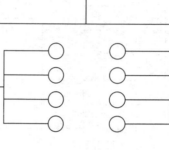

(d) Matrix Structure

FIGURE 5
Structures to deal with residual interdependencies

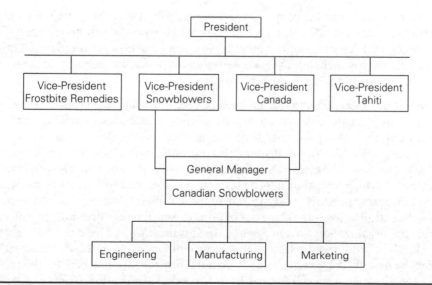

FIGURE 6
A permanent matrix structure in an international firm

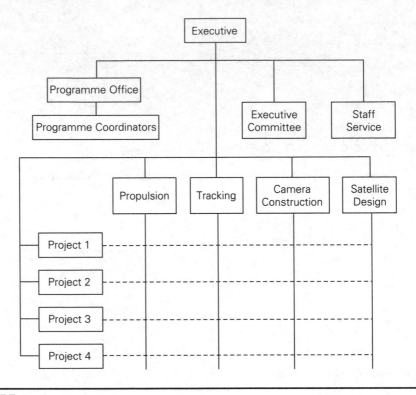

FIGURE 7
Shifting matrix structure in the NASA weather satellite programme
Source: Modified from Delbecq and Filley (1974: 16)

where the units and the people in them move around frequently. Shifting matrix structures are common in high-technology industries, which group specialists in functional departments for housekeeping purposes (process interdependencies, etc.) but deploy them from various departments in project teams to do the work, as shown for NASA in Figure 7.

● *Decentralization* refers to the diffusion of decision-making power. When all the power rests at a single point in an organization, we call its structure centralized; to the extent that the power is dispersed among many individuals, we call it relatively decentralized. We can distinguish *vertical decentralization* – the delegation of formal power down the hierarchy to line managers – from *horizontal decentralization* – the extent to which formal or informal power is dispersed out of the line hierarchy to non-managers (operators, analysts and support staffers). We can also distinguish *selective* decentralization – the dispersal of power over different decisions to different places in the organization – from *parallel* decentralization – where the power over various kinds of decisions is delegated to the same place. Six forms of decentralization may thus be described: (1) vertical and horizontal centralization, where all the power rests at the strategic apex; (2) limited horizontal decentralization (selective), where the strategic apex shares some power with the technostructure that standardizes everybody else's work; (3) limited vertical decentralization (parallel), where managers of market based units are delegated the power to control most of the decisions concerning their line units; (4) vertical and horizontal deccentralization, where most of the power rests in the operating core, at the bottom of the structure; (5) selective vertical and horizontal decentralization, where the power over different decisions is dispersed to various places in the organization, among managers, staff experts and operators who work in teams at various levels in the hierarchy; and (6) pure decentralization, where power is shared more or less equally by all members of the organization.

THE SITUATIONAL FACTORS

A number of 'contingency' or 'situational' factors influence the choice of these design parameters, and vice versa. They include the age and size of the organization; its technical system of production: various characteristics of its environment, such as stability and complexity; and its power system, for example, whether or not it is tightly controlled by outside influencers. Some of the effects of these factors, as found in an extensive body of research literature, are summarized below as hypotheses.

Age and Size

● *The older an organization, the more formalized its behaviour:* What we have here is the 'we've-seen-it-all-before' syndrome. As organizations age, they tend to repeat their behaviours: as a result, these become more predictable and so more amenable to formalization.

● *The larger an organization, the more formalized its behaviour:* Just as the older organization formalizes what it has seen before, so the larger organization formalizes what it sees often. ('Listen mister, I've heard that story at least five times today. Just fill in the form like it says.')

● *The larger an organization, the more elaborate its structure; that is, the more specialized its jobs and units and the more developed its administrative components:* As organizations grow in size, they are able to specialize their jobs more finely. (The big barbershop can afford a specialist to cut children's hair; the small one cannot.) As a result, they can also specialize – or 'differentiate' – the work of their units more extensively. This requires more effort at coordination. And so the larger organization tends also to enlarge its hierarchy to effect direct supervision and to make greater use of its technostructure to achieve coordination by standardization, or else to encourage more coordination by mutual adjustment.

● *The larger the organization, the larger the size of its average unit:* This finding relates to the previous two, the size of units growing larger as organizations themselves grow larger because (1) as behaviour becomes more formalized, and (2) as the work of each unit becomes more homogeneous, managers are able to supervise more employees.

● *Structure reflects the age of the industry from its founding:* This is a curious finding, but one that we shall see holds up remarkably well. An organization's structure seems to reflect the age of the industry in which it operates, no matter what its own age. Industries that pre-date the industrial revolution seem to favour one kind of structure, those of the age of the early railroads another, and so on. We should obviously expect different structures in different periods; the surprising thing is that these structures seem to carry through to new periods, old industries remaining relatively true to earlier structures.

Technical System

Technical system refers to the instruments used in the operating core to produce the outputs. (This should be distinguished from 'technology', which refers to the knowledge base of an organization.)

● *The more regulating the technical system – that is, the more it controls the work of the operators – the more formalized the operating work and the more bureaucratic the structure of the operating core:* Technical systems that regulate the work of the operators – for example, mass production assembly lines – render that work highly routine and predictable, and so encourage its specialization and formalization, which in turn create the conditions for bureaucracy in the operating core.

● *The more complex the technical system, the more elaborate and professional the support staff:* Essentially, if an organization is to use complex machinery, it must hire staff experts who can understand that machinery – who have the capability to design, select and modify it. And then it must give them considerable power to make decisions concerning that machinery and encourage them to use the liaison devices to ensure mutual adjustment among them.

● *The automation of the operating core transforms a bureaucratic administrative structure into an organic one:* When unskilled work is coordinated by the standardization of work processes, we tend to get bureaucratic structure throughout the organization, because a control mentality pervades the whole system. But when the work of the operating core becomes automated, social relationships tend to change. Now it is machines, not people, that are regulated. So the obsession with control tends to disappear – machines do not need to be watched over – and with it go many of the managers and analysts who were needed to control the operators. In their place come the support specialists to look after the machinery, coordinating their own work by mutual adjustment. Thus, automation reduces line authority in favour of staff expertise and reduces the tendency to rely on standardization for coordination.

Environment

Environment refers to various characteristics of the organization's outside context, related to markets, political climate, economic conditions, and so on.

● *The more dynamic an organization's environment, the more organic its structure:* It stands to reason that in a stable environment – where nothing changes – an organization can predict its future conditions and so, all other things being equal, can easily rely on standardization for coordination. But when conditions become dynamic – when the need for product change is frequent, labour turnover is high and political conditions are unstable – the organization cannot standardize but must instead remain flexible through the use of direct supervision or mutual adjustment for coordination, and so it must use a more organic structure. Thus, for example, armies, which tend to be highly bureaucratic institutions in peacetime, can become rather organic when engaged in highly dynamic, guerilla-type warfare.

● *The more complex an organization's environment, the more decentralized its structure:* The prime reason to decentralize a structure is that all the information needed to make decisions cannot be comprehended in one head. Thus, when the operations of an organization are based on a complex body of knowledge, there is usually a need to decentralize decision-making power. Note that a simple environment can be stable or dynamic (the manufacturer of dresses faces a simple environment yet cannot predict style from one season to another), as can a complex one (the specialist in perfected open heart surgery faces a complex task, yet knows what to expect).

● *The more diversified an organization's markets, the greater the propensity to split it into market-based units, or divisions, given favourable economies of scale:* When an organization can identify distinct markets – geographical regions, clients, but espcially products and services – it will be predisposed to split itself into high-level units on that basis, and to give each a good deal of control over its own operations (that is, to use what we called 'limited vertical decentralization'). In simple terms, diversification breeds divisionalization. Each unit can be given all the functions associated with its own markets. But this assumes favourable economies of scale: If the operating core cannot be divided, as in the case of an aluminium smelter, also if some critical function must be centrally coordinated, as in purchasing a retail chain, then full divisionalization may not be possible.

● *Extreme hostility in its environment drives any organization to centralize its structure temporarily:* When threatened by extreme hostility in its environment, the tendency for an organization is to centralize power, in other words, to fall back on its tightest coordinating mechanism, direct supervision. Here a single leader can ensure fast and tightly coordinated response to the threat (at least temporarily).

Power

● *The greater the external control of an organization, the more centralized and formalized its structure:* This important hypothesis claims that to the extent that an organization is controlled externally, for example by a parent firm or a government that dominates its external coalition – it tends to centralize power at the strategic apex and to formalize its behaviour. The reason is that the two most effective ways to control an organization from the outside are to hold its chief executive officer responsible for its actions and to impose clearly defined standards on it. Moreover, external control forces the the organization to be especially careful about its actions.

● *A divided external coalition will tend to give rise to a politicized internal coalition, and vice versa:* In effect, conflict in one of the coalitions tends to spill over to the other, as one set of influencers seeks to enlist the support of the others.

● *Fashion favours the structure of the day (and of the culture), sometimes even when inappropriate:* Ideally, the design parameters are chosen according to the dictates of age, size, technical system and environment. In fact, however, fashion seems to play a role too, encouraging many organizations to adopt currently popular design parameters that are inappropriate for themselves. Paris has its salons of haute couture; likewise New York has its offices of '*haute structure*', the consulting firms that sometimes tend to oversell the latest in structural fashion.

THE CONFIGURATIONS

We have now introduced various attributes of organizations – parts, coordinating mechanisms, design parameters, situational factors. How do they all combine?

We proceed here on the assumption that a limited number of configurations can help explain much of what is observed in organizations. We have introduced in our discussion six basic parts of the organization, six basic mechanisms of coordination, as well as six basic types of decentralization. In fact, there seems to be a fundamental correspondence between all of these sixes, which can be explained by a set of pulls exerted on the organization by each of its six parts, as shown in Figure 8. When conditions favour one of these pulls, the associated part of the organization becomes key, the coordinating mechanism appropriate to itself becomes prime, and the form of decentralization that passes power to itself emerges. The organization is thus drawn to design itself as a particular configuration. We list here and then introduce briefly the six resulting configurations, together with a seventh that tends to appear when no one pull or part dominates.

The Entrepreneurial Organization

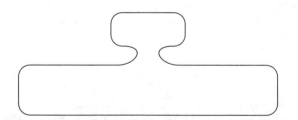

The name tells it all. And the figure above shows it all. The structure is simple, not much more than one large unit consisting of one or a few top managers, one of whom dominates by the pull to lead, and a group of operators who do the basic work. Little of the behaviour in the organization is formalized and minimal use is made of planning, training or the liaison devices. The absence of standardization means that the structure is organic and has little need for staff analysts. Likewise there are a few middle-line managers because so much of the coordination is handled at the top. Even the support staff is minimized, in order to keep the structure lean, the organization flexible.

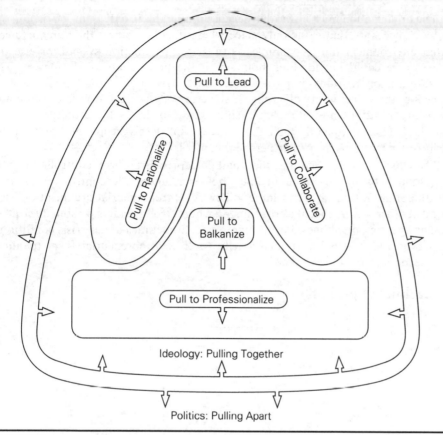

FIGURE 8
Basic pulls on the organization

Configuration	Prime Coordinating Mechanism	Key Part of Organization	Type of Decentralization
Entrepreneurial organization	Direct supervision	Strategic apex	Vertical and horizontal centralization
Machine organization	Standardization of work processes	Technostructure	Limited horizontal decentralization
Professional organization	Standardization of skills	Operating core	Horizontal decentralization
Diversified organization	Standardization of outputs	Middle line	Limited vertical decentralization
Innovative organization	Mutual adjustment	Support staff	Selected decentralization
Missionary organization	Standardization of norms	Ideology	Decentralization
Political organization	None	None	Varies

The organization must be flexible because it operates in a dynamic environment, often by choice since that is the only place where it can outsmart the bureaucracies. But that environment must be simple, as must the production system, or else the chief executive could not for long hold on to the lion's share of the power. The organization is often young, in part because time drives it towards bureaucracy, in part because the vulnerability of its simple structure often causes it to fail. And many of these organizations are often small, since size too drives the structure toward bureaucracy. Not infrequently the chief executive purposely keeps the organization small in order to retain his or her personal control.

The classic case is, of course, the small entrepreneurial firm, controlled tightly and personally by its owner. Sometimes, however, under the control of a strong leader, the organization can grow large. Likewise, entrepreneurial organizations can be found in other sectors too, like government, where strong leaders personally control particular agencies, often ones they have founded. Sometimes under crisis conditions, large organizations also revert temporarily to the entrepreneurial form to allow forceful leaders to try to save them.

The Machine Organization

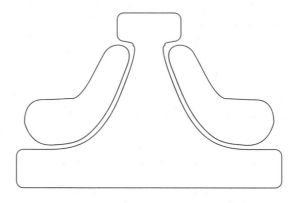

The machine organization is the offspring of the industrial revolution, when jobs became highly specialized and work became highly standardized. As can be seen in the figure above, in contrast to entrepreneurial organizations, the machine one elaborates is administration. First, it requires a large technostructure to design and maintain its systems of standardization, notably those that formalize its behaviours and plan its actions. And by virtue of the organization's dependence on these systems, the technostructure gains a good deal of informal power, resulting in a limited amount of horizontal decentralization, reflecting the pull to rationalize. A large hierarchy of middle-line managers emerges to control the highly specialized work of the operating core. But the middle-line hierarchy is usually structured on a functional basis all the way up to the top, where the real power of coordination lies. So the structure tends to be rather centralized in the vertical sense.

To enable the top managers to maintain centralized control, both the environment and the production system of the machine organization must be fairly simple, the latter regulating the work of the operators but not itself automated. In fact, machine organizations fit most naturally with mass production. Indeed, it is interesting that this structure is most prevalent in industries that date back to the period from the Industrial Revolution to the ealy part of the twentieth century.

The Professional Organization

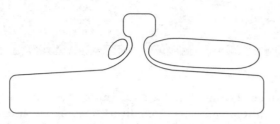

There is another bureaucratic configuration, but because this one relies on the standardization of skills rather than of work processes or outputs for its coordination, it emerges as dramatically different from the machine one. Here the pull to professionalize dominates. In having to rely on trained professionals – people highly specialized, but with considerable control over their work, as in hospitals or universities – to do its operating tasks, the organization surrenders a good deal of its power not only to the professionals themselves but also to the associations and institutions that select and train them in the first place. So the structure emerges as highly decentralized horizontally; power over many decisions, both operating and strategic, flows all the way down the hierarchy, to the professionals of the operating core.

Above the operating core we find a rather unique structure. There is little need for a technostructure, since the main standardization occurs as a result of training that takes place outside the organization. Because the professionals work so independently, the size of operating units can be very large, and few first line managers are needed. The support staff is typically very large too, in order to back up the high-priced professionals.

The professional organization is calld for whenever an organization finds itself in an environment that is stable yet complex. Complexity requires decentralization to highly trained individuals, and stability enables them to apply standardized skills and so to work with a good deal of autonomy. To ensure that autonomy, the production system must be neither highly regulating, complex nor automated.

The Diversified Organization

Like the professional organization, the diversified one is not so much an integrated organization as a set of rather independent entities coupled together by a loose administrative structure. But whereas those entities of the professional organization are individuals, in the diversified one they are units in the middle line, generally called 'divisions', exerting a dominant pull to Balkanize. This configuration differs from the others in one major respect: it is not a complete structure, but a partial one superimposed on the others. Each division has its own structure.

An organization divisionalizes for one reason above all, because its product lines are diversified. And that tends to happen most often in the largest and most

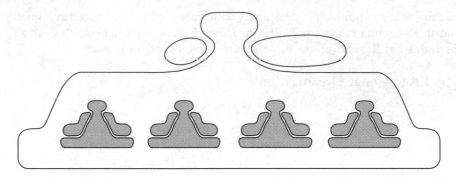

mature organizations, the ones that have run out of opportunities – or have become bored – in their traditional markets. Such diversification encourages the organization to replace functional by market-based units, one for each distinct product line (as shown in the diversified organization figure), and to grant considerable autonomy to each to run its own business. The result is a limited form of decentralization down the chain of command.

How does the central headquarters maintain a semblance of control over the divisions? Some direction supervision is used. But too much of that interferes with the necessary divisional autonomy. So the headquarters relies on performance control systems, in other words, the standardization of outputs. To design these control systems, headquarters creates a small technostructure. This is shown in the figure, across from the small central support staff that headquarters sets up to provide certain services common to the divisions such as legal counsel and public relations. And because headquarters' control constitutes external control, as discussed in the first hypothesis on power, the structure of the divisions tend to be drawn towards the machine form.

The Innovative Organization

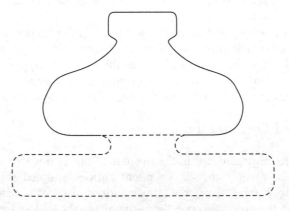

None of the structures so far discussed suits the industries of our age, industries such as aerospace, petrochemicals, think tank consulting and film-making. These organizations need above all to innovate in very complex ways. The bureaucratic structures are too inflexible, and the entrepreneurial one too centralized. These industries require 'project structures', ones that can fuse experts drawn from different specialties into smoothly functioning creative teams. That is the role of our fifth configuration, the innovative organization, which we shall also call 'adhocracy', dominated by the experts' pull to collaborate.

Adhocracy is an organic structure that relies for coordination on mutual adjustment among its highly trained and highly specialized experts, which it encourages by the extensive use of the liaison devices – integrating managers, standing committees and above all task forces and matrix structure. Typically, the experts are grouped in functional units for housekeeping purposes but deployed in small, market-based project teams to do their work. To these teams, located all over the structure in accordance with the decisions to be made, is delegated power over different kinds of decisions. So the structure becomes decentralized selectively in the vertical and horizontal dimensions, that is, power is distributed unevenly, all over the structure, according to expertise and need.

All the distinctions of conventional structure disappear in the innovative organization, as can be seen in the figure above. With power based on expertise, the line–staff distinction evaporates. With power distributed throughout the structure, the distinction between the strategic apex and the rest of the structure blurs.

These organizations are found in environments that are both complex and dynamic, because those are the ones that require sophisticated innovation, the type that calls for the cooperative efforts of many different kinds of experts. One type of adhocracy is often associated with a production system that is very complex, sometimes automated, and so requires a highly skilled and influential support staff to design and maintain the technical system of the operating core. (The dashed lines of the figure designate the separation of the operating core from the adhocratic administrative structure.) Here the projects take place in the administration to bring new operating facilities on line (as when a new complex is designed in a petrochemicals firm). Another type of adhocracy produces its projects directly for its clients (as in a think tank consulting firm of manufacturer of engineering prototypes). Here, as a result, the operators also take part in the projects, bringing their expertise to bear on them; hence the operating core blends into the administrative structure (as indicated in the figure above the dashed line). This second type of adhocracy tends to be young on average, because with no standard products or services, many tend to fail while others escape their vulnerability by standardizing some products or services and so converting themselves to a form of bureaucracy.[1]

The Missionary Organization

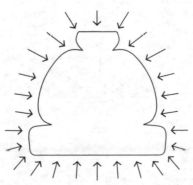

Our sixth configuration forms another rather distinct combination of the elements we have been discussing. When an organization is dominated by its ideology, its members are encouraged to pull together, and so there tends to be a loose division of labour, little job specialization, as well as a reduction of the various forms of differentiation found in the other configurations – of the strategic apex from the rest, of staff from line or administration from operations, between operators, between divisions, and so on.

What holds the missionary together – that is, provides for its coordination – is the standardization of norms, the sharing of values and beliefs among all its members. And the key to ensuring this is their socialization, effected through the design parameter of indoctrination. Once the new member has been indoctrinated into the organization – once he or she identifies strongly with the common beliefs – then he or she can be given considerable freedom to make decisions. Thus the result of effective indoctrination is the most complete form of decentralization. And because other forms of coordination need not be relied on, the missionary organization formalizes little of its behaviour as such and makes minimal use of planning and control systems. As a result, it has little technostructure. Likewise, external professional training is not relied on, because that would force the organization to surrender a certain control to external agencies.

Hence, the missionary organization ends up as an amorphous mass of members, with little specialization as to job, differentiation as to part, division as to status.

Missionaries tend not to be very young organizations – it takes time for a set of beliefs to become institutionalized as an ideology. Many missionaries do not get a chance to grow very old either (with notable exceptions, such as certain long-standing religious orders). Missionary organizations cannot grow very large *per se* – they rely on personal contacts among their members – although some tend to spin off other enclaves in the form of relatively independent units sharing the same ideology. Neither the environment nor the technical system of the missionary organization can be very complex, because that would require the use of highly skilled specialists, who would hold a certain power and status over others and thereby serve to differentiate the structure. Thus we would expect to find the simplest technical systems in these organizations, usually hardly any at all, as in religious orders or in the primitive farm cooperatives.

The Political Organization

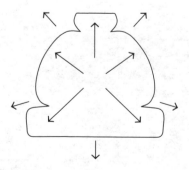

Finally, we come to a form of organization characterized, structurally at least, by what it lacks. When an organization has no dominate part, no dominant mechanism or coordination and no stable form of centralization or decentralization, it may have difficulty tempering the conflicts within its midst, and a form of organization called the *political* may result. What characterizes its behaviour is the pulling apart of its different parts, as show in the figure above.

Political organizations can take on different forms. Some are temporary, reflecting difficult transitions in strategy or structure that evoke conflict. Others are more permanent, perhaps because the organization must face competing internal forces (say, between necessarily strong marketing and production departments), perhaps because a kind of political rot has set in but the organization is sufficiently entrenched to support it (being, for example, a monopoly or a protected government unit).

Together, all these configurations seem to encompass and integrate a good deal of what we know about organizations. It should be emphasized however, that as presented, each configuration is idealized – a simplification, really a caricature of reality. No real organization is ever exactly like any one of them, although some do come remarkably close, while others seem to reflect combinations of them, sometimes in transition from one to another.

The first five represent what seem to be the most common forms of organizations; thus these will form the basis for the 'context' section of this book – labelled entrepreneurial, mature, diversified, innovation and professional. There, a reading in each chapter will be devoted to each of these configurations, describing its structure, functioning, conditions, strategy-making process and the issues that surround it. Other readings in these chapters will look at specific strategies in each of these contexts, industry conditions, strategy techniques, and so on.

The other two configurations – the missionary and the political – seem to be less common, represented more by the forces of culture and conflict that exist in all organizations than by distinct forms as such. Hence they will be discussed in the chapter that follows this one, 'Dealing with Culture and Power'.

[1] We shall clarify in a later reading these two basic types of adhocracies. Toffler employed the term adhocracy in his popular book *Future Shock*, but it can be found in print at least as far back as 1964.

6

DEALING WITH CULTURE AND POWER

Culture arrived on the management scene in the 1980s like a typhoon blowing in from the Far East. It suddenly became fashionable in consulting circles to sell culture like some article of organizational clothing, much as 'management by objectives' or 'total information systems' were once sold. What gave this subject most impetus was Peter and Waterman's *In Search of Excellence*. This depicted successful organizations as being rich in culture – permeated with strong and sustaining systems of beliefs. In our view– as in theirs – culture is not an article of fashion, but an intrinsic part of a deeper organization 'character'. To draw on definitions introduced earlier, strategy is not just an arbitrarily chosen *position*, nor an analytically developed *plan*, but a deeply entrenched *perspective* which influences the way an organization develops new ideas, considers and weights options, and responds to changes in its environment.

Culture thus permeates many critical aspects of strategy-making. But perhaps the most crucial realm is the way people are chosen, developed, nurtured, interrelated and rewarded in the organization. The kinds of people attracted to an organization and the way they can most effectively deal with problems and each other are largely a function of the culture a place builds – and the practices and systems which support it.

In some organizations, the culture may become so strong that it is best referred to as an 'ideology', which dominates all else. The first reading in this chapter, drawn from Mintzberg's book *Power in and around Organizations*, traces how such rich cultures evolve through three stages: their rooting in a sense of mission, their development through traditions and sagas, and their reinforcement through various forms of identifications. Mintzberg briefly considers the missionary-type organization introduced in Chapter 5 and then shows how other organizations, for example regular business firms, sometimes overlay rich cultures on their more conventional ways of operating.

The second reading, by Christopher Bartlett of the Harvard Business School and Sumantra Ghoshal, the third author of this book and a professor of international management at the London Business School, presents a biological metaphor in which formal structure represents the organizations' anatomy, while the interpersonal relationships and management processes are its physiology, and a shared vision together with a set of common norms and values are its psychology. They argue that to build organizational capability, large global firms must look beyond structure to the vision, values and processes to create 'a matrix in the minds of its managers'.

Up to this point, the ideas and concepts we have presented in the book, for the most part, have a functionalist orientation in which organizations are viewed as rather rational and cooperative instruments. Strategies, whether formulated analytically or allowed to emerge in some kind of a learning process, none the less serve the good of the organization at large, as do the associated structures, systems and culture. True Quinn's managers, for example, have consciously considered and dealt with potential resistance in creating and implanting their strategies. In doing so, they may have been forced to think in political terms. But the overt use of power and organized political action has largely been absent from our discussion.

An important group of thinkers in the field, however, have come to view the strategy process as an interplay of the forces of power, sometimes highly politicized. Rather than assuming that organizations are consistent, coherent and cooperative systems, tightly integrated to pursue certain traditional ends (namely the delivery of their products and services in the pursuit of profit, at least in the private sector), these writers start with quite different premises. They believe that organizations' goals and directions are determined primarily by the power needs of those who populate them. Their analyses raise all kinds of interesting and unsettled questions, such as: For whom does the organization really exist? For what purposes? If the organization is truly a political entity, how does one manage effectively in it? And so on. These are the issues we consider in the last two readings in this chapters.

No work in the literature sets this into perspective better than the famous study in the United States' response to the Cuban missile crisis by Graham Allison (1971) of Harvard's Kennedy School of Government. Allison believes that our conception of how decision-making proceeds in organizations can be considered from three perspectives: a 'rational actor' model (which is the concept he believes the American leaders had of the Soviets), an 'organizations process' model and a 'bureaucratic politics' model (both of which Allison thinks could have been used as well to improve America's understanding of the Soviets' behaviour). In the first model, power is embedded in a relatively rational and calculating centre of action, much as strategy-making was described in Chapter 3. In the second, it is entrenched in various organizational departments, each using power to further its own particular purposes. In the third model, 'politics' comes into full play as individuals and groups exercise their influence to determine outcomes for their own benefits.

The first of our two readings on power is drawn from Mintzberg's *Power in and around Organizations* book, and focuses on Allison's third model, with elements of his second. It considers the general force of politics in organizations, what it is and what political 'games' people play in organizations, and then the various forms taken by organizations that are dominated by such politics, the extreme one labelled the 'political arena'. This reading concludes with a discussion of when and why politics sometimes plays a functional role in organizations.

The second reading, also by Mintzberg, raises the issue of power at a more macro-level: for whom does or should the large business corporation exist? Mintzberg proposes a whole portfolio of answers around a 'conceptual horseshoe'. In so doing, he perhaps helps to reconcile some of the basic differences between those who view organizations as agents of economic competition and those who consider them to be instruments of the public will, or else as political systems in their own right. This reading also discusses the concept of social responsibility, one of the traditional topics covered in policy or strategy courses. But here the subject is treated not in a philanthropic or ethical sense, but as a managerial or organizational one. It also reviews the issues of corporate democracy, of regulation and pressure campaigns, and of 'freedom', as described by Milton Friedman.

● IDEOLOGY AND THE MISSIONARY ORGANIZATION*

HENRY MINTZBERG

We all know that $2 + 2 = 4$. But general systems theory, through the concept of synergy, suggests that it can also equal 5, that the parts of a system may produce more working together than they can apart. A flashlight and a battery add up to just so many pieces of hardware; together they form a working system. Likewise an organization is a working system which can entice from its members more than they would produce apart – more effort, more creativity, more output (or, of course, less). This may be 'strategic' – deriving from the way components have been combined in the organization. Or it may be motivational: The group is said to develop a 'mood', an 'atmosphere', to have some kind of 'chemistry'. In organizations, we talk of a 'style', a 'culture' a 'character'. One senses something unique when one walks into the offices of IBM; the chemistry of Hewlett-Packard just doesn't feel the same as that of Texas Instruments, even though the two have operated in some similar businesses.

All these words are used to describe something – intangible yet very real, over and above the concrete components of an organization – that we refer to as its *ideology*. Specifically, an ideology is taken here to mean a rich system of values and beliefs about an organization, shared by its members, that distinguishes it from other organizations. For our purposes, the key feature of such an ideology is its unifying power: It ties the individual to the organization, generating an *esprit de corps*, a 'sense of mission', in effect, an integration of individual and organizational goals that can produce synergy.

THE DEVELOPMENT OF AN ORGANIZATIONAL IDEOLOGY

The development of an ideology in an organization will be discussed here in three stages. The roots of the ideology are planted when a group of individuals band

*Adapted from Henry Mintzberg, *Power in and around Organizations* (copyright © Prentice-Hall, 1983), Chs. 11 and 21; used by permission of the publisher; based on a summary that appeared in *Mintzberg on Management: Inside Our Strange World of Organizations* (New York: Free Press, 1989).

together around a leader and, through a sense of mission, found a vigorous organization or invigorate an existing one. The ideology then develops over time through the establishment of traditions. Finally, the existing ideology is reinforced when new members enter the organization and identify with its system of beliefs.

Stage 1: The Rooting of Ideology in a Sense of Mission

Typically, an organization is founded when a single prime mover identifies a mission – some product to be produced, service to be rendered – and collects a group around him or her to accomplish it. Some organizations are, of course, founded by other means, as when a new agency is created by a government or a subsidiary by a corporation. But a prime mover often can still be identified behind the founding of the organization.

The individuals who come together don't do so at random, but coalesce because they share some values associated with the fledgling organization. At the very least they see something in it for themselves. But in some cases, in addition to the mission *per se* there is a 'sense of mission', that is, a feeling that the group has banded together to create something unusual and exciting. This is common in new organizations for a number of reasons.

First, unconstrained by procedure and tradition, new organizations offer wide latitude for manoeuvre. Second, they tend to be small, enabling the members to establish personal relationships. Third, the founding members frequently share a set of strong basic beliefs, sometimes including a sense that they wish to work together. Fourth, the founders of new organizations are often 'charismatic' individuals, and so energize the followers and knit them together. Charisma, as Weber (1969: 12) used the term, means a sense of 'personal devotion' to the leader for the sake of his or her personal qualities rather than formal position. People join and remain with the organization because of dedication to the leader and his or her mission. Thus the roots of strong ideologies tend to be planted in the founding of organizations.

Of course, such ideologies can also develop in existing organizations. But a review of the preceding points suggests why this should be much more difficult to accomplish. Existing organizations *are* constrained by procedures and traditions, many are *already* large and impersonal, and their *existing* beliefs tend to impede the establishment of new ones. None the less, with the introduction of strong charismatic leadership reinforced by a strong new sense of mission, an existing organization can sometimes be invigorated by the creation of a new ideology.

A key to the development of an organizational ideology, in a new or existing organization, is a leadership with a genuine belief in mission and an honest dedication to the people who must carry it out. Mouthing the right words might create the veneer of an organizational ideology, but it is only an authentic feeling on the part of the leadership – which followers somehow sense – that sets the roots of the ideology deep enough to sustain it when other forces, such as impersonal administration (bureaucracy) or politics, challenge it.

Stage 2: The Development of Ideology Through Traditions and Sagas

As a new organization establishes itself or an existing one establishes a new set of beliefs, it makes decisions and takes actions that serve as commitments and establish precedents. Behaviours reinforce themselves over time, and actions become infused with value. When those forces are strong, ideology begins to emerge in its own right. That ideology is strengthened by stories – sometimes called 'myths' – that develop around important events in the organization's past. Gradually the organization establishes its own unique sense of history. All of this – the precedents, habits, myths, history – form a common base of tradition, which the members of the organization share, thus solidifying the ideology. Gradually, in Selznick's (1957) terms, the organization is converted from an expendable 'instrument' for the accomplishment of externally imposed goals into an 'institution', a system with a life of its own. It 'acquires a self, a distinct identity'.

Thus B.R. Clark described the 'distinctive college', with reference particularly to Reed, Antioch and Swarthmore. Such institutions develop, in his words, an 'organizational saga', 'a collective understanding of a unique accomplishment based on historical exploits', which links the organization's present with its past and 'turns a formal place into a beloved institution' (1972: 178). The saga captures allegiance, committing people to the institution (B.R. Clark 1970: 235).

Stage 3: The Reinforcement of Ideology Through Identifications

Our description to this point makes it clear that an individual entering an organization does not join a random collection of individuals, but rather a living system with its own culture. He or she may come with a certain set of values and beliefs, but there is little doubt that the culture of the organization can weigh heavily on the behaviour he or she will exhibit once inside it. This is especially true when the culture is rich – when the organization has an emerging or fully developed ideology. Then the individual's *identification* with and *loyalty* to the organization can be especially strong. Such identification can develop in a number of ways:

- Most simply, identification occurs *naturally* because the new member is attracted to the organization's system of beliefs.

- Identification may also be *selected*. New members are chosen to 'fit in' with the existing beliefs, and positions of authority are likewise filled from among the members exhibiting the strongest loyalty to those beliefs.

- Identification may also be *evoked*. When the need for loyalty is especially great, the organization may use informal processes of *socialization* and formal programmes of *indoctrination* to reinforce natural or selected commitment to its system of beliefs.

- Finally, and most weakly, identification can be *calculated*. In effect, individuals conform to the beliefs not because they identify naturally with them nor because they even necessarily fit in with them, not because they have been socialized or indoctrinated into them, but simply because it pays them to identify with the beliefs. They may enjoy the work or the social group, may like the remuneration, may work to get ahead through promotion and the like. Of course, such identification is fragile. It disappears as soon as an opportunity calculated to be better appears.

Clearly, the higher up this list an organization's member identifications tend to be, the more likely it is to sustain a strong ideology, or even to have such an ideology in the first place. Thus, strong organizational belief systems can be recognized above all by the presence of much natural identification. Attention to selected identification indicates the presence of an ideology, since it reflects an organization's efforts to sustain its ideology, as do efforts at socialization and indoctrination. Some organizations require a good deal of the latter two, because of the need to instill in their new members a complex system of beliefs. When the informal processes of socialization tend to function naturally, perhaps reinforced by more formal programmes of indoctrination, then the ideology would seem to be strong. But when an organization is forced to rely almost exclusively on indoctrination, or worse to fall back on forms of calculated identification, then its ideology would appear to be weakening, if not absent to begin with.

THE MISSIONARY ORGANIZATION

While some degree of ideology can be found in virtually every organization, that degree can vary considerably. At one extreme are those organizations, such as religious orders or radical political movements, whose ideologies tend to be strong and whose identifications are primarily natural and selected. Edwards (1977) refers to organizations with strong ideologies as 'stylistically rich', Selznick (1957) as 'institutions'. It is the presence of such an ideology that enables an organization to have 'a life of its own', to emerge as 'a living social institution' (Selznick 1949: 10). At the other extreme are those organizations with relatively weak ideologies, 'stylistically barren', in some cases business organizations with strong utilitarian reward systems. History and tradition have no special value in these organizations. In the absence of natural forms of identification on the part of their members, these organizations sometimes try to rely on the process of indoctrination to integrate individual and organizational goals. But usually they have to fall back on calculated identifications and especially formal controls.

We can refer to 'stylistically rich' organizations as *missionaries*, because they are somewhat akin in their beliefs to the religious organizations by that name. Mission counts above all – to preserve it, extend it or perfect it. That mission is typically (1) clear and focused, so that its members are easily able to identify with it; (2) inspiring, so that the members do, in fact, develop such identifications; and (3) distinctive, so that the organization and its members are deposited into a unique niche where the ideology can flourish. As a result of their attachment to its mission, the members of the organization resist strongly any attempt to change it, to interfere with tradition. The mission and the rest of the ideology must be preserved at all costs.

The missionary organization is a distinct configuration of the attributes of structure, internally highly integrated yet different from other configurations. What holds this orgaization together – that is, provides for its coordination – is the standardization of its norms, in other words, the sharing of values and beliefs among its members. As was noted, that can happen informally, either through natural selection or else the informal process of socialization. But from the perspective of structural design the key attribute is indoctrination, meaning formalized programmes to develop or reinforce identification with the ideology. And once the new member has been selected, socialized and indoctrinated, he or she is accepted into the system as an equal partner, able to participate in decision-making alongside everyone else. Thus, at the limit, the missionary organization can achieve the purest form of decentralization: all who are accepted into the system share its power.

But that does not mean an absence of control. Quite the contrary. No matter how subtle, control tends to be very powerful in this organization. For here, the organization controls not just people's behaviour but their very souls. The machine organization buys the 'workers'' attention through imposed rules; the missionary organization captures the 'members'' hearts through shared values. As Jay noted in his book *Management and Machiavelli* (1970), teaching new Jesuit recruits to 'love God and do what you like' is not to do what they like at all but to act in strict conformance with the order's beliefs (1970: 70).

Thus, the missionary organization tends to end up as an amorphous mass of members all pulling together within the common ideology, with minimum specialization as to job, differentiation as to part, division as to status. At the limit, managers, staffers and operators, once selected, socialized and indoctrinated, all seem rather alike and may, in fact, rotate into each other's positions.

The traditional Israeli kibbutz is a classic example of the missionary organization. In certain seasons, everyone pitches in and picks fruit in the fields by day and then attends the meetings to decide administrative issues by night. Managerial positions exist but are generally filled on a rotating basis so that no one emerges with the status of office for long. Likewise, staff support positions exist, but they too tend to be filled on a rotating basis from the same pool of members, as are the operating positions in the fields. (Kitchen duty is, for example, considered drudgery which everyone must do periodically.) Conversion to industry has, however, threatened that ideology. As suggested, it was relatively easy to sustain the egalitarian ideology when the work was agricultural. Industry, in contrast, generally called for greater levels of technology, specialization and expertise, with a resulting increase in the need for administrative hierarchy and functional differentiation, all a threat to the missionary orientation. The kibbutzim continue to struggle with this problem.

A number of our points about the traditional kibbutz are summarized in a table developed by Rosner, which contrasts the 'principles of kibbutz organization' – classic missionary – with those of 'bureaucratic organization', in our terms, the classic machine:

Principles of Bureaucratic Organization	*Principles of Kibbutz Organization*
1. Permanency of office.	Impermanency of office.
2. The office carries with it impersonal, fixed privileges and duties.	The definition of office is flexible – privileges and duties are not formally fixed and often depend on the personality of the official.
3. A hierarchy of functional authorities expressed in the authority of the officials.	A basic assumption of the equal value of all functions without a formal hierarchy of authority.

Principles of Bureaucratic Organization	*Principles of Kibbutz Organization*
4. Nomination of officials is based on formal objective qualifications.	Officials are elected, not nominated. Objective qualifications are not decisive, personal qualities are more important in election.
5. The office is a full-time occupation.	The office is usually supplementary to the full-time occupation of the official. (Rosner, 1969)

We can distinguish several forms of the pure missionary organization. Some are *reformers* that set out to change the world directly – anything from overthrowing a government to ensuring that all domestic animals are 'decently' clothed. Other missionaries can be called *converters*, their mission being to change the world indirectly, by attracting members and changing them. The difference between the first two types of missionaries is the difference between the Women's Christian Temperance Union and Alcoholics Anonymous. Their ends were similar, but their means differed, seeking to reduce alcoholism in one case by promoting a general ban on liquor sales, in the other by discouraging certain individuals, namely joined members, from drinking. Third are the *cloister* missionaries who seek not to change things so much as to allow their members to pursue a unique style of life. The monasteries that close themselves off from the outside world are good examples, as are groups that go off to found new isolated colonies.

Of course, no organization can completely seal itself off from the world. All missionary organizations, in fact, face the twin opposing pressures of isolation and assimilation. Together these make them vulnerable. On one side is the threat of *isolation*, of growing ever inward in order to protect the unique ideology from the pressures of the ordinary world until the organization eventually dies for lack of renewal. On the other side is the threat of *assimilation*, of reaching out so far to promote the ideology that it eventually gets compromised. When this happens, the organization may survive but the ideology dies, and so the configuration changes (typically to the machine form).

IDEOLOGY AS AN OVERLAY ON CONVENTIONAL ORGANIZATIONS

So far we have discussed what amounts to the extreme form of ideological organization, the missionary. But more organizations have strong ideologies that can afford to structure themselves in this way. The structure may work for an Israeli kibbutz in a remote corner of the Negev desert, but this is hardly a way to run a Hewlett-Packard or a McDonald's, let alone a kibbutz closer to the worldly pressures of Tel Aviv.

What such organizations tend to do is overlay ideological characteristics on a more conventional structure – perhaps machine-like in the case of McDonald's and that second kibbutz, innovative in the case of Hewlett-Packard. The mission may sometimes seem ordinary – serving hamburgers, producing instruments and computers – but it is carried out with a good dose of ideological fervour by employees firmly committed to it.

Best known for this are, of course, certain of the Japanese corporations, Toyota being a prime example. Ouchi and Jaeger (1978: 308) contrast in the table reproduced below the typical large American corporation (Type A) with with its Japanese counterpart (Type J):

Type A (for American)	*Type J (for Japanese)*
Short-term employment	Lifetime employment
Individual decision-making	Consensual decision-making
Individual responsibility	Collective responsibility
Rapid evaluation and promotion	Slow evaluation and promotion
Explicit, formalized control	Implicit, informal control
Specialized career path	Non-specialized career path
Segmented concern	Holistic concern

Ouchi and Jaeger (1978: 309), in fact, make their point best with an example in which a classic Japanese ideological orientation confronts a conventional American bureaucratic one:

> [D]uring one of the author's visits to a Japanese bank in California, both the Japanese president and the American vice-presidents of the bank accused the other of being unable to formulate objectives. The Americans meant that the Japanese president could not or would not give them explicit, quantified targets to attain over the next three or six months, while the Japanese meant that the Americans could not see that once they understood the company's philosophy, they would be able to deduce for themselves the proper objective for any conceivable situation.

In another study, however, Ouchi together with Johnson (1978) discussed a native American corporation that does resemble the Type J firm (labelled 'Type Z'; Ouchi (1981) later published a bestseller about such organizations). In it, they found greater loyalty, a strong collective orientation, less specialization and a greater reliance on informal controls. For example, 'a new manager will be useless for at least four or five years. It takes that long for most people to decide whether the new person really fits in, whether they can really trust him.' That was in sharp contrast to the 'auction market' atmosphere of a typical American firm: It 'is almost as if you could open up the doors each day with 100 executives and engineers who had been randomly selected from the country, and the organization would work just as well as it does now' (1978: 302).

The trends in American business over several decades – 'professional' management, emphasis on technique and rationalization, 'bottom-line' mentality – missionary configuration has hardly been fashionable in the West, especially the United States. But ideology may have an important role to play there, given the enormous success many Japanese firms have had in head-on competition with American corporations organized in machine and diversified ways, with barren cultures. At the very least, we might expect more ideological overlays on the conventional forms of organizations in the West. But this, as we hope our discussion made clear, may be both for better and for worse.

MATRIX MANAGEMENT: NOT A STRUCTURE, A FRAME OF MIND*

By Christopher A. Bartlett and Sumantra Ghoshal

Top-level managers in many of today's leading corporations are losing control of their companies. The problem is not that they have misjudged the demands created by an increasingly complex environment and an accelerating rate of environmental change, nor even that they have failed to develop strategies appropriate to the new challenges. The problem is that their companies are organizationally incapable of carrying out the sophisticated strategies they have developed. Over the past 20 years, strategic thinking has far outdistanced organizational capabilities....

In recent years, as more and more managers recognized oversimplification as a strategic trap, they began to accept the need to manage complexity rather than seek to minimize it. This realization, however, led many into an equally threatening organizational trap when they concluded that the best response to increasingly complex strategic requirements was increasingly complex organizational structures.

The obvious organizational solution to strategies that required multiple, simultaneous management capabilities was the matrix structure that became so fashionable in the late 1970s and the early 1980s. Its parallel reporting relationships acknowledged the diverse, conflicting needs of functional, product and geographic management groups and provided a formal mechanism for resolving them. Its multiple information channels allowed the organization to capture and analyze external complexity. And its overlapping responsibilities were designed to combat parochialism and build flexibility into the company's response to change.

In practice, however, the matrix proved all but unmanageable – especially in an international context. Dual reporting led to conflict and confusion; the proliferation of channels created informational log-jams as a proliferation of committees and reports bogged down the organization; and overlapping responsibilities produced turf battles and a loss of accountability. Separated by barriers of distance, language, time and culture, managers found it virtually impossible to clarify the confusion and resolve the conflicts.

... For decades, we have seen the general manager as chief strategic guru and principal organizational architect. But as the competitive climate grows less stable and less predictable, it is harder for one person alone to succeed in that great visionary role. Similarly, as formal, hierarchical structure gives way to networks of personal relationships that work through informal, horizontal communication channels, the image of top management in an isolated corner office moving boxes and lines on an organization chart becomes increasingly anachronistic.

Paradoxically, as strategies and organizations become more complex and sophisticated, top-level general managers are beginning to replace their historical concentration on the grand issues of strategy and structure with a focus on the details of managing people and processes. The critical strategic requirement is not to devise the most ingenious and well-coordinated plan but to build the most viable and flexible strategic process; the key organizational task is not to design the most elegant structure but to capture individual capabilities and motivate the entire organization to respond cooperatively to a complicated and dynamic environment.

BUILDING AN ORGANIZATION

While business thinkers have written a great deal about strategic innovation, they have paid far less attention to the accompanying organizational challenges. Yet many companies remain caught in the structural-complexity trap, which paralyzes their ability to respond quickly or flexibly to the new strategic imperatives.

For those companies that adopted matrix structures, the problem was not in the way they defined the goal. They correctly recognized the need for a multidimensional organization to respond to growing external complexity. The problem was that they defined their organizational objectives in purely structural terms. Yet formal structure describes only the organization's basic anatomy. Companies must also concern themselves with organizational physiology – the systems and relationships that allow the lifeblood of information to flow through the organization. And they need to develop a healthy organizational psychology – the shared norms, values and beliefs that shape the way individual managers think and act.

The companies that fell into the organizational trap assumed that changing their formal structure (anatomy) would force changes in interpersonal relationships and decision processes (physiology), which in turn would reshape the individual attitudes and actions of managers (psychology).

But as many companies have discovered, reconfiguring the formal structure is a blunt and sometimes brutal instrument of change. A new structure creates new and presumably more useful managerial ties, but these can take months and often years to evolve into effective knowledge-generating and decision-making relationships. And since the new job requirements will frustrate, alienate or simply overwhelm so many managers, changes in individual attitudes and behaviour will likely take even longer.

As companies struggle to create organizational capabilities that reflect rather than diminish environmental complexity, good managers gradually stop searching for the ideal structural template to impose on the company from the top down. Instead, they focus on the challenge of building up an appropriate set of employee attitudes and skills and linking them together with carefully developed processes and relationships. In other words, they begin to focus on building the organization rather than simply on installing a new structure.

Indeed, the companies that are most successful at developing multidimensional organizations begin at the far end of the anatomy–physiology–psychology sequence.

Their first objective is to alter the organizational psychology – the broad corporate beliefs and norms that shape managers' perceptions and actions. Then, by enriching and clarifying communication and decision processes, companies reinforce these psychological changes with improvements in organizational physiology. Only later do they consolidate and confirm their progress by realigning organizational anatomy through changes in the formal structure.

No company we know of has discovered a quick or easy way to change its organizational psychology to reshape the understanding, identification, and commitment of its employees. But we found three principal characteristics common to those that managed the task most effectively:

1. The development and communication of a clear and consistent corporate vision.

2. The effective management of human resource tools to broaden individual perspectives and develop identification with corporate goals.

3. The integration of individual thinking and activities into the broad corporate agenda by means of a process we call co-option.

BUILDING A SHARED VISION

Perhaps the main reason managers in large, complex companies cling to parochial attitudes is that their frame of reference is bounded by their specific responsibilities. The surest way to break down such insularity is to develop and communicate a clear sense of corporate purpose that extends into every corner of the company and gives context and meaning to each manager's particular roles and responsibilities. We are not talking about a slogan, however catchy and pointed. We are talking about a company vision, which must be crafted and articulated with clarity, continuity and consistency: clarity of expression that makes company objectives understandable and meaningful; continuity of purpose that underscores their enduring importance; and consistency of application across business units and geographical boundaries that ensures uniformity throughout the organization.

Clarity

There are three keys to clarity in a corporate vision: simplicity, relevance and reinforcement. NEC's integration of computers and communications – C & C – is probably the best single example of how simplicity can make a vision more powerful. Top management has applied the C & C concept so effectively that it describes the company's business focus, defines its distinctive source of competitive advantage over large companies like IBM and AT & T, and summarizes its strategic and organizational imperatives.

The second key, relevance, means linking broad objectives to concrete agendas. When Wisse Dekker became CEO at Philips, his principal strategic concern was the problem of competing with Japan. He stated this challenge in martial terms – the United States had abandoned the battlefield; Philips was now Europe's last defence against insurgent Japanese electronics companies.. . .

The third key to clarity is top management's continual reinforcement, elaboration and interpretation of the core vision to keep it from becoming obsolete or abstract. Founder Konosuke Matsushita developed a grand, 250-year vision for his company, but he also managed to give it immediate relevance. He summed up its overall message in the 'Seven Spirits of Matsushita', to which he referred constantly in his policy statements. Each January he wove the company's one-year operational objectives into his overarching concept to produce an annual theme, which he then captured in a slogan. For all the loftiness of his concept of corporate purpose, he gave his managers immediate, concrete guidance in implementing Matsushita's goals.

Continuity

Despite shifts in leadership and continual adjustments in short-term business priorities, companies must remain committed to the same core set of strategic objectives and organizational values. Without such continuity, unifying vision might as well be expressed in terms of quarterly goals.

It was General Electric's lack of this kind of continuity that led to the erosion of its once formidable position in electrical appliances in many countries. Over a period of 20 years and under successive CEOs, the company's international consumer-product strategy never stayed the same for long. . . . The Brazilian subsidiary, for example, built its TV business in the 1960s until it was told to stop; in the early 1970s, it emphasized large appliances until it was denied funding; then it focused on housewares until the parent company sold off that business. In two decades, GE utterly dissipated its dominant franchise in Brazil's electrical products market.

Unilever, by contrast, made an enduring commitment to its Brazilian subsidiary, despite volatile swings in Brazil's business climate. Company chairman Floris Maljers emphasized the importance of looking past the latest political crisis or economic downturn to the long-term business potential. . . .

Consistency

The third task for top management in communicating strategic purpose is to ensure that everyone in the company shares the same vision. The cost of inconsistency can be horrendous. It always produces confusion and, in extreme cases, can lead to total chaos, with different units of the organization pursuing agendas that are mutually debilitating.

Philips is a good example of a company that, for a time, lost its consistency of corporate purpose. As a legacy of its wartime decision to give some overseas units legal autonomy, management had long experienced difficulty persuading North American Philips (NAP) to play a supportive role in the parent company's global strategies. The problem came to a head with the introduction of Philip's technologically first-rate videocassette recording system, the V2000. Despite considerable pressure from world headquarters in the Netherlands, NAP refused to launch the system, arguing that Sony's Beta system and Matsushita's VHS format were too well established and had cost, feature and system-support advantages Philips couldn't match. Relying on its legal independence and managerial autonomy, NAP management decided instead to source products from its Japanese competitors and market them under its Magnavox brand name. As a result, Philips was unable to build the efficiency and credibility it needed to challenge Japanese dominance of the VCR business....

But formulating and communicating a vision – no matter how clear, enduring and consistent – cannot succeed unless individual employees understand and accept the company's stated goals and objectives. Problems at this level are more often related to receptivity than to communication. The development of individual understanding and acceptance is a challenge for a company's human resource practices.

DEVELOPING HUMAN RESOURCES

While top managers universally recognize their responsibility for developing and allocating a company's scarce assets and resources, their focus on finance and technology often overshadows the task of developing the scarcest resource of all – capable managers. But if there is one key to regaining control of companies that operate in fast-changing environments, it is the ability of top management to turn the perceptions, capabilities and relationships of individual managers into the building blocks of the organization.

One pervasive problem in companies whose leaders lack this ability – or fail to exercise it – is getting managers to see how their specific responsibilities relate to the broad corporate vision. Growing external complexity and strategic sophistication have accelerated the growth of a cadre of specialists who are physically and organizationally isolated from each other, and the task of dealing with their consequent parochialism should not be delegated to the clerical staff that administers salary structures and benefit programmes. Top managers inside and outside the human resource function must be leaders in the recruitment, development, and assignment of the company's vital human talent.

Recruitment and Selection

The first step in successfully managing complexity is to tap the full range of available talent. It is a serious mistake to permit historical imbalances in the nationality or functional background of the management group to constrain hiring or subsequent promotion. In today's global marketplace, domestically oriented recruiting limits a company's ability to capitalize on its worldwide pool of management skill and biases its decision-making processes....

Not only must companies enlarge the pool of people available for key positions, they must also develop new criteria for choosing those most likely to succeed. Because past success is no longer a sufficient qualification for increasingly subtle, sensitive and unpredictable senior-level tasks, top management must become involved in a more discriminating selection process. At Matsushita, top management selects candidates for international assignment on the basis of a comprehensive set of personal characteristics, expressed for simplicity in the acronym SMILE: *s*pecialty (the needed skill, capability or knowledge); *m*anagement ability (particularly motivational ability); *i*nternational flexibility (willingness to learn and ability to adapt); *l*anguage facility; and *e*ndeavour (vitality, perseverance in the face of difficulty). These attributes are remarkably similar to those targeted by NEC and Philips, where top executives also are involved in the senior-level selection process.

Training and Development

Once the appropriate top-level candidates have been identified, the next challenge is to develop their potential. The most successful development efforts have three aims that take them well beyond the skill-building objectives of classic training programmes: to inculcate a common vision and shared values; to broaden management perspectives and capabilities; and to develop contacts and shape management relationships.

To build common vision and values, white-collar employees at Matsushita spend a good part of their first six months in what the company calls 'cultural and spiritual training'. They study the company credo, the 'Seven Spirits of Matsushita', and the philosophy of Konosuke Matsushita. Then they learn how to translate these internalized lessons into daily behaviour and even operational decisions. Culture-building exercises as intensive as Matsushita's are sometimes dismissed as the kind of Japanese mumbo jumbo that would not work in other societies, but in fact, Philips has a similar entry-level training practice (called 'organization cohesion training'), as does Unilever (called, straightforwardly, 'indoctrination').

The second objective – broadening management perspectives – is essentially a matter of teaching people how to manage complexity instead of merely to make room for it. To reverse a long and unwieldy tradition of running its operations with two- and three-headed management teams of separate technical, commercial and sometimes administrative specialists, Philips asked its training and development group to despecialize top management trainees. By supplementing its traditional menu of specialist courses and functional programmes with more intensive general management training, Philips was able to begin replacing the ubiquitous teams with single business heads who also appreciated and respected specialist points of view.

The final aim – developing contacts and relationships – is much more than an incidental by-product of good management development, as the comments of a senior personnel manager at Unilever suggest:

> By bringing managers from different countries and businesses together at Four Acres [Unilever's international management training college], we build contacts and create bonds that we could never achieve by other means. The company spends as much on training as it does on R & D not only because of the direct effect it has on upgrading skills and knowledge but also because it plays a central role in indoctrinating managers

into a Unilever club where personal relationships and informal contacts are much more powerful than the formal systems and structures.

Career-Path Management

Although recruitment and training are critically important, the most effective companies recognize that the best way to develop new perspectives and thwart parochialism in their managers is through personal experience. By moving selected managers across functions, businesses and geographic units, a company encourages cross-fertilization of ideas as well as the flexibility and breadth of experience that enable managers to grapple with complexity and come out on top.

Unilever has long been committed to the development of its human resources as a means of attaining durable competitive advantage. As early as the 1930s, the company was recruiting and developing local employees to replace the parent-company managers who had been running most of its overseas subsidiaries. In a practice that came to be known as '-ization', the company committed itself to the Indianization of its Indian company, the Australization of its Australian company, and so on.

Although delighted with the new talent that began working its way up through the organization, management soon realized that by reducing the transfer of parent-company managers abroad, it had diluted the powerful glue that bound diverse organizational groups together and linked dispersed operations. The answer lay in formalizing a second phase of the -ization process. While continuing with Indianization, for example, Unilever added programmes aimed at the Unileverization of its Indian managers.

In addition to bringing 300–400 managers to Four Acres each year, Unilever typically has 100–50 of its most promising overseas managers on short- and long-term job assignments at corporate headquarters. This policy not only brings fresh, close-to-the-market perspectives into corporate decision making but also gives the visiting managers a strong sense of Unilever's strategic vision and organizational values. In the words of one of the expatriates in the corporate offices, 'The experience initiates you into the Unilever Club and the clear norms, values and behaviours that distinguish our people – so much so that we really believe we can spot another Unilever manager anywhere in the world.'

Furthermore, the company carefully transfers most of these high-potential individuals through a variety of different functional, product and geographic positions, often rotating every two or three years. Most important top management tracks about 1,000 of these people – some 5 per cent of Unilever's total management group – who, as they move through the company, forge an informal network of contacts and relationships that is central to Unilever's decision-making and information-exchange processes.

Widening the perspectives and relationships of key managers as Unilever has done is a good way of developing identification with the broader corporate mission. But a broad sense of identity is not enough. To maintain control of its global strategies, Unilever must secure a strong and lasting individual commitment to corporate visions and objectives. In effect, it must co-opt individual energies and ambitions into the service of corporate goals.

CO-OPTING MANAGEMENT EFFORTS

As organizational complexity grows, managers and management groups tend to become so specialized and isolated and to focus so intently on their own immediate operating responsibilities that they are apt to respond parochially to intrusions on their organizational turf, even when the overall corporate interest is at stake. A classic example, described earlier, was the decision by North America Philip's consumer electronics group to reject the parent company's VCR system.

At about the same time, Philips, like many other companies, began experimenting with ways to convert managers' intellectual understanding of the corporate vision – in Philips's case, an almost evangelical determination to defend Western electronics against the Japanese – into a binding personal commitment. Philips concluded that it could co-opt individuals and organizational groups into the broader vision by inviting them to contribute to the corporate agenda and then giving them direct responsibility for implementation.

In the face of intensifying Japanese competition, Philips knew it had to improve coordination in its consumer electronics among its fiercely independent national organizations. In strengthening the central product divisions, however, Philips did not want to deplete the enterprise or commitment of its capable national management teams.

The company met these conflicting needs with two cross-border initiatives. First, it created a top-level World Policy Council for its video business that included key managers from strategic markets – Germany, France, the United Kingdom, the United States and Japan. Philips knew that its national companies' long history of independence made local managers reluctant to take orders from Dutch headquarters in Eindhoven – often for good reason, since much of the company's best market knowledge and technological expertise resided in its offshore units. Through the council, Philips co-opted their support for company decisions about product policy and manufacturing location.

Second, and more powerful, Philips allocated global responsibilities to units that had previously been purely national in focus. Eindhoven gave NAP the leading role in the development of Philips's projection television and asked it to coordinate development and manufacture of all Philips television sets for North America and Asia. The change in the attitude of NAP managers was dramatic.

A senior manager in NAP's consumer electronics business summed up the feelings of US managers: 'At last, we are moving out of the dependency relationship with Eindhoven that was so frustrating to us.' Co-option had transformed the defensive, territorial attitude of NAP managers into a more collaborative mind-set. They were making important contributions to global corporate strategy instead of looking for ways to subvert it....

THE MATRIX IN THE MANAGER'S MIND

Since the end of World War II, corporate strategy has survived several generations of painful transformation and has grown appropriately agile and athletic.

Unfortunately, organizational development has not kept pace, and managerial attitudes lag even further behind. As a result, corporations now commonly design strategies that seem impossible to implement, for the simple reason that no one can effectively element third-generation strategies through second-generation organizations run by first-generation managers.

Today, the most successful companies are those where top executives recognize the need to manage the new environmental and competitive demands by focusing less on the quest for an ideal structure and more on developing the abilities, behaviour and performance of individual managers....

• POLITICS AND THE POLITICAL ORGANIZATION*

HENRY MINTZBERG

How does conflict arise in an organization, why and with what consequences? Years ago, the literature of organizations avoided such questions. But in the last decade or so, conflict and politics that go along with it have become not just acceptable topics but fashionable ones. Yet these topics, like most others in the field, have generally been discussed in fragments. Here we seek to consider them somewhat more comprehensively, first by themselves and then in the context of what will be called the political organization – the organization that comes to be dominated by politics and conflict.

POLITICS IN ORGANIZATIONS

What do we mean by 'politics' in organizations? An organization may be described as functioning on the basis of a number of systems of influence: authority, ideology, expertise, politics. The first three can be considered legitimate in some sense: Authority is based on legally sanctioned power, ideology on widely accepted beliefs, expertise on power that is officially certified. The system of politics in contrast, reflects power that is technically illegitimate (or, perhaps more accurately, *a*legitimate), in the means it uses, and sometimes also in the ends it promotes. In other words, political power in the organization (unlike government) is not formally authorized, widely accepted or officially certified. The result is that political activity is usually divisive and conflictive, pitting individuals or groups against the more legitimate systems of influence and, when those systems are weak, against each other.

*Adapted from Henry Mintzberg, *Power in and around Organizations* (Copyright © Prentice-Hall, 1983), Chs. 13 and 23, used by permission of the publisher; based on a summary that appeared in *Mintzberg on Management: Inside Our Strange World of Organizations* (New York: Free Press, 1989).

POLITICAL GAMES IN ORGANIZATIONS

Political activity in organizations is sometimes described in terms of various 'games'. The political scientist Graham Allison, for example, has described political games in organizations and government as 'intricate and subtle, simultaneous, overlapping', but nevertheless guided by rules: 'some rules are explicit, others implicit, some rules are quite clear, others fuzzy. Some are very stable; others are ever changing. But the collection of rules, in effect, defines the game' (1971: 170). I have identified 13 political games in particular, listed here together with their main players, the main reasons they seem to be played, and how they relate to the other systems of influence:

- *Insurgency game:* usually played to resist authority, although can be played to resist expertise or established ideology or even to effect change in the organization; ranges 'from protest to rebellion' (Zald and Berger, 1978: 841), and is usually played by 'lower participants' (Mechanic, 1962), those who feel the greatest weight of formal authority.

- *Counterinsurgency game:* played by those with legitimate power who fight back with political means, perhaps with legitimate means as well (e.g. excommunication in the Church).

- *Sponsorship game:* played to build a power base, in this case by using superiors; individual attaches self to someone with more status, professing loyalty in return for power.

- *Alliance-building game:* played among peers – often line managers, sometimes experts – who negotiate implicit contracts of support for each in order to build a powerbase to advance selves in the organization.

- *Empire-building game:* played by line managers, in particular, to build power bases, not cooperatively with peers but individually with subordinates.

- *Budgeting game:* played overtly and with rather clearly defined rules to build power bases; similar to last game, but less divisive, since prize is resources, not positions or units *per se*, at least not those of rivals.

- *Expertise game:* non-sanctioned use of expertise to build power base, either by flaunting it or by feigning it; true experts play by exploiting technical skills and knowledge, emphasizing the uniqueness, criticality and irreplaceability of the expertise (Hickson *et al.*, 1971), also by seeking to keep skills from being programmed, by keeping knowledge to selves; nonexperts play at attempting to have their work viewed as expert, ideally to have it declared professional so they alone can control it.

- *Lording game:* played to build power base by 'lording' legitimate power over those without it or with less of it (i.e. using legitimate power in illegitimate ways); manager can lord formal authority over subordinate or civil servant over a citizen; members of missionary configuration can lord its ideology over outsiders; experts can lord technical skills over the unskilled.

- *Line versus staff game:* a game of sibling-type rivalry, played not just to enhance personal power but to defeat a rival; pits line managers with formal decision-making authority against staff advisers with specialized expertise; each side tends to exploit legitimate power in illegitimate ways.

- *Rival camps game:* again played to defeat a rival; typically occurs when alliance or empire-building games result in two major power blocs, giving rise to two-person, zero-sum game in place of *n*-person game; can be most divisive game of all; conflict can be between units (e.g. between marketing and production in manufacturing firm), between rival personalities, or between two competing missions (as in prisons split between custody and rehabilitation orientations).

- *Strategic candidates game:* played to effect change in an organization; individuals or groups seek to promote through political means their own favoured changes of a strategic nature; many play – analysts, operating personnel, lower-level managers, even senior managers and chief executives (especially in the professional configurations), who must promote own candidates politically before they can do so formally; often combines elements of other games – empire-building (as purpose of game), alliance-building (to win game), rival camps, line versus staff, expertise, and lording (evoked during game), insurgency (following game), and so on.

- *Whistle-blowing game:* a typically brief and simple game, also played to effect organizational change; privileged information is used by an insider, usually a lower participant, to 'blow the whistle' to an influential outsider on questionable or illegal behaviour by the organization.

- *Young Turks game:* played for highest stakes of all, not to effect simple change or to resist legitimate power *per se*, but to throw the latter into question, perhaps even to overthrow it, and institute major shift; small group of 'young Turks', close to but not at centre of power, seeks to reorient organization's basic strategy, displace a major body of its expertise, replace its ideology, or rid it of its leadership; Zald and Berger discuss a form of this game they call 'organizational coup d'état', where the object is 'to effect an unexpected succession' – to replace *holders* of authority while maintaining *system* of authority intact (1978: 833).

Some of these games, such as sponsorship and lording, while themselves technically illegitimate, can nevertheless *coexist with* strong legitimate systems of influence, as found for example in the machine and missionary type organizations; indeed, they could not exist without these systems of influence. Other political games, such as insurgency and young Turks – usually highly divisive games – arise in the presence of legitimate power but are *antagonistic to it*, designed to destroy or at least weaken it. And still others, such as rival camps, often arise when legitimate power is weak and *substitute for* it, for example in the professional and innovative type organizations.

The implication of this is that politics and conflict may exist at two levels in an organization. They may be present but not dominant, existing as an overlay in a more conventional organization, perhaps a kind of fifth column acting on behalf of some challenging power. Or else politics may be the dominant system of influence, and conflict strong, having weakened the legitimate systems of influence or having arisen in their weakness. It is this second level that gives rise to the type of organization we call *political*.

FORMS OF POLITICAL ORGANIZATIONS

What characterizes the organization dominated by politics is a lack of any of the forms of order found in conventional organizations. In other words, the organization is best described in terms of power, not structure, and that power is exercised in ways not legitimate in conventional organizations. Thus, there is no preferred method of coordination, no single dominant part of the organization, no clear type of decentralization. Everything depends on the fluidity of informal power, marshalled to win individual issues.

How does such an organization come to be? There is little published research on the question. But some ideas can be advanced tentatively. First, conflict would seem to arise in a circumscribed way in an organization, say between two units (such as marketing and production) or between an influential outside group and a powerful insider (such as between a part owner and the CEO). That conflict may develop gradually or it may flare up suddenly. It may eventually be resolved, but when it becomes intense, it may tend to spread, as other influencers get drawn in on one side or the other. But since few organizations can sustain intense political activity for long, that kind of conflict must eventually moderate itself (unless it kills off the organization first). In moderated form, however, the conflict may endure, even when it pervades the whole system, so long as the organization can make up for its losses, perhaps by being in a privileged position (as in the case of a conflict-ridden regulatory agency that is sustained by a government budget, or a politicized corporation that operates in a secure cartel).

What we end up with are two dimensions of conflict: first, moderate or intense; and second, confined or pervasive. A third dimension – enduring or brief – really combines with the first (intense conflict having to be typically brief, moderate conflict possibly enduring). Combining these dimensions, we end up with four forms of the political organization:

- *Confrontation*, characterized by conflict that is *intense*, *confined* and *brief* (unstable).

- *Shaky alliance*, characterized by conflict that is *moderate*, *confined* and possibly *enduring* (relatively stable).

- *Politicized organization*, characterized by conflict that is *moderate*, *pervasive* and possibly *enduring* (relatively stable, so long as it is sustained by privileged position).

- *Complete political arena*, characterized by conflict that is *intense*, *pervasive* and *brief* (unstable).[1]

One of these forms is called *complete* because its conflict is both intense and pervasive. In this form, the external influencers disagree among themselves; they try to form alliances with some insiders, while clashing with others. The internal activities are likewise conflictive, permeated by divisive political games. Authority, ideology and expertise are all subordinated to the play of political power. An organization so politicized can pursue no goal with any consistency. At best, it attends to a number of goals inconsistently over time, at worst it consumes all its energy in disputes and never accomplishes anything. In essence, the complete political arena is less a coherent organization than a free-for-all of individuals. As such, it is probably the form of political organization least commonly found in practice, or, at least, the most unstable when it does appear.

In contrast, the other three forms of political organization manage to remain partial, one by moderating its conflict, a second by containing it, and the third by doing both. As a result, these forms are more stable than the complete form and so are probably more common, with two of them in particular appearing to be far more viable.

In the *confrontational* form, conflict may be intense, but it is also contained, focusing on two parties. Typical of this is the takeover situation, where, for example, an outside stockholder tries to seize control of a closed system corporation from its management. Another example is the situation, mentioned earlier, of two rival camps in and around a prison, one promoting the mission of custody, the other that of rehabilitation.

The *shaky alliance* commonly emerges when two or more major systems of influence or centres of power must coexist in roughly equal balance. The symphony orchestra, for example, must typically combine the strong personal authority of the conductor (entrepreneurial orientation) with the extensive expertise of the musicians (professional orientation). As Fellini demonstrated so well in his film *Orchestra Rehearsal*, this alliance, however uncomfortable (experts never being happy in the face of strong authority), is nevertheless a necessary one. Common today is the professional organization operating in the public sector, which must somehow sustain an alliance of experts and government officials, one group pushing upward for professional autonomy, the other downward for technocratic control.

Our final form, the *politicized organization*, is characterized by moderate conflict that pervades the entire system of power. This would appear to describe a number of today's largest organizations, especially ones in the public sector whose mandates are visible and controversial – many regulatory agencies, for example, and some public utilities. Here it is government protection, or monopoly power, that sustains organizations captured by conflict. This form seems to be increasingly common in the private sector too, among some of the largest corporations that are able to sustain the inefficiencies of conflict through their market power and sometimes by their ability to gain government support as well.

THE FUNCTIONAL ROLE OF POLITICS IN ORGANIZATIONS

Little space need be devoted to the dysfunctional influence of politics in organizations. Politics is divisive and costly; it burns up energies that could instead go into the operations. It can also lead to all kinds of aberrations. Politics is often used to sustain outmoded systems of power, and sometimes to introduce new ones that are not justified. Politics can also paralyze an organization to the point where its effective functioning comes to a halt and nobody benefits. The purpose of an organization, after all, is to produce goods and services, not to provide an arena in which people can fight with one another.

What does deserve space, however, because they are less widely appreciated, are those conditions in which politics and the political organization serve a functional role.

In general, the system of politics is necessary in an organization to correct certain deficiencies in its other, legitimate systems of influence – above all to provide for certain forms of flexibility discouraged by those other systems. The other systems of influence were labelled legitimate because their *means* – authority, ideology or expertise – have some basis of legitimacy. But sometimes those means are used to pursue *ends* that are illegitimate (as in the example of the lording game, where legitimate power is flaunted unreasonably). In contrast, the system of politics, whose *means* are (by definition) illegitimate, can sometimes be used to pursue *ends* that are in fact legitimate (as in certain of the whistle-blowing and Young Turks games, where political pressures are used against formal authority to correct irresponsible or ineffective behaviours). We can elaborate on this in terms of four specific points.

First, politics as a system of influence can act in a Darwinian way to ensure that the strongest members of an organization are brought into positions of leadership. Authority favours a single chain of command; weak leaders can suppress strong subordinates. Politics, on the other hand, can provide alternative channels of information and promotion, as when the sponsorship game enables someone to leap over a weak superior (McClelland, 1970). Moreover, since effective leaders have been shown to exhibit a need for power, the political games can serve as tests to demonstrate the potential for leadership. The second-string players may suffice for the scrimmages, but only the stars can be allowed to meet the competition. Political games not only suggest who those players are but also help to remove their weak rivals from contention.

Second, politics can also ensure that all sides of an issue are fully debated, whereas the other systems of influence may promote only one. The system of authority, by aggregating information up a central hierarchy, tends to advance only a single point of view, often the one already known to be favoured above. So, too, does the system of ideology, since every issue is interpreted in terms of 'the word', the prevailing set of beliefs. As for the system of expertise, people tend to defer to the expert on any particular issue. But experts are often closed to new ideas, ones that developed after they received their training. Politics, however, by obliging 'responsible men . . . to fight for what they are convinced is right' (Allison, 1971: 145) encourages a variety of voices to be heard on any issue. And, because of attacks by its opponents, each voice is forced to justify its conclusions in terms of the broader good. That means it must marshal arguments and support proposals that can at least be justified in terms of the interests of the organization at large rather than the parochial needs of a particular group. As Burns has noted in an amusing footnote:

It is impossible to avoid some reference from the observations made here to F. M. Cornford's well known 'Guide for the Young Academic Politician'. Jobs 'fall into two classes, My Jobs and Your Jobs. My Jobs are public-spirited proposals, which happen (much to my regret) to involve the advancement of a personal friend, or (still more to my regret) of myself. Your Jobs are insidious intrigues for the advancement of yourself and your friends, spuriously disguised as public-spirited proposals.' (1961–2: 260)

Third, the system of politics is often required to stimulate necessary change that is blocked by the legitimate systems of influence. Internal change is generally threatening to the 'vested interest' of an organization. The system of authority concentrates power up the hierarchy, often in the hands of those who were responsible for initiating the existing strategies in the first place. It also contains the established controls, which are designed to sustain the *status quo*. Similarly, the system of expertise concentrates power in the hands of senior and established experts, not junior ones who may possess newer, more necessary skills. Likewise, the system of ideology, because it is rooted in the past, in tradition, acts as a deterrent to change. In the face of these resistances, it is politics that is able to work as a kind of 'invisible hand' – 'invisible underhand' would be a better term – to promote necessary change, through such games as strategic candidates, whistle-blowing and Young Turks.

Fourth and finally, the system of politics can ease the path for the execution of decisions. Senior managers, for example, often use politics to gain acceptance for their decisions, playing the strategic candidates game early in promoting proposals to avoid having to play the more divisive and risky counterinsurgency game later in the face of resistance to them. They persuade, negotiate and build alliances to smooth the path for the decisions they wish to make.

To conclude our discussion, while I am not personally enthusiastic about organizational politics and have no desire to live in a political organization, I do accept, and hope I have persuaded the reader to accept, that politics does have useful roles to play in a society of organizations. Organizational politics may irritate us, but it can also serve us.

• WHO SHOULD CONTROL THE CORPORATION?*

Henry Mintzberg

Who should control the corporation? How? And for the pursuit of what goals? Historically, the corporation was controlled by its owners – through direct control of the managers if not through direct management – for the pursuit of economic goals. But as shareholding became dispersed, owner control weakened; and as the corporation grew to very large size, its economic actions came to have increasing social consequences. The giant, widely held corporation came increasingly under the implicit control of its managers, and the concept of social responsibility – the voluntary consideration of public social goals alongside the private economic ones – arose to provide a basis of legitimacy for their actions.

*Originally published in the *California Management Review* (Autumn 1984), pp. 90–115, based on a section of Henry Mintzberg, *Power in and Around Organizations* (Prentice-Hall, 1983). Copyright © 1984 by The Regents of the University of California. Reprinted with deletions by permission of The Regents.

To some, including those closest to the managers themselves, this was accepted as a satisfactory arrangement for the large corporation. 'Trust it' to the goodwill of the managers was their credo; these people will be able to achieve an appropriate balance between social and economic goals.

But others viewed this basis of control as fundamentally illegitimate. The corporation was too large, too influential, its actions too pervasive to be left free of the direct and concerted influence of outsiders. At the extreme were those who believed that legitimacy could be achieved only by subjecting managerial authority to formal and direct external control. 'Nationalize it,' said those at one end of the political spectrum, to put ultimate control in the hands of the government so that it will pursue public social goals. No, said those at the other end, 'restore it' to direct shareholder control, so that it will not waver from the pursuit of private economic goals.

Other people took less extreme positions. 'Democratize it' became the rallying cry for some, to open up the governance of the large, widely held corporation to a variety of affected groups – if not the workers, then the customers, or conservation interests, or minorities. 'Regulate it' was also a popular position, with its implicit premiss that only by sharing their control with government would the corporation's managers attend to certain social goals. Then there were those who accepted direct management control so long as it was tempered by other, less formal types of influence. 'Pressure it,' said a generation of social activists, to ensure that social goals are taken into consideration. But others argued that because the corporation is an economic instrument, you must 'induce it' by providing economic incentives to encourage the resolution of social problems.

Finally, there were those who argued that this whole debate was unnecessary, that a kind of invisible hand ensures that the economic corporation acts in a socially responsible manner. 'Ignore it' was their implicit conclusion.

This article is written to clarify what has become a major debate of our era, *the* major debate revolving around the private sector: Who should control the corporation, specifically the large, widely held corporation, how, and for the pursuit of what goals? The answers that are eventually accepted will determine what kind os society we and our children shall live in. . ..

As implied earlier, the various positions of who should control the corporation, and how, can be laid out along a political spectrum, from nationalization at one end to the restoration of shareholder power at the other. From the managerial perspective, however, those two extremes are not so far apart. Both call for direct control of the corporation's managers by specific outsiders, in one case the government to ensure the pursuit of social goals, in the other case the shareholders to ensure the pursuit of economic ones. It is the moderate positions – notably, trusting the corporation to the social responsibility of its managers – that are furthest from the extremes. Hence, we can fold our spectrum around so that it takes the shape of a horseshoe.

Figure 1 shows our 'conceptual horseshoe', with 'nationalize it' and 'restore it' at the two ends. 'Trust it' is at the centre, because it postulates a natural balance of social and economic goals. 'Democratize it', 'regulate it', and 'pressure it' are shown on the left side of the horseshoe, because all seek to temper economic goals with social ones. 'Induce it' and 'ignore it', both of which favour the exclusive pursuit of economic goals, are shown on the right side.

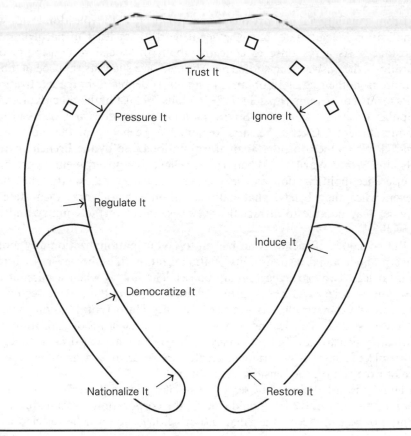

FIGURE 1
The conceptual horseshoe

This conceptual horseshoe provides a basic framework to help clarify the issues in this important debate. We begin by discussing each of these positions in turn, circling the horseshoe from left to right. Finding that each (with one exception) has a logical context, we conclude – in keeping with our managerial perspective – that they should be thought of as forming a portfolio from which society can draw to deal with the issue of who should control the corporation and how.

'NATIONALIZE IT'

Nationalization of the corporation is a taboo subject in the United States – in general, but not in particular. Whenever a major corporation runs into serious difficulty (i.e. faces bankruptcy with possible loss of many jobs), massive government intervention, often including direct nationalization, inevitably comes up as an option. This option has been exercised: US travellers now ride on Amtrak; Tennessee residents have for years been getting their power from a government utility; indeed, the Post Office was once a private enterprise. Other nations have, of course, been much more ambitious in this regard.

From a managerial and organizational perspective, the question is not whether nationalization is legitimate, but whether it works – at least in particular, limited circumstances. As a response to concerns about the social responsibility of large corporations, the answer seems to be no. The evidence suggests that social difficulties arise more from the size of an organization and its degree of bureaucratization than from its form of ownership (Epstein, 1977; Jenkins, 1976). On the other hand, contrary to popular belief in the United States, nationalization does not necessarily harm economic efficiency. Over the years, Renault has been one of the most successful automobile companies outside Japan; it was nationalized by the French government shortly after World War II. ... When people believe that government ownership leads to interference, politicization and inefficiency, that may be exactly what happens. However, when they believe that nationalization *has* to work, then state-owned enterprises may be able to attract the very best talent in the country and thereby work well.

But economic efficiency is no reason to favour nationalization any more than is concern about social responsibility. Nationalization does, however, seem to make sense in at least two particular circumstances. The first is when a mission deemed necessary in a society will not be provided adequately by the private sector. That is presumably why America has its Amtrak [and why Third World nations often create state enterprises]. ... The second is when the activities of an organization must be so intricately tied to government policy that it is best managed as a direct arm of the state. The Canadian government created Petrocan to act as a 'window' and a source of expertise on the sensitive oil industry.

Thus, it is not rhetoric but requirement that should determine the role of this position as a solution to who should control the corporation. 'Nationalize it' should certainly not be embraced as a panacea, but neither should it be rejected as totally inapplicable.

'DEMOCRATIZE IT'

A less extreme position – at least in the context of the American debate – is one that calls for formal devices to broaden the governance of the corporation. The proponents of this position either accept the legal fiction of shareholder control and argue that the corporation's power base is too narrow, or else they respond to the emergent reality and question the legitimacy of managerial control. Why, they ask, do stockholders or self-selected managers have any greater right to control the profound decisions of these major institutions than do workers or customers or the neighbours downstream?

This stand is not to be confused with what is known as 'participative management'. The call to 'democratize it' is a legal, rather than ethical one and is based on power, not generosity. Management is not asked to share its power voluntarily; rather, that power is to be reallocated constitutionally. That makes this position a fundamental and important one, *especially* in the United States with its strong tradition of pluralist control of its institutions.

The debate over democratization of the corporation has been confusing in part because many of the proposals have been so vague. We can bring some order to it by considering, in organizational terms, two basic means of democratization and two basic constituencies that can be involved. As shown in Figure 1, they suggest four possible forms of corporate democracy. One means is through the election of representatives to the board of directors, which we call *representative democracy*. The other is through formal but direct involvement in internal decision making processes, which we call *participatory democracy*. Either can focus on the workers ... or else on a host of outside interest groups, the latter giving rise to a *pluralistic* form of democracy. These are basic forms of corporate democracy in theory. With one exception, they have hardly been approached – let alone achieved – in practice. But they suggest where the 'democratize it' debate may be headed.

The European debate has focused on worker representative democracy. This ha[d], in some sense, been achieved in [the former] Yugoslavia, where the workers of all but the smallest firms elect[ed] the members of what [was] the equivalent of the American board of directors. In Germany, under the so-called *Mitbestimmung* ('codetermination'), the workers and the shareholders each elect half of the directors.

The evidence on this form of corporate democracy has been consistent, and it supports neither its proponents nor its detractors. Workers' representation on the board seems to make relatively little difference one way or the other. The worker representatives concern themselves with wage and welfare issues but leave most other questions to management. Worker-controlled firms (not unlike the state-owned ones) appear to be no more socially responsible than private ones. ...

On the other hand, worker representative democracy may have certain positive benefits. [The former] German Chancellor Helmut Schmidt is reported to have said that 'the key to [his] country's postwar economic miracle was its sophisticated system of workers' participation' (in Garson, 1977: 63). While no one can prove this statement, codetermination certainly does not seem to have done the German economy much

| | GROUPS INVOLVED | |
	Internal Employees	External Interest Groups
Board of Directors	Worker Representative Democracy (European style, e.g. co-determination or worker ownership)	Pluralistic Representative Democracy (American style, e.g. public interest directors)
Internal Decision-Making Process	Worker Participatory Democracy (e.g. works councils)	Pluralistic Participatory Democracy (e.g. outsiders on new product committees)

FOCUS OF ATTENTION

FIGURE 1
The four basic forms of corporate democracy

harm. By providing an aura of legitimacy to the German corporation and by involving the workers (at least officially) in its governance, codetermination may perhaps have enhanced the spirit of enterprise in Germany (while having little real effect on how decisions are actually made). More significantly, codetermination may have fostered greater understanding and cooperation between the managers and the union members who fill most of the worker seats on the boards....

...the embryonic debate over representative democracy in the United States has shown signs of moving in a different direction. Consistent with the tradition of pluralism in America's democratic institutions, there has been increasing pressure to elect outside directors who represent a wide variety of special interest groups – that is, consumers, minorities, environmentalists, and so on....

Critics ... have pointed out the problems of defining constituencies and finding the means to hold elections. 'One-person, one-vote' may be easily applied to electing representatives of the workers, but no such simple rule can be found in the case of the consumer or environmental representatives, let alone ones of the 'public interest'. Yet is amazing how quickly things become workable in the United States when Americans decide to put their collective mind to it. Indeed, the one case of public directors that I came across is telling in this regard. According to a Conference Board report, the selection by the Chief Justice of the Supreme Court of New Jersey of 6 of the 24 members of the board of Prudential Insurance as public directors has been found by the company to be 'quite workable' (Bacon and Brown, 1975: 48).... [See the associated box on 'The Power of the Board'.]

THE POWER OF THE BOARD

Proposals for representative democracy, indeed those for nationalization and the restoration of shareholder control as well, rest on assumptions about the power of the board of directors. It may, therefore, be worth considering at this point the roles that boards of directors play in organizations and the board's resulting powers.

In law, traditionally, the business of a corporation was to be 'managed' by its board. But of course, the board does no such thing. Managers manage, although some may happen to sit on the board. What, then, are the roles of the board, particularly of its 'outside' directors?

The most tangible role of the board, and clearly provided for in law, is to name, and of course to dismiss as well, the chief executive officer, that person who in turn names the rest of the management. A second role may be to exercise direct control during periods of crisis, for example when the management has failed to provide leadership. And a third is to review the major decisions of the management as well as its overall performance.

These three constitute the board's roles of control, in principle at least because there is no shortage of evidence that boards have difficulty doing even these effectively, especially outside directors. Their job is, after all, part-time, and in a brief meeting once in a while they face a complex organization led by a highly organized management that deals with it every day. The result is that board control tends to reduce to naming and replacing the chief executive, and that person's knowledge of that fact, nothing more. Indeed, even that power is circumscribed, because a management cannot be replaced very often. In a sense, the board is like a bee hovering near a person picking flowers. The person must proceed carefully, so as not to provoke the bee, but can proceed with the task. But if the bee does happen to be provoked, it only gets to sting once. Thus many boards try to know only enough to know when the management is not doing its job properly, so that they can replace it.

But if boards tend to be weaker than expected in exercising *control over* the organization, they also tend perhaps to be stronger than expected in providing *service to* the organization. Here board membership plays at least four other roles. First, it 'co-opts' influential outsiders: The organization uses the status of a seat on its board to gain the support of people important to it (as in the case of the big donors who sit on university boards). Second, board membership may be used to establish contacts for the organization (as when retired military officers sit on the boards of weapons manufacturing firms). This may be done to help in such things as the securing of contracts and the raising of funds. Third, seats on the board can be used to enhance an organization's reputation (as when an astronaut or some other type of celebrity is given a seat). And fourth, the board can be used to provide advice for the organization (as in the case of many of the bankers and lawyers who sit on the boards of corporations).

How much do boards serve organizations, and how much do they control them? Some boards do, of course, exercise control, particularly when their members represent a well-defined constituency, such as the substantial owner of a corporation. But, as noted, this tends to be a loose control at best. And other boards hardly do even that, especially when their constituencies are widely dispersed.

To represent everyone is ultimately to represent no one, especially when faced with a highly organized management that knows exactly what it wants. (Or from the elector's point of view, having some distant representative sitting on a board somewhere hardly brings him or her closer to control over the things that impinge on daly life – the work performed, the products consumed, the rivers polluted.) In corporations, this has been shown to be true of the directors who represent many small shareholders no less than those who represent many workers or many customers, perhaps even those who represent government, since that can be just a confusing array of pressure groups. These boards become, at best, tools of the organization, providing it with the variety of the services discussed above, at worst mere façades of formal authority.

Despite its problems, representative democracy is crystal clear compared with participatory democracy. What the French call 'autogestion' (as opposed to 'cogestion', or codetermination) seems to describe a kind of bottom-up, grass-roots democracy in which the workers participate directly in decision-making (instead of overseeing management's decisions from the board of directors) and also elect their own managers (who then become more administrators than bosses). Yet such proposals are inevitably vague, and I have heard of no large mass production or mass service firm – not even one owned by workers or a union – that comes close to this. . . .

What has impeded worker participatory democracy? In my opinion, something rather obvious has stood in its way; namely, the structure required by the very organizations in which the attempts have been made to apply it. Worker participatory democracy – and worker representative democracy too, for that matter – has been attempted primarily in organizations containing large numbers of workers who do highly routine, rather unskilled jobs that are typical of most mass production and service – what I have elsewhere called Machine Bureaucracies. The overriding requirement in Machine Bureaucracy is for tight coordination, the kind that can only be achieved by central adminstrators. For example, the myriad of decisions associated with producing an automobile at Volvo's Kalmar works in Sweden cannot be made by autonomous groups, each doing as it pleases. The whole car must fit together in a particular way at the end of the assembly process. These decisions require a highly sophisticated system of bureaucratic coordination. That is why automobile companies are structured into rigid hierarchies of authority. . . .

Participatory democracy *is* approached in other kinds of organizations . . . the autonomous professional institutions such as universities and hospitals, which have very different needs for central coordination. . . . But the proponents of democracy in organizations are not lobbying for changes in hospitals or universities. It is the giant mass producers they are after, and unless the operating work in these corporations becomes largely skilled and professional in nature, nothing approaching participative democracy can be expected.

In principle, the pluralistic form of participatory democracy means that a variety of groups external to the corporation can somehow control its decision-making processes directly. In practice, of course, this concept is even more elusive than the worker form of participatory democracy. To open up fully the internal decision-making processes of the corporation to outsiders would mean chaos. Yet certain very limited forms of outside participation would seem to be not only feasible but perhaps even desirable. . . . Imagine telephone company executives resolving rate conflicts with consumer groups in quiet offices instead of having to face them in noisy public hearings.

To conclude, corporate democracy – whether representative or participatory in form – may be an elusive and difficult concept, but it cannot be dismissed. It is not just another social issue, like conservation or equal opportunity, but one that strikes at the most fundamental of values. Ours has become a society of organizations. Democracy will have decreasing meaning to most citizens if it cannot be extended beyond political and judicial processes to those institutions that impinge upon them in their daily lives – as workers, as consumers, as neighbours. This is why we shall be hearing a great deal more of 'democratize it'.

'REGULATE IT'

In theory, regulating the corporation is about as simple as democratizing it is complex. In practice, it is, of course, another matter. To the proponents of 'regulate it', the corporation can be made responsive to social needs by having its actions subjected to the controls of a higher authority – typically government, in the form of a regulatory agency or legislation backed up by the courts. Under regulation, constraints are imposed externally on the corporation while its internal governance is left to its managers.

Regulation of business is at least as old as the Code of Hammurabi. In America, it has tended to come in waves. ...

To some, regulation is a clumsy instrument, which should never be relied upon; to others, it is a panacea for the problems of social responsibility. At best, regulation sets minimum and usually crude standards of acceptable behaviour; when it works, it does not make any firm socially responsible so much as stop some from being grossly irresponsible. Because it is inflexible, regulation tends to be applied slowly and conservatively, usually lagging public sentiment. Regulation often does not work because of difficulties in enforcement. The problems of the regulatory agencies are legendary – limited resources and information compared with the industries they are supposed to regulate, the cooption of the regulators by industries, and so on. When applied indiscriminately, regulation either fails dramatically or else succeeds and creates havoc.

Yet there are obvious places for regulation. A prime one is to control tangible 'externalities' – costs incurred by corporations which are passed on to the public at large. When, for example, costly pollution or worker health problems can be attributed directly to a corporation, then there seems to be every reason to force it (and its customers) to incur these costs directly, or else to terminate the actions that generate them. Likewise, regulation may have a place where competition encourages the unscrupulous to pull all firms down to a base level of behaviour, forcing even the well-intentioned manager to ignore the social consequences of his actions. Indeed, in such cases, the socially responsible behaviour is to encourage sensible regulation. 'Help us to help others', businessmen should be telling the government. ...

Most discouraging, however, is Theodore Levitt's revelation some years ago that business has fought every piece of proposed regulatory or social legislation throughout this century, from the Child Labour Act on. In Levitt's opinion, much of that legislation has been good for business – dissolving the giant trusts, creating a more honest and effective stock market, and so on. Yet, 'the computer is programmed to cry wolf' (Levitt, 1968: 83). ...

In summary, regulation is a clumsy instrument but not a useless one. Were the business community to take a more enlightened view of it, regulation could be applied more appropriately, and we would not need these periodic housecleanings to eliminate the excesses.

'PRESSURE IT'

'Pressure it' is designed to do what 'regulate it' fails to do: provoke corporations to act beyond some base level of behaviour, usually in an area that regulation misses entirely. Here, activists bring *ad hoc* campaigns of pressure to bear on one or a group of corporations to keep them responsive to the activists' interpretation of social needs. ...

'Pressure it' is a distinctively American position. While Europeans debate the theories of nationalization and corporate democracy in their cafés, Americans read about the exploits of Ralph Nader *et al.* in their morning newspapers. Note that 'pressure it', unlike 'regulate it', implicitly accepts management's right to make the final decisions. Perhaps this is one reason why it is favoured in America.

While less radical than the other positions so far discussed, 'pressure it' has nevertheless proved far more effective in eliciting behaviour sensitive to social needs ... [activist groups] have pressured for everything from the dismemberment of diversified corporations to the development of day care centres. Of special note is the class action suit, which has opened up a whole new realm of corporate social issues. But the effective use of the pressure campaign has not been restricted to the traditional activist. President Kennedy used it to roll back US Steel price increases in the early 1960s, and business leaders in Pittsburgh used it in the late 1940s by threatening to take their freight-haulage business elsewhere if the Pennsylvania Railroad did not replace its coal-burning locomotives to help clean up their city's air.

'Pressure it' as a means to change corporate behaviour is informal, flexible and focused; hence, it has been highly successful. Yet it is irregular and *ad hoc*, with different pressure campaigns sometimes making contradictory demands on management. Compared to the positions to its right on the horseshoe, 'pressure it', like the other positions to its left, is based on confrontation rather than cooperation.

'TRUST IT'

To a large and vocal contingent, which parades under the banner of 'social responsibility', the corporation has no need to act irresponsibly, and therefore there is no reason for it to either be nationalized by the state, democratized by its different constituencies, regulated by the government or pressured by activists. This contingent believes that the corporation's leaders can be trusted to attend to social goals for their own sake, simply because it is the noble thing to do. (Once this position was known as *noblesse oblige*, literally 'nobility obliges'.)

We call this position 'trust it', or, more exactly, 'trust the corporation to the goodwill of its managers', although looking from the outside in, it might just as well be called 'socialize it'. We place it in the centre of our conceptual horseshoe because it alone postulates a natural balance between social and economic goals – a balance which is to be attained in the heads (or perhaps the hearts) of responsible businessmen. And, as a not necessarily incidental consequence, power can be left in the hands of the managers; the corporation can be trusted to those who reconcile social and economic goals.

The attacks on social responsibility, from the right as well as the left, boil down to whether corporate managers should be trusted when they claim to pursue social goals; if so, whether they are capable of pursuing such goals; and finally, whether they have any right to pursue such goals.

The simplest attack is that social responsibility is all rhetoric, no action. E. F. Cheit refers to the 'Gospel of Social Responsibility' as 'designed to justify the power of managers over an ownerless system' (1964: 172). ...

Others argue that businessmen lack the personal capabilities required to pursue social goals. Levitt claims that the professional manager reaches the top of the hierarchy by dedication to his firm and his industry; as a result, his knowledge of social issues is highly restricted (Levitt, 1968: 83). Others argue that an orientation to efficiency renders business leaders inadept at handling complex social problems (which require flexibility and political finesse, and sometimes involve solutions that are uneconomic). ...

The most far reaching criticism is that businessmen have no right to pursue social goals. 'Who authorized them to do that?' asks Braybrooke (1967: 224), attacking from the left. What business have they – self-selected or at best appointed by shareholders – to impose *their* interpretation of the public good on society. Let the elected politicians, directly responsible to the population, look after the social goals.

But this attack comes from the right, too. Milton Friedman writes that social responsibility amounts to spending other people's money – if not that of shareholders, then of customers or employees. Drawing on all the pejorative terms of right-wing ideology, Friedman concludes that social responsibility is a 'fundamentally subversive doctrine', representing 'pure and unadulterated socialism', supported by businessmen who are 'unwitting puppets of the intellectual forces that have been undermining the basis of a free society these past decades'. To Friedman, 'there is one and only one social responsibility of business – to use its resources and engage in activities designed to increase its profits so long as it stays within the rules of the game' (1970). Let businessmen, in other words, stick to their own business, which is business itself.

The empirical evidence on social responsibility is hardly more encouraging. Brenner and Molander, comparing their 1977 survey of *Harvard Business Review* readers with one conducted 15 years earlier, concluded that the 'respondents are somewhat more cynical about the ethical conduct of their peers' than they were previously (1977: 59). Close to half the respondents agreed with the statement that 'the American business executive tends not to apply the great ethical laws immediately to work. He is preoccupied chiefly with gain' (p. 62). Only 5 per cent listed social responsibility as a factor 'influencing ethical standards' whereas 31 per cent and 20 per cent listed different factors related to pressure campaigns and 10 per cent listed regulation. ...

The modern corporation has been described as a rational, amoral institution – its professional managers 'hired guns' who pursue 'efficiently' any goals asked of them. The problem is that efficiency really means measurable efficiency, so that the guns load only with goals that can be quantified. Social goals, unlike economic ones, just don't lend themselves to quantification. As a result, the performance control systems – on which modern corporations so heavily depend – tend to drive out social goals in favour of economic ones (Ackerman, 1975). ...

In the contemporary large corporation, professional amorality turns into economic morality. When the screws of the performance control systems are turned tight ... economic morality can turn into social immorality. And it happens often: A *Fortune* writer found that 'a surprising number of [big companies] have been involved in blatant illegalities' in the 1970s, at least 117 of 1,043 firms studied (Ross, 1980: 57). ...

How, then, is anyone to 'trust it'?

The fact is that we have to trust it, for two reasons. First, the strategic decisions of large organizations inevitably involve social as well as economic consequences that are inextricably intertwined. The neat distinction between economic goals in the private sector and social goals in the public sector just doesn't hold up in practice. Every important decision of the large corporation – to introduce a new product line, to close an old plant, whatever – generates all kinds of social consequences. There is no such thing as purely economic decisions in big business. Only a conceptual ostrich, with his head deeply buried in the abstractions of economic theory, could possibly use the distinction between economic and social goals to dismiss social responsibility.

The second reason we have to 'trust it' is that there is always some degree of discretion involved in corporate decision-making, discretion to thwart social needs or to attend to them. Things could be a lot better in today's corporation, but they could also be an awful lot worse. It is primarily our ethics that keep us where we are. If the performance control systems favoured by diversified corporations cut too deeply into our ethical standards, then our choice is clear; to reduce these standards or call into question the whole trend toward diversification.

To dismiss social responsibility is to allow corporate behaviour to drop to the lowest level, propped up only by external controls such as regulation and pressure campaigns. Solzhenitsyn, who has experienced the natural conclusion of unrestrained bureaucratization, warns us (in sharp contrast to Friedman) that 'a society with no other scale but the legal one is not quite worthy of man... A society which is based on the letter of the law and never reaches any higher is scarcely taking advantage of the high level of human possibilities' (1978: B1).

This is not to suggest that we must trust it completely. We certainly cannot trust it unconditionally by accepting the claim popular in some quarters that only business can solve the social ills of society. Business has no business using its resources without constraint in the social sphere – whether to support political candidates or to dictate implicitly through donations how non-profit institutions should allocate their efforts. But where business is inherently involved, where its decisions have social consequences, that is where social responsibility has a role to play: where business creates externalities that cannot be measured and attributed to it (in other words, where regulation is ineffective); where regulation would work if only business would cooperate with it; where the corporation can fool its customers, or suppliers, or government through superior knowledge; where useful products can be marketed instead of wasteful or destructive ones. In other words, we have to realize that in many spheres we must trust it, or at least socialize it (and perhaps change it) so that we can trust it. Without responsible and ethical people in important places our society is not worth very much.

'IGNORE IT'

'Ignore it' differs from the other positions on the horseshoe in that explicitly or implicitly it calls for no change in corporate behaviour. It assumes that social needs are met in the course of pursuing economic goals. We include this position in our horseshoe because it is held by many influential people and also because its validity would preempt support for the other positions. We must, therefore, investigate it alongside the others.

It should be noted at the outset the 'ignore it' is not the same position as 'trust it'. In the latter, to be good is the right thing to do; in the present case, 'it pays to be good'. The distinction is subtle but important, for now it is economics, not ethics, that elicits the desired behaviour. One need not strive to be ethical; economic forces will ensure that social needs fall conveniently into place. Here we have moved one notch to the right on our horseshoe, into the realm where the economic goals dominate. . . .

'Ignore it' is sometimes referred to as 'enlightened self-interest', although some of its proponents are more enlightened than others. Many a true believer in social responsibility has used the argument that it pays to be good to ward off the attacks from the right that corporations have no business pursuing social goals. Even Milton Friedman must admit that they have every right to do so if it pays them economically. The danger of such arguments, however – and a prime reason 'ignore it' differs from 'trust it' – is that they tend to support the *status quo*: corporations need not change their behaviour because it already pays to be good.

Sometimes the case for 'ignore it' is made in terms of corporations at large, that the whole business community will benefit from socially responsible behaviour. Other times the case is made in terms of the individual corporation, that it will benefit directly from its own socially responsible actions. . . Others make the case for 'ignore it' in 'social investment' terms, claiming that socially responsible behaviour pays off in a better image for the firm, a more positive relationship with customers, and ultimately a healthier and more stable society in which to do business.

Then, there is what I like to call the 'them' argument: 'If we're not good, *they* will move in' – 'they' being Ralph Nader, the government, whoever. In other words, 'Be good or else.' The trouble with this argument is that by reducing social responsibility to simply a political tool for sustaining managerial control of the corporation in the face of outside threats, it tends to encourage general pronouncements instead of concrete actions (unless of course, 'they' actually deliver with pressure campaigns). . . .

The 'ignore it' position rests on some shaky ground. It seems to encourage average behaviour at best; and where the average does not seem to be good enough, it encourages the *status quo*. In fact, ironically, 'ignore it' makes a strong case for 'pressure it', since the whole argument collapses in the absence of pressure campaigns. Thus while many influential people take this position, we question whether in the realities of corporate behaviour it can really stand alone.

'INDUCE IT'

Continuing around to the right, our next position drops all concern with social responsibility *per se* and argues, simply, 'pay it to be good', or, from the corporation's point of view, 'be good only where it pays'. Here, the corporation does not actively pursue social goals at all, whether as ends in themselves or as means to economic ends. Rather, it undertakes socially desirable programmes only when induced economically to do so – usually through government incentives. If society wishes to clean up urban blight, then let its government provide subsidies for corporations that renovate buildings; if pollution is the problem, then let corporations be rewarded for reducing it.

'Induce it' faces 'regulate it' on the opposite side of the horseshoe for good reason. While one penalizes the corporation for what it does do, the other rewards it for doing what it might not otherwise do. Hence these two positions can be direct substitutes: pollution can be alleviated by introducing penalties for the damage done or by offering incentives for the improvements rendered.

Logic would, however, dictate a specific role for each of these positions. Where a corporation is doing society a specific, attributable harm – as in the case of pollution – then paying it to stop hardly seems to make a lot of sense. If society does not wish to outlaw the harmful behaviour altogether, then surely it must charge those responsible for it – the corporation and, ultimately, its customers. Offering financial incentives to stop causing harm would be to invite a kind of blackmail – for example, encouraging corporations to pollute so as to get paid to stop. And every citizen would be charged for the harm done by only a few.

On the other hand, where social problems exist which cannot be attributed to specific corporations, yet require the skills of certain corporations for solution, then financial incentives clearly make sense (so long, of course, as solutions can be clearly defined and tied to tangible economic rewards). Here, and not under 'trust it', is where the 'only business can do it' argument belongs. When it is true that only business can do it (and business has not done it to us in the first place), then business should be encouraged to do it. . . .

'RESTORE IT'

Our last position on the horseshoe tends to be highly ideological, the first since 'democratize it' to seek a fundamental change in the governance and the goals of the corporation. Like the proponents of 'nationalize it', those of this position believe that managerial control is illegitimate and must be replaced by a more valid form of external control. The corporation should be restored to its former status, that is, returned to its 'rightful' owners, the shareholders. The only way to ensure the relentless pursuit of economic goals – and that means the maximization of profit, free of the 'subversive doctrine' of social responsibility – is to put control directly into the hands of those to whom profit means the most.

A few years ago this may have seemed to be an obsolete position. But thanks to its patron saint Milton Friedman . . . it has recently come into prominence. Also, other forms of restoring it, including the 'small is beautiful' theme, have also become popular in recent years.

Friedman has written,

> In a free-enterprise, private-property system, a corporate executive is an employee of the owners of the business. He has direct responsibility to his employers. That responsibility is to conduct the business in accordance with their desires, which generally will be to make as much money as possible while conforming to the basic rules of the society, both those embodied in law and those embodied in ethical custom. (1970: 33)

Interestingly, what seems to drive Friedman is a belief that the shift over the course of this century from owner to manager control, with its concerns about social responsibility, represents an unstoppable skid around our horseshoe. In the opening chapter of his book *Capitalism and Freedom*, Friedman seems to accept only two possibilities – traditional capitalism and socialism as pracised in Eastern Europe. The absence of the former must inevitably lead to the latter:

> The preservation and expansion of freedom are today threatened from two directions. The one threat is obvious and clear. It is the external threat coming from the evil men in the Kremlin who promised to bury us. The other threat is far more subtle. It is the internal threat coming from men of good intentions and good will who wish to reform us. (1962: 20)

The problem of who should control the corporation thus reduces to a war between two ideologics – in Friedman's terms, 'subversive' socialism and 'free' enterprise. In this world of black and white, there can be no middle ground, no moderate position between the black of 'nationalize it' and the white of 'restore it', none of the grey of 'trust it'. Either the owners will control the corporation or else the government will. Hence: '"restore it" or else.' Anchor the corporation on the right side of the horseshoe, Friedman seems to be telling us, the only place where 'free' enterprise and 'freedom' are safe.

All of this, in my view, rests on a series of assumptions – technical, economic and political – which contain a number of fallacies. First is the fallacy of the technical assumption of shareholder control. Every trend in ownership during this century seems to refute the assumption that small shareholders are either willing or able to control the large, widely held corporation. The one place where free markets clearly still exist is in stock ownership, and that has served to detach ownership from control. When power is widely dispersed – among stockholders no less than workers or customers – those who share it tend to remain passive. It pays no one of them to invest the effort to exercise their power. Hence, even if serious shareholders did control the boards of widely held corporations (and one survey of all the directors of the *Fortune* 500 in 1977 found that only 1.6 per cent of them represented significant shareholder interests: L. Smith, 1978), the question remains open as to whether they would actually try to control the management. (This is obviously not true of closely held corporations, but these – probably a decreasing minority of the *Fortune* 500 – are 'restored' in any event.)

The economic assumptions of free markets have been discussed at length in the literature. Whether there exists vibrant competition, unlimited entry, open information, consumer sovereignty and labour mobility is debatable. Less debatable is the conclusion that the larger the corporation, the greater is its ability to interfere with these processes. The issues we are discussing centre on the giant corporation. It is not Luigi's Body Shop that Ralph Nader is after, but General Motors, a corporation that employs more than half a million people and earns greater revenues than many national governments.

Those who laid the foundation for conventional economic theory, such as Adam Smith and Afred Marshall, never dreamed of the massive amounts now spent for advertising campaigns, most of them designed as much for affect as for effect; of the waves of conglomeration that have combined all kinds of diverse businesses into single corporate entities; of chemical complexes that cost more than a billion dollars; and of the intimate relationships that now exist between giant corporations and government, as a customer and partner not to mention subsidizer. The concept of arm's length relationships in such conditions is, at best, nostalgic. What happens to consumer sovereignty when Ford knows more about its gas tanks than do its customers? And what does labour mobility mean in the presence of an inflexible pension plan, or commitment to a special skill, or a one-factory town? It is an ironic twist of conventional economic theory that the worker is the one who typically stays put, thus rendering false the assumption of labour mobility, while the shareholder is the mobile one, thus spoiling the case for owner control.

The political assumptions are more ideological in nature, although usually implicit. These assumptions are that the corporation is essentially amoral, society's instrument for producing goods and services, and, more broadly, that a society is 'free' and 'democratic' so long as its governmental leaders are elected by universal suffrage and do not interfere with the legal activities of businessmen. But many people – a large majority of the general public, if polls are to be believed – seem to subscribe to one or more assumptions that contradict these 'free enterprise' assumptions.

One assumption is that the large corporation is a social and political institution as much as an economic instrument. Economic activities, as noted previously, produce all kinds of social consequences. Jobs get created and rivers get polluted, cities get built and workers get injured. These social consequences cannot be factored out of corporate strategic decisions and assigned to government.

Another assumption is that society cannot achieve the necessary balance between social and economic needs so long as the private sector attends only to economic goals. Given the pervasiveness of business in society, the acceptance of Friedman's prescriptions would drive us toward a one-dimensional society – a society that is too utilitarian and too materialistic. Economic morality, as noted earlier, can amount to a social immorality.

Finally, the question is asked: Why the owners? In a democratic society, what justifies owner control of the corporation any more than worker control, or consumer control, or pluralistic control? Ours is not Adam Smith's society of small proprietors and shopkeepers. His butcher, brewer and baker have become Iowa Beef Packers, Anheuser-Bush and ITT Continental Baking. What was once a case for individual democracy now becomes a case for oligarchy. . . .

I see Friedman's form of 'restore it' as a rather quaint position in a society of giant corporations, managed economies and dispersed shareholders – a society in which the collective power of corporations is coming under increasing scrutiny and in which the distribution between economic and social goals is being readdressed.

Of course, there are other ways [than Friedman's] to 'restore it'. 'Divest it' could return the corporation to the business or central theme it knows best, restoring the role of allocating funds between different businesses to capital markets instead of central headquarters. Also, boards could be restored to positions of influence by holding directors legally responsible for their actions and by making them more independent of managers (for example, by providing them with personal staffs and by precluding full-time managers from their ranks, especially the position of chairman). We might even wish to extend use of 'reduce it' where possible, to decrease the size of those corporations that have grown excessively large on the basis of market or political power rather than economies of scale, and perhaps to eliminate certain forms of vertical integration. In many cases it may prove advantageous, economically as well as socially, to have the corporation trade with its suppliers and customers instead of being allowed to ingest them indiscriminately.[2]

I personally doubt that these proposals could be any more easily realized in today's society than those of Friedman, even though I believe them to be more desirable. 'Restore it' is the nostalgic position on our horseshoe, a return to our fantasies of a glorious past. In this society of giant organizations, it flies in the face of powerful economic and political forces.

CONCLUSION: IF THE SHOE FITS...

I believe that today's corporation cannot ride on any one position any more than a horse can ride on part of a shoe. In other words, we need to treat the conceptual horseshoe as a portfolio of positions from which we can draw, depending on circumstances. Exclusive reliance on one position will lead to a narrow and dogmatic society, with an excess concentration of power ... the use of a variety of positions can encourage the pluralism I believe most of us feel is necessary to sustain democracy. If the shoe fits, then let the corporation wear it.

I do not mean to imply that the eight positions do not represent fundamentally different values and, in some cases, ideologies as well. Clearly they do. But I also believe that anyone who makes an honest assessment of the realities of power in and around today's large corporations must conclude that a variety of positions have to be relied upon [even if they themselves might tilt to the left, right or centre of our horseshoe]. ...

I tilt to the left of centre, as has no doubt been obvious in my comments to this point. Let me summarize my own prescription as follows, and in the process provide some basis for evaluating the relevant roles of each of the eight positions.

First, 'trust it' or at least 'socialize it'. Despite my suspicions about much of the rhetoric that passes for social responsibility and the discouraging evidence about the behaviour of large contemporary organizations (not only corporations), I remain firmly convinced that without honest and responsible people in important places, we are in deep trouble. We need to trust it because, no matter how much we rely on the other positions, managers will always retain a great deal of power. And that power necessarily has social no less than economic consequences. The positions on the right side of our horseshoe ignore these social consequences while some of those on the left fail to recognize the difficulties of influencing these consequences in large, hierarchical organizations. Sitting between these two sets of positions, managers can use their discretion to satisfy or to subvert the wishes of the public. Ultimately, what managers do is determined by their sense of responsibility as individual members of society.

Although we must 'trust it', we cannot *only* 'trust it'. As I have argued, there is an appropriate and limited place for social responsibility – essentially to get the corporation's own house in order and to encourage it to act responsibly in its own sphere of operations. Beyond that, social responsibility needs to be tempered by other positions around our horseshoe.

Then 'pressure it', ceaselessly. As we have seen, too many forces interfere with social responsibility. The best antidote to these forces is the *ad hoc* pressure campaign, designed to pinpoint unethical behaviour and raise social consciousness about issues. The existence of the 'pressure it' position is what most clearly distinguishes the western from the eastern 'democracies'. Give me one Ralph Nader to all those banks of government accountants.

In fact, 'pressure it' underlies the success of most of the other positions. Pressure campaigns have brought about necessary new regulations and have highlighted the case for corporate democracy. As we have seen, the 'ignore it' position collapses without 'pressure it'. . . .

After that, try to 'democratize it'. A somewhat distant third in my portfolio is 'democratize it', a position I view as radical only in terms of the current US debate, not in terms of fundamental American values. Democracy matters most where it affects us directly – in the water we drink, the jobs we perform, the products we consume. How can we call our society democratic when many of its most powerful institutions are closed to governance from the outside and are run as hierarchies of authority from within?

As noted earlier, I have no illusions about having found the means to achieve corporate democracy. But I do know that Americans can be very resourceful when they decide to resolve a problem – and this is a problem that badly needs resolving. Somehow, ways must be found to open the corporation up to the formal influence of the constituencies most affected by it – employees, customers, neighbours, and so on – without weakening it as an economic institution. At stake is nothing less than the maintenance of basic freedoms in our society.

Then, only where specifically appropriate, 'regulate it' and 'induce it'. Facing each other on the horseshoe are two positions that have useful if limited roles to play. Regulation is neither a panacea nor a menace. It belongs where the corporation can abuse the power it has and can be penalized for that abuse – notably where externalities can be identified with specific corporations. Financial inducements belong, not where a corporation has created a problem, but where it has the capability to solve a problem created by someone else.

Occasionally, selectively, 'nationalize it' and 'restore it', but not in Friedman's way. The extreme positions should be reserved for extreme problems. If 'pressure it' is a scalpel and 'regulate it' a cleaver, then 'nationalize it' and 'restore it' are guillotines.

Both these positions are implicitly proposed as alternatives to 'democratize it'. One offers public control, the other 'shareholder democracy'. The trouble is that control by everyone often turns out to be control by no one, while control by the owners – even if attainable – would remove the corporation even further from the influence of those most influenced by it.

Yet, as noted earlier, nationalization sometimes makes sense – when private enterprise cannot provide a necessary mission, at least in a sufficient or appropriate way, and when the activities of a corporation must be intricately tied in to government policy.

As for 'restore it', I believe Friedman's particular proposals will aggravate the problems of political control and social responsibility, strengthening oligarchical tendencies in society and further tilting what I see as the current imbalance between social and economic goals. In response to Friedman's choice between 'subversive' socialism and 'free' enterprise, I say 'a pox on both your houses'. Let us concentrate our efforts on the intermediate positions around the horseshoe. However, other forms of 'restore it' are worth considering – to 'divest it' where diversification has interfered with capital markets, competition and economic efficiency; to '*dis*integrate it' vertically where a trading network is preferable to a managerial hierarchy; to strengthen its board so that directors can assess managers objectively; and to 'reduce it' where size represents a power game rather than a means to provide better and more efficient service to the public. I stand with Friedman in wishing to see competitive markets strengthened; it is just that I believe his proposals lead in exactly the opposite direction.

Finally, above all, don't 'ignore it'. I leave one position out of my portfolio altogether, because it contradicts the others. The one thing we must not do is ignore the large, widely held corporation. It is too influential a force in our lives. Our challenge is to find ways to distribute the power in and around our large organizations so that they will remain responsive, vital, and effective.

[1] I do not consider conflict that is moderate, confined and brief to merit inclusion under the label of political organization.

[2] A number of these proposals would be worthwhile to pursue in the public and para-public sectors as well, to divide up overgrown hospitals, school systems, social service agencies and all kinds of government departments.

CASE

2-1

THE PHILIPS GROUP 1987*

In his first videotaped message to the worldwide Philips organization since becoming president in April 1986, Cor van der Klugt opened with the following admonition:

> Philips must be profit-oriented. The top priority for Philips, and hence our main objective for the coming years, is profit.

He went on to enumerate four other major policy statements which were to provide the driving forces for achieving this objective:

> Philips must be globally oriented! Philips with its structure of product divisions and national organizations is ideally positioned to combine 'a global presence with local faces'.
>
> Philips must be a quality-driven, customer-oriented organization ... There is a growing percentage of our people who never see or 'smell' a customer in the marketplace.... A strong commitment in serving the customer must be cultivated at every level.
>
> Philips must be faster and even more innovation-oriented. Fifty per cent of the products marketed in the next five years do not exist today. Moreover, changes in the market succeed one another at ever shorter intervals. We must work faster.
>
> The Philips organization has to adapt itself. Which means we have to organize our internal activities on the basis of what I like to describe as contractual relationships. Product Divisions have the ultimate responsibility for products and profits.

In this last point, van der Klugt was signalling the coming change to organizational

---

*This case was prepared by Professors Francis J. Aguilar and Michael Y. Yoshino as a basis for class discussion rather than to illustrate either effective or ineffective handling of an administrative situation.

structure and to the managerial mindset that would be necessary for implementing Philips's new strategic thrust. By June 1987, van der Klugt had made or announced a number of sweeping changes which affected almost every aspect of how Philips would be managed. This proud company had turned down a new road as it approached its centennial milestone, making changes that would not be easily, if ever, reversed.

THE HISTORY OF PHILIPS

Philips was founded in 1891 by Gerard Philips, a Dutch engineer who had developed an inexpensive process to manufacture incandescent lamps. In 1987, N.V. Philips's Gloeilampenfabrieken was the fourth largest industrial company outside the United States and was reputedly the world's most widely known manufacturer of household appliances, television and radio sets, professional electronic equipment, lighting and related products. Exhibit 1 shows the company's product deliveries, geographic sales and value-added for 1986; Exhibit 2 presents group financial data for 1977–86.

The company had several hundred subsidiaries in 60 countries and operated plants in more than 40 countries (more than 380 plants in the world) manufacturing thousands of different products. It employed approximately 344,000 persons at the end of 1986.

Organization

Until 1940, Philips had been managed from Eindhoven, where R & D and financial control were centred. During World War II, Philips's subsidiaries, which were cut off from the Netherlands, began to operate independently. Following the war, Philips's management decided that the company could be rebuilt most successfully through its national organizations for several reasons. Most compelling were the severe trade restrictions imposed by European nations during the reconstruction period. Aside from tariff walls, the self-contained networks of plants in individual countries serving only local markets also minimized Philips's identity as a foreign company and enabled it to respond more effectively to local preferences. The war-weakened condition of the headquarters organization also facilitated decentralization.

Over the years, Philips had developed a matrix management structure to relate its many products with its broad geographical interests. Product policy throughout the world was the responsibility of 14 product divisions. This responsibility was to be exercised in consultation with the general managements of the national organizations.

The general management boards of more than 60 national organizations were responsible for operations and overall policies (in consultation with the product divisions) in each country. Most national organizations comprised a group of subsidiary companies ranging from pure marketing organizations to complete industrial enterprises.

A ten-man board of management was the top policy- and decision-making organ in the company. While the board members shared general management responsibility for the whole concern, each typically maintained special interest in one of the functional areas (e.g. R & D, sales, finance). Members of this board were selected by a 12-member supervisory board, which in turn was responsible to shareholders.

The board of management, the product divisions and the national organizations were supported by a number of staff departments and the research laboratories in Eindhoven and elsewhere. Exhibit 3 shows the broad structure of Philips's operating management organization for 1972.

Decision-Making

The management of Philips during the early 1970s was based on coordination and consultation among these major units. The complicated relations were described in the following account in the 12 January 1972 edition of *Business Week*:

> As Philips views its management process, Eindhoven's role is just to coordinate activities of the highly autonomous national organizations. Says one executive: 'Coordination does not mean giving orders. It means negotiation.'
>
> Much of the negotiating goes on between the product groups and the national companies, with the management board acting as referee and final arbiter, and even the management board operates by mutual agreement. . . . Even the simple matter of setting a sales target is negotiated, with the national company often setting a higher target than the product groups.

Coordination was also the practice within organizational units in Philips, where, typically, a manager in charge of commercial affairs and a manager in charge of technical activities shared responsibility for general leadership of the unit. This duumvirate form of management, found at all levels in the Philips organizations, had its origins when Anton Philips joined the firm as a salesman to complement his brother Gerard's talents as an engineer. Anton noted at a later date:

> From the moment I joined the company, the technical management and the sales management competed to outperform each other. Production tried to produce so much that sales would not be able to get rid of it; sales tried to sell so much that the factory would not be able to keep up. And this competition has always continued; sometimes the one is ahead, sometimes the other seems to be winning.

In many national organizations, a third person – the financial manager who was responsible for accounting and cost reporting activities – joined the commercial and technical managers to form a three-man Committee of Coordination and Direction.

The need to coordinate both within and among organizational units in making plans and deciding issues placed its own special demands on the Philips manager. As one executive explained in 1972:

> There is always a great deal of discussion and pressure from different directions working on the individual manager with respect to any major decision. I suppose one reason the system works is that when a man comes to work for Philips, more often than not, it is for life. I cannot think of an executive in our upper management levels who has not been with Philips since his twenties. During his time with the company, he will occupy a number of different positions in different divisions (a Dutchman will normally undertake at least one extended tour of foreign duty). This experience tends to foster a set of informal relationships among managers throughout the organization and an intuitive understanding as to what can be done and what cannot be done.

Another integrating device is the common working language. A man cannot reach a top position without being fluent in English and all key documents are prepared in English. This practice permits an easier coordination and communication of ideas and problems between our national groups than is possible in many multinational companies.

In addition to these unifying practices, there were several headquarters staff departments responsible for coordination within the concern. These included Industrial Coordination, Technical Efficiency and Organization, Commercial Prognoses and Planning, Accounting, Financial Affairs and External Relations.

FORCES FOR CHANGE

During the 1960s, the emphasis on national autonomy came increasingly into question as the firm's environment changed in several important respects. The creation and development of the European Common Market was to remove the trade barriers between many of Philips's most important production centres. This period also witnessed the advent of such items as the transistor and printed circuit, which called for large production runs to obtain efficient operations. Moreover, an increasing amount of electronic equipment was being produced by US (and later Japanese) competitors in the low-wage areas of the Far East and elsewhere.

In the early 1970s, Hendrick van Reimsdijk, the president at the time, created an Organization Committee to examine and redefine managerial relationships between product divisions (PDs) and national organizations (NOs). International Production Centres (IPCs) were organized to supply products to more than one national organization and thereby gain production economies of scale. With this change, PD managers began to control manufacturing operations for the first time.

Despite these moves, Philips's financial performance continued to be disappointing through the 1970s. Much of this result could be attributed to Europe's troubled economy, where Philips conducted the major part of its business. Already saddled with a high wage structure and an outdated production infrastructure, Europe was particularly hard hit by the oil crisis in 1973 and again in 1978. The rate of unemployment rose calamitously and with it the burden of welfare support.

Added to the sickly condition of its home territory, Philips found itself facing another challenge. As the 1970s wore on, the electronics field continued to change in character, driven in part by the nature of the technology and in part by the aggressive competitive drive of Japanese firms. By the early 1980s, Philips's management had come to the following general understanding of the role, nature and direction of the electronics business.

Role of Electronics

Electronics and information technology had become the driving force of the post-industrial age. By 1990, the electronics industry would employ between four and five million people to produce some $850 billion in products and software.

Nature of electronics

A salient characteristic of the electronics field was a trend towards integration. A clear-cut movement from components to ever-more encompassing systems dominated the technology proper. The rapid succession from semiconductors to integrated circuits, large-scale ICs, very large-scale ICs, and so on, since the early 1950s, provided a dramatic example of this evolution. At the same time, developments in electronics were affecting the development and use of optics, magnetics and other technologies. The net impact of these parallel developments for firms in the field was to increase greatly the scope and complexity of the required technological capabilities and the cost of new product innovations.

Another consequence of the increasing interplay of various technologies with electronics was the speed-up of product innovation. No longer could firms count on years of undisturbed profit-making for a successful product.

Evolving Competitive Situation

For Philips, with 63.3 per cent of its 1980 sales and 73.5 per cent of its assets in Europe, one of the more alarming developments was the gradual shift of the world's economic concentration from the Atlantic to the Pacific Basin, and with it the electronics business. This shift was pronounced for consumer electronics, a core business for Philips.

The competitive structure in consumer electronics was also experiencing strong integrating forces. No longer could individual firms act as independently of others in the field as had been true in earlier times. The following account about Philips's experience with the compact disc concept gave an indication of this development. According to R. van Meurs, senior director in charge of Consumer Electronics Compact Discs:

> One of the first things Philips wanted to do was to reach an agreement with competitors setting technical specification standards for the world. It was then necessary to get enough participants into the business to be able to give the market some assurance of the product's future viability. Philips also had to negotiate with the software suppliers – in this case, the record industry – to ensure that everyone received attractive future returns. In effect, a large collaborative effort had to be organized prior to launching this new product.
>
> Once launched, we could expect many new entrants, since innovations now can be copied in three to four months instead of the one to two years that had been true in former years. As a result, Philips could now hope for a maximum market share of 10 per cent to 15 per cent versus the 45 per cent to 50 per cent it had enjoyed in earlier times.

LAYING THE GROUNDWORK

By the time he had been appointed president of the company and chairman of the board of management on 1 January 1982, Wisse Dekker was convinced of the need to accelerate and extend the changes his predecessors, van Reimsdijk (1971–9) and Dr Rodenburg (1979–82), had begun. His sense of urgency was understandable; in

1981, the company's margin had fallen to less than 1 per cent. He later noted how he had gone about launching a programme of change:

> When I took over the company, the world saw us as a sleeping giant. The company had a great technological heritage, but it lacked aggressiveness and a marketing orientation, nor was it cost-competitive. I knew that the firm would have to be changed in ways that would be difficult for most of our management to accept.
>
> My first priority was to communicate a sense of urgency to our employees. I had to make clear to our generally comfortable staff that Philips could not continue to survive without dramatic changes.

As part of his communication campaign, Dekker began to speak out in public, an unprecedented move for this traditionally secretive company. He explained:

> I sought public visibility basically to send the message to my own employees. It's one thing to receive a message from management through company channels and quite something else to read it in the newspapers or hear it on television.

The message that Dekker sent was that Philips's resources were limited and that the company would have to increase its profitability. He announced the objectives for 1984: sales of 50 billion guilders; net profit of 1 billion guilders; and an inventory ratio decline by 10 per cent. He then began to redefine the Philips strategy and structure to achieve these goals.

Strategy

Dekker was the first to express explicitly Philips's commitment to a global strategy. He noted:

> The Japanese taught us the value of pursuing a global strategy with standard products. They had a tremendous cost advantage in being able to supply the world market from their factories at home. We were trying to compete on a country-by-country basis with all the additional costs associated with a fragmented operation.

In line with this new thinking, he pushed for manufacturing rationalization, creating more International Production Centres and closing many small, inefficient plants, particularly in Europe. The company's earlier efforts to divest businesses that were seen as falling outside its areas of primary interest were continued with the sale of such businesses as welding, energy cables, and furniture. At the same time, Philips continued acquiring ownership of business which fit the firm's new direction. These acquired interests included 35 per cent of Grundig (audio and video equipment) and Westinghouse Electric's lamp activities in the United States and Canada.

Somewhat of a departure from earlier practices was Dekker's recognition of the need for Philips to expand significantly its collaborative arrangements with other leading firms in the professional electronics sector. His reasoning, as stated by a senior executive, reflected the evolving nature of electronics technology:

> The functional expansion of electronic products also means that an ever increasing level of knowledge and skill are required to put one product or system on the market ... even the largest industrial research centres no longer have all the knowledge available in-house to be able to guarantee sufficient progress in every sector.

He also pointed to an important change in Philips's approach to such collaborations:

> Probably with Japanese examples in mind, Philips clearly shifted the emphasis when looking for cooperation arrangements. These are now sought with companies which have something to offer that Philips cannot develop itself, or cannot develop in time.

For 1982, the company reported a contract with Control Data Corporation (CDC) for the joint development of an optical storage system and an agreement with RCA and Intel for cooperation with respect to certain types of integrated circuits. The 1983 annual report announced an agreement with AT & T to cooperate in the field of public telephony and transmission, explaining:

> The high development costs in the field of digital telephone exchanges and the need to acquire a greater supporting structure were the reasons for embarking on a cooperative activity. The strong technological position of AT & T in the field of public telephony, together with Philips's competence in developing systems based on the CCITT specifications, our transmission technology and our international marketing experience, constitutes a good basis for the future.

In 1984, the arrangement with CDC was extended to include the manufacture and sale of optical discs and read-out equipment. In 1985, the CDC collaborative effort was folded into a 50–50 joint venture in optical media for consumer and professional applications with DuPont. Philips also established two joint-ventures with Kyocera Corporation – one for developing and manufacturing new interactive systems for use in the home and for its sale in Japan and another for introducing the Philips communication network system into the Japanese market – and a 50–50 joint venture with the Beijing Radio Factory to build an audio factory. In 1986, joint ventures were entered into with R.R. Donnelley & Sons (US) and Toppan Printing Company (Japan) to promote the development of software for interactive compact discs and with Willi Studer (Switzerland) for research and development relating to professional CD systems for radio and television studios.

Organization

Dekker also acted to revitalize the ponderous management structure. At the operating level, he continued Dr Rodenburg's initiative to replace the dual leadership arrangement (commercial and technical co-directors) which had been in place since the firm's founding with a single general manager. To revitalize a management board that he had characterized as 'too large, too distant and too uninvolved, where each person was almost a baron protective of his particular territory', Dekker reduced the number of members, brought in people with strong operating experiences and created subcommittees to deal with difficult issues.

In line with the new emphasis on global involvement, Dekker continued to 'tilt the matrix' away from national organizations by creating a Corporate Council on which the heads of product divisions would join the heads of the national organizations to discuss issues of importance to both. At the same time, product divisions were to play an increasingly important role in the firm's decision-making with respect to product design, manufacturing and research.

To facilitate change, a management-by-objectives system was introduced and emphasis on incentive compensation increased. Plants were closed and staff reduced through early retirement in an attempt to reduce costs.

In April 1986, van Riemsdijk reached the mandatory retirement age for chairman of the supervisory board and Dekker moved up to that position. His efforts to redefine the Philips strategy and structure would now be in the hands of Cor van der Klugt, his selected successor as president and chairmon of the board of management.

In his farewell speech, Dekker reminded Philips's 300 senior managers that the firm's performance in recent years had been less than satisfactory. He pointed to its slow growth and low profitability when compared to leading US and Japanese competitors, concluding with the admonition:

> We are still far from being where we want and would like to be. In just over four years, we shall be on the eve of our centennial anniversary. Shall we be able, in 1991, to celebrate the achievement of our objectives?

COR VAN DER KLUGT

More than one senior executive noted how the change in leadership seemed well suited to Philips's evolving needs. The two men were characterized as follows:

> Dekker was conceptual and a statesman. He sensed danger, sounded the alarm bell, and pointed the organization in a new direction for survival and success. Van der Klugt is an organization builder and a fighter. He likes to convince people and has the emotional force to bring about the needed changes.

Van der Klugt spoke of the change in leadership as one involving continuity with change:

> A new CEO steps into an ongoing process, inheriting many things that were started by his predecessor. He must build on the past, but needs to go beyond the past. In a way, each CEO is a new light in the firm's sky who must set the stage for the next decades.

The objectives set forth in his first message to the Philips organization were in large part a reaffirmation of earlier policies. But in specifying profits as the central measure and the product divisions as having the ultimate responsibility for achieving profits, the new president was beginning to impose his own imprint on developments. In his second videotaped message to the Philips organization, given in November 1986, he took another step defining his agenda and priorities in spotlighting the management of human resources, stating, 'People are our most important *resources*. The unavoidable conclusion is that human resources management is a strategic activity which demands top priority.' The speech went on to describe responsibilities and policies, and included among the firm's objectives: improving identification and guidance of young talent; improving management education, job rotation and international exchange; and creating challenging career prospects and an attractive organizational climate.

Major actions accompanied the words. In late 1986, van der Klugt terminated the US Philips trust, which had been given control of North American Philips during World War II. He explained:

> The United States is the largest and most sophisticated arena for a number of important electronics products. To compete, Philips needs to have a direct and clear cut presence there. The termination of the Trust accords with our global stategy, which for the future, requires a more integrated international organization capable of facing the challenge of worldwide competition.

No longer would North American Philips operate in a quasi-independent corporation.

At the same time, the management board had begun to refine corporate strategy. Henceforth, Philips would focus on selected sectors of electronics along with its large and profitable lighting business. Consumer electronics would continue as one area for emphasis because of the firm's strong market position in Europe. The increasing global character of consumer electronics products also offered Philips an opportunity to expand in other major markets through its already established worldwide organization.

Professional electronics would also remain an area of focus because of its importance as a place where 'technological push' was strongest. The professional user's willingness to experiment with new concepts and products made this sector a natural staging ground for new consumer electronics products.

A continued presence in components was also seen as critical since it was in this sector that the foundations were laid for new generations of systems and products. The rationale for this commitment was later described by a senior director:

> The American consumer electronics industry ... lost out completely because ... the production of essential components was left to the Far East. ... It is easy to guess what happened: the Far East, partly helped by high volume production for American customers, entered the American market with its own labels. The American industry was left standing.... The essential fact is that components development is creating new possibilities and that, if at all possible, we must endeavour to keep these new possibilities in our own hands.

In May 1987, van der Klugt announced a major restructuring: the Consumer Electronics, Components and Telecommunications and Data Systems product divisions were designated core-interlinked units; the lighting division was to become a core, stand-alone unit; and all other operating units were non-core. At the same time, the top management structure was to be reconstituted so as 'to enhance efficiency and flexibility ... reducing the number of levels of management in the organization'. Specifically, the board of management would be reduced in size and its policy-making responsibility would devolve on a newly created group management committee, comprising the remaining board members as well as the heads of the three core-linked product divisions and of key functional staffs. Exhibit 4 shows the new top management organizational structure.

In placing the core-linked unit managers on the group's policy-making body, the new structure completed the tilting of Philips's matrix in favour of the product divisions. So as to avoid any misunderstanding, the announcement went on to spell out this point: 'In the proposed organizational structure, the Philips Group will be directed primarily via the Product Divisions.'

Van der Klugt was later to comment on the dilemma that Philips faced in tilting the matrix:

> Competitive forces in electronics call for a global approach and that means that we must now emphasize product divisions with a global perspective. But we cannot afford to forget that national organizations are still very important, especially the large units such as those in Germany, France and the UK. The head of a national organization has an important presence in his community, enjoying considerable prestige and power. Our challenge is to combine the strengths of national organizations and product divisions. In my view, the answer is to let national organizations govern, but to let product divisions fight it out in the battlefield.

The policy of joining forces with other firms for non core businesses was put into practice almost simultaneously with its announcement. In May 1987, Philips reached an agreement with General Electric Company of Britain to combine their medical electronics businesses in a 50–50 joint venture. Negotiations were also underway with Whirlpool to combine their major appliance businesses.

To strengthen the firm's capital structure, Philips issued 20.75 million common shares in April 1987 to raise $480.6 million. According to Dick Snijders, Director of Corporate Finance, this had been the first time since 1962 that the Group had offered shares on a global basis. (In 1985, the Philips Group had offered 10 million shares in the US market.) He thought that the firm would continue to raise its equity base through small additional offers every two or three years.

On 18 August 1987, Philips offered $50 a share, or $610 million, for the 42 per cent of North American Philips that it did not already own. According to the press release, the company hoped to bring its US sales – already more than a quarter of its 55 billion guilder ($26 billion) total revenues – into line with the United States' share of the world market. A Philips spokesman in Eindhoven said that the acquisition was not related to the recent capital increase and that existing lines of credit would be used to finance the transaction.

If there had been any doubts in the Philips organization as to top management's commitment to a new strategy and structure, van der Klugt's bold moves were calculated to lay them to rest. He recognized, however, the formidable task before him to realign his people's attitudes and abilities in accordance with the new Philips:

> Categorizing businesses was a cultural shock. Everyone had always felt that they were part of the family. There was a strong sense that we had betrayed a number of our managers.
>
> The emphasis on profits is also foreign to our thinking. Sales volume had always been the measure of success. The difficulty in changing this thinking can perhaps be seen in the following experience. Soon after taking over, I began a campaign to cut our enormous overhead costs. Among other things, we discussed eliminating such things as 38 million guilders for corporate aircraft, $1\frac{1}{2}$ million guilders for cigarettes, and 4 million guilders for alcohol. Admittedly, these are small things, but they have a tremendous symbolic value. The reaction of many of my colleagues was that we were sacrificing the quality of life. What they failed to realize was that no quality of life can exist when there are no profits.

The importance van der Klugt attached to his people's attitudes and abilities was clearly indicated in his remark, 'A president can redirect a corporation only with the support of many senior managers and corporate staff.' The remainder of this case describes how the Philips' situation in 1987 appeared to various managers in the organization.

LIGHTING DIVISION

Philips was the largest producer of lighting in the world, with 1986 sales of about 7 billion guilders. The business was divided between consumer lamps, accounting for 45 per cent of this total, and professional lamps and fixtures, accounting for the rest. The industry was characterized as a profitable, low-growth business which was becoming increasingly global in nature. Technical content was changing: in the 1990's, about 20 per cent of lighting was expected to be connected with electronics (e.g. an electronic ballast to permit changing the intensity of fluorescent lamps).

In May 1987, the lighting division was instructed to submit concrete proposals to the board of management regarding just how it would be organized as an autonomous businesses enterprise. Y. Bouwkamp, the newly appointed senior managing director who had had a distinguished career in various national organizations, described how he viewed the challenge before him:

> The lighting division has been the most profitable operating unit in Philips and over the years has generated cash flow to fund other units. We have to find a way to operate as a separate business while taking advantage of the Group's strengths and also contributing to its other initiatives. We have engaged McKinsey to help us figure out how to deal with the various problems associated with such a change.
>
> Our objective is to maintain product leadership. We need to create a culture which would make people proud to work for lighting. Otherwise we run a risk of losing our best people to the core, interlinked electronics business units with their appeal as the Philips heartland.

Bouwkamp saw the present relationships between the lighting division and the national organization as unsatisfactory. He explained:

> Lighting is a protected business in many countries and can be very profitable. Because of this, lighting is often used to make up for any profit shortfalls a national organization might encounter. For example, it might choose to sacrifice market share for additional income, even though that might weaken us against an aggressive competitor. Or, if the lighting division is trying to build its forces, a national organization might veto adding people because it has a personnel hiring stop policy or has other priorities.
>
> In my view, we shall probably have to set up autonomous lighting organizations in the major countries. For the rest of the world, we would continue to use the Philips's national organizations as agents, provided they fulfill certain conditions and agree to specific turnover and profit goals. To be sure, such changes will not occur without controversy.

According to Bouwkamp, many of the existing Philips management information systems were designed to serve many purposes and as a result, were complicated and often inappropriate for lighting's specific needs. He saw a need to introduce new systems suitable for a global lighting organization. He also questioned the future role of Philips's Elcoma Division as a supplier of electronic components, noting that:

> Elcoma has more expertise with respect to ICs and electronics circuitry than with the power ICs suitable for high temperatures and the voltages associated with lighting. We might need to seek another source of components.

Bouwkamp held no illusions about the difficulties he would encounter in proposing the kind of changes he had in mind:

> A lot of people in Eindhoven are not ready to change. We are talking about the possibility of altering important responsibilities and power. One of the biggest battles will be to change the cash generating role that lighting has played in the past. It's not that I oppose funding other businesses. It's just that I would like to see lighting get full credit for its profits and an end to saddling it with charges of other operations.

Only partly in jest, Bouwkamp pointed out that it was lighting, the original Philips business, that was entitled to celebrate the centennial anniversary, adding:

> I like to think that under the new arrangement, it is really lighting that is divesting itself of all the other products that Philips has accumulated over the years.

MEDICAL SYSTEMS DIVISION

In June 1987, W. Stoorvogel, senior managing director of the Medical Systems Division, was engrossed in the job of extricating his operation from Philips and merging it with Picker International, a month after an agreement had been reached with General Electric Company (UK) to set up a 50–50 joint venture. The two businesses – making a wide range of medical diagnostic equipment, including X-ray machines, computer-aided tomography (CAT) scanners and magnetic resonance scanners – would have combined sales of $1.9 billion, giving the new entity world market share leadershop. (In July 1987, General Electric (US) recaptured the lead with its acquisition of Thomson's (France) medical electronics business.)

According to Stoorvogel, the new venture would benefit the Medical Systems Division in three ways. First, were the added resources that would be available to compete in a business with high fixed costs. For example, the division's R & D costs ran about 10 per cent compared with Philips's average of 7 per cent. The large service organization required in this business was also costly. Second, was the geographical complementarity of the two units. The Medical Systems Division's sales of about $1.3 billion were primarily in Europe; most of Picker International's revenues came from the United States. The US presence also put the division in closer touch with the major centre of medical electronics technological innovation. Third was a healthier management arrangement. Stoorvogel explained:

> It was difficult for a high-tech, professional business like ours to survive in the Philips matrix. We had to deal with noses pointed in too many different directions. A lot of energy was lost in the friction of making joint decisions. A rapidly developing business calling for large investment decisions really needs a single worldwide management.

The new ownership arrangement also posed several serious future problems for the Medical Systems Division. The difficulty the division had experienced in its relationships with the national organizations – whereby some NOs were not willing to invest in developing their markets and would handle only its most profitable products – was likely to be exacerbated by the organizational decoupling. The national organizations with their political clout played a critical role in selling the expensive equipment to the government-supported health programmes in Europe and elsewhere.

Another major problem facing Stoorvogel was to disentangle the medical products activities from the Philips operations. Many of its manufacturing, selling, technical and administrative functions had been interconnected in various ways with other Group activities to lessen costs. He expected that the new unit would continue to depend on Philips for legal and financing relationships and to tap into corporate research.

Stoorvogel also faced a morale problem. Many of the division's 11,000 people were upset by the termination of their direct relationships with Philips. There was also the threat of employee redundancy in the United States which would require some cutbacks in administration and sales. The new company, which still had no name, would require approval of the parents for major restructuring and for the selection of its CEO.

He agreed with the conclusion that the medical products business was not interlinked with other businesses in the Philips Group. What he did not understand was how top management had decided that it was not a core business in view of its high electronics technology and future growth potential.

HEADQUARTERS

While support for the changes underway had gained widespread support, no one expected them to be carried out easily. The company had a long and proven tradition, and the new approach laid out by Dekker and van der Klugt had to contend with the entrenched Philips' way of doing business. As one senior official observed:

> One of the new objectives is to focus on profits, but we are trained to think about turnover and market share. We are now supposed to think in global terms, but we have a strong country orienation. We are supposed to engage in strategic alliances, but we are conditioned to having one hundred percent control over our operations and to being boss. After four years, the mentality has not really changed.

A senior staff manager identified two other transitional problems:

> Headquarters has a staff of some 3,000 people, the PDs have about 2,500. Many of the headquarters staff will have to be reallocated to the product divisions. This move will be most painful for the staff associated with the board of management. This group of 1,200 will be considerably reduced. They will be transferred with the same pay but will suffer a loss in status.
>
> Reassigning key people in line with the shift in power from NOs to PDs and maintaining morale while making all the necessary job changes will also be a very difficult task. There has been a tradition at this company that the strongest people went to national organizations. Indeed, most of senior group management has come up through the NOs. Take van der Klugt as an example. He spent nineteen years in Chile, Uruguay and Brazil before returning to Eindhoven to join the board of management in 1978. So, whether true or not, there is a widely-shared perception that the quality of the managers in the NOs is higher than at the PDs. What this means, of course, is that the national organizations will not simply defer to the product divisions. Product division management must win the right to direct strategy on a worldwide basis.

Changing the relationship between product divisions and national organizations without unduly hampering Philips's ability to function smoothly during the next several years was clearly uppermost in everyone's mind. The nature of the difficulty was revealed in the following observation:

> Philips's management is based on intricate webs of relationships. These strong networks have been the glue that provided cohesion for almost a hundred years. Personal relationships involving power and status will not change easily or quickly. They are deeply rooted and entrenched.

Whether or not van der Klugt would succeed in transforming Philips to carry out its new global and focused strategy and whether or not Philips would achieve its profit margin of 4 per cent by 1991 remained to be seen. Failure, however, would not be for lack of trying, as a senior executive noted:

Van der Klugt will move with bold strokes. He knows that it would be a mistake to try to deal with nuances in communicating to the organization. Besides, he has four years to complete his programme before he reaches retirement age.

EXHIBIT 1
Commercial activities for 1986.

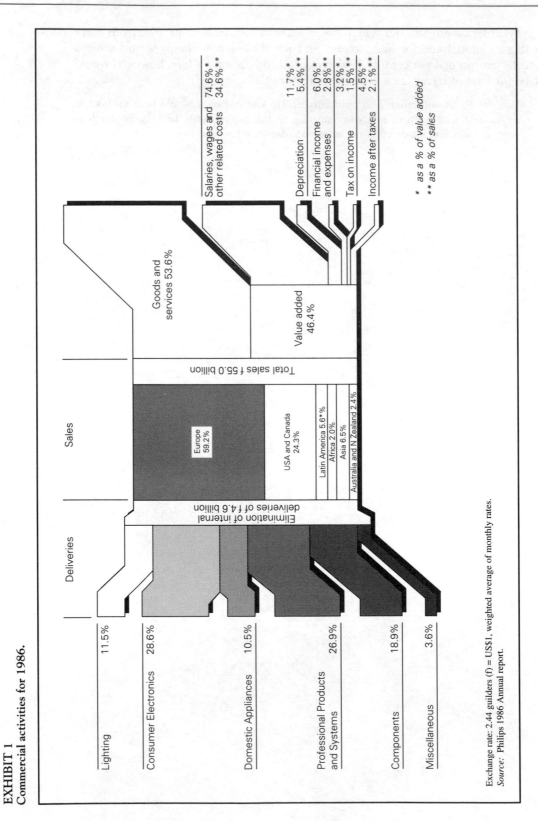

Exchange rate: 2.44 guilders (f) = US$1, weighted average of monthly rates.
Source: Philips 1986 Annual report.

EXHIBIT 2
Financial* and related information, 1977–86.

	1986	1985	1984	1983	1982	1981	1980	1979	1978	1977
Net Sales	55,037	60,045	53,804	46,183	42,991	42,411	36,536	33,238	32,658	31,164
Income from Operations	3,194	3,075	3,473	2,755	2,130	2,193	1,577	1,796	2,210	2,162
Net Income	1,015	919	1,113	647	453	357	328	564	651	583
as Percentage of										
Stockholders' Equity	6.3	5.6	6.9	4.9	3.4	3.0	2.7	5.0	6.0	5.6
Inventories	12,851	13,942	15,547	13,615	12,199	12,374	11,974	10,468	9,362	9,226
Accounts Receivable	13,992	15,094	14,825	12,963	11,258	11,081	10,370	9,636	9,370	8,465
Current Assets	28,167	30,770	31,964	28,266	24,879	24,748	23,687	21,417	20,009	19,155
Total Assets	50,630	52,883	54,535	47,758	43,295	42,730	39,647	35,150	31,967	31,108
Current Liabilities	18,453	19,693	19,781	17,601	15,747	15,198	14,204	12,121	11,229	10,397
Long-term Liabilities	13,840	14,609	15,108	12,503	11,395	11,755	11,028	10,192	8,719	8,851
Equity	18,337	18,581	19,646	17,654	16,153	15,777	14,415	12,837	12,019	11,860
Employees (000s)	344	346	344	343	336	348	373	379	388	384
Wages, Salaries	19,755	21,491	20,240	18,364	17,488	17,369	15,399	14,159	13,471	12,816

1986 Percentage of Total

Product Sector	Sales	Operating Income
Lighting	12	17
Consumer Electronics	31	23
Domestic Appliances	11	7
Professional Products	29	36
Components	13	8
Miscellaneous	4	9

Area	Sales	Operating Income
Netherlands	7	17
Europe (rest of)	52	59
USA/Canada	24	2
Latin America	6	13
Africa	2	1
Asia	7	7
Australia/NZ	2	–

*All amounts are expressed in millions of guilders unless otherwise stated. (The exchange rate on 1 October 1987 was 2.07 guilders=$1.) Due to factors such as consolidations and divestments, the stated amounts are not directly comparable over time.
Source: Philips Financial statements, 1986.

EXHIBIT 3
Company organization chart, 1972.

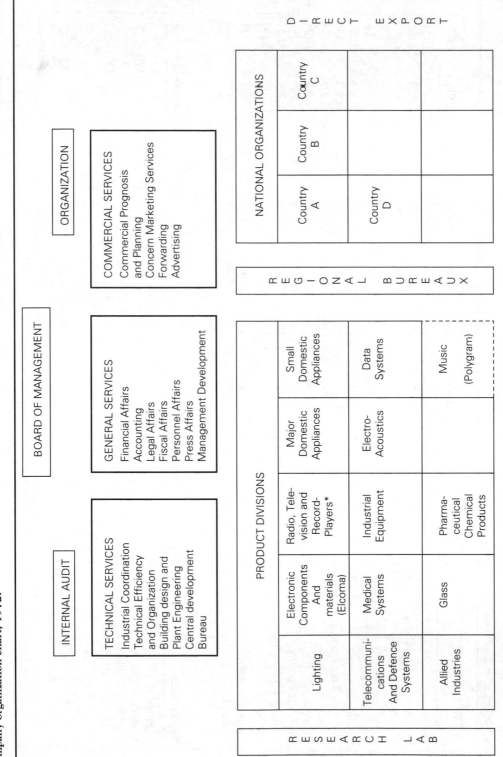

INTERNAL AUDIT

BOARD OF MANAGEMENT

ORGANIZATION

TECHNICAL SERVICES
Industrial Coordination
Technical Efficiency
and Organization
Building design and
Plant Engineering
Central development
Bureau

GENERAL SERVICES
Financial Affairs
Accounting
Legal Affairs
Fiscal Affairs
Personnel Affairs
Press Affairs
Management Development

COMMERCIAL SERVICES
Commercial Prognosis
and Planning
Concern Marketing Services
Forwarding
Advertising

RESEARCH LAB

PRODUCT DIVISIONS

Lighting	Electronic Components And materials (Elcoma)	Radio, Television and Record-Players*	Major Domestic Appliances	Small Domestic Appliances
Telecommunications And Defence Systems	Medical Systems	Industrial Equipment	Electro-Acoustics	Data Systems
Allied Industries	Glass	Pharmaceutical Chemical Products		Music (Polygram)

REGIONAL BUREAUX

NATIONAL ORGANIZATIONS

| Country A | Country B | Country C |
| Country D | | |

DIRECT EXPORT

Source: Philips charts and tables, 15 November 1972

EXHIBIT 4
Group management committee, 1 September 1987.

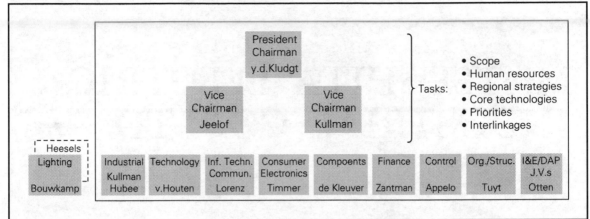

MATSUSHITA ELECTRIC INDUSTRIAL CO. LTD (MEI)*

They [Matsushita] believe in peace, brotherhood and market share. (*Fortune*, 31 October 1983)

In 1977, when Toshihiko Yamashita took over as its president, *Fortune* had described Matsushita Electric (MEI) as the 'most dazzling corporate success in Japan'. Almost a decade of his leadership had only enhanced that reputation. Compounded annual sales growth of 11.6 per cent between 1980 and 1985 had helped MEI move ahead of Philips, Siemens and Hitachi and emerge as the world's largest producer of customer electronics products, and the fourth largest electrical and electronics firm in the world, behind IBM, AT & T and GE. By 1985, Matsushita ranked 20th on *Fortune*'s list of the world's largest companies – up 26 places from the 1980 list.

Financially too, MEI had done extremely well. The company's 14.6 per cent annual growth in net profits between 1980 and 1985 had been well above those of its domestic rivals (see Exhibit 1), and had helped it accumulate a cash mountain of over $6.8 billion by the end of 1985. Its equity ratio of 47 per cent was unusually high for Japanese companies and 'qualified it as an international blue-chip company', according to Yamaichi Securities.

Yet, as Yamashita recognized, a new and different era had arrived. The dramatic rise in the value of the yen from 239 to the dollar in the 4th quarter of 1985 to 159

---

*This case was prepared by Raymond Oullet, Research Associate, under the supervision of Sumantra Ghoshal, Assistant Professor at INSEAD and Christopher A. Bartlett, Associate Professor at Harvard Business School. It is intended to be used as a basis for class discussion rather than to illustrate either effective or ineffective handling of an administrative situation.

a year later led to a 20 per cent decline in Matsushita's 1986 international sales compared with 1985. The company's highly centralized production system left it particularly vulnerable. The financial impact of the exchange rate changes was cushioned by the effect of what many observers called 'The Matsushita Bank'. In 1986, over 67 billion yen in dividend and interest income from its cash hoard contributed almost 10 per cent of pre-tax profits, obscuring the fact that operating margins of the company had steadily declined from the second quarter of 1985 (Exhibit 2). Of particular concern were the sales declines of 30 per cent in colour TV and 19 per cent in VCR, since these had been the products that had fuelled the company's dramatic growth in sales and profits in earlier years.

Yamashita was fighting hard to prevent decline in MEI, and had tied a great deal of importance to two programmes he had initiated to spearhead the necessary change. 'Operation localization' was a programme to shift more activities to Matsushita's vast overseas operations, and 'ACTION 86' was a broad-based effort to revitalize the company and shift its business emphasis. Were they appropriate responses? Would they work? Were they enough? These were the questions that filled Yamashita's mind in 1986.

BACKGROUND HISTORY OF MEI

Humble Beginning

In 1918, very few houses in Japan had electricity, and in those that did, the only source was usually a single ceiling outlet in one room. Electricity was distributed to other rooms by attaching a large and cumbersome cord to the outlet. That same year, Konosuke Matsushita, a 23-year-old inspector with the Osaka Electric Light Company, saw an opportunity to start his own business by solving that problem. Investing $100, he set up shop in his modest home to produce a double-ended socket which would make the extension cord easier to use. By 1922 the company had 50 employees and KM, as the founder came to be called, was ready for bigger and better things.

Strategic Foundation: Product Diversification and Domestic Dominance

Between 1923 and 1929, the company grew rapidly, primarily on the strength of a battery-powered bicycle lamp and an electric iron which established a 50 per cent market share despite its 30 per cent price premium. In 1931, the company made its first radio.

In 1935, a public share offer gave the company a total capital base of $2.9 million, and allowed rapid proliferation of high-volume products. Domestic fans and light bulbs were the next additions, followed by small motors for domestic appliances, then the appliances themselves. Production of black and white TV sets commenced in 1952 leading to an avalanche of new product introductions: transistor radios in 1957; stereos, tape recorders and air conditioners in 1958; driers and disposal units in 1959; colour TVs, dishwashers and electric cookers in 1960. By 1968, Matsushita had 5,000 products compared to about 80 at Sony.

Based on the strength of its large product portfolio, and wanting to by-pass the highly fragmented Japanese distribution system which provided little service and no customer education, Matsushita established a retail chain throughout Japan. By the late 1960s, a chain of 25,000 'National Shops', about 40 per cent of all electric appliance stores in Japan, was providing the company's full product line with a strong leadership position in domestic distribution (Sony, Matsushita's arch rival in the consumer electronics business, had only 4,000 exclusive shops). These shops also became the company's primary source for competitive and market intelligence and an important training ground for new employees.

But even its rapidly expanding product line and its excellent distribution system could not protect the company from the eventual slowdown in the phenomenal post-war expansion of the Japanese consumer electronics market. Exhibiting its normal flexibility, the company resorted to many different tactics to deal with the slowing growth – including sending assembly-line workers out into the markets as door-to-door salesmen – but eventually recognized that continued rapid expansion would be hard to achieve at home.

Cultural Foundation: Company Creed and the 250-Year Plan

As important as the product market evolution was the development of a unique culture and set of values that also shaped the company's subsequent growth and strategies. On 5 May 1932, the 14th anniversary of the company's founding, Konosuke Matsushita assembled his 162 employees and announced his business philosophy and a 250-year corporate plane, broken up into ten 25-year sections. 'I, myself and you assembled here are to carry out the first 25 years. Our successors will carry on exactly the same for another 25 years, and so on.' The business philosophy KM described that day has since been codified in the form of a company 'creed' and in the 'Seven precepts or spirits of Matsushita' (see Exhibit 3). Typically, the creed, the seven principles and the company song are woven into morning assemblies held in Matsushita facilities worldwide.

The values are deeply ingrained in the organization, however, and involve far more than rote repetition of principles as a morning ritual. During the first seven months on the job, all white-collar employees spend a good portion of their time in 'cultural and spiritual training'. They study the fuller philosophy of Konosuke Matsushita which underlies the creed and the seven spirits, much of which evolved as KM struggled to understand the role of business in society. (Some examples of his conclusions are presented in Exhibit 3.) At the conclusion of the formal programme, employees are grouped under a leader to continue discussions on how the philosophy translates into their daily responsibilities in the company. Furthermore, the personnel department in each of the company's different units conducts on-going 'spiritual training' to further reinforce and embed the corporate values.

To most Westerners and even some Japanese, the values and philosophies appeared so idealized as to be gimmicky. Yet, within the company, managers remained convinced of their importance. They were referred to frequently at all levels within the company and often became the basis for deciding on even the most operational issues.

Organizational Foundation: The Divisional Structure

In 1933, one year after he formulated the company's business philosophy, Konosuke Matsushita introduced the divisional structure in MEI, making it not only the first company in Japan to adopt this organizational form, but also an international pioneer. Plagued with poor health, KM felt he needed the ability to delegate more than was normal in traditional Japanese companies. He wanted to create an organization that would develop managers able to lead the company into the first phase of its ambitious long-term mission. The division structure he implemented was designed to allow easy identification of the performance of each division through unambiguously defined profit responsibilities while creating a 'small business' environment necessary to maintain its growth and flexibility.

Under his 'one product – one division' system, each product line was managed by a separate autonomous division which was expected to operate as if it was an independent corporation. When a new division was created, corporate management provided it with initial funds for establishing new assets and this was credited to the divisional balance-sheet as internal capital. In assessing the initial capital needs, working capital requirements were deliberately underestimated to motivate the division to work hard to retain and accumulate its earnings. Divisional profitability, measured after management fees to cover corporate overheads, direct charges for central services such as R & D, and interest on internal borrowings, was made public within the company. Performance expectations were uniform across the 36 business divisions regardless of the maturity of the market or the company's competitive position, and divisions in which operating profits fell below 4 per cent of sales for two successive years had the division manager replaced.

The corporate treasury operated essentially like a commercial bank. Divisions were required to deposit their excess funds and received normal market interest. All inter-divisional sales, the prices for which were set at market rates, were payable within 30 days and were settled by transfers of the relevant divisions' corporate deposits. Each division paid about 60 per cent of its net earnings as dividends to the headquarters, and was expected to finance all additional working capital and fixed asset requirements from the retained 40 per cent. Requests for additional corporate funds to meet expansion plans were submitted as loan applications to the central finance department which reviewed the proposals like a bank. Approved loans carried interest rates slightly higher than commercial bank rates and had to be repaid on first priority from subsequent division earnings.

This organizational system generated a high level of internal competition among divisions, and helped drive new product development which managers saw as their best way to maintain long-term growth and profitability. For example, the radio and the tape recorder divisions competed for the right to introduce a radio-cassette recorder. When corporate managers decided to allow the radio division to develop this product to compensate for its declining sales and earnings in a saturated world market, the tape recorder division was forced to find a new product to secure its own future. The result was the 'Karoake', a dual-track recorder that allowed amateurs to sing with pre-recorded music accompaiment, which became enormously popular in Japan. Similarly, the black and white television division developed CATV and computer display products to compensate for its maturing market. The need to fund new product development also drove managers to maximize performance of existing products. For example, the funds required to support the development of VTR made the video division extremely aggressive in maximizing sales of colour TV sets. To maintain this 'hungry spirit' in all divisions, whenever a new product established any significant volume potential, company policy was to create a separate division.

THE INTERNATIONALIZATION OF MATSUSHITA

On 5 May 1981, 50 years after the company's 'spiritual foundation day', 100,000 employees worldwide celebrated the beginning of the third section of the 250-year plan. Although the central theme of the third plan was to achieve 'true internationalization' of the company, the seed of overseas expansion had been sown much earlier.

Establishing the Base: Expanding Through Colour TV

In 1951, Konosuke Matsushita made his first trip to the United States and was extremely impressed with the sophistication and dynamism of the US market. In meetings with American manufacturers, he sought collaborations but found no takers. Returning to Japan via Europe he visited Philips where he met with a more positive response. On his first day back in Kodama City, he told his managers: 'To survive and to grow we have to become international not only in our operations but also in our outlook.'

The first task was to upgrade technology, and in 1952 MEI entered into a technology exchange and licensing agreement with Philips, which led to the formation of a joint venture producing electronic components in Japan. In 1953, the company opened a branch office in New York, and six years later, upgraded it to become MEI's first overseas company – Matsushita Electric Corporation of America (MECA). In following years, similar sales companies were established in Canada, Central and South America, and a number of nearby countries in Southeast Asia.

The international environment in which this expansion was taking place was in flux. Successive rounds of GATT negotiations continued to reduce trade barriers, while the introduction of containerization and supercargo ships were bringing down transportation costs. From its modest start exporting three black and white models, Matsushita made export of TV sets the base of its international expansion. With neither the contacts and past relationships necessary to get distribution through small specialty electrical stores where personal selling was the norm, nor the reputation or brand image to gain access to the traditional chains and retailers, Matsushita was forced to establish its products through different outlets and on the basis of aggressive pricing. Capitalizing on emerging changes in the distribution system in the United States and other Western countries, it sold primarily through the new mass merchandisers and discount chains, often private-branding its products specifically for these retailers.

In 1961, the company established its first overseas manufacturing facility in Thailand, and over the next decade opened many other such operations, primarily in the developing countries of East Asia and Central and South America. Top management explained that these affiliates were not established as part of a well-defined worldwide strategy (as they perceived subsidiaries of US and European MNCs as being), but were set up solely to comply with requests of host governments or local distributors. Most were simple assembly operations, which imported knockdown kits of components and sub-assemblies from the company's efficient Japanese plants. Later, as manufacturing costs rose in Japan, more and more production was transferred to efficient plants in low wage countries like Singapore, Puerto Rico and Mexico.

By the early 1970s, Matsushita found that its historically successful international strategy and the manufacturing infrastructure supporting it were being threatened by rising protectionist sentiments in the West. The first warnings came from the United States, where local manufacturers became concerned with the rapidly increasing sales of imported Japanese colour TVs, which had risen from 350,000 sets in 1967 to 880,000 (or 20 per cent of the market) the following year. Through their association, they filed an anti-dumping suit with the US Treasury Department. Although its worldscale plants in Singapore, Taiwan and other low-cost sources offered a means of circumventing the quotas that were subsequently established on Japanese exports, Matsushita felt obliged to respond to the political pressures more directly. In 1972 it established a colour TV plant in Canada; two years later it acquired Motorola's TV business and started manufacturing its Quasar sets in the United States; and in 1976 it built a plant in Cardiff (Wales), to supply the Common Market.

To build even broader ties with the national environments in which it operated, the company began making overtures to overseas capital markets. In 1971, Matsushita was listed on the New York Stock Exchange, and within two years listings had been secured in six more international financial centres, mostly in Europe. In 1975, its $100 million convertible bond float was rated AA by both Standard and Poor's and Moody's. Reflecting Matsushita's financial strength, the rating was subsequently upgraded to AAA by both companies.

Building Global Leadership: Dominating Through VCRs

More than anything else, it was the birth of the video cassette recorder (VCR) that propelled MEI into its mid-1980s position as the world's No. 1 consumer electronics company. The first commercially viable videotape recorder was launched in 1956 by Ampex, a California-based company which focused on broadcast applications. Engineers at Matsushita (as well as others at its own 50 per cent owned subsidiary JVC, and Sony) recognized the potential consumer application of this technology and, with some funding from MITI and the Japanese National Broadcasting Corporation (NHK), began modifying a prototype built on the Ampex design. Under the leadership of Dr Hiroshi Sugaya, a young physicist in the central research laboratory, the company developed a video head which became its key VCR development, and within six years Matsushita launched its commercial broadcast video recorder just in time for the Tokyo Olympics.

Following close on the heels of Sony, Matsushita introduced a consumer market version in 1966. Over the next seven years, the company developed several major technological breakthroughs, which it incorporated in successive new consumer VCR models, but again market acceptance was poor. The 1,400 workers in the new Okanyama plant – the first in the world dedicated solely to VCR production – were operating at well below the plant's 120,000 unit annual capacity, and corporate pressure was increasing to get this product out of the red.

In 1975, Sony introduced its new Betamax system and the following year JVC launched the VHS format. In 1977, with the urging of MITI which was concerned about the internally competing formats, Matsushita agreed to adopt the VHS standard, and the Okanyama plant was finally able to begin mass production of a successful VCR. Although the twenty years of losses created pressures within the profit-driven Matsushita system, the company's commitment to the product never flagged. The losses were 'tuition fees' as one manager described them, helping Matsushita refine its development and manufacturing capabilities, by responding to market feedback.

As was the practice in Matsushita, various members of the research team who had remained under Dr Sugaya's leadership had moved from the central labs to the product division and, finally, out to the plant as the task evolved from basic research to product development and finally to production engineering. Even when the new Okanyama plant was lying almost idle, the cadre of manufacturing engineers was kept together and assigned to 'research projects'. Expertise was continually sought from Matsushita engineers in other divisions working on related technologies or applications, such as solid state circuit design or tape cassette manufacture.

Having finally developed a commercially viable product, Matsushita and its subsidiary company JVC adopted a very aggressive policy in licensing the VHS technology to other manufacturers, signing up such leaders as Hitachi, Sharp, Mitsubishi and, later, Philips. An aggressive OEM policy ensured that companies like GE, RCA and later, Zenith, were also locked into the VHS format on units they sourced from Japan to market under their own brands. By building 'format volume' Matsushita hoped to make VHS the industry standard and lock in future sales. (See Exhibit 4 for a history of format market shares.)

The company quickly built production volumes to ensure it could accommodate the fast-growing worldwide demand. Capacity, which was only 205,000 units in 1977, was increased 33-fold to 6.8 million units by 1984 – a scale-up effort five times greater than the increases necessary in the boom days of colour TV production. Distribution channels that had been opened with TV products were now loaded up with the new product lines, and brand names and images that had been estalished to introduce the earlier consumer electronics products were used to sell the VCRs. The boom was reflected in the company's overseas sales growth of the early 1980s which increased a remarkable 52 per cent in 1980 (from 764 billion to 1,164 billion) then by a further 35 per cent in 1981 (to 1,575 billion), with most of the growth neing attributable to VCR exports. By 1985, VCR sales comprised an estimated 43 per cent of the company's total overseas volume (see Exhibit 5).

By concentrating all of the tremendous growth on its focused factories and its network of established suppliers in Japan, Matsushita was able to reap scale and experience benefits that allowed prices to drop by 50 per cent within five years of the product launch (see Exhibit 6). Meanwhile, product quality and reliability as measured by carefully monitored consumer return rates continued to rise as plant engineers constantly refined production processes and worked with the company's numerous internal and external suppliers to improve sourced components and subassemblies. As a result, by the mid-1980s, VCRs were contributing almost 30 per cent of the company's total sales, and an estimated 45 per cent of its profits (see Exhibits 7 and 8).

MANAGEMENT OF INTERNATIONAL OPERATIONS

Organizational Evolution

As much as anything else, it was Matsushita's strong tradition of profit centre responsibility that drove product divisions to leverage the capabilities of their efficient domestic plants through exports. Matsushita Electric Trading Company (METC), a separate corporate entity formed in 1935, provided the distribution contacts and logistical infrastructure that facilitated this export process. The formation of a branch sales office in New York in 1954 led to the creation of the Overseas Department in MEI headquarters. With the opening of more overseas offices, this department because the company's Overseas Division.

The existence of these two separate international management groups at MEI and METC created some confusion about the reporting relationship of the overseas companies. This became even more complex as offshore sourcing plants were established and began to link back to MEI's product divisions. In general, the company thought about its overseas companies in three groups. The A group were the wholly owned single product global sourcing plants such as the Singapore audio plant or the Hong Kong fan factory that reported primarily to the relevant product divisions of MEI and were tightly controlled by them. The B group were the multi-product sales and manufacturing subsidiaries like MELCOM, the Malaysian company, or National do Brazil, many of which were joint ventures, often producing a broad product line for their local markets. These companies reported to Corporate Overseas Management (COM), the MEI corporate group that had replaced the Overseas Division. The third group of offshore companies were the sales and marketing subsidiaries like the Argentinian and French companies that imported their products from Japan and from the global production centres. These reported to METC, the Trading Company (with the notable exception of the US sales companies which reported to COM, the corporate group).

In 1985, in an attempt to rationalize and clarify this situation, the 120 staff of COM were merged in to the 1,500 person METC organization (Exhibit 9). In addition to uniting Matsushita's overseas strategy, the purpose of the change was to speed up decision-making, decrease overall corporate costs and better integrate overseas sales and marketing operations.

Changing Systems

The tight division level systems and controls that were at the centre of Matsushita's domestic operations had not been transferred to the overseas companies with the same rigour. The ROI measures were rendered meaningless by the fact that the overseas companies were financed by the parent company, and the profit centre concept was undermined by the fact that the divisions received only a cost-based transfer price, and a modest 3 per cent royalty.

Increasingly, however, sales and profit numbers were consolidated and reviewed on a worldwide basis, and by the early 1980s, product divisions were receiving globally consolidated return on sales reports for their businesses. Formally, the financial statements of all foreign subsidiaries were consolidated in the accounts of METC whose performance, like that of other Matsushita units, was evaluated primarily on the basis of growth in sales and market share. The financial plans of newly established overseas companies normally required that they recover accumulated operating deficits and begin to make profits by the end of their third year of existence.

In addition to these administrative systems, the international operating controls were also changing. In the late 1960s and early 1970s, the ability of central product divisions to control overseas operations was greatly facilitated by the fact that offshore plants had equipment designed by the parent company, followed manufacturing procedures dictated by the centre, and used materials supplied from Matsushita's domestic plants. With increasing pressures for more local sourcing and independence, however, the divisions' overseas operations departments were unable to continue managing as directly or simply. Instead of controlling the inputs, they were forced to monitor output on a variety of dimensions (quality, productivity, inventory levels, etc.), tailoring the nature and number of such reporting systems to the size and maturity of the particular subsidiary.

Finally, the company began adding greater sophistication to its strategic planning systems. Upon assuming control in 1977, President Yamashita began introducing medium-term planning as a means of counterbalancing the short-term perspective created by the company's financial systems. At first these three-year plans were largely financially oriented and domestic in focus, but gradually Yamashita began asking for more qualitative data and began suggesting that plans be prepared for the worldwide business. By the mid-1980s, global product strategies began to appear in the three-year plans. The final strategy for a given business in a particular country was the outcome of negotiations between the MEI product division representing the global business strategy and the appropriate METC regional division which had prepared geographic strategies.

Headquarters–subsidiary relations

Tomio Koide, the managing director of Matsushita's subsidiary in Singapore described the way foreign subsidiaries are managed in the company:

> Headquarters–subsidiary relations in Matsushita is a process of 'hands-off' management: Japan gives a sales and a profit target and the subsidiary must achieve them. That is the only basis. As long as these targets are achieved, local management has complete autonomy on everything else. How many people are required, how much they should be paid, what other expenses should be incurred – they are all subsidiary decisions and nothing is told by Japan.

However, 'Mike' Matsuoka, the President of MELAC, the company's largest European production subsidiary in Cardiff (Wales) emphasized that failure to meet targets forfeits the freedom: 'Losses show bad health and invite many doctors from Japan who provide advice and support.'

There were many linkages between headquarters and subsidiaries, extending across all levels of the organization. For example, in the video department of MECA, the North American sales subsidiary, the vice-president was a veteran of Matsushita Electric Trading Company, and remained a member of its top management team that decided overall strategy for the North American market. As the vice-president of MECA, he implemented the strategy that he had helped to form. The department general manager was also an expatriate who had spent over ten years in the video product division of MEI and maintained close contacts with his former colleagues. Finally, the assistant manager in the department, the most junior expatriate in the subsidiary, had worked for five years in the central production plant in Japan and acted as the key link between the factory and the subsidiary.

The general managers of all foreign subsidiaries visited the company headquarters at least 2–3 times each year, and the heads of the larger subsidiaries travelled to Japan almost every month. Other key managers went to Japan at least annually. Each subsidiary also received numerous visits from senior corporate managers each year and major operations hosted at least one headquarters manager almost each day of the year. One headquarters manager estimated there were 5,500 trips from the parent company to overseas operations during 1985. Face-to-face meetings were a vital part of the company's style of operation. 'Figures are important, but the meetings are necessary to develop judgement,' said one senior manager. Telephone, telex and fax communication between headquarters and overseas subsidiaries was intensive. In particular, regular after-hours telephone calls between headquarters managers and their expatriate colleagues abroad represented a vital management link.

Foreign production subsidiaries were required to buy key components from within the company but could choose their internal source. In recent years, they gained more freedom to purchase minor and less critical parts from local vendors as long as quality standards could be assured. While they were expected to carry out all routine production tasks independently, corporate technical personnel became intimately involved when plans called for major expansion or change.

Sales subsidiaries, similarly, had some choice with regard to the products they sold. Each year the company held a two-week merchandising and product planning meeting, essentially a large internal trade show, in which all product divisions displayed the items that would be available during the following model year. Three to five managers from each sales subsidiary attended these week-long meetings to 'buy' the specific products they wanted for their local markets and also to suggest changes in product design. The ultimate decision on product choice, however, rested with corporate managers who could over-rule the subsidiary if introduction of a particular item in a particular market was thought to be of strategic importance to the company.

Transfer prices for products supplied from Japan were negotiated annually and increasingly took into account not only production costs but also the conditions prevailing in the subsidiary's market. In general, the plant was expected to absorb the effect of any changes in its costs during the year, while the subsidiary was expected to deal with changes in market conditions without modifying the transfer price.

Role of Expatriates

Matsushita had over 700 expatriate managers and technicians in its overseas operations, but defended that relatively high number by describing the complexity of their task. Not only did these managers have to transmit a complex and subtle philosophy, they also had to act as the communication links translating information about the overseas environment to headquarters and transferring the company's strategies and technologies to the local companies. In the words of one manager,

> This communication role almost always requires a manager from the parent company. Even if a local manager speaks Japanese, he would not have the long experience that is needed to build relationships and understand our management processes.

For this reason, there were a few senior positions that were typically reserved for expatriates, the most visible being that of the subsidiary general manager. 'The key task of the general manager', according to the GM of a major international production centre, 'is to translate the Matsushita philosophy to the local environment. To do that, you really have to have experienced the philosophy as it is practised in Japan.' Indeed, all headquarters employees assigned to foreign companies received additional training in the company's impressive Overseas Training Centre (OTC) before departing. A central focus of OTC was to ensure that expatriates had a deep understanding of the company's philosophy so they could adapt it appropriately to the culture to which they were transferring the philosophy.

Another position usually reserved for an expatriate was that of accounting manager. These individuals reported directly to the corporate accounting division at the headquarters, and were expected to 'mercilessly expose the truth' so that problems could be identified and acted upon quickly. These accounting managers formed a very well-defined cadre within the company, and received intensive on-the-job training at the headquarters for about nine years before taking up foreign assignments.

Technical managers were the third common expatriate roles, and were responsible for transferring product and process technologies. They also served as the product division's eyes and ears, translating local market needs to the engineering and development groups for development of new products and enhancement of existing models.

Most expatriate managers were posted abroad only once in their careers and spent between four and eight years in the same subsidiary. When assigned, each Japanese manager identified a senior colleague as his headquarters contact and counsellor, to keep him in touch with company changes, provide him with advice on official and personal matters, and arrange for an appropriate re-entry position. This mentor role supplemented the formal developmental responsibilities that rested with a senior manager in the employees' parent division, who evaluated and rewarded the expatriate, with the input of his local manager.

Socially, the expatriate groups spent much of their time together, and some local managers felt that key decisions were often taken off-hours, in these informal gatherings. However, considerable effort was made to keep local nationals in the foreign subsidiaries informed and involved. Key decisions would be taken at regular weekly management meetings, usually after lengthy discussion. Senior managers admitted that the impression that local managers could not achieve top-level decision-making positions had impeded recruitment in the past, but felt this problem was diminishing.

NEW CHALLENGES, NEW RESPONSES

Although he took charge at a time of unprecedented growth and profitability, by the mid-1980s Mr Yamashita had become increasingly concerned about Matsushita's long-term prosperity. In particular, he feared that the two growth engines of the company – international exports and the VCR product line – had both become vulnerable. He reminded his managers that despite the company's strong situation, leadership positions could be lost quickly.

> 'In 1956, Matsushita's sales were about half Hitachi's,' he said. 'But Hitachi failed to adjust to the times, and by 1973 Matsushita had overtaken it. Today, NEC's sales are about half of ours, but if we do not take action, we will be overtaken by NEC within ten years for sure.'

In Yamashita's view, in order to continue to grow, Matsushita first had to respond to the growing protectionist pressures that threatened the 50 per cent of sales that came from abroad. Second, it had to reduce its dependence on consumer electronics which also represented about half the volume and over 75 per cent of international sales. To reduce these risks and prepare for the future, Mr Yamashita set in motion a variety of different programmes and activities, but central to his plans were two core initiatives – Operation Localization and the ACTION programmes.

Operation Localization

From his earliest days as president of Matsushita, Mr Yamashita had been aware of rising protectionist sentiment in the world, and had urged his company to seek a better balance between exports from Japan, overseas local production, and exports from overseas companies to other countries. Despite his internal urgings and external statements, however, the company's foreign sales grew as fast as its transfer of production to offshore plants, and as it entered the 1980s with 50 per cent of its sales volume coming from abroad, it seemed unable to increase its offshore production levels beyond 10 per cent.

But pressure continued to mount and the flood of VCRs into Europe in the early 1980s triggered a response similar to the reaction in the US to colour TV imports a decade earlier.[1] In the United States, rising trade deficits were being hotly debated in Congress and a strong protectionist sentiment was gaining broad political support. Realizing he had to take a stronger stand, in 1982 Yamashita launched 'Operation Localization', that set an ambitious target of increasing overseas production to 25 per cent, or half overseas sales, by 1990. As a means to achieve this target he set out a programme of four localizations that he expected his overseas operations to follows – localization of personnel, technology, material and capital.

In personnel appointments, the objective was to increase the number of local nationals in key positions. For example, in the United States, while the chief executive of MECA was still Japanese, three of the six company presidents reporting to him were Americans; halfway around the world a similar pattern existed in Matsushita Electric (Taiwan) where the majority of production divisions were now headed by local Chinese managers. In each case, however, the local managers were supported by senior Japanese advisers who maintained a direct link with the parent company.

To localize technology and material, the company had tried to help its national companies to evolve from what the manager of the Overseas Operations Department of the TV Division termed 'Phase I and Phase II' operations to become 'Phase III' facilities. In contrast to the Phase I plant which is almost completely dependent on the parent for equipment, supplies and manufacturing technology, the Phase III company is one which has developed the expertise to source equipment locally, modify designs to meet local market needs and incorporate local components, and adapt corporate processes and technologies to accommodate these changes while maintaining the company's quality standards.

By transferring more assets and responsibilities abroad, by upgrading local management and technological capabilities and by giving national units more independence and autonomy, Yamashita hoped that Matsushita's overseas companies would develop more of the innovative capability and entrepreneurship which he had long admired in the national organizations of arch rival Philips. These subsidiaries of the giant Dutch multinational not only adapted central products and strategies to meet their local needs, but also used the technical and other resources available in their host countries to create new products that the company could use worldwide. In contrast, Matsushita subsidiaries historically had played the role of efficient implementers, adopting central products and strategies instead of taking the lead to create their own. Past efforts to develop technological capabilities abroad had failed due to the company's highly centralized R & D structure in Japan. For example, when it acquired Motorola's TV business in the United States, the local R & D group had been responsible for a number of major innovations both before the acquisition and also immediately afterwards. But this important local capability was lost when most of the American engineers resigned in response to what they felt to be excessive functional control from Japan. Yamashita was determined that the localization programme would solve such problems in the future.

But, despite important achievements in raising the local content of many of its overseas products, replacing expatriates with local nationals, and linking its overseas companies into their local financial markets, Matsushita was having difficulty evolving into the kind of truly international company it aspired to be. In an unusual move for a Japanese executive, Mr Yamashita showed his frustration in an interview with the London *Financial Times* when he expressed his unhappiness with the company's TV plant in Cardiff (Wales). The basic problem was, despite the transfer of substantial resources and the delegation of many responsibilities to the plant, it remained too dependent on the centre. He wanted to see it become more innovative and self-sufficient.

To support the localization thrust structurally, the foreign production subsidiaries which were earlier controlled by the product divisions of MEI were brought under the control of METC, thereby consolidating the company's international operations within one central administrative unit. Because MEI's product divisions received only 3 per cent royalties for foreign production against at least 10 per cent return on sales for exports from Japan, separating the foreign subsidiaries from MEI was considered important to prevent this factor from impeding the development of manufacturing capacity outside Japan. But opinions on the implementation of the localization programme were divided. Some subsidiary managers felt that localization could weaken their relationships with headquarters managers and reduce their access to central resources and expertise. If export income began contributing less, the central product division managers could give priority to domestic needs over foreign operations. A senior manager in one of the company's largest foreign subsidiaries voiced his concerns quite explicitly: 'Our main strengths lie in MEI's product divisions in Japan and we have to use those strengths to grow. Without them, we do not have a chance.' A senior headquarters manager raised another critical question:

> Given the low growth environment, foreign production must come at the cost of domestic production. What will that mean for employment in Japan? Protecting the interests of employees is one of our greatest moral commitments. We cannot sacrifice that for any reason.

Others voiced concerns about whether the company could maintain its innovative product development record and cost and quality advantages if control over R & D and production became more decentralized.

'ACTION' 86: Strategic Redirection at Home

In 1979, soon after taking over as president of MEI, Yamashita had initiated the first 'ACTION' programme aimed at revitalizing the company. The word ACTION was an acronym of six major thrusts envisaged in the programme: Act immediately, Cost reduction, Topical products, Imaginative marketing, Organization revitalization, New management strength. By drawing attention to the fact that over 65 per cent of Matsushita's revenues came from traditional consumer products most of which were entering the mature phase, the ACTION programme was aimed at refocusing the company in new and growing sectors such as semiconductors, robots, computers and other instruments for automated offices and factory floors. The company planned to build these new lines without dismantling the traditional ones. So large was this refocusing task that the programme had to be renewed in 1983 and again in 1986.

In 1986, Matsushita was already Japan's largest robot manufacturer, and the domestic leader in office automation products like the facsimile machines and push-button telephones. Besides producing its own PCs under the 'Panfacon' brand name in a joint venture with Fujitsu, the company also supplied IBM's 5550 personal computers on OEM basis. It has also begun to move aggressively into the area it called the 'new media': studio equipment for cable TV stations, big screen TV sets for stadium use, and telecommunication systems for home automation.

In the area of technology, Yamashita saw the central challenge this way:

> Lifecycles of products have become shorter and technological innovations more rapid. For example, the product costs of LSI becomes half in six months. If we cannot lead to develop products at the beginning, we will never catch up. R & D has become the key to success.

The company was strong in linear semiconductor technology, but not in digital technology which was essential in the new businesses. It also lagged behind such domestic competitors as Hitachi, NEC, Sharp, Fujitsu, Ricoh and Canon in technologies for computers and copiers, the two products that played key roles in office automation. To overcome these deficiencies, management had substantially increased the research budget from 200 billion yen (4.2 per cent of sales) in 1984 to 260 billion yen (5.7 per cent of sales) in 1986. Semiconductors, optical technology, computer and software, and new materials had been defined as the focal points for future research and in all four areas the company planned to become the technology leader rather than a mere application engineering specialist, shrugging off the 'Maneshita' (copy-cat) nickname its earlier strategy of technology followership had created. To make this technological leapfrog possible, MEI had joined Kyoto University in the development of high speed supercomputers, which were expected to be 100 times larger than those available from Cray Research, Fujitsu and IBM. It had also created four new research laboratories at a total cost of over ¥40 billion. And, in a symbolic gesture to emphasize the importance of R & D, President Yamashita had taken on the additional post of head of the central research laboratory.

But, according to Yamashita, by far the biggest challenge lay in revitalizing the Matsushita organization. In his view, the divisionalized organization had developed 'structural weaknesses'. In a period of low growth, the profitability-oriented responsibility accounting system was causing division managers to emphasize short-term results and to avoid risky development investments. Furthermore, competition among divisions impeded transfers of information, resources, and people across different parts of the organization. A large number of trained engineers was needed for the growing information equipment business and the company was facing difficulties in recruiting an adequate number of people at the entry level. The problem was particularly acute for software engineers the demand for whom in Japan far exceeded domestic supply. However, despite huge difficulties in recruiting scarce software engineers for the new information and communication businesses, internal competition made it difficult to transfer specialists from one division to another. Besides, with the integration of information technologies, new products were increasingly taking the form of multifunctional 'systems' rather than stand-alone equipment, and joint actions on the part of multiple divisions were becoming more and more essential. Under these circumstances, the invigorating force of divisional autonomy and interdivisional competition had become less important than the need for internal transfers, sharing and synergies.

Although there was strong organizational commitment for the ACTION programme, privately some managers expressed some doubts about such a major technological and strategic redirection. While supporting the need for acquiring new technologies, they feared that by de-emphasizing traditional products, the company might lose its competitiveness in its existing markets. They expected the consumer electronics business to re-emerge as a high growth sector in the 1990s with the advent of integrated home entertainment systems, and feared that unless Matsushita maintained its technological and market leadership in this business, it might be overtaken by companies like Sony and Philips, which continued to invest heavily for the development of such systems. Others believed that the autonomy and responsibility emphasized by the 'one product – one division' logic had allowed the company to respond quickly and flexibly to market changes, while motivating managers to work hard to increase revenues and reduce costs, and any significant change in the divisional structure might compromise Matsushita's culture and philosophy, undermining its source of strength.

The Situation in 1986

Many of Mr Yamashita's fears seemed to be justified in 1986 when sales declined 10 per cent and profits dropped by over 30 per cent compared to 1985. While domestic sales had remained flat, international sales had collapsed (Exhibit 10). The rising yen, deteriorating trade relations with China and increasing competition in the video market (particularly with the new Korean entrants) all contributed to the problem.

Meanwhile, overseas production levels were still stuck at about 10 per cent (although geographic mix was also shifting as shown in Exhibit 11) and the boom in VCR sales had kept the company dependent on that single product for a quarter of its sales. What the company was attempting was, to borrow *Fortune*'s colourful metaphor, 'to get the new giant to perch on the old giant's shoulders without both of them toppling over'. In early 1987, there were many who were wondering if the company could pull off such an astounding feat of strength, skill and balance.

EXHIBIT 1
Comparison of leading manufacturers of electrical and electronic products, 1985.

Corporation	Matsushita	Hitachi	Sony	IBM	GE	Philips
Sales ($million)	20,749	29,473	5,777	50,056	28,285	18,079
Net Profits ($million)	1,012	884	297	6,555	2,336	277
Net Assets ($million)	10,130	10,251	2,832	31,990	13,094	5,865
TOTAL ASSETS ($million)	21,452	30,378	6,841	52,634	26,432	19,202
Equity Ratio (%)	47.2	33.7	32.3	60.8	52.6	30.5
Average Annual Growth: 1980–5 (%)						
Sales	11.6	8.3	10.0	13.8	2.5	10.4
Net Profits	14.6	9.1	1.2	13.0	9.1	21.6

Source: Yamaichi Company Report 86-14, September 1986.

EXHIBIT 2
Net profit margin of MEI by quarter, 1983.

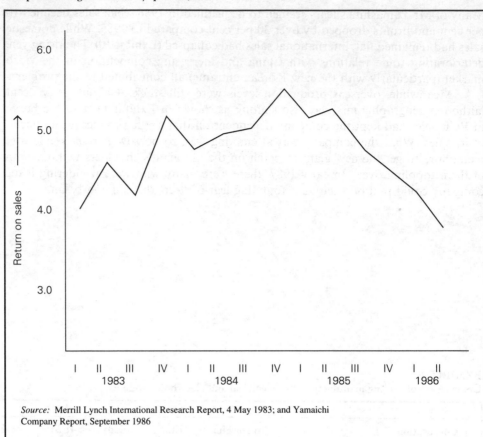

Source: Merrill Lynch International Research Report, 4 May 1983; and Yamaichi
Company Report, September 1986

EXHIBIT 3
Matsushita creed and philosophy: selected excerpts.

Matsushita Company Creed
Through our industrial activities, we strive to foster progress, to promote the general welfare of society, and to devote ourselves to furthering the development of world culture.

Seven Spirits of Matsushita
- Service through Industry
- Fairness
- Harmony and Cooperation
- Struggle for Progress
- Courtesy and Humility
- Adjustment and Assimilation
- Gratitude

KM's Business Philosophy (selected quotations)
- 'The purpose of an enterprise is to contribute to society by supplying goods of high quality at low prices in ample quantity.'
- 'Profit comes in compensation for contribution to society ... [it] is a result rather than a goal.'
- 'The responsibility of the manufacturer cannot be relieved until its product is disposed of by the end-user.'
- 'Unsuccessful business employs a wrong management. You should not find its causes in bad fortune, unfavourable surroundings or wrong timing.'
- 'Business appetite has no self-restraining mechanism .... When you notice you have gone too far, you must have the courage to come back.'

EXHIBIT 4
VCR production and market shares, 1981–4.

Company	Production Shares (%)				Market Shares (%)			
	1981	1982	1983	1984	1981	1982	1983	1984
VHS Group								
Matsushita (incl. JVC)	36.8	36.5	45.1	41.7	25.2	25.3	24.6	24.0
Hitachi	9.5	9.9	11.1	14.5	2.0	3.4	4.0	3.8
Sharp	6.8	7.2	8.5	9.1	1.2	1.5	3.0	3.5
Mitsubishi	3.2	3.0	3.4	4.4	1.0	1.0	2.0	2.0
RCA	–	–	–	–	28.0	22.0	16.0	16.0
GE	–	–	–	–	3.3	5.0	5.5	5.0
Others*	11.9	15.1	6.8	10.7	11.2	12.6	16.5	24.3
TOTAL VHS	68.2	71.7	74.9	80.4	71.9	70.8	71.6	78.6
Betamax Group								
Sony	17.9	14.1	11.8	9.1	14.2	13.0	7.0	6.5
Sanyo	9.2	9.5	7.7	5.5	2.6	4.0	5.0	5.0
Toshiba	4.2	4.1	3.6	3.3	1.5	1.0	1.2	1.5
Others**	0.5	0.6	2.0	1.7	6.0	4.1	2.6	–
TOTAL BETAMAX	31.8	28.3	25.1	19.6	24.3	22.1	15.8	13.0

*Includes Fisher, Philips (Magnavox, Sylvania, Philco), Zenith (from 1984), Montgomery Ward, J.C. Penny, Emerson, Akai, Tatung, Kenwood, etc.
**Contributed almost exclusively by Zenith, before switching to VHS in 1984.
Source: Michael Cusumano, 'Note on the VTR industry and market development: Japan, the US and Europe, Ca 1975–1985', Unpublished paper, Harvard Business School, May 1985.

EXHIBIT 5
Percentage contribution to total sales by product and region.

	Domestic %	Foreign %
1. Video Equipment		
VTR	13	43
Colour TV	8	11
Black and white TV	1	2
Total video	22	56
2. Audio Equipment	7	19
3. Home Appliances	24	6
4. Information/Industrial Equipment	19	6
5. Energy/Kitchen Appliances	8	2
6. Electrical Components	12	4
7. Others	8	7

Source: Author's estimates based on company balance sheet.

EXHIBIT 6
Matsushita's production and selling prices of VTRs, 1977–84.

	Production (in 000s units)	Average Price in Japan (in 000s yen)	Relative Production (1977 as base)	Relative Price (1977 as base)
1977	205	172	1.00	100
1978	526	144	2.56	82
1979	624	135	3.04	68
1980	1,273	127	6.21	64
1981	2,701	114	13.18	60
1982	3,520	98	17.17	54
1983	5,228	83	25.50	46
1984	6,860	73	33.46	39

EXHIBIT 7
Sales breakdown by divisions: 1981–5.

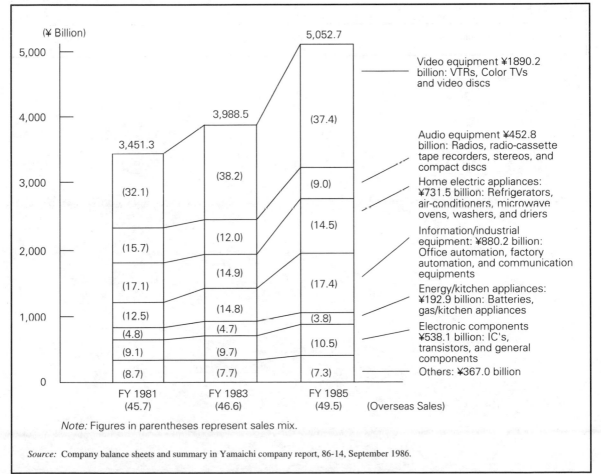

Note: Figures in parentheses represent sales mix.

Source: Company balance sheets and summary in Yamaichi company report, 86-14, September 1986.

EXHIBIT 8
Total profits contributed by various products.

% of Total Profits Contributed by:	1977	1978	1979	1980	1981	1982	1983	1984
1. Video Division								
VCR	4	9	16	26	39	44	44	45
Colour TV	22	20	17	16	11	10	10	9
Black and White TV	1	1	1	1	1	1	1	1
Total Video	27	30	34	43	51	55	55	55
2. Audio Division	17	14	10	11	10	8	7	7
3. Home Appliances	18	18	16	9	9	8	9	8
4. Information/ Industrial Equipment	14	16	16	14	12	12	13	13
5. Energy/Kitchen Appliances	8	8	9	8	5	6	6	6
6. Electronic Components	9	8	8	8	7	6	6	6
7. Others	8	7	7	7	6	5	5	5

Source: Merrill Lynch International Research Report, 4 May 1983.

EXHIBIT 9
Changes in Matsushita's headquarters organization for international companies.

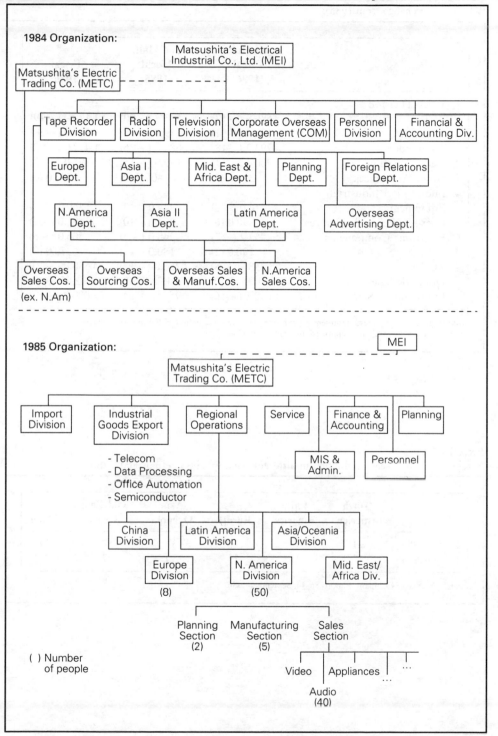

EXHIBIT 10
Operating results, 1986
(¥ billions; % change from 1985).

	1st Half: Fiscal 1986	2nd Half: Fiscal 1986	Fiscal 1986
1. Video Division			
VCR	586.8 (−18)	533.2 (−20)	1,120.0 (−19)
Colour TV	170.4 (−21)	139.6 (−38)	310.0 (−30)
Total video	793.2 (−18)	684.0 (−26)	1,477.0 (−22)
2. Audio Division	200.0 (−11)	195.0 (−15)	395.0 (−13)
3. Home Appliances	338.5 (4)	406.5 (0)	745.0 (2)
4. Information/Industrial			
Equipment	416.0 (−2)	444.0 (−3)	860.0 (−2)
5. Energy/Kitchen Appliances	99.0 (6)	99.0 (−10)	198.0 (−2)
6. Electronic Components	257.2 (−7)	248.0 (−5)	505.0 (−6)
7. Others	190.0 (2)	180.0 (−1)	370.0 (0)
TOTAL	2,293.9 (−8)	2,256.0 (−12)	4,550.0 (−10)
Domestic Sales	1,254.8 (0)	1,304.0 (0)	2,550.0 (0)
International Sales	1,048.1 (−16)	952.0 (−24)	2,000.0 (−20)

Note: Figures in parentheses represent growth rate over the same period of the previous year.
Source: Yamaichi Company Report, 86–14, September 1986.

EXHIBIT 11
Percentage of overseas production in different regions, 1985 actuals and 1988 plans.

	North America	Latin America	Europe	Asia Oceania	Mid-East Africa	China
Fiscal 1985	21	11	10	37	7	14
Fiscal 1988	19	11	11	30	7	22

Source: Yamaichi Company Report, 86–14, September 1986.

THE BODY SHOP INTERNATIONAL*

> Business people have got to be the instigators of change. They have the money and the power to make a difference. A company that makes a profit from society has a responsibility to return something to that society. (Anita Roddick, founder and managing director of The Body Shop)

'Let's face it, I can't take a moisture cream too seriously,' Anita Roddick, founder of The Body Shop, was fond of saying. 'What really interests me is the revolutionary way in which trade can be used as an instrument for change for the better.'[1] A heretical statement for the head of the fastest-growing company in the cosmetics industry. But then, ever since she started The Body Shop in 1976, Roddick had made a habit of going against the tide of the industry's established business practices.

The Body Shop did not advertise, avoided traditional distribution channels, spent as little as possible on packaging and used product labels to discuss ingredients and their properties rather than making miraculous claims for its products. Its products were based on all-natural ingredients, and were sold in refillable, recyclable containers. But the most unconventional of all, was The Body Shop's strong social message. As Roddick explained: 'Businesses are the true planetary citizens, they can push frontiers, they can change society. There hasn't been an ethical or philosophical code of behaviour for any business body ever, and I think it's going to have to change.'[2]

---

*This case was prepared by Professor Christopher A. Bartlett and Research Associates Kenton Elderkin and Krista McQuade as the basis for class discussion rather than to illustrate either effective or ineffective handling of an administrative situation. It is written from public sources only.

From a single storefront in 1976, The Body Shop had grown to 576 shops by 1991, trading in 38 countries and 18 languages. Worldwide retail sales from company stores and licensees were estimated at $391 million. Along the way, The Body Shop was voted UK Company of the Year in 1985, and UK Retailer of the Year in 1989. In addition, Roddick had been the Veuve Cliquot Businesswoman of the Year in 1985, and Communicator of the Year in 1987. In 1988, she was awarded the prestigious Order of the British Empire by Queen Elizabeth (who herself was rumoured to use The Body Shop's Peppermint Foot Lotion).

But in the early 1990s, some began wondering if The Body Shop's phenomenal run of success was fading. Could its unconventional retailing approach succeed in the highly competitive US market? Would its quirky organization and values be effective as it grew in size and scope? And could it survive the eventual departure of its founder?

ANITA RODDICK: THE ENTREPRENEUR

> The world of business has taught me nothing ... I honestly believe I would not have succeeded if I had been taught about business.[3] (Anita Roddick)

The Story of a Start-Up

Born to Italian-immigrant parents, Roddick (*née* Perella) grew up working in the family-owned café in Littlehampton, West Sussex. Trained in education, she taught briefly in a local elementary school before accepting a position as a library researcher for the *International Herald Tribune* in Paris. Next, she moved to Geneva, where she joined the United Nations International Labour Organization to work with issues of Third World women's rights. With money saved, she travelled throughout the South Pacific and Africa, developing a fascination along the way for the simplicity and effectiveness of the beauty practices of the women she encountered. As she came to know the properties of the ingredients they used to care for their skin and hair, Anita began experimenting with her own natural cosmetics.

Returning to England, she met Gordon Roddick, a Scots poet and adventurer who shared her love of travel. The birth of two daughters forced the Roddicks to settle down, and the couple decided to convert a Victorian house in Brighton into a hotel. In 1976, however, they sold their business so Gordon could fulfil a lifelong dream of trekking by horse from Buenos Aires to New York City – a journey that would take up to two years. Anita agreed to the plan ('Gordon never was a boring man') and, at 33, undertook to support the family. She had an idea for a shop that dated back to her travelling days.

With a £4,000 bank loan (approximately $6,000), Roddick developed a line of 25 skin and hair care products based on natural ingredients. Sourcing exotic ingredients like jojoba oil and rhassoul mud from a local herbalist, she prepared the first product batches on her kitchen stove and packaged them in the cheapest containers she could find – urine-sample bottles. Handwritten labels provided detailed information about the ingredients and their properties. A local art student designed her logo for £25. The Body Shop name – a tongue in cheek inspiration Anita took from car repair shops she had seen in the United States – turned out to be a potential liability when she located her first outlet in a small shop near a funeral parlour. When her new neighbour's solicitor threatened to sue unless she changed her shop's name, Roddick took the story to the local newspaper. The curiosity inspired by the subsequent article assured that her first day of business, 27 March 1976, was an unqualified success.

Roddick gradually developed a loyal clientele. Some found the natural products less irritating to sensitive skin; others liked their novel aromas and textures; and many just enjoyed the relaxed, honest shop environment. As the sole employee, Anita formulated new products, ran the store, purchased supplies, kept the books and constantly tried to draw attention to her business. (In one successful ruse, she sprinkled strawberry essence along the street leading to her door, in an attempt to lure customers by the pleasing aroma.)

After a successful summer, Roddick exchanged a half-share in her fledgling business: for a £4,000 investment by a local businessman, funding the opening of a second store. In April 1977, when Gordon returned (his horse had died in the Andes), he hit upon the idea of franchising as a way to continue expansion despite limited capital. When the first two franchises in nearby towns both succeeded, the Roddicks began receiving calls from other interested parties. The business began to take off.

Founding Concepts and Practices

From the beginning, the company was an extension of Anita Roddick's personal philosophy and convictions. Although these were not formalized early on, her intense involvement in the growing organization shaped its operations. Yet she freely acknowledged she 'didn't have a clue about business matters', and from the early days, Gordon managed the financial and administrative aspects.

Roddick's first goal for the company was simple: survival. 'The Body Shop style developed out of World War II mentality of shortages, utility goods and rationing', said Roddick. 'It was imposed by sheer necessity and the simple fact I had no money.'[4] To make her original selection look larger, for example, she offered each product in five sizes – creating a choice much appreciated by her customers. Due to a cash flow that prevented her buying more bottles, she created a refill service at a 15 per cent discount. This service subsequently appealed to a new generation of environmentally conscious consumers. Detailed labelling information had originally been necessary because of the products' unfamiliar ingredients, but later seemed totally in tune with a consumer awareness movement. Even the trademark Body Shop green colour – now so politically correct – was chosen originally because it was most effective in concealing the damp that showed through the walls of the first store. Roddick recalled:

> There was a grace we had when we started – the grace that you didn't have to bullshit and tell lies. We didn't know you could. We thought we had to be accountable. How do you establish accountability in a cosmetics business? We looked at the big companies. They put labels on the products. We thought what was printed on the label had to be truthful. I mean, we were really that naïve.[5]

In addition to the products, Roddick also strove to create a unique environment in her stores – one of honesty, excitement and fun. Rather than become over-sophisticated, she focused on the elements of what she called 'trading':

> You set up a business without any understanding of business vocabulary. If you throw away all those words, you have trading going on....It's just buying and selling, with an added bit for me, which is the magical arena where people come together – that is, the shop.... It's making your product so glorious that people don't mind buying it from you at a profit. Too many businesses have gotten distracted with management structures and . . . making money, that they've forgotten that they are just buyers and sellers. That's why I will never dilute the image of the shops. It's all just trading.[6]

Building on the Foundation

The Body Shop experienced phenomenal growth through the 1980s, expanding sales at a rate of 50 per cent (see Exhibit 1). In April 1984, when the stock was floated on London's Unlisted Securities market, it opened at 95 pence and closed that afternoon at 165 pence. In January 1986, when it obtained a full listing on the London Stock Exchange, the stock was selling at 820 pence and had become known as 'the shares that defy gravity'.* By February 1991, the company's market value stood at £350 million ($591 million).

The products and the stores had also evolved, but had remained true to the original concepts. Entering a Body Shop anywhere in the world, the customer experienced brightly-lit, open spaces, trimmed in dark green, with a black-and-white tiled floor. Neat stacks of black-capped, green-labelled plastic bottles lined wall shelves, their monotony broken by pyramids of brightly coloured soap bars or displays of natural loofah back scrubbers, potpourri and T-shirts. Cards in front of each display offered information about products with simple and descriptive names like Orchid Oil Cleansing Milk, Carrot Moisture Cream and Seaweed and Birch Shampoo. A self-service perfume bar featured natural oils that could be used either as perfume, or added as scents to a selection of non-perfumed lotions. The whole experience, in Roddick's vision, was designed to be 'theatre, pure and simple'.

Products were priced more expensively than mass merchandised cosmetics, but well under exclusive department store lines. Sales staff were trained to be friendly and knowledgeable, but never overbearing. Stacks of pamphlets provided information on a range of topics, from 'Hair, Who Needs It?', to 'The Body Shop Approach to Packaging' or 'Against Animal Testing'. In one corner, a giant product information manual described each product in detail. Noticeably lacking, for a cosmetics retail company, were any photographs of models with beautiful hair and perfect skin. Roddick was fond of saying that her concept of beauty was Mother Theresa not some bimbo: 'There are no magic potions, no miracle cures, no rejuvenating creams. Skin care products can do nothing more than cleanse, polish and protect. That's it. End of story.'[7]

---

*The Roddicks retained 30 per cent of the equity, Ian McGlinn, the source of the original £4,000 investment, held another 30 per cent, and an additional 7 per cent had been distributed to franchisees.

> It turned out that my instinctive trading values were dramatically opposed to the standard practices in the cosmetics industry. I look at what they are doing and walk in the opposite direction.[8] (Anita Roddick)

As she built her business, Roddick developed most of The Body Shop's unique operating practices and management policies to respond to opportunities she perceived. From product development to human resource management, The Body Shop had been described as 'innovative', 'daring' and even 'radical'. But there was no question it was successful (see Exhibit 2).

Franchising

Of the 576 shops worldwide, only 62 were company owned, but these served the important role of testing new products and marketing concepts, and sensing customer interests and trends. Roddick readily conceded that The Body Shop's rapid growth would not have been possible without the important external source of financing that franchising represented. Independently managed franchises allowed her to concentrate on the development of new product lines and the company's global vision, rather than issues of administration or personnel management. The franchise contract was for 5–10 years, and involved an investment of £150,000–£200,000 ($270,000–$360,000). The start-up cost included shop fittings, opening day stock, a percentage of the location's rent (The Body Shop maintained the lease) and a licensing fee of approximately £5,000 ($9,000) for The Body Shop name. The company chose the sites in high-traffic areas, and underperforming franchises were often relocated. Typically, it took a franchise two to three years to become profitable. Overseas, the company role was taken by a head franchisee appointed in each country.

Anita Roddick kept strict control over the franchising process – no small task with over 5,000 applicants at any one time. The process, which involved a personality test, a home visit and an assessment of the candidate's business acumen and attitude towards people and the environment, took as long as three years. Roddick always conducted the final interview, and was known for asking unexpected questions. ('How would you like to die?' 'Who is your favourite heroine in literature?') Her objective was to ensure that the image she developed for her company, and the principles it was based on, were not diluted through franchising. 'We choose as franchisees only people who are passionate about our product and our ides,' she explained.[9] Once selected, the candidate was required to undergo extensive training on product knowledge, merchandising and store operations.

Roddick felt that one reason why the cosmetics industry had become dishonest and exploitative was that it was dominated by men who traded on women's fears. She felt business practices could be improved substantially 'if they were guided by "feminine prinicples" – like love and care and intuition.'[10] As a consequence, she admitted to a preference for women as franchisees:

> What is wonderful about the company is that 90 per cent of the people running the shops are female, have no formal business training, and yet are brilliant retailers and brilliant business people. . . . This business is run by women. Policy decisions are made

by women, all the words are written by women, product development is controlled by women. So our customer, our female customer, believes that we have a covert understanding of women. It gives us an extraordinary edge. It's The Body Shop's secret ingredient.

Product Development and Production

Believing that the cosmetics industry had a lot to learn from the skin and hair care practices of women all over the world, Roddick spent 2–4 months of every year travelling to remote corners of the world, with an anthropologist. She was particularly fascinated by the rituals surrounding major life events such as birth, death and marriage. 'I ask them about their bodies inch by inch. "How do you clean your hair?" "What makes your skin soft?" "What makes your hair shine?"'[11]

In Sri Lanka, she saw women rubbing their faces with the skins of freshly cut pineapple, producing a fresh, clean look. Later, she learned that pineapple had an enzyme which acted to remove dead cells from the surface of the skin. This was translated into The Body Shop's Pineapple Face Wash. In the Polynesian islands, she saw women rubbing an untreated extract from the seeds of the cocoa plant into their hair to make shine. Cocoa butter was then incorporated into a number of products, making The Body Shop one of the world's largest importers of this raw material. In Ghana, she discovered Shea-butter oil, a product extracted from an African tree nut; in Hawaii, she learned of anfeltia conccina, a seaweed extract incorporated into her Seaweed and Birch Shampoo; in Japan, she picked up tsubaki oil, extracted from camellias.

Even back in England, Roddick would approach anyone, 'from taxi drivers, to shop assistants, to your mother-in-law' to inquire about personal care habits. She wrote to the chairman of Quaker Oats, in Chicago, to ask about the cosmetic properties of oatmeal. He sent her a formula for a protein extract which she discovered could be used in a range of products such as eye shadow and soap. After reading about huge stockpiles of powdered milk in UK warehouses, she telephoned the Milk Marketing Board for information, a conversation which resulted in The Body Shop's Milk Bath. Instead of market research, The Body Shop relied on direct customer ideas and feedback obtained through the widely used suggestion boxes located in each outlet, and six staff members catalogued and replied to ideas submitted.

Initially, product development had been driven by samples brought back in Anita's back pack, and the creativity of the herbalists she had worked with since the startup. Testing had been done on staff volunteers, and because ingredients had been used for centuries, risks were minimal. Eventually, the company employed an outside academic to test for toxicity and effectiveness, and finally, by 1990 established a formal research department in its corporate offices. There was some debate about the extent to which The Body Shop's products were 'natural', and the company acknowledged using some synthetic preservatives, ingredients derived from petrochemicals and artificial colours.

Although over 70 per cent of Body Shop products were supplied by outside contractors, the company hoped to increase its in-house manufacturing from 30 per cent to 50 per cent by the early 1990s. Most of its production occurred in Wick,

West Sussex, where the company had 320,000 square feet of production and warehouse space.

Marketing

It was hard to recognize that The Body Shop was competing in the cosmetics industry. Products were still packaged in plain plastic bottles with simple labels. There were no elaborate claims or promotions. And the products were never 'sale' priced. In an industry where 30 cents on every dollar of sales was typically devoted to advertising, Roddick was proud of the fact that her company had no marketing or advertising department. She despised the traditional marketing-intensive industry practices:

> [The cosmetics industry] makes its money through packaging and advertising, which together are 85 per cent of its costs. Charles Revlon, the founder of Revlon said, 'In the factory we make cosmetics, in the store we sell hope.' And he's right. The cosmetics industry is a dream machine.[12]

Roddick recognized the value of publicity, however, and by 1980 had hired a PR consultant. She openly courted the press, and by her own estimate, generated £2 million worth of free publicity in a year. She was a natural for the role: 'The press like us. I'm always available. I'm loud-mouthed and quotable.'[13]

Because the stores represented the company's primary marketing tool, Roddick used regular visits by regional managers to keep tight control over layout, literature, window displays and operating style. The company's Write Stuff Department – five writers and six graphic designers – created The Body Shop's constantly changing brochures and displays.

In 1990 when The Body Shop was nominated to the UK Marketing Hall of Fame, Roddick insisted her approach was only common sense: 'The trouble with marketing is that consumers are hyped out. The din of advertising and promotion has become so loud, they are becoming cynical about the whole process. What we have tried to do is establish credibility by educating our customers... It humanizes the company, and makes customers feel they are buying from people they know and trust.'[14]

Organization and Human Resources

As The Body Shop grew, so too did Roddick's recognition of the importance of maintaining the enthusiasm and commitment of her employees, 75 per cent of whom were women under 30:

> Most businesses focus all the time on profits, profits, profits ... I have to say I think that is deeply boring. I want to create an electricity and passion that bonds people to the company. You can educate people by their passions, especially young people. You have to find ways to grab their imagination. You want them to feel that they are doing something important ... I'd never get that kind of motivation if we were just selling shampoo and body lotion.[15]

Roddick constantly worked at communications within the company. Every shop had a bulletin board, a fax machine and a video player through which she bombarded staff with information on topics ranging from new products, or causes she supported, to reports on her latest trip or discussions of 'dirty tricks in the cosmetics industry'. The in-house video production company produced a monthly multilingual video magazine, *Talking Shop*, as well as training tapes and documentaries on social campaigns.

Roddick also encouraged upward communication through a suggestion scheme to DODGI (the Department of Damned Good Ideas), through regular meetings of a cross-section of staff, often at her home, and through a 'Red Letter' system which allowed any employee to bypass management and communicate directly with a director. But she was equally aware of the power of informal communication, and unabashedly tapped into the grapevine by planting rumours with the office gossips. She explained the motivation behind her intensive communications:

> What's imperative is the creation of a style that becomes a culture. It may be forced, it may be designed. But that real sense of change, that anarchy – I tell Gordon we need a Department of Surprises – we do whatever we must to preserve that sense of being different. Otherwise, the time will come when everyone who works for us will say The Body Shop is just like every other company.[16]

Roddick took advantage of her travel to visit stores regularly. She ensured she always looked as she was expected to – 'a mess', in her terms, wearing jeans and carrying a knapsack. Typically she told stories, joked about embarrassing moments in her travels, described new products or projects she was working on, and listened to employees' concerns.

She encouraged employees to 'think frivolously' and 'break the rules', and tied bonuses to innovative suggestions. She also introduced a system of two-way assessment, asking staff to evaluate their managers' effectiveness. She detested bureaucracy and kept meetings short by requiring participants to stand through them. Roddick explained:

> To be honest, I tend to encourage separateness and eccentricity because it gets me listened to when its non-threatening. I am desperate to keep the company divorced from the 'greed-is-good' spirit of the City [London's financial community]. For me, the bottom line is keeping my company alive in the most imaginative, breathless, honest way I can. I don't think in all the years I've been running this business there has been one meeting, except for the end-of-year results, where profit has been mentioned.[17]

Extending the family feeling, the company built a £1 million daycare facility for the young children of employees at its Littlehampton headquarters. The charge for this service was staggered by salary level; a worker earning £10,000 paid £30 per week, while one earning £20,000 paid £75 per week. Free daycare slots were offered to social service organizations for emergency placements.

As The Body Shop grew, Roddick saw the need to supplement communications with education. In 1986, it established a training centre in London and began offering courses on the company's products and philosophy, problem hair and skin care, and customer service. Soon, however, there were sessions on topics as diverse as sociology, urban survival, ageing in our society and AIDS. Any employee of the company or its franchisees could sign up, and all courses were free. 'You can train dogs,' explained Roddick. 'We wanted to *educate* and help people realize their own potential.'

THE BODY SHOP PHILOSOPHY

> All the Body Shops around the world form part of a whole that is held together by a common bond. It is underwritten by a common philosophy. This is the strong foundation on which a thriving and successful international company has been built. (Anita Roddick)

As The Body Shop became increasingly successful in a period often characterized as 'The Decade of Greed', Roddick kept pushing herself and others to define the appropriate role for their growing corporation. Going public did not seem to reduce the company's quirkiness as some had predicted. Indeed Roddick seemed little concerned about the investment community's view of The Body Shop, and routinely referred to investors in the stock as 'speculators':

> Most are only interested in the short term and quick profit; they don't come to our annual meetings and they don't respond to our communications. As far as I am concerned, I have no responsibility to these people at all.[18]

Indeed, The Body Shop's stock flotation marked a very different watershed for Anita Roddick:

> Since 1984, the year The Body Shop went public, as far as I am concerned, the business has existed for one reason only – to allow us to use our success to act as a force of social change, to continue the education of our staff, to assist development in the Third World, and above all, to help protect the environment.[19]

Environmental Consciousness

Long a critic of the environmental insensitivity of the cosmetics industry ('Its main products are packaging, garbage and waste,' she claimed), Roddick found in this area a natural focus for her redoubled commitment to a social agenda. Within months of the public stock issue, she had entered into an alliance with Greenpeace, and began campaigning through the shops to 'Save the Whales'. The link was natural since several Body Shop products were based on jojoba oil, a plant-based product which she argued could be substituted for the oil from sperm whales widely used in the cosmetics industry. Roddick soon heard from several franchisees concerned that the campaign was becoming 'too political'. She dismissed their protests.

Within a couple of years, disagreements with Greenpeace led Roddick to switch her primary allegiance to Friends of the Earth, jointly promoting awareness campaigns on acid rain, recycling and ozone layer depletion. Again, she turned over display windows to posters and distributed literature through the shops.

In 1986, the company set up a four-person Environmental Projects Department not only to coordinate the campaigning, but also to ensure that the company's own products and practices were environmentally sound. In addition to using biodegradable packaging and refilling 2 million containers annually, the company expanded its use of recycled paper, substituted reusable cases for cardboard shipping boxes and offered refunds on returned packaging. It also banned smoking in all its offices and shops, and provided bicycles at low prices to over 350 headquarters employees.

Feeling frustrated with the bureaucracy of Friends of the Earth, in 1987 Roddick decided that The Body Shop should define and implement its own environmental and social campaigns. She enjoyed the freedom of being able to pick her own issues and respond rapidly to crises.

Community Activity

About the same time, Roddick was looking for ways to become more active in the communities in which The Body Shop operated. As she put it, 'We had to neutralize the corrupting effect of our wealth by taking positive steps to ensure we remained a humane and caring company.' She set up a Community Care Department and began talking to franchisees about having every shop commit to a local need, and supporting it by allowing staff time off to work on the project.

Most responded positively, and soon shops worldwide were working with disabled centres, AIDS support groups and homeless programmes. But Roddick still fretted that some programmes were not imaginative enough, and some 'malingerers' remained uninvolved:

> If a shop didn't have a project and said, in effect, it didn't give a damn about the community, it was usually the franchisee speaking, not the staff.... If they absolutely refused to become involved, there was not much I could do – other than to make quite sure they did not get another shop.[20]

As she launched into the social and environmental projects, Roddick became sensitive to some associated risks. First, she didn't want to make potential customers feel guilty or overwhelmed by the campaigning. And second, she saw a risk that staff could become so enamoured with the causes that they neglected their 'trading' role.

Nor were the company's motivations always perceived positively. Indeed, some challenged The Body Shop's altruism, suspecting that it was part of a public relations campaign to create a desired image. An article in *Marketing* noted: 'There are times when Roddick's thirst for publicity seems almost insatiable. She has associated herself with every conscience-raising exercise from Third World development to a cheap condom campaign to curb the spread of AIDS.'[21]

Her response to such criticism varied from defensive to dismissive depending on her mood:

> Look, if I put our poster for Colourings [makeup] in the shop windows, that creates sales and profits. A poster to stop the burning of the rain forest does not. It creates a banner of values, it links us to the community, but it will not increase sales.[22]

> To cynics, altruism in business is disarming. But the bottom line is, you keep your staff – and good staff are hard to keep, especially in retail.[23]

> The absolute truth is that nothing of what we do ... is undertaken with an eye to our 'image' .... If there is a single motivation for what we do, it is, in the words of Ralph Waldo Emerson, 'to put love where our labour is'.[24]

Trade Not Aid

Her regular travels made Roddick acutely aware of the huge development needs that existed in the Third World; but her experience with the ILO in Geneva convinced her that aid programmes were not the answer. So, in 1987, she launched The Body Shop's 'Trade Not Aid' policy with the objective of 'creating trade to help people in the Third World utilize their resources to meet their own needs'. Eventually, she hoped to trade directly with those who grew or harvested all the raw ingredients The Body Shop used. By 1991 two major projects had been initiated.

Boys' Town Trust

During a visit to southern India in 1987, Roddick visited a group of farm communities set up by a British expatriate to train poor and homeless boys. Impressed, Roddick agreed to make Boys Town the primary supplier of Footsie Rollers – serrated pieces of acacia wood sold by The Body Shop as foot massagers. A price was calculated using first world wage rates – four times the local norm. Workers were paid local wages, with the balance being deposited in a trust account for each worker to receive as he left to start an independent life at the age of 16. Retail profits from the Footsie Rollers funded the boys' healthcare and education.

Returning home, she had little difficulty in raising the money required to open a new village, and in 1989 Anita and Gordon returned to India to set up The Body Shop Boys' Town with facilities to house and employ 85 boys. The success of that project led to other contracts to produce soap bags, woven baskets, Christmas cards and silk-screened T-shirts. Over the next three years, The Body Shop proudly reported that 3,000 jobs were created as the impact of the programmes' spread into surrounding communities. By 1990, Roddick had plans to establish Boys' Town Trusts in Mexico, Africa and Thailand.

Nepalese Paper

On a trip to Nepal, Roddick found entire villages unemployed as a result of a government limit on the harvest of the lokta shrub – the traditional source of material for their handmade paper. Needing a source of environmentally friendly paper, she saw the possibility of setting up another Trade Not Aid project. She brought in an expert who found alternative sources of paper fiber – water hyacinth, banana tree fiber and sugar cane, for example – and commited The Body Shop to an order for bags, notebooks and scented drawer liners, which allowed a large family paper factory to convert to the new production. In June 1989, this company bought the land needed for another papermaking factory, which employed 37 people. A portion of The Body Shop's profits were used to replant the area and another 10 per cent went to the Nepal Women's Association.

On the other side of the glowing success stories, however, were many frustrations, failures and even occasional disillusionment. The Boys' Town project, for example, ended in what Roddick described as 'a cruel deception'. After several years, managers discovered serious irregularities, including the fact that the Footsie Rollers were being made in local sweatshops for only a fraction of the price The Body Shop was paying. The contract was cancelled and relationships severed. A textile project in Bangladesh and a sponge sourcing venture in Turkey were also aborted due to various supply problems. Yet Roddick remained committed to Trade Not Aid, and was pursuing projects in Somalia, Malaysia, Philippines and Kenya.

The Soapworks Project

In 1989, Roddick turned the principles of her Trade Not Aid campaign to effecting change in what she termed 'Britain's own third world'. A visit to the depressed Glasgow suburb of Easterhouse, a 55,000-person slum with 37 per cent unemployment, resulted in the decision to locate a new 33,000 square foot soap factory in the town, despite the fact that it was almost 400 miles from the company's other facilities. She described her decision:

> It certainly would have been more conventional to set up the Soapworks factory near Littlehampton. But it's more fun, more motivating, and better for morale to do it here. It's not economic in terms of transport, but it's easier to inculcate our ideas here.[25]

Eight months and £1 million later, Soapworks opened, staffed by 16 of the community's chronically unemployed. After two weeks training, they returned to Easterhouse on Littlehampton wages – a third higher than local rates. By 1991, the payroll had reached 100, and eventually Soapworks was expected to provide a third of The Body Shop's worldwide soap needs. In early 1991, UK franchisees raised £26,000 ($45,000) to build a playground at the factory. Once the factory became profitable (expected in 1991), 25 per cent of after-tax profits were to be placed in a charitable trust for the purpose of benefiting the community.

The project generated much favourable publicity, including this reaction from the Confederation of British Industry (CBI) in Scotland:

> Mrs Roddick is to be congratulated for converting a thousand speeches into a million pounds worth of positive investment. This belies the myth that nothing can be done. This business leader is about to prove otherwise. We welcome this imaginative venture and hope it will be the first of many such enterprises which will bring money and jobs to deprived city areas.

There was indication, however, that some Easterhouse residents felt that The Body Shop had a patronizing and even exploitative attitude about Soapworks. When Roddick referred to the community as a location 'where angels fear to tread', for example, one observer remarked, 'To hear her speak . . . you might think The Body Shop was the only industrial employer in Easterhouse. But as you can see, her plant is on a small industrial estate surrounded by several busy factories.'[26]

In typical fashion, her response was, 'Cynics – up yours!' She hoped that she would inspire other firms worldwide to establish similar projects. In her view, 'The Body Shop will have failed by 50 per cent if we don't provide a role model for other companies.'[27]

Political Involvement

In the late 1980s, The Body Shop's social and environmental activities became increasingly political. Although the company had long required suppliers to vouch that their ingredients had not been tested on animals in the past five years, in 1989 it escalated its activities in this area. In response to a 1989 EC draft directive proposing that all cosmetics be tested on animals, Roddick mounted a massive media blitz and began a petition in her shops. With five million supporting signatures, the petition was influential in the Bill's eventual withdrawal.

Again, critics within the industry claimed that her cruelty-free platform was a marketing ploy. They pointed out that it was possible to adopt her five-year rule, yet still use ingredients tested on animals. Indeed, they claimed that most base cosmetics ingredients – including many used by The Body Shop – had originally been tested on animals. Roddick responded:

> Although we recognize that, realistically, most existing ingredients used in the cosmetics industry have been tested on animals by someone, somewhere, at sometime, we make sure that no animal testing is carried out by us or in our name.

Roddick's environmental concerns also became more political in nature as she became committed to the protection of the rain forests. After a visit to Brazil to attend a rally protesting the construction of a dam which would flood 15 million acres of rain forest, Roddick returned to England to take action. She held a franchisee meeting where she raised £200,000, initiated a 'Stop the Burning' poster campaign, and organized a petition which collected 1 million signatures in four weeks. Followed by a small media army, Roddick and 250 of her staff marched on the Brazilian Embassy in London and tried to deliver the sacks of protest letters to the ambassador. Several franchisees expressed concern about such high-profile political activity, and one wondered if The Body Shop was going into the 'rent-a-mob' business.

The Body Shop also began associating itself with several other organizations such as Amnesty International and FREEZE, the anti-nuclear weapons group. It was this latter campaign that finally brought a strong reaction from several franchisees who felt that Roddick should not be speaking for them on such issues:

> My first reaction was 'if you support nuclear weapons, what the hell are you doing in one of my shops?'. . . . But then I realized I did not necessarily have the right to speak for The Body Shop on every issue. . . . I accepted that principle – and completely ignored it. I have never been able to separate Body Shop values from my own personal values.[28]

Profit with Principle

Roddick acknowledged that she was on a mission to create 'a new business paradigm' – one in which companies accepted the responsibility that came with their economic power and became engines of social change. To implement her vision, however, she recognized she had to overcome two major impediments. Externally, she rejected the pressures of shareholders and the financial community to focus companies on profits to the exclusion of other objectives:

> The responsibility of business is not to create profits but to create live, vibrant, honorable organizations with real commitment to the community. . . . I certainly believe that companies should not be evaluated solely on their annual report and accounts.[29]

Equally threatening to Roddick was the growing complacency among employees as The Body Shop became larger, more widespread and more successful:

> What worries me now is that within the company there is an umbrella of corporate goodness which some people are hiding under, saying 'I work for The Body Shop, therefore I am sincere, good, caring, humane, and so on.' It really depresses me. . . . We talk about being lean and green, but I can see a fat cat mentality creeping in: paper being wasted, lights left on after meetings. What it comes down to is arrogance.[30]

THE US MARKET CHALLENGE

> 'It was Gordon's view that while the United States offered The Body Shop the greatest potential for growth, it also represented the greatest potential for disaster.'[31] (Anita Roddick)

In early 1991, observers wondered whether The Body Shop could maintain its phenomenal growth (see Exhibit 3). They pointed to the fact that sales in the United Kingdom, which represented 67 per cent of the company's total, had grown by only 1 per cent, after inflation and new store openings had been removed from the 1990 figures. Overseas, the company still had plenty of room to expand, but it was clear that its success would be tied to its ability to break into the $12 billion US cosmetics market. Gordon was particularly nervous about entering what had been described as 'a graveyard for British retailers'.

Entry into the US Market

Finally, in 1988, with over 200 stores in 33 countries, The Body Shop established its first toehold in the United States – a 50,000 square foot production and warehouse facility in Morristown, New Jersey. Under the direction of a British expatriate, who was previously the president of Unilever's fragrance subsidiary, twelve company-owned shops were opened on the East Coast. In mid-1990, the company began franchising, and by year's end, 37 shops – including 14 company-owned – had been opened. Anita Roddick explained the delay: 'We wanted to wait for two years to see how we would do.... We don't advertise. We've never gone into shopping malls, and we were terrified of those. The question was, "Were we good enough?"'[32] Due to the high cost of the initial infrastructure, however, the US operations were still running at a loss in 1991.

Challenges of the US Market

Whether the losses would continue or indeed, whether stores remained open, depended on how the company dealt with a different set of challenges. First, environmental concern had been less of a public issue in the United States during the 1980s, and it was not certain that The Body Shop's strong image and unfamiliar practices would appeal to them. A 1990 Price Waterhouse report commented:

> The link between common ideals and store loyalty is not yet proven.... Some customers may be willing to pay $3.00 for a bar of soap, knowing that some of the money is going to a worthy cause. Others will be turned off to a company that uses its profits to support such a bold political agenda. The diversity of the US market, in terms of consumer values and demand, and the vocal nature of dissident groups may make it difficult for The Body Shop to find a solid platform on which to build a business.[33]

Already Roddick had learned how difficult it was to transfer her values even within her organization. It was hard to recruit staff who embraced Body Shop values and could fit into what she called 'our quirky, zany, organization'. 'I thought our values were global,' she said, '... and that our image and style were so strong that they would be easily transferable across the Atlantic. I was wrong.'[34]

She was also amazed by how constrained business was in a country that epitomized the free enterprise system. The Food and Drug registrations, the various state and city regulations, and the lawyers' horror stories all made Roddick nervous about her decision. Under warnings about product liability and the likelihood of litigation, for example, she was advised not to offer a refill service in the United States. Lawyers also convinced her to drop her 'Against Animal Testing' logo on products for fear of retribution by the cosmetics industry. They really put the frighteners on us,' she said. 'We felt we had to modify our trading practices drastically.'[35]

Furthermore, some questioned whether The Body Shop's reliance on word-of-mouth promotion alone would be sufficient to build awareness in the communications-intensive US market, and to support an ever-increasing number of shop openings. Price Waterhouse calculated that The Body Shop would have to achieve sales of $685 million, in order to support its target of 1,500 shop openings by 1995. This implied a 17 per cent share of the top third of the cosmetics industry where it operated, and without advertising, analysts predicted that this would be a difficult challenge. David Altschiller, chief executive of the New York advertising agency handling the $10 million Liz Claiborne fragrance account, commented: 'It's very hard to cultivate awareness and familiarity among consumers here without media advertising. Many highly successful European concepts have fizzled ... when they're plunked down unadulterated in the American market.'[36] Roddick acknowledged the challenge: 'There's no example of anyone doing what we're doing in America and making it work.... I think I have to become slightly more eccentric and slightly more theatrical to get my point across.'[37]

Finally, The Body Shop's global success had not gone unnoticed in the cosmetics industry. Betting that the 'green consumer' population would continue to grow, many leading firms were introducing 'natural' lines, and revamping the look and the marketing pitch of their products. Revlon were marketing 'New Age Naturals' – a line of cosmetic products with names like Peppermint Skin Toner and Almond and Walnut Scrub. In 1990, Estée Lauder created Origins, a product line based on plant oils and extracts. It sold them in recycled (and recyclable) containers, and emphasized that no animal testing had been carried out on its ingredients within six years. Lauder planned to market this line in stand-alone stores, the first of which was scheduled to open in Cambridge, Massachusetts in mid-1991. And Leslie Wexner, founder of the hugely successful retailer, The Limited, had opened 42 Bath and Body Works shops. *Business Week* reported that Roddick was so concerned about the shops which looked 'astonishingly like Body Shops' that her lawyers were discussing the concern with The Limited. 'People think we're a flaky New Age company,' Roddick declared. 'But my God, we defend ourselves like lions.'[38]

As The Body Shop entered the 1990s, the price of 'the shares that defy gravity' seemed to reflect some of the uncertainty the company faced in its markets (see Exhibit 4). Adding to that uncertainty were questions about the future leadership of the company – a question that Anita seemed to share:

> Leadership of a company should encourage next generation not just to follow, but to overtake.... The complaint Gordon and I have is that we are not being overtaken by our staff.[39]

Yet for the first time, the Roddicks hinted that they may have been thinking of stepping back from their intense role at the centre of The Body Shop. Announcing the 1990 results. Gordon Roddick said:

> The thing we now have to do is reduce the dependence of the business on Anita and Gordon. You can either create a structure where the business is unable to do without you because you hang on to all the bits, or you can create a structure where they are pleased to see you, but they can do without you. That is our aim.[40]

For some, the vital question was whether the organization could indeed succeed without them.

APPENDIX

The Body Shop: A Timeline of Key Events and Milstones

1976 First shop opens in Brighton (March). Second shop opens in Chichester (November).

1977 First franchises granted.

1978 First franchisee outside the United Kingdom – in Belgium.

1984 The Body Shop goes public on the UK unlisted securities market in April.

1985 Anita Roddick selected as the Veuve Cliquot Business Woman of the Year.

1986 Save The Whale campaign launched with Greenpeace.
New £4 million headquarters and 320,000 square foot warehouse and production facility opened.
Environmental Projects Department and Body Shop training school established.

1987 Friends of the Earth campaign launched.
Jacaranda, the company's own independent video company, is established.
Named Company of the Year by the Confederation of British Industry (CBI).

1988 Queen awards Anita Roddick the Order of the British Empire (OBE).
The first US branch of The Body Shop opens in New York.
Soapworks, a 33,000 square foot soap factory, opens in Easterhouse, Scotland.

1989 The Body Shop is voted Retailer of the Uear.
'Stop the Burning' rainforest campaign launched.

1990 Against Animal Testing campaign is launched.
The first Body Shop opens in Tokyo.
Among many 1990 awards are the Queen's Award for Export, UK Hall of Fame Marketing Award, the Animalia Award for animal protection, the UK Environmental Management Award, the International Women's Forum Award, and the US Environmental Protection Agency's Environmental Achievement Award.

EXHIBIT 1
Key financial data for The Body Shop, 1984–90.
(£000s)

Year ended:	30/9/84	30/9/85	30/9/86	30/9/87	28/2/88[a]	28/2/89[b]	28/2/90
Turnover, of which:	4,910	9,362	17,394	28,476	73,007	55,409	84,840
Overseas	20%	21%	22%	25%	25%	25%	33%
United States					874	874	5,839
Profit before Taxes	1,044	1,929	3,451	5,998	15,243	11,232	14,508
Dividends	75	150	300	605	1,439		1,558
Transferred to Reserves	414	871	1,762	3,129	7,114		6,977
Tangible Fixed Assets	608	676	1,744	4,093	15,606	15,606	31,442
Net Current Assets	524	1,265	1,948	2,772	8,630	8,630	1,515
Long-term Liabilities	(320)	(258)	(230)	(120)	(239)	(239)	(5,991)
Minority Interests	–	–	(17)	(158)	(520)	(520)	(974)
Shareholders' Funds	812	1,683	3,445	6,587	23,477	23,477	25,992
Weighted Average Number of Shares (000s)	n/a	80,000	80,000	80,397	83,780	84,908	85,306
Number of Outlets							
United Kingdom	45	66	77	89	112	112	139
Overseas	83	102	155	186	255	255	318
TOTAL	128	168	232	275	367	367	457

[a] 74 weeks.
[b] 52 weeks.
Source: Body Shop annual reports.

EXHIBIT 2
Industry comparisons, 31 December 1990.

	The Body Shop	Industry Lower Quartile	Industry Median	Industry Upper Quartile
Return on Capital	43.6%	3.1%	16.5%	41.2%
Return on Total Assets	20.2%	−0.9%	6.8%	14.2%
Pre-tax Profit Margin	17.2%	0.0%	4.8%	10.5%
Sales/Total Assets	117.9%	111.8%	159.7%	192.9%
Average Remuneration	£10,424.5	£6,740.7	£9,000.0	£12,269.2
Sales/Employee	£66,782.6	£32,927.6	£50,483.9	£99,252.1

Source: ICC Online Ltd, *Financial Datasheets*, 5 November 1990.

EXHIBIT 3
Worldwide shop list, March 1991.

No. of Shops		Overseas History First Shops Opening In:	
Antigua	1	1978	Belgium (Brussels)
Australia	31		
Austria	5	1979	Sweden (Stockholm)
Bahamas	4		Greece (Athens)
Bahrain	1		
Belgium	4	1980	Canada (Toronto)
Bermuda	1		Iceland (Reykjavik)
Canada	87		
Cyprus	1	1981	Denmark (Copenhagen)
Denmark	5		Finland (Tampere)
Eire	5		Eire (Dublin)
Finland	11		
France	3	1982	The Netherlands (Leiden)
Germany	28		France (Paris)
Gibraltar	1		
Grand Cayman	1	1983	Australia (Melbourne)
Greece	14		Cyprus (Limassol)
Holland	23		Germany (Cologne)
Hong Kong	7		Singapore
Indonesia	1		Switzerland (Zurich)
Italy	22		UAE (Dubai)
Japan	1		

No. of Shops		Overseas History First Shops Opening In:	
Malta	1	1984	Hong Kong (Tsimshatsui/Kc)
Malaysia (E)	3		Italy (Catania/Sicily)
Malaysia (W)	7		Malaysia (Kuala Lumpur)
New Zealand	3		
Norway	13	1985	Bahamas (Nassau)
Oman	2		Bahrain (Manama)
Portugal	5		Norway (Oslo)
Qatar	1		
Saudi Arabia	6	1986	Austria (Vienna)
Singapore	6		Kuwait (Safat)
Spain	17		Oman (Muscat)
Sweden	30		Portugal (Lisbon)
Switzerland	18		Spain (Madrid)
Taiwan	3		
UAE	1	1987	Antigua (St. John's)
USA	39[a]		Saudi Arabia
			Malta (Sliema)
			Bermuda (Hamilton)
OVERSEAS	412		
UK & Channel Isles	174[b]	1988	USA (New York)
GRAND TOTAL	586		Gibraltar
			Taiwan (Taipei)
		1989	New Zealand (Wellington)
		1990	Indonesia
			Japan (Tokyo)

Number of countries we trade in: 38
Number of languages we trade in: 18

[a] Franchise 23, Company 14.
[b] Franchise 133, Company 41.
Source: The Body Shop Press Office.

EXHIBIT 4
Stock price movement, 1984–90 (£).

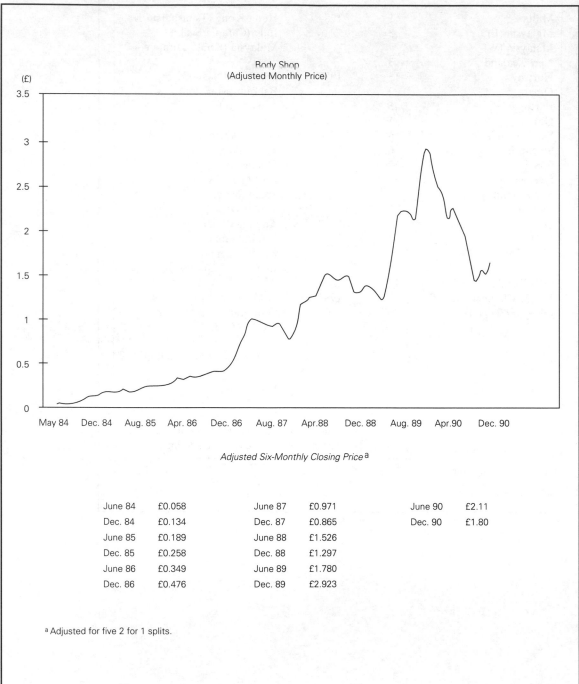

Body Shop
(Adjusted Monthly Price)

Adjusted Six-Monthly Closing Price [a]

June 84	£0.058	June 87	£0.971	June 90	£2.11
Dec. 84	£0.134	Dec. 87	£0.865	Dec. 90	£1.80
June 85	£0.189	June 88	£1.526		
Dec. 85	£0.258	Dec. 88	£1.297		
June 86	£0.349	June 89	£1.780		
Dec. 86	£0.476	Dec. 89	£2.923		

[a] Adjusted for five 2 for 1 splits.

Source: Interactive Data Corp.

ISS–INTERNATIONAL SERVICE SYSTEMS A/S*

With a turnover of 11.4 billion DKK (Danish kroner), equivalent to nearly $2 billion, and employing over 115,000 people in 17 countries spread around three continents, ISS is an anomaly in the world of mega-corporations. The company counts advanced technology, high levels of professional skills and a global brand image among its key sources of competitive advantage. It is not in the business of computers or pharmaceuticals, however, nor in packaged foods or luxury cosmetics. ISS, as described by Poul Andreassen, the company's president since 1962, 'is the world's largest and best cleaning service company'. In a highly fragmented industry in which the three key success factors are believed to be 'cost, cost and cost', ISS is rarely the low-cost vendor. Yet, in 1992, over 80 per cent of its worldwide revenues and over 92 per cent of its profits came from the 'mom and pop' business of daily office cleaning.

Poul Andreassen believes that opportunities for further development are practically unlimited for ISS:

> The business is ours to lose. Where ISS will be in the future all depends on ourselves because the market is out there. There is not a serious threat unless we are not doing what we're saying, what we believe in.

Sven Ipsen, the head of the Scandinavian division, which contributes half of ISS's

*This case was prepared by Mary Ackenhusen, Research Associate, under the supervision and guidance of Professor Sumantra Ghoshal. We are grateful to Sandeep Sander for helping to make this case possible. It is intended to be used as a basis for class discussion rather than to illustrate either effective or ineffective handling of an administrative situation.

Copyright © 1993, by INSEAD, Fontainebleau, France.

worldwide profit, concurs with this assessment:

> I see no major threats for ISS Scandinavia for the next 5 years apart from a severe recession. We operate with very small margins and we understand the market well enough to know which levers to pull if we begin to lose market share. We know where to go if we have to tighten our belt. I think we have a very flexible organization.

ISS's ambition is to continue improving its service levels so that, 'Some day, ISS and the word service will be synonymous just like Xerox and photocopying once were.' To achieve this vision, however, Andreassen believes that two key hurdles have to be first overcome.

In the second half of the 1980s, ISS achieved spectacular growth in both sales and profits: 17 per cent and 25 per cent, respectively, per annum. (See Exhibits 1–3 for financial information.) Yet, its relative profitability at 3 per cent of sales remained several percentage points lower than that of either ServiceMaster or BET, its two key competitors. Improving profitability is therefore the first priority:

> I have seen too many 'wheeler-dealer' companies grow rapidly only to go under for not taking quality seriously. They did not try to compile resources for product development, to build personnel development systems, or invest to create a modern way of managing their enterprises. To improve service quality, we must continue to make these investments. But for that, we must achieve 5 per cent profit before tax, at the least.

Second, ISS's admirable rate of growth has thus far come primarily from acquisitions. This strategy of acquisitive growth has reached its limit and the company's target of 15 per cent annual growth through the 1990s must now come from in-house developments. Given the size of the company, continued growth through acquisitions would require either too many small acquisitions or acquisitions of very large companies, both of which would entail unacceptable levels of risk. Importantly, there is a large amount of goodwill on the corporate balance sheet, thus, the new strategy of organic growth must achieve a consistent improvement in earnings per share in order to protect and enhance the value of ISS's stock.

While ample opportunities for organic growth remain available, the company needs to reassess its organizational approach and replenish its management skills to reorient itself to this new growth process. Many managers feel that the company is too conservative financially, and does not provide the funding necessary to build new businesses from scratch. However, this is where Andreassen sees growth and profitability improvement as two inseparably intertwined objectives:

> We've invested a lot of money over the years in management training and now is the time to show for it. We have got to come up and make the 5 per cent before tax. Then we will have a very important cash flow and can make available those funds the businesses need to grow.

ISS SPREADS ITS WINGS

ISS was created in 1901 by a Danish lawyer to provide security services for office buildings in Copenhagen. The company grew in the security business and, in 1934, it expanded its activities to include commercial cleaning. By the time Andreassen took over the management of the company in 1962, it had grown to 2,000 employees and 50 million DKK in sales. At this time, office cleaning was considered to be neither an attractive nor a sophisticated business. The margins were very low and the companies which served the market were almost entirely small businesses. Andreassen likes to emphasize how negatively people viewed their positions as cleaners by recalling experiences of employees who left their houses at 5 a.m. in full tennis garb, drove to their building sites and then changed into their cleaning clothes. They did not ever want the neighbours to know what they really did between 5 and 8 in the morning. Andreassen spent the next 30 years of his life working to mould ISS into a professionally managed service company which would combat the low-class image of the industry.

The 1960s: Professional Management

The market for commercial cleaning and security services was changing at the time Andreassen took over the management of ISS in the early 1960s. Companies were beginning to focus on their main lines of business and contracting out secondary activities such as cleaning, security and food service. This 'structural rationalization' trend supported Andreassen's personal philosophy that cleaning was a professional business and must be managed as such.

Before joining ISS, Andreassen had gained a degree in industrial engineering and then worked in positions ranging from time-study engineer to plant manager in several multinational companies including Remington Rand and SAS. In his new job, he immediately began applying some of the basic management techniques he had learned in a manufacturing environment to the cleaning business.

In his early days as president, Andreassen was somewhat surprised to find that the only information collected to measure the work of the cleaners was how much material (cleaning products) had been used. Since this comprised only 3 per cent of the cost of a contract and wages accounted for 65–70 per cent, Andreassen began his task of professionalizing ISS's operations by developing a system to plan the work better. The new planning system assured the job would be performed efficiently and to a given standard by specifying the work methods, the frequency of each task and how the various jobs were to be distributed among the workers. With this innovation, a cleaner now had a personalized job sheet of the tasks to be performed by him or her each day. The planning system also allowed ISS to bid accurately for new business.

The system remains a key tool at ISS in 1992 though it is now more sophisticated and computerized. When a tender offer is being prepared for a new site, a group of planners estimate the labour, equipment and material content by entering the building parameters, including the size of the area to be cleaned, types of floors, number of toilets, frequency of cleaning tasks, etc. into a special computer program developed by ISS. The program then calculates the estimated cost of the job using the pre-established standards for cleaning.

To address the efficiency of his workers, Andreassen implemented a combination of improvements to increase substantially the cleaning rate which stood at 40 m^2 per hour. Often the rate could be increased by improved tools such as better cleaning products, specially designed mops and dusters and new or additional machinery.

Likewise, the growing popularity of carpets in office buildings helped boost the productivity of the cleaning operators. By 1992, average cleaning rates had been improved to 250–350 m^2 per hour.

At the same time, Andreassen hired a chemical engineer to take responsibility for the technical function of developing and producing new cleaning products. Referring to the bad image of the cleaning business, Andreassen remembers that in 1962 when he placed an advertisement for this position in a Copenhagen paper, he had no responses because 'Who wants to be in the cleaning business?' In the end, he pressured a friend into taking the position. The result of this drive for state-of-the-art cleaning tools was the establishment in 1963 of a separate company, Darenas, under the ISS banner.

His next action was to break the company up into profit centres, units with full operational and financial responsibility. This change supported his philosophy that the most motivated managers were those who thought of the business as their own. To monitor these relatively autonomous business units, he adopted a financial reporting system, the Management Reporting System (MRS), which provided a detailed profit and loss statement, called the after-calculation, for each business unit (see Exhibit 4 for a sample report). This information was compiled monthly and the report was distributed to all senior managers of the company, including Andreassen.

The basis of the report was a cost accounting system starting at the contract level which deducted all direct costs such as material, equipment and wage costs for every cleaning contract against the contract's turnover, to figure the 'contract contribution'. Enabling management to understand their overhead costs, the expenses of each successive layer of management (i.e. branch, district and country) were subtracted to calculate CBI (contribution I), CBII and CBIII. CBIII was the operating profit earned by the business unit after all costs were deducted. Monthly, the budgeted direct costs were compared with the actual results using the after-calculation report, giving the unit manager immediate insight into the profitability of each job under his or her control.

The MRS had two major benefits. First, it focused at the smallest and most basic unit of performance, the cleaning contract and team, and provided the transparency necessary for corrective actions at that level. Second, this financial system became the basis for measuring a manager's success and identifying areas which needed improvement. Andreassen explains the value of the system:

> One of the most important ingredients of management is that all levels of management know exactly on which criteria to measure whether or not a manager is successful. This takes care of half of the management process as . . . one does not have to kick everybody around. [With MRS] people were well aware when they were successful, and they knew how to take corrective actions if they had bad results.

When ISS acquired a company, the implementation of this system was the priority management action in order to immediately improve profitability.

With the realization that people were his largest cost on a contract, Andreassen was convinced that he must focus his attention on the individuals doing the cleaning, the cleaners. Beyond his drive to improve the efficiency and standards of cleaning, Andreassen wanted to improve his employees' satisfaction with their work. Andreassen's mother had been a shop steward in a tobacco company and this gave him an appreciation for the feelings of workers who performed manual labour and a desire to improve their status.

Andreassen began improving his workforce's self-image by giving ISS employees an identity of which they could be proud. All ISS employees were given attractive uniforms with the ISS logo. All supervisors were given company cars with the ISS blue letters emblazoned on the side. Andreassen explained:

> We all need a certain degree of recognition. We want to identify with something . . . I want a cleaner to be able to point out to her children the smart white car in the street with its blue strips driving past, and say to them, 'This is my company.'

Likewise, Andreassen extended the existing training programmes for the cleaners and added new training programmes for his management to help them carry out the work in a professional manner. He recalls:

> At the time, there was a growing understanding of the importance of this type of work, that it had to be carried out in a professional manner and that the persons doing the work were entitled to wages on a level with the industrial workers. The work had to be done professionally in order for us to be able to develop the systems and methods . . . and this called for resources for both training and professional management.

This era was one of expansion within Scandinavia and the rest of Europe. ISS is believed to be the first cleaning company to have worked outside of its home country when it entered Sweden in the 1940s and Norway in the 1950s. In the 1960s, ISS increased its international presence by entering Germany, Switzerland, Holland and the United Kingdom through local acquisitions.

The 1970s: Service Management

By the early 1970s, ISS had a strong system of procedures and standards which assured high quality, efficient cleaning, but management realized that the market was beginning to demand more. As Sven Ipsen remembers:

> Earlier we thought that if we gave the customer the quality he wanted, shiny floors, clean lavatories, then he should be satisfied because that was what he paid for. Then we realized that we needed to not only focus on what we delivered as service, but how we delivered it.

ISS's new service philosophy was based on 'The Magic Formula' (see Exhibit 5). The thrust of the formula was that every market segment had unique characteristics, i.e. hospitals, schools or office buildings. Thus, the service package, including methods and product offerings, should reflect the needs of each segment. A unique delivery system for each segment was the most effective way of handling the different needs of the segment, yet the company could still be tied together by one identity, such as a common logo. Additionally, the company should carry the same culture for a high level of service throughout all aspects of the operation.

Thus, instead of the same workers cleaning hospitals, schools and other buildings using the same methods and equipment, there was a recognition of the difference in customer needs. This drove ISS to set up separate organizations to serve each of its markets. While before, the only separate groups were security, food service and cleaning, now cleaning was broken into groups to meet the special, different needs of offices, schools, hospitals and food (mainly abattoirs). The cleaners and managers received special training on the specific needs of these areas and remained dedicated to a market segment in order to build the experience and expertise needed to effectively serve customers in these segments.

Focused attention on specific market segments allowed ISS to leverage its knowledge of a customer's business with its onsite presence to offer special cleaning and other services. For example, in a supermarket, ISS would gain entrance to the customer through a contract to do traditional cleaning of the shop area and offices. Over time, after ISS had proved its professionalism in cleaning, it expanded its service offering to include special cleaning of the meat section, freezers, shopping carts or even air filters as well as non-cleaning tasks such as labelling, coffee-making, uniform cleaning, lighting and repair of shopping trolleys.

A key element of the 'Magic Formula' is to nurture the 'front line' which is the primary contact with the customer: the supervisors and workers. Close attention is paid to the hiring, training and retention of these employees. For example, in Denmark, all managers including the managing director, spend up to two days per month interviewing candidates for the cleaning operator position. Then, a video presentation of what a cleaner can expect from his or her job is shown to each candidate and a formal job bank is used to try to match cleaners to jobs, primarily based on location of the job relative to the cleaner's home.

The high turnover which is usually found in low-paid jobs such as cleaning (cleaners earn close to the bottom of the wage scale) has always been a concern to ISS. The actual turnover rate of ISS varies greatly between countries from 50 per cent to 100 per cent annually, depending somewhat on the tightness of the labour market in that country. As Andreassen explains:

> Many, perhaps 60 per cent of them will stay many years, a lot for 25 years . . . but the last 40 per cent is turning around 2 or 3 times. Some of that you cannot avoid because they are coming in to earn money for a wedding or other special event so they only stay a couple of months. Also we hire quite a few students.

ISS believes a good supervisor can reduce the turnover. Though the supervisors are responsible for training, quality control and scheduling of their work team, the most important part of their job is letting the cleaners know that they care. As described by one of the supervisors:

> The ISS advantage is that the supervisor is there for the people . . . that they can come to us for time, for a coffee. It's not always possible to help them, but they need someone to listen. If they know this, they'll work for a supervisor on Saturdays and Sundays.

The supervisor also serves as the primary customer contact, interacting with the customer daily to assure that he or she is satisfied with the service as well as to suggest added services which might be performed either regularly, such as more frequent waxing of the floors, or on a one-time basis, such as cleaning the telephones.

The company uses a whole array of formal reports and surveys to measure customer satisfaction, in addition to regular customer contact by the branch and district management, yet it is the supervisors who help most in differentiating ISS from the other cleaning companies. As one of the supervisors explained:

> Other cleaning companies are cheaper but they have less supervision. We supervisors

are a very good internal control system. Also, we are there for the customer, an on-site answer for all the customer's problems.

Service management layered on top of the professional methods and quality standards proved to be a successful formula which helped ISS to grow to be a 3 billion DKK business by the end of the 1970s. Contributing to this geographic and market growth, were the additional acquisitions of cleaning services in Europe, the purchase of Clorius, an energy control company, and its first expansion into North America through the purchase of a majority share in Prudential Building Maintenance Corporation of New York.

The 1980s: Strategic Planning

By the beginning of the 1980s, ISS was operating three continents and had ventured into a dozen specialized cleaning and related businesses. With the good fortune to have too many growth opportunities, both geographically and in the market, Andreassen decided it was time to guide the further development of ISS formally through the adoption of a strategic planning system.

The ISS 'team planning process' is a top-down, bottom-up participative system to develop detailed and integrated plans to support defined corporate objectives. The key elements of the plan answer the questions 'Where are we?' 'Where do we want to go?' 'How do we get there?' and 'Who does what and how?'. That is: status, goals, strategies and action plans. The process involves many team members at each level necessitating that it begin in April each year in order to finish by the end of October.

The team planning process begins with training for all participants new to the process to assure that everyone 'speaks the same language'. Starting from the top at the corporate level, a planning team is formed which will develop both qualitative and quantitative goals and objectives to be passed down to the next level, the divisions, as input to their plans. The divisons will also each have a team which will develop its mission, goals and objectives. This continues in the same manner down each of the levels of management and stops at the level of branch management within each country. Then the plans with the detailed proposals on how the various units expect to meet the corporate guidelines flow upward by management level with the lower level management plan becoming input for the next higher level. Therefore, each planning team at each level has two major planning sessions per year as the plans flow downward and then climb back up. To assure smooth communication of plans between levels, planning teams include members from the management level directly above and below.

The process is designed to complement the autonomy granted to the local operating managers with each level of management giving the level below it a framework of strategic guidelines. Andreassen and his management team place a high value on the process:

> The process holds our organization together and is the basis for our development and success.... It is the national leaders of ISS, with their teams, who contribute to the corporate strategy, the strategy for the development of each national unit, adapted not only to each country's particular personnel, social and legal conditions, but also the cultural and behavioural conditions. This complex task cannot be dealt with from behind a desk in Copenhagen.

The tool is credited for helping to build and maintain the ISS culture through extensive communication of mission, guidelines, rules and expectations.

Guided by this formal strategic planning process, ISS continued its growth throughout the 1980s by expanding the US cleaning business nationwide through acquisition, acquiring additional cleaning companies in Denmark, Sweden and Germany, sponsoring further acquisitions of energy companies under the Clorius umbrella and by acquiring a hospital service company, Mediclean, in United Kingdom.

The 1990s: Total Quality Management

Poul Andreassen does not worry about other service companies copying the ISS formula because he drives ISS continuously to develop new initiatives. He likes to say, 'Walking in the footsteps of somebody else will not put you in front.' To this end, ISS initiated a programme in 1991 to implement *Total Quality Management* as the next step for achieving service excellence. The TQM mission, as stated by the company, is to:

> Target the Group's functions and resources throughout the entire supply chain towards the creation of a perceived service quality which, as a minimum, fulfils the customers' demands and expectations, with the specific objectives of increasing customer satisfaction, reducing the loss of contracts, increasing sales to existing customers and reducing the staff turnover.

The primary two tools of TQM are extensive measurement systems in important areas, such as employee and customer satisfaction and work analysis. The objective of the work analysis is to improve the operational processes used in ISS by identifying every step of the current process backwards from the customer to the beginning of the ISS supply chain and then looking for ways to rationalize the process (process mapping). This extensive analysis will eventually be done for every activity within the company.

The TQM programme is envisaged to extend through 1995 for the training phase alone. To support this massive effort, a special subsidiary, ISS Quality Institute A/S, was established in 1992 near Copenhagen with its own managing director. One reason for the separate operating company was because a programme which was perceived to be a 'corporate programme' would not be easily accepted.

Still, various divisional and country managers had difficulties accepting the importance, as well as the 20 million DKK price tag, of TQM when Andreassen first introduced the idea. Even its supporters admit that when comparing this focus to the Service Management thrust of the 1970s, 'It looks like old wine in new bottles, to some extent.' One of the country managers comments that he has been providing quality all along, and remarks, 'You cannot turn a switch and say "Now we start TQM." What's TQM? It all comes through the people.'

As the concept grew to address other ISS needs beyond its stated objectives, its internal acceptance increased. TQM is now envisaged to be a marketing tool to other multinational corporations who are also embracing the concept in their own businesses; it is a means of enabling cleaners to more easily involve themselves in initiating and implementing new ideas, and it is an integration tool to hep transfer best practices between business units.

Flemming Schandorff, the managing director for the cleaning business in Denmark, is enthusiastic about TQM and feels it could make a real difference in the bottom line of his business:

> Every year we lose 140 million Danish kroner in turnover through loss of contracts to our competitors. We believe that after we have educated our people in TQM and begin monitoring the customer satisfaction index and the employee satisfaction index, we will be able to reduce that.

By the end of 1992, only the Scandinavian division had started the TQM training process. The other countries outside of Scandinavia, and some within Scandinavia, had taken a first step towards TQM by starting the process of achieving ISO 9000 certification, an international quality standard which assures documentation and consistency of process.

Although the European division did not expect to begin the TQM process for several years, one of the first tangible results of the TQM thrust occurred in this division in 1992 when the UK operation brought in the head of the ISS Quality Institute to convince the Heathrow airport management of the value of the ISS TQM programme. Primarily due to that competitive difference ISS subsequently won a cleaning contract for Terminal 1 at the airport. The TQM training for the employees involved in this contract began in 1993, ahead of the rest of the European division.

ISS in 1992

Traditional cleaning and maintenance made up 83 per cent of ISS 1992 revenues. The bulk of this activity was in daily office cleaning but other specialized activities included cleaning services for the food industry, hospitals, hotels, trains, shopping malls, as well as landscaping and snow removal. Additionally, ISS was active in security services (which it began divesting in the early 1990s), catering, linen service, uniform rental, the selling of cleaning products/equipment and energy services. (See Exhibits 6 and 7.)

The company is organized in four divisions: Scandinavia, Europe and Brazil, North America and Clorius. The Scandinavian management team runs the four Scandinavian countries and the European division includes all other European countries and Brazil. The North America 'division' only includes the United States and therefore the division and country management are one and the same. Clorius is an energy control equipment company which has an international scope (Exhibit 8). Geographically, Scandinavia contributed 45 per cent of 1992 turnover with Europe and Brazil and North America each producing 26 per cent.

ISS was by far the leading company in the four Scandinavian countries in 1992 with approximately 33 per cent of the contract market, i.e. the part of the cleaning market which is contracted to outside vendors. ISS was also the market leader in Austria and Greece. In the other European countries, ISS was much smaller relative to the largest local competitor. In the United States, the company's share was only 1 or 2 per cent of the contract market.

Beyond in-house cleaning, ISS's largest competition by far are the numerous, small cleaning companies which have the advantage of being substantially less expensive because of the minimal management and training overhead. There are only a few other multinational competitors which ISS competes with, one of which is ServiceMaster in the United States. This company provides only contract management services for cleaning. The workers who perform the service are the clients' own employees. The other significant multinational competitor is BET, who is active in professional cleaning in Europe as well as many other unrelated businesses. Within each country, there are often other strong competitors of significant size.

The ISS strategy for the first half of the 1990s is to concentrate on growth within the commercial cleaning market and to prioritize expansion within its current geographic base before going on to open new units in Asia and other parts of the world. Thus, ISS will continue to emphasize the traditional office cleaning market. Additionally, there are other higher value-added – and therefore more profitable – opportunities such as the cleaning of hospitals and the cleaning of food processing facilities that will be exploited in the markets where ISS already has a strong presence. Furthermore, there is a growing demand for single point service, i.e. one vendor who can either perform or coordinate total facility management (cleaning, security, catering, snow removal, etc.) as well as serve multinational companies across borders. ISS, as one of the few multinational cleaning and facility service companies in the world, seems to be ideally positioned to take advantage of this trend.

WITHIN THE CHINESE WALLS: THE BUSINESS UNIT

Andreassen has based the ISS organizational structure on the philosophy that the most efficient, profitable way to provide services is through small, stand-alone companies led by a local manager who is encouraged to think of the business as his or her own. Andreassen has intentionally erected a barrier around the operating units which he calls the 'Chinese Wall' to keep out top management. He explains its importance:

> Obviously the reason for its construction was that the Chinese wanted to keep the enemy out of their country . . . therefore they built this wall. Within this wall, they developed a culture entirely their own, and everyone knew it was outstanding. . . . That is why I think that if you have a business . . . these people should have their Chinese Wall around them. . . . They should not be managed from the top. The market should be left for them to develop. They should identify themselves with this market.

Thus, each national subsidiary of ISS is a legally separate company with the country manager carrying the title of managing director with his or her own board of directors. This board is normally staffed by key members of the country's management team, the head of the divisional management team, one or two outsiders who provide professional services to the country organization (i.e. the lawyer) and often another ISS country manager. The board meets three times a year to review budgets, potential acquisitions and any non-urgent policy decisions that need to be made.

The managing director's reports are typically several regional directors for the cleaning business and a director(s) heading up a special service such as Hospitals or Food. There are three usual levels of management under the regional director starting with the district manager who has overall responsibility for a specified geographical area within the country, the branch manager with responsibility for the profitability and quality of coverage for an even smaller geographical area, and the supervisor who has responsibility for the daily execution of one or a few specific contracts. See Exhibit 9 for a typical country organization.

The title 'managing director' is considered to be a valuable tool for attracting and keeping good country managers. Not only does the title and the legal structure reinforce the philosophy that the country organization is his or her own company, it also enables the country manager to more easily call on the managing directors of potential customers. The title gives both professional and social prestige to the country manager in what many would consider to be an unprestigious industry. The compensation package for each managing director is renegotiated each year and varies by country. Like most managing director positions in Europe, the package includes a car such as a high end BMW. This arrangement has enabled ISS to hire successful managers who might otherwise not have been interested in the company. Theo Buitendijk joined ISS as managing director in Holland in 1990 after working in a multinational oil company for 25 years. He remarks: 'Here it's more fun because I'm in charge of the whole thing. You can keep your independence as long as you meet your budget.' Similarly, David Openshaw used to work for ISS's largest competitor in Europe, BET, in a position with responsibility for £35 million turnover (1 pound = $1.76, 1991). Upon joining ISS, Openshaw became the managing director for a new ISS company whose mission was to build from scratch a cleaning operation in London. 'The one thing that attracted me was the promise that I would have my own business ... that I could run the business the way I wanted to run it.' In two years, he was proud to note that his turnover had reached £6 million.

In 1992, the country-level managing directors were being encouraged to create independent companies with their own managing directors within the country structure to focus only on Food or only on Hospitals. Taking the philosophy even further, Germany was in the process of establishing five additional independent companies under the country managing director to focus on daily office cleaning in the various regions of Germany. The key reason for breaking up the country units in this manner was to motivate and focus the managers of these segments.

This organizational philosophy imposed some additional costs in terms of additional management, audit and legal fees. For this reason, some country managers were resisting the push from corporate to develop the special service businesses as separate legal entities while they were too small to support the additional overhead. On the other hand, focused activities seemed to create more profit.

The head of the cleaning business in Denmark was not pleased when the decision was made to relieve him of his responsibility for hospital cleaning in Denmark in order to combine all the hospital business in Scandinavia under one company. Yet after this happened, as related by his boss, Sven Ipsen, 'His PBT is up by half a percent and his growth in turnover is better than before. He admits it's because of his new focus just on cleaning.'

Waldemar Schmidt, the head of the European group, is a longtime ISS manager who originally developed the Brazilian operation. From this experience and seeing how the European countries which he now manages have benefited from the 'own your company' approach, he comments, 'One can easily quantify the cost of creating smaller companies ... the value-added is something you must believe in.'

The success or failure of a country manager is viewed by ISS corporate almost exclusively in terms of financial results: his or her performance against profitability and growth targets. The profitability target is a minimum of 5 per cent profit before tax and the growth target generally ranges from 10–15 per cent, varying by country. The country manager's bonus is a reflection of these parameters.

The ISS requirement that its unit managers provide consistent financial returns often takes priority over any strategic objectives. Gerhard Marischka, the managing director of Austria, is one of ISS's 'stars' because he has averaged 16 per cent organic sales growth annually over the past three years and earned a profitability (before tax) above all other ISS countries, approaching 8 per cent in 1991 and 1992. Strategically, however, he has had to chart a path that has not always been consistent with the overall ISS priorities. He retains his profitable security business, for example, despite the divisional decision to quit that activity. He has also not developed any significant business in either of the targeted areas of special service, Hospitals or Food, which tend to be less profitable, at least initially.

Theo Buitendijk, the managing director of Holland who came to ISS in 1990 from Exxon, has tried to balance the financial and strategic objectives laid out by ISS divisional and corporate managements. By doubling his sales by acquisition between 1990 and 1991 without increasing overhead, he doubled his financial returns which allowed him to invest in building a new service area, Food. Though he is suffering a short-term drop in profitability before tax at the country level as he builds the food business, he believes it is the more profitable strategy for the long term. As a measure of his market success, in 1992, he was servicing 50 food contracts and was the market leader in that segment in Holland. In 1991, Holland reported a profit of 4.7 per cent and 5.4 per cent in 1992. Speaking from experience, Buitendijk comments:

> We as entrepreneurs are paid on results – that makes us risk-avoiders, not risk-takers. The system as it stands now doesn't stimulate focused attention to new areas . . . change is costly. Corporate says they accept the costs if you try new things . . . but I really don't know.

Within the challenging objective of meeting the financial plan, the managing directors have almost complete freedom to manage their business as they like. For example, Rolf Witt, the German managing director, quickly used his freedom to exploit the need for a service to dispose of building rubble when the former East Germany was first opened to the West. Using 'petty cash', he acquired a small concern in East Germany to perform this type of work. After a period, he made a tidy profit by selling off pieces of the company such as the vehicles which were bought by a concern in Poland. There are limits, however, to such freedom. When the former head of the Brazilian operation signed an agreement for a major acquisition committing ISS corporate resources without corporate approval, he was later asked to resign.

This local freedom also serves as a breeding ground for new ideas, when the investment can be justified at the operating unit level. Andreassen explains:

> With only 43 people at headquarters, it's clear that it is not from there that development springs. Our development is based on what goes on around us. . . . But we put a good deal of money into education and committee work. So you see, what we have here are companies working together, developing something new, under the leadership of

corporate management, a process involving all companies, a process which does not start at the top.

One of the most important innovations springing from an operating unit was the 5 Star training programme. It is originated in Brazil, but then was shared with Belgium and Austria, who greatly enhanced the programme. This key programme for supervisors and managers is now a part of the corporate human resources strategy. The five stars refer to the five levels of training (Exhibit 10) which cover the ISS philosophy, cleaning techniques, labour law, contract management, quality control, customer relations, employee relations and other key areas.

BUILDING BRIDGES: DIVISIONAL MANAGEMENT

The corporate management team at ISS has always been small because Andreassen 'dreads bureaucracy'. He feels that the primary role of the headquarters staff should be to:

> Procure the financial opportunities, check and control the company's development, and to create resources for the strategic development, training, R & D and marketing on an international basis. . . .. The number should be small at the headquarters office but they must be extremely qualified.

Thus, until 1989, Andreassen and his corporate staff of 50 people managed the ISS operations employing 100,000 people scattered across 16 countries. In 1989, the divisional level of management was added to reduce the span of control enough that the leadership of the company could work with the managing directors more closely. In 1992, the European division totalled 8 people, the Scandinavian division management numbered 22 people and the North American division, which also served as the country management team for the United States, totalled 40 people.

The majority of the staff are oriented towards the financial function, though there are also experts to provide advice on marketing, human resource management, quality, strategy and acquisitions. To support the management above the country level, each country pays a royalty of 1.5 per cent of turnover to ISS corporate of which 0.5 per cent is forwarded to the division management organization. Waldemar Schmidt, head of the European division, points to the performance improvement in Europe to prove the value-added of divisional management: the PBT for the countries within the division more than doubled from 2 per cent in 1989 to almost 5 per cent in 1991.

Strategy

Both Schmidt, the head of Europe and Ipsen, the head of Scandinavia, spend much of their time developing the strategy for their areas of the world and working individually with the country managers to develop their respective business plans. They also give a lot of thought to optimizing the organizational structure, such as creating or spinning off a new operating company at the right time. Though the divisional management team is very respectful of the autonomy of the local management, their mandate is to make the division greater than the sum of its parts, the countries. The corporate and divisional management can persuade and negotiate, but for the most part, the quest for entrepreneurial freedom seems to take priority over upper management directives. The Chinese Wall works.

One example of this is the freedom which the operating companies have when they choose a supplier for their cleaning products. The ISS operating company, Darenas, provides a full line of cleaning products, but the operating units are not required to buy them, though some formerly reluctant country managers have yielded to pressure to do so. In a similar vein, corporate or divisional-level strategic priorities are not normally pushed on a country manager who does not 'buy in'. That is why there were several countries in Europe who had little or no activity in Hospitals or Food in 1992, in spite of the corporate strategy to target these areas.

The country management can be a barrier to strategic plans from above, but there are also instances when the local manager finds the corporate strategy to be a barrier to his own initiative. The managing director of Mediclean, the UK hospital service company, saw an attractive opportunity to purchase an interest in a prepared food company which sells its product to the British National Health Service. He felt it would be a strong complement to the hospital catering business he provided. The investment was not approved by divisional management because 'Our strategy is not to invest in food manufacturing.' The managing director feels that if he had been the true owner of Mediclean, he would have risked his capital on the new venture. In the end, informal ties were made with the company that allow Mediclean to enjoy most of the sought-after benefits without any risk of capital.

The divisional management has taken the lead in developing the strategy and infrastructure to meet the emerging demand by customers for single-point facilities management. The European division became a partner in 1992 in a marketing company called 'Service Interface' which coordinates a number of service companies to provide an all-inclusive facility management contract. Beyond the cleaning service offered by ISS, the companies in the partnership provide catering, technical maintenance, waste management, textile services and security services. The idea has been well received in the UK market and Schmidt hopes to sell the idea to other countries in Europe. He comments, 'It's an interesting alternative to acquiring companies.'

The overall demand for such one-stop shopping was uncertain, however. The Scandinavian division provided a similar type of 'multi-service' to clients in the early 1990s by offering a complete ISS contract covering the range of available services: cleaning, security, catering, landscaping and textiles, with one contract manager and integrated billing. The programme was discontinued when it became evident that the majority of customers actually preferred dealing with multiple vendors so that they could leverage one against another to gain a better overall price. Additionally, customer decision-making often occurred in different parts of the organization for the various services that ISS was providing, making smooth coordination very difficult.

Measurement

The divisional management team is responsible for setting the targets for the MRS budget for each unit manager based on the corporate guidelines for the year as articulated during the planning process. These targets, such as sales growth, contribution margin and profit before tax, vary slightly by country and are always an improvement over the previous year's performance. This emphasis on the financials prompted one manager to exclaim, 'The only vision we get from above are numbers!'

Retained earnings which are accumulated by each operating company are not its own to keep. For historical reasons, ISS Scandinavia is an exception and enjoys the right to keep the balance of the earnings of its operating companies not paid out as dividends and to reinvest the funds as it chooses. The European division was not set up with this autonomy and therefore, in principle, its earnings are returned to corporate to be redistributed throughout ISS as headquarters sees fit.

There is some dissatisfaction with the policy which allows one division to keep its retained earnings. Its opponents believe that investment funds should be applied to the best opportunity within the entire corporation. As one manager remarked:

> When ISS Scandinavia bought the rest of the Finnish cleaning company in 1992, it was probably the best opportunity they had to grow their turnover ... but I think there were better investment opportunities in the European division where ISS has a very small presence.

The drive for continually improving financial returns combined with an extremely conservative approach to reinvesting in the local business is a source of frustration for some business unit managers. As one remarked:

> There is no extra money to develop a business on your own. I could expand more rapidly if I got some funding from corporate. It's easier to acquire a company [than grow internally] because corporate will provide that money.

Transferring Knowledge

ISS has several formal platforms which attempt to transfer best practices among operations and geographies. Until 1991, a group of all the senior management and managing directors (the *Top Management Conference*) within ISS met annually to discuss relevant issues. As the company grew, the group exceeded 100 people, making it hard to create a participative environment for sharing. Therefore, the divisions began holding a similar meeting several times a year with the appropriate participants within their division which limited the group to a more workable number.

In the last European Division TMC, attended by 30 managers, the group spent the first day discussing how to improve their business development capabilities by using Belgium's process as an example of one successful strategy. The second day was spent discussing methods to improve customer retention by learning from the progress that Holland had made in this area.

At the corporate level, and within the European and Scandinavian divisions, there are a number of committees which share information and make decisions on common systems. At the corporate level, the committees meet two to four times each year on the subjects of Quality, Strategy, Human Resources, Finance and Marketing to develop general policies in these areas. The membership of these committees is drawn primarily from the divisional and corporate management. Similar committees exist in many of the same functions at the divisional level to provide a forum for sharing ideas among countries. While some within ISS see the committee structure to be one of the few available mechanisms to share expertise within the company, others are less supportive of the system. One manager commented, 'The committees are not very well-liked. They're too expensive with no value.'

There is no formal mechanism for sharing ideas and practices between line managers below the country management level. While contact with other ISS managers outside their own country structure is limited for managers in staff functions (i.e. finance and sales), it is practically non-existent for line management. Thus, a district manager for office cleaning in Austria has no contact with his or her counterpart in the United Kingdom, for example. Explaining the difficulty of sharing new methods, one manager remarked, 'A new idea which appears in one country has to go all the way up through the division or even corporate and back down to another country to be shared.'

ISS had a matrix organization in the early 1980s of corporate-level product managers for each service segment such as Food and Hospitals whose mission was to transfer best practices across the operating units in different countries. Most of these product managers were young and inexperienced in the cleaning business; thus they spent much of their time 'publishing manuals'. The limitations of this approach to sharing best practices was revealed when the Hospital Service manual for Denmark was given to ISS in New York to assist them in their entry into the business. The New York management was disappointed to find that the education level of their workforce was not high enough to read the manuals and execute the complicated calculations used in the procedures. Results such as this one made it difficult to justify the value-added and, after a short time, the product manager positions were eliminated. In 1992, corporate management again proposed a matrix structure which would assign a product manager at the corporate level for two service areas. In part due to the last experience with this type of position, the division management opposed the proposal and it was dropped.

Communication within ISS seems to work best on an informal basis with the business unit managers reaping the most benefit when sharing their experiences in new service areas. Denmark has supported a significant amount of training of managers from other countries in the Food business, both in Denmark and in their home countries. An idea for a new vacuum cleaner which could be carried on the operator's back for cleaning trains travelled from Denmark back to the UK through a chance visit by a British manager. Yet, informal sharing does have its limits. As the Germany country manager explains: 'I would like to be aggressive on Food but I don't have enough knowledge. I can't ask Denmark to lend me a person for four weeks. The royalty [paid to corporate] doesn't cover that.' Nevertheless, he does not support the idea of paying for this service because, 'These things must work informally, colleague to colleague.'

The most successful example of transferring learning within ISS occurred when a very experienced and multilingual planner from Denmark spent several years travelling between offices in Europe giving advice to the operations and sharing his experiences. Also, helping to share ideas on a regular basis, ISS corporate publishes a quarterly newsletter, *ISS News*, which gives an indepth review of one country's business in each issue, as well as the key events happening throughout the rest of the ISS world. Within the countries, other newsletters update the employees on the latest happenings.

Beyond the organizational difficulties, the lack of a common language inhibits the sharing between countries. With the exception of the managing directors and their financial directors, the ability to speak the most likely common language, English, is often lacking, apart from in the United States, the United Kingdom and Scandinavia. This discourages common training and teamwork across countries in many cases. One manager, who has the experience to compare ISS's ability in this area with other multinational companies in other industries, feels that ISS managers have a lower level of multilingual ability than most multinational companies of its size.

Expertise

The division management provides mainly financial and marketing expertise to the countries. In the financial domain, the divisional financial director spends several days a year with each country performing an indepth audit of their financial records and systems. During this visit, and as needed throughout the year, he gives advice on such matters as cash management, insurance, reduction of debtor days, and other similar concerns. The divisional-level finance committee is also active in sharing financial tools between countries.

The marketing expertise at the divisional level was added in the late 1980s to assist the countries in meeting the challenge of organic growth. Several years later, all managing directors are not yet comfortable with the new emphasis in this area. As one managing director expressed:

> When I'm thinking of marketing, I'm saying ooh, it costs. I'm much more operations-oriented. All the problems my people are having today, I was through years ago. I have a much more open eye and ear for operations problems than marketing issues.

In recognition of the fact that most of the country managers had grown up with ISS, building their organizations through their expertise in operations, the two most recent country manager recruits in Holland and Belgium came from marketing and sales backgrounds in non-service industries.

The ISS sales and marketing function varies in strength and sophistication from country to country. In most country organizations, the two are combined into one function with the sales function being the stronger of the two. To target customers, an ISS salesman would typically drive through a neighbourhood, noting all large buildings which were not ISS clients and any new office buildings under construction. These potential customers would then be contacted by mail or telephone to try to set up a meeting to discuss the client's needs. In some countries, ISS is the only cleaning company to have a professional sales and marketing department.

The European divisional efforts to assist in the country marketing plans have been met with mixed feelings. Though the market data which the division provides is welcomed by the countries, the feeling is that marketing is a line function, not a staff position. One country manager commented, 'How can someone from the division help us write a marketing plan when they don't even know the market?'

In 1992, the European marketing director sponsored a study of the cleaning opportunities in the food processing segment within Europe. When the study showed a very attractive opportunity for ISS in this area, the European division proposed to its member countries that they aggressively go after the market with a pan-European salesman who could support and leverage the countries' individual efforts by selling to customers who have multiple food processing operations across Europe. This thrust met with strong resistance from the country management for a variety of reasons, but primarily because 'it was too much, too fast'.

Though Theo Buitendijk of Holland had the leading Food business in the European division, he opposed the plan. He argued that first everyone in Europe must get some experience in the industry so that they could properly support it. 'We must not sell hot air.' He remembers very well a contract he lost with a multinational in the Netherlands due to problems in the service provided by the Spanish ISS subsidiary with the same multinational client in Spain. In explanation, he says, 'In professional services, we sell confidence. My customer must believe in my blue eyes. We don't sell on our name in Europe, we're too small.'

Buitendijk feels that as long as ISS corporate promotes the virtues of high strategic autonomy at the country level, it will be a long time before ISS Europe can provide the consistent, high quality service in Food that he believes is needed to support a pan-European strategy. He suggests that if ISS wants to speed the implementation of these types of multiple-country strategies, 'They should direct or force us ... rather than leaving it up to each country manager.' In the end, the pan-European proposal was 'shelved' awaiting further market analysis and discussions. In spite of the lack of progress in Food, the European division was still working to market office cleaning services to multinationals across Europe.

The division management teams also provide other services which an individual country would not normally be able to support on its own. For example, the European division did a study for its countries to help them understand the impact of the 1992 Common Market in terms of labour law, health and safety, public sector policies and other areas relevant to the ISS operating companies.

Beyond his strategic, control and support roles, Schmidt feels the biggest help he can provide to his country managers is showing that he cares:

> It's very difficult with 25 companies to spend a lot of time with each. The most important thing is to show an interest, show that you care about them and their performance. When I receive the monthly management report, I often call people who do not even report to me and say 'well done'. When David Openshaw was struggling to build a business from scratch, I would send him a bottle of champagne every time his turnover increased by a million pounds ... I also try to notice when things aren't going so well and give a call to say 'What happened?'

Additionally, several managing directors have profited from the one-on-one assistance that divisional management has been able to provide during some rough times. When the managing director in Belgium, was hired in1989 from the pharmaceuticals industry, Ken Pepper, the European chief operations officer worked very closely with him for a year to turn the business around. Pepper was able to add value due to his many years in line management in the UK cleaning industry. He remembers that a big part of this help was in the role of a sounding board for his colleage as he tried to apply some of his marketing ideas from the pharmaceuticals industry to ISS's cleaning business.

AT THE HELM: POUL ANDREASSEN

In 1992, Poul Andreassen was preparing to retire as head of ISS within the next two years. He will leave a company which has been deeply imprinted with his management ideals. He feels satisfied with the role he has played in the first 30 years of his leadership because during that period he has laid down a network of values which have served ISS well. He explains:

> I was the right man at the right time … with the entrepreneurial personality and qualifications. I believe I had the right approach, maybe because of my [working-class] background.

Establishing Values

ISS has been built upon a few guiding principles laid down by Andreassen from his early days: financial conservatism, respect for workers and the professionalism of the industry. Though ISS has always functioned as an extremely decentralized organization, he has used 'centralized training and information functions to, more or less, instill in the people the same attitude to handling various situations'.

Andreassen characterizes ISS as a conservative company which 'doesn't like to speculate or go into risky businesses'. He points to the monthly MRS reports as an example of a conservative tool to keep the business on track. If the numbers did not make a good story, ISS would quickly get out of the business. ISS quit a number of business over the years, including restaurants in Scandinavia and cleaning operations in Australia and France because of negative returns. Andreassen claims that he has the patience to suffer some losses in businesses he knows, but not otherwise.

The message to the rest of ISS concerning how failures are handled is very clear because of the transparency of the MRS reports which are widely available within many levels of the company. Andreassen comments:

> We never cut a failure before everyone expects it. I mean everyone can see the MRS, month by month, year by year. I would say it's more the other reaction … if I have too much patience with a company, then the other people say, hey, wait a minute. We're not going to pay a lot of money for that other business to blow it.

He feels he allows a large margin for failure, though if someone fails too often, action must be taken.

> A manager shouldn't be afraid in a given situation to make his decisions, even if he doesn't know all the prerequisites. But then again, he has to accept the fact that there is a professional hazard involved if he wants to be a leader, that if he doesn't succeed he won't have the glory. He risks losing his stars.

The financial conservatism of ISS is one reason why large amounts of funding are not made to develop businesses from scratch. Andreassen is not against new investments of this type but he is very cautious; they must be backed by a budget and a plan. ISS's bad experience in France taught the company a strong lesson. He describes what ISS learned:

> You can't just say I want to go into this business – let me hire ten salesmen. I saw that in Security in France. Fifty salesman with all their allowances …. He got the 50 people

but certainly did not live up to the expectations for sales performance and revenue. So we had big losses and then he didn't want to stop. So it depends on how realistic the plans and profits are.

Andreassen points to the example of when David Openshaw started an ISS business from scratch in London to show that even a conservative financial policy can support the right investment:

> He came with a plan and a budget. We looked at the plan and said OK, go ahead. It's the third year now. If they come up with a plan and a budget, very few people have negative answers.

Andreassen holds his workforce in high regard and strongly believes in training as a lever for building professionalism in the firm and the industry:

> These people are trained which gives us an image, a profile in public that this is a modern company that is doing an important job. We try to build this image all the time. Not so much with lots of advertising, but by doing what we're doing. Training is also a demonstration of caring because it costs someone. People need to know that they're number 1, well-trained and to be told that, 'You're important and this is your company.'

The professional reputation Andreassen has built is recognized by the multinational clients that ISS seeks. In 1992, the company won a contract with Eastman Kodak for its whole industrial complex in Rochester, New York. The work had previously been performed by in-house employees. ISS was asked to make an offer for the job in an unusual situation where the job was not opened up for bidding. Andreassen attributes its 'win' with Kodak to be due to the ISS professional image and the fact that it is subscribing to the same TQM principles that Kodak espouses to its employees.

Challenge and Stretch

Andreassen sees his personal role as that of the innovator and challenger, not an administrator. His managers have complained in the past that he moves too fast, changing direction before they have implemented the first plan. Understanding that it takes a large company more time to move, his philosophy remains that, 'If you stop struggling for it, then nothing will happen.' Expanding on his personal management style, he continues:

> I like new ideas, I like to stir up new things, new concepts .... One of my best days is when they [the divisions or business units] ask me to come out and sit down and discuss for one or two days with them, where I challenge them .... But I say to them, 'This is what I am criticizing and this is what I recommend, but in the end, it is your choice.'

He sees no one management style which is essential for ISS's continued development, though he believes that there needs to be a good balance between entrepreneurship and management controls.

> As an innovator, I choose to have good planning administrators among the top executives around me. But another man could come in and be a planner or an economist, for instance, and run this company on a more bookkeeping approach. Then he would need to have some aggressive people underneath him to spark the innovation, as well as someone to judge what they're doing.

Though within ISS, the managing directors are commonly called entrepreneurs, Andreassen characterizes them differently:

> Those people are intrapreneurs, not entrepreneurs. The people that are willing to stay at ISS have more or less the same values as I ... that they like to grow and they have talents for making this happen, but not for their own money. From the start they like to be in a company where they have some control, where they're not on their own, they like to work for other people.

Foundation for the Future

Poul Andreassen sees no change in the ISS mission as the company continues its geographic and service expansion:

> ISS's mission is to be the international market leader, within our business areas, not only regarding our product areas but also how we manage a service company, how we treat and work with our employees, how we organize, how our customer service works, how we are conceived as an investment object.

He has worked with his management team to create a shared Vision 2000 for ISS to help drive its service and personnel development into the future. It includes services for the elderly, service in the private home market and increased partnering with the public sector.

Andreassen considers the TQM strategy to be critical to ISS's future. It will not only be a marketing tool, but more importantly, it will help integrate the ISS units through the communication which will have to take place to pursue quality:

> Training people, bringing them together, creates new ideas for new services. I think this is one of the most important benefits of TQM. The Quality Institute will be the driving wheel. The people in the special service companies will be in a group under the Quality Institute. No product management, but they themselves will have to say how can we improve our business, customer satisfaction, our value-added service.

Carrying the benefits of communication through training even further, Andreassen hopes to have an ongoing training programme beginning in 1994 for ISS top management at the Quality Institute to help establish a stronger network at the very top of the company.

> They will have to sit together for 14 days and get to know each other. And when they have a problem in San Francisco, they can call someone in Amsterdam, and say 'Hey John, can't you send me some ...'

The effort must wait until 1994, however, to avoid overwhelming the management agenda. With the restructuring of the special service companies, TQM and the 5 Star training programme all in full swing, in 1992, senior managers could not cope with another major initiative at the same time.

Andreassen feels comfortable about leaving ISS in someone else's hands. He expects his successor to be different from him and it is unclear whether he or she will come from within or outside of ISS. He is not concerned though because he has changed the image of cleaning from being a 'dirty business'.

> Now you can find somebody, I think you can find many, many people. Now it's a professional job. Still the top managers can choose between a beer brewery and tobacco

companies or food manufacturing. I think many would prefer that to coming here. But I certainly know people I would like to see and that would be interested to follow me in this job today. They would never have dreamed of it 10 or 15 years ago.

EXHIBIT 1
ISS income statement, 1990-2.
(DKKm)

	1992	1991	1990
Consolidated Turnover	11,356.0	11,805.7	9,610.1
Staff Costs	8,326.5	8,572.3	6,931.4
Cost of Goods Sold	783.6	929.8	835.9
Other Operating Costs	1,379.0	1,398.9	1,139.5
Depreciation	329.9	322.8	289.7
Operating Profit	537.0	581.9	413.6
Amortization of Goodwill	60.7	62.2	17.8
Income from Participating Interests	3.4	8.9	10.1
Interest Receivable and Similar Income	74.1	73.7	42.8
Interest Payable and Similar Charges	180.0	270.6	182.7
Interest Receivable (Payable), Net	(105.9)	(196.9)	(139.9)
Profit on Ordinary Operations	373.8	331.7	266.0
Other Income	35.1	10.6	103.8
Other Expenses	31.9	13.8	101.7
Other Income (Expenses), Net	3.2	(3.2)	2.1
Profit before Tax	377.0	328.5	268.1
Tax on Profit for the Year	105.9	82.0	62.5
Consolidated Profit	271.1	246.5	205.6
Minority Interests	(5.2)	(2.8)	(1.0)
ISS Consolidated Net Profit	265.9	243.7	204.6

Source: ISS Annual report, 1992.

EXHIBIT 2
ISS consolidated balance sheet, 31 December 1992.
(DKKm)

Assets	1992	
Fixed Assets		
Intangible assets		
Goodwill	990.0	
Development costs	7.8	
Leasehold improvements	47.0	
		1,044.8
Tangible assets		
Land and buildings	392.2	
Production plant	70.5	
Service equipment, vehicles and fixtures	751.9	
Assets under construction	53.3	
		1,267.9
Financial assets		
Investments in associated companies	4.4	
Other securities	18.3	
Other receivables	75.6	
		98.3
TOTAL FIXED ASSETS		2,411.0
Current Assets		
Stocks		254.9
Debtors		
Trade debtors	1,123.9	
Other debtors	249.9	
		1,373.8
Securities		89.4
Cash at bank and in hand		539.9
TOTAL CURRENT ASSETS		2,258.0
TOTAL ASSETS		4,669.0

Liabilities	1992	
Equity		
Share capital	432.9	
Reserves	564.6	
ISS Shareholders' Equity	997.5	
Minority Interests	129.8	
TOTAL CONSOLIDATED EQUITY		1,127.3
Provisions for Liabilities and Charges		
Deferred tax	101.4	
Other provisions	226.2	
TOTAL PROVISIONS		327.6
Long-term Creditors		
Bond loan	477.3	
Mortgage debt	35.0	
Bank loans and other debt	679.3	
TOTAL LONG-TERM CREDITORS		1,191.6
Short-term Creditors		
Bond loan	0	
Mortgage debt	1.4	
Bank loans and other debt	117.9	
Trade creditors and other debt	1,197.1	
Prepayments from customers	66.9	
Corporation tax	50.2	
Tax withholdings, VAT, etc.	545.7	
Dividend	43.3	
TOTAL SHORT-TERM CREDITORS		2,022.5
TOTAL PROVISIONS AND CREDITORS		3,541.7
TOTAL LIABILITIES		4,669.0

Source: ISS Annual Report, 1992.

EXHIBIT 3
ISS B-shares (1983 = 100).

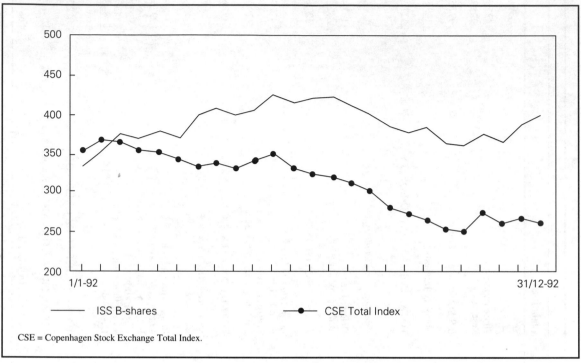

CSE = Copenhagen Stock Exchange Total Index.

EXHIBIT 4
Profit and loss statement.

ISS Servisystem Marischka											SA: 10 R: 1 D: 3	
Company No.: 412	Beträge in A.S.										Distriktmanager: Steinreiber Erich	
September 1992												

| | Month | | | | Year to Data | | | | Total Year | | | |
| | Budget | | Actual | | Budget | | Actual | | Budget | | Estim. | |
	%	Amount	%	Amount	%	Amount	%	Amount	%	Amount	%	Amount
Sales External	100.0	7,894	100.0	8,063	100.0	67,075	100.0	70,388	100.0	90,227	100.0	92,000
Sales to Sub-group co.s	0.0	0	0.0	0	0.0	0	0.0	0	0.0	0	0.0	0
Sales to Other ISS co.s	0.0	0	0.0	0	0.0	0	0.0	0	0.0	0	0.0	0
Sales to Other Groups co.s	0.0	0	0.0	0	0.0	0	0.0	0	0.0	0	0.0	0
TOTAL SALES	100.0	7,894	100.0	8,063	100.0	67,075	100.0	70,388	100.0	90,227	100.0	92,000
Net Wages	36.0	2,839	37.6	3,029	36.1	24,196	36.7	25,839	36.2	32,619	36.9	33,919
Additional Wages & Social Chg	26.3	2,077	27.7	2,233	26.4	17,724	27.1	19,063	26.5	23,883	27.2	25,024
TOTAL WAGES	62.3	4,916	65.3	5,262	62.5	41,920	63.8	44,902	62.6	56,502	64.1	58,943
Subcontractors	0.0	0	0.0	0	0.0	0	0.0	0	0.0	0	0.0	0
TOTAL WAGES + SUBCONTRACTORS	62.3	4,916	65.3	5,262	62.5	41,920	63.8	44,902	62.6	56,502	64.1	58,943
Transportation	2.2	173	2.1	173	2.2	1,502	2.3	1,592	2.2	2,027	2.3	2,151
Material Consumption	2.6	209	2.6	207	2.6	1,776	2.3	1,649	2.7	2,393	2.4	2,230
Machinery & Equipment	1.3	106	1.2	95	1.5	1,007	1.2	848	1.5	1,356	1.4	1,248
Supervision	5.1	400	3.6	292	5.1	3,388	3.9	2,777	5.1	4,599	4.2	3,850
Other Production Costs	1.1	88	0.9	70	1.2	790	1.0	683	1.2	1,049	1.1	970
TOTAL DIRECT PRODUCTION COSTS	74.6	5,892	75.6	6,099	75.1	50,383	74.5	52,451	75.3	67,926	75.4	69,392
CONTRACT CONTRIBUTION	25.4	2,002	24.4	1,964	24.9	16,692	25.5	17,937	24.7	22,301	24.6	22,608
Brarch Management	3.1	245	2.0	165	3.3	2,218	2.3	1,642	3.3	2,971	2.5	2,312
CONTRIBUTION I	22.3	1,757	22.3	1,799	21.6	14,474	23.2	16,295	21.4	19,330	22.1	20,296
District Planning Costs	0.0	0	0.0	0	0.0	0	0.0	0	0.0	0	0.0	0
District Stock Costs	0.0	0	0.0	0	0.0	0	0.0	0	0.0	0	0.0	0
District Sales Costs	0.0	0	0.0	0	0.0	0	0.0	0	0.0	0	0.0	0
District Office Costs	0.0	0	0.0	0	0.0	0	0.0	0	0.0	0	0.0	0
District Management	0.0	0	0.0	0	0.0	0	0.0	0	0.0	0	0.0	0
District Joint Costs	0.0	0	0.0	0	0.0	0	0.0	0	0.0	0	0.0	0
Reg. Management + Joint Costs	0.0	0	0.0	0	0.0	0	0.0	0	0.0	0	0.0	0
TOTAL DISTRICT + REGION COSTS	0.0	0	0.0	0	0.0	0	0.0	0	0.0	0	0.0	0
CONTRIBUTION II	22.3	1,757	22.3	1,799	21.6	14,474	23.2	16,295	21.4	19,330	22.1	20,296

Source: ISS Marischka.

EXHIBIT 5
The ISS magic formula.

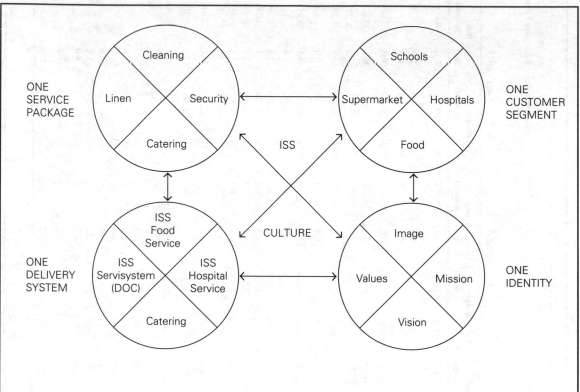

EXHIBIT 6
ISS activities.

	Cleaning and maintenance	Special services for the food industry	Special services for the health sector	Landscape management service	Sales of cleaning products and machinery	Security service	Linen service	Canteen service	Energy service	Other act.
Denmark	■	■	■	■	■	■	■	■	■	■
Sweden	■	■	■	■					■	■
Norway	■	■	■	■		■	■	■	■	■
Finland	■	■	■							■
United Kingdom	■	■	■	■	■				■	■
Germany	■	■		■						
Switzerland	■	■	■					■		■
Austria	■		■			■				
Hungary	■	■	■							
Slovenia	■		■							
Holland	■	■	■					■		
Belgium	■	■								
Greece	■					■				
Spain	■		■							
Portugal	■									
Brazil	■	■		■	■					■
United States	■			■	■				■	■

Source: ISS.

EXHIBIT 7
ISS results by division and service area, 1990-2.
(DK Km)

	1992	1991	1990
Results by Division			
Turnover			
Scandinavia	5,079	4,984	3,444
Europe & Brazil	2,943	3,341	2,924
North America	3,001	3,217	2,962
Clorius	323	250	258
Others	10	14	22
	11,356	11,806	9,610
Operating Profit			
Scandinavia	288	305	182
Europe & Brazil	159	177	155
North America	127	133	123
Clorius	21	16	(6)
Others	(58)	(49)	(40)
	537	582	414
Results by Service Area			
Turnover			
Cleaning and maintenance	9,432	9,449	7,303
Security services	795	963	926
Canteen/catering services	310	541	594
Sales of cleaning products and machinery	149	188	165
Linen services	329	341	339
Energy services	323	285	258
Others	18	39	25
	11,356	11,806	9,610
Operating Profit			
Cleaning and maintenance	498	539	330
Security services	57	56	52
Canteen/catering services	9	18	34
Sales of cleaning products and machinery	18	16	19
Linen services	34	32	28
Energy services	21	18	(6)
Others	(100)	(97)	(43)
	537	582	414

Source: ISS Annual report, 1992.

EXHIBIT 8
ISS organization, January 1993.

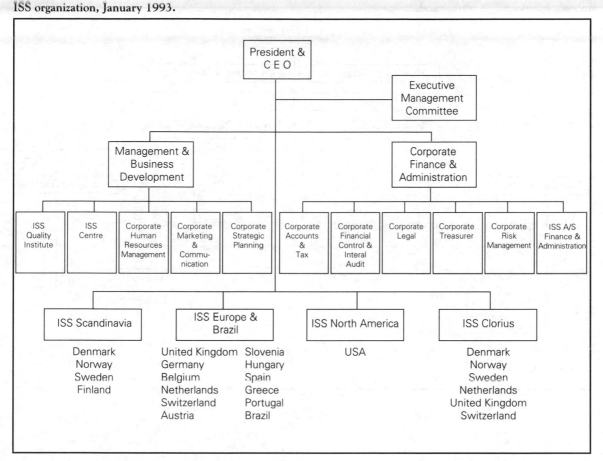

EXHIBIT 9
ISS organization: The Netherlands.

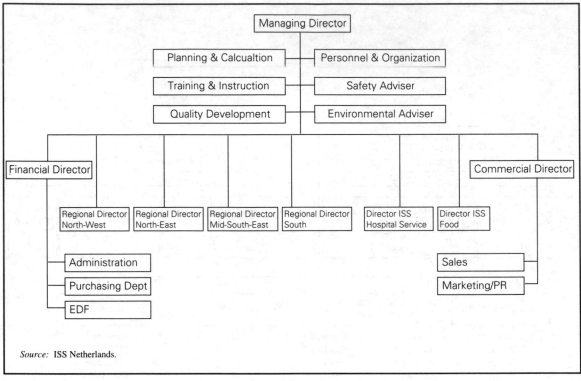

Source: ISS Netherlands.

EXHIBIT 10
Basic constituents for a five-star programme.

Subject	One Star	Two Star	Three Star
ISS Knowledge	Basic overview – local and international	Basic financial reports – structure, ownership, etc.	Vision, mission and strategy
Function of Job	Role, responsibilities and success criteria	Role responsibilities and success criteria	Role responsibilities and success criteria
Contract Control Systems	Labour: hours/wages, social costs, numbers	Staff turnover %'s and costs, materials, machinery	Contract profitability and contribution
Cleaning Systems	Basic work methods and material standards	Machinery and equipment usage	Chemicals, technology, equipment, materials-flow
Personnel Management	Recruitment and selection	Team-building and interpersonal skills	Basic pers. administration and the contract's labour relations
Risk Management, Health and Safety	Personal appearance, job safety, safety precautions and regulations. First aid	Hazard training and communications/signs, exits substances, storage	Loss control (both ISS and customer property) and insurance
Customer Relations	Attitudes and professionalism	Complaint handling/corrective action	Proactive customer relations on service quality
Quality Control	What is quality and why have it? What is a quality standard? Introduction to ISO 9000 where applicable	Quality: Inspection and maintaining, identifying shortfalls and reasons, corrective action. ISO 9000 responsibilities	Taking quality to consistent, uniform delivery; 100 per cent performance
Training Skills	On job – one-to-one skills training	Refresh	Group training skill
Leadership Techniques	Motivation	Communication	Problem-solving and decision-making in the HR arena **Extra Courses** Contract planning and rationalisation: An Introduction Basic overview of time management (personal & work related)

ALL COUNTRIES CAN ADD COURSE MATERIAL WHICH IS APPLICABLE TO THEIR OWN LOCAL MARKET

Subject	Four Star	Five Star
ISS Knowledge	Who's who? Local and international	ISS News: Company Progress: How to keep up to date: Local and international news: The communications channels
Financial Knowledge		Basic P/L, balance and budgets Negotiation skills
Management Skills	Basic MRS Handling meetings Problem-solving and decision-making	Delegation, appraisal skills Organizing
Sales	Customer care Selling add-ons	Customer relations Sales techniques and service department
Contract Review	Contract planning and rationalization	Contract analysis cycle
Human Resources	Employment law overview	Industrial relations
Training Development	Review training skills	Organizing, monitoring and assessing training

Polaroid started as a inventor's story on the classical model.[1] A superbly gifted inventor and scientist, Edwin Land, created Polaroid in 1937 and remained its chairman and director of research until 1982, when he stepped aside to pursue his research interests full time and be available as a consultant to Polaroid. Mr William McCune, CEO since 1980 and a longtime colleague and friend of Dr Land, had to reposition the company in light of some powerful new competitive forces.

EARLY HISTORY

Edwind Land never graduated from Harvard, preferring to form a company with one of his professors. His doctorate was honorary. But his attachment to research and invention was inseparable and ultimately led to his acquiring over 500 patents. Dr Land's innovative mind caused one associate to claim, in reference to Land's original instant photography work: '100 PhD's would not have been able to duplicate Land's feat in ten years of uninterrupted work.'[2] Yet Land develped the basic physical elements of this process within six months. Polaroid was actually founded on Land's invention of a light-polarizing sheet material, which filtered out all light except that vibrating in a single plane. Normally light waves vibrate in myriad planes as they

Case copyright © 1985 by James Brian Quinn.

Research associate, Penny C. Pacquette.

Case derived solely from secondary sources. Numbers in brackets indicate the reference page number for material from a previously footnoted source.

emanate from a source. By crossing these planes two polarized sheets could eliminate light or glare as desired.

Land's early efforts concentrated on manufacturing easily marketed products like sunglasses and scientific products. And almost from the beginning, his company earned a profit (2,154). In 1937 Land incorporated the company, selling common stock to the Rothschilds and Baron Schroder under an unusual agreement that allowed him to maintain control. The agreement gave Land power over a trust that held the majority of the stock (1,116). With this unusual beginning, Polaroid issued no long-term debt for years, financing itself internally and through stock issues. Among other innovations, Polaroid was one of the first public companies consciously to adopt a 'low-dividend' policy, offering its stockholders the opportunity of taking almost all their profits as capital gains. The company grew rapidly through the World War II period when it was a government supplier of specialized optical products.

But Land hoped to design his product into automobile headlights and windshields to reduce night driving glare (2,157). With windshields polarized in one direction and headlights in another, each driver would have a full view of the road ahead with no glare from oncoming lights. In 1947 although Detroit had successfully tested the headlight polarizing system, the automakers turned them down (2,157). The industry saw no practical way to equip the 33 million cars then on the roads and was concerned that owners of those vehicles might be handicapped by the somewhat brighter headlights needed on filter-equipped cars.

INSTANT PHOTOGRAPHY

The year 1947 started dismally, but all that changed in February when Land disclosed his now famous 60-second photographic process. Land's inspiration came one day during World War II, as he was taking pictures of his daughter. She had asked impatiently why she could not see the finished picture right away. The question triggered Land's fertile imagination. And he soon conceptualized the basic idea for his revolutionary product. But he worked three long years before the process produced a sufficiently acceptable result. The secret lay in a self-developing film packet. Once he achieved initial success with this, Land moved quickly (in 1947) to design a camera to handle the film. William McClune, then a Polaroid engineer, and several associates contributed a series of important early inventions to support Land's work (2,157). But this was only the beginning of a decades-long quest to develop improved films and cameras for instant photography.

The full requirements of the camera and film were beyond the financial capabilities of the young Polaroid Corporation, and it turned to outside contractors for much of its production. Protected by over 1,000 patents, Polaroid ultimately had Bell & Howell and US Time manufacture the camera, while Kodak supplied the negative film. Polaroid produced only the unique instant positive film and used its remaining manpower to market the camera.[3]

Sales grew from $1.5 million in 1947 to nearly $100 million by 1960. During this period Polaroid offered only black and white film – but vastly improved the quality of both its cameras and the film. It stayed strictly in the high (over $100) end of the camera market, while most of its potential competitors, including Kodak, scoffed at the idea of a large instant picture market (2,125). In fact, Kodak worked with Polaroid, helping the growing fledgling introduce the world's first instant colour film in 1963. This technological achievement spurred Polaroid's sales in the mid-1960s as Polaroid rode a burgeoning amateur photography market along with Kodak and its Instamatic line.

By 1963 Polaroid completely dominated the high-priced 'instant' camera field and began to eye the much larger inexpensive segment controlled by Kodak. The Polaroid Swinger – a black and white camera selling for under $20 – introduced in the autumn of 1965 was an immediate success.[4] Polaroid soon expaned its presence with the Big Swinger (in 1968) and Colorpak II in 1969. In each case, the new camera, priced within $5 of its predecessor, overwhelmed the former model, and large inventories of the older cameras were often sold below cost to discount houses.[4]

SX-70 AND SHOCKWAVES

Still, in this period Polaroid began to face some ominous problems. Its original patents for instant photography started to expire in 1965. While newer patents prevented immediate competition, other companies would be able to enter the instant picture market by 1970. And Polaroid's successful forays into the low price camera market had stimulated Kodak's interest in instant photography.[4]

In the early 1960s, Dr Land began organizing a project team to revolutionize instant photography and leapfrog past his competition into another fortress of patents. As Land's project team pushed both film technology and the camera design art (Land called it forced evolution) Polaroid became involved in such seemingly unrelated fields as integrated circuits and batteries. Polaroid's new products had such demanding standards that they required significant design and manufacturing cooperation with suppliers. During this period, talented Polaroid engineers often 'lived' with vendors to help them achieve new and rigorous design and production specifications. Virtually all of this project's work was performed without any market research except Polaroid's own confidence in knowing its customers' needs.[5]

Polaroid felt market research was only valid as a method of delineating an existing market, not for evaluating an entirely new concept. Land always held that Polaroid's product created the market, rather than the market dictating the product. This was in part why he could withstand the knee-buckling scepticism and delays that accompanied the introduction of the revolutionary SX-70 line. He later scoffed at those who 'couldn't see the potential of a $600 camera value marketed in the $100 range'.[6]

In 1972, this project ('Aladdin') bore its professed creation, the SX-70. The camera offered startling improvements over previous models. Its colour film literally developed before the customer's eyes. The distasteful refuse layers generated by the old 'peel apart' process were eliminated. And the camera itself was a marvel of optical engineering. The SX-70's development costs had been staggering; some estimates were as high as $600 million (including buildings) over its full duration.

Polaroid initiated another important shift along with the introduction of the SX-70. Because of the camera's sophistication and Kodak's impending instant camera introduction, Polaroid decided to manufacture and assemble the major components of the camera 'in house', as well as produce the negatives for its film. This decision not only required substantial investments in plant and equipment (over $200 million) between 1968 and 1972, but it strained the organization to adapt its highly unstructured management style to the routine operations of an assembly line.[7] The gamble also sent shockwaves down Wall Street, with many analysts doubting Polaroid's ability to maintain respectable earnings growth during this period (3,125).

In fact, the SX-70's introduction was plagued with bad luck. The national introduction was delayed until late 1973, while engineers scrambled to solve its problems. Production difficulties caused product shortages in most locales. The 1974 recession cut deeply into the SX-70's potential sales, as its high price ($180) kept it from the volume markets. At the same time there were complaints about the quality of the SX-70's innovative self-developing pictures, and the sale of other Polaroid models fell off more than expected. Profits for 1974 dropped to $28.4 million, down $23.4 million from the previous year.

Land Changes Roles

In January 1975 Dr Land stepped aside as president. Land wanted to get out of daily operations to concentrate on one of his favourite projects – instant movies – and he saw the need for a full-time operations manager. William McCune, who took over the presidency, was experienced in all phases of engineering and manufacturing and had spearheaded the project which removed Polaroid's colour negative manufacturing from Kodak's benevolent control. 'Bill' McCune had a warm, calm and relaxed manner even in crisis situations. Slim and greying, McCune understood the unique Polaroid organization and Dr Land's style well. He preferred to operate through consensus, but he was also demanding and wanted problems addressed. Said one executive at the time.

> 'He has known for years that certain things needed to be done around here, and now that he's got the charter he's doing them. ... We had been trying to get certain product decisions for as long as two years before Bill became president,' the executive added. 'The routine had been that one top guy thought this and another top guy thought that and the boss [Mr Land] was waffling. So we'd go back and get more data and do it all over again. Now Bill just says, "Okay, do it."[8]

McCune also removed some of the centralizing aura of Dr Land's style from operating decisions:

> McCune's orders are usually clear, but if they aren't I can say, 'Bill, what are you trying to tell me? Exactly what do you want me to do?' I would never dare ask Land that.[8]

A NEW ERA BEGINS

Polaroid faced its first direct competitor in 1975. Pint-sized Berkey Photo introduced an instant picture camera which used SX-70 film.[9] Polaroid's reaction was prompt and predictable; it immediately filed a patent infringement suit against Berkey. Despite this unexpected intruder into its domain. Polaroid rebounded to near record profits of $62.5 million in 1975. But the prospects of a much bloodier battle seemed in prospect when Kodak marketed its entry in April 1976. Instead, the entire instant photo market exploded. Even with Kodak initially grabbing 25 per cent of the market, Polaroid's sales grew to $950 million with record profits of $79.7 million by the end of 1976.

But the threat from the Rochester giant was lethal; and Polaroid, armed with its vast patent portfolio, pursued an injunction against Kodak to cease and desist from further manufacture of instant cameras and film. Similar actions in Canada and the United Kingdom temporarily prevented Kodak from offering its product, but Kodak's lawyers soon found a way out from each injunction.[9] Still, counter-punching effectively with Kodak, Polaroid's sales and profits grew while Kodak's instant camera division operated in the red.[10] Then from the east, a third challenger, Fuji Photo of Japan, reared its head and began its tentative probing of what had been Polaroid's exclusive domain only two years before.

As a partial counter to these entries, in 1977 Polaroid introduced instant movies. Dr Land had been determined to provide a moving picture complement to his instant still pictures. But the initial product entry, Polavision, was expensive ($699) and was positioned at the high end of a stagnant home movie market, representing only 10 per cent of the total photography market. Unlike SX-70, the camera and hardware were manufactured outside Polaroid. With his characteristic optimism, Dr Land entered the new field hoping to generate the same response that occurred 30 years before (9,45). As he had so many times before, Dr Land made the announcement of this new product dramatically at the 1976 stockholders' meeting (April 1977), a year before the product was to be fully available in the marketplace.

Unfortunately, Polavision was a striking failure in both technology and marketing – the very areas in which the company had been so strong,[11] and it was financially costly with three years of 'substantial' operating losses and a $68.5 million write off in 1979. But *Fortune* also noted,

> Polavision began in the late 1960s as part of Project Sesame, the code name the company used for experiments with film that is designed to be viewed by shining light through it (as opposed to film designed to produce printed pictures). One consolation for Polaroid is that Polavision is merely the first of the products that can be expected to grow out of Project Sesame ... Polaroid may have discovered a way to reduce the cost of manufacturing all instant color film ... In any case, there is an obvious application of the Polavision technology – instant slides.[11]

NEW COMPETITIVE FORCES

Instant cameras reached a peak of 41 per cent of the still photographic market in 1978, with Polaroid selling a record 9.4 million cameras worldwide. Confident of future growth, it launched an extensive capital expenditure programme to increase production of SX-70 cameras and film worldwide.[12] In 1979, after a 4-year growth of 41 per cent, the US camera market dropped 3 per cent.[13] Polaroid's unit sales plummeted more than 22 per cent just as its capital expansion projects neared completion. The worldwide recession of the following several years hurt the whole photographic industry, but even more so the instant cameras and films, which had always sold to lower income groups than those who bought conventional cameras.[14]

Polaroid fought to maintain and survive on its two-thirds share of the declining instant market. It introduced sonar automatic focusing, Time Zero Supercolor film, the Sun (light management system) cameras, and high-speed 600 ASA instant colour film. Kodak's share dropped from 40 per cent in 1978 to 30 per cent in 1982. But by 1982 Polaroid's instant still sales had fallen to an estimated 4 million units annually.

Fuji Photo's instant system was doing well in its Japanese home market, and Eastman upgraded its somewhat deficient instant line in 1982. In addition Kodak's new disc system had proved an immediate novelty and consumer success. Nimslo International had introduced a three-dimensional still process, but its market was generally considered a novelty.[15] Sony too had announced its all electronic Mavica camera and system, but in 1982 this required several cabinets of complex backup equipment to manipulate and display its images. Other important market trends are shown in Exhibits 2–7.

DIVERSIFICATION EFFORTS

Polaroid had for years marketed photographic products in non-consumer markets – such as instant cameras for use in hospitals and labs, microphotography cameras, panorama cameras, studio films, passport and driver's licence photo equipment and special event cameras.[16] As the amateur market for instant photography declined, the company began to devote more of its energies towards expanding such markets and breaking into well-established (non-photography-related) fields with spinoffs from its instant photographic and optical technology (such as a wafer thin battery, a filter for video display terminal screens, a curing agent for polyurethene, an anti-counterfeit labelling material, a sonar transducer and precision optical devices).[16]

These diversification efforts were beginning to bear fruit by mid-1982. Sales of such products constituted a growing percentage of Polaroid's revenues; although not yet the 50 per cent that represented the goal that *Business Week* had earlier reported.[17] Intensified development efforts in these areas were also paying off. The company's 1982 Annual Report stated:

> The new 35 mm Autoprocess color and black and white rapid access slide film system adds a new dimension to 35 mm photography and marks the first time Polaroid will be marketing products in a conventional film format for use in existing cameras and instruments. [Our prototype of a new low-cost business graphics system for use with the Apple II and IBM Personal Computers] consists of a menu-driven software program (supplied on a diskette) and a tri-color videoprinter which can produce 4 × 5 inch format color prints and 35 mm rapid-access color and black and white slides. These new Polaroid tabletop imaging and processing systems make Polaroid instant photography a part of the flow of immediate information in the office and laboratory. In their design, these self-contained systems become logical extensions of their host electronic imaging systems, and in operation they expand and complement the functions of those systems.

The graphics hardcopy system was an offshoot of Polaroid's 23 per cent stake in a small company, Image Resource Corp. But these endeavours did not remedy the decline of Polaroid's primary market and the failure of its Polavision product.

Polaroid saw its EPS drop from a high of $3.60 in 1978 to $0.95 in 1981. In the same period, return on assets fell from 9.2 per cent to 2.2 per cent and pre-tax profits as a per cent of sales went from 14.1 per cent down to 4.4 per cent.

MANAGEMENT AND ORGANIZATIONAL CHANGES

In April 1980, Bill McCune took over as CEO, and Land became chairman of the board and consulting director of Basic Research in Land Photography. Soon after he took office, Mr McCune began to change Polaroid's unique organization. *Business Week* had summarized some of the key philosophies under Dr Land as follows:

> Seldom, if ever, has a large American company so faithfully reflected the substance and style of one man as does Polaroid Corp. under Dr Edwin H. Land ... Land thrives on informality; thus, Polaroid has no organization chart. Land is almost compulsively secretive; so is Polaroid. Land believes manufacturing is an extension of research; Polaroid employees often follow such projects as the new SX-70 camera from laboratory to factory floor. Land works prodigious hours; so do key employees, who are resigned to taking phone calls from Land anytime.[18]

Other philosophies of Dr Land were still important factors in Polaroid's 1982 culture (See Appendix, p. 519.) Under Dr Land, Polaroid's commitment to research and development had dominated the organization's structure and approach. By providing exceptional work flexibility, Dr Land attempted to create an innovative atmosphere where the corporate structure did not interfere with employees' motivation. Major divisions were organized simply along functional lines (i.e. marketing, manufacturing). The heart of the corporation's creative capability was the research division headed by Dr Land. The manufacturing and operating divisions were coordinated by Mr McCune. A Management Executive Committee (MEC), comprised of Land, McCune, Julius Silver (corporate attorney) and the heads of the major divisions, served as a forum to discuss key aspects of corporate policy and to exchange information about major operating decisions.

McCune had coordinated the functional operations of the company. However, not being a detail man, he preferred to delegate to his young, aggressive divisional managers, who in turn assumed firm control over their areas and promoted strong divisional loyalties and even some degree of proprietary control over divisional information. All the division and senior managers were long-time Polaroid employees. And, although McCune could act as an effective coordinator and buffer, all understood that Land's word had been final on crucial issues, especially those associated with product offerings. In fact, Land had held strategic direction strictly to himself, and often pre-empted decisions or overturned operating management's consensus on issues of particular interest to him. Although no official organization chart existed prior to 1980, published information and informed outside observers estimated key relationships to be as shown in Exhibit 10. Some details about each major activity and player follows.

Manufacturing Division

Under the direction of I. M. 'Mac' Booth, this division had responsibility for domestic camera and film pack production as well as all negative film coatings. Labour-intensive operations such as the camera assembly were separated from the highly automated coating facilities for the negative and positive film production.

Polaroid had decided against consolidating all Boston area facilities into one giant Cambridge industrial complex, preferring to keep things in relatively smaller locations in Norwood, Needham, New Bedford, Freetown, and Waltham, Mass. It wanted to keep things more on a human and manageable scale, with workers having a greater opportunity to feel an integral part of what was happening. This dispersal also raised the company's profile in each community the way a single large Cambridge complex could not (6,191).

In 1980 Booth (age 49) was a rising star at Polaroid. Tough, hard-nosed and inquiring, he often became the 'devil's advocate' in top-level discussions. Booth had the difficult task of planning and operating the bulk of Polaroid's complex manufacturing facilities and coordinating them with the vagaries of the consumer marketplace and the magnificent spurts of inventiveness coming from Research. Booth believed in running a tight ship, was willing to experiment with new management techniques and prided himself on his capacities to select people. Booth had become the senior vice-president of manufacturing after successfully developing and operating the company's new negative film manufacturing facilities. He had earlier served as an assistant to McCune and enjoyed excellent relationships with the president.

Marketing Division

Since the company's early beginnings, its marketing division had always played an important role. Polaroid's innovative product line had required an aggressive and intelligent marketing programme which Edwin Land personally supported. In 1980 the division was headed by youthfully greying, dapper, soft-spoken Peter Wensberg (age 52) who had become senior vice-president in 1971. More philosophical than 'Mac' Booth in many ways, Wensberg liked to talk about the long-term market positioning and management needs of Polaroid amid a collection of historical instruments and nautical devices that artistically decorated his office. Nevertheless, within his division Wensberg was known as a hard driver. Along with Richard Young, head of Polaroid's International Division, Wensberg had been considered one of the three likely successors to Land, before McCune was named to the position (6,216). He had complete control over marketing and was a powerful force throughout the corporation. However, his non-technical background limited the depth of his influence in the more technical divisions.

The marketing division was responsible for all domestic marketing including advertising, customer service and marketing/sales. The marketing/sales department was divided into a consumer and an industrial product group with a separate sales force for each. Consumer products were distributed directly to large retail, department and discount stores and through selected wholesalers to smaller retail outlets. Polaroid's sales force handled both cameras and film supplies within their regional territories. Industrial products – designed for commercial photographers and industrial, scientific or medical applications – were sold through an industrial sales force or independent industrial agents. In addition, the marketing division also had its own market research, marketing planning, advertising, promotion, order processing, internal bookkeeping (etc.), groups.

Research Divisions

Since its inception Polaroid had been dominated by its research activities. And under Dr Land's leadership research continued to be a major focal point of the corporation. No absolute delineation existed between applied and pure research; however, separate divisions had been set up to specialize in those two functions. The applied research division, referred to as the technology division, carried most new new products or product improvements into production. It occasionally was responsible for manufacturing new products which either needed further design changes or whose market demand was not sufficient to justify transferring them to the huge manufacturing division. Dr Sheldon Buckler (age 49), who had originally worked in pure research and had participated in a number of Land's entrepreneurial projects, had served as the division's manager since 1972. Dr Land's great technical abilities and strong personality made this both a difficult and a highly rewarding role.

The research division worked primarily on more basic research projects and had fostered many major technological improvements in films and coatings. The division's close relations to Dr Land gave it extremely high-level support in dealing with other divisions. In fact, some claimed that Research often had the controlling hand in such relationships. President McCune had also had a long association with research. When Land had come up with his early inventions McCune had been the one who followed up and built them (6,216). In addition to McCune, research had served as an incubation ground for other senior managers, with three present members of the MEC – Drs Young, Buckler and Bloom – each having at one time been Land's assistant director of research.

Land had philosophically conceptualized Polaroid as an extension of the scientific laboratory. He wanted to move the concept of scientific experimentation into the industrial sphere, with the same absence of guilt attached to business as to laboratory failures. In fact the company's success really came back to continual experiments and recombinations of technical work and business ventures that at many points in time had indeed been stopped or looked like failures (6,184–5). Hence R & D teams were formed, dissolved and reformed with scientists and engineers fluidly following projects into development or production and then returning to the labs again.

Land believed in a strong relationship between the laboratory and the factory. In a manner reminiscent of Mao sending the intellectuals to the rice fields, he sometimes had research people 'operating machines'. He felt this exposure would give them a greater practical feel for their own theoretical work. In Land's vision, production was just a continuation of research and development, with McCune and Land participating (for example) in the design of machinery and components for SX-70 (6,190).

International Division

Dr Richard Young (age 54) had managed the International division with an independence and feistiness sometimes envied by the domestic managers. His entrepreneurial talents were put to work in the division when he was appointed its president in 1969 after a very successful career in the research division. By early 1980 international sales had grown to nearly 40 per cent of total corporate revenues and the division controlled all manufacturing and marketing outside the United States. The manufacturing capabilities of the division included positive film coating operations, camera and film pack assembly, and sunglass production. It relied on the US operation for batteries, negative film and other proprietary items, but used local contractors for other components. International had three manufacturing facilities – in Scotland, in Ireland and the Netherlands. The facilities in Scotland and the Netherlands were involved with most phases of production, whereas the plant in Ireland was strictly for film pack assembly. No research had been conducted by the division. Almost all of its products had been first introduced in the United States. And its product line had been essentially the same as the domestic unit's with some local adaptations to accommodate metric measures, special market conditions or local regulations.

In 1980 International marketed the full line of Polaroid products directly through wholly owned subsidiaries in some 20 countries.[19] It hired independent distributors in most other areas of the world. The sales force also had a line of sunglasses which was marketed along with its other products; otherwise the sales organization operated in a manner similar to the domestic group's.

International was reportedly the only profit centre within Polaroid in 1980. With this distinction, it seemed to operate somewhat more independently and aggressively within the corporation. Financial controls for all divisions were maintained by McCune and the finance division. Financial allocations had generally been based largely on the presentations of each functional group as reviewed by the finance division and the MEC. With the exception of major new products there had been little attempt to interrelate capital programmes between divisions. And there had been significant reluctance to develop integrated five-year plans among the divisions because of the entrepreneurial nature of the company and the uncertainty of the marketplace.

Staff Divisions

The remaining divisions represented specialized staff activities which supported the line manufacturing, research and marketing divisions. The largest were the engineering, finance and legal divisions – although there were also personnel, planning, systems analysis and public relations specialists at the corporate level. The company's accounting and financial controls tended to follow functional lines, with each division handling the bulk of its own detailed bookkeeping, systems development and data generation internally. Of course, the finance division specified the records and reports needed for corporate purposes and coordinated all contracts with outside capital sources.[20]

A Smorgasbord of Talent

Dr Land had used his flexible and creative organization as a 'smorgasbord of talent'. By selecting individuals with specific skills from any area in the corporation, Land could quickly assemble the highly diverse talents needed to handle desired tasks. For example, when he was confronted with an enormous project like 'Aladdin' (SX-70),

Land would reach into all his functional groups to gather the necessary people available within Polaroid. Then he would fill any gaps with outside specialists.

In such circumstances, Land reportedly maintained complete control over the project team's R & D activities, even to the information going to and from his team. Secrecy would often shroud his group's activities, and team members might purposely be kept isolated from nonessential contact with other groups in Polaroid. Land himself might be the only individual intimately aware of the entire project's work (6,210). He would call for additional support work as necessary, and tried to make sure that each research task was the responsibility of a particular individual, rather than diffused as 'an organizational responsibility'.

As the project's concept crystallized into more definite shape, moved into development or began scale-up, Dr Land transferred his attention increasingly to marketing the evolving product. Individual technical team members usually followed their element of the project through full scale-up and debugging before returning to their former jobs. But occasionally, a team researcher or engineer ended up managing manufacturing for the developed component.

Under Land's care and feeding the Polaroid organization responded dynamically – and somewhat amorphously – to changing conditions. Teams formed and reformed around problems (6,198). From the beginning Polaroid had encouraged employees to participate in decisions affecting their areas. In fact, innovation in organization and corporate human relations was a stated goal of the company. Employees were encouraged to take courses and advanced degrees at company expense. And many of Polaroid's more productive engineers were high school graduates or technicians who had never taken full-time university training. Formal organization constraints and authority relationships were kept to a minimum, and inconsistencies in managerial styles and even the corporation's functional setup were frequent. For example, digressions often arose when a development project moved into manufacturing or commercialization stages. At that point, the responsibility for the project's completion usually reverted to the team leader's division regardless of its function. Consequently, an applied research or engineering division might house manufacturing operations or a small commercial unit for some time. Eventually, however, the misplaced unit would be relocated to its proper functional area or occasionally operated as a small division more or less on its own.

Knowledgeable observers referred to the Polaroid organizations as a 'moving target'. The arrangement at any moment seemed to evolve naturally from the unstructured operational environment, and further adjustments might soon change any existing situation. The attached organizational charts indicate only those broad relationships which one could define from published data and external contacts with the company. And even these might change quickly with circumstances. There seemed to be substantial participation in decision making among affected parties *within* a division. But such participation *between* divisions was reportedly less common, and of course major interdivisional decisions had to be made at the very top level if substantial disagreements occurred.

The 1980 Reorganization

In October 1980, Mr McCune began to restructure the top level activities of Polaroid, although many of its *operating* philosophies remained unchanged. He stated:

Our goals are fourfold: to understand better our total potential, to encourage expanding fields such as our technical and industrial photographic businesses, to explore fields which are new for Polaroid such as batteries and the commercial chemical business; and to establish clear cut areas of responsibility for growth in both sales and profits.[21]

The office of the president was enlarged by the creation of four executive vice-presidents. These were Drs Buckler and Young, and Messrs Booth and Wensberg. Major departments were consolidated on a worldwide basis to recognize global needs more fully in such areas as marketing, finance, manufacturing and materials management.[21] This was widely recognized as the beginning of several phased moves which would ensure Polaroid's competitiveness and continued innovativeness in the 1980s. Mr McCune wanted to be ready to announce his final organization concept in 1982.

QUESTIONS

1. In light of its changing competitive situation, what should Polaroid's strategy have been in 1982? Why?

2. Design an organization suited to support this strategy. Draw an organization chart showing critical relationships down through the departmental level. Who should occupy each position at the division level or above? Why?

3. What control system is needed to make your strategy and organization effective? Define key measures at each level down to departments.

4. What other steps are necessary to implement your strategy?

APPENDIX

Polaroid Corporation Philosophy and Culture

In May 1967, Dr Land wrote down some key points of the Polaroid philosophy. These were still widely accepted in Polaroid in 1982:

> We have two basic products at Polaroid: (1) Products that are genuinely unique and useful, excellent in quality, made well and efficiently, so that they present an attractive value to the public and an attractive profit to the Company; (2) A worthwhile working life for each member of the Company – a working life that calls out the members' best talents and skills – in which he or she shares the responsibilities and the rewards.
>
> These two products are inseparable. The Company prospers most, and its members find their jobs most worthwhile, when its members are contributing their full talents and efforts to creating, producing, and selling products of outstanding merit (6,183).

In amplifying this Dr Land was quoted as saying,

> What we're after in America is an industrial society where a person maintains at work the full dignity he has at home. I don't mean that they will all be happy. They'll be unhappy – but in new, exciting, and important ways. [At Polaroid, people] would work happy for that time. Polaroid eliminated the time clock, provided extensive educational

opportunities inside and outside the company, and allowed employees to 'try out' for the other jobs if they thought they would be more satisfying (6,188–9).

In a *Harvard Business Review* article Dr Land further stated his philosophies:

I think whether outside science or within science there is no such thing as *group* originality or *group* creativity or *group* perspicacity.

I do believe wholeheartedly in the individual capacity for greatness, in one way or another in almost any healthy human being under the *right* circumstances; but being part of a group is, in my opinion, generally the *wrong* circumstance. Profundity and originality are attributes of single, if not singular, minds. Two minds may sometimes be better than one, provided that each of the two minds is working separately while the two are working together; yet three tend to become a crowd.[22]

Dr Land believed in mutual trust and commitment between employees and management; and he expected his people to actively participate in this opportunity:

EXHIBIT 1
Polaroid Corporation and subsidiary companies ten-year financial summary (unaudited),
year ended 31 December 1972–81
(US$ millions except per share data).

	1981	1980	1979
Consolidated Statement of Earnings			
Net Sales:			
United States	817.8	791.8	757.2
International	601.8	659.0	604.3
TOTAL NET SALES	1,419.6	1,450.8	1,361.5
Cost of Goods Sold	855.4	831.1	876.8
Marketing, Research, Engineering and Administrative			
Expenses	520.8	483.9	449.4
TOTAL COSTS	1,376.2	1,315.0	1,326.2
Profit from Operations	43.4	135.8	35.3
Other Income	49.2	25.4	13.3
Interest Expense	29.9	17.0	12.8
Earnings before Income Taxes	62.7	144.2	35.8
Federal, State and Foreign Income Taxes (credit)	31.6	58.8	(0.3)
Net Earnings	31.1	85.4	36.1
Earnings per Share	0.95	2.60	1.10
Cash Dividends per Share	1.00	1.00	1.00
Average Number of Shares (in millions)	32.9	32.9	32.9
Selected Balance Sheet Information			
Working Capital*	749.5	721.9	535.9
Net Property, Plant and Equipment	332.9	362.2	371.6
Total Assets*	1,434.7	1,404.0	1,253.7
Long-term Debt	124.2	124.1	–
Stockholders' Equity*	958.2	960.0	907.5
Other Statistical Data			
Additions to Property, Plant and Equipment	42.5	68.1	134.6
Depreciation	69.2	62.7	51.7
Payroll and Benefits	550.5	497.3	464.1**
Number of Employees, end of Year	16,784	17,454	18.416
Return on Equity* (two point average)	3.2%	9.1%	4.0%

*Years 1972 through 1980 have been restated to reflect implementation of Financial Accounting Standards Board Statement No. 43 'Accounting for Compensated Absences'.
**Restated.
Source: Polaroid Corporation, Annual report, 1981.

I don't regard it as normal for a human being to have an eight-hour day, with two long coffee breaks, with a martini at lunch, with a sleepy period in the afternoon and a rush home to the next martini. I don't think that can be dignified by calling it working, and I don't think people should be paid for it.[23]

In 1977 Dr Land reaffirmed his commitment to a high corporate ethic in Polaroid's Annual Report:

A company has as many aspects to its character as a person has, seeking fulfillment and self expression, power, friendship, creativity, immediate recognition and ultimate significance. It has a conscience and high purpose and moral standards and vulnerability. It can sin, feel guilty and repent, it can love and it can hate, it can build and it can destroy.... Recognition of the analogs of human characteristics in corporate life will in my opinion rejuvenate the economy, regenerate national self-respect, initiate an intellectual renaissance, and reward us all with a vast family of blessings which in our blindness we hold stubbornly at arm's length (9,3).

EXHIBIT 1
(Continued)

1978	1977	1976	1975	1974	1973	1972
817.4	645.8	586.7	495.6	487.3	493.1	417.5
559.2	416.1	363.3	317.1	270.0	192.4	141.8
1,376.6	1,061.9	950.0	812.7	757.3	685.5	559.3
778.3	575.7	511.8	467.9	485.2	358.0	260.1
418.2	337.3	294.9	237.0	239.3	251.6	236.7
1,196.5	913.0	806.7	704.9	724.5	609.6	496.8
180.1	148.9	143.3	107.8	32.8	75.9	62.5
20.3	19.0	14.4	16.8	13.4	14.2	13.5
5.9	6.4	3.3	1.3	1.1	0.3	0.8
194.5	161.5	154.4	123.3	45.1	89.9	75.2
76.1	69.2	74.7	60.7	16.7	38.0	32.7
118.4	92.3	79.7	62.6	28.4	51.8	42.5
3.60	2.81	2.43	1.91	0.86	1.58	1.30
0.90	0.65	0.41	0.32	0.32	0.32	0.32
32.9	32.9	32.9	32.9	32.9	32.9	32.8
609.5	589.6	546.4	475.1	402.0	380.1	341.7
294.8	225.9	198.2	203.3	224.3	228.3	224.5
1,276.0	1,076.7	959.0	843.7	777.8	751.0	661.2
–	–	–	–	–	–	–
904.3	815.5	744.6	678.4	626.3	608.4	566.2
115.0	68.7	33.9	21.8	40.0	40.3	44.6
43.0	39.5	38.3	39.1	39.6	35.3	32.0
421.4**	332.2**	289.6**	231.8**	223.2	191.3	160.2
20,884	16,394	14,506	13,387	13,019	14,227	11,998
13.8%	11.8%	11.2%	9.6%	4.6%	8.8%	7.7%

EXHIBIT 2
Comparative instant camera and film data, 1982
(US$ millions).

	Polaroid 1982			Kodak 1982
	Total	Non-amateur	Amateur	All Amateur
Sales	1,294	390	904	425
Cost of Goods	741	211	530	264
% of Sales	57.3%	54.0%	58.6%	62.0%
S & A	473	128	345	162
% of Sales	36.6%	32.8%	38.2%	38.2%
Operating Profit	80	51	29	(1)
Margins	6.2%	13.1%	3.2%	–

Source: Donaldson, Lufkin and Jenrette, *Research Bulletin*, 28 September 1983.

EXHIBIT 3
Manufacturers' shipments of photographic equipment and supplies, 1977–82.
($ millions)

	1977		1978		1979		1980		1981		1982	
	$	%	$	%	$	%	$	%	$	%	$	%
Sensitized Film and Paper	3,874.1	39.0%	4,489.7	39.0%	5,288.7	39.5%	6,706.7	42.3%	7,186.4	42.4%	7,652.9	41.3%
Prepared Photographic Chemicals	695.6	7.0	805.4	7.0	937.2	7.0	1,030.6	6.5	1,033.9	6.1	1,080.4	5.8
Micrographic Equipment	298.1	3.0	345.2	3.0	401.7	3.0	539.1	3.4	793.2	3.5	948.5	4.0
Motion Picture Equipment	198.7	2.0	230.1	2.0	267.8	2.0	269.5	1.7	220.3	1.3	298.3	1.6
Still Picture Equipment	993.7	10.0	1,150.6	10.0	1,405.9	10.5	1,442.8	9.1	1,271.2	7.5	1,466.5	7.9
Reprographic Equipment	3,876.8	39.0	4,485.0	39.0	5,087.7	38.0	5,866.3	37.0	6,644.0	39.2	7,310.4	39.4
TOTAL	9,937.0	100	11,506.0	100	13,389.0	100	15,855.0	100	16,949.0	100	18,557.0	100
Year to Year Change			15.8%		16.4%		18.4%		6.9%		9.5%	

Source: Lehman Brothers Kuhn Loeb, *The Photographic Products Market,* 4 August 1983.

EXHIBIT 4
US imports and exports of photographic equipment and supplies.

Estimated Product Breakdown (1979–82)
($ millions)

	1979			1980			1981			1982		
	Exports	Imports	Net	Exports	Imports	Net	Exports	Imports	Net	Exports	Imports	Net
Sensitized Film and Paper	1,074.2	390.7	683.5	1,349.9	532.7	817.2	1,346.1	567.1	779.0	1,234.9	607.7	627.2
Prepared Photographic Chemicals	133.9	6.7	127.2	137.8	9.1	128.7	133.3	9.5	123.8	135.6	8.0	127.6
Micrographic Equipment	77.3	1.6	75.7	90.9	1.9	89.0	110.0	5.0	105.0	86.1	2.7	83.4
Motion Picture Equipment	82.7	68.3	14.4	99.1	69.4	29.7	99.3	45.5	53.8	85.9	32.3	53.6
Still Picture Equipment	420.5	731.7	(311.2)	450.3	644.5	(194.2)	457.7	798.9	(341.2)	491.3	783.4	(292.1)
Reprographic Equipment	358.4	358.3	0.1	331.7	497.0	(165.3)	361.5	721.1	(359.6)	423.6	676.4	(252.8)
TOTAL	2,147.0	1,557.3	589.7	2,459.7	1,754.6	705.1	2,507.9	2,147.1	360.8	2,457.4	2,110.5	346.9

Source: Lehman Brothers Kuhn Loeb, *The Photographic Products Market,* 4 August 1983.

Estimated Regional Breakdown, 1979–82
($ millions)

	1979				1980				1981				1982			
	Exports		Imports		Exports		Imports		Exports		Imports		Exports		Imports	
	$	%	$	%	$	%	$	%	$	%	$	%	$	%	$	%
Europe	972.6	45.3%	294.3	18.9%	1,167.7	45.4%	352.7	20.1%	969.4	38.7%	329.7	15.3%	1,069.7	43.5%	373.2	17.7%
Canada	255.5	11.9	73.2	4.7	275.5	11.2	119.3	6.8	271.2	10.8	113.9	5.3	316.5	12.9	102.8	4.9
Latin America	188.9	8.8	1.6	0.1	206.6	8.4	1.8	0.1	376.2	15.0	1.8	0.1	287.5	11.7	3.0	0.1
Asia	298.5	13.9	1,175.7	75.5	332.1	13.5	1,272.1	72.5	491.9	19.6	1,669.9	77.8	529.8	21.6	1,622.0	76.9
Other	431.5	20.1	12.5	0.8	528.8	21.5	8.7	0.5	399.2	15.9	31.9	1.5	253.9	10.3	9.5	0.4
TOTAL	2,147.0	100.0%	1,557.3	100.0%	2,459.7	100.0%	1,754.6	100.0%	2,507.9	100.0%	2,147.1	100.0%	2,457.4	100.0%	2,110.5	100.0%

Source: Lehman Brothers Kuhn Loeb, *The Photographic Products Market,* 4 August 1983.

EXHIBIT 5
Estimated breakdown of still pictures taken by US consumers (millions of units).

	1977		1978		1979		1980		1981		1982	
	Units	% Chg.	Units	% Chg.	Units	% Chg.	Units	% Chg.	Units	% Chg.	Units	% Chg.
Colcur Print Negative	4,805	17.8%	6,010	25.1%	6,295	4.7%	6.645	5.6%	7.300	9.9%	7,950	8.9%
Slides (positive)	1,495	(4.4)	1,585	6.0	1,530	(3.5)	1,540	0.7	1,350	(12.3)	1,250	(7.4)
Instant	1,370	5.4	1,675	22.3	1,550	(7.5)	1,500	(3.3)	1,450	(3.3)	1,250	(13.8)
Black and White	660	(10.0)	600	9.1	575	(4.2)	565	(1.7)	525	(7.1)	500	(4.8)
TOTAL	8,330	8.5%	9,870	18.5%	9,950	0.8%	10,250	3.0%	10,625	3.7%	10,950	3.1%

Source: Lehman Brothers Kuhn Loeb, *The Photographic Products Market,* 4 August 1983.

EXHIBIT 6
Estimated US consumer purchases of film by type, 1978–82
(millions of units).

Film Type	1978	1979	1980	1981	1982	Change 1981–2
Instant B&W	18.8	12.8	7.9	5.8	4.4	(24.1)%
Instant Colour	119.6	124.1	124.2	126.0	110.9	(12.0)
35 mm B&W	26.7	21.2	25.3	23.0	18.6	(19.1)
35 mm Colour Slide	61.3	56.2	55.3	57.0	52.0	(8.8)
35 mm Colour Print	84.8	98.5	119.9	137.0	146.8	7.2
110 Cartridge B&W		18.4	14.0	10.0	13.9	39.0
110 Cartridge Colour	16.1	170.7	182.3	193.0	196.5	1.8
126 Cartridge B&W		14.3	9.2	8.0	9.0	12.5
126 Cartridge Colour	221.6	104.2	103.1	105.0	90.0	(14.3)
Disc					21.0	
Other Still B&W	20.0	8.2	6.9	6.7	6.5	(3.0)
Other Still Colour	44.4	17.8	13.4	15.0	13.2	(12.0)
Movie	35.3	27.5	26.8	22.0	19.0	(13.6)
TOTAL	648.6	673.9	688.3	708.5	701.8	(0.9)%

Source: Lehman Brothers Kuhn Loeb, *The Photographic Products Market*, 4 August 1983.

Estimated Breakdown of US Consumer Camera Sales
(000s units)

	1974	1975	1976	1977	1978
Cartridge*	8,590	8,630	9,050	9,250	10,200
35 mm (all types)	825	708	980	1,560	2,300
Instant	3,300	3,900	4,500	6,600	8,200
8 mm Movie	636	392	450	609	525
Other**	12	15	20	22	23
TOTAL	13,363	13,645	15,000	18,041	21,249

	1979	1980	1981	1982	Change 1981–2
Cartridge*	8,800	7,500	7,000	2,800	(60.0)%
Disc	–	–	–	3,900	–
35 mm (all types	2,600	2,900	3,400	3,700	8.8
Instant	6,600	5,700	5,000	4,500	(10.0)
8 mm Movie	300	230	180	100	(44.4)
Other**	30	33	36	35	(2.8)
TOTAL	18,330	16,363	15,616	15,035	(3.7)%

*110 and 126 combined.
**Roll and large format.
Source: Lehman Brothers Kuhn Loeb, *The Photographic Products Market*, 4 August 1983.

EXHIBIT 7
Polaroid Corporation comparative data, 1978–82
($ millions, millions of items).

	1977	1978	1979	1980	1981	1982
Sales						
Worldwide ($)	1,061.9	1,376.6	1,361.5	1,450.8	1,419.6	1,293.9
United States	645.8	817.4	757.2	791.8	817.8	752.5
Europe	274.2	364.9	383.3	436.8	369.2	333.2
Rest of World						
Including Asia	141.9	194.3	220.9	222.2	232.6	208.2
Worldwide (no. of units)						
Cameras	7.0+*	9.4	7.3	6.6	5.6	4.0
Film Packs	N/A	200+	205**	198**	194**	N/A
Tech/Ind Photo						
as % of Total $	N/A	N/A	N/A	25.30%	30%	33%
Financial ($)						
EPS	2.81	3.60	1.10	2.60	0.95	0.73
Dividends/Share	0.65	0.90	1.00	1.00	1.00	1.00
R&D Expense	88.9	86.5	109.6	114.0	121.4	118.4
Capital Expense	68.9	115.0	134.7	68.1	42.5	31.5
Advertising Expense	70.8	101.1	105.0	101.4	106.6	96.4
Return on Assets	8.6%	9.3%	2.9%	61.%	2.2%	1.8%
No. of Employees	16,394	20,884	18,416	17,454	16,784	14,540

N/A = Not available.
* *The Wall Street Journal*, 5 September 1980.
** Merrill Lynch Securities Research Report, 17 May 1982, p. 3.
Source: All data not otherwise noted drawn from Polaroid Corporation, annual reports, 1978–82.

EXHIBIT 8
Polaroid executive officers, 1981.

Name	Office	Age
Edwin H. Land	Chairman of the board	72
William J. McCune, Jr.	President and chief executive officer	66
I. M. Booth	Executive vice-president	50
Sheldon A. Buckler	Executive vice-president	50
Peter Wensberg	Executive vice-president	53
Richard W. Young	Executive vice-president	55
Milton S. Dietz	Senior vice-president	50
Charles Mikulka	Senior vice-president	68
Howard G. Rogers	Senior vice-president and director of research	66
Harvey H. Thayer	Senior vice-president, finance	54
Richard F. deLima	Vice-president and secretary	51
Julius Silver	Vice-president and chairman executive committee	81
Edward R. Bedrosian	Treasurer	49

Dr Land, founder of the company, served as chairman of the board, chief executive officer and director of research from 1937 to 1980. In 1980, Dr Land was re-elected chairman of the board and assumed the new position of consulting director of basic research in Land photography. He is the inventor of synthetic sheet polarizer for light and of one-step photography. He is the holder of numerous honorary degrees and has been the recipient of many awards from various professional societies.

Mr McCune joined the company in 1939 and has been a director since 1975. He was elected vice-president, engineering in 1954, vice-president, assistant general manager in 1963, executive vice-president in 1969, president and chief operating officer in 1975 and to his present positions as president and chief executive officer in 1980.

Mr Booth joined the company in 1958. He was elected assistant vice-president and assistant to the president in 1975, vice-president and assistant to the president in 1976, senior vice-president in 1977, and to his present position as executive vice-president in 1980.

Dr Buckler joined the company in 1964. He was elected assistant vice-president in 1969, vice-president, research division in 1972, group vice-president in 1975, senior vice-president in 1977 and to his present position as executive vice-president in 1980.

Mr Wensberg joined the company in 1958. He was elected assistant vice-president, advertising in 1966, vice-president, advertising in 1968, senior vice-president in 1971 and to his present position as executive vice-president in 1980.

Dr Young joined the company in 1962. He was elected vice-president, assistant director of research in 1963, senior vice-president in 1969 and to his present position as executive vice-president in 1980.

Mr Dietz joined the company in 1955. He was elected assistant vice-president in 1975, vice-president, engineering in 1977 and to his present position as senior vice-president in 1980.

Mr Mikulka joined the company in 1942. He was elected vice-president, patents in 1960 and to his present position as senior vice-president in 1975.

Mr Rogers joined the company in 1937. He was elected vice-president and senior research fellow in 1968, vice-president, senior research fellow and associate director of research in 1975, senior vice-president and associate director of research in 1979 and to his present positions as senior vice-president and director of research in 1980.

Mr Thayer joined the company in 1956. He was elected treasurer in 1970, vice-president and treasurer in 1971, vice-president, finance and treasurer in 1977 and to his present position as senior vice-president, finance in 1980.

Mr deLima joined the company as secretary in 1972. He was elected to his present positions as vice-president and secretary in 1975.

Mr Silver, a director and vice-president since 1937 and chairman of the executive committee, is also a partner in the firm of Silver & Solomon, the company's general counsel.

Mr Bedrosian joined the company in 1965, He was elected assistant treasurer in 1975 and to his present position as treasurer in 1980.

Source: Polaroid Corporation, *10K*, 1981.

EXHIBIT 9
Polaroid Corporation production facilities as of 1981.

Location	Function
Domestic	
Norwood, Mass.	Polarizer sheet production
Norwood, Mass.	Transparency film production
Norwood, Mass.	Camera assembly*
Waltham, Mass.	Battery assembly
Waltham, Mass.	Chemical production
Waltham, Mass	Film pack production
Waltham, Mass	Positive film production
Freetown, Mass.	Chemical production
Foreign	
Dumbarton, Scotland	Camera assembly, film pack assembly, positive film production, sunglass production
Enschede, Netherlands	Film pack assembly, positive film production, sunglass production
Newbridge, Ireland	Film pack assembly

*Highly labour intensive.
Source: Compiled from various annual reports.

EXHIBIT 10
Polaroid Corporation, 1980.

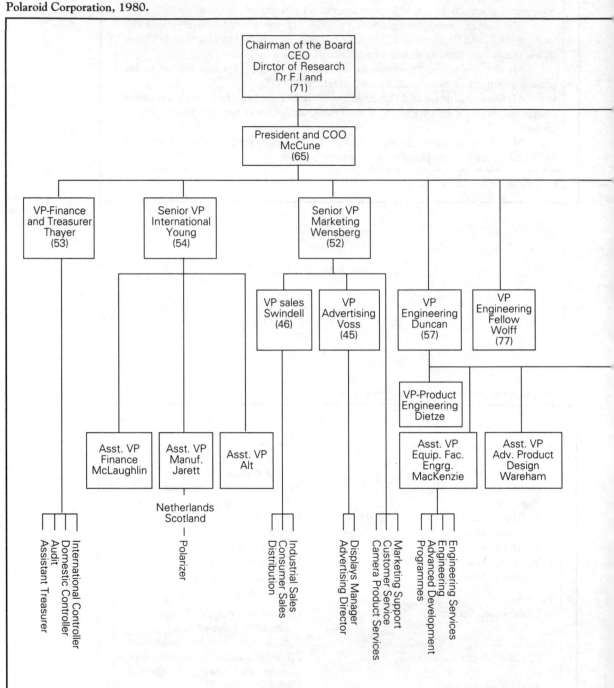

Note: Numbers in parentheses indicate the ages of the various executives.

Source: Approximate 1980, pre-reorganization, organizational chart drawn from various secondary sources. The company does not have an official organization chart.

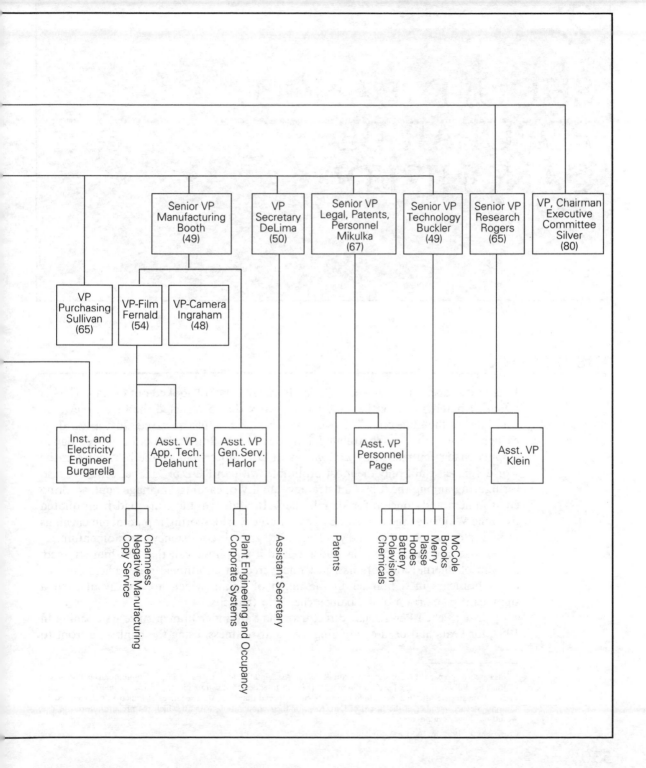

Senior VP
Manufacturing
Booth
(49)

VP
Secretary
DeLima
(50)

Senior VP
Legal, Patents,
Personnel
Mikulka
(67)

Senior VP
Technology
Buckler
(49)

Senior VP
Research
Rogers
(65)

VP, Chairman
Executive
Committee
Silver
(80)

VP
Purchasing
Sullivan
(65)

VP-Film
Fernald
(54)

VP-Camera
Ingraham
(48)

Inst. and
Electricity
Engineer
Burgarella

Asst. VP
App. Tech.
Delahunt

Asst. VP
Gen.Serv.
Harlor

Asst. VP
Personnel
Page

Asst. VP
Klein

Chamness
Negative Manufacturing
Copy Service

Plant Engineering and Occupancy
Corporate Systems

Assistant Secretary

Patents

McCole
Brooks
Merry
Plasse
Hodes
Battery
Polavision
Chemicals

2–6

SHOULD BANCO POPULAR BE CANONIZED?*

THE DILEMMA

Luis Valls Taberner, president of Banco Popular Español, looked out on calle Ortega y Gasset barely noticing the construction work that obstructed the lovely view. He was deep in thought, brooding over the news he had just received. Just a few days earlier a friend had congratulated him on Banco Popular's performance. Banco Popular had been named by *Euromoney* in December 1990 as 'the best bank in the world' for being not only the most profitable, with an ROE of 25.2 per cent, but also for figuring among the top 10 in strategy, quality of earnings, management, working environment and concern for shareholders. In addition, the bank had been quoted by Gene Walden as the best stock to own in the world, scoring top points in earnings growth, stock growth, dividend yield, dividend growth, consistency and momentum.[1]

That morning Luis Valls had received a telephone call that left him stunned. A team of internal auditors had just uncovered an enormous fraud scheme in one of its branches in Santander in the north of Spain, which apparently affected a significant proportion of the bank's clients in that city.

José ('Pepe') Pérez Díaz, director of the Santander branch since its opening in 1984, for years had been conducting irregular business, using the bank as a front to

---

*This case was prepared by Christina Johnson, Research Associate, under the supervision of Dominique Héau, Professor of Business Policy, as a basis for class discussion. It is not intended to illustrate either effective or ineffective handling of an administrative situation. We would like to extend a special thanks to the executives of Banco Popular and to Mr Giorgio Stecher, member of the Board of Directors, for their cooperation, without which the preparation of this case would not have been possible.

'legitimize' it. Having detected some anomalies in the branch's numbers, the Control and Audit Departments had sent a surprise audit team to investigate the situation. It seems they arrived too late, however. Before the authorities could be notified, the branch director had fled the country, leaving the bank with potential liabilities of up to Ptas 4,000 million.

He knew the news would be all over Spain in the evening papers and on television, and would have a very negative impact on the image of the bank. He wondered whether the incident had been merely an accident, a stroke of bad luck or whether it had occurred as a result of some fatal flaw in the organization he had worked so long and so hard to build.

Banco Popular was the sixth largest privately held commercial banking group in Spain, with total assets of Ptas 2.39 billion and capital of Ptas 131,013 million at year-end 1990.[2] The Banco Popular Group comprised the parent bank, five regional commercial banks (Banco de Andalucía, Banco de Castilla, Banco de Galicia, Banco de Vasconia and Banco de Crédito Balear), a merchant bank (Eurobanco), and several finance, leasing, factoring, investment estate subsidiaries which owned the premises housing the banking offices. Through its network of 1,662 branches throughout the country and its staff of 11,811 people, the Banco Popular Group served 7 per cent of the Spanish retail market in terms of deposits.[3]

Banco Popular stated that it was and wanted to remain essentially a retail bank with a domestic focus. Its objective was to target basically small and medium-sized companies (the PYME) and individuals. Therefore, outside of Madrid and Barcelona it had practically no relationship with the large corporate sector and had an insigificant presence in the capital markets. With the exception of 13 branches in France, whose specific function was to serve the needs of Spanish emigrants, and seven representative offices in Europe, the bank had an exclusively of national presence. Of the six major Spanish banks, it was the most retail-oriented and least international.

BACKGROUND HISTORY

Incorporated in Madrid in 1926 under the name of 'Banco Popular de los Previsotes del Porvenir', its name was shortened to Banco Popular Español (commonly known as 'Banco Popular') in 1947. During the first 20 years of its existence the bank's growth was conditioned by the adversities of the Spanish Civil War and World War II, the foundations for its development as a nationwide bank being laid only in the 1950s. In 1959 the government formulated a stabilization plan which triggered a golden age of economic expansion in Spain which lasted until 1974. During this period Banco Popular, like all Spanish banks, experienced considerable growth, its customer deposits rising from Ptas 8,576 million in December 1960 to Ptas 125,400 million at the end of 1974, a cumulative annual growth of 21.1 per cent.

Banco Popular's expansion was achieved mainly through the acquisition of five regional banks and through the development of its range of specialized services. In 1967, responding to rumours of the possible nationalization of large Spanish banks and to overcome regulatory restrictions on branching, Banco Popular created five holding companies (the Popularinsa companies) and transferred its share in the regional banks to these companies. This made it possible for the Banco Popular

Group to expand its branch network slowly in spite of government restrictions. These restrictions were finally lifted in 1974, and between 1976 and 1985 Banco Popular more than tripled its number of branches from 257 to 885.

In 1985 new legislation on portfolio companies was enacted making it advisable to merge the five Popularinsa companies into one. In 1986, under the pressure of a raid by the Spanish March Group, Banco Popular took steps to regain its ownership in Popularinsa and the two entities finally merged in September 1987.

In January 1988, reacting to several takeover attempts in the banking arena in Spain (some of these encouraged by the government), Banco Popular decided to strengthen the board's effective control capability by doubling the permitted number of directors from 22 to 40. The bank was determined to protect itself from a potential takeover by filling its board of directors with 'friendly sharks', people who concurred with the principles underlying the bank's management style and were prepared to invest significant amounts (no less than 0.5 per cent of its total capitalization) in the bank's shares. In order to facilitate the process of integrating new partners, Banco Popular revised its long-standing policy of non-intervention in the stock market and began buying significant lots of its own shares. At one point the bank held up to 5 per cent of its own stock in Treasury ('autocartera'), with the intention of offering it to the 'friendly sharks'. These measures were temporary and defensive in nature, and at no time involved interference with the market-driven, price-fixing process.

At this time the president, Luis Valls, had personally taken charge of finding attractive investors. He admitted: 'I used to go to the poor neighbourhoods on weekends to attend charity programmes. In 1988 I started going to the wealthy neighbourhoods, to get rich people to invest in our stock.'

A LOOK INSIDE BANCO POPULAR

The Bank's Management Policies and Objectives

> The prime corporate responsibility of a business enterprise is to generate added economic value. Discharge of this responsibility at Banco Popular involves pursuit of the goal of reaching and maintaining an adequate level of profit by rendering optimum service to the customers. Service and profit are the two pillars which guarantee the bank's survival and, accordingly, constitute its ultimate objective.[4]

In order to achieve this objective, Banco Popular conducted its business in accordance with the following management policies:

Treat the Customer as the Axis of all Business Activity...

Banco Popular subordinated its whole structure to its customers, considering them the principal part of the organization.[5] Its mission was thoroughly to satisfy the needs of its existing and prospective customers, and its organization was designed to facilitate this mission. Management believed that it had to anticipate the needs of its customers and have a portfolio of products ready before these customers realized what their needs really were. Supposedly, the bank was able to do this by singling out homogeneous customer groups (people that had similar financial needs and technical difficulties) and designing products to satisfy them.

...Providing Excellent Service...

A fundamental tenet of Banco Popular was to offer optimum service to its customers. Besides providing the full range of traditional products (in the form of credit and savings instruments) Banco Popular offered its client groups tailor-made solutions to specific problems:

> We are well aware that the strength of Banco Popular lies in its ability to win customers by providing overall service to homogeneous customer groups, and we therefore pay special attention to analyzing the problems and needs of such groups so as to design the most suitable products for each of them. This 'made-to-measure' tailoring always gives better results than ready-made articles.[6]

In this way the bank was able to transform a potentially sporadic customer into a steady one. 'Banco Popular is not just a bank; it is their bank'.[7]

The concept of personalized service was the key to the way the bank conducted its business. Management at Banco Popular insisted on personally knowing all its customers and made sure to inquire about their families and day-to-day activities. It was very important that such a close, intimate relationship be established so that the client's loyalty and complete trust could be obtained. In fact, in many small rural villages the branch manager was a 'confidant' for a number of people, advising them not only on their personal finances, but on their personal lives. In a small village not far from Madrid, for example, a client of the bank asked the local branch manager for advice on what to do about her 18-year-old daughter who had run off with a married man. Although he might have thought that this was none of his affair, he felt obliged to give his opinion and his moral support. It was all part of catering to the needs of the client. This personalized approach to banking earned Banco Popular its leadership position in rural Spain as well as the most loyal customer base of the large Spanish banks.

An interesting aspect of Popular's personalized approach was the fact that the group often had branches of both Banco Popular and one of its regional banks in the same town, sometimes on the same street block, competing with one another. This was done to respond to the preferences of customers. Some were fiercely loyal to Banco Popular. Others, perhaps from a sense of regional patriotism, greatly preferred to work with their regional bank, even though they knew that they both belonged to the same group.

Banco Popular further developed the concept of personalized service by setting up a customer service office where customers could present their complaints. No claim was ever left undealt with. Customers could complain directly to the president if they wanted to, as he would personally respond, endeavouring to clarify matters and provide full information to the customer concerned. The bank claimed to be eager to learn from its mistakes:

> By means of a thorough and dispassionate analysis of each and every claim made to the bank, it is possible to segregate those which are provoked by straightforward human errors, which to some extent are logical and correctable, from those which disclose organizational or structural shortcomings which must be made good so as to optimize our operations.[8]

It therefore kept a recording of all complaints received and problems experienced and published these every year in its '*Repertorio de Temas*'.

...stressing Profitability and Regularity...

Management at Banco Popular had traditionally had a policy of favouring profitability over growth. Its aim was to maintain regularity – 'the proper cruising speed, with no sudden accelerations or sharp braking' – in the conduct of its banking business. In implementing this policy, increases in net income had been achieved not only through increases in asset size, but also through higher returns on assets. While profits increased by 67 per cent between 1986 and 1989, assets increased only 38 per cent over the same period.

During 1990 Banco Popular was able to increase profits in spite of Banco de España's limitation on the growth of Spanish banks' loans of no more than 10 per cent. As credit was limited, banks charged higher interest rates and Popular was thus able to improve its intermediation margin. However, most of the other banks, who were bent on growing their deposit base, saw their intermediation margins decline as customers' funds had become so much more expensive as a result of the deposit war.[9]

Banco Popular's share in the deposits of the private sector increased only slightly during the period of June 1989 (the deposit war began in September) and December 1990 as it experienced marginal growth in this area compared to other banks, like Santander, whose deposit base grew 64 per cent.[10] The bank was able to keep its existing customer base, however, by exercising price discrimination, granting high interest rates only on demand and after lengthy negotiation with clients. In most cases it succeeded in paying less for deposits than its competitors because of the high quality and personalized nature of its service. In general its clients were not willing to take their business elsewhere for a mere 1/2 or 1 per cent more.

The bank also attempted to maximize its profitability by using innovative cash management techniques. With the help of its EDP systems, it carefully checked value dates of transactions and monitored the movement of funds to minimize idle cash, ensured minimum traffic time by standardizing check clearing and eliminated double counting of entries by removing from the daily balance sheet all 'in transit' operations. These techniques brought the bank huge savings by liberating over Ptas 10,000 million from double accounting entries and reducing idle cash by about Ptas 7,000 million. Cash management was not only conducted by the central administration, but was the concern of every officer and branch director. For example, a Madrid branch received a cheque for a considerable amount drawn on a Valencia-based bank in payment for a service. Under the normal system this cheque would take 7 days to clear. In terms of float, at an interbank rate of over 15 per cent, the bank stood to 'lose' a lot of money. Therefore an officer of Banco Popular flew to Valencia to cash the cheque, thus recovering six days of float for the bank.

...All the While Maintaining Liquidity, Asset Quality and a Strong Capital Position...

This policy was manifested in Banco Popular's asset and liability management, its low level of bad debt expense and its generous provisions for uncollectibles and country risk. Liquidity was ensured by maintaining a balance between loans and discounts and customers' deposits, and by limiting the bank's indebtedness to other financial institutions, which could be hazardous when interest rates were high and there was tension in the capital markets.

Banco Popular was actually a net lender in the interbank market, and was therefore protected from possible future liquidity crises. The bank made a point of keeping at least Ptas 100,000 million in the money market as a liquidity cushion. This way, when money market rates were very high, it would not be forced to cut credit, as many of its competitors did. The fact that Banco Popular never cut credit permitted it to charge higher rates than the competition.

To guarantee high asset quality, Banco Popular consistently made provisions for doubtful loans well above the required amount. It generally wrote off each year up to 50 per cent of the existing provisions, preferring to recognize a loss and possibly recover it later than to carry assets of dubious quality on its books. In line with this policy, the bank had made provisions for 97 per cent of its LDC portfolio by 31 December 1989. The bank also had strict credit policies. It had a well-diversified portfolio of loans, having set a ceiling (up to 3 per cent of the bank's capital base) for the credit provided to any one borrower in order to avoid concentration of risk in any one corporation or sector. In addition it established a ceiling for long-term credits (more than three years) of 15 per cent of the total loan portfolio.

Banco Popular stressed the importance of high solvency, and thanks to this policy its capitalization had long been above the average both in Spain and internationally. The bank's capital adequacy ratio at year-end 1989 was 11.86 per cent, well above the Bank for International Settlements' (BIS) required minimum of 8 per cent and higher even than Deutsche Bank's ratio of 11.5 per cent, which was the highest of the large international banks.[11]

...Providing Full Disclosure...

Banco Popular believed in complete transparency in management, both in-house and to the outside world. It implemented this policy by providing in its Annual reports and in its quarterly reports to shareholders much more detailed information than that ordinarily furnished by the world's leading banks. In fact, even when audits were still not obligatory for banks in Spain, Banco Popular had its financial statements audited by independent external auditors and had their reports published in its Annual report.

As a further application of this policy, the bank published each year and distributed to its shareholders the '*Repertorio de Temas*', a document which recorded and explained the mistakes that had been made during the year and the blows it had suffered, both in-house and outside.[12] It also published an '*Operations Review*', which analyzed all the problems and challenges the bank had experienced during the year and the measures that were taken to resolve them. In the 1990 document Popular applied a technique of self-analysis which, according to management, INSEAD had helped them develop. It stated all the current management criteria and all the internal criticisms of these criteria, and then proceeded to analyze both in the text of the document. Popular's management considered both these documents a 'periodic vaccination shot, to avoid . . . catching more serious diseases'.

In essence, full disclosure meant that every member of the bank's staff knew that the outcome of his or her decisions and actions could be made public. It was therefore a most effective mechanism of management control, ensuring honesty and efficiency in the bank's operations. This practice had earned Banco Popular the reputation of the bank with most transparency in its operations, and had made the media the bank's staunchest supporter.

In fact, Banco Popular was a master at public relations. It purportedly tried to maintain a very low profile by never advertising, claiming to avoid prestige and grandeur. In reality, however, the bank was notorious. It was a favourite of the press and the international financial analysts, and was widely publicized by both. The facts spoke for themselves – nobody could deny that Banco Popular did extremely well. But the bank's managers were also very convincing, and it was hard, even for the case writer, to remain objective about the professionalism with which the bank was run.

...Run the Business Conservatively...

Banco Popular believed in cautious and conservative decision-making. According to management, it did not follow market fads as it was 'wary of fashions in banking'. During the late 1980s, a period of feverish financial innovation in the Spanish markets, Banco Popular had preferred not to be the first in line, but instead to wait and see if it should move at all. In this way it had supposedly avoided losing a lot of money. An excellent example of this was the deposit war which the bank had chosen not to join. Between June 1989 and December 1990 Banco Popular's cost of funds increased by 21 per cent compared to an average of 29 per cent for the big six Spanish banks.

The bank preferred to concentrate on its core business which was commercial banking, taking deposits and lending to consumers and the PYME. It therefore held negligible positions in the stock and long-term debt markets, and steered clear of products with vague or unclear tax connotations, such as single-premium insurance policies and loan sales. This policy made it difficult for the bank quickly to expand its customer base, but ensured the loyalty and confidence of its existing customers. This fact is illustrated by the following incident:

> Not long ago, one branch manager proudly described at a managers meeting how he had recovered a major customer that, like the prodigal son, had been lured away by the high return on the single-premium insurance policies. The manager's pride however was not at the customer's return to the fold, but rather at the latter's comments upon returning: 'I'm coming back to your bank even though you pay lower rates than others because you were the only bank manager who told me the truth about the possible implications of the single-premium policies even though it could have cost you my business. I'll never doubt you again.'[13]

...Limiting risk and Avoiding Conflicts of Interest...

Unlike many of its competitors, Banco Popular tried to avoid conflicts of interest by sticking to its main line of business which was banking. While BBV, Banco Central and Banesto had large portfolios of industrial holdings and lent extensively to these companies, Popular had opted to invest only in its area of expertise. It therefore had no equity participation in the industrial sector, preferring not to involve itself in the governance of the companies it financed. It had withdrawn its representatives from the boards of its minority-owned investees long ago. Similarly (with the exception of a 1.5 per cent interest in Banco Commercial Portugues), the bank had no participations in any foreign financial institutions as it did not have an indepth knowledge of the markets in which these operated. In addition, the bank claimed to be strictly neutral in the field of politics, dealing on an equal footing with all the ideologies in Spain's constitutional spectrum. This way it was able to avoid being dragged down by any political disturbances or controversies.

...Participating in Cooperation Agreements...

Banco Popular understood that to meet genuinely the increasingly sophisticated demands of its customers and to embrace new customer groups it had to constantly enhance the content of its financial service package by adding new services and technology. Thus, it had a policy of actively cooperating with other entities to provide common services if and when the nature of such services, the means required and the costs involved, made it advisable to do so.

In Spain it cooperated with other banks and financial institutions to develop electronic banking and means of payment systems. In the field of electronic banking, Popular was in the forefront of developments, despite its smaller size relative to the other large Spanish banks. It had been the first bank in Spain to introduce Automatic Teller Machines (ATM), and in 1974 had the biggest network in Europe. Although its network was not the biggest in 1990, it participated with other banks in a number of common networks to provide maximum convenience to its customers. In the field of means of payment systems Banco Popular was also among the leading banks. In 1978 it had signed an agreement with VISA international for the issuance of credit cards and by 1990 had 10 per cent of the VISA market in terms of the number of cards issued and 7 per cent in terms of revenues. Popular also had agreements with MasterCard, Air Plus and Japan Credit Bureau, and was the only bank in Spain to offer its customers American Express cards. By 1990 it was second largest credit card issuer in Spain.

On the international front, the bank had set up a number of strategic alliances with top-line entities whose views about the future were in harmony with its own. The purpose of these alliances was to borrow specific product know-how and technology from these entities in order to offer new specialized financial services to the bank's customers in Spain. In return the bank gave the entity use of its branch network and its commercial action capability.

It had set up a joint venture with the German insurance group Allianz (the biggest insurance group in Europe) and its Italian subsidiary Riunione Adriatica de Sicurtà (RAS) to develop and market services in the life insurance and pension fund fields. It also established two joint ventures with the German bank Bayerische Hypothekem und Wechsel Bank (Hypo-bank) to develop wholesale mortgage loans and property leasing. In addition it set up a joint venture with the French Pelloux group to market real estate investment funds in Spain. Finally, it signed a commercial agreement with the Dutch bank Rabobank to share branch networks and attend the needs of their respective clients in the other's country.

In line with its desire to form a network of friendly investors, and thus protect it from possible raiders, Banco Popular succeeded in getting the above-mentioned entities to take equity participations in its capital. Thus Allianz owned 3.3 per cent of Banco Popular, Hypo-bank owned 1.7 per cent and Rabobank 1.25 per cent.

Banco Popular was also looking at possibilities in the capital markets, wholesale banking and stock market intermediation. Although it was open to all new opportunities in order to provide continually added value to its customers, the bank did not actively seek strategic alliances. Typically the foreign institution approached the bank with the purpose of using its branch network to establish a presence in Spain. Banco Popular was happy to consider the union as long as the institution fulfilled certain prerequisites which were: The foreign institution had to be bigger than the bank, extremely solid, a leader in its market and at the forefront of technology in its product offering, it also had to be willing to share risks with Banco Popular, taking an equity participation in the bank as well as the venture the two entities were jointly undertaking, and thus give the bank access to a business or market that alone it would be incapable of exploring; in addition, this institution would ideally have a large and solid client base to which the bank could offer its services and in this way mark a presence in the foreign country.

... The Bank Should be Independent ...

Banco Popular had always been fiercely independent and intended to remain so. It had been an ideal target in the past, being highly esteemed for its management and profitability record, and having a low P/E ratio (which meant its share had been underpriced in the stock market). In addition, until 1988 its board of directors had controlled less than 4 per cent of the stock, the rest of which had been widely spread among close to 100,000 shareholders.

Thanks to the measures taken in 1988 to protect the bank from raiders, in 1990 the board of directors controlled, directly or indirectly, nearly 40 per cent of the bank's stock. Over 40 per cent was held by a number of Spanish and foreign institutional investors and the rest was widely dispersed among more than 70,000 shareholders. Close to 45 per cent of the bank's capital was owned by foreigners, and this number was growing. The bank still had a low P/E ratio, but didn't seem to worry about it. Its managers claimed that this endemic undervaluation was not a reflection of the bank's performance or quality of management, but stemmed from its policy of not interfering in the stock market. Unlike most Spanish banks, Banco Popular did not hold positions in or speculate with its own shares.

Lately, some of the bank's managers had begun to worry about how long the Banco Popular would survive with the changing conditions in Spain's financial arena and the creation of the Single European Market. They felt that a plausible solution was to merge with another financial institution in order to achieve economies of scale by gaining sheer size. Drawing from the experience of other banks (notable Banco Bilbao Vizcaya), however, the benefits of size seemed inconclusive. The president, Luis Valls, claimed that he had nothing against mergers. In fact it had been suggested at one point by the Banco de España that Banco Popular and the Banco Hispano Americano merge. Valls commented: 'That is fine with me under two conditions: first that Hispano's branch managers report to our regional managers, and second that Hispano's headquarters be sold.' He left it clear that the bank was not going to change its policy of independence, at least not in the foreseeable future. In any event, this question would probably soon become a rhetorical one as rumours had it that Banco Hispano Americano might merge with Banco Central.

When asked how Banco Popular would be able to compete and maintain its position among the large commercial banks he replied that the banks that were merging would have to digest their merger. 'Like a siesta after a heavy lunch, this will take time.' He added that customers didn't like to work with only one bank. He therefore felt the bank's business would continue to prosper, because those that worked with the banks that merged would be looking for an alternative. There was the danger, however, that if another merger took place and only four big banks remained, Popular would be left out of the 'Club' of big banks for being too small. Valls, however, didn't think this would affect the business. He felt that the only thing that might be hurt was the bank's vanity 'Popular is the Switzerland of the Spanish banks.' Like the country, which was not included among the big seven industrial powers, Popular might be excluded from the 'Club'. He believed, nevertheless, that also like the country, it would continue doing extremely well.

...Separate Ownership and Management...

The bank had a long-standing policy of separating ownership and management, considering this an ideal formula for efficiency. Accordingly, decision-making power had traditionally rested on the board of directors (the administrative body) as opposed to the shareholders. Thus the board of directors was responsible for controlling and monitoring that the business was being run efficiently, and the actual management of the bank was done by professional executives, whose actions were not interfered or meddled with in any way.

This management policy was common to banks in countries like the United States and Germany, but was a fairly recent phenomenon in Spain, where banks had traditionally been run by the owning families. It was developed at Banco Popular to cure the bank of ills which had adversely affected its performance until 1953. Up to this date many directors had personally intervened in the hiring of staff, in employee promotions, in the granting of loans, in speculative operations, in setting up subsidiaries – in short, in practically all aspects of the banking business. Some of these directors were frankly unethical, using the bank's premises and facilities to conduct personal and/or family business.

...And Hire Exceptional People...

Banco Popular prided itself on hiring only very high quality people to be its future managers. Traditionally, Banco Popular had admitted the majority of its people at very young ages, 'still wearing shorts' as many managers put it. These boys, many still completing high school, would take very lowly jobs and slowly work their way up through the ranks. They saw the bank as a life-long career, and willingly became an integral part of the organization, part of the 'Banco Popular family'. Although many never obtained university degrees, they were said to be intelligent, motivated and very dedicated people who had a vocation to be bankers.

Since the mid-1980s the bank had instituted a policy of 'rejuvenating' its staff and upgrading its employees' professional capabilities in order to meet future demands:

> The bank only hires candidates who rate as exceptional in almost all variables, with capability for intuitive risk assessment and commercial skills, who accept job rotation, who are computer-numerate and who know English.[14]

This was true particularly of major locations such as Madrid and Barcelona, and in industrial and tourist areas where customers were more demanding and managerial rotation was more important. For small towns and rural areas Banco Popular expected its people to be affable and have a certain degree of humility in order to understand and be able to service the needs of small depositors. In these areas the bank wanted 'gente del pueblo' (town folk), not 'stars'. Perhaps most important of all, Banco Popular wanted people that had a vocation for banking and were interested in long-term careers. Thus the bank rarely took people in for middle management positions: promotion was from within.

The Bank's Customers

The bank's principal customer groups were the PYME and consumers. It was quite strong in the rural sector, the educational sector, the tourism sector, and also in the service to Spanish emigrants, where it boased a 25 per cent market share.

Banco Popular had an extensive retail network and had used its numerous branches to create very close bonds between itself and its customers. Over 1,000 of Banco Popular Group's 1,679 branches were located in rural areas in towns of fewer than 40,000 inhabitants and were very small, with no more than two to three staff. Although the rural sector was no longer the bank's principal business, the PYME and individuals in the metropolitan areas accounting for the bulk, it still represented approximately one third of the total, not at all an insignificant amount.

The strength of Popular's distribution network and its excellent customer relations had allowed it to maintain market share in the face of increasing competition from the high-yielding current accounts offered by its rivals.[15] By concentrating on consumers and smaller businesses, rather than on large industrial groupings like many of Big Six, Banco Popular had managed to achieve much higher margins than its competitors.

Its Segmentation Strategy...

Banco Popular was the first bank in Spain to segment its customers, and as a result was a leader in its segments of focus. It had a special group of marketing experts at the group level (the 'Dirección Comercial') which performed market studies to identify potential customer groups, and analyzed proposals originated at the branch level. This group never made impositions on the branches, but was there to help them. Its purpose was to give the branches the necessary tools to adequately meet customer needs, and to motivate them to attract new customer groups.

Although at Banco Popular segmentation had become quite sophisticated (especially during the 1980s), it had originally been purely intuitive. *De facto* segmentation began very early at Banco Popular. The bank was a latecomer in the Spanish market, having been established in the 1920s as a 'pseudo-insurance company which had a weak presence and a poor performance', becoming a commercial bank only in 1947 when it assumed its present name. By that time the Spanish market was completely dominated by the other big Spanish banks, like Banesto and Banco Central. Therefore, in order to survive, Banco Popular needed to find a niche where it could establish a presence and grow.

At that time Spanish banks served basically the large metropolitan areas, most of rural Spain being deprived of their services, as the Banco de España had restricted the expansion of branch networks. Thus Banco Popular saw the rural Spain as an avenue to grow and expand the banking market.

Since branching was restricted, Banco Popular decided to set up a network of correspondents ('corresponsales de radio'). These correspondents were typically tradesmen (pharmacists, grocers, butchers, etc.), who acted as agents for the bank, visiting people in their homes, both in their own villages and in the neighbouring hamlets (sometimes quite far away), taking deposits and performing other financial services. The bank would then pay these men a commission on the business they had generated. Periodically an officer of the bank would visit these correspondents, providing support and monitoring activity in the region. At one point Banco Popular had 4,000 correspondents representing it. These correspondents never officially became part of the bank. When the volume of business in a region warranted it, a branch was opened and the correspondent relationship was terminated. Although considerably reduced, the correspondent network still represented an important part of Banco Popular's business, with 800 correspondents accounting for about 10 per cent of its deposit base.

Banco Popular gained prominence in the Spanish banking sector by continuing this practice of singling out specific segments. The second group the bank identified and then consciously targeted was the Spanish emigrant population. This began in the 1960s which witnessed an exodus of Spanish labour to other European countries, notably France, where it was in high demand (because it was well qualified and considerably cheaper than local labour). The bank saw an opportunity in the handling of the remittances of these emigrants' earnings to family members left behind in Spain. By giving them special attention and personalized service, Banco Popular was able to develop a strong presence amid and gain the loyalty of these people. The bank became a leader in this segment, which, like the correspondents, represented about 10 per cent of its deposit base.

Other segments which were subsequently identified, and with which the bank then worked, were schools, travel agencies and airlines, service stations and transportation companies, car repair workshops and associations of independent professionals (like doctors and architects).

Schools were first identified as a possible segment through the Church, which possessed a huge amount of funds that could be deposited. Since the Catholic Church community was fundamentally responsible for the educational system, Banco Popular recognized a great opportunity in the handling of school receipts, and began targeting the school administrators to get the business. The bank was very successful in its endeavour and soon became the leading bank for the Spanish educational system. By 1990 Banco Popular had nearly 80 per cent of the religious orders and 75 per cent of their schools as customers, and issued some 10 million bills for them every school year. Although the bank failed in its attempt to gain the students' parents as a customer group (they already had solid banking relationships), it was able to capture the teachers and the students. It successfully negotiated the deposit of the teachers' payroll, and offered 'beginners' accounts' and educational material on the basics of managing an account to the students who would soon be going to university and would need to get by on their own.

The bank had been working with airlines and travel agencies since 1982 when it was chosen by IATA (after competing with the other large Spanish banks) to provide a clearing settlement service for airline tickets. Banco Popular was the only bank in Spain that offered this service (called BSP, or the Bank Settlement Plan), and was recognized internationally for the high operating quality and efficiency with which it delivered the service. As a result of this efficiency, Banco Popular won a second IATA contest to manage the payments to cargo agencies. By 1990 the bank worked with more than 50 per cent of the airlines and over 80 per cent of the travel agencies in Spain.

At about the same time as it started worked with travel agencies, Banco Popular discovered two other segments: service stations and car repair workshops. The sale of petrol to service stations in Spain was done by a state monopoly and the receipts were handled by very few banks, all shareholders of the monopoly. The service stations, in order to protect their interests and increase their bargaining power with the monopoly, grouped together and sought to offer their main clients (lorry drivers and transport companies) an instrument which would facilitate payment terms. This could not be a credit card, however, as the monopoly prohibited credit cards and the granting of discounts. They asked Banco Popular, an expert in means of payment services, to provide them with such an instrument. The bank came up with a special debit card for the stations' clients, whereby they could pay at sight without carrying cash. With this product Banco Popular was able to get not only the service stations as clients, but lorry drivers and transport companies as well.

Car repair workshops were identified as a potential segment through an agreement made with the Mutua Madrileña de Seguros (a Madrid-based insurance company) to centralize in Banco Popular all the payments made to their authorized shops. These shops were not obliged to become clients of the bank, but its service was considered so good and personalized that many of them were won over, and by year-end 1990 Banco Popular had about 1300 car repair workshops as clients.

Professional associations were a very new segment for Banco Popular: a commercial agreement being reached with the first group, the Association of Doctors, only in 1990. Through this agreement the bank gave the association special conditions in the remuneration of savings and the granting of credit, returned part of the commission on the volume generated by the VISA 'Affinity' card offered them, provided a Videotex service with a special database designed especially for doctors. This new segment was first identified in Madrid through the 'Colegio de Médicos'. Banco Popular already had a tradition in the educational sector with schools and had begun targeting colleges and universities. It saw the medical school as a possible vehicle to get the Doctors' Association as a client and thus opened a small branch office at the college and managed all the school's receipts and the medical students' payments. The bank was extending this business with the Madrid Medical School to medical schools throughout the country in the hope of getting doctors all over Spain as clients.

Banco Popular also began considering the possibility of working with the Architects' Association and the Lawyers' Association using the same methods as it did to gain the business of the Doctors' Association. In addition, the bank was looking to work with universities in the same way as it did with schools and negotiations with the University of Valencia were well under way.

...Competitive Benchmarking...

Banco Popular made a point of carefully observing the competition in everything to avoid making similar mistakes. According to the president, 'We observe our competition as if we were at the theatre, watching a play ... we do so secretively, always by surprise, so that we catch them unprepared.' An example of this was the establishment by Banco Hispano Americano of a branch office in Tokyo. The Japanese monetary authorities had, for a long time, only permitted banks to establish representative offices. When they authorized the opening of branches, Hispano jumped on the opportunity, without first evaluating whether or not the investment made economic sense. When management realized how much this move would cost the bank, they tried to pull out, but it was too late: the Japanese authorities wouldn't permit it. As a result, Hispano lost a lot of money.

Banco Popular also watched competition to get new ideas. For example, when the president of Bilbao Vizcaya announced the bank's intentions to distribute quarterly dividends, Banco Popular, seeing that the idea was a good one, anticipated Bilbao Vizcaya and was the first to introduce them.

...And Some Food for Thought...

In spite of Banco Popular's success, some managers were starting to feel that the momentum of the bank was waning, that it was beginning to show signs of fatigue in terms of its position in the market. The rural sector was no longer as big as it had been, as many people and businesses had moved to urban areas. With a smaller rural sector, the Cajas de Ahorro (savings banks) posed a much bigger threat to Banco Popular than they did before as they were competing for a smaller space and had stronger capital bases to do so.[16] The bank was not afraid of them, however, as they lacked the expertise in dealing with the PYME and homogeneous customer groups, having traditionally worked with individuals. Popular's personnel, on the other hand, had years of experience, and knew the customers thoroughly. It would take the *cajas* years to catch up.

According to management, Banco Popular had the most loyal customer base of the big six Spanish banks. They admitted, however, that only 30 per cent of the bank's customers were truly loyal, 20 per cent being semi-loyal and 50 per cent not loyal. It seemed, therefore, that the bank's lack of diversification could prove to be a real problem in terms of maintaining and growing the business. The fact that it lacked experience and know-how in investment banking might hurt Banco Popular, because customers (especially PYME) were becoming more and more sophisticated and demanding.

A few managers complained that the bank was even losing one of its key selling propositions which was the very personalized service it had traditionally offered. With the expansion of branch networks and the advance of information technology, some of the personalized touch was disappearing, as it was becoming impractical and too costly.

The Bank's Organizational Philosophy

Banco Popular was well aware that its success depended on the existence of a strong organizational philosophy and a total commitment to this philosophy.

> In a context where the physical environment and economic situation are similar, the differences in profitability, productivity and development among companies in the same industry arise essentially from differences in the abilities, attitudes and skills of their people, and from the autonomy of their managers with respect to responsibility, decision-making power and risk-acceptance.[17]

Dictated by a clear set of management policies, the bank's culture was 'endowed with internal coherence and unity' and was characterized by the following factors.

...Operational Decentralization...

Management at Banco Popular had been 'striving for years to be nimble in making appropriate organizational changes, so as to attain a structure which is simple, decentralized, flexible and horizontal, oriented to improving the service to customers'.[18] The bank's structure was flat and decentralized. There were only three layers of management, 19 regional managers and five general managers of banking subsidiaries forming the link between the branch managers and top management (the 'cúpula directiva central'). According to Ricardo Lacasa, general manager in charge of Specialized Banking, the bank was 'a federation of regional directorships', each one of them enjoying a great deal of autonomy. The reason for this is twofold. First, the bank's growth was in large part due to the acquisition of five regional banks, whose networks expanded together with Banco Popular's own network. These banks had their own personalities, which were mainly determined by the characteristics of the particular region in which they operated. For example, Banco de Castilla was mainly a rural bank as the Castilla region depended mainly on agriculture and livestock raising. Banco de Andalucía's business, on the other hand, was more diversified, agriculture still representing a significant portion of the business, but tourism and construction also playing important roles. Second, branch offices were regionalized to assure 'greater flexibility and a more thorough knowledge of the social and economic characteristics of each area so as to be able to respond promptly and efficiently to customers' needs'.[19]

As with the regions, the 1,662 branches enjoyed a good deal of autonomy, the degree varying from one branch to another according to the features of the business and needs posed by the clientele. In any event, each branch was run like a separate bank, having balance-sheet and profit and loss responsibility, and being subject to the obligations imposed by the monetary authorities as to mandatory ratios, provisions, etc. Branch managers thus felt the challenge, pleasure and headaches of running their own businesses. There was no fixed rule regarding how many branches should report to a regional manager. What was important was the maintenance of the necessary 'fluidity of communication and flexibility of supervision' at all times.

According to management, also implicit in the concept of operational decentralization, was that of unity of command. For this the regional manager, while providing a direct link between the CEO and the branch managers, was personally responsible for the attainment of the bank's overall objectives in his region. He had to analyze the directives he received and devise specific action plans and monitor their implementation in the branches under his command. Typically, the regional manager's responsibilities included both the standard banking business (funds, loans and services) and the general oversight of the operations of the branch offices under his command. The only matters outside his authority were the definition of general policies, cash control and management, institutional relations and certain special operations of particular importance or characteristics, all of which were reserved to the head office.

Not only was the operating part (the branch network) of the bank decentralized, but so was the back-office. In the late 1970s the central administrative offices, such as Accounting and Control, Information Systems, Credit Analysis and Marketing, which up till then had been organized as departments, were split up into small nuclei according to the functions they performed, each with their own budget to manage.

This permitted better control of costs, a rationalization of personnel and more rapid and effective communication within and between functional areas. It is also ensured less wasted time and duplicated work and resulted in a significant reduction in personnel and general costs during the 1980s. It is worthy of note that the administrative offices accounted for only 18 per cent of the bank's total headcount, compared with 30–5 per cent as an average for the international banks.

This operational decentralization – central to the bank's culture – was expected to assure service speed and flexibility, and contribute thereby to make Banco Popular the most efficiently run bank in Spain, according to analysts. 'Anything which brings where the decisions are made closer to where the business is generated is a step forward in the pursuit of efficiency.'[20]

...And Stringent Management Control...

To balance its decentralized structure, Banco Popular depended on tight control systems, using sophisticated analytical techniques and computer resources, to monitor day-to-day operations. This permitted effective budgeting and cost control, which, according to international business analysts, made Popular one of the most efficiently managed banks not only in Spain, but in the world.

Several methods of control were used in the bank. These included accounting methods, internal audit and quality control. Accounting Control was carried out by producing on a monthly basis a myriad of statements on the branch, region, bank and consolidated levels. These statements contained detailed breakdowns of all profit and loss accounts as well as balance sheet accounts, showing their evolution month by month and comparing them to the same month in the previous year. All statements contained historical information so comparisons could be made and any abnormality or problem could be easily identified and acted upon. In addition to these statements a report showing and comparing the operating margins of branches and regions, classifying them as 'below average' and 'average or above', was issued and served to promote competition between branches and regions.

The most important management report was the 'Informe Mensual de Valoración' ('IMV') which was prepared every month for each branch. In this report was included not only the balance sheet and profit and loss statement of each branch, but a detailed account of the branch's strengths and weaknesses. It was the envy of many banks, who were trying, without much success, to copy it. 'It took us over five years to teach our branches how to use this report and to understand its importance', claimed Juan Manuel García, Chief Controller of the Bank.

At Banco Popular these statements were ready at the latest by the 15th day of the following month. The other Spanish banks, that is, those that prepared monthly statements, were able to produce them at best with a delay of more than 30 days. Thus Banco Popular's reaction time to any problem or abnormality was at least one half of its competitors.

Banco Popular also took the internal audit function, a conventional method of control used by all banks, further than its competitors. Besides having an administrative manager in each branch to check and sign off all operations performed by the branch, the bank used a number of other methods of internal control. With the help of its EDP systems the bank was able to detect doubtful accounts ('dudosos técnicos') before they became bad debts and take the necessary corrective measures at the first signs of alert. It also monitored costs on a daily basis by instituting the 'FAX of the day' system. This system was instituted in 1984 and consisted of asking branch managers for an immediate justification of 'excessive' expenditures which had been identified through the central computer. The result was that branch managers became much more careful about their expenditures and the bank was able to save over Ptas 2,000 million in a five-year period. Unlike its competitors, Banco Popular also had its central office perform 'surprise' investigations of a branch or region. These 'surprise' audits were performed regularly, but without a specific timetable, so they could never be predicted.

Another management control system in place was one that ensured service quality. This quality control system began formally in 1976 with the first publishing of client complaints in the 'Repertorio de Temas'. Since then a Customer Service Office had been set up, acting as a *de facto* 'Ombudsman' for the bank. Other methods of quality control included a telephone audit, which checked up on how telephones were being answered and customers were being handled. By monitoring the speed with which information was communicated to the central computer, the control office could evaluate the efficiency with which clients were being served. By checking transaction codes the bank could tell how many clients did business with each branch on a daily basis and thus measure how well the branch was doing, and so on.

... Supported by Practical and Efficient Information Technology Systems ...

Banco Popular did not have the most advanced systems in Spain, but they were quite practical and compatible with the bank's structure. According to Angel Pesquera, director of Information Technology, 'IT systems should be a tool to facilitate the business and support the strategic policies of a company', which is precisely what they were meant to be at Banco Popular.

The bank had been a pioneer in office automation, installing the first system in Spain in 1968. However, it did not extend this system to its branch network as its competitors later did. Most of Banco Popular's competitors invested heavily during the early 1970s in centralized office automation systems, equipping their branches with workstations which were linked directly with the central computer. By 1975 these banks had workstations in most of their principal branches while Banco Popular had nothing. Since these centralized computer systems required massive investments which took a long time to pay off and depended heavily on the telecommunications network which at that time was expensive and inefficient, the bank decided to look for other alternatives.

In 1979 Banco Popular decided on a decentralized computer system using recently launched minicomputers, which had their own data processing capabilities and therefore did not need to be hooked up constantly to a central computer. This decentralized system had the advantage of being much less dependent on Spain's telephone lines (which were quite expensive and rather unreliable) and of requiring a much smaller central computer thus a much lower initial investment. Thus, it fit in very well with the bank's objective to maximize profitability. In addition, the decentralized system corroborated the bank's decentralized structure, permitting maximum autonomy for the branches.[21]

Although Banco Popular was late to install a branch-wide office automation system, it did not remain behind for long as its system had several advantages. Besides being much cheaper than its competitors' centralized systems, Banco Popular's decentralized system was much more flexible, so it could incorporate technological advances as they were made. For example in 1987, when the installation of the decentralized system was being completed, it began substituting its minicomputers with microcomputers, making the branches even more independent than they had been before. In addition, phone communications were getting better and less costly as a result of technological improvements made by the telephone company, making possible the installation of station to station lines between all of Banco Popular's branches. As each branch was equipped with an intelligent system and a phone line, they could communicate between themselves without depending on the central computer (the Host).[22] In fact, because of the flexibility of this system, Banco Popular had one of the most advanced and efficient treatments of accounting entries not only in Spain but also internationally, according to management. As most Spanish banks had installed centralized systems, they had obsolete hardware and software which were in urgent need of replacement, and their treatment of accounting entries was by and large antiquated and of poor quality.

Banco Popular's decentralized system had several disadvantages, however. In the first place it did not offer real-time information since contact was made with the Host only twice a day. Thus the bank could not offer its clients real time balance information as could the competition, who had centralized systems. Additionally, the banking business had developed in such a way that in 1990 46 per cent of the bank's transactions were realized outside of the branch network (as opposed to 10 per cent in 1979). These transactions included credit cards and other means of payment systems, interbank transactions, debt markets, etc., all of which depended on a centralized computer system with huge information-processing capabilities.

These problems prompted the bank to develop in 1989 an IT strategy. It set up a team of 24 people composed of its best Organization and IT experts to develop a state of the art IT system which would be put in place by 1994. The first step of the long-term strategic plan involved finding a supplier to develop a pilot system. Once the supplier was selected and the pilot system developed, six platforms were to be installed, national installation occurring only after the system proved successful.

The next major step involved installing a huge database in the Host computer where detailed client and market information could be stored. So, while the new platform was being developed and tested, Banco Popular would build its central database, only converting to the new system when the success of the new technology had been confirmed.

...Coherent Personnel Development and Unique Compensation Systems...

Although no formal training programmes were used, employees were gradually imbued with the bank's culture and management style through 'osmosis'. Introduction into Banco Popular was done basically in the 'sink or swim' fashion, and if new employees were not flexible enough to adapt to the bank's way of doing business, they didn't go very far in the organization. This is why there were very few women in management positions. The general consensus at Banco Popular was that women were generally not as flexible as was necessary to succeed at the bank.

Over the years those unable to adapt were weeded out. During the 1980s over 1,000 people had left the bank while only 200 were admitted, turning Banco Popular into a very lean organization. It must be noted, however, that this weeding-out process also turned the bank into an older organization, the average age of the managers rising from 34–35 to 45–46 years, putting it on almost equal footing with its competitors.

A typical career path for a manager at Banco Popular was as follows. Secondary school and university graduates would be hired in a branch as assistants, to perform administrative functions. They would be rotated in all of the functional areas of the branch (this could take up to 2–3 years) and if they showed a good deal of promise they would be promoted to first officer or even to *apoderado* (the first level of management in the bank) if they proved exceptional. From the position of *apoderado* an individual could become an *interventor* (the branch controller and administrative manager) or even a branch director in a smaller branch. Typically, a Banco Popular professional would spend at least 20 years as director in several different branches before becoming a regional director. Since the organization was so flat, only a few became regional directors and merely a handful reached the top.

All the bank's employees were monitored very closely, so that if they were good their performance could be promptly recognized and compensated. Besides good performance, an essential condition for progress in the bank was an individual's acceptance by his peers. One had to maintain good relations with everyone in order to succeed at Banco Popular. Promotions were not approved at the branch level but had to be referred to the regional manager and at times even top management. This was the only area in which the branches didn't have autonomy, the reason being to ensure that everyone got fair and equal treatment.

Banco Popular had a unique remuneration system which it had recently developed to adapt to the changing demands and expectations of its personnel. This system was offered to all managers, that is, all personnel of the level of *apoderado* and up. It was called the '*Pacto Individual*' (Individual Pact) and had experienced almost 100 per cent acceptance among all those that had been offered it. It was a very flexible system where there were no formal grades or levels to determine promotion or remuneration. Salary increases were given in absolute terms (not as a percentage of base salary) and according to merit (not according to pre-established ranges). True to its name, the individual pact was a private, tailor-made arrangement where the reviewer and the reviewee agreed on the terms. Nobody else knew of its content. This eliminated completely any problem of unfair treatment or discrimination. Nobody got a 'raw deal' or, on the contrary, a 'special boost'.

Below the *apoderado* level people were remunerated according to the *sueldo base*, the base salary set by the *Convenio Colectivo*, in line with agreement between the banks and the workers' unions. This base salary was quite low and very rigid, so employees only started earning a decent living when they reached the *apoderado* level. This posed a problem for the hiring of bright, ambitious university graduates, who might not be willing to 'invest' in their careers for 2–3 years. This problem became especially significant when new employees were asked to transfer outside their home towns. The bank did not help its employees with housing costs until they had gaining signing authority. Although Banco Popular was hard put to keep these young professionals, those that really had a vocation to be bankers and truly wanted to make a career in the bank stayed and in time were amply compensated for their patience.

...And a Participative Style of Management...

A unique feature of the Banco Popular organization was its Association of Managers. This body was set up in 1977 to maximize the involvement of the managers in the conduct of the bank's affairs, and its request to be represented on the board of directors was approved in 1981. According to management, it formed a veritable link between the shareholders and the managers of the bank and ensured that the managers were running the bank in the best interests of both parties. The Association of Managers was composed of 2,700 members which elected a *comisión permanente* of 40 members to represent them. This commission included all levels of management, from *apoderados* to regional managers to members of the *cúpula directiva*, and each representative had an equal voice. Besides the various meetings in the different regions and work locations, every quarter a general meeting was held at the headquarters of the bank where issues of every nature were discussed openly in the presence of the president.

> Roundtable working sessions are not held to congratulate ourselves on the bank's very good performance, with which we are quite familiar, nor to relish the laudatory news items about our management which habitually appear in the daily press and financial journals. On the contrary, our aim is to ensure that the well-deserved prestige is not lost, and to try to enhance it. The stationary contemplation of success is the starting-point for a headlong descent into failure.[23]

The Bank's Leadership

Luis Valls...

Luis Valls Taberner had joined Banco Popular as executive vice-president in 1956, becoming president in 1972. Although in 1991 the presidency of the bank was in the hands of two men, Luis and his brother Javier Valls, Luis was basically the one responsible for the presentday Banco Popular. The culture and management style of the bank reflected his own personal style.

Luis Valle was described as a very cultured and sophisticated man. He was an avid reader, having a special fascination for Machiavelli. According to a journalist for the Spanish magazine *Ranking* he was 'Cultured, extroverted in small circles, shy before the large public, cold as ice... "Machiavelli reincarnated", but his quasi-giocondan smile reveals a certain human essence.'[24] A 'numbered' member of Opus Dei, a powerful and influential religious group in Spain, he had never married. He was 64 years old and his whole life revolved around Banco Popular. A journalist for the Spanish magazine *El Futuro* observed:

> He seems removed from the rest of the world. His capacity for observation and an acute sense of smell make him follow with painstaking detail... the future of Popular's people ... not only those that work there, but also the clients and the shareholders in their relation with the Bank.[25]

It was Luis Valls who instituted the culture of service at Banco Popular. He believed firmly that the mission of the bank was to serve its clients, and that in order to do this properly the bank's managers had to know them and be near them at all times. Thus, as Banco Popular expanded its branch network in the late 1970s, Luis Valls modified its organizational structure, departing from the traditional hierarchical structure of the Spanish banks and creating a flat and flexible structure, where lines of communication would be short and reaction-time fast. Mr Valls was always reflecting on the bank's role in the market and what it should be doing in order to respond best to its client's needs. Accordingly, he often personally took charge of dealing with client complaints.

Everyone agreed that Luis Valls was the heart and mind of the bank and set the direction that it was to follow. He combined an ability to see the big picture with a remarkable capacity for observation, giving attention to the most minute detail. As a manager of Banco Popular said,

> The president is a distinctive man, he has an unusual ability to see into the future, free of prejudices and mental blocks. Like a champion chess player, he is able to see far ahead into the game, planning his 50th move. He does things others wouldn't do. He doesn't limit himself to the use of rules and norms, he doesn't use traditional logic or rationality, he uses intuition. He has a great practical sense. His intuition is not only instinctive, but derives from a summation of his experiences and observations. He is aware of everything; nothing escapes his eye.

He was also a very complex man. 'He is like a cryptic puzzle, multifaceted, unpredictable, difficult to decipher, difficult to synthesize. He is not a common mortal,' commented another manager. He abhorred traditional logic and openly 'persecuted' all those that tried to use it to run the bank's business. Although Mr Valls gave reasons for his decisions, his managers were rarely able to comprehend his motives. He was extremely subtle; his way of thinking and expressing himself departed from the ordinary. His word was doctrine, but he never used his authority to enforce it. He didn't need to. His managers had so much confidence in his judgement and in his vision that they knew their best alternative was not to question but to 'follow and everything will work out for the best'.

This was the way business was done at Banco Popular. Strategy was formulated by Luis Valls and executed by the managers. Although he delegated authority, believing strongly in the capabilities and the good judgement of the bank's managers, when it came to major decisions and changes of direction, he dictated them. The bank's managers just trusted and followed, knowing from experience that his intuition had always been accurate. An example of this was lending to LDC countries. In the late 1970s when all the international banks were feverishly lending huge sums of money to Latin America, expanding their businesses there or setting up new operations, Luis Valls decided to pull out of this area of the world. This came as a surprise to Banco Popular's managers who thought that lending to Latin America was a good business. Although they didn't necessarily agree with him at the time, they decided to trust his judgement. A few years later his instinct proved correct. In 1982 Mexico defaulted on its debt, initiating the Latin American debt crisis. Another example of Liuis Valls' acute sense of 'smell' concerned investments in industrial companies. During the Spanish banking crisis many banking concerns went bankrupt in large part because of their involvement with industry and other non-banking activities.[26]

...And the dual Presidency...

In 1989 Luis Valls named his brother, Javier Valls, president of Banco Popular. He had liked the idea of a dual presidency which Banco Bilbao Vizcaya had put in practice during the merger process, and decided to adopt it for Banco Popular. The motivation for a dual presidency was not the same, however.

Banco Vizcaya had adopted it as a temporary solution to the merging of two organizations with two different cultures and management teams, vying for the top positions. Luis Valls had two motivations. The first was to solve the problem of succession. Were he to die, no struggle for power would occur, as Banco Popular would already have a president. The second reason was ubiquity: the president would have twice the normal time to man the ship, and could be in two places at the same time.

Journalists were always eager to detect conflicts between the two presidents. It was hard to believe that a dual presidency could work so well at Banco Popular, when Banco Bilbao Vizcaya had had so many problems. According to Luis Valls the secret lay in the blood ties:

> We think alike, that is the secret. Furthermore, one of is always willing to compromise. We also make a point of never losing our sense of humour. Nothing is so important that one of us feels he must impose his point of view.

The dual presidency also worked because each president had his strong points, and they divided their tasks accordingly. Luis was responsible for the 'back office'. He worried about strategy and set the direction the bank was to follow. Javier, on the hand, was the 'man of the street'. He was responsible for the commercial aspects of the business. Having the knack for negotiations, he dealt with all the foreign investors, and attended the annual World Bank and IMF meetings as well as meeting with major international banks. For example, a few years back Banco Popular had purchased a Swiss bank, whose owner had suffered an accidental death. 'It wasn't murder or suicide, so we thought it was all right,' said Luis jokingly. After three years, however, Popular realized that it didn't understand the business, and so decided to sell it. After one year of arduous negotiations with the Dutch bank ABN, the sale was finally concluded. Javier took charge of the negotiations. Luis Valls admitted: 'I don't have the ability to negotiate, especially with the Dutch.'

IS SAINTHOOD STILL ATTAINABLE?

Luis Valls read carefully the report prepared by the special team dispatched to Santander to investigate the 'Pepe' situation. It stated:

> Between 1976 and 1990 Financial Audit and Internal Audit detected numerous anomalies in the manner in which Branch No. 1 of the city of Santander was being run. Among these the most salient are: Returned cheques, Past Due and Overdrawn loans, Large Sum Deposits not registered or accounted for in the computer. Masking of Overdrafts by temporarily debiting other accounts without express permission of depositors, etc. These committees concluded that the branch was in complete disorder, lacking important documents of every type, totalling lacking in compliance with the norms that affect the security of the Bank. The only point it had in its favour was the fact that it was extremely profitable. They added that they and regional management had warned the branch manager several times to 'clean up his act', but he had made feeble excuses and had obviously ignored them. We quote a report made by regional management to central control and general management in June 1987: The branch fails to apply the minimum

discipline in complying with the norms of the Bank, ignores the observations and instructions of regional management, does not inform of excesses and extra limitations, etc. . ... Since these attitudes can only bring losses to the Bank, we believe that somebody should intervene before they occur. It is evident that this report was not taken very seriously and that the recommended intervention is quite tardy, as we are now in April 1991, amost four years after the report was made.

The president was aghast. He was having a difficult time understanding why he had not been notified sooner, and how 'Pepe' had been able to defraud the bank and its customers for so long. Was the speed and effectiveness of communication which he was so proud of beginning to deteriorate at Banco Popular? How could his management team have let such an alarming report such as that one written in June 1987 pass without taking immediate remedial action? Were some managers becoming so concerned about the short-term results that they were willing to sacrifice the image, integrity and the long-term results of the bank? Was he, Luis Valls, losing control of the empire he had dedicated so much time and effort to build?

EXHIBIT 1
Schematic diagram of the organization of Banco Popular.

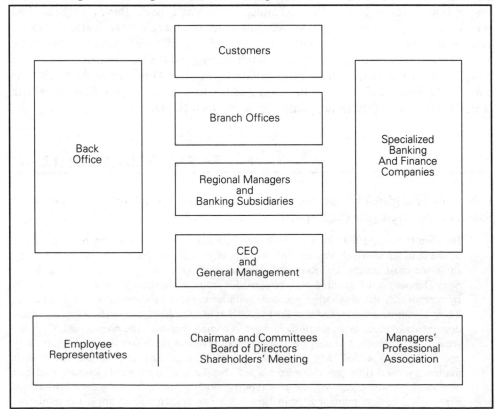

EXHIBIT 2
Evolution of bank intermediation margins*.

	The Bix Six Banks			
	1989		**1990**	
	June	**Dec.**	**June**	**Dec.**
The Bix Six	%	%	%	%
Financial Returns	10.97	11.09	11.75	11.83
Cost of Funds	6.36	6.58	7.36	7.60
Intermediation Margin	4.61	4.51	4.39	4.23
Bilbao-Vizcaya				
Financial Returns	11.31	11.36	11.97	11.87
Cost of Funds	6.48	6.70	7.37	7.58
Intermediation Margin	4.83	4.66	4.60	4.29
Banesto				
Financial Returns	10.37	10.59	11.35	11.44
Cost of Funds	6.15	6.50	7.62	7.94
Intermediation Margin	4.22	4.09	3.73	3.50
Central				
Financial Returns	10.66	10.51	11.48	11.44
Cost of Funds	6.62	6.48	6.95	7.12
Intermediation Margin	4.04	4.03	4.53	4.32
Hispano Americano				
Financial Returns	11.10	11.44	12.16	12.44
Cost of Funds	6.50	6.75	7.61	7.92
Intermediation Margin	4.60	4.69	4.55	4.52
Santander				
Financial Returns	11.02	11.22	11.42	11.61
Cost of Funds	6.46	6.91	7.83	8.01
Intermediation Margin	4.56	4.31	3.59	3.60
Popular				
Financial Returns	11.36	11.66	12.51	12.87
Cost of Funds	5.25	5.54	6.01	6.30
Intermediation Margin	6.11	6.12	6.50	6.57

*Percentage of average total assets.

EXHIBIT 3
Evolution of the deposits of the private sector
(Pesetas 000s millions).

| | The Big Six Banks and Banking Groups | | | | | | | |
| | 1989 | | | | 1990 | | | |
	June	%	Dec.	%	June	%	Dec.	%
Total Banks	17,658	100.0	18,272	100.0	19,612	100.0	20,401	100.0
Total Big Six Banks	9,332	52.8	9,911	54.2	10,772	54.9	11,214	55.0
Total Big Six Banking Groups	12,310	69.7	12,584	68.9	13,502	68.8	14,083	69.0
Bilbao Vizcaya	2,259	12.8	2,439	13.3	2,632	13.4	2,702	13.2
Bilbao Vizcaya Group*	3,625	20.5	3,483	19.1	3,653	18.6	3,771	18.5
Banesto	2,034	11.5	2,050	11.2	2,223	11.3	2,310	11.3
Central	1,717	9.7	1,825	10.0	1,856	9.5	1,969	9.7
Hispano Americano	1,391	7.9	1,426	7.8	1,503	7.7	1,562	7.7
Santander	1,093	6.2	1,362	7.5	1,682	8.6	1,798	8.8
Popular	838	4.7	809	4.4	876	4.5	873	4.3
Popular Group*	1,356	7.7	1,331	7.3	1,431	7.3	1,438	7.0

*Results of other groups do not differ significantly from those of their parent.

EXHIBIT 4
Excerpts from the *Repertorio de Temas*.

'Wanted to Pay but Couldn't'

A client owed Banco Popular more than Ptas 700,000 when he defaulted on his loan. The branch warned him that if he didn't begin paying, they would have to sue.

The client wrote to the president of the bank, explaining that he had defaulted because a serious illness had required of him significant expenditures which he was trying to recover from. 'I don't want to beg; I just ask that you give me time so that I can make up to you and your bank,' he said in his letter.

A manager, sent by the president, investigated the situation and confirmed the truth of the client's claims. With the help of the branch employees he was able to verify that actually the client did have financial difficulties generated by an illness, the treatment of which had required frequent and expensive travel because of the lack of adequate facilities in his home town.

The manager spoke to the client and, in accordance with the branch's decision, told him that the bank would wait until he was in a position to repay, just as he had asked the president.

'Complaint Based on a Poorly Written Document'

In February a client wrote to the president of Banco Popular asking for his intervention to resolve a problem originated six years earlier with a branch.

In 1984 the branch had demanded of the client the payment of outstanding debt relating to an unpaid loan. The client also owed the bank a credit of Ptas 350,000. At the time of debt recognition and liquidation, the branch globalized the amounts pending, including the loan, the credit, the interest due and all related expenditures, although the only concrete reference made was to the loan.

The client claimed, six years later, that he had asked the branch for clarifications and 'I received reasons which then sounded convincing ... but, with the passing of time, my son became suspicious and began investigating the matter, and we came to the conclusion that the amount paid to the branch for exceeded the amount actually owed'.

The president charged a manager with investigating the complaint. By analyzing all the documentation relating to the incident, the manager was able to confirm that the branch had charged the client Ptas 30,000 more than the amount really owed.

The manager spoke to the client who didn't accept the charges of Ptas 350,000 relating to the unpaid credit, only recognizing his indebtedness on the loan.

Soon afterwards, however, the client's lawyer wrote to the bank implicitly accepting the calculations the manager had come to and reclaiming 'the devolution of the quantity the bank recognizes it owes plus the corresponding legal interest'.

The bank found this petition just and credited the client with over Ptas 50,000.

EXHIBIT 5
Banco Popular's office automation system before 1987.

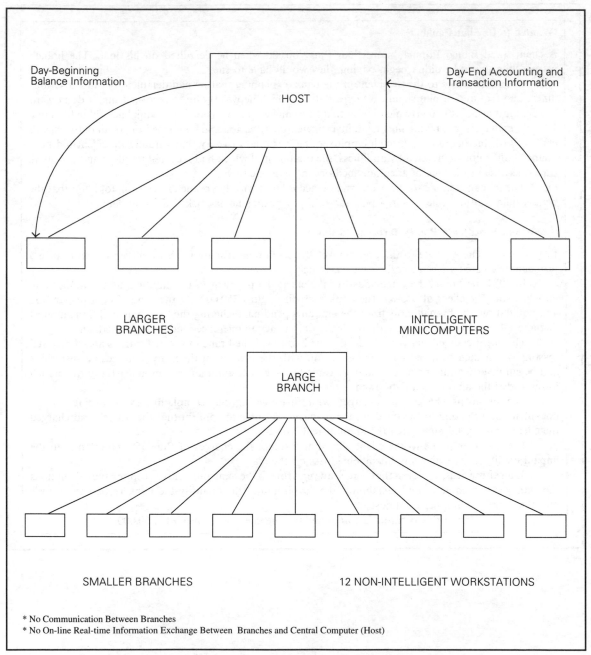

Day-Beginning
Balance Information

HOST

Day-End Accounting and
Transaction Information

LARGER
BRANCHES

INTELLIGENT
MINICOMPUTERS

LARGE
BRANCH

SMALLER BRANCHES

12 NON-INTELLIGENT WORKSTATIONS

* No Communication Between Branches
* No On-line Real-time Information Exchange Between Branches and Central Computer (Host)

EXHIBIT 6
Banco Popular's office automation system after 1987.
Still no on-line real-time information exchange between branches and host.

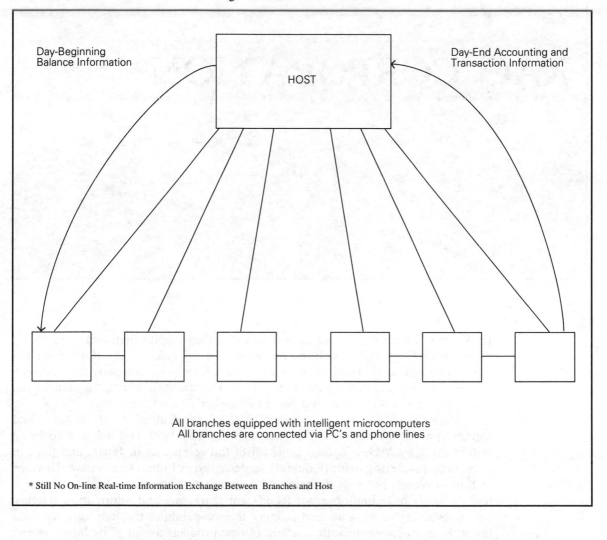

Day-Beginning
Balance Information

HOST

Day-End Accounting and
Transaction Information

All branches equipped with intelligent microcomputers
All branches are connected via PC's and phone lines

* Still No On-line Real-time Information Exchange Between Branches and Host

2–7

KAO CORPORATION*

Dr Yoshio Maruta introduced himself as a Buddhist scholar first, and as president of the Kao Corporation second. The order was significant, for it revealed the philosophy behind Kao and its success in Japan. Kao was a company that not only learned, but 'learned how to learn'. It was, in Dr Maruta's words, 'an educational institution in which everyone is a potential teacher'.

Under Dr Maruta's direction, the scholar's dedication to learning had metamorphosed into a competitive weapon which, in 1990, had led to Kao being ranked ninth by *Nikkei Business* in its list of top companies in Japan, and third in terms of corporate originality (Exhibit 1). As described by Fumio Kuroyanagi, Director of Kao's overseas planning department, the company's success was due not merely to its mastery of technologies nor its efficient marketing and information systems, but to its ability to integrate and enhance these capabilities through learning. As a result, Kao had come up with a stream of new products ahead of its Japanese and foreign competitors and, by 1990, had emerged as the largest branded and packaged goods company in Japan and the country's second largest cosmetics company.

Since the mid-1960s, Kao had also successfully used its formidable array of technological, manufacturing and marketing assets to expand into the neighbouring markets of Southeast Asia. Pitting itself against long-established multinationals like Procter & Gamble and Unilever, Kao had made inroads into the detergent, soap

*This case was prepared by Charlotte Butler, Research Assistant, and Sumantra Ghoshal, Associate Professor at INSEAD. It is intended to be used as the basis for class discussion, rather than to illustrate either effective or ineffective handling of an administrative situation.

and shampoo markets in the region. However, success in these small markets would not make Kao a global player, and since the mid-1980s, Kao had been giving its attention to the problem of how to break into the international markets beyond the region. There, Kao's innovations were being copied and sold by its competitors, not by Kao itself, a situation the company was keen to remedy. But would Kao be able to repeat its domestic success in the United States and Europe? As Dr Maruta knew, the company's ability to compete on a world-wide basis would be measured by its progress in these markets. This, then, was the new challenge to which Kao was dedicated: how to transfer its learning capability, so all-conquering in Japan, to the rest of the world.

THE LEARNING ORGANIZATION

Kao was founded in 1890 as Kao Soap Company with the prescient motto, 'Cleanliness is the foundation of a prosperous society.' Its objective then was to produce a high quality soap that was as good as any imported brand, but at a more affordable price for the Japanese consumer, and this principle had guided the development of all Kao's products ever since. In the 1940s Kao had launched the first Japanese laundry detergent, followed in the 1950s by the launch of dishwashing and household detergents. The 1960s had seen an expansion into industrial products to which Kao could apply its technologies in fat and oil science, surface and polymer science. The 1970s and 1980s, coinciding with the presidency of Dr Maruta, had seen the company grow more rapidly than ever in terms of size, sales and profit, with the launching of innovative products and the start of new businesses. Between 1982 and 1985 it had successfully diversified into cosmetics, hygiene and floppy disks.

A vertically integrated company, Kao owned many of its raw material sources and had, since the 1960s, built its own sales organization of wholesalers who had exclusive distribution of its products throughout Japan. The 1980s had seen a consistent rise in profits, with sales increasingly at roughly 10 per cent a year throughout the decade, even in its mature markets (Exhibit 2). In 1990, sales of Kao products had reached ¥620.4 billion ($3,926.8 million), an 8.4 per cent increase on 1989. This total consisted of laundry and cleaning products (40 per cent), personal care products (34 per cent), hygiene products (13 per cent), specialty chemicals and floppy disks (9 per cent) and fatty chemicals (4 per cent) (Exhibit 3). Net income had increased by 1.7 per cent, from ¥17.5 billion ($110 million) in 1989 to ¥17.8 billion ($112.7 million) in 1990.

Kao dominated most of its markets in Japan. It was the market leader in detergents and shampoo, and was vying for first place in disposable nappies and cosmetics. It had decisively beaten off both foreign and domestic competitors, most famously in two particular instances: the 1983 launch of its disposable nappy brand Merries which, within 12 months, had overtaken the leading brand, Procter & Gamble's Pampers and the 1987 launch of its innovative condensed laundry detergent, the aptly named Attack; as a result of which the market share of Kao's rival, Lion, had declined from 30.9 per cent (1986) to 22.8 per cent (1988), while in the same period Kao's share had gone from 33.4 per cent to 47.5 per cent.

The remarkable success of these two products had been largely responsible for Kao's reputation as a creative company. However, while the ability to introduce a continuous stream of innovative, high quality products clearly rested on Kao's repertoire of core competences, the wellspring behind these was less obvious: Kao's integrated learning capability.

This learning motif had been evident from the beginning. The Nagase family, founders of Kao, had modelled some of Kao's operations, management and production facilities on those of US corporations and in the 1940s, following his inspection of US and European soap and chemical plants, Tomiro Nagase II had reorganized Kao's production facilities, advertising and planning departments on the basis of what he had learned. As the company built up its capabilities, this process of imitation and adaptation had evolved into one of innovation until, under Dr Maruta, a research chemist who joined Kao in the 1930s and became president in 1971, 'Distinct creativity became a policy objective in all our areas of research, production and sales, supporting our determination to explore and develop our own fields of activity.'

The Paperweight Organization

The organizational structure within which Kao managers and personnel worked embodied the philosophy of Dr Maruta's mentor, the seventh century statesman Prince Shotoku, whose constitution was designed to foster the spirit of harmony, based on the principle of absolute equality; 'Human beings can live only by the Universal Truth, and in their dignity of living, all are absolutely equal.' Article 1 of his constitution stated that 'If everyone discusses on an equal footing, there is nothing that cannot be resolved.'

Accordingly, Kao was committed to the principles of equality, individual initiative and the rejection of authoritarianism. Work was viewed as 'something fluid and flexible like the functions of the human body', therefore the organization was designed to 'run as a flowing system' which would stimulate interaction and the spread of ideas in every direction and at every level (Exhibit 4). To allow creativity and initiative full rein, and to demonstrate that hierarchy was merely an expedient that should not become a constraint, organizational boundaries and titles were abolished.

Dr Maruta likened this flat structure to an old-fashioned brass paperweight, in contrast to the pyramid structure of Western organizations: 'In the pyramid, only the person at the top has all the information. Only he can see the full picture, others cannot. . . . The Kao organization is like the paperweight on my desk. It is flat. There is a small handle in the middle, just as we have a few senior people. But all information is shared horizontally, not filtered vertically. Only then can you have equality. And equality is the basis for trust and commitment.'

This organization practised what Kao referred to as 'biological self-control'. As the body reacted to pain by sending help from all quarters, 'If anything goes wrong in one department, the other departments should know automatically and help without having to be asked.' Small group activities were encouraged in order to link ideas or discuss issues of immediate concern. In 1987, for example, to resolve the problem of why Kao's Toyohashi factory could achieve only 50 per cent of the projected production of Nivea cream, workers there voluntarily formed a small team consisting of the people in charge of production, quality, electricity, process and machinery. By the following year, production had been raised to 95 per cent of the target.

In pursuit of greater efficiency and creativity, Kao's organization has continued to evolve. A 1987 programme introduced a system of working from home for sales people, while another will eventually reduce everyone's working time to 1,800 hours a year from the traditional level of 2,100 hours. Other programmes have aimed at either introducing information technology or revitalizing certain areas. 1971 saw the 'CCR movement', aimed at reducing the workforce through computerization. 'Total Quality Control' came in 1974, followed in 1981 by Office Automation. The 1986 'Total Cost Reduction' programme to restructure management resources evolved into the 'Total Creative Revolution', designed to encourage a more innovative approach. For example, five people who were made redundant following the installation of new equipment, formed, on their own initiative, a special task force team, and visited a US factory which had imported machinery from Japan. They stayed there for three months until local engineers felt confident enough to take charge. Over time, this group became a flying squad of specialists, available to help foreign production plants get over their teething troubles.

Managing Information

Just as Dr Maruta's Buddha was the enlightened teacher, so Kao employees were the 'priests' who learned and practised the truth. Learning was 'a frame of mind, a daily matter', and truth was sought through discussions, by testing and investigating concrete business ideas until something was learned, often without the manager realizing it. This was 'the quintessence of information. . .something we actually see with our own eyes and feel with our bodies'. This internalized intuition, which coincides with the Zen Buddhist phrase *kangyo ichijo*, was the goal Dr Maruta set for all Kao managers. In reaching it, every individual was expected to be a coach; both to himself and to everyone else, whether above or below him in the organization.

Their training material was information. And information was regarded not as something lifeless to be stored, but as knowledge to be shared and exploited to the utmost. Every manager repeated Dr Maruta's fundamental assumption: 'In today's business world, information is the only source of competitive advantage. The company that develops a monopoly on information, and has the ability to learn it continuously, is the company that will win, irrespective of its business.' Every piece of information from the environment was treated as a potential key to a new positioning, a new product. What can we learn from it? How can we use it? These were the questions all managers were expected to ask themselves at all times.

Access to information was another facet of Kao's commitment to egalitarinism: as described by Kuroyanagi, 'In Kao, the "classified" stamp does not exist.' Through the development of computer communication technologies, the same level of information was available to all: 'In order to make it effective to discuss subjects freely, it is necessary to share all information. If someone has special and crucial information that the others don't have, that is against human equality, and will deprive us and the organisation of real creativity.'

Every director and most salesmen had a fax in their home to receive results and news, and a bi-weekly Kao newspaper kept the entire company informed about competitors' moves, new product launches, overseas development or key meetings. Terminals installed throughout the company ensured that any employee could, if they wished, retrieve data on sales records of any product for any of Kao's numerous outlets, or product development at their own or other branches. The latest findings from each of Kao's research laboratories were available for all to see, as were the details of the previous day's production and inventory at every Kao plant. 'They can even', said Dr Maruta, 'check up on the president's expense account.' He believed that the increase in creativity resulting from this pooling of data outweighed the risk of leaks. In any case, the prevailing environment of *omnes flux* meant that things moved so quickly 'leaked information instantly becomes obsolete'.

The task of Kao managers, therefore, was to take information directly from the competitive environment, process it and, by adding value, transform it into knowledge or wisdom. Digesting information from the marketplace in this way enabled the organization to maintain empathy with this fast moving environment. The emphasis was always on learning and on the future, not on following an advance plan based on previous experience. 'Past wisdom must not be a constraint, but something to be challenged,' Dr Maruta constantly urged. Kao managers were discouraged from making any historical comparisons. 'We cannot talk about history,' said Mr Takayama, Overseas Planning Director. 'If we talk about the past, they [the top management] immediately become unpleasant.' The emphasis was rather, what had they learnt today that would be useful tomorrow? 'Yesterday's success formula is often today's obsolete dogma. We must continuously challenge the past so that we can renew ourselves each day,' said Dr Maruta.

'Learning through cooperation' was the slogan of Kao's R & D; the emphasis was on information exchange, both within and outside the department, and sharing 'to motivate and activate'. Glycerine Ether, for example, an emulsifier important for the production of Sofina's screening cream, was the product of joint work among three Kao laboratories. Research results were communicated to everyone in the company through the IT system, in order to build a close networking organization. Top management and researchers met at regular R & D conferences, where presentations were made by the researchers themselves, not their section managers. 'Open Space' meetings were offered every week by the R & D division, and people from any part of the organization could participate in discussions on current research projects.

A number of formal and informal systems were created to promote communication among the research scientists working in different laboratories. For example, results from Paris were fed daily into the computer in Tokyo. The most important of these communication mechanisms, however, were the monthly R & D working conferences for junior researchers which took place at each laboratory in turn. When it was their own laboratory's turn to act as host, researchers could nominate anyone they wished to meet, from any laboratory in the company, to attend that meeting. In addition, any researcher could nominate him or herself to attend meetings if they felt that the discussions could help their own work, or if they wanted to talk separately with someone from the host laboratory. At the meetings, which Dr Maruta often attended to argue and discuss issues in detail, researchers reported on studies in progress, and those present offered advice from commercial and academic perspectives.

The Decision Process

'In Kao, we try collectively to direct the accumulation of individual wisdom at serving the customer.' This was how Dr Maruta explained the company's approach to the decision process. At Kao, no one owned an idea. Ideas were to be shared in order to enhance their value and achieve enlightenment in order to make the right decision. The prevailing principle was *tataki-dai*; present your ideas to others at 80 per cent completion so that they could criticize or contribute before the idea became a proposal. Takayama likened this approach to heating an iron and testing it on one's arm to see if it was hot enough. 'By inviting all the relevant actors to join in with forging the task,' he said, 'we achieve *zo-awase*; a common perspective or view.' The individual was thus a strategic factor, to be linked with others in a union of individual wisdom and group strategy.

Fumio Kuroyanagi provided an illustration. Here is the process by which a problem involving a joint venture partner, in which he was the key person, was resolved:

> I put up a preliminary note summarizing the key issues, but not making any proposals. I wanted to share the data and obtain other views before developing a proposal fully.... This note was distributed to legal, international controllers to read ... then in the meeting we talked about the facts and came up with some ideas on how to proceed. Then members of this meeting requested some top management time. All the key people attended this meeting, together with one member of the top management. No written document was circulated in advance. Instead, we described the situation, our analysis and action plans. He gave us his comments. We came to a revised plan. I then wrote up this revised plan and circulated it to all the people, and we had a second meeting at which everyone agreed with the plan. Then the two of us attended the actual meeting with the partner. After the meeting I debriefed other members, discussed and circulated a draft of the letter to the partner which, after everyone else had seen it and given their comments, was signed by my boss.

The cross-fertilization of ideas to aid the decision process was encouraged by the physical lay out of the Kao building. On the 10th floor, known as the top management floor, sat the chairman, the president, four executive vice-presidents and a pool of secretaries (Exhibit 5). A large part of the floor was open space, with one large conference table and two smaller ones, and chairs, blackboards and overhead projectors strewn around: this was known as the decision space, where all discussions with and among the top management took place. Anyone passing, including the president, could sit down and join in any discussion on any topic, however briefly. This layout was duplicated on the other floors, in the laboratories and in the workshop. Workplaces looked like large rooms; there were no partitions, but again tables and chairs for spontaneous or planned discussions at which everyone contributed as equals. Access was free to all, and any manager could thus find himself sitting round the table next to the president, who was often seen waiting in line in Tao's Tokyo cafeteria.

The management process, thus, was transparent and open, and leadership was practised in daily behaviour rather than by memos and formal meetings. According to Takayama, top management 'emphasizes that 80 per cent of its time must be spent on communication, and the remaining 20 per cent on decision-making'. While top management regularly visited other floors to join in discussions, anyone attending a meeting on the 10th floor then had to pass on what had happened to the rest of his colleagues.

Information Technology

Information technology (IT) was one of Kao's most effective competitive weapons, and an integral part of its organizational systems and management processes. In 1982, Kao made an agreement to use Japan Information Service Co.'s VAN (Value-Added Networks) for communication between Kao's head office, its sales companies and its large wholesalers. Over time, Kao built its own VAN, through which it connected upstream and downstream via information linkages. In 1986 the company added DRESS, a new network linking Kao and the retail stores receiving its support.

The objective of this networking capability was to achieve the complete fusion and interaction of Kao's marketing, production and R & D departments. Fully integrated information systems controlled the flow of materials and products; from the production planning of raw materials to the distribution of the final products to local stores: no small task in a company dealing with over 1,500 types of raw materials from 500 different suppliers, and producing over 550 types of final products for up to 300,000 retail stores.

Kao's networks enabled it to maintain a symbiotic relationship with its distributors, the *hansha*. Developed since 1966, the Kao *hansha* (numbering 30 by 1990) were independent wholesalers who handled only Kao products. They dealt directly with 100,000 retail stores out of 300,000, and about 60 per cent of Kao's products passed through them. The data terminals installed in the *hansha* offices provided Kao with up-to-date product movement and market information, which was easily accessible for analysis.

Kao's Logistics Information System (LIS) consisted of a sales planning system, an inventory control system and an on-line supply system. It linked Kao headquarters, factories, the *hansha* and logistics centres by networks, and dealt with ordering, inventory, production and sales data (Exhibit 6). Using the LIS, each *hansha* sales person projected sales plans on the basis of a head office campaign plan, an advertising plan and past market trends. These were corrected and adjusted at corporate level, and a final sales plan was produced each month. From this plan, daily production schedules were then drawn up for each factory and product. The system would also calculate the optimal machine load, and the number of people required. An on-line supply system calculated the appropriate amount of factory stocks and checked the *hansha* inventory. The next day's supply was then computed and automatically ordered from the factory.

A computerized ordering system enabled stores to receive and deliver products within 24 hours of placing an order. Through a POS (point of sale) terminal, installed in the retail store as a cash register and connected to the Kao VAN, information on sales and orders was transmitted to the *hansha*'s computer. Via this, orders from local stores, adjusted according to the amount of their inventory, were transmitted to Kao's logistics centre, which then supplied the product.

Two other major support systems, KAP and RSS, respectively helped the wholesale houses in ordering, stocking and accounting, and worked with Kao's nine distribution information service companies: the Ryutsu Joho Service Companies (RJSs). Each RJS had about 500 customers, mainly small and medium-sized supermarkets who were too small to access real-time information by themselves. The RJSs were essentially consulting outfits, whose mandate was to bring the benefits of information available in Kao VAN to those stores that could not access the information directly. They guided store owners by offering analysis of customer buying trends, shelf space planning and ways of improving the store's sales, profitability and customer service. The owner of one such store commented: 'A Kao sales person comes to see us two or three times a week, and we chat about many topics. To me, he is both a good friend and a good consultant. . . I can see Kao's philosophy, the market trend and the progress of R & D holistically through this person.' According to Dr Maruta, the RJSs embodied Kao's principle of the information advantage: their purpose was to provide this advantage to store owners, and the success of the RJSs in building up the volume and profitability of the stores was ample evidence of the correctness of the principle.

Kao's Marketing Intelligence System (MIS) tracked sales by product, region and market segment, and provided raw market research data. All this information was first sifted for clues to customer needs, then linked with R & D 'seeds' to create new products. New approaches to marketing were sought by applying artificial intelligence to various topics, including advertising and media planning, sales promotion, new product development, market research and statistical analysis.

Additional information was provided by the Consumer Life Research Laboratory which operated ECHO, a sophisticated system for responding to telephone queries about Kao products. In order to understand and respond immediately to a customer's question, each phone operator could instantly access a video display of each of Kao's 500 plus products. Enquiries were also coded and entered into the computer system on-line, and the resulting database provided one of the richest sources for product development or enhancement ideas. By providing Kao with 'a direct window on the consumer's mind', ECHO enabled the company to 'predict the performance of new products and fine tune formulations, labelling and packaging'. Kao also used a panel of monitor households to track how products fitted into consumers' lives.

In 1989, Kao separated its information systems organization and established a distinct entity called Kao Software Development. The aim was to penetrate the information service industry which, according to Japan Information, was projected to reach a business volume of ¥12,000 billion ($80 billion) by the year 2000. In 1989, the market was ¥3,000 billion ($20 billion). One IBM sales engineer forecast, 'by 2000, Kao will have become one of our major competitors, because they know how to develop information technology, and how to combine it with real organization systems'.

In 1989 Kao's competitors, including Lion and Procter & Gamble, united to set up Planet Logistics, a system comparable to Kao's VAN. Through it, they aimed to achieve the same information richness as Kao. But Dr Maruta was not worried by this development. Irrespective of whatever information they collected, he believed that the competitors would not be able to add the value and use it in the same way as Kao did:

> As a company we do not spend our time chasing after what our rivals do. Rather, by mustering our knowledge, wisdom and ingenuity to study how to supply the consumer with superior products, we free ourselves of the need to care about the moves of our competitors. Imitation is the sincerest form of flattery, but unless they can add value to all that information, it will be of little use.

SOFINA

The development of Sofina was a microcosm of Kao's *modus operandi*. It illustrated the learning organization in action since it sought to create a product that satisfied the five principles guiding the development of any new offering: 'Each product must be useful to society. It must use innovative technology. It must offer consumers value. We must be confident we really understand the market and the consumers. And, finally, each new product must be compatible with the trade.' Until a new product satisfied all these criteria, it would not be launched on the market. At every stage during Sofina's creation, ideas were developed, criticized, discussed and refined or altered in the light of new information and learning by everyone involved, from Dr Maruta down.

The Sofina story began in 1965 with a 'vision'. The high quality, innovative product that finally emerged in 1982 allowed Kao to enter a new market and overtake well-established competitors. By 1990, Sofina had become the highest selling brand of comestics in Japan for most items except lipsticks.

The Vision

The vision, according to Mr Daimaru (the first director of Sofina marketing), was simple: to help customers avoid the appearances of wrinkles on their skin for as long as possible. From this vision an equally simple question arose: 'What makes wrinkles appear?' Finding the answer was the spring that set the Kao organization into motion.

Kao's competence until then had been in household and toiletry personal care products. However, Kao had long supplied raw materials for the leading cosmetics manufacturers in Japan, and had a technological competence in fats and soap that could, by cross-pollination, be adapted to research on the human skin. Accordingly, the efforts of Kao's R & D laboratories were directed towards skin research, and the results used in the company's existing businesses such as Nivea or Azea, then sold in joint venture with Beiersdorf. From these successes came the idea for growth that steered the development of Sofina.

The Growth Idea

The idea was to produce a new, high quality cosmetic that gave real value at a reasonable price. During the 1960s, there was a strong perception in the Japanese cosmetics industry that the more expensive the product, the better it was. This view was challenged by Dr Maruta, whose travels had taught him that good skin care products sold in the United States or Europe were not as outrageously expensive.

Yet in Japan, even with companies like Kao supplying high quality raw materials at a low price, the end-product was still beyond the reach of ordinary women at ¥10–20,000.

As a supplier of raw materials, Dr Maruta was aware of how well these products performed. He also knew that though cosmetics' prices were rising sharply, little was being spent on improving the products themselves, and that customers were paying for an expensive image. Was this fair, or good for the customer? Kao, he knew, had the capacity to supply high quality raw materials at low cost, and a basic research capability. Intensive research to develop new toiletry goods had led to the discovery of a technology for modifying the surface of powders, which could be applied to the development of cosmetics. Why not use these assets to develop a new, high quality, reasonably priced product, in keeping with Kao's principles?

To enter the new market would mean a heavy investment in research and marketing, with no guarantee that their product would be accepted. However, it was decided to go ahead; the product would be innovative and, against the emotional appeal of the existing competition in terms of packaging and image, its positioning would embody Kao's scientific approach.

This concept guided the learning process as Sofina was developed. It was found that integration of Kao's unique liquid crystal emulsification technology and other newly developed materials proved effective in maintaining a 'healthy and beautiful skin'. This led Kao to emphasize skin care, as opposed to the industry's previous focus on make-up only. All the research results from Kao's skin diagnosis and dermatological testing were poured into the new product and, as Dr Tsutsumi of the Tokyo Research Laboratory recalled, in pursuing problems connected with the product, new solutions emerged. For example, skin irritation caused by the new chemical was solved by developing MAP, a low irritant, and PSL, a moisturiser. By 1980, most of the basic research work had been done. Six cosmetics suitable for the six basic skin types had been developed, though all under the Sofina name.

During this stage, Kao's intelligence collectors were sent out to explore and map the new market environment. Information on products, pricing, positioning, the competition and above all, the customers, was analyzed and digested by the Sofina marketing and R & D teams, and by Kao's top management. Again and again Dr Maruta asked the same two questions: How would the new product be received? Was it what customers wanted?

The Growth Process

Test marketing began in September 1980, in the Shizuoka prefecture, and was scheduled to last for a year. Shizuoka was chosen because it represented 3 per cent of the national market and an average social mix; neither too rich nor too poor, too rural nor too urban. Its media isolation meant that television advertisements could be targeted to the local population, and no one outside would question why the product was not available elsewhere. The local paper also gave good coverage. In keeping with Kao's rule that 'the concept of a new product is that of its advertising', the Sofina advertisements were reasoned and scientific, selling a function rather than an image.

Sofina was distributed directly to the retail stores through the Sofina Cosmetics

Company, established to distinguish Sofina from Kao's conventional detergent business and avoid image blurring. No mention was made of Kao. Sofina's managers found, however, that retailers did not accept Sofina immediately, but put it on the waiting list for display along with other new cosmetics. The result was that by October 1980, Kao had only succeeded in finding 200 points of sale, against an objective of 600. Then, as the real parentage of Sofina leaked out, the attitude among retailers changed, and the Sofina stand was given the best position in the store. This evidence of Kao's credibility, together with the company's growing confidence in the quality and price of the product, led to a change of strategy. The 30-strong sales force was instructed to put the Kao name first and, by November, 600 outlets had been found.

Sofina's subsequent development was guided by feedback from the market. Direct distribution enabled Kao to retain control of the business and catch customer responses to the product at first hand. To Mr Masashi Kuga, Director of Kao's Marketing Research Department, such information 'has clear added value, and helps in critical decision-making'. During the repeated test marketing of Sofina, Kao's own market research service, formed in 1973 to ensure a high quality response from the market with the least possible distortion, measured the efficacy of sampling and helped decide on the final marketing mix. This activity was usually supported by 'concept testing, focus group discussions, plus product acceptance research'. Mr Daimaru visited the test market twice or three times each month and talked to consumers directly. Dr Maruta did the same.

Every piece of information and all results were shared by the Sofina team, R & D, Kao's top management, corporate marketing and sales managers. Discussions on Sofina's progress were attended by all of these managers, everyone contributing ideas about headline copy or other issues on an equal basis. Wives and friends were given samples and their reactions were fed back to the team.

From the reactions of customers and stores, Kao learnt that carrying real information in the advertisements about the quality of the product had been well received, despite differing from the normal emphasis on fancy packaging. This they could never have known from their detergent business. Another finding was the importance of giving a full explanation of the product with samples, and of a skin analysis before recommending the most suitable product rather than trying to push the brand indiscriminately. They also learned the value of listening to the opinion of the store manager's wife who, they discovered, often had the real managing power, particularly for cosmetics products.

Decisions were implemented immediately. For example, the decision to improve the design for the sample package was taken at 3.30 p.m., and by 6.30 p.m. the same day the engineer in the factory had begun redesigning the shape of the bottle.

The results of this test marketing, available to the whole company, confirmed the decision to go ahead with Sofina. Kao was satisfied that the product would be accepted nationally, though it might take some time. A national launch was planned for the next year. Even at this stage, however, Dr Maruta was still asking whether consumers and retail store owners really liked Sofina.

The Learning Extended

Sofina finally went on nationwide sale in October 1982. However, the flow of learning and intelligence gathering continued via the *hansha* and MIS. Kao, the *hansha*, the retailers and Sofina's customers formed a chain, along which that was a free, two-way flow of information. The learning was then extended to develop other products, resulting in production of the complete Sofina range of beauty care. In 1990, the range covered the whole market, from basic skin care to make-up cosmetics and perfumes.

In fact, the product did not achieve real success until after 1983. Dr Tsutsumi dated it from the introduction of the foundation cream which, he recalled, also faced teething problems. The test result from the panel was not good; it was too different from existing products and was sticky on application. Kao, however, knowing it was a superior product that lasted longer, persevered and used their previous experience to convert the stickiness into a strength: the product was repositioned as 'the longest lasting foundation that does not disappear with sweat'.

In the early 1980s, while market growth was only 2–3 per cent, sales of Sofina products increased at the rate of 30 per cent every year. In 1990, sales amounted to ¥55 billion, and Kao held 15.6 per cent of the cosmetics market behind Shiseido and Kanebo, though taken individually, Sofina brands topped every product category except lipsticks.

Within Japan, Sofina was sold through 12,700 outlets. According to Mr Nakanishi, director of the Cosmetics Division, the marketing emphasis was by that time being redirected from heavy advertising of the product to counselling at the point of sale. Kao was building up a force of beauty counsellors to educate the public of the benefits of Sofina products. A Sofina store in Tokyo was also helping to develop hair care and cosmetics products. A Sofina newspaper had been created which salesmen received by fax, along with the previous month's sales and inventory figures.

Knowledge gathered by the beauty advisers working in the Sofina shops was exploited for the development of the next set of products. Thus, Sofina 'ultra-violet' care, which incorporated skin lotion, UV care and foundation in one, was positioned to appeal to busy women and advertised as 'one step less'. The Sofina cosmetics beauty care consultation system offered advice by phone, at retail shops or by other means to consumers who made enquiries. From their questions, clues were sought to guide new product development.

A staff of Field Companions visited the retail stores to get direct feedback on sales. Every outlet was visited once a month, when the monitors discussed Kao products with store staff, advised on design displays and even helped clean up. Dr Maruta himself maintained an active interest. Mr Kuroyanagi described how Dr Maruta recently 'came down to our floor' to report that while visiting a certain town, he had 'found a store selling Sofina products, and a certain shade sample was missing from the stand'. He asked that the store be checked and the missing samples supplied as soon as possble.

Despite Sofina's success, Kao was still not satisfied. 'To be really successful, developing the right image is important. We've lagged behind on this, and we must improve.'

As the Sofina example showed, in its domestic base Kao was an effective and confident company, renowned for its ability to produce high quality, technologically advanced products at relatively low cost. Not surprising, then, that since the 1960s it had turned its thoughts to becoming an important player on the larger world stage. But could the learning organization operate effectively outside Japan? Could Kao transfer its learning capability into a very different environment such as the United

States or Europe, where it would lack the twin foundations of infrastructure and human resource? Or would internationalization demand major adjustments to its way of operating?

KAO INTERNATIONAL

When the first cake of soap was produced in 1890, the name 'Kao' was stamped in both Chinese characters and Roman letters in preparation for the international market. A century later, the company was active in 50 countries but, except for the small neighbouring markets of Southeast Asia, had not achieved a real breakthrough. Despite all its investments, commitment and efforts over 25 years, Kao remained only 'potentially' a significant global competitor. In 1988, only 10 per cent of its total sales was derived from overseas business, and 70 per cent of this international volume was earned in Southeast Asia. As a result, internationalization was viewed by the company as its next key strategic challenge. Dr Maruta made his ambitions clear; 'Procter and Gamble, Unilever and L'Oréal are our competitors. We cannot avoid fighting in the 1990s.' The challenge was to make those words a reality.

The Strategic Infrastructure

Kao's globalization was based not on a company-wide strategy, but on the product division system. Each product division developed its own strategy for international expansion and remained responsible for its worldwide results. Consequently, the company's business portfolio and strategic infrastructure varied widely from market to market.

Southeast Asia

As Exhibit 7 illustrates, Kao had been building a platform for production and marketing throughout Southeast Asia since 1964, when it created its first overseas subsidiary in Thailand. By 1990, this small initial base had been expanded, mainly through joint ventures, and the company had made steady progress in these markets. The joint ventures in Hong Kong and Singapore sold only Kao's consumer products, while the others both manufactured and marketed them.

One of Kao's biggest international battles was for control of the Asian detergent, soap and shampoo markets, against rivals like P & G and Unilever. In the Taiwanese detergent market, where Unilever was the long-established leader with 50 per cent market share, Kao's vanguard product was the biological detergent, Attack. Launched in 1988, Attack increased Kao's market share from 17 per cent to 22 per cent. Subsequently, Kao decided on local production, both to continue serving the local market and for export to Hong Kong and Singapore. Its domestic rival, Lion (stationary at 17 per cent) shortly followed suit. In Hong Kong, Kao was the market leader with 30 per cent share and in Singapore, where Colgate-Palmolive led with 30 per cent, had increased its share from 5 per cent to 10 per cent. Unilever, P & G and Colgate-Palmolive had responded to Kao's moves by putting in more human resources, and consolidating their local bases.

In Indonesia, where Unilever's historic links again made it strong, Kao, Colgate-Palmolive and P & G competed for the second position. In the Philippines, Kao had started local production of shampoo and liquid soap in 1989, while in Thailand it had doubled its local facilities in order to meet increasing demand. To demonstrate its commitment to the Asian market where it was becoming a major player, Kao had established its Asian headquarters in Singapore. In that market, Kao's disposable nappy Merrys had a 20 per cent share, while its Merit shampoo was the market leader.

North America

Step 1–Joint Venture

In 1976, Kao had embarked on two joint ventures with Colage-Palmolive Company, first to market hair care products in the United States, and later to develop new oral hygiene products for Japan. The potential for synergy seemed enormous; Colgate-Palmolive was to provide the marketing expertise and distribution infrastructure, Kao would contribute the technical expertise to produce a high quality product for the top end of the US market.

1977 saw a considerable exchange of personnel and technology, and a new shampoo was specially developed by Kao for the US consumer. Despite the fact that tests in three major US cities, using Colgate-Palmolive's state of the art market research methods, showed poor market share potential, the product launch went ahead. The forecasts turned out to be correct, and the product was dropped after 10 months due to Colgate-Palmolive's reluctance to continue. A Kao manager explained the failure thus:

> First, the product was not targeted to the proper consumer group. High price, high end-products were not appropriate for a novice and as yet unsophisticated producer like us. Second, the US side believed in the result of the market research too seriously and did not attempt a second try. . . . Third, it is essentially very difficult to penetrate a market like the shampoo market. Our partner expected too much short term success. Fourth, the way the two firms decided on strategy was totally different. We constantly adjust our strategy flexibly. They never start without a concrete and fixed strategy. We could not wait for them.

The alliance was dissolved in 1985. However, Kao had learnt some valuable lessons: about US marketing methods; about Western lifestyles; and, most of all, about the limitations of using joint ventures as a means of breaking into the US market.

Step 2–Acquisition

In 1988, Kao had made three acquisitions. In May, it bought the Andrew Jergens Company, a Cincinnati soap, body lotion and shampoo maker, for $350 million. To acquire Jergens' extensive marketing know-how and established distribution channels, Kao beat off 70 other bidders, including Beiersdorf and Colgate-Palmolive, and paid 40 per cent more than the expected price. Since then, Kao has invested heavily in the company, building a new multi-million dollar research centre and doubling Jergens's research team to over 50. Cincinnati was the home town of P & G, who have since seen Jergens market Kao's bath preparations in the US.

High Point Chemical Corporation of America, an industrial goods producer, was also acquired in 1988. As Kao's US chemical manufacturing arm, it had since begun 'an aggressive expansion of its manufacturing facilities and increased its market position'. The third acquisition, Info Systems (Sentinel) produced application products in the field of information technology.

In Canada, Kao owned 87 per cent of Kao-Didak, a floppy disk manufacturer it bought out in 1986. A new plant, built in 1987, started producing 3.5 inch and 5.25 inch diskettes, resulting in record sales of $10 million that same year. Kao viewed floppy disks as the spearhead of its thrust into the US market. As Mr Kuroyanagi explained: 'This product penetrates the US market easily. Our superior technology makes it possible to meet strict requirements for both quantity and quality. Our experience in producing specific chemicals for the floppy disk gives us a great competitive edge.' In what represented a dramatic move for a Japanese company, Kao relocated its worldwide head office for the floppy disk business to the United States, partly because of Kao's comparatively strong position there (second behind Sony) but also because it was by far the biggest market in the world. The US headquarters was given complete strategic freedom to develop the business globally. Under the direction of this office a plant was built in Spain.

Europe

Within Europe, Kao had built a limited presence in Germany, Spain and France. In Germany, it had established a research laboratory, and through its 1979 joint venture with Beiersdorf to develop and market hair care products, gained a good knowledge of the German market. The strategic position of this business was strengthened in 1989 by the acquisition of a controlling interest in Goldwell AG, one of Germany's leading suppliers of hair and skin care products to beauty salons. From studying Goldwell's network of beauty salons across Europe, Kao expected to expand its knowledge in order to be able to develop and market new products in Europe.

Kao's French subsidiary, created in January 1990, marked floppy disks, skin toner and the Sofina range of cosmetics. The research laboratory established in Paris that same year was given the leading role in developing perfumes to meet Kao's worldwide requirements.

Kao's vanguard product in Europe was Sofina, which was positioned as a high quality, medium-priced product. Any Japanese connection had been removed to avoid giving the brand a cheap image. While Sofina was produced and packaged in Japan, extreme care was taken to ensure that it shared a uniform global positioning and image in all the national markets in Europe. It was only advertised in magazines like *Vogue*, and sales points were carefully selected; for example in France, Sofina was sold only in the prestigious Paris department store, Galeries Lafayette.

Organizational Capability

Organizationally, Kao's international operations were driven primarily along the product division axis. Each subsidiary had a staff in charge of each product who reported to the product's head office, either directly or through a regional product manager. For example, the manager in charge of Sofina in Spain reported to the French office where the regional manager responsible for Sofina was located, and he

In turn reported to the director of the Divisional HQ in Japan. Each subsidiary was managed by Japanese expatriate managers, since Kao's only foreign resource was provided by its acquired companies. Thus, the German companies remained under the management of its original directors. However, some progress was made towards localization; in Kao Spain (250 employees) there were 'only six to ten Japanese, not necessarily in management'. Kao's nine overseas R & D laboratories were each strongly connected to both the product headquarters and laboratories in Japan through frequent meetings and information exchange.

Mr Takayama saw several areas that needed to be strengthened before Kao could become an effective global competitor. Kao, he believed 'was a medium-sized company grown large'. It lacked international experience, had fewer human resource assets, especially in top management and, compared with competitors like P & G and Unilever, had far less accumulated international knowledge and experience of Western markets and consumers. 'These two companies know how to run a business in the West and have well established market research techniques, whereas the westernization of the Japanese lifestyle has only occurred in the last 20 years,' he explained. 'There are wide differences between East and West in, for example, bathing habits, that the company has been slow to comprehend.'

Kao attempted to redress these problems through stronger involvement by headquarters' managers in supporting the company's foreign operations. Mr Kuroyanagi provided an insight into Kao's approach to managing its overseas units. He described how, after visiting a foreign subsidiary where he felt change was necessary, he asked a senior colleague in Japan to carry out a specific review. The two summarized their findings, and then met with other top management members for further consultation. As a result, his colleague was temporarily located in the foreign company to lead certain projects. A team was formed in Japan to harmonize with locals, and sent to work in the subsidiary. Similarly, when investigating the reason for the company's slow penetration of the shampoo market in Thailand, despite offering a technologically superior product, HQ managers found that the product positioning, pricing and packaging policies developed for the Japanese market were unsuitable for Thailand. Since the subsidiary could not adapt these policies to meet local requirements, a headquarters marketing specialist was brought in, together with a representative from Dentsu – Kao's advertising agent in Japan – to identify the source of the problem and make the necessary changes in the marketing mix.

Part of Mr Kuroyanagi's role was to act as a 'liaison officer' between Kao and its subsidiaries. Kao appointed such managers at headquarters to liaise with all the newly acquired companies in Europe and Asia; their task was to interpret corporate strategies to other companies outside Japan and ensure that 'We never make the same mistake twice.' He described himself as 'the eyes and ears of top management, looking round overseas moves, competitors' activities and behaviours and summarizing them'. He was also there to 'help the local management abroad understand correctly Kao as a corporation, and give hints about how to overcome the cultural gap and linguistic difficulties, how to become open, aggressive and innovative'.

Kao's 1990 global strategy was to develop 'local operations sensitive to each region's characteristics and needs'. As Mr Takayama explained, these would be able 'to provide each country with goods tailored to its local climate and customs, products which perfectly meet the needs of its consumers'. To this end, the goals of the company's research centres in Los Angeles, Berlin, Paris and Santiago de Compostela in Spain, had been redefined as: 'to analyze local market needs and characteristics and integrate them into the product development process', and a small market research unit had been created in Thailand to support local marketing of Sofina. Over time, Kao hoped, HQ functions would be dispersed to Southeast Asia, the United States and Europe, leaving to the Tokyo headquarters the role of supporting regionally based, locally managed operations by giving 'strategic assistance'. There were no plans to turn Jergens or other acquired companies into duplicate Kaos; as described by Dr Maruta 'We will work alongside them rather than tell them which way to go.'

The lack of overseas experience among Kao's managers was tackled via a new ¥9 billion training facility built at Kasumigaura. The 16-hectare campus, offering golf, tennis and other entertainment opportunities, was expected to enjoy a constant population of 200, with 10 days' training becoming the norm for all managers. To help Kao managers develop a broader and more international outlook, training sessions devoted considerable attention to the cultural and historical heritages of different countries. A number of younger managers were sent to Europe and the United States, spending the first year learning languages and the second either at a business school, or at Kao's local company offices.

'If you look at our recent international activity,' said Mr Kuroyanagi, 'we have prepared our stage. We have made our acquisitions. . . the basis for globalization in Europe, N. America and SE Asia has been facilitated. . . . We now need some play on that stage.' Kao's top management was confident that the company's R & D power, 'vitality and open, innovative and aggressive culture' would ultimately prevail. The key constraints, inevitably, were people. 'We do not have enough talented people to direct these plays on the stage.' Kao could not and did not wish to staff its overseas operations with Japanese nationals, but finding, training and keeping suitable local personnel was a major challenge.

Kao expected the industry to develop like many others until 'there were only three or four companies operating on a global scale. We would like to be one of these.' Getting there looked like taking some time, but Kao was in no rush. The perspective, Dr Maruta continually stressed, was very long-term, and the company would move at its own pace. 'We should not', he said,

> think about the quick and easy way, for that can lead to bad handling of our products. We must take the long term view. . . and spiral our activity towards the goal. . . . We will not, and need not hurry our penetration of foreign markets. We need to avoid having unbalanced growth. The harmony among people, products and world wide operations is the most important philosophy to keep in mind. . . only in 15 years will it be clear how we have succeeded.

EXHIBIT 1
The ranking of Japanese top companies, 1990.

1. Honda Motors	79.8
2. IBM-Japan	79.4
3. SONY	78.4
4. Matsushita Electrics	74.5
5. Toshiba	69.9
6. NEC	69.8
7. Nissan Motors	69.8
8. Asahi Beer	67.4
9. KAO	66.6
10. Yamato Transportation	66.4
11. Fuji-Xerox	66.3
12. Seibu Department Store	66.2
13. Suntory	65.8
14. Nomura Security	65.4
15. NTT (Nippon Telegraph & Telephone)	65.3
16. Omron	65.1
17. Ajinomoto	64.3
18. Canon	64.3
19. Toyota Motors	63.9
20. Ohtsuka Medicines	63.8

Notes: Points are calculated on the basis of the following criteria:
    1. The assessment by Nikkei Business Committee's member corporate originality, corporate vision, flexibility, goodness.
    2. The result of the researches among consumers.
Source: Nikkei Business, 9 April 1990.

EXHIBIT 2
The trend of Kao's performance.

Years Ended 31 March	1985	1986	1987	Billions of Yen 1988	1989	1990	Millions of US$ 1990
Net Sales	398.1	433.7	464.1	514.4	572.2	620.4	3,926.8
(increase)		+8.9%	+7.0%	+10.9%	+11.2%	+8.4%	
Operating Income	16.5*	19.853*	31.7	36.5	41.4	43.5	275.5
(increase)				+15.2%	+13.5%	+5.1%	
Net Income	9.4	10.5	12.9	13.4	17.5	17.8	112.7
(increase)		+12.3%	+22.5%	+4.2%	+30.4%	+1.7%	
Total Assets	328.3	374.4	381.0	450.4	532.3	572.8	3,625.5
Total Shareholders' Equity	114.4	150.9	180.2	210.7	233.8	256.6	1,624.1

Note: The US dollar amounts are translated, for convenience only, at the rate of ¥156=$1, the approximate exchange rate prevailing on 30 March 1990.
*Non-consolidated.

EXHIBIT 3
Review of operations.

Household Products

Personal care

Cosmetics

toilet soap, body cleansers, shampoo, hair rinse, hair care products, cosmetics and skin care products, toothpaste and toothbrushes

Net Sales (Yen billions)

90	183.7
89	176.7
88	158.9
87	133.3
86	115.0

0' 50' 100' 150' 200' 250'

34%

Laundry and Cleaning

laundry, kitchen and other household detergents, laundry finishing agents

Net Sales (Yen billions)

90	220.2
89	211.1
88	196.1
87	177.2
86	164.7

0' 50' 100' 150' 200' 250'

40%

Hygiene

sanitary products, disposable diapers, bath agents

Net Sales (Yen billions)

90	69.5
89	64.7
88	69.5
87	68.8
86	59.5

0' 50' 100' 150' 200' 250'

13%

Chemical Products

Fatty Chemicals

edible fats and oils, fatty acids, fatty alcohols, glycerine, fatty amines

Net Sales (Yen billions)

90	22.9
89	22.6
88	22.1
87	21.2
86	26.2

0' 50' 100' 150' 200' 250'

4%

Specialty Chemicals and Floppy Disks

surface active agents, polyurethane systems and additives, plasticizers for synthetic resins, polyester resins, floppy disks

Net Sales (Yen billions)

90	49.0
89	46.3
88	43.4
87	40.6
86	40.3

0' 50' 100' 150' 200' 250'

9%

Source: Kao Corporation Annual Report 1990, p.5.

EXHIBIT 4
Organizational structure.

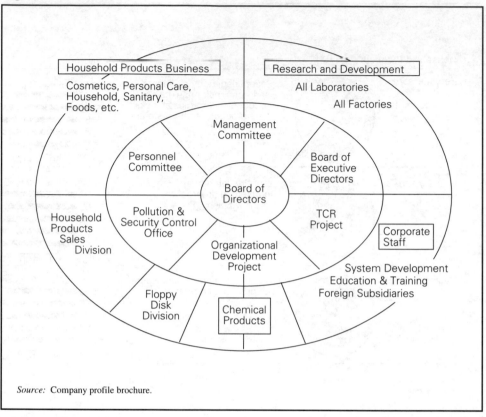

Source: Company profile brochure.

EXHIBIT 3
Layout of Kao offices.

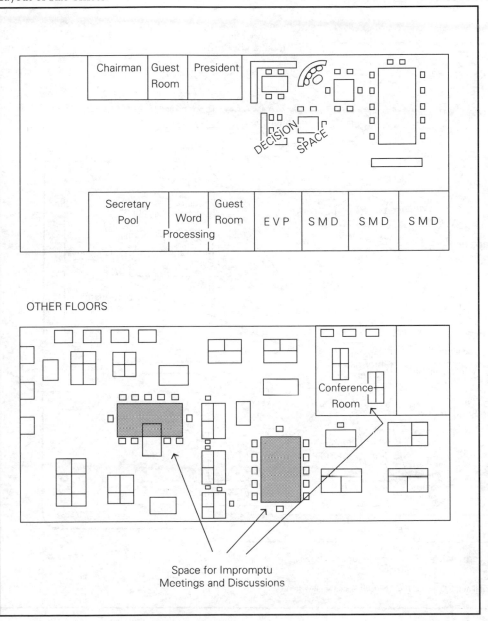

Space for Impromptu
Meetings and Discussions

EXHIBIT 6
Kao's information network.

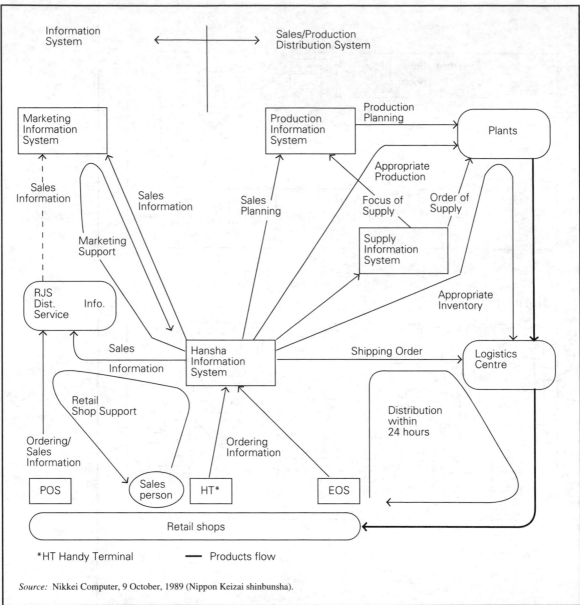

Source: Nikkei Computer, 9 October, 1989 (Nippon Keizai shinbunsha).

EXHIBIT 7
The history of Kao's internationalization.

Area	Company	Year	Capital	Main Products
Asia				
Taiwan	Taiwan Kao Co. Ltd	1964	90	Detergent, soap
Thailand	Kao Industrila Co. Ltd	1964	70	Hair care products
Singapore	Kao Private Ltd	1965	100	Sales of soap, shampoo, detergents
Hong Kong	Kao Ltd	1970	100	Sales of soap, shampoo, detergents
Malaysia	Kao Pte. Ltd	1973	45	Hair care products
Philippines	Philippinas Kao Inc.	1977	70	Fats and oils
Indonesia	P. T. PoleKao	1977	74	Surfactants
Philippines	Kao Inc.	1979	70	Hair care products
Indonesia	P. T. Dino Indonesia Industrial Ltd	1985	50	Hair care products
Malaysia	Fatty Chemical Sdn. Bdn.	1988	70	Alcohol
Singapore	Kao South-East Asia Headquarters	1988		
Philippines	Kao Co. Philippines Laboratory			
North America				
Mexico	Qumi-Kao S. A. de C. V.	1975	20	Fatty amines
	Bitumex	1979	49	Asphal
Canada	Kao-Didak Ltd	1983	89	Floppy disk
USA	Kao Corporation of America (KCOA)	1986	100	Sales of household goods
	High Point Chemical	1987	100 (KCOA)	Ingredients
	Kao Infosystems Company	1988	100 (KCOA)	Duplication of software
	The Andrew Jergens	1988	100 (KCOA)	Hair care products
USA	KCOA Los Angeles Laboratories			
Europe				
W. Germany	Kao Corporation GmbH	1986	100 (KCG)	Sales of household goods
	Kao Perfekta GmbH	1986	80 (KCG)	Toners for copier
	Guhl Ikebana GmnH	1986	50 (KCG)	Hair care products
Spain	Kao Corporation S. A.	1987	100	Surfactants
W. Germany	Goldwell AG	1989	100	Cosmetics
France	Kao Co. S. A. Paris Laboratories			
Spain	Kao Co. S. A. Barcelona Laboratories			
W. Germany	Kao Co. GmbH Berlin Laboratories			

SECTION THREE

CONTEXT

THE ENTREPRENEURIAL CONTEXT

The text of this book divides into two basic parts, although there are three sections. The first, encompassing Sections One and Two (Chs 1–6), introduces a variety of important *concepts* of organizations – strategy, the strategist, process, structure, systems, culture, power. The second, beginning here with Section Three, in Chapter 7, considers how these concepts combine to form major *contexts* of organizations. In effect, a context is a type of situation wherein can be found particular structures, power relationships, processes, competitive settings, and so on.

Traditionally, policy and strategy textbooks were divided into two very different parts – the first on the 'formulation' of strategy, the second on its 'implementation' (including discussion of structure, systems, culture, etc.). As some of the readings of Chapter 4 have already made clear, we believe this is often a false dichotomy: in many situations (that is, contexts), formulation and implementation can be so intertwined that it makes no sense to separate them. To build a textbook around a questionable dichotomy likewise makes no sense to us, and so we have instead proceeded by introducing all the concepts related to the strategy process first, before considering the various ways in which they might interact in specific situations.

There is no one best way to manage the strategy process. The notion that there are several possible good ways, however – various contexts appropriate to strategic management – was first developed by Mintzberg, in Chapter 5. In fact, his configurations of structure serve as the basis for determining the set of contexts we include here. These are as follows:

We begin in Chapter 7 with the *entrepreneurial* context. Here, a single leader takes personal charge in a highly dynamic situation, as in a new firm or a small one operating in a growing market, or even sometimes in a large organization facing crisis.

We next consider (Chapter 8) a contrasting context which often dominates large business as well as big government. We label it the *mature* context, although it might equally be referred to as the stable context or the mass production or mass service context. Here, rather formal structures combine with strategy-making processes which are predominantly planning and technique-oriented.

Third (Chapter 9), we consider the context of the *diversified* organization, which has become increasingly important as waves of mergers have swept across various economies in the West. Because product market strategies are diversified, the structures tend to be divisionalized, and the focus of strategy shifts to two levels: the corporate or portfolio level, and the divisional or business level.

Our fourth and fifth contexts (Chapters 10 and 11) are those of organizations largely dependent on specialists or experts. These contexts are called *professional* when the environment is stable, *innovation* when it is dynamic. Here responsibility for strategy-making tends to diffuse throughout the organization, sometimes even lodging itself at the bottom of the hierarchy. The strategy process tends to become quite emergent in nature.

The next context we consider (Chapter 12) is *international* – a particular dimension of the diversified context, which has become increasingly important over the last two decades. Geographic diversity requires multinational companies to manage the tension between the need for national responsiveness in each country and the countervailing need to integrate their worldwide operations, thereby adding an additional layer of complexity to their strategy process.

We complete our discussion of contexts (Chapter 13) with consideration of the problems of *managing change* from one of these contexts to another (often 'cultural revolution'), or from one major strategy and structure to another within a particular context.

In the chapter on each context, our intention was to include material that would describe all the basic concepts as they take shape in that context. We wished to describe the form of organizational structure and of strategic leadership found there, the nature of its strategy-making process, including its favoured forms of strategy analysis and its most appropriate types of strategies (generic and otherwise), its natural power relationships and preferred culture, and the nature of its competition and industry structure as well as the social issues that surround it. Unfortunately, appropriate readings on all these are not available – in part, we do not yet know all that we must about each context. But we believe that the readings that we have included in this section cover a good deal of the ground – enough to give a real sense of each different context.

Before beginning, we should warn you of one danger in focusing this discussion on contexts such as these: it may make the world of organizations appear to be more pat and ordered than it really is. Many organizations certainly seem to fit one context or another, as numerous examples will make clear. But none ever does so quite perfectly – the world is too nuanced for that. And then there are the many organizations that do not fit any single context at all. We believe, and have included arguments in a concluding chapter to this section, that the set of contexts altogether form a framework by which to understand better all kinds of organizations. But until we get there you should bear in mind that much of this material caricatures reality as much as it mirrors it.

Of course, such caricaturing is a necessary part of formal learning: like the librarian's need for a cataloguing system to store books, we all need frameworks of categories in which to store the confusing set of experiences that the world throws at us. That is what theory is. Without it, we would simply be overwhelmed – and paralyzed. Managers, for example, would never get anything done if they could not use such simplified frameworks to comprehend their experiences in order to act on them. As we suggested in the Introduction, paraphrasing Keynes's the 'practical' person who believes him or herself free of theory is simply the prisoner of some old theory buried deep in the subconscious mind. Moreover, as Miller and Mintzberg have argued in their paper 'The case for configuration', managers are attracted to a particular, well-defined context because that allows them to achieve a certain consistency and coherence in the design of their organization and so to facilitate its effective performance. Each context, as you will see, has its own logic, its own integrated way of dealing with its part of the world – that makes things more manageable.

This chapter of Section Three discusses the entrepreneurial context. At least in its traditional form, this encompasses situations in which a single individual, typically with a clear and distinct vision of purpose, directs an organization that is structured to be as responsive as possible to his or her personal wishes. Strategy-making thus resolves around a single brain, unconstrained by the forces of bureaucratic momentum.

Such entrepreneurship is typically found in young organizations, especially ones in new or emerging industries. Entrepreneurial visions tends to have a high potential payoff in these situations and may indeed be essential when there are long delays between the conception of an idea and its commercial success. In addition, in crisis situations a similar type of strong and visionary leadership may offer the only hope for successful turnaround. And it can thrive as well in highly fragmented industries, where small flexible organizations can move quickly into and out of specialized market niches, and so outmanoeuvre the big bureaucracies.

The word 'entrepreneurship' has also been associated recently with change and innovation within larger, more bureaucratic organizations – sometimes under the label 'intrapreneurship'. In these situations, it is often not the boss, but someone in an odd corner of the organization – a 'champion' for some technology or strategic issue – who takes on the entrepreneurial role. We believe, however, for reasons that will later become evident, that intrapreneurship better fits into our chapter on the innovation context.

To describe the structure that seems to be most logically associated with the traditional form of entrepreneurship, we open with material on the simple structure in Mintzberg's book *The Structuring of Organizations*. Combined with this is a discussion on strategy-making in the entrepreneurial context, especially with regard to strategic vision, based on two sets of research projects carried out at McGill University. In one, the strategies of visionary leadership were studied through biographies and autobiographies; in the other, the strategies of entrepreneurial firms were tracked across several decades of their histories. Then, to investigate the external situations that seem to be most commonly (although not exclusively) associated with the entrepreneurial context, we present excerpts from a chapter of Michael Porter's book *Competitive Strategy*, which focuses on emerging industries.

• THE ENTREPRENEURIAL ORGANIZATION*

HENRY MINTZBERG

Consider an automobile dealership with a flamboyant owner, a brand new government department, a corporation or even a nation run by an autocratic leader, or a school system in a state of crisis. In many respects, those are vastly different organizations. But the evidence suggests that they share a number of basic characteristics. They form a configuration we shall call the *entrepreneurial organization*.

THE BASIC STRUCTURE

The structure of the entrepreneurial organization is often very simple, characterized above all by what it is not: elaborated. As shown in the opening figure, typically it has little or no staff, a loose division of labour and a small managerial hierarchy. Little of its activity is formalized, and it makes minimal use of planning procedures or training routines. In a sense, it is non-structure; in my 'structuring' book, I called it *simple structure*.

Power tends to focus on the chief executive, who exercises a high personal profile. Formal controls are discouraged as a threat to the chief's flexibility. He or she drives the organization by sheer force of personality or by more direct interventions. Under the leader's watchful eye, politics cannot easily arise. Should outsiders, such as particular customers or suppliers, seek to exert influence, such leaders are as likely as not to take the organizations to a less exposed niche in the market place.

Thus, it is not uncommon in some entrepreneurial organizations for everyone to report to the chief. Even in ones not so small, communication flows informally, much of it between the chief executive and others. As one group of McGill MBA students commented in their study of a small manufacturer of pumps: 'It is not unusual to see the president of the company engaged in casual conversation with a machine shop mechanic. [That way he is] informed of a machine breakdown even before the shop superintendent is advised.'

* Adapted from *The Structuring of Organizations* (Prentice Hall, 1979, Ch. 17 on 'The simple structure'), *Power In and Around Organizations* (Prentice Hall, 1983, Ch. 20 on 'The autocracy'), and material on strategy formation from 'Visionary leadership and strategic management', *Strategic Management Journal*, (1989, co-authored with Frances Westley); see also 'Tracking strategy in an entrepreneurial firm', *Academy of Management Journal* (1982), and 'Researching the formation of strategies. The history of a Canadian lady, 1939–1976', in R. B. Lamb (ed.), *Competitive Strategic Management* (Prentice Hall, 1984), the last two co-authored with James A. Waters. A chapter similar to this appeared in *Mintzberg on Management: Inside Our Strange World of Organizations* (Free Press, 1989).

Decision-making is likewise flexible, with a highly centralized power system allowing for rapid response. The creation of strategy is, of course, the responsibility of the chief executive, the process tending to be highly intuitive, often oriented to the aggressive search for opportunities. It is not surprising, therefore, that the resulting strategy tends to reflect the chief executive's implicit vision of the world, often an extrapolation of his or her own personality.

Handling disturbances and innovating in an entrepreneurial way are perhaps the most important aspects of the chief executive's work. In contrast, the more formal aspects of managerial work – figurehead duties, for example, receive less attention, as does the need to disseminate information and allocate resources internally, since knowledge and power remain at the top.

CONDITIONS OF THE ENTREPRENEURIAL ORGANIZATION

A centrist entrepreneurial configuration is fostered by an external context that is both simple and dynamic. Simpler environments (say, retailing food as opposed to designing computer systems) enable one person at the top to retain so much influence, while it is a dynamic environment that requires flexible structure, which in turn enables the organization to outmanoeuvre the bureaucracies. Entrepreneurial leaders are naturally attracted to such conditions.

The classic case of this is, of course, the entrepreneurial firm, where the leader is the owner. Entrepreneurs often found their own firms to escape the procedures and

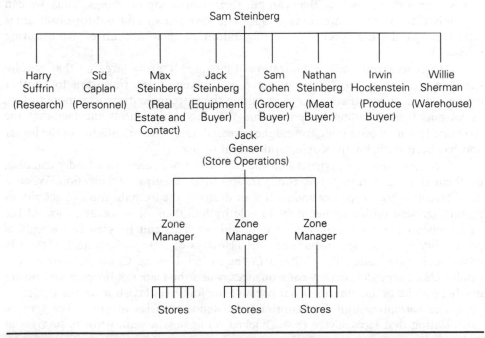

FIGURE 1
Organization of Steinberg's, an entrepreneurial firm (c. 1948)

control of the bureaucracies where they previously worked. At the helm of their own enterprises, they continue to loathe the ways of bureaucracy and the staff analysts that accompany them, and so they keep their organizations lean and flexible. Figure 1 shows the organigram for Steinberg's, a supermarket chain we shall be discussing shortly, during its most classically entrepreneurial years. Notice the identification of people above positions, the simplicity of the structure (the firm's sales by this time were of the order of $27 million), and the focus on the chief executive (not to mention the obvious family connections).

Entrepreneurial firms are often young and aggressive, continually searching for the risky markets that scare off the bigger bureaucracies. But they are also careful to avoid the complex markets, preferring to remain in niches that their leaders can comprehend. Their small size and focused strategies allow their structures to remain simple, so that the leaders can retain tight control and manoeuvre flexibly. Moreover, business entrepreneurs are often visionary, sometimes charismatic or autocratic as well (sometimes both, in sequence!). Of course, not all 'entrepreneurs' are so aggressive or visionary; many settle down to pursue common strategies in small geographic niches. Labelled the *local producers*, these firms can include the local restaurant, the town bakery, the regional supermarket chain.

But an organization need not be owned by an entrepreneur, indeed need not even operate in the profit sector, to adopt the configuration we call entrepreneurial. In fact, most new organizations seem to adopt this configuration, whatever their sector, because they generally have to rely on personalized leadership to get themselves going – to establish their basic direction, or *strategic vision*, to hire their first people and set up their initial procedures. Of course, strong leaders are likewise attracted to new organizations, where they can put their own stamp on things. Thus, we can conclude that most organizations in business, government and not-for-profit areas pass through the entrepreneurial configuration in their formative years, during *start-up*.

Moreover, while new organizations that quickly grow large or that require specialized forms of expertise may make a relatively quick transition to another configuration, many others seem to remain in the entrepreneurial form, more or less, as long as their founding leaders remain in office. This reflects the fact that the structure has often been built around the personal needs and orientation of the leader and has been staffed with people loyal to him or her.

This last comment suggests that the personal power needs of a leader can also, by themselves, give rise to this configuration in an existing organization. When a chief executive hoards power and avoids or destroys the formalization of activity as an infringement on his or her right to rule by fiat, then an autocratic form of the entrepreneurial organization will tend to appear. This can be seen in the cult of personality of the leader, in business (the last days of Henry Ford) no less than in government (the leadership of Stalin in the Soviet Union). Charisma can have a similar effect, though different consequences, when the leader gains personal power not because he or she hoards it but because the followers lavish it on the leader.

The entrepreneurial configuration also tends to arise in any other type of organization that faces severe crisis. Backed up against a wall, with its survival at stake, an organization will typically turn to a strong leader for salvation. The structure thus becomes effectively (if not formally) simple, as the normal powers of existing groups – whether staff analysts, line managers or professional operators, and so on, with their perhaps more standardized forms of control – are suspended to allow the chief to impose a new integrated vision through his or her personalized control. The leader may cut costs and expenses in an attempt to effect what is known in the strategic management literature as an *operating turnaround*, or else reconceive the basic product and service orientation, to achieve *strategic turnaround*. Of course, once the turnaround is realized, the organization may revert to its traditional operations, and, in the bargain, spew out its entrepreneurial leader, now viewed as an impediment to its smooth functioning.

STRATEGY FORMATION IN THE ENTREPRENEURIAL ORGANIZATION

How does strategy develop in the entrepreneurial organization? And what role does that mysterious concept known as 'strategic vision' play? We know something of the entrepreneurial mode of strategy making, but less of strategic vision itself, since it is locked in the head of the individual. But some studies we have done at McGill do shed some light on both these questions. Let us consider strategic vision first.

Visionary Leadership

In a paper she co-authored with me, my McGill colleague Frances Westley contrasted two views of visionary leadership. One she likened to a hypodermic needle, in which the active ingredient (vision) is loaded into a syringe (words) which is injected into the employees to stimulate all kinds of energy. There is surely some truth to this, but Frances prefers another image, that of drama. Drawing from a book on theatre by Peter Brook (1968), the legendary director of the Royal Shakespeare Company, she conceives strategic vision, like drama, as becoming magical in that moment when fiction and life blend together. In drama, this moment is the result of endless 'rehearsal', the 'performance' itself and the 'attendance' of the audience. But Brook prefers the more dynamic equivalent words in French, all of which have English meanings – 'repetition', 'representation' and 'assistance'. Frances likewise applies these words to strategic vision.

'Repetition' suggests that success comes from deep knowledge of the subject at hand. Just as Lord Olivier would repeat his lines again and again until he had trained his tongue muscles to say them effortlessly (Brook, 1968: 154), so too Lee Iococca 'grew up' in the automobile business, going to Chrysler after Ford because cars were 'in his blood' (Iacocca, 1984: 141). The visionary's inspiration stems not from luck, although chance encounters can play a role, but from endless experience in a particular context.

'Representation' means not just to perform but to make the past live again, giving it immediacy, vitality. To the strategist, that is vision articulated, in words and actions. What distinguishes visionary leaders is their profound ability with language, often in symbolic form, as metaphor. It is not just that they 'see' things from a new perspective but that they get others to so see them.

Edwin Land, who built a great company around the Polaroid camera he invented, has written of the duty of 'the inventor to build a new gestalt for the old one in the framework of society' (1975: 50). He himself described photography as helping 'to focus some aspect of [your] life'; as you look through the viewfinder, 'it's not merely the camera you are focusing: you are focusing yourself ... when you touch the button, what is inside of you comes out. It's the most basic form of creativity. Part of you is now permanent' (*Time*, 1972: 84). Lofty words for 50 tourists filing out of a bus to record some pat scene, but powerful imagery for someone trying to build an organization to promote a novel camera. Steve Jobs, visionary (for a time) in his promotion, if not invention, of the personal computer, placed a grand piano and a BMW in Apple's central foyer, with the claim that 'I believe people get great ideas from seeing great products' (in Wise, 1984: 146).

'Assistance' means that the audience for drama, whether in the theatre or in the organization, empowers the actor no less than the actor empowers the audience. Leaders become visionary because they appeal powerfully to specific constituencies at specific periods of time. That is why leaders once perceived as visionary can fall so dramatically from grace – a Steve Jobs, a Winston Churchill. Or to take a more dramatic example, here is how Albert Speer, arriving sceptical, reacted to the first lecture he heard by his future leader: 'Hitler no longer seemed to be speaking to convince; rather, he seemed to feel that he was experiencing what the audience, by now transformed into a single mass, expected of him' (1970: 16).

Of course, management is not theatre; the leader who becomes a stage actor playing a part he or she does not live, is destined to fall from grace. It is integrity – a genuine feeling behind what the leader says and does – that makes leadership truly visionary, and that is what makes impossible the transition of such leadership into any formula.

This visionary leadership is style and strategy, coupled together. It is drama, but not playacting. The strategic visionary is born and made, the product of a historical moment. Brook closes his book with the following quotation:

> In everyday life, 'if' is a fiction, in the theatre 'if' is an experiment.
> In everyday life, 'if' is an evasion, in the theatre 'if' is the truth.
> When we are persuaded to believe in this truth, then the theatre and life are one.
> This is a high aim. It sounds like hard work.
> To play needs much work. But when we experience the work as play, then it is not work any more.
> A play is play. (p. 157)

In the entrepreneurial organization, at best, 'theatre', namely strategic vision, becomes one with 'life', namely organization. That way leadership creates drama; it turns work into play.

Let us now consider the entrepreneurial approach to strategy formation in terms of two specific studies we have done, one of a supermarket chain, the other of a manufacturer of women's undergarments.

The Entrepreneurial Approach to Strategy Formation in a Supermarket Chain

Steinberg's is a Canadian retail chain which began with a tiny food store in Montreal in 1917 and grew to sales in the billion-dollar range during the almost 60-year reign of its leader. Most of that growth came from supermarket operations. In many ways. Steinberg's fits the entrepreneurial model rather well. Sam Steinberg, who joined his mother in the first store at the age of 11 and personally made a quick decision to expand it two years later, maintained complete formal control of the firm (including every single voting share) to the day of his death in 1978. He also exercised close managerial control over all its major decisions, at least until the firm began to diversify after 1960, primarily into other forms of retailing.

It has been popular to describe the 'bold stroke' of the entrepreneur (A. H. Cole, 1959). In Steinberg's we saw only two major reorientations of strategy in the 60 years, moves into self-service in the 1930s and into the shopping centre business in the 1950s. But the stroke was not bold so much as tested. The story of the move into self-service is indicative. In 1933 one of the company's eight stores 'struck it bad', in the chief executive's words, incurring 'unacceptable' losses ($125 a week). Sam Steinberg closed the store one Friday evening, converted it to self-service, changed its name from 'Steinberg's Service Stores' to 'Wholesale Groceteria', slashed its prices by 15–20 per cent, printed handbills, stuffed them into neighbourhood postboxes, and reopened on Monday morning. That's strategic change! But only once these changes proved successful did he convert the other stores. Then, in his words. 'We grew like Topsy.'

This anecdote tells us something about the bold stroke of the entrepreneur – 'controlled boldness' is a better expression. The ideas were bold, the execution careful. Sam Steinberg could have simply closed the one unprofitable store. Instead, he used it to create a new vision, but he tested that vision, however ambitiously, before leaping into it. Notice the interplay here of problems and opportunities. Steinberg took what most businessmen would probably have perceived as a *problem* (how to cut the losses in one store) and by treating it as a *crisis* (what is wrong with our *general* operation that produces these losses) turned it into an *opportunity* (we can grow more effectively with a new concept of retailing). That was how he got energy behind actions and kept ahead of his competitors. He 'oversolved' his problem and thereby remade his company, a characteristic of some of the most effective forms of entrepreneurship.

But absolutely central to this form of entrepreneurship is intimate, detailed knowledge of the business or of analogous business situations, the 'repetition' discussed earlier. The leader as conventional strategic 'planner' – the so-called architect of strategy – sits on a pedestal and is fed aggregate data that he or she uses to 'formulate' strategies that are 'implemented' by others. But the history of Steinberg's belies that image. It suggests that clear, imaginative, integrated strategic vision depends on an involvement with detail, an intimate knowledge of specifics. And by closely controlling 'implementation' personally, the leader is able to reformulate *en route*, to adapt the evolving vision through his or her own process of learning. That is why Steinberg tried his new ideas in one store first. And that is why, in discussing his firm's competitive advantage, he told us: 'Nobody knew the grocery business like we did. Everything has to do with your knowledge'. He added: 'I knew merchandise, I knew cost. I knew selling. I knew customers. I knew everything … and I passed on all my knowledge; I kept teaching my people. That's the advantage we had. They couldn't touch us'.

Such knowledge can be incredibly effective when concentrated in one individual who is fully in charge (having no need to convince others, not subordinates below, not superiors at some distant headquarters, nor market analysts looking for superficial pronouncements) and who retains a strong, long-term commitment to the organization. So long as the business is simple and focused enough to be comprehended in one brain, the entrepreneurial approach is powerful, indeed unexcelled. Nothing else can provide so clear and complete a vision, yet also allow the flexibility to elaborate and rework that vision when necessary. The conception of a new strategy is an exercise in synthesis, which is typically best carried out in a single, informed brain. That is why the entrepreneurial approach is at the centre of the most glorious corporate successes.

But in its strength lies entrepreneurship's weakness. Bear in mind that strategy for the entrepreneurial leader is not a formal, detailed plan on paper. It is a personal vision, a concept of the business, locked in a single brain. It may need to get 'represented', in words and metaphors, but that must remain general if the leader is to maintain the richness and flexibility of his or her concept. But success breeds a large organization, public financing and the need for formal planning. The vision must be articulated to drive others and gain their support, and that threatens the personal nature of the vision. At the limit, as we shall see later in the case of Steinberg's, the leader can get captured by his or her very success.

In Steinberg's, moreover, when success in the traditional business encouraged diversification into new ones (new regions, new forms of retailing, new industries), the organization moved beyond the realm of its leader's personal comprehension, and the entrepreneurial mode of strategy formation lost its viability. Strategy making became more decentralized, more analytic, in some ways more careful, but at the same time less visionary, less integrated, less flexible and, ironically, less deliberate.

Conceiving a New Vision in a Garment Firm

The genius of an entrepreneur like Sam Steinberg was his ability to pursue one vision (self-service and everything that entailed) faithfully for decades and then, based on a weak signal in the environment (the building of the first small shopping centre in Montreal), to realize the need to shift that vision. The planning literature makes a big issue of forecasting such discontinuities, but as far as I know there are no formal techniques to do so effectively (claims about 'scenario analysis' notwithstanding). The ability to perceive a sudden shift in an established pattern and then to conceive a new vision to deal with it appears to remain largely in the realm of informed intuition, generally the purview of the wise, experienced and energetic leader. Again, the literature is largely silent on this. But another of our studies, also concerning entrepreneurship, did reveal some aspects of this process.

Canadelle produces women's undergarments, primarily brassieres. It too was a highly successful organization, although not on the same scale as Steinberg's. Things were going well for the company in the late 1960s, under the personal leadership of Larry Nadler, the son of its founder, when suddenly everything changed. A sexual revolution of sorts was accompanying broader social manifestations, with bra burning a symbol of its resistance. For a manufacturer of brassieres the threat was obvious. For many many other women the miniskirt had come to dominate the fashion scene, making the girdle obsolete and giving rise to tights. As the executives of Canadelle put it, 'the bottom fell out of the girdle business'. The whole environment – long so receptive to the company's strategies – seemed to turn on it all at once.

At the time, a French company had entered the Quebec market with a light, sexy, moulded garment called 'Huit', using the theme, 'just like not wearing a bra'. Their target market was 15–20-year-olds. Though the product was expensive when it landed in Quebec and did not fit well in Nadler's opinion, it sold well. Nadler flew to France in an attempt to license the product for manufacture in Canada. The French firm refused, but, in Nadler's words, what he learned in 'that one hour in their offices made the trip worthwhile'. He realized that what women wanted was a more natural look; not no bra but less bra. Another trip shortly afterwards, to a sister American firm, convinced him of the importance of market segmentation by age and life-style. That led him to the realization that the firm had two markets, one for the more mature customer, for whom the brassiere was a cosmetic to look and feel more attractive, and another for the younger customer who wanted to look and feel more natural.

Those two events led to a major shift in strategic vision. The CEO described it as sudden, the confluence of different ideas to create a new mental set. In his words, 'all of a sudden the idea forms'. Canadelle reconfirmed its commitment to the brassiere business, seeking greater market share while its competitors were cutting back. It introduced a new line of more natural brassieres for the younger customers, for which the firm had to work out the moulding technology as well as a new approach to promotion.

We can draw on Kurt Lewin's (1951) three-stage model of unfreezing, changing and refreezing to explain such a Gestalt shift in vision. The process of *unfreezing* is essentially one of overcoming the natural defence mechanisms, the established 'mental set' of how an industry is supposed to operate, to realize that things have changed fundamentally. The old assumptions no longer hold. Effective managers, especially effective strategic managers, are supposed to scan their environments continually, looking for such changes. But doing so continuously, or worse, trying to use technique to do so, may have exactly the opposite effect. So much attention may be given to strategic monitoring when nothing important is happening that when something really does, it may not even be noticed. The trick, of course, is to pick out the discontinuities that matter, and as noted earlier that seems to have more to do with informed intuition than anything else.

A second step in unfreezing is the willingness to step into the void, so to speak, for the leader to shed his or her conventional notions of how a business is supposed to function. The leader must above all avoid premature closure – seizing on a new thrust before it has become clear what its signals really mean. That takes a special kind of management, one able to live with a good deal of uncertainty and discomfort. 'There is a period of confusion', Nadler told us, 'you sleep on it ... start looking for patterns ... become an information hound, searching for [explanations] everywhere'.

Strategic *change* of this magnitude seems to require a shift in mind-set before a new strategy can be conceived. And the thinking is fundamentally conceptual and inductive, probably stimulated (as in this case) by just one or two key insights. Continuous bombardment of facts, opinions, problems, and so on may prepare the mind for the shift, but it is the sudden *insight* that is likely to drive the synthesis – to bring all the disparate elements together in one 'Eureka'-type flash.

Once the strategist's mind is set, assuming he or she has read the new situation correctly and has not closed prematurely, then the *refreezing* process begins. Here the object is not to read the situation, at least not in a global sense, but in effect to block it out. It is a time to work out the consequences of the new strategic vision.

It has been claimed that obsession is an ingredient in effective organizations (Peters, 1980). Only for the period of refreezing would we agree, when the organization must focus on the pursuit of the new orientation – the new mind-set – with fully vigour. A management that was open and divergent in its thinking must now become closed and convergent. But that means that the uncomfortable period of uncertainty has passed, and people can now get down to the exciting task of accomplishing something new. Now the organization knows where it is going; the object of the exercise is to get there using all the skills at its command, many of them formal and analytic. Of course, not everyone accepts the new vision. For those steeped in old strategies, *this* is the period of discomfort, and they can put up considerable resistance, forcing the leader to make greater use of his or her formal powers and political skills. Thus, refreezing of the leader's mind-set often involves the unfreezing, changing and refreezing of the organization itself! But when the structure is simple, as it is in the entrepreneurial organization, that problem is relatively minor.

Leadership Taking Precedence in the Entrepreneurial Configuration

To conclude: entrepreneurship is very much tied up with the creation of strategic vision, often with the attainment of a new concept. Strategies can be characterized as largely deliberate, since they reside in the intentions of a single leader. But being largely personal as well, the details of those strategies can emerge as they develop. In fact, the vision can change too. The leader can adapt *en route*, can learn, which means new visions can emerge too, sometimes, as we have seen, rather quickly.

In the entrepreneurial organization, as shown in Figure 2, the focus of attention is on the leader. The organization is malleable and responsive to that person's initiatives, while the environment remains benign for the most part, the result of the leader's selecting (or 'enacting') the correct niche for his or her organization. The environment can, of course, flare up occasionally to challenge the organization, and then the leader must adapt, perhaps seeking out a new and more appropriate niche in which to operate.

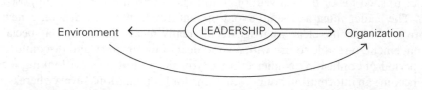

FIGURE 2
Leadership taking precedence in the entrepreneurial organization

SOME ISSUES ASSOCIATED WITH THE
ENTREPRENEURIAL ORGANIZATION

We conclude briefly with some broad issues associated with the entrepreneurial organization. In this configuration, decisions concerning both strategy and operations tend to be centralized in the office of the chief executive. This centralization has the important advantage of rooting strategic response in deep knowledge of the operations. It also allows for flexibility and adaptability: only one person need act. But this same executive can get so enmeshed in operating problems that he or she loses sight of strategy; alternatively, he or she may become so enthusiastic about strategic opportunities that the more routine operations can wither for lack of attention and eventually pull down the whole organization. Both are frequent occurrences in entrepreneurial organizations.

This is also the riskiest of organizations, hinging on the activities of one individual. One heart attack can literally wipe out the organization's prime means of coordination. Even a leader in place can be risky. When change becomes necessary, everything hinges on the chief's response to it. If he or she resists, as is not uncommon where that person developed the existing strategy in the first place, then the organization may have no means to adapt. Then the great strength of the entrepreneurial organization – the vision of its leader plus its capacity to respond quickly – becomes its chief liability.

Another great advantage of the entrepreneurial organization is its sense of mission. Many people enjoy working in a small, intimate organization where the leader – often charismatic – knows where he or she is taking it. As a result, the organization tends to grow rapidly, with great enthusiasm. Employees can develop a solid identification with such an organization.

But other people perceive this configuration as highly restrictive. Because one person calls all the shots, they feel not like the participants on an exciting journey, but like cattle being led to market for someone else's benefit. In fact, the broadening of democratic norms into the sphere of organizations has rendered the entrepreneurial organization unfashionable in some quarters of contemporary society. It has been described as paternalistic and sometimes autocratic, and accused of concentrating too much power at the top. Certainly, without countervailing powers in the organization the chief executive can easily abuse his or her authority.

Perhaps the entrepreneurial organization is an anachronism in societies that call themselves democratic. Yet there have always been such organizations, and there always will be. This was probably the only structure known to those who first discovered the benefits of coordinating their activities in some formal way. And it probably reached its heyday in the era of the great American trusts of the late nineteenth century, when powerful entrepreneurs personally controlled huge empires. Since then, at least in Western society, the entrepreneurial organization has been on the decline. None the less, it remains a prevalent and important configuration, and will continue to be so as long as society faces the conditions that require it: the prizing of entrepreneurial initiative and the resultant encouragement of new organizations, the need for small and informal organizations in some spheres and of strong personalized leadership despite larger size in others, and the need periodically to turn around ailing organizations of all types.

• COMPETITIVE STRATEGY IN EMERGING INDUSTRIES*

MICHAEL E. PORTER

Emerging industries are newly formed or reformed industries that have been created by technological innovations, shifts in relative cost relationships, emergence of new consumer needs, or other economic and sociological changes that elevate a new product or service to the level of a potentially viable business opportunity. ...

The essential characteristic of an emerging industry from the viewpoint of formulating strategy is that there are no rules of the game. The competitive problem in an emerging industry is that all the rules must be established such that the firm can cope with and prosper under them.

THE STRUCTURAL ENVIRONMENT

Although emerging industries can differ a great deal in their structures, there are some common structural factors that seem to characterize many industries in this stage of their development. Most of them relate either to the absence of established bases for competition or other rules of the game or to the initial small size and newness of the industry.

Common Structural Characteristics

Technological Uncertainty
There is usually a great deal of uncertainty about the technology in an emerging industry: What product configuration will ultimately prove to be the best? Which production technology will prove to be the most efficient? ...

Strategic Uncertainty
... No 'right' strategy has been clearly identified, and different firms are groping with different approaches to product/market positioning, marketing, servicing, and so on, as well as betting on different product configurations or production technologies. ... Closely related to this problem, firms often have poor information about competitors, characteristics of customers and industry conditions in the emerging phase. No one knows who all the competitors are, and reliable industry sales and market share data are often simply unavailable, for example.

High Initial Costs but Steep Cost Reduction
Small production volume and newness usually combine to produce high costs in the emerging industry relative to those the industry can potentially achieve. ... Ideas come rapidly in terms of improved procedures, plant layout, and so on, and employees

---

achieve major gains in productivity as job familiarity increases. Increasing sales make major additions to the scale and total accumulated volume of output produced by firms. ...

Embryonic Companies and Spin-Offs

The emerging phase of the industry is usually accompanied by the presence of the greatest proportion of newly formed companies (to be contrasted with newly formed units of established firms) that the industry will ever experience. ...

First-Time Buyers

Buyers of the emerging industry's product or service are inherently first-time buyers. The marketing task is thus one of inducing substitution, or getting the buyer to purchase the new product or service instead of something else. ...

Short Time-Horizon

In many emerging industries the pressure to develop customers or produce products to meet demand is so great that bottlenecks and problems are dealt with expediently rather than as a result of an analysis of future conditions. At the same time, industry conventions are often born out of pure chance. ...

Subsidy

In many emerging industries, especially those with radical new technology or that address areas of societal concern, there may be subsidization of early entrants. Subsidy may come from a variety of government and nongovernment sources. ... Subsidies often add a great degree of instability to an industry, which is made dependent on political decisions that can be quickly reversed or modified. ...

Early Mobility Barriers

In an emerging industry, the configuration of mobility barriers is often predictably different from that which will characterize the industry later in its development. Common early barriers are the following:

- proprietary technology,
- access to distribution channels,
- access to raw materials and other inputs (skilled labour) of appropriate cost and quality,
- cost advantages due to experience, made more significant by the technological and competitive uncertainties,
- risk, which raises the effective opportunity cost of capital and thereby effective capital barriers.

... The nature of the early barriers is a key reason why we observe newly created companies in emerging industries. The typical early barriers stem less from the need to command massive resources than from the ability to bear risk, be creative technologically, and make forward-looking decisions to garner input supplies and distribution channels. ... There may be some advantages to late entry, however. ...

Strategic Choices

Formulation of strategy in emerging industries must cope with the uncertainty and risk of this period of an industry's development. The rules of the competitive game are largely undefined, the structure of the industry unsettled and probably changing, and competitors hard to diagnose. Yet all these factors have another side – the emerging phase of an industry's development is probably the period when the strategic degrees of freedom are the greatest and when the leverage from good strategic choices is the highest in determining performance.

Shaping Industry Structure

The overriding strategic issue in emerging industries is the ability of the firm to shape industry structure. Through its choices, the firm can try to set the rules of the game in areas like product policy, marketing approach, and pricing strategy. ...

Externalities in Industry Development

In an emerging industry, a key strategic issue is the balance the firm strikes between industry advocacy and pursuing its own narrow self-interest. Because of potential problems with industry image, credibility, and confusion of buyers ... in the emerging phase the firm is in part dependent on others in the industry for its own success. The overriding problem for the industry is inducing substitution and attracting first-time buyers, and it is usually in the firm's interest during this phase to help promote standardization, police substandard quality and fly-by-night producers, and present a consistent front to suppliers, customers, government and the financial community....

It is probably a valid generalization that the balance between industry outlook and firm outlook must shift in the direction of the firm as the industry begins to achieve significant penetration. Sometimes firms who have taken very high profiles as industry spokespersons, much to their and the industry's benefit, fail to recognize that they must shift their orientation. As a result, they can be left behind as the industry matures. ...

Changing Role of Suppliers and Channels

Strategically, the firm in an emerging industry must be prepared for a possible shift in the orientation of its suppliers and distribution channels as the industry grows in size and proves itself. Suppliers may become increasingly willing (or can be forced) to respond to the industry's special needs in terms of varieties, service and delivery. Similarly, distribution channels may become more receptive to investing in facilities, advertising, and so forth in partnership with the firms. Early exploitation of these changes in orientation can give the firm strategic leverage.

Shifting Mobility Barriers

As outlined earlier ... the early mobility barriers may erode quickly in an emerging industry, often to be replaced by very different ones as the industry grows in size and as the technology matures. This factor has a number of implications. The most obvious is that the firm must be prepared to find new ways to defend its position and must not rely solely on things like proprietary technology and a unique product variety on which it has succeeded in the past. Responding to shifting mobility barriers may involve commitments of capital that far exceed those that have been necessary in the early phases.

Another implication is that the *nature of entrants* into the industry may shift to more established firms attracted to the larger and increasingly proven (less risky) industry, often competing on the basis of the newer forms of mobility barriers, like scale and marketing clout. ...

Timing Entry

A crucial strategic choice for competing in emerging industries is the appropriate timing of entry. Early entry (or pioneering) involves high risk but may involve otherwise low entry barriers and can offer a large return. Early entry is appropriate when the following general circumstances hold:

- Image and reputation of the firm are important to the buyer, and the firm can develop an enhanced reputation by being a pioneer.

- Early entry can initiate the learning process in a business in which the learning curve is important, experience is difficult to imitate, and it will not be nullified by successive technological generations.

- Customer loyalty will be great, so that benefits will accrue to the firm that sells to the customer first.

- Absolute cost advantages can be gained by early commitment to supplies of raw materials, distribution chennels, and so on. ...

Tactical Moves

The problems limiting development of an emerging industry suggest some tactical moves that may improve the firm's strategic position:

- Early commitments to suppliers of raw materials will yield favourable priorities in times of shortages.

- Financing can be timed to take advantage of a Wall Street love affair with the industry if it happens, even if financing is ahead of actual needs. This step lowers the firm's cost of capital. ...

The choice of which emerging industry to enter is dependent on the outcome of a predictive exercise such as the one described above. An emerging industry is attractive if its ultimate structure (not its *initial* structure) is one that is consistent with above-average returns and if the firm can create a defendable position in the industry in the long run. The latter will depend on its resources relative to the mobility barriers that will evolve.

Too often firms enter emerging industries because they are growing rapidly, because incumbents are currently very profitable, or because ultimate industry size promises to be large. These may be contributing reasons, but the decision to enter must ultimately depend on a structural analysis. ...

8

THE MATURE CONTEXT

In this chapter, we focus on one of the more common contexts for organizations. Whether we refer to this by its form of operations (usually mass production or the mass provision of services), by the form of structure adopted (machine-like bureaucracy), by the type of environment it prefers (a stable one in a mature industry) or by the specific generic strategy often found there (low cost), the context tends to be common and to give rise to a relatively well-defined configuration.

The two readings on what we shall refer to as the *mature* context cover the different aspects and examine some of the problems and opportunities of functioning in this realm. The first reading, on the machine organization, from Mintzberg's work, describes the structure for this context as well as the environment in which it tends to be found, and also investigates some of the social issues surrounding this particular form of organization. This reading also probes the nature of the strategy making process in this context. Here we can see what happens when large organizations accustomed to stability suddenly have to change their strategies dramatically. The careful formal planning, on which they tend to rely so heavily in easier times, seems ill-suited to dealing with changes that may require virtual revolutions in their functioning. A section of this reading thus considers what can be the role of planners when their formal procedures fail to come to grips with the needs of strategy-making.

The second reading is a chapter from Michael Porter's book *Competitive Strategy* on how to deal with the transition to industry maturity. It describes the environment of this context and also probes some of its favoured strategies, notably what Porter calls cost leadership.

• THE MACHINE ORGANIZATION*

HENRY MINTZBERG

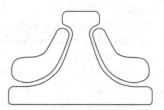

A national post office, a custodial prison, an airline, a giant automobile company, even a small security agency – all these organizations appear to have a number of characteristics in common. Above all, their operating work is routine, the greatest part of it rather simple and repetitive; as a result, their work processes are highly standardized. These characteristics give rise to the machine organizations of our society, structures fine-tuned to run as integrated, regulated, highly bureaucratic machines.

THE BASIC STRUCTURE

A clear configuration of the attributes has appeared consistently in the research: highly specialized, routine operating tasks; very formalized communication throughout the organization; large-size operating units; reliance on the functional basis for grouping tasks; relatively centralized power for decision-making; and an elaborate administrative structure with a sharp distinction between line and staff.

The Operating Core and Administration

The obvious starting point is the operating core, with its highly rationalized work flow. This means that the operating tasks are made simple and repetitive, generally requiring a minimum of skill and training, the latter often taking only hours, seldom more than a few weeks and usually in-house. This in turn results in narrowly defined jobs and an emphasis on the standardization of work processes for coordination, with activities highly formalized. The workers are left with little discretion, as are their supervisors, who can therefore handle very large spans of control.

* Adapted from *The Structure of Organizations* (Prentice Hall, 1979), Ch. 18 on 'The machine bureaucracy': also *Power In and Around Organizations* (Prentice Hall, 1983), Chs. 18 and 19 on 'The instrument' and 'The closed system'; the material on strategy formation from 'Patterns in strategy formation', *Management Science* (1978): 'Does planning impede strategic thinking? Tracking the strategies of Air Canada, from 1937–1976' (co-authored with Pierre Brunet and Jim Waters), in R. B. Lamb and P. Shrivastava (eds), *Advances in Strategic Management*, Volume IV (JAI Press, 1986); and 'The mind of the strategist(s)' (co-authored with Jim Waters), in S. Srivastva (ed.), *The Executive Mind* (Jossey-Bass, 1983); the section on the role of planning, plans and planners is drawn from a book in process on strategic planning. A chapter similar to this appeared in *Mintzberg on Management: Inside Our Strange World of Organizations* (Free Press, 1989).

To achieve such high regulation of the operating work, the organization has need for an elaborate administrative structure – a fully developed middle-line hierarchy and technostructure – but the two are clearly distinguished.

The managers of the middle line have three prime tasks. One is to handle the disturbances that arise in the operating core. The work is so standardized that when things fall through the cracks, conflict flares, because the problems cannot be worked out informally. So it falls to managers to resolve them by direct supervision. Indeed, many problems get bumped up successive steps in the hierarchy until they reach a level of common supervision where they can be resolved by authority (as with a dispute in a company between manufacturing and marketing that may have to be resolved by the chief executive). A second task of the middle-line managers is to work with the staff analysts to incorporate their standards down into the operating units. And a third task is to support the vertical flows in the organization – the elaboration of action plans flowing down the hierarchy and the communication of feedback information back up.

The technostructure must also be highly elaborated. In fact this structure was first identified with the rise of technocratic personnel in early nineteenth-century industries such as textiles and banking. Because the machine organization depends primarily on the standardization of its operating work for coordination, the technostructure – which houses the staff analysts who do the standardizing – emerges as the key part of the structure. To the line managers may be delegated the formal authority for the operating units, but without the standardizers – the cadre of work-study analysts, schedulers, quality control engineers, planners, budgeters, accountants, operations researchers and many more – these structures simply could not function. Hence, despite their lack of formal authority, considerable informal power rests with these staff analysts, who standardize everyone else's work. Rules and regulations permeate the entire system. The emphasis on standardization extends well beyond the operating core of the machine organization, and with it follows the analysts' influence.

A further reflection of this formalization of behaviour are the sharp divisions of labour all over the machine organization. Job specialization in the operating core and the pronounced formal distinction between line and staff have already been mentioned. In addition, the administrative structure is clearly distinguished from the operating core; unlike the entrepreneurial organization, here managers seldom work alongside operators. And they themselves tend to be organized along functional lines, meaning that each runs a unit that performs a single function in the chain that produces the final outputs. Figure 1 shows this, for example, in the organigram of a large steel company, traditionally machinelike in structure.

All this suggests that the machine organization is a structure with an obsession – namely, control. A control mentality pervades it from top to bottom. At the bottom, consider how a Ford Assembly Division general foreman described his work:

> I refer to my watch all the time. I check different items. About every hour I tour my line. About six thirty, I'll tour labour relations to find out who is absent. At seven, I hit the end of the line. I'll check paint, check my scratches and damage. Around ten I'll start talking to all the foremen. I make sure they're all awake. We can't have no holes, no nothing.

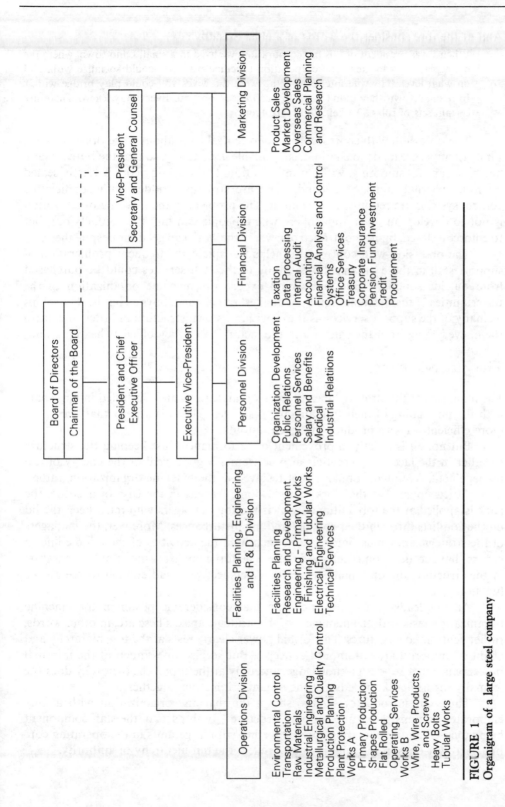

FIGURE 1
Organigram of a large steel company

And at the top, consider the words of a chief executive:

> When I was president of this big corporation, we lived in a small Ohio town, where the main plant was located. The corporation specified who you could socialize with, and on what level. (His wife interjects: 'Who were the wives you could play bridge with.'). In a small town they didn't have to keep check on you. Everybody knew. There are certain sets of rules. (Terkel, 1972: 186, 406)

The obsession with control reflects two central facts about these organizations. First, attempts are made to eliminate all possible uncertainty, so that the bureaucratic machine can run smoothly, without interruption, the operating core perfectly sealed off from external influence. Second, these are structures ridden with conflict; the control systems are required to contain it. The problem in the machine organization is not to develop an open atmosphere where people can talk the conflicts out, but to enforce a closed, tightly controlled one where the work can get done despite them.

The obsession with control also helps to explain the frequent proliferation of support staff in these organizations. Many of the staff services could be purchased from outside suppliers. But that would expose the machine organization to the uncertainties of the open market. So it 'makes' rather than 'buys'. That is, it envelops as many of the support services as it can within its own structure in order to control them, everything from the cafeteria in the factory to the law office at headquarters.

The Strategic Apex

The managers at the strategic apex of these organizations are concerned in large part with the fine-tuning of their bureaucratic machines. Theirs is a perpetual search for more efficient ways to produce the given outputs.

But not all is strictly improvement of performance. Just keeping the structure together in the face of its conflicts also consumes a good deal of the energy of top management. As noted, conflict is not resolved in the machine organization; rather, it is bottled up so that the work can get done. And as in the case of a bottle, the cork is applied at the top. Ultimately, it is the top managers who must keep the lid on the conflicts through their role of handling disturbances. Moreover, the managers of the strategic apex must intervene frequently in the activities of the middle line to ensure that coordination is achieved there. The top managers are the only generalists in the structure, the only managers with a perspective broad enough to see all the functions.

All this leads us to the conclusion that considerable power in the machine organization rests with the managers of the strategic apex. These are, in other words, rather centralized structures: The formal power clearly rests at the top; hierarchy and chain of authority are paramount concepts. But so also does much of the informal power, since that resides in knowledge, and only at the top of the hierarchy does the formally segmented knowledge of the organization come together.

Thus, our introductory figure shows the machine organization with a fully elaborated administrative and support structure – both parts of the staff component being focused on the operating core – together with large units in the operating core but narrower ones in the middle line to reflect the tall hierarchy of authority.

CONDITIONS OF THE MACHINE ORGANIZATION

Work of a machine bureaucratic nature is found, above all, in environments that are simple and stable. The work associated with complex environments cannot be rationalized into simple tasks, and that associated with dynamic environments cannot be predicted, made repetitive and so standardized.

In addition, the machine configuration is typically found in mature organizations, large enough to have the volume of operating work needed for repetition and standardization, and old enough to have been able to settle on the standards they wish to use. These are the organizations that have seen it all before and have established standard procedures to deal with it. Likewise, machine organizations tend to be identified with technical systems that regulate the operating work, so that it can easily be programmed. Such technical systems cannot be very sophisticated or automated (for reasons that will be discussed later).

Mass production firms are perhaps the best-known machine organizations. Their operating work flows through an integrated chain, open at one end to accept raw materials, and after that functioning as a sealed sysyem that processes them through sequences of standardized operations. Thus, the environment may be stable because the organization has acted aggressively to stabilize it. Giant firms in such industries as transportation, tobacco and metals are well known for their attempts to influence the forces of supply and demand by the use of advertising, the development of long-term supply contacts, sometimes the establishment of cartels. They also tend to adopt strategies of 'vertical integration', that is, extend their production chains at both ends, becoming both their own suppliers and their own customers. In that way they can bring some of the forces of supply and demand within their own planning processes.

Of course, the machine organization is not restricted to large, or manufacturing, or even private enterprise organizations. Small manufacturers – for example, producers of discount furniture or paper products – may sometimes prefer this structure because their operating work is simple and repetitive. Many service firms use it for the same reason, such as banks or insurance companies in their retailing activities. Another condition often found with machine organizations is external control. Many government departments, such as post offices and tax collection agencies, are machine bureaucratic not only because their operating work is routine but also because they must be accountable to the public for their actions. Everything they do – treating clients, hiring employees, and so on – must be seen to be fair, and so they proliferate regulations.

Since control is the forte of the machine bureaucracy, it stands to reason that organizations in the business of control – regulatory agencies, custodial prisons, police forces – are drawn to this configuration, sometimes in spite of contradictory conditions. The same is true for the special need for safety. Organizations that fly airplanes or put out fires must minimize the risks they take. Hence they formalize their procedures extensively to ensure that they are carried out to the letter: A fire crew cannot arrive at a burning house and then turn to the chief for orders or discuss informally who will connect the hose and who will go up the ladder.

MACHINE ORGANIZATIONS AS INSTRUMENTS AND CLOSED SYSTEMS

Control raises another issue about machine organizations. Being so pervasively regulated, they themselves can easily be controlled externally, as the *instruments* of outside influencers. In contrast, however, their obsession with control runs not only up the hierarchy but beyond, to control of their own environments, so that they can become *closed systems* immune to external influence. From the perspective of power, the instrument and the closed system constitute two main types of machine organizations.

In our terms, the instrument form of machine organization is dominated by one external influencer or by a group of them in concert. In the 'closely held' corporation, the dominant influencer is the outside owner; in some prisons, it is a community concerned with the custody rather than the rehabilitation of prisoners.

Outside influencers render an organization their instrument by appointing the chief executive, charging that person with the pursuit of clear goals (ideally quantifiable, such as return on investment or prisoner escape measures), and then holding the chief responsible for performance. That way outsiders can control an organization without actually having to manage it. And such control, by virtue of the power put in the hands of the chief executive and the numerical nature of the goals, acts to centralize and bureaucratize the internal structure, in other words, to drive it to the machine form.

In contrast to this, Charles Perrow, the colourful and outspoken organizational sociologist, does not quite see the machine organization as anyone's instrument:

> Society is adaptive to organizations, to the large, powerful organizations controlled by a few, often overlapping, leaders. To see these organizations as adaptive to a 'turbulent', dynamic, very changing environment is to indulge in fantasy. The environment of most powerful organizations is well controlled by them, quite stable, and made up of other organizations with similar interests, or ones they control. (1972: 199)

Perrow is, of course, describing the closed system form of machine organization, the one that uses its bureaucratic procedures to seal itself off from external control and control others instead. It controls not only its own people but its environment as well: perhaps its suppliers, customers, competitors, even government and owners too.

Of course, autonomy can be achieved not only by controlling others (for example, buying up customers and suppliers in so-called vertical integration) but simply by avoiding the control of others. Thus, for example, closed system organizations sometimes form cartels with ostensible competitors or, less blatantly, diversify markets to avoid dependence on particular customers, finance internally to avoid dependence on particular financial groups, and even buy back their own shares to weaken the influence of their own owners. Key to being a closed system is to ensure wide dispersal, and therefore pacification, of all groups of potential external influence.

What goals does the closed system organization pursue? Remember that to sustain centralized bureaucracy the goals should be operational, ideally quantifiable. What operational goals enable an organization to serve itself, as a system closed to external influence? The most obvious answer is growth. Survival may be an indispensable goal and efficiency a necessary one, but beyond those what really matters here is making the system larger. Growth serves the system by providing greater rewards for its insiders – bigger empires for managers to run or fancier private jets to fly, greater programs for analysts to design, even more power for unions to wield by virtue of having more members. (The unions may be external influencers, but the management can keep them passive by allowing them more of the spoils of the closed system.) Thus the classic closed system machine organization, the large, widely held industrial corporation, has long been described as oriented far more to growth than to the maximization of profit *per se* (Galbraith, 1967).

Of course, the closed system form of machine organization can exist outside the private sector too, for example in the fundraising agency that, relatively free to external control, becomes increasingly charitable to itself (as indicated by the plushness of its managers' offices), the agricultural or retail cooperative that ignores those who collectively own it, even government that becomes more intent on serving itself than the citizens for which it supposedly exists.

The communist state, at least up until very recently, seemed to fit all the characteristics of the closed system bureaucracy. It had no dominant external influencer (at least in the case of the Soviet Union, if not the other East Euroean states, which were its 'instruments'). And the population to which it is ostensibly responsible had to respond to its own plethora of rules and regulations. Its election procedures, traditionally offering a choice of one, were similar to those for the directors of the 'widely held' Western corporation. The government's own structure was heavily bureaucratic, with a single hierarchy of authority and a very elaborate technostructure, ranging from state planners to KGB agents. (As James Worthy (1959: 77) noted, Frederick Taylor's 'Scientific Management had its fullest flowering not in America but in Soviet Russia'.) All significant resources were the property of the state – the collective system – not the individual. And, as in other closed systems, the administrators tend to take the lion's share of the benefits.

SOME ISSUES ASSOCIATED WITH THE MACHINE ORGANIZATION

No structure has evoked more heated debate than the machine organization. As Michel Crozier, one of its most eminent students, has noted:

> On the one hand, most authors consider the bureaucratic organization to be the embodiment of rationality in the modern world, and, as such, to be intrinsically superior to all other possible forms of organizations. On the other hand, many authors – often the same ones – consider it a sort of Leviathan, preparing the enslavement of the human race. (1964: 176)

Max Weber, who first wrote about this form of organization, emphasized its rationality; in fact, the word *machine* comes directly from his writings (see Gerth and Mills, 1958). A machine is certainly precise; it is also reliable and easy to control; and it is efficient – at least when restricted to the job it has been designed to do.

Those are the reasons many organizations are structured as machine bureaucracies. When an integrated set of simple, repetitive tasks must be performed precisely and consistently by human beings, this is the most efficient structure – indeed, the only conceivable one.

But in these same advantages of machinelike efficiency lie all the disadvantages of this configuration. Machines consist of mechanical parts; organizational structures also include human beings – and that is where the analogy breaks down.

Human Problems in the Operating Core

James Worthy, when he was an executive of Sears, wrote a penetrating and scathing criticism of the machine organization in his book *Big Business and Free Men*. Worthy traced the root of the human problems in these structures to the 'scientific management' movement led by Frederick Taylor that swept America early in the twentieth century. Worthy acknowledged Taylor's contribution to efficiency, narrowly defined. Worker initiative did not, however, enter into his efficiency equation. Taylor's pleas to remove 'all possible brain work' from the shopfloor also removed all possible initiative from the people who worked there: the 'machine has no will of its own. Its parts have no urge to independent action. Thinking, direction – even purpose – must be provided from outside or above.' This had the 'consequence of destroying the meaning of work itself', which has been 'fantastically wasteful for industry and society', resulting in excessive absenteeism, high worker turnover, sloppy workmanship, costly strikes and even outright sabotage (1959: 67, 79, 70). Of course, there are people who like to work in highly structured situations. But increasing numbers do not, at least not *that* highly structured.

Taylor was fond of saying, 'In the past the man has been first; in the future the system must be first' (in Worthy 1959: 73). Prophetic words, indeed. Modern man seems to exist for his systems; many of the organizations he created to serve him have come to enslave him. The result is that several of what Victor Thompson (1961) has called 'bureaupathologies' – dysfunctional behaviour of these structures – reinforce each other to form a vicious circle in the machine organization. The concentration on means at the expense of ends, the mistreatment of clients, the various manifestations of worker alienation – all lead to the tightening of controls on behaviour. The implicit motto of the machine organization seems to be, 'When in doubt, control.' All problems have to be solved by the turning of the technocratic screws. But since that is what caused the bureaupathologies in the first place, increasing the controls serves only to magnify the problems, leading to the imposition of further controls, and so on.

Coordination Problems in the Administrative Centre

Since the operating core of the machine organization is not designed to handle conflict, many of the human problems that arise there spill up and over, into the administrative structure.

It is one of the ironies of the machine configuration that to achieve the control it requires, it must mirror the narrow specialization of its operating core in its administrative structure (for example, differentiating marketing managers from manufacturing managers, much as salesmen are differentiated from factory workers).

This, in turn, means problems of communication and coordination. The fact is that the administrative structure of the machine organization is also ill-suited to the resolution of problems through mutual adjustment. All the communication barriers in these structures – horizontal, vertical, status, line/staff – impede informal communication among managers and with staff people. 'Each unit becomes jealous of its own prerogatives and finds ways to protect itself against the pressure or encroachments of others' (Worthy, 1950: 176). Thus narrow functionalism not only impedes coordination; it also encourages the building of private empires, which tends to produce top-heavy organizations which can be more concerned with the political games to be won than with the clients to be served.

Adaptation Problems in the Strategic Apex

But if mutual adjustment does not work in the administrative centre – generating more political heat than cooperative light – how does the machine organization resolve its coordination problems? Instinctively, it tries standardization, for example, by tightening job descriptions or proliferating rules. But standardization is not suited to handling the nonroutine problems of the administrative centre. Indeed, it only aggravates them, undermining the influence of the line managers and increasing the conflict. So to reconcile these coordination problems, the machine organization is left with only one coordinating mechanism, direct supervision from above. Specifically, non-routine coordination problems between units are 'bumped' up the line hierarchy until they reach a common level of supervision, often at the top of the structure. The result can be excessive centralization of power, which in turn produces a host of other problems. In effect, just as the human problems in the operating core become coordination problems in the administrative centre, so too do the coordination problems in the administrative centre become adaptation problems at the strategic apex. Let us take a closer look at these by concluding with a discussion of strategic change in the machine configuration.

STRATEGY FORMATION IN THE MACHINE ORGANIZATION

Strategy in the machine organization is supposed to emanate from the top of the hierarchy, where the perspective is broadest and the power most focused. All the relevant information is to be sent up the hierarchy, in aggregated, MIS-type form, there to be formulated into integrated strategy (with the aid of the technostructure). Implementation then follows, with the intended strategies sent down the hierarchy to be turned into successively more elaborated programmes and action plans. Notice the clear division of labour assumed between the formulators at the top and the implementors down below, based on the assumption of perfectly deliberate strategy produced through a process of planning.

That is the theory. The practice has been shown to be another matter. Drawing on our strategy research at McGill University, we shall consider first what planning really proved to be in one machinelike organization, how it may in fact have impeded strategic thinking in a second, and how a third really did change its strategy. From there we shall consider the problems of strategic change in machine organizations and their possible resolution.

Planning as Programming in a Supermarket Chain

What really is the role of formal planning? Does it produce original strategies? Let us return to the case of Steinberg's in the later years of its founder, as large size drove this retailing chain towards the machine form, and as is common in that form, towards a planning mode of management at the expense of entrepreneurship.

One event in particular encouraged the start of planning at Steinberg's: the company's entry into capital markets in 1953. Months before it floated its first bond issue (stock, always non-voting, came later), Same Steinberg boasted to a newspaper reporter that 'not a cent of any money outside the family is invested in the company.' And asked about future plans, he replied: 'Who knows? We will try to go everywhere there seems to be a need for us.' A few months later he announced a $5 million debt issue and with it a $15 million five-year expansion programme, one new store every two months for a total of 30, the doubling of sales, new stores to average double the size of existing ones.

What happened in those ensuing months was Sam Steinberg's realization, after the opening of Montreal's first shopping centre, that he needed to enter the shopping centre business himself to protect his supermarket chain and that he could not do so with the company's traditional methods of short-term and internal financing. And, of course, no company is allowed to go to capital markets without a plan. You can't just say: 'I'm Sam Steinberg and I'm good', though that was really the issue. In a 'rational' society, you have to plan (or at least appear to do so).

But what exactly was that planning? One thing for certain: It did not formulate a strategy. Sam Steinberg already had that. What planning did was justify, elaborate and articulate the strategy that already existed in Sam Steinberg's mind. Planning operationalized his strategic vision, programmed it. It gave order to that vision, imposing form on it to comply with the needs of the organization and its environment. Thus, planning followed the strategy-making process, which had been essentially entrepreneurial.

But its effect on that process was not incidental. By specifying and articulating the vision, planning constrained it and rendered it less flexible. Sam Steinberg retained formal control of the company to the day of this death. But his control over strategy did not remain so absolute. The entrepreneur, by keeping his vision personal, is able to adapt it at will to a changing environment. But by being forced to programme it, the leader loses that flexibility. The danger, ultimately, is that the planning mode forces out the entrepreneurial one; procedure replaces vision. As its structure became more machinelike, Steinberg's required planning in the form of strategic programming. But that planning also accelerated the firm's transition toward the machine form of organization.

Is there, then, such a thing as 'strategic planning'? I suspect not. To be more explicit, I do not find that major new strategies are formulated through any formal procedure. Organizations that rely on formal planning procedures to formulate strategies seem to extrapolate existing strategies, perhaps with marginal changes in them, or else copy the strategies of other organizations. This came out most clearly in another of our McGill studies.

Planning as an Impediment to Strategic Thinking in an Airline

From about the mid-1950s, Air Canada engaged heavily in planning. Once the airline was established, particularly once it developed its basic route structure, a number of factors drove it strongly to the planning mode. Above all was the need for coordination, both of flight schedules with aircraft, crews and maintenance, and of the purchase of expensive aircraft with the structure of the route system. (Imagine someone calling out in the hangar: 'Hey, Fred, this guy says he has two 747s for us; do you know who ordered them?') Safety was another factor: The intense need for safety in the air breeds a mentality of being very careful about what the organization does on the ground, too. This is the airlines' obsession with control. Other factors included the lead-times inherent in key decisions, such as ordering new airplanes or introducing new routes, the sheer cost of the capital equipment, and the size of the organization. You don't run an intricate system like an airline, necessarily very machinelike, without a great deal of formal planning.

But what we found to be the consequence of planning at Air Canada was the absence of a major reorientation of strategy during our study period (up to the mid-1970s). Aircraft certainly changed – they became larger and faster – but the basic route system did not, nor did markets. Air Canada gave only marginal attention, for example, to cargo, charter, and shuttle operations. Formal planning, in our view, impeded strategic thinking.

The problem is that planning, too, proceeds from the machine perspective, much as an assembly-line or a conventional machine produces a product. It all depends on the decomposition of analysis: You split the process into a series of steps or component parts, specify each, and then by following the specifications in sequences you get the desired product. There is a fallacy in this, however. Assembly-lines and conventional machines produce standardized products, while planning is supposed to produce a novel strategy. It is as if the machine is supposed to design the machine; the planning machine is expected to create the original blueprint – the strategy. To put this another way, planning is analysis oriented to decomposition, while strategy making depends on synthesis oriented to integration. That is why the term 'strategic planning' has proved to be an oxymoron.

Roles of Planning, Plans, Planners

If planning does not create strategy, then what purpose does it serve? We have suggested a role above, which has to do with the programming of strategies already created in other ways. This is shown in Figure 2, coming out of a box labelled strategy formation – meant to represent what is to planning a mysterious 'black box'. But if planning is restricted to programming strategy, plans and planners none the less have other roles in play, shown in Figure 2 and discussed alongside that of planning itself.

Role of Planning

Why do organizations engage in formal planning? The answer seems to be: not to create strategies, but to programme the strategies they already have, that is, to

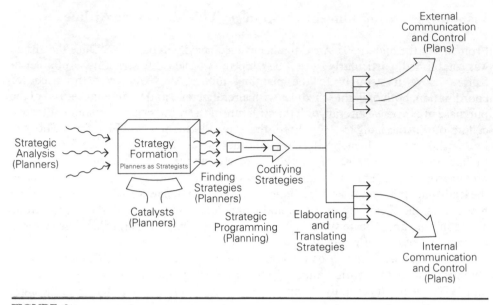

FIGURE 2
Specific roles of planning, plans, planners

elaborate and operationalize the consequences of those strategies formally. We should really say that *effective* organizations so engage in planning, at least when they require the formalized implementation of their strategies. Thus strategy is not the *consequence* of planning but its starting point. Planning helps to translate the intended strategies into realized ones, taking the first step that leads ultimately to implementation.

This *strategic programming*, as it might properly be labelled, can be considered to involve a series of steps, namely the *codification* of given strategy, including its clarification and articulation, the *elaboration* of that strategy into substrategies, *ad hoc* action programmes, and plans of various kinds, and the *translation* of those substrategies, programmes and plans into routine budgets and objectives. In these steps, we see planning as an analytical process which takes over after the synthesis of strategic formation is completed.

Thus formal planning properly belongs in the *implementation* of strategy, not in its formulation. But it should be emphasized that strategic programming makes sense when viable intended strategies are available, in other words when the world is expected to hold still while these strategies unfold, so that formulation can logically precede implementation, and when the organization that does the implementing in fact requires clearly codified and elaborated strategies. In other circumstances, strategic programming can do organizations harm by pre-empting the flexibility that managers and others may need to respond to changes in the environment, or to their own internal processes of learning.

Roles of Plans

If planning is programming, then plans clearly serve two roles. They are a medium for communication and a device for control. Both roles draw on the analytical character of plans, namely, that they represent strategies in decomposed and articulated form, if not quantified then often at least quantifiable.

Why programme strategy? Most obviously for coordination, to ensure that everyone in the organization pulls in the same direction, a direction that may have to be specified as precisely as possible. In Air Canada, to use our earlier example, that means linking the acquisition of new aircraft with the particular routes that are to be flown, and scheduling crews and planes to show up when the flights are to take off, and so on. Plans, as they emerge from strategic programming as programmes, schedules, budgets, and so on, can be prime media to communicate not just strategic intention but also the role each individual must play to realize it.

Plans, as communication media, inform people of intended strategy and its consequences. But as control devices they can go further, specifying what role departments and individuals must play in helping to realize strategy and then comparing that with performance in order to feed control information back into the strategy-making process.

Plans can help to effect control in a number of ways. The most obvious is control of the strategy itself. Indeed, what has long paraded under the label of 'strategy planning' has probably had more to do with 'strategic control' than many people may realize. Strategic control has to do with keeping organizations on their strategic tracks: to ensure the realization of intended strategy, its implementation as expected, with resources appropriately allocated. But there is more to strategic control than this. Another aspect includes the assessment of the realization of strategies in the first place, namely, whether the patterns realized corresponded to the intentions specified beforehand. In other words, strategic control must assess behaviour as well as performance. Then the more routine and traditional form of control can come in to consider whether the strategies that were in fact realized proved effective.

Roles of Planners

Planners, of course, play key roles in planning (namely, strategic programming), and in using the resulting plans for purposes of communication and control. But many of the most important things planners do have little to do with planning or even plans *per se*. Three roles seem key here.

First, planners can play a role in finding strategies. This may seem curious, but if strategies really do emerge in organizations, then planners can help to identify the patterns that are becoming strategies, so that consideration can be given to formalizing them, that is, making them deliberate. Of course, finding the strategies of competitors – for assessment and possible modified adoption – is also important here.

Second, planners play the roles of analysts, carrying out *ad hoc* studies to feed into the black box of strategy-making. Indeed, one could argue that this is precisely what Michael Porter proposes with his emphasis on industry and competitive analysis. The *ad hoc* nature of such studies should, however, be emphasized because they feed into a strategy-making process that is itself irregular, proceeding on no schedule and following no standard sequence of steps. Indeed, regularity in the planning process can interfere with strategic thinking, which must be flexible, responsive and creative.

The third role of the planner is as a catalyst. This refers not to the traditional role long promoted in the literature of selling formal planning as some kind of religion, but to encourage strategic *thinking* throughout the organization. Here the planner encourages *informal* strategy-making, trying to get others to think about the future in a creative way. He or she does not enter the block box of strategy-making so much as ensure that the box is occupied with active line managers.

A Planner For Each Side of the Brain

We have discussed various roles for planning, plans and planners, summarized around the block box of strategy formation in Figure 2. These roles suggest two different orientations for planners.

On one hand (so to speak), the planner must be a highly analytical, convergent type of thinker, dedicated to bringing order to the organization. Above all, this planner programmes intended strategies and sees to it that they are communicated clearly and used for purposes of control. He or she also carries out studies to ensure that the managers concerned with strategy formation take into account the necessary hard data that they may be inclined to miss and that the strategies they formulate are carefully and systematically evaluated before they are implemented.

On the other hand, there is another type of planner, less conventional, a creative, divergent thinker, rather intuitive, who seeks to open up the strategy-making process. As a 'soft analyst', he or she tends to conduct 'quick and dirty' studies, to find strategies in strange places and to encourage others to think strategically. This planner is inclined towards the intuitive processes identified with the brain's right hemisphere. We might call him or her a *left-handed planner*. Some organizations need to emphasize one type of planner, others the other type. But most complex organizations probably need some of both.

Strategic Change in an Automobile Firm

Given planning itself is not strategic, how does the planning-oriented machine bureaucracy change its strategy when it has to? Volkswagenwerk was an organization that had to. We interpreted its history from 1934 to 1974 as one long cycle of a single strategic perspective. The original 'people's car', the famous 'Beetle', was conceived by Ferdinand Porsche; the factory to produce it was built just before the war but did not go into civilian automobile production until after. In 1948, a man named Heinrich Nordhoff was given control of the devastated plant and began the rebuilding of it, as well as of the organization and the strategy itself, rounding out Porsche's original conception. The firm's success was dramatic.

By the late 1950s, however, problems began to appear. Demand in Germany was moving away from the Beetle. The typically machine-bureaucratic response was not to rethink the basic strategy – 'It's OK' was the reaction – but rather to graft another piece onto it. A new automobile model was added, larger than the Beetle but with a similar no-nonsense approach to motoring, again air-cooled with the engine in the back. Volkswagenwerk added position but did not change perspective.

But that did not solve the basic problem, and by the mid-1960s the company was in crisis. Nordhoff, who had resisted strategic change, died in office and was replaced by a lawyer from outside the business. The company then underwent a frantic search for new models, designing, developing or acquiring a whole host of them with engines in the front, middle and rear; air- and water-cooled; front- and rear-wheel drive. To paraphrase the humorist Stephen Leacock, Volkswagenwerk leaped onto its strategic horse and rode off in all directions. Only when another leader came in, a man steeped in the company and the automobile business, did the firm consolidate itself around a new strategic perspective, based on the stylish front-wheel drive, water-cooled designs of one of its acquired firms, and thereby turn its fortunes around.

What this story suggests, first of all, is the great force of bureaucratic momentum in the machine organization. Even leaving planning aside, the immense effort of producing and marketing a new line of automobiles locks a company into a certain posture. But here the momentum was psychological, too. Nordhoff, who had been the driving force behind the great success of the organization, became a major liability when the environment demanded change. Over the years, he too had been captured by bureaucratic momentum. Moreover, the uniqueness and tight integration of Volkswagenwerk's strategy – we labelled it Gestalt – impeded strategic change. Change an element of a tightly integrated Gestalt and it *dis*integrates. Thus does success eventually breed failure.

Bottleneck at the Top

Why the great difficulty in changing strategy in the machine organization? Here we take up that question and show how changes generally have to be achieved in a different configuration, if at all.

As discussed earlier, unanticipated problems in the machine organization tend to get bumped up the hierarchy. When these are few, which means conditions are relatively stable, thinks work smoothly enough. But in times of rapid change, just when new strategies are called for, the number of such problems magnifies, resulting in a bottleneck at the top, where senior managers get overloaded. And that tends either to impede strategic change or else to render it ill considered.

A major part of the problem is information. Senior managers face an organization decomposed into parts, like a machine itself. Marketing information comes up one channel, manufacturing information up another, and so on. Somehow it is the senior managers themselves who must integrate all that information. But the very machine bureaucratic premise of separating the administration of work from the doing of it means that the top managers often lack the intimate, detailed knowledge of issues necessary to effect such an integration. In essence, the necessary power is at the top of the structure, but the necesssary knowledge is often at the bottom.

Of course, there is a machinelike solution to that problem too – not surprisingly in the form of a system. It is called a management information system, or MIS, and what it does is combine all the necessary information and package it neatly so that top managers can be informed about what is going on – the perfect solution for the overloaded executive. At least in theory.

Unfortunately, a number of real-world problems arise in the MIS. For one thing, in the tall administrative hierarchy of the machine organization, information must pass through many levels before it reaches the top. Losses take place at each one. Good news gets highlighted while bad news gets blocked on the way up. And 'soft' information, so necessary for strategy information, cannot easily pass through, while much of the hard MIS-type information arrives only slowly. In a stable environment, the manager may be able to wait; in a rapidly changing one, he or she cannot. The president wants to be told right away that the firm's most important customer was seen playing golf yesterday with a main competitor, not to find out six months later in the form of a drop in a sales report. Gossip, hearsay, speculation – the softest kinds of information – warn the manager of impeding problems; the MIS all too often records for posterity ones that have already been felt. The manager who depends on an MIS in a changing environment generally finds himself or herself out of touch.

The obvious solution for top managers is to bypass the MIS and set up their own informal information systems, networks of contacts that bring them the rich, tangible, instant information they need. But that violates the machine organization's presuppositions of formality and respect for the chain of authority. Also, that takes the managers' time, the lack of which caused the bottleneck in the first place. So a fundamental dilemma faces the top managers of the machine organization as a result of its very own design: in times of change, when they most need the time to inform themselves, the system overburdens them with other pressures. They are thus reduced to acting superficially, with inadequate, abstract information.

The Formulation/Implementation Dichtomy

The essential problem lies in one of the chief tenets of the machine organization, that strategy formation must be sharply separated from strategy implementation. One is thought out at the top, the other then acted out lower down. For this to work assume two conditions: first, that the formulator has full and sufficient information, and second, that the world will hold still, or at least change in predictable ways, during the implementation, so that there is no need for *re*formulation.

Now consider why the organization needs a new strategy in the first place. It is because its world has changed in an unpredictable way, indeed may continue to do so. We have just seen how the machine bureaucratic structure tends to violate the first condition – it misinforms the senior manager during such times of change. And when change continues in an unpredictable way (or at least the world unfolds in a way not yet predicted by an ill-informed management), then the second condition is violated too – it hardly makes sense to lock in by implementation a strategy that does not reflect changes in the world around it.

What all this amounts to is a need to collapse the formulation/implementation dichotomy precisely when the strategy of machine bureaucracy must be changed. This can be done in one of two ways.

In one case, the formulator implements. In other words, power is concentrated at the top, not only for creating the strategy but also for implementing it, step by step, in a personalized way. The strategist is put in close personal touch with the situation at hand (more commonly a strategist is appointed who has or can develop that touch) so that he or she can, on one hand, be properly informed and, on the other, control the implementation *en route* in order to reformulate when necessary. This, of course, describes the entrepreneurial configuration, at least at the strategic apex.

In the other case, the implementers formulate. In other words, power is concentrated lower down, where the necessary information resides. As people who are naturally in touch with the specific situations at hand take individual actions – approach new customers, develop new products, etc. – patterns form, in other words, strategies emerge. And this describes the innovative configuration, where strategic initiatives often originate in the grass roots of the organization, and then are championed by managers at middle levels who integrate them with one another or with existing strategies in order to gain their acceptance by senior management.

We conclude, therefore, that the machine configuration is ill-suited to change its fundamental strategy, that the organization must in effect change configuration temporarily in order to change strategy. Either it reverts to the entrepreneurial form, to allow a single leader to develop vision (or proceed with one developed earlier), or else it overlays an innovative form on its conventional structure (for example, creates an informed network of lateral teams and task forces) so that the necessary strategies can emerge. The former can obviously function faster than the latter; that is why it tends to be used for drastic *turnaround*, while the latter tends to proceed by the slower process of *revitalization*. (Of course, quick turnaround may be necessary because there has been no slow revitalization.) In any event, both are characterized by a capacity to *learn* – that is the essence of the entrepreneurial and innovative configurations, in one case learning centralized for the simpler context, in the other, decentralized for the more complex one. The machine configuration is not so characterized.

This, however, should come as no surprise. After all, machines are specialized instruments, designed for productivity, not for adaptation. In Hunt's (1970) words, machine bureaucracies are performance systems, not problem-solving ones. Efficiency is their forte, not innovation. An organization cannot put blinders on its personnel and then expect peripheral vision. Managers here are rewarded for cutting costs and improving standards, not for taking risks and ignoring procedures. Change makes a mess of the operating systems: change one link in a carefully coupled system, and the whole chain must be reconceived. Why, then, should we be surprised when our bureaucratic machines fail to adapt?

Of course, it is fair to ask why we spend so much time trying to make them adapt. After all, when an ordinary machine becomes redundant, we simply scrap it, happy that it served us for as long and as well as it did. Converting it to another use generally proves more expensive than simply starting over. I suspect the same is often true for bureaucratic machines. But here, of course, the context is social and political. Mechanical parts don't protest, nor do displaced raw materials. Workers, suppliers and customers do, however, protest against the scrapping of organizations, for obvious reasons. But that the cost of this is awfully high in a society of giant machine organizations will be the subject of the final chapter of this book.

Strategic Revolutions in Machine Organizations

Machine organizations do sometimes change, however, at times effectively but more often it would seem at great cost and pain. The lucky ones are able to overlay an innovative structure for periodic revitalization, while many of the other survivors somehow manage to get turned around in entrepreneurial fashion.

Overall, the machine organizations seem to follow what my colleagues Danny Miller and Peter Friesen (1984) call a 'quantum theory' of organization change. They pursue their set strategies through long periods of stability (naturally occurring or

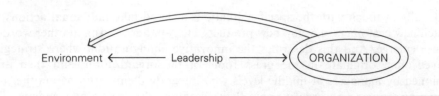

FIGURE 3
Organization takes precedence

created by themselves as closed systems), using planning and other procedures to do so efficiently. Periodically these are interrupted by short bursts of change, which Miller and Friesen characterize as 'strategic revolutions' (although another colleague, Mihaela Firsirotu (1985), perhaps better labels it 'strategic turn-around as cultural revolution').

Organization Taking Precedence in the Machine Organization

To conclude, as shown in Figure 3, it is organization – with its systems and procedures, its planning and its bureaucratic momentum – that takes precedence over leadership and environment in the machine configuration. Environment fits organization, either because the organization has slotted itself into a context that matches its procedures, or else because it has forced the environment to do so. And leadership generally falls into place too, supporting the organization, indeed often becoming part of its bureaucratic momentum.

This generally works effectively, though hardly non-problematically, at least in times of stability. But in times of change, efficiency becomes ineffective and the organization will falter unless it can find a different way to organize for adaptation.

All this is another way of saying that the machine organization is a configuration, a species, like the others, suited to its own context but ill-suited to others. But unlike the others, it is the dominant configuration in our specialized societies. As long as we demand inexpensive and so necessarily standardized goods and services, and as long as people continue to be more efficient than real machines at providing them, and remain willing to do so, then the machine organization will remain with us – and so will all its problems.

• THE TRANSITION TO INDUSTRY MATURITY*

MICHAEL E. PORTER

As part of their evolutionary process, many industries pass from periods of rapid growth to the more modest growth of what is commonly called industry maturity ... industry maturity does not occur at any fixed point in an industry's development, and it can be delayed by innovations or other events that fuel continued growth for industry participants. Moreover, in response to strategic breakthroughs, mature industries may regain their rapid growth and thereby go through more than one transition to maturity. With these important quantifications in mind, however, let us consider the case in which a transition to maturity is occurring. ...

INDUSTRY CHANGE DURING TRANSITION

Transition to maturity can often signal a number of important changes in an industry's competitive environment. Some of the probable tendencies for change are as follows:

1. *Slowing growth means more competition for market share.* With companies unable to maintain historical growth rates merely by holding market share, competitive attention turns inward towards attacking the shares of the others. ... Not only are competitors probably going to be more aggressive, but also the likelihood of misperceptions and 'irrational' retaliation is great. Outbreaks of price, service and promotional warfare are common during transition to maturity.

2. *Firms in the industry increasingly are selling to experienced, repeat buyers.* The product is no longer new but an established, legitimate item. Buyers are often increasingly knowledgeable and experienced, having already purchased the product, sometimes repeatedly. The buyers' focus shifts from deciding whether to purchase the product at all to making choices among brands. Approaching these differently oriented buyers requires a fundamental reassessment of strategy.

3. *Competition often shifts towards greater emphasis on cost and service.* As a result of slower growth, more knowledgeable buyers and usually greater technological maturity, competition tends to become more cost- and service-oriented. ...

4. *There is a topping-out problem in adding industry capacity and personnel.* As the industry adjusts to slower growth, the rate of capacity addition in the industry must slow down as well or overcapacity will occur. ... [But the necessary] shifts in perspective rarely occur in maturing industries, and overshooting of industry capacity relative to demand is common. Overshooting leads to a period of overcapacity, accentuating the tendency during transition toward price warfare. ...

5. *Manufacturing, marketing, distributing, selling and research methods are often undergoing change.* These changes are caused by increased competition for market share, technological maturity, and buyer sophistication. ...

6. *New products and applications are harder to come by.* Whereas the growth phase may have been one of rapid discovery of new products and applications, the ability to continue product change generally becomes increasingly limited, or the costs and risks greatly increase, as the industry matures. This change requires, among other things, a reorientation of attitude towards research and new product development.

7. *International competition increases.* As a consequence of technological maturity, often accompanied by product standardization and increasing emphasis on costs, transition is often marked by the emergence of significant international competition. ...

8. *Industry profits often fall during the transition period, sometimes temporarily and sometimes permanently.* Slowing growth, more sophisticated buyers, more emphasis on market share and the uncertainties and difficulties of the required strategic changes usually mean that industry profits fall in the short run from the levels of the pre-transition growth phase. ... Whether or not profits will rebound depends on the level of mobility barriers and other elements of industry structure. ...

9. *Dealers' margins fall, but their power increases.* For the same reaons that industry profits are often depressed, dealers' margins may be squeezed and many dealers may drop out of business – often *before* the effect on manufacturers' profits is noticeable. ... Such trends tighten competition among industry participants for dealers, who may have been easy to find and hold in the growth phase but not upon maturity. Thus, dealers' power may increase markedly.

SOME STRATEGIC IMPLICATIONS OF TRANSITION

... Some characteristic strategic issues often arise in transition. These are presented as issues to examine rather than generalizations that will apply to all industries; like humans, all industries mature a little differently. Many of these approaches can be a basis for the entry of new firms into an industry even though it is mature.

Overall Cost Leadership Versus Differentiate Versus Focus – The Strategic Dilemma Made Acute by Maturity

Rapid growth tends to mask strategic errors and allow most, if not all, companies in the industry to survive and even to prosper financially. Strategic experimentation is high and a wide variety of strategies can coexist. Strategic sloppiness is generally exposed by industry maturity, however. Maturity may force companies to confront, often for the first time, the need to choose among the three generic strategies described (in Chapter 4 of this text). It becomes a matter of survival.

Sophisticated Cost Analysis

Cost analysis becomes increasingly important in maturity to (1) rationalize the product mix and (2) price correctly.

Rationalizing the Product Mix
... a quantum improvement in the sophistication of product costing is necessary to allow pruning of unprofitable items from the line and to focus attention on items either that have some distinctive advantage (technology, cost, image, etc.) or whose buyers are 'good' buyers. ...

Correct Pricing

Related to product line rationalization is the change in pricing methodology that is often necessary in maturity. Although average-cost pricing, or pricing the line as a whole rather than as individual items, may have been sufficient in the growth era, maturity often requires increased capability to measure costs on individual items and to price accordingly. ...

We might summarize this and the other points in this section by saying that an enhanced level of 'financial consciousness' along a variety of dimensions is often necessary in maturity, whereas in the developmental period of the industry areas such as new products and research may have rightly held centre stage. ...

Process Innovation and Design for Manufacture

The relative importance of process innovations usually increases in maturity, as does the payoff for designing the product and its delivery system to facilitate lower-cost manufacturing and control. ...

Increasing Scope of Purchases

Increasing purchases of existing customers may be more desirable than seeking new customers. ... Such a strategy may take the firm out of the industry into related industries. This strategy is often less costly than finding new customers. In a mature industry, winning new customers usually means battling for market share with competitors and is consequently quite expensive. ...

Buy Cheap Assets

Sometimes assets can be acquired very cheaply as a result of the company distress that is caused by transition to maturity. A strategy of acquiring distressed companies or buying liquidated assets can improve margins and create a low-cost position if the rate of technological change is not too great. ...

Buyer Selection

As buyers become more knowledgeable and competitive pressures increase in maturity, buyer selection can sometimes be a key to continued profitability. Buyers who may not have exercised their bargaining power in the past, or had less power because of limited product availability, will usually not be bashful about exercising their power in maturity. Identifying 'good' buyers and locking them in ... becomes crucial.

Different Cost Curves

There is often more than one cost curve possible in an industry. The firm that is *not* the overall cost leader in a mature market can sometimes find new cost curves which may actually make it a lower-cost producer for certain types of buyers, product varieties or order sizes. This step is key to implementing the generic strategy of focus. ...

Competing Internationally

A firm may escape maturity by competing internationally where the industry is more favourably structured. Sometimes equipment that is obsolete in the home market can be used quite effectively in international markets, greatly lowering the costs of entry there. ...

STRATEGIC PITFALLS IN TRANSITION

In addition to failure to recognize the strategic implications of transition described above, there is the tendency for firms to fall prey to some characteristic strategic pitfalls:

1. *A company's self-perceptions and its perception of the industry.* Companies develop perceptions or images of themselves and their relative capabilities ('we are the quality leader'; 'we provide superior customer service'), which are reflected in the implicit assumptions that form the basis of their strategies. ... These self-perceptions may be increasingly inaccurate as transition proceeds, buyers' priorities adjust and competitors respond to new industry conditions. Similarly, firms have assumptions about the industry, competitors, buyers and suppliers which may be invalidated by transition. Yet altering these assumptions, built up through actual past experience, is sometimes a difficult process.

2. *Caught in the middle.* The problem of being caught in the middle described [earlier] is particularly acute in transition to maturity. Transition often squeezes out the slack that has made this strategy viable in the past.

3. *The cash trap – investments to build share in a mature market.* Cash should be invested in a business only with the expectation of being able to remove it later. In a mature, slow-growing industry, the assumptions required to justify investing new cash in order to build market share are often heroic. Maturity of the industry works against increasing or maintaining margins long enough to recoup cash investments down the road, by making the present value of cash inflows justify the outflows. Thus businesses in maturity can be cash traps, particularly when a firm is not in a strong market position but is attempting to build a large market share in a maturing market The odds are against it.

    A related pitfall is placing heavy attention on revenues in the maturing market instead of on profitability. This strategy may have been desirable in the growth phase, but it usually faces diminishing returns in maturity. ...

4. *Giving up market share too easily in favour of short-run profits.* In the face of the profit pressures in transition, there seems to be a tendency for some companies to try to maintain the profitability of the recent past – which is done at the expense of market share or by forgoing marketing, R&D and other needed investments, which in turn hurts future market position. ... A period of lower profits may be inevitable while industry rationalization occurs, and a cool head is necessary to avoid over-reaction.

5. *Resentment and irrational reaction to price competition ('we will not compete on price')*. It is often difficult for firms to accept the need for price competition after a period in which it has not been necessary. ...

6. *Resentment and irrational reaction to changes in industry practices ('they are hurting the industry')*. Changes in industry practices, such as marketing techniques, production methods and the nature of distributor contracts are often an inevitable part of transition. They may be important to the industry's long-run potential, but there is often resistance to them. ...

7. *Overemphasis on 'creative', 'new' products rather than improving and aggressively selling existing ones*. Although past success in the early and growth phases of an industry may have been built on research and on new products, the onset of maturity often means that new products and applications are harder to come by. It is usually appropriate that the focus of innovative activity should change, putting standardization rather than newness and fine-tuning at a premium. Yet this development is not satisfying to some companies and is often resisted.

8. *Clinging to 'higher quality' as an excuse for not meeting aggressive pricing and marketing moves of competitors*. High quality can be a crucial company strength, but quality differentials have a tendency to erode as an industry matures. ... Yet it is difficult for many companies to accept the fact that they do not possess the highest-quality product or that their quality is unnecessarily high.

9. *Overhanging excess capacity*. As a result of capacity overshooting demand, or because of capacity increases that inevitably accompany the plant modernization required to compete in the mature industry, some firms may have some excess capacity. Its mere presence creates both subtle and unsubtle pressures to utilize it, and it can be used in ways that will undermine the firm's strategy. ...

9

THE DIVERSIFIED CONTEXT

A good deal of evidence has accumulated on the relationship between diversification and divisionalization. Once organizations diversify their product or service lines, they tend to create distinct structural divisions to deal with each distinct business. This relationship was perhaps first carefully documented in the classic historical study by Alfred D. Chandler, *Strategy and Structure: Chapters in the history of the great American enterprise* (1962). Chandler traced the origins of diversification and divisionalization in Du Pont and General Motors in the 1920s which were followed later by other major firms. A number of other studies elaborated on Chandler's conclusions; these are discussed in the readings of this chapter.

The first reading, drawn from Mintzberg's work on structuring, probes the structure of divisionalization – how it works, what brings it about, what intermediate variations of it exist and what problems it poses for organizations that use it and for society at large. It concludes on a rather pessimistic note about conglomerate diversification and about the purer forms of divisionalization. The second reading, also by Mintzberg, extends his discussion on business-level generic strategies in Chapter 3 to the corporate level by suggesting how a company can elaborate, extend or reconceive its core business.

As diversification became an especially popular strategy among large corporations in the 1960s and 1970s, a number of techniques were developed to analyze strategies at the corporate level. Among the most widely used were a number labelled 'portfolio', which viewed the businesses of a diversified company as a collection of investments whose return could be optimized by properly balancing their growth and maturity characteristics and by redeploying investments and cash flows among them.

Perhaps the best known and most widely used of such portfolio models is the 'growth share matrix' described in the second reading of this chapter, by Bruce Hendersen, who built up the Boston Consulting Group in good part on the popularity of this technique. We should warn you that this model has been sharply criticized for, among other things, creating self-fulfilling prophecies by labelling businesses with simplistic funding roles. Many of the other models we have presented in this book have been or can be blamed for similar acts of omission or commission. These arguments emphasize a broader message, one well worth bearing in mind throughout management education: 'No management model can safely substitute for analysis and common sense.' While techniques such as the experience curve and competitive and portfolio analysis can be very useful in understanding critical relationships and in making sure one touches all the right bases, they provide no substitutes for a thorough-going intellectual and intuitive understanding of the full complexity of a company's unique capabilities in its particular environment. Many of these cannot be captured in numerical analyses, but abide in the minds and motivations of the people in the organization.

Aspects of the diversified organization, particularly in its more conglomerate form, thus come in for some heavy criticism in this chapter. The next reading takes up that torch too, but it quickly turns to the more constructive questions of how to use strategy to combine a cluster of different businesses into an effective corporate entity. This is Michael Porter's award-winning *Harvard Business Review* article, 'From competitive advantage to corporate strategy'. Porter discusses in a most insightful way various types of overall corporate strategies, including portfolio management, restructuring, transferring skills and sharing activities (the last two referred in his 1985 book *Competitive Advantage* as 'horizontal strategies', the former dealing with 'intangible', the latter 'tangible' interrelationships among business units, and conceived in terms of his value chain: see pp. 72–4).

● THE DIVERSIFIED ORGANIZATION*

HENRY MINTZBERG

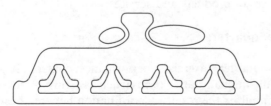

THE BASIC DIVISIONALIZED STRUCTURE

The diversified organization is not so much an integrated entity as a set of semi-autonomous units coupled together by a central administrative structure. The

* Adapted from *The Structuring of Organizations* (Prentice Hall, 1979), 1979), Ch. 20 on 'The divisionalized form'. A chapter similar to this appeared in *Mintzberg on Management: Inside Our Strange World of Organizations* (Free Press, 1989).

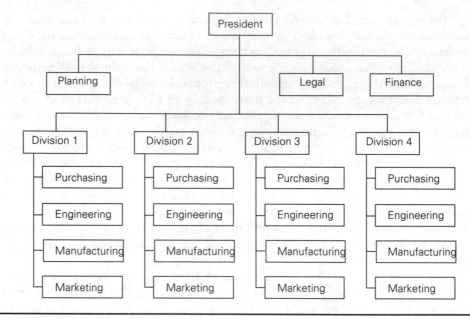

FIGURE 1
Typical organigram for a divisionalized manufacturing firm

units are generally called *divisions*, and the central administration, the *Headquarters*. This is a widely used configuration in the private sector of the industrialized economy; the vast majority of the *Fortune* 500, America's largest corporations, use this structure or a variant of it. But, as we shall see, it is also found in other sectors as well.

In what is commonly called the 'divisionalized' form of structure, units, called 'divisions', are created to serve distinct markets and are given control over the operating functions necessary to do so, as shown in Figure 1. Each is therefore relatively free of direct control by headquarters or even of the need to coordinate activities with other divisions. Each, in other words, appears to be a self-standing business. Of course, none is. There *is* a headquarters, and it has a series of roles that distinguish this overall configuration from a collection of independent businesses providing the same set of products and services.

Roles of the Headquarters

Above all, the headquarters exercises performance control. It sets standards of achievement, generally in quantitative terms (such as return on investment or growth in sales), and then monitors the results. Coordination between headquarters and the divisions thus reduces largely to the standardization of outputs. Of course, there is some direct supervision – HQ managers have to have personal contact with and knowledge of the divisions. But that is largely circumscribed by the key assumption in this configuration that if the division managers are to be responsible for the performance of their divisions, they must have considerable autonomy to manage them as they see fit. Hence there is extensive delegation of authority from headquarters to the level of division manager.

Certain important tasks do, however, remain for the headquarters. One is to develop the overall *corporate* strategy, meaning to establish the portfolio of businesses in which the organization will operate. The headquarters establishes, acquires, divests and closes down divisions in order to change its portfolio. Popular in the 1970s in this regard was the Boston Consulting Group's 'growth share matrix', where corporate managers were supposed to allocate funds to divisions on the basis of their falling into the categories of dogs, cash cows, wildcats and stars. But enthusiasm for that technique waned, perhaps mindful of Pope's warning that a little learning can be a dangerous thing.

Second, the headquarters manages the movement of funds between the divisions, taking the excess profits of some to support the greater growth potential of others. Third, of course, the headquarters, through its own technostructure, designs and operates the performance control system. Fourth, it appoints and therefore retains the right to replace the division managers. For a headquarters that does not directly manage any division, its most tangible power when the performance of a division lags – short of riding out an industry downturn or divesting the division – is to replace its leader. Finally, the headquarters provides certain support services that are common to all the divisions – a corporate public relations office or legal counsel, for example.

Structure of the Divisions

It has been common to label divisionalized organizations 'decentralized'. That is a reflection of how *certain* of them came to be, most notably Du Pont early in this century. When organizations that were structured functionally (for example, in departments of marketing, manufacturing and engineering, etc.) diversified, they found that coordination of their different product lines across the functions became increasingly complicated. The central managers had to spend great amounts of time intervening to resolve disputes. But once these corporations switched to a divisionalized form of structure, where all the functions for a given business could be contained in a single unit dedicated to that business, management became much simpler. In effect, their structures became *more* decentralized, power over distinct businesses being delegated to the division managers.

But more decentralized does not mean *decentralized*. The word refers to the dispersal of decision-making power in an organization, and in many of the diversified corporations much of the power tended to remain with the few managers who ran the businesses. Indeed, the most famous case of divisionalization was one of relative *centralization*: Alfred P. Sloan introduced the divisionalized structure to General Motors in the 1920s to *reduce* the power of its autonomous business units, to impose systems of financial controls on what had been a largely unmanaged agglomeration of different automobile businesses.

In fact, I would argue that it is the *centralization* of power within the divisions that is most compatible with the divisionalized form of structure. In other words, the effect of having a headquarters over the divisions is to drive them towards the machine configuration, namely a structure of centralized bureaucracy. That is the structure most compatible with headquarters control, in my opinion. If true, this would seem to be an important point, because it means that the proliferation of the diversified configuration in many spheres – business, government and the rest – has the effect of driving many sub-organizations towards machine bureaucracy, even where that configuration may be inappropriate (school systems, for example, or government departments charged with innovative project work).

The explanation for this lies in the standardization of outputs, the key to the functioning of the divisionalized structure. Bear in mind the headquarters' dilemma: to respect divisional autonomy while exercising control over performance. This it seeks to resolve by after-the-fact monitoring of divisional results, based on clearly defined performance standards. But two main assumptions underlie such standards.

First, each division must be treated as a single integrated system with a single, consistent set of goals. In other words, although the divisions may be loosely coupled with each other, the assumption is that each is tightly coupled internally.[1]

Second, these goals must be operational ones, in other words, lend themselves to quantitative measurement. But in the less formal configurations – entrepreneurial and innovative – which are less stable, such performance standards are difficult to establish, while in the professional configuration, the complexity of the work makes it difficult to establish such standards. Moreover, while the entrepreneurial configuration may lend itself to being integrated around a single set of goals, the innovative and professional configurations do not. Thus, only the machine configuration of the major types fits comfortably into the conventional divisionalized structure, by virtue of its integration and its operational goals.

In fact, when organizations with another configuration are drawn under the umbrella of a divisionalized structure, they tend to be forced towards the machine bureaucratic form, to make them conform with *its* needs. How often have we heard stories of entrepreneurial firms recently acquired by conglomerates being descended upon by hordes of HQ technocrats bemoaning the loose controls, the absence of organigrams, the informality of the systems? In many cases, of course, the very purpose of the acquisition was to do just this, tighten up the organization so that its strategies can be pursued more pervasively and systematically. But other times, the effect is to destroy the organization's basic strengths, sometimes including its flexibility and responsiveness. Similarly, how many times have we heard of government administrators complaining about being unable to control public hospitals or universities through conventional (meaning machine bureaucratic) planning systems?

This conclusion is, in fact, a prime manifestation of the hypothesis that concentrated external control of an organization has the effect of formalizing and centralizing its structure, in other words, of driving it towards the machine configuration. Headquarters' control of divisions is, of course, concentrated; indeed, when the diversified organization is itself a *closed system*, as I shall argue later many tend to be, then it is a most concentrated form of control. And, the effect of that control is to render the divisions its *instruments*.

There is, in fact, an interesting irony in this, in that the less society controls the overall diversified organization, the more the organization itself controls its individual units. The result is increased autonomy for the largest organizations coupled with decreased autonomy for their many activities.

To conclude this discussion of the basic structure, the diversified configuration is represented in the opening figure, symbolically in terms of our logo, as follows. Headquarters has three parts: a small strategic apex of top managers, a small technostructure to the left concerned with the design and operation of the performance control system, and a slightly larger staff support group to the right to provide support services common to all the divisions. Each of the divisions is shown below the headquarters as a machine configuration.

CONDITIONS OF THE DIVERSIFIED ORGANIZATION

While the diversified configuration may arise from the federation of different organizations, which come together under a common headquarters umbrella, more often it appears to be the structural response to a machine organization that has diversified its range of product or service offerings. In either case, it is the diversity of markets above all that drives an organization to use this configuration. An organization faced with a single integrated market simply cannot split itself into autonomous divisions; the one with distinct markets, however, has an incentive to create a unit to deal with each.

There are three main kinds of market diversity – product and service, client, and region. In theory, all three can lead to divisionalization. But when diversification is based on variations in clients or regions as opposed to products or services, divisionalization often turns out to be incomplete. With identical products or services in each region or for each group of clients, the headquarters is encouraged to maintain central control of certain critical functions, to ensure common operating standards for all the divisions. And that seriously reduces divisional autonomy and so leads to a less than complete form of divisionalization.

Thus, one study found that insurance companies concentrate at headquarters the critical function of investment, and retailers concentrate that of purchasing, also controlling product range, pricing and volume (Channon, 1975). One need only look at the individual outlets of a typical retail chain to recognize the absence of divisional autonomy: usually they all look alike. The same conclusion tends to hold for other businesses organized by regions, such as bakeries, breweries, cement producers and soft drink bottlers: Their 'divisions', distinguished only by geographical location, lack the autonomy normally associated with ones that produce distinct products or services.

What about the conditions of size? Although large size itself does not bring on divisionalization, surely it is not coincidental that most of America's largest corporations use some variant of this configuration. The fact is that as organizations grow large, they become inclined to diversify and then to divisionalize. One reason is protection: large organizations tend to be risk-averse – they have too much to lose – and diversification spreads the risk. Another is that as firms grow large, they come to dominate their traditional market, and so must often find growth opportunities elsewhere, through diversification. Moreover, diversification feeds on itself. It creates a cadre of aggressive general managers, each running his or her own division, who push for further diversification and further growth. Thus, most of the giant corporations – with the exception of the 'heavies', those with enormously high fixed-cost operating systems, such as the oil or aluminium producers – not only were able to reach their status by diversifying but also feel great pressures to continue to do so.

Age is another factor associated with this configuration, much like size. In larger organizations, the management runs out of places to expand in its traditional markets; in older ones, the managers sometimes get bored with the traditional markets and find diversion through diversification. Also, time brings new competitors into old markets, forcing the management to look elsewhere for growth opportunities.

As governments grow large, they too tend to adopt a kind of divisionalized structure. The central administrators, unable to control all the agencies and departments directly, settle for granting their managers considerable autonomy and then trying to control their results through planning and performance controls. Indeed, the 'accountability' buzzword so often heard in governments these days reflects just this trend – to move closer to a divisionalized structure.

One can, in fact, view the entire government as a giant diversified configuration (admittedly an oversimplification, since all kinds of links exist among the departments), with its three main coordinating agencies corresponding to the three main forms of control used by the headquarters of the large corporation. The budgetary agency, technocratic in nature, concerns itself with performance control of the departments; the public service commission, also partly technocratic, concerns itself with the recruiting and training of government managers; and the executive office, top management in nature, reviews the principal proposals and initiatives of the departments.

In the preceding chapter, the communist state was described as a closed-system machine bureaucracy. But it may also be characterized as the ultimate closed system diversified configuration, with the various state enterprises and agencies its instruments, machine bureaucracies tightly regulated by the planning and control systems of the central government.

STAGES IN THE TRANSITION TO THE DIVERSIFIED ORGANIZATION

There has been a good deal of research on the transition of the corporation from the functional to the diversified form. Figure 2 and the discussion that follows borrow from this research to describe four stages in that transition.

At the top of Figure 2 is the pure *functional* structure, used by the corporation whose operating activities form one integrated, unbroken chain from purchasing through production to marketing and sales. Only the final output is sold to the customers[2] Autonomy cannot, therefore, be granted to the units, so the organization tends to take on the form of one overall machine configuration.

As an integrated firm seeks wider markets, it may introduce a variety of new end-products and so shift all the way to the pure diversified form. A less risky alternative, however, is to start by marketing its intermediate products on the open market. This introduces small breaks in its processing chain, which in turn calls for a measure of divisionalization in its structure, giving rise to the *by-product* form. But because the processing chain remains more or less intact, central coordination must largely remain. Organizations that fall into this category tend to be vertically integrated, basing their operations on a single raw material, such as wood, oil or

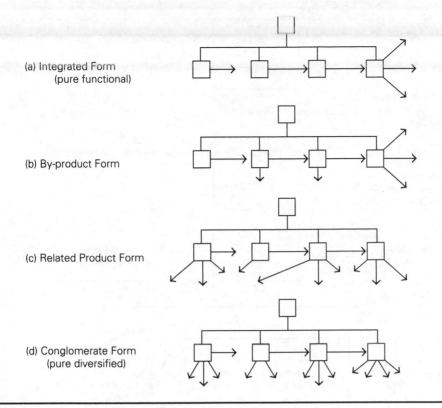

(a) Integrated Form
(pure functional)

(b) By-product Form

(c) Related Product Form

(d) Conglomerate Form
(pure diversified)

FIGURE 2
Stages in the transition to the pure diversified form

aluminium, which they process to a variety of consumable end-products. The example of Alcoa is shown in Figure 3.

Some corporations further diversify their by-product markets, breaking down their processing chain until what the divisions sell on the open market becomes more important than what they supply to each other. The organization then moves to the *related-product* form. For example, a firm manufacturing washing machines may set up a division to produce the motors. When the motor division sells more motors to outside customers than to its own sister division, a more serious form of divisionalization is called for. What typically holds the divisions of these firms together is some common thread among their products, perhaps a core skill or technology, perhaps a central market theme, as in a corporation such as 3M that likes to describe itself as being in the coating and bonding business. A good deal of the control over the specific product-market strategies can now revert to the divisions, such as research and development.

As a related-product firm expands into new markets or acquires other firms with less regard to a central strategic theme, the organization moves to the *conglomerate* form and so adopts a pure diversified configuration, the one described at the beginning of this reading. Each division serves its own markets, producing products unrelated to those of the other divisions – chinaware in one, steam shovels in a second, and so on.[3] The result is that the headquarters planning and control

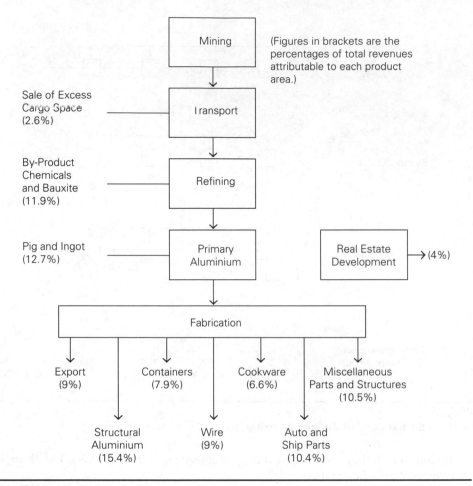

FIGURE 3
By-product and end-product sales of Alcoa.
Source: Rumelt (1974: 21). Percentages for 1969 prepared by Richard Rumelt from data from company's reports

system becomes simply a vehicle for regulating performance, and the headquarters staff can diminish to almost nothing – a few general and group managers supported by a few financial analysts with a minimum of support services.

SOME ISSUES ASSOCIATED WITH THE DIVERSIFIED ORGANIZATION

The Economic Advantages of Diversification?

It has been argued that the diversified configuration offers four basic advantages over the functional structure with integrated operations, namely an overall machine configuration. First, it encourages the efficient allocation of capital. Headquarters can choose where to put its money and so can concentrate on its strongest markets, milking the surpluses of some divisions to help others grow. Second, by opening up opportunities to run individual businesses, the diversified configuration helps to train general managers. Third, this configuration spreads its risk across different markets, whereas the focused machine bureaucracy has all its strategic eggs in one market basket, so to speak. Fourth, and perhaps most important, the diversified configuration is strategically responsive. The divisions can fine-tune their bureaucratic machines while the headquarters can concentrate on the strategic portfolio. It can acquire new businesses and divest itself of old, unproductive ones.

But is the single machine organization the correct basis of comparison? Is not the real alternative, at least from society's perspective, the taking of a further step along the same path, to the point of eliminating the headquarters altogether and allowing the divisions to function as independent organization? Beatrice Foods, described in a 1976 *Fortune* magazine article, had 397 different divisions (Martin, 1976). The issue is whether this arrangement was more efficient than 397 separate corporations.[4] In this regard, let us reconsider the four advantages discussed earlier.

In the diversified corporation, headquarters allocates the capital resources among the divisions. In the case of 397 independent corporations, the capital markets do that job instead. Which does it better? Studies suggest that the answer is not simple.

Some people, such as the economist Oliver Williamson (1975; 1985), have argued that the diversified organization may do a better job of allocating money because the capital markets are inefficient. Managers at headquarters who know their divisions can move the money around faster and more effectively. But others find that arrangement more costly and, in some ways, less flexible. Moyer (1970), for example, argued early on that conglomerates pay a premium above stock market prices to acquire businesses, whereas the independent investor need pay only small brokerage fees to diversify his or her own portfolio, and can do so easier and more flexibly. Moreover, that provides the investor with full information on all the businesses owned, whereas the diversified corporation provides only limited information to stockholders on the details inside its portfolio.

On the issue of management development, the question becomes whether the division managers receive better training and experience than they would as company presidents. The diversified organization is able to put on training courses and to rotate its managers to vary their experience; the independent firm is limited in those respects. But if, as the proponents of diversification claim, autonomy is the key to management development, then presumably the more autonomy the better. The division managers have a headquarters to lean on – and to be leaned on by. Company presidents, in contrast, are on their own to make their own mistakes and to learn from them.

On the third issue, risk, the argument from the diversified perspective is that the independent organization is vulnerable during periods of internal crisis or economic slump; conglomeration offers support to see individual businesses through such periods. The counter-argument, however, is that diversification may conceal bankruptcies, that ailing divisions are sometimes supported longer than necessary, whereas the market bankrupts the independent firm and is done with it. Moreover, just as diversification spreads the risk, so too does it spread the consequences of that risk. A single division cannot go bankrupt; the whole organization is legally responsible for its debts. So a massive enough problem in one division can pull down the whole organization. Loose coupling may turn out to be riskier than no coupling!

Finally, there is the issue of strategic responsiveness. Loosely coupled divisions may be more responsive than tightly coupled functions. But how responsive do they really prove to be? The answer appears to be negative: this configuration appears to inhibit, not encourage, the taking of strategic initiatives. The problem seems to lie, again, in its control system. It is designed to keep the carrot just the right distance in front of the divisional managers, encouraging them to strive for better and better financial performance. At the same time, however, it seems to dampen their inclination to innovate. It is that famous 'bottom line' that creates the problem, encouraging short-term thinking and shortsightedness; attention is focused on the carrot just in front instead of the fields of vegetables beyond. As Bower has noted,

> [T]he risk to the division manager of a major innovation can be considerable if he is measured on short-run, year-to-year, earnings performance. The result is a tendency to avoid big risk bets, and the concomitant phenomenon that major new developments are, with few exceptions, made outside the major firms in the industry. Those exceptions tend to be single-product companies whose top managements are committed to true product leadership. ... Instead, the diversified companies give us a steady diet of small incremental change. (1970: 194)

Innovation requires entrepreneurship, or intrapreneurship, and these, as we have already argued, do not thrive under the diversified configuration. The entrepreneur takes his or her own risks to earn his or her own rewards; the intrapreneur (as we shall see) functions best in the loose structure of the innovative adhocracy. Indeed, many diversified corporations depend on those configurations for their strategic responsiveness, since they diversify not by innovating themselves but by acquiring the innovative results of independent firms. Of course, that may be their role – to exploit rather than create those innovations – but we should not, as a result, justify diversification on the basis of its innovative capacity.

The Contribution of Headquarters

To assess the effectiveness of conglomeration, it is necessary to assess what actual contribution the headquarters makes to the divisions. Since what the headquarters does in a diversified organization is otherwise performed by the various boards of directors of a set of independent firms, the question then becomes, what does a headquarters offer to the divisions that the independent board of directors of the autonomous organization does not?

One thing that neither can offer is the management of the individual business. Both are involved with it only on a part-time basis. The management is, therefore, logically left to the full-time managers, who have the required time and information. Among the functions a headquarters *does* perform, as noted earlier, are the establishment of objectives for the divisions, the monitoring of their performance in terms of these objectives, and the maintenance of limited personal contacts with division managers, for example to approve large capital expenditures. Interestingly, those are also the responsibilities of the directors of the individual firm, at least in theory.

In practice, however, many boards of directors   notably, those of widely held corporations – do those things rather ineffectively, leaving business managements carte blanche to do what they like. Here, then, we seem to have a major advantage to the diversified configuration. It exists as an administrative mechanism to overcome another prominent weakness of the free-market system, the ineffective board.

There is a catch in this argument, however, for diversification by enhancing an organization's size and expanding its number of markets, renders the corporation more difficult to understand and so to control by its board of part-time directors. Moreover, as Moyer has noted, one common effect of conglomerate acquisition is to increase the number of shareholders, and so to make the corporation more widely held, and therefore less amenable to director control. Thus, the diversified configuration in some sense resolves a problem ot its own making – it offers the control that its own existence has rendered difficult. Had the corporation remained in one business, it might have been more narrowly held and easier to understand, and so its directors might have been able to perform their functions more effectively. Diversification thus helped to create the problem that divisionalization is said to solve. Indeed, it is ironic that many a diversified corporation that does such a vigorous job of monitoring the performance of its own divisions is itself so poorly monitored by its own board of directors!

All of this suggests that large diversified organizations tend to be classic closed systems, powerful enough to seal themselves off from much external influence while able to exercise a good deal of control over not only their own divisions, as instruments, but also their external environments. For example, one study of all 5,995 directors of the *Fortune* 500 found that only 1.6 per cent of them represented major shareholder interests (L. Smith, 1978) while another survey of 855 corporations found that 84 per cent of them did not even formally require their directors to hold any stock at all (Bacon, 1973: 40)!

What does happen when problems arise in a division? What can a headquarters do that various boards of directors cannot? The chairman of one major conglomerate told a meeting of the New York Society of Security Analysts, in reference to the headquarters vice-presidents who oversee the divisions, that 'it is not too difficult to coordinate five companies that are well run' (in Wrigley, 1970: V78). True enough. But what about five that are badly run? What could the small staff of administrators at a corporation's headquarters really do to correct problems in that firm's thirty operating divisions or in Beatrice's 397? The natural tendency to tighten the control screws does not usually help once the problem has manifested itself, nor does exercising close surveillance. As noted earlier, the headquarters managers cannot manage the divisions. Essentially, that leaves them with a choice. They can either replace the division manager or they can divest the corporation of the division. Of course, a board of directors can also replace the management. Indeed, that seems to be its only real prerogative; the management does everything else.

On balance, then, the economic case for one headquarters versus a set of separate boards of directors appears to be mixed. It should, therefore, come as no surprise that one important study found that corporations with 'controlled diversity' had better profits than those with conglomerate diversity (Rumelt, 1974). Overall, the pure diversified configuration (the conglomerate) may offer some advantages over a weak system of separate boards of directors and inefficient capital markets, but most of those advantages would probably disappear if certain problems in capital markets and boards of directors were rectified. And there is reason to argue, from a social no less than an economic standpoint, that society would be better off trying to correct fundamental inefficiencies in its economic system rather than encourage private administrative arrangements to circumvent them, as we shall now see.

The Social Performance of the Performance Control System

This configuration requires that headquarters control the divisions primarily by quantitative performance criteria, and that typically means financial ones – profit, sales growth, return on investment, and the like. The problem is that these performance measures often become virtual obsessions in the diversified organization, driving out goals that cannot be measured – product quality, pride in work, customers well served. In effect, the economic goals drive out the social ones. As the chief of a famous conglomerate once remarked, 'We, in Textron, worship the god of New Worth' (in Wrigley, 1970: V86).

That would pose no problem if the social and economic consequences of decisions could easily be separated. Governments would look after the former, corporations the latter. But the fact is that the two are intertwined; every strategic decision of every large corporation involves both, largely inseparable. As a result, its control systems, by focusing on economic measures, drive the diversified organization to act in ways that are, at best, socially unresponsive, at worst, socially irresponsible. Forced to concentrate on the economic consequences of decisions, the division manager is driven to ignore their social consequences. (Indeed, that manager is also driven to ignore the intangible economic consequences as well, such as product quality or research effort, another manifestation of the problem of the short-term, bottom-line thinking mentioned earlier.) Thus, Bower found that 'the best records in the race relations area are those of single-product companies whose strong top managements are deeply involved in the business' (1970: 193).

Robert Ackerman, in a study carried out at the Harvard Business School, investigated this point. He found that social benefits such as 'a rosier public image ... pride among managers ... an attractive posture for recruiting on campus' could not easily be measured and so could not be plugged into the performance control system. The result was that

> ... the financial reporting system may actually inhibit social responsiveness. By focusing on economic performance, even with appropriate safeguards to protect against sacrificing long-term benefits, such a system directs energy and resources to achieving results measured in financial terms. It is the only game in town, so to speak, at least the only one with an official scoreboard. (1975: 55, 56)

Headquarters managers who are concerned about legal liabilities or the public relations effects of decisions, or even ones personally interested in broader social issues, may be tempted to intervene directly in the divisions' decision-making process to ensure proper attention to social matters. But they are discouraged from doing so by this configuration's strict division of labour: divisional autonomy requires no meddling by the headquarters in specific business decisions.

As long as the screws of the performance control system are not turned too tight, the division managers may retain enough discretion to consider the social consequences of their actions, if they so choose. But when those screws are turned tight, as they often are in the diversified corporation with a bottom-line orientation, then the division managers wishing to keep their jobs may have no choice but to act socially unresponsively, if not actually irresponsibly. As Bower has noted of the General Electric price-fixing scandal of the 1960s, 'a very severely managed system of reward and punishment that demanded yearly improvements in earnings, return and market share, applied indiscriminately to all divisions, yielded a situation which was – at the very least – conducive to collusion in the oligopolistic and mature electric equipment markets' (1970: 193).

The Diversified Organization in the Public Sphere

Ironically, for a government intent on dealing with these social problems, solutions are indicated in the very arguments used to support the diversified configuration. Or so it would appear.

For example, if the administrative arrangements are efficient while the capital markets are not, then why should a government hesitate to interfere with the capital markets? And why shouldn't it use those same administrative arrangements to deal with the problems? If Beatrice Foods really can control those 397 divisions, then what is to stop Washington from believing it can control 397 Beatrices? After all, the capital markets don't much matter. In his book on 'countervailing power', John Kenneth Galbraith (1952) argued that bigness in one sector, such as business, promotes bigness in other sectors, such as unions and government. That has already happened. How long before government pursues the logical next step and exercises direct controls?

While such steps may prove irresistible to some governments, the fact is that they will not resolve the problems of power concentration and social irresponsibility but rather will aggravate them, but not just in the ways usually assumed in Western economics. All the existing problems would simply be bumped up to another level, and there increase. By making use of the diversified configuration, government would magnify the problems of size. Moreover, government, like the corporation, would be driven to favour measurable economic goals over intangible social ones, and that would add to the problems of social irresponsibility – a phenomenon of which we have already seen a good deal in the public sector.

In fact, these problems would be worse in government, because its sphere is social, and so its goals are largely ill-suited to performance control systems. In other words, many of the goals most important for the public sector – and this applies to not-for-profit organizations in spheres such as health and education as well – simply do not lend themselves to measurement, no matter how long and how hard public officials continue to try. And without measurement, the conventional diversified configuration cannot work.

There are, of course, other problems with the application of this form of organization in the public sphere. For example, government cannot divest itself of subunits quite so easily as can corporations. And public service regulations on appointments and the like, as well as a host of other rules, preclude the degree of division manager autonomy available in the private sector. (It is, in fact, these central rules and regulations that make governments resemble integrated machine configurations as much as loosely coupled diversified ones, and that undermine their efforts at 'accountability'.)

Thus, we conclude that, appearances and even trends notwithstanding, the diversified configuration is generally not suited to the public and not-for-profit sectors of society. Governments and other public-type institutions that wish to divisionalize to avoid centralized machine bureaucracy may often find the imposition of performance standards an artificial exercise. They may thus be better off trying to exercise control of their units in a different way. For example, they can select unit managers who reflect their desired values, or indoctrinate them in those values, and then let them manage freely, the control in effect being normative rather than quantitative. But managing ideology, even creating it in the first place, is no simple matter, especially in a highly diversified organization.

In Conclusion: A Structure on the Edge of a Cliff

Our discussion has led to a 'damned if you do, damned if you don't' conclusion. The pure (conglomerate) diversified configuration emerges as an organization perched symbolically on the edge of the cliff, at the end of a long path. Ahead, it is one step away from disintegration – breaking up into separate organizations on the rocks below. Behind it is the way back to a more stable integration, in the form of the machine configuration at the start of that path. And ever hovering above is the eagle, representing the broader social control of the state, attracted by the organization's position on the edge of the cliff and waiting for the chance to pull it up to a higher cliff, perhaps more dangerous still. The edge of the cliff is an uncomfortable place to be, perhaps even a temporary one that must inevitably lead to disintegration on the rocks below, a trip to that cliff above, or a return to a safer resting place somewhere on that path behind.

● GENERIC CORPORATE STRATEGIES*

HENRY MINTZBERG

In Chapter 3 we examined three sets of strategies – for locating, then distinguishing, the core business. These are appropriate for the business level. After locating the core business in a given industry, the strategist answers the business-level question of 'How do we compete successfully in this industry?' by distinguishing and elaborating the core business.

* This reading is an abbreviated version of Henry Mintzberg, 'Generic strategies: Toward a comprehensive framework', in *Advances in Strategic Management*, Vol. 5 (Greenwich, CT: JAI Press, 1988), pp. 1–67. Reproduced with permission of the publisher.

Next comes the question of what strategies of a generic nature are available to extend and reconceive that core business. These are approaches designed to answer the corporate-level question, 'What business should we be in?'

EXTENDING THE CORE BUSINESS

Strategies designed to take organizations beyond their core business can be pursued in so-called vertical or horizontal ways, as well as combinations of the two. 'Vertical' means backward or forward in the operating chain, the strategy being known formally as 'vertical integration', although why this has been designated vertical is difficult to understand, especially since the flow of product and the chain itself are almost always drawn horizontally! Hence this will here be labelled chain integration. 'Horizontal' diversification (its own geometry no more evident), which will be called here just plain diversification, refers to encompassing within the organization other, parallel businesses, not in the same chain of operations.

Chain Integration Strategies

Organizations can extend their operating chains downstream or upstream, encompassing within their own operations the activities of their customers on the delivery end or their suppliers on the sourcing end. In effect, they choose to 'make' rather than to 'buy' or sell. *Impartation* (Barreyre, 1984; Barreyre and Carle, 1983) is a label that has been proposed to describe the opposite strategy, where the organization chooses to buy what it previously made, or sell what it previously transferred.

Diversification Strategies

Diversification refers to the entry into some business not in the same chain of operation. It may be *related* to some distinctive competence or asset of the core business itself (also called *concentric* diversification); otherwise, it is referred to as *unrelated* or *conglomerate*, diversification. In related diversification, there is evident potential synergy between the new business and the core one, based on a common facility, asset, channel, skill, even opportunity. Porter (1985: 323–4) makes the distinction here between 'intangible' and 'tangible' relatedness. The former is based on some functional or managerial skill considered common across the businesses, as in a Philip Morris using its marketing capabilities in Kraft. The latter refers to businesses that actually 'share activities in the value chain' (p. 323), for example, different products sold by the same sales force. It should be emphasized here that no matter what its basis, every related diversification is also fundamentally an unrelated one, as many diversifying organizations have discovered to their regret. That is, no matter what is common between two different businesses, many other things are not.

Strategies of Entry and Control

Chain integration or diversification may be achieved by *internal development* or *acquisition*. In other words, an organization can enter a new business by developing it itself or by buying an organization already in that business. ... Both internal development and acquisition involve complete ownership and formal control of the diversified business. But there are a host of other possible strategies, as follows:

Strategies of Entry and Control

Fuel ownership and control	• Internal Development
	• Acquisition
Partial ownership and control	• Majority, minority
	• Partnership, including
	– Joint venture
	– Turnkey (temporary control)
Partial control without ownership	• Licensing
	• Franchising
	• Long-term contracting

Combined Integration–Diversification Strategies

Among the most interesting are those strategies that combine chain integration with business diversification, sometimes leading organizations into whole networks of new businesses. *By-product diversification* involves selling off the by-products of the operating chain in separate markets, as when an airline offers its maintenance services to other carriers. The new activity amounts to a form of market development at some intermediate point in the operating chain. *Linked diversification* extends by-product diversification: one business simply leads to another, whether integrated 'vertically' or diversified 'horizontally'. The organization pursues its operating chain upstream, downstream, sidestream; it exploits pre-products, end-products and by-products of its core products as well as of each other, ending up with a network of businesses, as illustrated in the case of a supermarket chain in Figure 1. *Crystalline diversification* pushes the previous strategy to the limit, so that it becomes difficult and perhaps irrelevant to distinguish integration from diversification, core activities from peripheral activities, closely related businesses from distantly related ones. What were once clear links in a few chains now metamorphose into what looks like a form of crystalline growth, as business after business gets added literally right and left as well as up and down. Here businesses tend to be related, at least initially, through internal development of core competences, as in the 'coating and bonding technologies' that are common to so many of 3M's products.

Withdrawal Strategies

Finally there are strategies that reverse all those of diversification: organizations cut back on the businesses they are in. 'Exit' has been one popular label for this, withdrawal is another. Sometimes organizations *shrink* their activities, cancelling long-term licences, ceasing to sell by-products, reducing their crystalline networks. Other times they abandon or *liquidate* businesses (the opposite of internal development), or else they *divest* them (the opposite of acquisition).

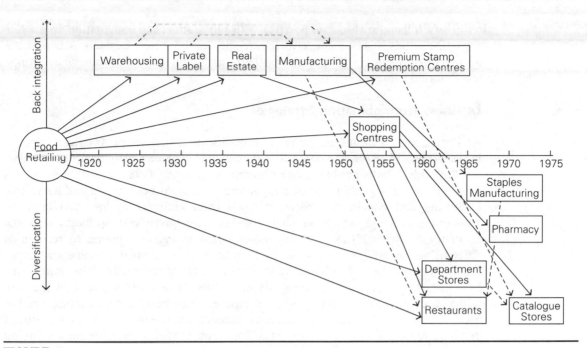

FIGURE 1
Linked diversification on a time scale – the case of the Steinberg chain
Source: From Mintzberg and Waters (1982: 490)

RECONCEIVING THE CORE BUSINESS(ES)

It may seem strange to end a discussion of strategies of ever more elaborate development of a business with ones involving reconception of the business. But in one important sense, there is a logic to this: after a core business has been identified, distinguished, elaborated and extended, there often follows the need not just to consolidate it but also to redefine it and reconfigure it – in essence, to reconceive it. As they develop, through all the waves of expansion, integration, diversification, and so on, some organizations lose a sense of themselves. Then reconception becomes the ultimate form of consolidation: rationalizing not just excesses in product offerings or markets segments or even new businesses, but all of these things together and more – the essence of the entire strategy itself. We can identify three basic reconception strategies:

Business Redefinition Strategy

A business, as Abell (1980) has pointed out, may be defined in a variety of ways – by the function it performs, the market it serves, the product it produces. All businesses have popular conceptions. Some are narrow and tangible, such as the canoe business, others broader and vague, such as the financial services business. All such definitions, no matter how tangible, are ultimately concepts that exist in the minds of actors and observers. It therefore becomes possible, with a little effort and imagination, to *redefine* a particular business – reconceive the 'recipe' for how that business is conducted (Grinyer and Spender, 1979; Spender, 1989) – as Edwin Land did when he developed the Polaroid camera.[5]

Business Recombination Strategies

As Porter notes, through the waves of diversification that swept American business in the 1960s and 1970s, 'the concept of synergy has become widely regarded as passé' – a "nice idea" but one that rarely occurred in practice' (1985: 317–18). Businesses were elements in a portfolio to be bought and sold, or, at best, grown and harvested. Deploring that conclusion, Porter devoted three chapters of his 1985 book to 'horizontal strategy', which we shall refer to here (given our problems with the geometry of this field) as *business recombination strategies* – efforts to recombine different businesses in some way, at the limit to reconceive various businesses as one. Businesses can be recombined tangibly or only conceptually. The latter was encouraged by Levitt's 'Marketing Myopia' (1960) article. By a stroke of the pen, railroads could be in the transportation business, ball-bearing manufacturers in the friction reduction business. Realizing some practical change in behaviour often proved much more difficult, however. But when some substantial basis exists for combining different activities, a strategy of business recombination can be very effective. There may never have been a transportation business, but 3M was able to draw on common technological capabilities to create a coating and bonding business.[6] Business recombination can also be more tangible, based on shared activities in the value chain, as in a strategy of *bundling*, where complementary products are sold together for a single price (e.g. automobile service with the new car). Of course, *unbundling* can be an equally viable strategy, such as selling 'term' insurance free of any investment obligation. Carried to their logical extreme, the more tangible recombination strategies lead to a 'systems view' of the business, where all products and services are conceived to be tightly interrelated.

Core Relocation Strategies

Finally we come full circle by closing the discussion where we began, on the location of the core business. An organization, in addition to having one or more strategic positions in a marketplace, tends to have what Jay Galbraith (1983) calls a single 'centre of gravity', some conceptual place where is concentrated not only its core skills but also its cultural heart, as in a Procter & Gamble focusing its efforts on 'branded consumer products', each 'sold primarily by advertising to the homemaker and managed by a brand manager' (1983: 13). But as changes in strategic position take place, shifts can also take place in this centre of gravity, in various ways. First, the organization can move *along the operating chain*, upstream or downstream, as did General Mills 'from a flour miller to a related diversified provider of products for the homemaker'; eventually the company sold off its flour milling operation altogether (Galbraith, 1983: 76). Second, there can be a shift *between dominant functions*, say from production to marketing. Third is the shift *to a new business*, whether or not at the same stage of the operating chain. Such shifts can be awfully demanding, simply because each industry is a culture with its own ways of thinking and acting. Finally, is the shift *to a new core theme*, as in the reorientation from a single function or product to a broader concept, for example when Procter & Gamble changed from being a soap company to being in the personal care business.

This brings us to the end of our discussion of generic strategies – our loop from locating a business to distinguishing it, elaborating it, extending it and finally reconceiving it. We should close with the warning that while a framework of generic strategies may help to think about positioning an organization, use of it as a pat list may put that organization at a disadvantage against competitors that develop their strategies in more creative ways.

● THE PRODUCT PORTFOLIO* (GROWTH-SHARE MATRIX OF THE BOSTON CONSULTING GROUP)

BRUCE D. HENDERSON

To be successful, a company should have a portfolio of products with different growth rates and different market shares. The portfolio composition is a function of the balance between cash flows. High-growth products require cash inputs to grow. Low-growth products should generate excess cash. Both kinds are needed simultaneously.

Four rules determine the cash flow of a product:

1. Margins and cash generated are a function of market share. High margins and high market share go together. This is a matter of common observation, explained by the experience curve effect.

2. Growth requires cash input to finance added assets. The added cash required to hold share is a function of growth rates.

3. High market share must be earned or bought. Buying market share requires additional investment.

4. No product market can grow indefinitely. The payoff from growth must come when the growth slows, or it will not come at all. The payoff is cash that cannot be reinvested in that product.

Products with high market share and slow growth are 'cash cows' (see Figure 1). Characteristically, they generate large amounts of cash, in excess of the reinvestment required to maintain share. This excess need not, and should not, be reinvested in those products. In fact, if the rate of return exceeds the growth rate, the cash *cannot* be reinvested indefinitely, except by depressing returns.

Products with low market share and slow growth are 'dogs'. They may show an accounting profit, but the profit must be reinvested to maintain share, leaving no cash throwoff. The product is essentially worthless, except in liquidation.

---

* Originally published in *Henderson on Corporate Strategy* (Cambridge, MA: Abt Books. Copyright © 1979) pp. 163–6, reprinted by permission of the author and the publisher.

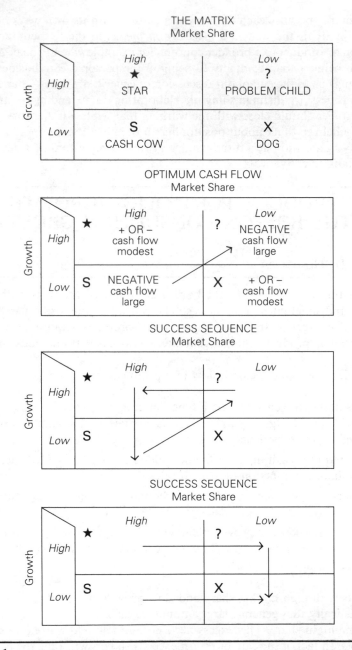

FIGURE 1
Boston Consulting Group growth-share matrix.

All products eventually become either a 'cash cow' or a 'dog'. The value of a product is completely dependent upon obtaining a leading share of its market before the growth slows.

Low market-share, high-growth products are the 'problem children'. They almost always require far more cash than they can generate. If cash is not supplied, they fall behind and die. Even when the cash is supplied, if they only hold their share, they are still dogs when the growth stops. The 'problem children' require large added cash investment for market share to be purchased. The low market-share, high-growth product is a liability unless it becomes a leader. It requires very large cash inputs that it cannot generate itself.

The high-share, high-growth product is the 'star'. It nearly always shows reported profits, but it may or may not generate all of its own cash. If it stays a leader, however, it will become a large cash generator when growth slows and its reinvestment requirements diminish. The star eventually becomes the cash cow – providing high volume, high margin, high stability, security – and cash throwoff for reinvestment elsewhere.

The payoff for leadership is very high indeed, if it is achieved early and maintained until growth slows. Investment in market share during the growth phase can be very attractive   if you have the cash. Growth in market is compounded by growth in share. Increases in share increase the margin. Higher margin permits higher leverage with equal safety. The resulting profitability permits higher payment of earning after financing normal growth. The return on investment is enormous.

The need for a portfolio of businesses becomes obvious. Every company needs products in which to invest cash. Every company needs products that generate cash. And every product should eventually be a cash generator; otherwise, it is worthless.

Only a diversified company with a balanced portfolio can use its strengths to truly capitalize on its growth opportunities. The balanced portfolio has:

- 'Stars', whose high share and high growth assure the future.
- 'Cash cows', that supply funds for that future growth.
- 'Problem children', to be converted into 'stars' with the added funds.

'Dogs' are not necessary. They are evidence of failure either to obtain a leadership position during the growth phase, or to get out and cut the losses.

● FROM COMPETITIVE ADVANTAGE TO CORPORATE STRATEGY*

MICHAEL E. PORTER

Corporate strategy, the overall plan for a diversified company, is both the darling and the stepchild of contemporary management practice – the darling because CEOs have been obsessed with diversification since the early 1960s, the stepchild because almost no consensus exists about what corporate strategy is, much less about how a company should formulate it.

A diversified company has two levels of strategy: business unit (or competitive) strategy and corporate (or companywide) strategy. Competitive strategy concerns how

---

* Originally published in the *Harvard Business Review* (May–June 1987) and winner of the McKinsey Prize for the best in the *Review* in 1987.

to create competitive advantage in each of the businesses in which a company competes. Corporate strategy concerns two different questions: what businesses the corporation should be in and how the corporate office should manage the array of business units.

Corporate strategy is what makes the corporate whole add up to more than the sum of its business unit parts.

The track record of corporate strategies has been dismal. I studied the diversification records of 33 large, prestigious US companies over the 1950–86 period and found that most of them had divested many more acquisitions than they had kept. The corporate strategies of most companies have dissipated instead of created shareholder value.

The need to rethink corporate strategy could hardly be more urgent. By taking over companies and breaking them up, corporate raiders thrive on failed corporate strategy. Fuelled by junk bond financing and growing acceptability, raiders can expose any company to takeover, no matter how large or blue chip. ...

A SOBER PICTURE

... My study of 33 companies, many of which have reputations for good management, is a unique look at the track record of major corporations. ... Each company entered an average of 80 new industries and 27 new fields. Just over 70 per cent of the new entries were acquisitions, 22 per cent were start-ups and 8 per cent were joint ventures. IBM, Exxon, Du Pont and 3M, for example, focused on start-ups, while ALCO Standard, Beatrice and Sara Lee diversified almost solely through acquisitions. ...

My data paint a sobering picture of the success ratio of these moves. ... I found that on average corporations divested more than half their acquisitions in new industries and more than 60 per cent of their acquisitions in entirely new fields. Fourteen companies left more than 70 per cent of all the acquisitions they had made in new fields. The track record in unrelated acquisitions is even worse – the average divestment rate is a startling 74 per cent. Even a highly respected company like General Electric divested a very high percentage of its acquisitions, particularly those in new fields. ... Some [companies] bear witness to the success of well-thought-out corporate strategies. Others, however, enjoy a lower rate simply because they have not faced up to their problem units and divested them. ...

I would like to make one comment on the use of shareholder value to judge performance. Linking shareholder value quantitatively to diversification performance only works if you compare the shareholder value that is with the shareholder value that might have been without diversification. Because such a comparison is virtually impossible to make, my own measure of diversification success – the number of units retained by the company – seems to be as good an indicator as any of the contribution of diversification to corporate performance.

My data give a stark indication of the failure of corporate strategies.[7] Of the 33 companies, six had been taken over as my study was being completed. ... Only the lawyers, investment bankers and original sellers have prospered in most of these acquisitions, not the shareholders.

PREMISSES OF CORPORATE STRATEGY

Any successful corporate strategy builds on a number of premisses. These are facts of life about diversification. They cannot be altered, and when ignored, they explain in part why so many corporate strategies fail.

- *Competition Occurs at the Business Unit Level.* Diversified companies do not compete; only their business units do. Unless a corporate strategy places primary attention on nurturing the success of each unit, the strategy will fail, no matter how elegantly constructed. Successful corporate strategy must grow out of and reinforce competitive strategy.

- *Diversification Inevitably Adds Costs and Constraints to Business Units.* Obvious costs such as the corporate overhead allocated to a unit may not be as important or subtle as the hidden costs and constraints. A business unit must explain its decisions to top management, spend time complying with planning and other corporate systems, live with parent company guidelines and personnel policies and forgo the opportunity to motivate employees with direct equity ownership. These costs and constraints can be reduced but not entirely eliminated.

- *Shareholders Can Readily Diversify Themselves.* Shareholders can diversify their own portfolios of stocks by selecting those that best match their preferences and risk profiles (Salter and Weinhold, 1979). Shareholders can often diversify more cheaply than a corporation because they can buy shares at the market price and avoid hefty acquisition premiums.

These premisses mean that corporate strategy cannot succeed unless it truly adds value – to business units by providing tangible benefits that offset the inherent costs of lost independence and to shareholders by diversifying in a way they could not replicate.

PASSING THE ESSENTIAL TESTS

To understand how to formulate corporate strategy, it is necessary to specify the conditions under which diversification will truly create shareholder value. These conditions can be summarized in three essential tests:

1. *The attractiveness test:* The industries chosen for diversification must be structurally attractive or capable of being made attractive.
2. *The cost-of-entry test:* The cost of entry must not capitalize all the future profits.
3. *The better-off test:* Either the new unit must gain competitive advantage from its link with the corporation, or vice versa.

Of course, most companies will make certain that their proposed strategies pass some of these tests. But my study clearly shows that when companies ignored one or two of them, the strategic results were disastrous.

How Attractive Is the Industry?

In the long run, the rate of return available from competing in an industry is a function of its underlying structure. An attractive industry with a high average return on investment will be difficult to enter because entry barriers are high, suppliers and buyers have only modest bargaining power, substitute products or services are few and the rivalry among competitors is stable. An unattractive industry like steel will have structural flaws, including a plethora of substitute materials, powerful and price-sensitive buyers and excessive rivalry caused by high fixed costs and a large group of competitors, many of whom are state supported.

Diversification cannot create shareholder value unless new industries have favourable structures that support returns exceeding the cost of capital. If the industry doesn't have such returns, the company must be able to restructure the industry or gain a sustainable competitive advantage that leads to returns well above the industry average. An industry need not be attractive before diversification. In fact, a company might benefit from entering before the industry shows its full potential. The diversification can then transform the industry's structure.

In my research, I often found companies had suspended the attractiveness test because they had a vague belief that the industry 'fit' very closely with their own business. In the hope that the corporate 'comfort' they felt would lead to a happy outcome, the companies ignored fundamentally poor industry structures. Unless the close fit allows substantial competitive advantage, however, such comfort will turn into pain when diversification results in poor returns. Royal Dutch Shell and other leading oil companies have had this unhappy experience in a number of chemicals businesses, where poor industry structures overcame the benefits of vertical integration and skills in process technology.

Another common reason for ignoring the attractiveness test is a low entry cost. Sometimes the buyer has an inside track or the owner is anxious to sell. Even if the price is actually low, however, a one-shot gain will not offset a perpetually poor business. Almost always, the company finds it must reinvest in the newly acquired unit, if only to replace fixed assets and fund working capital.

Diversifying companies are also prone to use rapid growth or other simple indicators as a proxy for a target industry's attractiveness. Many that rushed into fast-growing industries (personal computers, video games and robotics, for example) were burned because they mistook early growth for long-term profit potential. Industries are profitable not because they are sexy or high-tech; they are profitable only if their structures are attractive.

What Is the Cost of Entry?

Diversification cannot build shareholder value if the cost of entry into a new business eats up its expected returns. Strong market forces, however, are working to do just that. A company can enter new industries by acquisition or start-up. Acquisitions expose it to an increasingly efficient merger market. An acquirer beats the market if it pays a price not fully reflecting the prospects of the new unit. Yet multiple bidders are commonplace, information flows rapidly and investment bankers and other intermediaries work aggressively to make the market as efficient as possible. In recent years, new financial instruments such a junk bonds have brought new buyers into the market and made even large companies vulnerable to takeover. Acquisition premiums are high and reflect the acquired company's future prospects – sometimes too well. Philip Morris paid more than four times book value for Seven-Up Company, for example. Simple arithmetic meant that profits had to more than quadruple to sustain the pre-acquisition ROI. Since there proved to be little Philip Morris could add in marketing prowess to the sophisticated marketing wars in the soft drink industry, the result was the unsatisfactory financial performance of Seven-Up and ultimately the decision to divest.

In a start-up, the company must overcome entry barriers. It's real catch-22 situation, however, since attractive industries are attractive because their entry barriers are high. Bearing the full cost of the entry barriers might well dissipate any potential profits. Otherwise, other entrants to the industry would have already eroded its profitability.

In the excitement of finding an appealing new business, companies sometimes forget to apply the cost-of-entry test. The more attractive a new industry, the more expensive it is to get into.

Will the Business Be Better Off?

A corporation must bring some significant competitive advantage to the new unit, or the new unit must offer potential for significant advantage to the corporation. Sometimes, the benefits to the new unit accrue only once, near the time of entry, when the parent instigates a major overhaul of its strategy or installs a first-rate management team. Other diversification yields ongoing competitive advantage if the new unit can market its product, through the well-developed distribution system of its sister units, for instance. This is one of the important underpinnings of the merger of Baxter Travenol and American Hospital Supply.

When the benefit to the new unit comes only once, the parent company has no rationale for holding the new unit in its portfolio over the long term. Once the results of the one-time improvement are clear, the diversified company no longer adds value to offset the inevitable costs imposed on the unit. It is best to sell the unit and free up corporate resources.

The better-off test does not imply that diversifying corporate risk creates shareholder value in and of itself. Doing something for shareholders that they can do themselves is not a basis for corporate strategy. (Only in the case of a privately held company, in which the company's and the shareholder's risk are the same, is diversification to reduce risk valuable for its own sake.) Diversification of risk should only be a by-product of corporate strategy, not a prime motivator.

Executives ignore the better-off test most of all or deal with it through arm waving or trumped-up logic rather than hard strategic analysis. One reason is that they confuse company size with shareholder value. In the drive to run a bigger company, they lose sight of their real job. They may justify the suspension of the better-off test by pointing to the way they manage diversity. By cutting corporate staff to the bone and giving business units nearly complete autonomy, they believe they avoid the pitfalls. Such thinking misses the whole point of diversification, which is to create shareholder value rather than to avoid destroying it.

CONCEPTS OF CORPORATE STRATEGY

The three tests for successful diversification set the standards that any corporate strategy must meet; meeting them is so difficult that most diversification fails. Many companies lack a clear concept of corporate strategy to guide their diversification or pursue a concept that does not address the tests. Others fail because they implement a strategy poorly.

My study has helped me identify four concepts of corporate strategy that have been put into practice – portfolio management, restructuring, transferring skills and sharing activities. While the concepts are not always mutually exclusive, each rests on a different mechanism by which the corporation creates shareholder value and each requires the diversified company to manage and organize itself in a different way. The first two require no connections among business units; the second two depend on them. ... While all four concepts of strategy have succeeded under the right circumstances, today some make more sense than others. Ignoring any of the concepts is perhaps the quickest road to failure.

Portfolio Management

The concept of corporate strategy most in use is portfolio management, which is based primarily on diversification through acquisition. The corporation acquires sound, attractive companies with competent managers who agree to stay on. While acquired units do not have to be in the same industries as existing units, the best portfolio managers generally limit their range of businesses in some way, in part to limit the specific expertise needed by top management.

The acquired units are autonomous and the teams that run them are compensated according to unit results. The corporation supplies capital and works with each to infuse it with professional management techniques. At the same time, top management provides objective and dispassionate review of business unit results. Portfolio managers categorize units by potential and regularly transfer resources from units that generate cash to those with high potential and cash needs. ...

In most countries, the days when portfolio management was a valid concept of corporate strategy are past. In the face of increasingly well-developed capital markets, attractive companies with good managements show up on everyone's computer screen and attract top dollar in terms of acquisition premium. Simply contributing capital isn't contributing much. A sound strategy can easily be funded; small to medium-size companies don't need a munificent parent.

Other benefits have also eroded. Large companies no longer corner the market for professional management skills; in fact, more and more observers believe managers cannot necessarily run anything in the absence of industry-specific knowledge and experience. ...

But it is the sheer complexity of the management task that has ultimately defeated even the best portfolio managers. As the size of the company grows, portfolio managers need to find more and more deals just to maintain growth. Supervising dozens or even hundreds of disparate units and under chain-letter pressures to add more, management begins to make mistakes. At the same time, the inevitable costs of being part of a diversified company take their toll and unit performance slides while the whole company's ROI turns downward. Eventually, a new management team is installed which initiates wholesale divestments and pares down the company to its core businesses. ...

In developing countries, where large companies are few, capital markets are undeveloped, and professional management is scarce, portfolio management still works. But it is no longer a valid model for corporate strategy in advanced economies. ... Portfolio management is no way to conduct corporate strategy.

Restructuring

Unlike its passive role as a portfolio manager, when it serves as banker and reviewer, a company that bases its strategy on restructuring becomes an active restructurer of business units. The new businesses are not necessarily related to existing units. All that is necessary is unrealized potential.

The restructuring strategy seeks out undeveloped, sick or threatened organizations or industries on the threshold of significant change. The parent intervenes, frequently changing the unit management team, shifting strategy or infusing the company with new technology. Then it may make follow-up acquisitions to build a critical mass and sell off unneeded or unconnected parts and thereby reduce the effective acquisition cost. The result is a strengthened company or a transformed industry. As a coda, the parent sells off the stronger unit once results are clear because the parent is no longer adding value, and top management decides that its attention should be directed elsewhere. ...

When well implemented, the restructuring concept is sound, for it passes the three tests of successful diversification. The restructurer meets the cost-of-entry test through the types of company it acquires. It limits acquisition premiums by buying companies with problems and lacklustre images or by buying into industries with as yet unforeseen potential. Intervention by the corporation clearly meets the better-off test. Provided that the target industries are structurally attractive, the restructuring model can create enormous shareholder value. ... Ironically, many of today's restructurers are profiting from yesterday's portfolio management strategies.

To work, the restructuring strategy requires a corporate management team with the insight to spot undervalued companies or positions in industries ripe for transformation. The same insight is necessary to actually turn the units around even though they are in new and unfamiliar businesses. ...

Perhaps the greatest pitfall ... is that companies find it very hard to dispose of business units once they are restructured and performing well. ...

Transferring Skills

The purpose of the first two concepts of corporate strategy is to create value through a company's relationship with each autonomous unit. The corporation's role is to be a selector, a banker and an intervenor.

The last two concepts exploit the interrelationships between businesses. In articulating them, however, one comes face-to-face with the often ill-defined concept of synergy. If you believe the text of the countless corporate annual reports, just about anything is related to just about anything else! But imagined synergy is much more common than real synergy. GM's purchase of Hughes Aircraft simply because cars were going electronic and Hughes was an electronics concern demonstrates the folly of paper synergy. Such corporate relatedness is an *ex post facto* rationalization of a diversification undertaken for other reasons.

Even synergy that is clearly defined often fails to materialize. Instead of cooperating, business units often compete. A company that can define the synergies it is pursuing still faces significant organizational impediments in achieving them.

But the need to capture the benefits of relationships between businesses has never been more important. Technological and competitive developments already link many businesses and are creating new possibilities for competitive advantage. In such sectors as financial services, computing, office equipment, entertainment and health care, interrelationships among previously distinct businesses are perhaps the central concern of strategy.

To understand the role of relatedness in corporate strategy, we must give new meaning to this often ill-defined idea. I have identified a good way to start – the value chain. Every business unit is a collection of discrete activities ranging from sales to accounting that allow it to compete. I call them value activities. It is at this level, not in the company as a whole, that the unit achieves competitive advantage.

I group these activities in nine categories. *Primary* activities create the product or service, deliver and market it, and provide after-sale support. The categories of primary activities are inbound logistics, operations, outbound logistics, marketing and sales, and service. *Support* activities provide the input and infrastructure that allow the primary activities to take place. The categories are company infrastructure, human resource management, technology development and procurement.

The value chain defines the two types of interrelationships that may create synergy. The first is a company's ability to transfer skills or expertise among similar value chains. The second is the ability to share activities. Two business units, for example, can share the same sales force or logistics network.

The value chain helps expose the last two (and most important) concepts of corporate strategy. The transfer of skills among business units in the diversified company is the basis for one concept. While each business unit has a separate value chain, knowledge about how to perform activities is transferred among the units. For example, a toiletries business unit, expert in the marketing of convenience products, transmits ideas on new positioning concepts, promotional techniques and packaging possibilities to a newly acquired unit that sells cough syrup. Newly entered industries can benefit from the expertise of existing units, and vice versa.

These opportunities arise when business units have similar buyers or channels, similar value activities like government relations or procurement, similarities in the broad configuration of the value chain (for example, managing a multi-site service organization), or the same strategic concept (for example, low cost). Even though the units operate separately, such similarities allow the sharing of knowledge. ...

Transferring skills leads to competitive advantage only if the similarities among businesses meet three conditions:

1. The activities involved in the businesses are similar enough that sharing expertise is meaningful. Broad similarities (marketing intensiveness, for example, or a

common core process technology such as bending metal) are not a sufficient basis for diversification. The resulting ability to transfer skills is likely to have little impact on competitive advantage.

2. The transfer of skills involves activities important to competitive advantage. Transferring skills in peripheral activities such as government relations or real estate in consumer goods units may be beneficial but is not a basis for diversification.

3. The skills transferred represent a significant source of competitive advantage for the receiving unit. The expertise or skills to be transferred are both advanced and proprietary enough to be beyond the capabilities of competitors. ...

Transferring skills meets the tests of diversification if the company truly mobilizes proprietary expertise across units. This makes certain the company can offset the acquisition premium or lower the cost of overcoming entry barriers.

The industries the company chooses for diversification must pass the attractiveness test. Even a close fit that reflects opportunities to transfer skills may not overcome poor industry structure. Opportunities to transfer skills, however, may help the company transform the structures of newly entered industries and send them in favourable directions.

The transfer of skills can be one time or ongoing. If the company exhausts opportunities to infuse new expertise into a unit after the initial post-acquisition period, the unit should ultimately be sold. ...

By using both acquisitions and internal development, companies can build a transfer-of-skills strategy. The presence of a strong base of skills sometimes creates the possibility for internal entry instead of the acquisition of a going concern. Successful diversifiers that employ the concept of skills transfer may, however, often acquire a company in the target industry as a beachhead and then build on it with their internal expertise. By doing so, they can reduce some of the risks of internal entry and speed up the process. Two companies that have diversified using the transfer-of-skills concept are 3M and PepsiCo.

Sharing Activities

The fourth concept of corporate strategy is based on sharing activities in the value chains among business units. Procter & Gamble, for example, employs a common physical distribution system and sales force in both paper towels and disposable nappies. McKesson, a leading distribution company, will handle such diverse lines as pharmaceuticals and liquor through super-warehouses.

The ability to share activities is a potent basis for corporate strategy because sharing often enhances competitive advantage by lowering cost or raising differentiation. ...

Sharing activities inevitably involves costs that the benefits must outweigh. One cost is the greater coordination required to manage a shared activity. More important is the need to compromise the design or performance of an activity so that it can be shared. A salesperson handling the products of two business units, for example, must operate in a way that is usually not what either unit would choose were it independent. And if compromise greatly erodes the unit's effectiveness, then sharing may reduce rather than enhance competitive advantage. ...

Despite ... pitfalls, opportunities to gain advantage from sharing activities have proliferated because of momentous developments in technology, deregulation and competition. The infusion of electronics and information systems into many industries creates new opportunities to link business. ...

Following the shared-activities model requires an organization context in which business unit collaboration is encouraged and reinforced. Highly autonomous business units are inimical to such collaboration. The company must put into place a variety of what I call horizontal mechanisms – a strong sense of corporate identity, a clear corporate mission statement that emphasizes the importance of integrating business unit strategies, an incentive system that rewards more than just business unit results, cross-business-unit task forces, and other methods of integrating.

A corporate strategy based on shared activities clearly meets the better-off test because business units gain ongoing tangible advantages from others within the corporation. It also meets the cost-of-entry test by reducing the expense of surmounting the barriers to internal entry. Other bids for acquisitions that do not share opportunities will have lower reservation prices. Even widespread opportunities for sharing activities do not allow a company to suspend the attractiveness test, however. Many diversifiers have made the critical mistake of equating the close fit of a target industry with attractive diversification. Target industries must pass the strict requirement test of having an attractive structure as well as a close fit in opportunities if diversification is to ultimately succeed.

CHOOSING A CORPORATE STRATEGY

... Both the strategic logic and the experience of the companies I studied over the last decade suggest that a company will create shareholder value through diversification to a greater and greater extent as its strategy moves from portfolio management towards sharing activities. ...

Each concept of corporate strategy is not mutually exclusive of those that come before, a potent advantage of the third and fourth concepts. A company can employ a restructuring strategy at the same time it transfers skills or shares activities. A strategy based on shared activities becomes more powerful if business units can also exchange skills. ...

My study supports the soundness of basing a corporate strategy on the transfer of skills or shared activities. The data on the sample companies' diversification programmes illustrate some important characteristics of successful diversifiers. They have made a disproportionately low percentage of unrelated acquisitions, *unrelated* being defined as having no clear opportunity to transfer skills or share important activities. ... Even successful diversifiers such as 3M, IBM and TRW have terrible records when they strayed into unrelated acquisitions. Successful acquirers diversify into fields, each of which is related to many others. Procter & Gamble and IBM, for example, operate in 18 and 19 interrelated fields respectively, and so enjoy numerous opportunities to transfer skills and share activities.

Companies with the best acquisition records tend to make heavier-than-average use of start-ups and joint ventures. Most companies shy away from modes of entry besides acquisition. My results cast doubt on the conventional wisdom regarding start-ups. ... successful companies often have very good records with start-up units, as 3M, P&G, Johnson & Johnson, IBM and United Technologies illustrate. When a company has the internal strength to start up a unit, it can be safer and less costly to launch a company than to rely solely on an acquisition and then have to deal with the problem of integration. Japanese diversification histories support the soundness of start-up as an entry alternative.

My data also illustrate that none of the concepts of corporate strategy works when industry structure is poor or implementation is bad, no matter how related the industries are. Xerox acquired companies in related industries, but the businesses had poor structures and its skills were insufficient to provide enough competitive advantage to offset implementation problems.

An Action Programme

... A company can choose a corporate strategy by:

1. Identifying the interrelationships among already existing business units. ...
2. Selecting the core businesses that will be the foundation of the corporate strategy. ...
3. Creating horizontal organizational mechanisms to facilitate interrelationships among the core businesses and lay the groundwork for future related diversification. ...
4. Pursuing diversification opportunities that allow shared activities, ...
5. Pursuing diversification through the transfer of skills if opportunities for sharing activities are limited or exhausted. ...
6. Pursuing a strategy restructuring if this fits the skills of management or no good opportunities exist for forging corporate interrelationships. ...
7. Paying dividends so that the shareholders can be the portfolio managers. ...

Creating a Corporate Theme

Defining a corporate theme is a good way to ensure that the corporation will create shareholder value. Having the right theme helps unite the efforts of business units and reinforces the ways they interrelate as well as guides the choice of new businesses to enter. NEC Corporation, with its 'C&C' theme, provides a good example. NEC integrates its computer, semiconductor, telecommunications and consumer electronics businesses by merging computers and communication.

It is all too easy to create a shallow corporate theme. CBS wants to be an 'entertainment company', for example, and built a group of businesses related to leisure time. It entered such industries as toys, crafts, musical instruments, sports teams and hi-fi retailing. While this corporate theme sounded good, close listening revealed its hollow ring. None of these businesses had any significant opportunity to share activities or transfer skills among themselves or with CBS's traditional broadcasting and record businesses. They were all sold, often at significant losses, except for a few of CBS's publishing-related units. Saddled with the worst acquisition record in my study, CBS has eroded the shareholder value created through its strong performance in broadcasting and records.

Moving from competitive strategy to corporate strategy is the business equivalent of passing through the Bermuda Triangle. The failure of corporate strategy reflects the fact that most diversified companies have failed to think in terms of how they really add value. A corporate strategy that truly enhances the competitive advantage of each business unit is the best defence against the corporate raider. With a sharper focus on the tests of diversification and the explicit choice of a clear concept of corporate strategy, companies' diversification track records from now on can look a lot different.

---

[1] Unless, of course, there is a second layer of divisionalization, which simply takes this conclusion down another level in the hierarchy.

[2] It should be noted that this is in fact the definition of a functional structure: Each activity contributes just one step in a chain toward the creation of the final product. Thus, for example, engineering is a functionally organized unit in the firm that produces and markets its own designs, while it would be a market organized unit in a consulting firm that sells its design services, among other, directly to clients.

[3] I wrote this example here somewhat whimsically before I encountered a firm in Finland with divisions that actually produce, among other things, the world's largest icebreaker ships and fine pottery!

[4] The example of Beatrice was first written as presented here in the 1970s, when the company was the subject of a good deal of attention and praise in the business press. At the time of this revision, in 1988, the company is being dis assembled. It seemed appropriate to leave the example as first presented, among other reasons to question the tendency to favour fashion over investigation in the business press.

[5] MacMillan refers to the business redefinition strategy as 'reshaping the industry infrastructure' (1983: 18), while Porter calls it 'reconfiguration' (1985: 518–23), although his notion of product *substitution* (273–314) could sometimes also constitute a form of business redefinition.

[6] Our suspicion, we should note, is that such labels often emerge after the fact, as the organization seeks a way to rationalize the diversification that has already taken place. In effect, the strategy is emergent.

[7] Some recent evidence also supports the conclusion that acquired companies often suffer eroding performance after acquisition. See Frederick M. Scherer, 'Mergers, sell-offs and managerial behavior', in *The Economics of Strategic Planning*, ed. Lacy Glenn Thomas (Lexington, MA: Lexington Books, 1986), p. 143, and David A. Ravenscraft and Frederick M. Scherer, 'Mergers and managerial performance', paper presented at the Conference on Takeovers and Contests for Corporate Control, Columbia Law School, 1985.

THE PROFESSIONAL CONTEXT

While most large organizations draw on a variety of experts to get their jobs done, there has been a growing interest in recent years in those organizations whose work, because it is highly complex, is organized primarily around experts. These range from hospitals, universities and research centres to consulting firms, space agencies and biomedical companies.

This context is a rather unusual one, at least when judged against the more traditional contexts discussed in previous chapters. Both its strategic processes and its structures tend to take on forms quite different from those presented earlier. Organizations of experts, in fact, seem to divide themselves into two somewhat different contexts. In one, the experts work in rapidly changing situations that demand a good deal of collaborative innovation (as in the biotechnology or semiconductor fields); in the other, experts work more or less alone in more stable situations involving slower-changing bodies of skill or knowledge (as in law, university teaching and accounting). This chapter takes up the latter, under the label of the 'professional' context; the next chapter discusses the former under the label of 'innovation'.

We open this chapter with a description of the type of organization that seems best suited to the context of the more stable application of expertise. Taken from Mintzberg's work, primarily his original description of 'professional bureaucracy', it looks at the structure of the professional organization, including its important characteristic of 'pigeonholing' work, the management of professionals, the unusual nature of strategy in such organizations (drawing from a paper Mintzberg co-authored with Cynthia Hardy, Ann Langley and Janet Rose), and some issues associated with these organizations.

The second reading in this chapter, published in the *Sloan Management Review* and written by David Maister, focuses on one particular instance of the professional context, but one that has become an increasingly important career option for management students: the professional service firm. Maister describes how companies in businesses like consulting, investment banking, accounting, achitecture and law manage the interactions between revenue generation, compensation and staffing to ensure long-term balanced growth.

Overall, these two readings suggest that the traditional concepts of managing and organization simply do not work as we move away from conventional mass production – which has long served as the model for 'one best way' concepts in management. Whether it be highly expert work in general or service work subjected to new technologies and skills in particular, our thinking has to be opened up to some very different needs. Peter Drucker has, in a widely discussed article ('The coming of the new organization', *Harvard Business Review*, Jan.–Feb. 1988), argued the case that work in general is becoming more skilled and so structures of organizations in general are moving towards what we would call the professional form. While we would not go that far – we maintain our 'contingency' view of different needs for different contexts – we do believe this is becoming a much more important form of organization.

● THE PROFESSIONAL ORGANIZATION*

HENRY MINTZBERG

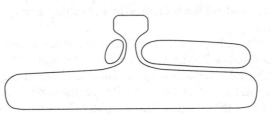

An organization can be bureaucratic without being centralized. This happens when its works is complex, requiring that it be carried out and controlled by professionals, yet at the same time remains stable, so that the skills of those professionals can be perfected through standardized operating programmes. The structure takes on the form of *professional* bureaucracy, which is common in universities, general hospitals, public accounting firms, social work agencies and firms doing fairly routine engineering or craft work. All rely on the skills and knowledge of their operating professionals to function; all produce standardized products or services.

* Adapted from *The Structuring of Organizations* (Prentice Hall, 1979), Ch. 19 on 'The professional bureaucracy'; also *Power In and Around Organizations* (Prentice Hall, 1983), Ch. 22 on 'The meritocracy'; the material on strategy formation from 'Strategy formation in the university setting', co-authored with Cynthia Hardy, Ann Langley and Janet Rose, in J. L. Bess (ed.) *College and University Organization* (New York University Press, 1984). A chapter similar to this one appeared in *Mintzberg on Management: Inside Our Strange World of Organizations* (Free Press, 1989).

The Work of the Professional Operators

Here again we have a tightly knit configuration of the attributes of structure. Most important, the professional organization relies for coordination on the standardization of skills, which is achieved primarily through formal training. It hires duly trained specialists – professionals – for the operating core, then gives them considerable control over their own work.

Control over their work means that professionals work relatively independently of their colleagues but closely with the clients they serve – doctors treating their own patients and accountants who maintain personal contact with the companies whose books they audit. Most of the necessary coordination among the operating professionals is then handled automatically by their set skills and knowledge – in effect, by what they have learned to expect from each other. During an operation as long and as complex as open-heart surgery, 'very little needs to be said [between the anaesthesiologist and the surgeon] preceding chest opening and during the procedure on the heart itself... [most of the operation is] performed in absolute silence' (Gosselin, 1978). The point is perhaps best made in reverse by the cartoon that shows six surgeons standing around a patient on an operating table with one saying, 'Who opens?'

Just how standardized the complex work of professionals can be is illustrated in a paper read by Spencer before a meeting of the International Cardiovascular Society. Spencer notes that an important feature of surgical training is 'repetitive practice' to evoke 'an automatic reflex'. So automatic, in fact, that this doctor keeps a series of surgical 'cookbooks' in which he lists, even for 'complex' operations, the essential steps as chains of 30–40 symbols on a single sheet, to 'be reviewed mentally in sixty to 120 seconds at some time during the day preceding the operation' (1976: 1179, 1182).

But no matter how standardized the knowledge and skills, their complexity ensures that considerable discretion remains in their application. No two professionals – no two surgeons or engineers or social workers – ever apply them in exactly the same way. Many judgements are required.

Training, reinforced by indoctrination, is a complicated affair in the professional organization. The initial training typically takes place over a period of years in a university or special institution, during which the skills and knowledge of the profession are formally programmed into the students. There typically follows a long period of on-the-job training, such as being a junior register in medicine or articling in accounting, where the formal knowledge is applied and the practice of skills perfected. On-the-job training also completes the process of indoctrination, which began during the formal education. As new knowledge is generated and new skills develop, of course (so it is hoped) the professional upgrades his or her expertise.

All that training is geared to one goal, the internalization of the set procedures, which is what makes the structure technically bureaucratic (structure defined earlier as relying on standardization for coordination). But the professional bureaucracy differs markedly from the machine bureaucracy. Whereas the latter generates its own standards – through its technostructure, enforced by its line managers – many of the standards of the professional bureaucracy originate outside its own structure, in the self-governing associations its professionals belong to with their colleagues from other institutions. These associations set universal standards, which they ensure are taught by the universities and are used by all the organizations practising the profession. So whereas the machine bureaucracy relies on authority of a hierarchical nature – the power of office – the professional bureaucracy emphasizes authority of a professional nature – the power of expertise.

Other forms of standardization are, in fact, difficult to rely on in the professional organization. The work processes themselves are too complex to be standardized directly by analysts. One need only try to imagine a work-study analyst following a cardiologist on rounds or timing the activities of a teacher in a classroom. Similarly, the outputs of professional work cannot easily be measured and so do not lend themselves to standardization. Imagine a planner trying to define a cure in psychiatry, the amount of learning that takes place in a classroom, or the quality of an accountant's audit. Likewise, direct supervision and mutual adjustment cannot be relied upon for coordination, for both impede professional autonomy.

The Pigeonholing Process

To understand how the professional organization functions at the operating level, it is helpful to think of it as a set of standard programmes – in effect, the repertoire of skills the professionals stand ready to use – that are applied to known situations, called contingencies, also standardized. As Weick notes of one case in point, 'schools are in the business of building and maintaining categories' (1976: 8). The process is sometimes known as *pigeonholing*. In this regard, the professional has two basic tasks: (1) to categorize, or 'diagnose', the client's need in terms of one of the contingencies, which indicates which standard programme to apply, and (2) to apply, or execute, that programme. For example, the management consultant carries a bag of standard acronymic tricks: MBO, MIS, LRP, OD. The client with information needs gets MIS; the one with managerial conflicts, OD. Such pigeonholing, of course, simplifies matters enormously; it is also what enables each professional to work in a relatively autonomous manner.

It is in the pigeonholing process that the fundamental differences among the machine organization, the professional organization and the innovative organization (to be discussed next) can best be seen. The machine organization is a single-purpose structure. Presented with a stimulus, it executes its one standard sequence of programmes, just as we kick when tapped on the knee. No diagnosis is involved. In the professional organization, diagnosis is a fundamental task, but one highly circumscribed. The organization seeks to match a predetermined contingency to a standardized programme. Fully open-ended diagnosis – that which seeks a creative solution to a unique problem – requires the innovative form of organization. No standard contingencies or programmes can be relied upon there.

The Administrative Structure

Everything we have discussed so far suggests that the operating core is the key part of the professional organization. The only other part that is fully elaborated is the support staff, but that is focused very much on serving the activities of the operating core. Given the high cost of the professionals, it makes sense to back them up with as much support as possible. Thus, universities have printing facilities, faculty clubs, alma mater funds, publishing houses, archives, libraries, computer facilities and many, many other support units.

The technostructure and middle-line management are not highly elaborated in the professional organization. They can do little to coordinate the professional work. Moreover, with so little need for direct supervision of, or mutual adjustment among, the professionals, the operating units can be very large. For example, the McGill Faculty of Management functions effectively with 50 professors under a single manager, its dean, and the rest of the university's academic hierarchy is likewise thin.

Thus, the diagram at the beginning of this chapter shows the professional organization, in terms of our logo, as a flat structure with a thin middle line, a tiny technostructure, but a fully elaborated support staff. All these characteristics are reflected in the organigram of a university hospital, shown in Figure 1.

Coordination within the administrative structure is another matter, however. Because these configurations are so decentralized, the professionals not only control their own work but they also gain much collective control over the administrative decisions that affect them – decisions, for example, to hire colleagues, to promote them and to distribute resources. This they do partly by doing some of the administrative work themselves (most university professors, for example, sit on various administrative committees) and partly by ensuring that important administrative posts are staffed by professionals or at least sympathetic people appointed with the professionals' blessing. What emerges, therefore, is a rather democratic administrative structure. But because the administrative work requires mutual adjustment for coordination among the various people involved, task forces and especially standing committees abound at this level, as is in fact suggested in Figure 1.

Because of the power of their professional operators, these organizations are sometimes described as inverse pyramids, with the professional operators on top and the administrators down below to serve them – to ensure that the surgical facilities are kept clean and the classrooms well supplied with chalk. Such a description slights the power of the administrators of professional work, however, although it may be an accurate description of those who manage the support units. For the support staff – often more numerous than the professional staff, but generally less skilled – there is no democracy in the professional organization, only the oligarchy of the professionals. Such support units as housekeeping in the hospital or printing in the university are likely to be managed tightly from the top, in effect as machinelike enclaves within the professional configuration. Thus, what frequently emerges in the professional organization are parallel and separate administrative hierarchies, one democratic and bottom-up for the professionals, a second machinelike and top-down for the support staff.

The Roles of the Administrators of Professional Work

Where does all this leave the administrators of the professional hierarchy, the executive directors and chiefs of the hospitals and the presidents and deans of the universities? Are they powerless? Compared with their counterparts in the entrepreneurial and machine organizations, they certainly lack a good deal of power. But that is far from the whole story. The administrator of professional work may not be able to control

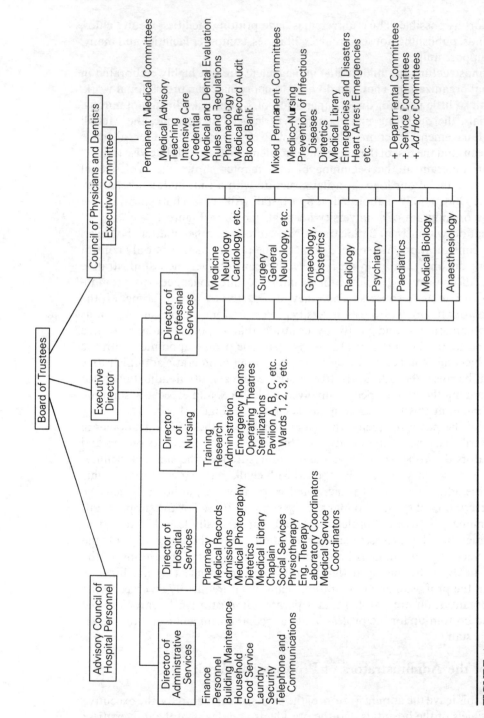

FIGURE 1
Organization of a university hospital

Board of Trustees

Advisory Council of Hospital Personnel

Council of Physicians and Dentists
Executive Committee

Executive Director

Director of Administrative Services

Finance
Personnel
Building Maintenance
Household
Food Service
Laundry
Security
Telephone and Communications

Director of Hospital Services

Pharmacy
Medical Records
Admissions
Medical Photography
Dietetics
Medical Library
Chaplain
Social Services
Physiotherapy
Eng. Therapy
Laboratory Coordinators
Medical Service Coordinators

Director of Nursing

Training
Research
Administration
Emergency Rooms
Operating Theatres
Sterilizations
Pavilion A, B, C, etc.
Wards 1, 2, 3, etc.

Director of Professinal Services

Medicine
Neurology
Cardiology, etc.

Surgery
General
Neurology, etc.

Gynaecology,
Obstetrics

Radiology

Psychiatry

Paediatrics

Medical Biology

Anaesthesiology

Permanent Medical Committees

Medical Advisory
Teaching
Intensive Care
Credential
Medical and Dental Evaluation
Rules and Regulations
Pharmacology
Medical Record Audit
Blood Bank

Mixed Permanent Committees

Medico-Nursing
Prevention of Infectious Diseases
Dietetics
Medical Library
Emergencies and Disasters
Heart Arrest Emergencies
etc.

+ Departmental Committees
+ Service Committees
+ *Ad Hoc* Committees

the professionals directly, but he or she does perform a series of roles that can provide considerable indirect power.

First, this administrator spends much time handling disturbances in the structure. The pigeonholing process is an imperfect one at best, leading to all kinds of jurisdictional disputes between the professionals. Who should perform mastectomies in the hospitals, surgeons who look after cutting or gynaecologists who look after women? Seldom, however, can one administrator impose a solution on the professionals involved in a dispute. Rather, various administrators must often sit down together and negotiate a solution on behalf of their constituencies.

Second, the administrators of professional work – especially those at higher levels – serve in key roles at the boundary of the organization, between the professionals inside and the influencers outside: governments, client associations, benefactors, and so on. On the one hand, the administrators are expected to protect the professionals' autonomy, to 'buffer' them from external pressures. On the other hand, they are expected to woo those outsiders to support the organization, both morally and financially. And that often leads the outsiders to expect these administrators, in turn, to control the professions, in machine bureaucratic ways. Thus, the external roles of the manager – maintaining liaison contacts, acting as figurehead and spokesman in a public relations capacity, negotiating with outside agencies – emerge as primary ones in the administration of professional work.

Some view the roles these administrators are called upon to perform as signs of weakness. They see these people as the errand boys of the professionals, or else as pawns caught in various tugs of war – between one professional and another, between support staffer and professional, between outsider and professional. In fact, however, these roles are the very sources of administrators' power. Power is, after all, gained at the locus of uncertainty, and that is exactly where the administrators of professionals sit. The administrator who succeeds in raising extra funds for his or her organization gains a say in how they are distributed; the one who can reconcile conflicts in favour of his or her unit or who can effectively buffer the professionals from external influence becomes a valued, and therefore powerful, member of the organization.

We can conclude that power in these structures does flow to those professionals who care to devote effort to doing administrative instead of professional work, so long as they do it well. But that, it should be stressed, is not *laissez-faire* power; the professional administrator maintains power only as long as the professionals perceive him or her to be serving their interests effectively.

CONDITIONS OF THE PROFESSIONAL ORGANIZATION

The professional form of organization appears wherever the operating work of an organization is dominated by skilled workers who use procedures that are difficult to learn yet are well defined. This means a situation that is both complex and stable – complex enough to require procedures that can be learned only through extensive training yet stable enough so that their use can become standardized.

Note that an elaborate technical system can work against this configuration. If highly regulating or automated, the professionals' skills might be amenable to rationalization, in other words, to be divided into simple, highly programmed steps that would destroy the basis for professional autonomy and thereby drive the structure to the machine form. And if highly complicated, the technical system would reduce the professionals' autonomy by forcing them to work in multidisciplinary teams, thereby driving the organization toward the innovative form. Thus the surgeon uses a scalpel, and the accountant a pencil. Both must be sharp, but both are otherwise simple and commonplace instruments. Yet both allow their users to perform independently what can be exceedingly complex functions.

The prime example of the professional configuration is the personal service organization, at least the one with complex, stable work not reliant on a fancy technical system. Schools and universities, consulting firms, law and accounting offices and social work agencies all rely on this form of organization, more or less, so long as they concentrate not on innovating in the solution of new problems but on applying standard programmes to well-defined ones. The same seems to be true of hospitals, at least to the extent that their technical systems are simple. (In those areas that call for more sophisticated equipment – apparently a growing number, especially in teaching institutions – the hospital is driven towards a hybrid structure, with characteristics of the innovative form. But this tendency is mitigated by the hospital's overriding concern with safety. Only the tried and true can be relied upon, which produces a natural aversion to the looser, innovative configuration.)

So far, our examples have come from the service sector. But the professional form can be found in manufacturing too, where the above conditions hold up. Such is the case of the craft enterprise, for example, the factory using skilled workers to produce ceramic products. The very term *craftsman* implies a kind of professional who learns traditional skills through long apprentice training and then is allowed to practise them free of direct supervision. Craft enterprises seem typically to have few administrators, who tend to work, in any event, alongside the operating personnel. The same would seem to be true for engineering work oriented not to creative design so much as to modification of existing dominant designs.

STRATEGY FORMATION IN THE PROFESSIONAL ORGANIZATION

It is commonly assumed that strategies are formulated before they are implemented, that planning is the central process of formulation, and that structures must be designed to implement these strategies. At least this is what one reads in the conventional literature of strategic management. In the professional organization, these imperatives stand almost totally at odds with what really happens, leading to the conclusion either that such organizations are confused about how to make strategy, or else that the strategy writers are confused about how professional organizations must function. I subscribe to the latter explanation.

Using the definition of strategy as pattern in action, strategy formation in the professional organization takes on a new meaning. Rather than simply throwing up our hands at its resistance to formal strategic planning, or, at the other extreme, dismissing professional organizations, as 'organized anarchies' with strategy-making processes as mere 'garbage cans' (March and Olsen, 1976) we can focus on how decisions and actions in such organizations order themselves into patterns over time.

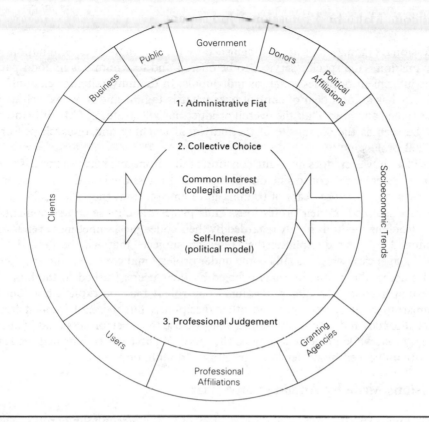

FIGURE 1
Three levels of decision-making in the professional organization

Taking strategy as pattern in action, the obvious question becomes, which actions? The key area of strategy-making in most organizations concerns the elaboration of the basic mission (the products or services offered to the public); in professional organizations, we shall argue, this is significantly controlled by individual professionals. Other important areas of strategy here include the inputs to the system (notably the choice of professional staff, the determination of clients and the raising of external funds), the means to perform the mission (the construction of buildings and facilities, the purchase of research equipment, and so on), the structure and forms of governance (design of the committee system, the hierarchies, and so on), and the various means to support the mission.

Were professional organizations to formulate strategies in the conventional ways, central administrators would develop detailed and integrated plans about these issues. This sometimes happens, but in a very limited number of cases. Many strategic issues come under the direct control of individual professionals, while others can be decided neither by individual professionals nor by central administrators, but instead require the participation of a variety of people in a complex collective process. As illustrated in Figure 2, we examine in turn the decisions controlled by individual professionals, by central administrators and by the collectivity.

Decisions Make by Professional Judgement

Professional organizations are distinguished by the fact that the determination of the basic mission – the specific services to be offered and to whom – is in good part left to the judgement of professionals as individuals. In the university, for example, each professor has a good deal of control over what is taught and how, as well as what is researched and how. Thus the overall product-market strategy of McGill University must be seen as the composite of the individual teaching and research postures of its 1,200 professors.

That, however, does not quite constitute full autonomy, because there is a subtle but not insignificant constraint on that power. Professionals are left to decide on their own only because years of training have ensured that they will decide in ways generally accepted in their professions. Thus professors choose course contents and adopt teaching methods highly regarded by their colleagues, sometimes even formally sanctioned by their disciplines; they research subjects that will be funded by the granting agencies (which usually come under professional controls); and they publish articles acceptable to the journals refereed by their peers. Pushed to the limit, then, individual freedom becomes professional control. It may be explicit freedom from administrators, even from peers in other disciplines, but it is not implicit freedom from colleagues in their own discipline. Thus we use the label 'professional judgement' to imply that while judgement may be the mode of choice, it is informed judgement, mightily influenced by professional training and affiliation.

Decisions Made by Administrative Fiat

Professional expertise and autonomy, reinforced by the pigeonholing process, sharply circumscribe the capacity of central administrators to manage the professionals in the ways of conventional bureaucracy – through direct supervision and the designation of internal standards (rules, job descriptions, policies). Even the designation of standards of output or performance is discouraged by the intractable problem of operationalizing the goals of professional work.

Certain types of decisions, less related to the professional work *per se*, do however fall into the realm of what can be called administrative fiat, in other words, become the exclusive prerogative of the administrators. They include some financial decisions, for example, to buy and sell property and embark on fund raising campaigns. Because many of the support services are organized in a conventional top-down hierarchy, they too tend to fall under the control of the central administration. Support services more critical to professional matters, however, such as libraries or computers in the universities, tend to fall into the realm of collective decision-making, where the central administrators join the professionals in the making of choice.

Central administrators may also play a prominent role in determining the procedures by which the collective process functions: what committees exist, who gets nominated to them, and so on. It is the administrators, after all, who have the time to devote to administration. This role can give skilful administrators considerable influence, however indirect, over the decisions made by others. In addition, in times of crisis, administrators may acquire more extensive powers, as the professionals become more inclined to defer to leadership to resolve the issues.

Decisions Make by Collective Choice

Many decisions are, however, determined neither by administrators nor by individual professionals. Instead they are handled in interactive processes which combine professionals with administrators from a variety of levels and units. Among the most important of these decisions seem to be ones related to the definition, creation, design and discontinuation of the pigeonholes, that is, the programmes and departments of various kinds. Other important decisions here include the hiring and promotion of professionals and, in some cases, budgeting and the establishment and design of the interactive procedures themselves (if they do not fall under administrative fiat).

Decision-making may be considered to involve the three phases of *identification* of the need for a decision, *development* of solutions and *selection* of one of them. Identification seems to depend largely on individual initiative. Given the complexities of professional work and the rigidities of pigeonholding, change in this configuration is difficult to imagine with an initiating 'sponsor' or 'champion'. Development may involve the same individual but often requires the efforts of collective task forces as well. And selection tends to be a fully interactive process, involving several layers of standing commiittees composed of professionals and administrators, and sometimes outsiders as well (such as government representatives). It is in this last phase that we find the full impact and complexity of mutual adjustment in the administration of professional organizations.

Models of Collective Choice

How do these interactive processes in fact work? Some writers have traditionally associated professional organizations with a *collegial* model, where decisions are made by a 'community of individuals and groups, all of whom may have different roles and specialties, but who share common goals and objectives for the organization' (Taylor, 1983: 18). *Common interest* is the guiding force, and decision-making is therefore by consensus. Other writers instead propose a *political* model, in which the differences of interest groups are irreconcilable. Participants thus seek to serve their *self-interest*, and political factors become instrumental in determining outcomes.

Clearly, neither common interest nor self-interest will dominate decision processes all the time; some combination is naturally to be expected. Professionals may agree on goals yet conflict over how they should be achieved; alternatively, consensus can sometimes be achieved even where goals differ – Democrats do, after all, sometimes vote with Republicans in the US Congress. In fact, we need to consider motivation, not just behaviour, in order to distinguish collegiality from politics. Political success sometimes requires a collegial posture – one must cloak self-interest in the mantle of the common good. Likewise, collegial ends sometimes require political means. Thus, we should take as collegial any behaviour that is *motivated* by a genuine concern for the good of the institution, and politics as any behaviour driven fundamentally by self-interest (of the individual or his or her unit).

A third model that has been used to explain decision-making in universities is the *garbage can.* Here decision-making is characterized by 'collections of choices looking for problems, issues and feelings looking for decision situations in which they may be aired, solutions looking for issues to which they might be an answer, and decision makers looking for work' (Cohen, March and Olsen, 1972: 1). Behaviour is, in other words, non-purposeful and often random, because goals are unclear and the means to achieve them problematic. Furthermore, participation is fluid because of the cost of time and energy. Thus, in place of the common interest of the collegial model and the self-interest of the political model, the garbage can model suggests a kind of *disinterest*.

The important question is not whether garbage can processes exist – we have all experienced them – but whether they matter. Do they apply to key issues or only to incidental ones? Of course, decisions that are not significant to anyone may well end up in the garbage can, so to speak. There is always someone with free time willing to challenge a proposal for the sake of so doing. But I have difficulty accepting that individuals to whom decisions are important do not invest the effort necessary to influence them. Thus, like common interest and self-interest, I conclude that disinterest neither dominates decision processes nor is absent from them.

Finally, *analysis* may be considered a fourth model of decision-making. Here calculation is used, if not to select the best alternative, then at least to assess the acceptability of different ones. Such an approach seems consistent with the machine configuration, where a technostructure stands ready to calculate the costs and benefits of every proposal. But, in fact, analysis figures prominently in the professional configuration too, but here carried out mostly by professional operators themselves. Rational analysis structures arguments for communication and debate and enables champions and their opponents to support their respective positions. In fact, as each side seeks to pick holes in the position of the other, the real issues are more likely to emerge.

Thus, as indicated in Figure 2, the important collective decisions of the professional organization seem to be most influenced by collegial and political processes, with garbage can pressures encouraging a kind of haphazardness on one side (especially for less important decisions) and analytical interventions on the other side encouraging a certain rationality (serving as an invisible hand to keep the lid on the garbage can, so to speak!).

Strategies in the Professional Organization

Thus, we find here a very different process of strategy-making, and very different resulting strategies, compared with conventional (especially machine) organizations. While it may seem difficult to create strategies in these organizations, due to the fragmentation of activity, the politics and the garbage can phenomenon, in fact the professional organization is inundated with strategies (meaning patterning in its actions). The standardization of skills encourages patterning, as do the pigeonholing process and the professional affiliations. Collegiality promotes consistency of behaviour; even politics works to resist changing existing patterns. As for the garbage can model, perhaps it just represents the unexplained variance in the system; that is, whatever is not understood looks to the outside observer like organized anarchy.

Many different people get involved in the strategy-making process here, including administrators and the various professionals, individually and collectively, so that the resulting strategies can be very fragmented (at the limit, each professional pursues his or her own product-market strategy). There are, of course, forces that encourage some overall cohesion in strategy too: the common forces of administrative fiat, the broad negotiations that take place in the collective process (for example, on new tenure regulations in a university), even the forces of habit and tradition, at the limit ideology, that can pervade a professional organization (such as hiring certain kinds of people or favouring certain styles of teaching or of surgery).

Overall, the strategies of the professional organization tend to exhibit a remarkable degree of stability. Major reorientations in strategy – 'strategic revolutions' – are discouraged by the fragmentation of activity and the influence of the individual professionals and their outside associates. But at a narrower level, change is ubiquitous. Inside tiny pigeonholes, services are continually being altered, procedure redesigned and clientele shifted, while in the collective process, pigeonholes are constantly being added and rearranged. Thus, the professional organization is, paradoxically, extremely stable at the broadest level and in a state of perpetual change at the narrowest one.

SOME ISSUES ASSOCIATED WITH THE PROFESSIONAL ORGANIZATION

The professional organization is unique among the different configurations in answering two of the paramount needs of contemporary men and women. It is democratic, disseminating its power directly to its workers (at least those lucky enough to be professional). And it provides them with extensive autonomy, freeing them even from the need to coordinate closely with their colleagues. Thus, the professional has the best of both worlds. He or she is attached to an organization yet is free to serve clients in his or her own way, constrained only by the established standards of the profession.

The result is that professionals tend to emerge as highly motivated individuals, dedicated to their work and to the clients they serve. Unlike the machine organization, which places barriers between the operator and the client, this configuration removes them, allowing a personal relationship to develop. Moreover, autonomy enables the professionals to perfect their skills free of interference, as they repeat the same complex programmes time after time.

But in these same characteristics, democracy and autonomy, lie the chief problems of the professional organization. For there is no evident way to control the work, outside of that exercised by the profession itself, no way to correct deficiencies that the professionals choose to overlook. What they tend to overlook are the problems of coordination, of discretion and of innovation that arise in these configurations.

Problems of Coordination

The professional organization can coordinate effectively in its operating core only by relying on the standardization of skills. But that is a loose coordinating mechanism at best; it fails to cope with many of the needs that arise in these organizations. One need is to coordinate the work of professionals with that of support staffs. The professionals want to give the orders. But that can catch the support staffs between the vertical power of line authority and the horizontal power of professional expertise. Another need is to achieve overriding coordination among the professionals themselves. Professional organizations, at the limit, may be viewed as collections of independent individuals who come together only to draw on common resources and support services. Though the pigeonholing process facilitates this, some things inevitably fall through the cracks between the pigeonholes. But because the professional organization lacks any obvious coordinating mechanism to deal with these, they inevitably provoke a great deal of conflict. Much political blood is spilled in the continual reassessment of contingencies and programmes that are either imperfectly conceived or artificially distinguished.

Problems of Discretion

Pigeonholing raises another serious problem. It focuses most of the discretion in the hands of single professionals, whose complex skills, no matter how standardized, require the exercise of considerable judgement. Such discretion works fine when professionals are competent and conscientious. But it plays havoc when they are not. Inevitably, some professionals are simply lazy or incompetent. Others confuse the needs of their clients with the skills of their trade. They thus concentrate on a favoured programme to the exclusion of all others (like the psychiatrist who thinks that all patients, indeed all people, need psychoanalysis). Clients incorrectly sent their way get mistreated (in both senses of that word).

Various factors confound efforts to deal with this inversion of means and ends. One is that professionals are notoriously reluctant to act against their own, for example, to censure irresponsible behaviour through their professional associations. Another (which perhaps helps to explain the first) is the intrinsic difficulty of measuring the outputs of professional work. When psychiatrists cannot even define the words *cure* or *healthy*, how are they to prove that psychoanalysis is better for schizophrenics than is chemical therapy?

Discretion allows professionals to ignore not only the needs of their clients but also those of the organization itself. Many professionals focus their loyalty on their profession, not on the place where they happen to practise it. But professional organizations have needs for loyalty too – to support their overall strategies, to staff their administrative committees, to see them through conflicts with the professional associations. Cooperation is crucial to the functioning of the administrative structure, yet many professionals resist it furiously.

Problems of Innovation

In the professional organization, major innovation also depends on cooperation. Existing programmes may be perfected by the single professional, but new ones usually cut across the established specialties – in essence, they require a rearrangement of the pigeonholes – and so call for collective action. As a result, the reluctance of the professionals to cooperate with each other and the complexity of the collective processes can produce resistance to innovation. These are, after all, professional *bureaucracies*, in essence, performance structures designed to perfect given programmes in stable environments, not problem-solving structures to create new programmes for unanticipated needs.

The problems of innovation in the professional organization find their roots in convergent thinking, in the deductive reasoning of the professional who sees the specific situation in terms of the general concept. That means new problems are forced into old pigeonholes, as is excellently illustrated in Spencer's comments: 'All patients developing significant complications or death among our three hospitals ... are reported to a central office with a narrative description of the sequence of events, with reports varying in length from a third to an entire page.' And six to eight of these cases are discussed in the one-hour weekly 'mortality–morbidity' conferences, including presentation of it by the surgeon and 'questions and comments' by the audience (1976: 1181). An 'entire' page and 10 minutes of discussion for a case with 'significant complications'! Maybe that is enough to list the symptoms and slot them into pigeonholes. But it is hardly enough even to begin to think about creative solutions. As Lucy once told Charlie Brown, great art cannot be done in half an hour; it takes at least 45 minutes!

The fact is that great art and innovative problem solving require *inductive* reasoning – that is, the inference of the new general solution from the particular experience. And that kind of thinking is *divergent*: it breaks away from old routines or standards rather than perfecting existing ones. And that flies in the face of everything the professional organization is designed to do.

Public Responses to These Problems

What responses do the problems of coordination, discretion and innovation evoke? Most commonly, those outside the profession see the problems as resulting from a lack of external control of the professional and the profession. So they do the obvious: try to control the work through other, more traditional means. One is direct supervision, which typically means imposing an intermediate level of supervision to watch over the professionals. But we have already discussed why this cannot work for jobs that are complex. Another is to try to standardize the work or its outputs. But we also discussed why complex work cannot be formalized by rules, regulations or measures of performance. All these types of controls really do, by transferring the responsibility for the service from the professional to the administrative structure, is destroy the effectiveness of the work. It is not the government that educates the student, not even the school system or the school itself; it is not the hospital that delivers the baby. These things are done by the individual professional. If that professional is incompetent, no plan or rule fashioned in the technostructure, no order from any administrator or government official, can ever make him or her competent. But such plans, rules, and orders can impede the competent professional from providing his or her service effectively.

Are there then no solutions for a society concerned about the performance of its professional organizations? Financial control of them and legislation against irresponsible professional behaviour are obviously in order. But beyond that, solutions must grow from a recognition of professional work for what it is. Change in the professional organization does not *sweep* in from new administrators taking office to announce wide reforms, or from government officials intent on bringing the professionals under technocratic control. Rather, change *seeps* in through the slow process of changing the professionals – changing who enters the profession in the first place, what they learn in its professional schools (norms as well as skills and knowledge), and thereafter how they upgrade their skills. Where desired changes are resisted, society may be best off to call on its professionals' sense of public responsibility or, failing that, to bring pressure on the professional associations rather than on the professional bureaucracies.

• BALANCING THE PROFESSIONAL SERVICE FIRM*

DAVID H. MAISTER

The topic of managing professional service firms [PSF] (including law, consulting, investment banking, accountancy, architecture, engineering and others) has been relatively neglected by management researchers. ... Yet in recent years large (if not giant) PSFs have emerged in most of the professional service industries. ...

The professional service firm is the ultimate embodiment of that familiar phrase 'our assets are our people'. Frequently, a PSF tends to sell to its clients the services of particular individuals (or a team of such individuals) more than the services of the firm. Professional services usually involve a high degree of interaction with the client, together with a high degree of customization. Both of these characteristics demand that the firm attract (and retain) highly skilled individuals. The PSF, therefore, competes in two markets simultaneously: the 'output' market for its services and the 'input' market for its productive resources – the professional workforce. It is the need to balance the often conflicting demands and constraints imposed by these two markets that constitutes the special challenge for managers of the professional service firm.

This [reading] explores the interaction of these forces inside the professional service firm, and examines some of the major variables that firm management can attempt to manipulate in order to bring these forces into balance. The framework employed for this examination is shown in Figure 1, which illustrates the proposition that balancing the demands of the two markets is accomplished through the firm's economic and organizational structures. All four of these elements – the two markets and the two structures – are tightly interrelated. By examining each in turn, we shall attempt to identify the major variables which form the links shown in Figure 1. First [we shall] examine the typical organizational structure of the firm; second, [we shall] explore the economic structure and its relation to other elements. [We] shall then consider the market for professional labour, and finally discuss the market for the firm's services. As we shall see, successful PSF management is a question of balance among the four elements of Figure 1.

* Originally published in *Sloan Management Review* (Autumn 1982). Copyright © Sloan Management Review Association 1982. Reproduced with deletions by permission of the *Review*.

THE ORGANIZATIONAL STRUCTURE OF THE PSF

The archetypal structure of the professional service firm is an organization containing three professional levels which serve as a normal or expected career path. In a consulting organization, these levels might be labelled junior consultant, manager and vice-president. In a CPA firm they might be referred to as staff accountant, manager, and partner. Law firms tend to have only two levels, associate and partner, although there is an increasing tendency in large law firms to recognize formally what has long been an informal distinction between junior and senior partners. Whatever the precise structure, nearly all PSFs have the pyramid form shown in Figure 2.

There is nothing magical about the common occurrence of three levels (a greater or lesser number may be found), but it is instructive to consider other organizations that have this pattern. One example is the university which has assistant professors,

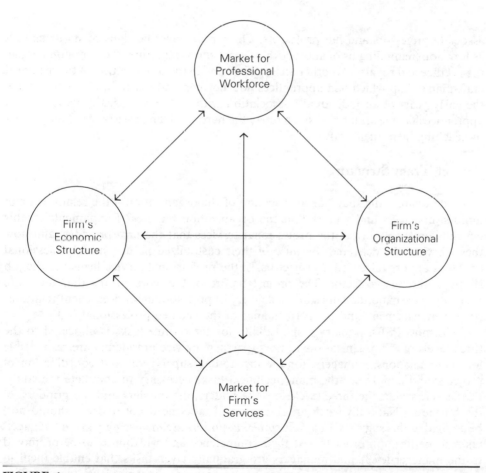

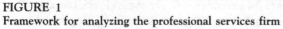

FIGURE 1
Framework for analyzing the professional services firm

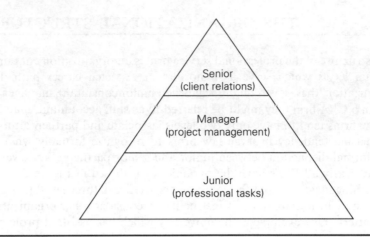

FIGURE 2
The professional pyramid

associate professors and full professors. These ranks may be signs of status as well as function (reminding us of another three-level status structure: the common people, the peerage and royalty). Another analogy is found in the organization of the medieval craftsman's shop which had apprentices, journeymen and master craftsmen. Indeed, the early years of an individual's association with a PSF are usually viewed as an apprenticeship: the senior craftsmen repay the hard work and assistance of the juniors by teaching them their craft.

Project Team Structure

What determines the shape or architecture of the organization – the relative mix of juniors, managers and seniors that the organization requires? Fundamentally, this depends on the nature of the professional services that the firm provides, and how these services are delivered. Because of their customized nature, most professional activities are organized on a project basis: the professional service firms are the job shops of the service sector. The project nature of the work means that there are basically three major activities in the delivery of professional services: client relations, project management, and the performance of the detailed professional tasks.

In most PSFs, primary responsibility for these three tasks is allocated to the three levels of the organization: seniors (partners or vice-presidents) are responsible for client relations; managers, for the day-to-day supervision and coordination of projects; and juniors, for the many technical tasks necessary to complete the study. In the vernacular, the three levels are 'the finders, the minders and the grinders' of the business.[1] Naturally, such an allocation of tasks need not (indeed, should not) be as rigid as this suggests. In a well-run PSF, juniors are increasingly given 'manager' tasks to perform (in order to test their competence and worthiness to be promoted to the manager level), and managers are gradually given tasks that enable them to develop client relations skills to prepare for promotion to the senior level. Nevertheless, it is still meaningful to talk of 'senior tasks', 'manager tasks' and 'junior tasks'.

Capacity Planning

The required shape of the PSF is thus primarily influenced by the mix of client relations, project management and professional tasks involved in the firm's projects. If the PSF is a job shop, then its professional staff members are its 'machines' (productive resources). As with any job shop, a balance must be established between the types of work performed and the number of different types of 'machines' (people) that are required. The PSF is a 'factory', and the firm must plan its capacity. ...

THE ECONOMICS OF THE PSF

Most professional service firms are partnerships; some are corporations. Regardless of the precise form, however, certain regularities in the economic structure are observable. For example, since most PSFs have few fixed assets, they only require capital to fund accounts receivable and other working capital items. Consequently, the vast majority of revenues are disbursed in the form of salaries, bonuses and net partnership profits. A typical division of revenues might be 33 per cent for professional salaries, 33 per cent for support staff and overheads, and 33 per cent for senior (or shareholder) salary compensation. However, in some PSFs, partnership salary and profits might rise to 50 per cent or more, usually corresponding to lower support staff and overhead costs.

Generating Revenues

If revenues are typically disbursed in this way, how are they generated? ... The relevant variable is, of course, the billing rate – the hourly charge to clients for the services of individuals at different levels of the hierarchy. The ratio between the lowest and highest rates ... in some firms it can exceed 3 or 4 to 1. ... The 'rewards of partnership' come only in part from the high rates that top professionals can charge their clients. Partners' rewards are also derived, in large part, from the firm's ability, through its project team structure, to leverage the professional skills of the seniors with the efforts of juniors. As the managing senior of a top consulting firm obsrved, 'How is it that a young MBA, straight from graduate school, can give advice to top corporate officers?' The answer lies in the synergy of the PSF's project team. Acting independently, the juniors could not 'bill out' the results of their efforts at the rates that can be charged by the PSF. The firm can obtain higher rates for the juniors' efforts because they are combined with the expertise and guidance of the seniors. ...

The Billing Multiple
It is also instructive to compare the net weighted billing rate to compensation levels within the firm. This (conventional) calculation is known as the billing multiple, and is calculated (for either the firm or an individual) as the billing rate per hour divided by the total compensation per hour. ... the average multiple for most firms is between 2.5 and 4.

The appropriate billing multiple that the firm can achieve will, of course, be influenced by the added value that the firm provides and by the relative supply and demand conditions for the firm's services. The market for the firm's services will determine the fees it can command for a given project. The firm's costs will be determined by its ability to deliver the service with a 'profitable' mix of junior, manager and senior time. ... However, if it can find a way to deliver the service with a higher proportion of juniors to seniors, it will be able to achieve lower costs and hence a higher multiple. The project team structure of the firm is, therefore, an important component of firm profitability.

The billing multiple is intimately related to the breakeven economics of the firm. If total professional salaries are taken as an amount \$Y, and support staff and overhead cost approximate, say, an equivalent amount \$Y, then breakeven will be attained when the firm bills \$2Y. This could be attained by charging clients a multiple of 2 for professional services, but only if all available time was billed out. If the firm wishes to break even at 50 per cent target utilization (a common figure in many PSFs), then the required net billing multiple will be 4. ...

THE PSF AND THE MARKET FOR PROFESSIONAL LABOUR

One of the key characteristics of the PSF is that the three levels (junior, manager, senior) constitute a well-defined career path. Individuals joining the organization normally begin at the bottom, with strong expectations of progressing through the organization at some pace agreed to (explicitly or implicitly) in advance. While this pace may not be a rigid one ('up or out in X years'), both the individual and the organization usually share strong expectations about what constitutes a reasonable period of time. Individuals that are not promoted within this period will seek greener pastures elsewhere, either by their own choice or career ambitions or at the strong suggestion of those who do not consider them promotable. Intermediate levels in the hierarchy are not considered by the individual or the organization as career positions. It is this characteristic, perhaps more than any other, that distinguishes the PSF from other types of organizations.

Promotion Policy

While there are many considerations that attract young professionals to a particular firm, career opportunities within the firm usually play a large role. Two dimensions of this rate of progress are important: the normal amount of time spent at each level before being considered for promotion and the 'odds of making it' (the proportion promoted). These promotion policy variables perform an important screening function. Not all young professionals are able to develop the managerial and client relations skills required at the higher levels. While good recruiting procedures may reduce the degree of screening required through the promotion process, they can rarely eliminate the need for the promotion process to serve this important function. The 'risk of not making it' also serves the firm by placing pressure on junior personnel to work hard and succeed. This pressure can be an important motivating tool in light of the discretion which many PSF professionals have over their working schedules.

Accommodating Rapid Growth

... What adjustments can be made to allow faster growth? Basically, there are four strategies. First, the firm can devote more attention and resources to its hiring process so that a higher proportion of juniors can be routinely promoted to managers. (In effect, this shifts the quality of personnel screen from the promotion system to the hiring system, where it is often more difficult and speculative.) Second, the firm can attempt to hasten the 'apprenticeship' process through more formal training and professional development programmes, rather than the 'learn by example' and mentoring relationships commonly found in smaller firms and those growing at a more leisurely pace. In fact, it is the rate of growth, rather than the size of the firm, which necessitates formal development programmes.[2] ...

The third mechanism that the firm can adopt to accelerate its target growth rate is to make use of 'lateral hires': bringing in experienced professionals at other than the junior level. In most PSFs, this strategy is avoided because of its adverse effect on the morale of junior personnel, who tend to view such actions as reducing their own chances for promotion. Even if these have been accelerated by the fast growth rate, juniors will still tend to feel that they have been less than fairly dealt with.

Modifying the project team structure is the final strategy for accommodating rapid growth without throwing out of balance the relationships between organizational structure, promotion incentives and economic structure. In effect, the firm would alter the mix of senior, manager and junior time devoted to a project. This strategy will be discussed in a later section.

Turnover

... In most PSF industries, one or more firms can be identified that have a high target rate of turnover (or alternatively, choose to grow at less than their optimal rate). Yet individuals routinely join these organizations knowing that the odds of 'making it' are very low. Such 'churning' strategies have some clear disadvantages and benefits for the PSF itself. One of the benefits is that the firm's partners (or shareholders) can routinely earn the surplus value of the juniors without having to repay them in the form of promotion. The high turnover rate also allows a significant degree of screening so that only the 'best' stay in the organization. Not surprisingly, firms following this strategy tend to be among the most prestigious in their industry.

This last comment gives us a clue as to why such firms are able to maintain this strategy over time. For many recruits, the experience, training and association with a prestigious firm compensate for poor promotion opportunities. Young professionals view a short period of time at such a firm as a form of 'post-postgraduate' degree, and often leave for prime positions they could not have achieved (as quickly) by another route. Indeed, most of the prestigious PSFs following this strategy not only encourage this, but also provide active 'outplacement' assistance. Apart from the beneficial effects that such activities provide in recruiting the next generation of juniors, such 'alumni/ae' are often the source of future business for the PSF when they recommend that their corporate employers hire their old firm (which they know and understand) over other competitors. The ability to place ex-staff in prestigious positions is one of the prerequisites of a successful churning strategy. ...

THE MARKET FOR THE FIRM'S SERVICES

The final element in our model is the market for the firm's services. We have already explored some of the ways in which this market is linked to the firm's economic structure (through the billing rates the firm charges) and to the organizational structure (though the project team structure and target growth rate).

We still must add to our model one of the most basic linkages in the dynamics of the PSF: the direct link between the market for professional labour and the market for the firm's services. The key variable that links these two markets is the quality of professional labour that the firm requires and can attract. Earlier, when we considered the factors that attract professionals to a given PSF, we omitted a major variable that often enters into the decision process: the types of projects undertaken by the firm. Top professionals are likely to be attracted to the firm that engages in exciting or challenging projects, or that provides opportunities for professional fulfilment and development. In turn, firms engaged in such projects need to attract the best professionals. It is, therefore, necessary to consider different types of professional service activity.

Project Types

While there are many dimensions which may distinguish one type of professional service activity from another, one in particular is crucial: the degree of customization required in the delivery of the service. To explore this, we will characterize professional service projects into three types: 'Brains', 'Grey Hair' and 'Procedure'.

In the first type (Brains), the client's problem is likely to be extremely complex, perhaps at the forefront of professional or technical knowledge. The PSF that targets this market will be attempting to sell its services on the basis of the high professional craft of its staff. In essence, this firm's appeal to its market is 'hire us because we're smart'. The key elements of this type of professional service are creativity, innovation and the pioneering of new approaches, concepts or techniques – in effect, new solutions to new problems. [See next chapter on the innovative context.]

Grey Hair projects may require highly customized 'output', but they usually involve a lesser degree of innovation and creativity than a Brains project. The general nature of the problem is familiar, and the activities necessary to complete the project may be similar to those performed on other projects. Clients with Grey Hair problems seek out PSFs with experience in their particular type of problem. The PSF sells its knowledge, its experience, and its judgement. In effect, it is saying: 'Hire us because we have been through this before. We have practice in solving this type of problem.'

The third type of project (Procedure) usually involves a well-recognized and familiar type of problem, at least within the professional community. While some customization is still required, the steps necessary to accomplish this are somewhat programmatic. Although clients may have the ability and resources to perform the work itself, they may turn to the PSF because it can perform the service more efficiently; because it is an outsider; or because the clients' staff capabilities may be employed better elsewhere. In essence, the PSF is selling its procedures, its efficiency, and its availability: 'Hire us because we know how to do this and can deliver it effectively.'

Project Team Structure

One of the most significant differences between the three types of projects is the project team structure required to deliver the firm's services. Brains projects are usually denoted by an extreme job-shop operation, involving highly skilled and highly paid professionals. Few procedures are routinizable: each project is a 'one-off.' Accordingly, the opportunities for leveraging the top professionals with juniors are relatively limited. Even though such projects may involve significant data collection and analysis (usually done by juniors), even these activities cannot be clearly specified in advance and require the involvement of at least middle-level (project management) professionals on a continuous basis. Consequently, the ratio of junior time to middle-level and senior time on Brains projects tends to be low. The project team structure of a firm with a high proportion of Brains projects will tend to have a relatively low emphasis on juniors, with a corresponding impact on the shape of the organization.

Since the problems to be addressed in Grey Hair projects are somewhat familiar, some of the tasks to be performed (particularly the early ones) are known in advance and can be specified and delegated. More juniors can be employed to accomplish these tasks, which are then assembled and jointly evaluated at some middle stage of the process. Unlike the 'pure job-shop' nature of Brains projects, the appropriate process to create and deliver a Grey Hair project more closely resembles a disconnected assembly line.

Procedure projects usually involve the highest proportion of junior time relative to senior time, and hence imply a different organizational shape for firms that specialize in such projects. The problems to be addressed in such projects, and the steps necessary to complete the analysis, diagnosis and conclusions, are usually sufficiently well established so that they can be easily delegated to junior staff (with supervision). Whereas in Grey Hair projects senior or middle-level staff must evaluate the results of one stage of the project before deciding how to proceed, in Procedure projects the range of possible outcomes for some steps may be so well known that the appropriate responses can be 'programmed'. The operating procedure takes on even more of the characteristics of an assembly line.

While the three categories described are only points along a spectrum of project types, it is a simple task in any PSF industry to identify types of problems that fit these categories. The choice that the firm makes in its mix of project types is one of the most important variables available to balance the firm. As we have shown, this choice determines the firm's project team structure, thereby influencing significantly the economic and organizational structures of the firm.

CONCLUSIONS: BALANCING THE PROFESSIONAL SERVICE FIRM

Figure 3 summarizes our review of the four major elements involved in balancing the PSF and the major variables linking these elements. What may we conclude from this review? Our discussion has shown that the four elements are, indeed, tightly linked. The firm cannot change one element without making corresponding changes in one or more of the other three. ...

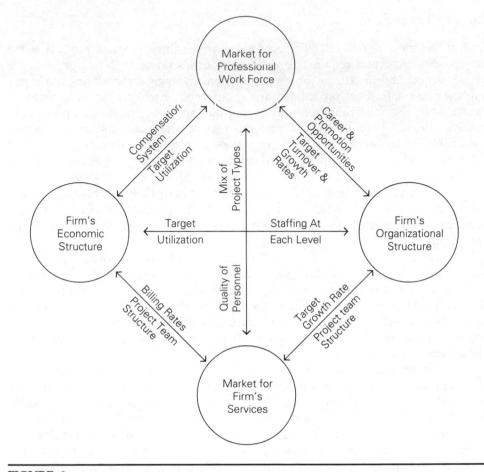

FIGURE 3
Balancing the professional services firm

In performing these balance analyses, the firm must distinguish between the 'levers' (variables that it controls) and the 'rocks' (variables substantially constrained by the forces of the market). ...

Perhaps the most significant management variable is the mix of projects undertaken and the implications this has for the project team structure. This variable is a significant force in influencing the economics of the firm, its organizational structure, and both markets. The project team structure as defined in this article (i.e the average or typical proportion of time required from professionals at different levels) has not been a variable that is routinely monitored by PSF management. However, as we have shown, its role in balancing the firm is critical.

It is possible, and not uncommon, for the firm's project team structure to change over time. If it is possible to deliver the firm's services with a greater proportion of juniors, this will reduce the costs of the project. Competition in the market will, over time, require the firm to seek lower costs for projects, thus creating opportunities for more juniors to be used on projects that required a high proportion of senior time in the past. Projects that, in the past, had Brains or Grey Hair characteristics may be accomplished as Procedure projects in future years.[3]

When considering new projects to undertake, it is usually more profitable for the firm to engage in a project similar to one recently performed for a previous client. The knowledge, expertise and basic approaches to the problem that were developed (often through significant personal and financial investment) can be capitalized upon by applying them to a similar or related problem. Frequently, the second project can be billed out to the client at a similar (or only slightly lower) rate, since the client perceives (and receives) something equally custom-tailored: the solution to his or her problem. However, the savings in PSF costs in delivering this customization are not all shared with the client (if, indeed, any are). The firm thus makes its most money by 'leading the market': selling a service with reproducible, standardizable elements as a fully customized service at a fully customized price.

Unfortunately, even before the market catches up and refuses to bear the fully customized price, the firm may encounter an internal behaviour problem. While it is in the best interest of the firm to undertake similar or repetitive engagements, often this does not coincide with the desires of the individuals involved. Apart from any reasons of status, financial rewards or fulfilment derived from serving the clients' needs, most individuals join PSFs to experience the professional challenge and variety and to avoid routine and repetition. While individuals may be content to undertake a similar project for the second or third time, they will not be for the fourth, sixth, or eighth. Yet it is in the interest of the firm (particularly if the market has not yet caught up) to take advantage of the experience and expertise that it has acquired. One solution, of course, is to convert the past experience and expertise of the individual into the expertise of the firm by accepting a similar project, but utilizing a greater proportion of juniors on it. Besides requiring a lesser commitment of time from the experienced seniors, this device serves to train the juniors.

For all these reasons, we might suspect that the proportion of juniors to seniors required by the firm in a particular practice area will tend to increase over time. If this is allowed to proceed without corresponding adjustments in the range of practice areas, the project team structure of the firm will be altered, causing significant impacts on the economics and organization of the firm. The dangers of failing to monitor the project team structure are thus clearly revealed. Examples of this failure abound in many PSF industries. One consulting firm that learned how to increasingly utilize junior professionals began to aggressively hire new junior staff. After a reasonable period of time for the promotion decision, the firm realized that, at its current growth rate, it could not promote its 'normal' proportion of promotion candidates: it did not need as many partners and managers in relation to the number of juniors it now had. Morale and productivity in the junior ranks suffered. ... Successful PSF management is a question of balance.

---

[1] This characterization is, of course, simplified. Additional 'levels' or functions can be identified at both the top and bottom of the pyramid. To the top we can add those individuals responsible for managing the firm (rather than managing projects). At the bottom of the pyramid lie both 'non-professional' support staff and trainees.

[2] Speeding the development of individuals so that the firm can grow faster is, of course, not the only role for formal training programmes. They can also be a device to allow the firm to hire less (initially) qualified and hence lower wage individuals, thereby reducing its cost for juniors.

[3] This argument suggests that there is a 'lifecycle' to professional 'products' in the same way that such cycles exist for tangible products.

11

THE INNOVATION CONTEXT

Although often seen as a high-technology event involving inventor-entrepreneurs, innovation may, of course, occur in high or low technology, product or service, large or small organizational situations. Innovation may be thought of as the *first reduction to practice* of an idea in a culture. The more radical the idea, the more traumatic and profound its impact will tend to be. But there are no absolutes. Whatever is most new and difficult to understand becomes the 'high technology' of its age. As Jim Utterback of MIT is fond of pointing out, the delivery of ice was high technology at the turn of the century, later it was the production of automobiles. By the same token, 50 years from now, electronics and space stations may be considered mundane.

Our focus here, however, is not on innovation *per se*, but on the innovation context, that is the situation in which steady or frequent innovation of a complex nature is an intrinsic part of the organization and the industry segment in which it chooses to operate. Such organizations depend, not just on a single entrepreneurial individual, but on teams of experts moulded together for 'intrapreneurship'.

The innovation context is one in which the organization often must deal with complex technologies or systems under conditions of dynamic change. Typically, major innovations require that a variety of experts work towards a common goal, often led by a single champion or a small group of committed individuals. Much has been learned from research in recent years on such organizations. While this knowledge may seem less structured than that of previous chapters, several dominant themes have emerged.

This chapter opens with a description of the fifth of Mintzberg's structures, here called the innovative organization, but also referred to as 'adhocracy'. This is the structure that, as noted, achieves its effectiveness by being inefficient. This reading probes into the unusual ways in which strategies evolve in the context of work that is both highly complex and highly dynamic. Here we see the full flowering of the notion of emergent strategy, culminating in a description of a 'grassroots' model of the process. We also see here a strategic leadership less concerned with formulating and then implementing strategies than managing a process through which strategies almost seem to *form* by themselves.

The second reading of this chapter, James Brian Quinn's 'Managing innovation: Controlled chaos', another winner of the McKinsey prize for the best *Harvard Business Review* article, this in 1985, suggests how the spirit of adhocracy and strategy formation as a learning process can be integrated with some of the formal strategic processes of large organizations. To achieve innovativeness, other authors have advocated adhocracy with little or no reliance on planning. Quinn suggests that blending broad strategy planning with a consciously structured adhocracy gives better results. This reading also brings back the notion of 'intrapreneurship', first mentioned in the introduction to Chapter 7 on the entrepreneurial context. When it is successful – intrapreneurship – implying the stimulation and diffusion of innovative capacity throughout a larger organization, with many champions of innovations – tends to follow most of Quinn's precepts. As such, it seems to belong more to this context than the entrepreneurial one, which focuses on organizations highly centralized around the initiatives of their single leaders, whether or not innovative.

• THE INNOVATIVE ORGANIZATION*

HENRY MINTZBERG

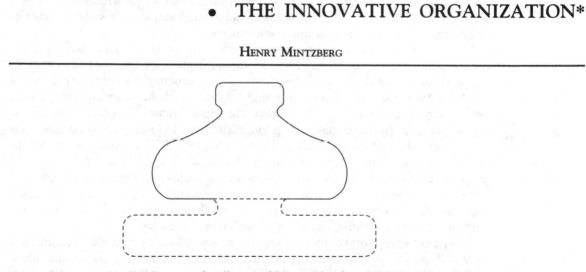

None of the organization forms so far discussed is capable of sophisticated innovation, the kind required of a high-technology research organization, an avant-garde film company or a factory manufacturing complex prototypes. The entrepreneurial

* Adapted from *The Structuring of Organizations* (Prentice Hall, 1979), Ch. 21 on the adhocracy, on strategy formation from 'Strategy formation in an adhocracy', co-authored with Alexandra McHugh, *Administrative Science Quarterly* (1985: 160–97), and 'Strategy of design: A study of "architects in co-partnership"', co-authored with Suzanne Otis, Jamal Shamsie and James A. Waters, in J. Grant (ed.), *Strategy Management Frontiers* (JAI Press, 1988). A chapter similar to this one appeared in *Mintzberg on Management: Inside Our Strange World of Organizations* (Free Press, 1989).

organization can certainly innovate, but only in relatively simple ways. The machine and professional organizations are performance, not problem-solving types, designed to perfect standardized programmes, not to invent new ones. And although the diversified organization resolves some problem of strategic inflexibility found in the machine organization, as noted earlier it too is not a true innovator. A focus on control by standardizing outputs does not encourage innovation.

Sophisticated innovation requires a very different configuration, one that is able to fuse experts drawn from different disciplines into smoothly functioning *ad hoc* project teams. To borrow the word coined by Bennis and Slater in 1964 and later popularized in Alvin Toffler's *Future Shock* (1970), these are the *adhocracies* of our society.

THE BASIC STRUCTURE

Here again we have a distinct configuration of the attributes of design: highly organic structure, with little formalization of behaviour; specialized jobs based on expert training; a tendency to group the specialists in functional units for house-keeping purposes but to deploy them in small project teams to do their work; a reliance on teams, on task forces and on integrating managers of various sorts in order to encourage mutual adjustment, the key mechanism of coordination, within and between these teams; and considerable decentralization to and within these teams, which are located at various places in the organization and involve various mixtures of line managers and staff and operating experts.

To innovate means to break away from established patterns. Thus the innovative organization cannot rely on any form of standardization for coordination. In other words, it must avoid all the trappings of bureaucratic structure, notably sharp divisions of labour, extensive unit differentiation, highly formalized behaviours and an emphasis on planning and control systems. Above all, it must remain flexible. A search for organigrams to illustrate this description elicited the following response from one corporation thought to have an adhocracy structure: '[W]e would prefer not to supply an organization chart, since it would change too quickly to serve any useful purpose.' Of all the configurations, this one shows the least reverence for the classical principles of management, especially unity of command. Information and decision processes flow flexibly and informally, wherever they must, to promote innovation. And that means overriding the chain of authority if need be.

The entrepreneurial configuration also retains a flexible, organic structure, and so is likewise able to innovate. But that innovation is restricted to simple situations, ones easily comprehended by a single leader. Innovation of the sophisticated variety requires another kind of flexible structure, one that can draw together different forms of expertise. Thus the adhocracy must hire and give power to experts, people whose knowledge and skills have been highly developed in training programmes. But unlike the professional organization, the adhocracy cannot rely on the standardized skills of its experts to achieve coordination, because that would discourage innovation. Rather, it must treat existing knowledge and skills as bases on which to combine and build new ones. Thus the adhocracy must break through the boundaries of conventional specialization and differentiation, which it does by assigning problems not to individual experts in preestablished pigeonholes but to multidisciplinary teams that merge their efforts. Each team forms around one specific project.

Despite organizing around market-based projects, the organization must still support and encourage particular types of specialized expertise. And so the adhocracy tends to use a matrix structure: Its experts are grouped in functional units for specialized house-keeping purposes – hiring, training, professional communication, and the like – but are then deployed in the project teams to carry out the basic work of innovation.

As for coordination in and between these project teams, as noted earlier standardization is precluded as a significant coordinating mechanism. The efforts must be innovative, not routine. So, too, is direct supervision precluded because of the complexity of the work: Coordination must be accomplished by those with the knowledge, namely the experts themselves, not those with just authority. That leaves just one of our coordinating mechanisms, mutual adjustment, which we consider foremost in adhocracy. And, to encourage this, the organization makes use of a whole set of liaison devices, liaison personnel and integrating managers of all kinds, in addition to the various teams and task forces.

The result is that managers abound in the adhocracy: functional managers, integrating managers, project managers. The last-named are particularly numerous, since the project teams must be small to encourage mutual adjustment among their members, and each, of course, needs a designated manager. The consequence is that 'spans of control' found in adhocracy tend to be small. But the implication of this is misleading, because the term is suited to the machine, not the innovative configuration: the managers of adhocracy seldom 'manage' in the usual sense of giving orders; instead, they spend a good deal of time acting in a liaison capacity, to coordinate the work laterally among the various teams and units.

With its reliance on highly trained experts, the adhocracy emerges as highly decentralized, in the 'selective' sense. That means power over its decisions and actions is distributed to various places and at various levels according to the needs of the particular issue. In effect, power flows to wherever the relevant expertise happens to reside – among managers or specialists (or teams of those) in the line structure, the staff units, and the operating core.

To proceed with our discussion and to elaborate on how the innovative organization makes decisions and forms strategies, we need to distinguish two basic forms that it takes.

The Operating Adhocracy

The *operating adhocracy* innovates and solves problems directly on behalf of its clients. Its multidisciplinary teams of experts often work under contract, as in the think-tank consulting firm, creative advertising agency or manufacturer of engineering prototypes.

In fact, for every operating adhocracy, there is a corresponding professional bureaucracy, one that does similar work but with a narrower orientation. Faced with a client problem, the operating adhocracy engages in creative efforts to find a novel solution; the professional bureaucracy pigeonholes it into a known contingency to which it can apply a standard programme. One engages in divergent thinking aimed at innovation, the other in convergent thinking aimed at perfection. Thus, one theatre company might seek out new avant-garde plays to perform, while another might perfect its performance of Shakespeare year after year.

A key feature of the operating adhocracy is that its administrative and operating work tend to blend into a single effort. That is, in *ad hoc* project work it is difficult to separate the planning and design of the work from its execution. Both require the same specialized skills, on a project-by-project basis. Thus it can be difficult to distinguish the middle levels of the organization from its operating core, since line managers and staff specialists may take their place alongside operating specialists on the project teams.

Figure 1 shows the organigram of the National Film Board of Canada, a classic operating adhocracy (even though it does produce a chart – one that changes frequently, it might be added). The Board is an agency of the Canadian federal government and produces mostly short films, many of them documentaries. At the time of this organigram, the characteristics of adhocracy were particularly in evidence: It shows a large number of support units as well as liaison positions (for example, research, technical and production coordinators), with the operating core containing loose concurrent functional and market groupings, the latter by region as well as by type of film produced and, as can be seen, some not even connected to the line hierarchy!

The Administrative Adhocracy

The second type of adhocracy also functions with project teams, but toward a different end. Whereas the operating adhocracy undertakes projects to serve its clients, the *administrative adhocracy* undertakes projects to serve itself, to bring new facilities or activities on line, as in the administrative structure of a highly automated company. And in sharp contrast to the operating adhocracy, the administrative adhocracy makes a clear distinction between its administrative component and its operating core. That core is *truncated* – cut right off from the rest of the organization – so that the administrative component that remains can be structured as an adhocracy.

This truncation may take place in a number of ways. First, when the operations have to be machinelike and so could impede innovation in the administration (because of the associated need for control), it may be established as an independent organization. Second, the operating core may be done away with altogether – in effect, contracted out to other organizations. That leaves the organization free to concentrate on the development work, as did NASA during the Apollo project. A third form of truncation arises when the operating core becomes automated. This enables it to run itself, largely independent of the need for direct controls from the administrative component, leaving the latter free to structure itself as an adhocracy to bring new facilities on line or to modify old ones.

Oil companies, because of the high degree of automation of their production process, are in part at least drawn toward administrative adhocracy. Figure 2 shows the organigram for one oil company, reproduced exactly as presented by the company (except for modifications to mask its identity, done at the company's request). Note the domination of 'Administration and Services', shown at the bottom of the chart;

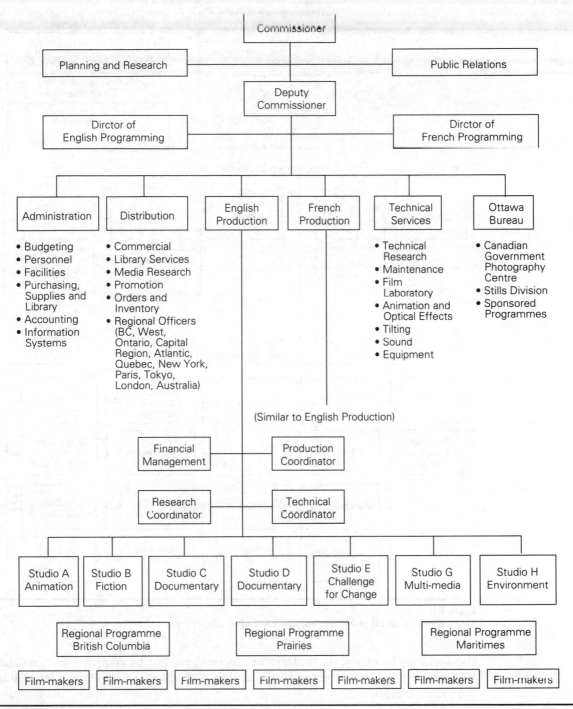

FIGURE 1
The National Film Board of Canada: an operating adhocracy (c. 1975, used with permission). *Note:* No lines shown on original organigram connecting regional programmes to studio or film-makers

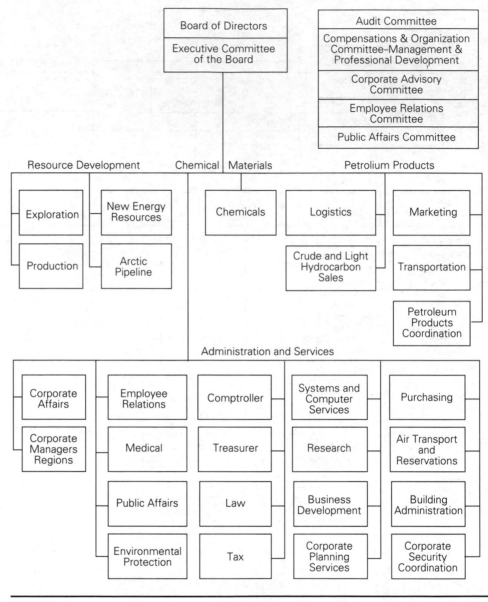

FIGURE 2
Organigram of an oil company: an administrative adhocracy

the operating functions, particularly 'production', are lost by comparison. Note also the description of the strategic apex in terms of standing committees instead of individual executives.

The Administrative Component of the Adhocracies

The important conclusion to be drawn from this discussion is that in both types of adhocracy the relation between the operating core and the administrative component is unlike that in any other configuration. In the administrative adhocracy, the operating core is truncated and becomes a relatively unimportant part of the organization; in the operating adhocracy, the two merge into a single entity. Either way, the need for traditional direct supervision is diminished, so managers derive their influence more from their expertise and interpersonal skills than from formal position. And that means the distinction between line and staff blurs. It no longer makes sense to distinguish those who have the formal power to decide from those who have only the informal right to advise. Power over decision-making in the adhocracy flows to anyone with the required expertise, regardless of position.

In fact, the support staff plays a key role in adhocracy, because that is where many of the experts reside (especially in administrative adhocracy). As suggested, however, that staff is not sharply differentiated from the other parts of the organization, not off to one side, to speak only when spoken to, as in the bureaucratic configurations. The other type of staff, however, the technostructure, is less important here, because the adhocracy does not rely for coordination on standards that it develops. Technostructure analysts may, of course, be used for some action planning and other forms of analysis – marketing research and economic forecasting, for example – but these analysts are as likely to take their place alongside the other specialists on the project teams as to stand back and design systems to control them.

To summarize, the administrative component of the adhocracy emerges as an organic mass of line managers and staff experts, combined with operators in the operating adhocracy, working together in ever-shifting relationships on *ad hoc* projects. Our logo at the head of this reading shows adhocracy with its parts mingled together in one amorphous mass in the middle. In the operating adhocracy, that mass includes the middle line, support staff, technostructure and operating core. Of these, the administrative adhocracy excludes just the operating core, which is truncated, as shown by the dotted section below the central mass. The reader will also note that the strategic apex of the figure is shown partly merged into the central mass as well, for reasons we shall present in our discussion of strategy formation.

The Roles of the Strategic Apex

The top managers of the strategic apex of this configuration do not spend much time formulating explicit strategies (as we shall see). But they must spend a good deal of their time in the battles that ensue over strategic choices and in handling the many other disturbances that arise all over these fluid structures. The innovative configuration combines fluid working arrangements with power based on expertise, not authority. Together those breed aggressiveness and conflict. But the job of the managers here, at all levels, is not to bottle up that aggression and conflict so much as to channel them to productive ends. Thus, the managers of adhocracy must be masters of human relations, able to use persuasion, negotiation, coalition, reputation and rapport to fuse the individualistic experts into smoothly functioning teams.

Top managers must also devote a good deal of time to monitoring the projects. Innovative project work is notoriously difficult to control. No MIS can be relied on to provide complete, unambiguous results. So there must be careful personal monitoring of projects to ensure that they are completed according to specifications, on schedule and within budget (or, more likely, not excessively late and not too far in excess of cost estimates).

Perhaps the most important single role of the top management of this configuration (especially the operating adhocracy form) is liaison with the external environment. The other configurations tend to focus their attention on clearly defined markets and so are more or less assured of a steady flow of work. Not so the operating adhocracy, which lives from project to project and disappears when it can find no more. Since each project is different, the organization can never be sure where the next one will come from. So the top managers must devote a great deal of their time to ensuring a steady and balanced stream of incoming projects. That means developing liaison contacts with potential customers and negotiating contracts with them. Nowhere is this more clearly illustrated than in the consulting business, particularly where the approach is innovative. When a consultant becomes a partner in one of these firms, he or she normally hangs up the calculator and becomes virtually a full-time salesperson. It is a distinguishing characteristic of many an operating adhocracy that the selling function literally takes place at the strategic apex.

Project work poses related problems in the administrative adhocracy. Reeser asked a group of managers in three aerospace companies, 'What are some of the human problems of project management?' Among the common answers: '[M]embers of the organization who are displaced because of the phasing out of [their] work ... May have to wait a long time before they get another assignment at as high a level of responsibility' and 'the temporary nature of the organization often necessitates "make work" assignments for [these] displaced members' (1969: 463). Thus senior managers must again concern themselves with a steady flow of projects, although in this case, internally generated.

CONDITIONS OF THE INNOVATIVE ORGANIZATION

This configuration is found in environments that are both dynamic and complex. A dynamic environment, being unpredictable, calls for organic structure; a complex one calls for decentralized structure. This configuration is the only type that provides both. Thus we tend to find the innovative organization wherever these conditions prevail, ranging from guerrilla warfare to space agencies. There appears to be no other way to fight a war in the jungle or to put the first man on the moon.

As we have noted for all the configurations, organizations that prefer particular structures also try to 'choose' environments appropriate to them. This is especially clear in the case of the operating adhocracy. Advertising agencies and consulting firms that prefer to structure themselves as professional bureaucracies seek out stable environments; those that prefer the innovative form find environments that are dynamic, where the client needs are difficult and unpredictable.[1]

A number of organizations are drawn towards this configuration because of the dynamic conditions that result from very frequent product change. The extreme case is the unit producer, the manufacturing firm that custom-makes each of its products to order, as in the engineering company that produces prototypes or the fabricator of extremely expensive machinery. Because each customer order constitutes a new project, the organization is encouraged to structure itself as an operating adhocracy.

Some manufacturers of consumer goods operate in markets so competitive that they must be constantly changing their product offerings, even though each product may itself be mass produced. A company that records rock music would be a prime example, as would some cosmetic and pharmaceutical companies. Here again, dynamic conditions, when coupled with some complexity, drive the organization toward the innovative configuration, with the mass production operations truncated to allow for adhocracy in product development.

Youth is another condition often associated with this type of organization. That is because it is difficult to sustain any structure in a state of adhocracy for a long period – to keep behaviours from formalizing and thereby discouraging innovation. All kinds of forces drive the innovative configuration to bureaucratize itself as it ages. On the other hand, young organizations prefer naturally organic structures, since they must find their own ways and tend to be eager to innovate. Unless they are entrepreneurial, they tend to become intrapreneurial.

The operating adhocracy is particularly prone to a short life, since it faces a risky market which can quickly destroy it. The loss of one major contract can literally close it down overnight. But if some operating adhocracies have short lives because they fail, others have short lives because they succeed. Success over time encourages metamorphosis, driving the organization towards a more stable environment and a more bureaucratic structure. As it ages, the successful organization develops a reputation for what it does best. That encourages it to repeat certain activities, which may suit the employees who, themselves aging, may welcome more stability in their work. So operating adhocracy is driven over time toward professional bureaucracy to perfect the activities it does best, perhaps even toward the machine bureaucracy to exploit a single invention. The organization survives, but the configuration dies.

Administrative adhocracies typically live longer. They, too, feel the pressures to bureaucratize as they age, which can lead them to stop innovating or else to innovate in stereotyped ways and thereby to adopt bureaucratic structure. But this will not work if the organization functions in an industry that requires sophisticated innovation from all its participants. Since many of the industries where administrative adhocracies are found do, organizations that survive in them tend to retain this configuration for long periods.

In recognition of the tendency for organizations to bureaucratize as they age, a variant of the innovative configuration has emerged – 'the organizational equivalent of paper dresses or throw-away tissues' (Toffler, 1970: 133) – which might be called the 'temporary adhocracy'. It draws together specialists from various organizations to carry out a project, and then it disbands. Temporary adhocracies are becoming increasingly common in modern society: the production group that performs a single play, the election campaign committee that promotes a single candidate, the guerrilla group that overthrows a single government, the Olympic committee that plans a single games. Related is what can be called the 'mammoth project adhocracy', a giant temporary adhocracy that draws on thousands of experts for a number of years to carry out a single major task, the Manhattan Project of World War II being one famous example.

Sophisticated and automated technical systems also tend to drive organizations toward the administrative adhocracy. When an organization's technical system is sophisticated, it requires an elaborate, highly trained support staff, working in teams, to design or purchase, modify and maintain the equipment. In other words, complex machinery requires specialists who have the knowledge, power and flexible working arrangements to cope with it, which generally requires the organization to structure itself as an adhocracy.

Automation of a technical system can evoke even stronger forces in the same direction. That is why a machine organization that succeeds in automating its operating core tends to undergo a dramatic metamorphosis The problem of motivating bored workers disappears, and with it goes the control mentality that permeates the structure; the distinction between line and staff blurs (machines being indifferent to who turns their knobs), which leads to another important reduction in conflict; the technostructure loses its influence, since control is built into the machinery by its own designers rather than having to be imposed on workers by the standards of the analysts. Overall, then, the administrative structure becomes more decentralized and organic, emerging as an adhocracy. Of course, for automated organizations with simple technical systems (as in the production of hand creams), the entrepreneurial configuration may suffice instead of the innovative one.

Fashion is most decidedly another condition of the innovative configuration. Every one of its characteristics is very much in vogue today: emphasis on expertise, organic structure, project teams, task forces, decentralization of power, matrix structure, sophistocated technical systems, automation and young organizations. Thus, if the entrepreneurial and machine forms were earlier configurations, and the professional and the diversified forms yesterday's, then the innovative is clearly today's. This is the configuration for a population growing ever better educated and more specialized, yet under constant encouragement to adopt the 'systems' approach – to view the world as an integrated whole instead of a collection of loosely coupled parts. It is the configuration for environments that are becoming more complex and more insistent on innovation, and for technical systems that are growing more sophisticated and more highly automated. It is the only configuration among our types appropriate for those who believe organizations must become at the same time more democratic and less bureaucratic.

Yet despite our current infatuation with it, adhocracy is not the structure for all organizations. Like all the others, it too has its place. And that place, as our examples make clear, seems to be in the new industries of our age – aerospace, electronics, think-tank consulting, research, advertising, film-making, petrochemicals – virtually all of which experienced their greatest development since World War II. The innovative adhocracy appears to be the configuration for the industries of the last half of the twentieth century.

STRATEGY FORMATION IN THE INNOVATIVE ORGANIZATION

The structure of the innovative organization may seem unconventional, but its strategy making is even more so, upsetting virtually everything we have been taught to believe about that process.

Because the innovative organization must respond continuously to a complex, unpredictable environment, it cannot rely on deliberate strategy. In other words, it cannot predetermine precise patterns in its activities and then impose them on its work through some kind of formal planning process. Rather, many of its actions must be decided upon individually, according to the needs of the moment. It proceeds incrementally, to use Charles Lindblom's words, it prefers 'continual nibbling' to a 'good bite' (1968: 25).

Here, then, the process is best thought of as strategy *formation*, because strategy is not formulated consciously in one place so much as formed implicitly by the specific actions taken in many places. That is why action planning cannot be extensively relied upon in these organizations: Any process that separates thinking from action – planning from execution, formalization from implementation – would impede the flexibility of the organization to respond creatively to its dynamic environment.

Strategy Formation in the Operating Adhocracy

In the operating adhocracy, a project organization never quite sure what it will do next, the strategy never really stabilizes totally but is responsive to new projects, which themselves involve the activities of a whole host of people. Take the example of the National Film Board. Among its most important strategies are those related to the content of the 100 or so mostly short, documentary-type films that it makes each year. Were the Board structured as a machine bureaucracy, the word on what films to make would come down from on high. Instead, when we studied it some years ago, proposals for new films were submitted to a standing committee, which included elected film-makers, marketing people and the heads of production and programming – in other words, operators, line managers and staff specialists. The chief executive had to approve the committee's choices, and usually did, but the vast majority of the proposals were initiated by the film-makers and the executive producers lower down. Strategies formed as themes developed among these individual proposals. The operating adhocracy's strategy thus evolves continuously as all kinds of such decisions are made, each leaving its imprint on the strategy by creating a precedent or reinforcing an existing one.

Strategy Formation in the Administrative Adhocracy

Similar things can be said about the administrative adhocracy, although the strategy-making process is slightly neater there. That is because the organization tends to concentrate its attention on fewer projects, which involve more people. NASA's Apollo project, for example, involved most of its personnel for almost ten years.

Administrative adhocracies also need to give more attention to action planning, but of a loose kind – to specify perhaps the ends to be reached while leaving flexibility to work out the means *en route*. Again, therefore, it is only through the making of specific decisions – namely, those that determine which projects are undertaken and how these projects unfold – that strategies can evolve.

Strategies None the Less

With their activities so disjointed, one might wonder whether adhocracies (or either type) can form strategies (that is, patterns) at all. In fact, they do, at least at certain times.

At the Film Board, despite the little direction from the management, the content of films did converge on certain clear themes periodically and then diverge, in remarkably regular cycles. In the early 1940s, there was a focus on films related to the war effort. After the war, having lost the *raison d'être* as well as its founding leader, the Board's films went off in all directions. They converged again in the mid-1950s around series of films for television, but by the late 1950s were again diverging widely. And in the mid-1960s and again in the early 1970s (with a brief period of divergence in between), the Board again showed a certain degree of convergence, this time on the themes of social commentary and experimentation.

This habit of cycling in and out of focus is quite unlike what takes place in the other configurations. In the machine organization especially, and somewhat in the entrepreneurial one, convergence proves much stronger and much longer (recall Volkswagenwerk's concentration on the Beetle for twenty years), while divergence tends to be very brief. The machine organization, in particular, cannot tolerate the ambiguity of change and so tries to leap from one strategic orientation to another. The innovative organization, in contrast, seems not only able to function at times without strategic focus, but positively to thrive on it. Perhaps that is the way it keeps itself innovative – by periodically cleansing itself of some of its existing strategic baggage.

The Varied Strategies of Adhocracy

Where do the strategies of adhocracy come from? While some may be imposed deliberately by the central management (as in staff cuts at the Film Board), most seem to emerge in a variety of other ways.

In some cases, a single *ad hoc* decision sets a precedent which evokes a pattern. That is how the National Film Board got into making series of films for television. While a debate raged over the issue, with management hesitant, one film-maker slipped out and made one such series, and when many of his colleagues quickly followed suit, the organization suddenly found itself deeply, if unintentionally, committed to a major new strategy. It was, in effect, a strategy of spontaneous but implicit consensus on the part of its operating employees. In another case, even the initial precedent-setting decision wasn't deliberate. One film inadvertently ran longer than expected, it had to be distributed as a feature, the first for the organization, and as some other filmmakers took advantage of the precedent, a feature film strategy emerged.

Sometimes a strategy will be pursued in a pocket of an organization (perhaps in a clandestine manner, in a so-called 'skunkworks'), which then later becomes more broadly organizational when the organization, in need of change and casting about for new strategies, seizes upon it. Some salesman has been pursuing a new market, or some engineer has developed a new product, and is ignored until the organization has need for some fresh strategic thinking. Then it finds it, not in the vision of its leaders or the procedures of its planners, not elswehere in its industry, but hidden in the bowels of its own operations, developed through the learning of its workers.

What then becomes the role of the leadership of the innovative configuration in making strategy? If it cannot impose deliberate strategies, what does it do? The answer is that it manages patterns, seeking partial control over strategies but otherwise attempting to influence what happens to those strategies that do emerge lower down.

These are the organizations in which trying to manage strategy is a little like trying to drive an automobile without having your hands on the steering wheel. You can accelerate and brake but cannot determine direction. But there do remain important forms of control. First the leaders can manage the *process* of strategy-making if not the content of strategy. In other words, they can set up the structures to encourage certain kinds of activities and hire the people who themselves will carry out these activities. Second, they can provide general guidelines for strategy – what we have called *umbrella* strategies – seeking to define certain boundaries outside of which the specific patterns developed below should not stray. Then they can watch the patterns that do emerge and use the umbrella to decide which to encourage and which to discourage, remembering, however, that the umbrella can be shifted too.

A Grass-roots Model of Strategy Formation

We can summarize this discussion in terms of a 'grass-roots' model of strategy formation, comprising six points.

1.   *Strategies grow initially like weeds in a garden, they are not cultivated like tomatoes in a hothouse.* In other words, the process of strategy formation can be overmanaged; sometimes it is more important to let patterns emerge than to force an artificial consistency upon an organization prematurely. The hothouse, if needed, can come later.

2.   *These strategies can take root in all kinds of places, virtually anywhere people have the capacity to learn and the resources to support that capacity.* Sometimes an individual or unit in touch with a particular opportunity creates his, her, or its own pattern. This may happen inadvertently, when an initial action sets a precedent. Even senior managers can fall into strategies by experimenting with ideas until they converge on something that works (though the final result may appear to the observer to have been deliberately designed). At other times, a variety of actions converge on a strategic theme through the mutual adjustment of various people, whether gradually or spontaneously. And then the external environment can impose a pattern on an unsuspecting organization. The point is that organizations cannot always plan where their strategies will emerge, let alone plan the strategies themselves.

3.   *Such strategies become organizational when they become collective, that is, when the patterns proliferate to pervade the behaviour of the organization at large.* Weeds can proliferate and encompass a whole garden; then the conventional plants may look out of place. Likewise, emergent strategies can sometimes displace the existing deliberate ones. But, of course, what is a weed but a plant that wasn't expected? With a change of perspective, the emergent strategy, like the weed, can become what is valued (just as Europeans enjoy salads of the leaves of America's most notorious weed, the dandelion!).

4.   *The processes of proliferation may be conscious but need not be; likewise they may be managed but need not be.* The processes by which the initial patterns work their way through the organization need not be consciously intended, by formal leaders or even informal ones. Patterns may simply spread by collective action, much as plants proliferate themselves. Of course, once strategies are recognized as valuable, the processes by which they proliferate can be managed, just as plants can be selectively propagated.

5. *New strategies, which may be emerging continuously, tend to pervade the organization during periods of change, which punctuate periods of more integrated continuity.* Put more simply, organizations, like gardens, may accept the biblical maxim of a time to sow and a time to reap (even though they can sometimes reap what they did not mean to sow). Periods of convergence, during which the organization exploits its prevalent, established strategies, tend to be interrupted periodically by periods of divergence, during which the organization experiments with and subsequently accepts new strategic themes. The blurring of the separation between these two types of periods may have the same effect on an organization that the blurring of the separation between sowing and reaping has on a garden – the destruction of the system's productive capacity.

6. *To manage this process is not to preconceive strategies but to recognize their emergence and intervene when appropriate.* A destructive weed, once noticed, is best uprooted immediately. But one that seems capable of bearing fruit is worth watching, indeed sometimes even worth building a hothouse around. To manage in this context is to create the climate within which a wide variety of strategies can grow (to establish flexible structures, develop appropriate processes, encourage supporting ideologies, and define guiding 'umbrella' strategies) and then to watch what does in fact come up. The strategic initiatives that do come 'up' may in fact originate anywhere, although often low down in the organization, where the detailed knowledge of products and markets resides. (In fact, to be successful in some organizations, these initiatives must be recognized by middle-level managers and 'championed' by combining them with each other or with existing strategies before promoting them to the senior management.) In effect, the management encourages those initiatives that appear to have potential, otherwise it discourages them. But it must not be too quick to cut off the unexpected: sometimes it is better to pretend not to notice an emerging pattern to allow it more time to unfold. Likewise, there are times when it makes sense to shift or enlarge an umbrella to encompass a new pattern – in other words, to let the organization adapt to the initiative rather than vice versa. Moreover, a management must know when to resist change for the sake of internal efficiency and when to promote it for the sake of external adaptation. In other words, it must sense when to exploit an established crop of strategies and when to encourage new strains to displace them. It is the excesses of either – failure to focus (running blind) or failure to change (bureaucratic momentum) – that most harms organizations.

I call this a 'grass-roots' model because the strategies grow up from the base of the organization, rooted in the solid earth of its operations rather than the ethereal abstractions of its administration. (Even the strategic initiatives of the senior management itself are in this model rooted in its tangible involvement with the operations.)

Of course, the model is overstated. But no more so than the more widely accepted deliberate one, which we might call the 'hothouse' model of strategy formulation. Management theory must encompass both, perhaps more broadly labelled the *learning* model and the *planning* model, as well as a third, the *visionary* model.

I have discussed the learning model under the innovative configuration, the planning model under the machine configuration, and the visionary model under the entrepreneurial configuration. But in truth, all organizations need to mix these approaches in various ways at different times in their development. For example, our discussion of strategic change in the machine organization concluded, in effect, that they had to revert to the learning model for revitalization and the visionary model for turnaround. Of course, the visionary leader must learn, as must the learning organization evolve a kind of strategic vision, and both sometimes need planning to programme the strategies they develop. And overall, no organization can function with strategies that are always and purely emergent; that would amount to a complete abdication of will and leadership, not to mention conscious thought. But none can function either with strategies that are always and purely deliberate; that would amount to an unwillingness to learn, a blindness to whatever is unexpected.

Environment Taking Precedence in the Innovative Organization

To conclude our discussion of strategy formation, as shown in Figure 3, in the innovative configuration it is the environment that takes precedence. It drives the organization, which responds continuously and eclectically, but does nevertheless achieve convergence during certain periods.[2] The formal leadership seeks somehow to influence both sides in this relationship, negotiating with the environment for support and attempting to impose some broad general (umbrella) guidelines on the organization.

If the strategist of the entrepreneurial organization is largely a concept attainer and that of the machine organization largely a planner, then the strategist of the innovative organization is largely a *pattern recognizer*, seeking to detect emerging patterns within and outside the strategic umbrella. Then strategies deemed unsuitable can be discouraged while those that seem appropriate can be encouraged, even if that means moving the umbrella. Here, then, we may find the curious situation of leadership changing its intentions to fit the realized behaviour of its organization. But that is curious only in the perspective of traditional management theory.

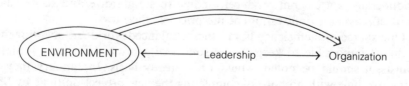

FIGURE 3
Environment taking the lead in adhocracy

SOME ISSUES ASSOCIATED WITH THE
INNOVATIVE ORGANIZATION

Three issues associated with the innovative configuration merit attention here: its ambiguities and the reactions of people who must live with them, its inefficiencies, and its propensity to make inappropriate transitions to other configurations.

Human Reactions to Ambiguity

Many people, especially creative ones, dislike both structural rigidity and the concentration of power. That leaves them only one configuration, the innovative, which is both organic and decentralized. Thus they find it a great place to work. In essence, adhocracy is the only structure for people who believe in more democracy with less bureaucracy.

But not everyone shares those values (not even everyone who professes to). Many people need order, and so prefer the machine or professional type of organization. They see adhocracy as a nice place to visit but no place to spend a career. Even dedicated members of adhocracies periodically get frustrated with this structure's fluidity, confusion and ambiguity. 'In these situations, all managers some of the time and many managers all the time, yearn for more definition and structure' (Burns and Stalker, 1966: 122–3). The managers of innovative organizations report anxiety related to the eventual phase-out of projects; confusion as to who their boss is, whom to impress to get promoted; a lack of clarity in job definitions, authority relationships, and lines of communication; and intense competition for resources, recognition and rewards (Reeser, 1969). This last point suggests another serious problem of ambiguity here, the politicization of these configurations. Combining its ambiguities with its interdependencies, the innovative form can emerge as a rather politicized and ruthless organization – supportive of the fit, as long as they remain fit, but destructive of the weak.

Problems of Efficiency

No configuration is better suited to solving complex, ill-structured problems than this one. None can match it for sophisticated innovation. Or, unfortunately, for the costs of that innovation. This is simply not an efficient way to function. Although it is ideally suited for the one-of-a-kind project, the innovative configuration is not competent at doing *ordinary* things. It is designed for the *extra*ordinary. The bureaucracies are all mass producers; they gain efficiency through standardization. The adhocracy is a custom producer, unable to standardize and so be efficient. It gains its effectiveness (innovation) at the price of efficiency.

One source of inefficiency lies in the unbalanced workload, mentioned earlier. It is almost impossible to keep the personnel of a project structure – high priced specialists, it should be noted – busy on a steady basis. In January they may be working overtime with no hope of completing the new project on time; by May they may be playing cards for want of work.

But the real root of inefficiency is the high cost of communication. People talk a lot in these organizations; that is how they combine their knowledge to develop new ideas. But that takes time, a great deal of time. Faced with the need to make a decision in the machine organization, someone up above gives an order and that is that. Not so in the innovative one, where everyone must get into the act – managers of all kinds (functional, project, liaison), as well as all the specialists who believe their point of view should be represented. A meeting is called, probably to schedule another meeting, eventually to decide who should participate in the decision. The problem then gets defined and redefined, ideas for its solution get generated and debated, alliances build and fall around different solutions, until eventually everyone settles down to the hard bargaining over which one to adopt. Finally a decision emerges – that in itself is an accomplishment – although it is typically late and will probably be modified later.

The Dangers of Inappropriate Transition

Of course, one solution to the problems of ambiguity and inefficiency is to change the configuration. Employees no longer able to tolerate the ambiguity and customers fed up with the inefficiency may try to drive the organization to a more stable, bureaucratic form.

That is relatively easily done in the operating adhocracy, as noted earlier. The organization simply selects the set of standard programmes it does best, reverting to the professional configuration, or else innovates one last time to find a lucrative market niche in which to mass produce, and then becomes a machine configuration. But those transitions, however easily effected, are not always appropriate. The organization came into being to solve problems imaginatively, not to apply standards indiscriminately. In many spheres, society has more mass producers than it needs; what it lacks are true problem-solvers – the consulting firm that can handle a unique problem instead of applying a pat solution, the advertising agency that can come up with a novel campaign instead of the common imitation, the research laboratory that can make the really serious breakthrough instead of just modifying an existing design. The television networks seem to be classic examples of bureaucracies that provide largely standardized fare when the creativity of adhocracy is called for (except, perhaps, for the newsrooms and the specials, where an *ad hoc* orientation encourages more creativity).

The administrative adhocracy can run into more serious difficulties when it succumbs to the pressures to bureaucratize. It exists to innovate for itself, in its own industry. Unlike the operating adhocracy, it often cannot change orientation while remaining in the same industry. And so its conversion to the machine configuration (the natural transition for administrative adhocracy tired of perpetual change), by destroying the organization's ability to innovate, can eventually destroy the organization itself.

To reiterate a central theme of our discussion throughout this section: In general, there is no one best structure; in particular, there may be at a cost of something forgone, so long as the different attributes combine to form a coherent configuration that is consistent with the situation.

• MANAGING INNOVATION: CONTROLLED CHAOS*

JAMES BRIAN QUINN

Management observers frequently claim that small organizations are more innovative than large ones. But is this commonplace necessarily true? Some large enterprises are highly innovative. How do they do it? ... This article [reports on a] $2\frac{1}{2}$-year worldwide study ... [of] both well-documented small ventures and large US, Japanese and European companies and programmes selected for their innovation records. ... More striking than the cultural differences among these companies are the similarities between innovative small and large organizations and among innovative organizations in different countries. Effective management of innovation seems much the same, regardless of national boundaries or scale of operations.

There are ... many reasons why small companies appear to produce a disproportionate number of innovations. First, innovation occurs in a probabilistic setting. A company never knows whether a particular technical result can be achieved and whether it will succeed in the marketplace. For every new solution that succeeds, tens to hundreds fail. The sheer number of attempts – most by small-scale entrepreneurs – means that some ventures will survive. The 90 per cent to 99 per cent that fail are distributed widely throughout society and receive little notice.

On the other hand, a big company that wishes to move a concept from invention to the marketplace must absorb all potential failure costs itself. This risk may be socially or managerially intolerable, jeopardizing the many other products, projects, jobs and communities the company supports. Even if its innovation is successful, a big company may face costs that newcomers do not bear, like converting existing operations and customer bases to the new solution.

By contrast, a new enterprise does not risk losing an existing investment base or cannibalizing customer franchises built at great expense. It does not have to change an internal culture that has successfully supported doing things another way or that has developed intellectual depth and belief in the technologies that led to past successes. Organized groups like trade unions, consumer advocates and government bureaucracies rarely monitor and resist a small company's moves as they might a big company's. Finally, new companies do not face the psychological pain and the economic costs of laying off employees, shutting down plants and even communities, and displacing supplier relationships built with years of mutual commitment and effort. Such barriers to change in large organizations are real, important and legitimate.

The complex products and systems that society expects large companies to undertake further compound the risks. Only big companies can develop new ships or locomotives; telecommunication networks; or systems for space, defence, air traffic control, hospital care, mass foods delivery or nationwide computer interactions. These large-scale projects always carry more risk than single-product introductions. A

* Originally published in the *Harvard Business Review* (May–June 1985): winner of the McKinsey prize for the best article in the *Review* in 1985. Copyright © 1985 by the President and Fellows of Harvard College; all rights reserved. Reprinted with deletions by permission of the *Harvard Business Review*.

billion-dollar development aircraft, for example, can fail if one inexpensive part in its 100,000 components fails.

Clearly, a single enterprise cannot by itself develop or produce all the parts needed by such large new systems. And communications among the various groups making design and production decisions on components are always incomplete. The probability of error increases exponentially with complexity, while the system innovator's control over decisions decreases significantly – further escalating potential error costs and risks. Such forces inhibit innovation in large organizations. But proper management can lessen these effects.

OF INVENTORS AND ENTREPRENEURS

A close look at innovative small enterprises reveals much about the successful management of innovation. Of course, not all innovations follow a single pattern. But my research – and other studies in combination – suggest that the following factors are crucial to the success of innovative small companies:

Need Orientation

Inventor-entrepreneurs tend to be 'need or achievement oriented'. They believe that if they 'do the job better', rewards will follow. They may at first focus on their own view of market needs. But lacking resources, successful small entrepreneurs soon find that it pays to approach potential customers early, test their solutions in users' hands, learn from these interactions, and adapt designs rapidly. Many studies suggest that effective technological innovation develops hand-in-hand with customer demand (Von Hippel, 1982: 117).

Experts and Fanatics

Company founders tend to be pioneers in their technologies and fanatics when it comes to solving problems. They are often described as 'possessed' or 'obsessed', working towards their objectives to the exclusion even of family or personal relationships. As both experts and fanatics, they perceive probabilities of success as higher than others do. And their commitment allows them to persevere despite the frustrations, ambiguities and setbacks that always accompany major innovations.

Long Time-Horizons

Their fanaticism may cause inventor-entrepreneurs to underestimate the obstacles and length of time to success. Time-horizons for radical innovations make them essentially 'irrational' from a present value viewpoint. In my sample, delays between invention and commercial production ranged from 3 to 25 years.[3] In the late 1930s, for example, industrial chemist Russell Marker was working on steroids called sapogenins when he discovered a technique that would degrade one of these, diosgenin, into the female sex hormone progesterone. Buy processing some 10 tons of Mexican yams in rented and borrowed lab space, Marker finally extracted about four pounds of diosgenin and started a tiny business to produce steroids for the laboratory market. But it was not until 1962, over 23 years later, that Syntex, the company Marker founded, obtained FDA approval for its oral contraceptive.

For both psychological and practical reasons, inventor-entrepreneurs generally avoid early formal plans, proceed step-by-step, and sustain themselves by other income and the momentum of the small advances they achieve as they go along.

Low Early Costs

Innovators tend to work in homes, basements, warehouses or low-rent facilities whenever possible. They incur few overhead costs; their limited resources go directly into their projects. They pour nights, weekends, and 'sweat capital' into their endeavours. They borrow whatever they can. They invent cheap equipment and prototype processes, often improving on what is available in the marketplace. If one approach fails, few people know; little time or money is lost. All this decreases the costs and risks facing a small operation and improves the present value of its potential success.

Multiple Approaches

Technology tends to advance through a series of random – often highly intuitive – insights frequently triggered by gratuitous interactions between the discoverer and the outside world. Only highly committed entrepreneurs can tolerate (and even enjoy) this chaos. They adopt solutions wherever they can be found, unencumbered by formal plans or PERT charts that would limit the range of their imaginations. When the odds of success are low, the participation and interaction of many motivated players increase the chance that one will succeed.

A recent study of initial public offerings made in 1962 shows that only 2 per cent survived and still looked like worthwhile investments 20 years later.[4] Small-scale entrepreneurship looks efficient in part because history only records the survivors.

Flexibility and Quickness

Undeterred by committees, board approvals and other bureaucratic delays, the inventor-entrepreneur can experiment, test, recycle and try again with little time lost. Because technological progress depends largely on the number of successful experiments accomplished per unit of time, fast-moving small entrepreneurs can gain both timing and performance advantages over clumsier competitors. This responsiveness is often crucial in finding early markets for radical innovations where neither innovators, market researchers, nor users can quite visualize a product's real potential. For example, Edison's lights first appeared on ships and in baseball parks; Astroturf was intended to convert the flat roofs and asphalt playgrounds of city schools into more human environments; and graphite and boron composites designed for aerospace unexpectedly found their largest markets in sporting goods. Entrepreneurs quickly adjusted their entry strategies to market feedback.

Incentives

Inventor-entrepreneurs can foresee tangible personal rewards if they are successful. Individuals often want to achieve a technical contribution, recognition, power or sheer independence, as much as money. For the original, driven personalities who create significant innovations, few other paths offer such clear opportunities to fulfil all their economic, psychological, and career goals at once. Consequently, they do not panic or quit when others with solely monetary goals might

Availability of Capital

One of America's great competitive advantages is its rich variety of sources to finance small, low-probability ventures. If entrepreneurs are turned down by one source, other sources can be sought in myriads of creative combinations.

Professionals involved in such finances have developed a characteristic approach to deal with the chaos and uncertainty of innovation. First, they evaluate a proposal's conceptual validity: If the technical problems can be solved, is there a real business there for someone and does it have a large upside potential? Next, they concentrate on people: Is the team thoroughly committed and expert? Is it the best available? Only then do these financiers analyze specific financial estimates in depth. Even then, they recognize that actual outcomes generally depend on subjective factors, not numbers (Pence, 1982).

Timeliness, aggressiveness, commitment, quality of people and the flexibility to attack opportunities not at first perceived are crucial. Downside risks are minimized, not by detailed controls, but by spreading risks among multiple projects, keeping early costs low, and gauging the tenacity, flexibility and capability of the founders.

LARGE-COMPANY BARRIERS TO INNOVATION

Less innovative companies and, unfortunately, most large corporations operate in a very different fashion. The most notable and common constraints on innovation in larger companies include the following:

Top Management Isolation

Many senior executives in big companies have little contact with conditions on the factory floor or with customers who might influence their thinking about technological innovation. Since risk perception is inversely related to familiarity and experience, financially oriented top managers are likely to perceive technological innovations as more problematic than acquisitions that may be just as risky but that will appear more familiar (Hayes and Garvin, 1982: 70: Hayes and Abernathy, 1980: 67).

Intolerance of Fanatics

Big companies often view entrepreneurial fanatics as embarrassments or trouble-makers. Many major cities are now ringed by companies founded by these 'non-team' players – often to the regret of their former employers.

Short Time-Horizons

The perceived corporate need to report a continuous stream of quarterly profits conflicts with the long time spans that major innovations normally require. Such pressures often make publicly owned companies favour quick marketing fixes, cost-cutting and acquisition strategies over process, product or quality innovations that would yield much more in the long run.

Accounting Practices

By assessing all its direct, indirect, overhead, overtime and service costs against a project, large corporations have much higher development expenses compared with entrepreneurs working in garages. A project in a big company can quickly become an exposed political target, its potential net present value may sink unacceptably, and an entry into small markets may not justify its sunk costs. An otherwise viable project may soon founder and disappear.

Excessive Rationalism

Managers in big companies often seek orderly advance through early market research studies or PERT planning. Rather than managing the inevitable chaos of innovation productively, these managers soon drive out the very things that lead to innovation in order to prove their announced plans.

Excessive Bureaucracy

In the name of efficiency, bureaucratic structures require many approvals and cause delays at every turn. Experiments that a small company can perform in hours may take days or weeks in large organizations. The interactive feedback that fosters innovation is lost, important time windows can be missed and real costs and risks rise for the corporation

Inappropriate Incentives

Reward and control systems in most big companies are designed to minimize surprises. Yet innovation, by definition, is full of surprises. If often disrupts well-laid plans, accepted power patterns and entrenched organizational behaviour at high costs to many. Few large companies make millionaires of those who create such disruptions, however profitable the innovations may turn out to be. When control systems neither penalize opportunities missed nor reward risks taken, the results are predictable.

HOW LARGE INNOVATIVE COMPANIES DO IT

Yet some big companies are continuously innovative. Although each such enterprise is distinctive, the successful big innovators I studied have developed techniques that emulate or improve on their smaller counterparts' practices. What are the most important patterns?

Atmosphere and Vision

Continuous innovation occurs largely because top executives appreciate innovation and manage their company's value system and atmosphere to support it. For example, Sony's founder, Masaru Ibuka, stated in the company's 'Purposes of Incorporation' the goal of a 'free, dynamic, and pleasant factory ... where sincerely motivated personnel can exercise their technological skills to the highest level'. Ibuka and Sony's chairman, Akio Morita, inculcated the 'Sony spirit' through a series of unusual policies: hiring brilliant people with non-traditional skills (like an opera singer) for high management positions, promoting young people over their elders, designing a new type of living accommodation for workers and providing visible awards for outstanding technical achievements.

Because familiarity can foster understanding and psychological comfort, engineering and scientific leaders are often those who create atmospheres supportive of innovation, especially in a company's early life. Executive vision is more important than a particular management background – as IBM, Genentech, AT&T, Merck, Elf Aquitaine, Pilkington and others in my sample illustrate. CEOs of these companies value technology and include technical experts in their highest decisions circles.

Innovative managements – whether technical or not – project clear, long-term visions for their organizations that go beyond simple economic measures. ... Genentech's original plan expresses [such a] vision: 'We expect to be the first company to commercialize the [rDNA] technology, and we plan to build a major profitable corporation by manufacturing and marketing needed products that benefit mankind. The future uses of genetic engineering are far reaching and many. Any product produced by a living organism is eventually within the company's reach.'

Such visions, vigorously supported, are not 'management fluff', but have many practical implications.[5] They attract quality people to the company and give focus to their creative and entrepreneurial drives. When combined with sound internal operations, they help channel growth by concentrating attention on the actions that lead to profitability, rather than on profitability itself. Finally, these visions recognize a realistic time frame for innovation and attract the kind of investors who will support it.

Orientation to the Market

Innovative companies tie their visions to the practical realities of the marketplace. Although each company uses techniques adapted to its own style and strategy, two elements are always present: a strong market orientation at the very top of the company and mechanisms to ensure interactions between technical and marketing people at lower levels. At Sony, for example, soon after technical people are hired, the company runs them through weeks of retail selling. Sony engineers become sensitive to the ways retail sales practices, product displays and non-quantifiable customer preferences affect success. ...

From top to bench levels in my sample's most innovative companies, managers focus primarily on seeking to anticipate and solve customers' emerging problems.

Small, Flat Organizations

The most innovative large companies in my sample try to keep the total organization flat and project teams small. Development teams normally include only six or seven key people. This number seems to constitute a critical mass of skills while fostering maximum communication and commitment among members. According to research done by my colleague, Victor McGee, the number of channels of communication increases as $n[2^{n-1}-1]$. Therefore:

For team size	=	1	2	3	4	5	6
Channels	=	1	2	9	28	75	186
		7	8	9	10	11	
		441	1,016	2,295	5,110	11,253	

Innovative companies also try to keep their operating divisions and total technical units small – below 400 people. Up to this number, only two layers of management are required to maintain a span of control over seven people. In units muxh larger than 400, people quickly lose touch with the concept of their product or process, staffs and bureaucracies tend to grow, and projects may go through too many formal screens to survive. Since it takes a chain of yeses and only one no to kill a project, jeopardy multiplies as management layers increase.

Multiple Approaches

At first one cannot be sure which of several technical approaches will dominate a field. The history of technology is replete with accidents, mishaps and chance meetings which allow one approach or group to emerge rapidly over others. Leo Backelund was looking for a synthetic shellac when he found Bakelite and started the modern plastics industry. At Syntex, researchers were not looking for an oral contraceptive when they created 19-nonprogesterone, the precursor to the active ingredient in half of all contraceptive pills. And the microcomputer was born because Intel's Ted Hoff 'happened' to work on a complex calculator just when Digital Equipment Corporation's PDP8 architecture was fresh in his mind.

Such 'accidents' are involved in almost all major technological advances. When theory can predict everything, a company has moved to a new stage, from development to production. Murphy's law works because engineers design for what they can foresee; hence what fails is what theory could not predict. And it is rare that the interactions of components and subsystems can be predicted over the lifetime of operations. For example, despite careful theoretical design work, the first high-performance jet engine literally tore itself to pieces on its test stand, while others failed in unanticipated operating conditions (like an Iranian sandstorm).

Recognizing the inadequacies of theory, innovative enterprises seem to move faster from paper studies to physical testing than do non-innovative enterprises. When possible, they encourage several prototype programmes to proceed in parallel. ... Such redundancy helps the company cope with uncertainties in development, motivates people through competition, and improves the amount and quality of information available for making final choices on scale-ups or introductions.

Developmental Shoot-outs

Many companies structure shoot-outs among competing approaches only after they reach the prototype stages. They find this practice provides more objective information for making decisions, decreases risk by making choices that best reflect marketplace needs, and helps ensure that the winning option will move ahead with a committed team behind it. Although many managers worry that competing approaches may be inefficient, greater effectiveness in choosing the right solution easily outweighs duplication costs when the market rewards higher performance or when large volumes justify increased sophistication. Under these conditions, parallel development may prove less costly because it both improves the probability of success and reduces development time.

Perhaps the most difficult problem in managing competing projects lies in reintegrating the members of the losing team. If the company is expanding rapidly or if the successful project creates a growth opportunity, losing team members can work on another interesting programme or sign on with the winning team as the project moves toward the marketplace. For the shoot-out system to work continuously, however, executives must create a climate that honours highly-quality performance whether a project wins or loses, reinvolves people quickly in their technical specialties or in other projects, and accepts and expects rotation among tasks and groups. ...

Skunkworks

Every highly innovative enterprise in my research sample emulated small company practices by using groups that functioned in a skunkworks style. Small teams of engineers, technicians, designers and model-makers were placed together with no intervening organizational or physical barriers to developing a new product from idea to commercial prototype stages. In innovative Japanese companies, top managers often worked hand in hand on projects with young engineers. Surprisingly, *ringi* decision-making was not evident in these situations. Soichiro Honda was known for working directly on technical problems and emphasizing his technical points by shouting at his engineers or occasionally even hitting them with wrenches!

The skunkworks approach eliminates bureaucracies, allows fast, unfettered communications, permits rapid turnaround times for experiments, and instils a high level of group identity and loyalty. Interestingly, few successful groups in my research were structured in the classic 'venture group' form, with a careful balancing of engineering, production and marketing talents. Instead, they acted on an old truism: introducing a new product or process to the world is like raising a healthy child – it needs a mother (champion) who loves it, a father (authority figure with resources) to support it and paediatricians (specialists) to get it through difficult times. It may survive solely in the hands of specialists, but its chances of success are remote.

Interactive Learning

Skunkworks are as close as most big companies can come to emulating the highly interactive and motivating learning environment that characterizes successful small ventures. But the best big innovators have gone even farther. Recognizing that the random, chaotic nature of technological change cuts across organizational and even institutional lines, these companies tap into multiple outside sources of technology as well as their customers' capabilities. Enormous external leverages are possible. No company can spend more than a small share of the world's $200 billion devoted to R&D. But like small entrepreneurs, big companies can have much of that total effort cheaply if they try.

In industries such as electronics, customers provide much of the innovation on new products. In other industries, such as textiles, materials or equipment suppliers provide the innovation. In still others, such as biotechnology, universities are dominant, while foreign sources strongly supplement industries such as controlled fusion. Many R&D units have strategies to develop information for trading with outside groups and have teams to cultivate these sources. Large Japanese companies have been notably effective at this. So have US companies as diverse as Du Pont, AT&T, Apple Computer and Genentech.

An increasing variety of creative relationships exist in which big companies participate – as joint ventures, consortium members, limited partners, guarantors of first markets, major academic funding sources, venture capitalists, spin-off equity holders, and so on. These rival the variety of inventive financing and networking structures that individual entrepreneurs have created.

Indeed, the innovative practices of small and large companies look ever more alike. This resemblance is especially striking in the interactions between companies and customers during development. Many experienced big companies are relying less on early market research and more on interactive development with lead customers. Hewlett-Packard, 3M, Sony and Raychem frequently introduce radically new products through small teams that work closely with lead customers. These teams learn from their customers' needs and innovations and rapidly modify designs and entry strategies based on this information.

Formal market analyses continue to be useful for extending product lines, but they are often misleading when applied to radical innovations. Market studies predicted that Haloid would never sell more than 5,000 xerographic machines, that Intel's microprocessor would never sell more than 10 per cent as many units as there were minicomputers, and that Sony's transistor radios and miniature television sets would fail in the marketplace. At the same time, many eventual failures such as Ford's Edsel, IBM's FS system, and the supersonic transport were studied and planned exhaustively on paper, but lost contact with customers' real needs.

A STRATEGY FOR INNOVATION

The flexible management practices needed for major innovations often pose problems for established cultures in big companies. Yet there are reasonable steps managers in these companies can take. Innovation can be bred in a surprising variety of organizations, as many examples show. What are its key elements?

An Opportunity Orientation

In the 1981–83 recession, many large companies cut back or closed plants as their 'only available solution'. Yet I repeatedly found that top managers in these companies took these actions without determining first hand why their customers were buying from competitors, discerning what niches in their markets were growing or tapping the innovations their own people had to solve problems. These managers foreclosed innumerable options by defining the issue as cost-cutting rather than opportunity-seeking. As one frustrated division manager in a manufacturing conglomerate put it: 'If management doesn't actively seek or welcome technical opportunities, it sure won't hear about them.'

By contrast, Intel met the challenge of the last recession with its '20 per cent solution'. The professional staff agreed to work one extra day a week to bring innovations to the marketplace earlier than planned. Despite the difficult times, Intel came out of the recession with several important new products ready to go – and it avoided layoffs.

Entrepreneurial companies recognize that they have almost unlimited access to capital and they structure their practices accordingly. They let it be known that if their people come up with good ideas, they can find the necessary capital – just as private venture capitalists or investment bankers find resources for small entrepreneurs.

Structuring for Innovation

Managers need to think carefully about how innovation fits into their strategy and structure their technology, skills, resources and organizational commitments accordingly. A few examples suggest the variety of strategies and alignments possible:

> Hewlett-Packard and 3M develop product lines around a series of small, discrete, freestanding products. These companies form units that look like entrepreneurial start-ups. Each has a small team, led by a champion, in low-cost facilities. These companies allow many different proposals to come forward and test them as early as possible in the marketplace. They design control systems to spot significant losses on any single entry quickly. They look for high gains on a few winners and blend less successful, smaller entries into prosperous product lines.
>
> Other companies (like AT&T or the oil majors) have had to make large system investments to last for decades. These companies tend to make longterm needs forecasts. They often start several programs in parallel to be sure of selecting the right technologies. They then extensively test new technologies in use before making systemwide commitments. Often they sacrifice speed of entry for long-term low cost and reliability.
>
> Intel and Dewey & Almy, suppliers of highly technical specialities to EOMs, develop strong technical sales networks to discover and understand customer needs in depth. These companies try to have technical solutions designed into customers' products. Such companies have flexible applied technology groups working close to the marketplace. They also have quickly expandable plant facilities and a cutting edge technology (not necessarily basic research) group that allows rapid selection of currently available technologies.

Dominant producers like IBM or Matsushita are often not the first to introduce new technologies. They do not want to disturb their successful product lines any sooner than necessary. As market demands become clear, these companies establish precise price-performance windows and form overlapping project teams to come up with the best answer for the marketplace. To decrease market risks, they use product shoot-outs as close to the market as possible. They develop extreme depth in production technologies to keep unit costs low from the outset. Finally, depending on the scale of the market entry, they have project teams report as close to the top as necessary to secure needed management attention and resources.

Merck and Hoffman-LaRoche, basic research companies, maintain laboratories with better facilities, higher pay, and more freedom than most universities can afford. These companies leverage their internal spending through research grants, clinical grants, and research relationships with universities throughout the world. Before they invest $20 million to $50 million to clear a new drug, they must have reasonable assurance that they will be first in the marketplace. They take elaborate precautions to ensure that the new entry is safe and effective, and that it cannot be easily duplicated by others. Their structures are designed to be on the cutting edge of science, but conservative in animal testing, clinical evaluation and production control.

These examples suggest some ways of linking innovation to strategy. Many other examples, of course, exist. Within a single company, individual divisions may have different strategic needs and hence different structures and practices. No single approach works well for all situations.

Complex Portfolio Planning

Perhaps the most difficult task for top managers is to balance the needs of existing lines against the needs of potential lines. This problem requires a portfolio strategy much more complex than the popular four-box Boston Consulting Group matrix found in most strategy texts. To allocate resources for innovation strategically, managers need to define the broad, long-term actions within and across divisions necessary to achieve their visions. They should determine which positions to hold at all costs, where to fall back, and where to expand initially and in the more distant future.

A company's strategy may often require investing more resources in current lines. But sufficient resources should also be invested in patterns that ensure intermediate and long-term growth; provide defences against possible government, labour, competitive or activist challenges; and generate needed organizational, technical and external relations flexibilities to handle unforeseen opportunities or threats. Sophisticated portfolio planning within and among divisions can protect both current returns and future prospects – the two critical bases for that most cherished goal, high price/earnings ratios.

AN INCREMENTALIST APPROACH

Such managerial techniques can provide a strategic focus for innovation and help solve many of the timing, coordination and motivation problems that plague large, bureaucratic organizations. Even more detailed planning techniques may help in guiding the development of the many small innovations that characterize any successful business. My research reveals, however, that few, if any, major innovations result from highly structured planning systems. [Why?] ...

The innovative process is inherently incremental. As Thomas Hughes says, 'Technological systems evolve through relatively small steps marked by an occasional stubborn obstacle and by constant random breakthroughs interacting across laboratories and borders' (Hughes, 1984: 83). A forgotten hypothesis of Einstein's became the laser in Charles Townes's mind as he contemplated azaleas in Franklin Square. The structure of DNA followed a circuitous route through research in biology, organic chemistry, X-ray crystallography and mathematics towards its Nobel prize-winning conception as a spiral staircase of [base pairs]. Such rambling trails are characteristic of virtually all major technological advances.

At the outset of the attack on a technical problem, an innovator often does not know whether his problem is tractable, what approach will prove best and what concrete characteristics the solution will have if achieved. The logical route, therefore, is to follow several paths – though perhaps with varying degrees of intensity – until more information becomes available. Now knowing precisely where the solution will occur, wise managers establish the widest feasible network for finding and assessing alternative solutions. They keep many options open until one of them seems sure to win. Then they back it heavily.

Managing innovation is like a stud poker game, where one can play several hands. A player has some idea of the likely size of the pot at the beginning, knows the general but not the sure route to winning, buys one card (a project) at a time to gain information about probabilities and the size of the pot, closes hands as they become discouraging, and risks more only late in the hand as knowledge increases. ...

Chaos Within Guidelines

Effective managers of innovation channel and control its main directions. Like venture capitalists, they administer primarily by setting goals, selecting key people and establishing a few critical limits and decision points for intervention rather than by implementing elaborate planning or control systems. As technology leads or market needs emerge, these managers set a few – most crucial – performance targets and limits. They allow their technical units to decide how to achieve these, subject to defined constraints and reviews at critical junctures.

Early bench-scale project managers may pursue various options, making little attempt at first to integrate each into a total programme. Only after key variables are understood – and perhaps measured and demonstrated in lab models – can more precise planning be meaningful. Even then, many factors may remain unknown; chaos and competition can continue to thrive in the pursuit of the solution. At defined review points, however, only those options that can clear performance milestones may continue. ...

Even after selecting the approaches to emphasize, innovative managers tend to continue a few others as smaller scale 'side bets' or options. In a surprising number of cases, these alternatives prove winners when the planned option falls.

Recognizing the many demands entailed by successful programmes, innovative companies find special ways to reward innovators. Sony gives 'a small but significant' percentage of a new product's sales to its innovating teams. Pilkington, IBM and 3M's top executives are often chosen from those who have headed successful new product entries. Intel lets its Magnetic Memory Group operate like a small company, with special performance rewards and simulated stock options. GE, Syntex and United Technologies help internal innovators establish new companies and take equity positions in 'non-related' product innovations.

Large companies do not have to make their innovators millionaires, but reward should be visible and significant. Fortunately, most engineers are happy with the incentives that Tracy Kidder (1981) calls 'Playing pinball' – giving widespread recognition to a job well done and the right to play in the next exciting game. Most innovative companies provide both. ...

MATCH MANAGEMENT TO THE PROCESS

... Executives need to understand and accept the tumultuous realities of innovation, learn from the experiences of other companies, and adapt the most relevant features of these others to their own management practices and cultures. Many features of small company innovators are also applicable in big companies. With top-level understanding, vision, a commitment to customers and solutions, a genuine portfolio strategy, a flexible entrepreneurial atmosphere and proper incentives for innovative champions, many more large companies can innovate to meet the severe demands of global competition.

[1] I like to tell a story of the hospital patient with an appendix about to burst who presents himself to a hospital organized as an adhocracy: 'Who wants to do another appendectomy? We're into livers now,' as they go about exploring new procedures. But the patient returning from a trip to the jungle with a rare tropical disease had better beware of the hospital organized as a professional bureaucracy. A student came up to me after I once said this and explained how hospital doctors puzzled by her bloated stomach and not knowing what to do took out her appendix. Luckily, her problem resolved itself, some time later. Another time, a surgeon told me that his hospital no longer does appendectomies.

[2] We might take this convergence as the expression of an 'organization's mind' – the focusing on a strategic theme as a result of the mutual adjustments among its many actors.

[3] A study at Battelle found an average of 19.2 years between invention and commercial production. Battelle Memorial Laboratories, 'Science, technology, and innovation'. Report to the National Science Foundation, 1973; also Dean (1974: 13).

[4] Business Economics Group, W. R. Grace & Co., 1983.

[5] Thomas J. Allen (1977) illustrates the enormous leverage provided such technology accessors (called 'gatekeepers') in R&D organizations.

THE INTERNATIONAL CONTEXT

This chapter focuses on the strategy process of companies whose activities stretch across national borders. Operating in an international rather than a domestic arena presents managers of these companies with many new opportunities. Having worldwide operations not only gives a company access to new markets and specialized resources, it also opens up new sources of information to stimulate future product development. And it broadens the options of strategic moves and countermoves the company might make in competing with its domestic or more narrowly international rivals. However, with all these new opportunities comes the challenge of managing strategy, organization and operations that are innately more complex, diverse and uncertain:

The first reading in this chapter, by George Yip, who teaches at the University of California in Los Angeles, focuses on the strategic aspects of managing in an international context. Yip's views on 'global strategy' reflect the same orientation of industrial organization economics that influenced Porter's work: in deciding on markets to participate in, products and services to offer and location of specific activities and tasks, managers must analyze the 'globalization drivers' in their industries and find the right strategic fit.

In the second reading, Christopher Bartlett and Sumantra Ghoshal deal with the organizational aspects of managing in the international context. To operate effectively on a worldwide basis, Bartlett and Ghoshal suggest, companies must learn to differentiate how they manage different businesses, countries and functions, create interdependence among units instead of either dependence or independence, and focus on coordination and cooption rather than control. The key to such organizational capability lies in the same elements of shared vision and values that they had described in their article in Chapter 4, as essential for 'building a matrix in managers' minds'.

GLOBAL STRATEGY … IN A WORLD OF NATIONS?*[1]

GEORGE S. YIP

Whether to globalize and how to globalize have become two of the most burning strategy issues for managers around the world. Many forces are driving companies around the world to globalize by expanding their participation in foreign markets. Almost every product market in the major world economies – computers, fast food, nuts and bolts – has foreign competitors. Trade barriers are also falling; the … United States/Canada trade agreement and the … 1992 harmonization in the European Community are the two most dramatic examples. Japan is gradually opening up its long barricaded markets. Maturity in domestic markets is also driving companies to seek international expansion. This is particularly true of US companies that, nourished by the huge domestic market, have typically lagged behind their European and Japanese rivals in internationalization.

Companies are also seeking to globalize by integrating their worldwide strategy. Such global integration contrasts with the multinational approach whereby companies set up country subsidiaries that design, produce, and market products or services tailored to local needs. This multinational model (also described as a 'multi-domestic strategy') is now in question (Hout *et al.*, 1982). Several changes seem to increase the likelihood that, in some industries, a global strategy will be more successful than a multi-domestic one. One of these changes, as argued forcefully and controversially by Levitt (1983), is the growing similarity of what citizens of different countries want to buy. Other changes include the reduction of tariff and non-tariff barriers, technology investments that are becoming too expensive to amortize in one market only, and competitors that are globalizing the rules of the game.

Companies want to know how to globalize – in other words, expand market participation – and how to develop an integrated worldwide strategy. As depicted in Figure 1, three steps are essential in developing a total worldwide strategy:

- Developing the core strategy – the basis of sustainable competitive advantage. It is usually developed for the home country first.
- Internationalizing the core strategy through international expansion of activities and through adaptation.
- Globalizing the international strategy by integrating the strategy across countries.

Multinational companies know the first two steps well. They know the third step less well since globalization runs counter to the accepted wisdom of tailoring for national markets (Douglas and Wind, 1987).

This article makes a cast for how a global strategy might work and directs managers toward opportunities to exploit globalization. It also presents the

---

* Originally published in the *Sloan Management Review* (Autumn 1989). Copyright © *Sloan Management Review* 1989. Reprinted with deletions by permission of the *review*.

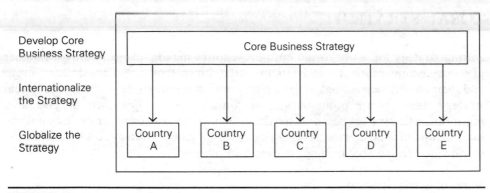

FIGURE 1
Total global strategy

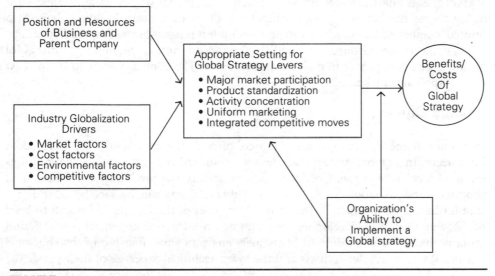

FIGURE 2
Framework of global strategy forces

drawbacks and costs of globalization. Figure 2 lays out a framework for thinking through globalization issues.

Industry globalization drivers (underlying market, cost and other industry conditions) are externally determined, while global strategy levers are choices available to the worldwide business. Drivers create the potential for a multinational business to achieve the benefits of global strategy. To achieve these benefits, a multinational business needs to set its *global strategy levers* (e.g. use of product standardization) appropriately to industry drivers, and to the position and resources of the business and its parent company. The organization's ability to implement the strategy affects how well the benefits can be achieved.

WHAT IS GLOBAL STRATEGY?

Setting strategy for a worldwide business requires making choices along a number of strategic dimensions. Table 1 lists five such dimensions or 'global strategy levels' and their respective positions under a pure multi-domestic strategy and a pure global strategy. Intermediate positions are, of course, feasible. For each dimension, a multi-domestic strategy seeks to maximize worldwide performance by maximizing local competitive advantage, revenues or profits; a global strategy seeks to maximize worldwide performance through sharing and integration.

Market Participation

In a multi-domestic strategy, countries are selected on the basis of their stand-alone potential for revenues and profits. In a global strategy, countries need to be selected for their potential contribution to globalization benefits. This may mean entering a market that is unattractive in its own right, but has global strategic significance, such as the home market of a global competitor. Or it may mean building share in a limited number of key markets rather than undertaking more widespread coverage. ... The Electrolux Group, the Swedish appliance giant, is pursuing a strategy of building significant share in major world markets. The company aims to be the first global appliance maker. ...

Product Offering

In a multi-domestic strategy, the products offered in each country are tailored to local needs. In a global strategy, the ideal is a standardized core product that requires minimal local adaptation. Cost reduction is usually the most important benefit of product standardization. ... Differing worldwide needs can be met by adapting a standardized core product. In the early 1970s, sales of the Boeing 737 began to level off. Boeing turned to developing countries as an attractive new market, but found initially that its product did not fit the new environments. Because of the shortness of runways, their greater softness and the lower technical expertise of their pilots, the planes tended to bounce a great deal. When the planes bounced on landing, the brakes failed. To fix this problem, Boeing modified the design by adding thrust to

TABLE 1   Globalization Dimensions/Global Strategy Levers

Dimension	Setting for Pure Multi-domestic Strategy	Setting for Pure Global Strategy
Market participation	No particular pattern	Significant share in major markets
Product offering	Fully customized in each country	Fully standardized worldwide
Location of value-added activities	All activities in each country	Concentrated – one activity in each (different) country
Marketing approach	Local	Uniform worldwide
Competitive moves	Stand-alone by country	Integrated across countries

the engines, redesigning the wings and landing gear, and installing tyres with low pressure. These adaptations to a standardized core product enabled the 737 to become the best selling plane in history.

Location of Value-Added Activities

In a multi-domestic strategy, all or most of the value chain is reproduced in every country. In another type of international strategy – exporting – most of the value chain is kept in one country. In a global strategy, costs are reduced by breaking up the value chain so each activity may be conducted in a different country. ...

Marketing Approach

In a multi-domestic strategy, marketing is fully tailored for each country, being developed locally. In a global strategy, a uniform marketing approach is applied around the world, although not all elements of the marketing mix need be uniform. Unilever achieved great success with a fabric softener that used a globally common positioning, advertising theme and symbol (a teddy bear), but a brand name that varied by country. Similarly, a product that serves a common need can be geographically expanded with a uniform marketing programme, despite differences in marketing environments.

Competitive Moves

In a multi-domestic strategy, the managers in each country make competitive moves without regard for what happens in other countries. In a global strategy, competitive moves are integrated across countries at the same time or in a systematic sequence: a competitor is attacked in one country in order to drain its resources for another country or a competitive attack in one country is countered in a different country. Perhaps the best example is the counterattack in a competitor's home market as a parry to an attack on one's own home market. Integration of competitive strategy is rarely practised, except perhaps by some Japanese companies.

Bridgestone Corporation, the Japanese tyre manufacturer, tried to integrate its competitive moves in response to global consolidation by its major competitors. ... These competitive actions forced Bridgestone to establish a presence in the major US market in order to maintain its position in the world tyre market. To this end, Bridgestone formed a joint venture to own and manage Firestone Corporation's worldwide tyre business. This joint venture also allowed Bridgestone to gain access to Firestone's European plants.

BENEFITS OF A GLOGBAL STRATEGY

Companies that use global strategy levers can achieve one or more of these benefits. ...

- cost reductions,
- improved quality of products and programmes,

- enhanced customer preference,
- increased competitive leverage.

Cost Reductions

An integrated global strategy can reduce worldwide costs in several ways. A company can increase the benefits from economies of scale by *pooling production or other activities* for two or more countries. Understanding the potential benefit of these economies of scale, Sony Corporation has concentrated its compact disc production in Terre Haute, Indiana, and Salzburg, Austria.

A second way to cut costs is by *exploiting lower factor costs* by moving manufacturing or other activities to low-cost countries. This approach has, of course, motivated the recent surge of offshore manufacturing, particularly by US firms. For example, the Mexican side of the US–Mexico border is now crowded with *maquiladoras* – manufacturing plants set up and run by US companies using Mexican labour.

Gobal strategy can also cut costs by *exploiting flexibility*. A company with manufacturing locations in several countries can move production from location to location on short notice to take advantage of the lowest costs at a given time. Dow Chemical takes this approach to minimize the cost of producing chemicals. Dow uses a linear programming model which takes account of international differences in exchange rates, tax rates and transportation and labour costs. The model comes up with the best mix of production volume by location for each planning period.

An integrated global strategy can also reduce costs by *enhancing bargaining power*. A company whose strategy allows for switching production among different countries greatly increases its bargaining power with suppliers, workers and host governments. ...

Improved Quality of Products and Programmes

Under a global strategy, companies focus on a smaller number of products and programmes than under a multi-domestic strategy. This concentration can improve both product and programme quality. Global focus is one reason for Japanese success in automobiles. Toyota markets a far smaller number of models around the world than does General Motors, even allowing for its unit sales being half that of General Motors's. ...

Enhanced Customer Preference

Global availability, serviceability and recognition can enhance customer preference through reinforcement. Soft drink and fast food companies are, of course, leading exponents of this strategy. Many suppliers of financial services, such as credit cards, must have a global presence because their service is travel-related. ...

Increased Competitive Leverage

A global strategy provides more points from which to attack and counterattack competitors. In an effort to prevent the Japanese from becoming a competitive nuisance in disposable syringes, Becton Dickinson, a major US medical products company, decided to enter three markets in Japan's backyard. Becton entered the Hong Kong, Singapore and Philippine markets to prevent further Japanese expansion (Cvar, 1986).

DRAWBACKS OF GLOBAL STRATEGY

Globalization can incur significant management costs through increased coordination, reporting requirements and even added staff. It can also reduce the firm's effectiveness in individual countries if overcentralization hurts local motivation and morale. In addition, each global strategy lever has particular drawbacks.

A global strategy approach to *market participation* can incur an earlier or greater commitment to a market than is warranted on its own merits. Many American companies, such as Motorola, are struggling to penetrate Japanese markets, more in order to enhance their global competitive position than to make money in Japan for its own sake.

Product standardization can result in a product that does not entirely satisfy any customers. When companies first internationalize, they often offer their standard domestic product without adapting it for other countries and suffer the consequences. ...

A globally standardized product is designed for the global market but can seldom satisfy all needs in all countries. For instance, Canon, a Japanese company, sacrificed the ability to copy certain Japanese paper sizes when it first designed a photocopier for the global market.

Activity concentration distances customers and can result in lower responsiveness and flexibility. It also increases currency risk by incurring costs and revenues in different countries. Recently volatile exchange rates have required companies that concentrate their production to hedge their currency exposure.

Uniform marketing can reduce adaptation to local customer behaviour. For example, the head office of British Airways mandated that every country use the 'Manhattan Landing' television commercial developed by advertising agency Saatchi and Saatchi. While the commercial did win many awards, it has been criticized for using a visual image (New York City) that was not widely recognized in many countries.

Integrated competitive moves can mean sacrificing revenues, profits or competitive position in individual countries, particularly when the subsidiary in one country is asked to attack a global competitor in order to send a signal or to divert that competitor's resources from another country.

FINDING THE BALANCE

The most successful worldwide strategies find a balance between overglobalizing and underglobalizing. The ideal strategy matches the level of strategy globalization to the globalization potential of the industry. ...

INDUSTRY GLOBALIZATION DRIVERS

To achieve the benefits of globalization, the managers of a worldwide business need to recognize when industry globalization drivers (industry conditions) provide the opportunity to use global strategy levers. These drivers can be grouped in four categories: market, cost, governmental and competitive. Each industry globalization driver affects the potential use of global strategy levers. ...

Market Drivers

Market globalization drivers depend on customer behaviour and the structure of distribution channels. These drivers affect the use of all five global strategy levers.

Homogeneous Customer Needs
When customers in different countries want essentially the same type of product or service (or can be so persuaded), opportunities arise to market a standardized product. Understanding which aspects of the product can be standardized and which should be customized is key. In addition, homogeneous needs make participation in a large number of markets easier because fewer different product offerings need to be developed and supported.

Global Customers
Global customers buy on a centralized or coordinated basis for decentralized use. The existence of global customers both allows and requires a uniform marketing programme. There are two types of global customers: national and multinational. A national global customer searches the world for suppliers but uses the purchased product or service in one country. National defence agencies are a good example. A multinational global customer also searches the world for suppliers, but uses the purchased product or service in many countries. The World Health Organization's purchase of medical products is an example. Multinational global customers are particularly challenging to serve and often require a global account management programme. ...

Global Channels
Analogous to global customers, channels of distribution may buy on a global or at least a regional basis. Global channels or middlemen are also important in exploiting differences in prices by buying at a lower price in one country and selling at a higher price in another country. Their presence makes it more necessary for a business to rationalize its worldwide pricing. Global channels are rare, but regionwide channels are increasing in number, particularly in European grocery distribution and retailing.

Transferable Marketing
The buying decision may be such that marketing elements, such as brand names and advertising, require little local adaptation. Such transferability enables firms to use uniform marketing strategies and facilitates expanded participation in markets. A worldwide business can also adapt its brand names and advertising campaigns to make them more transferable, or, even better, design global ones to start with.

Offsetting risks include the blandness of uniformly acceptable brand names or advertising and the vulnerability of relying on a single brand franchise.

Cost Drivers

Cost drivers depend on the economics of the business; they particularly affect activity concentration.

Economies of Scale and Scope
A single-country market may not be large enough for the local business to achieve all possible economies of scale or scope. Scale at a given location can be increased through participation in multiple markets combined with product standardization or concentration of selected value activities. Corresponding risks include rigidity and vulnerability to disruption. ...

Learning and Experience
Even if economies of scope and scale are exhausted, expanded market participation and activity concentration can accelerate the accumulation of learning and experience. The steeper the learning and experience curves, the greater the potential benefit will be. Managers should beware, though, of the usual danger in pursuing experience curve strategies – overaggressive pricing that destroyed not just the competition but the market as well. Prices get so low that profit is insufficient to sustain any competitor.

Sourcing Efficiencies
Centralized purchasing of new materials can significantly lower costs. ...

Favourable Logistics
A favourable ratio of sales value to transportation cost enhances the company's ability to concentrate production. Other logistical factors include non-perishability, the absence of time urgency and little need for location close to customer facilities. ...

Differences in Country Costs and Skills
Factor costs generally vary across countries; this is particularly true in certain industries. The availability of particular skills also varies. Concentration of activities in low-cost or high-skill countries can increase productivity and reduce costs, but managers need to anticipate the danger of training future offshore competitors. ...

Product Development Costs
Product development costs can be reduced by developing a few global or regional products rather than many national products. The automobile industry is characterized by long product development periods and high product development costs. One reason for the high costs is duplication of effort across countries. The Ford Motor Company's 'Centres of Excellence' programme aims to reduce these duplicating efforts and to exploit the differing expertise of Ford specialists worldwide. As part of the concentrated effort, Ford of Europe is designing a common platform for all compacts, while Ford of North America is developing platforms for the replacement of the mid-sized Taurus and Sable. This concentration of design is estimated to save

'hundreds of millions of dollars per model by eliminating duplicative efforts and saving on retooling factories' (*Business Week*, 1987).

Governmental Drivers

Government globalization drivers depend on the rules set by national governments and affect the use of all global strategy levers.

Favourable Trade Policies

Host governments affect globalization potential through import tariffs and quotas, non-tariff barriers, export subsidies, local content requirements, currency and capital flow restrictions, and requirements on technology transfer. Host government policies can make it difficult to use the global levers of major market participation, product standardization, activity concentration, and uniform marketing; they also affect the integrated-competitive moves lever. . . .

Compatible Technical Standards

Differences in technical standards, especially government-imposed standards, limit the extent to which products can be standardized. Often, standards are set with protectionism in mind. Motorola found that many of their electronics products were excluded from the Japanese market because these products operated at a higher frequency than was permitted in Japan.

Common Marketing Regulations

The marketing environment of individual countries affects the extent to which uniform global marketing approaches can be used. Certain types of media may be prohibited or restricted. For example, the United States is far more liberal than Europe about the kinds of advertising claim that can be made on television. The British authorities even veto the depiction of socially undesirable behaviour. For example, British television authorities do not allow scenes of children pestering their parents to buy a product. . . .

Competitive Drivers

Market, cost and governmental globalization drivers are essentially fixed for an industry at any given time. Competitors can play only a limited role in affecting these factors (although a sustained effort can bring about change, particularly in the case of consumer preferences). In contrast, competitive drivers are entirely in the realm of competitor choice. Competitors can raise the globalization potential of their industry and spur the need for a response on the global strategy levers.

Interdependence of Countries

A competitor may create competitive interdependence among countries by pursuing a global strategy. The basic mechanism is through sharing of activities. When activities such as production are shared among countries, a competitor's market share in one country affects its scale and overall cost position in the shared activities. Changes in that scale and cost will affect its competitive position in all countries dependent on the shared activities. Less directly, customers may view market position in a lead country as an indicator of overall quality. Companies frequently promote a product as, for example, 'the leading brand in the United States'. Other competitors then need to respond via increased market participation, uniform marketing or integrated competitive strategy to avoid a downward spiral of sequentially weakened positions in individual countries.

In the automobile industry, where economies of scale are significant and where sharing activities can lower costs, markets have significant competitive inter-dependence. As companies like Ford and Volkswagen concentrate production and become more cost-competitive with the Japanese manufacturers, the Japanese are pressured to enter more markets so that increased production volume will lower costs. Whether conscious of this or not, Toyota has begun a concerted effort to penetrate the German market: between 1984 and 1987, Toyota doubled the number of cars produced for the German market.

Globalized Competitors

More specifically, matching or pre-empting individual competitor moves may be necessary. These moves include expanding into or within major markets, being the first to introduce a standardized product, or being the first to use a uniform marketing programme.

The need to pre-empt a global competitor can spur increased market participation. In 1986, Unilever, the European consumer products company, sought to increase its participation in the US market by launching a hostile takeover bid for Richardson-Vicks Inc. Unilever's global archrival, Procter & Gamble, saw the threat to its home turf and outbid Unilever to capture Richardson-Vicks. With Richardson-Vicks's European system, P&G was able to greatly strengthen its European positioning. So Unilever's attempt to expand participation in a rival's home market backfired to allow the rival to expand participation in Unilever's home markets.

In summary, industry globalization drivers provide opportunities to use global strategy levers in many ways. Some industries, such as civil aircraft, can score high on most dimensions of globalization (Yoshino, 1986). Others, such as the cement industry, seem to be inherently local. But more and more industries are developing globalization potential. Even the food industry in Europe, renowned for its diversity of taste, is now a globalization target for major food multinationals.

Changes over Time

Finally, industry evolution plays a role. As each of the industry globalization drivers changes over time, so too will the appropriate global strategy change. For example, in the European major appliance industry, globalization forces seem to have reversed. In the late 1960s and early 1970s, a regional standardization strategy was successful for some key competitors (Levitt, 1983). But in the 1980s the situation appears to have turned around, and the most successful strategies seem to be national (Badenfuller et al., 1987).

In some cases, the actions of individual competitors can affect the direction and pace of change; competitors positioned to take advantage of globalization forces will want to hasten them. ...

MORE THAN ONE STRATEGY IS VIABLE

Although they are powerful, industry globalization drivers do not dictate one formula for success. More than one type of international strategy can be viable in a given industry.

Industries Vary Across Drivers

No industry is high on every one of the many globalization drivers. A particular competitor may be in a strong position to exploit a driver that scores low on globalization. ... The hotel industry provides examples both of successful global and successful local competitors.

Global Effects are Incremental

Globalization drivers are not deterministic for a second reason: the appropriate use of strategy levers adds competitive advantage to existing sources. These other sources may allow individual competitors to thrive with international strategies that are mismatched with industry globalization drivers. For example, superior technology is a major source of competitive advantage in most industries, but can be quite independent of globalization drivers. A competitor with sufficiently superior technology can use it to offset globalization disadvantages.

Business and Parent Company Position and Resources are Crucial

The third reason that drivers are not deterministic is related to resources. A worldwide business may face industry drivers that strongly favour a global strategy. But global strategies are typically expensive to implement initially even though great cost savings and revenue gains should follow. High initial investments may be needed to expand within or into major markets, to develop standardized products, to relocate value activities, to create global brands, to create new organization units or coordination processes and to implement other aspects of a global strategy. The strategic position of the business is also relevant. Even though a global strategy may improve the business's long-term strategic position, its immediate position may be so weak that resources should be devoted to short-term, country-by-country improvements. Despite the automobile industry's very strong globalization drivers, Chrysler Corporation had to deglobalize by selling off most of its international automotive businesses to avoid bankruptcy. Lastly, investing in non-global sources of competitive advantage, such as superior technology, may yield greater returns than global ones, such as centralized manufacturing.

Organizations Have Limitations

Finally, factors such as organization structure, management processes, people and culture affect how well a desired global strategy can be implemented. Organizational differences among companies in the same industry can, or should, constrain the companies' pursuit of the same global strategy. ...

• MANAGING ACROSS BORDERS: NEW ORGANIZATIONAL RESPONSES*

Christopher A. Bartlett and Sumantra Ghoshal

... [R]ecent changes in the international operating environment have forced companies to optimize *efficiency, responsiveness* and *learning* simultaneously in their worldwide operations. To companies that previously concentrated on developing and managing one of these capabilities, this new challenge implie[s] not only a total strategic reorientation but a major change in organizational capability as well.

Implementing such a complex, three-pronged strategic objective would be difficult under any circumstances, but in a worldwide company the task is complicated even further. The very act of 'going international' multiplies a company's organizational complexity. Typically, doing so requires adding a third dimension to the existing business- and function-oriented management structure. It is difficult enough balancing product divisions that bring efficiency and focus to domestic product market strategies with corporate staffs whose functional expertise allows them to play an important counterbalance and control role. The thought of adding capable, geographically-oriented management – and maintaining a three-way balance of organizational perspectives and capabilities among product, function and area – is intimidating to most managers. The difficulty is increased because the resolution of tensions among product, function and area managers must be accomplished in an organization whose operating units are often divided by distance and time, and whose key members are separated by culture and language.

FROM UNIDIMENSIONAL TO MULTIDIMENSIONAL CAPABILITIES

Faced with the task of building multiple strategic capabilities in highly complex organizations, managers in almost every company we studied[2] made the simplifying assumption that they were faced with a series of dichotomous choices. They discussed the relative merits of pursuing a strategy of national responsiveness as opposed to one based on global integration; they considered whether key assets and resources should be centralized or decentralized; and they debated the need for strong central control versus greater subsidiary autonomy. How a company resolved these dilemmas typically reflected influences exerted and choices made during its historical development. In telecommunications, ITT's need to develop an organization responsive to national political demands and local specification differences was as important to its survival in the pre- and post-World War II era as was NEC's need to build its highly centralized technological manufacturing and marketing skills and resources in order to expand abroad in the same industry in the 1960s and 1970s.

When new competitive challenges emerged, however, such unidimensional biases became strategically limiting. As ITT demonstrated by its outstanding historic success and NEC showed by its more delayed international expansion, strong *geographic*

* Originally published in *Sloan Management Review* 43 (Autumn 1987). Reprinted with deletions by permission of the *Review*.

management is essential for development of dispersed responsiveness. Geographic management allows worldwide companies to sense, analyze and respond to the needs of different national markets.

Effective competitors also need to build strong *business management* with global product responsibilities if they are to achieve global efficiency and integration. These managers act as champions of manufacturing rationalization, product standardization and low-cost global sourcing. (As the telecommunications switching industry globalized, NEC's organizational capability in this area gave it a major competitive advantage.) Unencumbered by either territorial or functional loyalties, central product groups remain sensitive to overall competitive issues and become agents to facilitate changes that, though painful, are necessary for competitive viability.

Finally, a strong, worldwide *functional management* allows an organization to build and transfer its core competencies – a capability vital to worldwide learning. Links between functional managers allow the company to accumulate specialized knowledge and skills and to apply them wherever they are required in the worldwide operations. Functional management acts as the repository of organizational learning and as the prime mover for its consolidation and circulation within the company. It was for want of a strongly linked research and technical function across subsidiaries that ITT failed in its attempt to coordinate the development and diffusion of its System 12 digital switch.

Thus, to respond to the needs for efficiency, responsiveness and learning *simultaneously*, the company must develop a multidimensional organization in which the effectiveness of each management group is maintained *and* in which each group is prevented from dominating the others. As we saw in company after company, the most difficult challenge for managers trying to respond to broad, emerging strategic demands was to develop the new elements of multidimensional organization without eroding the effectiveness of their current unidimensional capability.

OVERCOMING SIMPLIFYING ASSUMPTIONS

For all nine companies at the core of our study, the challenge of breaking down biases and building a truly multidimensional organization proved difficult. Behind the pervasive either/or mentality that led to the development of unidimensional capabilities, we identified three simplifying assumptions that blocked the necessary organizational development. The need to reduce organizational and strategic complexity has made these assumptions almost universal in worldwide companies, regardless of industry, national origin or management culture.

- There is a widespread, often implicit assumption that roles of different organizational units are uniform and symmetrical; different businesses should be managed in the same way, as should different functions and national operations.

- Most companies, some consciously, most unconsciously, create internal inter-unit relationships on clear patterns of dependence or independence, on the assumption that such relationships *should* be clear and unambiguous.

- Finally, there is the assumption that one of corporate management's principal tasks is to institutionalize clearly understood mechanisms for decision making and to implement simple means of exercising control.

Those companies most successful in developing truly multidimensional organizations were the ones that challenged these assumptions and replaced them with some very different attitudes and norms. Instead of treating different businesses, functions and subsidiaries similarly, they systematically *differentiated* tasks and responsibilities. Instead of seeking organizational clarity by basing relationships on dependence or independence, they built and managed *interdependence* among the different units of the companies. And instead of considering control their key task, corporate managers searched for complex mechanisms to *coordinate and coopt* the differentiated and interdependent organizational units into sharing a vision of the company's strategic tasks. These are the central organizational characteristics of what we described in the earlier article as transnational corporations – those most effective in managing across borders in today's environment of intense competition and rapid, often discontinuous change.

FROM SYMMETRY TO DIFFERENTIATION

.... Just as they saw the need to change symmetrical structures and homogeneous processes imposed on different businesses and functions, most companies we observed eventually recognized the importance of differentiating the management of diverse geographic operations. Despite the fact that various national subsidiaries operated with very different external environments and internal constraints, they all traditionally reported through the same channels, operated under similar planning and control systems and worked under a set of common and generalized mandates.

Increasingly, however, managers recognized that such symmetrical treatment can constrain strategic capabilities. At Unilever, for example, it became clear that Europe's highly competitive markets and closely linked economies meant that its operating companies in that region required more coordination and control than those in, say, Latin America. Little by little, management increased the product coordination groups' role in Europe until they had direct line responsibility for all operating companies in their businesses. Elsewhere, however, national management maintained its historic line management role, and product coordinators acted only as advisers. Unilever has thus moved in sequence from a symmetrical organization to a much more differentiated one: differentiating by product, then by function and finally by geography. ...

But Unilever is far from unique. In all of the companies we studied, senior management was working to differentiate its organizational structure and processes in increasingly sophisticated ways. For example. ... Procter & Gamble is differentiating the roles of its subsidiaries by giving some of them responsibilities as 'lead countries' in product strategy development, then rotating that leadership role from product to product. ... Thus, instead of deciding the overall roles of product, functional and geographic management on the basis of simplistic dichotomies such as global versus domestic businesses or centralized versus decentralized organizations, many companies are creating different levels of influence for different groups as they perform different activities. Doing this allows the relatively underdeveloped management perspectives to be built in a gradual, complementary manner rather than in the sudden, adversarial environment often associated with either/or choices. Internal heterogeneity has made the change from unidimensional to multidimensional organization easier by breaking the problem up into many small, differentiated parts and by allowing for a step-by-step process of organizational change.

FROM DEPENDENCE OR INDEPENDENCE TO INTERDEPENDENCE

.... New strategic demands make organizational models of simple inter-unit dependence *or* independence inappropriate. The reality of today's worldwide competitive environment demands collaborative information-sharing and problem-solving, cooperative support and resource-sharing, and collective action and implementation. Independent units risk being picked off one-by-one by competitors whose co-ordinated global approach gives them two important strategic advantages – the ability to integrate research, manufacturing and other scale-efficient operations, and the opportunity to cross-subsidize the losses from battles in one market with funds generated by profitable operations in home markets or protected environments. ...

On the other hand, foreign operations totally dependent on a central unit must deal with problems reaching beyond the loss of local market responsiveness. ... They also risk being unable to respond effectively to strong national competitors or to sense potentially important local market or technical intelligence. This was the problem Procter & Gamble's Japan subsidiary faced in an environment where local competitors began challenging P&G's previously secure position with successive, innovative product changes and novel market strategies, particularly in the disposable nappies business. After suffering major losses in market share, management recognized that a local operation focused primarily on implementing the company's classic marketing strategy was no longer sufficient; the Japanese subsidiary needed the freedom and incentive to be more innovative. Not only to ensure the viability of the Japanese subsidiary, but also to protect its global strategic position, P&G realized it had to expand the role of the local unit and change its relationship with the parent company to enhance two-way learning and mutual support.

But it is not easy to change relationships of dependence or independence that have been built up over a long history. Many companies have tried to address the increasing need for inter-unit collaboration by adding layer upon layer of administrative mechanisms to foster greater cooperation. Top managers have extolled the virtues of teamwork and have even created special departments to audit management response to this need. In most cases these efforts to obtain cooperation by fiat or by administrative mechanisms have been disappointing. The independent units have feigned compliance while fiercely protecting their independence. The dependent units have found that the new cooperative spirit implies little more than the right to agree with those on whom they depend.

Yet some companies have gradually developed the capability to achieve such cooperation and to build what Rosabeth Kanter calls an 'integrative organization'.[3] Of the companies we studied, the most successful did so not by creating new units, but by changing the basis of the relationships among product, functional, and geographic management groups. From relations based on dependence or independence, they moved to relations based on formidable levels of explicit, genuine inter-dependence. In essence, they made integration and collaboration self-enforcing by making it necessary for each group to cooperate in order to achieve its own interests....

Procter & Gamble ... in Europe, for example, [has] formed a number of

Eurobrand teams for developing product-market strategies for different product lines.[4] Each team is headed by the general manager of a subsidiary that has a particularly well-developed competence in that business. It also includes the appropriate product and advertising managers from the other subsidiaries and relevant functional managers from the company's European headquarters. ...

In observing many such examples of companies building and extending interdependence among units, we were able to identify three important flows, which seem to be at the centre of the emerging organizational relationships. Most fundamental was the product interdependence which most companies were building as they specialized and integrated their worldwide manufacturing operations to achieve greater efficiency, while retaining sourcing flexibility and sensitivity to host country interests. The resulting *flow of parts, components and finished goods* increased the interdependence of the worldwide operations in an obvious and fundamental manner.

We also observed companies developing a resource interdependence that often contrasted sharply with earlier policies that had either encouraged local self-sufficiency or required the centralization of all surplus resources. ...

Finally, the worldwide diffusion of technology, the development of international markets and the globalization of competitive strategies have meant that vital strategic information now exists in many different locations worldwide. Furthermore, the growing dispersion of assets and delegation of responsibilities to foreign operations have resulted in the development of local knowledge and expertise that has implications for the broader organization. With these changes, the need to manage the *flow of intelligence, ideas and knowledge* has become central to the learning process and has reinforced the growing interdependence of worldwide operations, as P&G's Eurobrand teams illustrate.

It is important to emphasize that the relationships we are highlighting are different from the interdependencies commonly observed in multi-unit organizations. Traditionally, MNC managers have attempted to highlight what has been called 'pooled interdependence' to make subunit managers responsive to global rather than local interests. (Before the Euroteam approach, for instance, P&G's European vice-president often tried to convince independent-minded subsidiary managers to transfer surplus generated funds to other, more needy subsidiaries, in the overall corporate interest, arguing that, 'Someday when you're in need they might be able to fund a major product launch for you'.)

As the example illustrates, pooled interdependence is often too broad and amorphous to affect day-to-day management behaviour. The interdependencies we described earlier are more clearly reciprocal, and each unit's ability to achieve its goals is made conditional upon its willingness to help other units achieve their own goals. Such interdependencies more effectively promote the organization's ability to share the perspectives and link the resources of different components, and thereby to expand its organizational capabilities.[5]

FROM CONTROL TO COORDINATION AND COOPTION

The simplifying assumptions of organizational symmetry and dependence (or independence) had allowed the management processes in many companies to be dominated by simple controls – tight operational controls in subsidiaries dependent on the centre, and a looser system of administrative or financial controls in decentralized units. When companies began to challenge the assumptions underlying organizational relationships, however, they found they also had to adapt their management processes. The growing interdependence of organizational units strained the simple control-dominated systems and underlined the need to supplement existing processes with more sophisticated ones. Furthermore, the differentiation of organizational tasks and roles amplified the diversity of management perspectives and capabilities and forced management to differentiate management processes.

As organizations became, at the same time, more diverse and more interdependent, there was an explosion in the number of issues that had to be linked, reconciled, or integrated. The rapidly increasing flows of goods, resources and information among organizational units increased the need for *coordination* as a central management function. But the costs of coordination are high, both in financial and human terms, and coordinating capabilities are always limited. Most companies, though, tended to concentrate on a primary means of coordination and control – the company's way of doing things. ...

In [a number of] companies, we saw a ... broadening of administrative processes as managers learned to operate with previously underutilized means of coordination. Unilever's heavy reliance on the socialization of managers to provide the coordination 'glue' was supplemented by the growing role of the central product coordination departments. In contrast, NEC reduced central management's coordination role by developing formal systems and social processes in a way that created a more robust and flexible coordinative capability.

Having developed diverse new means of coordination, management's main task is carefully to ration their usage and application. ... it is important to distinguish where tasks can be formalized and managed through systems, where social linkages can be fostered to encourage informal agreements and cooperation, and where the coordination task is so vital or sensitive that it must use the scarce resource of central management arbitration. ...

We have described briefly how companies began to ... differentiat[e] roles and responsibilities within the organization. Depending on their internal capabilities and on the strategic importance of their external environments, organizational units might be asked to take on roles ranging from that of strategic leader with primary corporate-wide responsibility for a particular business or function, to simple implementer responsible only for executing strategies and decisions developed elsewhere.

Clearly, these roles must be managed in quite different ways. The unit with strategic leadership responsibility must be given freedom to develop responsibility in an entrepreneurial fashion, yet must also be strongly supported by headquarters. For this unit, operating controls may be light and quite routine, but coordination of information and resource flows to and from the unit will probably require intensive involvement from senior management. In contrast, units with implementation responsibility might be managed through tight operating controls, with standardized systems used to handle much of the coordination – primarily of goods flows. Because the tasks are more routine, the use of scarce coordinating resources could be minimized.

Differentiating organizational roles and management processes can have a fragmenting and sometimes demotivating effect, however. Nowhere was this more clearly illustrated than in the many companies that unquestioningly assigned units the 'dog' and 'cash cow' roles defined by the Boston Consulting Group's growth-share matrix in the 1970s.[6] Their experience showed that there is another equally important corporate management task, which complements and facilitates coordination effectiveness. We call this task *cooption*: the process of uniting the organization with a common understanding of, identification with, and commitment to the corporation's objectives, priorities and values.

A clear example of the importance of cooption was provided by the contrast between ITT and NEC managers. At ITT, corporate objectives were communicated more in financial than in strategic terms, and the company's national entities identified almost exclusively with their local environment. When corporate management tried to superimpose a more unified and integrated global strategy, its local subsidiaries neither understood nor accepted the need to do so. For years they resisted giving up their autonomy, and management was unable to replace the interunit rivalry with a more cooperative and collaborative process.

In contrast, NEC developed an explicitly defined and clearly communicated global strategy enshrined in the company's 'C&C' motto – a corporate-wide dedication to building business and basing competitive strategy on the strong link between computers and communications. For over a decade, the C&C philosophy was constantly interpreted, refined, elaborated and eventually institutionalized in organizational units dedicated to various C&C missions (e.g the C&C Systems Research Laboratories, the C&C Corporate Planning Committee and eventually the C&C Systems Division). Top management recognized that one of its major tasks was to inculcate the worldwide organization with an understanding of the C&C strategy and philosophy and to raise managers' consciousness about the global implications of competing in these converging businesses. By the mid-1980s, the company was confident that every NEC employee in every operating unit had a clear understanding of NEC's global strategy as well as of his or her role in it. Indeed, it was this homogeneity that allowed the company to begin the successful decentralization of its management processes.

Thus the management process that distinguished transnational organizations from simpler unidimensional forms was one in which control was made less dominant by the increased importance of interunit integration and collaboration. These new processes required corporate management to supplement its control role with the more subtle tasks of coordination and cooption, giving rise to a much more complex and sophisticated management process.

SUSTAINING A DYNAMIC BALANCE: ROLE OF THE 'MIND MATRIX'

Developing multidimensional perspectives and capabilities does not mean that product, functional and geographic management must have the same level of influence on all key decisions. Quite the contrary. It means that the organization must possess a differentiated influence structure – one in which different groups have different roles for different activities. These roles cannot be fixed but must change continually to respond to new environmental demands and evolving industry characteristics. Not only is it necessary to prevent any one perspective from dominating the others, it is equally important not to be locked into a mode of operation that prevents reassignment of responsibilities, realignment of relationships and rebalancing of power distribution. This ability to manage the multidimensional organization capability in a flexible manner is the hallmark of a transnational company.

In the change processes we have described, managers were clearly employing some powerful organizational tools to create and control the desired flexible management process. They used the classic tool of formal structure to strengthen, weaken or shift roles and responsibilities over time, and they employed management systems effectively to redirect corporate resources and to channel information in a way that shifted the balance of power. By controlling the ebb and flow of responsibilities, and by rebalancing power relationships, they were able to prevent any of the multidimensional perspectives from atrophying. Simultaneously, they prevented the establishment of entrenched power bases.

But the most successful companies had an additional element at the core of their management processes. We were always conscious that a substantial amount of senior management attention focused on the *individual* members of the organization. NEC's continual efforts to inculcate all corporate members with a common vision of goals and priorities; P&G's careful assignment of managers to teams and task forces to broaden their perspectives; Philips's frequent use of conferences and meetings as forums to reconcile differences; and Unilever's extensive use of training as a powerful socialization process and its well-planned career path management that provided diverse experience across businesses, functions, and geographic locations – all are examples of companies trying to develop multidimensional perspectives and flexible approaches at the level of the individual manager.

What is critical, then, is not just the structure, but also the mentality of those who constitute the structure. The common thread that holds together the diverse tasks we have described is a managerial mindset that understands the need for multiple strategic capabilities, that is able to view problems from both local and global perspectives, and that accepts the importance of a flexible approach. This pattern suggests that managers should resist the temptation to view their task in the traditional terms of building a formal global matrix structure – an organizational form that in practice has provel extraordinarily difficult to manage in the international environment. They might be better guided by the perspective of one top manager who described the challenge as 'creating a matrix in the minds of managers'.

Our study has led us to conclude that a company's ability to develop transnational organizational capability and management mentality will be the key factor that separates the winners from the mere survivors in the emerging international environment.

[1] My framework, developed in this article, is based in part on M. E. Porter's (1986) pioneering work on global strategy. Bartlett and Ghoshal (1987) define a 'transnational industry' that is somewhat similar to Porter's 'global industry'.

[2] The findings presented in this article are based on a three-year research project on the organization and management of multinational corporations. Extensive discussions were held with 250 managers in nine of the world's largest multinational companies, in the United States, Europe and Japan. Complete findings are presented in *Managing across Borders: The transnational solution* (Boston: Harvard Business School Press, 1988).

[3] See R. M. Kanter, *The Change Masters* (New York: Simon & Schuster, 1983).

[4] For a full description of the development of Eurobrand in P&G, see C. A. Bartlett, 'Procter & Gamble Europe: Vizir launch' (Boston: Harvard Business School, Case Services # 9-384-139).

[5] The distinction among sequential, reciprocal and pooled interdependencies has been made in J. D. Thompson, *Organizations in Action* (New York: McGraw-Hill, 1967).

[6] See P. Haspeslagh, 'Portfolio planning: Uses and limits', *Harvard Business Review*, January– February 1982, pp. 58–73.

THE CONTEXT
OF CHANGE

Strategy itself is really about continuity, not change: it is concerned with imposing stable patterns of behaviour on an organization, whether these take the form of intentions in advance that become deliberate strategies, or actions after the fact that fall into the consistent patterns of emergent strategies. But to manage strategy is frequently to manage change – to recognize when a shift of a strategic nature is possible, desirable, necessary, and then to act.

Managing such change is generally far more difficult than it may at first appear. The need for major strategic reorientation occurs rather infrequently, and when it does, it means moving from a familiar domain into a less well-defined future where many of the old rules no longer apply. People must often abandon the roots of their past successes and develop entirely new skills and attitudes. This is clearly a frightening situation – and often, therefore, the most difficult challenge facing a manager.

The causes of such change also vary, from an ignored steady decline in performance which ultimately demands a 'turnaround' to a sudden radical shift in a base technology which requires a reconceptualization of everything the organization does; from the gradual shifts into the next stage of an organization's 'lifecycle' to the appearance of a new chief executive who wishes to put his or her personal stamp on the organization. The resulting strategic alignments may also take a variety of forms, from a shift of strategic position within the same industry to a whole new perspective in a new industry. Some changes require rapid transitions from one structural configuration to another, as in a machine organization which, having diversified into new businesses, suddenly switches to a divisionalized form of structure, while others are accompanied by slower structural change, as when a small entrepreneurial firm grows steadily towards a larger, mature company. Each transition has its own management prerequisites and problems.

The two readings in this chapter cover the aspects of organizational change, presenting material on what stimulates them in the first place, what forms they can take and how they can and should be managed in differing situations. The readings appropriately cap the earlier chapters of this book: on strategy and its formation, structure and systems, power and culture, and the various contexts in which these come together. Major changes typically involve them all. Configuration, so carefully nurtured in earlier chapters, turns out to be a double-edged sword, promoting consistency on the one hand, but sometimes discouraging change on the other.

The first reading seeks to bring some closure to our discussion of the different configurations of structure presented in the last five chapters. Called 'Beyond configuration: Forces and forms in effective organizations', it is, in a sense, Mintzberg's final chapter of his book on structure, except that it was written recently, after that book first appeared. It seeks to do just what its title says: make the point that while the different structural forms (configurations) of the last chapters can help us to make sense of, and to manage in, a complex world, there is also a need to go beyond the configuration, to consider the nuanced linkages between these various forms. This he proposes be done by treating all the forms as a framework of forces that act on every organization and whose contradictions need to be reconciled. By so doing, we can begin to see the weaknesses in each form as well as the times when an organization is better off to design itself as a combination of two or more forms. Some organizations, to use a metaphor introduced in this reading, achieve greater effectiveness by playing 'organizational LEGO' – creating their own form rather than letting themselves be put together like a jigsaw puzzle into a standard form. Finally, this reading discusses how the forces of ideology (representing cooperation – pulling together) and of politics (representing competition – pulling apart) work both to promote change and also to impede it, and how the contradictions among these two must also be reconciled if an organization is to remain effective in the long run.

In the second reading. John Stopford of the London Business School and Charles Baden-Fuller of the University of Bath present a specific model of how a company can rejuvenate itself. The key challenge, these authors believe, lies in rebuilding corporate entrepreneurship, and they describe a four-step process of renewal, which starts with galvanizing the top team to create a commitment to change. In the next phase, the company must simplify both its businesses and its organization so as to create the base for the third step of building new skills, knowledge and resources. Then, in the final step, the company can restart the growth engine by leveraging the new sources of advantage it has created. Overall, this model of change builds directly on the arguments of C. K. Prahalad and Gary Hamel in the first section on strategy, and is quite consistent with Quinn's views on strategies for change with which we started on this journey of mapping the strategy process.

● BEYOND CONFIGURATION: FORCES AND FORMS IN EFFECTIVE ORGANIZATIONS*

Henry Mintzberg

Charles Darwin once made the distinction between 'lumpers' and 'splitters'.[1] Lumpers categorize; they are the synthesizers, prone to consistency. Once they have pigeonholed something into one box or another, they are done with it. To a lumper in management, strategies are generic, structures are types, managers have a style (X, Y, Z. 9–9, etc.). Splitters nuance; they are the analyzers, prone to distinction. Since nothing can ever be categorized, things are never done with. To a splitter in management, strategies, structures and styles all vary infinitely.

I believe a key to the effective organization lies in this distinction, specifically in its simultaneous acceptance and rejection (which themselves amount to lumping and splitting). Both are right and both are wrong. Without categories, it would be impossible to practise management. With only categories, it could not be practised effectively.

For several years I worked as a lumper, seeking to identify types of organizations. Much as in the field of biology, I felt we in management needed some categorization of the 'species' with which we dealt. We long had too much of 'one best way' thinking, that every organization needed every new technique or idea that came along (like MBO or formal planning or participate management). Thus, in my books on structure and power, I developed various 'configurations' of organizations. My premiss was that an effective organization 'got it all together' as the saying goes – achieved consistency in its internal characteristics, harmony in its processes, fit with its context.

But then, a student of mine, Alain Noël, came along and asked me a question that upset this nice lumping. He wanted to know whether I was intending to play 'jigsaw puzzle' or 'LEGO' with all the elements of structure and power that I described in those books. In other words, did I mean all these elements of organizations to fit together in set ways – to create known images – or were they to be used creatively to build new ones? I had to answer that I had been promoting jigsaw puzzle, even if I was suggesting that the pieces could be combined into several images instead of the usual one. But I immediately began to think about playing 'organizational LEGO'. All of the anomalies I had encountered – all those nasty, well-functioning organizations that refused to fit into one or another of my neat categories – suddenly became opportunities to think beyond configuration. I could become a splitter too.

This reading is presented in the spirit of playing 'organizational LEGO'. It tries to show how we can use splitting as well as lumping to understand what makes organizations effective as well as what causes many of their fundamental problems.

* Adapted from a chapter of this title in *Mintzberg on Management: Inside Our Strange World of Organizations* (Free Press. 1989); an article similar to this was published in the *Sloan Management Review* (Winter, 1991).

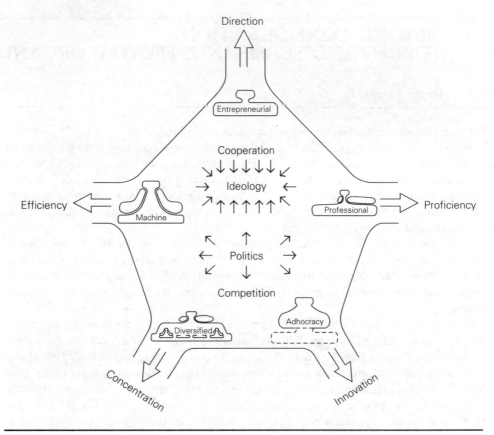

FIGURE 1
Integrating pentagon of forces and firms

FORMS AND FORCES

I shall refer to the configurations of organizations as *forms*. The original five of my structure book – here labelled entrepreneurial, machine, diversified, professional and adhocracy – are laid out at the nodes of pentagon, shown in Figure 1.

Many organizations seem to fit naturally into one or another of these categories, *more or less*. We all know the small aggressive entrepreneurial firm, the perfectly machinelike Swiss hotel, the diversified conglomerate, the professional collegial university, the freewheeling intrapreneurial Silicon Valley innovator. But some organizations do not fit, much to the chagrin of the lumpers. And even many that may seem to, on closer examination reveal curious anomalies. It is difficult to imagine a more machinelike organization than McDonald's; why then, does it seem to be rather innovative, at least in its own context? And why is it that whenever I mention to an executive group about a 3M or a Hewlett-Packard as innovative in form, someone from the audience leaps up to tell me about their tight control systems? Innovative adhocracies are not supposed to rely on tight controls.

All this, of course, pleases the splitters. 'Come on, Henry,' a colleague chided me recently, 'in my consulting practice I never see any one of these forms. I can find all of them in all serious organizations.' To him, organizations float around the inside of my pentagon; they never make it to any one node. In response, therefore, to the valid claims of the splitters, I recently added *forces* to the pentagon, shown as arrows emanating out from each of the forms. In other words, every form can be thought to represent a force too:

- First is the force for *direction*, repemesented by the entrepreneurial form, for some sense of where the organization must go. Without such direction – which today is apt to be called 'strategic vision', years ago 'grand strategy' – the various activities of an organization cannot easily work together to achieve common purpose.

- Next is the force for *efficiency*, represented by the machine form, for ensuring a viable ratio of benefits gained to costs incurred. Without some concern for efficiency, all but the most protected of organizations must eventually falter. Efficiency generally means standardization and formalization; often it reduces to economy. In current practice, it focuses on rationalization and restructuring, among other things.

- Across from the force for efficiency is the force for *proficiency*, represented by the professional form, for carrying out tasks with high levels of knowledge and skill. Without proficiency, the difficult work of organizations – whether surgery in the hospital or engineering in the corporation – just could not get done.

- Below efficiency is the force for *concentration*, represented by the diversified form, for individual units in an organization to concentrate their efforts on particular markets that it has to serve. Without such concentration, it becomes almost impossible to manage an organization that is diversified.

- At the bottom right of the pentagon is the force for *innovation*, represented by the adhocracy form. Organizations need central direction and focused concentration and they need efficiency and proficiency. But they also need to be able to learn, to discover new things for their customers and themselves – to adapt and to innovate.

I have so far left out the two forms from my book on power. We can certainly find examples of the missionary organization, as in the traditional Israeli kibbutz. Likewise, some regulatory agencies, sometimes even business corporations, become so captured by conflict for a time that they come to look like political organizations. But these forms are relatively rare, at least compared with the other five, and so I prefer to show them only as forces (placed in the middle of the pentagon for reasons to be discussed later).

- Ideology represents the force for *cooperation*, for 'pulling together' (hence the arrows focus in towards the middle).

- And politics represents the force for *competition*, for 'pulling apart' (hence the arrows flare out).

To recap to this point, we have two views of organizational effectiveness. One, for the lumpers, concentrates on a *portfolio of forms*, from which organizations are encouraged to choose if they wish to become effective. The other, for the splitters, focuses on a *system of forces*, with which organizations are encouraged to play in order to become effective.

The basis of my argument here is that both views are critical to the practice of management. One represents the most fundamental forces that act on organizations: All serious organizations experience all seven of them, at one time or another if not all the time. And the other represents the most fundamental forms that organizations can take, which some of them do some of the time. Together, as conceived on the pentagon, these forces and forms appear to constitute a powerful diagnostic framework by which to understand what goes on in organizations and to prescribe effective change in them.

My argument here will proceed as follows. First, I suggest that when one force dominates an organization, it is drawn toward a coherent, established form, described as *configuration*. That facilitates its management, but also raises the problem of *contamination*, which must be dealt with. When no one force dominates, the organization must instead function as a balanced *combination* of different forces, including periods of *conversion* from one form to another. But combination raises the problem of *cleavage*, which must also be dealt with. Both contamination and cleavage require the management of *contradiction*, and here the catalytic forces of the middle of the pentagon come into play: cooperation and competition both help to deal with it. But these two forces are themselves contradictory and so must be balanced as well. Put this all together and you get a fascinating game of jigsaw puzzle-cum-LEGO. It may seem difficult, but bear with me; reading it here will prove a lot easier than managing it in practice. And it may even help!

CONFIGURATION

When one force dominates the others, based on an organization's particular needs or perhaps just the arbitrary exercise of power, then we should look for the organization to fall close to one of the nodes, to take the form of one of our configurations, more or less. But these configurations are really pure types, what Mac Weber once labelled 'ideal types' (in Gerth and Mills, 1958). We must first ask whether they really do exist in practice.

In one sense, these configurations do not exist at all. After all, they are just words and pictures on pieces of paper, caricatures that simplify a complex reality. No serious organization can be labelled a pure machine or a pure innovator, and so on. On the other hand, managers who have to make decisions in their heads cannot carry reality around their either. They carry simplifications, called theories or models, of which these forms are examples. We must, therefore, turn to a second question: whether the forms are useful, real or not. And again I shall answer yes and no.

While no configuration ever matches a real organization perfectly, some do come remarkably close, as in the examples of the machinelike Swiss hotel or the freewheeling silicon valley innovator cited earlier. Species exist in nature in response to distinct ecological niches, likewise configurations evolve in human society to serve distinct needs. The Swiss hotel guest wants no surprises – no jack-in-the-box popping up when the pillow is lifted, thank you – just pure predictability, the efficiency of that wake-up call at 8:00, not 8:07. But in the niche called advertising, the client that gets no surprises may well take its business to another agency.

My basic point about configuration is simple: when the form fits, the organization is well advised to wear it, at least for a time. With configuration, an organization achieves a sense of order, of integration. There is internal consistency, synergy among processes, fit with the external context. It is the organization without configuration, much like the person without distinct character, who tends to suffer the identity crises.

Outsiders appreciate configuration; it helps them to understand an organization. We walk into a McDonald's and we know immediately what drives it; likewise a Hewlett-Packard. But more important is what configuration offers the managers: it makes an organization more manageable. With the course set, it is easier to steer, also to deflect pressures that are peripheral. No configuration is perfect – the professional one, for example, tends to belittle its clients and the machine one often alienates its workers – but there is something to be said for consistency. Closely controlled workers may not be happier than autonomous ones, but they are certainly better off than ones confused by quality circles in the morning and time study engineering in the afternoon. Better to have the definition and discipline of configuration than to dissipate one's energies trying to be all things to all people.

Moreover, much of what we know about organizations in practice applies to specific configurations. There may not be any one best way, but there are certainly preferred ways in particular contexts, for example time study in the machine organization and matrix structure in the innovative one.

Thus for classification, for comprehension, for diagnosis and for design, configuration seems to be effective. But only so long as everything holds still. Introduce the dynamics of evolutionary change and, sooner or later, configuration becomes ineffective.

Contamination by Configuration

In harmony, consistency and fit lies configuration's great strength. Also its debilitating weakness. The fact is that the dominant force sometimes dominates to the point of undermining all the others. For example, in a machine organization, the quest for efficiency can almost totally suppress the capacity for innovation, while in an adhocracy organization, it is the need to express some modicum of efficiency that often gets suppressed. I call this phenomenon *contamination*, although it might just as easily be called Lord Acton's dictum: among the forces of organizations too, power tends to corrupt and absolute power corrupts absolutely. For example, the story of medical care in the United States could well be described as the contamination of efficiency by proficiency. No one can deny the primacy of proficiency – who would go to a hospital that favours efficiency – but certainly not to the extent that it has been allowed to dominate.

Machine organizations recognize this problem when they put their research and development facilities away from head office, to avoid the contaminating effects of the central efficiency experts. Unfortunately, while lead may block X-rays, there is no known medium to shield the effects of a dominant culture. The controller drops by, just to have a look: 'What, no shoes?' Of course, the opposite case is also well known. Just ask the members of an innovative organization who's the most miserable person in adhocracy. Whenever I do this in a workshop with such an organization, the inevitable reply is a brief silence followed by a few smiles, then growing laughter as everyone turns to some poor person cowering in the corner. Of course, it's the controller, the victim of adhocracy's contamination. He or she may wear shoes, but that hardly helps him or her keep the lid on all the madness.

Contamination is another way of saying that a configuration is not merely a structure, not even merely a power system: each is a culture in its own right. Being machinelike or innovative is not just a way of organizing, it's a way of life!

Of course, given the benefits claimed for configuration, contamination may seem like a small price to pay for being coherently organized. True enough. Until things go out of control.

Configuration Out of Control

A configuration is geared not only to a general context but also to specific conditions – for example, a particular leader in an entrepreneurial organization, even a particular product and market in a machine one. Thus, when the need arises for change, the dominating force may act to hold the organization in place. Then other forces must come into play. But if contamination has worked its effects, the other forces are too weak. And so the organization goes out of control. For example, a machine organization in need of a new strategy may find available to it neither the direction of an entrepreneurial leader nor the learning of intrapreneurial subordinates. And so its internal consistency gets perpetuated while it falls increasingly out of touch with its context.

In addition, each configuration is also ccapable of driving itself out of control. That is to say, each contains the seeds of its own destruction. These reside in its dominating force, and come into play through the effects of contamination. With too much proficiency in a professional organization, unconstrained by the forces of efficiency and direction, the professionals become overindulged (as in many of today's universities), just as with too much technocratic regulation in a machine organization, free of the force for innovation, there arises an obsession with control (as in far too much contemporary industry and government).

My colleagues, Danny Miller and Manfred Kets de Vries (1987), have published an interesting book about *The Neurotic Organization*. They discuss organizations that become dramatic, paranoid, schizoid, compulsive and depressive. In each case, a system that may once have been healthy has run out of control. Very roughly, I believe these five organizational neuroses correspond to what tends to happen to each of the five forms. The entrepreneurial organization tends to go out of control by becoming dramatic, as its leader, free of the other forces, takes the system off on a personal ego trip. The machine organization seems predisposed to compulsion once its analysts and their technocratic controls take over completely. Those who have worked in universities and hospitals well understand the collective paranoid tendencies of professionals, especially when free of the constraining forces of administration and innovation. I need not dwell on the depressive effects of that obsession with the 'bottom line' in the diversified organization; the results on morale and innovation of the turning of the financial screws are now widely appreciated. As for the adhocracy organization, its problem is that while it must continually innovate, it must also exploit the benefits of that innovation. One requires divergent thinking, the other convergent. Other forces help balance that tension; without them, the organization can easily become schizoid.

In effect, each form goes over the edge in its own particular way, so that behaviours that were once functional when pursued to excess become dysfunctional. This is easily seen on our pentagon. Remove all the arrows but one at any node, and the organization, no longer anchored, flies off in that direction.

Containment of Configuration

Thus I conclude that truly effective organizations do not exist in pure form. What keeps a configuration effective is not only the dominance of a single force but also the constraining effects of other forces. They keep it in place. I call this *containment*. For example, people inclined to break the rules may feel hard pressed in the machine organization. But without some of them, the organization may be unable to deal with unexpected problems. Similarly, administration may not be the strongest in the professional organization, but when allowed to atrophy, anarchy inevitably results as the absolute power of the professionals corrupts them absolutely. Thus, to manage configuration effectively is to exploit one form but also to reconcile the different forces. But how does the effective organization deal with the contradiction?

COMBINATION

Configuration is a nice thing when you can have it. Unfortunately, some organizations all of the time and all organizations some of the time cannot. They must instead balance competing forces.

Consider the symphony orchestra. Proficiency is clearly a critical force, but so too is direction: such an organization is not conceivable without highly skilled players as well as the strong central leadership of a conductor. The Russians apparently tried a leaderless orchestra shortly after their revolution, but soon gave it up as unworkable.

I shall use the word *combination* for the organization that balances different forces. In effect, it does not make it to any one node of the pentagon but instead finds its place somewhere inside.

How common are combinations as compared with configurations? To some extent the answer lies in the eyes of the beholder: what looks to be a relatively pure form to one person may look like a combination of forces to another. Still, it is interesting to consider how organizations appear to intelligent observers. For several years now, we have sent McGill MBA students out to study organizations in the Montreal area, having exposed them, among other things, to the five forms of organizations. At the end of the year, I have circulated a questionnaire asking them to categorize the organization they studied as one of the forms, a combination of two or more, or neither. In just over half the cases – 66 out of 123 – the students felt that a single form fitted best. They identified 25 entrepreneurial, 13 machine, 11 diversified, 9 adhocracy and 8 professional. All the rest were labelled combinations – 17 different ones in all. Diversified machines were the most common (9), followed by adhocracy professionals (8), entrepreneurial professionals (6) and entrepreneurial machines (5).[2]

Kinds of Combination

Combinations themselves may take a variety of forms. They may balance just two main forces or several; these forces may meet directly or indirectly; and the balance may be steady over time, or oscillate back and forth temporarily.

When only two of the five forces meet in rough balance, the organization might be described as a *hybrid* of two of our forms. This is the case of the symphony orchestra, which can be found somewhere along the line between the entrepreneurial and professional forms. Organizations can, of course, combine several of the forces in rough balance as well. In fact, five of the McGill student groups identified combinations of three forms and another a combination of four forms.

Consider Apple Computers. It seems to have developed under its founder, Steve Jobs, largely as an adhocracy organization, to emphasize new product development. The next CEO, John Sculley, apparently felt the need to temper that innovation with greater focus, to give more attention to efficiency in production and distribution. When I presented this framework at an executive programme a couple of years ago, an employee of Apple Canada saw other things going on in his operation too: he added an entrepreneurial form in sales due to a dynamic leader, professional forms in marketing and training to reflect the skills there, and another adhocracy form in a new venture unit. Organizations that experience such multiple combinations are, of course, the ones that must really play LEGO.

Then there is the question of how the different forces interact. In some cases, they function on a direct, steady basis; in others, they can be separated as to place or time. The combination in the symphony orchestra must be close and pervasive – leadership and professional skill meet regularly, face to face. In organizations like Apple, however, whose different units may reflect different forces, they can act somewhat independently of each other. In fact, some organizations are lucky enough to be able to achieve almost complete buffering between units representing different forces. In newspapers, for example, the more professional editorial function simply hands over its camera-ready copy to the machinelike plant for production, with little need for interaction.

Finally, in contrast to the combinations maintained on a steady-state basis are those that achieve balance in a dynamic equilibrium over time – power oscillates between the competing forces. In this regard, Richard Cyert and James March (1963) some years ago wrote about the 'sequential attention to goals' in organizations, when conflicting needs are attended to each in their own turn – for example, a period of innovation to emphasize new product development followed by one of consolidation to rationalize product lines. (Might Apple Computers simply be in one of these cycles, the innovation of Jobs have been replaced by the consolidation of Sculley, or will Sculley himself be able to get the organization to balance these two forces?)

Cleavage in Combinations

Necessary as it may sometimes be, all is not rosy in the world of combination, however. If configuration encourages contamination, which can drive the organization out of control, then combination encourages *cleavage*, which can have much the same effect. Instead of one force dominating, two or more confront each other to the point of paralyzing the organization.

In effect, a natural fault line exists between any two opposing forces. Pushed to the limit, fissures begin to open up. In fact, Fellini made a film on exactly this with my favourite example. Called *Orchestra Rehearsal*, It is about musicians who revolt against their conductor, and so bring about complete anarchy, followed by paralysis. Only then do they become prepared to cooperate with their leader, who, they realize, is necessary for their effective performance.

But one need not turn to allegories to find examples of cleavage. It occurs commonly in most combinations, for example, in business in the battles between the R&D people who promote new product innovation and the production people in favour of stabilizing manufacturing for operating efficiency. Cleavage can, of course, be avoided when the different forces are separated in time or place, as in the newspaper. But not all organizations with combinations are so fortunate.

Combination of one kind or another is necessary in every organization. The nodes of our pentagon, where the pure configurations lie, are only points, imaginary ideals. Indeed, any organization that reaches one is already on its way out of control. It is the inside of the pentagon that has the space; that is where the effective organization must find its place. Some may fall close to one of the nodes, as configuration, more or less, while others may sit between nodes as combinations. But, ultimately, configuration and combination are not so very different, one representing more of a tilt in favour of one force over others, the other more of a balance between forces. In other words, there must always be the splitting of grey between the black and white of lumping. The question thus becomes again: how does the effective organizational deal with the contradiction?

CONVERSION

So far our discussion has suggested that an organization finds its place in the pentagon and then stays there, more or less. But, in fact, few organizations get the chance to stay in one place forever: their needs change, and they must therefore undergo *conversion* from one configuration or combination to another.

Any number of external changes can cause such a conversion. An innovative organization may chance upon a new invention and decide to settle down in machine form to exploit it. Or a previously stable market may become subject to so much change that machine forms must become innovative. Some conversions are, of course, temporary, as in a machine organization in trouble that becomes entrepreneurial for a time to allow a forceful leader to impose new direction on it (usually called 'turnaround'). This seems to describe Chrysler's experience when Iacocca first arrived, also that of SAS when Carlzon took over.

Cycles of Conversion

Of particular interest here is another type of conversion, however, somewhat predictable in nature because it is driven by forces intrinsic to the organization itself. Earlier I discussed the seeds of destruction contained in each configuration. Sometimes they destroy the organization, but at other times they destroy only the configuration, driving the organization to a more viable form. For example, the entrepreneurial form is inherently vulnerable, dependent as it is on a single leader. It may work well for the young organization, but with ageing and growth a dominant need for direction may be displaced by that for efficiency. Then conversion to the machine form becomes necessary – the power of one leader must be replaced but that of administrators.

The implication is that organizations often go through stages as they develop – *if* they develop – possibly sequenced into so-called lifecycles. In fact, I have placed the forces and forms on the pentagon to reflect the most common of these, with the simple, early states near the top and the more complex ones lower down.

What appears to be the most common lifecycle, especially in business, occurs around the left side of the figure. Organizations generally begin life in the entrepreneurial form, because start-up requires clear direction and attracts strong leaders. As they grow and develop, many settle into the machine form to exploit increasingly established markets. But with greater growth, established markets eventually become saturated, and that often drives the organization to diversify its markets and then divisionalize its structure, taking it finally to the bottom left of our pentagon. Those organizations highly dependent on expertise, however, will instead go down the right side of the pentagon, using the professional form if their services are more standardized or the adhocracy form if these are more creative. (Some ahocracy organizations eventually settle down by converting to the professional form, where they can exploit the skills they have developed, a common occurrence, for example, in the consulting business.)

Ideology is shown above politics on the pentagon because it tends to be associated with the earlier stages of an organization's life, politics with the later ones. Any organization can, of course, have a strong culture, just as any can become politicized. But ideologies develop rather more easily in young organizations, especially with charismatic leadership in the entrepreneurial stage, whereas it is extremely difficult to build a strong and lasting culture in a mature organization. Politics, in contrast, typically spreads as the energy of a youthful organization dissipates with age and its activities become more diffuse. In fact, time typically blunts ideology as norms rigidify into procedures and beliefs become rules; then political activity tends to rise in its place. Typically, it is the old and spent organizations that are the most politicized; indeed, it is often their political conflict that finally kills them.

Cleavage in Conversion

Conversions may be necessary, but that does not make them easy. Some are, of course; they occur quickly because a change is long overdue, much as a supersaturated liquid, below freezing point, solidifies the moment it is disturbed. But most conversions require periods of transition, prolonged and agonizing, involving a good deal of conflict. Two sides battle, usually an 'old guard' committed to the *status quo* challenged by a group of 'Young Turks' in favour of the change. As Apple Computer grew large, for example, a John Sculley intent on settling it down confronted a Steve Jobs who wished to maintain its freewheeling style of innovation.

As the organization in transition sits between its old and new forms, it becomes, of course, a form of combination, with the same problems of cleavage. Given that the challenge is to the very base of its power, there can be no recourse to higher authority to reconcile the conflict. Once again, then, the question arises: how does the effective organization deal with the contradiction?

CONTRADICTION

The question of how to manage contradiction has been the concluding point of each of the sections of this reading. I believe the answer lies in the two forces in the centre of our pentagon. Organizations that have to reconcile contradictory forces, especially in dealing with change, often turn to the cooperative force of ideology or the competitive force of politics. Indeed, I believe that these two forces themselves represent a contradiction that must be managed if an organization is not to run out of control.

I have placed these two forces in the middle of the pentagon because I believe they commonly act in ways different from the other five. It is true that each can dominate an organization, and so draw it towards a missionary or political form, but more commonly I believe that these forces act differently. While the other forces tend to infiltrate parts of an organization (for example, direction in senior management, efficiency in accounting), and so isolate them, these tend instead to *infuse* the entire organization. Thus I refer to them as *catalytic*, noting that one tends to be centripetal, drawing behaviour inwards toward a common core, and the other centrifugal, driving behaviour away from any central place. I shall argue that both can act to promote change, also to prevent it, either way sometimes rendering an organization more effective, sometimes less.

Cooperation through Ideology

Ideology represents the force for cooperation in an organization, for collegiality and consensus. People 'pull together' for the common good – 'we' are in this together.

I use the word ideology here to describe a rich culture in an organization, the uniqueness and attractiveness of which binds the members tightly to it. They commit themselves personally to the organization and identify with its needs.

Such an ideology can infuse any form of organization. It is often found with the entrepreneurial form, because, as already noted, organizational ideologies are usually created by charismatic leaders. But after such leaders move on, these ideologies can sustain themselves in other forms too. Thus we have the ideological machine that is McDonald's and the ideological adhocracy built up by Messrs Hewlett and Packard. And one study some years ago (B. R. Clark, 1970) described 'distinctive' colleges, such as Swarthmore and Antioch – professional forms infused with powerful ideologies.

Ideology encourages the members of an organization to look inward – to take their lead from the imperatives of the organization's own vision, instead of looking outward to what comparable organizations are doing. (Of course, when ideology is strong, there are no comparable organizations!) A good example of this is Hewlett Packard's famous 'next bench syndrome' – that the product designer receives his or her stimulus for innovation, not from the aggregations of marketing research reports, but from the need of a particular colleague at the next bench.

This looking inward is represented by the direction of the halo of the arrows of cooperation on the pentagon. They form a circle facing inward, as if to shield the organization from outside influences. Organizational ideology above all draws people to cooperate with each other, to work together to take the organization where all of them, duly indoctrinated into its norms, believe it must go. In this sense, ideology should be thought of as the spirit of an organization, the life force that infuses the skeleton of its formal structure.

One important implication of this would appear to be that the infusion of an ideology renders any particular configuration more effective. People get fired up to pursue efficiency or proficiency or whatever else drives the organization. When this happens to a machine organization – as in a McDonald's, very responsive to its customers and very sensitive to its employees – I like to call it a 'snappy bureaucracy'. Bureaucratic machines are not supposed to be snappy, but ideology changes the nature of their quest for efficiency. This, of course, is the central message of the Peters and Waterman (1982) book, *In Search of Excellence*, that effectiveness is achieved not by opportunism, not even by clever strategic positioning but by a management that knows exactly what it must do ('sticks to its knitting') and then does it with the fervour of religious missionaries ('hands on, value-driven').

There seems to be another important implication of this: ideology helps an organization to manage contradiction and so to deal with change. The different forces no longer need conflict in quite the same way. As an organization becomes infused with ideology, parts that reflect different forces can begin to pull together. As a result, forces that normally dominate or oppose each other begin to work together, thereby reducing contamination and cleavage and so facilitating adaptation.

I have always wondered why its is that McDonald's, so machinelike, is so creative in its advertising and new product development. Likewise, if 3M and Hewlett Packard really do conform largely to the adhocracy model, why do they have those tight control systems? I suspect we have the answer here. Their strong cultures enable these organizations to reconcile forces that work against each other in more ordinary organizations. People behind these different forces develop a grudging respect for one another: when it matters, they actively cooperate for the common good. 'Old Joe, over there, that nut in R&D: we in production sometimes wonder about him. But we know this place could never function without him.' Likewise in the great symphony orchestra, the musicians respect their conductor because they know that without him they could never produce beautiful music.

Such organizations can more easily reconcile their opposing forces because what matters to their people is the organization itself, not any of its particular parts. If it is IBM you believe in over and above marketing finesse or technical virtuosity *per se*, then when things really matter you will suspend your departmental rivalries to enable IBM to adapt. Great organizations simply pull together when they have to, because they are rooted in great systems of beliefs.

In his popular book, *Competitive Strategy*, Michael Porter (1980) warns about getting 'stuck in the middle' between a strategy of 'cost leadership' and one of 'differentiation' (one representing the force for efficiency, the other including quality as well as innovation). How, then, has Toyota been able to produce such high-quality automobiles at such reasonable cost? Why didn't Toyota get stuck in the middle?

I believe that Porter's admonition stems from the view, prevalent in American management circles throughout this century and reflected equally in my own case for configuration, that if an organization favours one particular force, then others must suffer. If the efficiency experts have the upper hand, then quality gets slighted; if it is the elite designers who get their way, productive efficiency must lag; and so on. This may be true so long as an organization is managed as just a collection of different parts – a portfolio of products and functions. But when the spirit of ideology infuses the bones of its structure, an organization takes on an integrated life of its own and contradictions get reconciled. In Toyota, for example, one has the impression that each individual is made to feel like the embodiment of the entire system, that no matter what job one does, it helps to make Toyota great. Is that not why the assembly workers are allowed to shut down the line: each one is treated as a person capable of making decisions for the good of Toyota. Thus the only thing that gets stuck in the middle at Toyota is the conventional management thinking of the West!

I have so far discussed the reconciliation of contradictory forces between people and units. But even more powerful can be the effect of reconciling these forces within individuals themselves. That is what the concept of infusion really means. It is not the researchers who are responsible for innovation, not the accountants for efficiency; everyone internalizes the different forces in carrying out his or her own job. In metaphorical terms, it is easy to change hats in an organization when all are emblazoned with the same insignia.

Limits to Cooperation

Overall, then, ideology sounds like a wonderful thing. But all is not rosy in the world of culture either. For one thing, ideologies are difficult to build, especially in established organizations, and difficult to sustain once built. For another thing, established ideologies can sometimes get in the way of organizational effectiveness.

The impression left by a good deal of current writing and consulting notwithstanding, ideology is not there for the taking, to be plucked off the tree of management technique like just another piece of fashionable fruit. As Karl Weick has argued, 'A corporation doesn't *have* a culture. A corporation *is* a culture. That's why they're so horribly difficult to change' (in Kiechel, 1984: 11). The fact is that there are no procedures for building ideologies, no five easy steps to a better culture. At best, those steps overlay a thin veneer of impressions that washes off in the first political storm; at worst, they destroy whatever is left of prevailing cultural norms. I believe that effective ideologies are built slowly and patiently by committed leaders who establish compelling missions for their organizations, nurture them and care deeply about the people who perform them.

But even after an ideology is established, the time can come – indeed, usually does eventually – when its effect is to render the organization ineffective, indeed sometimes to the point of destroying it. This is suggested in the comment above that ideologies are 'so horribly difficult to change'.

Just as I argued that ideology promotes change, by allowing an organization to reconcile contradictory forces, now I should like to argue the opposite. Ideology discourages change by forcing everyone to work within the same set of beliefs. In other words, strong cultures are immutable: they may promote change within themselves but they themselves are not to be changed. Receiving 'the word' enables people to ask all kinds of questions but one: the word itself must never be put into question.

I can explain this in reference to two views of strategy, as position and as perspective. In one case, the organization looks down to specific product-market positions (as depicted in Michael Porter's work), in the other it looks up to a general philosophy of functioning (as in Peter Drucker's earlier writings about the 'concept of a business'). In this regard, I like to ask people in my management seminars whether Egg McMuffin was a strategic change for McDonald's. Some argue yes, of course, because it brought the firm into the breakfast market. Others dismiss this as just a variation in product line, pure McDonald's, just different ingredients in a new package. Their disagreement, however, concerns not the change at McDonald's so much as their implicit definition of strategy. To one, strategy is position (the breakfast market), to the other it is perspective (the McDonald's way). The important point here is that change *within* perspective – change at the margin, to new position – is facilitated by a strong culture, whereas change *of* perspective – fundamental change – is discouraged by it. (Anyone for McDuckling à l'Orange?) The very ideology that makes an organization so adaptive within its niche undermines its efforts to move to a new niche.

Thus, when change of a fundamental nature must be made – in strategy, structure, form, whatever – the ideology that may for so long have been the key to an organization's effectiveness suddenly becomes its central problem. Ideology becomes a force for the *status quo*; indeed, because those who perceive the need for change are forced to challenge it, the ideology begins to breed politics!

To understand this negative effect of ideology, take another look at the pentagon. All those arrows of cooperative ideology face inward. The halo they form may protect the organization, but at the possible expense of isolating it from the outside world. In other words, ideology can cause the other forces to atrophy: direction comes to be interpreted in terms of an outmoded system of beliefs, forcing efficiency, proficiency and innovation into ever narrower corners. As the other arrows of the figure disappear, those of ideology close in on the organization, causing it to *implode*. That is how the organization dominated by the force of ideology goes out of control. It isolates itself and eventually dies. We have no need for the extreme example of a Jonestown to appreciate this negative consequence of ideology. We all know organizations with strong cultures, which, like that proverbial bird, flew in ever diminishing circles until they disappeared up their own rear ends!

Competition through Politics

If the centripetal force of ideology, ostensibly so constructive, turns out to have a negative consequence, then perhaps the centrifugal force of politics, ostensibly so destructive, may have a positive one.

Politics represents the force for competition in an organization, for conflict and confrontation. People pull apart for their own needs. 'They' get in our way.

Politics can infuse any of the configurations or combinations, exacerbating contamination and cleavage. Indeed, both problems were characterized as intrinsically conflictive in the first place; the presence of politics for other reasons simply encourages them. The people behind the dominant force in a configuration – say, the accountants in a machine organization or the experts in a professional one – lord their power over everyone else, while those behind each of the opposing forces in a combination relish any opportunity to do battle with each other to gain advantage. Thus, in contrast to a machinelike Toyota pulling together is the Chrysler Iaccoca entered pulling apart; the ideology of an innovative Hewlett-Packard stands in contrast to the politics of a NASA during the *Challenger* tragedy; for every 'distinctive' college there are other 'destructive' ones.

Politics is generally a parochial force in organizations, encouraging people to pursue their own ends. Infusing the parts of an organization with the competitive force of politics only reinforces their tendency to fly off in different directions. At the limit, the organization dominated by politics goes out of control by *exploding*. Nothing remains at the core – no central direction or even set of concentrations and no integrating ideology, and therefore, no directed effort at efficiency or proficiency or innovation.

In this respect, politics may be a more natural force than ideology in organizations. That is to say, organizations left alone seem to pull apart rather more easily than they pull together. Getting a system of human beings to cooperate, on the other hand, seems to require continual effort on the part of a dedicated management.

Benefits of Competition

But we cannot dismiss politics as merely divisive. The constructive role that politics can play in an organization is suggested by the very problems of ideology. If pulling together discourages people from addressing fundamental change, then pulling apart may become the only way to ensure that happens.

Change is fundamental to an organization because it upsets the deeply rooted status quo. Most organizations have such a *status quo*, reinforced especially by the forces of efficiency, proficiency and ideology, all designed to promote development within an established perspective. Thus, to achieve fundamental change in an organization, particularly one that has achieved configuration and more so when that is infused with ideology, generally requires challenge of the established forces, and that means politics. In the absence of entrepreneurial or intrapreneurial capabilities, and sometimes despite them, politics may be the only force available to stimulate the change. The organization must, in other words, pull apart before it can again pull together. Thus, it appears to be an inevitable fact of life in today's organizations that a great deal of the most significant change is driven, not by managerial insight or specialized expertise or ideological commitment, let alone the procedures of planning, but by political challenge.

I conclude that both politics and ideology can promote organizational effectiveness as well as undermine it. Ideology infused into an organization can be a force for revitalization, energizing the system and making its people more responsive. But that same ideology can also hinder fundamental change. Likewise, politics often impedes necessary change and wastes valuable resources. But it can also promote important change that may be available in no other way, by enabling those who realize the need for it to challenge those who do not. There thus remains one last contradiction to reconcile in our story, between ideology and politics themselves.

Combining Cooperation and Competition

My final point is that the two catalytic forces of ideology and politics are themselves contradictory forces which have to be reconciled if an organization is to remain truly effective in the long run. Pulling together ideologically infuses life energy into an organization; pulling apart politically challenges the *status quo*; only by encouraging both can an organization sustain its viability. The centripetal force of ideology must contain and in turn be contained by the centrifugal force of politics. That is how an organization can keep itself from imploding or exploding – from isolating itself, on one hand, and going off in all directions, on the other. Moreover, maintaining a balance between these two forces – in their own form of combination – can discourage the other forces from going out of control. Ideology helps secondary forces to contain a dominant one; politics encourages them to challenge it. All of this – politics tempering the insularity of ideology, ideology restraining the divisiveness of politics, and both helping to limit the destructive power of the other forces – is somewhat reminiscent of that old children's game (with extended rules!): paper (ideology) covers scissors (politics) and can also help cover rocks (the force for efficiency), while scissors cut paper and can even wedge rocks out of their resting places.

Let me turn one last time to the arrows of the pentagon to illustrate. Imagine first the diverging arrows of competition contained within the converging circle of cooperation. Issues are debated and people are challenged, but only within the existing culture. The two achieve an equilibrium, as in the case of those Talmudic scholars who fight furiously with each other over the interpretation of every word in their ancient books yet close ranks to present a united fromt to the outside world. Is that not the very behaviour we find in some of our most effective business corporations, IBM among others? Or reverse the relationship and put the arrows pulling apart outside those of the halo pulling together. Outside challenges keep a culture from closing it on itself.

Thus, I believe that only through achieving some kind of balance of these two catalytic forces can an organization maintain its effectiveness. That balance need not, however, be one of steady state. Quite the contrary, I believe it should constitute a dynamic equilibrium over time, to avoid constant tension between ideology and politics. Most of the time, to be preferred is the cooperative pulling together of ideology, contained by a healthy internal competition, so that the organization can pursue its established perspective with full vigour. But occasionally, when fundamental change becomes necessary, the organization has to be able to pull apart vigorously through the competitive force of politics. That seems to be the best combination of these two forces.

COMPETENCE

To conclude, what makes an organization truly effective? Two views tend to dominate much of the current management literature. I like to call them 'Peterian' and

'Porterian'. Tom Peters implores managers to 'stick to their knitting' and to be 'hands on, value-driven', among other best ways, while Michael Porter insists that they use competitive analysis to choose strategic positions that best match the characteristics of their industries. To Porter, effectiveness resides in strategy, while to Peters it is the operations that count – executing any strategy with excellence.

While agreeing that being effective depends on doing the right thing as well as doing things right, as Peter Drucker put it years ago, I believe we have to probe more deeply to find out what really makes an organization truly effective. We need to understand what takes it to a viable strategy in the first place, what makes it excellent there, and how some organizations are able to sustain viability and excellence in the face of change.

Let me close the reading by summarizing five increasingly developed views of organizational effectiveness.

Convergence

First is the *convergence* hypothesis. 'One best way' is its motto, the single lens its image. There is a proper way to view, and so to design, an organization. This is usually associated with the machine form. A good structure is one with a rigid hierarchy of authority, with spans of control no greater than six, with heavy use of strategic planning, MIS, and whatever else happens to be in the current fashion of the rationalizers. In *In Search of Excellence*, in contrast, Peters and Waterman argued that ideology was the key to an organization's success. While we cannot dismiss this hypothesis – sometimes there *are* proper things to do in most if not all organizations – we must take issue with its general thrust. Society has paid an enormous price for 'one best way' thinking over the course of this century, on the part of all its organizations that have been drawn into using what is fashionable rather than functional. We need to look beyond the obvious, beyond the convergence hypothesis.

Congruence

Beyond convergence is the *congruence* hypothesis, 'it all depends' being its motto, the buffet table its image. Introduced in organization theory in the 1960s, it suggests that running an organization is like choosing dinner from such a table – a little bit of this, a little bit of that, all selected according to specific needs. Organizational effectiveness thus becomes a question of matching a given set of internal attributes, treated as a kind of portfolio, with various situational factors. The congruence hypothesis has certainly been an improvement, but like a dinner plate stacked with an old assortment of foods, it has not been good enough.

Configuration

An so the *configuration* hypothesis was introduced. 'Getting it all together' is its motto, the jigsaw puzzle its image, the lumpers its champions. Design your organization as you would do a jigsaw puzzle, fitting all the pieces together to create a coherent, harmonious picture. There is certainly reason to believe that organizations succeed in good part because they are consistent in what they do; they are certainly easier to manage that way. But, as we have seen, configuration has its limitations too.

Contradiction

While the lumpers may like the configuration hypothesis, splitters prefer the *contradiction* hypothesis. Manage the dialectic, the dynamic tension, is their call, perhaps 'to each his own' their motto, the tug of war their image. They point to the common occurrence of combinations and conversions, where organizations are forced to manage contradictory forces. This is an important hypothesis, together with that of configuration (in their own dynamic tension) certainly an important clue to organizational effectiveness. But still it is not sufficient.

Creation

The truly great organization transcends all of the foregoing while building on it to achieve something more. It respects the *creation* hypothesis. Creativity is its forte, 'understand your inner nature' is its motto, LEGO its image. The most interesting organizations live at the edges, far from the logic of conventional organizations, where as Raphael (1976: 5–6) has pointed out in biology (for example, between the sea and the land, or at the forest's edge), the richest, most varied, and most interesting forms of life can be found. These organizations invent novel approaches that solve festering problems and so provide all of us with new ways to deal with our world of organizations.

• THE CRESCENDO MODEL OF REJUVENATION*

CHARLES BADEN-FULLER AND JOHN M. STOPFORD

Is rejuvenation really possible? How does a business paralyzed by years of turmoil and failure and constrained by limited resources create a vibrant organization committed to entrepreneurship? Unless the organization is frugal and produces some short-term results, it risks losing support from its many stakeholders. But short-term results alone are not enough; longer-term survival must be sought. A start must be made to initiate a form of entrepreneurial behaviour that increases the chances of durable recovery. As one chairman said, 'We have put in new controls and financial disciplines that have stanched the hemorrhaging, cut costs, and returned us, temporarily, to profit. That's the easy part. Getting some momentum going is much harder'. ...

THE CRESCENDO MODEL

We regard building corporate entrepreneurship as the essential ingredient for lasting rejuvenation. ... The task is difficult and often subtle. To ensure that all the attributes of entrepreneurship are diffused throughout an organization, the business must avoid the 'quick fixes' so beloved by many. ... massive capital investment programmes, aggressive but shallow attempts to force total quality management, or re-engineering, or 'cultural immersion' are usually ineffective if undertaken with insufficient attention to the issues we raised. The quick fix rarely delivers any long-term sustainable reward for, like the Tower of Babel, it falls if its foundations are insecure. The way forward must carry the whole organization to be self-sustaining.

Rebuilding a mature organization takes time; it cannot be done with a leap. It is, for example, seldom clear at the outset, because of information gaps, just where the business should be heading. Even when the direction has become clear, the details of the twists and turns in the road ahead can remain fog-bound. Experimentation is necessary to test the feasibility of ideas. Too early commitment to a new direction can be unduly risky. A way has to be found to build consistently and to link newfound strengths before real and lasting transformation can be achieved.

While there are many routes mature businesses might take, the experience of [firms] can be distilled to identify one path, which we feel is more sure than many others. It is a four-stage renewal process, an orchestrated crescendo. Crescendo is a musical term meaning 'a gradual increase in volume'. Our renewal process is also gradual, requiring many steps over many years. The crescendo has to be managed and momentum for change established to allow businesses to reach for ever more challenging targets.

... we address the question of how businesses can get started and shrug off the stasis that has plagued so many mature firms. To place that start in context and show where we are heading, we begin with a brief summary of the overall model ...

Four Stages for Rejuvenation
1. Galvanize: create a top team dedicated to renewal.
2. Simplify: cut unnecessary and confusing complexity.
3. Build: develop new capabilities.
4. Leverage: maintain momentum and stretch the advantages.

Galvanize

Although it seems obvious to begin by creating a top team dedicated to renewal, this vital stage is often overlooked. Rejuvenation is not the fixing up of a few activities or functions that have gone awry; it is the process of changing every part of an organization and the way its functions, territories and various groups interact. No individual, not even the chief executive, alone can achieve this magnitude of change, but at the start it requires leadership from the top team. Such commitment carries important positive messages to the whole organization, for without that commitment those who labour in the firm become demoralized or frustrated.

To galvanize the top team, the agenda for action needs to be drawn up carefully. At the start, detailed plans of action are neither necessary nor wise. Instead, there must be a broad understanding of the issues and a belief that progress will be achieved only by many small steps. There is serious danger in the early stages that top management will either try to buy its way out of difficulties with overgrandiose schemes, such as investing in expensive, state-of-the-art technology which few in the organization understand, or spend too much time chasing culture change programmes and not enough time initiating action.

Simplify

Simplifying the business helps change managers' and workers' perceptions of what has been wrong and what new actions are required. Like clearing the rubbish from an overgrown garden, cutting some activities is a necessary precursor to building something new. Removing outdated control systems and incorrect data helps eliminate the causes of resistance to change. Simplifying the business concentrates scarce resources on a smaller agenda and so increases the chances of gaining positive results in the short to medium term. Simplification also signals to outside stakeholders – owners, suppliers, customers, bankers and employers alike – that something positive is being attempted.

Actions to simplify the task and provide focus for the effort are no more than temporary measures. They must be regarded as work to provide a 'beachhead' in complex industry structures that can be defended while work to build new strengths can proceed.

Build

In the third stage, which overlaps the second, the organization must set about building new advantages for later deployment as the business breaks out of the beachhead. It is at this stage that corporate rather than individual entrepreneurship must be developed. Beginning with raised aspirations to do better and resolve old problems, in the course of time new challenges need to be articulated, which will help all to work to a common purpose. That purpose, expressed in terms of visions and a direction for progress, is typically phrased in terms that all can understand. Making progress along the chosen path requires managers to experiment and to discover what can work and what fails.

Experiments, of necessity have to be small at the start: resources are limited, knowledge about possibilities uncertain and the risks seem immense. As some experiments pay off, momentum should increase to the point where major investments in new technology for delivering the product or service may be required. Learning may also start slowly, though ordinarily some parts of the organization progress more quickly than others. Over time the organization must invest in deepening existing skills and acquiring new ones, developing new systems, data bases and knowledge. Alongside these initiatives, teamwork must be developed, first on a small scale to deal with essential tasks, but then growing across the whole organization and extending along the supply chain. The momentum created helps build the values that underpin the crucial ingredient of the will to win.

Leverage

The final stage is leveraging advantages and maintaining momentum. As the organization grows in competitive strength, it can expand the sphere of its operations into new markets, new products and new parts of the value chain. Leveraging capabilities can be by acquisition, alliances or internal moves so that the business can extend its newfound advantages to a much wider sphere of activities. Pressures for expansion must be balanced against the danger of too much complexity slowing down the pace of innovation and forcing the organization to a standstill.

We label the rejuvenation process a *crescendo* to emphasize that the four stages are not discrete steps, but rather activities which merge into each other as the magnitude of change increases over time. The reality of all organizations is messy, confusing and complex. In the building of corporate entrepreneurship, activities in one department or at one level of the organizationa may proceed faster and more effectively than others. Moreover, organizations do not rejuvenate only once: they may need to do so repetitively. The challenges of one period may be resolved, but those of the next may again require organizational change.

The rejuvenation steps are summarized in Figure 1. The arrows are drawn as lines, though in practice progress is usually made in loops of learning. The dance to the crescendo of music is the samba. *One step back to take two steps forward* describes how organizations proceed—and it is exactly what happens with simplification and building. Let us use an analogy: renovators of old buildings know full well that the plaster has to come off the walls if a rotten structure is to be repaired. ... it is rarely possible to fix it without spoiling the decorations. ...

We emphasize that in the early simplifying stage of renewal, cutting may have to be radical. The contraction can be tangible, for example, cutting out parts of the product range, geographic territory or stages of the value chain; it can also be less tangible, for example, eliminating systems and procedures. Even profitable activities may have to be dropped if they distract attention and deflect resourcss from building the new 'core'.

In building, progress is best achieved by many small initiatives, because resources are limited. Small steps spread the risks and prevent the organization from betting everything on one initiative. As rejuvenation proceeds, the risks become better understood and progress more secure, allowing the steps to get bigger. Small steps also allow the organization to encourage initiatives from below and help build an entrepreneurial culture. Whereas instructions for surgery are imposed from the top, it is the bottom-up flow of ideas and actions that accelerates the convalescence and return to fighting fitness.

We stress that organizations need a long time to rejuvenate. It takes years to build a truly entrepreneurial company. Like builders of houses, who spend almost two-thirds of the cost and time below ground digging foundations and preparing the

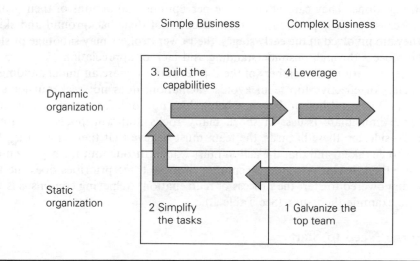

FIGURE 1
Critical path for corporate renewal

site, effective organizations that aim to become entrepreneurial also have to sink deep foundations; rushing for the quick-fix solution is unlikely to result in long.term rewards. ...

GALVANIZING THE TOP TEAM

Rejuvenating a mature organization is impossible without commitment from the top. As we pointed out at the end of Chapter 5, many mature organizations show signs of life with innovative actions being taken in parts, and include many able individuals who are committed to change. Entrepreneurial individuals generally labour in isolated groups. They are unable to make the connections essential to altering the path of the organization, for that requires linkages across functions and territories, which cannot be achieved without the backing of top management.

Initial moves are often made by a new chief executive, and in all the firms we studied, the CEO played a vital and decisive role. The effective ones, however, did not act alone; they all realized the importance of teams. ...

Building a top team dedicated to change provides continuity and reduces the risks that the process will falter if one person leaves. In several of our organizations the chief executive changed without loss of momentum. ...

Effective top teams span all the key functions. Rejuvenation involves changing the way in which the functions work and the way in which they relate. An effective top team must have a real understanding of the functions so that it understands what is technically possible, what is required by customers, suppliers, the workforce and other stakeholders. Without shared knowledge within the team, there can be no intuition, which is vital for the business.

The need to involve the key functions also ensures the involvement of the vital power brokers of the organization. Functional or territorial heads carry weight in getting things done. They can influence the perceptions and actions of their group, perhaps because of their position but often because of their background and skills. Unless they are involved in the early stages, the power brokers may sabotage or slow down the process through misunderstanding and lack of appreciation.

For rejuvenation, all members of the top team must share an understanding of the problem. An effective top team avoids vacillation, does not seek outsiders to resolve its problems (although they may help), does not look for a quick fix or shirk dealing with immediate issues. In short, many rocks and whirlpools have to be avoided. To sidestep these hazards, the team must believe that there is a crisis, that action has to be taken, and that the action must extend throughout the organization. Only where there is real common acceptance of these three priorities does the top team feel empowered to start the process of rejuvenation. Achieving consensus is not easy, so we examine the issues. (See Table 1.)

Sensing the Need to Start

What triggers actions that can lead to rejuvenation? Why is correct sensing so critical to generating a sense of urgency? Earlier, we discussed the difficulty of recognizing

TABLE 1   Galvanizing the top team

Limiting perceptions	Galvanizing perceptions
The problem we face is temporary.	There is a crisis and the issues are major and fundamental.
We must move slowly to avoid upsetting the existing order.	There is a sense of urgency. Change must be set into motion even if we do not know exactly where we are going.
It is someone else's fault that we are in trouble.	We must understand *why* we are in the mess, so that we, the top team, can lead the way forward.
The problems lie in specific areas of the organization; they are not widespread.	Firm-wide change is needed across functions, territories and hierarchy.
The financial figures tell us what is wrong.	We have to look behind the figures to find out where the markets are going and the needed capabilities.

crises in a form that can lead to action and the even more serious problem of using the recognition of an opportunity as a way of focusing energies to change behaviour. It is one thing to bring together a top team, quite another to have it share, collectively, a sense that change is imperative. We use the word sense advisedly, because at the earliest stages only rarely do hard data indicate a clear direction; information by itself seldom 'proves' or 'disproves' any action.

Consider what can happen when managers sense the signals for change. They may seem so vague that they are effectively ignored. They may point to solutions that are beyond current capabilities, they can provoke responses of general concern, but the actions are little more than tinkering with the symptoms. More precise signals can also be ignored, even when the solutions are within capabilities, because the team has yet to share a common will to respond. The issue of the urgency is also embodied in the message. Managers may feel that they have plenty of time and allow other agendas to preoccupy them. Alternatively, an urgent message may seem to be so complex that appropriate responses are hard to calculate.

We found that all the top teams of rejuvenating firms had experienced many of these difficulties before they could commit themselves to collective internal action. Often, we found top teams working to exhaust all the 'obvious' actions before they could perceive the need to consider more radical approaches to transform the business as a whole. Rational calculations of partial response to complex challenges can be used, perhaps unwittingly, to perpetuate the inertia of maturity. The problem is exacerbated when the agenda is so complex that team members cannot agree on priorities. ...

It is important to appreciate that the data in signals for change need to be interpreted for others, particularly when they are weak. Consider the assessment of competitors, so commonly undertaken by top management. Measures of competition may cover profitability, productivity, reliability or customer acceptance. Generally, a few competitors are doing better on some if not all the measures, but many may be similar to a given organization and some may be doing worse. Should this fact be seen as a trigger for action or a signal for complacency? Unless someone has high aspirations and a sense of danger, complacency prevails. ... there are always those who believe that poor performance, be it in profits or some other measure, can be excused: 'It is not our fault.' Worse yet, competitor benchmarking studies can be used to justify the status quo. One mature firm that later went out of business went so far as to reject a study that indicated the need for a fundamental change of approach. In the words of one director, it was 'obviously fallacious. If this was possible, we would be doing it already.'

There are many other reasons why managers may fail to react to changing circumstance. Mature organizations can become trapped in an illusion bred of undue focus on accounting profits. Of necessity, accounting figures can register only what has happened, not what is about to happen; when confronted by 'satisfactory' profits, many top groups ignored other signals indicating declining competitiveness. ...

Only a few of our rejuvenators did the obvious thing at the start, that is, establish measures that heighten the sense of urgency to deal with emergent problems before they become serious. Wise and successful organizations broaden their measures of performance to include specific indicators of relative achievement of financial and non-financial goals. A broader and more balanced scorecard helps top teams in general, and chief executives in particular, to anticipate where trouble might strike. It amplifies the weak signals that forewarn of danger and diminishes those signals which encourage complacency. If the top team does not anticipate it, the organization may be submerged and unable to retrieve itself when the real crisis arrives.

Triggers for Action

Sensing impending doom is not always sufficient to induce action. Although it comes late in the day, falling profitability seems to be the most common trigger for inducing a sufficient enough sensing of urgency and crisis that actions to cure the roots of the problem can be instituted. ...

Must firms wait for a financial crisis before top managers do more than tinker with some of the parts? Though harder to do, it is possible for individuals to anticipate a looming crisis and initiate corrective action before it is too late or too expensive to try. It is relatively easier for that to happen when an individual has the power to act. The awareness may come first to shareholders, who appoint a new chief executive to carry the message, or the chief executive may be prescient. It is more difficult when the messages come from outside and are heard by individual managers without power. Dealings with suppliers, customers, bankers and innumerable others can highlight the problem and stir up action within isolated groups. But when that happens, action to change business fundamentally usually has to wait until there is a chief executive who listens and buys into the possibilities.

...it is possible to anticipate a real crisis. Those who have done so have been able to take positive action at less cost than would have been incurred had they procrastinated. In such instances, hindsight seems to show repetitively that the actions taken were less risky than a policy of standing still. But before the event, the risks may have appeared large.

Empowering Management

Bringing together a top team and making its members realize that there is a crisis is not enough to start rejuvenation: the team must believe that it has the power and the responsibility to do something. It is necessary that certain aspects of the problem are appreciated by the top team: that the problem is not limited to a single part of the organization, that the quick fix does not work. The top team must also appreciate that it does not have to know all the answers before it can act. Its job is to chart the direction ahead and enlist the aid of others in finding durable solutions. It is tempting to suggest that the realization comes quickly, but the truth is that appreciation comes gradually.

   ... managers of mature organizations are often keen to fasten blame on others. Sometimes they blame the environment, poor demand, overfussy customers, adverse exchange rates, even the weather. Sometimes they blame the decisions of previous top management and sometimes the failure of current middle management to implement decisions made by the top team. While an element of blame may rightly be attached to these groups, in all cases top management showed insufficient appreciation of the issues at stake. Progress can take place only when team members appreciate the extent of a problem and realize that they, and only they, are ultimately responsible for its organization's failures. More important, only the top team can lead the organization out of its mess.

   It is also common for senior managers to perceive that the problems (and hence the solutions) lie in a single function or part of their organization. Blaming particular functions, territories or groups is often unhelpful, as the crisis reflects failures of the whole organization. For example, when high-cost products are also poor quality, the production department is usually blamed. Such finger-pointing is naive, for rarely is production alone to blame for poor quality. It may be that production, not being told by the service department which failures occur most frequently, is trying to improve the wrong elements. Distribution may be at fault, damaging goods in transit. Purchasing may be paying insufficient attention to ensuring that suppliers provide quality components, and marketing may insist on designs that are difficult and expensive to produce. Quality at low cost can be achieved only when all functions work closely together. ...

   The dawning realization that the problems are serious and that the causes extend beyond a single function to all parts of the organization is one step on the road towards taking necessary corrective actions. But before effective action can be initiated, hard choices among many alternatives must be made. Here the chief executive has the central role of holding the ring as people test their intuition against always imperfect data. Lacking hard evidence, a top team always has members with competing senses of priority. And lacking anything more than a common will to be positive, the debates can all too readily become unproductive without firm leadership.

CHOOSING EFFECTIVE ACTION

Some top teams choose to manage their way forward by exhaustive analysis of the alternatives they can perceive at the time of crisis. Others feel their way by trying solutions and discovering what does and does not work. Still others examine the experience of other organizations. And often all these approaches are combined. However choices are made, there are many false paths and blind alleys, which can seduce and lull management into thinking that it is effectively dealing with the issues at hand.

The steps that we suggest mark out the most effective path of action are in stark contrast to other actions we observe. Simplification involves cutting to conserve resources, revealing a new core and pointing the way forward. The subsequent building, later described in detail, lays new foundations for the entrepreneurial organization and requires an extended time perspective. These measured steps contrast with the following alternatives, which many have taken and which fail to address key issues effectively: scrapping everything and starting afresh – rather than saving what is of value; looking to outsiders to alleviate a problem – as a substitute for internal action; vacillation among extreme directives issued by top management – paralyzed uncomprehending top management; large-scale investments in state-of-the-art technology and systems at the initial stages – quick fix or big hit, and culture change programmes without parallel actions – denying that there is an immediate crisis. These issues are discussed more fully below.

Scrap Everything and Start Afresh

Consider first the problem of those Cassandras who argue that it is hopeless to try to rejuvenate – better to give up without a struggle and go elsewhere. Their pessimistic views can be justified if *all* the alternatives are more costly and more risky. Only if all else fails must an organization be extinguished.

One US company seeking the rejuvenation of an existing operation a waste of time. Instead of tackling the deep-seated problems in its Midwest plants, it moved the whole operation to the South, leaving its past behind. In so doing, the company abandoned many skilled and loyal workers who might have been capable of adapting to new working methods faster than it took to train a brand new workforce and at less cost. The Japanese experience of buying US facilities and doubling or trebling productivity in under a year illustrates that the possibility of rejuvenation often exists. Their experience also confirms that faster returns may come from renewal rather than greenfield initiatives, a point often overlooked by those in a hurry to 'get something going'.[3]

Sometimes, to be sure, troubled organizations do not have the option of a clean start elsewhere. Even though they might wish to walk away, the owners may not be able to afford the exit costs. They may also face severe union opposition and the resistance of politicians and local government officials. In such cases, management is obliged to try to find a middle way, regardless of how many Cassandras argue that the effort will be in vain.

Seeking Outside Support

For years, many European chemical companies, particularly the Italian giants, the French and Belgians, and even the British ICI, perceived the problems of their industry as being caused by government's failure to manage demand in the economy and allowing the Middle Eastern countries power over oil prices. In these firms, top management consistently lobied governments for support to resolve their problems and failed to take internal initiatives. ICI, one of the bigger culprits, was also one of the first to break out of the vicious circle and realize that internal action was necessary. A galvanized top management led the way, and ten years later, in better shape than many of its European counterparts, it is still trying to pull its organization around....

Lest we be accused of ignoring politics and reality, we fully recognize that all organizations have a role to lobby and put their case to government, and all need to watch and influence events. However, we draw a distinction between this approach and those failing organizations which do nothing for themselves while waiting to be rescued by the white knight of outside support. The first puts the role of public policy in perspective, while the second fails in the duties of management.

Top-down Directives that Address Symptoms, Not causes

Many top managers seem to believe that issuing orders from the top and expecting immediate responses is the best way to start things going. ... this is unlikely to instil corporate entrepreneurship. As a sense of crisis looms, if statements from the top become hysterical, they can be met by inaction or lack of results from below. Vacillation is usually another sign that top management is not really in control and does not understand either the causes of a problem or how to respond effectively. Seldom can top-down directives do more than preserve yesterday's 'formula'. ...

Going for the Big Hit

The recognition that an organization is far behind in its capabilities can drive top management to seek a quick fix. At the beginning of the renewal process there is a temptation to spend money on modern capital by buying state-of-the-art factories, service delivery systems or other forms of technology. Typically, consultants or other outsiders have suggested that such investments permit a firm to catch up with its industry leaders. Usually the investments are large, take several years to build and commit the organization to a single unchangeable route for the future. There is often an absence of understanding in the organization of how the new technology works, and certainly a lack of appreciation for all the issues it involves. At the early stages of rejuvenation, big programmes are dangerous, not least because most of the organization's resources are bet on a single course.

For the mature organization in crisis, the arrival of massive amounts of new capital, new computers or new systems without a corresponding building of a skill-base risks disasters. All our rejuvenators discovered, if they did not already know, that skills have to be built in tandem with investment in hardware. Without the proper skills and awareness throughout the whole organization, the investments are misused or underused. Little progress is made either in delivering financial results or building a competitive edge. Worse, the spirit of entrepreneurial enthusiasm with its characteristics of learning and experimentation may be repressed. ...

We should make it clear that large investment programmes can pay off handsomely when undertaken by firms that have gained entrepreneurial capabilities. When organizations have built their internal skills and processes, they can leverage new investments effectively. ...

Culture Change Programmes without Cooresponding Action

If the big hit is dangerous because it squanders resources, takes unnecessary risks and does not build a new organization, the culture change programme goes to the opposite extreme. It is certainly true that mature organizations need to change their culture if they are to become entrepreneurial, but many mistakenly believe that the culture has to be changed before actions for improvement can be taken, or that culture change is sufficient in itself. A culture change programme without action is very risky because it denies the existence of a crisis and takes the organization's attention away from the necessity for immediate action. Moreover, it fails to appreciate the most obvious fact that organizations change only through actions because actions reflect and alter beliefs.

Our finding echoes the observations of Tom Peters and Robert Waterman [1982], who noted that effective organizations had a bias for action. Their point was that unless action is taken, progress cannot be made. Their message is highly appropriate for rejuvenating organizations. We found a surprising number of firms investing heavily in changing the culture of their organizations without ensuring that deliberate progress was made in the specification of the actual tasks. ...

Rejuvenating a business does require a culture change, but change must be linked to action. Our research suggests that effective culture change requires managers to deal with tasks. Thus, abolishing the executive dining room at [one firm] did help, but only because it reinforced other important initiatives dealing with productivity and quality. In many organizations, quality circles and the like are introduced, and it seems that those which work well are those which have short-term tangible goals as well as long-term ones. Grand schemes for change without action seldom work....

The Quick Fix: TQM or Process Reengineering

All our rejuvenators subscribed in one way or another to aspects of total quality management (TQM) and all have re-engineered their processes, occasionally several times over. But what they did ... bore little relation to those peddlers of snake oil who claim instant results.

A few less careful proponents of TQM or process engineering (or the equivalent) portray complex philosophies as quick-fix solutions. They understate the investment in the time, energy and effort required to yield results. In their desire for speed, they fail to stress the need to teach the organization the skills to ensure that the process can be continued and typically do not build a proper foundation for lasting success. Not surprisingly, recent surveys of organizations that took up the TQM fad in the 1980s show that many have been disappointed and stopped earlier initiatives.[4] To be sure, there have been successes, but we suggest that they have probably been organizations which were either far down the rejuvenation road or, like our mature firms, patient and persistent ones. We forecast the same for process re-engineering.

Claims by consultants that process re-engineering can deliver a ten-fold improvement come as no surprise. ... But boasts that such progress is achieved quickly do not ring true. Long before the recent fad, we observed mature firms attempting such rapid engineering without preparation and failing. ...

THE WAY FORWARD

To go forward, the mature firm aspiring to rejuvenate must galvanize and build a top team committed to action. Crucial choices need to be made about the scope of the firm and how and where it will compete. In addition, action must be taken to start the building of entrepreneurship, which we assert is necesssary for renewal and any higher aspirations. Some businesses have found that outside stakeholders can play a role. One such group is the top team of a business that is part of a holding company or parent organization. ...

There may be a gap in cultural perceptions on these matters about what is and is not effective. Where many US managers espouse the value of directives from the very top and point to the benefits of the resulting focus and speed of change, many we spoke to across Europe adopted a different perspective. Those whose job it was to look after a whole portfolio often preferred to work on encouraging managers to embrace the values of creativity, innovation and challenge to conventions without specifying the actions or processes. Many set challenging targets, but some who regarded their approach as slower and harder to control, bet that the end-results would be much more durable.

There is no way we know of to resolve the issue of which is the superior approach. Both have good and bad points and both are dependent on the climate of attitudes into which such initiatives are introduced. The difference of opinion, however, serves to reinforce the point we made at the start ... real transformation of a business cannot begin in earnest without the regognition by its top managers that a new direction must be found.

[1] See F. Darwin (ed.), *The Life and Letters of Charles Darwin* (London: John Murray, 1887), p. 105.

[2] The high incidence of entrepreneurial forms may be thought to reflect the students' bias towards studying small organizations, but I think not. There exist many more small organizations, in business and elsewhere, than large ones, usually entrepreneurial in nature. Of the larger ones, I would expect the machine form to predominate in any western society. As for the incidence of combinations, I personally believe that the diversified and adhocracy forms are the most difficult to sustain (the former a conglomerate with no links between the divisions, the latter a very loose and freewheeling structure), and so these should be most common in hybrid combinations. Also some of the hybrids reflect common transitions in organizations, especially from the entrepreneurial to the machine form, as I shall discuss later.

[3] The West German approach to rebuilding East Germany also has the appearance of trying to start afresh: old factories are demolished, workers dismissed and the new owners act as if they are setting up greenfield sites. For an academic view of when it is best to start afresh, see M. T. Hannan and J. Freeman, 'Structural inertia and organizational change' in K. S. Cameron, R. I. Sutton and D. A. Whetten, (eds), *Readings in Organizational Decline* (Cambridge, Mass.: Ballinger, 1988).

[4] See, for instance, the studies by Arthur D. Little in the United States and A. T. Kearney in the United Kingdom as reported in *The Economist*, 18 April 1992.

3–1

CARTIER: A LEGEND OF LUXURY

PAST: THE BIRTH AND GROWTH OF A LEGEND

In 1817, a man named Pierre Cartier returned from the Napoleonic Wars and opened a shop in Marais, Paris's artisan quarter, where he sculpted powder horns and decorative motifs for firearms. His son, Louis-François (1819–1904) adapted to the more peaceful and prosperous times of the Restoration by becoming first the apprentice and later, in 1847, the successor of Monsieur Picard, a 'maker of fine jewellery, novelty fashion and costume jewellery'. In 1859, Louis-François opened a shop on the Boulevard des Italiens, flanked by the favourite cafés of the smart set. He soon attacted the attention and patronage of the Princess Eugénie, cousin of Napoleon III and soon to become Empress of France.

Alfred Cartier took over from his father, Louis-François, in 1874. In the turbulent decade following the collapse of the Second Empire and the revolt of the communards, the company survived by selling the jewels of La Barucci, a famous courtesan of the time, in London. Like his ancestors, Alfred adapted to changing times and the whims of a new set of customers, the wealthy bourgeois, adding *objets d'art*, clocks, snuff boxes and fob watches to his range of wares. His son, Louis, became his associate in 1898.

This case was prepared by François-Xavier Huard and Charlotte Butler, Research Associates, under the supervision of Sumantra Ghoshal, Associate Professor at INSEAD. It is intended to be used as a basis for class discussion rather than to illustrate either effective or ineffective handling of an administrative situation.
Copyright © 1990, by INSEAD-CEDEP, Fontainebleau, France. Revised 1992.
Financial support from the INSEAD Alumni Fund European Case Programme is gratefully acknowledged.

Louis Cartier

> Cartier ... the subtle magician who breaks the moon into pieces and captures it in threads of gold. (Jean Cocteau)

Louis brought to the firm his 'creativity, his commercial genius and an extraordinary dynamism'. Full of curiosity, passionately interested in artistic and technical innovation, Louis introduced platinum into jewellery settings, making them lighter and easier to wear, and showed a distinctive flair for design. His was the inspiration for new items such as the watch with a geometric hull, designed for his friend, the Brazilian pilot Santos Dumont. The jewellery designer Jeanne Toussaint (1887–1978) added her creativity to that of Louis. The result was the famous animal collection, including the beast that was to become Cartier's best-known international trade-mark, the fabulous jewelled panther.

Cartier moved to the Place Vendôme, home of the greatest names in jewellery, but Louis had no intention of allowing Cartier to become just another jewellery firm. The clockmaker, Jaeger and Lalique, the goldsmith and luxury glass manufacturer, both worked for him. At the 1925 World Fair, it was clear that rather than cling to the company of traditional jewellers, Louis preferred to mix with people from other creative fields, such as the couturiers Lanvin and Louis's father-in-law, Worth.

With his brothers, Louis opened shops in London (1902) and New York (1908), while at the Court of St Petersburg he established Cartier as a rival to Fabergé. Cartier ruled over the crowned heads of Europe, 'the jeweller of kings and the King of jewellers'. Royal warrants came from Edward VII of England (Louis created 27 diadems for his coronation), Alphonse XII of Spain and Charles of Portugal.

In the early decades of the 20th century, Cartier reached its apogee. There was not a monarch, business tycoon or film star who was not a client. Louis even conquered the literary world, designing the swords carried by authors such as Mauriac, Duhamel, Maurois and Jules Romains for their enrolment as members of the Académie Française. And it was Jean Cocteau who, in 1922, inspired Louis to create his famous ring composed of three interlocking circles, a magical symbol in Indian legend.

But Louis' descendants were to live through less glorious times. The Second World War engulfed many of the clients who had been the mainstay of the great jewellery houses and, after four generations of entrepreneurial, successful Cartiers, the firm seemed to lose its sense of direction. The New York store was sold, amid some dispute and discord within the family.

In 1964, a man came knocking at the door of the legendary jewellers. He was a manufacturer of mass-produced cigarette lighters, an inventive spirit who had applied all the latest technical refinements to the development of a new product. To mark the event, he wanted to decorate this new product with silver and christen it with one of the great names of the jewellery establishment. Rejected by other jewellers, he made his way to Cartier.

Robert Hocq

Robert Hocq was the head of Silver Match. A self-educated man, his dreams were forged among the machines in his workshop. Trailing behind the great names of Dupont and Dunhill, Silver Match had adopted the 'copied from America' style of the new consumer society, furnishing disposable lighters to the mass market. Positioned in the middle range, the Silver Match lighters were sold through tobacco shops.

Robert Hocq had defined the market he was aiming for – the gap between his current products and the 'super luxury' of Dunhill and Dupont. All that his lighters needed was 'a little something' that would elevate them to the realm of 'authentic' luxury goods. And in a world of plastic and cheap imitations, he needed the guarantee that only a name associated with true luxury could provide. Whether prompted by the need for money or the memory of past innovatons, in 1968 Cartier agreed to grant Hocq a temporary licence.

The lighter's original design, a simple column in the Greek architectural style encircled by a ring, was slowly elaborated. Two radical innovations were incorporated. First, its oval shape was a direct descendant of Louis Cartier's favourite form, then quite unknown in the world of lighters. Second, Robert Hocq introduced the use of butane gas. The sale of gas cartridges would be a lucrative sideline even though, for the moment, clients were more accustomed to using liquid fuel.

To commercialize the new product, Le Briquet Cartier S.A. was established. The lighters were to be sold through the same outlets as Silver Match, a network of retailers. By 1968, the deal had been finalized and Robert Hocq turned to the task of finding the right person to sell his Cartier lighter.

Alain Perrin

The candidate who entered Robert Hocq's office did so in response to an advertisement he had seen in the paper. The meeting began at six o'clock in the evening, and ended at midnight over an empty bottle of whisky. Alain Perrin often exhausted those around him whether at home, at the 12 schools he attended or during the long nights of his student days. He had arm-wrestled with Johnny Halliday, dined with the Beatles and, in short, led the Parisian life of insouciance of the 1960s generation. Born into a family of scientists, he dreamt only of a business career. While at the Ecole des Cadres he imported Shetland sweaters for his friends. Skipping classes to race all over trading sweaters for farmers' old furniture, he earned the nickname 'King Pullover'.

After the death of his father in 1965, Alain Perrin directed his ebullient energy towards more serous objectives. He returned to college to finish his studies and then began work in a paper recycling company. Bored by this, he started his own company dealing in antiques. One shop led to another, and finally to three.

In May 1969, he was still only 26.

On the road, a suitcase of the new Cartier lighters in his hand, Perrin visited those existing Silver Match clients who seemed best suited to the new product's image; wholesalers and fine tobacco stores or civettes. The lighter was an immediate success. The civettes gave it star billing; to be able to handle a Cartier product was tantamount to selling real jewellery. In competing with traditional jewellers, this gave them a long-sought legitimacy.

All profits were reinvested by Hocq in order to acquire the permanent and exclusive right to the Cartier name. His relations with Cartier grew ever closer.

Hocq's activities were not confined to lighters. Two days after Cartier acquired a 70 carat diamond in a New York sale, Richard Burton bought it for 14.5 million francs as a gift for Elizabeth Taylor. Cartier's profit on the deal was minimal but the publicity surrounding the sale was invaluable. Orchestrated by Hocq, the event was a media coup for Cartier.

In 1971, backed by a group of financiers, Robert Hocq bought the jewellery business and the Paris and London shops from the Cartier family. In 1976, he bought back the New York store. Alain Dominique Perrin became general manager of the lighter division.

Must Lighters

In 1972, the trademark 'les Must de Cartier' was born.

When the lighters were first launched in December 1969, Robert Hocq was discussing the project with a colleague. Tapping a magazine advertisement, Hocq asked him 'Cartier . . . what exactly does Cartier mean to you.' In English, the man answered: 'Cartier is a must, Sir.' At the time, the reply baffled Hocq, but several years later he remembered the incident.

> Modern man has a need to let the world know that he has succeeded. To do this, he needs to be able to buy symbols of social prestige. True luxury objects produced by the great jewellers cannot give him the recognition he yearns for, since they are exclusively one-of-a-kind.

> Must lighters are the materialization of social status.

In 1974, following the example of Dupont, Cartier pens joined the lighters in shop windows. Whereas the lighter was, by its very nature, connected with tobacco shops, pens opened up new distribution channels. In 1975, the addition of leather goods opened up yet another.

With the Cartier pen–lighter duo, stores were no longer selling an object but a prestige concept. At the same time, Cartier was anxious to expand distribution of its jewellery. However, although lighters and pens could hold their own amidst displays of necklaces and rings in neighbourhood jewellery stores, Cartier jewels were simply not meant to be surrounded by the ordinary and anonymous.

Exclusive Cartier boutiques were created. In them, under the slogan 'Les Must de Cartier' and set against the rich bordeaux red chosen for the line, Cartier jewels were displayed to advantage. Later on, leathers, lighters and pens too were shown against this same distinctive setting. Strict guidelines defined the product mix, decoration and service which each distributor had to provide. Cartier then began sending inspectors round to monitor discreetly that these conditions were being respected.

The Must line was not to everyone's taste. The very select Comité Colbert excluded Cartier from its membership and shortly afterwards, Cartier withdrew from the Syndicat de Haute Joaillerie, the organisation of fine jewellers which represented the most prestigious houses of the Place Vendôme. For a time, relations between 'that cowboy Perrin' and the other jewellers were strained.

In 1973, Cartier founded a new company under the emblem 'Les Must de Cartier', to be kept entirely separate from its jewellery interests. Alain Perrin became its President. Concerned that too much of the jewellery business was concentrated in the Paris area (65% of sales), he convinced Robert Hocq that the concept and products should be exported.

> I needed to move from the state of an elegantly sleepy retailer to that of a young, contemporary, international concern, capable of creating products for a world-wide market, and not just Paris, London or New York.

Once a year, Alain Perrin travelled round the world. In ten to twelve stops from the Middle East to Australia, from Hong Kong to the United States, he picked up orders and sold the universality of the Must concept.

Must Watches

Buying back the New York store in 1976 led to a new activity. As a jeweller, Cartier made a sold gold watch: the Tank. Its reputation (which went back to Louis Cartier) had inspired innumerable imitations. The American market in particular was infested by a plague of watches in plated brass, copies of the Tank. For 500 or 1,000 francs, an imitation of the real thing (costing 10,000 to 15,000 francs) could be bought. Even the New York store, long out of the control of the Cartier family, was selling this type of imitation.

To end these shoddy practices, Alain Dominique Perrin fought fire with fire. He brought out a vermeil watch, based on an original model. This meant that for only 2,000 francs more than the price of a cheap imitation, people could buy themselves a real Cartier watch, a true descendant of the masterpieces created by Louis Cartier in solid gold and brilliants.

The extension of the luxury Must line into watches allowed Cartier to surpass Dupont. From then on, Cartier's line of lighters, pens, leathers and watches were always displayed quite separately. Retailers had to reserve 'a space within a space' for them in their stores and the style of presenting the goods had to be in keeping with (and directly inspired by) the Must boutiques.

Perfume

The idea of launching a perfume, planned for 1981, presented a dilemma. On the one hand, the very nature of the product contradicted Cartier's expressed wish to limit itself to 'lasting products which clients covet and to which they become attached'. Cartier had originally resolved only to produce objects that were 'never thrown out'. On the other hand, perfume was inevitable. Historically, it had been the first diversification channel for every luxury brand, and constituted the most obvious path in the public mind. A further problem was how to launch the perfume – and hence follow in the footsteps of most other luxury brands – without breaking another of Cartier's golden rules: 'Avoid what is already being done.'

Cartier's product managers came up with the idea of a 'case/refill'. The case was conceived as an object in the Cartier tradition, lasting for ever and never going out of fashion – an expensive product, priced well above the competition – while the refill, in utilitarian plastic, would be priced well below the competition for the same quantity of perfume. The bevelled shape of the refill would ensure that it could not stand upright or be used without the case. And sale of the perfume to a client without a case would be forbidden.

The idea seemed simple yet seductive. Opposition came from market specialists, who did not believe that it would work. Previous similar attempts, albeit limited, had failed. But Cartier's marketing team felt that the 'Cartier' cachet would overcome any reservations in the perfume market, and that the very novelty of the case, 'a totally new gift idea', would open up a whole new area of marketing. Perrin decided to go ahead with the launch. It was an immediate success.

At a later date, having legitimized its entry into the perfume market, Cartier brought out its perfume in a classic bottle, with a leather pouch. It was presented as a 'travel' version.

> In the luxury market, it's the survival of the fittest. You have to have the largest market share and be the most creative. Then you can do as you like with the market.

Transition

In 1979, Robert Hocq was run over and killed by a car while crossing the Place Vendôme. His daughter Nathalie became head of the group until 1981, when she moved to the United States. At that time, the Must collection represented a turnover of 250 million francs. The same year, Must and Cartier Joaillier merged, regrouping under the name Cartier International. Alain Dominique Perrin became President of the Board of Directors.

In 1983, Cartier was acquired by the Richemont group, a 3.3 billion Swiss francs tobacco and luxury goods conglomerate of South African origin.

PRESENT: THE FORCES OF CREATIVITY

On becoming President of the company following the Richemont takeover in 1983, Alain Perrin announced to *Business Week*, 'By 1990, we'll show a turnover of 300 million dollars'. The actual turnover in 1990 reached US$950 million, representing an average annual growth rate of 27% per year over ten years (Exhibit 1). Consolidated sales, including other brands acquired or under licence, amounted to US$1.350 billion. A 1990 McKinsey study evaluated the world luxury market at US$50 billion in retail sales, thus giving the Cartier brand 4% of sales – the largest for any single brand – in a highly fragmented market.

In jewellery, representing 25% of its turnover, Cartier is one of the world leaders after the US firm Winston. It is number one in the sale of luxury watches (40% of the market and 550,000 annual sales), and deluxe leather goods (10% of turnover) with 1.6 million articles sold in 1989 (Exhibit 2).

According to Alain Perrin, creativity is the engine that has powered Cartier to this spectacular success. For him, it is the soul, the very essence of the group. Under Perrin, the lifeblood of the company is derived from the friction between a series of dualities. Thus, creation at Cartier is yesterday's memory, juxtaposed with today's insights into the environment. Perrin loves to cultivate such disequilibrium because 'It forces us to move forwards'.

> One of the best sources of profit is creativity. Creativity is what? It is doing something your competitors do not do. Or doing it first. Or doing it stronger or better. Everything that is creative contains a plus on something . . . and creativity is the backbone of Cartier.

Product Development

The design for every new Cartier product is discussed and prepared according to a very precise process involving all the 200 people working at Cartier International. The launch of a product takes 2–3 years. A 'product plan' three years ahead of the launch describes the evolution of the line: one major launch per year and spin-offs from each major project.

Nothing is launched until Perrin is convinced Cartier can 'do it right': 'I'd rather lose one year than introduce a half-baked concept.'

Once the designs have been selected, the Drafting Department elaborates models and prototypes 'while stressing quality and keeping in constant contact with the creator'. In order to reproduce the audacity of the designs, technical creativity is added to artistic imagination:

> The oval pen was a real brain teaser, one which the best specialists in the business refused to touch when we consulted them. It took us two years to bring out the product, since we had to design and produce our own cartridge. We patent designs every year.

Such creativity rests on this paradox: 'Each product is an exceptional creation, but we invent nothing.'

The Old

Cartier's past is where the search for present creativity begins. Each new product launched has its ancestor among the collections of chalk and pastel drawings made by Louis Cartier and represents: 'the spirit of creation and the style of Cartier, adapted to our time and to the trends we are setting for the future'.

At the turn of the century, a piece of Cartier jewellery destined for the mistress of a client was accidentallly delivered to his wife. To avoid a repetition of this error, Cartier began to keep exhaustive records on clients, the models they chose and the gems used. These records became Cartier's archives:

> The first lesson a product manager has to learn is how to navigate his or her way through our archives. In this treasure trove, we search for ideas which will fall onto fertile ground, germinate, ripen and one day, when the time is right, be launched onto a market which is not quite ready for it.

While looking at an archive photograph of the governor of Marrakesh and at the massive watch that Louis Cartier had made for him, Alain Perrin predicted that 'One day we'll have to launch a watch like that.' Today, 'the Pasha watch is one of our star products, and has brought large watches back into fashion'. Perrin had already delved into the archive's rich seam of ideas for the Must line. When he became president, its use became systematic. Consequently, the company began to develop lines whose names – Santos, Panthère, Pasha, Cougar – owed nothing to the American culture of the 1960s and 1970s that dominated elsewhere.

... And The New

Cartier's business is to be a trend-setter not a follower; 'to influence people in their behaviour, in their choice, in their taste . . . . Other companies follow customers; but customers follow Cartier'. To do this, 'We spend a lot of time and money on surveying the market and the competition ... on getting the information that will lead us to understand and make decent forecasts on trends.'

Perrin has files on each of his major competitors going back twenty years. 'I know more about them than they do about themselves'. He even has 'people making window checks on competitors' products all over the world, all the year round'.

> Starting from concrete information on competition, on distribution, on consumption, on people's choices, on political trends, on fashion, all these ingredients at the end give us the quality of information that we need to be able to create a product which we know will be fashionable, and have an influence on the culture of the year 2000.

Image

For Perrin, brand image is the basis of an effective marketing strategy. 'Luxury, for the client and the manufacturer alike, means communicating around a brand in the same way that jewellery communicates around a gem.' But promotion should be based on the name and image of the company rather than the product.

> Our brand name was built very slowly, and it's set in concrete. We survive economic, political and regional conflicts without disturbance. Crises seem to stimulate the market for high value added products. In recent years we have even witnessed a growing demand for relatively old Cartier jewels. This is unhoped-for support for our image.

Perrin is proud of Cartier's pioneering marketing methods. 'We were the first to use heavy marketing, the first to communicate in the way we do, the first to use heavy public relations to create events around culture, promote artists, and probably the first to succeed in controlling our distribution as we did.' He enjoys manipulating the opposite marketing poles of secrecy and publicity.

Secrecy ...

Through secrecy about past events affecting the company, Cartier is able to protect its legend.

> One of our strengths is our ability to maintain a certain mystery about the economic entity which is the company. We bring magic and dreams to consumers who don't want to see their favourite brands discussed in the media, and lacking any sense of the romantic.

According to Perrin, breaching this secrecy could bring the luxury industry crashing down. Thus, he regards going public as a sure way to perdition. 'Waging public battles on the floor of the stock exchange is a serious error for the luxury goods sector. It kills the magic. My craft is to make money with magic.' Luxury businesses who go public 'risk losing their soul. A luxury business has nothing to gain from seeing its name indiscriminately positioned in alphabetical order in the daily quotations listing.'

... And Publicity

But then again, 'Cartier is a name which lives in the news.' The luxury goods sector is an important consumer of publicity. Cartier's public relations department has a team of 20 people, and each new product launch is accompanied by astounding creative pageantry, courtesy of a company called Delirium.

Undoubtedly, Perrin himself is Cartier's best communication tool. A high-profile figure, he is photographed everywhere; beside Elton John on his French tour, at the launch of the 'restos du coeur' (soup kitchens set up by the French comedian, the late Coluche), on the slopes of a fashionable ski resort, at a Red Cross benefit or attending a conference at HEC (a leading French business school). Another powerful weapon is Cartier's universal implantation:

'I remember', notes a competitor, 'finding myself in a tiny airport deep in the heart of Venezuela. The very first thing I saw as I got off the plane and entered the makeshift building was a Cartier watch.'

Cartier files all the magazine photos or articles which mention its name, or that of one of its products. Its picture gallery includes the tennis player Jimmy Connors, Dynasty star Linda Evans, French film star Jean-Paul Belmondo, Pakistan's Prime Minister Benazir Bhutto, and also 'rogues' such as Libya's President Ghadafi, the ex-gangster Mesrine, giving his companion a Cartier necklace just hours before being shot down by the police. The sale of the Duchess of Windsor's jewels 'among which ours were prominent' also served Cartier well. Another famous picture shows Perrin perched on the top of a steamroller, the day in 1981 when he destroyed 4,000 counterfeit Cartier watches. The defence of the Cartier name against counterfeiters costs the company nearly US$3.5 million a year.

Cartier has created its own highly effective communication and marketing weapon: the use of sponsorship and culture:

By marrying Cartier with contemporary art we seduced the anti-luxury and anti-uniform population. We also seduced the media which, since 1981, had been cool towards the luxury goods industry. By positioning the firm in the future rather than in the past, we at last managed to reach a younger clientèle.

Most famous is the 'Cartier Foundation for Contemporary Art', a cultural centre established just outside Paris in response to a 1983 market survey which found that young people were interested in contemporary art, and that 70 per cent of those attending exhibitions were less than 25 years old. A meeting place, as well as an exhibition and seminar centre, the Foundation hosts young artists from across the world and offers them financial support. Exhibitions have included a retrospective dedicated to the 'Solex', the little moped symbolizing a whole generation of young Frenchmen and women, and another on the cars of Enzo Ferrari.

Sponsorship is an impressive form of communication. It unites Cartier's employees around an adventure which attracts both the media and the public across the world. Patronage costs Cartier 30 to 40 million francs a year. But it earns us media coverage worth 200 to 250 million francs.

Marketing

Perhaps Perrin's trickiest balancing act has been to maintain Cartier's image as an elite purveyor of expensive luxuries, while thriving in the mass markets of watches, wallets and pens.

Exclusivity ...

At the fusion of Cartier Joaillers and Les Must in 1981, demarcation lines were established to keep the Must line clearly separate. In the company's London office in Bond Street, 'Must people worked upstairs, Cartier people downstairs.' To compensate for the Must 'wide distribution' image and to keep the Cartier name close to its roots, the 'high jewellery' business was relaunched. By developing a line of 'signed' jewels with extremely limited editions, Cartier strengthened its presence in the US$50,000–$100,000 market segment (the top of the jewellery market goes above US$100,000).

One of Cartier's principles is never to test any of its products commercially. 'Our products, whether we are talking about a piece of fine jewellery or a Must pen, must be exclusive. There has to be a "certain something" that makes them stand out, something that goes against the norms. We do "anti-marketing."

... and Volume Sales

With the Must line I was perfectly conscious that by producing thousands of watches or pens instead of one-of-a-kind objects, I was running the risk of affecting the image of our company. If it is true that men and women wish to call attention to themselves by having a Cartier lighter or pen or sunglasses, it is also true that they wish to be recognised as part of an exclusive milieu and not as just anyone.

Quality must never be sacrificed. 'The same care must be exercised over each of the 300 operations necessary to the making of a lighter as in the 1400 hours it took to make the Odin necklace (US$600,000). Industrial quality has to stand comparison with the traditional, painstaking care of the individual craftsman. Cartier's workshop has 67 craftsmen, setters, polishers and jewellers, three times more than most leading jewellers.'

Cartier's success in watchmaking illustrates the manipulation of these contradictions. Cartier's adversary was Rolex, whose massive sporty wrist-watches in steel and gold had set the trend. Alain Perrin felt that a watch of equal quality, but with more creative lines and more style could become an effective rival to the Swiss brand. Through his efforts, a large clientèle was now familiar with luxury products. Their appetites whetted, they were demanding more .... However, he also believed that the Must line would not be strong enough to compete against Rolex. The Must concept, used and re-used since 1972, risked becoming stale through repetition.

Perrin decided that henceforth, Cartier would develop its exclusive collections under a generic name taken from Cartier's history. 'I was going to put products inspired by the exclusive designs of Louis Cartier within the reach of thousands of people.'

On 20 October, 1978 twenty Mystère jets brought Cartier's guests to Paris's Le Bourget airport from the four corners of the world. Among them were Jacky Ickx, Ursula Andress and Santos Dumont's grandson. They were to be present at the launch of the 'Santos Dumont', a wristwatch with a shape inspired by the famous aviator's watch. The first watch to have screws on its body, it was 'immediately copied by the competition'. In 1981, it was followed by another success, the first moonphase Pasha watch.

In 1990, Cartier overtook Rolex as the world leader in luxury timepieces.

Distribution

> We had to get Cartier out of the temple . . . . We had to shake Cartier out of its retailer's lethargy in order to make it a profitable luxury goods company, distributing internationally.

'Leaving the Temple'

Cartier's journey into the light had begun when Perrin set off round the tobacconists with his suitcase full of lighters. The move signalled Cartier's move away from the discreet salons of the jewellers and its entry into the wider world of the gift shop.

By December 1989, 33 per cent of Cartier's revenues (15 per cent of volume) came from its network of 135 stores. The rest came from concessions. Cartier used its profits gradually to purchase all the distributors controlling its 7,500 name-brand points of sale. This takeover was complete by 1990.

In Japan, Cartier entered the market early in 1971 by renting the usual corner spaces in hotels and department stores. By 1989, Cartier had bought an entire building, cancelled the contract with its importer and in its place established a joint venture (Cartier controlling 51 per cent of the shares) to manage the 16 Japanese points of sale:

> It's the only way to consolidate our margins and control our brand name. The retail margin accumulated with the gross margin is what makes us profitable. But more importantly, it's the assurance that the name will be represented as it ought to be, whether it's in Melbourne, Madrid or Paris.

Logistics

In the mind 1980s, Cartier was confronted by an almost total blockage of its logistics system. 'We were no longer able to guarantee supplies, but at the same time we were troubled by an inrease in intermediary inventory. Our network took some hard knocks.' Cartier responded by reinforcing the coordination between sales and production and introducing a sophisticated computer system. This system was designed around 13 months sales projections and was piloted from Freiburg in Switzerland by Cartier's General Agent (Switzerland is a duty-free zone where products can be circulated quickly with the minimum of customs formalities.) Freiburg, Cartier's central supplier, manages all plant deliveries and covers subcontractors supplying all 22 sales affiliates. It then centralizes the statistics needed to update sales and manufacturing plans.

Freiburg also controls the customer service file. 'We have to be able to repair all our models, including those we no longer produce. After-sales service is assured indefinitely. It's a valuable contact with clients and it makes them return to our stores.' Product maintenance costs Cartier 7 million dollars each year, and represents 240,000 repairs.

Strategy

Focus ...

Cartier is one of the very rare luxury houses that will not allow any licensing of its name (with the exception of the development of a brand of cigarettes, a decision imposed by the holding company which also owns Rothmans). Perrin will never develop a new line simply because there is a market for it. Except for scarves, he has not ventured into the fashion businesses. 'There is no Cartier make-up, clothes, shoes or ties, and as long as I am here there never will be.'

> Cartier could do what the other luxury houses do: a little bit of everything. We haven't wanted that, since every name has strict limits. Our business is gems, jewellery, watch making, lighters, pens.

... And Diversification

On the other hand, 'We have developed all of our traditional products. Now, Cartier is condemned to external growth.' Acquisitions will prevent the Cartier name becoming over-exposed and besides, 'If there is something that can add to the group, it is better to buy it than to leave it to you competitors'.

Every acquisition is designed 'to consolidate our leadership in the luxury leadership'. Thus, in 1988, Cartier bought the two Swiss watch-makers, Baume & Mercier (70,000 watches per year in a market segment close to that of the Must line) and Piaget (17,000 watches in an exclusive market 'more than Rolls Royce, maybe Lagonda'). They were, says Perrin, 'sleeping beauties'. He has separated the two 'for their own good. I don't want them to talk to each other any more'. Cartier also acquired the distinguished jewellers Aldebert (80 million FF in annual sales), which has seven stores in Paris, Cannes and Monte Carlo.

Since 1989, Cartier has held a 6 per cent share in Yves Saint Laurent, the high fashion firm for which it had produced a line of jewellery. A contract with Ferrari allows Cartier to go beyond the defined limits of luxury goods, as it did years ago with cigarette lighters (Exhibit 3).

> We wanted to introduce our expertise, our distribution, our know-how into the male and female accessory businesses. The deals also set a kind of barrier at the bottom of the pyramid .... With Ferrari and Yves St Laurent we have got the market share we could not have got with the Cartier name.

> We will go no further in diversification, which has remained relatively restrained.

Management

> If you decentralize creativity too much, it is no longer creativity, it's a mess ... the information must come from the satellites, from the subsidiary or from the markets, but the final decision must come from one man.

Absolutism ...

Under Perrin, absolutism lives on in France. 'In a company with a strong name, a strong personality, the president must be in charge.'

Perrin is the ultimate arbiter of what is produced by the firm. It is he who decides which products will be launched, he who examines, refuses or approves each of the 1,200 designs submitted to him by the marketing department, he who pulls apart each product before its launch. 'I am', he says, 'that kind of man. I want to participate in the daily life of this company and I do it .... I participate very much in the creativity, in the production, in the quality. I am an active executive.' But all these choices are, he maintains, 'the choices of any good manager ... anybody could be Alain Perrin at the head of Cartier':

> At Cartier, we are a management team. I can disappear tomorrow morning.... My management people are very able to go on .... The team is built around Cartier, not around me .... It took twenty years, but there is no recipe .... It is by finding the people to match .... It is the quality of these people which guarantees our growth.

Observers note a sense of shared excitement among a workforce embarked on 'the adventure at Cartier'. 'Everyone sees him, and he enters anyone's office at any time. Ask anyone here and you'll get the impression that they know him personally. They'll tell you, "his greatest assets are his attentiveness to others and his great generosity".'

Such a direct relationship can cause difficulties. It is an area where Perrin's balancing act has occasionally failed. When Perrin took over the management of Cartier, he was assisted by an executive committee composed of the 15 managers responsible for different areas of the company. However, Cartier's expansion rendered this system increasingly difficult, whereupon Perrin appointed a general manager. Unsurprisingly, Perrin's direct, impulsive and omnipresent management style had trouble accommodating this new structure and so he modified it, transforming the General Manager into a Vice President. Three General Managers were then appointed to run the operational functions of Marketing, Finance and Operations (coordinating the sales affiliates from Freiburg).

Perrin also has a group of close advisers, 'people who have been with me for a long while, between about six and twelve years'. They help him with his top management tasks of creation, communication and production and have been selected because 'I found in them all the qualities that I don't think I could find in myself. So let's say I am always looking for complementary colleagues.' He also uses them as 'a task force to check and control what is being completed and achieved on the operational side'.

Any occasional conflicts between the normal line organization and his advisory group, Perrin sees as another source of creative energy. 'A company without conflict is a company without life .... If you take it the positive way, a conflict must end up with something creative. So I believe in conflicts.' His role is to 'be the referee' of this 'calculated chaos', so that it does not result in paralysis.

> If you know how to manage conflict, it ends up being very constructive.

... And Autonomy
At the same time, Perrin insists that 'a company is not only a money machine' but 'a mosaic of men and women ... a place where people live together .... And the relationships that you have to create inside a company are human relationships, they give everyone the opportunity to express themselves.' One of Cartier's great successes has been 'in motivating people .... And you cannot motivate the 4,600 people working for Cartier if you don't give them the absolute conviction that a soul exists ...'

At Cartier, this soul is composed of 'the partners plus the management', and before taking any final decision, the top man 'must take the time and go round the world if necessary, and listen to the partners'.

At Cartier, it is 'natural for many, many people around me in this company to come up with a new concept .... They can always try, they know they can try ....

The art of management is to put the ideas of others together. Creativity is something you manage exactly like an industry.'

Perrin believes that 'everybody has within himself a fantastic power of creation and of interpretation.' The modern executive is 'one who knows how to use what is inside the brain of the people, not only what he knows, not only his techniques, but his power of creation.'

'The secret of Cartier', says Perrin, 'is that we try to extract something from everybody, and give everybody the chance to participate in the creation.' And by this, he means not just the product, but 'the way you decorate a new office, the way you organise a new factory, a new distribution network . . . . I like to have creative meetings, and this is the way we work.'

> You must allow people the freedom to express themselves. I very often say in meetings, and we all do the same, express yourself. If you say something stupid don't worry, we will let you know. But I prefer people to say ten stupid things, because the eleventh one will be the idea.

FUTURE: A NEW TEMPLE

In 1990, Cartier International was installed in its new offices on the rue François 1er in Paris. Housed in one of the city's grandest former private residences, Cartier is within striking distance of the large foreign luxury shops on the avenue Montaigne, and demonstrably a long way from the old-style jewellers of the Place Vendôme. All its stores will eventually be transformed along the same lines as this new corporate headquarters.

A considerable investment programme will see the renovation of the boutiques. There will be room for leisurely browsing, as well as intimate alcoves in which to personalize private sales. Luminous window displays in green, ivory and mushroom tones will be reduced in size and show only a few items. The centrepiece will be a column decorated in gold leaf, against which some of Cartier's most exclusive jewels will be thrown into sharp relief.

The next generation of acolytes in the Cartier temple is also being assured. Recruitment is based on student placements. Every year, 100 students work in the company, vying to fill 20 positions. In 1990, Cartier created a sales school, Sup de Luxe, which will train salespeople from the stores as well as distributors of Cartier products.

Perrin prefers managers who have 'experienced the terrain'. 'The manager who is only a technocrat and who has never gone out into the field, talked to a client or gone to a factory and talked to the workers, worked with them, understood how to transform a piece of steel into a watch . . . understood what the process of production is really like, as well as distribution . . . is somebody who is less complete.'

> When you hire four guys D-day, and after two years look at them, one has been everywhere and knows everybody, and this is the one you are going to promote right away . . . . One day, the fact that he has learnt so much from all kinds of horizons will help him have a broader view and have this famous intuition, the power to make a decision . . . . The others are already stuck in one direction, doing what they do best.

Global Strategy

The expansion of Cartier outside France began in the 1970s, with the export of the Must concept. By 1991, Cartier was present in 123 countries with 145 boutiques and a network of 10,000 concessions. Cartier spread early to Hong Kong (1969) and Japan (1971). At the time, few believed there could be a market for Cartier's products in the Far East.

To fight off the competition in Hong Kong, Cartier played its cultural card and launched the 'Cartier Master Series' in 1988. The first year was 'an unbelievable success'. By 1990, Hong Kong had five boutiques and 114 retailers and was one of Cartier's three regular international launching pads, along with Paris and New York.

And yet, Perrin is clear that Cartier will never stray too far from its heartland. 'We must be strong at home. America represents 20%, of which the greater part is the United States, and Asia 25%.' Since 1983, Cartier has gradually pulled back from the Middle East market (only 3% in 1990, which left the company less exposed to the effects of the Gulf War) (Exhibit 4).

> Our European penetration is a voluntary strategy. Europe is the origin of luxury. It is a product of our culture. I believe that the market most loyal to the artistic professions is the one that has conceived them. I will always ensure that Europe never represents less than 50%. Most of the major names have chosen the opposite strategy and Asia claims between 60% and 80% of their revenues. But who can guarantee that there won't be a reversal in the Asian market?

In the early 1990s, Cartier looks to expand into Eastern Europe. Openings are planned in Budapest, Warsaw, Prague and Moscow. The Cartier name is already known in Hungary. At the turn of the century, Louis Cartier directed the company from a palace in Budapest, where he lived for six months of the year while pursuing an affair with the beautiful Hungarian woman who became his second wife.

Meanwhile, Cartier is strengthening its position in the American market. A consumer research firm was commissioned for a study to identify areas with the most highly paid populations. Shops will be opening in San Diego, San Jose, Phoenix . . . 'We're going to places where money flows like ice in the sun . . .'

Integrated Manufacturing

Perrin sees the integration of its industrial facilities as Cartier's next major strategic challenge. The process will be led from Saint Imier in Switzerland, the headquarters of Cartier's industrial arm, CTL (Luxury Technology Company).

With the exception of a few smaller outfits and its jewellery workshop, Cartier has hitherto lacked the means to manufacture its other products. Some of them, such as glasses frames (introduced in 1983 and manufactured by Essilor) and perfumes, are subcontracted to major industrial companies. For the rest, Cartier depends on networks of small local craftsmen who have traditionally supplied the fashion and luxury goods industry. Paris is rich in such craftsmen, who are closely tied to the greatest names in jewels. Cartier's leather goods are produced in France, Italy and Spain. Nothing comes from the Far East.

In 1988, Cartier completely integrated its cigarette lighter and pen production by opening a plant in Freiburg (100 employees) and another in Franconville (200 employees).

Next, 'We decided that the artisan watch manufacturing in Switzerland should be integrated, as this activity accounts for more than 40% of sales.' Relations with the watch-makers, to whom Cartier subcontracted 80 per cent of its watch-making business, had been strained. 'Respect for deadlines among some of our subcontractors had deteriorated drastically. The big companies are fighting to dominate a network of manufacturers who are themselves struggling to keep up with the expansion of the business.'

In 1989, Cartier invested in a 50 per cent shareholding in Cristallor, the watch-case manufacturing affiliate of Ebel (a very exclusive Swiss manufacturer and a long-time Cartier subcontractor). With Piaget and Baume & Mercier, Cartier also acquired two manufacturing companies, Prodor and Complications. Further additions have resulted in an industrial armoury which Perrin hopes will make Cartier invincible first in watches, and then in jewellery. Since October 1991, the majority of watches made by the company have been assembled at the plant in Saint Imier. As a result, Cartier has reversed the proportion of watches it subcontracts.

In the future, Cartier will be able to manufacture 75 per cent of its production, the remaining 25 per cent will give the company flexibility.

> This push towards integration allows us to consolidate our margins and our quality, and affirms our leadership.

By a twist of fate, Piaget and Rolex face each other on opposite sides of the street in Geneva. Alain Perrin likes to feel the vibrations from his closest rival so nearby. 'In 1991', he predicted, 'the battle will really start.'

The future of the luxury industry, considers Perrin, will be 'in the hands of two or three or four groups, no more'. The names that will dominate? 'Cartier, of course, as number one. Chanel. Vuitton. Dior. Yves St Laurent. Dunhill. Hermès...'

Cartier is planning a three-pronged strategy: to reinforce its presence where it is already strong; to expand in Eastern Europe and, in anticipation of 1993 and the end of duty-free shopping, to open shops in every European airport. These will become 'centres of luxury products, at the expense of alcohol, tobacco and perfume'. But even as he describes the changes to prepare for the future, Perrin is equally emphatic about the inherent continuity and timelessness of the company.

> There is no significant change in the spirit of Cartier between 1847 and 1990, and there will be none by 2000 or 3000.... Cartier has been the companion of all the success stories of the world for 150 years. As long as the world is the world, that success story will never cease.

EXHIBIT 1
Cartier: rate of growth, 1985–90

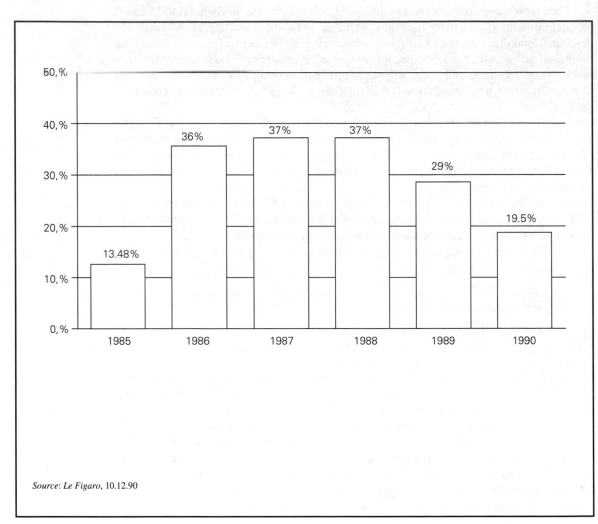

Source: *Le Figaro*, 10.12.90

EXHIBIT 2
Cartier sales by product.

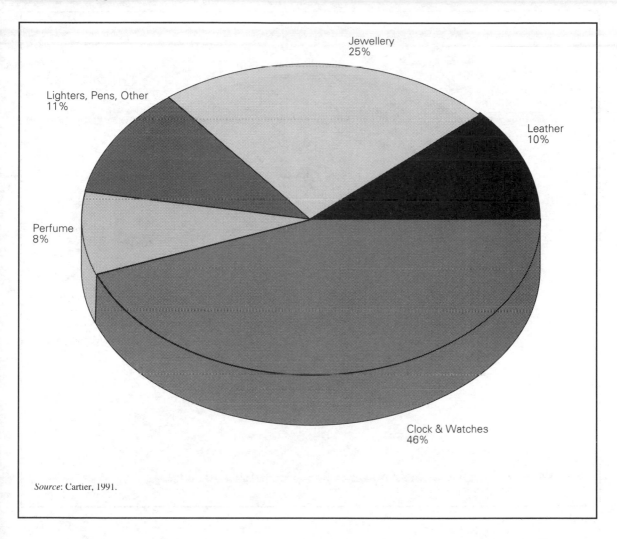

Jewellery
25%

Lighters, Pens, Other
11%

Leather
10%

Perfume
8%

Clock & Watches
46%

Source: Cartier, 1991.

EXHIBIT 3
Cartier: sales by brands

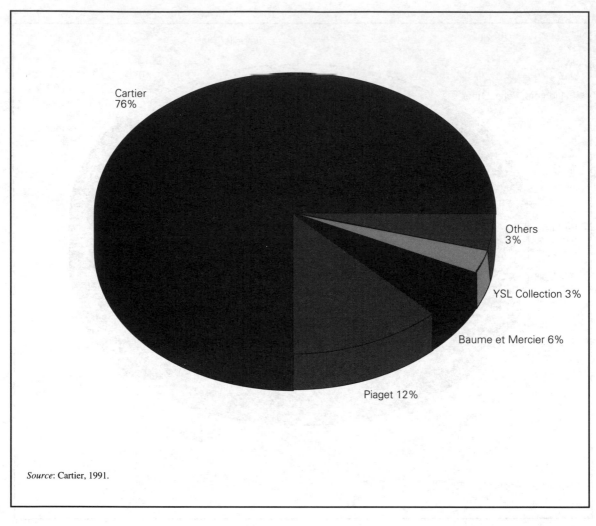

Cartier
76%

Others
3%

YSL Collection 3%

Baume et Mercier 6%

Piaget 12%

Source: Cartier, 1991.

EXHIBIT 4
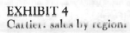

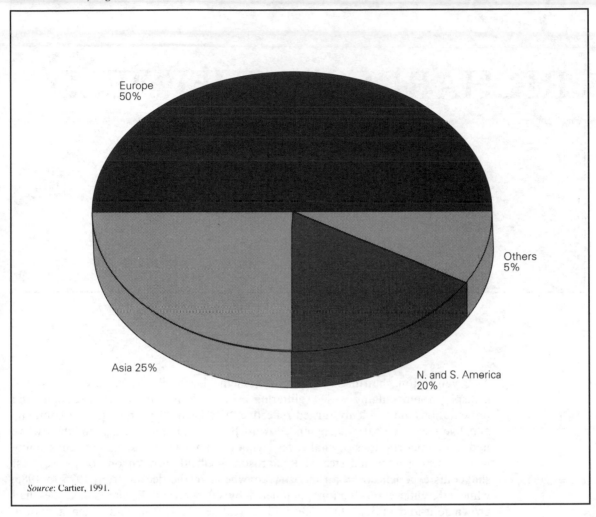

Europe
50%

Others
5%

Asia 25%

N. and S. America
20%

Source: Cartier, 1991.

CASE

3–2

RICHARDSON SHEFFIELD

As Bryan Upton, chairman of Richardson Sheffield, proudly showed a visitor around a display room bulging with a glittering array of knives in countless designs and presentations, he suddenly turned reflective, 'I've been 30 years with this company and I've seen my share of ups and downs. But I can't think of a time when we've had more opportunities or challenges facing us'. This was quite a statement coming from a person who had steered Richardson Sheffield through one of the severest shakeouts experienced by an industry anywhere. In the decade from 1975 to 1985, while UK cutlery production plummeted by 60 per cent, Richardson's sales had grown four-fold and profits eight-fold in real terms. Upton had taken a mature industrial operation in a nineteenth-century industry and turned it into a growth company.

Yet his mixture of optimism and concern was understandable. In 1989, Richardson was poised on the threshold of a major international expansion which could continue the growth trajectory through the 1990s. But would the ongoing transformation in the organization and the nature of the business facilitate or impede that future growth?

This case was prepared by Professor Christopher A. Bartlett and Research Associate Ashish Nanda as the basis for class discussion rather than to illustrate either effective or ineffective handling of an administrative situation. It draws on *The Richardson Sheffield Story*, by R.M. Grant and C. Baden Fuller (London Business School Case Series No. 2, 1987). Copyright © 1992, by the President and Fellows of Harvard College. All rights reserved.

INDUSTRY AND COMPANY BACKGROUND

Although the industry environment and business situations that Upton encountered over his 33 years with Richardson had been extraordinarily challenging, he had somehow negotiated himself and his company through the turbulence remarkably successfully.

The UK Cutlery Industry

The cutlery industry in Sheffield which pre-dated the Industrial Revolution, grew with the worldwide reputation of its quality silverware until it employed 30,000 people in the 1950s. Soon thereafter, however, increasingly informal lifestyles shrank the demand for silverware. In addition, mass production of stainless steel cutlery helped manufacturers in the Far East build an increasingly dominant position in the world market. Even within the UK market, by the mid-1980s imports had captured over 50 per cent of the market by value, and a much larger share in units. As a result, by 1989 industry employment had plunged to 2,500 in Sheffield (see Exhibit 1). Within this devastated industry, only a few segments, such as silverplated tableware and kitchen knives, had survived by focusing on quality.

  The kitchen knife segment was highly fragmented, with two dominant suppliers – Richardson Sheffield and Kitchen Devils. Kitchen Devils had become the largest manufacturer of kitchen knives in Britain during the 1970s. It was acquired by Wilkinson Sword in 1984; Wilkinson Sword was in turn acquired by British Match, which was then bought out by Swedish Match. Later, Fiskar of Finland bought the knives and scissors division from Swedish Match. Kitchen Devils had lost its momentum as a consequence of all these moves and, by the mid-1980s, its business had stagnated.

Richardson's Rebirth: The Scalpel and the Hammer

Founded in 1839, Richardson Sheffield remained a family company until 1956, when Jerome Hahn, an American, acquired a 51 per cent share. Hahn wanted a captive blade supplier to supply his US-based cutlery company, Regent Sheffield.

  When Hahn visited Richardson Sheffield in 1959, he asked a young employee named Bryan Upton if he had any suggestions on improving productivity. Upon had left school in 1945 at the age of 13. After 14 years as a die sinker in the cutlery industry, he joined Richardson as a 'progress chaser', a job requiring him to coordinate with nine chargehands to match production with order requirements. As Upton later recalled, 'I told Jerry Hahn that the chargehands were not productive, and were obstructing smooth factory operations. Senior executives told him I was crazy, but he still made me works manager and told me to try out my ideas.' Upton immediately replaced the chargehands with three others. 'They worked better than the nine ever had,' he recalled, 'and they went on to have lifetime careers with our company.'

  By 1960, Hahn owned 100 per cent of the company. Committed to building it, he drew no salary and took no dividends, reinvesting all profits in the business. However, problems at Richardson persisted, and in 1966, Hahn appointed Upton as managing director. He immediately stopped uncontrolled spending and instead concentrated on increasing productivity. To keep management lean, Upton recruited an active board of three nonexecutive directors in finance, sales and external relations. Their expertise supplemented his manufacturing experience.

Gordon Bridge, the finance director, felt that Hahn and Upton ideally complemented each other:

> Jerry was a brilliant systems man. He introduced labour and steel utilization control systems, and imposed the discipline of part numbers and standard costs for every item in the plant. The systems let him review an entire business, spot the mistakes, identify solutions and come up with great ideas. Eighty per cent of his ideas were unworkable, but 20 per cent were phenomenal! But Jerry couldn't run the business. Bryan, on the other hand, went deep into the operating details of the business. While Jerry was like a scalpel with his keen mind and sarcasm, Bryan was like a hammer with his dogged determination and direct forcefulness. Hahn was the ideas man and Upton was the action man – a great team!

THE DEVELOPING BUSINESS CAPABILITIES

Richardson's evolution from a commodity blade supplier to a manufacturer and marketer of a distinctive line of kitchen knives was driven by Upton's belief in continuous upgrading in production and engineering, aggressive product development and focusing on the customers.

Productivity-driven Engineering

When Upton took over in 1966, operators sitting astride their grindstones pulled blades across the wheels. Motivated by piecework pay, they would produce about 700 blades a day. To bring about change, Upton got rid of piecework ('a constant source of tension and dispute that reduced our flexibility and willingness to change') and closed down the knife assembly operations ('We had to concentrate on making blades right before we could pay attention to handles and assembly'). Upton then focused on improving the blade production process, reinvesting most of the earnings in modifying and upgrading equipment. 'I didn't want to risk having a machine supplier take ideas he developed with us and sell them to our competitors, so we developed our own equipment,' he said.

Existing operations were semi-automated, largely through the use of electro-mechanical systems. Central to this effort was Bob Russell, a young engineer whom Upton tapped to head up the development process. Russell recalled:

> Our blade-grinding machines cut the operation from a 35-second manual job to a five-second automatic cycle. Better still, one operator could supervise five or six machines. These were pretty simple, straightforward machines, but by the time we'd built 100, making marginal improvements on each one we built, we had the design very refined. That's how most improvements have happened here – gradually and continuously.

When this technology appeared to be reaching its limit, Upton recruited David Williams, a young engineer who had been experimenting with the possibility of applying electronics and computer-based systems to cutlery manufacturing. When Williams joined as manufacturing systems manager in 1985, Upton focused Russell's responsibilities more on machine installation and the civil engineering tasks of plant expansion. Gordon Bridge commented:

> We were a mechanical and pneumatic manufacturer, but Bryan foresaw the increasing need for electronics and robotics. So far, David and his small team have developed and installed electronic sensors that tell the operator when to change grinding wheels, computer controls that monitor the output and quality by machine, and automated grinding and polishing techniques that reduce labour input in these key operations.

By 1989, the company had 50 computer-controlled, edge-grinding machines monitored by eight operators, with each machine producing 6,000 blades a day. Williams was proud of the progress he and his team had been able to achieve. 'There are probably only 30 other production monitoring systems like this in the country,' he said scanning a monitor screen that showed what each machine on the shopfloor was doing at that moment. 'Most of the others are in high-tech or high-capital process industries. We have the only one in the cutlery industry.' Williams and his team had won a British Machinery award in 1988 for an electronically controlled scalloping machine that improved the grinding unit's productivity by 100 per cent.

Bryan Upton reflected on the central importance of this process development effort: 'What distinguishes us from the rest of the industry is that we are engineers, not cutlers. As a result, we have been able to continuously improve our operating efficiencies – sometimes very dramatically' (see Exhibit 2).

Innovation-driven Product Development

In 1979, Jerry Hahn presented a challenge to Bryan Upton which triggered a major change in Richardson's strategy. Hahn knew that Sears was looking for a supplier that could produce a unique kitchen knife – one that never needed sharpening. On his next visit to England, he asked Upton if he could develop and manufacture such a product. 'If you can,' he said, 'I have a great name for it – the Laser knife.'

Working with a variety of blade angles, edges and tiny serrations, Upton and his development team finally came up with a product they felt was truly a breakthrough. In typical fashion, they developed a new model of grinding machine to produce the special blade. To show their confidence, they backed the product with a 25-year guarantee; the reaction of British store buyers, however, was one of complete lack of interest. They already had strong brands, they told Richardson. Upton was fighting mad and took his crusade to the national press:

> I told them that here was a major technical innovation – the sharpest knife in the world – developed and manufactured in Britain, and the stores were turning us away. That did the trick. Without spending a penny on advertising, we got massive coverage and the stores were forced to stock Laser. The knife sold extremely well from the start, and by 1989, Richardson has secured 45 per cent of the domestic knives market.

It did not take foreign competitors long to see the product's success and copy it. Richardson responded by improving the Laser's design and performance. In 1982, it introduced Laser 5 and, four years later, Laser 7. The company was planning to introduce Laster 10 in 1990.

With the success of Laser, the company accelerated its shift from blade producer to knife manufacturer. In the early 1980s, Richardson was buying 25 per cent of the plastic knife handles produced by Elford Plastics, a nearby manufacturer, and Upton and Bridge decided they should buy the company. A quick review convinced Jerry Hahn of the merits of the idea and, in April 1984, the deal was consummated. This spurred another round of innovation focused on the handle. 'We realized that there was a fashion element to our business also,' said Upton, 'so we began experimenting with different handle colours and shapes. They were a great success.'

To cope with the surge in its knife business, the company had purchased a 140,000 square foot factory site in 1986 which it used exclusively for knife assembly. About half of the blades it was making were now being turned into knives. That same year, Richardson overtook Kitchen Devils as the UK market leader and became the largest supplier of kitchen knives in Western Europe. The success of the Laser knife encouraged the company to think about extending the product line, and by 1989 designs had been finalized for a line of Laser scissors.

Customer-driven Marketing

The development of the Laser knife thrust Richardson into the mainstream of consumer marketing in the 1980s. But, even when the company was basically a blade producer supplying other knife manufacturers, it had developed a strong market consciousness. The concern for customer responsiveness was ingrained into every member of the company, in what were known as 'Upton's four golden rules'. Upton explained:

> A letter received today must be answered today, a sample requested today must be ready today, telexes and faxes must be responded to in minutes, and if the customer needs delivery tomorrow, he'll get it tomorrow. This quick response is appreciated by our customers and often means the difference in getting an order.
>
> For example, seven days before our Christmas shutdown, Shell asked us to supply 80,000 knives to Ireland on four day's notice. We were just coming out of the rush period, and some thought we could never make it. But we accepted the order and delivered. No competitor can match that performance. As a result, we got a repeat order.

However, it had taken many years to convert Richardson from a blade supplier to a customer-sensitive knife marketer. Not surprisingly, the effort started at the shopfloor level, as Production Manager Denise Ogden explained:

> Since my earliest days, Mr Upton constantly stressed that our edge is our customer orientation, and for those of us in the factory that means quick reaction and attention to quality. Everybody understands and there is a strong belief here that we have to keep improving if we are to remain the leaders.

As part of his ongoing effort to expand the company's knife business, in 1975 Upton hired Kathy Sanchez as customer liaison and asked her to start exploring the international market. Sanchez recalled:

> I began doing some simple, basic things, like corresponding in German with German agents. After a visit to the Cologne trade fair in 1976, I became convinced we could do very well internationally and Bryan supported my initiatives. I looked up the business

directory, and wrote personal letters to 300 traders all over the world, enclosing our prices and catalogues. Our export sales rose dramatically, and we won the Queen's award for export achievement in 1986. Today, 60 per cent of our sales are overseas.

But Upton was wary of sophisticated marketing practices. When Laser was introduced, he relied heavily on the product's superior performance and Richardson's basic customer orientation to sell it. He remarked:

> We didn't need a marketing staff or an advertising campaign. We had a great product, and Laser was a terrific brand name. Then we got excellent free publicity to bring it to public attention and get it in the stores, and we had the drive of Kathy Sanchez whom I had promoted to sales director.

THE DISTINCTIVE WORK ENVIRONMENT

'Central to our success', said Bryan Upton, 'are our continual attention to engineering and production, our hands-on management style, and the quality of our people.' The following pages describe a few of Richardson's unique organizational characteristics.

Upton's Management Style

A newspaper article once described Bryan Upton as a man 'who never says no to an order, and never takes no for an answer'. In his straightforward Yorkshire manner he confessed, 'I am not an easy person to get along with. But I am not difficult. I'm just demanding!' He looked at himself as a hands-on manager. 'Even as the chief executive of the company', he said, 'I will unload lorries on the dock, if need be. I'm often the first in, and the last out. I believe in leadership by example.'

Within the company, he was viewed as a mix of coach, controller and company conscience. For example, on one of his frequent shopfloor rounds, he saw knife blades that had been dropped near a machine. He took some 10 pence coins from his pocket, threw them on the floor and, in full hearing of the workers, asked the supervisor, 'Would you leave these coins lying on the floor? Well these blades are worth much more!'

Upton's attention to detail was legendary. 'When Bryan visits the shopfloor,' remarked a production executive, 'he doesn't just pass through – he pokes around, and he sees things you have missed. He knows a lot more about the business than I do and he has answers for every problem. More often than not, he's right, but sometimes it gets frustrating. His style is direct and he'll beat you over the head every day with an awful lot of common sense. You sometimes may not like him, but in the end you respect him.'

Organization Culture and Values

Many of Richardson's organizational norms and management practices had been deeply influenced by the leader's management style – his bias for action, attention to detail, commitment to customer service and dedication to the company had all ben absorbed into the company culture. Said one executive:

> Byran personalizes the culture of our company. In order to survive here, you have got to be very open and have a sunny personality, yet be able to work under pressure and give and take with Bryan and others. Those who are quiet or sensitive are so unhappy that they have to leave. And yet, we have built a great team here. Many in the company would walk through fire for Bryan. He is very enthusiastic and his enjoyment of what he is doing is very infectious. You see Kathy Sanchez, Bob Russell, Tony Seagrave, Denise Ogden, and others who have moulded themselves very much in Bryan's image.

Sanchez had risen rapidly within the company based on her hard work, skills, dedication and toughness – all attributes Upton admired. These skills also brought results, and in 1987 she won an award as Salesperson of the Year from the British Sales and Marketing Association. Sanchez acknowledged:

> I have consciously copied Bryan's style. It works, although for a long time I found it difficult to delegate responsibility. But, as work has increased, I have had to form priorities, I have had to identify key people and put my faith in them.

A sales executive confirmed her view:

> Kathy strives for the best, and she expects 110 per cent from you. Like Bryan Upton, she is a very hardworking person, and the company is a big part of her life – perhaps too big. Both of them are approachable, they teach you, they back you up on crazy schemes, they are always motivating people, bringing people into their projects. But they will also give you a 'rocket' if you have made a mistake.

As a result, Richardson's work environment was most often referred to as 'demanding' and usually involved very high time commitment of its executives. 'I work more than 60 hours a week', said one manager, 'because the expectation is that everything has to be done immediately. Sometimes it is tiring, and I find myself wondering if it is worth it.' Bryan Upton himself warned prospective employees, 'It is not only you, but your spouses and your families may have to sacrifice, too.'

The work pressure was felt in all parts of the company. David Williams, the manufacturing systems manager, felt that Bryan Upton subjected him to time pressures and deadlines inappropriate for a development laboratory. 'I have learned to take the flak from these people and do what I can at my pace,' he said. 'But, it can be hard when long-term development projects are turned on and off depending on the latest crisis.' Another term often used by managers to describe their work environment was 'unstructured'. Said one:

> We have an active, even unsociable culture, and people who revel in unstructured situations, and are self-motivated and pressure-driven, will do well here. When I joined the company, I was depressed that people didn't have time to meet with me. I later realized that they hold off to see if the new person is going to stay. However, once you're on board, this company works like a family. But you are not mollycoddled – you have to be self-directed. It's fun if you like living on your adrenaline.

Human Resources Management

Cutlery was a low-paid seasonal industry, traditionally dominated by relatively low-skilled female employees. Richardson employed between 250 and 450 workers, many on short-term contracts. Average earnings for such workers were about £100 ($155) a week. Richardson had deskilled operations to simplify recruiting and training in an environment of fairly high labour turnover. Absenteeism ran at about 15 per cent.

Upton was philosophically opposed to the idea of a personnel department, believing that matters relating to people should be managed by those who had responsibility for them. Consequently, all personnel functions were handled by line managers who were responsible for the recruitment, development and deployment of people in their respective departments. Management was developed from within where possible, and recruited from outside when inside capabilities were lacking. Upton described how he selected people who would fit into this unique environment:

> I interview all candidates for management positions, and my criteria are straightforward. First, the person should be ready to work 24 hours a day for the company. Second, the person should be very flexible since there are no sharp lines between jobs here. Third, he or she should be able to react quickly. Finally, the person should really believe from within that the business exists to serve the customer. Given all this, I tell prospective employees to join us only if they feel that they need to come here more than we need them to come.
>
> I can tell a lot about a candidate very quickly. If you walk slow and talk slow, you will not get in my office. If you are overweight, chances are you will not be employed. I may give you a page with dots on it and ask you to draw circles around them. If you are not fast, you are out. We don't need capable people as much as we need those who are quick and responsive.

One prominent aspect of Upton's management approach was his deep interest in the development of those working with him. He explained:

> I feel I have a natural ability to spot and develop talent that it right for this company. For example, when Kathy Sanchez joined us in the customer liaison role 13 years ago, I noticed that she was unbelievably bright. I kept giving her increasing responsibilities, and today she is our direct of sales and marketing. Denise Ogden is another good example. She joined this company as a worker when she was 15 years old, and today she is a production manager. These are people we have been able to develop in the company, knowing our business, and the way we manage. It's a huge asset.

Denise Ogden had risen rapidly on the basis of her deep commitment to the company, unswerving sense of purpose, and strict discipline. She looked on Bryan Upton as a teacher and a role model:

> I came here 16 years ago straight from school, and Mr Upton has taught me everything I know. He made me aware that the most important task is to ensure that orders and samples go out on time, so that the customers are served well. If he asked me for a sample, I knew he wanted it not the same day, but within 15 minutes. He taught me how to manage people, I learned to keep watch on my workers, be aware of where they were, and what was happening at any moment.

One manager described a recent incident when a young worker had left footprints on a wall when he climbed up to get supplies from a high shelf. Ogden made him walk through the plant to get a bucket of water and clean off the footprints while all his co-workers watched. 'It was a great lesson in production floor cleanliness,' he observed, 'but it was a lesson in discipline Denise had learned painfully some 15 years earlier. As a young line worker, she had taken rivets from the plant and tossed them at a friend on her way home. Bryan had called in the police to talk to her, and that public humiliation shook her up and sent a lesson to the others.'

Although the company had been very successful in developing talent internally, there were no formal training programmes or career development schemes. It was all done through capable people being given new – often additional – responsibility. Gordon Bridge gave an example:

> Our marketing manager left us recently. We have not replaced him. Instead, we had the marketing assistant report directly to Kathy. He is under tremendous pressure to take over much of the work of his previous boss, but he also has a great opportunity. We have succeeded in the past in management development by the 'pressure cooker' method.

The company also had no hesitation in redeploying those it felt could do better in another position, or firing those who were not contributing. Bryan Upton gave an example of how he tried to fit people and jobs:

> Tony Seagrave was in charge of our production for many years, but with all the changes, the pressure was getting too much for him, so I moved him to special projects. He's now in a niche where he can contribute much more and where he will eventually be much happier because of that.

'I used to come in at 6.00 in the morning and leave at 10.00 in the night,' recalled Seagrave, 'and I'd come in on Sundays to do the production planning. I had my finger in everything. Then, three years ago, Bryan shifted me to special projects.'

Richardson's worker turnover was quite low. Most management turnover occurred within the first few months of employment as people decided whether they liked the Richardson environment, and the company decided whether they could contribute. Bryan Upton commented:

> Turnover in the sales department has been high. Kathy Sanchez is a very demanding person. One UK sales manager who came to us with a good record at Kellogg and Duracell was with us only four weeks. He and Kathy had gone with a salesman to a meeting with an important customer. After the meeting, Kathy let him have it in front of the salesman. She asked why he had forgotten whom he had met at the previous meeting, why he had not brought along a notebook, why he had let her control the meeting, and why he had no price list readily available. When she finished, he told her he was quitting.

Sanchez gave her perspective on the turnover issue:

> One reason for our high turnover may be recruitment of people who are poorly matched to our requirements. Our standards are quite different and our jobs are much less structured than in most companies. It is very difficult to find the kind of committed people we demand, and some people just cannot take our pace physically. What seems a high turnover is really an initial weeding out of misfits.

RECENT CHANGES, NEW CHALLENGES

In the late 1980s, several internal and external developments were converging to challenge some of the basic strategic directions and organizational foundations Bryan Upton had laid over the previous two decades.

International Expansion

The first major change was occurring in Richardson's markets. As European market harmonization approached, management began looking towards continental Europe. 'After 1992, German and French manufacturers will try to enter the UK', said Bryan Upton, 'and the comptitive game will become much tougher.'

In 1988 and 1989, Richardson established small sales branches in Germany, France and Scandinavia. Although these branches were growing steadily, it was a difficult task penetrating further into new markets, slower than the rapid expansion direct exports had brought earlier. Established supplier relationships, local differences in product preferences, and parochial national attitudes all represented important entry barriers. Upton and Bridge acknowledged it would be difficult to continue on their current growth trajectory without taking bold new steps. But there were sceptics who questioned whether this strongly Sheffield-rooted company with its unique culture and style had the management capability to grow into a much larger or much more diverse organization.

The McPherson's Takeover

In 1986, Jerry Hahn sold his US and UK cutlery companies to McPherson's Ltd, an Australia-based company which was diversifying out of its core industrial metals business into consumer products, mainly housewares. After the acquisition, the consumer products division was split into regional offices with McPherson's consumer group taking responsibility for Asia-Pacific, the Regent Sheffield unit covering North America, and Richardson Sheffield handling Europe.

McPherson's had developed the Wiltshire Staysharp line of knives, which came in scabbards with tungsten carbide insets that sharpened the knife edge each time the blade was withdrawn or replaced. Because of its design and its higher price, Staysharp required more sophisticated marketing than the impulse-buy Laser with its 'never-needs-sharpening' concept. In order to launch the Staysharp line in the United Kingdom, Richardson established its first-ever, five-person marketing department and went in for heavy TV advertising. (Exhibit 3 describes Richardson's principal products; Exhibit 4 provides financial information.)

After the McPherson's takeover, Richardson augmented its top management group. In particular, they felt it was important to fill the top production manager's job, to build a stronger marketing organization, and to reinforce the financial control staff. Richardson implemented these changes over the next few yeas. By 1989, a new production director had been hired and integrated into the management, and a McPherson's financial manager had been added to the staff. However, the new marketing manager has lasted only two years, running into a conflict of management styles with Upton and Sanchez. Sanchez was made directly responsible for marketing also in her new position as director of sales and marketing.

When Richardson's non-executive board was dissolved after its acquisition, Upton persuaded Gordon Bridge to become a full-deputy managing director. Then, in 1988 when Upton was appointed chairman, Bridge succeeded him as managing director. (See Exhibit 5.)

With the change in ownership and leadership, many wondered if Richardson Sheffield could, or indeed should, continue to remain the same company. Some newer executives had started pushing to formalize systems and tighten policies. The financial analyst was working to upgrade what he termed 'rather primitive' management information and costing systems. And the production director was asking the sales department for periodic forecasts by product so he could better plan production. On the other hand, some older employees were concerned by what they saw as a dilution of company values. Bob Russell, chief engineer, reflected:

> As we've grown, personal commitment has diffused. We are split into tiny domain, and there are little managers sitting in little offices instead of managing the work. We're not knit together like we were, and as a result, there's not the same loyalty to the company. Just as bad is the red tape and paperwork that is creeping in. I hate the cost systems and analyses that delay us without improving productivity. Yet, despite the fancy systems, the floodgates have been opened on overhead costs.

Yet, Kathy Sanchez was optimistic about the future:

> The key is retaining our team's overriding commitment to the company. It has given us freedom, opportunities, and enthusiasm. There is an energy – a fire – which used to come from Jerry Hahn, which comes from Bryan, and which now is within me and others in the next generation. That's the vital element that will keep pushing us to think of new and better ways to build this company.

LOOKING TO THE FUTURE

There was a widespread feeling that Richardson Sheffield faced a momentous point in its history. One executive suggested:

> We will either burst through this phase or fall back. If we can adapt by becoming truly professional and multinational, our horizons are fantastic. But our management must decouple from the operational details so they can guide us strategically. The alternative is that Richardson remains the size management is comfortable with.

Gordon Bridge described the challenge:

> We can't continue to run an operation of this size and complexity through personal intervention. We have to develop more managers who think and act like Bryan – managers with a hands-on instinct. To do that, I have got to stop Bryan from taking unnecessary responsibility.

Bryan Upton saw the situation simply:

> Like a Liverpool football club, we've learned that it's very hard getting to the top of the first division. But we also understand it's even harder staying there. We're at the top of the league in this knife business, and we are determined to stay there.

EXHIBIT 1
The cutlery industry in the United Kingdom

The cutlery industry can be divided into table cutlery, kitchen knives, and scissors and razors. The scissors and razors market is excluded from these tables.

A UK Manufacturers' Production of Table Cutlery and Kitchen Knives

	1975	1983	1984	1985	1986	1987
Gross Index of Production						
(1980 = 100)	160	73.8	75.0	74.5	66.6	65.5
Production (£ million at manufacturer sale price)						
Table Cutlery		19.9	20.0	21.7	20.5	21.3
Kitchen Knives		6.4	9.7	10.6	12.4	17.8

B Export and Import of Cutlery (£million at manufacturer's sale price)

	1983	1984	1985	1986	1987
Kitchen Knives:					
Export	3.5	4.4	4.7	6.0	5.7
Import	2.4	2.3	2.4	3.6	3.2
Table Cutlery:					
Export	10.0	9.0	8.9	9.2	8.7
Import	14.7	18.8	21.3	19.7	25.8

EXHIBIT 2
Richardson's cost and productivity data.

A Summary of Productivity Data, 1975–88[a]

Year	Revenue	Profit (£000s)	Stocks	Capital	Labour Cost/ Revenue (%)	Employees
1975	752	44	91	280	17.1	103
1976	1,113	42	196	324	15.6	112
1977	1,595	107	327	408	12.6	120
1978	2,422	254	503	662	11.9	134
1979	2,222	199	703	843	12.2	155
1980	2,446	210	703	1,074	12.2	160
1981	2,698	227	783	1,292	11.0	159
1982	3,458	263	823	1,537	11.0	176
1983	5,059	410	1,130	1,955	11.4	221
1984	7,000	554	1,417	2,302	9.5	339
1985	8,683	856	2,147	2,626	8.5	338
1985[b]	4,826	942	2,428	3,531	9.5	367
1987	11,751	2,124	3,303	10,879	8.9	410
1988	17,268	1,693	4,287	11,809	8.9	442

Note: Profit figure is before interest and tax.
[a] Data have been disguised.
[b] Data for six months.

B Costs and Expenses as Percentage of Revenue, 1989 Data[c]

Revenue	100
Less:	
Materials	37
Labour	9
Production Expenses	10
TOTAL DIRECT EXPENSES	56
Gross Profit	44
Selling Expenses	19
Distribution	5
General Administration	11
Net Profit (before interest and tax)	9

[c] Data have been disguised.

EXHIBIT 3
Richardson Sheffield's product range.

Range	Product	Features
Laser Knives		25-year guarantee.
	Laser	Original knives with hardwood handles, brass compression rivets and stainless steel blades. Also available in wooden blocks and gift sets.
	Laser 5	Made of permanently bonded, contoured polypropylene handles. The knife had a dishwasher-resistant ink marking. Also available in polystyrene wall racks, wooden wall racks, steak sets, dishwasher-safe polystyrene blocks and wooden blocks.
	Laser 7	Laser 7 knives had three rivets, instead of the two in Laser knives. Their blades were made of thicker gauge steel and their handles were of pakkawood.
	Laser 2000	Satin finish and PTFE non-stick coating.
Wiltshire Staysharp	Knives-900	Tailor-made sharpening scabbards. Dishwasher-safe polypropylene handles.
	Knives-1200	Tailor-made sharpening scabbards. Rosewood handles with brass reinforcing rivets.
	Scissors	Scissors in sharpening scabbards.
Sabatier Knives	Sabatier 1	High-quality professional knives with steel bolsters and hand-crafted blades.
	Sabatier 2	Professional knives at a lower price, with aluminium bolsters.
Others		10-year guarantee.
	Kitchen King	Range of precision ground knives.
	Prestwood	Hollow ground blades and hardwood handles.
	Cuisine	Satin finish stainless steel blades with hardwood handles and brass compression rivets.
	Supersharp	Dishwasher-safe, stainless steel blades and polypropylene handles with decorative studs.
	Carlton	Unbreakable polypropylene handles.
	Thrifty	Lowest priced, but dishwasher-safe.
	Snac-Pac	Knife, fork and spoon set, complete with salt and pepper shakers.

EXHIBIT 4
Financial performance of Richardson Sheffield.

	6/87	6/88
Profit and Loss Statement (£000s)		
Sales	11,751	17,268
Gross Profit	5,372	6,997
Less: Overheads	3,248	5,304
Net Profit (Loss) before Interest and Tax	2,124	1,693
Balance Sheet (£000s)		
Capital, Reserve and Liabilities:		
Capital and Reserves	469	1,428
Profit after Tax, Current Year	–	430
Creditors	3,071	3,539
Taxation	1,309	953
Loan – Bank	5,000	5,000
– McPherson's	–	1,100
McPherson's Ltd	1,209	(79)
TOTAL	11,058	12,004
Short-term Debt	(179)	(195)
TOTAL	10,879	11,809
Assets:		
Debtors	2,202	2,059
Stock	3,301	4,287
Plant and Machinery – Net	1,691	1,852
Land and Buildings – Net	1,682	1,784
Investments	2	2
Intangibles	185	165
Goodwill	1,816	1,650
TOTAL	10,879	11,809

Note: £1 = $1.55 in June 1989.

EXHIBIT 5
Organization chart of Richardson Sheffield, 1989.

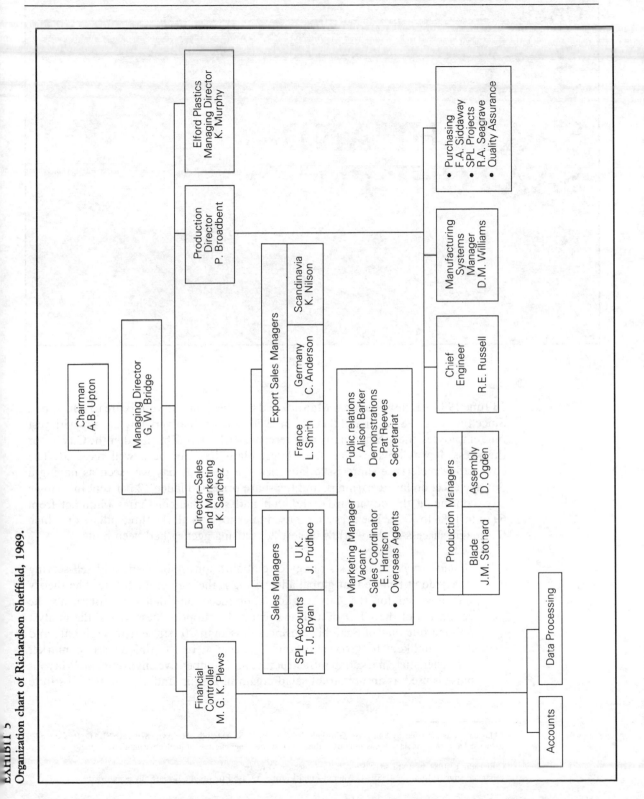

18 June 1988 was not a day that Maurice and Charles Saatchi would care to remember. Since the start of Saatchi and Saatchi in 1970 as a small advertising agency with just nine employees, the brothers had never received such a rebuff from either the City . . . or the press. It was obvious that their latest plans had not been well received. The convertible preference share issue launched the previous day was seen as having a dilutive effect on future earnings, and the share price had fallen 12 per cent in a single day, continuing the downward trend that had seen Saatchi shares plummet from 697p in 1986 to 372p. The press had raised questions on all the three pillars on which the magic success of the world's largest advertising agency had been built:

1. *Globalization:* 'Saatchi's strategy of globalization is simplistic and self-serving – they don't believe that global advertising is the way of the future. The theory was invented for the City's sake,' announced one daily, paraphrasing the comments of the CEO of a rival agency. To support these views, the analyst pointed out that of Saatchi's business, less than 20 per cent was 'global', and it was unlikely to grow substantially because of the differences in market characteristics, marketing infrastructure and competitive environment. 'Mayonnaise is used as an upmarket salad cream in Britain and as a butter substitute

*This case was prepared by Sumantra Ghoshal, Professor at INSEAD and Alice Avis, MBA, INSEAD. It is intended to be used as a basis for class discussion rather than to illustrate either effective or ineffective handling of an administrative situation.
Copyright © 1989, by INSEAD-CEDEP, Fontainebleau, France.
Financial support from the INSEAD Alumni Fund European Case Programme is gratefully acknowledged.

in the United States. Although the UK is moving towards the US, differences in the product's lifecycle and use patterns will continue to require different campaigns in the two markets.'

2.   *Diversification:* 'The concept of an integrated marketing services company may be attractive to smaller firms, but the big multinational clients see little benefit in buying a full package from one company since there is limited cost saving, and probably some inconsistency in quality within the integrated group.' This comment in a major business weekly contrasted sharply with Saatchi's strategy of becoming the world-wide leader in the business of providing 'know-how' – a broad term used by the company to refer to advertising, marketing services, management consulting, litigation services and information technology – and their continued acquisition blitz to implement this strategy. Sceptics questioned not just the concept but also its implementation: some of the company's recent acquisition moves 'smacked of a firm that had run out of ideas', declared the *Financial Times*.

3.   *Decentralization:* Also under challenge was Saatchi's system of decentralized management that led to each affiliated company operating as autonomous units with local management having full responsibility for profit and growth. As described by an ex-employee of the company, 'Because of decentralization, they haven't developed any system for information sharing, or cross-referrals . . . their organizational approach prevents them from leveraging their positions in different markets and activities.'

As the brothers met in Maurice's office, it was clear to both that each of these issues had to be addressed urgently so as to restore clients' and investors' confidence in the company they had built up from scratch and in which they now owned less than 3 per cent of the equity. This required immediate attention to three crucial questions.

First, the company's vision of a global agency was premissed on the promise of superior efficiency and service. Yet, trading margins in the communications division were falling as costs grew faster than revenues. Ways had, therefore, to be found to leverage the company's global reach in this business into specific sources of extra margins or customer benefits, and necessary changes had to be made in the division's strategy and systems to ensure that these potential benefits actually passed through to the bottom line.

Second, some urgent decisions had to be taken for the consulting business too. Vic Miller, head of the company's consulting division, firmly believed that the business had the potential for contributing significant profits, but it needed considerable up-front investments in acquisitions and for hiring and training of new personnel. Because of a combination of falling trading margins, a heavy debt burden accumulated to finance earlier acquisitions, and a miserable price:earnings ratio that had fallen from 26 to 7 and was now less than half of many lesser rivals, these investments had become increasingly difficult to finance. A clear vision and a credible strategy were necessary to prevent further erosion in the competitive position of this business which both brothers felt was central to their ambition of building the 'world's greatest service supermarket'.

And finally, the company's organization and its management systems also needed close scrutiny. Was the overall structure appropriate for the strategy it had adopted?

Were the right administrative processes in place to manage the company's diverse, dispersed and complex businesses? Was the corporate organization playing the right roles and managing the right tasks? One analyst had recently described the organization as Saatchi's Achilles' heel. It was up to the brothers to make the changes necessary to make it the engine of the company's recovery and renewal.

THE ADVERTISING INDUSTRY

'When I attempt to tell others of the current state of the advertising agency business, it reminds me of nothing so much as Alice attempting to explain her presence in Wonderland: "I can't explain myself, I'm afraid, sir," said Alice, "because I'm not myself, you see." Certainly, the agency business is having difficulties explaining itself, because it is not itself, at least not in a way anyone in the business for more than a couple of years would recognize . . . . We have altered not only the nature of the agency business so that for the first time we are perceived, unhappily, as just another business. . . but the fundamental structure of the business as well.'

C. Peebler, CEO
Bozell, Jacobs, Kenyon & Eckhardt

The factor that most strongly influenced the dramatic transformation of the advertising agency business in the 1980s was what the press often described as the 'tidal wave from Britain'. Up to the late 1970s, the industry was dominated by a few large American companies both in terms of market share and creative talent, and Madison Avenue in New York was the undisputed advertising capital of the world. Saatchi and Saatchi changed this traditional structure of the industry, not only by its own explosive growth through acquisitions and its creative excellence, but also by the UK imitators it spawned. Whereas in 1978 there was not a single UK holding company among the top 20 agency groups world-wide, by 1988 there were four. Saatchi and Saatchi were the first of these British 'new wave' agencies: new wave referring to the formula of maintaining continuous earnings growth so as to maintain a high P/E ratio, using the resulting financial muscle to buy market share through aggressive acquisitions, and leveraging these acquisitions to boost earnings by imposing strong financial controls, introducing new creative products, and motivating management through extremely generous performance-related incentive systems.

THE AGENCY BUSINESS

Traditionally, advertising agencies had four functional areas: planning and research, account handling, creative design and media planning and purchasing. It was a worldwide custom for agencies to be remunerated with a 15 per cent commission on the media placed. A client move towards negotiated commission rates had recently led to an average rate below 15 per cent. With the exception of the very small companies, agencies rarely competed on price, though this was changing under growing competitive pressures. Historically, creative reputation, individual personalities, planning facilities and resources in terms of an international network and marketing services were the main selection criteria for the clients.

The planning and research function had the responsibility for providing information on which the agency would develop an advertising strategy for the client. Quality of the planning department was, therefore, often a key basis for differentiation among the different agencies. While planning expenses were part of the standard fee for regular campaigns, they were paid for separately on a fee basis for new product development projects or consumer behaviour analysis. For many agencies, such fee-based remuneration accounted for about a quarter of total income.

The main task of the media department was to plan and buy media. A company's effectiveness at media purchase was often measured by independent research houses commissioned by the clients. A good media department could save clients as much as 20 per cent on their media spends. Effective media buying was partly a function of an agency's clout as large agencies enjoyed some advantages in negotiating with media owners. But it was also a function of the negotiating skills of the buyer, and relatively smaller agencies such as Dorland in the United Kingdom often outperformed larger agencies such as Saatchi in media buying.

An agency's costs were mostly related to its personnel. For UK-based agencies, for example, salaries accounted for about 60 per cent of costs, while office and general administration contributed 36 per cent, and depreciation only 4 per cent. In the United States, salaries tended to be higher and accounted for between 65 and 70 per cent of total costs for agencies of comparable size. As a result, the average profit margins of agencies were lower in the United States – about 8 per cent of revenues compared to about 13 per cent in the United Kingdom. Among the different functional areas, the creative design department typically accounted for 30–40 per cent of total personnel costs, while planning and account handling contributed 20–30 per cent, and media planning and buying contributed 10–15 per cent.

MARKET TRENDS

The American multinational agencies who traditionally dominated the market were not known for their creative brilliance. Despite this, they had maintained their market positions by appealing to the large advertisers – the multinational packaged goods companies – who, being risk-averse, preferred to deal with the established agencies. Although the work of the 'hot shop' agencies was admired, their more limited resources in terms of marketing services and media buying leverage, and the controversial nature of some of their advertising, confined them to a niche or, at most, a ranking below the top ten in most national markets.

The success of the 'new wave' agencies in the 1980s could be partly attributed to the high growth of the industry. During 1980–7, advertising expenditures grew at a real rate of 5.2 per cent per annum. This strong growth was due to a number of reasons. The rise in import penetration in North America and Europe in major industries such as consumer durables and cars had a positive effect on advertising since imported products typically required higher advertising spends to obtain distribution and to build customer franchise. General increase in consumer spending, rapid concentration in retail power and the subsequent rise of private label products were some of the other contributory factors.

In 1988, the prospects for future growth looked promising, even though the situation varied a great deal from country to country (see Exhibit 1). The United States, which accounted for about 55 per cent of the market, was expected to be the slowest growth sector with an estimated real growth of only 1.3 per cent in 1988, slowing further in 1989. This was in part a reflection of the increasing shift of advertising expenditures in the United States into below the line and local promotions.

Europe was expected to remain buoyant, benefiting from the increase in competition in preparation for the single market of 1992. Besides, the European market was also much less mature. As Exhibit 1 shows, advertising as a percentage of GNP was much lower in Europe than in the United States, and the trend had been upwards in recent years as companies realized the increasing importance of investing in branding in a tougher competitive arena.

The easing of restrictions on television advertising and the development of new media opportunities, as European cable and satellite channels started up, were also expected to boost advertising spends. In 1987, Europe accounted for 24 per cent of the worldwide advertising market, with the United Kingdom alone accounting for about 5 per cent. Growth in real terms was forecast at 6–8 per cent for 1988 and 4–6 per cent in 1989.

The Asia Pacific market was dominated by Japan, the second largest national market after the United States. In 1987, Japan accounted for 13 per cent of worldwide advertising expenditure with a nominal increase of 12.7 per cent predicted for 1988 and 6 per cent for 1989. Western agencies, however, had found this market to be almost impenetrable. Unlike any other major market, the Japanese advertising industry was completely dominated by a handful of large and powerful domestic agencies: the two largest accounting for 42 per cent of billings, and the top 10 controlling 64 per cent. Not a single Western agency was included in the top ten. However, Young and Rubicam, the largest agency in the world, and some others such as McCann Erickson and DMB&B had set up joint-venture agreements with some of the top ranking Japanese agencies. Saatchi operated independently in Japan, but ranked 30th with less than 1 per cent of the total market.

In the Pacific region, the growth forecast for some of the emerging economies such as Malaysia and India looked promising. Little could be predicted with any level of accuracy with regard to the Latin American region because of fluctuations in the dollar to which the national economies were highly sensitive, and because of hyperinflation.

KEY COMPETITORS

As described earlier, in the late 1980s, the advertising industry was in the midst of a major transformation. Its boundaries were being redefined and its overall structure was changing rapidly. This transformation was in part a result of the broader trend of consolidation and rationalization among some of the most advertising-intensive businesses in the world. The wave of international acquisitions and mergers in beverages, food, pharmaceuticals and other consumer product industries and the tendency of the merged companies to retain a single agency on a worldwide basis had led to the demise of many medium-sized advertising companies and to a polarization of the industry into a few mega-agencies and a large number of specialized boutiques.

The restructuring was being driven by the British pack with both Saatchi and WPP at the foreground. But the Americans were also launching a counter-attack as evidenced by the mega-merger of BBDO and DDB Needham in 1986 to form the Omnicom group and D'Arcy McManus and Masius with Benton and Bowles in 1985. Exhibit 2 lists the major advertising groups and provides some data on their revenues and profitability in 1987. Exhibit 3 shows their ranking in each of the world's ten largest advertising markets.

Saatchi and Saatchi derived 80 per cent of its profits from advertising and marketing services, and the balance from consultancy. Its aim was to boost the consulting business so as to contribute 50 per cent of profits within five years. The company had two worldwide advertising networks and ten independent agencies. The two networks, Saatchi and Saatchi and Backer Spielvogel Bates ranked numbers 2 and 3 respectively on a worldwide basis, behind Young and Rubicam. The company had developed a strong presence in each of the world's top ten advertising markets with a top five ranking in each with the notable exception of Japan. The main problem the group faced in the advertising arm was inconsistency in quality and reputation among the subsidiary companies. The flagship agency in the United Kingdom still enjoyed an excellent reputation for its creative talent but its subsidiaries in the United States and in some of the European countries had recently faced some criticism for mediocre quality.

The group had diversified strongly into management services. It had a number 6 ranking among public relations firms in the United States and was among the top 5 in the United Kingdom with a good worldwide coverage. In sales promotion and direct marketing, it was one of the five largest companies, with strong presence in the United States and United Kingdom, but with patchy coverage in the rest of the world. It had made one significant acquisition in the United States to develop a presence in the field of market research, but was not represented in this activity in any other country. In 1984, the company had declared its intention to build a major presence in the management consultancy field and to become one of the five leading players in each segment of this business. Since then it had made a number of acquisitions to meet this goal, but most of them were relatively small and significant gaps remained in terms of both geographic and functional coverage.

Dentsu was the largest of the Japanese agencies and enjoyed an unprecedented 29 per cent share of its home market. Despite its size, it had no presence outside Japan except for its share in HDM, a relatively small international agency ranked 15th on a worldwide basis that was jointly owned by Havas Publicis Conseil, a French company, Young and Rubicam, and Dentsu. Unlike the other top ranking agencies, Dentsu had grown organically, fuelled by the strong growth of its clients. With many Japanese manufacturers eager to enter Europe before 1992, there was speculation that Dentsu might soon set up a European base.

The Interpublic Group consisted of three agency networks: Lintas, McCann-Ericsson Worldwide, which were the 6th and 8th largest agencies respectively, and Lowe Marschalk. The agency had excellent international coverage, particularly in the developing countries. It had won a number of prized accounts because of this strength. For example, McCann won the business of Coca-Cola on a worldwide basis on the strength of the quality of the work it initially did for Coke in Brazil. Foreign billing represented 60 per cent of its total revenues, up from 55 per cent in 1986. The group had strong client links and a record of excellent financial performance, but suffered from a reputation of having only mediocre creative talent.

The Omnicom Group was formed in the spring of 1986 through the merger of two US-based agencies – DDB Needham and BBDO – which ranked 4th and 12th respectively on a worldwide basis. The merger was largely a response to the British invasion of the US market. Initial performance of the group, however, was unsatisfactory. In contrast to the 14.3 per cent growth of Saatchi, or to that of 20.7 per cent registered by Interpublic, Omnicom grew by only 9.2 per cent in 1987. DDB Needham dropped 12.9 per cent in gross income, while BBDO registered only a slight increase of 1.4 per cent.

The group was diversified both geographically and functionally. However, it was weak in some important sectors, particularly in the United Kingdom, Canada, France and Japan. Although it offered over 43 types of marketing communications, the companies were small and mainly US-based. The group's objectives were to fill out its areas of regional weaknesses, and to offer the client a full range of integrated marketing services.

WPP was run by Martin Sorrell, the finance director of Saatchi and Saatchi between 1977 and 1986. The group emerged as a major force in 1987 after its hostile takeover of JWT group – the fourth largest advertising agency at the time. Prior to the takeover, WPP was a marketing services company consisting of 18 small firms that had been acquired in the previous 18 months.

WPP had major presence in all the areas of advertising, marketing services and public relations. In the JWT takeover, it also acquired Hill and Knowlton, the world's largest PR firm. The company, then a loss-maker, had since been turned around to make a reasonable profit in 1988. WPP was also perhaps the strongest of the major groups in marketing services and one of its strategic priorities was to consolidate further this strength by building an extensive international network to support this activity.

In its management orientation, WPP was highly focused on financial performance. As described by the *Economist,* 'Neither group [Saatchi and Saatchi and WPP] has any nostalgia for the tradition of undisciplined accounting in the advertising business. Mr Sorrell is proud to call WPP a financial brand . . . . Financial professionals find Mr Sorrell's strategy easier to follow. He is doing what they like most – turning around wayward companies . . . . Before its takeover by WPP, [JWT's] operating margins were running at 4 per cent. The agency's target now was the industry average of 10 per cent by 1991.' By 1988, Sorrell had already achieved a margin of 8.1 per cent, and industry analysts confidently predicted that he would achieve at least 9 per cent by the end of 1989.

The factor which could hinder WPP's progress was its high level of debt. In the year ending 1987, it had a net debt of £107.3 million, with an estimated deferred payment of £194.7 million. As a result, its cashflows were mortgaged out for five years into the future and the company had very limited borrowing capacity left for any further acquisitions.

THE GROWTH OF SAATCHI AND SAATCHI:
STRATEGIC FOUNDATION

In 1970 Maurice Saatchi quit his job to join his brother Charles in setting up an advertising agency. Until then the two brothers had pursued very different careers. Charles left school at 18 and became one of the top copywriters in a leading London agency before leaving to set up his own creative consultancy. Maurice, meanwhile, went to the London School of Economics and then joined the Haymarket publishing group as promotions manager for *Campaign,* the advertising industry's trade paper.

The agency, a metamorphosis of Charles's creative consultancy, started with £1 million of billings, £25,000 in financial backing, and nine employees, all under 27 and entirely creative except for Maurice Saatchi and Tim Bell, an old friend and associate of the two brothers. From this modest beginning, by 1986, it had grown to be one of the world's largest advertising groups, with billing of £2 billion spread over 57 countries and 10,000 employees (see Exhibit 4). Behind this almost incredible achievement lay a set of beliefs that the two brothers shared and which they pursued with both courage and vigour throughout the period. Second, they believed that careful attention to financial strategy was key to developing and implementing a growth-oriented business strategy. Third, they were fully committed to the concept of globalization of markets and, therefore, to the vision of a global agency. Finally, they saw advertising as one element of a broader management services business and believed that clients would reward a company that offered them the facility of one stop shopping for their diverse needs.

Big could be beautiful

The structure of the advertising industry had been stable over decades as a result of both client inertia and the norms and customs of the business. Traditionally, client turnover had been low and only about 2 per cent of accounts moved from one agency to another during any particular year. This was partly due to risk-aversion among the major advertisers, but switching costs were also believed to be high because of the investments both the agency and the client had to make in establishing close working relationships that were necessary for building shared understanding of the role of advertising in supporting the client's business. These long-term agency–client relationships were also supported by a set of well-established industry norms. Like accountants, doctors and lawyers, advertising agencies were not expected to solicit business unless invited by the client, nor to promote themselves obtrusively. IPA, the industry association, was the protector of these norms which were seen as integral to the creative mystique of advertising that made it different from a 'mere business'.

The Saatchi brothers were convinced from the start that size was an extremely important source of competitive advantage in the business. Economies of scale or cost-sharing were part of the benefits: the primary advantages lying in centralized research and information departments, in production, and in sharing of corporate overhead and research expenses. But perhaps the most important advantage of size was not scale *per se* or cost-sharing but market power. Volume gave visibility and, thereby, the ability to attract good personnel and clients – it got an agency on the pitch list. It also ensured clout in media buying. Besides, size also gave an agency the flexibility to invest in developing new products, to take risks and to build highly specialized capabilities.

The brothers realized that the existing rules of the game were stacked against fast growth of a new agency. Therefore, they decided not to play to those rules. Charles set aside one day a week to promote the agency. He announced new business wins, controversial campaigns and pitches they had been involved in. This ensured that the name Saatchi and Saatchi was on the front page of *Campaign* every week. Maurice broke the rule of no solicitation: he began each working day by making 25 cold calls to leading clients of competing agencies. The company also refused to join the IPA.

Ultimately, however, the business did not offer a potential of organic growth that would satisfy the ambitious and impatient Saatchi's. Acquisitions were the only route to the express lane and it was primarily in this arena that Saatchi and Saatchi created a new legacy in the advertising industry.

Besides making his 25 cold calls a day, Maurice had also developed a habit of corresponding regularly if in somewhat of an unusual manner with the heads of the other agencies. The letters tended to be short, courteous and to the point: 'I am sure this will be the last thing on your mind but I wondered if you felt it would make sense to dispose of your company,' so they began. These letters were mailed to most of the agencies of the day both large and small.

By 1974, the company had made several acquisitions, moving into France, Belgium and Holland, and buying three regional agencies in the United Kingdom. With the exception of Notley Advertising and E.G. Dawes, these acquisitions were relatively unsuccessful. However, they boosted the agency's growth and taught them a great deal about what to do and not do in future takeovers.

The first headline winning acquisition of Saatchi's came in 1975 with the reverse takeover of Garland-Compton, the 11th largest UK agency with billings of £17.4 million. A subsidiary of Compton Advertising in the United States, Garland-Compton was twice the size of Saatchi, with blue chip clients but lacking in creativity and strong financial management. It was just what the Saatchis needed to gain first division status so as to be able to attract the risk-averse large consumer product companies which had so far been beyond their reach. It also gave the company a public quotation which later proved to be the principal tool for future growth. Furthermore, the brothers were paid to receive the benefits: they gained a 35 per cent stake in the merged company and were paid £400,000 by Compton Advertising who thought they were taking over Saatchi and Saatchi and merely retaining the brothers as local managers of the merged business. Charles and Maurice thought differently. *Campaign* were briefed and the headline that Friday read 'Saatchi swallows up the Compton Group'. The two agencies were merged in Garland-Compton's offices, creating the 4th largest UK agency with billings of £30 million. Tim Bell was installed as managing director with the brothers planning the business strategy. Advising the Saatchi brothers on the Compton deal was a 31-year-old Harvard MBA, Martin Sorrell, who then worked for James Gulliver, head of the food conglomerate Argyll. Shortly after the deal he was signed up to join the company and remained with the Saatchis until 1986, playing a vital role in the success of their acquisitions and in developing investor relations.

From 1975 to 1979, the company focused on leveraging the Compton client base to achieve an astounding organic growth rate of 26 per cent per annum (nominal) and become the number one agency in the United Kingdom. A string of outstanding creative successes fuelled this growth. First, the 'pregnant man' advertisement for the British Health Education Council and then the 'Labour isn't working' advertisement for the election campaign of the British Conservative Party made them a household name. Although new business came more easily than at the beginning, the Saatchis were not prepared to relax their efforts. The agency now had a team of 5-6 people devoted to chasing new accounts and, as a result, managed to get major advertisers such as IBM, British Petroleum, Nestlé and Sainsbury on their client list. As a former employee described, 'Whenever Maurice read in the press that a client was reviewing his account, the first reaction was "Right, who knows him? Get on the phone, now." The second response was to kick the new business director in the . . . for not getting us on the shortlist beforehand.'

Between 1979 and 1985, the company grew by another 20-fold through both strong organic growth and also a string of acquisitions that ran up to a rate of about one per month during 1985. The most significant of these acquisitions were those of Garrott Dorland Crawford in 1981 and of Compton Advertising in the United States in 1982. The first gave Saatchi a second strong agency in the United Kingdom, and the second provided direct access to the corporate advertising budgets of the large US multinational companies.

There were many, however, who contested Saatchi's faith in the advantages of size. Large advertisers saw the trend of increasing concentration in the agency business as a threat, and some of them were prepared to counteract by either buying an agency and converting to in-house production of advertising services or switching to smaller agencies. They believed that large institutions were not conducive to carrying out an essentially creative task. They also believed that, by definition, senior management involvement in client service had to decline as an agency grew in size and, as the chairman of Procter and Gamble pointed out, there was 'no such thing as an agency business other than its service to clients'. Some analysts even argued that in professional services businesses, diseconomies of scale soon exceeded economies of scale, and local operations with more than 100–50 employees incurred more costs than benefits. Fears of conflict of interest were also raised since large agencies often dealt with more than one competitor in a particular industry. These criticisms were increasingly gathering force and 66 per cent of companies surveyed by *Advertising Age* in 1986 were negative about the trend toward mega-agencies.

Focus on Financial Strategy

Few agencies before Saatchi and Saatchi had tried the acquisition route to growth. The main problem was getting access to capital. The large multinational agencies, mainly American, were on low price:earnings ratios (P/E) of 4–5. This was a reflection of the stock markets' opinion of the poor quality of their earnings because of weak financial management and because of the fact that most of their assets were intangibles – key employees and clients – who could walk out of the door at any time. On such low P/Es, it was difficult to raise sufficient cash. On the other hand, the new start-up agencies were typically partnerships and had only very limited access to the capital markets.

Saatchi's got access to the capital market when they acquired Garland-Compton, then the only listed agency in the United Kingdom. At the time of acquisition, Garland-Compton had a P/E of 4. By maintaining effective communication and otherwise ensuring good investor relations and by showing consistently high profitability, Saatchi's drove this ratio up to 20. At the core of their outstanding growth lay the strategy of acquiring low P/E companies on the strength of their own high P/E, which in turn boosted their earnings per share (EPS) growth and increased the city's confidence in their stock.

To make this strategy work, they developed a particular approach to structuring the financial arrangements of their acquisitions. Payments for acquisitions were made contingent to the owners meeting profit targets over a period of five years after the acquisition. For example, in the Garrott Dorland Crawford acquisition, Saatchi's paid only £1.4 million up-front and the balance of about £5.6 million was contracted to be paid over the next five years from internally generated cash flows, subject to profit targets being met by the local managers. Exactly the same formula was followed for the Compton acquisition with $30 million paid immediately and payment of the balance $24.8 million made contingent on profit performance over the next five years. In each case, the initial payment was raised by a matching share issue. This financing method allowed Saatchi's to boost earnings quickly, as the earnings of the acquired agency were included immediately in the company's financial reports while only a part of the purchase price was actually paid.

A significant portion of any agency acquisition is goodwill. In the United States, goodwill has to be amortised over a 40-year period which results in dilution of EPS. The treatment of goodwill in the United Kingdom, however, allows a company to write it off against reserves rather than amortising it. This helped Saatchi's since, unlike their American competitors, they could maintain high earnings growth despite successive acquisitions. This financial strategy also motivated managers of acquired companies to cut costs with an iron hand to earn their profit-related bonuses. However, it might also have affected essential investments: as described by Victor Miller, the Arthur Anderson executive Saatchi hired to run its consulting division, 'investments after the earn-out period typically had some catching up to do'.

Vision of a Global Agency

By the mid-1980s, the theme of globalization of markets was being hotly debated around the world. Much of this debate focused on an article written by Professor Theodore Levitt of the Harvard Business School in which he claimed that the days of the traditional multinational corporation, which adjusts its products and practices to suit national or regional preferences, were nearing an end. According to Professor Levitt, a new 'Republic of Technology' was relentlessly homogenizing the world's preference structures and the result was the emergence of global markets for highly standardized products which the modern global corporation exploited by selling 'the same thing in the same way everywhere'. By so doing, they created enormous economies of scale in production, distribution, marketing, and management.

> By translating these benefits into reduced world prices, they could decimate competitors who still lived in the disabling grip of the old assumptions of how the world worked.

Saatchi and Saatchi embraced this concept of globalization fully, and positioned themselves as the champion of the global advertising agency. Such an agency, they claimed, could enjoy a number of clear advantages. First, because of their global information systems, they could help their clients market their products globally by identifying similar customer segments across national boundaries. Second, they could exploit economies of scale in their own operations such as media buying and production, and pass those savings on to the clients. Third, they could have the organizational structure and systems in place to service a global account effectively. In essence, Saatchi's belief in the future of the global agency rested on their belief that international companies would increasingly coordinate their marketing activities on a global basis so as to help standardize their brand image and marketing messages. The use of a global agency would then become mandatory, both to achieve this rationalization and standardization in their marketing approach, and also to realize savings in executive time and facilitate the transfer of information and knowledge about a brand across countries.

As an evidence of their commitment to this philosophy, Saatchi's put Professor Levitt on their board and also took out large advertisements in leading newspapers such as the *Wall Street Journal* and the *Financial Times* extolling the benefits of global advertising. As a proof, they referred to their enormously successful 'Manhattan Landing' commercial for British Airways. Produced at a cost of about half a million dollars, this 90-second television commercial was shown in 45 countries with no change except for identical voiceovers in seven languages. On the negative side, they also pointed out their own earlier loss of the Black and Decker account when the company moved to a standard commercial in a number of countries for their small power tools. For the want of an integrated global network, Saatchi's could not service such a requirement at that time. Since then, many other major advertisers such as Procter and Gamble, Coca-Cola and Remington had begun to demand such a global network as a precondition for considering to work with an agency.

While acknowledging the differences in tastes or media regulations among different national markets, Saatchi's highlighted that those differences were, on the one hand, declining over time and, on the other, being bypassed by developments such as the emergence of pan-European satellite TV that were not subject to national rules and regulations. Besides, they also asserted many other advantages from being a global firm such as access to multiple national capital markets (Saatchi shares were listed in five) and the ability to attract the best talents around the world, irrespective of where they lived or preferred to live.

This philosophy of globalization was not without its detractors, however. In the first instance, many rivals questioned Saatchi's commitment to this philosophy and saw it as a fashionable garb used for *ex-post* justification of the company's opportunistic actions. As described by the CEO of a major rival new wave agency in the United Kingdom:

> to play the EPS game, Saatchi's had to begin acquiring American companies both because there were no more large UK agencies to acquire and also because there were a number of agencies in the US with good client lists and low share prices. All the talk about globalization was a good rationalization for actions taken merely in response to client losses and to maintain growth in earnings per share.

Others discounted Saatchi's talk about global information systems or global media discounts. 'It's garbage, and they haven't invested in developing any system for information sharing or superior research facilities. They conduct worldwide studies but that's not an advantage since all multinational agencies do that,' claimed an ex-employee of the company. 'It's in their interest to promote the idea of a global media discount, but it's such a small part of media spend that they never give out a figure.'

Others raised more fundamental questions about the appropriateness or even feasibility of global advertising. They believed that Saatchi's underemphasized the continued importance of national differences: 'You can't sell Levi's jeans with the same campaign in the US and in Europe. In the US, jeans are seen much less as a fashion garment geared at the younger generation,' said a senior marketing manager in a large British consumer products company. Even within Europe, he pointed out, local campaigns were necessary in most markets to maximize effectiveness of media spend because of differences in media availability and legal restrictions (see Exhibit 5). 'Advertising is about as close as you can get to a cultural thing in business, and country differences in cultural preferences are not about to go away just on the say so of some starry-eyed Harvard professor.' To support this claim, he referred to the differences in national advertising for even such celebrated global brands as Coca-Cola and Marlboro: 'You want to show girls playing volleyball in bikinis in Saudi Arabia? Actually, the trend is in the other direction. As I read in a Harvard case, Campbell Soup is going away from even national advertising in the US, and is moving towards regional advertising in the different areas of the country to respond to the specific composition of local ethnic groups, their tastes, and to seasonal fluctions.'

One-Stop Shopping for Management Services

The fourth pillar of the strategic foundation of Saatchi and Saatchi was their vision of providing one-stop shopping for all the management services a company required. They believed that clients would be increasingly interested in integrated offers where a number of services such as advertising, public relations and promotional activities were all coordinated as a package. They claimed that by providing such diversified services within one umbrella, they could provide the benefits of greater consistency and lower costs. Following this belief, Saatchi's expanded their portfolio of activities in two stages. First, between 1980 and 1984, they diversified, through both organic development and acquisitions, from advertising to marketing services, including sales promotion, direct marketing, public relations and sponsorship. Next, following their 1984 acquisition of Hay consultants, they further expanded into the areas of strategy and management information systems consulting and executive recruitment and compensation. As described by Maurice Saatchi, the company's ultimate ambition was 'to put together a global service-supermarket that would combine Saatchi's advertising skills, McKinsey's consulting capabilities, the accounting expertise of Arthur Andersen, and the financial clout of Goldman Sachs.'

The company justified its diversification into marketing services on both strategic and financial grounds. More and more purchase decisions were being made by customers at the point of sale in less and less time. Marketeers were therefore trying to maximize the effectiveness of all elements of the promotional mix including packaging design, sales promotion, and so on. While previously these marketing services were performed in-house, the need to become more sophisticated about their usage had caused a shift to specialist consultants. With only 2 per cent and 8 per cent respectively of sales promotion budget of UK and US companies being handled by outside consultancies in 1987, this was seen as a potentially profitable and high growth business in its own right.

Furthermore, inflation in media costs far outstripped retail price inflation, thereby leading to a shift from advertising to promotional spend which had become more cost effective. For example, in 1977, promotional expenditures accounted for 47 per cent and 58 per cent of total spend in the United Kingdom and United States respectively. By 1987, the shares had gone up to 55 per cent and 68 per in the two countries. Expansion into these areas was therefore seen as necessary to compensate for the ultimate slowdown or, possibly, actual decline in advertising billings.

Saatchi's also claimed the benefit of considerable synergy between marketing services and advertising activities. There was the obvious potential for cross-referrals of clients, but there was also the possibility of attracting top professionals in one field on the strength of the company's reputation in the other. As a tangible evidence in support of their various justifications for diversification, the company often pointed out that between 1986 and 1987, the number of clients they served in three or more functions had increased from 30 to 128.

While many external analysts basically accepted these arguments for diversifying into marketing services, some of them remained unconvinced about the justification for entering into management consulting. The brothers justified this diversification on a number of grounds. Consulting was a high-growth high-profit sector which had many similarities and potential synergies with the advertising business. Effective management of creative and highly skilled professionals was the main challenge in both businesses. It was also a fragmented, nationally focused industry with global customers that the brothers believed was ripe for the same magic of globalization that they had applied so successfully to transform the advertising business. Besides, the major accounting firms were rapidly building up consulting practices of their own and if they could do so, why couldn't an advertising agency?

Detractors, however, marshalled an equally powerful array of contrary arguments. Although the client company might be the same, the actual client within the company was often different for marketing and management consulting. Furthermore, while the reputation of Saatchi and Saatchi could attract clients and personnel for the related marketing services areas, they believed it would be of limited value in consulting. This would make cross-selling difficult, particularly in the absence of any strong client benefits. They also feared that strong differences in the professional cultures of advertising and consulting would impede organizational integration and thereby prevent the company from exploiting any potential synergies even if they were theoretically available.

IMPLEMENTING THE STRATEGY: THE SAATCHI ORGANIZATION

The Saatchi and Saatchi organization was structured into two main division: consulting and communications (see Exhibit 6). There were two parallel worldwide agencies within the communications division: the flagship agency of Saatchi and Saatchi which included Compton and DFS, Backer Spielvogel Bates, and Dorland. The smaller agencies and service companies were also kept separate and the company had deliberately avoided any moves toward rationalization and merger among the different acquired companies despite, for example, owning 11 different advertising agencies in New York alone.

The group headquarters was exceptionally small for the size of operations that reported to it. There were only about 50 people in the headquarters responsible, at the corporate level, for accounting, financing, public relations and business development. Through luck, good judgement and persuasiveness, the brothers had assembled an outstanding team of senior managers in the headquarters organization all of whom played important roles in shaping the agency, both financially and strategically. With his charm and ease with clients, Tim Bell was instrumental in getting the company access to mega-clients, and also in maintaining the group's public relations and image within the United Kingdom. He, for example, was responsible for bagging the Tory election account. Martin Sorrell was a brilliant financier who gained the confidence of the City, masterminded the acquisition deals, and developed the financing tools and corporate control systems. Jeremy Sinclair was one of the few to have stayed with the company for over 17 years. He was an exceptionally creative copywriter and was responsible for many of the agency's award winning campaigns. Anthony Simmonds Gooding was the architect of the company's organizational system which, in its own way, was as distinct as its strategic vision and financial approach and, in the opinion of some analysts, almost as important a factor behind the company's outstanding performance.

Fundamentally, the organizational systems and management processes in Saatchi's were structured with some clear delineation of the roles and tasks of local management in each of the affiliated companies and central management at the headquarters. Further, efforts were also underway to superimpose a new set of administrative mechanisms on top of these local and central management processes so as to develop a truly worldwide coordination capability.

Local Entrepreneurship: Decentralized Responsibilities

The company believed that autonomy was essential for promoting creativity and entrepreneurship in an agency. Further, in an industry infested with strong personalities, eccentric artists and prima donnas, autonomy was essential for keeping key personnel. Therefore, Saatchi's had developed a strong organizational philosophy of decentralizing both strategic and operational responsibilities fully to each affiliated agency. Local management had full responsibility for profit and growth of their unit, and had complete freedom to pursue those objectives in any manner they chose. Such a management system sat very well with the company's acquisition policy of making payment on a part of the acquisition price contingent on future performance of an acquired company and, in fact, was essential to make such a payment system credible to managers (many of whom were also partners) of those companies.

The principle of decentralization was not limited to the relationship between the group headquarters and the different companies, but was extended further down to the relationships among and even within each company. For example, there were no systems for cross-referrals among the different companies, nor any incentives for any one company to refer a client to another company within the family. Each company was, in turn, divided into a number of groups, each of which was treated as an independent profit centre and had its own P&L accounts. These groups enjoyed relatively complete operating freedom, and there were no systems in place for information sharing among them. As one manager described, 'One can always find some sources of synergy between almost any two groups, and there is an urge to exploit them. But managing those synergies also carries certain costs, much of which are not visible. How do you value the loss of commitment of a key manager, or dilution of the sense of personal responsibility and achievement?'

From 1987, however, the company was trying to adopt the idea of lead countries. The plan was to nominate a country that had developed some specialization in a certain field because of its client portfolio as an expert in that field, with their expertise available to be drawn upon by other agencies worldwide. For example, France was designated as the lead country for the financial services industry, Germany for electricals, and the United Kingdom for retailing. It was made clear, however, that sharing of such expertise was entirely voluntary and no formal incentives were provided to either the supplying or the receiving agency.

Central Value-Added: Financial Planning and Control

In sharp contrast to this strategic and operational decentralization, the financial planning and control systems of the company were highly centralized. These systems were rigidly defined, uniform throughout the group and each company had to adopt them with almost no discretion for any change at the local level. In fact, the financial control function was separated from all other operations, and was run directly from the headquarters on a worldwide basis.

For example, the Communications Division had two finance officers in the corporate headquarters to whom the finance directors of each company reported directly. The finance managers of each group within each company, similarly, reported to the company finance director and not to local managements. The main task of this finance group was to help each company prepare very detailed annual revenues, costs and profit budgets, and to maintain extremely rigorous monitoring of the performance of each company against those budgets.

Each agency had to forecast its billings 3 and 12 months ahead, and actual billings were reviewed against these forecasts on a monthly basis. In the event of any negative variances due to unforeseeable circumstances, the agency was expected to make up for the loss by exploiting some other opportunity. Costs were monitored on more than 50 different categories, and all variances from budget in either billings or costs were reported to the corporate headquarters as soon as they could be reasonably predicted or, at the latest, by the end of the month. Profitability of each client account was similarly monitored through a system that accounted for all time spent on the client and full costs rather than on the basis of contribution margin. Cash balances of each company were monitored daily and were consolidated on a worldwide basis each day into a single corporate account.

Traditionally, in most agencies, corporate responsibilities were handled by executives who had made their careers in advertising. They were effectively the line managers. Despite creative excellence, not all these managers were equally trained or motivated to manage the business for profit and growth. By separating the finance function from the rest of the business, Saatchi and Saatchi were able to design and implement a strong planning and financial control system which was administered by accountants and finance specialists. Some industry observers believed that this financial control system was among the most important benefits that Saatchi brought to an acquired company. For example, in one year after its acquisition by Saatchi, the Hay group improved its operating margins from 11.5 per cent to 14 per cent. In part, this system was also the main source of the company's credibility in the financial markets. As described by an analyst in Goldman Sachs, 'One of the problems in covering the agencies as an analyst is that they are run by agency people. They don't run these businesses as businesses should be run. The Saatchis were unique in that.'

Global Coordination: Worldwide Account Management

Saatchi and Saatchi's philosophy of a global agency rested on the claim that such an agency could link and leverage its own resources in different markets and thereby provide a worldwide coordination capability as an unique service to its global clients. In pursuit of this capability, the company had begun to install a system for worldwide account management. A single manager in the agency that served the headquarters of a multinational client was often designated as the worldwide account director and carried the responsibility of developing and supporting the client's business for all the services that the agency could provide in any country.

The main tasks of the account director were two-fold: to attract the client's business in those countries where they used a different agency, and to coordinate multi-country campaigns. Given the philosophy of decentralization within the Saatchi organization (which was often mirrored in the client organization also), the role of the account director was that of a consultant and coordinator rather than that of a line manager. The effectiveness of this role, therefore depended on the incumbent's expertise on the client's businesses and products, and on his or her ability to establish personal credibility among managers in different countries in both Saatchi and the client organizations by transferring information and acting as a catalyst for cross-fertilization of ideas. It was hoped that, over time, the Saatchi account director would often stay longer on the job than many of the relevant brand managers in the headquarters and national subsidiaries of the client company and could therefore serve as a lynchpin in consolidating the client's own knowledge of the brand and in developing the appropriate global advertising strategy. Besides, the account director was also expected to act as the client's champion within Saatchi and to ensure that the agency developed the required capabilities and resources to provide the best possible services to meet the client's present and future needs.

As of 1988, the global account management system was in a very early stage of implementation, and the jury was out on its effectiveness. There were some clear tensions between the agency's emphasis on decentralized profit responsibility and its desire to maintain worldwide coordination in client servicing. It was not yet clear how the inevitable tradeoffs between local interests of a particular unit and the global interests of the company could be handled and no formal systems were yet in place to either measure the profitability of a client on a worldwide basis or to compensate any particular unit for services it might render or sacrifices it might make to support the business of another.

NEW CHALLENGES: THE SITUATION IN 1988

> We have pushed our luck too hard in the City and Wall Street. Finally, our luck turned against us. (A Saatchi employee who preferred to remain unnamed)

As the Saatchi brothers were among the first to admit, the Saatchi phenomenon was a product of a right set of ideas, applied in the right industry, at the right time, implemented with the right dose of daring and the right quota of luck. Of this success cocktail, by 1988, the last element had perhaps begun to run out.

Loss of Key Personnel

The most visible symbol of the changing fortunes of the company was the departure of Tim Bell and Martin Sorrell. Highly ambitious and entrepreneurial, both wanted to have their own businesses and were frustrated at the brothers' unwillingness to give them their own operations – with significant equity stakes – within the Saatchi umbrella. Bell left to join Lowe Howard-Spink, one of the new wave agencies which Saatchi had spawned in the United Kingdom. Sorrell started WPP which, after the dramatic and highly visible hostile takeover of J. Walter Thompson, had already become the fourth largest advertising group in the world and was close on the heels of Saatchi for the mantle of global leadership. The City viewed Sorrell's departure with particular concern: as an investment banker pointed out, 'Sorrell and the brothers were a good combination. He knew what was a good deal and what was a good price – he tempered the brothers' ambition so that their actions made commercial sense.'

While these changes at the top affected the group's external credibility and internal morale, the problems were compounded by two major moves the company made subsequently. The first was the acquisition of Ted Bates. The second was the abortive bid for the Midland Bank and then Hill Samuel, the merchant bank.

New Mega-Moves

Ted Bates was the third largest agency worldwide and one of the most profitable, with a pre-tax profit to income ratio of 16.8 per cent compared with an average of under 10 per cent for major quoted US agencies. Acquisition of Ted Bates was an irresistible deal for the brothers: in one fell swoop it would make them the largest agency group in the world. In May 1986 they bought the agency for $450 million of which they paid $400 million in cash up-front. As against a book value per share of $390, they paid $893.5. As a Bates executive described, 'We picked the largest figure we could think of and they accepted.'

The financial market's reaction was highly negative. Most analysts criticized the brothers for paying too much and also for giving up the use of contingent earn-outs. There was also a big client backlash and Bates lost $450 million worth of billings due to conflicting accounts with other Saatchi agencies. Internal power struggles further weakened the agency and 8 of of the 10 directors resigned. Most significant of these losses was that of Brian Jacoby, the chairman, who had been a strong cementing force within the agency and also an important link with many blue chip clients.

To stem the losses and to help the agency pick up new business, Saatchi's merged it with Baker and Spielvogel. Carl Spielvogel was given the mandate for instilling a new strategic direction in the agency and for injecting new creative talent. but, while this move helped recoup the billing losses through new business development, the company never quite regained the confidence of the financial market (see Exhibit 7).

The second move caused a much more serious dent to the company's reputation. In 1988, the brothers tried to bid for the Midland Bank, the third largest banking company in Britain. If successful, this would have been their most ambitious deal yet. At the time of the attempt, Saatchi and Saatchi was capitalized at around $1 billion while Midland Bank was capitablized at $2 billion. Like the advertising industry, the banking industry too was highly fragmented and was moving towards rationalization and globalization helped by technology and deregulation of the financial markets. Maurice saw the parallel and believed that since they had 'successfully globalized the advertising industry', they could do the same in another service business.

Investors thought very differently. 'The concept of globalization, howsoever neatly packaged, would not solve Midland's immediate problem – that of Latin American debt,' declared one analyst. 'This is something that Maurice hadn't thought of . . . . When Sorrell left Saatchi's strategy went out of the window. The brothers did not want to bother themselves with small businesses such as PR agencies and sales promotion – they wanted the mega-deals, whether they made any sense or not.' As a result of almost universal disapproval of the move, the glamour stock fell sharply, and took Hill Samuel, another declared acquisition target, out of the brothers' reach.

The Challenge Ahead

Since these abortive bids, Maurice no longer talked of financial service. As declared in the shareholders' meeting in April 1988, the goal was scaled back to becoming the leading management services company in the world, with 50 per cent of revenues each from consulting and communications. The consulting wing was to be developed by Vic Miller, who had been hired away from his previous position as the managing director of Arthur Anderson's international division. The new issue of 6.75 per cent convertible preference shares on 17 June 1988 was in pursuance of this revised strategy. Resorting to what was essentially a debt instrument eschewing the traditional equity financing route was itself an acknowledgement on Maurice's part of the cooling of the company's relationship with the City. The lukewarm reaction to even such a conservative financial approach suggested that the company had to find some way to regain investors' confidence so as to be able to fund the next phase of their strategic evolution.

EXHIBIT 1
The advertising industry: market size and growth.

Market	Expenditures in 1987 ($m)	Real Growth 1980–7 (%)	Share of GDP (%)	Growth Forecast 1988 (%)	Growth Forecast 1989 (%)
Top Ten Countries					
USA	90,539	4.0	1.6	7.5	6.1
Japan	21,961	3.5	0.8	12.7	6.0
UK	9,457	5.8	1.4	15.7	11.0
W. Germany	8,836	2.5	0.9	4.6	4.5
France	5,926	6.9	0.7	13.8	12.2
Canada	4,562	3.2		7.0	7.8
Italy	4,171	11.0	0.6	19.1	14.0
Spain	3,346	13.4	1.4	23.9	25.9
Australia	2,720	3.9		8.4	10.3
Holland	2,358	2.0	1.1	0.2	0.7
TOTAL TOP TEN	153,876	5.2			
Rest of the World					
Rest of Europe	8,140				
Rest of South East Asia	4,398				
Latin America	4,799			10.4	8.3
Africa	1,473			10.4	8.3
WORLDWIDE TOTAL	172,685			10.0	7.6

EXHIBIT 2
Top agency holding groups worldwide, 1987.

Ranking 1983	1987	Billings $m	Income $m	Ros %	Nationality
8	1 Saatchi & Saatchi	11,360	1,685	14.8	UK
2	2 Dentsu	6,780	N/A	N/A	Japan
1	3 Interpublic	6,620	993	15.0	US
N/A	4 Omnicom	6,270	896	14.3	US
N/A	5 WPP	5,950	893	15.0	UK
6	6 Ogilvy	5,040	724	14.4	US
4	7 Young & Rubicam	4,910	736	15.0	US
11	8 Hakuhodo	2,900	N/A	N/A	Japan
N/A	9 Eurocom	2,760	N/A	N/A	France
13	10 D'Arcy Masius B & B	2,494	371	14.0	US
12	11 Grey	2,462	369	15.0	US
10	12 Leo Burnett	2,462	369	15.0	US
9	13 FCB	2,300	344	15.0	US
N/A	14 WCRS/Belier	1,630	230	14.1	UK/FRA
N/A	15 HDM	1,380	204	14.8	US/Japan
N/A	16 Bozell, Jacobs, K & E	1,330	185	13.9	US
N/A	17 LoweHSpink & Bell	1,270	N/A	N/A	UK

N/A: because did not exist in 1983.
Source: Advertising Age.

EXHIBIT 3
Advertising industry rankings worldwide, 1987.

	USA	Japan	UK	West Germany	France	Canada	Italy	Spain	Australia	Holland
Dentsu	–	1	–	22*	4*	–	21*	8*	–	19*
Young & Rubicam	1	17*	5	6	8	3	4	15	5	2
Saatchi & Saatchi	2	30	1	9	11	11	8	10	17	7
B&B	5	–	2	7	20	13	20	1	1	1
BBDO	3	–	27	1	21	27	7	5	2	17
Ogilvy & Mather	4	39	6	4	13	1	10	13	6	3
McCann Erickson	13	9*	11	3	14	–	1	2	8	8
JWT	7	14	3	8	17	2	5	3	12	18
Hakuhodo	–	2	–	37	–	–	–	–	–	–
Lintas	12	–	15	2	7	2	9	4	14	4
Holding Group										
Saatchi & Saatchi	1	N/A	1	3	8	N/A	6	1	3	3
Interpublic	3	–	2	1	5	1	3	2	2	
Omnicom	2	–	13	2	7	–	2	1	1	

*HDM: Dentsu owns 33⅓ per cent. Y&R owns 33⅓ per cent +joint venture.

EXHIBIT 4
Saatchi and Saatchi Plc
(£million).

	1971	1972	1973	1974	1975	1976	1977	1978	1979	1980	1981	1982	1983	1984	1985	1986	1987
Turnover[c]	13.7	17.1	21.1	22.8	28.9	35.2	42.6	59.1	71.5	84.7	102.1	258.3	603.2	855.4	1,307.4	2,087.0	3,954.2
Revenue										13.2	17.1	39.6	101.8	147.0	301.6	443.9	773.8
Pre-tax Profit	0.1	0.4	0.6	0.6	0.8	1.0	1.3	1.9	2.5	3.0	3.6	5.5	11.2	18.3	40.5	70.1	124.1
Post-tax Profit[d]						0.4	0.5	0.6	0.8	1.0	1.5	2.6	6.0	11.4	21.7	37.4	69.6
Goodwill[e]							0.1	0.1	0.1	0.1	0.3	0.5	0.6	1.0	3.7	14.9	
US GAAP Post-tax Profit						0.4	0.5	0.5	0.6	0.9	1.1	2.1	5.2	9.0	15.0	22.5	33.1
EPS adj. for Impact a Rights Issue (87)							2.1	3.2	4.1	5.2	6.7	9.4	13.1	22.2	31.6	38.2	43.9
Current Assets Including Cash and Investments						7.1	9.0	13.2	14.8	18.8	32.8	92.9	123.7	193.9	336.8	739.8	763.9
Investments						1.7	2.7	3.6	5.2	6.2	9.7	31.4	26.9	59.7	132.3	189.0	215.9
Current Liabilities						7.0	8.2	11.9	13.6	17.3	30.7	86.3	120.1	174.4	266.3	692.3	744.6
Fixed Assets						0.8	0.9	1.1	2.1	2.5	3.6	12.0	15.8	21.6	32.0	119.4	133.5
Goodwill						1.8	1.7	1.2	1.3	1.4	6.0	20.4	25.4	39.2	177.2	402.1	151.5
Long-term Liabilities						0.1	–	–	–	0.2	–	17.8	17.8	38.4	100.3	124.0	
Capital[e]	0.1				0.2	2.2	2.5	2.6	2.6	3.1	7.2	34.1	38.2	66.3	249.8	598.1	
Acquisition Cost						0.0	0.0	0.3	0.5	0.3	1.7	16.4	11.8	16.1	152.3	443.2	78.6
Contingent Liabilities[f]						N/A	N/A	2.0	N/A	N/A	6.0	16.0	21.0	N/A	80.0	164.0	154.0
Capital Raised[g]	0.03	N/A	N/A	N/A	N/A	0.0	0.0	0.0	0.0	0.0	3.0	25.2	0.0	19.5	174.3	392.0	61.5
Average Employees	11					507	521	644	744	730	777	1,486	3,049	3,748	6,226	9,774	15,630
Offices	1	1	2	4	6	6	6	7	8	8	9	66	71		91	150	–
Countries	1	1	2	3	4	1	1	1	2	2	2	37	40		54	57	58
Market Rank in Advertising Industry																	
UK	N/A	N/A	26	13	4	4	4	4	2	1	1	1	1	1	1	1	1
Europe (incl. UK)	N/A	N/A	N/A	N/A	N/A	4	4	4	–	2	1	1	1	1	1	1	1
USA	–	–	–	–	–	–	–	–	–	–	–	13	7	6	5	1	1
World	N/A	N/A	N/A	N/A	N/A	N/A	N/A	N/A	N/A	N/A	N/A	9	8	7	5	1	1

[a] Includes Ted Bates and other acquisitions for part of the year only.
[b] Estimate.
[c] Billings and non-advertising fees.
[d] UK accounting, after-tax, minority, exceptional and preference items, but before goodwill.
[e] In 1986 Saatchi & Saatchi wrote off £507.1 million of goodwill against reserves. Included here for comparative purposes only.
[f] Estimate of maximum future liability.
[g] Includes £100 million of 6.3 per cent convertible preferred stock in 1986.

EXHIBIT 5
Current regulations on TV advertising in Europe.

Country	TV Households (million)	No. of Channels Accepting Advertising	Total Ad. Mins. p/week	Specific Features/Comments	Restrictions
Austria	2.78	2	280	Limits on no. of spots for a brand p/month. Bookings taken in October for the following year.	Tobacco, spirits banned. Beer, wines, pharmaceuticals restricted.
Belgium	3.50	3	926	Channels broadcast in Flemish and French in the 2 regions. General spots.	Tobacco, alcohol banned. State TV only carries non-commercials.
Denmark	2.20	–	–	New advertising financed channel being launched with 70 minutes per week.	–
Finland	1.80	3	310	Booking period 6 months ahead.	Political parties, religious groups, alcohol, undertakers, slimming drugs, tobacco are banned.
France	20.50	6	1,194	All channels accept advertising.	Alcohol, tobacco, press, cinema, shows and retailers are banned on TV.
Greece	3.00	2	399	Two state-owned stations providing national commercial coverage.	Pharmaceutical products and cigarettes are banned.
Ireland	0.92	2	882	National TV broadcast on two channels. 59% of homes receive BBC/ITV from the UK.	Cigarettes and spirits banned.
Italy	18.53	350+	7,189	Three state-owned channels. Over 350 commercial channels.	Tobacco is the only ban for independent TV stations.
Netherlands	5.32	2	246	Advertising is managed by an	Tobacco is banned.
Norway	1.55	–	–	Commercials not allowed.	All TV advertising.
Portugal	2.42	2	608	Both state run channels funded by advertising.	Tobacco banned. Alcohol allowed after 22.00 hours.
Spain	10.33	2	704	Only two state run channels offer national coverage although 3 regionals accepts advertising.	Tobacco, alcohol banned.
Sweden	3.33	–	–	Commercials not allowed on TV.	All TV advertising.
Switzerland	2.49	1	150	One state owned station consisting of 3 regionals serving the major language groups.	Alcohol, medicine, tobacco, religion, politics.
Turkey	6.00	2	224	Supply still inadequate, bookings made at beginning of the year.	Alcohol, medicine, tobacco, religion, politics are banned.
United Kingdom	20.60	3	1,354	Three majors of ITV, Channel 4 and TV-A.M.	Tobacco, spirits are banned.
W. Germany	25.34	4	451	Demand high, bookings made in Sept. for following year.	Tobacco, prescription drugs are banned.

Source: Advertising Age/James Capel.

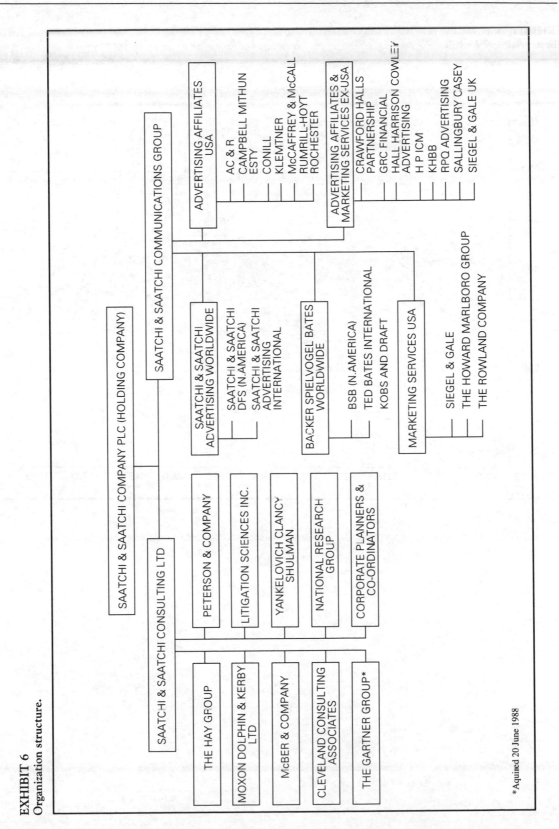

EXHIBIT 6
Organization structure.

The chart shows the following organization structure:

SAATCHI & SAATCHI COMPANY PLC (HOLDING COMPANY)

Under the holding company:

SAATCHI & SAATCHI CONSULTING LTD
- THE HAY GROUP
  - MOXON DOLPHIN & KERBY LTD
- PETERSON & COMPANY
  - McBER & COMPANY
- LITIGATION SCIENCES INC.
- YANKELOVICH CLANCY SHULMAN
- NATIONAL RESEARCH GROUP
  - CLEVELAND CONSULTING ASSOCIATES
- CORPORATE PLANNERS & CO-ORDINATORS
  - THE GARTNER GROUP*

SAATCHI & SAATCHI COMMUNICATIONS GROUP

- **SAATCHI & SAATCHI ADVERTISING WORLDWIDE**
  - SAATCHI & SAATCHI DFS (N.AMERICA)
  - SAATCHI & SAATCHI ADVERTISING INTERNATIONAL
- **BACKER SPIELVOGEL BATES WORLDWIDE**
  - BSB (N.AMERICA)
  - TED BATES INTERNATIONAL
  - KOBS AND DRAFT
- **MARKETING SERVICES USA**
  - SIEGEL & GALE
  - THE HOWARD MARLBORO GROUP
  - THE ROWLAND COMPANY

- **ADVERTISING AFFILIATES USA**
  - AC & R
  - CAMPBELL MITHUN
  - ESTY
  - CONILL
  - KLEMTNER
  - McCAFFREY & McCALL
  - RUMRILL-HOYT
  - ROCHESTER

- **ADVERTISING AFFILIATES & MARKETING SERVICES EX-USA**
  - CRAWFORD HALLS PARTNERSHIP
  - GRC FINANCIAL
  - HALL HARRISON COWLEY ADVERTISING
  - H P ICM
  - KHBB
  - RPQ ADVERTISING
  - SALLINGBURY CASEY
  - SIEGEL & GALE UK

*Aquired 20 June 1988

EXHIBIT 7
Share price 1979 – 89.

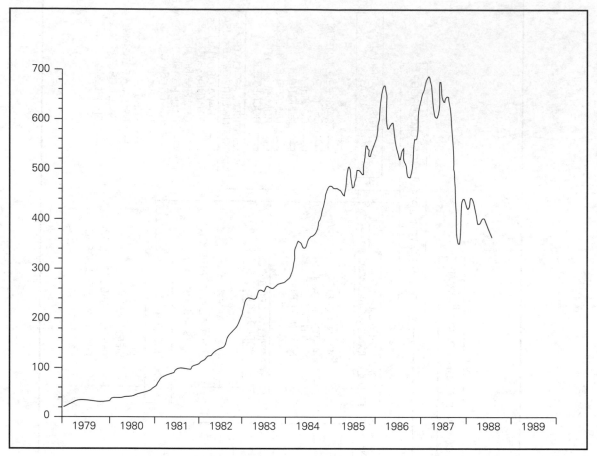

3–4

ANDERSEN CONSULTING (EUROPE): ENTERING THE BUSINESS OF BUSINESS INTEGRATION

A partner in Andersen Consulting defined its business as 'helping clients manage complexity'. As information systems technology progressed over the decades, Andersen emerged as the world's largest information systems consulting company through 'analyzing and then systematizing business's current information requirements into commodity products and then quickly proceeding to the next tier of complexity'. According to Terry Neill, head of services for the company's UK office: 'Andersen's greatest challenge is constant commoditization of its products and services. Our success depends on our ability to stay ahead of the commoditization envelope.'

In the 1940s, Andersen's expertise lay in designing the complex and manual accounting processes required in corporations to meet the increased reporting demanded by the Securities and Exchange Commission (SEC) in the United States. The business had become routine by the 1950s with many companies able to do the work as efficiently and cost-effectively as Andersen, but by this time Andersen had moved on to the next emerging business system requirement which had never been done before: payroll systems. These had become commonplace by the 1960s and the firm had proceeded on to the development and integration of computerized accounting and payroll systems. Likewise, with the introduction of personal computers, networks and fast-paced change in the capability of hardware and software, the 1970s and

This case was prepared by Mary Ackenhusen, Research Associate, under the supervision of Sumantra Ghoshal, Associate Professor at INSEAD. It is intended to be used as a basis for class discussion rather than to illustrate either effective or ineffective handling of an administrative situation.
Copyright © 1992, by INSEAD, Fontainebleau, France.
Financial support from the INSEAD Alumni Fund European Case Programme is gratefully acknowledged.

1980s offered a constant stream of new opportunities as the company's clients struggled to exploit these new technologies to manage the increasing complexity of their businesses.

The emerging business integration market, described by Andersen as the clients' need for an integrated business, information and people strategy, was the company's target for the 1990s. Building from its unequalled strength in systems integration, Andersen sought to broaden its capabilities so as to be able to help clients formulate and implement strategic thrusts, which encompassed all activities and functions on an integrated basis.

This new business vision presented an enormous challenge for the company. While there was a broad agreement among the senior partners about the need for pursuing the business integration market, there were considerable differences of opinion on how to implement the strategy without sacrificing the strengths inherent in Andersen's traditional organizational values and management processes. There were also some significant differences in the market structures in different countries which called for a delicate balancing between the need for a coherent worldwide business integration strategy and the demand for different implementation approaches to suit the context of different national operations. Further, the thrust into the business integration market also required the development of two new skill areas – namely, strategy and change management – and the seamless integration of those skills into the existing organizations which supported Andersen's unique strengths in systems integration and information technology. To integrate the client's business, Andersen needed first to integrate its own business, which could prove to be the most difficult task the company had faced yet.

ARTHER ANDERSEN AND COMPANY

In 1913, Arthur Andersen, the son of Scandinavian immigrant parents, purchased a small audit firm in Chicago which had since grown into the major accounting and consulting firm of Arthur Andersen. Andersen's vision was to establish 'a firm that will do more than routine auditing . . . a firm where we can measure our contribution more by the quality of the services rendered than by whether we are getting a good living out of it.' For more than three-quarters of a century, his philosophies have continued to influence the firm's culture as well as the profession of accounting as a whole.

Andersen wanted to build a practice with intelligent, well-trained people, but he could not find them through the profession's traditional method of hiring high school and commercial school graduates. At this time he was also teaching accounting at Northwestern (a major US business school) and he began recruiting his brightest students. This meant he had to pay more for his staff, but he found that the extra productivity and comprehensive understanding of business they brought with them was worth the higher cost. Andersen also started the then unheard of practice of paying his employees during their training period. In other accounting firms, the employee paid the firm during this period of apprenticeship.

Andersen ingrained in his company the concept that the client always came first, regardless of personal sacrifice – evenings and weekends were not sacred. 'The client deserves our best, regardless.' To help support this philosophy, Andersen initiated the practice of paying his employees overtime in the face of strong criticism from the major accounting firms of the day.

Extensive professional training, which became a well-known distinguishing feature of the company, had its roots in the 1920s. Training was strongly advocated by Andersen, beginning with mandatory lectures given by him and by other senior partners several times a week in the office and expanding to a rigorous course developed in the 1940s designed to teach common standards to all US Andersen employees. From the beginning, these courses were taught by insiders. It was Andersen's belief that 'lectures should be given by men in our own organization who have pedagogical inclinations because these men [understand] our methods and procedures.'

The culture built by Andersen was one of inscrutable professional honesty even at the cost of losing a client. He always said that if the staff 'thought straight and talked straight', they would earn the respect of clients. According to former CEO Duane Kullberg, 'Those remain words we live by – not simply a hand-me-down slogan.'

The firm outpaced market growth in the 1950s and 1960s, expanding internationally and domestically through a mixture of a few high-quality acquisitions and the establishment of new offices. This period also saw the beginnings of the consulting arm of the business which helped fuel growth in the 1970s when the market for audit began to stagnate. The consulting business continued to be the major impetus for growth through the 1980s.

Andersen Consulting

The origins of the Andersen Consulting practice lay in the industrial engineering function sponsored by the firm's founder, the purpose being to 'show the strong or weak points in company position or management, and seek to correct such weak spots'. This function was given second priority to the audit business through the 1940s until, in 1951, Joe Glickauf, an influential partner, built a copy of an advanced design computer which had been developed at the University of Pennsylvania. When he presented it to the partners with his vision of what it could mean for the future of business systems, they voted to give full support to the development of the area. The implementation of an automated payroll system at GE in 1952 was Andersen's first computer-based project – it is believed to be the first commercial application of a computer.

Since the 1950s, Andersen's consulting business has grown quickly with the advancement of information technology and its capabilities. The strong culture and training infrastructure established by Arthur Andersen for the accounting practice have proved to be key strengths in this business also. Initially, clients came from the customer base in the audit business but by 1990 their share had declined to less than 20 per cent. By 1990, Andersen Consulting had emerged as the largest player in information systems consulting and was, in fact, the largest consulting company in the world, with over 20,000 professionals, operating in more than 50 countries. Worldwide revenues of $1.9 billion represented a compounded annual growth rate of 30 per cent between 1985 and 1990 (see Exhibit 1). The company designed and implemented large-scale information systems and provided all associated services including programming and training of client personnel. Andersen also developed and marketed its own proprietary software and was an increasingly active player in the business of facilities management (i.e. managing computer operations outsources by its clients).

Andersen the man always stressed homogeneity within Andersen the firm, with his maxim, 'one firm, one voice'. Continuous reinforcement of this principle through standardized training and extensive formalization of work procedures positioned the firm for consistent service and methods across all offices and all countries. By the late 1980s, maintenance of the 'one firm' concept became increasingly difficult as Andersen began to branch off into two distinctly different businesses – audit and tax on the one hand, and consulting on the other – with vastly different professional norms, market structures, business approaches and compensation levels in the two activities. Matters came to a head with the increasing demand of consulting partners for remuneration consistent with the significantly higher profitability and growth of the consulting practice, and in 1988 the two businesses were formally separated into two division. The consulting arm was renamed Andersen Consulting and was given the freedom to develop its own compensation system and management structure (Exhibit 2). While a 24-member board of partners retained responsibility for providing oversight of the company as a whole, both strategic business units now had significant strategic and operational autonomy so that each could respond most effectively to its own market and business needs.

Andersen Consulting (Europe, Middle East, Africa and India)

Andersen Consulting in Europe, the Middle East, Africa and India (EMEAI) emerged as a separate entity when the management of the tax/audit and consulting businesses was divided. In 1990, Andersen EMEAI had offices in 18 countries staffed with 6,500 professionals who generated total 1,990 billings of $695 million. This made it the largest consultancy in Europe in terms of gross revenues. The EMEAI practice had been growing at a rate of 28 per cent per year in people terms over the preceding five years.

The Andersen organization (see Exhibit 3 for the EMEAI organizational structure) was built around a geographic base of country practices. A matrix structure including industry functions, specialty skills and functional skills was overlaid on top of this legally autonomous aggregation of national practices, creating an organization of considerable complexity.

Each country, or country group, was managed by a country managing partner who had reporting to him or her three industry sector heads and several heads of specialty skill or functional areas. The three industry sectors were Financial Services, Industrial and Consumer Products, and Government and Services. The number and types of speciality and functional heads depended on the size and expertise of the office and included strategy and change management. Every professional in a country reported to either an industry, specialty skills, or functional head. Additionally, larger countries often had a varying number of industry subsector heads (e.g. oil and gas) and functional managers (e.g. logistics). These partners had no direct reports and reported into one of the industry sectors.

Each country was responsible for effectively utilizing its professionals to meet annual, and multi-annual, fee and productivity targets. A country managing partner's most important job was the management of his or her people resource to assure they were either utilized within the country practice or loaned out to support a job outside the country practice and therefore still effectively utilized.

Vernon Ellis, the managing partner of EMEAI, was based in the United Kingdom. Each country managing partner reported to him, as did the European heads of each of the three industry sectors and the heads of the specialty and functional skill areas. These regional sector or functional managers were responsible for practice leadership which included setting strategy and assisting in the staffing and execution of projects in their respective areas, and were linked to their counterparts in the country offices through what were referred to as 'dotted line relationships'.

THE ANDERSEN WAY

While all professional service firms assert that people are their key asset, at Andersen Consulting this assertion was translated into a set of institutionalized practices that lay at the core of what was often described both within and outside the company as the 'Andersen way'. The company invested heavily in building the capabilities of its people and the systems which supported them. These assets were then effectively leveraged through the project team structure to provide value to the client.

Building Capabilities: Developing People

The training infrastructure was one of the key distinguishing features of Andersen. Every new employee worldwide was required to take a six-week course, Computer Application Programming School (CAPS), taught in Andersen's luxurious St Charles (Illinois) Education facility which was referred to, not inappropriately, as 'the university'. This rigorous course taught the fundamentals of computer applications and programming through intensive work sessions designed to simulate project work at a client site. Eighty-hour weeks and the requirement of business attire throughout the programme made the simulation realistic and also emphasized that 'at Andersen, training is a serious business.' The same methods were used to teach liberal arts majors and engineers alike in the Andersen methodology of systems design and implementation. As one senior partner described:

> CAPS is a real shock at first . . . you wonder how you'll be able to keep up, it is very intense . . . but then you find that everyone is in this together and you begin working as a team helping each other to pull through. And since then, this group has been my main network within the company. The experience created a career-long bond with these cohorts.

Andersen Consulting educated all its professionals in a uniform approach to each aspect of a job whether it was systems design, programming, project management or writing a proposal for new business. The tools were designed to eliminate any ambiguity in the nuts and bolts of a project. This common tool set embodied in numerous, thick reference manuals was used worldwide to assure consistency in firm performance and to enhance the ability of consultants from different countries and disciplines to work together. In combination, the uniform training programme at St

Charles with the immense documentation tools provided the core of Andersen's success in management information consulting: the ability to hire new undergraduates and in six weeks turn them into productive, billable programmers.

Training continued throughout a professional's career with a standardized system that required everyone to spend nearly 1,000 hours over a five-year period in training, undertaking a pre-specified set of courses at pre-designated intervals (see Exhibit 4). All training still conformed to Andersen's original contention that the best teacher came from within, allowing the more senior professionals to impart their learning to the new recruits. All offices of the company around the world were allocated a fixed number of hours of training they had to staff and faculty roles were allocated within the office among partners and other experienced staff. The internal faculty was supplied with standard material for teaching their classes, but was also encouraged to embellish their sessions with examples from their most recent assignments. These new case stories were then incorporated into the teaching material that was provided to the next faculty for the same sessions. Approximately £35,000 were spent on a new employee in the first five years and an extraordinary 10 per cent of Andersen's revenue was allocated to professional training. Internally, training was emphasized as an important benefit of working for Andersen: 'Your skills aren't just good news for the client. After training with Andersen Consulting, you could work for anyone, anywhere or you could work for yourself.'

The majority of Andersen's recruiting historically had been targeted at young undergraduates directly out of university. Each recruit had to undergo extensive interviewing and the objective was to seek out bright achievers who could best be 'moulded' into the Andersen pattern with the expectation of a long career in the firm. Recruiting was a major activity for all professionals at Andersen's including the partners. Likewise, the developing and nurturing of new recruits was an important part of upper management's role. Andersen partners were involved in subordinate development through a formal counselling programme. Each new employee was assigned a counselling partner upon arrival and met with this partner every six months to discuss performance, career interests and other pertinent topics. Each partner counselled 20–30 professional personnel.

The typical career path with Andersen Consulting began with 1–2 years as an assistant consultant working mainly on large systems integration projects as a programmer, with regular formal and informal training in information technology and business skills. The next 3–5 years as a senior consultant were spent broadening technical and business skills in client engagements with more specialized training. In 5–8 years, a professional could be expected to take on the role of project manager and in 9–12 years, most recruits still with the firm would be expected to become a partner.

Like universities, Andersen followed the up or out principles of a meritocracy: each individual either performed well and moved up the ladder, or left the firm, opening up opportunities for those behind in the queue. The evaluation process was tough: only 50–60 per cent of new professional recruits would become a manager and perhaps 10 per cent would ever become a partner.

Assistant and senior consultants were evaluated on their performance every three months by their project managers. The evaluations were taken very seriously by both sides and were a valuable tool for performance improvements. Theoretically, project managers were evaluated themselves every six months by their project partner, but these often turned into self-evaluations due to limited partner time for the process. Consultant and manager compensation was strictly based on merit, though the range between an outstanding performer and a satisfactory performer was less than in other comparable companies. There was no bonus or profit-sharing below the partner level.

To facilitate personal development and professional contacts, Andersen Consulting prided itself on its vast and varied methods of communication within the firm. Every industry, functional and country group had at least one newsletter which helped the fast-paced professionals stay on top of new projects, successes and issues in their areas of interest. Likewise, these groups often sponsored conferences and circulated files of interesting papers on current issues. For those consultants with a wide area of interest, oversaturation, not lack of communication, was the problem.

The continuous training at St Charles and the European centre in Eindhoven (Holland) provided professional and social stimulation. To help retain a small firm feeling, personnel groups of 100–200 people were formed solely for the purpose of regular social gatherings. Upward communication with the partners was also facilitated through informal partner/manager dinners held on a regular basis.

The end-result was a strong cultural 'glue' which helped Andersen employees to understand each others' objectives, methods and motivations across offices and functions. They grew up together after college with the same experiences and values. As one manager remarked:

> It's hard for outsiders to work for Andersen. They just don't know our vocabulary, our systems. While those who grow up in Andersen can carry out a task based on one sentence directions, an outsider will be lost. Andersen's can think alike.

Other firms in the industry expressed both their envy and their scorn for this strong internal homogeneity by the label 'Andersen Androids', which was almost a source of pride within the company.

Leveraging Capabilities: Managing Project Teams

The project team was the main organizational unit of Andersen for leveraging the capabilities of its people to deliver value to the client. Each team was made up of at least one partner, one manager and a number of junior level consultants, and utilized the worldwide network of experts to participate on the team or advise. The ratio of partner time to consultant time attributed to the project determined the economics of the project and therefore, of the firm. At Andersen, the partner to consultant ratio was very low with, for example, only 180 partners out of 6,500 professionals in EMEAI, which resulted in high compensation for the partners leveraged off the large base of associate and senior consultants. Somewhat offsetting the favourable economics of a high consultant to partner ratio, target utilization rates were lower than the industry norm due to the emphasis on training and other forms of personnel development. Target rates for partner, manager and consultant levels were 50 per cent, 75 per cent and 80 per cent respectively. Nevertheless, this ability to leverage the expertise of partners across a large base of consultants was why Andersen partners were among the most highly compensated in the industry. (See Exhibit 5 to review the economics of a typical professional service firm.)

A project manager was chosen by the partner managing the case based on skills, past experience and availability. The company had a database detailing each professional's skills and experience by industry and client, as well as his or her current assignment and availability. Partners complained, however, that it was too hard to codify all the important characteristics of a team player and the database was typically used only as a last resort. The personal networks of the partners were often more important for selecting project managers and later staffing the teams.

With the partner's guidance, the project manager built the team and provided day-to-day management in the execution of the project. To staff a project, the manager would call on the worldwide resources of Andersen to get the proper fit. For example, for a project at Jaguar, the UK office, which had done relatively little work in the automotive field, borrowed personnel from the Paris office which had worked extensively with Renault and Peugeot. The manager was also responsible for meeting budget and time commitments and for the professional development of team members. People management was a very important part of this job.

Availability was the key to forming a team and therefore the scheduling database, which detailed was who available and when, was the most utilized formal database within Andersen. Each consultant was expected to be 80 per cent utilized on client projects with the other 20 per cent of his or her time being spent in training, other personal development activities, or downtime. The Andersen culture would rarely allow someone to be pulled from a case before its completion: the client's needs came before the business's. Therefore, there was a relatively limited pool of available talent to be placed on a team and there were considerable pressures to utilize anyone not currently on a team. Though Andersen professionals had some latitude in choosing projects which met their own career development needs, most conceded that the system did not and probably could not be expected to support this objective fully.

Providing Stewardship: The Role of Partners

Partners at Andersen spent 50 per cent of their time on case work, 25 per cent selling new projects and 25 per cent on development of subordinates. The partners were seen as the entrepreneurs of the business because they traditionally developed their own portfolio of business based on their own contacts and interests.

Each partner owned a piece of the firm and participated in the management of the firm on a one-person, one-vote basis. According to one partner, 'This is how we challenge sacred cows. Ownership is a great driver of arguments and strong opinions.'

Partners shared costs on a worldwide basis. Partner income was determined by a distribution formula based on the number of his or her units. Unit allocations were set by a partner committee which evaluated business generated, business performed, development of personnel, teamwork, practice leadership, unique skills and other areas. Practice management partners evaluated all partners working for them and other partners could contribute to the review process as they felt appropriate. All management partners were evaluated by a comprehensive process of upward evaluation which was set up to be non-attributable, though many partners chose to discuss their feedback with the management partners they were evaluating. All partners received a listing of the unit allocations of every other partner in the world. Though there was an appeal process, it was rarely used. In general, the partners approved of the fairness of the evaluation and compensation systems. As described by one, 'It may not be perfect every year, but over a period of time, everyone seems to get what they are due.'

The partners saw themselves as the stewards of the firm who should continue to strengthen the firm for those who would follow. Sacrificing immediate personal income for the long-term benefit of the firm was a cherished norm. The first international expansion of the Company in 1957 provides a good example. The proposal to open new offices in Paris, London and Mexico was brought to the partners' meeting after the profits for the year had already been disbursed to them. Client needs required immediate opening of these offices, and the partners decided to pay back 40 per cent of their income so that the firm could expand even though many of them would not serve in the company long enough to reap the benefits. Likewise, year after year, the partners continued to approve the tremendous investment in the training of future generation of Andersens. When a partner retired he took with him only his initial capital investment in the firm, and no appreciation or goodwill accumulated over his period of partnership. One partner reflected, 'The style of the organization is set by high quality people with high values which we pass on to the next generation. It's a strong cultural influence.'

THE BUSINESS OF BUSINESS INTEGRATION

The informational technology (IT) consulting business could be divided into two broad segments. The first segment, also the larger and the more traditional of the two, was the IT professional services market that included custom software development, consulting, education and training, and systems operations. The other more complex segment was the systems integration market which was when one company took the technical and administrative responsibility for tying together information networks potentially involving multiple hardware and software vendors and multiple corporate functions. Systems integration projects usually ranged from $1–10 million in the commercial sector, but could go as high as $100 million for large-scale government projects.

In 1989, the IT professional service market for Europe exceeded $15 billion and was growing at the rate of 20 per cent per year. The 1994 market size was expected to approach $39 billion of which 68 per cent was attributed to custom software development. The systems integration market was only $1.9 billion in 1989 but was expected to grow to $6 billion by 1994 (over 30 per cent per year), with over half of this revenue coming from associated consulting services. In comparison, the systems integration market in the United States had grown to $8.8 billion by 1990 and was expected to grow to $20.5 billion by 1995.

Both the size and growth rate made the systems integration and professional services markets very enticing to most key competitors in the information field. The high growth rate was attributable to the decentralization of in-house information systems departments, fast-paced technological changes with the associated new product introductions, the externalization of in-house corporate services and the ongoing restructuring of major industrial markets.

European competition in such attractive markets was stiff and was continuing to attract new entrants. In professional services, the market was quite fragmented with the key competitors being IBM (5.3 per cent), Cap Gemini Sogeti, the French software multinational (4.7 per cent), and Volmac, a Dutch software company which received 90 per cent of its revenues from the Netherlands (2.0 per cent). Andersen was ranked number 13 with a 0.8 per cent market share. The top three competitors in systems integration and their European market shares were IBM (12.5 per cent), Cap Gemini Sogeti (11.8 per cent) and Andersen Consulting (10.2 per cent). (See Exhibit 6 for other competitors.)

Many of these companies also competed in the related businesses of facilities management and packaged software. Facilities management was an important market because it could often be an entry into a systems integration project; likewise it helped systems integration firms hone their technical skills. Packaged software was important because many clients demanded standardized solutions from a vendor before they would consider a later purchase of professional services. Andersen Consulting had become quite active in both markets.

From Systems Integration to Business Integration

The systems integration market had been experiencing serious quality problems as projects fell short of client expectations in functionality, cost and completion deadlines. It was increasingly believed that the potential of IT could not be realized until a firm had a clear business strategy to direct the use of IT and had made the necessary organizational changes to IT to support a new way of doing business. Overlay of new IT capabilities on existing business practices rarely yielded the potential or expected benefits: the real pay-off lay in utilizing the new technology to support fundamental redirection of busness strategy and management processes. This realization was the driving force behind the need for an integrated business philosophy and hence the potential of a business integration consulting market as the next level of complexity beyond the systems integration market.

According to Andersen's preliminary market research, only a few European clients recognized the need to better integrate their functional consulting requirements to produce an integrated business strategy through the engagement of one firm. Nevertheless, the company felt confident the market was going that way and had decided to build the competencies and infrastructure to exploit what they expected to be the new opportunity of the 1990s.

Key competitors in the emerging business integration market were potentially the same as in the systems integration market, with the addition of the general consulting firms. The traditional software and hardware companies such as Cap Gemini, IBM and DEC were considered to be strong competitors with perhaps unequalled technical expertise but lacking in project management skills. Systems integrators like SD-Scicon and Sema, two European based companies specializing in software services and integration, were also seen to be technically strong and further along in the task of building the needed project management skills. The large accounting firms were serious competitors in terms of project management skills, with less perceived competence in technical areas. Lastly, the general consulting firms, McKinsey, PA Consulting and others, had excellent reputations for their ability to develop and implement corporate strategies, easy access to corporate board rooms, some experience in systems design, but minimal systems implementation experience.

Many of these companies had already begun to prepare for an expanded business integration market by taking action to broaden their skill base or geographic scope through mergers, acquisitions and alliances. IBM had taken minority positions in numerous companies with large European market shares, and Andersen had developed numerous strategic alliances with companies such as DEC, IBM and Sun Microsystems. SEMA and SD-Scicon were both results of recent mergers.

Andersen's Entry into Business Integration

The need to link an IT project to the rest of the business was not a new concept to Andersen though it was not formally recognized as Andersen's strategic thrust under the name of 'business integration' until 1988. Even before formal recognition of the strategy, specialists were being groomed in two key areas where Andersen did not yet have a reputation and skill base, namely Strategy and human resource Change Management. In 1987, these became the separate practice areas of Strategic Services and Change Management. Shortly thereafter, the formal concept of business integration with its associated four bubble graphic (see Exhibit 7) was adopted by Andersen Consulting, who described business integration as:

> A seamless combination of skills from each of the four areas: strategy, technology, operations and people. In developing business solutions it [is] necessary to consider all four areas and select in the appropriate balance, using different proportions in different situations. [This requires] people who are not narrowly based in a single discipline but who combine knowledge and understanding of each of these different areas.

In support of the four functions, four centres of excellence were formed: Strategic Services, Chanage Management, Operations and Information Technology. The Strategic Services group worked with clients to develop and implement successful strategies in all areas of corporate activity. The Change Management group worked with organizations to position their people, processes and technology to master change with maximum benefits. The Operations group helped clients develop effective day-to-day processes including implementation of JIT systems, plant re-layouts, quality assurance systems, etc., and the Information Technology group contained very specialized hardware and software experts to assist in implementing state-of-the-art customer solutions. For most country organizations, only Strategic Services and Change Management were distinct skill sets; Operations and Information Technology were still located within other functional or industry groups.

These specialty areas were geared to building up repeat and continuous experience in their respective areas of a world class nature. The IT generalist background of a standard Andersen consultant was deemed unsuitable to efficiently support these specialty areas to the level needed to compete in the emerging business integration market. As described by Vernon Ellis:

> You could try to produce a complete Renaissance man but it is impossible these days. The business world is too complex .... We need both generalists and specialists. Some people will be in just one bubble, some in the middle of all the bubbles, and some at specific intersections.

In numbers, these specialists were few compared to the rest of Andersen. In 1989/90, there were 170 strategy specialists and 290 change specialists within EMEAI. The majority of Andersen professionals were the IT generalists (the 'engine room', as described by one consultant) in the middle of the graphic bubble chart – although the vast majority of these 'IT generalists' specialized in an industry or industry sector. IT generalists were the people doing the execution and had a 'delivery mechanism' skill set. They were expected to have a good general business understanding of each of the specialists areas as well as a thorough knowledge of the IT area, Andersen's traditional strength. The project manager's challenge was to glue the expertise of the specialists and the business understanding of the generalists together into a successful project team.

The Experience at National Power

A business integration case often developed through an evolutionary process. As described by Vernon Ellis, 'Usually we start with one aspect of a project and hopefully it broadens into a business integration project. Our aim is not to sell more work but to make sure the end result is better implementation.'

National Power in the United Kingdom was recently given the mandate to privatize, and called on Andersen Consulting to assist them in this major operational, organizational and cultural change. Tim Forrest, who was also the industry head for Oil and Gas/Energy in Europe, served as the partner on the initial engagement.

The team was composed of 15 Andersen consultants and included specialists from each of the centres of excellence. Forrest estimated that the project fell into the four areas of business integration as follows: Strategy (10–15 per cent), Information Technology (40–50 per cent), Operations (25 per cent) and Change Management (15 per cent).

The first three months were spent deciding on the new mission of the company. The objectives articulated by National Power upon engaging Andersen were: (1) to become a cost-effective supplier of electricity, (2) to take advantage of market opportunities and (3) to diversify into new businesses to optimize revenue.

Tim Forrest gave his view on what Andersen offered as strategic input to this mission:

> It was really to make the strategy work. It was partly to flesh out the ideas they had, because they were very conceptual. Within each area, there were myriads of things that needed to be done in every part of the organization. The Strategic Services people talked to a variety of National Power managers at different levels to get some specific definitions of what the company would do differently in the future and to ascertain what it would take to do those things differently.

In evaluating the contribution of the Change Management personnel, Forrest commented:

> Initially they were focused on IT because the IT department had been 1,200 people two years ago. At the beginning of the year it was split three ways . . . 300 was all that was left . . . . Basically they were in a very depressed state, they didn't know what the company was trying to do . . . . They didn't understand the IT strategy or the business strategy, so initially the Change Management people were very much focused on talking to as

many senior people as they could within the IT department to find out what their concerns were.... Once they got these people reasonably motivated and fired up, they then started to optimize the communication the other way [to the user community].

The technology and operations content of National Power was the type of work that Andersen had specialized in for many years. After developing strategic objectives, critical success factors and key performance indicators for each area, elaborate IT systems and operational systems were designed in the areas of Work Management, Inventory Management, Operational Information and Project Management Systems.

In evaluating the relationship between the various Centres of Excellence and the generalist practice, Time Forrest stated:

The core of the business is still the same [the IT/Operations concentration]. Change Management helps us to do lots of things we've done for the last 20 years, only we now do them very much better. There's nothing particularly new about Change Management . . . they're extremely good at forcing us to think more about cultural change and the impact of technology on people . . . quite honestly, the strategy input is a bit the same, or at least on many projects it is like that. Strategy is forcing the project team to think, well what are we really trying to do with this system? . . . In relation to our main practice, it is the discipline that helps us do our main job better.

THE CHALLENGE OF MANAGING COMPLEXITY

By 1990, the strategy of business integration had been well-communicated and widely accepted within Andersen, though there were some different internal views on how the company was pursuing the market. Vernon Ellis recognized this lack of clarity:

There are still conferences and debates on the strategy, which reflects an emerging understanding with no clear answer yet. We may be actually facing dichotomies to a certain extent which are not capable of resolution.

Balancing Conflicting Demands

At the core of these dichotomies lay the conflicting needs for building best-in-class capabilities in each of the skill areas needed to support the business integration strategy and the demand for integrating those skills internally in a matter that would provide Andersen with some competitive advantage over the scores of other companies targeting the same opportunity. As described by Terry Neill:

We are the best in the business systems piece. What goes with strategy or change is that we have to be the best in each piece. In strategy, there are established leaders like McKinsey and our challenge is to develop a reputation as good as theirs. The change management business is still fragmented, just like the IT marketplace in the 1960s and 1970s, with small 'guru' style firms and individuals. We are doing the same thing in change management that we did there.

Gerard Van Kemmel, managing partner of France, agreed:

I don't believe clients will buy a business integration project unless the supplier is the most skilled and best value in each area. Otherwise, a customer will hire the best firms and integrate themselves.

The other internal viewpoint stressed the importance of integrating the functional pieces of a customer solution.

> I don't think we want our strategic services practice to be the same as McKinsey's. We want the market to accept that we do strategic services work, but if that was all we had, we would be no better than McKinsey. I think that's why the integration bit, the fact that we can talk readily across into the other areas, and that we offer the portfolio, is a very strong message. Otherwise, we could just divide the building into four wings and put McKinsey down one wing, Andersen down another wing, someone who was good at change in another wing, and then some technology experts down the fourth wing.

And, while the two perspectives were not necessarily contradictory, their operational implications were not easy to reconcile. As described by an external industry analyst:

> If you want to be the best in each piece, you have to grow each activity separately – specialize each group with the most challenging assignments dedicated to its particular area. If you want to really integrate, you need to develop a different model of what strategy and change is all about, redefining them from the perspective of integrated delivery. Best-in-class specialization and effective integration require not just different structures and management processes, but even different definitions and visions of what each bubble represents.

Further, some differences of views still lingered on the right balance between allowing individual partners and local practices the freedom to develop their businesses entrepreneurially, identifying and exploiting local opportunities, and the need for pursuing a coherent world-wide business integration strategy. As described by Ellis:

> Historically, our partners have been entrepreneurs and that is how Andersen has been so successful. Partners built their own practices based on their skills, interests and contacts. They managed the projects start to fnish. Now we need a different approach. A world-wide strategy requires that the partner finds the best person for each job, and often than person may not be him. We need a change in the partner mindset.

Terry Neill also suggested that perhaps there was a need to consider some fundamental organizational changes to adapt to the new strategic approach,

> Everyone here is a doer – that's our style – but sometimes we don't have enough people fully dedicated to thinking things through and that, sometimes, shows up. We have had occasional false starts. Perhaps we need a dedicated internal strategy and planning group – with young partners spending two or three years in the role – in much the same way as officers in the military spend short periods in staff roles as a key part of their career development.

Responding to National Differences

The corporate vision of business integration was not always mirrored at the country operating level. For example, the UK and French offices pursued the business integration market with varied implementation strategies due to the competitive and cultural differences of the two markets and historical differences in the two practices.

The French information technology market was the most developed in the world in terms of percentage of GNP spent on IT and was also the largest market in Europe. The market structure reflected a much clearer dichotomy between IT and business consulting. In the IT area, the market had several large world-class competitors such as Cap Gemini and Sema who were able to compete successfully with Andersen on a cost basis. From this 'IT only' view of the French market, Andersen was sometimes seen as a small player. In contrast, it was historically very strong in the sector of management consulting.

By some measures, the United Kingdom was the third largest IT market in Europe and also very competitive. Andersen was very successful in the United Kingdom because the market was willing to pay a relatively high rate due to the perception of extra value being added when performed by an 'integrator'. This meant that Andersen could often command significantly higher rates in the United Kingdom than France for IT work. On the other hand, Andersen's UK competitors would often try to position Andersen as IT consultants so as to undermine the market perception of Andersen's strengths in the business consulting area.

Culturally, in France, the corporate IT function was perceived to be of lesser stature than in the United Kingdom, where the top IT job was a key management position charged with helping the company integrate its business and information technology strategies. In France, the position of IT director was not seen to be the way to the top – top positions in corporations were reserved for the graduates of the elite *grandes écoles* system, a group to which the IT directors did not typically belong. The IT director had little or no voice in corporate strategy and top management issues. The result was that IT directors ran a relatively insular and controlled world without top management interference. When they hired consultants they looked for firms who were cheap, had a flexible workforce, and most importantly, would allow them full control of the project. A successful consultant in France would never go around the IT director to top management.

These market differences led to very different recruiting and development systems in the two countries. To develop and maintain the French strength in management consulting, the French office had always recruited from the *grandes écoles* educational system. These individuals were trained in the fundamentals of IT through the traditional Andersen course work (CAPS, etc.) but were only required to work in IT for a very limited time period (6–12 months) after which they were assigned to the management consulting practice.

The majority of Andersen employees in the French office focused on the IT business were not recruited from the *grandes écoles*. They were on different pay scales – although these were significantly in excess of their French IT competitors. One career track within this organization did draw from the *grandes écoles* system; these were the employees who helped integrate the IT business with management consulting when needed and who were the future partners of the IT business.

In contrast, the United Kingdom had always been much stronger in the IT business and recruited to develop and maintain this skill. Recruits came from the top British schools, were trained in the Andersen methodology, and were then required to work in systems design and programming for 3–5 years.

Because of these competitive, cultural and historical differences, the French and UK national organizations pursued some very different approaches in implementing the business integration strategy. The UK implementation replicated the corporate vision as laid out by Ellis. The course centres of excellence were integrated at the country level to present a 'seamless combination of skills' to the clients. The Strategy and Change Management areas were distinct organizations reporting into the Services industry subsector. The professional development infrastructure was the same for all professionals in terms of training requirements, salary structure and promotion opportunities.

The French model maintained separate organizations for the information technology business – Ingénierie Informatique – and the management consulting business – Stratégie and Management. Within Stratégie and Management, there was a very successful stand-alone practice in Change Management. The Strategic Services function was not a separate area within the management consulting arm because the French management felt their professionals were well-schooled in strategy, making it unnecessary to develop this expertise in a separate group. Although the two organizations sometimes sold their services separately, more than 80 per cent of their work was for common clients.

While recognizing that the French model was very different from the corporate blueprint, local management strongly believed that their approach was better suited at least for the French market. First, a distinct IT organization showed a commitment to Andersen's core expertise in information technology with a focus on productivity and skills. Second, the structure recognized the French market's IT business dichotomy and made IT directors more comfortable because they could deal with a separate consulting group as they always had in the past. Third, the structure allowed for recruitment of people with different profiles and expectations and made it possible for the company to remain as a cost-effective competitor in the traditional IT business while protecting the high-quality image necessary for success in the management consulting and business integration fields. Lastly, it allowed clients easily to buy only one service from Andersen (just IT or just consulting) as a stand-alone piece of work and to do the business integration themselves.

The long-term vision of how Andersen's strategy should be developed also varied between the two country offices. The United Kingdom was organized by three main industry groups – Financial Markets, Products and Services. A fourth division, Integration Services, housed specialist technology, software and systems management skills. The UK practice had three further centres of excellence – Strategy and Change Management, housed in Services, and Operations/Logistics, housed in Products. The French vision planned for a centre of excellence structure within each of the three industry groups (Financial Services, Products, and Services) as soon as each area had enough critical mass to justify the organization.

Developing New Capabilities

Of the four centres of excellence, the newly formalized areas of Strategic Services and Change Management were still establishing themselves both internally and externally. Change Management was challenged to establish a distinct skill set for itself. Its historical roots were to provide training to clients in support of large complex systems being installed by Andersen. However, since 1988, Change Management's scope had expanded rapidly to reflect the cultural and organizational challenges of major transformational change in large organizations. Change Management was defined in three practice areas: Technology Assimilation which supported the training and education needed to ensure that the expected benefits of major IT investments were fully delivered; Knowledge Transfer which covered training in all its aspects, including the use of training technologies; and Organization Change which included the strategic and tactical aspects of process and organizational change.

Much of Andersen's Change Management work in 1988 and 1989 was still in the training area (Knowledge Transfer) but the balance was rapidly changing as partners recognized the key role of the people and change dimensions in executing Andersen's business integration strategy. Because the Change Management market subsector was very fragmented with few large players, cost was an important element of competition.

Strategic Services marketed the following services in support of business integration: strategic management studies, competitive/industry analysis, market and sales planning, operational planning, information technology strategy and organizational strategy and change management. In reality, most Strategic Services work seemed to have an operational bent. As one partner described the practice:

> Most of the strategy work, after all, is concerned with sorting out strategies to optimize a business, rather than what company should I go and acquire in the marketplace. In other words, it's what I would call internal strategic consulting, rather than external strategy consulting.

Some partners had expressed concerns about the potential overlaps between the Change Management and Strategy skill sets as Change Management moved into organizational change work. Others shared Terry Neill's view:

> Executing our business integration vision requires that we be able to mobilize project teams with a portfolio of skills in systems, strategy, process and change management. We need world class skills in each dimension and the ability to bring them together for a client without the client having to concern himself about divisions which could be created by the internal structures of Andersen Consulting. We now have a dozen large high quality UK clients where we are making business integration a working reality. These companies are seeing the value of the skills portfolio and that will accelerate the removal of internal barriers. We are winning with those organizations who see the skills of strategy and execution being inextricably intertwined.

To fill the specialist needs, Andersen broke with its tradition of hiring recent graduates and 50 per cent of the centre of excellence hires were brought in as experienced 'outsiders' at senior and manager levels, while the other 50 per cent came from within the firm or were recruited at an MBA level from the outside. In general, Strategic Services recruited MBAs from top business schools, and Change Management brought in experienced individuals from the fields of organization change, industrial psychology and education. Though Andersen prided itself on growing organically and not through acquisition, a small manufacturing consulting firm was acquired in 1988 in the United Kingdom to enhance the skill base of the Operations specialty practice.

The new recruiting model and acquisition strategy required a rapid build-up of expertise and internal training. Some partners felt that Andersen made a slow start in this area. Nevertheless, good progress was made in 1990 and 1991 in building training and methodologies for the emerging Change Management and Strategy skill sets. Andersen's ability to roll out and deploy new training and approaches quickly and effectively was seen by several partners as the key to success in delivering on the business integration vision. On-the-job training was somewhat hindered because project opportunities for inexperienced newly trained specialists could only grow at the rate at which Andersen was succeeding in taking its business integration strategy to the market.

Absorbing a large number of outsiders was a significant challenge for a firm whose strong cultural roots were passed on from one generation of recruits to the next through the institutionalized mechanisms represented in the 'Andersen way'. Normally, similar training, work tools, experiences and ways of thinking made a team work smoothly. With the development of specialists within the centres of excellence, some of the common parameters were diluted. These outsiders came in at middle management levels with different ideals and methods weakening the cultural glue that had traditionally bound together a team of Andersen consultants.

The more experienced professionals hired from the 'outside' did not view the traditional Andersen training programme as an appropriate initiation for a senior employee. A recent MBA from a top institution recruited into Strategic Services was required to take the full six-week CAPS course at St Charles and then work for several months on a systems project – the typical progression for an undergraduate recruit. His view was that the requirement added no value, and he did not think it compared favourably to the first few months of strategy work that his counterparts at the strategy boutiques experienced. Likewise, a newly hired senior manager in Change Management who had refused to participate in the six-week course said, 'I would quit before I would take the CAPS course!'

Furthermore, there was a concern within the Strategic Services practice that the Andersen compensation/development philosophy was hampering their ability to recruit and retain top individuals. They felt there was a need to at least approach some of the benefits which were found at their competitor's shops. Base compensation was on par with the competition, but in the boom times for strategy consulting in the 1980s, some partners felt that Andersen's unwillingness to have bonuses might have put the firm at some disadvantage in recruiting. On the other hand, Andersen grew by nearly 40 per cent in the United Kingdom in 1991 while most of its competitors were laying off large numbers of people. Most felt that its approach was thus vindicated – especially since so many strategy consultants from other firms applied to join Andersen, partly because of its rapidly growing reputation in the strategy area.

The generalists, in contrast, complained that the recently recruited specialists did not know how to do things in the 'Andersen way' and did not want to take the time to learn. The opinion of a member of the Change Management group who had come through the traditional Andersen career path was, 'If you change the infrastructure and make it different than the rest of Andersen, the result will be a loss of trust.' Another generalist consultant agreed, 'We're somewhat suspicious of the Strategic Services and Change Management types, especially if they are an external hire but even if they were moved from the IT area of the practice.'

A specialist in the Change Management field saw the tension between the groups differently, 'Although less than 50 per cent of our consulting practice is now in the US, our origins in the Midwest leave strong cultural values. We tend not to appreciate gurus or luminaries. Apartness, or individual aggrandizement, is neither revered, rewarded nor encouraged.'

The result of these difficulties was that the turnover in Strategic Services and

Change Managements was higher than for the firm in general. Consequently, Andersen had begun to fine-tune the profile of a successful outside hire to more closely match the characteristics of an Andersen undergraduate recruit and the traditional Andersen culture. Additionally, the mandatory computer-based training that all Andersen recruits had been required to take in the past at St Charles was shortened, and in some cases waived, for outside manager-level recruits. There was no formal policy in this area, but increasing flexibility seemed to be the direction in which Andersen was heading.

Integrating the Multinational Network

Andersen saw one of its competitive advantages to be its ability to serve a multinational client, or a client who would like to become multinational, through its own network of multinational offices to provide an integrated, pan-European, or even worldwide, solution. This service created a need within Andersen for professionals who embodied a multinational perspective in terms of language, culture and business knowledge. As one partner explained:

> There are very few [companies] who can pull into a project the resources from around the world. I've got over 20,000 people, and somewhere in the world we can find that somebody who really does understand a particularly difficult problem.

But as Andersen grew in size and organizational complexity, the firm was finding it increasingly difficult to take advantage of its enormous people resources to develop, identify, and effectively utilize this multinational specialist. As expressed by Terry Neill:

> A key impediment could become our ability to share knowledge quickly. In the past we have done it entirely by the personal network . . . now we're too big to do this. We need to improve our own IT network. But we also need to protect and improve our informal human network. Both are difficult, but both are challenges we must respond to urgently.

After an individual was identified as being needed on a project team, the country manager had to agree to release the individual. Because the country manager was responsible for his or her own profits, and these specialists tended to be very effective on national cases, deployment of people to regional or worldwide project teams was becoming more and more a source of conflict. There were incentives within the partnership evaluation system which measured how well each partner supported the multinational practice needs, but in reality, it was recognized that country interests came first.

Andersen was also finding it hard to hire and develop enough consultants who wanted and had the ability to participate in multinational cases. Language and cultural differences were difficult to overcome and many consultants preferred not to work outside their local area.

In 1991, a pilot programme was introduced in the Strategic Services area to try to better develop and manage the valuable multinational specialist resource. Breaking from the traditional structure in which all professionals reported within a geographic region, a multinational specialist team was formed, which had a small centralized core in one country and a network of specialists located in various other countries, all reporting directly to the head of the team. As expressed by Bill Barnard, the partner in charge of Market Development for Europe who developed the programme:

> In areas where we have very few specialists, we can't afford to have them only work in one country. We need to move them into different countries to work multinationally which causes conflicts with the country managers. Some conflict is good but we need to protect these people and to help them get repeat experience and develop their skill sets. Otherwise, their experience gets lost.

Andersen also attacked this problem by trying to hire and develop people who liked multinational activity and by stressing in the education process that international relocation was part of the job. A human resource programme introduced in 1990 supported a small group of individuals for development through exchange programmes across Europe. Nevertheless, Bill Barnard predicted that it would take until the end of the century before Andersen worked as a truly integrated European operation.

EXHIBIT 1
Anderson Consulting financial summary.

	Worldwide			EMEAI		
	Net Revenues ($MM)	Partners	Professionals	Net Revenues ($MM)	Partners	Professionals
1991	2,256	755	21,668	908	191	7,751
1990	1,850	692	18,188	663	172	6,263
1989	1,433	586	15,373	465	143	4,974
1988	1,106	529	12,009	360	123	3,743
1987	828	469	9,231	236	108	2,858

Source: Company document.

EXHIDIT 2
Worldwide organization.

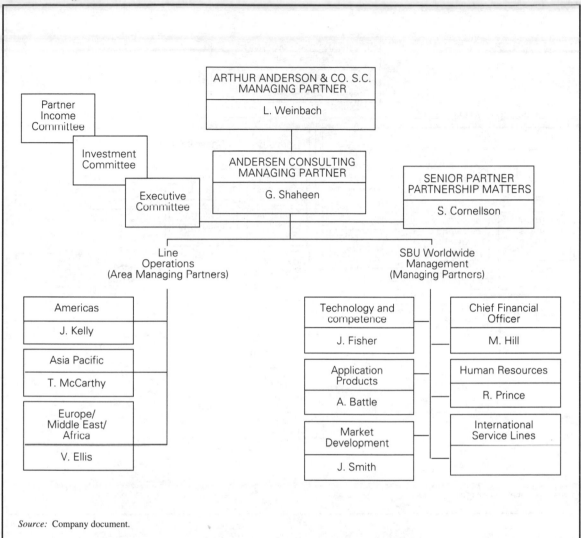

Source: Company document.

EXHIBIT 3
Anderson Consulting EMEAI organization.

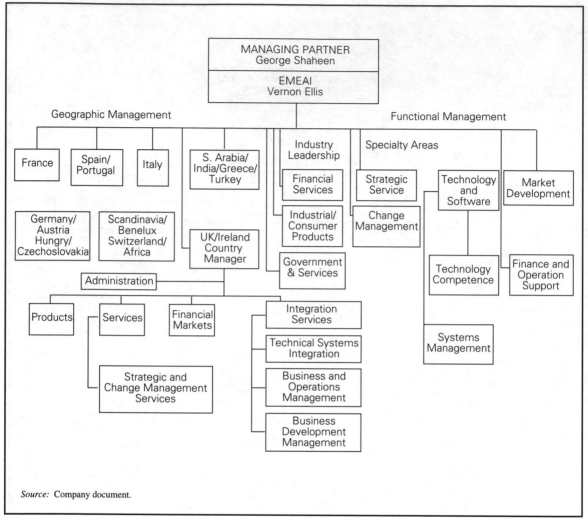

Source: Company document.

EXHIBIT 1
Graduate to manager.

Mandatory experience	Month 6–60	Minimum training hours
Orientation/SFC/CAPS		240
Basic accounting course		24
Programming/testing		
Introduction to financial and management information		24
		72
Business practices		138
Systems installation		
Programming supervision		
Detailed design		
System testing		
Conversion preparation		
Hardware/software evaluation		
Systems design		118
PSD – technical design		
– functional design		
Installation planning, organization and cost benefit analysis		
Elective schools/courses		280 approx
Special study		
Client service school		63
Information planning		
		259

Source: Company document.

EXHIBIT 5
Economics for typical professional service firm.

	Relative Number of Professionals By Level	Relative Net Billings per Head By Level	Relative Compensation of Professionals By Level
Consultant	100	100	100
Manager	40	156	250
Partner	20	208	633

Key Assumptions:
1. Target utilization: Consultant (90%), Manager (75%), Partner (75%).
2. Relative net billing per head = Relative billing rate/Hours × utilization rate × available hours;
   Relative billing rate/hours: Associate (100), Manager (187), Partner (250).
3. Relative Compensation = salary + bonus.
Source: 'Professional Service Firm Management', D. Maister, 1985.

EXHIBIT 6
IT professional services and systems integration (Europe) – key competitors.

Company	1988 European Prof. Services Est. Revenue ($m)	1988 European Prof. Services Market Share (%)	1988 European Systems Integr. Est. Revenue ($m)	1988 European Systems Integr. Market Share (%)	1989 World Revenue ($m)	1989 World Profit ($m)	Revenue CAGR (%) 1986–9	Profit CAGR (%) 1986–9
IBM	660	5.3	190	12.5	62,710	3,758	6.3	–7.8
Cap Gemini	590	4.7	180	11.8	1,202	89.4	34	40
Volmac	245	2.0	1	1	283	53	12[2]	4.1[2]
Finsiel	225	1.8	1	1	625	N/A	N/A	N/A
Sema	220	1.8	80	5.3	478	18	55	44
Bull	220	1.8	35	2.3	5,890	–48	23	N/A
Olivetti	200	1.6	45	2.9	7,406	166	7.3	–29
Unysis	180	1.4	55	3.6	10,097	–639	11	–145
Digital	140	1.1	1	1	12,742	1,073	19	20
SD-Scicon	140	1.1	85	5.6	462	5	66	3
Andersen	105	0.8	155	10.2	1,442	N/A	31	N/A
Logica	75	0.6	65	4.3	280	20	29	42
Siemens	80	0.6	65	4.3	32,398	836	8	2
Others	9,470	75	962	63	27	–	–	–
TOTAL	12,550	100	1,520	100				

1. Market share is insignificant and included in 'others'.
2. CAGR is 1987–9.
Source: Company document.

EXHIDIT 7
The business of business intergration.

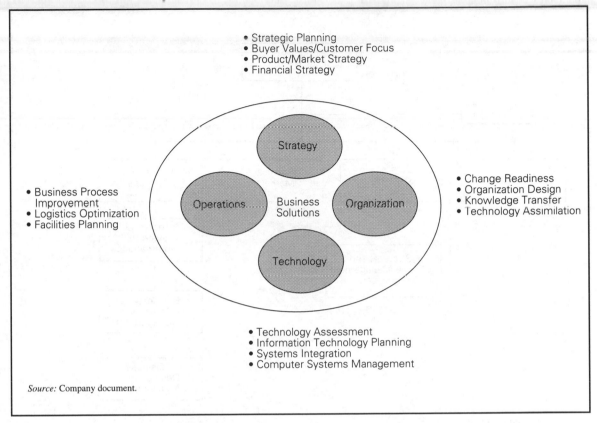

- Strategic Planning
- Buyer Values/Customer Focus
- Product/Market Strategy
- Financial Strategy

- Business Process Improvement
- Logistics Optimization
- Facilities Planning

- Change Readiness
- Organization Design
- Knowledge Transfer
- Technology Assimilation

Strategy

Operations   Business Solutions   Organization

Technology

- Technology Assessment
- Information Technology Planning
- Systems Integration
- Computer Systems Management

Source: Company document.

EXHIBIT 8
Anderson Consulting UK Ireland.

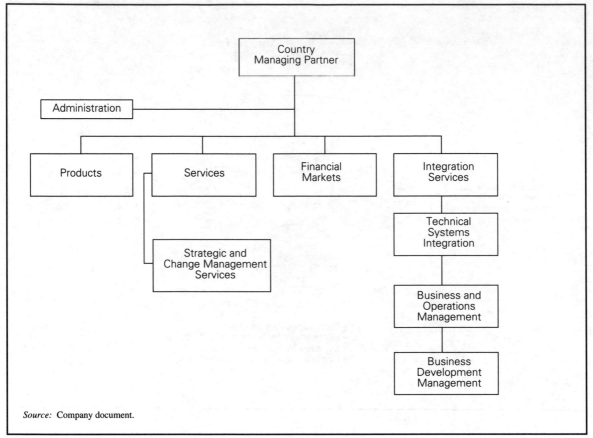

Source: Company document.

EXHIBIT 9
France.

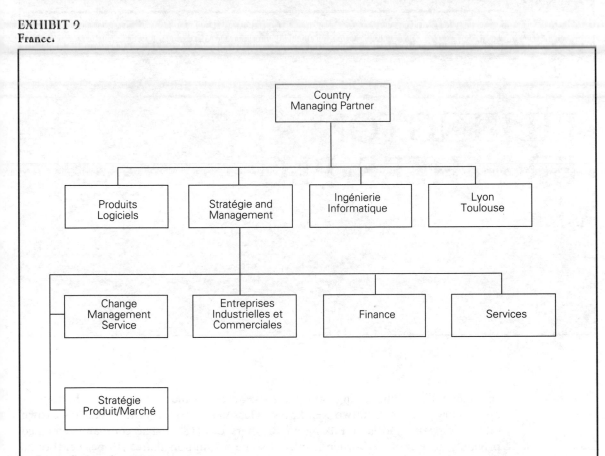

Source: Company document.

PILKINGTON BROTHERS PLC

In 1826 William Pilkington – son of a surgeon-cum-wine and spirit merchant-cum-apothecary – joined with two well-known glassmakers to form the St Helen's Crown Glass Company and later Pilkington Brothers Ltd (1894). The company remained privately held until 1970 when it offered some 5.7 million shares (10 per cent) of its stock to the public. Then in 1973, after being honoured as British Businessman of the Year, (Sir Harry) Lord Pilkington – the fourth generation direct descendant of the founder to head the company – retired. From 1974 to 1981 the company's next chairman, Sir Alastair Pilkington – scientist, inventor, professional manager, but not a lineal descendant of the ownership group – led the company's transition to a diversified, worldwide, technology-leading glass company. In 1981 when Sir Alastair stepped down as CEO, Pilkington's new management team had to design its strategies for a vastly changed world.

EARLY HISTORY

In 1894 Pilkington was the only British producer of both plate and sheet (window) glass, and it had diversified into other flat glasses. Because plate glass processes were so capital-intensive, manufacturing was centralized at Pilkington's original St Helens

Case copyright © 1989, by James Brian Quinn.
Research assistant, Allie J. Quinn.
The generous support of the International Management Institute, Geneva, Switzerland, is gratefully acknowledged.
The generous cooperation of Pilkington Brothers is gratefully acknowledged.

location, where all needed raw materials – coal, limestone, dolomite, alkali and iron-free sand – were abundant within reasonable distance.

Flat Glass Technology

The basic processes for making flat glass had remained substantially the same from the 1700s to the early 1900s. *Sheet* glass was drawn into a ribbon through a (slotted) block floating on the surface of the melted glass inside a glass furnace. The ribbon passed vertically upward through an asbestos roller, a lehr which relieved stresses in the glass, and then into a cutting room where the cooled, hardened glass was cut and stacked. The process produced a good, inexpensive window glass, but output was limited to relatively thin sheets of glass, subject to inhomogeneities and optical distortion.[1]

These properties were unacceptable for mirrors, automobile windows and the large windows increasingly used for retail displays and architectural effects. *Plate* glass was required to meet these demands. To make plate, molten glass was rolled into a plate with a waffled surface and then, in a discontinuous process, was ground and polished until both surfaces were smooth and parallel. Grinding required several stages using a series of very large grinding wheels or discs, with successfively finer abrasive surfaces. Polishing was done with buffers and various powdered rouges. Gigantic factories and huge process investments were required. Because of this, plate manufacture slowly became concentrated in the hands of a few producers. And even these could survive only in countries with large markets.

Then in the early 1920s Ford Motor Company began to develop a flow process for continuous rolling of plate. At the same time, and quite independently, Pilkington had developed a continuous grinding process to replace the disc process. Pilkington stepped in to provide the needed technical expertise, joined its development capabilities with Ford, and in 1923 – combining continuous rolling with continuous grinding – installed the industry's first continuous plate manufacturing process (at St Helens). Twelve years later Pilkington pioneered a machine (the 'twin') to grind both sides of a plate glass ribbon simultaneously. The machine ranked as one of the world's finest examples of large-scale precision engineering, and gave Pilkington world technological leadership in the manufacture of quality flat glass.

FLOAT GLASS DEVELOPMENT

Even the twin grinding process for making plate had substantial drawbacks. Tremendous equipment investments (of $30–$40 million) and sizeable markets were required to support a single glass furnace and its associated plate line. Costs of operating and maintaining a grinding and polishing line were very high. Up to 800 people were necessary to keep a line operating continuously. Some 15–20 per cent of the glass ribbon was ground away in the finishing processes. A plant discharged enough abrasives, polishing rouges and glass to build waste mountains reminding one of the slag heaps of the steel industry. Plants were hundred of yards long. The noise level of grinders, transfer machinery and crashing cullet was formidable. And repairs often required costly shutdowns or dangerous work in the grinding pits underneath the glass ribbon.

Many dreamed of combining the continuous flow, fire polish and inexpensiveness of sheet with the distortion-free quality of polished plate. But the secret eluded the industry until the late 1950s when Lionel Alexander Bethune (Alastair) Pilkington (later Sir Alastair Pilkington, FRS) developed the float glass process. An intense and impatient but thoroughly gracious man, Alastair had joined the company in 1947 after graduation from Cambridge with a degree in mechanical engineering and service in the Royal Artillery in World War II. He started in the sheet works technical development group, moved into plate works technical development, and by 1949 was production manager at the Doncaster works. At Doncaster Sir Alastair started some original experimental work involving interactions of glass and molten metals.

The Invention

Sir Alastair later described how he arrived at the basic idea for float glass:

> One quickly became aware that grinding and polishing was an extremely cumbersome way of making glass free from distortion. [You could see] that the window glass process produced a beautiful surface, which glass naturally has because it is a liquid. What you wanted to do was preserve the natural brilliance of molten glass and form it into a ribbon which was free from distortion. If you could do this you would have done something quite important .... A large part of innovation is, in fact, becoming aware of what is really desirable. [Then you] are ready in your mind to germinate the seed of a new idea .... You also must want to invent. This is terribly important. I don't know why, but I have always wanted to invent something.
>
> I was able to do some thinking about that time [June 1952] because I was bored. I had been very busy [in production operations at Doncaster and had been] brought back to work under the Technical Director .... I was actually consciously bored. This gave me time to think about the problem .... The idea came to me when I was helping my wife to wash up, but it had nothing to do with the act of washing up. It was just one of those moment when your mind is able to think and then it was sort of 'bang' – like that. Indeed the final solution was very similar to the original idea, though it was an awful long journey from the concept to making saleable glass.[2]

Stage I – Experimentation

Alastair quickly drew up some sketches of the new process, which the Engineering Development Group converted into working drawings. The Board gave verbal approval to the project, and within three months a $70,000 pilot plant was built and operational. Fortunately, some technical people were available for reassignment just then. Alastair – with a team of several engineers, a foreman and workman sworn to secrecy – essentially knocked a hole in the side of a remote rolled glass furnace and tried to pour molten glass onto a bed of molten tin. He described this stage as follows:

> We got the cheapest flow of glass we could find in the company. At the earliest possible moment we made a box for the molten tin. The first one leaked like a sieve because we

heated the tin by immersed tubes. We had to make gland joints at the end, and I can tell you molten tin goes through any gland joint. It just poured all over the ground. But it showed you could take a ribbon of glass, pass it over tin, at a relatively high temperature, and produce bright parallel surfaces. [The only answer] we wanted out of Stage I was: did the process look promising? Or would we crash up against some basic chemical or physical laws which would prevent the process from operating.

The Pilkington Board decided to give the project the highest possible priority so that either success or failure would be decided as early as possible. My own greatest fear was that float would drag on for years being a near success; interesting enough to justify further work but never quite achieving satisfactory results.[3]

After some six months it appeared that it would be feasible to 'fire finish' glass by floating it on a bath of molten tin. Once the process could be properly controlled, the bottom surface of the glass should be absolutely flat because it rested on the flat surface of the liquid tin. Natural forces of gravity and surface tension would tend to make the top surface flat too. And the glass should be of uniform thickness, with both surfaces completely parallel. There appeared to be no insurmountable barriers to achieving such results. But the process was far from producing commercial quality glass.

Still an important choice – that of tin as the support medium – had been made and was never changed. Only gallium, indium and tin met the strict physical requirements for the process. The support medium had to be liquid from 1,100°F to over 1,900°F, the range necessary for melting and forming glass. The medium had to be more dense than glass. It needed a low vapour pressure at the 1,900°F end of the temperature range to avoid excess vaporization and contamination of the glass or the process. Finally the medium must not chemically combine with the glass during processing and had to be available at a reasonable price. Tin was the most attractive alternative on almost all counts. (See Exhibit 1A.)

Stage II – Pilot Plants

Stage II was to make a ribbon 12 inches wide under controlled atmospheric conditions. The experimental team hoped to learn more about controlling the quality of the glass. A new pilot plant was built in early 1954 to allow long enough runs to analyze and hopefully correct faults in the process. But technological problems were formidable. Upon exposure to the atmosphere the tin oxidized and produced a crystalline scale on the surface of the glass. A carefully selected and maintained inert atmosphere slowly began to alleviate this problem. But other technical challenges rose to take its place. Because of the company's expertise in forming a glass ribbon through rollers, the team initially chose this method to flow the molten glass onto the tin surface. (See Exhibit 1B.) But tin vapours condensed on the water-cooled rollers, which then imparted surface imperfections to the tin. Unless the tin was extremely pure it also reacted with the glass. Ultimately, the team had to purify the tin well beyond the highest specifications for laboratory quality tin. Finally, the glass source, a rolled glass furnace for making patterned glass, did not provide molten glass of sufficient quality to judge just how well the process was working. Some $46,000 was charged against revenues for the 12 inch experimental line, but no commercial quality glass was produced.

Still, progress was encouraging, and the team came upon one substantial bit of good fortune. When the glass was held for 1 minutes at the 1,900°F temperature needed to eliminate its surface irregularities, a combination of surface tension and gravity effects caused it to form at an equilibrium thickness of 7 mm (0.275 in). By applying a tractive force from the annealing kiln (lehr) the glass might be thinned to 6.5 mm and sold as nominal $\frac{1}{4}$ in glass. As Sir Alastair later said, 'This was a fantastic stroke of luck.' Some 60 per cent of Pilkington's plate sales at that time were in the $\frac{1}{4}$ in thickness.

In June 1953, upon the retirement of Mr J. Meikle (former senior production director), Alastair Pilkington at age 33 became head of Pilkington's plate production and a subdirector of the company. He also continued to head the float glass experimental team. Despite the lack of progress in producing commercial quality glass, the board continued its confidence in the project, and in autumn 1954 agreed to build a new pilot plant capable of producing a 30 in ribbon of glass. This experimental line was designed and built in the incredibly short span of only three months at a cost of $140,000. Molten glass for the line came from the same rolled plate tank as before. The glass made by the process was better than sheet for distortion, but its bubble count would have made it unsaleable as plate.

Although roller forming of the glass into a ribbon had appeared more favourable at the outset, the development team continued a parallel project on the alternative possibility of pouring the glass directly onto tin. This approach would avoid roller contamination, but in experimental work tin compounds formed to contaminate the glass. Other major problems of glass flow, ribbon formation and oxygen and sulphur contamination also persisted. These and high bubble counts from the rolled plate source kept the glass from approaching commercial quality. Nevertheless the technical team's enthusiasm and morale were very high. Sir Alastair said, 'It was almost a crusade. Chaps were literally taken off on stretchers from heat exhaustion, yet came back for more . . . . We all thought the major faults in the glass were due to the glass source, not to the float process.'

About this time the Board came to a very important decision. Float glass would only be launched on the world if it could replace plate glass. If float merely provided an improved sheet glass, it would occupy a peculiar position between two glasses with well-established positions, one of which (sheet) had very low margins. In describing this decision Sir Alastair said:

> The forum for the decision was the Executive Committee of the Board. I was clearly a party to the decision and remember the discussions, but it is difficult to locate an exact moment when the decision was made. It was sometime during the discussions about whether to put down a production scale plant. There were no detailed calculations of such things as the ultimate capital implications of the process or its effects on our overall capital structure. Nevertheless, over a period of time a consensus crystallized with great clarity. This evolved from a series of formal and informal discussions among the members of the Executive Committee and the Board.
>
> Once arrived at, I don't think anyone had any doubt this was the right decision. On the other hand, as technical director I was very disturbed to be expected to make such a tremendous jump forward in one enormous leap. It would have been easier for the technical group to learn about the process while making a better quality of sheet, then launch ourselves up the ladder from sheet to plate.

Phase III – The 100 Inch Line

By April 1955 the three small pilot facilities had cost the company some $1.5 million. At this time Alastair Pilkington presented the board a requisition for another $1.96 million to modify a redundant plate glass furnace and go to a full-scale production line capable of producing a 100 in ribbon. On it he hoped to achieve float glass of commercial quality. The cost of operating this full-scale line would be £100,000 ($280,000) per month.

At that time 3 mm sheet glass sold for 3.34 pence (3.9 cents) per ft^2, while 6 mm plate sold for 21.28 pence (24.9 cents) per ft^2. Calculations showed the cost of float, if successful, would be closer to sheet than to plate. Sir Alastair later recalled:

> The early tests had been encouraging on surface quality and parallelism. But we didn't draw up any PERT charts or statements of probability. Nor did we run out detailed financial figures other than project costs. We knew if we could bring it through it would certainly be a world beater . . . . I suppose one should be able to face reality about a major development. But the reality may be difficult to bear in the early stages. You have to live it a bit from year to year.
>
> In the case of float, the figure are intriguing. It eventually took float 12 years to break even on cash flows. At one time it had a negative cash flow of £7 million ($19.6 million). Yet float was a commercial success immediately after we had solved its process problems. That's just how long it takes. If you went to an accountant and said, 'I've got a great idea to create a massive negative cash flow for certain, and it may – if it's a great success – break even on its cash flows in 12 years,' you wouldn't find many accountants who'd say 'that's exactly what I want.'
>
> But you can't look at development only on the basis of cash flows. If your company never does undertake major projects, then your standing is much lower. Some companies make things happen. They take really strategic decisions. Others aren't prepared to take big risks to [possibly] achieve great rewards.

The board approved the expenditure, and Alastair's team modified an existing plate glass line at the Cowley Hill works. Cowley Hill people were used to change. Many had seen continuous rolling, continuous grinding and polishing, and twin grinding introduced. But the 100 in line immediately encountered enormous troubles. Many of the faults the team had attributed to the poor quality glass source on the 30 in line were actually caused by the float process. The controlled atmosphere then in use still did not maintain a clean glass–tin interface. But the biggest problems occurred in transferring the molten glass onto the tin. Contamination and bubbles plagued the process. Tin oxide condensed on the water-cooled surfaces of the rollers metering the glass onto the tin, and this became imprinted on the glass surface. After some time the team made the momentous decision to move to direct pouring, even though this process was still unproved.[4]

In the early experiments with direct pouring the refractory spout dipped into the tin to provide a smooth glass contact. (See Exhibit 1C.) The chemical erosion on the refractory spout at the glass/tin interface was very rapid and contaminated the process. Glass that had been in touch with the refractory spout and then touched the tin bath created optical distortions called 'music lines' in the glass. Removing the spout from the tin and pouring with a 'free fall' of glass cured the interface wear problem. (See Exhibit 1D.) But the 'music lines' doggedly persisted. Finally the team understood the scientific problems involved and made some key inventions to keep glass which touched the spout from contaminating the whole ribbon.

The team attacked each problem one at a time even though the process might be producing unsalable glass for a half dozen reasons at once. While they slowly solved other contamination problems, bubbles continued to appear in the glass. For 14 months the 100 in line ran 24 hours per day producing useless glass. Every month Alastair had to go to the board to request another £100,000 ($280,000) to continue. He says of this period, 'One of my records which will never be beaten is that of making more continuously unsaleable glass than anyone in the history of the glass industry.'

As technical director, Alastair discussed progress three times daily with the development team. Production executives in the plant were kept well informed. 'We wanted the people who would operate the process to welcome it, not have it landed on them,' said Sir Alastair. In addition, each morning Alastair would meet with the chief project engineer, Barradell Smith, to lay out strategy for the day:

> I took him away from the noise of the crashing cullet so he could have a chance to think. A large pilot plant running 24 hours a day creates great stress and urgency. Glass making goes on around the clock; it never lets up. The heat and crashing glass is unbelievably disconcerting. We would discuss results, what was needed ahead, how the morale of the people was holding up. Every month I would write up a project report for the board and ask for another £100,000. For 7 years it was an apologia as to why we weren't making saleable glass, trying to explain the innumerable faults which occurred. But no single fault persisted. This is why we went ahead. When they would ask, 'Can you make saleable glass?' I would answer: 'I don't know, but nothing has proved it's impossible.' I couldn't recommend that we stop, because we had no reason to stop.
>
> The board was remarkably understanding throughout all this. But it was very difficult for me at times. As the development leader I had to be an optimist and see problems as challenges to be overcome. I think this is crucial to the success of any development. As a board member I had to be cold, analytical and objective. It was hard to fulfil both roles.[5]

Magic and Agony

Finally a magical day came. In mid-1958, the process suddenly made its first saleable glass. Unknown to the development team an accident had gone the right way for them. The pouring spout structure was in poor condition. Finally the spout's back broke, and the structure sagged badly in the middle. The bubbles which had plagued the process of 14 long months miraculously disappeared. The result was a beautiful plate of glass, which now came pouring off the line at a rate of roughly a thousand tons a week.

Fortunately, Pilkington could dispose of this vast outpouring. It quickly made arrangements with Triplex – in which Pilkington then owned a substantial interest – to sell the glass as windshields to British automotive companies. Triplex first tested the glass to ensure that it met their own strict standards. Then, because the surface characteristics of float plate differed slightly from those of ground plate, Triplex and Pilkington also let a few key procurement and quality control people in the automotive industry know that they were using 'a new process'. Otherwise the nature of the process was entirely secret. Pilkington actually sold over a million square feet of float glass before it publicly announced the process in January 1959. 'One thing we were good at was security,' said Sir Alastair. 'People easily fail to understand that the greatest secret about a new process is not how to do it, but that it can be done.' The process was a complete surprise to the industry. Even after the announcement, there were sceptics in other companies who wouldn't believe what had been accomplished.

Later in 1959 the float line was shut down for long overdue maintenance. The line was then carefully rebuilt with all that had been learned from the experimental line. There was agonizing disappointment when the new line was started up. The bubbles and crystals once again appeared. For several more months the team traced down every possible cause of the problem. Using a model in which silicone oil represented the glass and lead nitrate took the place of tin, they identified certain factors associated with the broken spout as keys to success. With new knowledge of the process the development team both captured the good features of the broken spout and designed a way to feed any contaminated glass to the edges of the ribbon. Although much more work was necessary, the process ultimately became self-cleaning and could run continuously for years without a shutdown for repairs.

The company had spent some £7.5 million ($21 million) over seven years. And it had chewed up more than 100,000 tons of glass. But in late 1959 Pilkington could make a glass of quality suitable for the market.

A STRATEGY FOR FLOAT

In October 1958 when the 100 in line was just beginning to produce saleable plate, the board formed a Directors Flat Glass Committee 'to consider the broad issues of flat glass policy both in the present and the future'. The committee (composed of all the executive directors associated with float glass: Sir Harry (Lord) Pilkington, Arthur Pilkington, Alastair Pilkington, J. B. Watt and D. V. Phelps) discussed all aspects of flat (rolled, sheet, wired, plate, etc.) glass strategy worldwide, but by far the most important issue was float.

The Directors Flat Glass Committee tried to raise all the key issues about float. How should Pilkington use its technological advantage? What would its impact be on existing lines, competition, investments? How would float affect exports, employment, facilities depreciation and tax structures, and so on? Not many detailed staff or financial projections were involved at this stage. Instead, the Committee dominantly tried to deal in broad concepts, to identify alternative routes and think through the potential consequences of each route for some ten years ahead. Sir Alastair later said, 'You would be surprised how it sharpens your mind to be told you are only to think about the future.' Members consciously tried to bring out different sides of each issue. At one stage, the Committee even hired a second patent attorney, gave him three of the people most knowledgeable about float, and invited him to attack the patent prepared (but not yet submitted) by the company's regular patent counsel. This helped sharpen and strengthen the ultimate application.

An interesting part of the deliberation was a series of process improvements made in the sheet glass division. Goaded by process on float, sheet glass engineers found a number of ways to improve the quality and lower the cost of their processes. In fact, for a while, the sheet and float glass teams were actively in competition with each other. The Directors Flat Glass Committee had to weigh the potential impact of these and future changes in sheet and plate technology.

They quickly agreed that float would surpass sheet's quality, but that it would not be sufficiently better than existing plate to demand a premium price because of its quality. On the other hand, a float line would ultimately more than halve labour requirements; it would lower energy costs by about 50 per cent; the 15–25 per cent of glass ground away in earlier processes would be saved, as would be the cost of abrasives and rouges; equipment investment would be about one-third the (then) $40 million cost of a conventional line; production space requirements would drop by over 50 per cent; and process interruption costs would virtually disappear. The Committee could not forecast the exact dimensions of these advantages. But it was clear that the process, if successful, would substantially lower existing plate costs. One director even predicted that float would be cost competitive with sheet by 1967–8, but this opinion was not widely shared.

DECISION POINT

What should Pilkington's introduction strategy be? Should it license anyone? If so, whom? In what order? If not, how should it exploit float? What should have been the key considerations?

PATENTS AND LICENSING

Pilkington's goal was to see that float occupied its 'right place' in the marketplace, to strengthen Pilkington's own position as a manufacturer, and to consolidate and extend Pilkington's own manufacturing interests throughout the world. Lord Pilkington later described certain key aspects of the resulting strategy as follows:

> We had the great benefit of time to decide upon our strategy. A great deal was said about ethics: that it was not our job to deliberately deny any existing glass competitor the opportunity of living in competition with us. I don't think we were shortsighted or rapacious .... There was a great deal of investment worldwide in plate, and people needed to have time to write off this plant or convert over. The alternative was chaotic disruption of a great industry.

Eventually Pilkington decided to license, and licensees quickly lined up, until by the mid-1960s substantially all plate manufacturers used the process and royalty income began to roll in to Pilkington. But licensing was not all a bed of roses. Sir Alastair described a chastening experience from this period:

> In the early sixties I was summoned with great urgency to a licensee's plant where an incredible thing was happening. The whole float bath was bubbling like a saucepan of boiling water. A unit which is normally calmer than a millpond was apparently on the verge of volcanic eruption! [The glass itself resembled Swiss cheese.] ... We were absolutely stumped. We had never seen anything like it and had no immediate answer .... Eventually we found that a thermal pump had been created in the bath because of the size of the pores in the refractory brick from which the bath was built.[4] Once the refractory brick was replaced the bath quieted down immediately.

After 1962, despite such temporary setbacks, *every new* plate glass facility built in the world used the float process. By 1968 float costs had become competitive with sheet glass in certain thicknesses. But float had much superior quality, and sheet manufacturers began to deluge the company with licence applications. Since there were 20–30 times as many sheet manufacturers as there were plate producers, this created important policy dilemmas for Pilkington.

By 1974 the float glass process had virtually replaced polished plate glass worldwide. The plate glass industry had invested over £400 million (approximately $1 billion) in the process. 23 manufacturers in 13 countries (including Russia) operated some 51 float plants under Pilkington licences, and float costs were very sensitive to scale of operations. Plants had to produce at least 2,000 tones of glass per week to be economical, and modern plants produced 5,000 T/wk. Many of the OPEC countries, possessing sand and fuel, wanted the process. But these and other developing countries did not have large enough national markets to support a plant.

Nevertheless, a long development process was required before float could make a full range of commercial thicknesses. By the mid-1970s float's thickness range was 2.3–25 mm, with other thicknesses being made experimentally. And float had become cost-competitive with sheet in thinner sections. Through 1981 development and experimentation on float continued. Sir Alastair noted,

> Every time you made a move, you needed to optimize the plant for that particular thickness, width or speed. It was a long, long learning process. How does the tin flow? How does it return through the bath? How does the constantly changing viscosity of the glass interact with the process? I don't know how many times I heard people over the years say, 'We're just about on the limits of speeds, or thickness, or something.' Most times I said, 'Rubbish! What you really mean is you've got to learn more or invent a new technique. You've reached the limits of your experience, not fundamental scientific limits.'

Float opened new realms of chemical challenges to Pilkington's glass technologists. For example, they learned to introduce metal ions into the top surface of float glass. During the float process these ions were electrically attracted towards the tin bath. This penetration created a tinted plate extremely valuable in architectural and automotive uses. The technique, called Electrofloat, allowed the process to be switched from clear to tinted glass and back again in a fraction of the time needed for other processes. In 1967, Pilkington's Triplex subsidiary began work on its 'Ten-Twenty' laminated glass for automobile windshields. This special plate made up from panels of thin float glass with a plastic interlayer was designed to greatly reduce laceration injuries in accidents. Pilkington hoped it would replace much of the 'toughened' glass used for windshields throughout the world. A special high strength, low weight, Ten-Twenty (10/20) was developed for advanced aircraft. This led to Triplex receiving the Queen's Award for Industry in 1974.

CONSOLIDATION AND DIVERSIFICATION

In 1929 Pilkington and Triplex – the largest British safety glass producer – had formed a joint company, Triplex Northern, to produce laminate glass. In 1955 Pilkington and Triplex Safety Glass agreed that the latter should acquire Pilkington's

51 per cent interest in Triplex (Northern) for which Pilkington received a block of Triplex Safety Glass shares. After 1955 Pilkington purchased Triplex stock at a steady rate as it came on the market, until in February 1965, Triplex became a subsidiary.

By 1967 Triplex controlled 85–90 per cent of the English automotive safety glass market. Its main competitor was British IndesTructo Glass (BIG), which was controlled by four major auto companies. In early 1967 Triplex discussed with BIG's controlling owner the mutual advantages of a merger. Triplex took over BIG, and terminated all production in BIG's works in July 1967. But Pilkington and Triplex agreed with the automobile companies and the British Board of Trade that they would at all times maintain adequate capacity to meet the users' forecast demands.

Optical and Specialty Glasses

Through its acquisition of Chance Brothers (1951) Pilkington had extended its entry into optical glass. In 1957, the optical business of both companies was merged into the Chance-Pilkington Optical Works. In 1966 a further company, Pilkington Perkin-Elmer (later Pilkington P. E. Ltd.) was set up to develop and produce electro-optical systems including specialized glasses for laser optics.

1971 saw the formation of the Chance-Propper Company to manufacture microscope slides, medical, surgical and laboratory equipment. In addition to ophthalmic glasses and lens systems, Chance Brothers had also led the company into television tubes, decorative glassware and glass tubing for the fluorescent and incandescent light fields. In 1974 Pilkington added the Michael Birch group – lens prescriptions, sunglasses, safety glasses and a microfilm equipment company. In 1977–8 it acquired Barr and Stroud, a UK maker of periscopes and precision defence products and SOLA, an Australian-based maker of plastic ophthalmic lenses. But the Monopolies Commission blocked its bid for UK Optical, the dominant British supplier of spectacle frames and glass lenses. In 1980–1, the electro-optical and ophthalmic businesses (including Pilkington's successful light-sensitive Reactolite spectacles) were thought to each have revenues of over £30 million.

Fiberglass Products

Chance had been making glass fibers near Glasgow since the late 1920s. Pilkington acquired an interest in this activity in 1938 and eventually purchased the company from Chance Brothers. The company, reorganized as Fiberglass Ltd in 1962–3, extended its operations in the United Kingdom and abroad. In 1971 Fiberglass Ltd announced the development of Cem-FIL fiber, the first glass fiber capable of enduring for any period as a reinforcement of Portland cement. This product, jointly developed with the British National Research Development Corporation (NRDC), offered the possibility of lightweight, high-strength, concrete construction techniques not hitherto possible. The glass provided the tensile strength concrete lacked, and it avoided the weight, bulk and chemical oxidation problems inherent in steel reinforcing. As an alkali-resistant fiber, Cem-FIL could replace asbestos in many of its uses. The development was a major breakthrough in glass chemistry, but in 1981 was only slowly working its way into a conservative marketplace.

Many of these successful diversifications became substantial businesses. But none compared in tonnage with the flat glass field. Here specialized glasses using float were developed for endless new uses: tinted windows, light-sensitive panes, special high-impact safety glass for vehicles, electroconducting glass for de-icing, and specialized glass for air conditioning uses all entered the market. Perhaps the greatest potential impact lay in architectural glasses. Glass plates could be hung or suspended together to provide a wall with uninterrupted visibility. Pilkington's Armourplate glass was developed for high impact uses like doors or squash court walls. And solar control or insulated glasses provided new opportunities for energy conservation in construction.

The company also had its failures, largely in the field of pressed glass operations. While some were relatively small – pavement lights, glass blocks for buildings, and battery boxes – in 1975 the company had to withdraw from the television tube glass market after considerable investment. A high level of Japanese tube imports and a recession in the United Kingdom were given as the primary causes for withdrawal.

But the biggest disappointment was the late 1970s commercial failure of 10/20 windshield glass. The glass removed about 98 per cent of risk of lacerations or head injuries from automobile windshield accidents. When hit by an object, the glass broke into fine particles that literally did not cut. Yet the plastic interlayer was strong enough to prevent a body going through the screen, and flexible enough to minimize brain injury. Still Pilkington could not get car manufacturers to pay the 15 per cent premium price over ordinary safety glass that made it economic to produce 10/20. Safety was not a great selling point, and the oil price increase put a premium on lightness and consequent fuel economy. The manufacturers said they could not pass costs on to consumers. Sir Alastair commented, 'The programme was one of those clear technical successes, but a commercial failure – most disappointing to all of us.'

Geographical Expansion

In 1946 Pilkington had no glass production facilities outside the United Kingdom except a partly owned activity in Argentina. The 1950s and 1960s saw a great international expansion abroad. In 1951 Canada and South Africa started sheet production, followed by India (1965), Australia (1963) and New Zealand (1964). Vasa, in Argentina, became a subsidiary. Safety glass plants opened in New Zealand (1953), Australia (1965), Rhodesia (1961). During the same period the company acquired interests in other companies in Nigeria (1964), Mexico (1965), South Africa (1965), Sweden (1968) and Venezuela (1973). By 1981 Pilkington had nine float plants in other countries. (See Exhibit 2.) It had 25,000 employees and £515 million in sales overseas versus 20,000 people and £377 million in sales in the United Kingdom. Approximately one half of the company's net trading assets were outside the United Kingdom. Exhibit 2 summarizes Pilkington's production operations outside the United Kingdom.

MANAGEMENT STYLE CHANGES

Through the 1970s much of St Helens depended on Pilkington for employment. And the Pilkington family was conscious of this trust. Young Pilkingtons were looked over carefully before they entered the company and, once in, were expected to work doubly hard. Family members developed personal contacts with employees by living in the town and visiting the works regularly. The company had provided pension funds and hospital services, long before these were common in industry. The family also built and endowed theatres and recreation clubs for its employees in St Helens. There was a personal touch too. For a long while, retired employees had been given vegetable seeds for their gardens and coal to warm them during the harsh Midlands winters. The company threw an annual employee party complete with dog shows, parachute jumping, and the like which someone described as 'the finest blowout north of London'.

A strong sense of morality and responsibility pervaded the company. As one director said,

> I think certainly the moral side does weigh with the company. If one runs a business one is to some extent one's brother's keeper. I think the company would still regard itself as being in business for something more than just money making, in the sense that it takes long-term views, and a long-term view is obviously that you have to look after your human capital as well as your money. It isn't just what you do this year that matters, but what you are working on that is going to bear fruit in ten years' time. It is important that the company is not only profitable, but also has a 'heart'.[6]

In the mid-1970s, there were some 15,000 people in the St Helens 'family', many of them new members. General Board members were seen less regularly at the works. And lines of communication from shopfloor to top management began to seem much longer. Diversification had led to anomalies between workers in different jobs and places.[7] And small incidents sometimes caused irritations. In a small community like St Helens, one of these suddenly – a man's pay cheque had been miscalculated, an error that was quickly corrected – amplified into a strike in early 1970. When management's hurt and shock subsided, the company recovered and learned from the strike. There were more formal procedures for negotiations and wage structures. Industrial relations professionals were brought into the corporate offices of Pilkington. And both union and management groups said relations improved markedly after the confrontation.

Regimes Change

During this difficult period another matter which would vastly affect the company's future had been quietly resolved: Pilkington Brothers became a public company in 1970. As Lord Pilkington said, 'Modern taxation makes it very difficult to either pass on the wealth you have accumulated or keep it in the company. And without a public market for the stock, death duties could place large individual shareholders in an impossible cash bind.'

Lord Pilkington had originally intended to retire on his 65th birthday which occurred in April 1970, right in the middle of the strike. But it was agreed that he should stay in order to pilot the change from private to public status and should retire after the annual meeting in 1973, when Sir Alastair Pilkington became chairman for a period of distinguished leadership, ending in 1981.

Sir Alastair continued the important processes of professionalizing and de centralizing Pilkington's management. Of his era he said:

I think the company started to take a much wider view of itself in the world – in processes, products and geography. I think it moved much more consciously to feeling that it could think out the future it wished to have, define what it meant by success in the future, and then lay out a route toward it. The company moved from feeling that it would essentially deal with situations and opportunities as they arose. We felt that we should create the future, rather than react to external circumstances.

I am very strong on people and on success definition. My own feeling is that unless you decide where you want to go, you never arrive there. I don't set goals for other people. That is one of their key jobs – to define their goals, define success. I set goals for myself. I will set goals for the company, but not for other people. I set the company goals in my own mind, and then they come out in discussions. But I don't sort of lay them down. I've never taken a major decision without consulting my colleagues. It would be unimaginable to me, unimaginable. I can't even see any point to it. Firstly, they help me make a better decision in most cases. But secondly, if they know about it and agree with it, they'll back it. Otherwise, they might challenge it, not openly, but subconsciously.

Throughout Alastair wanted to avoid diversifications or any other moves that led to mediocrity. He said, 'I'm absolutely obsessional on the subject of excellence. If you are going to work on a worldwide basis, you must have excellence. One of our most important policy statements was that we would only take on things where we intended to match or lead the world's best performers.'

The 1981 Situation

by 1981 the company had changed substantially. Like others in the industry, Pilkington's volume had grown throughout the world. Capacity expanded by a factor of 3 times from 1971 to 1981. See Exhibits 3 and 3A. Pilkington had large new facilities outside the United Kingdom in Germany, Sweden, Australia and Mexico. While other glass companies conglomerated and diversified into almost anything, in 1980 Pilkington bought Germany's Flachglas for £141 million. *The Paper Clip* described how the new partners matched up: Pilkington had sales of £629 million for 1980 and 35,000 employees while Flachglas had sales (unconsolidated) of £219 million for 1979 from raw glass (approximately 35 per cent) insulating glass (25 per cent), safety glass (25 per cent), plastics and other (approximately 15 per cent) with 7,900 employees. In justifying further acquisitions in the industry, Antony Pilkington, who took over as a chairman from Sir Alastair said, 'If you are technologically excellent, you can maintain your position in your chosen market. Glass is not as narrow a field as some imagine.'

Both parties moved carefully into the merger which had taken four years from concept to reality. The specific opportunity ultimately arose when BSN-Gervais-Danone, a French food company, decided to sell a large part of its glass-making operations. Many bizarre twists accompanied the purchase in which Pilkington could not – for competitive reasons – even investigate the facilities it was about to buy. For example, at the last moment due to legal considerations Pilkington had to come up with £28 million extra to up the percentage of stock bought from 55 to 62 per cent. Then Pilkington had to learn to deal with the dual board and labour representation structures of German companies. But benefits accrued within a few months as Flachglas profits helped offset Pilkington's UK trading losses and Pilkington found new work practices to improve the productivity of its domestic plants. One special aspect of the merger was the fit between Pilkington's strength in process research and Flachglas's strength in product development.[8] The acquisition made Pilkington the largest flat glass manufacturer in the world.

This degree of diversification had worked well. Licence fees and overseas operations – and importantly the Flachglas group's profits – had bolstered Pilkington's lagging fortunes during the sharp downturn in Britain's 1981–2 economy. The company's UK problems were compounded by a flood of glass imports from Europe, and the worldwide recession of those years. Pilkington's share of the UK flat glass market plummeted from 80 per cent to a little over two-thirds in 1981–2.

The European market was rapidly being restructured. Guardian, one of the most efficient operators in the industry, built a new plant in Luxembourg, turning over its stock 10 times a year and reportedly making 20 per cent on its capital before interest. Asahi Glass of Japan took over BSN's losing Belgium and Dutch plants, and PPG bought its French units. (The new structure is outlined in Exhibit 3A.) Much capacity was added while glass industry workforces plummeted – down 4,000 for St Gobain and 3,000 for Pilkington in two years. Asahi controlled 50 per cent of Japan's glass industry and was as efficient as Guardian. But the marketplace for flat glass in their period was over 50 per cent in building and 20 per cent in automobiles, both industries depressed by high interest rates. Overall demand was growing only 1 per cent per year.

Although only 20 per cent of Pilkington's flat glass output went to other divisions for processing, its optical business had moved steadily 'down stream' through acquisitions. This division's growth rate led to its split into two divisions (ophthalmic and electro-optical) of some £30 million sales each in 1981. After 15 years of technical work, fiber optics were slowly working their way into advanced technology applications, and Pilkington's sunlight-sensitive Reactolite spectacles were a great market success, especially in Japan. Many of these new high-tech businesses reported directly to Pilkington's technical board member, Dr Oliver, who commented that, 'Pilkington is still as prepared as ever to commit itself to long cycle developments like "integrated optics" which may some day provide an optical replacement for silicon chips. Bread on the water for 1995,' was the way he described such investments. 'Waiting is the name of the game in high technology.'[9]

Against this background of great success and increasing pressures, Pilkington's new management team – under tall, elegant and marketing-experienced Antony Pilkington – had to arrive at its new strategies for the 1980s.

QUESTIONS

1. What do you think of the way the float glass development project was managed?

2. What were the critical factors Pilkington should have considered when it arrived at its float strategy? What should it have done about these?

3. What crucial issues face the company at the end of the case? What should Antony Pilkington do?

EXHIBIT 1

A. Criteria Determining the choice of a Support Metal for the Float Bath

	Melting Point °C	Boiling Point °C	Estimated Density at 1050°C g cm⁻³	Vapour Pressure at 1027°C Torr
Required	<600	>1050	>2.5	>0.1
Bismuth	271	1680	9.1	27
Gallium	30	2420	5.5	7.6×10^{-3}
Indium	156	2075	6.5	7.9×10^{-2}
Lithium	179	1329	0.5	55
Lead	328	1740	9.38	1.9
Thallium	303	1460	10.9	16
Tin	232	2623	6.5	1.9×10^{-4}

B. The Roller Pouring Process

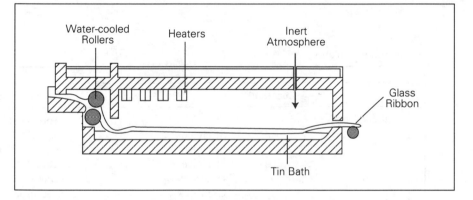

C. Direct Pouring with Spout Dipped Into the Tin Bath

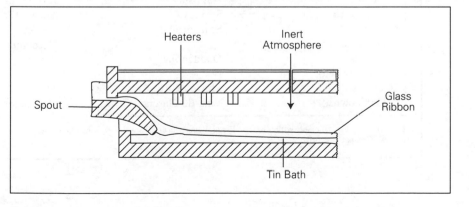

Source: L.A.B. Pilkington, 'Review lecture: The float glass process' The Royal Society, 13 February 1969. Reproduced by special permission

EXHIBIT 1 (cont.)

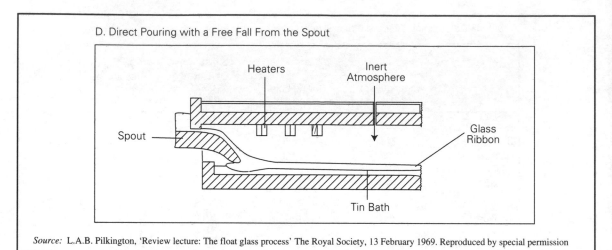

D. Direct Pouring with a Free Fall From the Spout

Source: L.A.B. Pilkington, 'Review lecture: The float glass process' The Royal Society, 13 February 1969. Reproduced by special permission

EXHIBIT 2
Pilkington float plants.

Location		Date of Start-Up
United Kingdom	St Helens	April 1962
	St Helens	July 1963
	St Helens	September 1972
	St Helens	April 1981
Germany	Gladbeck	March 1974
	Gladbeck	December 1976
	Weiherhammer	October 1979
Sweden	Halmstad	July 1976
South Africa	Springs	April 1977
Canada	Scarborough	February 1967
(49% owned)		December 1970
Australia	Dandenong	February 1974
(50% owned)		
ICO	Mexico City,	
(35% owned)	Villa de Garcia	November 1981

Plants (owned in partnership with others) in Brazil, Venezuela and Taiwan were scheduled to start up during 1982.
Source: Company records.

EXHIBIT 3
Clear flat glass saleable capacity, world excluding the communist bloc, 1971 vs. 1981.

(000s tonnes per annum)	1971 Float/Plate	Sheet	Total	1981 Fleet	Sheet	Total
North America	1,488	714	2,202	3,869	35	3,904
Europe	1,048	1,842	2,890	3,896	588	4,484
Australasia (incl. Japan and India)	280	1,058	1,338	1,301	793	2,094
Africa		68	68	115	37	152
Middle East		114	114		365	365
South America	45	263	308	94	505	599
TOTAL	2,861	4,059	6,920	9,275	2,323	11,598

The 1981 data excludes the three most recently opened float tanks, one in Europe (Luxguard), one in the Middle East (Turkey Sise), and one in Mexico.
Source: Company records supplied during interview.

EXHIBIT 3A
Two years of dramatic change in Europe.

	Number of Float Lines		Capacity (tons per day)	
Saint-Gobain	11.5	11.5	5,500	6,000
Pilkington	4	8	1,750	4,750
PPG	1	3	500	1,650
Asahi Glass	nil	2	nil	1,300
SIV (Italian govt.)	1.5	1.5	700	770
Luxguard	nil	1	nil	500
BSN-Gervais-Danone	7	nil	4,150	nil
TOTAL	25	27	12,600	14,970

Source: La Compagnie de Saint-Gobain, in *Financial Times*, 25 January 1982.

EXHIBIT 4
Pilkington Brothers PLC, 1981.

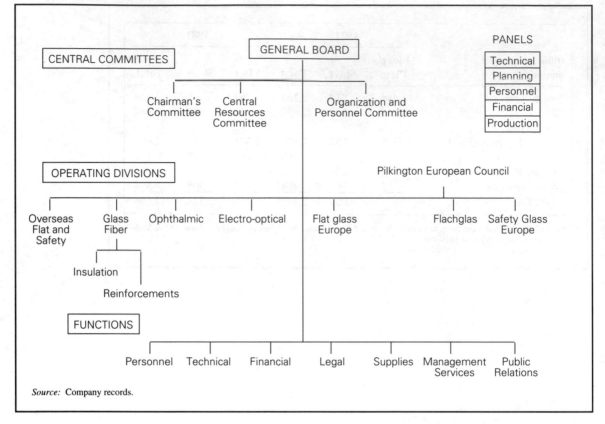

Source: Company records.

EXHIBIT 5
Pilkington Brothers PLC: changes since 1961
(£ millions).

	1961	1971	1981
Group turnover			
Historical	58	123	786
In 1981 money terms	230	300, of which $\frac{2}{3}$ UK, $\frac{1}{3}$ overseas	786, of which $\frac{1}{3}$ UK, $\frac{2}{3}$ overseas
Group assets			
Historical	36	120	1,200
In 1981 money terms	150	300, of which $\frac{3}{4}$ UK, $\frac{1}{4}$ overseas	1,200, of which $\frac{1}{2}$ UK, $\frac{1}{2}$ overseas

Source: Compiled from company records.

EXHIBIT 6
Group financial record for the years ended 31 March 1978 82
(£ millions).

	1978	1979	1980	1981	1982
Sales:					
Sales to Outside Customers	469.5	548.8	629.0	786.8	958.9
Profits:					
Trading Profit	42.6	50.5	49.0	48.2	26.7
Licensing Income	32.8	37.9	37.0	35.3	39.4
Related Companies and Other Income Less Interest	(3.7)	1.9	5.4	(2.5)	(12.7)
Group Profit before Taxation	71.7	90.3	91.4	81.0	53.4
Taxation	36.3	42.7	20.5	32.2	49.9
Group Profit after Taxation	35.4	47.6	70.9	48.8	3.5
Profit Attributable to Shareholders of Pilkington Brothers PLC	34.1	45.7	68.8	36.3	10.7
Dividends (net of taxation)	7.2	9.8	14.8	17.6	17.6
Profit/(loss) Retained in the Business	26.9	35.9	54.0	18.7	(6.9)
Assets Employed:					
Land, Buildings, Plant and Equipment, Less Depreciation	338.4	385.6	455.3	852.0	924.7
Investments in Related and Other Companies	35.8	49.1	53.1	60.6	70.6
Net Current Assets (before deducting bank overdrafts)	162.8	193.6	263.4	239.5	262.3
Assets Employed	537.0	628.3	771.8	1,152.1	1,257.6
Financed by:					
Ordinary Share Capital	62.2	124.4	155.8	167.7	167.7
Retained Profits and Reserves	300.9	298.5	426.1	568.4	624.0
	363.1	422.9	581.9	736.1	791.7
Minority Interests in Subsidiary Companies	21.6	20.8	29.5	138.2	120.0
Loan Capital and Bank Overdrafts	129.3	156.2	136.0	235.0	300.5
Deferred Taxation and Deferred Income	23.0	28.4	24.4	42.8	45.4
TOTAL FUNDS INVESTED	537.0	628.3	771.8	1,152.1	1,257.6

3–6

PROCTER & GAMBLE EUROPE: VIZIR LAUNCH

There were three critical decisions facing Procter & Gamble's (P&G) senior management in June 1981 as they reviewed the German test market results for Vizir, the new heavy duty liquid (HDL) detergent:

1. Should they follow the recommendation of Wolfgang Berndt and his German team and authorize a national launch on the basis of four months of test results? Or should they wait until final test market results were in, or perhaps even rethink their entire HDL product strategy?

2. If and when the decision was taken to launch Vizir, to what extent could this be considered a European rather than just a German product? If a coordinated European rollout was planned, to what degree should the company standardize its product formulation, packaging, advertising and promotion?

3. Finally, what organizational implications would these decisions have? For example, to what extent should individual country subsidiary managers retain the responsibility to decide when and how this new product would be introduced in their national market?

This case was prepared by Assistant Professor Christopher A. Bartlett as the basis for class discussion rather than to illustrate either effective or ineffective handling of an administrative situation. Proprietary data have been disguised, but key relationships are preserved.

PROCTER AND GAMBLE: COMPANY BACKGROUND

To understand anything in P&G, one had to appreciate the company's strong and long-established culture, which was reflected in the corporate values, policies and practices. The following sections outline how the company saw itself in each of these areas.

Corporate Values

Established in 1837 by two men of strong religious faith and moral conviction, P&G soon had developed an explicit set of corporate standards and values. From their earliest contact, prospective employees were told of P&G's firm belief that the interests of the company were inseparable from those of its employees. Over the years, this broad philosophy had been translated into a variety of widely shared management norms, such as the following:

- P&G should hire only good people of high character.
- P&G must treat them as individuals with individual talents and life goals.
- P&G should provide a work environment that encourages and rewards individual achievement.

The shared beliefs soon became part of the company's formal management systems. General managers would tell you they were evaluated on the achievements in three areas: volume, profit and people. P&G also tried to attract people willing to spend their entire career with the company. Promotions were made from within, and top management was chosen from career P&G people rather than from outside the company.

Management Policies

Over its almost 150-year history, P&G had also accumulated a broad base of industrial experience and business knowledge. Within the company, this accumulated knowledge was seen as an important asset and a great deal of it had been formalized and institutionalized as management principles and policies. In the words of the chairman, Ed Harness: 'Though our greatest asset is our people, it is the consistency of principle and policy that gives us direction.'

It was in the marketing area that these operating principles and management policies were the most strategically important for a company with a reputation as a premier consumer marketer. One of the most basic policies was that P&G's products should provide 'superior total value' and should meet 'basic consumer needs'. This resulted in a strong commitment to research to create products that were demonstrably better than the competition in blinds tests. (In the words of one manager, 'Before you can launch a new brand, you must have a win in a white box.')

Furthermore, P&G believed strongly in the value of market research. In a business where poorly conceived new product launches could be very expensive and sometimes not very successful, continuous and detailed market research was seen as insurance against major mistakes. Ed Harness had described their market research objectives as being 'to spot a new trend early, then lead it'.

For similar reasons, P&G also believed in extensive product and market testing before making major brand decisions. Having spotted a trend through market research, the company typically spent two or three years testing the product and the marketing strategy it had developed before committing to a full-scale launch. One paper goods competitor said of them: 'P&G tests and tests and tests. They leave no stone unturned, no variable untested. You can see them coming for months and years, but you know when they get there, it is time for you to move.'

Finally, P&G believed that through continual product development and close tracking of consumer needs and preferences, brands could be managed so that they remained healthy and profitable in the long term. Their rejection of the conventional product lifecycle mentality was demonstrated by the fact that Ivory Soap was over 100 years old, Crisco shortening was more than 70, and Tide detergent more than 35, yet each was still a leader in its field.

Organization Practices

In addition to strong corporate values and clear management principles, the P&G culture was also characterized by well-established organization practices and processes. Its internal operations had been described as thorough, creative and aggressive by some, and as slow, risk-averse and rigid by others. There was probably an element of truth in both descriptions, and there were organizational characteristics that were central to the company's operations.

Perhaps the most widely known of P&G's organizational characteristics was its legendary brand manager structure. Created in 1931, the brand management system was designed to provide each branch with management focus, expertise and drive at a low level in the organization. By legitimizing and even reinforcing the internal competition that had existed since Camay Soap was launched in competition with Ivory in 1923, the brand manager system tended to restrict lateral communication. This resulted in a norm among P&G managers that information was shared on a 'need to know' basis only.

While the brand manager system may have impaired lateral communication, vertical communication within P&G was strong and well established. Proposals on most key issues were normally generated at the lower levels of management, with analysis and recommendations working their way up the organization for concurrence and approval. In P&G, top management was intimately involved in most large decisions (e.g. all new brand launches, capital appropriations in excess of $100,000 and personnel appointment and promotion decisions three levels down). Although the approval system could be slow and at times bureaucratic (one manager claimed that a label change on Head and Shoulders shampoo had required 55 signatures), it was designed to minimize risk in the very risky and expensive consumer marketing business. Once a project was approved, it would have the company's full commitment. As one manager said, 'Once they sign off [on the new brand launch], they will bet the farm.'

A third characteristic of the P&G management process was that proposals were committed to paper, usually in the form of one- or two-page memos. The purpose was to encourage thoroughness and careful analysis on the part of the proposal originators, and objectivity and rationality on the part of the managers who reviewed the document. Written documents could also flow more easily through the organization, building support or eliciting comments and suggestions.

P AND G INTERNATIONAL: EUROPEAN OPERATIONS

Expansion Principles

Although P&G had acquired a small English soap company in 1926, it was not until the postwar years that the company built a substantial European presence. In 1954 a French detergent company was acquired; two years later, a Belgian plant was opened; and by the end of the decade P&G had established operations in Holland and Italy. A Swiss subsidiary served as a worldwide export centre. In the 1960s, subsidiaries were opened in Germany, Austria, Greece, Spain and the Scandinavian countries. The European Technical Centre (ETC) was established in Brussels in 1963, to provide R&D facilities and a small regional management team.

By 1981 Europe represented about 15 per cent of P&G's $11 billion worldwide sales, with almost all of that substantial volume having been built in the previous two and a half decades. The German and UK subsidiaries were the largest, each representing about one-fifth of the company's European sales. France and Italy together accounted for another 30 per cent and Belgium, Holland, Spain, Austria and Switzerland together made up the balance.

As international operations grew, questions arose as to how the new foreign subsidiaries should be managed. As early as 1955, Walter Lingle, P&G's Overseas Vice-President, had laid down some important principles, which guided the company's subsequent development abroad. Recognizing that consumer needs and preferences differed by country, Lingle emphasized the importance of acquiring the same intensive knowledge of local consumers as was required in the United States. Lingle said: 'Washing habits ... vary widely from country to country. We must tailor products to meet consumer demands in each nation. We cannot simply sell products with US formulas. They won't work – they won't be accepted.'

But Lingle insisted that the management policies and practices that had proved so successful for P&G in the United States would be equally successful overseas. He said: 'The best way to succeed in other countries is to build in each one as exact a replica of the US Procter & Gamble organization as it is possible to create.'

European Industry and Competitive Structure

From their earliest exposure to the European market for laundry detergents, US managers realized how important the first of these principles would be. Washing habits and market structures not only differed from the familiar US situation, but also varied from one country to the next witin Europe. Among the more obvious differences in laundry characteristics were the following:

- Typical washing temperatures were much higher in Europe, and the 'boil wash' (over 60°C) was the norm in most countries. However, lower washing temperatures were commonplace in some countries where washing machines did not heat water (e.g. United Kingdom) or where hand-washing was still an important segment (e.g. Spain, Italy).

- European washing machines were normally front-loading with a horizontal rotating drum – very different from the US norm of an agitator action in a top-loaded machine. The European machine also had a smaller water capacity (3–5 gallons versus 12–14 gallons) and used a much longer cycle (90–120 minutes versus 20–30 minutes).

- Europeans used more cottons and fewer synthetics than Americans, and tended to wear clothes longer between washes. Average washing frequency was 2–3 times per week versus 4–5 times in the United States. Despite the lower penetration of washing machines, much higher detergent use per load resulted in the total European laundry detergent consumption being about 30 per cent above the US total.

Market structures and conditions were also quite different from the United States, and also varied widely within Europe, as illustrated by the following examples:

- In Germany, concentration ratios among grocery retailers were among the highest in the world. The five largest chains (including co-ops and associations) accounted for 65 per cent of the retail volume, compared with about 15 per cent in the United States. In contrast, in Italy, the independent corner shop was still very important, and hypermarkets had not made major inroads.

- Unlimited access to television similar to the United States, was available only in the United Kingdom (and even there was much more expensive). In Holland, each brand was allowed only 46 minutes of TV commercial time per annum; in Germany and Italy, companies had to apply for blocks of TV time once a year. Allocated slots were very limited.

- National legislation greatly affected product and market strategies. Legislation in Finland and Holland limited phosphate levels in detergent; German laws made coupons, refunds and premium offers all but impossible; elsewhere local laws regulated package weight, labelling and trade discounts.

The competitive environment was also different from P&G's accustomed market leadership position in the United States. In Europe, P&G shared the first-tier position with two European companies, Unilever and Henkel. By the early 1970s each company claimed between 20 per cent and 25 per cent of the European laundry detergent market. P&G's old domestic market rival, Colgate, had a 10 per cent share and was in a second tier. At a third level were several national competitors. Henkel was present in most European markets but strongest in Germany, its home market; Unilever was also very international, dominating in Holland and the United Kingdom; Colgate's presence in Europe was patchier, but it had built up a very strong position in France. National companies typically were strong at the lower priced end of their local markets.

Each company had it own competitive characteristics. Unilever had long been a sleeping giant, but by the mid-1970s was becoming much more aggressive. Henkel was a strong competitor and could be relied on to defend its home market position tenaciously. Colgate was trying to elbow its way in, and tended to be more impulsive and take bigger risks, often launching new products with only minimal testing. As a result, P&G's market share varied by national market.

Laundry Detergent Market

($million)

	Total market	P&G share
Germany	950	200
United Kingdom	660	220
France	750	160
Italy	650	140
Spain	470	90
TOTAL EUROPE	3,750	950

By the mid-1970s, the rapid growth of the previous two decades had dropped to a standstill. Not only did the oil crisis add dramatically to costs, but almost simultaneously, washing machines approached the 85 per cent penetration rate many regarded as saturation point. In the late 1970s, volume was growing at 2 per cent per annum. As market growth slowed, competitive pressures increased.

P&G Europe's Strategy and Organization

These differences in consumer habits, market conditions and competitive environment led to the development of strong national subsidiaries with the responsibility for developing products and marketing programmes to match the local environment. Each subsidiary was a miniature Procter & Gamble, with its own brand management structure, its own product development capability, its own advertising agencies and, typically, its own manufacturing capability. The subsidiary general manager was responsible for the growth of the business and the organization. (See Exhibit 1.)

Most subsidiaries faced a major task of establishing P&G in the basic detergent and soap business in their national market. General managers typically tried to select the best volume and profit opportunity from the more than 200 products in the company's portfolio. The general manager of the Italian subsidiary described the choices he faced when he took over in 1974:

> Given the limits of P&G Italy's existing brands (a laundry detergent, a bar soap and a recently acquired coffee business), we had to build our volume and profit, and broaden our base. The choices we had were almost limitless. Pampers had been very successful in Germany and Belgium, but Italy couldn't afford such an expensive launch; Motiv, a new dishwashing liquid was being launched in France and Germany, but we were unconvinced of its potential here; Mr Propre (Mr Clean in the United States) was successful in three European countries, but competition in Italy was strong; finally we decided to launch Monsavon, the French bar soap. It represented an affordable new product launch in a traditionally good profit line.

Each of the country general managers reported to Tom Bower, an Englishman who had headed up P&G's European operations since 1961. Bower had a reputation as an entrepreneur and an excellent motivator. He believed that by selecting creative and entrepreneurial country general managers and giving them the freedom to run their business, results would follow. The strategy had been most successful for P&G, and sales and profits had grown rapidly throughout the 1960s and into the early 1970s. Growth had been aided by P&G's entry into new national markets and new product categories, and by the rapid growth of the core detergent business with the penetration of washing machines into European homes.

Tom Bower made sure that his small headquarters staff understood that they were not to interfere unduly in subsidiary decisions. Primarily, it was the subsidiary general manager's responsibility to call on ETC if there was a problem.

When Tom Bower retired in 1975, his successor, Ed Artzt, was faced with a situation quite different from the one that existed in the 1950s and 1960s. As growth slowed, competition intensified, prices weakened and profits dipped. Artzt felt that if profit and sales growth were to be rekindled, the diverse country operations would have to be better coordinated.

Over the next five years, under his leadership, the role of ETC took on new importance. (Exhibit 1 shows an abbreviated organization chart.) If increased competition was leading to declining margins, more emphasis must be placed on controlling costs, and Artzt moved to strengthen the ETC finance manager's role. The finance manager described the problems:

> Largely because of duplication of marketing and administrative groups in each subsidiary, our overhead expense per unit was almost 50 per cent higher than in the US parent. We needed to get it under control. Our problem was that we couldn't get meaningful or comparable costs by subsidiary. Our introduction of better cost and reporting systems helped put pressure on subsidiaries to control their costs. It had a very beneficial effect.

Artzt was also concerned about the slowing of innovation in P&G Europe, and felt that part of the sales and profit problem was due to the fact that too few new products were being developed, and those that were were not being introduced in a coordinated manner. Under the strong leadership of Wahib Zaki, Artzt's new R&D manager, ETC's role in product development took a dramatic shift.

Previously, each subsidiary was responsible for initiating its own local product development. These groups drew on the company's basic technology from the United States, as modified by ETC. The R&D group in a subsidiary the size of France was around 30, while Germany's technical staff was perhaps twice that size. Responding to its own local market, the subsidiary defined and developed products with the appropriate characteristics, perhaps calling on ETC for specialized technical support or backup. There was no requirement for a subsidiary to use standard formulations or technology. As a result, Ariel detergent had nine different formulas Europe-wide, having been positioned diversely as a low- and a high-suds powder, and for low- and high-temperature usage, depending on the country.

The problem with developing products in this way, concluded Zaki, was that there was insufficient focus, prioritization or strategic direction for the work. As a result, the strong technical capabilities housed in the European Technical Centres as well as in the United States were not being fully or effectively utilized. Furthermore, their efforts were not being appreciated by local country management, who tended to view the Technical Centre as a high-cost, perfectionist group, which did not respond rapidly enough to market needs.

Zaki sought to change this by having ETC take a stronger leadership role in R&D and by assuming responsibility for coordinating the new product development efforts among the subsidiaries. He felt the time had come where this was possible. His analysis indicated that habit differences between countries were narrowing and no longer justified product differences of the type that then existed from one country to another. He felt the need to establish priorities, to coordinate efforts and, to the extent possible, to standardize products across Europe. To achieve these goals he needed the involvement and cooperation of the subsidiaries.

In 1977, Zaki reorganized European R&D, creating European technical teams to work on Eurobrands. In his vision, Eurobrands were to be superior to the previous local brands in every country, without compromising the performance of the products, and at an affordable cost. The objective was to focus the resources of the total European R&D community around key brands and to define a long-term European approach to product development.

As roles became clearer, the ETC technical groups were seen as being the developers of new technologies ('putting the molecules together', as one described it), while the subsidiaries took responsibility for testing and refining the products in the field. After a couple of painful years, the new process seemed to be working. 'Lead countries' were named for each of the key products thereby giving more local subsidiary responsibility and ownership for the development process, and also to ensure ongoing coordination among subsidiaries. Transfer of technical staff between ETC and subsidiaries further encouraged the interdependence and cooperation.

An experimental attempts at 'Europeanization' in marketing, however, had been less successful. In a break from the philosophy of product adaptation, a group of managers in Cincinnati had concluded that 'a baby is a baby' worldwide, and that the laborious market-by-market evaluations necessary for cleaning products would not be needed for disposable nappies. In line with this decision, it was decided to gain experience by managing key elements of Pampers (such as product and copy strategy) on a Europe-wide basis. A senior manager was transferred from the German subsidiary where Pampers had been launched in 1974 to ETC where he was given responsibility for leading key activities on Pampers in all subsidiaries. The brand promotion manager responsible for Pampers in France at the time recalled the experiment:

> As soon as it was known I would be principally working with the European Pampers manager in ETC and not the subsidiary GM, my local support dried up. I couldn't get a brand manager or even an assistant to work with me. The French subsidiary manager was preoccupied with the Motiv (dishwashing liquid) launch, and was trying to regain leadership with Ariel (laundry powder). The Pampers situation was a disaster. Eventually Pampers was given back to the subsidiaries – it was the only way to get their support.

This experience conveyed a very important lesson to P&G's top management. It appeared that while coordination and planning could be effectively centralized and implemented on a European basis, the day-to-day management of the business had to continue to be executed at the local subsidiary level.

In 1980, Ed Artzt was transferred back to Cincinnati as executive vice-president of P&G, and Charlie Ferguson was named Group VP, Europe. Ferguson had a reputaton as an energetic, creative and intelligent manager who got things done.

Impressed by the effectiveness of the European approach to technical development, Ferguson was convinced that a similar approach could succeed in product marketing.

With the encouragement and support of his boss, Ed Artzt, who remained a strong advocate of Europeanization, Charlie Ferguson began to test the feasibility of developing European brands and marketing strategies. In pursuing the Eurobrand concept, as it was becoming known, Artzt and Ferguson saw Vizir, the new heavy duty liquid being prepared for launch in Germany, as being a good test case.

THE VIZIR PROJECT

Product Development

Following Lever's success in the United States with a product called Wisk, in 1974 P&G launched Era as their entrant in the fast-growing heavy duty liquid (HDL) detergent segment. As a late entrant, however, they were unable to match Wisk's dominant share. P&G managers watching developments from Europe realized that if the HDL product concept was transferable to their market, the first company to stake out the territory would have a major advantage. The success of liquids in other product categories (e.g. household cleansers), the trend towards low temperature washes and the availability of liquid product plant capacity all provided additional incentives to proceed with the project.

ETC initiated its HDL project in late 1974, and as a first step tested the US product Era against European powders in a small-scale test panel. Given the differences in laundry habits on either side of the Atlantic, it was not surprising that Era was evaluated poorly. The problems reported by the panel related not only to the product's washing performance (e.g. whitening ability, suds level), but also to its form. European washing machines were built with drawers that allowed different powdered products (pre-treatment, main wash detergent, fabric softener) to be activated at different times in the typical 90-minute cycle. To win acceptance of a laundry liquid would be difficult. First, consumers would have to be convinced that this product would achieve similar results; then their established behaviours would have to be changed.

Undeterred, a group at ETC began to work on a HDL product that would be more suited to European laundry practices. It was with high hopes and considerable corporate visibility that the modified European HDL product was placed in six full-scale blind tests in Germany, France and the United Kingdom. The results were disastrous in all tests. Given the high level of internal expectations that had been created, many P&G insiders felt that the product was dead, since it would be impossible to rebuild internal support and credibility.

However, the scientists at ETC were convinced that they should be able to capitalize on the intrinsic ability of a liquid detergent to incorporate three times the level of surfactants compared to a powder. (The surfactant is the critical ingredient that removes greasy stains.) The challenge was to compensate for the shortcomings of the HDL that offset this important advantage. Unlike US products, European powdered detergents normally contained enzymes (to break down proteins) and bleach (to oxidize stains) in addition to builders (to prevent redisposition of dirt), phosphates (to soften water) and surfactants. Unfortunately, it was not then possible to incorporate enzymes and bleach in a liquid detergent, and it was this limited capability that was behind the new product's blind test failure in Europe.

The challenge of overcoming these deficiencies excited P&G's scientists at ETC and in the United States. Eventually, they were able to patent a method to give enzymes stability in liquid form. Soon afterwards, a bleach substitute that was effective at lower temperatures was developed. The product modifications showed in improving consumer blind test results. In late 1976, the new HDL product won a blind test against the leading French powder, Ariel; the following year it won against Persil, the German market leader. Although the successes were sufficient to establish a HDL brand group in Germany, the project was still on a very shaky ground within P&G.

In early 1977, Colgate began test marketing Axion, a HDL formula that was similar to its US product, Dynamo. Axion showed excellent initial results, gaining almost a 4 per cent share in three months. However, sales declined from this peak and within 18 months Colgate closed down the test market and withdrew the product.

Meanwhile, P&G's reseach team had developed three important additional breakthroughs: a fatty acid that provided similar water softening performance to phosphate, a suds suppressant so the product would function in European drum washing machines, and a patented washing machine anti-corrosion ingredient. By 1979, European development efforts had shifted to product aesthetics, and the search began for perfumes compatible with the newly formulated *HDL-Formula SB* as it was known.

Meanwhile, Henkel had reformulated their market leading powder and relaunched it as New Persil. Blind tests against New Persil in early 1980 were a breakeven. Finally, in October 1980 with a new fragrance, Procter's Formula SB won a blind test against New Persil by 53 to 47. The product's superiority was confirmed in subsequent tests against the main competitive powders in France (58 to 42 win for Formula SB) and in the United Kingdom (61 to 39 win).

Now, the German brand group was ready to recommend a full-scale test market. During the previous 18 months they had cleared the proposed brand name (Vizir), appointed an advertising agency (Grey), designed packaging (bottles and labels) and collected and analyzed the masses of consumer and market data that were necessary to justify any new product launched in P&G. Management up to the highest level was interested and involved. Although an initial capital approval had been received for $350,000 to buy moulds and raw materials, the test market plan for Berlin was expected to involve a further investment of $1.5 million plus $750,000 for original advertising production and research. A national launch would involve an additional $1.5 million in capital investment and $16 million in marketing costs and would pay out in about three years if the product could gain a 4 per cent market share. A Europe-wide launch would be 5 or 6 times that amount.

While Germany decided to proceed with the test market, a great deal of uncertainty still surrounded Vizir. There were some in the company who questioned whether it made sense to launch this product at all in Germany, particularly with the proposed marketing positioning and copy strategy. Others were less concerned about the German launch but were strongly opposed to the suggestion that Vizir be made a Eurobrand and launched in all key European markets.

Vizir Launch Decision

One issue that had resulted in some major concern in P&G's senior management related to Vizir's positioning in the detergent market. Its strength was that it gave superior cleaning performance on greasy stains at low temperatures, and (following the product improvements) matched powder performance on enzymatic stains and whiteness. The problem was that P&G's Ariel, the leading low temperature laundry powder in Germany, made similar performance claims, and it was feared that Vizir would cannibalize its sales. So close were their selling propositions that two separate agencies operating independently produced almost identical commercials for Vizir and Ariel in early 1981 (Exhibit 2).

Some defenders of Vizir argued that the product had to be positioned in this way, since this was the promise that had resulted in high trials during the Axion test. To position it as a pre-treatment product would severely limit its sales potential, while to emphasize peripheral benefits like fabric care or softness would not have broad appeal. They argued that it had to be seen as a mainwash product with superior cleaning performance at lower temperatures.

Another concern being expressed by some managers was that P&G was creating a product segment that could result in new competitive entries and price erosion in the stagnant heavy duty detergent market. Liquids were much easier to make than powders and required a much smaller capital investment. ('For powders, you need a detergent tower – liquids can be made in a bath tub', according to one manager.) Although P&G had patented many of its technological breakthroughs, they were a less effective barrier to entry than might be expected. One product development manager explained:

> Our work on Vizir was very creative, but not a very effective barrier to competition. Often it's like trying to patent a recipe for an apple pie. We can specify ingredients and compositions in an ideal range or a preferred range, but competitors can copy the broad concepts and work around the patented ranges. And, believe me, they are all monitoring our patents! Even if they don't (or can't) copy our innovations, there are other ways to solve the problems. If enzymes are unstable in liquid form, you could solve that by dumping in lots of enzymes so that enough will still be active by the estimated usage data.

If capital costs were low, and products could be imitated (at least partially), the concern was that new entrants could open up a market for 'white labels' (generic products). Without the product or the market development costs of P&G they probably could undercut their prices. P&G's pricing strategy had been to price at an equivalent 'cost-per-job' as the leading powders. This pricing strategy resulted in a slightly higher gross profit margin for Vizir compared to powders. The pricing decision was justified on two grounds: a premium price was required to be consistent with the product's premium image, and also to avoid overall profit erosion, assuming that Vizir would cannibalize some sales of the company's low temperature laundry detergent brands.

At this time P&G was a strong No. 2 in the German detergent market – the largest in Europe. Henkel's leading brand, Persil, was positioned as an all-temperature, all-purpose powder, and held a 17 per cent share.[1] P&G's entrant in the all-temperature segment was Dash, and this brand had $5\frac{1}{2}$ per cent share. However, the company's low-temperature brand, Ariel, had a share of 11 per cent and was a leader in this fast-growing segment, far ahead of Lever's Omo ($1\frac{1}{2}$ per cent) and Henkel's new entrant, Mustang ($2\frac{1}{2}$ per cent).

The final argument of the opponents was that even ignoring these risks there were serious doubts that this represented a real market opportunity. P&G's marketing of its HDL in the United States had not been an outstanding success. Furthermore Colgate's experience with their European test market had been very disappointing.

In early 1981, an interesting article was published which concluded that it would be difficult for a liquid to compete in the European heavy duty detergent field. The paper, presented to an industry association congress in September 1980 by Henkel's director of product development and two other scientists, concluded that heavy duty liquids would continue to expand their penetration of the US market, due to the less demanding comparison standard of American powder detergents, and also to the compatibility of HDLs with American washing practices. In Europe, by contrast, the paper claimed that liquids were likely to remain specialty products with small market share (1 per cent compared to 20 per cent in the United States). This limited HDL market potential was due to the superiority of European powder detergents, and the different European washing habits (higher temperatures, washing machine characteristics, etc.).

While managers in Brussels and Cincinnati were wrestling with these difficult strategic issues, the brand group in Germany was becoming increasingly nervous. They were excited by the product and committed to its success. Initial test market readings from Berlin were encouraging (see Exhibit 3) but they were certain that Henkel was following Vizir's performance in Berlin as closely as they were. The product had now been in development and testing for seven years, and the Germany group felt sure that Henkel knew their intentions and would counterattack swiftly and strongly to protect their dominant position in their home market. By the early summer, rumours were beginning to spread in the trade that Henkel was planning a major new product. Henkel salesmen had been recalled from vacation and retailers were being sounded out for support on promotional programmes.

On three separate occasions the German group presented their analysis of the test market and their concerns about a pre-emptive strike; but on each occasion it was decided to delay a national launch. Senior management on both sides of the Atlantic explained it was just too risky to invest in a major launch on the basis of 3 or 4 months of test results. Experience had shown that a one-year reading was necessary to give a good basis for such an important decision.

Eurobrand Decision

Another critical issue to be decided concerned the scope of the product launch. Within P&G's European organization, the budding Eurobrand concept, whereby there would be much greater coordination of marketing strategies of brands in Europe, was extremely controversial. Some thought it might conflict with the existing philosophy that gave country subsidiary managers the freedom to decide what products were most likely to succeed in their local market, in what form, and when.

The primary argument advanced by Artzt and Ferguson and other managers with similar views, was that the time was now ripe for a common European laundry detergent. While widely differing washing practices between countries had justified up until now, national products tailored to local habits, market data indicated a converging trend in consumer laundry habits (see Exhibit 4).

Others were quick to point out that despite the trends, there were still huge differences in washing habits which were much more important than the similarities at this stage. For example, Spain and Italy still had a large handwash segment; in the United Kingdom and Belgium top loading washers were still important; and in Southern Europe, natural fibre clothing still predominated. Besides, the raw statistical trends could be misleading. Despite the trend to lower temperature washing, even in Germany over 80 per cent of housewives still used the boilwash (over 60°C) for some loads. In general, they regarded the boilwash as the standard by which they judged washing cleanliness.

Some subsidiary managers also emphasized that the differences went well beyond consumer preferences. Their individual market structures would prevent any uniform marketing strategy from succeeding. They cited data on differences in television cost and access, national legislation on product characteristics and promotion tool usage, differences in distribution structure and competitive behaviour. All these structural factors would impede standardization of brands and marketing strategies Europe-wide.

The second point Artzt and Ferguson raised was that greater coordination was needed to protect subsidiaries' profit opportunities. (However, they emphasized that subsidiary managers should retain ultimate profit responsibility and a leadership or concurrence role in all decisions affecting their operations.)

Increasingly, competitors had been able to imitate P&G's new and innovative products and marketing strategies, and pre-empt them in national markets where the local subsidiary was constrained by budget, organization or simple poor judgement from developing the new product category or market segment. For example, Pampers had been introduced in Germany in 1973, but was not launched in France until 1978. Meanwhile in 1976, Colgate had launched a product called Calline (a literal French translation of Pampers) with similar package colour, product position and marketing strategy, and had taken market leadership. Late introduction also cost Pampers market leadership in Italy. The product was just being introduced in the United Kingdom in 1981. An equally striking example was provided by Lenor. This new brand was launched in 1963 in Germany, creating a new fabric softener product category. It quickly became an outstanding market success. Nineteen years later, Lenor made its debut in France as the No. 3 entrant in the fabric softener category, and consequently faced a much more difficult marketing task.

Artzt and Ferguson were determined to prevent recurrences of such instances. Particularly for new brands, they wanted to ensure that product development and introduction were coordinated to ensure a consistent Europe-wide approach, and furthermore, that marketing strategies were thought through from a European perspective. This meant thoroughly analyzing the possibility of simultaneous or closely sequenced European product introductions.

At the country level, many were quick to point out that since the company wanted to keep the subsidiary as a profit centre, the concept was not feasible. To establish a new brand, and particularly to create a new product category like disposable nappies was an incredibly expensive and often highly risky proposition.

Many country general managers questioned whether they should gamble their subsidiary's profitability on costly, risky new launches, especially if they were not at all convinced their local market was mature enough to accept it. In many cases they had not yet completed the task of building a sound base in heavy and light duty detergents, and personal products. They felt that their organization should not be diverted from this important task.

The third set of arguments put forward by the advocates of the Eurobrand concept related to economics. They cited numerous examples: the fact that there were nine different Dash formulas in Europe; Mr Clean (known as M. Propre, Meister Proper, etc.) was sold in nine different sizes Europe-wide. To go to a single formula, standard size packs and multilingual labels could save the company millions of dollars in mould costs, line downtime for changeovers, sourcing flexibility, reduced inventory levels, etc.

Other managers pointed out that the savings could easily be offset by the problems standardization would lead to. The following represent some of the comments made at a country general managers' meeting at which Charlie Ferguson raised the Eurobrand issue for discussion:

> We have to listen to the consumer. In blind tests in my market that perfume cannot even achieve breakeven.

> The whole detergent market is in 2 kg packs in Holland. To go to a European standard of 3 kg and 5 kg sizes would be a disaster for us.

> We have low phosphate laws in Italy that constrain our product formula. And we just don't have hypermarkets like France and Germany where you can drop off pallet loads.

One general manager put it most forcefully in a memo to ETC management:

> There is no such things as a Eurocustomer so it makes no sense to talk about Eurobrands. We have an English housewife whose needs are different from a German hausfrau. If we move to a system that allows us to blur our thinking we will have big problems.
>
> Product standardization sets up pressures to try to meet everybody's needs (in which case you build a Rolls Royce that nobody can afford) and countervailing pressures to find the lowest common denominator product (in which case you make a product that satisfies nobody and which cannot compete in any market). These pressures probably result in the foul middle compromise that is so often the outcome of committee decision.

Organization Decision

The strategic questions of whether to launch Vizir, and if so on what scale, also raised some difficult questions about the existing organization structure and internal decision-making processes. If product market decisions were to be taken more in relation to Europe-wide strategic assessments and less in response to locally perceived opportunities, what implications did that have for the traditional role and responsibility of the country general manager? And if the Eurobrand concept was accepted, what organizational means were necessary to coordinate activities among the various country subsidiaries?

By the time Charlie Ferguson became vice-president of P&G Europe, the non-technical staff in ETC had grown substantially, from the 20 or so people that used to work with Tom Bower in the early 1970s. Ferguson was convinced that his predecessor, Ed Artzt, had been moving in the right direction in trying to inject a Europe-wide perspective to decisions, and in aiming to coordinate more activities among subsidiaries. He wanted to reinforce the organizational shift by changing the responsibilities of the three geographic division managers reporting to him.

In addition to their existing responsibilities for several subsidiaries, Ferguson gave each of these managers Europe-wide responsibility for one or more lines of business. For example, the division manager responsible for the UK, French, Belgian and Dutch subsidiaries was also given responsibility for packaged soaps and detergents Europe-wide. Although these roles were clearly coordinative in nature, the status and experience of these managers meant that their advice and recommendations would carry a good deal of weight, particularly on strategic and product planning issues.

Following this change, for the first time clear, Euro-wide objectives and priorities could be sent by line of business, product group or brand. Not surprisingly, some country subsidiary managers wondered whether their authority and autonomy were being eroded. Partly to deal with this problem, and partly because the division managers had neither the time nor the resources to manage their product responsibilities adequately, Ferguson created the Eurobrand Team concept.

Borrowing from the successful technical team concept, each key brand would have a team with a 'lead country'. The lead country would coordinate the analysis of opportunities for the standardization of the product, its promotion and packaging and for the simplification of the brand's management by coordinating activities and eliminating needless duplication between subsidiaries.

The main forum for achieving this would be the Eurobrand Team meetings. Chaired by the appropriate brand manager from the lead country, these teams would be composed of brand and advertising managers from all other countries marketing this product (called contributing countries), as well as appropriate ETC functional managers (technical, advertising, buying, manufacturing, etc.) and the European division manager responsible for that product group. Thus, a typical team might have 20–30 members in all.

At the subsidiary level, the proposal received mixed reviews. Some saw the teams as a good way to have increased local management participation in Eurobrand decisions. These individuals saw the European technical teams as evidence such an approach could work, and felt it represented a far better solution than having such decisions shaped largely by an enlarged staff group at ETC. Another group saw the Eurobrand Teams as a further risk to the autonomy of the country manager. Some also saw it as a threat to intersubsidiary relations rather than an aid. One general manager from a smaller country subsidiary explained:

> When a big, resource-rich subsidiary like Germany is anointed with the title of Lead Country, I am concerned that they will used their position and expertise to dominate the teams. I believe this concept will generate further hostility between subsidiaries. Pricing and volume are the only tools we have left. The general manager's role has been compromised.

Another concern was that team meetings would not be an effective decision-making forum. With individual subsidiaries still responsible for and measured on their local profitability, it was felt that participants would go in with strongly held parochial views that they would not be willing to compromise. Some claimed that because the teams' roles and responsibilities were not clear it would become another time-consuming block to decision-making rather than a means to achieve progress on Eurobrands. A subsidiary general manager commented:

> The agenda for the Eurobrand Teams is huge, but its responsibilities and powers are unclear. For such a huge and emotionally charged task, it is unrealistic to expect the 'brand manager of the day' to run things. The teams will bog down and decisions will take forever. Our system is all checks and no balances. We are reinforcing an organization in which no one can say yes – they can only veto. With all the controls on approvals, we've lost the knack to experiment.

At least one manager at ETC voiced his frustration directly: 'If we were serious [about standardization], we would stop paying lip service, and tell everyone "Like it or not, we're going to do it".'

Charlie Ferguson remained convinced that the concept made sense, and felt that *if* Vizir were to be launched and *if* it were to be considered a Eurobrand, it might provide a good early test for Eurobrand Teams.

EXHIBIT 1
Abbreviated organization chart : Proctor & Gamble Europe.

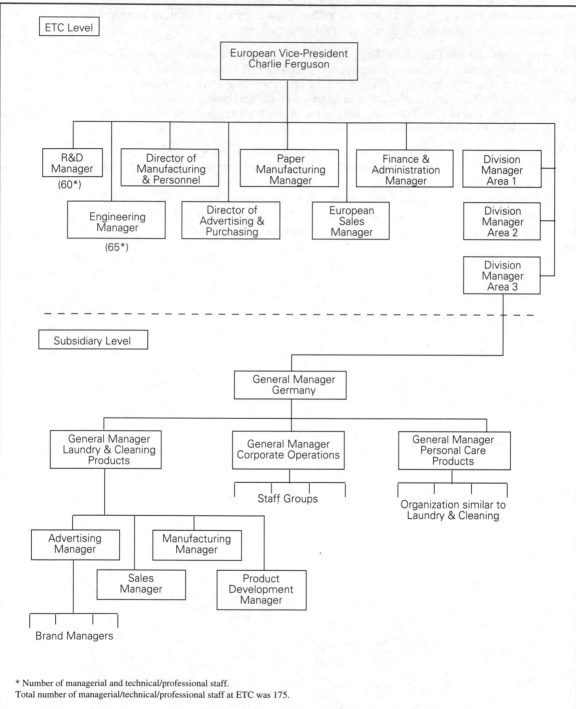

* Number of managerial and technical/professional staff.
Total number of managerial/technical/professional staff at ETC was 175.

EXHIDIT 2
Comparative scripts. Vizir and Ariel commercials.

Vizir ('Peter's Pants') (Woman in laundry examining newly washed pants on her son)	*Ariel* ('Helen Hedy') (Woman in laundry holding daughter's blouse)
Announcer: Hey, Peter's things look pretty nice. *Woman:* Thanks. *Announcer:* Too bad they're not completely clean. *Woman:* What? *Announcer:* There's still oily dirt from his bicycle. *Woman:* I can't boil modern fabrics. And without boiling they don't get cleaner. *Announcer:* Oh yes! Here is Vizir, the new liquid detergent Vizir, the liquid powder that gets things cleaner. Without boiling! *Woman:* Bicycle oil will come out? Without boiling? *Announcer:* Yes, one cap of Vizir in the main wash and on tough soiling pour a little Vizir on directly. Then wash. Let's test Vizir against boilwash powder. These make-up stains were washed in powder at 60° – not clean. On top we put this unwashed dirty towel, then pour on Vizir. Vizir's liquid power penetrates the dirt and dissolves it, as well as the stain that boilwash powder left behind. *Woman:* Incredible. The bicycle oil – gone! Without boiling. Through and through cleaner. *Announcer:* Vizir – liquid power to get things cleaner.	*Announcer:* Looks beautifully clean again, doesn't it? *Helen:* Yes, sure. *Announcer:* Also close up? *Helen:* Well, no. When you really look up close – that's gravy. A stain like that never comes out completely. *Announcer:* Why is that? *Helen:* Because you just can't boil these modern things. I can't get Barbel's blouse really clean without boiling. *Announcer:* Then use Ariel. It can clean without boiling. *Helen:* Without boiling? Even these stains? That I want to see. *Announcer:* THE TEST: With prewash and mainwash at low temperature we are washing stubborn stains like egg and gravy. The towel on the right had Ariel's cleaning power. *Helen:* Hey, it's really true. The gravy on Barbel's blouse is completely gone. Even against the light – deep down clean. All this without boiling. *Announcer:* Ariel – without boiling, still clean!

EXHIBIT 3
Selected test market results: Vizir Berlin test market.

A. Total Shipments and Share

	Shipments: MSU (Volume Index)		Share (%)	
	Actual	Target	Actual	Target
February	4.6	1.8		1.8
March	5.2	2.5	2.2	2.7
April	9.6	4.5	5.2	3.4
May	3.1	3.1	3.4	

B. Consumer Research Results

Use and Awareness (At 3 months; 293 responses)	Vizir	Mustang*
Ever Used (%)	28	22
Past 4 weeks	15	9
Ever Purchased	13	15
Past 4 weeks	8	6
Twice or more	4	NA
Brand on Hand	15	11
Large sizes	3	5
Advertising Awareness	47	89
Brand Awareness	68	95

Attitude Data (At 3 months; including sample only users)	Vizir	Mustang*
Unduplicated Comments On:		
whiteness, brightness, cleaning or stain removal	65/11**	58/8**
cleaning or stain removal	49/8	52/4
cleaning	12/2	17/NA
stain removal	37/6	35/NA
odour	30/4	15/3
effect on clothes	7/–	13/6
form (liquid)	23/11	NA

*Mustang was a recently launched Henkel low-temperature powder on which comparable consumer data was available. It was judged to have been only moderately successful, capturing 2½ per cent market share compared to Ariel's 11 per cent share as low-temperature segment leader.

**Number of unduplicated comments, favourable/unfavourable about the product in user interviews (e.g. among Vizir users interviewed, 65 commented favourably about whiteness, brightness, cleaning or stain removal, while 11 commented negatively about one or more of those attributes).

EXHIBIT 4
Selected market research data.

A. Selected Washing Practices

	Germany		UK		France		Italy		Spain	
	1973	1978	1973	1978	1973	1978	1973	1978	1973	1978
Washing Machine Penetration										
% Households with Drum Machines	76	83	10	26	59	70	70	79	24	50
Washing Temperature										
≤60° (including handwash)	51	67	71	82	48	68	31	49	63	85
>60°	49	33	29	18	52	32	69	51	37	15
Fabric Softener Use										
% Loads with Fabric Softener	68	69	36	47	52	57	21	35	18	37

B. Selected Consumer Attitude Data (German Survey Only)

Laundry Cleaning Problems (% respondents claim)*	Grease-Based	Bleach-Sensitive	Enzyme-Sensitive
Most Frequent Stains (%)	61	53	34
Desired Improvement (%)	65	57	33
in washes ≤60°	78	53	25
in washes >60°	7	36	65

*Do not add to 100 per cent because multiple responses allowed.

3–7

ELECTROLUX: THE ACQUISITION AND INTEGRATION OF ZANUSSI

In recounting the story of Electrolux's acquisition of Zanussi, Leif Johansson, head of Electrolux's major appliance division, had reasons to feel pleased. Through a combination of financial restructuring and operating improvements Zanussi had, in only three years since the acquisition, gone from a massive loss of L.120 billion in 1983 to a tidy profit of L.60 billion in 1987* – a turnaround that had astounded outside analysts, and was perhaps a shade more impressive than the expectations of even the extreme optimists within Electrolux. More important still was the progress made in integrating Zanussi strategically, operationally and organizationally within the Electrolux group, while protecting its distinct identity and reviving the fighting spirit that had once been the hallmark of the proud Italian company. Having been the first to suggest to President Anders Scharp that Electrolux should buy financially troubled Zanussi, Johansson had a major personal stake in the continued success of the operation.

By early 1988, however, the task was far from complete. Not everything was going well at Zanussi: the company had recently lost some market share within Italy to Merloni, its arch rival, which had taken over domestic market leadership following its acquisition of Indesit, another large Italian producer of household appliances.

This case was prepared by Dag Andersson, Nicola De Sanctis, Beniamino Finzi and Jacopo Franzan under the supervision of Sumantra Ghoshal and Philippe Haspeslagh, Associate Professors at INSEAD. It is intended to be used as a basis for class discussion rather than to illustrate either effective or ineffective handling of an administrative situation. The cooperation of the Electrolux company and its executives is gratefully acknowledged.
*$1 = L. 1170 = SEK 5.85 (*International Financial Statistics*, December, 1987).

There had been some delays in Zanussi's ambitious programme for plant automation. Moreover, a recent attitude survey had shown that, while the top 60 managers of Zanussi fully supported the actions taken since the acquisition, the next rung of 150 managers felt less motivated and less secure. It was not clear whether these problems were short-term in nature and would soon be resolved, or whether they were the warning signals for more basic and fundamental maladies.

Though Leif Johansson felt that it would be useful to review the integration process, his own concerns were focused on what the next stage of the battle for global leadership would be. The industry was changing rapidly with competitors like Whirlpool and Matsushita moving outside their home regions. At the same time some local European comptitors like GEC-Hotpoint in the United Kingdom and Merloni (Ariston) in Italy were making aggressive moves to expand their shares in a relatively low-growth market. The Zanussi takeover, coupled with the subsequent acquisition of White Consolidated in the United States, had catapulted Electrolux to the top of the list of the world's largest producers of household appliances. The challenge for Johansson now was to mould all the acquired entities into an integrated strategy and organization that would protect this leadership role and leverage it into a profitable worldwide operation.

In 1962, Electrolux was on a downward curve. Profits were falling and the company had not developed any significant in-house research and development capability. Compared with other appliance manufacturers such as Philips, Siemens, GEC and Matsushita, it had a limited range of products: the core business was made up of vacuum cleaners and absorption-type refrigerators. These refrigerators were increasingly unable to compete with the new compressor-type refrigerators developed by the competitors, and sales of the once highly successful lines of vacuum cleaners were rapidly declining.

That same year ASA, a company in the Wallenberg network (an informal grouping of major Swedish companies in which the Wallenbergs – the most influential business family in Sweden – had some equity shares) sold Electro-Helios to Electrolux for shares and thereby became a major shareholder. Electro-Helios was a technological leader in compressor-type refrigerators and a significant producer of freezers and cooking-ranges. This led to a major expansion of Electrolux's role in the Swedish household appliance market, but the company found itself in financial difficulty again due to rapid expansion of production capacity during a period of severe economic downturn.

In 1967 Hans Werthén was appointed CEO of Electrolux. In the next two decades he and the other two members of what was known as the 'Electrolux Troika', Anders Scharp and Gösta Bystedt, would manage to develop the company from a relatively small and marginal player in the business into the world's largest manufacturer of household appliances.

GROWTH THROUGH ACQUISITIONS

At the core of the dramatic transformation of Electrolux was an aggressive strategy of expansion through acquisition. At the beginning, Electrolux concentrated on acquiring firms in the Nordic countries, its traditional market, where the company already had a dominant market share. Subsequent acquisitions served not only to strengthen the company's position in its household appliance activities, but also to broaden its European presence and open the way to entirely new product areas. Exhibit 1 illustrates Electrolux's major acquisitions between 1964 and 1988.

With more than 200 acquisitions in 40 countries, and 280 manufacturing facilities in 25 countries, the Electrolux Group had few equals in managing the acquisition and integration processes. The company generally bought competitors in its core businesses, disposing of operations which either failed to show long-term profit potential or appeared to have a better chance of prospering under the management of another company. In addition, Electrolux always tried to ensure that there were sufficient realizable assets available to help finance the necessary restructuring of the acquired company. Thus, from the early 1970s to 1988, the group made capital gains of more than SEK 2.5 billion from selling off idle assets.

At the same time, flexibility had been maintained in order to pick up new product areas for further development. A typical example of this was the chainsaw product line which came with the acquisition of the Swedish appliance manufacturer Husqvarna in 1978. By developing this product line through acquisitions and in-house development, Electrolux emerged as one of the world's leading chainsaw manufacturers with about 30 per cent of the global market. Another example was provided by the new business are of outdoor products (consisting mainly of forestry and garden products), which had been grown from the small base of the Flugmo lawnmower business through the acquisition of firms like Poulan/Weed Eater in the United States and Staub/Bernard Moteur in France.

The two most notable departures from the strategy of buying familiar businesses had been the 1973 acquisition of Facit, a Swedish office equipment and electronics maker, and the 1980 purchase of Gränges, a metal and mining company. Both companies were in financial trouble. Electrolux had difficulty in fully mastering Facit. After having brought the profit up to a reasonable level, it was sold off to Ericsson in 1983. The borrowing necessary to buy Gränges, combined with the worldwide economic downturn and rising interest rates, pushed Electrolux into a sobering two-year (1981–3) decline of its profit margin. However, through the Gränges takeover Electrolux also acquired new businesses for future growth. An example was the manufacturing of seat belts, now concentrated in the subsidiary Electrolux Autoliv. Nevertheless, the acquisition of Gränges would be the last diversifying acquisition.

Even though Electrolux had dealt with a large number of acquisitions, specific companies were seldom targeted. In the words of Anders Scharp, 'You never choose an acquisition; opportunities just come.' The company made it their practice to simulate what the merger combination with other companies would result in should they come up for sale. The financial aspects of an acquisition were considered to be very important. The company usually ensured that it paid less for a company than the total asset value of the company, and not for what Electrolux would bring to the party.

Based on their experience, managers at Electrolux believed that there was no standard method for treating acquisitions: each case was unique and had to be dealt with differently. Typically, however, Electrolux moved quickly at the beginning of the integration process. It identified the key action areas and created task forces consisting of managers from both Electrolux and the acquired company in order to address each of the issues on a time-bound basis. Such joint task forces were believed to help foster management confidence and commitment and create avenues for reciprocal information flows. Objectives were clearly specified, milestones were identified, and the first phase of integration was generally completed within 3–6 months so as to create and maintain momentum. The top management of an acquired company was often replaced, but the middle management was kept intact. As explained by Anders Scharp, 'The risk of losing general management competence is small when it is a poorly performing company. Electrolux is prepared to take this risk. It is, however, important that we do not change the marketing and sales staff.'

ELECTROLUX PRIOR TO THE ACQUISITION OF ZANUSSI

The activities of the Electrolux group in 1984, prior to the acquisition of Zanussi, covered 26 product lines within five business areas, namely: household appliances, forestry and garden products, industrial products, commercial services and metal and mining (Gränges). Total sales revenue had increased from SEK 1.1 billion in 1967 to SEK 34.5 billion in 1984. The household appliance area (including white goods, special refrigerators, floor-care products and sewing machines) accounted for approximately 52 per cent of total Group Sales in 1984. Gränges was the second largest area with nearly 21.5 per cent of total sales. The third area, industrial products, provided heavy equipment for food services, semi-industrial laundries and commercial cleaning.

By the 1980s Electrolux had become one of the world's largest manufacturers of white goods with production facilities in Europe and North America and a small presence in Latin America and the Far East. The Group's reliance on the Scandinavian markets was still considerable: more than 30 per cent of sales came from Sweden, Norway and Denmark. European sales, focusing mainly on Scandinavia and Western Europe, constituted 65 per cent of total Group sales. The United States had emerged as the single most important market with 28.9 per cent (1987) of total sales.

Electrolux's household appliances were manufactured in plants with specialized assembly-lines. Regional manufacturing operations were focused on local brands and designs and established distribution networks. Sales forces for the various brands had been kept separate, though support functions such as physical distribution, stocking, order-taking and invoicing might be integrated. With increasing plant automation and product differentiation, the number of models and the value product in any given plant had risen sharply. As described by Anders Scharp, 'We recognized that expansion means higher volumes, which create scope for rationalization. Rationalization means better margins, which are essential to boost our competitive strength.'

One important characteristic of Electrolux was the astonishingly small corporate headquarters at Lilla Essingen, 6 km outside the centre of Stockholm, and the relatively few people who worked in central staff departments. The size of headquarters was a direct outcome of the company's commitment to decentralization: 'I believe that we have at least two hierarchical levels fewer than other companies of the same size,' said Scharp, 'and all operational matters are decentralized to the subsidiaries.' However, most strategic issues such as investment programmes and product range decisions were dealt with at headquarters. The subsidiaries were considered to be profit centres and were evaluated primarily on their returns on net assets as compared with the targets set by the corporate office. Presidents of the diversified subsidiaries reported directly to Scharp, while others reported to the heads of the different product lines.

THE ACQUISITION OF ZANUSSI

In June 1983, Leif Johansson, the 32-year-old head of Electrolux's major appliance division, received a proposal from Mr Candotti, head of Zanussi's major appliance division in France, from whom he had been 'sourcing' refrigerators for the French market. The proposal called for the investment of a small amount of money in Zanussi so as to secure future supplies from the financially troubled Italian producer. The next day Johansson called Anders Scharp to ask 'Why don't we buy all of it?', thereby triggering a process that led to the largest acquisition in the history of the household appliance industry and in the Swedish business world.

Zanussi

Having begun in 1916 as a small workship in Pordenone, a little town in north-east Italy, where Antonio Zanussi produced a few wood-burning cookers, Zanussi had grown by the early 1980s to be the second largest privately owned company in Italy with more than 30,000 employees, 50 factories and 13 foreign sales companies. Most of the growth came in the 1950s and 1960s under the leadership of Lino Zanussi, who understood the necessity of having not only a complete range of products but also a well-functioning distribution and sales network. Lino Zanussi established several new factories within Italy and added cookers, refrigerators and washing-machines to the product range. In 1958 he launched a major drive to improve exports out of Italy and established the first foreign branch office in Paris in 1962. Similar branches were soon opened in other European countries and the first foreign manufacturing subsidiary, IBELSA, was set up in Madrid in 1965. Through a series of acquisitions of Italian producers of appliances and components, Zanussi became one of the most vertically integrated manufacturers in Europe, achieving full control over all activities ranging from component manufacturing to final sales and service. It is rumoured that, during this period of heady success, Zanussi had very seriously considered launching a takeover bid for Electrolux, then a struggling Swedish company less than half Zanussi's size.

The company's misfortunes started in 1968 when Lino Zanussi and several other company executives died in an aircrash. Over the next fifteen years the new management carved out a costly programme of unrelated diversification into fields such as colour televisions, prefabricated housing, real estate and community centres. The core business of domestic appliances languished for want of capital, while the new businesses incurred heavy losses. By 1982, the company had amassed debts of over L 1,300 billion and was losing over L 100 billion a year on operations. (See Exhibit 2 for the consolidated financial statements during this period.)

Between 1982 and 1984, Zanussi tried to rectify the situation by selling off many of the loss-making subsidiaries, reducing the rest of the workforce by over 4,400 people, and focusing on its core activities. However, given the large debt burden and the need for substantial investment in order to rebuild the domestic appliance business, a fresh injection of capital was essential and the company began its search for a partner.

THE ACQUISITION PROCESS

The process of Electrolux's acquisition of Zanussi formally commenced when Enrico Cuccia, the informal head of Mediobanca and the most powerful financier in Italy, approached Hans Werthén on 30 November 1983, about the possibility of Electrolux rescuing Zanussi from impending financial collapse. It was not by chance that the grand old man of Mediobanca arrived in Sweden. Mr Cuccia had close links to the Agnelli family – the owners of Fiat, the largest industrial group in Italy – and the proposal to approach Electrolux came from Mr Agnelli, who wanted to save the second largest private manufacturing company in his country. As a board member of SKF, the Swedish bearing manufacturer, Agnelli had developed a healthy respect for Swedish management and believed that Electrolux alone had the resources and management skills necessary to turn Zanussi around.

In the meanwhile, Electrolux had been looking around for a good acquisition to expand its appliance busines. Its efforts to take over AEG's appliance business in Germany had failed because the conditions stipulated for the takeover were found to be too restrictive. Later, Electrolux had to back away from acquiring the TI group in the United Kingdom because of too high a price-tag. Zanussi now represented the best chance for significant expansion in Europe. 'It was a very good fit,' recalled Anders Scharp. 'There were not many overlaps: we were strong where Zanussi was weak, and vice versa.' There were significant complementarities in products, markets and opportunities for vertical integration. For example, while Electrolux was well established in microwave ovens, cookers and fridge-freezers, Zanussi was Europe's largest producer of 'wet products' such as washing-machines, traditionally a weak area of Electrolux. Similarly, while Electrolux had large market shares in Scandinavia and Switzerland where Zanussi was almost completely absent, Zanussi was the market leader in Italy and Spain, two markets that Electrolux had failed to crack. Zanussi was also strong in France, the only market where Electrolux was losing money, and had a significant presence in Germany where Electrolux had limited strength, except in vacuum cleaners. Finally, while Electrolux historically had avoided vertical integration and sourced most of its components externally, Zanussi was a vertically integrated company with substantial spare capacity for component production that Electrolux could profitably use.

From 30 November 1983 to 14 December 1984, the date when the formal deal was finally signed, there ensued a 12-month period of intense negotiation in which, alongside the top management of the two companies, Gianmario Rossignolo, the

Chairman of SKF's Italian subsidiary, took an increasingly active role. The most difficult parts of the negotiations focused on the following three issues:

Union and Workforce Reduction

At the outset, the powerful unions at Zanussi were opposed to selling the company to the 'Vikings from the North'. They would have preferred to keep Zanussi independent with a government subsidy, or to merge with Thomson of France. They also believed that under Electrolux management all important functions would be transferred to Sweden, thereby deskilling the Italian company and reducing local employment opportunities.

In response to these concerns, Electrolux guaranteed that all Zanussi's important functions would be retained within Italy. Twenty union leaders were sent from Sweden to Italy to reassure the Italians. The same number of Italian union leaders were invited to Sweden to observe Electrolux's production system and labour relations. Initially, Mr Rossignolo signed a letter of assurance to the unions on behalf of Electrolux confirming that the level of employment prevailing at that time would be maintained. Soon thereafter, however, it became obvious that Zanussi could not be made profitable without workforce reductions. This resulted in difficult re-negotiations. It was finally agreed that within three months of the acquisition Electrolux would present the unions with a three-year plan for investments, and reductions in personnel. Actual retrenchments would have to follow the plan, subject to its approval by the unions.

Prior Commitments of Zanussi

A number of problems were posed by certain commitments on the part of Zanussi. One major issue was SELECO, an Italian producer of television sets. A majority of shares in SELECO were held by REL, a government holding company, and the rest were owned by Zanussi and Indesit. Zanussi had made a commitment to buy REL's majority holdings of SELECO within a period of five years ending in 1989. Electrolux had no interest in entering the television business, but finally accepted this commitment despite considerable apprehension.

Another major concern was the unprofitable Spanish appliance company IBELSA, owned by Zanussi. Zanussi had received large subsidies from the Spanish government against a commitment to help restructure the industry in Spain, and heavy penalties would have to be paid if the company decided to pull out. Once again, Electrolux had to accept these terms despite concern about IBELSA's long-term competitiveness.

Nevertheless, there was one potential liability that Electrolux refused to accept. In the later stages of the negotiations, an audit team from Electrolux discovered that a previous managing director of Zanussi had sold a large amount of equipment and machinery to a German company and had then leased them back. This could potentially lead to severe penalties and large fines, as the actions violated Italian foreign exchange and tax laws. Electrolux refused to proceed with the negotiations until the Italian government had promised not to take any punitive action in this case.

Financial Structure and Ownership

Electrolux was not willing to take over majority ownership pf Zanussi immediately since it would then be required to consolidate Zanussi into group accounts, and the large debts would have major adverse effects on the Electrolux balance sheet and share prices. Electrolux wanted to take minority holdings without relinquishing its claim to majority holdings in the future. To resolve this issue, a consortium was organized which included prominent Italian financial institutions and industrial companies such as Mediobanca, IMI, Crediop and a subsidiary of Fiat. The consortium took on a large part of the shares (40.6 per cent), with another 10.4 per cent bought by the Friuli region. This allowed Electrolux to remain at 49 per cent. While the exact financial transactions were kept confidential since some of the parties opposed any payment to the Zanussi family, it is believed that Electrolux injected slightly under $100 million into Zanussi. One third of that investment secured the 49 per cent shareholding, and the remainder went towards debentures which could be converted into shares at any time to give Electrolux a comfortable 75 per cent ownership. An agreement with over 100 banks which had some form of exposure to Zanussi assured a respite from creditors, freezing payments on the Italian debt until January 1987. At the same time the creditors made considerable concessions on interest payments.

One of the most important meetings in the long negotiation process took place in Rome on 15 November 1984, when, after stormy discussions between the top management of Electrolux and the leaders of the Zanussi union, a document confirming Elextrolux's intention to acquire Zanussi was jointly signed by both parties. During the most crucial hour of the meeting, Hans Werthén stood up in front of the 50 union leaders and declared: 'We are not buying companies in order to close them down, but to turn them into profitable ventures ... and we are not Vikings, who were Norwegians, anyway.'

THE TURNAROUND OF ZANUSSI

It was standard Electrolux practice to have a broad but clear plan for immediate post-acquisition action well before the negotiation process for an acquisition was complete. Thus, by August 1984, well before the deal was signed in December, a specific plan for the turnaround and the eventual integration of Zanussi was drawn up in Stockholm. As stated by Leif Johansson, 'When we make an acquisition, we adopt a centralized approach from the outset. We have a definite plan worked out when we go in and there is virtually no need for extended discussions.' In the Zanussi case, the general approach had to be amended slightly since a feasible reduction in the employment levels was not automatic. However, clear decisions were taken to move the loss-making production of front-loaded washing-machines from France to Zanussi's factory in Pordenone. On the other hand, the production of all top-loading washing-machines was to be moved from Italy to France. In total, the internal plan anticipated shifting production of between 600,000 and 800,000 product units from Electrolux and subcontractors' plants to Zanussi, thereby increasing Zanussi's capacity utilization. Detailed financial calculations led to an expected cost savings of SEK 400,000–500,000 through rationalization. Specific plans were also drawn up to achieve a 2–3 per cent reduction in Zanussi's marketing and administrative costs by integrating the organization of the two companies in different countries.

IMMEDIATE POST-ACQUISITION ACTIONS

On 14 December, a matter of hours after signing the final agreement, Electrolux announced a complete change in the top management of Zanussi. The old board, packed with nominees of the Zanussi family, was swept clean and Mr Gianmario Rossignolo was appointed as chairman of the company. An Italian, long-experienced in working with Swedish colleagues because of his position as chairman of SKF's Italian subsidiary, Rossignolo was seen as an ideal bridge between the two companies with their vastly different cultures and management styles. Carlo Verri, who was managing directors of SKF's Italian subsidiary, was brought in as the new managing director of Zanussi. Rossignolo and Verri had turned around SKF's Italian operations and had a long history of working together as a team. Similarly, Hans Werthén, Anders Scharp, Gösta Bystedt and Lennart Ribohn joined the reconstituted Zanussi board. The industrial relations manager of Zanussi was the only senior manager below the board level to be replaced. The purpose was to give a clear signal to the entire organization of the need to change working practices.

Consistent with the Electrolux style, a number of task forces were formed immediately to address the scope of integration and rationalization of activities in different functional areas. Each team was given a specific time period to come up with recommendations. Similarly, immediate actions were initiated in order to introduce Electrolux's financial reporting system within Zanussi, the clear target being to have the system fully in place and operative within six months from the date of the acquisition.

Direct steps were taken at the business level to enhance capacity utilization, reduce costs of raw materials and components purchased, and revitalize local sales.

1. *Capacity utilization:* It was promised that Electrolux would source 500,000 units from Zanussi including 280,000 units of household appliances, 200,000 units of components and 7,500 units of commercial appliances. This sourcing decision was given wide publicity both inside and outside the company, and a drive was launched to achieve the chosen levels as soon as possible. By 1985, 70 per cent of the target had been reached.

2. *Cost-cutting in purchases:* Given that 70 per cent of production costs were represented by raw materials and purchased components, an immediate programme was launched to reduce vendor prices. The assumption was that vendors had adjusted their prices to compensate for the high risk of supplying to financially distressed Zanussi and should lower their prices now that that risk was eliminated. A net saving of 2 per cent on purchases was achieved immediately. Over time about 17 per cent gains in real terms would be achieved, not only for Zanussi, but also for Electrolux.

3.   *Revitalizing sales:* Local competitors in Italy reacted vigorously to the announcement of Electrolux's acquisition of Zanussi. Anticipating a period of inaction while the new management took charge, they launched an aggressive marketing programme and Zanussi's sales slumped almost immediately. After consulting with Electrolux, the new management of Zanussi responded with a dramatic move of initially extended trade credit from 60 to 360 days under specified conditions. Sales surged immediately and the market was assured once and for all that 'Zanussi was back'.

AGREEMENT WITH THE UNIONS

In the next phase, starting from February 1985, the new management turned its attention to medium and long-term needs. The most pressing of these was to fulfil a promise made to the unions before the acquisition: the presentation of a complete restructuring programme. This programme was finalized and discussed the with union leaders on 28 March 1985, at the Ministry of Industry in Rome. It consisted of a broad analysis of the industry and market trends, evaluation of Zanussi's competitive position and future prospects, and a detailed plan for investments and workforce reduction. The meeting was characterized by a high level of openness on the part of management. Such openness, unusual in Italian industrial relations, took the unions by surprise. In the end, after difficult negotiations, the plan was signed by all the parties on 25 May.

The final plan provided for a total reduction of the workforce by 4,848 employees (the emergency phone number in Italy!) to be implemented over a three-year period (2,850 in 1985, 850 in 1986 and 1,100 in 1987) through early retirement and other incentives for voluntary exit. In 1985, as planned, the workforce was reduced by 2,800.

Paradoxically, from the beginning of 1986 a new problem arose. With business doing well and export demands for some of the products strong, a number of factories had to resort to overtime work and even hired new skilled workers, whilst at the same time the original reduction plans continued to be implemented. Management claimed that there was no inconsistency in these actions since the people being laid off lacked the skills that would be needed in the future. With the prospect of factory automation clearly on the horizon, a more educated and skilled workforce was necessary and the new hirings conformed to these future needs. Some of the workers resisted, and a series of strikes followed at the Porcia plant.

Management decided to force the issue and brought out advertisements in the local press to highlight the situation publicly. In the new industrial climate in Italy, the strategy proved effective and the strikes ended. In 1987, the company made further progress in its relationship with the unions. In a new agreement, wage increases were linked to productivity and no limits were placed on workforce reductions. Further, it was agreed that the company could hire almost 1,000 workers on a temporary basis, so as to take advantage of the subsidy provided by the government to stimulate worker training through temporary employment. It was clear that Zanussi management benefited significantly from the loss of union power that was a prominent feature of the recently changed industrial scene in Italy. However, its open and transparent approach also contributed to the success by gaining the respect of trade union leaders, at both the company and national levels.

STRATEGIC TRANSFORMATION: BUILDING COMPETITIVENESS

The new management recognized that, in order to build durable competitive advantage, more basic changes were necessary. The poor financial performance of the company before the acquisition was only partly due to low productivity, and sustainable profits could not be assured through workforce reduction alone. After careful analysis, three areas were chosen as the focal points for a strategic transformation of Zanussi: improving production technology, spurring innovations and new product development, and enhancing product quality.

Improving Production Technology

Recalling his first visit to Zanussi, Halvar Johansson, then head of Electrolux's technical R&D, commented: 'What we found on entering Zanussi's factories was, in many respects, 1960s technology! The level of automation was far too low, especially in assembly operation. We did not find a single industrial robot or even a computer either in the product development unit or in the plant. However, we also discovered that Zanussi's engineers and production personnel were of notably high standards.' As part of a broad programme to improve production technology, Electrolux initiated an investment programme of L.340 billion to restructure Zanussi's two major plants at Susegana and Porcia.

The Susegana restructuring proposal foresaw an investment of L.100 billion to build up the facility into a highly automated, high-capacity unit able to produce 1.2 million refrigerators and freezers a year. The project was expected to come on stream by the end of 1988. The Porcia project anticipated a total investment of about L.200 billion to build a highly automated, yet flexible plant capable of producing 1.5 million washing-machines per year. This project, scheduled for completion in 1990, was the largest individual investment project in the history of the Electrolux group. When on stream it would be the largest washing-machine factory in the world. Both projects involved large investments to build flexibility through the use of CAD-CAM systems and just-in-time production methodology. As explained by Carlo Verri, 'The automation was primarily to achieve flexibility and to improve quality, and not to save on labour costs.'

Implementation of both the projects was somewhat delayed. While the initial schedules may have been over-optimistic, some of the delays were caused by friction among Zanussi and Electrolux engineers. The Electrolux approach of building joint teams for implementation of projects was seen by some Zanussi managers as excessive involvement of the acquiring company in tasks for which the acquired company had ample and perhaps superior capabilities. Consequently, information flows were often blocked, resulting in, for example, a more than one-year delay in deciding the final layout of the Susegana factory. The delays were a matter of considerable concern to the top management of Electrolux. On the one hand, they felt extensive involvement of Electrolux's internal consultants to be necessary for effective implementation of the projects, since Zanussi lacked the requisite expertise. On the other hand, they acknowledged Zanussi's well-established engineering skills and the need to provide the local engineers with the opportunity to learn and to prove themselves. They also worried about whether the skill-levels of the local workforce could be upgraded in time for operating the new units and looked for ways to expedite the training process.

Innovation and New Product Development

Zanussi had built its strong market presence on the reputation of being an innovator. This ability had, unfortunately, languished during the lean period. Both Rossignolo and Verri placed the greatest emphasis on reviving the innovative spirit of the company, and projects that had idled for years due to lack of funds were revitalized and assigned high priority.

The results were quite dramatic and a virtual torrent of new product ideas emerged very quickly. The most striking example was a new washing-machine design – the 'Jet System' – which cut detergent and water consumption by a third. The product was developed within only 9 months and the new machine was presented at the Cologne Fair in February 1986. Through a direct television link with Cologne, Carlo Verri himself presented the assembly line at Pordenone where the 'Jet System' was to be mass produced. By July 1986, demand for the new machine had reached the level of 250,000 per year and the company was facing delivery problems.

While the 'Jet System' was the most visible outcome of the new emphasis on innovation, other equally important developments were in the pipeline. For example, the company developed a new rotary compressor to replace the reciprocating compressors that were being used in refrigerators. A major drive was also underway to improve product design and features through the introduction of IC chips. Interestingly, most of these proposals came not from the sophisticated and independent research centre of the company, but from development groups located within the line organizations which produced the products. How to maintain the momentum of innovation was a major concern for Verri, particularly as the company moved into the larger and more complex projects necessary for significant technological breakthroughs.

Enhancing Product Quality

Quality enhancement was viewed as the third leg of the strategy for long-term revitalization of Zanussi. At Electrolux, high quality was viewed as an essential means of achieving the primary objectives of the company: satisfied customers, committed employees and sound profitability. Zanussi had a good reputation for quality, but the standards had slackened during the turmoil faced by the company for almost a decade prior to the acquisition. Committed to the policy that quality levels must be the same within the group no matter where a product was produced, Electrolux initiated a major drive to enhance product quality at Zanussi and set extremely ambitious targets to reduce failure rates and post-sales service requirements. The targets were such that incremental improvements did not suffice for their attainment and a new approach towards quality was necessary. The technical staff of Electrolux provided requisite guidance and assistance and helped set up the parameters for a series of quality improvement programmes launched by Zanussi.

Carlo Verri was involved in these programmes on an almost day-to-day basis. First, he headed the working group that set up the basic policy on quality for the entire Zanussi organization. In accordance with this policy, a Total Quality (TQ) project was started in May 1986 and a series of education and training programmes were introduced in order to diffuse the new philosophy and policy to all company employees. Supplier involvement was an integral part of the TQ project. As described by Verri,

> Supplier involvement was crucial. Zanussi's suppliers had to demonstrate their commitment to effective quality control. This meant that all the procedures for quality assurance, for tracking down failures etc., had to be approved by us. In other words, suppliers had to have the capability to provide self-certification for the quality of their products. They had to provide service within days rather than weeks, given that our plants were becoming automated. Our gains in flexibility and quality through new production techniques could be lost if the suppliers did not become equally efficient.

ORGANIZATIONAL REVITALIZATION: CHANGING ATTITUDES

One of the biggest challenges faced in the turnaround process lay in the area of revitalizing the Zanussi organization. During the troubled years the management process at Zanussi had suffered from many aberrations. Conflicts had become a way of life, and information flow within the organization had become severely constrained. Most issues were escalated to the top for arbitration, and the middle management had practically no role in decision making. Front-line managers had become alienated because of direct dealings between the workers and senior managers via the union leaders. Overall, people had lost faith in the integrity of the system, in which seniority and loyalty to individuals were seen as more important than competence or commitment to the company.

In addition, the acquisition had also created a strong barrier of defensiveness within the Zanussi organization. In its own acquisitions Zanussi typically eliminated most of the middle management in the acquired companies. As the acquired company it expected similar actions from Electrolux. Moreover, some Zanussi managers were not convinced of any need for change. They believed that Zanussi's financial problems were caused not by any strategic, operational or organizational shortcomings, but by the practices of the previous owners, including diversion of overseas profits through a foreign holding company on Luxembourg.

Finally, most of the managers were also concerned that both Rossignolo and Verri, with their backgrounds in the Italian subsidiary of a Swedish company, 'were closer to Stockholm than to Pordenone'.

In an attempt to overcome these barriers, Verri and the entire executive management group at Zanussi participated in a number of team-building sessions that were facilitated by an external consultant. These meetings gave rise to a number of developments that constituted the core of the organizational revitalization of Zanussi.

Statement of Mission, Values and Guiding Principles

One of the direct outcomes of the team-building meetings was a statement of Mission, Values and Guiding Principles developed to serve as the charter for change (see Exhibit 3). The statement identified the four main values of the company: to be close to the clients and satisfy them through innovation and service; to accept challenges and develop a leader mentality; to pursue total quality not only in production but in all areas of activity; and to become a global competitor by developing an international outlook. Apart from these specific points, the statement also confirmed the new management's commitment to creating a context that would foster transparent and coherent behaviour at both the individual and company levels under all circumstances. As described by Rossignolo, 'We adopted the Swedish work ethic – everybody keeps his word and all information is correct. We committed ourselves to being honest with the local authorities, the trade unions and our customers. It took some time for the message to get across, but I think everybody had got it now.'

Management Development Workshops

In order to improve the flow of information among senior managers and to co-opt them into the new management approach, a set of management development workshops was organized. The 60 most senior managers of Zanussi, including Verri, participated in each of three two-day workshops that were held between November 1985 and July 1986. The next tier of 150 middle managers of the company were subsequently exposed to the same programme.

Middle Management Problems

An organizational climate survey in 1987 revealed an interesting problem. The top 60 managers of the company confirmed strong support for the mission statement and the new management style. Conversely, the 150 middle managers, who seemed to feel threatened by the changes, appeared considerably less enthused. Their subordinates – about 1,000 front-line managers and professional employees like the top management, fully approved the change and demanded greater involvement. In response to this problem, it was decided that the 60 top managers should establish direct communication with the 1,000 front-line managers, by-passing the middle management when necessary. The decision was made known within the organization and a clear signal was sent to the middle managers that they should get on board or else they would risk missing the boat. At the same time, a special training programme was launched for the front-line managers and professional employees in order to broaden their management skills and outlook.

Structural Reorganization

Before the acquisition, Zanussi was organized in five 'sectors', with the heads of each sector reporting to the managing director. The sectors, in turn, controlled the operating companies in their business areas. In practice, the sector managers were closely involved with the day-to-day operations of the companies under their charge. Both the managing director at the corporate level, and the different sector managers had strong staff organizations to support their activities.

Verri abandoned the sector concept, even though the operating companies continued to report to the former sector managers who were now called managing directors. However, staff at the sector level were virtually eliminated and the operating companies were given full responsibility and authority for taking all operating-level decisions. Similarly, staff at the corporate level were also reduced very substantially, and the heads of planning, finance and control, organization and human resources, general administration, and legal and public affairs all reported directly to Verri. The four managing directors, the five heads of major corporate staff departments, and Verri constituted the executive management group of Zanussi. As chairman, Rossignolo concentrated primarily on external relations.

INTEGRATION OF THE TWO COMPANIES

As described by Leif Johansson, 'With the acquisition of Zanussi, the Electrolux group entered a new era. In several respects we were able to adopt a completely new way of thinking.' Much of the new thinking emerged from the discussions and recommendations of the task forces that had been appointed, involving managers from both companies, to look at specific opportunities for integrating the activities of the two organizations. In total, eight such task forces were formed: two each for components, product development and commercial appliances, and one each for the marketing function and management development. Each of these task forces had met 3 to 4 times, typically for half a day each time. Their recommendations formed the basis for the actions that were taken to integrate the production and sales operations of the two companies, rationalize component production, and develop specialization in product and brand development within the entire Electrolux group. At the level of individuals, a bridge had been built between the top management of Electrolux and the senior management team of Zanussi, and further actions were underway for creating similar understanding and mutual respect among managers lower down in the two organizations.

ELECTROLUX COMPONENTS GROUP (ECG)

Following Electrolux's acquisition of White Consolidated in the United States in March 1986, an international task force consisting of managers from Electrolux, White and Zanussi was created to explore the overall synergies that could be exploited within the activities of the three companies. The task force concluded that integration opportunities were relatively limited at the level of finished products because of factors such as differences in customer preferences and technical standards and the high transportation costs.

However, at the component level there were many similarities in the needs of the three companies, implying greater scope for standardization and production rationalization. As a result of this analysis, the Electrolux Component Group was formed at the beginning of 1987 as part of the newly created industrial products division at Electrolux. The group was made responsible for the coordination and development of all strategic components used by Electrolux worldwide. Since over 50 per cent of the group's component production came from Zanussi, Verri was appointed head of this group in addition to his responsibilities as managing director of Zanussi, and the group headquarters were located in Turin, Italy. In order to preserve and enhance the competitiveness of the component sector, it was decided that 50 per cent of the component group's sales must be made to outside parties and at least 20 per cent of the internal requirement for components must be sourced from outside the newly formed group.

INTEGRATION OF PRODUCTION

At Electrolux, production, sales and marketing had traditionally been integrated market by market. After the acquisition of Zanussi, all these activities will be reorganised into international product divisions and national marketing/sales companies.

The larger volumes from the combined operations made it feasible to switch to a system in which large-scale specialised plants, equipped with flexible manufacturing technology, would each produce a single product for the entire European market. This new 'one product – one factory' strategy was exemplified by the new plants in Susegana and Porcia. Each of the product divisions carried full responsibility not only for manufacturing, but also for development and internal marketing of their products. In order to coordinate long-term development among these 43 divisions, three coordinators were appointed for 'wet', 'hot' and 'cold' products respectively. Based in Stockholm without staff, each of these coordinators would be on the road most of the time.

INTEGRATION OF SALES/MARKETING

Similarly, it was decided to create single umbrella companies over the separate sales/marketing organizations in all countries. Given the longstanding history of competition between the Electrolux and Zanussi organizations, this would turn out to be a difficult and complex process. It was planned that in each country the stronger organization would absorb the weaker one. This did not mean, however, that the head of the larger organization in each country would automatically receive the top slot in the combined organization. A number of complaints arose on both sides over this issue, which became a source of much irritation. For example, it was because of this that Candotti, who had been the first to approach Electrolux for investment in Zanussi, resigned. In what remained a source of considerable frustration, Zanussi continued to operate through directly controlled sales companies in Germany, France, Denmark and Norway.

Coordination among the marketing companies was achieved through an equally lean coordinating structure reporting to Leif Johansson, with an Italian manager coordinating all European countries and a Swedish manager looking after the rest of the world.

To facilitate operational coordination between sales and production, a number of new systems were developed. One, the Electrolux Forecasting and Supply System (EFS), involved the automatic coordination of sales forecasts and delivery orders. By 1988 computer links with EFS would be established in all European Sales subsidiaries and factories. The Zanussi evaluation system was changed to that of Electrolux, in which both sales and factories were assessed on the basis of return on net assets (RONA) rather than on a profit and cost basis. An overall RONA target of 20 per cent was set for the Group as a whole.

BRAND POSITIONING AND PRODUCT DEVELOPMENT

One of the consequences of Electrolux's history of international expansion through acquisitions was a proliferation of brands, not only in Europe but also in the United States, where the acquisition of White had brought a number of brands. The task of coordinating these brands, some of which were local, others regional, and a few international, would fall to the two marketing coordinators, working closely with Leif Johansson and a task force involving product styling and marketing managers. The challenge was complicated by the fact that even the international brands did not always have the same position from market to market. Zanussi, for example, was not a brand name in Italy itself, where its products sold as 'Rex'. And its image in Sweden was not nearly as upscale and innovative as in other countries like the United Kingdom.

The approach chosen in Europe was to group the brands in four brand-name families, each targeted at a particular customer profile and destined to become a separate design family. Two of these families would be international brands, based respectively on Electrolux and Zanussi and the other two would regroup a number of local brands. The goal was to develop an integrated pan-European strategy for each brand-name family. For the international brands, the stategy would involve high-scale production of standardized products in focused factories and coordinated positioning and marketing across different countries. For the families representing a collection of national brands, the products would again be standardized as far as possible so as to allow manufacturing on a regional scale; but each brand would be 'localized' in its country through positioning, distribution, promotion and service.

MUTUAL RESPECT AND UNDERSTANDING AMONG PEOPLE

Since the acquisition Anders Scharp, Lennart Ribohn and Leif Johansson had ensured that they jointly visited Pordenone at least once every two months for a two-day review of Zanussi's activities and progress. Hans Werthén and Gösta Bystedt also visited Zanussi, though much less frequently. The visitors would typically spend some time touring one or another of Zanussi's facilities and then move on to pre-planned meetings with Zanussi's top management. Over time these meetings had built a strong bridge of mutual respect between the two groups and helped diffuse some of the early apprehensions. As described by a senior manager of Zanussi,

> The top management of Electrolux really understands numbers. They look at a few key numbers and immediately grasp the essentials. That was very good training for us – we had the habit of analyzing and analyzing, without coming to any conclusions . . . . Besides, the top two or three people in Electrolux have the ability of immersing themselves in a particular problem and coming up with a solution and an implementation plan. They are also so obviously excited by what they do, their enthusiasm is very contagious.

For most senior managers at Zanussi these meetings provided stronger evidence than could any words that the top management of Electrolux did not consider the acquisition as a conquest but rather as a partnership. 'We have had a lot of exchanges, and have learnt a lot from them, but we have not had a single Swedish manager imposed on top of us here.'

At the next level of management the joint task forces had helped build some relationships among individuals, but the links were still weak and apprehensions remained. 'We don't know them, but our concern is that the next level of Electrolux managers may be more bureaucratic and less open. To them we might be a conquest,' said a senior manager of Zanussi. 'In the next phase of integration, we must develop bridges at the middle and I frankly do not know how easy or difficult that might be.'

Future Requirements

Whereas the acquisition of Zanussi and White Consolidated had catapulted Electrolux into a clear lead in the industry, the race was far from over. After initially failing to reach agreement with Philips in 1987, Whirlpool had come back in early 1988 agreeing to buy out 53 per cent of Philips's appliance operations as a first step to taking full control. Upon full completion Whirlpool would have paid or assumed debt totalling $1.2 billion for activities which in 1987 were generating $70 million pre-tax pre-interest income on sales of $2 billion. The Japanese had started moving outside South East Asia. In the meantime, local European competitors such as GEC and Merloni were ensuring good returns and, more importantly, were gaining back market share.

All of this was taking place in a mature industry highly dependent on replacement demand. Industry analysts expected that, even in a moderately growing economy, appliance shipments would be on a downward trend for the next couple of years. Given the concentration of buyers and the shift toward specialized retailers, raw materials price increases were more and more difficult to pass on.

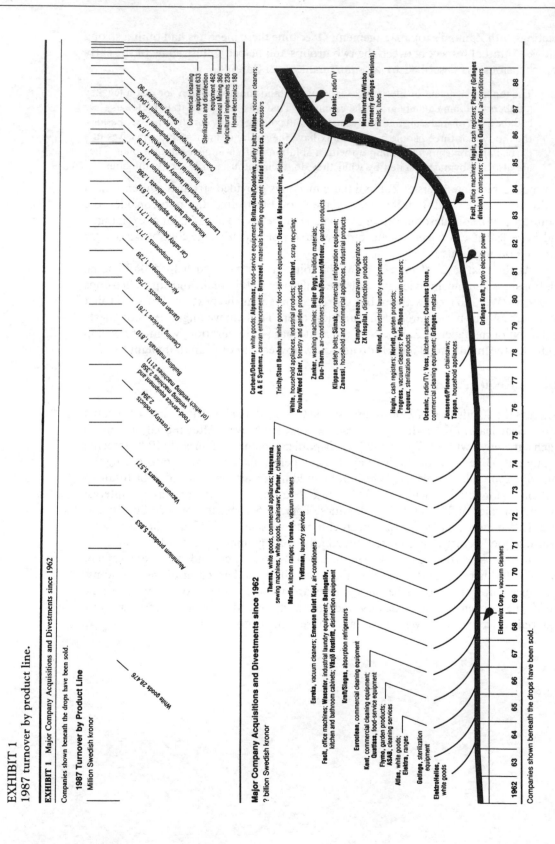

EXHIBIT 1
1987 turnover by product line.

EXHIBIT 1 Major Company Acquisitions and Divestments since 1962

Companies shown beneath the drops have been sold.

1987 Turnover by Product Line
Million Swedish kronor

White goods 28,476
Aluminum products 5,853
Vacuum cleaners 5,571
Forestry products 2,394
Food-service equipment and vending machines 2,356 (of which vending machines 211)
Building materials 1,810
Cleaning services 1,761
Garden products 1,756
Air-conditioners 1,739
Components 1,717
Car safety equipment 1,711
Leisure appliances 1,619
Kitchen and bathroom cabinets 1,286
Laundry services and goods protection 1,258
Industrial laundry equipment 1,132
Commercial refrigeration equipment 1,074
Materials handling equipment White 1,040
Sewing machines 790
Commercial cleaning equipment 633
Sterilization and disinfection equipment 462
International Mining 360
Agricultural implements 236
Home electronics 180

Major Company Acquisitions and Divestments since 1962
? billion Swedish kronor

Companies shown beneath the drops have been sold.

EXHIBIT 2
Consolidated financial statements for the Zanussi group.

Consolidated Income Statement for Zanussi Group (SEK millions)

	1980	1981	1982	1983
Sales	3,826	4,327	4,415	5,240
Operating Cost	−3,301	−3,775	−3,957	−4,654
Operating Income before Depreciation	525	552	458	585
Depreciation	−161	−98	−104	−130
Operating Income after Depreciation	364	454	354	455
Financial Income	192	330	284	279
Financial Expenses	−407	−489	−647	−627
Income after Financial Items	149	295	−9	108
Extraordinary Items	−53	−228	−223	81
Income before Appropriations	96	67	−232	189
Appropriations	−53	−42	−409	−382
Income before Taxes	43	25	−641	−193
Taxes	−7	−7	−10	−10
Net Income	36	18	−651	−203

Consolidated Balance Sheet for Zanussi Group (SEK millions)

	1980	1981	1982	1983
Current Assets (excl. inventory)	1,559	1,987	1,811	2,108
Inventory	965	1,054	999	955
Fixed Assets	1,622	1,539	2,366	2,902
TOTAL ASSETS	4,146	4,580	5,176	5,966
Current Liabilities	1,590	1,832	1,875	2,072
Long-term Liabilities	1,273	1,441	1,864	2,349
Reserves	259	301	472	627
Shareholders' Equity	1,024	1,006	965	918
TOTAL LIABILITIES AND SHAREHOLDERS' EQUITY	4,146	4,580	5,176	5,966

EXHIBIT 3
Mission values and guiding principles of Zanussi.

Mission

To become the market leader in Europe, with a significant position in other world areas, in supplying homes, institutions and industry with systems, appliances, components and after-sales services.

　　To be successful in this mission, the company and management legitimization must be based on the capability to be near the customer and satisfy his needs; to demonstrate strength, entrepreneurship and creativity in accepting and winning external challenges; to offer total quality on all dimensions, more than the competition; and to be oriented to an internal vision and engagement.

Vision

Our basic values, ranked, are:

1. To be near the customer;
2. To accept challenges;
3. To deliver total quality;
4. With an international perspective.

Our central value, underlying all of the above, is transparence, which means that Zanussi will reward behaviour which is based on constantly transparent information and attitudes, safeguarding the interests of the company.

Guiding principles

1. A management group is legitimized by knowing what we want, pursuing it coherently, and communicating our intent in order to be believable.
2. Shared communication means shared responsibility, not power and status index.
3. The manager's task is managing through information and motivation, not by building 'power islands'.
4. Time is short: the world will not wait for our 'perfect solutions'.
5. Strategic management implies:

   - Professional skills;
   - Risk-taking attitudes and the skill to spot opportunity;
   - Integration with the environment and the organisation, flexibility and attention to change;
   - Identification with the mission of the firm, and helping in the evolution of a culture that supports it;
   - Team work ability;
   - Skill in identifying strengths and weaknesses.

Policies to be developed

Specific policies were being developed in the following areas to support the implementation of the above mission, values and guiding principles: personnel, image and public relations, administration, purchasing, asset control, legal representation, R & D and innovation, and information systems. Members of senior management were assigned responsibility for developing policies in each of these areas, with completion expected by the end of 1986.

EXHIBIT 4
Electrolux Group key data.

1. Group Sales and Employees Worldwide

	Sales SEKm	No. of Employees		Sales SEKm	No. of Employees
Nordic Countries:			*North America:*		
Sweden	11,128	29,456	USA	19,488	29,750
Denmark	1,735	3,078	Canada	1,580	2,150
Norway	1,505	1,299		21,068	31,900
Finland	1,445	1,563			
	15,813	35,396			

	Sales SEKm	No. of Employees		Sales SEKm	No. of Employees
Rest of Europe:			*Latin America:*		
Great Britain	6,377	10,589	Brazil	302	6,215
France	5,098	8,753	Venezuela	208	1,032
West Germany	4,045	3,317	Peru	181	750
Italy	3,684	15,282	Colombia	104	1,865
Switzerland	1,818	1,814	Mexico	66	1,735
Spain	1,445	2,851	Ecuador	34	232
Netherlands	1,238	1,016	Guatemala	24	31
Belgium and			Others	443	198
Luxembourg	913	1,040		1,362	12,058
Austria	392	958			
Portugal	96	193			
Others	604	41			
	25,710	45,854			

	Sales SEKm	No. of Employees		Sales SEKm	No. of Employees
Asia:			*Africa:*		
Japan	707	1,175		414	
Saudi Arabia	215	738			
Hong Kong	152	1,340			
Philippines	150	525			
Kuwait	147	2,220		Sales SEKm	No. of Employees
Taiwan	119	2,178			
Malaysia	72	1,833			
Thailand	56	15	*Oceania:*		
Singapore	50	556	Australia	497	2,216
Jordan	28	137	New Zealand	114	557
Lebanon	22	35	Others	14	
Others	720	1,729		625	2,773
	2,438	12,481	TOTAL	67,016	140,462

EXHIBIT 4
(Continued).

2. Sales by Business Area

	1987 SEKm	1986 SEKm	1985 SEKm	% of Total Sales of 87
Household Appliances	39,487	31,378	19,200	58.6
Commercial Appliances	5,619	4,250	3,348	8.3
Commercial Services	2,893	2,504	2,266	4.3
Outdoor Products	4,475	2,909	2,990	6.6
Industrial Products	11,784	9,087	9,232	17.5
Building Components	3,172	2,962	2,652	4.7
TOTAL	67,430	53,090	39,688	100.0

3. Operating Income after Depreciation by Business Area

	1987 SEKm	1986 SEKm	1985 SEKm	% of Total Sales of 87
Household Appliances	2,077	1,947	1,589	49.2
Commercial Appliances	484	349	260	11.4
Commercial Services	169	172	132	4.0
Outdoor Products	421	241	373	10.0
Industrial Products	910	474	657	21.5
Building Components	164	138	126	3.9
TOTAL	4,225	3,321	3,137	100.0

SCANDINAVIAN AIRLINES SYSTEM (SAS) IN 1988

When the SAS Group's financial results for the fiscal year 1986/7 were released, it marked the trinational transport group's sixth profitable year in a row and their best year ever, with a net operating income of SEK 1.6 billion on revenues of SEK 23.9 billion. This was a huge improvement over the situation in 1981, when losses were mounting and the airline was rapidly losing market share. (A summary of the company's recent financial results, along with relevant exchange rates, are shown in Exhibit 1.) Much of the credit for the company's dramatic turnaround was ascribed to Jan Carlzon, who succeeded Carl-Olov Munkberg as president and CEO in 1981 and quickly initiated a number of major changes in the airline and its associated companies. He reoriented SAS towards the business travel market and gave top priority to customer service. This involved a complete reorganization of the company and a major decentralization of responsibility. As a result, SAS had become the leading carrier of full-fare traffic in Europe. Carlzon had joined SAS as executive vice-president in 1980, after serving as president of Linjeflyg, the Swedish domestic airline. Previously, he had been managing director of the SAS tour subsidiary Vingresor.

Despite these successes, and dramatic as they were, the company still faced considerable threats and many analysts questioned whether it could survive as a viable competitor in the increasingly global and competitive airline industry. Its

This case was prepared by Ronald Berger Lefèbure, Johnny Jorgensen and David Staniforth, INSEAD MBA candidates 1988, under the supervision of Sumantra Ghoshal, Associate Professor at INSEAD. It is intended to be used as a basis for class discussion rather than to illustrate either effective or ineffective handling of an administrative situation.
Copyright © 1988, by INSEAD-CEDEP, Fontainebleau, France.

population base of only 17 million spread out over a large area was too small by itself to support a comprehensive international traffic system. In addition, its geographic location at the periphery of Europe was a disadvantage when compared to Western Europe's densely populated areas.

The most pressing problem was the airline's operating costs, which were among the highest in the industry (see summary in Exhibit 2). It was estimated that labour charges accounted for 35 per cent of SAS's total costs, compared with only 25 per cent for the major US carriers since deregulation, and 18 per cent for the large Asian airlines. The evolution of the US 'mega-carriers' was a major concern, since they eyed Europe as an area for continued expansion.

Senior managers of the company were fully aware of these challenges. In discussing future developments in the airline industry, and SAS's role in particular, Helge Lindberg, group executive vice-president, noted:

> I doubt very much that SAS can survive alone as a major inter-continental airline. We need to expand our traffic system in order to compete with major European carriers having much larger population bases, as well as with the major American and Asian carriers who maintain considerably lower operating costs. We need to develop with other partners a global traffic system with daily connections to the important overseas destinations. The nature of our industry is such that if you are not present in the market the day the customers wish to travel, the business is lost. Another priority is to reduce our costs. Our social structure in Scandinavia leaves us with one of the highest personnel costs in the industry, coupled with the fact that increased emphasis on service caused us to lose our traditional budget consciousness over the past few years. A third major issue is to develop a competitive distribution system, a problem we are about to solve in partnership with Air France, Iberia and Lufthansa, with the so-called Amadeus system.

THE TURNAROUND

Sweden, Denmark and Norway had always shared a common interest in creating an ambitious air service, both to link their scattered communities and to ensure a role for Scandinavia among the world's international airlines. They first considered a joint airline in the 1930s when all three countries wanted to establish a route to America. No firm agreement was reached until 1940 however, when they decided to operate a joint service between New York and Bergen, on Norway's west coast. This plan was unfortunately scuttled by the German invasion three days later.

The Bermuda conference on international air travel in 1946 put an end to any hopes of true freedom of the air, and served to underline the importance of developing a common airline in order to establish a stronger world presence. The three countries agreed on an ownership structure, and in the summer of 1946 a DC-4 lifted off from Stockholm bound for Oslo and New York bearing the Scandinavian Airlines System name. Sweden controlled 3/7 of the new airline and Norway and Denmark 2/7 each, with ownership split 50/50 between the respective governments and private interests.

SAS gained a strong foothold in the European market – at the expense of the Germans who were forbidden from establishing their own airline – and quickly developed a worldwide route network. The airline established numerous firsts in the early years of worldwide air travel, beginning with the Swedish parent company ABA in 1945, who were the first to re-establish trans-Atlantic service after the war. SAS pioneered the Arctic route in 1954 with a flight from Copenhagen to Los Angeles via Greenland, and in 1957 inaugurated trans-polar service to Tokyo, cutting travel time by half. The Scandinavians were the first to operate the French Caravelle, introducing twin-engine jet travel within Europe, and worked with Douglas Aircraft to develop the ultra-long-range DC-8-62, capable of flying non-stop to the US west coast and Southeast Asia. A list of the airline's major milestones is shown in Exhibit 3. SAS had often looked for overseas partners, and purchased 30 per cent of Thai Airways International in 1959. This stake was bought back by the Thai government in 1977, but the two airlines had since entered into a cooperative service agreement.

The 1960s and early 1970s were the golden years for the airline. Apart from 1972 when profits shrank to US$8 million due to currency fluctuations, average annual net profits from 1969 to 1975 were between $15 million and $20 million. In the late 1970s, the second oil shock had a severe effect on profits, and the airline sustained considerable losses in 1979/80 and 1980/1.

SAS had developed close relationships with Swissair and KLM. An agreement between the three airlines (the KSSU agreement) was signed in 1969 with the objective of strengthening technical cooperation and jointly assessing any new aircraft entering the market. For example, it was agreed that SAS would be responsible for overhauling the Boeing 747 engines of all three airlines, while the other partners performed other joint maintenance activities.

Although the trinational airline had generally functioned smoothly, there had been some problems among the constituent groups, particularly when Denmark joined the EC in 1973. This underlying rivalry was reflected in Norway by the statement, 'SAS is an airline run by the Swedes for the benefit of the Danes', in reference to the airline's head office on Stockholm and its main traffic hub at Kastrup airport in Copenhagen. None the less, the larger traffic base and increased bargaining power afforded by the union had helped to make SAS a major world airline.

Problems Facing SAS in 1981

When Jan Carlzon assumed the presidency of SAS in August 1981, he realized that major changes would have to be made to restore the airline and associated companies to profitability, and to meet the growing challenges of an increasingly competitive industry. After 17 profitable years, the SAS group had declared operating losses of SEK 63.1 million and SEK 51.3 million in fiscal years 1979/80 and 1980/1 respectively. This dramatic decline had given rise to rumours that the three constituent countries were considering disbanding SAS and running their own separate airlines.

In addition to the problems that beset the industry – the international recession, higher interest rates and fuel costs, overcapacity and less regulated competition – specific problems had plagued SAS in recent years. The airline had been losing market share, even in its home territory; its fleet mix and route network did not meet market needs; and its reputation for service and punctuality had deteriorated. For example, on-time performance (defined as percentage of arrivals within 15 minutes of schedule) had slipped from over 90 per cent to 85 per cent, a major drop by airline standards.

In addition, many regular travellers from Norway and Sweden were increasingly avoiding transitting through Copenhagen's troublesome Kastrup airport – SAS's major hub – in favour of more attractive and efficient terminals at Amsterdam, Frankfurt or Zurich. Under the umbrella of regulation, bad habits had developed within the company's management ranks. Carlzon felt that SAS, like most airlines, had allowed itself to become too enamoured with technology – new aircrafts, new engines – often at the cost of meeting the customers' needs. They had become a product-driven airline instead of being a service-driven one. A typical example was the acquisition of the state-of-the-art Airbus A300 aircraft in the late 1970s. These larger planes required high load factors to be profitable and this necessitated lower flight frequencies – not in the best interests of customers who needed frequent and flexible flight schedules. In the past, customers had been willing to plan their trips according to a particular airline's schedule, and had even been willing to sacrifice some time to do so, since air travel was still somewhat of a novelty. The market had since changed, and experienced travellers now chose flights to suit their travel plans, not vice versa. 'In the past, we were operating as booking agents and aircraft brokers,' said Carlzon. 'Now we know, if we want the business we must fight for it like the "street fighters" of the rough-and-tumble American domestic market.'

New Strategy – 'The Businessman's Airline'

Faced with the situation of a stagnant market, general overcapacity in the industry, and continuing loss of market share to competitors, Carlzon recognized that a new strategy was necessary to turn SAS around. In a similar situation when he was the president of Linjeflyg, Carlzon had decided to increase flight frequency and cut fares dramatically in order to improve aircraft utilization and boost load factors. These actions had proved to be very successful, and profitability had improved substantially. However, the market SAS operated in was quite different from that of Linjeflyg, and it was not clear that a similar strategy could be applied successfully. Another option was to initiate a major cost-reduction programme aimed at obtaining a better margin from a declining revenue base. This strategy would have required significant staff cuts, fleet reduction and an overall lower level of flight frequency and service.

In the airline industry, the most stable market segment was the full-fare paying business traveller who provided the vast majority of revenues. First class travel within Europe was declining, mainly because businesses could not justify the extra expense, especially during a recession. All the major, scheduled airlines were after the business traveller, and some had created a separate 'business' class priced at a 10-20 per cent premium over economy, which offered many of the amenities of first class.

SAS chose the strategy of focusing on the business traveller. As described by Helge Lindberg, then executive vice-president – commercial, 'although other options were considered, we quickly decided there was no alternative but to go after the business traveller segment with a new product which offered significant advantages over the competition'. In the words of Jan Carlzon: 'We decided to go after a bigger share of the fullfare paying pie.'

There were a number of risks involved in this strategy. Increasing investment to provide an improved level of service at a time of mounting losses could bankrupt the airline if revenues did not improve sufficiently. On the other hand, if investment were the way to go, perhaps it could be better spent on more efficient aircraft so as to reduce costs. Another concern was that differentiating the product could alienate the tourist class passengers, especially among Scandinavian customers, who might resent any increase in passenger 'segregation'. In spite of these considerable risks, management increased expenditures and staked the future of the airline on their ability to woo the European business traveller away from the competition.

As a result, first class was dropped and 'EuroClass' was introduced, offering more amenities than competing airlines' business classes, but at the old economy fare. (A similar service, First Business Class, was introduced on intercontinental routes, where first class was retained.) Thus any passenger paying full-fare would be entitled to this new service, which included separate check-in, roomier seating, advance seat selection, free drinks and a better in-flight meal. The other European airlines reacted strongly. Air France saw EuroClass as a serious threat to its own 'Classe Affaires', which cost 20 per cent more than economy, and at one point refused to book any EuroClass fares on its reservation system. Other airlines protested to their local government authorities, but to no avail, and the new fare structures were allowed to remain. SAS backed up the new service with the largest media advertising campaign ever launched by the airline (see Exhibit 4).

In conjunction with the new EuroClass services, a drive was launched to improve flight schedules and punctuality. The aircraft fleet mix was modified in order to meet the demands of increased flight frequency. The recently acquired, high-capacity Airbus aircraft were withdrawn from service and leased to SAS's Scanair charter subsidiary since they were not suitable for the frequent, non-stop flights, which the new schedule demanded. For the same reason some Boeing 747s were replaced by McDonnell Douglas DC-10s, and the older DC-9s were refurbished instead of being replaced since they were of the right size for the new service levels.

On certain short distance routes such as Copenhagen–Hamburg, a new 'EuroLink' concept was introduced. This involved substituting 40 passenger Fokker F-27s for 110 passenger DC-9s and doubling flight frequencies to provide a more attractive schedule. In short, the previous high fixed-cost, high capacity fleet was changing into a lower fixed-cost, high frequency one. This evolution of the SAS fleet is shown in Exhibit 5.

Every effort was made to differentiate the business traveller product as much as possible from the lower priced fares. In this respect, 'Scanorama' lounges were introduced at many of the airports served by SAS in an effort to improve service further. These lounges were for the exclusive use of the full-fare paying passenger and offered telephones and telex machines and a more relaxing environment to the business traveller. A joint agreement with the Danish Civil Aviation Authority was reached to invest in refurbishing Kastrup airport to bring it up to competitive standards. The objective was to make Kastrup Europe's best airport by the end of the decade.

The introduction of these new products and related services represented a change in the overall philosophy of SAS. All tasks and functions within the organization were examined. If the business traveller benefited from a particular service or functions, it was maintained or enhanced, otherwise it was cut back, or dropped altogether. Managers were urged to look upon expenses as resources; to cut those that didn't contribute to revenue, but not to hesitate in raising those that did. Administrative costs were slashed 25 per cent, but at the same time an extra SEK 120 million was invested on new services, facilities, aircraft interiors and other projects that affected the passengers directly. As a result, annual operating costs were increased by SEK

55 million at a time of deep deficits and continuing losses. Furthermore, these additional investments for improved service delayed the acquisition of new, more efficient aircraft to replace the ageing DC-9 fleet.

The results of this new strategy were dramatic. Full-fare paying passenger traffic rose over 8 per cent in the first year, and profits rose to SEK 448 million for the 81/2 fiscal year. In punctuality, SAS improved on-time performance to 93 per cent, a record in Europe. The share of full-fare paying passengers rose consistently, and by 1986, it had risen to 60 per cent, giving SAS the highest proportion of any airline in Europe. Accompanying this change in passenger mix were impressive profit gains. In 1986, SAS turned in the third best profit performance among the world's major airlines with a net operating profit of SEK 1.5 billion. (A comparison of financial and operating results of major world airlines is shown in Exhibit 6.)

Corporate Cultural Revolution

Due in part to the protected, stable growth environment, the SAS organization was not ready to meet new competitive challenges without a major restructuring. Previously, the reference point had been fixed assets and technology, with an emphasis on return on investment, centralized control and orders from top management. Across the board cost-cutting was the usual approach to improve profits and to adapt to changing market conditions. The customer interface had been neglected. As described by a senior manager of the company,

> In those days, many employees felt that passengers were a disturbing element they had to contend with, rather than the ones who were in fact paying their salary. Taking control of a situation, and bypassing the regulations in order to please a customer were not the things to do in SAS.

Thus personal initiative was discouraged, and adherence to the company policy manuals was the norm. A large corporate staff was needed to run this bureaucracy, with layers of middle management to follow up directives from the top. Throughout the organization the morale of employees was low and the level of cooperation among them, such as between ground staff and air crews, was not always the best. 'There was a feeling of helplessness, and a fear for the future of the company,' remarked an SAS pilot when asked to comment on the situation prevailing prior to 1981.

A transformation 'from bureaucrats to businessmen' was essential, and an emphasis on the customer was needed. A major reorientation had been contemplated by Carlzon's predecessor, Carl-Olov Munkberg, but it was felt that implementation of a new organization would be more effective under a new CEO. 'New brooms sweep clean,' remarked Carlzon in relating his decision to replace or relocate 13 of the 14 executives in the management team of SAS. Helge Lindberg, the sole survivor in the top management team, was put in charge of the day-to-day running of the airline. Lindberg's extensive knowledge and experience was valued by Carlzon, who saw him as a 'bridge between old and new', and a valuable asset now that the time for change had arrived.

In the past, SAS had focused on instructions, thereby limiting potential contributions from the employees. A key element of the cultural revolution under Carlzon was a new emphasis on information instead of instructions. The practical implications of this were that any employee in the 'front line' (i.e. in the SAS/customer interface) should have the decision-making power necessary to do, within reasonable limits, whatever that person felt appropriate to please the customer. Each 'moment of truth', when the customer encountered the service staff, would be used to its full potential so as to encourage repeat business. 'Throw out the manuals and use your heads instead!' was the message from Lindberg. The underlying assumptions, made explicit throughout the organization, were that an individual with information could not avoid assuming responsibility and that hidden resources were released when an individual was free to assume responsibility instead of being restricted by instructions.

Some of the tools used by Carlzon in the reorganization were personal letters and several red booklets (*Carlzon's Little Red Books*) distributed to all employees. In these booklets the company's situation and its goals were presented in very simple language, using cartoon-like drawings to emphasize their importance (see examples in Exhibit 7). Some employees found this form of communication too simple, but overall, the response was very positive. In his first year Carlzon spent approximately half his time travelling, meeting SAS employees all over the world. This made it very clear to everyone that management was deeply committed to turning things around, and helped to implement the changes quickly.

Education was considered necessary to reap the full benefits of the new organization, and both managers and front-line staff were sent to seminars. The courses for the front-line personnel were referred to by many as the 'learn-to-smile seminars', but the real benefits probably resulted more from the participants' perception that the company cared about its employees, than from the actual content of the courses.

Certain problems were encountered in the process of change. Confusion and frustration were typical reactions of many middle managers when they suddenly found themselves bypassed by the 'front line', on the one hand, and by the top management, on the other. 'You can't please everyone, and some people will have to be sacrificed,' said an SAS manager when asked to comment on this problem. Cross-training of employees to perform several tasks was attempted, but met with resistance from the unions. An example was the 'turnaround' check – a visual check of the aircraft performed between each flight. This could very well be done by the pilots, but the mechanics' union insisted upon this task being done by their people, resulting in higher operating costs.

Another problem was that the first reorientation had short-term goals, and when these were achieved, the early momentum diminished. By 1984 SAS had received the 'Airline of the Year' award from the Air Transport World magazine, and its financial situation had improved dramatically. These factors led to a feeling of contentment, and people started to fall back into old habits. Demands for salary increases were again raised. Some people thought that SAS was now out of danger, and wanted to harvest the fruits of hard work. Small 'pyramids' started to crop up in the organization, and it became evident that the problems in the middle management were not solved. 'The new culture was taking roots, but we had problems keeping up the motivation,' noted Lindberg.

Consequently, a 'second wave' of change was launched, and new goals with a much longer time horizon were outlined. Management wanted to prepare the company for the coming liberalization in the airline industry, and ensure a level of profitability sufficient to meet upcoming fleet replacement needs. The ultimate goal was for SAS to be the most efficient airline in Europe by 1990.

THE SECOND WAVE

SAS wanted to integrate the various elements of the travel package offered to the business traveller: to develop a full service product for the full-fare paying passenger. In the words of Lindberg: 'We wanted to be a full service, door-to-door travel service company. We aimed to offer a unique product which we could control from A to Z.' To meet this objective, the SAS service chain concept was established by creating a distribution system and network of services that met the needs of the business travellers, from the time they ordered their tickets to the time they got back home. This meant that the development of a hotel network, reservation system and credit card operation were decisive for the company's future.

SAS International Hotels (SIH)

In 1983, SIH became a separate division within the SAS Group. A new concept, the SAS Destination Service – 'ticket, transport and hotel package' – was introduced in September 1985. SAS market research indicated that ground transportation and hotel reservations ranked high among the needs of business travellers. Indeed, surveys also indicated that more than 50 per cent of the Scandinavian business travellers had no prior knowledge of the hotels where they had been booked, and thus would appreciate the standards and facilities guaranteed by the SAS Destination Service. The hotels where guaranteed reservations could be made under this scheme totalled 80, and the chain, already one of the biggest in the world, was marketed as SAS Business Hotels. With this new service, passengers were able to order airline tickets, ground transportation and confirmed hotel reservations with one telephone call.

At each SAS destination where public transport from the airport to the city centre was time-consuming or complicated, a door-to-door limousine service was made available at reasonable prices to full-fare paying passengers. A helicopter shuttle service was introduced for travellers transferring between New York's Kennedy and LaGuardia airports. Many of the hotels featured SAS Airline Check-in. This meant that passengers could check their luggage and obtain boarding passes before leaving the hotel in the morning, and then go directly to the gate at the airport for afternoon or evening departures. With the creation of the SAS Destination Service, a complete door-to-door transport service was offered, and it reflected SAS's conviction that, to a large extent, the battle for full-fare paying passengers would be won on the ground. The total product had to be seen as an integrated chain of services for the business travel market, including reservations, airport limousines, EuroClass, hotels, car rentals, airline check-in at the hotel, hotel check-in at the airport, airport lounges and the SAS 24-hour telephone hot-line.

SAS Reservation System

SAS was facing a rising number of reservation transactions: one million in 1980, and two million in 1983. This demand created the need for an integrated information system, and a network able to accept higher access without increasing the response time. To respond to this need, the company introduced a new reservation system in 1984. Developed at a cost of over SEK 250 million, the new system had more than 13,000 terminals around the world which were connected with SAS's centralized computing centre. The company believed that innovative and aggressive applications of computerized information and communication technology would decide which airlines would survive. The strategy was to ensure that SAS products found the shortest and least expensive access to the market, either directly or via travel agencies. Management believed that the company had to retain independence from credit card companies and the huge distribution systems of the major US airlines. By creating its own information and communication system to assure continued direct access to markets, SAS would have control of the complete purchase process.

Controversy over ticket distribution had increased in Europe and European carriers manoeuvred to protect their national markets. The threat of competition from the US systems and the danger of losing control of the distribution process forced Europe's major airlines to improve and update their computer reservation systems. A summary of the major American systems can be found in Exhibit 8. In 1987, SAS joined a CRS study group formed by Air France, Lufthansa and Iberia. Later that year, the group announced its intention to develop one of the world's largest and most complete reservation and distribution systems. Known as AMADEUS, the system was expected to provide travel agencies with product and service information, reservation facilities for a worldwide array of airlines, hotels, car rentals, trains, ferries, and ticketing and fare quoting systems. Representing a total investment of US$270 million, the system was scheduled to be operational in mid-1989, and was expected to handle 150 million annual booking transactions. Finnair (Finland), Braathens SAFE (Norway), Air Inter and UTA (France) had joined the AMADEUS group by the end of 1987. A competing system, known as GALILEO, was also announced in 1987 grouping, among others, British Airways, KLM, Swissair, Alitalia and Austrian Airlines.

Credit Cards

In 1986, through the acquisition of Diners Club Nordic, SAS took over franchise rights in the Nordic countries for the Diners Club card, which had 150,000 card-holders in Scandinavia, Finland and Iceland. The annual sale of hotels and transport services was a multi-billion Kronor business in Scandinavia. SAS alone sold SEK 11 billion worth of airline tickets in Scandinavia during its 1984/5 fiscal year. Credit card purchases accounted for 13 per cent of these sales, and the share was steadily rising. The credit card acquisition was seen as an important element in SAS's distribution strategy, being a practical tool for the business traveller.

SAS Service Partner (SSP)

SSP, an SAS subsidiary in the catering business, was expanded from 12 international airline flight kitchens to an enterprise with more than 7,000 employees in over 100 locations. The subsidiary operated in 13 countries from the United States to Japan, delivering 18 million airline meals a year. SSP was made up of a group of independent companies in airline catering and the international restaurant business. In 1984, SSP catered to more than 100 airlines, operated flight kitchens for several others, and ran airport restaurants in all three Scandinavian countries as well as in England and Ireland. It had a separate unit for its Saudi Arabian business, which was expected to have possibilities for growth in the Middle and Far East. In the early 1980s, Chicago had been chosen as the entry point in a planned expansion among US airports. Despite the cyclical nature of the airline business, the subsidiary had remained consistently profitable. SAS believed that more and more airlines would concentrate on operating aircrafts, and leave service industry tasks like catering to specialist companies. British Airways was an example, having handed over its short/medium haul catering at London's Heathrow airport to SSP.

Other Related Activities

SAS had also begun to offer a dedicated service to US magazine publishers wishing to distribute their products in Europe. The airline offered a fast freight and delivery service at a reasonable price through a single distribution system, and management believed this to be a growing market. This new activity allowed otherwise unused cargo capacity to be put to productive use.

The role of Vingresor, an SAS subsidiary since 1971, and Sweden's largest tour operator, was also expanded considerably. All-inclusive tours on charter flights from Sweden and Norway remained the basic service offered. Additional service products such as Vingresor's resorts with hotels in Europe and Africa had been developed, as well as a travel programme including the Vingresor family concept.

New Group Structure

In March 1986, SAS was reorganized into five independent business units: the airline, SAS Service Partner, SAS International Hotels, SAS Leisure (Vingresor) and SAS Distribution (see Exhibit 9). The rationale was that each of these businesses faced very different strategic demands and, therefore, each was required to have its own management team to allow for more aggressive business development in an increasingly competitive climate. The same philosophy was pushed further down the line: for example, the new organization restructured the airline's route sectors into separate business units functioning as independent profit centres. The SAS Group management, consisting of the chief executive officer, three executive officers and three executive vice-presidents representing Denmark, Norway and Sweden, was expected to focus primarily on overall development of the SAS Group's business areas.

It had been planned to introduce the new organization as early as 1984, but Carlzon had felt that the time was not ripe because the airline was involved in a public debate on air safety and there were problems with various trade union groups. 'Now, I fear we might have waited too long. It has become clear that the two jobs cannot be combined. The burdens of the day-to-day operation of the airline and work on the future development of it and other business units are simply too heavy,' he commented in 1986.

1988: FACING THE FUTURE

Looking ahead to the turn of the century, management of SAS was concerned about the future of the company. The globalization trend in the airline industry was gaining momentum, exemplified by the actions of giants like British Airways and American Airlines. BA had made it clear that it did not intend to stop growing after its acquisition of British Caledonian and the so-called 'marketing merger' with United Airlines, in which the two carriers agreed to coordinate flight schedules and marketing programmes, offer joint fares and share terminals in four US cities. American Airlines was moving into Europe, having recently closed a leasing deal covering 40 new wide-body aircrafts. 'Globalization is inevitable,' commented Carlzon. 'Nobody will fly European unless we have a shake-out and become more efficient.' This underlined the threat of being relegated to a regional carrier, and SAS's need to unite with other airlines to create a 'Pan-European' system.

Aircraft replacement was another threat to SAS. The average age of its 60-strong DC-9 fleet (exclusive of the new MD-80s) was 25 years, and a forthcoming EC directive on noise levels could, if put into effect in 1992, ground 30 aircrafts. The required investment in new aircraft was estimated at SEK 40 billion over the next decade, which translated into one new plane per month from 1988 until the year 2000. This process of replacement had started, with the purchase of nine Boeing 767s for trans-Atlantic traffic. To be able to finance these projects, the airline had to attain a gross profit level of 13 per cent (before depreciation), compared to 11 per cent in 1986. This increase was difficult to achieve in an increasingly competitive environment and one in which SAS had a cost disadvantage with respect to other airlines.

Partnerships or mergers with other airlines was clearly an attractive option, but the company had been frustrated in its attempts to develop such relationships. In the spring of 1987, SAS entered into negotiations with Sabena of Belgium with the goal of merging the operations of the two companies. Sabena was 52 per cent state-owned and the Belgian government had expressed an interest in selling part of its holding to the private sector. With US$3.3 billion in sales, the merged carrier would have been Europe's fourth largest. Sabena chairman Carlos Van Rafelghem had stated that any accord with SAS would involve combining medium and long-distance networks in a system based on hubs in Copenhagen and Brussels. The negotiations failed, however, mainly on the issue of the degree of integration. SAS wanted to include all of Sabena's operations, including hotels and catering, while the Belgian carrier was only interested in merging the airline systems.

In the autumn of that same year, SAS launched a bid to acquire a major shareholding in British Caledonian Airways. SAS was eager to expand its traffic base and gain access to BCal's American, African and Middle East destinations, and to the carrier's Gatwick Airport hub outside London. A battle for control with British

Airways ensued, with BA emerging the winner, having £250 million, more than double the original bid. A major issue during the takeover battle was the implication of SAS gaining control of a British airline. The question of national control was important because of bilateral agreements. If Bcal were deemed to be non-British, the foreign partner in an agreement might revoke the airline's licences on routes to that country.

By the middle of 1988, it was clear to the corporate management of SAS that while past actions had led to a sound base for the future, they were not sufficient by themselves to ensure long-term viability of the company. Within the rapidly changing environment, a new thrust was necessary, and had to be found without much delay.

EXHIBIT 1
SAS Group financial and operating results, 1977/8–86/7.

Financial Summary Group:	77/8	78/9	79/80	80/1	81/2	82/3	83/4	84/5	85/6	86/7
SEK millions										
Operating Revenue	7,050	8,066	9,220	10,172	12,807	15,972	18,005	19,790	21,585	23,570
Operating Expenses	(6,437)	(7,551)	(8,920)	(9,664)	(11,895)	(14,696)	(16,415)	(18,256)	(19,369)	(21,524)
Depreciation	(347)	(360)	(391)	(430)	(474)	(483)	(545)	(574)	(863)	(1,126)
Financial & Extra Items	(140)	(7)	28	(129)	10	(192)	(77)	57	162	443
Net Operating Income	126	148	(63)	(51)	448	601	968	1,017	1,515	1,963
Exchange Rate – SEK/$US	4.60	4.15	4.17	5.61	6.28	7.83	8.70	7.40	6.91	6.40

Revenue by Business Area:	82/3 (%)	83/4 (%)	84/5 (%)	85/6 (%)	86/7 (%)
SEK millions					
SAS Airline Consortium	12,600 (79)	14,151 (79)	15,434 (78)	16,495 (76)	17,510 (73)
SAS International Hotels	732 (5)	843 (5)	948 (5)	1,083 (5)	1,230 (5)
SAS Service Partner	1,681 (11)	2,049 (11)	2,393 (12)	2,712 (13)	3,223 (14)
SAS Leisure (Vingresor)	1,311 (8)	1,474 (8)	1,537 (8)	1,897 (9)	2,379 (10)
Other	456 (3)	460 (3)	390 (2)	415 (2)	730 (3)
Group Eliminations	(808) (−5)	(972) (−5)	(912) (−5)	(1,017) (−5)	(1,202) (−5)
TOTAL	15,972 (100)	18,005 (100)	19,790 (100)	21,585 (100)	23,870 (100)

Income by Business Area:	82/3 (%)	83/4 (%)	84/5 (%)	85/6 (%)	86/7 (%)
SEK millions					
SAS Airline Consortium	461 (77)	729 (75)	811 (80)	1,207 (80)	1,453 (87)
SAS International Hotels	14 (2)	21 (2)	67 (7)	72 (5)	73 (4)
SAS Service Partner	75 (12)	15 (2)	81 (8)	123 (8)	180 (11)
SAS Leisure (Vingresor)	41 (7)	43 (4)	81 (8)	133 (9)	141 (8)
Other	17 (3)	5 (1)	(15) (−1)	(31) (−2)	(99) (−6)
Group Eliminations	(25) (−4)	(21) (−2)	(7) (−1)	(22) (−1)	(85) (−5)
Extraordinary Items	18 (3)	176 (18)	−1 (0)	34 (2)	0 (0)
TOTAL	601 (100)	968 (100)	1,017 (100)	1,516 (100)	1,663 (100)

Operating Statistics SAS Airline:	77/8	78/9	79/80	80/1	81/2	82/3	83/4	84/5	85/6	86/7
Cities Served	98	102	103	105	99	93	91	88	89	85
Kilometers Flown (mill)	123	124	120	113	113	120	124	125	136	N/A
Passengers (thou)	7,886	8,669	8,393	8,413	8,861	9,222	10,066	10,735	11,708	N/A
Cabin Load Factor (%)	56.4%	59.9%	59.4%	60.9%	63.6%	65.5%	67.2%	67.2%	66.2%	68.5%
Employees	16,010	16,755	17,069	16,425	16,376	17,101	17,710	18,845	19,773	N/A

Source: Annual Reports.

EXHIBIT 2
Comparison of airline operating costs.
(US cents per available tonne-kilometre)

Airline	1982	1983	1984	1985	1986
Singapore Airlines	36	36	33	32	30
British Caledonian	37	37	29	35	38
United Airlines	39	39	38	44	40
KLM	35	29	26	35	44
Pan American	34	36	38	36	N/A
British Airways	40	38	31	37	44
Delta	42	43	43	45	44
Lufthansa	51	44	40	53	57
Swissair	54	47	41	53	58
Sabena	53	43	44	56	63
SAS	53	53	50	65	76

Source: Company Annual Reports.

EXHIBIT 3
SAS milestones.

1946 – 31 July–1 August
DDL, DNL and SILA found SAS for the operation of intercontinental services to North and South America.

1946 – 17 September
Route to New York opened.

1946 – 30 November
Route to South America opened.

1948 – 18 April
ABA, DDL and DNL form ESAS to coordinate European operions.

1948 – 1 July
SILA and ANA amalgamated.

1949 – 26 October
Route to Bangkok opened.

1950 – 1 October
ABA, DDL and DNL transfer all operations to SAS in accordance with a new Consortium Agreement dated 8 February 1951, with retroactive effect.

1951 – 18 April
The Bangkok route is extended to Tokyo.

1951 – 19 April
Route to Nairobi is inaugurated.

1952 – 19 November
First transatlantic flight by commercial airliner.

1953 – 8 January
The Nairobi route is extended to Johannesburg.

1954 – 15 November
Polar route to Los Angeles inaugurated.

1956 – 9 May
Pre-war route to Moscow reopened.

1957 – 24 February
Inauguration of North Pole short-cut to Tokyo.

1957 – 2 April
SAS participates in formation of Linjeflyg.

1957 – 4 April
Route opened to Warsaw.

1957 – 16 April
First flight to Prague.

1958 – 6 October
Agreement of cooperation signed by SAS and Swissair.

1959 – 24 August
SAS and Thai Airways Co. establish THAI International.

1960 – 2 July
Monrovia added to South Atlantic Network.

1961 – 1 October
SAS Catering established as subsidiary.

1962 – 15 May
Inauguration of all-cargo service to New York.

1963 – 4 May
Route opened across top of north Norway to Kirkenes.

1963 – 2 November
First service to Montreal.

1964 – 2 April
Route to Chicago inaugurated.

1965 – 5 April
Non-stop service New York–Bergen begun.

1966 – 2 September
Inauguration of service to Seattle via Polar route.

1967 – 4 November
Opening of *Trans-Asian Express* via Tashkent to Bangkok and Singapore.

1968 – 31 March
Dar-Es-Salaam added to East African network.

1968 – 1 November
Route opened to Barbados and Port-of-Spain in West Indies.

1970 – 18 February
KSSU agreement ratified.

1971 – 3 April
Trans-Siberian Express to Tokyo inaugurated.

1971 – 1 November
SAS participates in formation of Danair.

1972 – 5 April
Route to East Berlin opened.

1972 – 24 May
New York–Stavanger route opened.

1973 – 4 November
All-cargo express route opened to Bangkok and Singapore.

1973 – 6 November
Dehli added to Trans-Orient route.

1975 – 2 September
Inauguration of Svalbard route, world's northernmost scheduled service.

1976 – 21 April
Route opened to Lagos.

1977 – 7 April
Kuwait added to Trans-Orient route.

1977 – 2 November
Opening of Gothenburg–New York route.

Source: 'The SAS Saga', Anders Buraas, Oslo 1979.

EXHIBIT 4
Example of EuroClass advertisment.

SAS Advertisment:

> 'Of the eight major airlines competing in Sweden for European traffic, five do not give you separate check-in and seating, separate cabin or free drinks. Of the three remaining airlines, two do not give you extra room or larger seats. Only one airline in Europe has EuroClass which gives you more service and comfort for the economy fare.'

Lufthansa Advertisment:

> 'You can still fly first class in Europe!'

Source: Advertising Age 1981

EXHIBIT 5
Evolution of SAS's fleet.

Aircraft Type*		Seat Capacity	1977/8	1978/9	1979/80	1980/1	1981/2	1982/3	1983/4	1984/5	1985/6	1986/7
Boeing 747		405	3	4	4	5	5	3	5	5	2	0
Airbus Industries	A300	242	0	0	2	4	1	1	0	0	0	0
McDonnell-Douglas	DC-10-30	230	5	5	5	5	5	5	6	8	9	11
McDonnell-Douglas	DC-8-62	N/A	5	5	2	3	3	3	3	3	3	0
	DC-8-63	170	5	3	4	2	2	2	3	2	2	0
McDonnell-Douglas	DC-9-21	75	9	9	9	9	9	9	9	9	9	9
	DC-9-33	(freight)	2	2	2	2	2	2	2	2	2	2
	DC-9-41	110/122	45	49	49	49	49	49	49	49	49	49
	DC-9-81	133	0	0	0	0	0	0	0	0	6	3
	DC-9-82	156	0	0	0	0	0	0	0	0	6	3
	DC-9-93	133	0	0	0	0	0	0	0	0	0	4
Fokker F-27		40	0	0	0	0	0	0	4	6	9	9
TOTAL			74	77	77	79	76	74	80	84	97	100

*Aircraft owned or leased by SAS which were leased to other operators are not included in this table.
Source: Company annual reports.

EXHIBIT 6
Comparison of major world airlines' statistics.

1986 World Airline Operating & Financial Statistics

Passengers	(000s)	RPKs	(000,000s)
1. Aeroflot	115,727	1. Aeroflot	188,056
2. United	50,690	2. United	95,569
3. American	45,983	3. American	78,499
4. Eastern	42,546	4. Eastern	56,164
5. Delta	41,062	5. Delta	50,480
6. TWA	24,636	6. TWA	48,100
7. All Nippon	24,503	7. Northwest	46,346
8. Piedmont	22,800	8. British Airways	41,405
9. US Air	21,725	9. Japan Air Lines	38,903
10. Continental	20,409	10. Pan American	34,844
22. SAS	11,700	30. (est) SAS	12,471

Fleet Size	(No. Aircraft)	Employees	
1. Aeroflot	2,682	1. Aeroflot	500,000
2. United	368	2. American	51,661
3. American	338	3. United	49,800
4. Northwest	311	4. Eastern	43,685
5. Eastern	289	5. Federal Express[a]	43,300
6. Delta	253	6. Delta	38,901
7. Continental	246	7. British Airways	37,810
8. CAAC (China)	241	8. Air France	35,269
9. TWA	167	9. Lufthansa	34,905
10. Republic	165	10. Northwest	33,250
18. SAS	106	22. SAS	19,773

Operating Revenue	(US $000,000s)	Operating Profit	(US $000,000s)
1. United	6,688	1. American	392
2. American	5,857	2. Federal Express[a]	365
3. Air France	4,747	3. SAS	260
4. Japan Air Lines	4,578	4. Delta	225
5. Eastern	4,522	5. Cathay Pacific	206
6. Delta	4,496	6. Swissair	200
7. Northwest	3,598	7. Northwest	167
8. TWA	3,181	8. US Air	164
9. Federal Express[a]	2,940	9. Continental	143
10. Pan American	2,580	10. KLM	131
11. SAS	2,387		

[a] Freight only.
Source: Air Transport World, June 1987.

EXHIBIT 7
Examples from *Carlzon's Little Red Book.*

Hopeless odds.
When we looked around a year ago, our hopes of 'getting our nose up' were sinking. Demand had stopped increasing. We could no longer get ourselves rich, i.e. there was less hope for continued growth and thus automatically increased revenues. The competition got harder. How could we survive?

EXHIBIT 7
(continued).

Certain competitors 'throw in the towel'.
At the time when SAS achieves its best result ever, the majority in the airline industry are doing poorly. The IATA companies are this year losing around US$ 2 billion! But they should be making a profit of US$ 3 billion (7.5 per cent of turnover) to have a chance of meeting their future aircraft investments. From this we can draw two conclusions:

- SAS is not like the other IATA companies. Our result is nothing less than a world sensation.

- The IATA companies will probably fight for their lives in the future - just as we started to do a year and a half ago. They will probably use all their force to beat us in the coming rounds.

Note: Translation from Swedish by casewriters
Source: SAS

EXHIBIT 8
Selected operating data for US CRS systems.

	Sabre (American)	Apollo (United)	System One (Texas Air)	Pars (TWA/NWA)	Datas II (Delta)
Terminals: USA	54.800	40.688	21.450	17.907	9.600
abroad	316	330	100	352	300
Subscriber Locations	13.018	8.944	6.350	4.816	3.100
% Total Agency Sales Processed Jan–June 1986[a]	43	30.1	8.5	8.5	4.1
% US RPMs of Airlines Jan–May 1987	14.136	17.124	19.212	17.766	12.317
1986 Revenues	$336 m	$318 m	N/A	N/A	N/A
1986 Profits	$412 m	N/A	N/A	N/A	N/A
Airline Booking Fees					
–basic	$1.75	$1.85	$1.75	$1.75	$1.50
–direct access	$2.00	$1.85	$1.75	$1.75	$1.50
Direct Access Airlines as of July 1987	13	30	20	13	5
Current Strengths:	Size: depth of data: most	Size: depth of data	Aggressiveness	International pricing; large number installed in corporations; flexibility	

Notes:
[a] USA only, Sabre estimate.
[b] American is the only airline reporting publicly; Apollo estimate as published previously by the author and not disputed by the company.
Sources: CRS vendors; *Travel Weekly; Aviation Daily; Travel and Tourism Analyst,* author's estimates.

EXHIBIT 9
SAS group structure.

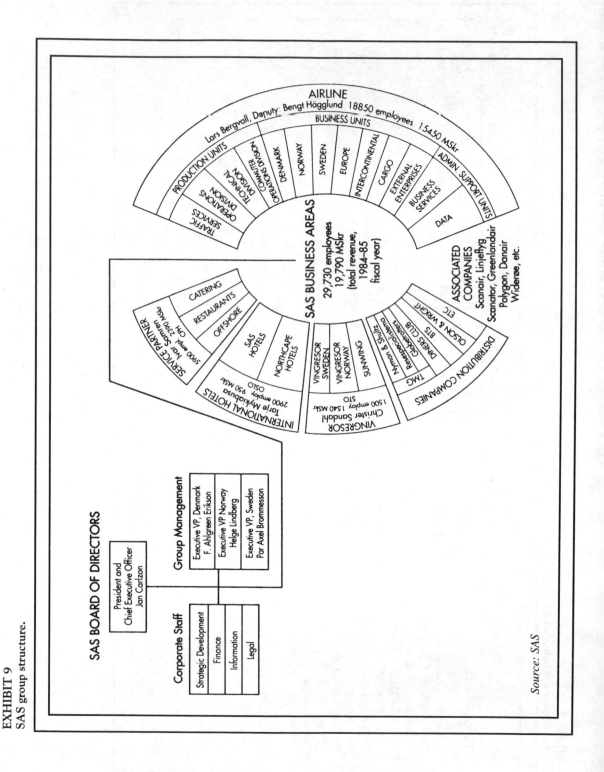

Source: SAS

DAIMLER-BENZ HOLDING: RESTRUCTURING AND CULTURE CHANGE

'Tents instead of Palaces' should have been the title of our brochure. In my opinion, this expresses well the concept of our restructuring aims

Speaking with just a touch of regret that his suggestion had not been adopted, Reinhard Krebs, vice-president, corporate executive management development, alluded with his metaphor to the title of the new brochure, *Free Spaces (Freiräume)*. It contained the future framework and guidelines regarding the organizational restructuring of the Daimler-Benz Holding that had started on 1 January 1993. The new structures were to be in place within the space of two years.

Despite not having his way with the title, Reinhard Krebs referred with pride and enthusiasm to *Free Spaces*, which was the product of long deliberations and many hours of work not only for the members of the board but also the 2,700 strong holding. In putting together its contents, they all had to take account of the fact that what could have once been described as the strengths of the corporation, namely, an organization built on functional lines, a clear understanding of the individual's tasks, a strong hierarchy to support decision-making and a company ethos that somehow made its 'employees' special, not to say privileged, now stood in the way of modernization.

During the previous 18 months, the holding had finally been forced to acknowledge, like so many other headquarters of large corporations before, that its

*This case was prepared by Gerda Rossell, Research Assistant, under the supervision of Todd Jick, Associate Professor at INSEAD. It is intended to be used as a basis for class discussion rather than to illustrate either effective or ineffective handling of an administrative situation. Partial support for this case was provided by the International Consortium for Executive Development Research.

organizational structure, its management and its day-to-day operations were no longer appropriate for leading a Daimler-Benz Company whose size and products had drastically changed in the course of time and which was facing increasingly tough economic realities.

In 1993, the holding presided over an empire which, over the space of a century, had mushroomed into the tenth largest industrial conglomeration in Europe and the biggest manufacturer and employer in Germany. It was also the first German company to list its shares on the New York Stock Exchange later that same year. At the same time, however, the domestic as well as the foreign media reported almost daily the corporation's unexpected but increasing difficulties with global and German recession, representing just some of the side-effects of monetary and socio-economic/political problems following the collapse of the USSR and the reunification of Germany. In April 1993, Gerhard Liener, the finance director of the corporation, forecast a fall in profits of between 25 and 30 per cent for the current financial year (see also Exhibit 1).

Until the 1980s, Daimler-Benz had enjoyed great success in building high-quality world-class cars, and the company's image and size had evolved accordingly. However, within the five years that followed, the product range had expanded to embrace everything from 'roadster to toaster', including such diverse items as washing machines, defence material and rails. This expansion had entailed growing administrative and managerial challenges and initial attempts to bring effectiveness and efficiency to an increasingly cumbersome organizational apparatus had not succeeded. The creation of the Daimler-Benz holding in 1989, seemed the right new framework for the administration, management and also the integration of the new technological concern.

By 1991, the board as well as the staff of the holding had to concede, however, that in its present structure it could not even adequately fulfil the role it had been designed for. 'Top-heavy', 'hydrocephalus', wre the terms used to describe the organization which was basically still run in the image of the Daimler-Benz Company of ten years before. In order to eradicate what had become an overly hierarchical structure, a 'too many chiefs' syndrome and an often nine-months' decision-making process, a totally new management concept was required, in tandem with a changed attitude.

Edzard Reuter, chairman of the Daimler-Benz AG since 1987, may have already had a somewhat similar vision when he played a decisive role in choosing the architectural model for the new buildings in Stuttgart-Möhringen, the seat of the holding. At the time of their inauguration in 1989, however, Reuter's vision was not recognized. Instead, people felt disappointed by the arrangement of ten interlinking 3–6 storey office buildings, certainly modest compared to the mighty concrete and glass monoliths so loved by other German industrial giants for their headquarters. The German press felt that the architecture lacked concept, seemed only 'fitting for accountants', that the complex resembled, if anything, a 'comfortable and bourgeois sedan'. The Mercedes star had been deprived of its place on an appropriately huge structure dominating the skyline from afar and had to resign itself to the comparatively low-impact central tower housing the CEO's offices. Just like the poster in Reuter's office, however, portraying a huge dinosaur and subtitled 'History is full of giants that couldn't adapt', these may have been portentous signs that the German conglomerate was becoming aware of the need for change, not only in answer to its organizational growth but also with a view to an inevitably different future.

By the end of 1992, a new company restructuring model had been agreed, which was to involve functional/operational changes as well as changes in ethos, culture and mentality. The new model attempted to do away with an outdated and counterproductive culture which had become more akin to that of a public administration than that of a living and growing enterprise. It would construct a flatter organizational hierarchy in support of a new, greater emphasis on individual 'know-how, creativity and strengths'. As it was described, 'networking through cross-departmental team work and better planning, organization, communication and coordination' would provide shorter routes for reporting and decision-making thereby guaranteeing more flexibility in processing tasks and solving problems.

As with any such drastic reorganizations, there were initially great uncertainties. Would it be possible to overturn such a deep-rooted 'palatial' culture? Would two years be enough time to plant and bring to fruition the concept of 'working in tents' and once achieved, what would it be like afterwards? Would it be better? Would it finally persuade the corporate businesses that the 'new' management holding was, indeed, capable of leading an integrated technology concern?

Reinhard Krebs, too, was aware of the difficulties that lay ahead, but there was no doubt in his mind about the necessity for such changes:

> So far we have been working as if each and every one of us lived in his own palace, we have erected high walls around us, embellished our areas with status symbols. We need to tear those palaces down, get rid of the status symbols. We must no longer hide behind walls. We need to start working with tents, which can easily be moved, put up and taken down when and wherever the need arises. This will encourage communication and facilitate cooperation

DAIMLER-BENZ – THE BACKGROUND

> Daimler-Benz Classic built up layers upon layers of management, like an onion. (D-B executive)

> It was like working in the French state in the Middle Ages, the king on top, and a steep hierarchy down to the bottom. (D-B manager)

When the original firms of Daimler and Benz merged in 1926, no one could have foreseen the huge success that the new company would eventually enjoy, as it did not really put its mark on the German automobile market until the 1960s when, finally defining its market niche of high-quality cars and upgrading its truck section through various alliances and associations, Mercedes-Benz established the basis for its growing success over the years to come.

As the manufacturing plants spread over the southwestern German regions, so the workforce grew and a business empire was in the making. The company possessed a unique organizational culture, characterized by a prevalence of status and accompanying symbols and a steep hierarchical structure. Staff were recruited largely from the surrounding regions, trained internally and they slowly worked their way up through the ranks. The company developed the image of a 'paternal employer', which paid good salaries, provided good benefits and a comfortable pension plan. Many employees and workers, starting at Daimler-Benz, were sure of a good job throughout their working lives until retirement.

Middle management was, in general, responsible for a small number of subordinates. Loyalty and hard work were rewarded with promotion, but if a higher post was not available, 'one created a title and gave them two subordinates', as one member of staff remembered. This system propagated reporting levels, from the lowest managers, via department managers, chief department managers, department directors, experts, chief expert, directors, etc. up to board members. As the company grew, so did the hierarchies.

Apart from titles and personnel, other status symbols represented an important part of the reward system. It was said that one could tell the position of Daimler-Benz employees not only by the type of their company cars, but also by the quality of the chair covers in their offices. It was emphasized by several managers, however, that this was not just a policy to satisfy Daimler-Benz personnel. It was also a public relations exercise: 'Clients were used to the fact, that a manager or department director drove a certain car and had his title printed on his visiting card. If the title were no longer there, if he suddenly drove a smaller car, he would not get the attention and the service he was entitled to because they probably would have thought he had been demoted. This was especially important with contacts from abroad.'

This culture also fostered a concept of authority strictly related to position. One manager remembered that there was:

> a strong feeling for authority by position. The time of talking in a meeting related 90 per cent of the time to the position they had. The higher the rank, the more they talked. The lower the position, the more they listened. This military order of command had been very strong in this culture – and still was, in many ways.

During the 1980s, turnover and profits grew (see Exhibit 2). Throughout this period, however, car production grew more complex, high technology became an increasing factor in development and design, and the Japanese competition began to make inroads, albeit small, into the automobile market. Daimler-Benz began to turn its thoughts to diversification. In 1985, it started on the road towards acquiring new technology, spending an estimated DM 8 billion buying or setting up companies in a wide range of industries: aerospace, including defence (DASA = MTU,[1] TST,[2] Messerschmitt-Boelkow-Blohm, Airbus and Fokker); electronics, rails transport and household goods (AEG); and financial services and software. Reuter rejected various accusations of 'wanting to link the unlinkable' by retorting that 'We felt, looking right into the next century, that we should set the course for new growth possibilities in case the motor business stagnates.'[3]

In July 1986, forced by the changed circumstances, the new Daimler-Benz Group undertook a rigorous reorganization of its company structure. It was one of the biggest organizational challenges the company had experienced. Its reported aim was to create closer cooperation and know-how transfer throughout the group.

The new scheme involved, first, reshuffling and extending the executive board. Until then, the structures defined that each board member was responsible for functions like finance and management, personnel, research and development, materials procurement, production, distribution and capital investment. No area of responsibility according to product group had existed. The new board system therefore established separate divisions for cars and commercial vehicles as well as the head of the three newly acquired companies of AEG, MTU and Dornier. Second, it tackled areas where changes had become necessary:

- Daimler-Benz had little experience in the field of diversification and divisional management.
- There was also a need for developing managerial skills, a gap which was to be filled by recruiting staff across the divisional range and providing appropriate training.
- There was general agreement that Daimler-Benz was a company with an international image, but that the internationalism related to its world-wide exports. There were very few manufacturing plants outside Germany and, principally, it was 'very Germany-oriented'.

'Structure and synergy' committees composed of key board members and various working groups were set up with the aim of coordinating change, preventing overlap between the different divisions while ensuring technological transfer. For some people, however, this was not the answer to rationalizing the collaboration between the four groups. As one corporate director complained:

> Steering committees with board members are only necessary if things don't work. Where additional capabilities need to be developed for new programs, as in some of the technology 'synergy points', coordination from Stuttgart is of course needed .... Where expertise already exists, Daimler should rely on its partners instead of creating new co-ordinating bodies above them.

Underneath all these new activities, however, the old Daimler-Benz 'classic' organization and culture was not affected by the reorganization. On the contrary, despite the desire to keep their individual organization models, the new corporate businesses were forced to adapt to the Daimler-Benz structure which, especially for the research and development divisions, had disadvantages. As one R & D manager comments, 'It may have been fitting for Mercedes, but in terms of research it had become a severe obstacle, an obstruction to the independence of the researchers . . . through these long strict procedures with seven management levels.' An employee at one of the divisions complained that 'people just followed the official channels, they did not dare take decisions on their own without the approval of their superiors.' Even one-day business trips abroad had to have the authorization of a board member. If the challenges for the corporate board were those of creating synergy, coordinating strategies, know-how and research, clearly, the existing organization would have to be overhauled more drastically.

DAIMLER-BENZ – THE HOLDING

It was time to shift from a concentration on operations towards one of strategies. The understanding of the role of management units *vis-à-vis* those of business units remained unclear and there was still an overlap of undefined activities. (Gerd Woriescheck, senior vice-president, Corporate Executive Management Development)

Following the example of many other corporations, which through growth, mergers or acquisitions, had outgrown their existing company structures, Daimler-Benz started to look at concepts of a headquarters, a nerve centre capable of directing and administering the new corporate units. As one manager remembered, 'with the acquisitions of AEG and the establishment of DASA, this holding concept came along'. A 'classic' holding, however, which looked after the resources and left its divisions to run their businesses, would not provide the right framework. How could four individual corporate divisions become an integrated technological corporation and what role should the Daimler-Benz AG play in its new form and how should it differ in its duties from D-B classic?

In 1988, the decision was made in favour of a management holding. It was structured into four corporate functions: The chairman of the board of management, finance and procurement, personnel, and research and technology. (See also Exhibit 3.) Its official role was set out as 'developing future projects and strategic goals for the Corporation and taking ... initiatives in the development of new areas of activity .... The holding coordinates and advises the Corporate Units. Concepts and measures are developed through collaboration in project work and working teams' (D-B recruitment brochure, 1991).

In the words of one employee, the four crucial areas of responsibility were in practical terms defined as 'First, to focus the strategies of Daimler-Benz – the right strategies. Second, it [the holding] was to create a synergy between the various DB companies to watch over the portfolio. Third, it was to provide an administrative centre whose function would be neutral. Fourth, its specific task was to be the centre of financial administration and to coordinate research and development.'

The initial holding staff of approximately 3,000 were made up for the most part of research and technology personnel. 'Daimler-Benz had acquired not only the new corporate units but also their integral research divisions. It was decided very quickly to gather all these research divisions together and allocate them to the holding ... in order to coordinate the activities and eradicate overlap,' explained an R & D manager. One of the consequences of this concentration of R & D activities was that the total number of holding personnel had, by 1993, been reduced to 2,700. A further 400 jobs were to be cut over the following three years.

It did not take long to find out that the strategies and policies of the new holding still did not marry easily with the existing organizational and management structures. The holding had to deal with four very different corporate units. Under the D-B classic system, projects, in order to be accepted, not only had to go to the board of the holding, but also to the board(s) of the various corporate units concerned which in turn passed them up and down their own hierarchical ladders. One member of the personnel department stated with exasperation that 'projects were passed upwards, sideways, downwards, upwards again, sideways, etc., taking up to nine months to receive their final OK.' Therefore, months passed before decisions were made. The holding was no longer able to serve its ultimate customers, the corporate units efficiently, many of whose staff had not only been against a holding concept from the outset, but also against pooling their R & D activities under such an umbrella.

One manager commented that 'it [the holding] had been too little customer-oriented . . . a new system was needed.' Gerd Woriescheck, senior vice-president, corporate executive management development, was also of the opinion that:

> from our point of view, were were not delivering things directly to the market, to our ultimate customers: our corporate units. I think that it took the corporate units a long time to talk to us and to work with us because we had such a long decision-making process in the holding . . . . The holding should not have been so slow that the corporate units were prevented from operating.

For many, the biggest problem was that of non-communication as 'each person saw only himself and his immediate area'. The 'palatial' boundaries continued to be strong, inhabited by people with a 'garden allotment' attitude. Although the centralization of finance worked well (33 businesses were financially dealt with by the holding), there was a general feeling that the holding did not live up to its management concept. Some managers even questioned the concept of the holding: 'this type of holding has disadvantages because it requires a hierarchical structure . . . always prone to hierarchies . . . . We have to make a continual effort to fight bureaucracy.' For others, the reasons for the severe shortcomings were more fundamental in that 'we just took a slice out of Mercedes-Benz and transplanted it to headquarters'. One manager said that nothing had really changed:

> The D-B holding . . . was a natural outgrowth of Mercedes, not formed differently – same culture, same mentality, i.e. 'the bigger my staff the more power I have'. But in a holding company, you need a more consultant-type executive.

THE RESTRUCTURING

> It is not the old structure minus one [reporting] level. It's not a cost-reduction exercise due to company difficulties. It is an entirely different approach. (Günther Sauder, executive human resources policies.)

> Most people avoided making or admitting mistakes, or learning from mistakes. We want to create a culture where mistakes are possible and acknowledged. (Gerd Woriescheck.)

In April 1991, as Woriescheck recalled, on the occasion of a board meeting, Reuter put the question forward 'whether the old structure we inherited from Daimler-Benz AG was the right one for the new tasks and duties of the holding and the management planning'. Woriescheck and Rolf Hanssen, senior vice-president, corporate planning and strategy, were given the task of formulating an organizational structure which would be appropriate for all the new tasks of the holding. The questions also arose as to who would ultimately be responsible for authorizing and implementing a new structure. Reuter decided that it would be the whole board (including the heads of the corporate units) who would review the various stages of the process and put the final stamp of approval on the finished project.

As a first step, a task force (Arbeitskreis Führungsstruktur und Personalent-wicklung) was set up which included Hanssen and Woriescheck and a further five members from planning and controlling, and personnel. The task force decided that the restructuring process should not be managed with the aid of an external consultant;

instead it should be steered internally on two levels: top-down, through the board and the task force, and also, more importantly, in consultation with the holding staff. 'The task force considered how to incorporate a broader sample of other people's opinions in its final decisions...' Although it was not a totally democratic process, for Woriescheck, it was a first step away from the 'usual authoritarian' style.

The task force decided to create a consulting group, composed of various members from all departments, which met every three weeks with members of the task force to discuss the restructuring process and forthcoming proposals. These members were chosen at random, independent of whether they were known to be for or against restructuring. Any attempts to influence the balance of opinions, and therefore any decision-making, were rejected. As one of the members recalls: 'Any attempt by any superior to send those people who, he thought, would represent his own opinion failed.' Nevertheless, when asked afterwards, members of the consulting group commented with dissatisfaction on this consultation and decision-making process. Although it was conceded that the task force had made a valiant attempt at involving as many people as possible in the time-span allocated, they felt nevertheless aggrieved that the *'vox populi'* procedure had not lived up to its promise of a more bottom-up democratic involvement. Some members of the consulting group felt 'people had not been involved in the optimum way, neither during the discussions nor on implementation. Somebody worked it out... our opinions did not matter', that it could have been possible 'to consider the needs of others.'

By April 1992, Woriescheck and Hanssen had their initial outline ready, which they presented to the board. The board gave the green light to submit a final plan. As Woriescheck remembered, 'We worked towards 1 September to develop a concept of the reorganization. On that day, the board gave its okay for the holding to be structured according to this concept.' The task force then talked to the departments to discuss and prepare with them the final changes to be implemented. The final presentation to the board was made in December 1992 and approved. The restructuring was to start on 1 January 1993 and, in exceptional cases, would extend over two years. Where the final structures could not be adopted immediately, an intermediate structure was to be in place after the first year, and during that time job evaluations, redundancies and shifts in personnel would be dealt with.

THE MODEL

In search of a new model, the holding had realized that, above all, the changed role of management in the holding needed to be addressed. Managers' tasks were no longer operations-related. Instead, their functions increasingly involved service-oriented and coordinating activities, with a heightened emphasis on the role of 'consulting' (there is no word in the German language for 'facilitating'). Increased competition, changed markets and economics demanded quicker and more decisive actions and reactions. A flatter hierarchy and 'networking' were the answers in that they allowed immediate communications and competence in dealing with complex tasks. In the words of members of the task force:

We had to change the attitude...we needed to work together without borders. My vision was to find new forms of working together in a fluid way and for that we had to bring forward creative people who wanted to cross borders and network constructively.

We had to reduce the gaps between the people working on the issues and the people deciding the issues .... People had to work with less supervision. They had to build their own networks - otherwise they would never be able to complete their work. They have got to talk directly to people, explain their ideas, etc.

There were four major changes (see Exhibits 4 and 5):

1. *Reporting levels.* Instead of the four management reporting levels (the reduction to four had already been a result of the previous reorganizations), there would be only three below the board. Titles were abolished. Managers now belonged to one of three management groups: directorate, upper management, management. Under the new model, posts were evaluated according to two dimensions: the reporting level and the management grades.

2. There would be distinct emphases on management knowledge and subject knowledge. This would be expressed in a strict separation between *management posts* and *expert posts*. However, both manager and expert had equal status and would both be represented in all three management groups. Their only difference related to the competences required for a post. A management post required competence in leadership and coordination, whereas an expert post necessitated a higher degree of specialist subject expertise. Management and expert posts were also interchangeable, i.e. if a given project required it, a manager with specialist subject knowledge could become an expert. An expert could also acquire management competence through project leadership or further training.

3. Through the reduction of reporting levels, managers were given now an *increased number of subordinates,* not counting assistants and secretaries. Whereas the previous ratio had been on average 1:2, 1:4 and 1:6, it would now range from a minimum of 1:6 to that of 1:10, and even more.

    Without subordinates, experts would have increased 'free spaces', i.e. to look for and take on more responsibilities in their specialist fields.

4. *Status symbols* were eradicated. Company cars were no longer assigned according to status but staff could choose from a range of cars available. Specific titles would be abolished and managers and experts would be known as *Leiter* (Head of). Promotion into a higher management group could not take place on the basis of, for example, higher qualifications while still occupying the same post, but would have to be connected to another, higher post.

The flattening of hierarchies, cross-departmental collaboration and an increase in 'free spaces' also meant that projects would no longer be delayed by a long and cumbersome hierarchical decision-making process. Project teams, composed of members from various departments, and headed by a team leader from one of the management groups were to ensure that this process was dealt with more speedily and efficiently (see also Exhibit 6).

The elimination of one reporting level and the reshuffling of posts and competences necessitated a regrading of posts and re-evaluation of salaries. This was done with the help of a special HAY procedure by which key personnel would be interviewed and their new tasks analyzed. The results were adapted summarily for the remainder of the staff involved. It was forecast that 67 jobs would be eliminated, but people would not be made redundant. This would be achieved either through attrition, redeployment or people leaving of their own accord.

The restructuring process had not gone unnoticed by the German press and public, who had always taken a great interest in Daimler-Benz. This was not just another large corporation; over the years it had almost become a barometer of the German economy. It came as no surprise, therefore, that, in November 1992, the Daimler-Benz member of the board for human resources, Wolfgang Hirschbrunn, went to the press and talked about the restructuring of the holding to reporters of *Capital*, a major German business magazine, in which he outlined the holding's projects for the two years to come:

CAPITAL: On 1 January 1993, the Daimler-Benz holding will give itself a new management structure. Is the organization, as it exists today, no longer manageable?

HIRSCHBRUNN: Our structure, as it is now, dates back to the old 'Daimler' and consequently, one encounters repeatedly the hierarchical thinking of the former automobile company. The new structure is intended to propagate more intensively the new corporate spirit.

CAPITAL: You needed three years to notice and correct this?

HIRSCHBRUNN: You cannot saddle all the horses at the same time. This means that in our case we could not build a new corporate *and* a management structure simultaneously. One has to wait for a shift of perspective in the staff. Only then is it possible to work on the structures.

CAPITAL: What is it, in concrete terms, that you want to reform?

HIRSCHBRUNN: Up to now we have had a clear four-level hierarchical structure. Each level has to report to the next higher. Only the highest management level, the directors, report directly to the Board. This we want to change radically. First, there will only be three future reporting levels incorporating management, expert and project posts. In parallel, there will continue to exist a demarcation according to directors, upper management and management groups. This might mean in practical terms that a member of the management group is in charge of a project on the first reporting level and reports to a director.

CAPITAL: In other words, you want to break up the Daimler authoritarian management style which was very much oriented towards command and execution?

HIRSCHBRUNN: We have not been that authoritarian for a long time. In spite of this, we would like to effect a totally new management approach. The job of the superior is no longer to control the work of his staff, but to define objectives and to merely check whether these are being attained. Furthermore, he no longer needs to have expert knowledge of each area: his staff will have expert competence.

CAPITAL: What are your aims for this new management structure in the holding?

HIRSCHBRUNN: Employees are to take on more responsibility. Nobody should be able to hide behind his superior. Each member of staff should act entrepreneurially and in order to do this he will receive the necessary free space from now on. Furthermore, we have to finish with the box mentality and improve internal communication.

CAPITAL: This will certainly motivate some members of staff. For others, however, this must have come as a shock as jobs will have to be sacrificed to these reforms.

HIRSCHBRUNN: Job reduction is not the primary objective of the reforms. Due to the new alignment of jobs, posts will, of course, become redundant. In this respect, each manager knows that his budget will be smaller next year. But we make no specific demands, each sector decides independently. Most members of staff support the reforms anyway because they have already taken the initiative and work together beyond hierarchical barriers and spheres of competence.

CAPITAL: Which reporting level do you want to eradicate?

HIRSCHBRUNN: We cannot tell you this because our new organization will be totally different, without comparison. We are even considering whether under the new structure we should maintain job titles. In any case, we will get rid of the company car hierarchy; those times where one could divine somebody's rank from his type of car are gone.

THE IMPACT

It is working well and we are much more autonomous. There are still hitches, but it will be a matter of six months or so before they are ironed out. (Finance executive)

I don't see an advantage in the new organization in my area. I now have to establish in more detail how we work together. (Another finance executive)

By July 1993, six months into the restructuring process, it was too early to take a reasonable measure of the success of the new model, but the offices of the Daimler-Benz holding were visibly full of activity and energy. Managers were more than usually occupied with meetings, discussing implementation procedures and implications for their own departments.

For the research and technology divisions, the impact of the restructuring had been, from the beginning, less significant. Indeed, the general comment had been 'Where are the differences for us?' One of the reasons was that prior to the holding restructuring, in 1991, the research divisions had already reduced the reporting levels to three (although four management grades remained and reporting levels and management grades were not separated). Their projects also required a great deal of cooperation between various departments and, as one researcher remembers, 'channels of decision-making could always be circumvented'. In fact, it could happen that a small research unit reported directly to the board, and as such did not have to pass through the various hierarchies for signatures and authorizations.

For others, however, initial reactions were mixed. In the short time that the holding staff had been working under the new model, the personnel experienced feelings of uncertainty. Despite the enthusiasm shown by the board, some personnel expressed their reservations about the time factor of the whole exercise, in that for them the 'top-down introduction was too rushed'. Others thought that considering the significance of such an undertaking, too little thought had been given to the implementation process. As one manager commented: 'I am not happy with the amount of time I have been given for this. I am not getting enough support from my people, no feedback from the task force.' Another made the point that: 'the restructuring is a milestone towards innovation, but the new model has to be put into practice by top management too, it has to be seen to be exercised daily by the top, and this is a process which cannot be finished in two years.'

From the outset, it had been clear to the Daimler-Benz leadership that additional tools were needed to underpin the restructuring process. In order to assist departments and their staff in changing not only their working procedures but also their personal attitudes, workshops and seminars were planned. Furthermore, the process of consultation and discussions was maintained in the form of continuing fora and round tables, the first of which took place in March 1993, three months into the restructuring process.

This meeting involved 200 people. Ten tables were placed in a large room and around each one 20 members of staff were seated. The occasion was to take stock, to discuss the initial problems and difficulties encountered during the previous weeks. Each table had a moderator who, after the discussion, summarized the findings of his particular table. Everybody was encouraged to talk openly, a process which for many who had worked for some time under the old hierarchical system was difficult, as it meant not only criticizing but also being seen to criticize. As one of the participants comments: 'Before 1993, there was criticism, but it was never in the open, never to the face of the persons it was directed at.' But, as Woriescheck pointed out, people started to learn that 'ideas were not "more correct" just because they came from a high level. They [the executives] had always thought that it was their job to know better. "The higher level is always right" has been a central theme in German history.'

The internal holding report of this forum focused on the major points of concern:

- *Lack of Overall Progress:* There was an impression that not much had been achieved thus far, that the reorganization had been 'built around personalities' and that everything continued much as before. There was a danger of the old culture overshadowing the new management structure, creating a 'shadow organization'.

- *Role Confusion:* There was confusion about the new roles of managers and experts. 'What is the difference between experts and managers? What do experts and managers do? Is there a new management concept and if so, what is it? Expert and manager posts appear to be equal only on paper. Due to the levelling process of expert and managing posts, experts felt they had lost out, that they no longer had the possibility of delegating.'

- *Lack of Cooperation and Coordination:* 'Free spaces' could only be sought and developed with the cooperation of colleagues and superiors, which was not always the case. And without coordination, conflicts and/or redundant actions would occur.

In addition to the above points of concern, the report duly took account of the fact that these were very early days and that 'the essential was still to come'. It then recommended more top-down leadership, more flexibility within departments, more personnel rotations between departments and increased communication on further actions. It was also recommended that there should be a right to vote on changes proposed during future team discussions and forums.

For some, working with the previous structure and hierarchy may have been cumbersome, but it had nevertheless contained a certain element of security.

In interviews with executives and managers in July 1993, uncertainties about the new evaluation of jobs and salaries and dissatisfaction with the abolition of titles, status symbols and perks still persisted. A number of staff members who had been with the company for a long time, had worked their way up through the ranks, and, in their middle age, were proud of what they had achieved, seemingly found it more difficult to adapt to the changes. 'I feel I have earned this and why should I now be deprived of it?' said one older manager. 'If a customer now sees my visiting card with just "*Leiter*" [Head of] on it, what is he to think, especially when he sees that I am also driving a less prestigious car.' These grievances, however, were also expressed by the young members of staff.

Vis-à-vis the concept of a future flatter hierarchy, the exchange of an expert function for new and increased managing responsibilities, or remaining an expert but without a department, managers were filled with doubts about whether they could adapt to the new structure. As one of them commented: 'The job of the manager, even though it was about staff management, has always had a functional aspect. He himself undertook those functions.'

A finance executive, who had previously been a functional manager and head of department, asked himself whether this restructuring model was the right one for him and his department. Previously, he had a staff responsibility of four, worked in an orderly hierarchy and reported to a director who then reported to the board. He was an expert at his job. Under the new structure, he had become directly responsible to the board, but saw himself deprived of his expert functions and put in the role of a manager with his number of subordinates then reaching ten. For him, his new objectives of 'further developing his area and tasks, to oversee implementation of objectives, to hasten communication, to structure and steer processes' meant that he was no longer able to supervise the work of his department: 'I was too far away from the content of the work. I have to judge the work of the experts from a distance, to make decisions by plausibility, not by knowing what they are actually doing.' He had little time now for 'working hands-on, solving problems' and could no longer 'look into the nitty-gritty'. Instead, he found that managing a large number of subordinates was a difficult role to adapt to. In his eyes, managing was 'a tool', not a job in itself. Under the new model he had lost control, be it over internal matters:

> In the new approach, there is too much delegation of the entire responsibility to the middle or lower level. If you want to have a subordinate who takes responsibility, who wants to fill up the free spaces in order to make decisions, that is all very nice, but what is it doing to the manager?

Or in dealing with external affairs:

> When contacts are used to dealing with high-level management and suddenly they have to talk to someone on the phone whom they don't know, who has no title and who is in charge of millions of Deutschmark transactions – what impression will that give?

However, despite uncertainties, criticisms and dissatisfaction, there existed a continuing recognition of the importance of change accompanied by a determination to see the process through. One executive remarked, 'The change is very big for me;

it will be more successful than anything else.' He spoke with great conviction about the new policies of networking and 'free spaces': 'The new structure is the first stage in the restructuring process. We will be more successful than in the past in all aspects of our business. I can now communicate more directly.'

Another finance executive from the outset had been very much in favour of restructuring. He felt that, finally, through cutting reporting levels, the lower and middle management had to do the tasks they were paid for:

> These people have to earn their money . . . and now through the elimination of reporting levels, responsibility has shifted downwards . . . and people who perhaps had been paid too much for what they did in the past, would now have tasks and responsibilities according to their salaries.

This executive now belonged to the upper management group and had five subordinates who were part of the management group. This number would increase to eight or nine, due to departmental reorganization. The initial difficulties, which the new way of working entailed, for him were only teething problems which would soon be overcome. Although project schedules had become tighter, staff was already learning to become more conscious of priorities and efficiency:

> Time pressure has made work scheduling much tighter and one can deal with about eighty percent of one's workload. Things have to be sorted, i.e. I have to do this now and the rest can wait. I see this as positive, that one has to make one's own decisions as to what is important and what can be done later. Time will show which is more important and which is not.

However, he was also of the opinion that the 'physical removal of hierarchies would not totally eliminate bureaucratization'. Instead, it would be achieved by changing previous traditions, habits and mentalities. It was a learning process; while one would make mistakes one would learn from them.

> We have always worked in a hierarchy. In my job as boss, I have previously ironed out the mistakes of others, i.e. I have worked on their strengths, and when I saw that in such and such an area there were weaknesses, then I did the work myself. This kind of 'cover-up' to ensure continuous quality no longer exists.

He himself could not be excluded from that learning process. He had to adapt to the same new working procedures in relation to his own superior who would soon manage 12 subordinates:

> Until now, when I had difficulties, I would consult him. But he no longer has the necessary time. Now I have to do things myself and if there are difficulties afterwards, then I have learnt that perhaps I cannot do this myself and we will have to find a different solution.

THE FUTURE

> The organization has to change in such a way that people do not suffer. We have to tell them that you used to work in a centralized way, but now we work decentralized, and while we used to quarrel with people, now we have to find a way to work together. (Finance executive)

> We have to do more in project management . . . find new ways . . . of being entrepreneurs.
> (Personnel executive)

By July 1993, the restructuring process had entered its sixth month and there was clearly a lot to be done by December 1994. When asked at that time about their future expectations, executives commented that, basically, the need for change had been recognized and that the process, despite its detractors, enjoyed general support. This said, they identified various areas which required additional emphasis, perhaps even additional measures.

As to the implementation process, this needed to be speedier and better directed. One executive thought:

> It was essential to create more instruments. If you do not get a critical speed, the process tends to slow down and come to a dead stop . . . It is just not good enough to set up an organization – people are still the same. I wish the process were led by the Personnel Department. They can identify people as corporate culture formers, multiplicators of a more modern culture. Just go through the ranks and start with two or three. The multiplicator would bring it up to 50 people. Just do it.

Another executive put the emphasis on: 'finding highly talented potential leaders. I want to involve these people in this process . . . I would like a steering group – these people must be members of the steering group – to find credible forms of transmitting this change.' Others felt that, so far, the leadership had not set enough examples in working with the new model and that the process thereby was in danger of losing its credibility: 'It [the restructuring] must become much more integrated in the day-by-day activities of management, in the contacts with colleagues . . . . Changes cannot be ordered top-down. What has to come from top down are living examples.'

It was also pointed out by one executive that, under the new model, the parameters of a job were contantly shifting, depending on the tasks to be undertaken, which required excellent specialist knowledge and a higher level, as well as a broader range, of qualifications. In the shorter term, personnel could receive further training in areas where certain capacities and knowledge were lacking, but, ultimately, it was a question of flexibility:

> What was done well in the development phase, but not flawlessly in the realization phase, was the extent of rigidity. You should be rigid in working out the principle, but when you implement it on a living company with a strong –albeit questionable – culture, then I feel one should have been more flexible than we were. The rigidity led many people to an attitude of resignation – I have to do it, but I don't believe in it – because although the principle is good, it has not been adapted well to individual circumstances.

There was general consensus, however, on various aspects of the restructuring which would have very positive consequences for the holding and its corporate units beyond 1994. There was no doubt in anyone's mind that departments would eventually evolve as entrepreneurial entities, with their own accountability and profit centres. Furthermore, new project management and networking concepts would lead towards 'centres of excellence', which would be beneficial for all sectors. One executive spoke for all:

> We must build centres of excellence . . . . If, for example, it is a question of financial problem solving, one could talk to someone who is strong in that field and say to him,

you will do that, because you have the capacity. For a different problem, one goes to someone else who has the necessary capacities specific to that problem.

The ultimate goal for him as for others, however, was more efficient working relations with the Corporate units.

We should act as advisors, maybe appoint certain people in the Holding reponsible for certain areas in the Corporate Units. These people could act as contacts in order to assist them .... We need to promote a strategy whereby the Corporate Units can see that cooperation is of mutual benefit.

At the end of 1993, Gerd Woriescheck and Rolf Hanssen were to report back to the board with the new job evaluations and salary structures in place. The remainder of the process was to be achieved in 1994.

EXHIBIT 1
First quarter results
(DM).

	1993	1992	Change %
Group			
Net Profit (millions)	20	480	−96
Sales (billions)	18.39	22.79	−19
Total Employees	367,508	393,390	−7
Mercedes-Benz			
Car Division			
Sales (billions)	7.12	10.16	−30
Production (units)	94,473	153,738	−39
Truck Division			
Sales (billions)	5.41	6.41	−16
Production (units)	55,853	76,110	−27
AEG (electronics)			
Sales (billions)	2.21	2.38	−7
DASA Aerospace			
Sales (billions)	2.85	3.18	−10
Debis (services)			
Sales (billions)	2.07	1.74	+19

Source: Wall Street Journal, 14/15 May 1993

EXHIBIT 2
Daimler-Benz Corporation.

Year	Employees	Turnover (DM m)	Profit (DM m)
1984	199.872	43.505	1.104
1985	231.077	52.409	1.682
1986	319.965	65.498	1.767
1987	326.288	67.475	1.782
1988	338.749	73.495	1.702
1989	368.226	76.293	1.700*
1990	376.785	85.500	1.795
1991	379.252	95.010	1.942
1992	382.633	98.549	1.451

* Figure adjusted for comparison.

Source: Daimler-Benz AG company reports.

EXHIBIT 3

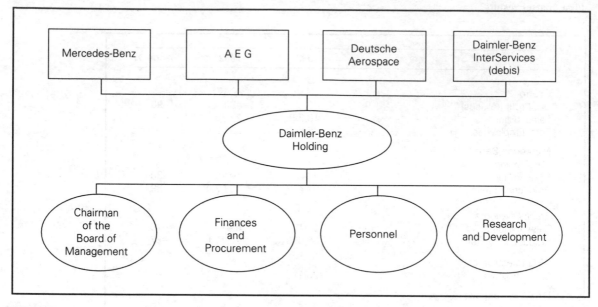

EXHIBIT 4

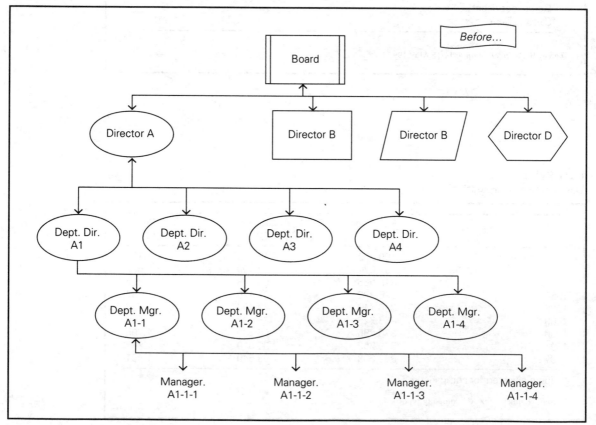

EXHIBIT 5

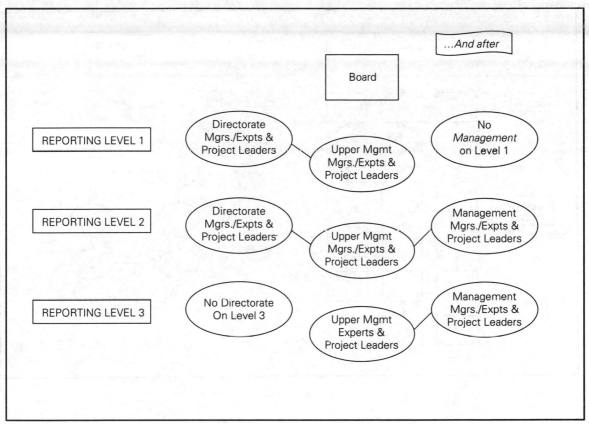

EXHIBIT 6

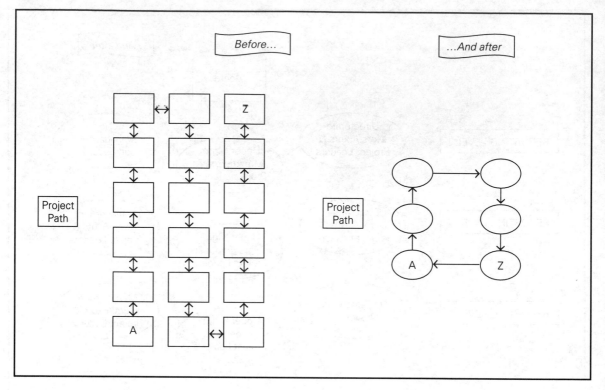

CASE NOTES

1-2

1. Cabotage is the freedom of a truck driver registered in one EC country to collect and deliver loads between two points inside another EC country.

1-3

1. In 1990 on average $1 = 1.7 Dfl. (Dutch Guilder) and 1 ECU = 2.3 Dfl.

1-4

1. The Spanish monetary unit, valued at Ptas/US$ = 154.15 on 1 January 1986, and Ptas/US$ = 109.00 on 1 January 1988.
2. Salomon Brothers, 'The Spanish Commercial Banks', September 1989.
3. These failed banks represented 46 per cent of the existing commercial banks in 1977 and 20 per cent of total deposits in the banking system. *Source*: Caminal, Gual and Vives, 'Competition in Spanish Banking', Discussion Papers of the Centre for Economic Policy Research, vol. 314, 1989, p. 9; Kleinwort Benson Securities, 'The Big Six Spanish Banks', 21 June 1990
4. Another consequence of the Spanish banking crisis was the government's adoption in May 1988 of capital adequacy requirements ranking among the most stringent in the world. Accordingly, the Spanish banking system was subsequently regarded as highly solvent.
5. Caminal, Gual and Vives (1989: 16).
6. In fact, they had been prevented from offering time deposits of more than two years, until 1973.
7. Crédit Lyonnais (established in 1875), Lloyd's Bank (1915), Société Générale (1919), and Banca Nazionale del Lavoro (1941).
8. Gabriel Hawawini and Eric Rajendra, 'The transformation of the European financial services industry: From fragmentation to integration', Leonard N. Stern School of Business, New York University, 1990.
9. Damien Neven, 'Structural adjustment in retail banking', in *European Banking in the 1990's,* ed. Jean Dermine (Oxford: Basil Blackwell, 1990), p. 171.
10. *Ibid.,* p. 165.
11. This informal cartel manifested itself in regular 'club' meetings between the CEOs of the 'Big Seven' banks. These banks held very cordial relations, much to the chagrin of the government, which favoured fierce competition between them. According to Luis Valls Taberner, CEO of Banco Popular Español (the smallest of the seven), these banks were 'united with respect to the government and competitive with respect to the market'.
12. Banco de España, *Boletín Económico,* November 1989.
13. *The Banker,* June 1988.
14. Under the terms of the EC's proposed Second Coordination Directive of January 1988, any bank authorized by its home member state would be entitled to provide a wide range of banking services in any other EC country. However, the host countries would retain discretion regarding rules on liquidity, business conduct and investor protection. *Source:* Caminal, Gual and Vives, 'Competition in Spanish Banking', p. 266.

15. 'Shock treatment', *International Management*, February 1991, pp. 62–7.
16. See Table 5 for the financial highlights of the 'Big Six' in December 1990.
17. *Financial Times*, 18 May 1988, p. 32
18. *Ibid.*, 24 February 1989, p. 24
19. i.e. the percentage of deposits banks are obliged to lodge with the Central Bank.
20. *Financial Times*, 4 February 1991, p. 21.
21. Cinco Días, 19 February 1990, p. 12.
22. *Euromoney*, September 1990, Special Supplement, pp. 18–19.
23. Dinero y Negocios, 12 October 1990, p. 11; Handelsblatt, 15 October 1990, p. 12.
24. 'Las Cajas de Ahorro Resisten el Primer Asalto', Actualidad Económica, 21 May 1990, pp. 138–42.
25. Dinero y Negocios, 14 February 1990, p. 1.
26. *Financial Times*, 10 January 1991, p. 1.
27. 'Shock treatment', *International Management*, February 1991, pp. 62–7.

1-5

1. *L'Obs Economie*, 6–12 July 1989, p. 54.
2. *L'Usine Nouvelle*, 15 June 1989, p. 12
3. *Forbes*, 9 June 1980.
4. *Ibid.*
5. *Le Figaro*, 8 June 1989.
6. BSN Company Report, Prudential Bache Capital Funding.
7. *Le Provençal*, 21 January 1989.

1-6

1. A. Palmeri, 'The internationalization of fashion', address to securities analysts, January 1987.
2. The biographical notes in the preceding paragraphs are adapted from 'Profiles – being everywhere', *The New Yorker*, 10 November 1986, pp. 53–74.
3. *Ibid.*, p. 58.
4. 'Benetton: Bringing European chic to Middle America', *Business Week*, 11 June 1984, p. 60.
5. 'Benetton takes on the world,' *Fortune*, 13 June 1983, p. 116.
6. *Wall Street Journal Europe*, 24 June 1986.
7. *The New Yorker, op. cit.*, p. 63.

8. *Fortune, op. cit.*, p. 119.
9. *Financial Times*, 23 May 1986.
10. *Ibid.*
11. *Ibid.*

1-9

1. T. Sakiya *Honda Motor: The Men, The Management, The Machines*. Kodansha International Ltd, Tokyo, 1982.
2. S. Sanders, *Honda: The Man and His Machines*, Little Brown, Boston, 1974.
3. Data in this section drawn in part from Richard Pascale, 'Perspectives on strategy', *California Management Review*, Spring 1984.
4. R. Guest, 'The quality of work life in Japan …'. *Hokudai Economic Papers*, Tokyo, Vol. XII, 1982–3.
5. 'America's new No. 4 automaken – Honda'. *Fortune*, 28 October 1985.
6. 'Toyota's fast lane', *Business Week*, 4 November 1985.
7. 'Honda the market guzzler', *Fortune*, 20 February 1984.

1-10

1. The Council of Mutual Economic Assistance (CMEA or Comecon) was formed in 1949 by the Soviet Union and the then Communist states in Eastern and Central Europe to divert trade away from western nations and achieve a greater degree of self-sufficiency among Communist nations. At that time, Comecon included the USSR, Bulgaria, Czechoslovakia, East Germany, Hungary, Poland, and Romania.
2. In 1989, \$1 = DM 1.88; in 1990, \$1 = DM 1.62.
3. Convertibility referred to the right of an enterprise to obtain foreign exchange to pay for imports, with no restrictions from a government or central bank. Under 'internal convertibility', on the other hand, any legal import could be paid for by bringing zlotys to a bank with the invoice for import. Thereafter, the bank paid for the invoice in foreign exchange, converted at the official rate.
4. The grey market, also known as 'parallel imports', referred to trade in legal goods and services that took place outside the channels normally controlled by distributors or company-owned sales subsidiaries.

5. BIS Mackintosh Ltd in *Electronic-World-News*, 23 July 1990, p. 6

6. In Czechoslovakia, the Koruna or Crown was devalued several times in 1990 and 1991. For this reason, sales forecasts were often denominated in hard currencies. In 1990, \$1 = Austrian Sch 11.4.

7. *The Economist*, 26 January 1991.

8. *Living in Europe*, 18 May 1990.

9. *Le Point*, June 1990.

10. Landor Associates.

11. 'A survey of electronics', *The Economist*, 13 April 1991, pp. 10–11

2-2

1. European imports of VCRs from Japan in the period 1978–82 rose as follows: 1978: 275,000; 1979: 555,000; 1980: 1,449,000; 1981: 2,855,000; 1982: 5,250,000. Strong pressure from Philips, trying to establish its own technology standard and its own European manufacturing base, caused several governments to impose limits on the Japanese imports.

2-3

1. Tim Blanks, 'Anita Roddick', *Toronto Life Magazine* (Autumn 1988): 90.

2. Mary Blume, 'Anita Roddick: more than skin deep', *International Herald Tribune* (12 September 1988).

3. Anita Roddick, *Body and Soul* (New York: Crown Publishers, 1991), pp. 19–21.

4. *Ibid.*

5. Burlingham, 'This Woman has changed business forever', *Inc.* (June 1988), p. 44.

6. Deborah Cowley, 'The woman from The Body Shop', *Reader's Digest* (September 1987): 41.

7. Roddick, *op. cit.*, 10.

8. *Ibid.*, 19–20.

9. Jules Arbose, 'The natural formula that's making The Body Shop a winner', *International Management* (July 1986): 37.

10. Roddick, *op. cit.*, 17.

11. Sandra Lane, 'Body work', *GH* (November 1987): 185.

12. Jon Steinberg, 'The body biz', *Ms* (September 1988): 50.

13. Mark Chipperfield, 'Body baroness dispenses with tradition', *Marketing* (April 1988): 31.

14. Roddick, *op. cit.*, 21

15. Burlingham, *op. cit.*, 42.

16. *Ibid.*, 45.

17. Blume, *op. cit.*

18. Roddick, *op. cit.*, 22.

19. *Ibid.*, 24.

20. *Ibid.*, 154.

21. Chipperfield, *op. cit.*, 51.

22. Burlingham, *op. cit.*, 42.

23. Anne Ferguson, 'Soapworks', *Management Today* (May 1989): 99.

24. Roddick, *op. cit.*, 161.

25. James Buxton, 'Tackling the sump', *Financial Times* (30 May 1989): 23.

26. *Ibid.*, 23.

27. *Ibid.*, 23.

28. Roddick, *op. cit.*, 123.

29. *Ibid.*, 252.

30. *Ibid.*, 221–2.

31. *Ibid.*, 132.

32. Christina Robb, 'Whole-earth beauty', *The Boston Globe* (15 September 1990): 15.

33. Cathy S. Dybdahl, 'The Body Shop', *Management Horizons*, Issue 4 (April 1990).

34. Roddick, *op. cit.*, 135.

35. *Ibid.*, 134.

36. Connie Wallace, 'Lessons in marketing – from a maverick', *Working Woman* (October 1990): 84.

37. Blanks, *op. cit.*, 86.

38. Laura Zinn, 'Whales, human rights, rain forests – and the heady smell of profits', *Business Week* (15 July 1991): 115.

39. Roddick, *op. cit.*, 227.

40. John Thorhill, 'Roddicks opt for a lighter touch on the body', *Financial Times* (4 November 1990): 23.

2-6

1. Gene Walden, 'The 100 best stocks to own', 1991, Dearborn Financial Publishing Inc.

2. Ptas/US\$ = 96.5.

3. *El País*, 9 October 1990.

4. Banco Popular Español, 1990 Annual report, p. 64
5. See Exhibit 1 for a diagram of the bank's organizational chart.
6. Banco Popular Español, *1988 Organization and Operations Review*, p. 7.
7. Banco Popular Español, *1990 Operations Review*, p. 15.
8. Banco Popular Español, *1988 Organization and Operations Review*, p. 8.
9. See Exhibit 2 and the Note on the Spanish banking industry.
10. See Exhibit 3.
11. 'Europe's reluctant superbanks', *The Economist*, 5 January, 1991, p. 59.
12. See Exhibit 4.
13. Banco Popular Español, *1990 Operations Review*, p. 13.
14. Banco Popular Español, *1990 Annual report*, p. 65.
15. See the note on the Spanish banking industry.
16. *Ibid*.
17. Banco Popular Español, *Organization and Operations Review*, p. 22.
18. Manuel Martin, 'Banco Popular readies itself for 1993', p. 4, Berlin, April 1989.
19. Banco Popular Español, *1988 Organization and Operations Review*, p. 13
20. *Ibid*., p. 11
21. See Exhibit 5 for an illustration of Banco Popular's IT system before 1987.
22. See Exhibit 6 for an illustration of the Bank's IT system after 1987.
23. Banco Popular Español, *1988 Organization and Operations Review*, p. 31.
24. 'Lo Pequeño es Eficaz', *Ranking*, May 1991, p. 197.
25. 'Ser Diferente es Rentable', *El Futuro*, October 1990, pp. 79–82.
26. See the note on the Spanish banking industry.

3-5

1. L.A.B. Pilkington, 'Review lecture, the float glass process,' The Royal Society, London, 13 February 1969.
2. J.J. Ermenc, Interview with Sir Alistair Pilkington, 25 June 1968, edited transcript, Dartmouth College, Hanover, New Hampshire.
3. Sir Alistair Pilkington, Speech to Toledo Glass & Ceramics Award Cermony, 21 January 1963.
4. Sir Alistair Pilkington, 'Float: An application of science, analysis, and judgement, Turner Memorial Lecture,' *Glass Technology*, August 1971.
5. Interview with James Brian Quinn, Spring 1978. All other quotations from Pilkington employees came from this same series of interviews unless otherwise footnoted.
6. T. Lane and K. Roberts, *Strike at Pilkingtons*, Collins/Fontana, London, 1971.
7. *Report of Joint Inquiry*, Dept of Employment and Productivity, HMSO, p. 10.
8. *The Paper Clip*, Ford Glass Ltd, Toronto, Ontario, Number 28–62, 22 June 1982.
9. *Financial Times*, 11 June 1982, p. 16.

3-6

1. These share data related to the total detergent market (including dishwashing liquid). The heavy duty segment (i.e. laundry detergent) represented about two-thirds of this total.

3-9

1. Maschinen-und Turbinen-Union.
2. Telefunken System Technik.
3. *Financial Times*, 30 July 1987.

BIBLIOGRAPHY FOR READINGS

ABELL, D.F., *Defining the Business. The starting point of strategic planning*, Englewood Cliffs, N.J.: Prentice Hall, 1980.

ACKERMAN, R.W., *The Social Challenge to Business*, Cambridge, MA: Harvard University Press, 1975.

AGUILAR, F.J., *Scanning the Business Environment*, New York: Macmillan, 1967.

ALLEN, T.J., *Managing the Flow of Technology*, Cambridge: MIT Press, 1972.

ALLISON, G.T., *Essence of Decision: Explaining the Cuban missile crisis*, Boston: Little, Brown, 1971.

ANSOFF, H.I., *Corporate Strategy: An analytic approach to business policy for growth and expansion*, New York. McGraw-Hill, 1965.

ARGYRIS, C. and D.A. SCHON, *Organizational Learning: A theory of action perspective*, Reading, MA: Addison-Wesley, 1978.

ASHBY, W.R., *Design for a Brain*, London: Chapman & Hall, 1954.

ASTLEY, W.G. and C.J. FOMBRUN, 'Collective strategy: social ecology of organizational environments', *Academy of Management Review*, 1983: 576–87.

BACON, J., *Corporate Directorship Practices: Membership and committees of the board*, Conference Board and American Society of Corporate Secretaries, Inc., 1973.

BADENFULLER, C. *et al.*, 'National or global? The study of company strategies and the European market for major appliances', London Business School Centre for Business Strategy, Working Paper series no. 28 (June 1987).

BARREYRE, P.Y., 'The concept of "impartition" policy in high speed strategic management', Working Paper, Institut d'Administration des Entreprises, Grenoble, 1984.

—— and M. CARLE, 'Impartition policies: Growing importance in corporate strategies and applications to production sharing in some worldwide industries', Paper Presented at Strategic Management Society Conference, Paris, 1983.

BARTLETT, C.A. and S. GHOSHAL, 'Managing across borders: New strategic requirements', *Sloan Management Review*, Summer 1987: 7–17.

BOSTON CONSULTING GROUP, *Strategy Alternatives for the British Motorcycle Industry*, London: Her Majesty's Stationery Office, 1975.

BOWER, J.L., 'Planning within the firm', *The American Economic Review:* 1970: 186–94.

BOWMAN, E.H., 'Epistemology, corporate strategy, and academe', *Sloan Management Review:* Winter 1974: 35–50.

BRAYBROOKE, D., 'Skepticism of wants, and certain subversive effects of corporations on American values', in S. Hook (ed.), *Human Values and Economic Policy*, New York: New York University Press, 1967.

—— and C.E. LINDBLOM, *A Strategy of Decision: Policy evaluation as a social process*, New York: Free Press, 1963.

BRENNER, S.N. and E.A. MOLANDER, 'Is the ethic of business changing?' *Harvard Business Review*, January–February 1977: 57– 71.

BROOK, P., *The Empty Space*, Harmondsworth, Middlesex: Penguin Books, 1968.

BRUNSSON, N., 'The irrationality of action and action rationality: Decisions, ideologies, and organizational actions', *Journal of Management Studies,* 1982(1): 29–44.

BURNS, T., 'The directions of activity and communication in a departmental executive group', *Human Relations,* 7, 1954: 73–97.

——, 'Micropolitics: Mechanisms of institutional change', *Administrative Science Quarterly:* December 1961: 257–81.

—— and G.M. STALKER, *The Management of Innovation,* 2d edn, London: Tavistock, 1966.

BUSINESS WEEK. 'Japan's strategy for the 80's', December 14, 1981: 39–120.

CHANDLER, A.D., *Strategy and Structure: Chapters in the history of the industrial enterprise,* Cambridge, Mass.: MIT Press, 1962.

CHANNON, D.F., 'The strategy, structure and financial performance of the service industries', Working Paper, Manchester Business School, 1975.

CHEIT, E.F., 'The new place of business: Why managers cultivate social responsibility', in E.F. Cheit (ed.), *The Business Establishment,* New York: John Wiley. 1964.

CHRISTENSON, C.R., K.R. ANDREWS and J.L. BOWER, *Business Policy: Text and Cases,* Homewood, Ill.: Richard D. Irwin, 1978.

CLARK, B.R., *The Distinctive College: Antioch, Reed and Swarthmore,* Chicago: Aldine, 1970.

——, 'The organizational saga in higher education', *Administrative Science Quarterly,* 1972: 178–84.

COHEN, M.D., MARCH, J.E. and OLSEN, J.P., 'A garbage can model of organizational choice', *Administrative Science Quarterly,* 1972, 17: 1–25.

COLE, A.H., *Business Enterprise in its Social Setting,* Cambridge, Mass.: Harvard University Press, 1959.

COPEMAN, G.H., *The Role of the Managing Director,* London: Business Publications, 1963.

CROZIER, M., *The Bureaucratic Phenomenon,* Chicago: University of Chicago Press, 1964.

CVAR, M.R., 'Case studies in global competition', in M.E. Porter (ed.) *Competition in Global Industries,* Boston: Harvard Business School Press.

CYERT R.M. and J.G. MARCH, *A Behavioral Theory of the Firm,* Englewood Cliffs, N.J.: Prentice Hall, 1963.

DAVIS, R.T., *Performance and Development of Field Sales Managers,* Boston: Harvard Business School, 1957.

DEAN, R.C., 'The temporal mismatch: Innovation's pace vs. management's time horizon', *Research Management,* May 1974: 13.

DELBECQ, A. and A.C. FILLEY, *Program and Project Management in a Matrix Organization: A case study,* Madison, Wis.: University of Wisconsin, 1974.

DOUGLAS, S.P. and Y. WIND, 'The myth of globalization', *Columbia Journal of World Business,* Winter 1987: 19–29.

DRUCKER, P.F., *The Practice of Management,* New York: Harper & Row, 1954

——, *Management: Tasks, responsibilities, practices,* New York: Harper & Row, 1974.

EDWARDS, J.P., 'Strategy formulation as a stylistic process', *International Studies of Management and Organization,* Summer 1977: 13–27.

EPSTEIN, E.M., 'The social role of business enterprise in Britain: An American perspective; Part II', *The Journal of Management Studies,* 1977: 281–316.

ESSAME, H., *Patton: A study in command,* New York: Charles Scribner's Sons, 1974.

EVERED, R., *So What Is Strategy?* Working Paper, Naval Postgraduate School, Monterey, 1980.

FARAGO, L., *Patton: Ordeal and triumph,* New York: I. Obolensky, 1964.

FIRSIROTU, M., 'Strategic turnaround as cultural revolution: The case of Canadian National Express', doctoral dissertation, Faculty of Management, 1985.

FOCH, F., *Principles of War,* translated by J. DeMorinnni, New York: AMS Press, 1970. First published London: Chapman & Hall, 1918.

FORRESTER, J.W., 'Counterintuitive behavior of social systems', *Technology Review,* January 1971: 52–68.

FRANKLIN, B., *Poor Richard's Almanac,* New York: Ballantine Books, 1977. First published, Century Company, 1898.

FRIEDMAN, M., *Capitalism and Freedom,* Chicago: University of Chicago Press, 1962.

——, 'A Friedman doctrine: The social responsibility of business is to increase its profits', *The New York Times Magazine.* 13 September 1970.

FUSHIMI, T., 'Matsushita Electric Industrial Co. Ltd. – Divisional management control', Keio Business School, Japan, February 1987.

GALBRAITH, J.K., *American Capitalism: The concept of countervailing power,* Boston: Houghton Mifflin, 1952.

——, *The New Industrial State,* Boston: Houghton Mifflin, 1967.

GALBRAITH, J.R., *Organization Design,* Reading, Mass.: Addison-Wesley, 1977.

——, 'Strategy and organization planning', *Human Resource Management*, 1983: 63–77.

GARSON, G.D., 'The codetermination model of worker's participation: Where is it leading?' *Sloan Management Review*, Spring 1977: 63–78.

GERTH, H.H. and C. WRIGHT MILLS (eds.) *From Max Weber: Essays in sociology*. New York: Oxford University Press, 1958.

GLUECK, W.F., *Business Policy and Strategic Management*, New York: McGraw Hill, 1980.

GOSSELIN, R., *A Study of the Interdependence of Medical Specialists in Quebec Teaching Hospitals*, PhD thesis, McGill University, 1978.

GREEN, P., *Alexander the Great*, New York: Frederick A. Praeger, 1970.

GRINYER, P.H. and J.C. SPENDER, *Turnaround – Management recipes for strategic success*, New York: Associated Business Press, 1979.

GUEST, R.H., 'Of time and the foreman', *Personnel*, May 1956: 478–86.

HART, B.H.L., *Strategy*, New York: Frederick A. Praeger, 1954.

HAYES, R.H. and W.J. ABERNATHY, 'Managing our way to economic decline', *Harvard Business Review*, July–August 1980: 67–77.

—— and D.A. GARVIN, 'Managing as if tomorrow mattered', *Harvard Business Review*, May–June 1982: 70–9.

HICKSON, D.J., C.A. LEE, R.E. SCHNECK and J.M. PENNINGS, 'A strategic contingencies' theory of intraorganizational power', *Administrative Science Quarterly*, 1971: 216–29.

HOFER, C.W. and D. SCHENDEL, *Strategy Formulation: Analytical concepts*, St Paul, Minn.: West Publishing, 1978.

HOMANS, G.C., *The Human Group*, New York: Harcourt Brace, 1950.

HOUT, T., M.E. PORTER and E. RUDDEN, 'How global companies win out', *Harvard Business Review*, September–October 1982: 98–108.

HUGHES, T., 'The inventive continuum', *Science 84*, November 1984.

HUNT, R.G., 'Technology and organization', *Academy of Management Journal*, 1970: 235–52.

IACOCCA, L. with W. NOVAK, *Iacocca: An autobiography*, New York: Bantam Books, 1984.

IRVING, D., *The Trail of the Fox*, New York: E.P. Dutton, 1977.

JAMES, D.C., *The Years of MacArthur, 1941–1945*, Boston: Houghton Mifflin, 1970.

JAY, A., *Management and Machiavelli*, New York: Penguin Books, 1970.

JENKINS, C., *Power at the Top*, Westport, Conn.: Greenwood Press, 1976.

JOMINI, A.H., *Art of War*, translated by G.H. Mendell and W.P. Craighill, Westport, Conn.: Greenwood Press, 1971. Original Philadelphia: J.B. Lippincott, 1862.

KATZ, R.L., *Cases and Concepts in Corporate Strategy*, Englewood Cliffs, N.J.: Prentice Hall. 1970.

KIDDER, T., *The Sould of a New Machine*, Boston: Little, Brown, 1981.

KIECHEL, W. III. 'Sniping at strategic planning (interview with himself)', *Planning Review*, May 1984: 8–11.

KRAAR, L., 'A Japanese champion fights to stay on top', *Fortune*, December 1972: 94 103.

LAND, E., 'People should want more from life . . .', *Forbes*, 1 June 1975.

LAPIERRE, L., 'Le changement stratégique: Un rêve en quête de réel', PhD Management Policy course paper, McGill University, Canada, 1980.

LENIN, V.I., *Collected Works of V.I. Lenin*, edited and annotated, New York: International Publishers, 1927.

LEVITT, T., 'Marketing Myopia', *Harvard Business Review*, July–August 1960: 45–56.

——, 'Why business always loses', *Harvard Business Review*, March–April 1968: 81–9.

——, 'Marketing success through differentiation – of anything', *Harvard Business Review*, January–February 1980: 83–91.

——, 'The globalization of markets', *Harvard Business Review*, May–June 1983: 92–102.

LEWIN, K., *Field Theory in Social Science*, New York: Harper & Row, 1951.

LINDBLOM, C.E., 'The science of "Muddling Through"', *Public Administration Review*, 1959: 79–88.

——, *The Policy-Making Process*, Englewood Cliffs, N.J.: Prentice Hall, 1968.

LODGE, G.C., *The New American Ideology*, New York: Alfred A. Knopf, 1975.

MACE, M.L. and G.G. MONTGOMERY, *Management Problems of Corporate Acquisitions*, Boston: Harvard Business School, 1962.

MACMILLAN, A.C., 'Preemptive strategies', *Journal of Business Strategy*, Fall 1983: 16–26.

MAJONE, G., 'The use of policy analysis', in *The Future and the Past: Essays on programs*. Russell Sage Foundation Annual Report, 1976–7.

MAO TSE-TUNG, *Selected Military Writings, 1928–1949*, San Francisco: China Books, 1967.

MARCH, J.G. and J.P. OLSEN, *Ambiguity and Choice in Organizations*, Bergen, Norway: Universitets-forlaget, 1976.

———, and H.A. SIMON, *Organizations*, New York: John Wiley, 1958.

MARTIN, L.C., 'How Beatrice foods sneaked up on $5 Billion', *Fortune*, April 1976: 119–29.

MATLOFF, M. and E.M. SNELL, *Strategic Planning for Coalition Warfare (1941–42)*, Washington, DC: Office of Chief of Military History, Department of the Army, 1953.

MCCLELLAND, D.C., 'The two faces of power', *Journal of International Affairs*, 1970: 29–47.

MCDONALD, J., *Strategy in Poker, Business and War*, New York: W.W. Norton, 1950.

MECHANIC, D., 'Sources of power of lower participants in complex organizations', *Administrative Science Quarterly*, 1962: 349–64.

MILLER, D. and P.H. FRIESEN, 'Archetypes of strategy formulation', *Management Science*, May 1978: 921–33.

———, *Organizations: A quantum view*, Englewood Cliffs, N.J.: Prentice Hall, 1984.

———, *Unstable at the Top*, New York: New American Library, 1987.

MINTZBERG, H., 'Research on strategy-making', *Academy of Management Proceedings*, 1972: 90–4.

———, *The Nature of Managerial Work*, New York: Harper & Row, 1973.

———, 'Generic strategies: Toward a comprehensive framework', *Advances in Strategic Management*, Vol. 5, pp. 1–67, Greenwich, CT:JAI Press, 1988.

——— and J.A. WATERS, 'Tracking strategy in an entrepreneurial firm', *Academy of Management Journal*, 1982: 465–99.

———, 'Of strategies, deliberate and emergent', *Strategic Management Journal*, 1985: 257–72.

MONTGOMERY, B.L., *The Memoirs of Field-Marshal The Viscount Montgomery of Alamein*, Cleveland: World Publishing, 1958.

MOYER, R.C., 'Berle and Means revisited: The conglomerate merger', *Business and Society:* Spring 1970: 20–9.

NAPOLEON, I., 'Maximes de guerre', in T.R. Phillips (ed.), *Roots of Strategy*. Harrisburg, Pa.: Military Service Publishing, 1940.

NEUSTADT, R.E., *Presidential Power: The Politics of Leadership*. New York: John Wiley, 1960.

NODA, Y. and K. YOSHIDA, 'Matsushita Electric Industrial Co. Ltd.', Company Report 86–14, Yamichi Securities Co. Ltd, Tokyo, September 1986.

OUCHI, W.G., *Theory Z*, Reading, Mass.: Addison-Wesley, 1981.

——— and A.M. JAEGER, 'Type Z organization: Stability in the midst of mobility', *Academy of Management Review*, 1978: 305–14.

PENCE, C.C., *How Venture Capitalists Make Venture Decisions*, Ann Arbor, Mich.: UMI Research Press, 1982.

PERROW, C., *Organizational Analysis: A sociological review*, Belmont, Calif.: Wadsworth, 1970.

———, *Complex Organizations: A critical essay*, New York: Scott, Foresman, 1972.

PETERS, T.J., 'A style for all seasons', *Executive*, Summer 1980: 12–16.

——— and R.H. WATERMAN, *In Search of Excellence: Lessons from America's best run companies*, New York: Harper & Row, 1982.

PHILLIPS, T.R. (ed.), *Roots of Strategy*. Harrisburg, Pa.: Military Service Publishing, 1940.

PORTER, M.E., *Competitive Strategy: Techniques for analysing industries and competitors*, New York: Free Press, 1980.

———, *Competitive Advantage: Creating and sustaining superior performance*, New York: Free Press, 1985.

———, 'Competition in global industries: A conceptual framework', in M.E. Porter (ed.), *Competition in Global Industries*, Boston: Harvard Business School Press, 1986.

PURKAYASTHA, D., *Note on the Motorcycle Industry – 1975*, Copyrighted Case, Harvard Business School, 1981.

———, *Strategies for Change: Logical incrementalism*, Homewood, Ill.: Richard D. Irwin, 1980.

RAPHAEL, R., *Edges*, New York: Alfred A. Knopf, 1976.

RAPOPORT, C., 'Matsushita sits atop an $11 billion cash mountain', *Boston Globe*, 13 July 1986.

REESER, C., 'Some potential human problems in the project form of organization', *Academy of Management Journal*. 1969: 459–67.

ROSENBLOOM, R. and M. CUSUMANO, 'Technological pioneering and competitive advantage: birth of the VCR industry', *California Management Review*, Vol. 29, No. 4 Summer 1987: 51–76.

ROSNER, M., *Principle Types and Problems of Direct Democracy in the Kibbutz*, Working Paper,

Social Research Centre on the Kibbutz, Givat Haviva, Israel, 1969.

ROSS, I., 'How lawless are the big companies?' *Fortune*, 1 December 1980: 56–64.

RUMELT, R.P., 'Evaluation of Strategies: theory and models', in D. Schendel and C.W. Hofer, *Strategic Management*, Boston: Little, Brown, 1979, pp. 196–212.

——, 'A teaching plan for strategy alternatives for the British motorcycle Industry', in *Japanese Business: Business policy*, New York: The Japan Society, 1980.

SAKIYA, T., 'The story of Honda's founders', *Asahi Evening News*, June–August 1979.

——, *Honda Motor: The men, the management, the machines*, Tokyo, Japan: Kadonsha International, 1982.

SALTER, M.S. and W.A. WEINHOLD, *Diversification through Acquisition*, New York: Free Press, 1979.

SAYLES, L.R., *Managerial Behavior: Administration in complex organizations*, New York: McGraw-Hill, 1964.

SCHELLING, T.C., *The Strategy of Conflict*, 2nd edn, Cambridge, MA: Harvard University Press, 1980.

SELZNICK, P., *TVA and the Grass Roots*, Berkeley: University of California Press, 1949.

——, *Leadership in Administration: A sociological interpretation*, New York: Harper & Row, 1957.

SHUBIK, M., *Games for Society, business, and War: Towards a theory of gaming*, New York: Elsevier, 1975.

SIMON, M.A., 'On the concept of organizational goals', *Administrative Science Quarterly*, 1964–5: 1–22.

SLOANE, L., 'Panasonic's president pursues growth goals', *The Wall Street Journal*, 17 March 1982.

SMITH, L., 'The boardroom is becoming a different scene', *Fortune*, 8 May 1978: 150–88.

SMITH, L., 'Matsushita looks beyond consumer electronics', *Fortune*, 31 October 1983: 96–104.

SMITH, W.R., 'Product differentiation and market segmentation as alternative marketing strategies', *Journal of Marketing*, July 1956: 3–8.

SNODDAY, R., 'Matsushita warns over Welsh TV plant', *Financial Times*, 7 June 1985.

SPEER, A., *Inside the Third Reich*. New York: Macmillan, 1970.

SPENCER, F.C., 'Deductive reasoning in the lifelong continuing education of a cardiovascular surgeon', *Archives of Surgery*, 1976: 1177–83.

SPENDER, J.-C., *Industry Recipes: The nature and sources of managerial judgement*, London: Basil Blackwell, 1989.

STAFF, 'Matsushita to shift more output to foreign plants', *Financial Times*, 18 June 1981.

——, 'Matsushita', Company publication, Matsushita Electric Industrial Co. Ltd, Osaka, 1983a.

——, 'Matsushita Electric Industrial Company', *International Research Report*, Merrill Lynch, 4 May 1983b.

——, 'Matsushita tunes up its marketing machine', *The Economist*, 3 August 1985: 66–7.

——, 'Matsushita Electric Industrial Company', *International Herald Tribune*, 26 May 1987.

STEVENSON, W., *A Man Called Intrepid: The Secret War*, New York: Harcourt Brace Jovanovich, 1976.

STEWART, R., *Managers and Their Jobs*, London: MacMillan, 1967.

SUN TZU, *The Art of War*, translated by S.B. Griffith, New York: Oxford University Press, 1963. Original 500 B.C.

TAKAHASHI, K. and H. ISHIDA, 'The Matsushita Electric Industrial Co. Ltd. – Management control systems', Keio University, Japan, distributed by Intercollegiate Case Clearing House, Soldier's Field, Boston (Case no. 9-378-922), undated.

TAKEUCHI, H. and I. NONAKA, 'The new product development game', *Harvard Business Review*, January–February 1986: 137–46.

TAYLOR, W.H., 'The nature of policy making in universities', *The Canadian Journal of Higher Education*, 1983: 17–32.

TERKEL, S., *Working*, New York: Pantheon Books, 1972.

THOMPSON, J.D., *Organizations in Action*, New York: McGraw-Hill, 1967.

THOMPSON, V.A., *Modern Organizations*, New York: Alfred A. Knopf, 1961.

TILLES, S., 'How to evaluate corporate strategy', *Harvard Business Review*, July–August 1963: 111–21.

TOFFLER, A., *Future Shock*, New York: Bantam Books, 1970.

TREGOE, B. and I. ZIMMERMAN, *Top Management Strategy*, New York: Simon & Schuster, 1980.

TUCHMAN, B.W., *The Guns of August*, New York: Macmillan, 1962.

URBAN, G.L., R. CARTER, S. GASKIN, and Z. MUCHA, 'Market share rewards to pioneering brands', *Management Science*, 6 June 1986: 645–59.

VANCIL, R.F., 'Strategy formulation in complex organizations', *Sloan Management Review,* Winter 1976: 1–18.

—— and P. LORANGE, 'Strategic planning in diversified companies', *Harvard Business Review,* January–February 1975: 81–90.

VARNER, V.J. and J.I. ALGER (eds.), *History of the Military Art: Notes for the course,* West Point, N.Y.: U.S. Military Academy, 1978.

VON BÜLOW, D.F., *The Spirit of the Modern System of War,* translated by C.M. deMartemont, London: C. Mercier, 1806.

VON CLAUSEWITZ, C., *On War,* translated by M. Howard and P. Paret, Princeton, N.J.: Princeton University Press, 1976.

VON HIPPEL, E., 'Get new products from customers', *Harvard Business Review,* March–April 1982: 117–22.

VON NEUMANN, J. and O. MORGENSTERN, *Theory of Games and Economic Behavior,* Princeton, N.J.: Princeton University Press, 1944.

WEBER, M., 'The three types of legitimate rule', translated by H. Gerth, in A. Etzioni (ed.), *A Sociological Reader on Complex Organizations,* New York: Holt, Rinehart and Winston, 1969.

WEICK, K.E., 'Educational organizations as loosely coupled systems', *Administrative Science Quarterly,* 1976: 1–19.

WHITE, T.H., *In Search of History: A personal adventure,* New York: Warner Books, 1978.

WILLIAMSON, O.E., *Markets and Hierarchies: Analysis and antitrust implications,* New York: Free Press, 1975.

——, *The Economic Institutions of Capitalism,* New York: Free Press, 1985.

WISE, D., 'Apple's new crusade', *Business Week,* 26 November 1984.

WORTHY, J.C., 'Organizational structure and employee morale', *American Sociological Review,* 1950: 169–79.

——, *Big Business and Free Men,* New York: Harper & Row, 1959.

WRIGLEY, L., 'Diversification and divisional autonomy', DBA dissertation, Graduate School of Business Administration, Harvard University, 1970.

YOSHINO, M.Y., 'Global competition in a salient industry: The case of civil aircraft', in M.E. Porter (ed.), *Competition in Global Industries,* Boston: Harvard Business School Press, 1986.

YOUNG, D., *Rommel: The Desert Fox,* New York: Harper & Row, 1974.

ZALD, M.N. and M.A. BERGER, 'Social movements in organizations: *Coup d'etat,* insurgency, and mass movements', *American Journal of Sociology,* 1978.

NAME INDEX

SUBJECT INDEX